FROMMER'S
DOLLARWISE GUIDE TO ENGLAND & SCOTLAND

by Darwin Porter

1983-1984 Edition

Published by Frommer/Pasmantier Publishers
A Simon & Schuster Division of
Gulf & Western Corporation
1230 Avenue of the Americas
New York, NY 10020

ISBN 0-671-44791-2

Manufactured in the United States of America

*Although every effort was made to ensure the accuracy
of price information appearing in this book,
it should be kept in mind that prices
can and do fluctuate in the course of time.*

CONTENTS

MAPS

Acknowledgment

We wish to acknowledge the field research of Mr. and Mrs. Peter J. E. Barnes of London, England, and the editorial assistance of Margaret Foresman, of Key West, Florida.

To Stanley Haggart

Britain's VAT

On June 18, 1979, Great Britain raised its standard Value Added Tax (called VAT for short) from 8% to 15%. Most Common Market countries already have a tax similar to VAT (France, for example, a paralyzing 23%). In Britain, hotel rates and meals in restaurants are now taxed 15%. This extra VAT charge will show up on your bill unless otherwise stated. It is in addition to the service charge. Should the service charge be 15%, you will, in effect, be paying 30% higher than the prices quoted. The service charges, if included as part of the bill, are also taxable!

As part of an energy-saving scheme, the British government has also added a special 25% tax on gasoline ("petrol")!

Inflation Alert!!!

It is hardly a secret that a wave of inflation has battered the countries of northern Europe, and Britain has been hard hit. The author of this book has spent laborious hours researching to try and ensure the accuracy of prices appearing in this guide. As we go to press, I believe we have obtained the most reliable data possible. However, in a system that in 1982 alone saw one London hotelier raise his prices three times in one season, I cannot offer guarantees for the tariffs quoted. In the lifetime of this edition—particularly its second year (1984)—the wise traveler will add *at least* 20% to the prices quoted.

A Question of Borders

England and Scotland have changed their counties or "shires," carving out new ones, such as Humberside, and cutting up big ones, such as Yorkshire. Greater London has gobbled up many land areas of neighboring counties such as Surrey. The famous counties of Angus and Perthshire are now called "Tayside." However, many jolly innkeepers are keeping their old addresses—and threaten to continue to do so! In the transition there may be some confusion.

DOLLARWISE GUIDE TO ENGLAND AND SCOTLAND

The Reason Why

ENGLAND, AND SCOTLAND, too, sent her children across the waves to settle North America, Australia, New Zealand, and a host of other lands. Today the offspring of those children are returning to visit their mother lands at a rate that is practically an invasion.

What's the big attraction?

England, as in Restoration days, has thrown out the Puritan and is experimenting in all sorts of imaginative, creative ways. Vigorous and exciting changes are taking place, and England today is, in a word, fun. The island may be small, but, like Mighty Mouse, it packs a powerful punch.

On the other hand, Scotland fulfills romantic myths—a land of shimmering lochs, pepper-pot towers and crow-stepped castles, clans with bagpipes, and balladeers. Scotland is very different from England. When English people go to Scotland, they are, in effect, "going abroad."

Connecting you with the life forces of both countries is one of the aims of this book.

We have set for ourselves the formidable task of seeking out the best of England and Scotland and condensing it between the covers of a guide. The best includes not only descriptions of hotels, restaurants, pubs, and nightspots, but descriptions of cities, towns, and sightseeing attractions. Part of the philosophy of this book is based on the fact that the best need not be the most expensive. Hence, our ultimate aim—beyond that of familiarizing you with the offerings of merrie old England and romantic Scotland—is to stretch your dollar power, to show you that you need not always pay scalper's prices for charm, top-grade comfort, and food.

In this guide, we'll devote a great deal of attention to the tourist meccas of London, Edinburgh, Stratford-upon-Avon, and Oxford. But these ancient cities and towns are not the full "reason why" of the book. Important as they are, they simply do not fully reflect the complexity and diversity of both countries. Unlike most nations of Europe, England and Scotland defy a clear, logical, coherent plan of sightseeing. Both lands are a patchwork quilt of treasures, with many of the most scenic items tucked away in remote corners—

an Elizabethan country estate in Devon, a half-timbered thatched cottage by the sea in Cornwall, a Regency manor in the Lake District, an old whitewashed coaching inn at Loch Ness.

Meeting the English and the Scots is perhaps the most important reason for making the trip. If possible, try to arrive with few preconceived ideas. For example, generalizing about the character of the English in a land filled with "soopah" swinging dukes, Cockney porters, Rudyard Kipling adventurers, and Miss Marple–type ladies is fraught with hazards. Suffice it to say, they'll surprise you—particularly if you think of the English as a cold, snobbish, withdrawn people. A few visits to the haunts of Soho, or to a local pub for a "lager and lime," or even a look at the racy London tabloids, will cure you of stereotypes.

SOME NEW REASONS WHY: It may be presumptuous to give you "reasons why" to go to England and Scotland. Dozens may have already occurred to you, ranging from doing a brass rubbing on a church floor to tracing your ancestors to determine if you're descended from royalty or highwaymen. We'll merely add a few you may not have thought of:

To go pub crawling

The English pub is a unique institution. Its special charms will win you instantly, making you abandon the jaded cocktail hour forever. You can begin your crawl in the heart of Piccadilly Circus, eating "bangers and mash" with the young "blokes" from the East End in a "chirpy" Victorian atmosphere; then proceed to a pub in "The City" in the footsteps of Samuel Johnson, with Boswell writing down every word: "This man (Lord Chesterfield) I thought had been a Lord among wits; but, I find, he is only a wit among Lords"; then on to exclusive Belgravia to mix with London bluebloods in the stamping ground of the Iron Duke himself; finally, end your adventure with elegantly dressed operagoers in a pub off Covent Garden, Eliza Doolittle territory.

But don't stop there. You can go all over England, staking out your own "local"—be it the Mermaid in Rye, basking in its associations with a band of cutthroat smugglers, the Hawkhurst Gang; the Fox & Hounds on the outskirts of Southampton where you'll drink the legendary mead from a silver mazer (the Saxons considered it an elixir); the Ship Inn in Exeter, beloved ("next to mine own shippe") by Sir Francis Drake; and finally, the Sloop, an artists' pub at St. Ives on the Cornish coast, where you're likely to hear some Welsh folk singing.

To discover if Victoria was a wicked old witch or a nice old lady

Perhaps no woman in history ever dominated an era—at least symbolically—as much as the Empress of India and the Queen of Great Britain and the Dominions. One historian wrote: "She seemed the richest and most impressive monarch since Cyrus the Great or Augustus Caesar." Interest in her today hasn't dimmed—nor has controversy about her. Wherever you go in England, her influence permeates the air. At a theater club in London, members still drink a mock toast to the chubby queen, whose influence on morality still affects some people even today.

To sample the country life

Involve yourself in the rural life, the very heart of England. There's still quite a bit of it left. Dine in an ancient hall with a walk-in fireplace (inglenook), eat off an old blackened oak table, gobble up huge portions of roast beef and Yorkshire pudding, followed by hot deep-dish fruit pies smothered in thick Devonshire cream. At night crawl into a Tudor four-poster and dream of the England of yore. The next day go for a walk through a meadow, down a crooked lane lined with hedges and wild roses, until you eventually find your way to a tiny hamlet and ruined castle, with a tall stone tower and surrounding moat. Later go to one of the nearby inns where you can order a pint of cider in a pewter mug, sit in a 300-year-old settle, and listen to and talk to the villagers.

To be lord or lady of the manor

Burdened with taxes, the descendants of the privileged class are having to rent out their estates to paying guests. Many of the grand homes have been discreetly turned into manor house hotels that usually, for the price of a good seat at a Broadway show, will house you in a spacious room and provide three bountiful meals a day. By all means, take advantage of this unique opportunity to act the lord or lady of the manor—playing croquet on the well-rolled green, riding horseback, attending a hunt ball, fishing for speckled trout, having afternoon tea in a formal garden.

DOLLARWISE—WHAT IT MEANS: This is a guidebook giving specific, practical details (including prices) about the hotels, restaurants, pubs, sightseeing attractions, and nightlife of England and Scotland. First-class to rock-bottom-budget establishments have been documented and described, from the elegant May Fair Hotel in London to a bed-and-breakfast house in an old fishing village in Scotland. Each establishment has been judged by the strict yardstick of value.

The major focus of the book is on the average voyager who'd like to patronize the almost wholly undocumented establishments of England and Scotland—that is, the second-class hotels and some of the better, although less heralded, restaurants where you can often get a superb dinner.

The sights of England and Scotland have been set forth in what we believe is a human, personal, and practical style. In both England and Scotland, the bewildered visitor is faced with a staggering number of attractions from the most catholic collection of art and artifacts in the world (the British Museum), to George Washington's ancestral home, to Anne Hathaway's Cottage of Stratford-upon-Avon, to some of the Scottish castles where Mary Queen of Scots lived during her brief, tragic reign.

What the Dollarwise Guide attempts is to lead the reader through the maze of important sights, such as the Tower of London and Edinburgh Castle, then introduce him or her to a number of lesser known locales, such as the little hamlets, flint churches, and historic houses of East Anglia, perhaps the mellow old towns of the Scottish "Borders." The hours and prices of admission to these attractions have been detailed.

SOME DISCLAIMERS: No restaurant, inn, hotel, guest house, or shop paid to be mentioned in this book. What you read are personal recommendations—in many cases, proprietors never knew their establishments were being investigated.

A word of warning: Unfortunately, prices change, and they rarely go downward, at least not in Britain. The government does not control hotel prices, as is customary in Spain and Italy. Nearly all British hotels are fond of quoting a rate of "from so many pence up," and many establishments simply refuse to quote anything else. The hotelier, anxious about inflation or a sudden tax imposed by the government, doesn't want to commit himself or herself too far in advance to a specific price. However, the "from" rate often—but not always—means the average price you're likely to be charged.

Always, when checking into a hotel, inquire about the price—and agree on it. This policy can save much embarrassment and disappointment when it comes time to settle the tab. In no circumstances can you invariably demand to be charged the price quoted in this book, although every effort has been made to state the accurate tariff as much as it was foreseeable when this guide was published.

This guide is revised every other year, yet even in a book that appears fresh every year it may happen that that cozy little family dining room changes colors, blossoming out with cut-velvet walls and dining tabs that include the decorator's fee and the owner's new Bentley. It may be that some of the people, animals, and settings we've described are no longer there or have been changed beyond recognition.

AN INVITATION TO READERS: Like all the Dollarwise books, *Dollarwise Guide to England and Scotland* hopes to maintain a continuing dialogue between its author and its readers. All of us share a common aim—to travel as widely and as well as possible, at the best value for our money. And in achieving that goal, your comments and suggestions can be of tremendous help. Therefore, if you come across a particularly appealing hotel, restaurant, store, even sightseeing attraction, please don't keep it to yourself. We'll send free copies of the next edition of *this* book to readers whose suggestions are used. Unfortunately, we cannot send copies of other guides to other countries published in the series, but only the book in which your specific recommendation appears. The solicitation for letters applies not only to new establishments, but to hotels or restaurants already recommended in this guide. The fact that a listing appears in this edition doesn't give it squatter's rights in future publications. If its services have deteriorated, its chef grown stale, its prices risen unfairly, whatever, these failings should be known. Even if you enjoyed every place and found every description accurate—that, too, can cheer many a gray day. Send your comments to Darwin Porter, c/o Frommer/Pasmantier Publishers, 1230 Avenue of the Americas, New York, NY 10020.

1. The $15-a-Day Travel Club—How to Save Money on All Your Travels

In just a few paragraphs, you'll begin your exploration of England and Scotland. But before you do, you may want to learn how to save money on all your trips and travels; by joining the $15-a-Day Travel Club, now in its 20th successful year of operation.

The Club was formed at the urging of readers of the $-a-Day Books and the Dollarwise Guides, many of whom felt that such an organization could bring financial benefits, continuing travel information, and a sense of community to economy-minded travelers in all parts of the world.

In keeping with the budget concept, the membership fee is low and is immediately exceeded by the value of your benefits. Upon receipt of U.S. $14

(U.S. residents), or $16 (Canadian, Mexican, and other foreign residents) to cover one year's membership, we will send all new members by return mail (book rate) the following items:

(1) The latest edition of any *two* of the following books (please designate in your letter which two books you wish to receive).

Europe on $20 a Day
Australia on $20 a Day
England and Scotland on $25 a Day
Greece on $20 a Day
Hawaii on $25 a Day
Ireland on $25 a Day
Israel on $25 & $30 a Day
Mexico on $20 a Day
New Zealand on $20 & $25 a Day
Scandinavia on $25 a Day
South America on $25 a Day
Spain and Morocco (plus the Canary Is.) on $25 a Day
Washington, D.C. on $25 a Day

Dollarwise Guide to the Caribbean (including Bermuda and the Bahamas)
Dollarwise Guide to Canada
Dollarwise Guide to Egypt
Dollarwise Guide to England and Scotland
Dollarwise Guide to France
Dollarwise Guide to Germany
Dollarwise Guide to Italy
Dollarwise Guide to Portugal (plus Madeira and the Azores)
Dollarwise Guide to California and Las Vegas
Dollarwise Guide to Florida
Dollarwise Guide to New England
Dollarwise Guide to the Southeast and New Orleans
(Dollarwise Guides discuss accommodations and facilities in all price ranges, with emphasis on the medium-priced.)

How to Beat the High Cost of Travel
(This practical guide details how to save money on absolutely all travel items—accommodations, transportation, dining, sightseeing, shopping, taxes, and more. Includes special budget information for seniors, students, singles, and families.)

Museums in New York
(A complete guide to all the museums, historic houses, botanic gardens, zoos, and libraries in New York City. Profusely illustrated with over 200 handsome photographs.)

The Urban Athlete
(The ultimate sports guide to New York City and environs.)

Where to Stay USA
(By the Council on International Educational Exchange, this extraordinary guide is the first to list accommodations in all 50 states that cost anywhere from $3 to $25 per night.)

The Speak Easy Phrase Book
(The four most useful languages—French, German, Spanish, and Italian —all in one convenient, easy-to-use phrase guide.)

(2) A one-year subscription to an 8-page tabloid newspaper **The Wonderful World of Budget Travel** which brings you the latest money-saving travel information—the kind of information you'd have to pay over $25 a year to obtain elsewhere. This consumer-conscious publication also provides some very special services to readers: **Traveler's Directory** (a list of members all over the world who are willing to provide hospitality to other members as they pass through their home cities); **Share-a-Trip** (requests from members for travel companions who can share costs and help avoid the burdensome single supplements); and **Readers Ask ... Readers Reply** (travel questions from members to which other members reply with authentic firsthand information).

(3) A copy of **Arthur Frommer's Guide to New York,** a newly revised pocket-size guide to hotels, restaurants, night spots, and sightseeing attractions in all price ranges throughout the New York area.

(4) Your personal membership card, which entitles you to purchase through the Club all Arthur Frommer Publications for a third to a half off their regular retail prices during the term of your membership.

So why not join this hardy band of international budgeteers now and participate in its exchange of travel information and hospitality? Simply send your name and address, together with your membership fee of $14 (U.S., residents), or $16 (Canadian, Mexican, and other foreign residents) in U.S. currency to: $15-a-Day Travel Club, Inc., 1230 Avenue of Americas, New York, NY 10020. Remember to specify which *two* books in section (1) above you wish to receive in your initial package of members' benefits. Or, if you prefer, use the last page of this book, simply checking off the two books you want and enclosing $14 or $16 in U.S. currency. All foreign residents please pay by international postal money order in U.S. funds or by a check drawn on a U.S. bank.

Chapter I

GETTING THERE

1. Plane Economics
2. By Ship
3. Traveling Within Britain

A FEW YEARS AGO this chapter was fairly simple to write, because, prior to 1979, airfares were strictly regulated by the International Air Transport Association (IATA) and therefore uniform: if British Airway's round-trip fare from New York to London was $628, let's say, then you could be sure that Pan Am, TWA, Air India, and the rest offered the identical fare.

Since deregulation under the Carter administration, such simplicity and uniformity have disappeared as the airlines have competed fiercely with one another for air traffic. To many destinations, an airline now proposes a fare structure; another airline then files a competing and different fare structure. A process of jockeying occurs which may or may not result in a uniform price structure for all airlines flying to that particular city.

It all adds up to chaos—but often *beneficial* chaos for the alert traveler willing to study and consider all the various alternative fares available. The key to bargain airfares is to shop around.

1. Plane Economics

It's never been cheaper—and more complicated—to fly to London. In what follows we'll try to unravel the current options available by classifying the fares according to their basic function.

Please note that all fares appearing on these pages are those available at press time and are subject to change and/or government approval. Doublecheck all fares with the airlines or your travel agent.

LEAST EXPENSIVE "REGULAR" FARES: Currently your cheapest options with the regular airlines fall into two categories.

Standby Fares

Every airline flying to London offers standby fares sold at the airport on the day of departure, and subject to availability. You'll have to chance (in many cases, you can call the airline the night before to find out what those chances are) waiting hours to find out whether you're confirmed, and being "stranded" for one to several days on the return leg of your trip.

If you're emotionally ready to hazard those risks and your travel plans are flexible enough, then you can take advantage of the lowest "regular" fares available. British Airways offers standby seats between New York and London at a round-trip price of $408 in basic season, $494 peak season (May 15 through September 14). The same standby opportunities to London are available on Delta from Atlanta for $630 round trip in basic and $735 in peak. Pan Am has a standby fare from New York to London of $494 in basic, $544 in peak season.

Super-Apex

The most heavily used fare to London is the Super-Apex, known also (by British Airways) as the "Dollar Stretcher." It's valid for a stay abroad of from seven days to six months, must be purchased at least 21 days in advance of your outbound flight to London, and with slight variations among the airlines, is priced from New York round trip to London at $435 in low season, $628 in high season, and $549 in shoulder.

THE EXPENSIVE FARES: If you can't take advantage of any of the above fares, which should be unlikely, here are the regular round-trip fares offered by British Airways from New York to London: economy—$522 basic, $636 shoulder, $682 peak; club—$1044 low season, $1244 peak; (747) super-club—$1300 low season, $1500 peak; first class—$3380 all year; and Concorde—$3874 all year.

LOW-COST MIAMI TO LONDON FARES: With fares as much as 56% below its competitors, **Air Florida**, the fastest growing airline in the United States, offers the lowest unrestricted fares for reserved seats between Miami and London.

Air Florida's unrestricted one-way coach fare is $262 off-peak (January 1 to March 31 and November 1 to December 14), and $320 peak (June 1 to August 31). In shoulder season (September 1 to October 31, April 1 to May 31, and December 15 to 31), the one-way fare is $284. There are no advance purchase or maximum-minimum-stay requirements, and meals are included.

Air Florida also offers standby fares of $209 one way in low season, $236 in shoulder, and $261 in high.

Air Florida passengers arriving at London's Gatwick Airport can take trains departing every 15 minutes from Gatwick's BritRail Station, one floor beneath the airport terminal, to London's Victoria Station.

A NEWARK TO GATWICK BARGAIN: British Airtours has scheduled a series of reasonably priced twice per week flights. Their sample fares for the 1982-83 winter season are $245 one way standby, $325 standard Economy, and $549 Super Apex. There are no advance purchase or minimum stay requirements. For more details call toll free 800/243-8588, or 203/622-1008.

BRITISH AIRWAYS: British Airways planes take off from New York City, Boston, Chicago, Detroit, Miami, San Francisco, Los Angeles, Philadelphia, Washington, D.C., Seattle, Anchorage, Montréal, and Toronto; naturally, they offer the greatest number of flights to the United Kingdom of any airline.

Another major advantage of flying British Airways: it is the only carrier with daily service from the U.S. and Canada to Scotland and the Midlands (the planes on these flights land at Prestwick and Manchester). Many budget-minded visitors like to take advantage of the less expensive fares to these cities, and then tour their way down to London. Prestwick, of course, is the perfect point for starting such a tour, and it is also a gateway to Northern Ireland. Manchester is, among other things, the natural gateway to Wales.

There are British Airways offices in cities throughout the United States, and there are thousands of travel agents as well, who are authorized to book you on a flight. The British Airways offices, and their staffs, are unusually well qualified to discuss touring in Britain and to make whatever arrangements— hotels, sightseeing, escorted bus trips, and the like—you need.

2. By Ship

Traveling to England by ship is only for those who crave a sea experience —either on a luxury liner, with resort-level facilities, or else on a more relaxed, time-consuming freighter. For traveling by air is both quicker and cheaper.

Here is a brief description of some of the major services offered from the Atlantic seaboard to various ports in England (most often Southampton, where you'll pay a small debarkation fee):

Cunard Line, 555 Fifth Ave., New York, NY 10017 (tel. 212/880-7500), boasts the *Queen Elizabeth 2* as its flagship—self-styled, quite accurately, as "the most advanced ship of the age." It is the only ocean liner providing regular transatlantic service—23 sailings from April to November—between New York and Cherbourg, France, and Southampton, England. Designed for super cruises, the *Queen Elizabeth 2* is reaching a younger market, those leery of the traditional liner-type crossing. Hence, you'll find four swimming pools, a sauna, nightclubs, a theater with a balcony, an art gallery, cinemas, even chic boutiques.

The vessel is a two-class ship, with both first and transatlantic classes. Each class has a number of public rooms for its exclusive use. However, most public rooms, such as the Casino, are used in common.

Throughout the year lively and fascinating entertainment is provided aboard. Called "Festival of Life," a series introduces you to such personalities as Lauren Bacall, Lillian Gish, or Clive Barnes.

The prices quoted are per person, but based on double occupancy. Fares are extremely complicated, so if you don't live in New York, it's suggested you call a Cunrad representative on their toll-free number (tel. 800/221-4700).

On the Air/Sea passage, you go over by ship, returning by air (British Airways) by one of 15 gateways. In all, you're given an air allowance of $500. In thrift season, you pay a minimum fare of $1095 transatlantic, $2075 first class; in intermediate, $1260 transatlantic, $2265 first class; and in high season, $1330 transatlantic, $2390 first class. In addition, you must pay a port tax of $45 in transatlantic, $54 in first class.

Another ticket is known as One-Way Free Sailing. That is, you pay for a one-way ticket by ship, but you get your return by ship included "free." Of course, you have to adjust your sailing dates to Cunard's. Usually there are 12 departures annually. If you depart in low season but return in high season, you'll still have to pay the more expensive fare. Minimum fares in thrift season are $1395 transatlantic, $2160 first class; in intermediate, $1525 transatlantic, $2365 first class; and in high season, $1600 transatlantic, $2490 first class.

Perhaps you'll be interested in excursion rates. One-way minimum fares in thrift season are $930 transatlantic, $1765 first class; in intermediate, $1070 transatlantic, $1925 first class; in high, $1130 transatlantic, $2030 first class.

The minimum one-way Youth Fare is $445, plus port tax, and this is available in transatlantic class only. A person, however, will share a double room, even a "quad," with someone of his or her own age.

Tours include the European Weekender, which is a week's vacation combining a *QE2* crossing and a weekend in London or Paris. The minimum transatlantic fare to London is $1149, rising to $2154 in first class. The minimum transatlantic fare to Paris is $1299, going up to $2304 in first class.

In addition, discount programs include special excursions throughout the year. These complicated and often changing dates will be provided by writing Cunard or else dealing directly with your travel agent.

3. Traveling Within Britain

BY TRAIN: There is something magical about traveling on a train in Britain. You sit in comfortable compartments, on upholstered seats, next to the reserved and well-dressed British; you're served your meal in the dining car like an aristocrat; and the entire experience can become a relaxing interlude.

You should, of course, be warned that *your Eurailpass is not valid on trains in Great Britain.* But the cost of rail travel in England, Scotland, Northern Ireland, and Wales can be quite low—particularly if you take advantage of certain cost-saving travel plans, some of which can only be purchased in North America, before leaving for Great Britain.

BritRail Pass

This pass gives unlimited rail travel in England, Scotland, and Wales, and is valid on all British Rail routes, on Lake Windermere steamers, and on Sealink ferry services to the Isle of Wight. It is not valid on ships between Great Britain and the continent, the Channel Islands, or Ireland. A seven-day **economy class pass,** as of 1982, cost $107 for one person, rising to $147 in first class, for U.S. travelers. Canadians, on the same arrangement, pay $123 in economy, $169 in first class. A one-month pass costs $243 (U.S.) and $279 (Canadian) in economy, rising to $317 (U.S.) and $365 (Canadian) in first class. Children under 4 years of age travel free, and children from 5 to 15 pay approximately half fare.

BritRail also offers a **Youth Pass** to people ages 16 to 25. On this arrangement, U.S. citizens pay $93 for a seven-day pass while Canadians are charged $107. On the Youth Pass ticket, seats are in the economy section only. It's also possible to purchase a Youth Pass for one month, costing $215 (U.S.) and $247 (Canadian).

BritRail and Youth Passes cannot be obtained in Britain, but should be secured before leaving North America either through travel agents or by writing or visiting BritRail Travel International, 630 Third Ave., New York, NY 10017; 510 West Sixth St., Los Angeles, CA 90014; or 333 North Michigan Ave., Chicago, IL 60601. Canadians can write to BritRail Travel International, 55 Eglinton Ave., East Toronto M4P 1G8, ON; or 409 Granville St., Vancouver V6C 1T2, BC.

BritRail Passes do not have to be predated. Validate your pass at any British Rail station when you start your first rail journey.

If you plan to travel heavily on the European and/or British railroads, you will do well to secure the latest copy of the Thomas Cook Continental Timetable of European Railroads. This comprehensive, 500-plus-page timetable lists all of Europe's mainline rail services with great detail and accuracy. It is available exclusively in North America from Forsyth Travel Library, PO Box 2975, Shawnee Mission, KS 66201 at a cost of $15.95 including postage.

COUNTIES OF ENGLAND & WALES

1. TYNE AND WEAR
2. CLEVELAND
3. LANCASHIRE
4. MERSEYSIDE
5. GREATER MANCHESTER
6. WEST YORKSHIRE
7. SOUTH YORKSHIRE
8. CHESHIRE
9. SALOP
10. STAFFORD
11. DERBY
12. NOTTINGHAM
13. HEREFORD AND WORCESTER

14. WEST MIDLANDS
15. WARWICK
16. LEICESTER
17. NORTHAMPTON
18. GWENT
19. GLOUCESTER
20. BEDFORD

21. BUCKINGHAM
22. HERTFORD
23. AVON
24. WILTSHIRE
25. BERKSHIRE
26. SURREY
27. WEST SUSSEX
28. EAST SUSSEX
29. WEST GLAMORGAN
30. MID GLAMORGAN
31. SOUTH GLAMORGAN

Britrail Seapass—Continent

In general terms, purchasers of a BritRail Pass wishing to travel one way or round trip between Britain and Ireland and Britain and continental Europe by Sealink services can purchase an extension of their BritRail Pass carrying one or two coupons, according to requirements. The one-way fare to continental Europe, for example, is $50 (U.S.) or $58 (Canadian); a single journey is half the round-trip price. A round trip to Ireland costs $74 (U.S.) or $86 (Canadian); a single journey again is one half the round-trip price.

Furthermore, if the appropriate supplement is paid, the coupons are valid for all services operated by Sealink or Seaspeed, and are not tied to the validity of the associated BritRail Pass. For example, a traveler may arrive in Ireland, use one coupon for the journey to London, stay several days, validate the BritRail Pass and travel for its duration, and then return to London for another period of time before traveling from London to a continental European port.

Special Bargain Fares

British Rail from time to time offers special round-trip fares for optional travel and weekend travel, which may only be purchased in Great Britain. Because of the changing nature of these fares and facilities, it is not possible to give advance information about them to travelers from abroad. Information can be obtained from travel agents and British Rail stations in Great Britain.

If you're in London, and want more information on transportation rates, schedules, or facilities, go to the **British Rail Travel Centre,** 4–12 Lower Regent Street, S.W.1 (tel. 839-4343), only a few minutes' walk from Piccadilly Circus. You can also make reservations and purchase rail tickets there and at British Rail Travel Centres at Oxford Street, Victoria Street, the Strand, King William Street, Heathrow Airport, and the main London stations.

CAR RENTALS: No doubt about it—the best way to see the real England and Scotland is to travel by car. It gives you the freedom to visit that out-of-the-way antique shop that doesn't know about tourist prices, and to picnic wherever you like. And for two or more persons, economy can be a major advantage of traveling by car.

There are many car-rental services available in England and Scotland, including **Hertz, National, Kemwel,** and **Avis.** There are also dozens of British-owned car-rental firms, most of them charging rates to match their American competitors.

Hertz is particularly well represented with major branches at both airports, Heathrow (tel. 01/897-3349) and Gatwick (tel. 02/933-0555). In case your car, rented in London, runs into trouble, other major branches are found at such strategic locations throughout the country as Cambridge, Brighton, and Edinburgh (Scotland). When making a reservation, inquire if the unlimited-mileage rates of three days or more are still available. All Hertz cars are fitted with radios, and you can rent both manual and automatic transmission.

Godfrey Davis Europcar, Davis House, Wilton Road, S.W. 1 (tel. 828-7700), is well equipped for those who plan to cover part of their travels by train and part by car, having in excess of 70 offices at rail stations and more than 160 other locations, including 19 airports. They offer such bargains as a weekend cost-cutter when a small Ford rents for £32 ($62.40), plus VAT, from Friday at 5 p.m. to Monday at 9 a.m. with 500 miles free. Excess miles are 9p (18¢) a mile. Cost-cutters are from set locations only.

Driving Requirements

To drive a car in Britain, your passport and your own driver's license must be presented along with your deposit; no special British license is needed. The prudent driver will secure a copy of the *British Highway Code,* available from almost any stationer or news agent.

Although not mandatory, a membership in one of the two major auto clubs in England can be helpful: the **Automobile Association** and the **Royal Automobile Club.** The headquarters of the AA are at Fanum House, Basingstoke, Hampshire (tel. Basingstoke 20123); the RAC offices are at 83 Pall Mall, London, S.W.1 5HW (tel 01/839-7050). Membership in one of these clubs is usually handled by the agent from whom you rent your car. Upon joining, you'll be given a key to the many telephone boxes you see along the road, so that you can phone for help in an emergency.

BUSES IN ENGLAND: For the traveler who wants to see the country as even a train cannot reveal it, but who can't afford to rent a car, the old, reliable, and inexpensive (at least half the cost of railway fares) bus offers a fine form of transportation. While the trains do go everywhere, passing through towns and villages, they rarely bring you into contact with country life, and they almost never carry you across the high (main) streets of the villages, as the buses do. Moreover, distances between towns in England are usually short, so your chances of tiring are lessened. Every remote village is reachable by a bus.

The express motorcoach network covers the greater part of Britain. It links villages, towns, and cities with frequent schedules, convenient timetables, and efficient operation in all seasons. Most places off the main route can be easily reached by stopping and switching to a local bus. Fares are relatively cheap, making travel on the express motorcoach network economical.

The departure point from London for most of the bus lines is **Victoria Coach Station,** which is a block up from Victoria Railroad Station. You'll be well advised to have reservations for the express buses; the locals can usually be boarded on the spot.

Britexpress Travel Card

The great advantage of this card is that the five or ten days of travel it allows do not have to be consecutive. It means that a client can travel by coach between London and Edinburgh one way for £4 ($7.80) or £5 ($9.75), depending on the duration of the travelcard purchased, compared with £8.50 ($16.58), the normal single fare. As you will appreciate, this travelcard offers value for money.

The card allows you to travel by express coach between 60 cities and towns in Britain. You purchase the card unvalidated. If you don't use it, 80% of its cost will be refunded at the sales office where you bought it.

A five-day ticket costs £22 ($42.90) for adults, £17 ($33.15) for students 14 to 26 years of age. However, a ten-day card goes for £33 ($64.35) for adults, £28 ($54.60) for students. Children under 14 pay only half fare. Tariffs, incidentally, are estimated.

Green Line Buses

For trips to the immediate suburbs of London, and the towns nearby, you needn't go to Victoria Coach Station, however. Most of the spots are serviced by the Green Line coaches, which you can board throughout the city wherever you see green bus signs. To the south, these buses go as far as Reigate, Westerham, East Grinstead, and Tunbridge Wells, all 30 to 40 miles from the center of London. To the north, they go as far as Dunstable, Luton, Hitchin, or Bishops Stortford—all around 20 to 25 miles from Piccadilly Circus. To the west, they reach Guildford, High Wycombe, Windsor, and Aylesbury, within 20 to 40 miles from London. And to the east, they go to Brentwood, Grays, or Gravesend, approximately 15 to 26 miles from the center of London.

A Golden Rover Ticket costs £2.50 ($4.88) per person, purchased as you board your first bus. Pick up a map of the system to plan your journey. An **Outback Ticket**, off-peak day return, will save up to 40% on two tickets.

Wanderbus gives an unlimited-mileage ticket which costs adults about £3 ($5.85) per day and £2 ($3.90) for children, and can be used on some 20 national carriers (especially those around London), including Green Line, except on the Heathrow/Gatwick airport link.

Heathrow/Gatwick Green Line link, so useful for interlining passengers, costs £3 ($5.85) for a single ticket during the day. Children under 5 years of age travel free. However, from midnight to 5 a.m., the cost goes up to £6 ($11.70). All tickets can be purchased from the London Transport Office at the Heathrow Airport underground station.

For more precise information on the Green Line routes, fares, and schedules, write to the **London Country Bus Services Ltd.,** Lesbourne Road, Reigate, Surrey RH2 7LE (tel. Reigate 7442411).

Find a green-and-white sign mounted on a metal post, and stop the bus by signaling with your left hand.

Country Buses

The Country Bus Lines ring the heart of London. They never go into the center of London, although they hook up with the routes of the red buses and the Green Line coaches which do. You can get free maps of Country Buses from London Country Bus Services Ltd., Bell Street, Reigate, Surrey (see above). For more information about this form of touring, refer to "One-Day Trips from London," Chapter IV.

MOTORCYCLES: These are real money savers in this land of steep gas prices, if you don't mind getting drenched occasionally. **Rent-A-Scooter,** 7 Broadwell Parade, Broadhurst Gardens, N.W.6 (tel. 624-8491 and 328-4060; nearest underground, West Hampstead), has Hondas and gives free unlimited mileage, plus free safety helmets and free membership in the Royal Automobile Club which gives roadside assistance anywhere in the British Isles. These cycles go up to 200 miles per gallon. The one-seater Honda Moped rents for £3 ($5.85) per day or £15 ($29.25) per week, with a £30 ($58.50) deposit. A 400-cc motorcycle can cost from £12 ($23.40) per day or £60 ($117) per week, requiring a £50 ($97.50) deposit. A valid license endorsed for motorcycles is required for every vehicle except a Honda Moped, for which only a car license is necessary. Advance reservations are advised.

BIKES: This is the cheapest transportation apart from that you walk on. You can rent bikes by the day or by the week from a number of businesses, such as **Rent-a-Bike,** Kensington Student Centre, Kensington Church Street, W.8 (tel. 937-6089).

Another popular place to rent a bike is **Savile's Stores,** 97 Battersea Rise, Battersea, S.W.11 (tel. 228-4279), which has been renting out bikes for more than 70 years. Stan Savile's father started the company back in 1912! Prices are

£8 ($15.60) per week, which is about half the charge of most of its competitors. This firm is not only the cheapest but also the most reliable bike-rental company we can find. A deposit of £10 ($19.50) is required with a passport, £20 ($39) without. Padlocks are provided free, and insurance costs £1 ($1.95) for any one rental period. It's closed all day Wednesday.

DAY CRUISES ON THE THAMES: This is a venture for those who have visited London before, and want to spend a day—or even a week—cruising the Thames. The idea is to show overseas visitors a side of England they might not otherwise see.

The craft used are slipper-stern river day launches, designed especially for their elegance and grace. They are privately owned, and this is not an advertised hire service. The boats have awnings in case of rain.

Passengers are collected from their London hotel in the morning by car and driven to Runnymede where they embark. There they cruise downstream through Runnymede Fields past Magna Carta Island, where King John is reputed to have signed the famous document. Then they turn upstream and cruise through Windsor, under the shadow of the castle, Eton College, and Bray, to Maidenhead, so popular in Edwardian times with young sportsmen and their ladies.

Lunch is taken either as a picnic while moored in some quiet backwater or else in a riverside hotel or pub. At Maidenhead, Skindles Hotel grounds run down to the river, making it a popular stopping-off place.

Passengers then turn downstream again during the afternoon, disembarking at Windsor Town Quay within yards of the railway station. From there, the journey back to London is quick, cheap, and easy.

The cost for up to five people is £85 ($165.75). A picnic lunch is provided at an extra cost of £5 ($9.75) per person.

Extended cruises can be arranged to suit the time available and the passengers' inclination. The journey from Oxford to Hampton Court takes three or four days, but shorter or longer cruises can be planned. They are carefully arranged so that not more than four or five hours a day are spent traveling. There is time for everyone to go ashore and explore riverside towns and villages, shop for antiques, walk in the fields, or talk to the locals in pubs.

Overnight accommodation must be arranged in advance, as many of the riverside hotels are small, although they do provide accommodations with private facilities. All are personally selected and offer good food with a fine standard of accommodation. Baggage is transferred between hotels by taxi, as there is no room for cabin trunks in the dayboats.

Passengers are transferred from and to London at the start and finish of the cruise. They are expected to pay their own overnight expenses and all meals during the day.

These extended cruises cost £85 ($165.75) per day for up to six persons, excluding all meals and accommodations.

Advance booking is essential. Write to **Peter J. E. Barnes,** Willow Point, Friary Island, Wraysbury, near Staines, Middlesex TW19 5JR (tel. Wraysbury 2259).

SELF-DRIVE HOUSEBOATS AND HOTEL BOATS: At various places on the Thames, it's possible to rent a self-drive houseboat (the English call them river cruisers). Using this unique form of sightseeing—ideal for a family—you can visit Hampton Court, Windsor Castle, the city of Oxford, and stop off at attractive riverside towns, known for their antique shops. The Thames Valley abounds in restaurants and pubs. The facilities on these boats vary, but you can usually expect to find a gas cooker with an oven, hot and cold water, cooking utensils and cutlery, a refrigerator, blankets and pillows, and chemical toilets. The larger boats are also equipped with showers. Navigational aids, other than a map of the river, aren't needed.

Houseboats are also available on the Norfolk Broads and on much of the network of canals covering the country.

The bulk of the self-drive cruisers on the Thames, and on the canal network throughout the country, are available through **Boat Enquiries Ltd.,** 43 Botley Rd., Oxford (tel. Oxford 727288). Their free colorful brochure features self-drive boats on the Thames, the canals, the Severn, the Avon, and the Norfolk Broads. Boats vary in size from 2 to 12 persons and most are suitable for operation by novices. This agency is also one of the main sources of information on hotel boats on Britain's inland waterways. Here clients book single, twin, or double cabins aboard a floating hotel. Food and service are included. The maximum number of guests aboard such boats is 12, and passengers come from all over the world. This is an ideal way to overcome jet lag.

When you book, you can get a plan of the boat you're to have and a description of its facilities—many have showers, even TV if you wish, and all contain hot and cold running water, toilets, and central heating. In addition, the boatyard will often arrange (upon request) a supply of victuals for your breakfast and other meals. All are fully equipped with bed and table linen, dishcloths, cutlery, cooking utensils, and crockery.

The **Captain Webb,** a converted Dutch yacht-barge, is arguably the most comfortable hotel boat cruising the royal river, taking a week to travel from Windsor down to Greenwich. It was no accident that two royal residences, so often mentioned in history books, are the start and finish of the cruise.

Paul Waterman and his wife Gaynor, with their crew of three, have set out to show you "another Britain," combining history-by-the-river with today-by-the-river. Old-fashioned English pubs are visited; the new National Theatre or the Royal Opera House will entertain you; and a city walkabout (taxis provided for nonwalkers) will cover the alleyways and back streets so often missed in professional tours. Not all meals are served on board. Some you enjoy in inns where people like Boswell, Johnson, and Goldsmith used to meet, talk, and eat in the 18th century. Or perhaps you'll visit a 17th-century inn written about by Dickens.

The meals served on board are a gastronomic tour of the country— London pie, Glamorgan sausage, Devon lamb, Gloucester rolls—all skillfully prepared by Gaynor Waterman and her assistant. Wine is provided, and in the evening the separate tables in the dining saloon are converted into one long Captain's Table. Often entertainment is brought on board—perhaps the local Pearly King and Queen, real Cockney characters, maybe the Morris Dancers. The whole adds up to a relaxed and novel experience, remarkable for the ease with which you make friends and learn new things.

Cabins are well fitted and quiet, with a shower and toilet en suite. Beds are twins or doubles with duvets (blankets on request). All meals and wine, transport from your hotel at the start and finish of the voyage, entertainment, and any other transportation during the cruise is included in the cost of £640 ($1248) per person for the seven days, commencing on Sunday and ending on the following Saturday afternoon. Your hotel accommodation before and afterward is, of course, not included.

For bookings and information, write to **Another Britain,** Shepperton Marina, Felix Lane, Shepperton, Middlesex TW17 8NJ (tel. Walton-on-

TOURIST AREAS

Thames 48105). In the U.S.A. and Canada, simply call toll free at 800/286-0129, and the service will link you free with the office in England, five hours ahead of New York time.

PLANNING YOUR ITINERARY: If you plan to drive yourself around the countryside, you can save the cost in gas by having Peter Barnes prepare a route, including road numbers, the places you want to see, and suggestions for overnight accommodations and places to eat. His vast experience touring the country on behalf of the British Tourist Authority and leading his own tours enables him to produce a driveable itinerary.

Just send your check for $25 (U.S.) for the first seven days, plus another $3.75 per day thereafter, with a brief description of what you hope to see and do, and the itinerary will be mailed to you. Of course, it helps him to know what you've already seen and don't want to do, too. You must submit your request at least eight weeks before your departure from home.

Mr. Barnes also provides a London orientation tour—a nonstop trip by car around the places of major interest, as well as some others which visitors rarely see, along with personal commentary. The cost is $140 (U.S.) for the seven-hour tour, and as many as four passengers can go along for the ride. Lunch in a pub or restaurant is extra.

A day's guided tour to Oxford, Windsor, Hampton Court, Cambridge, Stratford-upon-Avon, or Salisbury and Stonehenge costs around $160 (U.S.) for up to four passengers.

For small parties, Mr. Barnes will plan an itinerary, book accommodations, and personally escort two or more day tours by private car or minibus throughout the island. You must make up your own group, however. The cost of six or seven passengers is around $300 (U.S.) per person per week for Mr. Barnes's services and transport. Accommodations, meals, and admission charges are extra, but for this figure you get 1400 miles of touring.

For those who need to stretch their golfing muscles, there are several courses around London, including Wentworth, Royal Ascot, and Moor Park, along with the less formal Datchet. Club rental and caddy can be arranged, and Peter Barnes will collect you from your London hotel, smooth your way at the clubhouse, and return you to London after half a day's exercise. The cost is £30 ($58.50), plus greens fees, and club and caddy rental. For the buff, complete tours of the courses of England and Scotland can be arranged.

For more information, write to **Peter Barnes**, Willow Point, Friary Island, Wraysbury, near Staines, Middlesex TW19 5JR (tel. Wraysbury 2259).

Part One

ENGLAND

LONDON: HOTELS FOR EVERY BUDGET

LONDON IS A HYBRID, a gathering place for people from the far corners of a once-great Empire. Both the country gentry and the blue-collar worker from the provinces visit London somewhat in the mood of going abroad.

The true Londoner, usually from the East End, is called a Cockney, the name for a person born within the sound of the Bow Bells, the chimes of a church in Cheapside. But the city is also the home of the well-bred English lady who has had to sell her family estate of 400 years and take meager lodgings in Earl's Court; of the expatriate Hollywood actress living in elegance in a Georgian town house; of the islander from Jamaica who comes seeking a new life and ends up collecting fares on one of London's red double-decker buses; of the young playwright from Liverpool whose art reflects the outlook of the working class.

Cosmopolitan or not. Europe's largest city is still like a great wheel, with Piccadilly Circus at the hub and dozens of communities branching out from it. Since London is such a conglomeration of sections—each having its own life

(hotels, restaurants, pubs)—the first-time visitor may be intimidated until he gets the hang of it. In this chapter, we'll concentrate on the so-called West End, although nobody has been able to come up with a satisfactory explanation as to what that entails. For the most part, a visitor will live and eat in the West End, except when he or she ventures into the old and historic part of London known as "The City," or goes on a tour to the Tower of London, or seeks lodgings in the remote villages such as Hampstead Heath.

The East End—the docks, the homes of the Cockney working class, the commercial and industrial districts—is rarely visited by tourists, except the more adventurous travelers bent on discovering the true London.

A LIVABLE METROPOLIS: The government has moved strongly against pollution. For example, residents can't burn anything but smokeless fuel. The legendary smog that once hung over the city is gone. When a trout was caught in the Thames, it made headlines in the world press. Nostalgia buffs miss the fogs, but eight million Londoners are getting 50% more winter sunshine than they used to.

In this day of energy crisis and inflation, London has many problems she's yet to tackle. But she has made inroads to create a better city in which to live.

She's wrinkled with age and was severely scarred by the war, but her presence is impressive. Tradition is maintained in the face of world change and upheaval. Mutton-chopped veterans of World War I still exist—hiding behind the Dickensian, dark-mahogany walls of their gentlemen's clubs, poring over the memoirs of long-forgotten generals.

But they are clichés. London today is filled with vital people, both young and old, pursuing their interests. Gambling clubs, discos, strip shows, and experimental theater make London an adventure all night long, as art galleries, museums, curiosity shops, and historic monuments fill the day.

THE HOTEL OUTLOOK: The hotel picture has changed drastically since the 19th century, when the Hotel Victoria had only four bathrooms for its 500 guests. London now offers accommodations to satisfy all purposes, tastes, and pocketbooks—ranging from the deluxe suites to army cots that rent to students in hostels.

One or two hotels sprout up every year, and others are on the drawing boards. For too long London hotels seemed lost in the days of Victoria (many still are). Now, increased pressure from overseas has brought about a discernible upgrading. Of course, in the name of progress, Edwardian architectural features have often given way to the worst and most impersonal of modern; and showers (even bedrooms) are placed in broom closets best left to serve their original functions. Nevertheless, a hotel revolution is in the air, as evidenced by low-budget town-house hotels now forced to install central heating.

Before launching into actual recommendations, I should issue a . . .

Warning: July and August are the vacation months in England, when nearly two-thirds of the population—every Jaguar maker, Liverpudlian dockworker, and Manchester textile worker—strikes out for a long-awaited holiday. Many head for the capital, further exacerbating what has become a crowded hotel situation. That doesn't mean you won't get a room if you should arrive at this peak time. There are so many hotels nowadays you can almost always find a room, but perhaps not in the price bracket you want.

When the holidays are over, the season in London begins, lasting through October. Even in September and October, as in June, low-budget hotels are tight—although nothing like they are in the peak summer months. It is recommended that you nail down a reservation before arriving in London. If you're a personal shopper who doesn't like to book a blind date, then by all means arrive early to begin your search for a room. Many of the West End hotels have vacancies, even in peak season, between 9 a.m. and 11 a.m., but by noon they are often packed solidly again with fresh arrivals.

In the sections to follow, we'll explore all the major districts of the English capital of interest to visitors. But first we'll devote our attention to the pressing problem of finding a room—be it the Oliver Messel Suite at "The Dorch" or a beautifully decorated, comfortable guest house—privately owned—near Kensington Gardens and Hyde Park.

All hotels, motels, inns, and guest houses in Britain, with four bedrooms or more (including self-catering accommodations), are required to display notices showing minimum and maximum overnight charges. The notice must be displayed in a prominent position in the reception area or at the entrance. The prices shown *must* include any service charge and *may* include VAT, and it must be made clear whether or not these items are included. If VAT is not included, then it must be shown separately. If meals are provided with the accommodation, this must be made clear, too. If prices are not standard for all rooms, then only the lowest and highest prices need be given.

1. Deluxe Hotels.

For the lucky few who can afford them, we'll lead off with a selection of luxury hotels, some of which are among the finest in the world.

Connaught Hotel, Carlos Place, W.1 (tel. 499-7070), perhaps more than any other hotel in London captures an elegant old English atmosphere. It ranks at the top with Claridge's for prestige and character. Its position is supreme, in the center of Mayfair, two short blocks from both Berkeley and Grosvenor Squares. The Connaught is a 19th-century architectural treasure house of a way of life fast disappearing. It's a brick structure, with a formal Rolls-Royce entrance, and its tall French windows overlook two curved, tree-lined streets.

As you enter, the staircase reminds you of an estate in the English countryside. Throughout the hotel you'll find excellent antiques, such as in the drawing room with its formal fireplace, soft lustrous draperies at high windows, and bowls of fresh flowers. The cost of staying here is the same year round: a single with bath from £50 ($97.50) to £65 ($126.75), a double with bath from £80 ($156) to £105 ($204.75), inclusive of VAT. All meals are extra, and the service charge is 15%. The bedrooms vary in size but all are furnished with well-selected antiques and tasteful reproductions. All of the rooms have well-equipped bathrooms and niceties galore. It is imperative to reserve well in advance.

The paneled bar-lounge is old-school-tie conservative; the fashionable (everybody from movie stars to bestselling novelists) dining room is also wood paneled, but it glitters with mirrors and crystal. The chef has perfected the English cuisine and a selection of French dishes. The b. ving and attentive waiters, the fresh flowers, set the proper mood. A semi-table d'hôte luncheon is offered for £20 ($39) to £25 ($48.75), depending on your choice of a main course.

At four o'clock at the Connaught guests head for the circular sun room just off the entry lounge, where the English ritual of afternoon tea is practiced at its best, with all the proper accoutrements.

The Connaught is constantly taking top awards for its restaurant.

The Dorchester, Park Lane, W.1. (tel 629-8888), faces Hyde Park on the fringe of Mayfair. Built and opened in 1931, it enjoys many of the benefits of early 20th-century design, with large rooms and bathrooms. A big refurbishing program of the public rooms on the first floor has recently been completed. Paris-based decorator Alberto Pinto was responsible for the bar, the Terrace Restaurant, and the promenade. The bar, decorated with mirrors and ceramics, is London's smart meeting place, particularly in the evening when guests relax to piano music. The new promenade, which extends from the lobby through the old lounge to the ballroom entrance, provides elegant and comfortable seating accommodation for afternoon tea or for cocktails before lunching or dining.

The new Terrace Restaurant, with a view across Hyde Park and discreet dining alcoves on one side, is a sophisticated, beautiful room open for dinner only, with dancing on Friday and Saturday. Bruncheon is served here on Sunday. The traditional Grill Room serves only the best of English dishes.

The Oliver Messel Suite is as popular as ever, and his penthouse and Pavilion Room for small parties have been refurbished exactly as he originally designed them. All the rooms and suites in the hotel are tastefully decorated in different colors and styles. Singles start at £65 ($126.75) and doubles at £85 ($165.75), including tax and service. The Dorchester offers numerous amenities, such as valet and maid service, hairdressing salons, a florist, in-house films, and radio and television in every room.

Ritz Hotel, Piccadilly, W.1 (tel. 493-8181), along with its namesake on the Place Vendome in Paris, made the word "Ritzy" synonymous in the English vernacular with luxury. Of the Ritz in the "other city," a French writer once said, "It isn't a hotel, it isn't even a big hotel, it's a monument." Much the same can be said of the London Ritz. For the incurable romanticist, it remains the leading choice in the capital; seemingly cut off from busy Piccadilly, especially if you get a room overlooking Green Park. The Ritz world is one of sparkling crystal, gleaming gilt, rich Italian marble, all dear to the heart of the Edwardian *école des beaux arts.*

After two years of renovation, Cunard Leisure has restored the lovely old place to much of its former elegance. Many of the old staff have remained, and the Ritz today is still the finest place in London to order afternoon tea in bone-china cups, accompanied by a selection of finger sandwiches, including cucumber and smoked salmon and especially made french pastries. The re-painting, cleaning, and recovering have been much in the original scheme, the way Cesar Ritz would have wanted it back in 1906—a predominantly pastel world of apricot, pink, dusty rose, and cream with gold-leafed molding, cupids and garlands, and potted palms.

Staying here costs from £58.65 ($114.37) in a single, from £83.95 ($163.70) to £101.20 ($197.34) in a twin, VAT and service included. Each bedroom has its own character, generally furnished in an old-fashioned manner, the champagne brocade with beige or pale blue seemingly preferred by every generation of English aristocracy. Everybody from Jacqueline Onassis to Mick Jagger is discreetly slipped in without fanfare. Victorian brass beds, cara-marble fireplaces, and crystal lighting fixtures are found in many of the bedrooms.

The public rooms are spacious and dramatic. The restaurant has been refurbished, its elegant Louis XVI decor of the 1900s restored to its former splendor. It lies at the far end of the gallery. On the way there you'll pass The Bar at the Ritz, famous for its exotic cocktails, and the Palm Court where tea is served. It's like a stage setting, an oval-shaped room dominated by a gold-leafed statue, *La Source,* adorning the fountain.

The Savoy, The Strand, W.C.2 (tel. 836-4343), is a landmark. Lucius Beebe maintained that its position has "ranked with the great hotels of all time." He went on to say that it "is perfumed with an aura lingering from the rich and regal England of Edward VII." The London institution looks to Richard D'Oyly Carte, the Victorian impresario who managed the first Gilbert and Sullivan operas, as its founding father. Through it have walked many of the famous personages of yesterday and today, everybody from the Divine Sarah, to acting partners Dame Ellen Terry and Sir Henry Irving, to rock stars.

Its position is choice, right on the Strand overlooking the Thames and adjacent to the new Covent Garden Market redevelopment. The lounges of the Savoy are comfortable and restrained, with intimate nooks. Bedrooms are skillfully planned and furnished with color-coordinated accessories; the furnishings are a blend of antiques, an eclectic combination of such pieces as gilt mirrors, Queen Anne chairs, and Victorian sofas. Singles cost from £85 ($165.75), doubles from £110 ($214.50), VAT and service charge included. Every chambermaid, every waiter, is groomed for attentive service; the Savoy has long been a training ground for employees desiring to learn top-level hotel service. The Savoy Grill and the Savoy Restaurant are world famous.

Churchill, Portman Square, W.1 (486-5800), is a 500-room luxury hotel in Mayfair. It's leased for 99 years to a subsidiary of the Loew's chain and Yankee know-how in design and taste are combined here with the best of traditional London hotel keeping. Interior designer Ellen Lehman McCluskey has dipped into England's great periods to give the hotel style and flair. At No. 10, a restaurant, the decor is Regency, the tented effect reminiscent of the field headquarters of the Iron Duke; all is glamorous, with much gilt and marble, columns and Egyptian-style paintings. You dine in a simpler fashion in the Greenery, with its skylit roof. Drinks are served in the swank Churchill Bar, where soft piano music plays in the background; afternoon tea is taken in the sunken lounge. The bedrooms tastefully blend traditional pieces with classic modern. Every room has individually controlled temperature, two phones (one in the bath), radio, TV, and bath. Singles rent for £54 ($105.30); doubles. £30 ($58.50); plus service and VAT.

Brown's, Dover street and Albermarle Street, W.1 (tel. 493-6020), is the London base of many of the gentry who desert their stuffy manors for "the season" in the capital, quietly booking into their "usual" room. They know that Brown's resists the brassy new and doesn't appeal to flashy tourists.

This traditional hotel was the creation of Lord Byron's manservant, James Brown, who wanted to go into business for himself. He accepted "fine gentlemen only." The location is appropriate—in Mayfair, just off Berkeley Square. The rates for a single room with private bath are £59 ($115.05) and from £75 ($146.25) for a twin-bedded room with a bath. A suite, including a sitting room, twin-bedded room, a single, and a private bath, is from £130 ($253.50). Family rooms consisting of two rooms and one private bath, for three persons, go from £98 ($191.10). Two rooms with one private bath to accommodate four persons costs from £120 ($234).

The bedrooms vary considerably, and are a tangible record of the past history of England. Even the wash basins are semiantiques. The rooms have restrained taste, with good soft beds and telephones. The lounges on the street floor are inviting and cozy. There's a paneled lounge for the drinking of "spirits," another for afternoon tea.

The dining room has a quiet dignity and unmatched service. À la carte meals are served, plus a set luncheon menu at £13.50 ($26.33).

HOTELS IN THREE PRICE RANGES

After this look at life at the top, we'll now discuss our remaining recommendations, the bulk of those in this guide. These establishments are divided into districts, such as Mayfair, Belgravia, Bloomsbury. All of the hotels have one thing in common: they are less expensive than the deluxe, but even they reveal wide price differences. Therefore, we've broken them down into categories, beginning with the upper bracket, with first-class amenities. The medium-priced range follows with a listing of the best of London's moderately priced hotels with or without private baths. In this category a full English breakfast is usually (but not always) included in the rates quoted. Finally, for those who want to keep travel costs bone-trimmed, we'll list budget-range choices wherever possible. Establishments in this category are most often converted town houses with only a handful of rooms with private baths, if any.

First-class hotels in London have generally abandoned the time-honored English tradition of serving you a full English breakfast (bacon and eggs) for the price of the room. The hotels in the medium-priced range are a toss-up—the majority still maintain this custom, although many establishments rely on skimpy continental fare instead of the works.

Most budget hotels in London, with many exceptions, still provide a full English breakfast for the price of the room. Because the policy of charging extra for breakfast is so erratic, always inqure before checking in.

Further, nearly all upper and middle-bracket hotels, and even some budget accommodations, charge a service fee ranging from 10% to 15%. Again, inquire about all such hidden extras *before* checking in so as to avoid a surprise when the bill's presented.

2. St. James's

This section, the beginning of Royal London, starts at Piccadilly Circus and moves southwest. It's frightfully convenient, as the English say, enclosing a number of important locations such as American Express on Haymarket, many of the leading stores (Burberry's of raincoat wear), and Buckingham Palace (see Royal London in Chapter IV).

It basks in its associations with royalty—it was the "merrie monarch" himself, Charles II, the famous skirt chaser (Nell Gwynne the favorite), who founded St. James's Park. And it was in St. James's Palace that his father, Charles I spent his last troubled night, awaiting his beheading the following morning. At one time the palace was a hunting lodge of Henry VIII and his wife of the moment, Anne Boleyn.

For the traditionalist in particular, living in the heart of aristocratic London has many advantages—none more important than its well-run and discriminating hotels themselves. Their number is limited, but their addresses are most fashionable, just as they were in the society heyday of the 18th century.

THE UPPER BRACKET: Cavendish Hotel, Jermyn Street, S.W.1 (tel. 930-2111), has an old name, but a new body with a lively spirit. It was built in 1966 on the site of the old Cavendish, the subject of numerous stories about the days of Edward VII, when it was thronged with theatrical and royal personages. The hotel grew to fame under its colorful proprietor Rosa Lewis, known as "The Duchess of Jermyn Street" in a biography written about her. In the St. James's district ("Royal London"), just off Piccadilly and a five-minute walk from Pall Mall, this former landmark has been transformed into an ultra-contemporary

WESTMINSTER, WHITE HALL, ST. JAMES'S & VICTORIA

hotel. Its first two floors are devoted to shops, lounges, restaurants, bars, and the 250-bedroom tower is set back, rising above it. Tube: Piccadilly Circus.

The rooms are bright and airy, with wall-to-wall curtains, a sitting area, and TV. Double-thickness windows keep out traffic noises. All rooms have private baths. A single rents for £55 ($107.25), doubles from £73 ($142.35).

The second-floor lounge and drinking bar are approached by a curious "floating staircase." The Sub Rosa bar-lounge, named in honor of the former proprietor, captures some of the flavor of the Edwardian era with brass lamps and black tufted banquettes. The Cavendish Restaurant is suitable for an after-theater supper (special menu from 11:30 p.m. to 7 a.m.) and also offers an alternative menu in the style of *cuisine minceur* (cooking without fats) during the lunch and dinner service.

The **Goring Hotel,** Beeston Place, Grosvenor Gardens, S.W.1 (tel. 834-8211), achieves the seemingly impossible—it provides the charm of traditional, dignified English living, but at the same time offers all modern comforts. Hotelier Goring built the establishment in 1910 with "revolutionary ideas"— that is, that every room should have a private bath, foyer, and central heating. His grandson, George Goring, continues to provide top service.

The 100 rooms (here they are called apartments) rent for £45 ($87.75) in a single, £58 ($113.10) in a double or twin. Rates include color TV, service, and VAT. The most practical way of lodging at the Goring is to take the half-board rate (breakfast and dinner) for £55 ($107.25) per person. You can have a three-course table d'hôte luncheon for £8 ($15.60) and dinner from £9.50 ($18.53). The menu includes such selections as fine duckling pâté, calf's liver with bacon and onions, venison, and roast boned best end of lamb. In the paneled drawing room, afternoon teas are served by a butler from a trolley. Many prefer to enjoy this ritual in the adjacent sunroom, with its view of the rear gardens and a new bar situated by the window. The Goring's situation is choice—close to Victoria Station, a ten-minute walk to Westminster Abbey and the Houses of Parliament. Tube: Victoria Station.

Stafford Hotel, 16 St. James's Pl., S.W.1 (tel. 493-0111), is left over from Edwardian days, hidden away from the pulse beat of Piccadilly, near Green Park. You'll need either a compass, divining rod, or the aid of an oldtime hack driver to locate it. The hotel can be entered via St. James's Place or else through the more colorful Blue Ball Yard (but only when the hotel's cocktail bar is open). Many of the original architectural details remain, although it has been brought up to date with contemporary amenities. All the bedrooms—described by an English friend as "comfy and homey"—have private bathrooms. A single rents for £61 ($118.95), a double for £77 ($150.15) to £86 ($167.70), plus VAT and service. Breakfast is also extra. A restaurant serving both lunch and dinner is on the premises. The Stafford is often used by those who need a place near court, as well as the embassy and political life of London. Tube: Piccadilly Circus.

Duke's Hotel, 35 St. James's Pl., S.W.1 (tel 491-4840), is a small, turn-of-the-century hotel in the St. James's district, only a five-minute walk from Piccadilly, a hundred feet or so from Green Park (which abuts Buckingham Palace) and near St. James's Palace. A bit of leftover Victorian architecture, it sits on a postage stamp square lit by gas lamps and adorned with flowers. It's all pure Regency, and frequented mainly by gentry who avoid the large impersonal hotels and gravitate to an establishment where the staff knows their quirks ("Welcome back, Lady Cooper-Plympton, will you want your morning tea at the usual time?").

There is central heating throughout, every bedroom has its own private bath and direct-dial telephone, and each suite is named after a duke. A single rents for £51 ($99.45), a double or twin for £80 ($156), inclusive of service and VAT. A 25% discount is offered on all accommodations on Friday and Saturday night. Light refreshments are available in a charming little bar or in the sitting room at all times. Main meals are served in the St. James's Room restaurant from 12:30 to 2:30 p.m. and from 6:30 to 10:30 p.m. Room service functions 24 hours a day. Tube: Piccadilly Circus.

Royal Westminster, Buckingham Palace Road, S.W.1 (tel. 834-1821), has one of the most fashionable addresses in London, within minutes of Buckingham Palace (in fact, this hotel is passed during the Changing of the Guard). A shining concrete and glass structure, the Royal Westminster charges from £55 ($107.25) in a double or twin, £45 ($87.75) in a single. Rates are inclusive of service charge and VAT, although breakfast is extra. Each bedroom is spacious, with many fine touches; you get private baths, radio and TV, and there's a free ice machine on every floor. Thatcher's, the Royal Westminster's à la carte restaurant, is designed on a charming English rustic theme and offers an English and international menu appealing to business persons and visitors alike. The attractive cocktail bar, conveniently situated next to Thatcher's Restaurant, is ideal for a relaxing prelunch or dinner drink. Light refreshments and drinks are also served to residents in the comfortable, elegant lounge-bar, adjacent to the reception. The notable feature of the hotel is its collection of 18 "royal suites," each portraying a different theme—you go from Braganza and Botticelli to Victoria and Gladstone to Sayonara to Du Barry. Tube: Victoria Station.

THE MEDIUM-PRICED RANGE: Hamilton House, 62 Warwick Way, S.W.1 (tel. 821-7113), is composed of early Victorian houses, joined and recently modernized. James Burns, the owner, was born in Pimlico, a few yards from the hotel. Since buying the property with his Danish wife, who was a TWA stewardess, he has constantly improved the facilities. There are now 45 rooms of which 30 have private baths and toilets, renting for £32 ($62.40) per night, breakfast and tax included. All rooms have telephone, radio, and TV. There is a residents' bar on the premises, and a fine restaurant for 60 people. Open to the public, it serves traditional English dishes and American fast foods. American guests are particularly welcome. Tube: Piccadilly Circus.

3. Piccadilly Circus

If you want to be in the middle of the West End, right at Piccadilly Circus and Leicester Square, then the following will appeal to you. Most of London's theaters, Soho, Regent Street, and many famous restaurants and pubs will be at your doorstep.

THE MEDIUM-PRICED RANGE: Regent Palace Hotel, Piccadilly Circus (tel. 734-7000), is one of the largest hotels in Europe. It's a mammoth establishment, some 1068 rooms, all with hot and cold running water (i.e., without private baths) and color TV. There is no more centrally located hotel in London—in fact, some of its rooms overlook the Eros statue on Piccadilly Circus. It charges £22.50 ($43.88) for a single, £34 ($66.30) for a double. Prices include a continental breakfast. Best of all, there is plenty of well-brewed coffee, an item which makes the Palace popular with North Americans. Facilities include a booking office for theaters and concerts, pressing, cleaning, and laundry service, shops for gifts, clothing, jewelry, and confectionery, and a hairdressing salon. Within the building is a Grill Room and an all-you-can-eat

Carvery. A third restaurant, Garry's Coffee Shop, is open until 1:30 a.m. Tube: Piccadilly Circus.

4. The Strand and Covent Garden

Beginning at Trafalgar Square, the Strand runs east into Fleet Street. Londoners used to be able to walk along the Strand and see the Thames, but the river has receded. In the 17th century, the elegant and wealthy built their homes on the Strand, their gardens stretching to the Thames. But today it's changing to something less grand—flanked as it is with theaters, shops, hotels, and such landmarks as Somerset House.

Peaceful lanes jut off from the Strand, leading to the Victoria Embankment Gardens along the river. Opposite the gardens is Cleopatra's Needle, an Egyptian obelisk, London's oldest (and dullest) monument. You might want to stroll along the river if weather permits. You may also want to book a hotel along the Strand.

THE UPPER BRACKET: The **Waldorf Hotel,** Aldwych, W.C.2 (tel. 836-2400), is our choice for travelers on a theater binge. It's not only surrounded by some of the best theaters in the West End, but lies within a quick walk of many of the most visited sights—the Old Curiosity Shop of Dickens fame (just around the corner), the National Gallery, Horse Guards Parade, Trafalgar Square, and Piccadilly. Buses to the Tower of London stop outside the hotel, and tube stations are only a few minutes away.

The Waldorf, with its now-rare Edwardian colonnade, retains the elegance of yesteryear. The 310 bedrooms, from suites to singles, are well furnished. The price of a single is £47 ($91.65); a double or twin is £58 ($113.10). All have private bathrooms, and VAT is included. Tube: Aldwych.

The **Drury Lane Hotel,** 10 Drury Lane, High Holborn, W.C.2 (tel. 836-6666), a Grand Metropolitan hotel, is a concrete and glass structure in the heart of theaterland. Once you're inside its confines, however, the atmosphere is relaxed and subdued, suggesting neither a chain hotel nor one of such severe modernity as the facade might indicate. Built with terraced gardens and its own plaza, the hotel is a self-contained entity. All of its 128 spacious bedrooms have good views and are furnished in a subtle, harmonious fashion, with many luxurious touches, such as individually controlled central heating, color TVs, even 24-hour room service. Singles range from £40 ($78), doubles from £56 ($109.20). Tariffs include VAT and service. All the bedrooms have fully tiled baths kept sparkling clean. The decor in the public rooms successfully uses green and beige, and plants evoke a garden atmosphere. Maudie's Restaurant is named after Sir Osbert Lancaster's famous arbiter-of-chic cartoon character Maudie Littlehampton, and offers a French cuisine. Maudie's Bar makes a good posttheater rendevous. Tube: High Holborn.

Strand Palace Hotel, The Strand, W.C.2 (tel. 836-8080), is ideally situated for those who want to be in the theater district, near points such as Trafalgar Square, yet within a block of the Thames Embankment. Rooms have baths, wall-to-wall draperies, innerspring mattresses, comfortable furnishings. Sunbright colors contrast vividly with chalk-white walls. Behind the scenes is a staff of more than 400 standing by to provide personalized service. Rates are £33 ($64.35) in a single, £42 ($81.90) in a double or twin, and £48 ($93.60) in a triple. VAT and service are included, and all rooms have private baths or showers.

One of the assets of the Strand Palace is its restaurants, including a Carvery where every day but Sunday you can gorge yourself on England's finest roasts at £7.50 ($14.63) per person. There's also the 369 Strand, a coffeeshop which attracts show people. Favored also is the intimate Mask Bar, with a collection of Saul Steinberg cartoons decorating the wall. To complete the dining possibilities, there is La Pizzerie, where you can select from an à la carte menu. Tube: The Strand.

5. Westminster

This section has been the seat of British government since the days of Edward the Confessor. Dominated by the Houses of Parliament and Westminster Abbey, Parliament Square symbolizes the soul of England. Westminster is a big name to describe a large borough of England, including Whitehall, headquarters of many government offices. A good part of the sprawling area in and around Victoria Station with its many budget hotels is also a part of Westminster. Known as the gateway to the continent, Victoria Station is where you get boat trains to Dover and Folkestone for that trip across the Channel. The area also has other advantages: the Green Line Coach Station and the Victoria Coach Station are just five minutes from Victoria. From the bus stations, you can board many a Green Line coach for the suburbs. And an inexpensive bus tour of London departs from a point on Buckingham Palace Road, just behind Victoria Station. From Grosvenor Gardens, you can get a bus direct to Heathrow Airport, and from Victoria Station, trains to Gatwick Airport.

THE MEDIUM-PRICED RANGE: Dolphin Square, Dolphin Square, S.W.1 (tel. 834-3800), is what dollarwise is all about. One of the largest blocks of flats (apartments) in all of Europe, it offers one of the best values in the city. The location, if not prestigious, is interesting—set back from Thames-bordering Grosvenor Road, between Chelsea and the Tate Gallery. Its past closed-door policy has changed to admit transient guests, many of whom want to create an instant home in London. To do so, you can book, say, a one-room apartment with a double bed for £45 ($87.75) nightly. A two-room apartment with twin beds goes for £50 ($97.50). Three- and four-room apartments are available also. You get handsome reductions with minimum stays of one week, even better bargains if you stay a month. Besides the fully equipped and furnished apartments, all of which have color TV, guest rooms, including early-morning tea and biscuits, are also rented at £12.50 ($24.38) in a single, £20 ($39) in a double, plus VAT. Dolphin Square was created to provide luxury living and has a vast inner courtyard and lots of gardens and lawns. The reception lounge is impressive, and a restaurant overlooking the heated swimming pool serves meals from breakfast until after the theater is out. Luxurious sauna baths for both men and women are available. For those who want to go English all the way, eight squash courts beckon. It's best reached by taxi.

St. Ermin's Hotel, Caxton Street, S.W.1 (tel. 222-7888), is the supreme choice for those who love opulent Victoriana. The palatial hotel, with a formal courtyard entry, was created for distinguished visitors from the world over—sultans, maharajahs, etc.—who had business to transact with the government. Modernization hasn't destroyed the splendor, certainly not in public rooms such as the front reception lounge, with its curving balcony and marble staircase.

The bedrooms vary considerably in size—some of them cavernous—and degree of modernization (many of the restyled singles and doubles have sleek, Nordic-inspired furnishings, with desks, television, bedside lights, and telephones). A single with bath goes for £37 ($72.15). You pay £48 ($93.60) in a double or twin, also with bath. Rates include a continental breakfast, VAT, and service. Installations of more recent vintage include the Caxton Bar and Caxton Grill, the latter a contemporary setting for such traditional English fare as steak and chops, steak-and-kidney pie, Scottish salmon, and Welsh lamb.

The hotel is opposite New Scotland Yard, halfway between Victoria Station and Big Ben. Tube: St. James's Park.

St. James Hotel, Buckingham Gate, S.W.1 (tel. 834-2360), is another great old Victorian hotel built in the heart of diplomatic London, only a few minutes' walk from 10 Downing Street, Whitehall, and the Houses of Parliament. Like St. Ermin's, the St. James clings to the glory of the past. A world unto itself, it is an ornate group of brick buildings with a courtyard. Its towers make for spacious sunny bedrooms.

The bedrooms—520 in all—have been streamlined and contain built-in headboards, private baths, and radios. The rooms vary in size and degree of modernization (indicate your needs when reserving). All the following rates include service, VAT, and continental breakfast. A bathless single goes for £18 ($35.10), £27 ($52.65) with a bath or shower. With a bath or shower a double or twin rents for £33 ($64.35). The American Diner is open till 11:30 p.m. You can order succulent roasts at the Baron Carver until 10 p.m., beginning at £6.50 ($12.68), including appetizer and dessert. Tube: St. James's Park.

Ebury Court, 26 Ebury St., S.W.1 (tel. 730-8147), was created out of a group of small town houses. You notice the country-house flavor right away; it's brightly painted (turquoise and white), with railings to match and flower-filled window boxes. The little reception rooms are informal and decorated with flowery chintz and quite good antiques. Best of all, it has a cordial and informal staff. The hotel is close to the airline terminals. Terms quoted include an English breakfast and VAT. The rate in a single ranges from £24 ($46.80) to £26 ($50.70), from £35 ($68.25) in a bathless twin-bedded room or a double. Doubles with private bathrooms cost from £44 ($85.80). Each of the rooms has hot and cold running water, as well as a telephone and radio. An asset is the night porter, handy for late arrivals. In the small restaurant, you can order either a lunch or dinner.

The A1 bus which goes to Heathrow every 20 minutes leaves from Grosvenor Gardens, which are approximately 1½ minutes from Ebury Court. Porters from the hotel will help visitors with their luggage on a trolley if required. Guests can apply for temporary membership in the hotel club which allows them access to the bar. Tube: Victoria Station.

6. Chelsea

This stylish district stretches along the Thames, south of Hyde Park, Brompton, and South Kensington. Beginning at Sloane Square, it runs westward toward the periphery of Earl's Court and Brompton. Its spinal cord: King's Road, center for boutique hopping. The little streets and squares on either side of King's Road have hundreds of tiny cottages used formerly by the toiling underprivileged of the 18th and 19th centuries (although Carlyle lived there—see "Homes of Famous Writers and Artists" in Chapter IV). Now, except for Belgravia and Mayfair, Chelsea couldn't be more chic. To become a part of the scene, you can, like Carlyle, "take up abode" in one of the following recommendations.

THE UPPER AND MEDIUM-PRICED RANGE: 11 Cadogan Gardens, Sloane Square, S.W.3 (tel. 730-3426), is a Victorian house—or four—converted into comfortable service apartments, single rooms, doubles, and suites. It is well furnished and elegant. Bed and an English breakfast, served in the rooms with morning papers of the guest's choice, costs £37 ($72.15) to £45 ($87.75) in a single, £55 ($107.25) in a double. Suites go for £75 ($146.25) for two. There is no license for liquor, but the porters will gladly send out for a bottle. TV can be arranged in your room at a small extra cost. Laundry and dry cleaning as well as shoe cleaning can be taken care of. Theater tickets, car rentals, and sightseeing excursions are in the hands of the porters. Charles Harbord is the owner, and his managers, Alan Eyers and Mark A. Fresson, will look after you.

Fenja Hotel, 69 Cadogan Gardens, Sloane Square, S.W.3 (tel. 589-1183), is an unusually interesting town house which has maintained much of its individualistic architecture. Some modern amenities have been slipped in, including a tiny elevator between a pair of marble pillars in the entry. A true English way of living is maintained here, and the atmosphere is quiet (no children), the clientele discriminating. Many embassy personnel stay here, along with owners of country manors who like to spend a season in London. Mr. and Mrs. Kaulback charge from £23 ($44.85) to £27 ($52.65) in a single, from £32 ($62.40) in a double, the more expensive tariffs for those rooms with private baths. The rates include VAT, service, and a continental breakfast. The rooms are cheerily furnished, and each contains a radio or TV (if requested), plus a telephone and central heating. Tube: Sloane Square.

Sloane Hall, 6 Sloane Gardens, S.W.1 (tel. 730-9206), is an authentic 1888 Victorian mansion converted by Derek R. Jones to accommodate visitors, especially families. Some rooms have private baths and all have hot and cold running water. A few rooms accommodate as many as five persons in two doubles and one single. The chambers are pleasantly furnished, renting for £13 ($25.35) in a single. Doubles without bath go for £19 ($37.05) to £21 ($40.95), increasing to £23 ($44.85) with bath. Rates include breakfast and VAT. Breakfast is provided in a paneled room which doubles as a lounge with color TV. Courtesy tea and coffee are available at all times in all bedrooms.

Willett Hotel, 32 Sloane Gardens, S.W.1 (tel. 730-0634), opening onto the gardens, is a 19th-century town house with many architectural curiosities, including a Dutch-style roof and varying styles of bay windows. It's an intimate hotel with many luxurious and stylish features. Each of the pleasantly decorated bedrooms has a radio, TV, dressing table, and facilities for making coffee or tea. Best of all is the full English breakfast served in a club-style room with black leather chairs. Most of the accommodations contain private baths. Including breakfast, singles rent for £20 ($39); doubles and twins, £24 ($46.80) to £30 ($58.50). An extra single bed in a family room costs an additional £8 ($15.60). Tube: Sloane Square.

THE BUDGET RANGE: Culford Hall, 7 Culford Gardens, off Sloane Square, S.W.3 (tel 581-2211), is a small, well-run hotel in one of the most fashionable parts of Chelsea. It's quiet, comfortable, and attractively furnished with contemporary pieces. Singles without bath cost from £12 ($23.40) nightly, and bathless doubles go from £18 ($35.10). However, the double rate in a unit with private bath and TV begins at £21 ($40.95). Breakfast, at no extra charge, is served in the rooms (which contain phones and radios). However, VAT is added. The rooms have won the approval of many a visiting American, who cited the shaving outlets, the intercom, the good beds, central heating, and cleanliness. The hotel attracts people connected with embassies, universities, airlines, and foreign office personnel. The atmosphere is friendly. A short walk from the hotel will take you to some of the best restaurants along King's Road.

7. Belgravia and Knightsbridge

Belgravia, south of Hyde Park, is the so-called aristocratic quarter of London, challenging Mayfair for grandness. It reigned in glory along with Queen Victoria, but today's aristocrats are likely to be the top echelon in foreign embassies, along with a rising new money class of actors and models.

Belgravia is near Buckingham Palace Gardens and Brompton Road. Its center is Belgrave Square, one of the more attractive plazas in London. A few town houses once occupied by eminent Edwardians have been discreetly turned into moderately priced hotels (others were built specifically for that purpose). For those who prefer a residential address, Belgravia is choice real estate.

Adjoining Belgravia is Knightsbridge, another top residential and shopping district of London. Just south of Hyde Park, Knightsbridge is close in character to Belgravia, although much of this section to the west of Sloane Street, is older—dating back in architecture and layout to the 18th century. Several of the major department stores, such as Harrods, are here (take the Piccadilly subway line to Knightsbridge). Since Knightsbridge is not principally a hotel district, our recommendations are limited.

THE UPPER AND MEDIUM-PRICED RANGE: The **London Belgravia Hotel**, 20 Chesham Pl., S.W.1 (tel. 235-6040), is a 1971 hotel entry, in Belgravia, home of most of London's diplomatic corps. Eleven stories, nearly all glass, rise from its foundation, and provide airy, well-lit bedrooms. Each room contains color TV, a bath with a shower-tub combination, and air conditioning. The rooms are luxuriously comtemporary. You even get a telephone in your tiled bath, 24-hour room service, and a helpful concierge. A single costs £52 ($101.40), and a double or twin is £69 ($134.55), including VAT and service. Breakfast is extra. On the premises is the Terrace Restaurant opening from Pont Street. The decor is cool, and the menus both practical and inexpensive. VAT is included in the prices. At lunchtime, three fixed-price meals and a superb buffet are offered. The specialty is rib of beef on the trolley. Tube: Sloane Square.

Wilbraham Hotel, Wilbraham Place, off Sloane Street, S.W.1 (tel. 730-8296), is as dyed-in-the-wool British as you can get. On this quiet little street, just a few hundred yards from busy Sloane Square, three Victorian town houses have been joined together as one hotel. The hotel has two intimate sitting rooms and a reception hall. There are 57 rooms in all, plus 34 baths. Depending on the plumbing, singles range from £18 ($35.10) to £21 ($40.95); doubles, £26 ($50.70), the latter a deluxe chamber. VAT is added, and breakfast is also extra. The Wilbraham owns a choice little restaurant, Le Beurre Fondu, serving both luncheons and dinners.

The **Cadogan Hotel,** Sloane Street, S.W.1 (tel. 235-7141), is a colorful Edwardian hotel, one of the few older hotels in London whose modernization has not been destructive. Untouched is its fussy belle époque facade, corner towers, and mansard roof. Its interior architecture, designed by the Adam brothers, is also untouched, although brightened by red velvet and gilt. The furnishings are traditional, as seen in the lounge, with its gold, mirrored, and colored walls and ceilings. The lounge leads to the Lillie Langtry Bar, which was once part of the London home of "Jersey Lily," mistress of Edward VII. The bedrooms have been modernized and provide plenty of comfort. Singles with bath start at £48 ($93.60), doubles and twins at £58 ($113.10), including service. Breakfast is extra. Oscar Wilde was arrested in one of the suites, by the way, a fact recorded in a poem by John Betjeman. Tube: Sloane Square.

Capital Hotel, Basil Street, Knightsbridge, S.W.3 (tel. 589-5171), is one of the most personalized hotels in the West End. Small and modern, it's a stone's throw from Harrods. The proud owner, David Levin, sat down and listed all the niceties he could offer guests. For example, it's one of the few hotels anywhere that will provide an emergency pack for the stranded traveler —robe, toothbrush, razor. From the modest lobby, an elevator will take guests to each floor, each corridor and staircase being treated as an art gallery, with original oil paintings. In all, 60 rooms are offered, the singles having more space than the doubles. The furniture is handmade, with color-coordinated fabrics. Singles rent for £55 ($107.25). Doubles go for £60 ($117) to £70 ($136.50). The Capital Restaurant is among the finest in London, offering such exquisitely prepared main dishes as filet de canard (duckling) aux choux rouges and carré d'agneau persillé. Fresh vegetables are used, and a sachertorte is often the featured dessert. Tube: Knightsbridge.

Basil Hotel, Basil Street, Knightsbridge, S.W.3 (tel. 581-3311), has long been a favorite little hotel of discerning British, who make an annual pilgrimage to London to shop at Harrods and perhaps attend the Chelsea Flower Show. This Edwardian charmer, totally unmarred by pseudo-modernization, is managed by Stephen Korany, who prefers guests who can appreciate his highly individualistic hotel. The open mahogany staircase seems ideal as a setting for the entrance line of a drawing room play: "You're just in time for tea, Braddie." There are several spacious and comfortable lounges, appropriately furnished with 18th- and 19th-century decorative accessories. Off the many rambling corridors are smaller sitting rooms.

The pleasantly furnished bedrooms are priced according to size and location. Single rooms range from £28 ($54.60) to £42 ($81.90), the latter with private baths. Doubles without bath go for £45 ($87.75), increasing to £58 ($113.10) with bath. The dining room serves a three-course lunch for about £7 ($13.65), and dinner is around the same price. Candlelight and piano music recreate the atmosphere of a bygone era. The Upstairs Restaurant is suitable for lighter meals and snacks, and the Downstairs Wine Bar serves a wide selection of wines and inexpensive food. Tube: Knightsbridge.

The Diplomat, 2 Chesham St., off Belgrave Square, S.W.1 (tel. 235-1544), provides an opportunity to stay in the converted town house of a lord. As such, it attracts many high-ranking military officers, diplomats (in honor of its name-sake), and professional persons. Many of the original architectural features have been retained. The entrance is marble floored, and the circular staircase is illuminated by a frieze-covered dome. All rooms have appropriately tasteful furnishings as well as private baths, phones, color televisions, and radios. Singles range from £19 ($37.05) and doubles start at £28 ($54.60). VAT is added, and breakfast at no extra charge is served in the rooms. Tube: Sloane Square.

Knightsbridge Hotel, 10 Beaufort Gardens, S.W.3 (tel. 589-9271), sand-wiched between the restaurants and fashionable boutiques of Beauchamp Place and Harrods, still retains the feeling of a traditional British hotel. On a tree-lined square that is peaceful and tranquil, and free from traffic, it has a subdued Victorian charm. The place is small—only 18 bedrooms—and personally run by the manager, Robert A. Novella. Units have phones, radios, and central heating, and there's a lounge with a color "telly" and a bar on the premises. Most expensive are rooms with private baths, costing £18.70 ($36.47) in a single, from £32 ($62.40) in a twin. The best for the budget are the bathless specials—from £14.50 ($28.28) in a single and from £20 ($39) in a twin. A family room with shower for three guests rents for about £39 ($76.05) per night. All tariffs include a continental breakfast and VAT, although a 12% service charge is added. Tube: Knightsbridge.

THE BUDGET RANGE: Bucks Hotel, 33 Beaufort Gardens, S.W.3 (tel. 584-5252), is the product of architectural evolution. Originally converted from two Georgian houses, the hotel has recently been completely renovated right down to the entrance doors. Each of the 34 rooms has either a private bath or shower. Visitors can relax in the attractive bar, the comfortable lounge, or the small, pleasant garden. The rooms are cozy, not large, but well furnished. Carpeting and central heating are used throughout. The B&B rate begins at £26 ($50.70) in a single, rising to £37 ($72.15) in a double, including a full English breakfast, VAT, and service. Tube: Knightsbridge.

Claverley House Hotel, 13–14 Beaufort Gardens, Knightsbridge, S.W.3 (tel. 589-8541), offers fair value for the dollar, considering its chic location. Many guests are regulars, including two millionaires who drop in occasionally. The hotel has been extensively renovated and decorated. Fifteen of its 31 rooms have private baths, although none contains a toilet. The cost of a room with bath or shower is from £12.50 ($24.38) to £13.50 ($26.33) for a single, from £18.50 ($36.08) to £20.50 ($39.98) for a double- or twin-bedded room, includ-ing VAT, service, and an English breakfast. Tube: Knightsbridge.

8. Kensington, South Kensington, and Earl's Court

Although the Royal Borough draws its greatest number of visitors from shoppers (Kensington High Street), it also attracts with a number of fine, medium-priced hotels, for the most part on Kensington Gardens. In Victoria's day, the rows of houses along Kensington Palace Gardens were inhabited by millionaires (although Thackeray also lived there). Today the houses are oc-cupied largely by ambassadors.

South Kensington, south of Kensington Gardens and Hyde Park, is essen-tially a residential area, not as elegant as that bordering Belgravia and

Knightsbridge. However, the section is rich in museums, and it has a number of colleges.

Staying in South Kensington has much to recommend it. Besides its proximity to the Kensington museums, such as the Victoria and Albert, the area encompasses Albert Hall, and is within walking distance of Kensington Gardens and Harrods department store. At the South Kensington station, you can catch trains for Kew Gardens and the Thames River town of Richmond.

For the most part, the hotels in this area recall yesterday more than today, although contemporary furnishings and modern amenities are grudgingly creeping in. It's an ideal spot for the traditionalist.

Earl's Court, below Kensington and bordering the western half of Chelsea, is one of the most popular middle-class hotel and rooming-house districts. A 15-minute subway ride from Earl's Court station will take you into the heart of Piccadilly, via either the District of Picadilly Lines. The bus from Grosvenor Gardens to Heathrow Airport stops on Cromwell Road, outside the Penta Hotel.

THE UPPER BRACKET: Kensington Palace Hotel, De Vere Gardens, W.8 (tel. 937-8121), although built in 1951, now rates as one of London's "newest," having been comprehensively refurbished and remodeled. It is ideally situated just opposite Kensington Gardens and two minutes' walk from Kensington High Street shopping center. The elegant and spacious foyer is decorated with a Regency theme. For formal wining and dining, there is the Kensington Chelsea Piano Bar and Restaurant which offers a comprehensive menu. More relaxed meals can be taken in the continental atmosphere of the Pavilion Coffee House. The 320 bedrooms have stylish, color-coordinated decor, and each has its own bathroom, radio, and TV. Singles rent from £38.50 ($75.08) nightly, with doubles going for £49 ($95.55). Tube: High Street Kensington.

Royal Kensington, 380 Kensington High St., W.14 (tel. 603-3333), supplies a near-luxurious accommodation at less-than-luxurious prices. It's in the Kensington area, near parks, museums, and shopping. You can enjoy the comforts of the handsomely styled bedrooms which include color TV, individually controlled air conditioning, and direct-dial telephones with bathroom extensions. Singles go for £35 ($68.25), and doubles or twins are £43 ($83.85), including service. VAT and a continental breakfast are extra. The Flaming Ox Restaurant offers a choice of steaks or flambés, while in the coffeeshop you can have a light snack. Twenty-four-hour room service and garage space are available. Tube: High Street Kensington.

De Vere Hotel, Hyde Park Gate, W.8 (tel. 584-0051). I always like this place because you can have tea in the Adam drawing room overlooking Kensington Gardens. Representing classic Victorian architecture, it's been around London for a long time and is an enduring favorite. Much of its original character and charm have been preserved; however, the building is completely modernized and up to date. For rent are 84 attractively decorated and tastefully furnished bedrooms, each with private bath, radio, and color TV. Some of the smaller rooms are in an annex, accessible through the main building of the hotel. In a single, the charge is £28 ($54.60) nightly, going up to £38 ($74.10) in a double, these tariffs including VAT and a continental breakfast. Tube: High Street Kensington.

THE MEDIUM-PRICED RANGE: Bailey's Hotel, Gloucester Road, S.W.7 (tel. 373-8131), to quote the management, was a "firm favourite with the squirearchy" when it was built back in the 1880s—but now caters to the visitor, both foreign and domestic, along with budding executives. This brick corner establishment in South Kensington, with its formal arched entrance and mansard roof, was one of those first revolutionary hotels to install an "ascending room"—that is, an elevator. The ground floor is paneled in oak, mixing antiques with reproductions. All 155 bedrooms have a private bathroom/shower, remote-control color TV, radio, direct-dial telephones, and facilities including wake-up calls, messages, and an electronic door-locking system. The hotel has finished an extensive upgrading program, and many amenities have been added, such as automatic elevators, a good coffeeshop, a hotel bar, and a wine bar, with a restaurant specializing in foreign food. There's also a fully computerized reservation and billing system. Single rooms are £28 ($54.60), and twin rooms are £34 ($66.30) per night. All prices include VAT and service. Tube: Gloucester Road.

Number Sixteen 16 Sumner Pl., S.W.7 (tel. 589-5232), is considered a luxury "pension" in central London. Just off Old Brompton Road, it's a three-minute walk to the South Kensington underground station. Michael Watson is the creator of this offbeat hotel, built in 1860, which is much patronized by people in the performing arts. The hotel, which now comprises 15, 16, and 17 Sumner Pl., is classically Victorian, with high-ceilinged period rooms converted to self-contained bed-sitting accommodations, with private shower/bathrooms (some of them have tubs as well). Rooms are decorated with antiques and Victorian pieces, along with pictures, Hans Holbein prints, and lithographs. Mr. Watson prefers guests who will stay more than a night or two. Singles range from £20 ($39) to £26 ($50.70), doubles and twins from £29 ($56.55) to £48 ($93.60).

Milestone Hotel, Kensington Court, W.8 (tel. 937-0991), is a great old building facing Kensington Gardens. There's an ornate roof with decorative gables and chimneys, plus large bay windows. The decor is modified neoclassic, the best example the glass-ceilinged dining room with its paneled walls, red draperies, and red chairs. The bedrooms, each with radio and telephone, are spacious. A bathless single rents for £16 ($31.20); a single with bath is £22 ($42.90). Bathless doubles or twins range from £26 ($50.70). A twin with bath costs £32 ($62.40). Rates include service and tax, although breakfast is extra. Tube: High Street Kensington.

The Town House, 44–48 West Cromwell Rd., S.W.5 (tel. 373-4546), is a small, privately owned place made over from three Victorian houses. Friendly and informal, it is well suited to younger visitors. All rooms have hot and cold running water, radio, and phone, and most are also equipped with shower and toilet. Color TV is standard in most units or else available at a small extra charge in others. There is a cozy, comfortable bar-lounge and a larger games bar with dartboard, pool table, fruit machines, dominos, backgammon, and bridge.

Singles range in price from £19 ($37.05) to £20 ($39) a night, and doubles or twins run from £29 ($56.55) to £32 ($62.40), these tariffs including service and a continental breakfast, although VAT is extra. The staff also offers some family rooms. Laundry and dry-cleaning can be taken care of, and there's also a Telex service available to guests.

Breakfast can be served in your room or else in the main dining room. Snacks are available throughout the day, and in the evenings a three-course dinner is offered, costing from £7.50 ($14.63). The fare is simple, traditional English cookery. Tube: Gloucester Road.

The Regency Hotel, 100–105 Queen's Gate, S.W.7 (tel. 370-4595), is a skillful conversion of six lively old houses to provide 200 simply furnished, comfortable rooms with bathroom or shower, color TV, radio, and telephone. There are elevators to all floors and 24-hour porterage. The high-ceilinged, warm red-walled dining room serves a set lunch or dinner, three courses for around £6 ($11.70). They also do a limited à la carte menu where a meal will cost around £12 ($23.40) per person. The bar is large and cheerfully decorated with green walls, dark wood, and button chairs, and serves coffee, tea, and sandwiches as well as drinks. The tariffs are a very good value at £21 ($40.95) single, £28 ($54.60) twin or double, £35 ($68.25) triple, including a continental breakfast, service, and VAT. South Kensington museums are close by. In addition, the underground stations at South Kensington and Gloucester Road, with direct link to Heathrow Airport, are just a five-minute walk away.

Albany Hotel, Barkston Gardens, S.W.5 (tel. 370-6116), has combined five Victorian town houses on tree-shaded Barkston Gardens—secluded, yet only one minute from Earl's Court Road and conveniently near underground and bus service to Heathrow Airport. Rebuilding and tasteful furnishing have transformed these former private residences into attractive public places in which to stay. Most of the 100 rooms contain private bath and toilet, and all have color TV, radio, and telephone. A single without bath rents for £13.50 ($26.33); a single with bath £18.75 ($36.56); a bathless twin or double, £20 ($39); a double or twin with bath £28.50 ($55.58). These tariffs include a continental breakfast, service, and VAT. Highly popular is an old-style pub, with a beamed ceiling, rough brick walls, and Windsor chairs. The dining room is stylish and airy. Tube: Earl's Court.

Burns Hotel, Barkston Gardens, S.W.5 (tel. 373-3151), stands near its sister, the already-recommended Albany. Small and intimate, it was once the home of Ellen Terry (1848–1928), who was especially acclaimed for her Shakespearean roles and was also known for her correspondence with G. B. Shaw. Most of the rooms overlook the trees of Barkston Gardens. Singles rent for £15 ($29.25) to £18 ($35.10) nightly, doubles or twins for £23 ($44.85) to £ 28 ($54.60). The higher tariffs are for private baths. Tariffs include VAT, service, and a full English breakfast. You can also use the sauna at the nearby Albany. Tube: Earl's Court.

Airways Hotel, 16 Collingham Rd., S.W.5 (tel. 373-1075), is a neat, bandbox-modern hotel, in Earl's Court opposite the Airbus stop. It's only a short block away from the heavy Cromwell Road traffic, where finding a quiet room is almost impossible. Its bedrooms are as compact and as utilitarian as some motels in America—built-in headboards, radios, telephones, dressing tables. Every room has a private bath. The rates, including a continental breakfast, in a single are £18.70 ($36.47), £30 ($58.50) in a double or twin, including a continental breakfast, service, and VAT. One of the reasons for staying here is the ease with which you can settle in—you can check in anytime, day or night. On the premises is a restaurant serving lunch and dinners. Tube: Earl's Court.

Onslow Court Hotel, 109–113 Queen's Gate, S.W.7 (tel. 589-6300), is a long-established family hotel. The plain but comfortable rooms have color TV, telephone, and central heating, and there is an elevator to all floors. Many units have private bathrooms as well. A single goes from £17 ($33.15) to £22 ($42.90), a double from £26 ($50.70) to £36 ($70.20). If you're traveling with children, an extra bed can be brought in at £8 ($15.60) per night. All rates include a full breakfast, VAT, and service. The hotel is not licensed, but they are quite happy for you to bring your own supplies of wine or liquor. They have a good range of mixes and sodas and will provide ice for you in your room. A coffeeshop offers both snacks and full meals. Tube: South Kensington.

Stanhope Court Hotel, 46–52 Stanhope Gardens, S.W.7 (tel. 370-2161), belongs to the same group as the previously recommended Onslow Court. The facilities offered are the same. This place looks out over a delightful London square garden just off Cromwell Road and around the corner from the Gloucester Road underground station. Rates are the same as for the Onslow Court and, in fact, reservations can be made through the central reservations office, The North Hotels, 58 Cromwell Rd., London S.W.7 5BZ (tel. 589-1212). This is an advantage, as it saves your having to try a second hotel if the first one is full. The group has several other hotels in the area which are totally adequate, but from a point of view of location and facilities these two are the ones I recommend the most. The chain is owned by a Quaker, Sir Cyril Black. Hence the lack of bars.

Eden Plaza, 68–69 Queensgate, S.W.7 (tel. 370-6111), completed in 1972, is an attractive, white-painted corner building, offering bedrooms furnished in modern style and tastefully decorated. An elevator carries guests to all floors, where bedrooms with double glazing await them. Other amenities include color TV sets, along with private baths and showers. The cost in a single is £24 ($46.80), rising to £34 ($66.30) in a twin or double. These tariffs include a full English breakfast, service, and VAT. Families might like to inquire about one of the three-bedded rooms, also with private baths, going for £40 ($78) nightly. Both business people and vacationers meet in the cocktail lounge and bar, and later go to the restaurant, offering a continental and English cuisine. On the ground level are such additional facilities as a sauna, massage room, and solarium. The location is near Hyde Park, close to the London Air Terminal, and convenient for shoppers heading for such emporiums as Harrods and Selfridges. Tube: Gloucester Road.

THE BUDGET RANGE: Strathmore House, 12 Strathmore Gardens, W.8 (tel. 229-3063). You'd never guess this is a hotel. There's no sign, only a street number, and its location near Embassy Row and Kensington Palace makes it appear like a private town house. It's a corner house, with a low wall and shrubbery. Mr. and Mrs. Haskell, the proprietors, charge from £7.50 ($14.63) to £9 ($17.55) per person per night inclusive, according to length of stay. Terms include a complete English breakfast, but don't expect private baths. The bed-sitting rooms, opening off the central hallway, are large and comfortable. There are some nice old pieces mixed in with the nondescript furniture, and the total effect is homey and immaculate. You get hot and cold running water in the rooms, as well as the free use of the corridor baths. Breakfast is brought to your room, and you have a gas ring and kettle so you can make your own tea or coffee. Tube: Notting Hill Gate.

Princes Lodge Hotel, Prince of Wales Terrace, W.8 (tel. 937-6306), is a family hotel in the literal meaning of the word. A number of rooms have been specially designed to accommodate families; there are also family suites, rooms for parents and children separated by private bath. There are day and night "baby-watching" and "child-minding" services; the hotel has cribs and cots. Large families are never met with a sigh here, but are always given a welcoming smile. Singles range in price from £8 ($15.60) to £18 ($35.10), and doubles go from £12 ($23.40) to £28 ($54.60). The difference in price depends on location, plumbing, and season, and all tariffs include a continental breakfast, service, and VAT. The Princes Lodge is opposite Kensington Palace Gardens. Tube: High Street Kensington.

Vicarage Private Hotel, 10 Vicarage Gate, W.8 (tel. 229-4030), is the domain of Ellen and Martin Diviney, who charge £9 ($17.55) per person double occupancy, and £10 ($19.50) in a single. All rates include breakfast, and as of November 1 charges are reduced slightly. The rooms have pleasant furnishings. All have water basins, and there's a good supply of showers. Mrs. Diviney makes each breakfast individually, and introduces her guests to each other. Vicarage Gate is handy for boutiques and restaurants on Kensington Church Street, and a laundromat is nearby. The nearest tube stops are Kensington High and Notting Hill Gate.

Clearlake Hotel, 19 Prince of Wales Terrace, W.8 (tel. 937-3274), is an ideal family hotel on a residential street facing Kensington Gardens. Remodeled from a row of early Victorian houses, the hotel offers every possible convenience for the traveler weary of typical hotel life. You can, of course, rent the comfortable single and double rooms, costing from £7.50 ($14.63) to £14 ($27.30) for one, or from £15 ($29.25) to £25 ($48.75) for two persons. However, the real finds are the two-room apartments with bath and kitchen housing up to four persons for anywhere from £22 ($42.90) to £35 ($68.25) nightly, and three-room apartments with baths and separate kitchens, accommodating four persons at a cost of £27 ($52.65) to £40 ($78). All rooms and suites have color TV sets. If you don't use the room's cooking facilities, you get your breakfast free. Andrew Herskovitz and his wife, Diana, have been managers here for many years. Tube: High Street Kensington.

Mr. and Mrs. A. Demetriou, 9 Strathmore Gardens, W.8 (tel. 229-6709), operate this small, privately owned guest house very close to Kensington Gardens and Hyde Park. Reader Joseph A. Wilson, a sergeant in the army, wrote, "They are without a doubt the most helpful, courteous, and gracious pair of hosts you could ever have the good fortune to meet. These kind people went out of their way to make me feel at home. The accommodations were immaculately clean. To use a cliché, 'You could literally eat off the floor.' " Beautifully kept and decorated, the rooms are rented at a rate of £9 ($17.55) per person for a bed and a full English breakfast served in an often-sun-filled basement dining room. Tube: Notting Hill Gate.

Hotel One Two Eight, 128 Holland Rd., W.14 (tel. 602-3395), is a somewhat offbeat place at which to live, located as it is in Holland Park to the north of Kensington High Street and to the south of Holland Park Avenue. Here the converted town houses still retain spacious gardens in the rear. The white facade of the hotel greets you with its small wrought-iron balconies and abundant flowers in summer. Of the 36 colorful, well-equipped bedrooms, 13 have private showers and 16 have private showers and toilets. All have bed lights, radio, and telephone. Rates, including a complete English breakfast, are as follows: from £20 ($39) to £26 ($50.70) in a double, from £15 ($29.25) to £19 ($37.05) in a single, depending on the plumbing. Ask the owners, Mr. and Mrs. D. Novakovic, for one of the quieter rooms in the rear. Besides two guest lounges with a communal TV, and a breakfast room, guests in the warmer months can also enjoy the rear garden, with its large lawn, stone walls, and towering trees. Tube: Shepherd's Bush.

Camellia Hotel, 16 Longridge Rd., S.W.5 (tel. 373-3848), lies in an unspoiled section of Kensington, on the better side of Earl's Court Road. The exterior is graced with an abundance of flowers in boxes and urns and baskets hanging from the windows. The lounge and breakfast room are made more inviting with Austrian pine furnishings. Central heating and color television add to the amenities. Singles cost £9 ($17.55). Doubles with private bath go for £17 ($33.15), although a few with hot and cold running water rent for £15 ($29.25). A continental breakfast, VAT, and service are included. A full English breakfast is available at an extra charge. Tube: Earl's Court.

Hotel 167, 167 Old Brompton Rd., S.W.5 (tel. 373-0672), is a converted corner town house, maintaining its Victorian architectural features, although the decor has been considerably updated by Christina Rasmus, a Finnish designer. In clean, comfortable rooms, the hotel charges £12.24 ($23.87) in a bathless single, £18.35 ($35.78) in a bathless double or twin, and £20.18 ($39.35) in a double or twin with private shower. Prices are inclusive of a continental breakfast, VAT, and service. A short walk from the hotel will take you to boutique-strewn King's Road. Tube: Gloucester Road.

READER'S HOTEL SELECTION: "I stayed in a delightful family hotel, **Coronet Hotel,** 59 Nevern Square, Earl's Court (tel. 373-6396), in a quiet residential area of London. Being well within walking distance of the underground, buses, exhibitions, and museums, it is an ideal base for any type of overseas visitor wishing to see and do as much as possible during a short stay. I found the rates offered most acceptable, and the accommodation of a very high standard. A single rents for £12.50 ($24.38), a bathless twin or double for £16.50 ($32.16), and a twin or double with private bath or shower for £20 ($39). A full English breakfast is included in all prices, and the service is personal and friendly. The proprietors are Mr. and Mrs. James, who ensure that the needs of their guests are attended to with promptness and courtesy. Tube: Earl's Court" (W. Bowker, Manama, Bahrain).

9. Bayswater

North of Bayswater Road, west of Hyde Park and north of Kensington Gardens, is Bayswater, another unofficial district of London, with many well-recommended, moderately priced hotels, plus a number of low-budget bed-and-breakfast lodgings. Many of these former town houses, converted into hotels, date back to the days when Bayswater spelled the good life to a prosperous, upper middle class. Some of the town houses, often lined up in rows, open onto pleasant squares. Serving Bayswater Road are buses 12, 88, and 289. Both the Central and District undergrounds run to Bayswater tube station.

THE MEDIUM-PRICED RANGE: **Portobello,** 22 Stanley Gardens, W.11 (tel. 727-2777), makes us green with envy, as it fulfills a secret desire to take over a couple of antiquated, threadbare, 19th-century town houses and restore them to their former luster. Under the leadership of Tim Herring, his wife Cathy, and designer Julie Hodgess, a 30-room miracle was created. It has all that cool sophistication that goes with an eclectic collection of furnishings harmoniously blended. A single room costs £30 ($58.50), although you can request a single cabin (very small) at £24 ($46.80); a double room, £35 ($68.25); a twin-bedded room, £42 ($81.90)—all plus VAT and service. A continental breakfast is provided in your room and included in the cost. Each bedroom has a private bath, as well as color TV and individually controlled air conditioning. Natural wood pieces are upholstered in bright colors, an oval gilt mirror in the lounge hangs over a gleaming white marble fireplace, and the reception area echoes the Edwardian era. Shuttered doors in the bedrooms hide do-it-yourself equipment for preparing light fare and mixing drinks. At a beautiful restaurant, again designed by Julie Hodgess, good food and drink can be obtained at any hour. There is no room service. Tube: Notting Hill Gate.

Henry the Eighth, 19 Leinster Gardens, W.2 (tel. 262-0117), is a glamorous remake of an older, more conservative hotel. Its fine facade, with Ionic-style columns, and the lime trees out front have been preserved, and inside the restoration has been carried out with good taste. The lounges and dining rooms open onto a covered courtyard, with its own heated swimming pool and semi-tropical plants; the entry lounge has a ceiling-high wall of modern ceramic

sculpture and a collage from London University. The "Strikes 1926" Restaurant specializes in a large variety of hamburgers, also providing steaks. The bedrooms are most attractive; each has push-button control of radio, color TV, lights and maid service. Some contain sofa beds, making for a bed-sitting room arrangement. Singles go for £22 ($42.90), doubles or twins for £30 ($58.50). All units contain showers and toilets, and rates include a continental breakfast, VAT, and service. The hotel is just north of Hyde Park. Tube: Queensway.

Post House, 104 Bayswater Rd., W.2 (tel. 262-4461), contains nine floors of ultramodern rooms. It's across from Kensington Gardens, and most of its studio-style bedrooms open onto the park. The hotel is ideal for those who are impatient with London's antiquated accommodations, and prefer a neat, new, streamlined look. All of the 175 bedrooms (air conditioning in the front rooms) have private baths, as well as telephones, color TV sets, and radios. A single is £32 ($62.40); a double, £42 ($81.90)—including service and tax. Breakfast is extra. On the second floor is a restaurant. The hotel has a free car park. Tube: Queensway.

The **Senator Hotel,** Westbourne Terrace, W.2 (tel. 262-4521), is a remake of one of London's classic old hotels; it lies just a few minutes north of Hyde Park and close to Oxford Street. Although the front is traditional, the interior is contemporary. Many of the bedrooms, for example, are duplexes, with narrow stairs leading from your sitting room to the sleeping area and bath. A single room with private bath goes for £20.50 ($39.98), £28 ($54.60) in a double or twin with bath. All rooms have color TV included in the price, as are a continental breakfast and service, although VAT is extra. A lower-level dining room is "ye olde England"—wood settles, Windsor chairs, trestle tables, and decorative bric-a-brac. Tube: Bayswater.

Cordova House Hotel, 14–16 Craven Hill, Lancaster Gate, W.2 (tel. 723-1065), was once a pair of Regency town houses lying north of Kensington Gardens. It's now been converted into an informal establishment which is one of the best run hotels in the area. All the redecorated rooms contain private baths and toilets, and single rates are £18 ($35.10); doubles £23 ($44.85)—including VAT and a continental breakfast. There is no service charge. The hotel offers an intimate bar. Tube: Paddington.

The **Royal Bayswater Hotel,** 122 Bayswater Rd., W.2 (tel. 229-8887), is a charming economy hotel overlooking Hyde Park. The friendly atmosphere, comfortable rooms, and reasonable prices attract the visitor who is looking for high standards at moderate prices. The 36 rooms are modern, tastefully furnished, with wall-to-wall carpets, private bath/showers, central heating, and radios. Wardrobe space is adequate, and there's a built-in "vanitory unit" with specially lit mirror. Tea- or coffee-making facilities are available in all rooms. The hotel charges no service tax as there is none, except for room cleaning. Every meal is additional at the contemporary restaurant on the premises. Singles with bath rent for £18.50 ($36.08), a double with bath going for £28.50 ($55.58). Tube: Queensway.

THE BUDGET RANGE: Garden Court Hotel, 30–31 Kensington Gardens Square, W.2 (tel. 229-2553), is run by Mr. and Mrs. Stefan Lis, who fled Poland during the war. The family found this old town house on a private garden square and began the long task of making it the homelike hotel it is today. For the occupants of a bathless double room, the B&B charge is £20 ($39), plus VAT. Most of the rooms are singles, renting for £13 ($25.35) to £15 ($29.25), the latter with private showers, but families may be interested in one of the four triple rooms ranging in price from £26.50 ($51.68) to £30 ($58.50), the latter with private bath. The ten double rooms with private bath cost from £22 ($42.90) nightly. Each room has a water basin, along with telephone, radio, and intercom. You'll enjoy meeting and talking with guests from many lands who frequent the Garden Court; there's a bar-television lounge on the ground floor, where you can lower the stock of beer on hand and hear candid opinions about world affairs. Tube: Queensway.

READERS' HOTEL SELECTION: "**Redland House Hotel**, 52 Kendal St., Hyde Park, W.2 (tel. 723-7118), is a double town house just off Edgware Road. The proprietors are Mr. and Mrs. H. Newlands, who charge £13 ($25.35) for singles, £12 ($23.40) per person for doubles or twins, plus VAT. This is just at the edge of the W.1 area. A two-minute walk from buses serving the Strand, this is a first-rate choice for budgeting time as well as money. Nearby are teashops and a variety of restaurants, plus laundromats. Further, one can walk to Oxford and Regent Streets and the parks. Redland House is attractive, clean, centrally heated, and most efficiently operated. No private baths are available, but there are ample facilities near all rooms. Reservations are desirable; in our experience inquiries were promptly answered. It is but a short walk to Selfridges and the Marble Arch tube stop, but the Newlandses point out that using buses saved money. They are Welsh, intelligent, and interesting people. The establishment is well ordered and quiet for sleeping" (Mr. and Mrs. Arthur Thurner, Chicago, Ill.).

10. Paddington and Little Venice

Another popular hotel area, particularly for budget travelers, is the Paddington section, around Paddington Station, just to the northwest of Kensington Gardens and Hyde Park. Here you'll be within walking distance of the great Marble Arch, the entrance to Hyde Park. The main Paddington avenue, Sussex Gardens, has been known for years to pence-shy travelers who seek out its bed-and-breakfast houses. But as more and more town houses are being razed on Sussex Gardens to make way for expensive flats, Norfolk Square is gaining importance as the area in which to shop for budget hotels. Allowed to deteriorate after World War II, the square was formerly one of the most prestigious squares of London, especially in the reign of Victoria when the eminent built large, beautiful town houses ideal for big families, maids, and nannies.

On the periphery of Paddington is an unofficial district dubbed Little Venice, a seldom-visited hideaway off Edgware Road, north of Paddington Station. Little Venice gets its name because two branches of the Grand Union canal meet at Blomfield Road and Warwick Avenue. Bus 6 from the West End runs to Warwick Avenue, or else you can take the Bakerloo line to the Warwick Avenue station. From this district, you can book a ride on Jason's boat through Regent's Park, or board a boat in summer to the London Zoo.

THE MEDIUM-PRICED RANGE: Colonnade Hotel, 2 Warrington Crescent, W.9 (tel. 286-1052), is an imposing town house in a pleasant residential area, just a block from the Warwick Avenue tube station. Owned and managed for some 35 years by the Richards family, the hotel is run in a personal and friendly manner. The bedrooms are spacious (some with balconies), and are equipped with either private bath/shower or hot and cold water. The rates, including a full English breakfast, are: £16 ($31.20) in a single without bathroom, £24 ($46.80) in a bathless double. For a single with private bath, the charge is £20 ($39) to £28 ($54.60); for a double with private bath, £28 ($54.60) to £35 ($68.25). Special suites are priced at £35 ($68.25) single and £45 ($87.75) double. VAT is extra, and tipping is left to your discretion. Mr. Richards emphasizes: "Every bedroom, bathroom, and corridor is centrally heated 24 hours a day of every day from the first chill wind of autumn until the last breath of retreating winter, even in summer if necessary." He's installed a water-softening plant as well. All rooms have TV, video, radio, telephone, hair driers, and electrically heated trouser presses. Seven have four-poster beds.

READER'S HOTEL SELECTION: "We stayed at the **Dylan Hotel,** 14 Devonshire Terrace, Lancaster Gate, W.2 (tel. 723-3280). The rates with breakfast are from £18 ($35.10) to £22.50 ($43.88) in a double, the latter with private shower or bath, plus a toilet. Singles rent from £11 ($21.45) to £13 ($25.35). The rooms are large, cheery, and very clean, and the breakfast more than adequate. The hotel has been redecorated and recarpeted from top to bottom. Accommodations have radio intercoms, shaver points, and central heating. Guests gather in the lounge to watch color TV. The hotel is convenient to the Paddington underground and Hyde Park" (Ann Calhoun, Los Angeles, Calif.).

11. St. Marylebone

Below Regent's Park, northwest of Piccadilly Circus, is the district of St. Marylebone (pronounced Mar-li-bone), a residential section which faces Mayfair to the south and extends north of Marble Arch. A number of simple but gracious town houses in this section are being converted into private hotels. Many visitors arriving in London in peak season without a reservation go hotel shopping in this relatively undiscovered area, letting the crowds fight it out in Bloomsbury.

THE UPPER BRACKET: Cumberland Hotel, Marble Arch. W.1 (tel. 262-1234), will please those who want to be in the center—at Marble Arch, at the corner of Hyde Park, with its Speakers' Corner, and at the beginning of Oxford Street and Mayfair. It's a modern, well-equipped hotel, which in North America would be described as a top-notch business persons' place. You may get lost in the corridors, as the Cumberland is a colossus, containing 900 bedrooms. Those rooms are furnished with built-in units, bedside lights, TV sets, telephones, radios, private baths with showers, color television, trouser pressers, mini-bars, and small sitting areas. The rates include service charge and VAT. From April to October, a twin-bedded room rents for £57 ($111.15), a single for £44 ($85.80). Off-season prices are lower.

A plus is the ownership: Trusthouse Forte. Also, in the hotel is one of the best bargain restaurants in the capital, the all-you-can-eat Carvery, costing from £8 ($15.60). And there's a quick-meal coffeeshop. The hotel's other restaurant, Wyvern, offers traditional recipes from the 18th and 19th centuries. Specialties include such dishes as sirloin steak in "wow wow sauce," a recipe which includes pickled walnuts, capers, and port. Another offering is sole with prawn sauce, based on a dish devised by the head cook to Queen Victoria in the first year of her marriage to Albert. Yet another specialty is salamagundy, a salad from *The British Housewife,* a book published in 1749. Tube: Marble Arch.

THE MEDIUM-PRICED RANGE: Hotel Concorde, 50 Great Cumberland Pl., Marble Arch. W.1 (tel. 402-6169), is a five-story brick building with a carriageway leading through to a quaint mews, little houses once reserved for servants, but now attracting the chic. The location is prestigious, just off a park and within walking distance of Marble Arch. The nightly charges, with VAT and a continental breakfast included, are £24 ($46.80) in a single with full bath, £30 ($58.50) in a twin or double with bath. The rooms are attractively furnished, with color TVs, and the lounge has a mixture of antiques and leather

chairs. Three-course table d'hôte meals begin at £6 ($11.70). Tube: Marble Arch.

Bryanston Court Hotel, Great Cumberland Place, Marble Arch, W.1 (tel. 262-3141), is three 19th-century town houses joined together by a central reception lounge, decorated with Delft Blue canvas. Just off restful Bryanston Square, with its well-tended gardens and trees, the hotel is only a short walk from Marble Arch and a rarity in central London in that it maintains a moderate price level. It is furnished with a good combination of antiques and traditional pieces. All rooms have bath or shower. Singles rent for £27 ($52.65), doubles or twins for £34 ($66.30), and triples for £40 ($78), these tariffs including a continental breakfast, service, and VAT. It's a good choice year round, as it's centrally heated, and each room has a radio and telephone. Tube: Marble Arch.

THE BUDGET RANGE: **Merryfield House**, 42 York St., off Baker Street, W.1 (tel. 935-8326), is a refreshingly pleasant remake of a 19th-century pub, the Lord Keith. Ale drinkers of old would look askance at the bright facade and the flower boxes filled with red geraniums. Owned by Mr. and Mrs. G. K. Tyler-Smith, the hotel is a haven for those who cling to the old English ways. Resisting continental breakfasts, the manager, Bridget, serves a "jolly good breakfast" right in your room. Radio and TV can be had on request. According to the season and location, doubles (no twins or singles) range in price from £22 ($42.90) to £25 ($48.75), and every room has its own private bath and toilet. The house is small enough so that a tiny staff can keep everything shiny, polished, scrubbed, and laundered. The location is also convenient for budget-conscious shoppers, as it lies near Selfridges and Marks and Spencers. York Street is just two blocks south of Marylebone Road. Tube: Baker Street.

12. Mayfair

Mayfair, bounded by Piccadilly, Hyde Park, and Oxford and Regent Streets, is an elegant section of London. Luxury hotels exist side by side with Georgian town houses and swank shops. Here are the parks, names, and streets that have snob appeal the world over, including Grosvenor Square (pronounced Grov-nor) and Berkeley Square (pronounced Bark-ley). If you can't afford Claridge's try:

THE UPPER BRACKET: **May Fair Hotel**, Berkeley Street, W.1 (tel. 629-7777), is a remade, redecorated hotel that's a world unto itself. The circular cantilevered lobby staircase sets the pace. If you're not of international celebrity material, and can't afford either the Maharajah or Monte Carlo Suites, then you may settle for one of the decorator bedrooms. Those I've inspected have been colorfully and tastefully conceived. All the bedrooms contain private baths, and rent for £50 ($97.50) to £65 ($126.75) in a single, £70 ($136.50) to £85 ($165.75) in a double, service included. All rooms have color TV. A new bedroom wing with a high standard of luxury has been added.

There are two major restaurants: Chateaubriand, with its excellent French cuisine, and the Beachcomber, with its Polynesian atmosphere and cuisine (dancing to two bands until 2 a.m.). In addition, there's a coffeehouse, really a grill, open from 10 a.m. until midnight. The facilities seem endless: bars, a movie house that operates as a private club (but is available to all hotel residents), a theater, and the Palm Beach Casino Club next door. Tube: Piccadilly Circus.

The **Europa,** Grosvenor Square, W.1 (tel. 493-1232), right by the American Embassy, is one of the leading hotels in the Grand Metropolitan Hotel chain. Its bedrooms, nearly 300 in all, have been furnished in the modern manner, in good taste, with an emphasis placed on simplicity. All rooms have private baths. Singles rent for £45 ($87.75); doubles or twins, £60 ($117). VAT is extra. Facilities include color TV, radios, and central heating. On the premises are the well-known Diplomat Restaurant and the Coffee Exchange. Tube: Bond Street.

THE MEDIUM-PRICED RANGE: Piccadilly Hotel, Piccadilly, W.1 (tel. 734-8000), is a union of the old and new. A classically designed building with a contemporary entrance, it is just one minute from Piccadilly Circus and close to many of London's fine stores. Opened in the spring of 1908, the hotel has attracted kings, queens, and ministers of state among other celebrated guests. Built at a tremendous cost, it became famous in the '20s for its tea dances. The bedrooms, 290 in all, have been modernized and furnished with Danish-style utilitarian furniture. A single with bath rents from £43 ($83.85), a twin with bath from £56 ($109.20). You can help yourself to succulent roasts from the Carver's Table Restaurant, where visitors can admire the magnificent Australian oak paneling. The Lounge Bar also creates an atmosphere of bygone days. Tube: Piccadilly Circus.

The **Londoner** and **Clifton Ford,** Welbeck Street, W.1 (tel. 935-4442), stand next to each other and share a joint reservation service. They are members of the Grand Metropolitan chain, dedicated to rejuvenating aging London hotels. Tucked away in Mayfair, off Wigmore Street (near Cavendish Square and Wigmore Hall), the hotels are excellent remakes of older buildings. Spaciousness is the mood, especially in the clean-cut and uncluttered reception areas. The bedrooms have been furnished in shipshape Nordic fashion. Each one has its own shower bath. Singles rent for £30 ($58.50), doubles for £40 ($78). A continental breakfast, VAT, and service are included. All rooms have TV, radio and 24-hour room service. At the Londoner, Oliver's Tavern serves traditional English dishes, and in the Chesterfield Room the martinis are dry. Tube: Bond Street.

13. Bloomsbury

To the northeast of Piccadilly Circus, beyond Soho, is Bloomsbury, a world unto itself. It is, among other things, the academic heart of London, where you'll find London University, several other colleges, the British Museum, and many bookstores. Despite its student overtones, the section is fairly staid and quiet. Its reputation has been fanned by such writers as Virginia Woolf (it figures in her novel, *Jacob's Room*). She and her husband, Leonard, were once the unofficial leaders of a coterie of artists and writers known as the Bloomsbury Group, nicknamed Bloomsberries.

The exact heart of Bloomsbury is difficult to pinpoint. There are those who say it is Russell Square, with its university buildings, private homes, and hotels. Others feel it is the nearby British Museum. Still others are convinced it's the sprawling University of London, which also contains the Royal Academy of Dramatic Art on Gower Street. In any case there are at least four other old tree-filled squares—Bloomsbury, Bedford, Gordon, and Tavistock—each one an oasis of green in the midst of some of London's finest buildings. The unquestioned northern border is Euston Road, with its three railway stations—

St. Pancras, King's Cross, and Euston—and its southern border is New Oxford Street.

THE UPPER BRACKET: Hotel Russell, Russell Square, W.C.1 (tel. 837-6470), is a late Victorian hotel facing the gardens of Russell Square and within easy reach of theaters and shopping. It is run by Trusthouse Forte and offers 300 rooms, all with private baths or showers. Rates for a single are from £37 ($72.15) and from £48 ($93.60) for a twin. The public rooms have been refurbished, and include an excellent restaurant which offers a full range of dishes and a Gaiety Bar with quick grills and drinks at pub prices in an Edwardian atmosphere. The King's Bar has become one of London's most popular lounge bars. In the restaurant, you can order a continental breakfast at £3.20 ($6.24) or an English one at £5 ($9.75). Other facilities include a theater ticket agency, secretarial services, and a car-rental agency. Tube: Russell Square.

THE MEDIUM-PRICED RANGE: "Y" Hotel, 112 Great Russell St., W.C.1 (tel. 637-1333), is actually a modern hotel in the heart of London. Single rooms with shower rent for £21 ($40.95) a night, prices rising to £30 ($58.50) in a double or twin-bedded room with shower. It was built by the London Central Young Men's Christian Association for men and women of all ages. At the Oxford Street end of Tottenham Court Road, this new "Y" Hotel may not be like any you've ever seen before. Its facilities include squash courts, a gymnasium, a swimming pool, a shop, and an underground garage for car parking. Other facilities include a lounge and bar, plus a restaurant. Every bedroom has a private shower and bath, central heating, color TV, and radio. The furnishings are up to date and comfortable, and there's even wall-to-wall carpeting. Tube: Russell Square.

THE BUDGET RANGE: Lonsdale Hotel, 9–10 Bedford Pl., W.C.1 (tel. 636-1812), is a Regency town house, within the shadow of the British Museum. It's elegantly positioned on one of the most attractive tree-lined streets in London, midway between Russell and Bloomsbury Squares. It is a particular favorite of professors and scientists from the continent who find it a convenient place to stay while researching at the museum. The B&B rate in a double or twin is £25 ($48.75), although singles pay £15 ($29.25), including VAT. There is no other charge. All rooms have razor outlets, and central heating assures cozy warmth. The hotel is privately owned and has a little garden in the rear. Tube: Russell Square.

READERS' HOTEL SELECTION: "Staunton Hotel (B&B), 13–15 Gower St., W.C.1 (tel. 580-2740), stands near the British Museum and many shops. It is also convenient to good city transportation. The rooms are very clean, and the breakfast is excellent. The rate is £8 ($15.60) per person (lower off-season). Mr. and Mrs. W. G. D. Morgan permitted us to leave luggage while on other tours, keeping the lodgings for us upon our return. Anxious to please, they are personable proprietors. Tube: Russell Square" (Mr. and Mrs. Samuel C. Levin, Chicago, Ill.).

14. Euston Station and King's Cross

Accommodations generally less expensive than those we have been considering so far can be found in these rather nondescript sections just a few blocks north of Bloomsbury. The hotels here are mainly around three large railway stations—Euston, St. Pancras, and King's Cross—and they are serviced by three tube stations. King's Cross, Euston, and Euston Square.

THE MEDIUM-PRICED RANGE: Kennedy Hotel, Euston, Cardington Street, N.W.1 (tel. 387-4400), opened in 1968 and is perhaps the most American-inspired hotel in London. Next to Euston Station, it is a gray building with a drive-in entrance. Inside, everything is bright and you'll find top-grade accommodations with many touches of luxury. Yet the prices are moderate— £29 ($56.55) in a single with bath, £38 ($74.10) in a double with bath. A continental breakfast is included. The rooms are expertly designed, with innerspring mattresses, TV, and air conditioning throughout. Decorator fabrics and colors are used—even the lamps are stylish.

EUSTON ST. PANCRAS
KING'S CROSS

The hotel's novelty is its Planters Restaurant. A profusion of greenery, full air conditioning, and an intriguing decor make this an attractive place to enjoy anything from a cup of coffee to a three-course meal with wine.

London Ryan, Gwynne Place, King's Cross Road, W.C.1 (tel. 278-2480), is one of London's new efficiency hotels, where there are no hidden extras. Everything in the bedrooms is streamlined and self-contained, that is, complete private baths, direct-dial telephones, TV, radios, color television, free in-house movies, and central heating. Even your continental breakfast is served in your chamber. From April to October, singles rent from £27.50 ($53.63), twins from £37.50 ($73.13), and triples from £45 ($87.75). These charges include a continental breakfast, service, and VAT. Facilities include a restaurant, a shop, Victorian Bar, and a private 50-car park. The location is convenient, near King's Cross railway and tube station, in back of Sadler's Wells, and within walking distance of the Dickens house.

15. On the Fringe

SOUTHEAST LONDON: Time was when no one would think of building a hotel in unchic Elephant and Castle, across the Thames in Southeast London. But this is a new day and a new London—and here it is . . .

The Budget Range

London Park Hotel, Brook Drive, S.E. 11 (tel. 735-9191), is an enormous warehouse across the Thames that has been completely overhauled and turned into a streamlined modern hotel. It now boasts 380 bedrooms, most with showers or tubs, plus a large restaurant, coffeeshop, and two bars. Rooms are very comtemporary and contain built-in headboards with telephones and radios (some even have "baby-listening" devices). Bathless singles go for £12.50 ($24.38), increasing to £14.50 ($28.28) with private bath or shower. In a twin-bedded or double-bedded room, the cost is £21.50 ($41.93) nightly, rising to £24.50 ($47.78) with private bath or shower. Prices include a full English breakfast and VAT. There are fast elevators, express laundry and dry-cleaning service, and a theater ticket bureau. Meal prices are low for London: a set lunch is £6 ($11.70); a set dinner, from £7 ($13.65). Numerous buses pass by the hotel, and there's a tube stop at Elephant and Castle.

HAMPSTEAD: The old village of Hampstead, sitting high on a hill, is the most desirable residential suburb of London. The village borders a wild heathland, which contains sprawling acres of wooded dells and fields of heather. Yet the Northern Line of the underground reaches the edges of the heath, making it possible for Londoners to enjoy isolated countryside while living only 20 minutes from city center. These advantages have caused many young artists to discover what Keats could have told them years ago—Hampstead is the place to live. The little Georgian houses have never received so much attention and love as they get now.

The Budget Range

Sandringham Hotel, 3 Holford Rd., N.W.3 (tel. 435-1569). You'd never guess this is a hotel, because it stands on a residential street in one of the best parts of London. After getting off at the Hampstead tube station, you walk up the hill past interesting shops, pubs, and charmingly converted houses. Shortly, at the Turpin Restaurant, you turn right into Hampstead Square which leads into Holford Road. A high wall and trees screen the house from the street (if you have a car, you can park in the driveway). It is a well-built, centrally heated house, and the comfortable rooms often house professional people who want to be near the center of London, yet retain the feel of rural life. The B&B charge is £9.50 ($18.53) in a single, increasing to £17 ($33.15) in a twin or double if bathless, but rising to £19 ($37.05) with private bath. A few triple rooms rent for £21 ($40.95). The breakfast room overlooks a walled garden; from the upper rooms you have a panoramic view over the heath of the center of London. You'll find a homelike lounge furnished with a color TV. Owners Mr. and Mrs. Dreyer and their two sons live on the premises.

SWISS COTTAGE: If you prefer life on a tree-lined residential street in north London, the following choice may appeal to you. It lies only ten minutes by underground from the heart of the West End.

Swiss Cottage Hotel, 4 Adamson Rd., N.W.3 (tel. 722-2281). This is rather an intriguing sort of place, an elegant family house furnished with paintings and antique furniture, Persian rugs, and chandeliers. The glass-fronted reception desk contains a fine collection of porcelain figures, and each bedroom has an old-fashioned bureau or writing desk. The lounge boasts a fine grand piano, a select place for afternoon tea. There is a pleasant quiet bar and a handsome dining room where a la carte meals are served.

Behind the hotel is a small formal town garden with trees, ferns, and geraniums, plus the Tea House area. This is the honeymoon suite, but you need not be on honeymoon to rent it. Bedrooms in the main hotel are very comfortable and, except for some singles, have modern showers or bathrooms. All have TV and telephone. The whole place is centrally heated. Singles go from £23 ($44.85) to £41 ($79.95) for sole occupancy of a large double with bathroom. Doubles are £34 ($66.30) to £46 ($89.70) and the Tea House rents for £64 ($124.80). All rates include a full breakfast and VAT. Tube: Swiss Cottage.

FULHAM: This is a pleasant part of West London. A tree-lined road stretches from St. Ethelred's Church (that's the bus stop you should ask for) to Bishop's Walk, a shady park running down to the river where in the afternoons a band often plays. And just around the corner is Fulham Palace, home of the bishop of London. In such a setting you're likely to discover London's most elegant B&B.

Off Fulham Palace Road, which runs from Hammersmith to Putney Bridge, at 10 Doneraile St., Fulham, S.W.6 (tel. 731-2192), **Lady Hartley** has two comfortable doubles available at £18 ($35.10) single occupancy, £25 ($48.75) double occupancy. In this elegant Edwardian house, renovated by Lady Hartley herself, you can come and go as you please.

The rooms are well furnished with comfortable beds. Guests share a bathroom but have their own tea- and coffee-making equipment. Knowing North American tastes, Lady Hartley willingly provides ice for your drinks.

Guests have the use of the front room to sit in, and this is where breakfast with hot croissants is served. Lady Hartley decided to take in guests purely because she and her two pug dogs enjoy meeting people. She does all she can to make you comfortable.

NEAR HEATHROW: For those who arrive exhausted after an overnight flight to Heathrow, but have enough energy still left to rent a self-drive car and head north to Lincoln and York, this is just far enough to go.

Elstree Moat House, Barnet Bypass (A1), Borehamwood, Elstree (tel. 953-1622), sits beside the A1 to the north, some 15 miles from Heathrow and London's West End. The original building dates from the 16th century, but much has been added and modernized to provide a very pleasant motel. Furnished with oak paneling and reproductions of antiques, all 60 bedrooms contain baths, color TVs, radios, telephones, and tea- and coffee-making facilities. Single occupancy costs £32 ($62.40). In a double or twin, the rate is £40 ($78). There are also rooms for three persons at £47 ($91.65). All tariffs include service, VAT, and a large English breakfast. The candlelit, oak-beamed dining room serves well-prepared meals and hot grills, and there are also two bars which provide snacks besides the usual range of drinks. Facilities include an Olympic-size swimming pool. Close by is St. Albans and the remains of the Roman city of Verulanium. Also nearby is Ayot St. Lawrence where Sir George Bernard Shaw lived.

AT GATWICK: Gatwick Hilton Hotel, London Gatwick Airport, Horley, Surrey, RH6 0LL (tel. Crawley 518080), a deluxe, five-floor hotel of the Hilton group, is the airport's most convenient resting place. A covered footbridge links the hotel and air terminal with a five-minute walk. You can also obtain porterage to the airport, and there are trolleys and electric cars if you can't cope with the walk.

A desk in the airport's arrival hall allows you to check your baggage and register, then catch the express city-link train into London to return later to your hotel room where your baggage awaits you.

The most dramatic part of the hotel is the first-floor lobby, where a glass-covered portico rises through four floors, containing a full-scale replica of the de Havilland Gypsy Moth airplane *Jason,* used by Amy Johnson on her solo flight from England to Australia in 1930. The reception is close by, an area of much greenery, trees, flowering shrubs, and trailing ivy and fig.

There is a well-equipped health club with a sauna, massage room, and swimming pool, along with other temptations available to guests. On the ground floor is the Garden Restaurant, serving both English and continental dishes. Opening for breakfast at 7 a.m., it serves dinner until 11 p.m. It has an open kitchen where you can see your meal prepared, and the decor consists of cane chairs, red carpet, and a fawn and white color scheme, with masses of green plants. Three courses are priced from £4.50 ($8.78) to £12 ($23.40). The Jockey Club Bar, with its masculine, Edwardian decor, is mainly for drinking, although sandwiches are available. Or there is the cozy Amy's Bar Lounge, where light refreshments are available 24 hours a day.

Rooms have the amenities expected of a Hilton: full air conditioning and double-glazing, phone, radio, and color TV with a full-length feature film shown daily in addition to normal stations (plus a mini-bar). Laundry and dry cleaning are returned within the day if collected by 9 a.m. Rates range from £40 ($78) to £51 ($99.45) in a single, from £48 ($93.60) to £58 ($113.10) in a double, including VAT and service.

There is, as well, a barber and a hairdressing salon, and plenty of parking space is provided. Business people will find excellent facilities here.

16. Alternatives to Hotels

STAYING WITH A FAMILY: At least ten agencies in Britain can arrange stays with a private family, either in London or in the country. As much as is possible, interests are matched. This program is an intriguing way to involve yourself in the social life of a country, seeing it from the inside. Also it's a great bargain. Some agencies limit themselves to teenagers, others welcome older readers.

Try one of the following: **Family Friendships Service,** 22 Palmerston Crescent, Palmers Green, London N.13 (tel. 882-5572), arranges accommodations with families in both London and throughout the United Kingdom (ages 12 and over), at prices that begin at £22.50 ($43.88) per week for B&B, rising to £70 ($136.50) weekly, according to locations and requirements. Often meals are possible. The service is run by Dr. and Mrs. Strawson-Sykes. He is a problems consultant to industry.

Or perhaps **Host & Guest Service,** 529a King's Rd., S.W.6 (tel. 731-5340), will provide a place for you at a cost that begins at £35 ($68.25) weekly for B&B and £49 ($95.55) with evening meals, added. Write or call Mrs. Rutter.

In addition, **Family Holidays,** 2 Kirklands Ave., Baildon, Shipley, Yorkshire (tel. Bradford 584-848), owned by Douglas Cummins, has a well-screened list of Britishers who ordinarily don't accept paying guests and who are not accessible from any other source. These include professional people, owners of London apartments or country estates. Upon application, you'll receive information about your host, his or her interests, age, and family. The cost of all accommodations is the same: about £50 ($97.50) per person weekly for full board. Mr. Cummins adds a 15% service charge, and you'll pay no more. There's even an arrangement for what to do if you and your host don't get on too well.

E.T.S., 9 Norbury Ave., Thronton Heath, CR4 8AH (tel. 653-8467), arranges accommodations throughout the year for any length of visit with selected families living in the southwest suburbs of London. These locations are about 15 to 18 minutes by suburban train to the center of London, and there are also frequent buses. These pleasant residential suburbs have many recreational and cultural facilities. There is also good train service from Heathrow and Gatwick Airports. Accommodation is also available in various other towns in the United Kingdom. London fees: Accommodations including English breakfast, booking fee, and tax cost £6 ($11.70) per night. For visits of one to three nights, there is a surcharge of £3.50 ($6.83) per person. An evening meal is available at an additional cost of £2.25 ($4.39) per person per night.

Hotel and Personal Accommodation Ltd., 10 Lower Belgrave St., S.W.1 (tel. 730-6181), will find suitable hotel accommodations for you in London and throughout the United Kingdom. As an alternative to a hotel, this agency can arrange short-term accommodation in serviced apartments, but only in the London area. Apartments in central London are all of first-class standard, and those in the suburbs are of economy standard. Try to give as much notice as possible, stating dates, types of rooms, standard, area required, and your maximum budget. This company charges no fees.

ACCOMMODATION SERVICE: The **London Tourist Board,** at 26 Grosvenor Gardens, Victoria, S.W.1 (tel. 730-0791), will make same-day bookings in a wide range of accommodations, from guest houses to hotels, for a basic price of £4.50 ($8.78) per person, including bed, breakfast, and VAT. At this price, however, the accommodation would be shared in a guest house or a hostel. Singles are available, beginning at £7.50 ($14.63). The board performs this service from its information centers at Victoria Station and at Heathrow underground station. You're charged a small booking fee regardless of the number of persons in your party, plus a refundable deposit. In addition, the centers supply information on accommodations at campsites and in dormitories, plus other types of accommodations below the minimum price of £4.50 ($8.78). However, staff members will not book such accommodations through their centers.

LIVING LIKE A LORD AND LADY: If you have always wanted to spend the night inside a castle, **Country Homes and Castles**, 138a Piccadilly, W.1 (tel. 491-2584), may be able to arrange just the suitable abode for you. More than 250 houses, ranging from cottages to historic manor houses to turreted fortresses, are available to paying guests through this program. Since the owners naturally vary in their interests, ages, and professional backgrounds, the agency makes every effort to match you with suitable hosts so that both will benefit from an enjoyable experience.

The organization will arrange a one- or two-night stay in a single house to fit in with your travel plans, or it will try to plan a complete tour with stops throughout the country, bearing in mind your personal interests. Prices for accommodations range from £85 ($165.75) to £155 ($302.25) per couple per night. The rate includes drinks, dinner with wine, accommodations with private bath, and breakfast. All payments are made in advance to the agent so that you can enjoy your guest-host relationship without embarrassment. Make arrangements through **Sue Duncan**, 6265 Courtside Dr. N.W., Norcross, GA 30092 (tel. 404/448-2185).

STAY ON A FARM: Country Farm Holidays, The Place, Ham Lane, Powick, Worcester (tel. Worcester 830899). For two or three nights or longer in the country, all you have to do is get in touch with Country Farm Holidays which will fit you up with a lovely Elizabethan farm in Salop, amid paneled walls and old oak beams, or with a 15th-century moated farmhouse in Suffolk where you can enjoy the country life, dinner, bed, and breakfast for as little as £11 ($21.45) a night per person. They have a wide selection of attractive and often historic farms on their books, and will give you details of how to get there, what to see and do. Many of the places allow guests to help with the animals and the working of the farm. They also have a list of self-catering cottages and apartments available for rentals of seven nights or more, sleeping from two to ten persons in comfort. Prices vary, obviously, but in June four to five persons can have an accommodation for around £70 ($136.50) for seven nights, including VAT.

YOUR OWN APARTMENT: The **South London Tourist Accommodation,** 428 Southcroft Rd., Streatham, S.W.16 (tel. 769-3225), is a family-run business, serving some 5000 visitors to London yearly who are looking for nice and inexpensive "self-catering" accommodation. Michael or John Slade will try to provide you with a fully equipped, private, clean, cozy, modern flatlet, flat, or house, depending on the number in your party and your needs for seven days or more. Mini-flatlet prices start at £80 ($156) a week. Family mini-flatlets are from £95 ($185.25) a week. Accommodations are in quiet, pleasant suburbs only about five miles from the center of London, reached by excellent public transport service. Upon arrival you will be presented with a free "Welcome Pack" containing: bus and train maps, things to do, places to see, and how to get there. Advance bookings can be made. Discounts are available if you mention that you obtained the address from the Arthur Frommer *Dollarwise Guide to England and Scotland*. The bureau also offers a free pickup service from the local station to take you to the accommodation upon arrival. The offices are open Monday through Friday from 9 a.m. to 4 p.m. and Saturday from 9 a.m. until noon; closed Sunday and bank holidays. A free airmail brochure by return mail is available upon request. If you do not have time to book, simply telephone the bureau when you arrive. The staff will usually be able to help you. Rentals are for a minimum of seven days, plus any number of additional days or weeks you require, and start on any day and end on any day. No lease is required, no extra fees, no fuss—in fact, it's as simple as booking into a hotel, but it only costs about half the price of comparable accommodations.

The **Regency Suites,** 130 Queen's Gate, S.W.7 (tel. 370-4242), are well-furnished apartments. Style varies from rather masculine brown leather buttoned chairs, indoor plants, and sober carpeting to warm apricot and white net curtains, flowery armchairs, and soft lights. The kitchens are fully equipped with modern electrical appliances and kitchen utensils, the glass is good, and all the china comes from Wedgwood. The penthouse suites even have a dishwasher to cope with your entertaining program, and all suites are serviced daily. There is 24-hour porterage as well. A wide range of provision shops are just around the corner so you should have to lack for nothing. Several of the larger apartments have their own terraces, equipped with garden furniture and electrically operated sunblinds. All have direct-dial telephone and a doorlock with at TV monitor. There is remote-control TV in all bedrooms and in the lounges. Bathrooms are well equipped, and all line is provided. A studio flat with large reception and bedroom, bath, and kitchen costs from £180 ($351) per week; a double room, lounge, kitchen, and bath from £250 ($487.50). Three-room flats run from £340 ($663) per week; and the penthouses, each with enormous living rooms, three bedrooms each with bath, kitchen, and entrance lobby, are from £1200 ($2340) per week. All rates include VAT and service, and rentals of 22 days or more are preferred. Tube: Gloucester Road.

Draycott House, 10 Draycott Ave., S.W.3 (tel. 584-4659), and its fellow block, 41 Draycott Pl., just across the street, offer what may seem the ultimate in the way of facilities. The old London houses are well converted to provide self-contained luxury apartments and studio flats, furnished in Edwardian style but with modern kitchens and bathrooms. All have private telephone lines and color TV. There are a resident porter and housekeeper, plus maid service five days a week. On your arrival the refrigerator will be stocked with basic provisions, and daily milk and newspapers will be delivered to you. Garage parking is also available. Rates compare very favorably with London hotels. A two-bedroom apartment is about £500 ($975) per week, and a three-bedroom apartment from £625 ($1218.75) to £675 ($1316.25) per week. Studios and one-bedroom apartments range from £225 ($438.75) to £350 ($682.50) per week. No service charge or VAT is added. The rub is that minimum rental is for three weeks. Miss Linda Coulthard is the resident administrator, young and highly experienced in the travel, hotel, and catering industry. In addition to the more domestic details, they can provide Telex, secretarial and translation services, and rental of video equipment for the business person, and will recommend eating places.

HOUSE SWAPPING: This custom is becoming more and more popular among those who spend three weeks or more in Great Britain. In exchange for a caretaker for your New York apartment or California bungalow, you might end up in a vine-covered country cottage.

Home from Home, Oasland's House, 4 Broad Lane, Cottenham, Cambridge, CB4 4SW (tel. 0954/50673), has about 700 properties on their books in the United Kingdom, Europe, U.S.A., and Canada. They have a very simple application form, and for a subscription fee of £17 ($33.15), they will send you a list of properties suitable to your needs, as well as hints to make your exchange smooth and trouble-free. They require payment in sterling, or if you pay in any other currency, they will convert at current rates and add £2 ($3.90).

FOR GOLFERS ONLY: The Golfers Club was started in 1893. It has now opened its doors to overseas members, and an annual subscription of £20 ($39) will give you access to more than 50 golf clubs in England and Scotland, as well as privileged greens fees of around half the normal rates. Membership also permits you to use the Sloane Club in London where accommodations are available at around £18 ($35.10) a night. The 400 or so United Kingdom members will arrange introductions for overseas visitors in the particular area they are visiting. Matches and friendly games are also arranged, and members will even help in lending clubs and equipment. Members are often able to obtain concessionary rates for car rental, restaurants, and hotels. The club also makes up special golf packages for aficionados of the game. Write to Golfers Club, International House, Windmill Road, Sunbury-on-Thames, Middlesex (tel. 09327/85666).

LONDON: RESTAURANTS AND PUBS

WHEN QUEEN ELIZABETH I was released from the Tower, with her stiff neck intact, she feasted on loin of pork and overcooked English peas. Up until the last few years, most of the English agreed with Queen Bess's idea of a feast, sometimes varying the peas with gray cabbage and boiled-to-death brussels sprouts. But the England of Elizabeth I is not the England of Elizabeth II, as your palate will quickly reveal to you if you sample some of the wares in the upcoming restaurants.

A new wave of skilled cooking, inspired by the continent and visitors' demands, has swept the country, but is most noticeable in London. Of course, the trend toward continental dishes is not without its pretensions. As novelist-historian-gourmet Raymond Postgate pointed out, boiled beef and carrots are still served, passed off as "la pièce de boeuf salée londonienne." A striking feature of the dining scene in London and the country is the emergence of the personality restaurant—that is, a dining spot based on the character, charm, and individual recipes of one exceptional chef.

Many Americans accustomed to spices and mixing and blending of foods find English cooking dull. Of course, the French show their disdain by calling anything plain, boiled, or cooked in the blandest way possible "à l'anglaise." However, simplicity doesn't mean bad food, and it's good to keep that in mind as you dine in London and elsewhere in England and Scotland.

All restaurants and cafés in Britain are required to display the prices of the food and drink they offer, in a place where the customer can see them before entering the eating area. If an establishment has an extensive à la carte menu, the prices of a representative selection of food and drink currently available must be displayed as well as the table d'hôte menu, if one is offered. Charges for service and any minimum charge or cover charge must also be made clear. The prices shown must be inclusive of VAT.

1. The Top Restaurants

Waltons, 121 Walton St., S.W.3 (tel. 584-0204). Dish after dish reflects the professionalism, enthusiasm, and creative skill of a fine chef, Shamus Barrett, a Scotsman. He is inspired. Not only is the cooking inventive, but the presentation is enchanting against a backdrop of an intimate modern decor. For an utterly delightful dining experience, go upstairs first and order an apéritif while looking over the menu leisurely.

As you're shown to your seat, you pass through a setting that blends Trianon gray with buttercup yellow and mauve tiles. The china is Royal Copenhagen: the cutlery, Georg Jensen.

A four-course dinner is featured at prices ranging from £20 ($39). I'd suggest beginning with the green vegetable pâté or else a pâté of hare and wood pigeon, if either of these openers is featured on the night of your visit. Main courses are likely to include rainbow trout poached in a whisky cream sauce, saffron chicken (based on an 18th-century recipe), or chicken suprême, even collops (fried slices of meat) in the pan. Although the prices are among the loftiest in the United Kingdom, the quality of the service and cuisine seem to merit them. You must make a reservation unless you plan to appear unannounced with the Queen of England on your arm.

This dinner of four courses, with international dishes, is served daily, except Sunday. However, you might prefer "Simply Waltons" at £7.50 ($14.63), a light lunch which changes frequently (again, not on Sunday.) A three-course luncheon menu at £13 ($25.35) is featured daily except Sunday as well. On Sunday the traditional English weekend lunch of roast meats is offered for £7 ($13.65) and a three-course dinner for £12 ($23.40). In addition to the regular dinner, a late supper, costing £7 ($13.65), is presented after the theater, including a selection of principal dishes along with petit fours. VAT and service are extra. The extensive wine list offers 90 château-bottled clarets from a wide range of vintages at reasonable prices. Thirty red burgundies are listed and champagne features extensively with 35 labels always available. Warre's 1963 port is decanted daily, and a full list of liqueurs and single vintage cognac from the House of Hine is always obtainable. The restaurant is open for luncheon from 12:30 to 2:30 p.m. (last order) and for dinner from 7:30 to 11:30 p.m.

Parkes and Mr. Benson's Bar, 5 Beauchamp Pl., S.W.3 (tel. 589-1390), is the pioneer of the new sort of gourmet restaurants that have sprung up in London; it has turned its back on the classic, dignified setting, the traditional French cooking, and has forged ahead to create a unique cuisine. Founded in the '50s by the late Ray Parkes, it was subsequently taken over by his assistant, Tom Benson, who not only carries on, but improves standards yearly.

It's on a short street of boutiques off Brompton Road, reached by a deceivingly small entrance. Inside is a *Town & Country* setting for portraying appetizing foods.

There are three intimate rooms for dining. Your host, Peter Dunn, will usher you to an upper-level drinking lounge where menu selections are made. A set dinner goes for £18 ($35.10), although if you order à la carte expect to spend from £24 ($46.80), including wine. The menu is highly personal and just a few dishes are prepared daily; the combinations reflect great imagination. A recent sampling: blackberry melon, or figs and smoked salmon as appetizers, followed by mussels in Pernod sauce or else asparagus and nut soup. Main dishes include boned chicken with spinach and almonds sole or crab en croûte, and roast partridge. Accompanying such plates is a green salad or a cheese pâte and freshly made herb bread. Among dessert listings, you're likely to find a grapefruit sorbet, and other items to tempt you. Last, you'll be served coffee and bittersweets. Dinner is from 7:30 to 11 p.m., except Saturday and Sunday. Lunch, offered from 12:15 to 2:45 p.m., features a shorter menu. Tube: Knightsbridge.

Carrier's, 2–4 Camden Passage, The Angel, N.1 (tel. 226-5353), is the special domain of Robert Carrier, one of the leading cookbook writers in the British Isles. His restaurant is in a tiny antique row district of Islington, where little shops and booths are crammed to the ceiling with antiques and bric-a-brac. Everybody makes the trip, and Mr. Carrier proves a point—if you serve exciting food, the world will find its way to your door.

To simplify matters, both the lunch and dinner have set prices, the former costing from £13.75 ($26.81), the latter from £16 ($31.20), both plus VAT. In addition, the chef also does a three-course club luncheon menu at £9 ($17.55) per head, plus wine, a 12¼% service charge, and VAT. He also does a three-course supper menu at £10 ($19.50) per head, plus wine, service, and VAT (available from 10:30 p.m.). Appetizers are likely to include the house specialty, brandade of smoked trout. You might follow with leek and pumpkin soup. For your main course, you can make selections from "the open fire" or else "the great dish of the day." All the main dishes are served with a choice of gratin Dauphinois or saffron rice, as well as a green salad with herb dressing. A dessert treat, when featured, is a cold chocolate soufflé. The wine list is modest, but sufficient. Carrier's is open Monday through Saturday from 12:30 to 2:30 p.m. and from 7:30 till 11:30 p.m. Tube: Angel.

2. The West End

We'll begin the pleasant task of exploring the cuisine in the major districts of the West End:

ST. JAMES'S: In the former playground of royalty is a well-recommended French restaurant.

The Upper Bracket

A l'Ecu de France, 111 Jermyn St., S.W.1 (tel. 930-2837), offers the quintessence of French cuisine. It's not cheap, but then you wouldn't expect it to be. A short block from Piccadilly, the restaurant attracts Londoners with bowlers and briefcases, as well as numerous well-heeled visiting French diners. The atmosphere is traditional, without ostentation. Pillars with mirrors reflect the dark walls in discreet lighting. There's a relaxing atmosphere with a touch of elegance. On the right of the menu, there is a prix-fixe luncheon choice for £10 ($19.50). A set dinner is offered on Saturday and Sunday only at £15 ($29.25). Otherwise, dinner is à la carte, and prices range from £22 ($42.90). Singled out for special praise are the coquilles St-Jacques (scallops baked in their shells), the crêpe de volaille (poultry) princess, and the boeuf en croûte (filet of beef cooked in pastry and served with truffle sauce). The veal served in a delicate wine sauce is outstanding. There is a good selection of desserts, including soufflé aux liqueurs and gâteau fromage. Sunday dinner hours are from 7 to 10:30 p.m. Weekday hours are from 12:30 to 2:30 p.m. and from 6:30 to 11:15 p.m. No lunch is served on Saturday or Sunday. Tube: Piccadilly Circus.

PICCADILLY CIRCUS: Garish, neon, crowded, but exciting Piccadilly Circus keeps time with the heartbeat of a mighty city. Here, from all sections of the city, come the aristocrat, the housewife, the revolutionary, the government official, the secretary, the pimp, the financier. They converge around the statue of Eros.

Much of your London activity will center here, so finding the right restaurant is important, as many establishments are unabashed tourist traps or sleazy joints. The following restaurants have been selected not only for the quality of their food but because they offer the best value for the money.

The Upper Bracket

The **China Garden**, 66 Brewer St., W.1 (tel. 437-6500), is probably the most sophisticated and richly adorned Chinese restaurant in the West End. The bar entrance is dramatically conceived, with a stairway railed with brass bamboo poles leading down to the softly lit dining room, the stage center of which is reserved for dancing. The mood is set for a seductive evening, and the lure is the food, an authentically prepared selection of more than 200 dishes.

Owner Tong Wong has carefully planned various groups of meals for one to four persons. For example, a dinner for two ranges from £7.50 ($14.63) to £10 ($19.50) per person. Among the more interesting items on the à la carte menu are sharkfin soup at £4.20 ($8.19) and Peking duck, £17 ($33.15) for four persons, including all the trimmings. The chef also does an excellent dish of prawns in sesame seed (called elephant eye) for £4.20 ($8.19). A good selection of desserts includes a toffee apple or a toffee banana, £2.50 ($4.88) for two persons. The restaurant is open daily, except Sunday, from noon to 2:30 p.m. and from 6 p.m. to 1 a.m. Tube: Piccadilly Circus.

The Budget Range

Richoux of London, 172 Piccadilly, W.1 (tel. 493-2204), is a restaurant with a fresh clean decor, along with attractive serving girls in starched aprons and caps. Comfortable, well-arranged tables give a degree of privacy. It is open from 9 a.m. to 1 a.m., seven days a week.

Breakfast can be a simple juice and scrambled eggs or a big brunch-type meal. Throughout the day the waitresses serve omelets. House specialties are steak-and-kidney pie and a chicken-and-mushroom vol-au-vent. There's also a variety of well-stuffed sandwiches, everything from club to smoked salmon.

Afternoon tea sees hot scones brought out, along with strawberry jam and freshly whipped cream. Pastries from the trolley include a chocolate fudge cake. All prices include VAT, but service is extra. The smallest tab is likely to be £2.50 ($4.88), although, depending on what you order, you can spend from £8 ($15.60) for a big meal here. Tube: Piccadilly Circus.

The Granary, Albemarle Street, W.1 (tel. 493-2978), is open from 10 a.m. to mid-evening, serving throughout this time a good variety of hot dishes, all of which have a real home-cooked flavor. For prices ranging from £1.60 ($3.12) to £2.10 ($4.10), you can order such dishes as cauliflower with cheese or beef Stroganoff. Salads are also available. Everything can be taken in foil containers to eat elsewhere. (Remember, no VAT is charged for food carried away.) A number of desserts and homemade cakes are offered at 80p ($1.56) a serving. A meal averages £3 ($5.85), including a glass of wine. Tube: Piccadilly Circus.

The Carvery, on the ground floor of the Regent Palace Hotel, Glasshouse Street, W.1 (tel. 734-7000), is just 20 feet from Piccadilly Circus. Who'd think that for £8 ($15.60) you could have all that your plate can hold of fabulous roasts and be able to go back for seconds, even thirds? Yet that's the policy of this renowned, all-you-can-eat establishment, a winner with visitors seeking rib-sticking food. The first course, perhaps a large slice of chilled melon, is served at your table. After that, you can go to the buffet table, where roast prime ribs of beef (choice of rare or well done), Yorkshire pudding, roast leg of Southdown lamb with mint sauce, and a roast leg of pork with apple sauce are spread before you.

You carve the meat yourself, slicing off as much as you want, although carvers stand by to assist and give instructions on how to wield the knife. You can then heap your heated plate with buttered peas, roast potatoes, new carrots, and gravy. In another area is a display of cold joints and assorted salads—whatever is in season. A plate of fresh fruit and a pitcher of thick cream are brought in for dessert, or you can select from the dessert trolley such delights as meringue or chocolate and pineapple gâteaux, perhaps a strawberry mousse. Well-brewed coffee for "afters" is included in the price. The Carvery is open Monday to Saturday from noon to 3 p.m. and 5:30 to 9 p.m., and on Sunday from 12:30 to 2:30 p.m. and 6 to 9 p.m. Tube: Piccadilly Circus.

Good news department: There are many more Carvery establishments in London, with the same policy and the same menu. One is within the Tower Hotel, an ideal place to lunch when you visit the Tower of London. The tab here will run £9.50 ($18.53), however. Then there is one at the Strand Palace Hotel, on the Strand. Here the decor is fetching: black tufted booths, a wood-paneled ceiling, decorative artifacts on the walls, a huge old wine press, modern paintings, Italian engravings, and converted baroque kerosene lanterns. At the Cumberland Hotel, at Marble Arch, the Carvery is more clublike, with tables on two levels, where you dine in low-lit, seductive atmosphere. It's convenient for Paddington and the West End area. A Carvery is also at the Kingsley Hotel, Bloomsbury Way, close to the British Museum.

Hard Rock Café, on Piccadilly at Hyde Park Corner, W.1 (tel. 629-0382), is as close as London comes to having a roadhouse diner or truck stop, reminiscent of the American South. Naturally, two Americans, one from Memphis, the other from Chicago, opened it. Popular with the young English, it is open from noon to the early hours of the morning. Pop music is played in the background. The Hard Rock soup of the day goes for 85p ($1.66). A half-pound "Down Home" double-burger is served for £3.20 ($6.24), including a salad. Hot chili (in winter) and crackers is priced at £3 ($5.85). Ice cream is home-made, costing £1.20 ($2.34) a dish. Still immensely popular, the café often has a long line waiting outside to get in. Tube: Piccadilly Circus.

LEICESTER SQUARE: Named for the Earl of Leicester, and once the site of the home of Sir Joshua Reynolds, Leicester Square has since become the movie center of London. The 19th-century square is a congested area of stores, theaters, movie houses, even churches. It also has some inexpensive restaurants and pubs (popular with West End actors) in its little offshoot lanes and alleyways.

The Medium-Priced Range

London Swiss Centre Restaurant, New Coventry Street, W.1 (tel. 734-1291), is a showcase four-in-one restaurant where Switzerland wins friends and influences palates. Opened in 1968 and dedicated to bettering people-to-people relationships between England and Switzerland, this group of restaurants prepares Swiss cuisine with consummate skill. You can dine either in the Chesa,

Rendez-Vous, Taverne, or the Locanda. Hot meals are served until midnight. The Chesa is the most expensive, the Locanda and Taverne medium priced, and Rendez-Vous the cheapest.

In the Taverne, the excellent cheese fondue is served for £4.50 ($8.78). In the Locanda Swiss and Italian dishes, including pasta, are presented. The informal Rendez-Vous serves an interesting range of snacks and light meals as well as hamburgers and steak tartare. Finally, in the Chesa you can enjoy specialties such as Züri-Gschnätzlets, a spectacular émincé of veal served with rösti potatoes, £7 ($13.65).

There is also an Imbiss for snacks, open seven days a week, 8:30 a.m. to 11:30 p.m. (on Sunday from 11:30 a.m. to 11:30 p.m.). Tube: Leicester Square.

J. Sheekey Ltd., 29–31 St. Martin's Court, W.C.2 (tel. 240-2565), is an 1896 restaurant-fishbar that over the years has been a gathering place for show people (autographed celebrity photos on the wall). Trying to get a table may make you feel like a salmon going upstream, but it's worth it. Sheekey serves a pre- and after-theater meal. For a beginning, we'd suggest the smoked fish pâté for £1.30 ($2.54). A regular dish of the day, such as fish pie, is usually offered at about £3.15 ($6.14). Naturally, the chef features jellied eels, costing £4.75 ($9.26). Most fish dishes are either grilled or poached. The large Dover sole, at this writing, goes for £6 ($11.70). The restaurant is open Monday through Saturday from 12:30 to 3 p.m. and from 5:30 to 11:30 p.m. It faces the stage doors of the Albury and Wyndham's theaters. Tube: Leicester Square.

Manzi's, 1–2 Leicester St., off Leicester Square, W.C.2 (tel. 734-0224), is London's oldest seafood restaurant. Here you can get that jellied eel you've heard so much about, or else real Dover sole which overflows your platter. This lively Soho seafood restaurant doesn't waste much effort on decor, but the fish is fresh and it's proved so reliable that a loyal clientele has patronized Manzi's for years. Perhaps the waiters aren't English any more, but otherwise the recipes are much the same. You can begin with a prawn cocktail at £1.50 ($2.93) or perhaps half a dozen Whitstable oysters at £4 ($7.80). Recently I sampled the legendary jellied eels at £2.20 ($4.29); fresh sardines, £2.20 also; and crab salad, £4.20 ($8.19). Other recommendable courses include the Dover sole at £6 ($11.70) and grilled turbot, £6 also. If you don't prefer the ground-floor restaurant, then you can ask to go up to the Cabin Room on the next floor. Hours are from noon to 2:40 p.m. and from 5:30 till 11:45 p.m. Tube: Leicester Square.

San Martino, 46 St. Martin's Lane, W.C.2 (tel. 240-2336), is a typical Italian eating place, the entrance hall with its enormous mouthwatering display of cold delicacies leading to the lounge where a piano softly plays while you sip your apéritif. They do a set pre- or post theater meal for £7.50 ($14.63), offering a choice of appetizers, followed by osso buco, a cold buffet, grilled trout, or chicken with two vegetables, then fruit salad, trifle, cassata, or crème caramel, and coffee.

The regular à la carte menu has a wide range of appetizers, including an enormous plate of mixed hors d'oeuvres of sardine, squid, whitebait, vegetables, and salads. This is to be avoided if you plan a substantial main course. There are the usual spaghetti, cannelloni, and lasagne dishes. Main courses include fagottino San Martino, and veal filets with cheese and ham filling and wine and mushroom sauce. There is also a good trolley of desserts. House wine is around £5.50 ($10.73) a bottle, or you can choose from a selection of more expensive Italian vintages. The price of a meal generally runs from £9 ($17.55) to £12 ($23.40). The restaurant is open Monday to Friday for lunch from noon to 3 p.m., and then from 5:30 to 11:30 p.m. for dinner. It's closed on Saturday for lunch and on Sunday. Tube: Leicester Square.

ON THE STRAND: In another major geographic and tourist center, the Strand, you'll probably want to consider what we view as the most English restaurant in the world:

The Medium-Priced Range

Simpson's-in-the-Strand, 100 The Strand, W.C.2 is more an institution than a restaurant. All this very Victorian place needs is an Empire; it has everything else—Adam paneling, crystal, and an army of grandly formal waiters hovering about—in all, an atmosphere reminiscent of a gentleman's club. On most visitors' lists there is this notation: "See the changing of the guard, lunch at Simpson's." It's that popular. Consequently, you must call in advance for reservations (tel. 836-9112).

There is one point most diners agree on: Simpson's serves the best roasts (joints) in London. Huge roasts are trolleyed to your table by faithful retainers and you can have slabs of beef carved off and served with traditional Yorkshire pudding. The classic dishes are: roast sirloin of beef, roast saddle of lamb with red currant jelly, roast Aylesbury duck with apple sauce, sausage and mash, and steak, kidney, and mushroom pie. All dishes include the near-legendary Simpson's cabbage, as well as potatoes and rolls. Remember to tip the carver so you won't get one of those frightening, contemptuous British stares. The classic dessert is the boiled treacle roll. Men should wear jackets and ties. A complete meal will cost about £14 ($27.30). Lunch is from noon to 3 p.m., dinner from 6 to 10 p.m. Tube: The Strand.

Joe Allen's, 13 Exeter St., W.C.2 (tel. 836-0651), has invaded London with his red-checked tablecloths and spinach salad, not to mention barbecued ribs and bowls of chili. Londoners, of course, by now are long familiar with American invasions, so Mr. Allen didn't create a revolution. The decor is actually an improvement on its New York namesake, the London Restaurant appearing more openly inviting. I even enjoy the food better in the English eatery. The food is solid, reliable, uninspired, but, on the other hand, rarely disappointing. Try the familiar specialties: black bean soup, barbecued ribs, the regular spinach salad, a bowl of chili, calf liver and onions, and the really tasty carrot cake. Expect to spend at least £6 ($11.70). The items of the day are listed on a blackboard menu. Naturally, show business posters adorn the walls. Service is by friendly waiters and waitresses who just may be out-of-work actors and actresses. The guests are often people connected with the world of the theater. Joe Allen's is open until 1 a.m. every day (till midnight on Sunday). The bar closes from 3 to 5:30 p.m. (from 2 to 7 p.m. on Sunday). Tube: The Strand.

The Budget Range

Lyons Corner House, 450 The Strand, W.C.2 (tel. 930-9381), is a whisper from the past. Once Lyons Corner Houses were much more prominent, having fed hungry Londoners for decades. This white-fronted place with gold trimmings offers a wide variety of fast food and traditional English dishes at reasonable prices. Meals are served by a new generation of waitresses known, as their predecessors were, as "Nippies," for the way they get around among the tables. Dressed in black frocks and natty white aprons, they serve hamburgers, eggs on toast, toasted cheese, welsh rarebit—all the familiar snacks—in the coffeeshop on the ground floor, along with soft drinks, tea, or coffee throughout the day.

The Garden Restaurant serves more substantial meals, including steak and french fries, roast chicken and vegetables, fried fish and chips. In the evening they offer a set Dine and Wine menu when £5.75 ($11.22) will buy you a cocktail and a quarter bottle of wine. On Sunday the Brunch and Wine menu at £6 ($11.70) includes wine and a cocktail. Children enjoy the same menu, but with a soft drink, for £4.50 ($8.78). The establishment is open from 10 a.m. to 11 p.m. daily. Alcoholic drinks can only be served during licensing hours. Tube: The Strand.

COVENT GARDEN: In 1970, London's flower, fruit, and veg market celebrated its 300th anniversary. But Auld Lang Syne should have been the theme song that day, as the historic, congested market was transferred in 1974 to a $7.2-million, 64-acre site at Nine Elms, in the suburb of Vauxhall, 2½ miles away, across the Thames.

Covent Garden dates from the time when the monks of Westminster Abbey dumped their surplus home-grown vegetables there. In 1670 Charles II granted the Earl of Bedford the right to "sell roots and herbs, whatsoever" in the district. The king's mistress, Nell Gwynne, once peddled oranges on Drury Lane (and later appeared on the stage of the **Drury Lane Theatre**).

Before that, in the 1630s, Inigo Jones designed the square. He hoped to complete a plaza in the Florentine style, but the work on it got bogged down. Even his self-tabbed handsomest barn in England, **St. Paul's Covent Garden,** burned down in the late 18th century and was subsequently rebuilt. The English actress, Dame Ellen Terry (noted in particular for her letters to G. B. Shaw), is buried there, incidentally. St. Paul's eastern face looks down on the market where Pygmalion's Professor Higgins met his "squashed cabbage leaf," Eliza Doolittle.

Also in the area is the **Royal Opera House** on Bow Street, housing the Royal Ballet and the Royal Opera Company. On nearby Russell Street, Samuel Johnson met his admirer, Boswell, and coffeehouses in the district were once patronized by Addison and Steele. Just as chicly dressed people once flocked to Les Halles in Paris to have onion soup, so London revelers used to drop in at Covent Garden's pubs to drink with Cockney barrow boys in the early dawn hours. The tradition will be sadly missed.

Covent Garden has now been turned into a commercial and entertainment district, complete with restaurants, hotels, and a convention center. Conservationists won a major battle in 1973, when the Department of Environment ruled that 250 buildings near the market site be preserved as historic, plus 80 already designated. What Londoners set out to achieve was something like the preserved character of Bourbon Street in New Orleans.

An old cabbage warehouse was reopened as the Jubilee Market. Monday is the antique market, and Saturday and Sunday are the days of a crafts market. Cockney costermongers (vegetable traders) have moved in in force, including Barry Teeden, the fastest apple polisher in the business, and Ginger Hurd, purveyor of jellied eels.

There are new exclusive clubs here, such as the **Zanzibar** and the **Rock Garden.** The **Blitz** offers snacks, and **Brahms and Liszt** offers drinks.

And the area has begun to attract art galleries, such as the Acme, the Hammond Lloyd, the Covent Garden, and the William Drummond. A new plant shop, the Neal Street, specializes in Chinese vases used as planters.

It's appropriate that art galleries should be returning to Covent Garden. In the 18th century it was a beehive of artists, including Lely and Kneller (famous portrait painters, the latter of whom is buried at St. Paul's Church, around the corner). Others who lived here were Thornhill, Richard Wilson, Fuseli, Daniel Mytens, the sculptor Roubiliac, Zoffany, and Flaxman. The American painter Benjamin West also lived here after he got out of jail for trying to study in London during the Revolution.

The Upper Bracket

Inigo Jones, 14 Garrick St., W.C.2 (tel. 836-6456), offers a mainly French menu and superbly cooked fresh vegetables, in a romantic setting, a former stained-glass studio in Covent Garden. It appears that you're arriving at a chapel door. During the reconstruction of the building, five stained-glass windows were discovered, and they were used decoratively in the present establishment. Listening to gentle harpsichord music, you are served while seated on a soft brown woolen banquette placed against a rough-textured brick wall. Filtered light focuses on wooden carved gargoyles and saints placed on the walls. Service by waiters in leather aprons is friendly and efficient. It's costly, but then you would expect it to be. For a beginning, why not one of the soups in the £2.05 ($4) to £4.50 ($8.78) range? For a main dish, we'd recommend the boned saddle of English lamb, baked in puff pastry, £24.20 ($47.19) for two persons although you may prefer Dover sole meunière at £12.70 ($24.77). As a side course, I especially like the shredded lettuce and spinach salad with bacon at £2.20 ($4.29). The restaurant is closed for lunch on Saturday and all day Sunday. Otherwise, hours are from 12:30 to 2:30 p.m. and from 6 to 11:45 p.m. Tube: Covent Garden.

The Medium-Priced Range

Poons of Covent Garden, 41 King St., W.C.2 (tel. 240-1743), is one of the best Chinese restaurants in London. The place is run by Wai-Lim (Bill) and his wife, Cecilia Poon. Mr. Poon's great-great-grandfather cooked for the Chinese emperors, and succeeding generations of the family have all interested themselves in traditional Chinese cookery. The decor is reminiscent of *The World of Suzie Wong.* Tables surround an island see-through kitchen which has been the subject of some controversy. I personally like it, as it's fascinating to stand and watch the chefs go through their intricate steps. The house specializes in wind-dried meat, including sausage, which is quite different in flavor from smoked. Two of the most recommendable courses include Poons special crispy duck from £9 ($17.55) and Poons special wind-dried meat with seasonal greens at £4.80 ($9.36). For a beginning, you might select the sharkfin broth at £2.80 ($5.46) or the bird's-nest soup at £2.80 also. Other preferred specialties include Poons special crispy chicken (one half) for £6 ($11.70), and sweet-and-sour pork based on an original recipe, £3.80 ($7.41).

If you're a serious and dedicated gourmet of the Chinese cuisine, as are many people these days, you'll find Poons willing to provide you with some rare and delectable specialties, providing you give them 24 hours' notice. Ever had stewed duck's feet with fish lips? Cecilia Poon is usually on hand to explain the niceties of the menu and to discuss the ingredients of any particular dish. They also do a set lunch at £11 ($21.45) for two persons, £16.50 ($32.16) for three persons, or £22 ($42.90) for four diners. The restaurant is open from noon to midnight daily except Sunday. Tube: Covent Garden.

Rules, 35 Maiden Lane, off the Strand, W.C.2 (tel. 836-5314), dates back to 1798 when it made its debut as an oyster bar. Over its long and legendary history, it has been the steady haunt of actors and actresses, newspaper columnists, and barristers. In the Gay '90s, the Prince of Wales (later Edward VII) was its most famous patron, accompanied, as always, by the Jersey Lily. The prince dined on the second floor, now the Edward VII Room. Pictures of Lillie hang in the alcove where they used to sit. Another alcove honors Charles Dickens, who used to dine and do some of his writing at Rules. The restaurant is under the care of John Shrimpton.

You enter via the front bar, with its red plush settees. The walls are hung with cartoons George Whitelaw did in the '20s and '30s. Rules specializes in dishes such as jugged hare, grilled Dover sole, grouse, steak, and kidney pie, and Rules duckling, the latter served for two persons. In season, hare soup is a specialty. Apple and blackberry pie with fresh cream makes a good finish. Meals begin at £10 ($19.50) per person, plus the cost of your drink. Reservations are important, and a pretheater dinner is available between 6 and 7:30 p.m. Rules is open for lunch and dinner Monday to Friday, and dinner only on Saturday. The restaurant is closed on Sunday and bank holidays. Tube: Covent Garden.

Boulestin, 25 Southampton St., W.C.2 (tel. 836-7061). This famous old restaurant, founded by Marcel Boulestin, the first Fleet Street restaurant critic, more than half a century ago has had a facelift. It's reached by a side door which goes down into the basement beneath a bank. The decor is warmly gold and tortoiseshell. Sober pictures of cattle and deer adorn the walls in a very British manner, but the menu is entirely French. Appetizers include soups and pâtés, although you'll have to pay around £4 ($7.80) for the more elaborate appetizers. For a main course, I'd recommend such dishes as filets de sole à la vapeur de vermouth at £7.50 ($14.63), and noix de carré d'agneau sur lit d'oignons blanc at £6.50 ($12.68). Desserts include salad de fruits brouillés, £2.50 ($4.88), mousses, and sorbets, and there is a wide choice of house wines (half bottles are available). VAT is included in the prices quoted, although a 15% service charge is added. The restaurant serves Monday to Friday from noon to 2:30 p.m. and from 7 to 11:15 p.m. (from 7 to 11:15 p.m. only on Saturday). Tube: Covent Garden.

Tuttons, 11–12 Russell St., W.C.2 (tel. 836-1167), sits on the side of Covent Garden's piazza with wide windows overlooking the square and the Opera House. The restaurant has stone floors and clean wooden tables. It opens from 9 a.m. for breakfast, with fresh hot croissants, works through morning coffee, lunch, and tea to dinner, closing around 11:30 p.m. The atmosphere is businesslike, and the service quick and cheery. Various quiches go for £1.50 ($2.93) to £2.25 ($4.39), pâtés and mousses for £1.40 ($2.73). Main courses include steak-and-kidney pie at £3.40 ($6.63), game pie and salad at £3.20 ($6.24), and salmon trout mayonnaise at £5.50 ($10.73). Desserts start at 75p ($1.46) and rise to £1.30 ($2.54) for profiteroles. Down below the snackbar is another restaurant, serving gazpacho at £1.30 ($2.54) or oyster pâté at £1.60 ($3.12). A Barnsley chop costs £5 ($9.75); rump steak with bananas, £5.50 ($10.73); and a baby chicken in mushroom sauce, £4.20 ($8.19). Downstairs, where it's better to reserve a table for dinner as it gets quite full, the restaurant is open from noon to 2:30 p.m. and 5:30 to 11:30 p.m. daily except Sunday. The street-level restaurant is open seven days a week from 11 a.m. to 12:30 a.m. the following morning. Tube: Covent Garden.

The more expensive list includes salmon and turbot pâté, fresh raw vegetables, and artichokes with taramasalata. Then roast saddle of venison, rack of lamb, filet of beef, or poached turbot. Desserts include fruit fools and mousses, apple and hazelnut tart, Nesselrode pudding, or various sorbets. There is Stilton cheese and coffee. The Grange is open Monday to Friday from 12:30 to 2:30 p.m. and from 7:30 to 11:30 p.m.; on Saturday from 6:45 to 11:30 p.m. Closed Sunday. Tube: Covent Garden.

The Budget Range

Penny's Place, 6 King St., W.C.2 (tel. 836-4553), is a wine and food bar in an old Victorian pub still with the mirrors and the antique mahogany woodwork. Snacks include various pâtés, crab, taramasalata, crab vol-au-vents, onion soup, quiches, chili, spare ribs, and chicken liver at £1.50 ($2.93) to £1.75 ($3.41). There is a wide selection of wines, a glass costing around 60p ($1.17). The place is open from 11 a.m. to 3 p.m. and from 5:30 to 11 p.m. Closed Sunday. There is live music on Friday and Saturday nights. Tube: Covent Garden.

Calabash Restaurant, 38 King St., W.C.2 (tel. 836-1976), is the only African restaurant in London, underneath the Africa Centre. A simply furnished place with a bar, it has an informal atmosphere. Dishes from all over Africa are offered, with fish and chicken a specialty. Pepperpot soup with bread costs £1.20 ($2.34). Also offered are Egusi (Nigerian) beef stew with melon seeds; spinach, dried shrimps, and fresh peppers; firire of fish (Senegal) with tomato sauce and potatoes; Nyama yo Phika (Malawi) beef stew with sweet peppers; or stew from the Ivory Coast with okra in palm oil—each going for £2.80 ($5.46). Pineapple fritters with rum round off the meal at £1.30 ($2.54). The restaurant is open Monday to Friday from noon to 3 p.m. and from 6:30 to 11 p.m.; on Saturday from 6:30 to 11 p.m. Closed Sunday. Tube: Covent Garden.

READER'S RESTAURANT SELECTION: "Food for Thought, 31 Neal St., W.C.2 (tel.836-0239), is a small place with inexpensive vegetarian food. Better go at odd hours—perhaps in the middle of the afternoon. Otherwise, it's likely to be crowded. Everybody ends up sitting with and often talking with everybody else. It's most congenial. The establishment is a basement café in the heart of the theater and movie district. From the Covent Garden tube station, walk along Neal Street toward Shaftesbury Avenue. The restaurant will be in the second block on the left. It's open Monday through Friday from noon to 8 p.m. The price of a meal for two is around £6 ($11.70) (Vicki Banks, London, England).

HIGH HOLBORN: In "legal London," you can join barristers, solicitors, and law clerks at the following recommendation.

The Budget Range

My Old Dutch, 132 High Holborn, W.C.1 (tel. 242-5200), is a cheerful, friendly place, resembling a Dutch kitchen with scrubbed pine tables at which you can be served 101 different pancakes—all enormous—on huge Delft plates. Fillings and garnishes include cheese, meats, and vegetables, as well as sweet fillings such as Adam's Downfall—that is, figs and avocado. The cost of an average meal is around £3.50 ($6.83). If you don't want a pancake, you can order a cold platter of meat and a salad. Fresh ground coffee and hot chocolate are available to wash it all down. My Old Dutch stays open from noon to midnight Sunday through Wednesday, and noon to 1 a.m. on Thursday, Friday, and Saturday. Tube: Holborn.

WESTMINSTER: Our dining expedition to Westminster begins in one of London's famous fish houses:

The Medium-Priced Range

Overton's, 4 Victoria Buildings, S.W.1 (tel. 834-3774), may not have been visited by Queen Victoria (it was founded in her day), but her image is indelibly imprinted on this second-floor restaurant overlooking Victoria Station (another branch is at 5 St. James's). The specialties of the house, the fish dishes, are worth getting excited about. If it swims, Overton's has it. You can devour some Whitstable oysters for £9 ($17.55) per dozen. Main-dish specialties include sole Overton at £7.75 ($15.11) and poached halibut at £6 ($11.70). The bisque de homard at £1.75 ($3.41) is a good beginning, and desserts begin at £1.25 ($2.44). You can order a carafe of wine for £1.75 ($3.41) to £6 ($11.70). A little oyster bar adjoins the main restaurant. The place is closed on Sunday. Tube: Victoria Station.

Bumbles, 16 Buckingham Palace Rd., S.W.1 (tel. 828-2903), gives you a chance to dine just 300 yards from Buckingham Palace. John D. Forbes places emphasis on cooking originality, above-average but moderately priced food, and gracious service by young women once described as "very sweet." There is a full wine list, including English wines, from £4.50 ($8.78) including VAT. The staff will make menu suggestions. Serving hours are Monday to Friday from noon to 2:15 p.m. and from 6 p.m. to midnight (last orders at 10:30 p.m.). Saturday hours are from 6 p.m., with the last orders placed at 10:30 p.m. The restaurant is closed all day Sunday and on bank holidays.

Both luncheon and supper choices are written on a super-large sheet of brown wrapping paper. Bumbles soup of the day costs £1.20 ($2.34), followed by a large selection of main courses, which average about £4.50 ($8.78) in price. On my most recent visit I enjoyed a leg of lamb stuffed with mushrooms, onions, and rosemary, then roasted and cut into steaks, caramelized with red-currant jelly and served with sauteed potatoes and cauliflower. Tube: Victoria Station.

Le Steak Nicole, 72–73 Wilton Rd., S.W.1 (tel. 834-7301), is a bistro run on French lines, with tables placed on the pavement in summer. There's a tiny dining room on the ground floor and more room in the basement. You can have your usual "tipple" at the bar while deliberating about your meal. Try a Kir, white wine and cassis, or one of the essentially French apéritifs, St. Raphael or Suze, so as not to destroy your tastebuds.

The owners, Graham Collard and Tony Clane, offer entrecôte cooked as you wish, cut finely in strips, and often served in a creamy garlic sauce (no garlic if you say so beforehand), with unlimited french fries and a choice of two salads (a green one with french dressing and a raw vegetable one with vinaigrette). Desserts include caramelized oranges, or else you may prefer just cheese and coffee. An average two-course meal, along with a half bottle of wine, goes for £8 ($15.60). VAT and service are extra. The restaurant serves from noon to 2:30 p.m. Monday to Friday, and from 6:30 to 11 p.m. Monday to Saturday. Tube: Victoria Station.

Pomegranates, 94 Grosvenor Rd., S.W.1 (tel. 828-6560). The owner of this basement restaurant, Patrick Gwynn-Jones, has traveled far and collected dishes from throughout the world. Asian and Indonesian delicacies vie for a place on the menu with European dishes, spiced pickled salmon with sweet mustard sauce, leg of lamb with herbs, veal kidneys deviled lightly. The decor is purely European—soft amber lights, mirrors, and well-laid tables. Bread is baked fresh twice a day, and vegetables are cooked when fresh, adding to the pleasure of a good meal. You should get away for about £18 ($35.10) a person, including wine, but if you start in on the more exotic dishes or the luscious desserts—grapefruit and gin sorbet, honey and brandy ice cream—it will probably cost more. The place is open for lunch from 12:30 to 2:15 p.m. Monday to Friday, and for dinner from 7:30 to 11:15 p.m. Monday to Saturday. There is a very good wine list and some reasonable house wines. A set lunch of three courses costs from £7.50 ($14.63), excluding wines. It's best reached by taxi.

BELGRAVIA: Belgravia after dark used to be a gastronomic wilderness. Happily, that situation has changed.

The Medium-Priced Range

Drones, 1 Pont St., S.W.1 (tel. 235-9638), was labeled by one newspaper columnist the "unofficial club for the bright people, at least half of whom seem to know each other." David Niven & Friends launched this two-floor restaurant, and its reputation for charm and chic has long ago spread. Reservations are imperative, preferably a day in advance. There's no elaborate menu, no fancy sauces, just simple but good food. At lunch have the Droneburger at £2.70 ($5.27), a favorite. For dinner, the calf liver with bacon is delicious (have it cooked pink if you prefer). As an appetizer, the chef's pâté poivre vert is worthy. A main-dish specialty is the chili. My heartiest recommendation goes to the sole à la Drones with prawns and truffles, £7 ($13.65). Hot apple pie and fresh pineapple vie for your attention in the dessert department. The menu is wisely limited, and it never changes, although plats du jour are featured. My latest meal, not including wine selection, cost £11 ($21.45).

You sit on bentwood armchairs with green velvet cushions at white wrought-iron tables. The simple white walls are perfect foils for oil paintings and framed copies of children's comics and magazines. Try to get a table downstairs. If you're lingering in the bar while waiting for a table (a likely possibility), take a look at the collection of movie-star photos. But John Wayne as a baby is hardly recommended as an appetizer! Open seven days a week, Drones serves lunch from 12:30 to 3 p.m. and dinner from 7:30 p.m. to midnight. Tube: Sloane Square.

Papillon, at the Chelsea Holiday Inn, Sloane Street, S.W.1 (tel. 235-4377), is a restaurant built around the pool. In good weather the clear roof rolls back for al fresco eating. Around the pool are bamboo tables and chairs. A piano player entertains in the evening, and on Sunday a jazz band plays from noon to 4 p.m. when those who come to eat and drink may also use the pool free. If not jazz, you are likely to hear country and western, perhaps a steel band. A wide menu of appetizers is offered, then omelets, lasagne, or spaghetti. Steaks and grills are served with french fries, baked or croquette potatoes, or rice. A mixed grill Chelsea is a specialty.

If this is all too much for you, hamburgers are also served. Sandwiches, too, are filling, and you can have a very ample snack meal, a club sandwich, steak sandwich, or buck rarebit (cheese with fried egg on top). Ordering à la carte is likely to cost you from £4 ($7.80) to £12 ($23.40). In addition, there is a buffet from which you can choose as much as you like for £8.50 ($16.58), including a glass of wine. There is always a roast, plus two other hot dishes, cold meats, pies, and salads. The place is fully licensed and specializes in an impressive list of cocktails and apéritifs. All prices include VAT and service. Tube: Sloane Square.

KNIGHTSBRIDGE–BROMPTON ROAD: After splurging at the high-priced shops of Knightsbridge, these choices will make you feel better:

The Medium-Priced Range

Shezan, 16 Cheval Pl., off Montpelier Street, S.W.7 (tel. 589-7918), is generally considered the finest Pakistani restaurant in London, and I heartily concur. In a cul-de-sac behind Harrods, this brick-and-tile establishment in Kensington turns out exquisite dishes from its clay tandoor ovens. By all means, order murgh tikka lahori (marinated tandoori chicken), which is usually served slightly pink and is delicious. Another specialty is bhuna gosht (lamb cooked with tomatoes and spices). Tandoori charcoal barbecues and grills are usually priced at £2.85 ($5.56), and most kebabs begin at £2.85 also. The tandoori breads are excellent, especially roti, a dark whole-wheat bread. Expect to spend from £8 ($15.60) for a complete meal. The restaurant is one of the most sophisticated in the city, and the service is flawless. Lunch is from noon to 3 p.m. and dinner from 7 p.m. to midnight. Closed Sunday and bank holidays. Tube: Knightsbridge.

In a small street, just off Knightsbridge, the **Upper Crust,** 9 William St., S.W.1 (tel. 235-8444), is a modest, simply decorated country sort of place with bare brick walls, wheel-back chairs, and warm lights. Pies, rather obviously, are the house specialty, and they are served filled with steak and giblets, savory chicken, curried fish, and a magnificent steak and pickled walnut. Main dishes are accompanied by fresh country bread and herb butter, plus a selection of fresh seasonal vegetables. Cold dishes with salads are also available. Puddings have a definitely old-world air, including traditional plum with custard or Yorkshire pudding with mincemeat. A three-course meal, including cover charge, a glass of wine, and coffee, is around £7.50 ($14.63). The Franks family, who own and run the place, have a secret in that Mr. Franks also owns the superbly entitled butchershop, Wainwright and Daughter. Naturally, they select meat of prime quality for their restaurant showcase. Hours are 11:30 a.m. to 3 p.m. and 6 to 11 p.m., Monday to Saturday. On Sunday, hours are only from 6 to 11 p.m. Tube: Knightsbridge.

Paper Tiger, 10 and 12 Exhibition Rd., S.W. 7 (tel. 584-3737). The dishes here are Szechuan rather than Peking cuisine, more spiced and beginning to be closer to Malaysian dishes than the blander Japanese ones. At this basement restaurant in South Kensington, you can order a Szechuan feast. Dishes include "bang-bang" sesame chicken salad, pickle soup, prawns, pork and peppers, chili chicken, and bamboo shoots. A less piquant Peking feast for the same price includes duck with trimmings, sweet-and-sour pork, chicken and almonds, fried dumplings, and hot-and-sour soup.

There is an extensive à la carte menu of reasonably priced dishes—spicy soups, entrees such as seaspice chicken shreds with peppers, chicken with yellow bean sauce and almonds, and lemon chicken. Vegetable dishes include stir-fried bean sprouts and Mother-Ma's hot pork mince and bean curd. Toffee apples and bananas are the featured desserts, followed by Chinese tea or coffee.

Lunchtimes they have platters—pork loin slices, meat and noodles, sweet-and-sour pork, beef slices and spring onions. In the off-season, they have a gourmet winter menu, including a sharp Chinese salad, a fish dish, spring rolls and wonton, three meat dishes (chicken, pork, and lamb), vegetables, rice, and a dessert. You should go there to sample the house specialty, aromatic crispy duck with pancakes, hoisin, and cucumber, or with green ginger and spring onions. A set lunch or dinner costs £18 ($35.10) for two persons. Ordering à la carte will run about £11 ($21.45) per person. Lunch is served from noon to 2:30 p.m.; dinner from 7 p.m. to 1 a.m. Tube: Knightsbridge.

The Budget Range

Great American Disaster, Beauchamp Place, S.W.3 (tel. 589-0992), is the answer to the fervent hope that someday the English would get to taste what a real hamburger is like. A few years ago, a curly-haired young North American finally succeeded in shaming the English "pseudo-burgers" by giving London a true American burger. Reportedly, some 2000 burgers were rejected before the final achievement was created with a sesame bun. The press call GAD "the apotheosis of the hamburger." The original Disaster is at 335 Fulham Rd., S.W.10, but the one at Beauchamp Place is much more fashionable and interesting. An exterior sign shows a man jumping presumably from a high building with a calendar in hand dated October 29, 1929. Uncle Sam is pondering, and King Kong is holding an airplane. Inside the restaurant, the tables are tightly packed, crowded, and noisy, the service cheerful. A quarter-pound hamburger with french fries, is the most popular item, although you can order the half-pound Disaster special with french fries, too. Barbecued spare ribs with GAD sauce, french fries, and coleslaw is another favorite; and home-made American apple pie is the most popular dessert. A two-course meal with a lager will cost from £3.80 ($7.41) to £6 ($11.70) per person. Tube: Knightsbridge.

Harveys, the rooftop restaurant above Harvey Nichols store, S.W.1 (tel. 235-5000, ext. 149 for table reservations), is a light, airy place among the rooftops of Knightsbridge. In summer you can eat in the open air, but there is also a large restaurant inside. The day starts with an English breakfast at 9:30 a.m., costing £3.50 ($6.83), or just tea or coffee at about 75p ($1.46). The staff serves morning coffee, luncheon, and then afternoon tea until 5:30 p.m. when the store closes (6:30 p.m. on Wednesday).

There is a selection of appetizers, then you choose your main dish from the long buffet of hot dishes or from the salad table. The meal ends with dessert or cheese and coffee. The cost is around £7 ($13.65) unless you have an omelet with one of the many fillings, salad, and vegetables for £4 ($7.80). Wine by the glass is £1 ($1.95). They also do a real old cream tea £2.15 ($4.19) with homemade scones, strawberry jam, and clotted Devon cream to revive the flagging shopper. Waitresses offer pleasant service in this nice atmosphere. It's rather Knightsbridge and British. Tube: Knightsbridge.

KENSINGTON: If Meg didn't ask you to stay to dinner at Kensington Palace, you'll be just as happy with:

The Medium-Priced Range

Flanagans, 11 Kensington High St., W.8 (tel. 937-2519), recaptures the splendor of turn-of-the century dining. One of London's bounciest restaurants, it offers bountiful food in a fun-loving atmosphere. It's a trip back through the years to a world of handlebar mustaches, cut-velvet walls, a honky-tonk piano player, gas lights, sawdust on the floor—and the inevitable sing-alongs. All the Florrie Forde favorites are aired here, everything from "Has Anybody Seen Kelly?" to "Flanagan" itself.

The pièce de résistance is Lobster Lillie Langtry, Edward VII's favorite. The shelled lobster is sauteed in chablis with tarragon and thyme and covered with a piquant cream sauce, then sprinkled with parmesan cheese and grilled. The Dover sole is so huge it extends over the edges of your plate; it is accompanied by a large helping of french fries. For an adventure in old English fare, order the homemade game pie, with mashed potatoes, and perhaps a side dish of pease pudding, for those who want to go Cockney all the way. A large dish of Irish stew, big enough for two, is a popular item. For an appetizer, there's an order of cockles, and for dessert, the original golden sponge pudding. A three-course meal, with a half liter of wine, costs from £8.50 ($16.58). The original Flanagans is at 100 Baker St., W.1. Both are open from noon to 3 p.m. and from 6 p.m. to midnight, daily. Just mind your manners, and "Please Do Not Expectorate." Tube: High Street Kensington.

The Budget Range

Fu Tong, 29 Kensington High St., W.8 (tel. 937-1293). On recommendation I tried Mr. Shin Sun Chin's delightful Chinese restaurant and found it to be, in my opinion, one of the best in town. The comfortable booths offer a great degree of privacy. However, the bell button on your table will bring the waiter in a moment. Hot towels come between courses, and when you become a regular, you will be presented with your own chopsticks engraved with your name. The cuisine is Cantonese/Peking style, and all the usual dishes are available. If you want Peking duck or another complicated dish, order it when you reserve your table or you'll have a wait when you arrive. The average meal is £7 ($13.65), and there is a minimum charge of £4.50 ($8.78) per person, plus a 50p (98¢) cover and 15% service. It is open seven days a week from noon to 11:30 p.m. Tube: High Street Kensington.

SOUTH KENSINGTON: When you're exhausted from South Kensington's museums, try a feast at the following:

The Upper Bracket

Eleven Park Walk, 11 Park Walk, S.W.10 (tel. 352-3449), is a high-key, airy, two-level restaurant, with a winding staircase for "entrances." Coming down that staircase nightly is a bevy of chic Londoners, including many from the art, fashion, and photographic worlds. A smart establishment, modern and beautiful, it is a haven for the sophisticated and glamorous. In addition to being seen, you can also order some good food. Even the service is friendly.

The restaurant serves mainly Italian dishes, beginning with minestrone primavera, and a number of good pasta dishes, principally taglierini verdi. Fish specialties include calamari fritti and sea bass with herbs. Main meat courses include roast baby chicken, bollito misto with green sauce, quail cooked in white wine, saltimbocca, and calf liver veneziana. For dessert, try crêpes soaked in Tía Maria. A three-course meal, including half a liter of wine, goes for £14 ($27.30) per person and up. Hours are from 12:30 to 3 p.m. and 7 p.m. to midnight. Closed Sunday. It's best reached by taxi.

The Medium-Priced Range

Chanterelle, 119 Old Brompton Rd., S.W.7 (tel. 373-5522), used to be a part of the South Kensington Public Library. But times have changed. The smell is not of old books, but of highly original English and continental cookery in a restrained setting of wood paneling. The personable Stewart Grimshaw oversees the restaurant, and his partner, Fergus Provan, organizes the kitchen. They are open every day of the week for both lunch and dinner, including Sunday when the set lunch goes for £7 ($13.65). The à la carte menu changes every three weeks, and it is supplemented by a fixed-price lunch of three courses for £6 ($11.70). On one recent occasion, we enjoyed watercress soup, beef braised with black walnuts, and a grape-and-orange salad. The à la carte menu is likely to include such well-prepared items as huntsman's beef, saddle of rabbit with mustard and shallots, and pigeon. A cold soufflé is velvety smooth. Desserts and ices are luscious in flavor and texture. VAT is included in all prices, which usually come to £14 ($27.30) for an à la carte meal at night. Wines are limited but well selected, the house wine going for £4.25 ($8.29). Reservations are necessary. Dinner is nightly from 7 p.m. to midnight. Tube: South Kensington.

The Budget Range

Chompers, 2 Exhibition Rd., S.W. 7 (tel. 589-8947), is probably the oldest established bistro in town. It boasts an art nouveau decor, but doesn't get lost in its stage setting. Chompers serves good food prepared on the premises at moderate prices, a meal costing from £8 ($15.60). Helpings are generous. You can order barbecued spare ribs, onion soup, and pâté maison. The main-course specialties include chicken ratatouille, kidneys in sherry, and trout with capers. Chompers sells a lot of filet and sirloin steak. The chef's specialties are sirloin with Stilton cheese and garlic butter, or a filet with Stilton and garlic butter. Chompers is open for dinner from 6 p.m. to 1 a.m. Monday to Saturday (on Sunday from 6 p.m. to midnight), and for lunch seven days a week from noon to 2:30 p.m. On Sunday it offers lunch. Reservations at this fully licensed restaurant are recommended between 8 and 10:30 p.m. Tube: South Kensington.

ST. MARYLEBONE: In Mar-li-bone you're in for a treat when you visit:

The Medium-Priced Range

The Baker & Oven, 10 Paddington St., W.1 (tel. 935-5072), may be in an out-of-the-way neighborhood, but it's a big success—a little corner bakery, with a sales shop converted into a tavern with a genuine pub atmosphere. The neighborhood people mingle with the fashionable West End visitors. Meals are served in the cellar kitchens, attractively done in a rustic style. The very English food often pleases the most critical; the portions are enormous, the tabs moderate. With a bit of luck, you'll be given a bare wooden table in one of the brick cove-ceilinged nooks, the former ovens.

The onion soup is a fine beginning at 95p ($1.85), as is the country pâté at £1.25 ($2.44). For the main course, there are several good choices, including roast Aylesbury duckling with stuffing and applesauce for £4.25 ($8.29) and jugged hare with red currant jelly, £4.75 ($9.26). All entrees include vegetables. For dessert, you can order a thoroughly English hot fruit pie and cream at £1.25 ($2.44). The restaurant is open Monday to Friday from noon to 3 p.m. and from 6:30 to 11 p.m. On Saturday, it's open only in the evenings. Tube: Baker Street.

London Steak Houses, Ltd., with its main offices at Cadby Hall, W.14 (tel. 603-2040), operates ten restaurants in metropolitan London, all with similar menus and prices, but with varying decors. The restaurant at 116 Baker St., W.1 (tel. 935-1932) is an attractive example, with small tables stretched in a single row through a long, narrow room decorated cheerfully in green and lemon yellow. Simulated gaslight plays across the oak-beamed ceiling. Framed French magazine prints add interest to the walls. The menu is extensive, with plenty of beef, pork, and seafood dishes available. Steak is, of course, the specialty, with rump, sirloin, and filet steaks offered in three sizes: standard, medium, and large. Steak Diane, served with shallots and parsley, is a specialty. Vegetables are extra. Appetizers include fresh avocado stuffed with prawns. After an enjoyable repast, you can enjoy a cup of rich coffee, accompanied by a complementary tray of sugared Turkish delights. An average meal will run £8 ($15.60), plus a minimum of £2 ($3.90) for wine. A three-course set meal, with a choice from ten appetizers and ten main dishes, costs only £7.50 ($14.63). All London Steak Houses are open for lunch and dinner every day of the week.

READERS RESTAURANT SELECTION: "We discovered a restaurant in London where we had one of the best meals we've ever eaten. It's **Trattoria Parioli**, 129 Crawford St., W.1 (tel. 935-3791), just around the corner one block south of the Baker Street tube station. The menu is à la carte, no service charge included, and there is one of those mysterious cover charges. Nevertheless, we had everything—soup, entree, a magnificent salad, excellent pasta, dessert, coffee, and the fine house white wine—all for about £11 ($21.45) per person, including tax and tip. It's gourmet Italian, with fine service, an attractive decor, and even the ubiquitous Muzak was soft" (Patricia Muller, Denver, Colo.).

NOTTING HILL GATE: From a gourmet treat to fish 'n' chips, your choice in this area is wide ranging.

The Upper Bracket

Leiths, 92 Kensington Park Rd., W.11 (tel. 229-4481). Prudence Leith, a lovely young woman from South Africa, has brought her culinary talents to the most unlikely Notting Hill Gate district of London, a few blocks from the Portobello Road Market and near the Portobello Hotel. Pru, as she is called, discovered "how good food could really be" when she worked as an *au pair* girl in a French family. In time, she studied at the Cordon Bleu in Paris and also at the Cordon Bleu in London. Nowadays she relies on her managing director, French-born Jean-Baptiste Reynaud, who was a chef by trade until joining her as a manager in 1973, to produce the menus and to maintain the established high quality. Like the Four Seasons in New York, there are four seasonal menus. A fixed-price meal costs £23 ($44.85), including service and VAT. One recent spring menu included such dishes as trout stuffed with chicken and ham, tarragon chicken, stuffed quail in pastry, and poached salmon with a hollandaise sauce. There is an ambitious wine list. To end your meal, you can make a selection from the dessert trolley, perhaps a lemon soufflé. The restaurant is open daily from 7:30 p.m. to midnight. Tube: Notting Hill Gate.

The Medium-Priced Range

Hungry Viking, 44 Ossington St., W.2 (tel. 727-3311), is a modern restaurant on a street of mews houses. You descend past flower-draped boxes into a Scandinavian parlor, where waitresses in national costume will help you select from a gigantic smörgåsbord for a set price of £8.50 ($16.58). It's called the traditional Viking table, and includes the usual array of delicacies, such as prawns, herring, smoked fish, aspics, salads, cheeses, and meats, both hot and cold. The salads are especially good. The amount of food you can eat is your own capacity. The restaurant is closed on Monday but open otherwise Tuesday to Saturday from 6:30 to 11 p.m. (Sunday, 7 to 11 p.m.). Tube: Queensway or Notting Hill Gate.

The Budget Range

Geale's, 2 Farmer St., W.8 (tel. 727-7969), is worth the investment in a subway ride to the western part of London if you're seeking some of the best fish and chips in the English capital—all at prices for around £2.50 ($4.88). The fish is bought fresh daily, and it's not greasy as it is in most establishments in London. Cod, haddock, and plaice are the featured mainstays of the menu. This corner restaurant, at the end of a mews street, is owned by Christopher A. Geale, who is proud, and rightly so, of his offerings. The place is run on very informal lines, and is open Tuesday to Saturday from noon to 3 p.m. and from 6 to 11 p.m. Tube: Notting Hill Gate.

MAYFAIR: Stick a few extra pounds in your pocket and join the swells for a memorable meal in Mayfair (less expensive Mayfair restaurants coming up, too):

The Upper Bracket

Langan's Brasserie, Stratton Street, W.1 (tel. 493-6437), has maintained its popularity since its opening in late 1976. Owned by restaurateur Peter Langan and actor Michael Caine, along with the chef de cuisine, Richard Shepherd, the café is reminiscent of a Parisian bistro. The walls are covered with pictures, and the combination of overhead fans and potted palms creates a 1930s atmosphere. A complete meal, including wine, VAT, and service, comes to about £16 ($31.20). The long menu always has a good choice of English dishes, such as kipper pâté and roast joints and pies, along with the classic French dishes. Live music is played during the dinner hour. Lunch is served Monday to Friday from 12:30 to 3 p.m. and dinner is offered from 7 p.m. to midnight, Monday through Friday. On Saturday, hours are from 8 p.m. to 1 a.m., and the restaurant is closed on Sunday. Upstairs is a more intimate dining room with silver service, although prices are the same as downstairs. The Venetian decor was the work of Patrick Proctor, the artist. Tube: Green Park.

Café-Royal Grill Room, 68 Regent St., W.1 (tel. 930-2473). One columnist called the Café Royal "champagne-from-slipper" country. And so it is. Mirrored walls, painted ceilings, a sea of white linen and plush red velvet—enough to warm the heart of Oscar Wilde, one of its most illustrious former patrons. But then nearly everybody famous, including Noël Coward, at one time or another since 1865 has dined at the Café Royal. The wine list continues to merit acclaim, remaining as comprehensive as ever. Get ready for a mile-long list Frank Harris called "The best on earth!" The food? A well-prepared haute cuisine. The ingredients are high quality, the vegetables fresh. The menu features such dishes as filets de sole sur le plat, Rochellaise (filets of sole braised with vermouth, tarragon, shallots, and sliced fresh tomatoes, pan reduced with butter, and covered with hollandaise sauce); and mignonettes d'agneau élysée (prime leg of lamb, sauteed in butter, coated with a madeira and port sauce with foie gras, chicken liver, and noisette potatoes). The restaurant offers a Sunday brunch at a set price of £8.95 ($17.45), plus a 12½% service charge. My most recent meal started with a soup of the day and was followed by a kipper, then scrambled eggs, mushrooms, kidney, tomato, and bacon washed down by a bottle of Pouilly Fuisse (an extra charge). Of course, "lashings" of toast were included, along with Cooper's Oxford marmalade and coffee. Whistler used to sign his bill with the mark of a butterfly. The brunch, from noon to 2:30 p.m., is frequented by a wide variety of Londoners—some rounding out a night's revelry. It's an amusing break in a London Sunday. Tube: Piccadilly Circus.

Bentley's, 11–15 Swallow St., W.1 (tel. 734-4756), is one of the most prestigious fish restaurants in London; tradition permeates the place. There's a certain type of Mayfair gentleman, with bowler and cane, who heads for Bentley's at sunset. There, standing at the shellfish bar, he slowly and deliberately downs one oyster after another, a ritual unchanged in years. Then he fades away, seemingly having no life before or after swallowing those oysters until he shows up the following evening.

This clublike restaurant is on a tiny street connecting Regent Street with Piccadilly (a three-minute walk from Piccadilly Circus). On the ground floor, you'll find the Oyster Bar, usually crowded with people feasting on the riches from Bentley's oyster beds near Colchester, Essex. Upstairs is a dining room filled with devotees of good fish dishes. A half-dozen oysters go for £5 ($9.75), but you may prefer iced lobster soup, the house specialty, at £2.10 ($4.10). Each weekday, there's a different specialty from the chef. On Monday, it's a sole Véronique, poached in white wine and garnished with grapes, for £6.60 ($12.87). You'll find exciting menu selections from the scampi, scallop, lobster, mussel, plaice, trout, turbot, and sole families. Scottish salmon, grilled or poached, comes to £8.50 ($16.58), and the lobster thermidor, £9.50 ($18.53). Less expensive offerings include the scampi meunière for £6 ($11.70). Prices include VAT. Closed Sunday. Tube: Piccadilly Circus

The Medium-Priced Range

Gaylord, 16 Albemarle St., W.1 (tel. 629-9802), has established an enviable reputation among local connoisseurs of Indian cuisine in spite of its relative youth—it just opened in 1974. An elegant Oriental atmosphere pervades the restaurant, creating an air of festive expectancy. The ornate hanging lamps, the gold-studded door, and the unusual glass ceiling imported from India set off the rich color scheme of royal purple and gold. And the delicacies upon which you dine do not disappoint you.

So many regional dishes are available that one hardly knows where to begin. The restaurant features three different types of regional cooking: Tandoori centers on the tandoor, an oven of Indian clay which is used for cooking foods while retaining the flavor and natural moisture. A good example of this cooking style is tandoori fish, at £2.95 ($5.75).

Mughlai cooking dates from the Moghul period of Indian history in which exotic dishes were prepared with rich combinations of spices. If you like curried foods, you may wish to try the chicken noor jehani, a chicken, minced lamb, and egg dish cooked in a thick curry sauce, at £2.55 ($4.97).

Kashmiri specialties frequently include combinations of lamb and yogurt, as exemplified in the roghan josh, pieces of lamb cooked alternately between smoking butter and beaten yogurt to develop a unique flavor, costing £2.60 ($5.07). Vegetarian entrees are also available for about £1.45 ($2.83). As a dessert treat, try an Indian delicacy from the trolley, for £1.15 ($2.24). All prices include VAT. The Gaylord is open daily for lunch and dinner. Tube: Piccadilly Circus.

Restaurant Café Jardin, 10 Lancashire Court, 122 New Bond St., W.1 (tel. 493-2896). In a tiny passageway between two shops on fashionable Bond Street, a courtyard with baytrees in tubs leads to the unobtrusive door to this charming basement restaurant. On the ground floor is a bar with mirrors and stools, then a winding stairway leads to the cellar where tables crowd the walls. The decor is enhanced by potted plants, bamboo screens, mirrors, and lights. The manager, Jean-Louis Commeureuc, is forever in attendance, and the cuisine is essentially French although the chef is an Englishman, Alan Bird.

They have two daily menus at £5.95 ($11.60) and £7.95 ($15.50) for three courses. Appetizers are very good. The main dish of either menu is a fricassee of chicken, sauteed beef with onions and mushrooms, and braised beef with green peppers. Fresh vegetables are included, and the meal finishes with a dessert from the tray. The à la carte choices include crayfish tails cooked in cream and served in a pastry case, chopped lobster with poached egg and cheese soufflé, and baked avocado with crab and smoked salmon stuffing. Much emphasis is laid on fresh fish dishes, including mousseline of sole with lobster sauce, fresh brill, and the day's fish fresh from the market (except Monday) cooked in whatever way you ask.

There are grills and steaks—try the tournedos with beef marrow and red wine sauce. A three-course average meal finishing with dessert or cheese will cost about £11 ($21.45), with the house wine at about £4.50 ($8.78) a bottle. There is a 12½% service charge added to the bill and a cover charge of 50p (98¢). Its a very busy place most days, and service tends to be slow but your meal will be worth waiting for. Tube: Bond Street.

Coconut Grove, 3–5 Barrett St., W.1 (tel. 486-5269), is a bright, shiny restaurant at the end of St. Christopher's Place, just off Oxford Street. Upstairs you'll find a decor of brown wood and pink napery, along with green frondy plants. There are more seats downstairs, and in summer, tables tumble onto the pavement to accommodate tired and thirsty shoppers. Find a table or seat at the bar and relax with a margarita, a Mississippi Mule, or perhaps a Singapore Sling. For a long, frosty glass, you'll pay £2.60 ($5.07).

Then choose a meal from a bewildering list of dishes with an international flavor. Guacamole, eggs Benedict, and chili vie with deep-fried potato skins with sour cream and chives or brie baked in almonds and served with hot garlic bread. The dozen or so salads include Waldorf and Caesar, and the chef's salad is called "indescribable." A 16-ounce T-bone is another popular item, served with fries and the vegetable of the day. You might also select lamb kebab with tomatoes and onions, perhaps a hamburger. Desserts are luscious, including hot pecan pie and deep apple pie. Expect to spend from £10 ($19.50). VAT is included, but not service. The Grove is open seven days a week from noon to 1 a.m. Tube: Bond Street.

The Budget Range

Cranks Health Food Restaurant, Marshall Street, W.1 (tel. 437-9431), around the corner from Carnaby Street, took its name from "cranks." But instead of the colloquial meaning of an eccentric, impractical person, the restaurant defines the word as those "who have the courage to pursue a line of thinking against the general stream of orthodox belief." Their "line," by the way, is excellent—the best of homemade soups, fresh fruit salads, homemade fruit pies, pastries, and cakes, and breads made from whole-meal, compost-grown, stone-ground English flour. Cranks became famous when it operated on Carnaby Street, and first drew its young health-conscious clientele. The food-reform restaurant even tempts full-fledged carnivores by its fresh-tasting selections—such as the mix-it-yourself salad platter at lunch. If you've got a small waist, you can order a bowl of choice salads from the main buffet counter for £1 ($1.95), although if you've already lost the battle of the bulge, you may prefer a large bowl at £2 ($3.90). Homemade cakes range from 30p (59¢). Cranks serves the best tiger's milk and dandelion coffee in town. It's open Monday to Friday from 10 a.m. to 8:30 p.m., on Saturday from 10 a.m. to 4:30 p.m.

Cranks Health Food Restaurants are also in two large London stores—Peter Robinsons, on Oxford Circus, and Heals, Tottenham Court Road. More recently a branch has been opened in Covent Garden Market which specializes in Cranks take-out food, a small food and juice bar, and downstairs a wholegrain shop. Tube: Piccadilly Circus.

Justin de Blanc, 54 Duke St., W.1 (tel. 629-3174), stands just off Oxford Street by Selfridges. It serves breakfast, then runs into lunchtime when it is very popular with tired shoppers. Choose your meal from a variety of hot dishes: lamb and eggplant casserole, barbecued spare ribs, or roast beef and three vegetables. The dishes of the day are written over the bar, and it can be quite a problem to select among them. The array of salads, rice and celery, cucumber and yogurt, orange and beetroot go for around £2.75 ($5.36) for a large plateful. Desserts are all homemade, including fruit pies, cheesecakes, and fruit salad. They bake their own bread, and the fresh granary rolls are tempting. Meals cost from £6 ($11.70). A glass of wine costs 75p ($1.46). It is open from 8:30 a.m. to 3:30 p.m., then from 4:30 to 9:30 p.m. on weekdays (on Saturday from 9 a.m. to 3:30 p.m. only). Closed on Sunday. Tube: Bond Street.

SOHO: This wedge-shaped section of narrow lanes and crooked streets is the main foreign quarter of London, where the city's best international restaurants reside. The life of the continent echoes throughout Soho. Large numbers of French people are found here, and so are Italians and all other European nationalities, as well as Orientals.

One writer wrote of Gerrard Street: "The smell of pickled ginger and roast duckling seeps from restaurant doors. The men scurry into stores from afternoon games of fan-tan and mah-jongg. A lilting twang of Chinese rock 'n' roll envelops the downtown street." Gerrard Street has succeeded in becoming London's Chinatown. Strip shows and honky-tonk clubs have given way to Chinese restaurants and bookstores keeping you informed of the latest developments in Hong Kong and the wisdom of Mao.

Soho starts at Piccadilly Circus, spreading out like a peacock and ending at Oxford Street. One side borders the theater center on Shaftesbury Avenue. From Piccadilly Circus, walk northeast and you'll come to Soho, to the left of Shaftesbury. This jumbled section can also be approached from the Tottenham Court Road tube station. Walk south along Charing Cross Road and Soho will be to your right.

The Upper Bracket

The Ivy, 1–5 West St., W.C.2 (tel. 836-4751). It's difficult to concentrate on the top-notch French cuisine here; diners are too busy star gazing in what is often a celebrity-filled dining spot. The Ivy is strong on tradition, an entrenched London restaurant since World War I. In the past it drew such regulars as Prime Ministers Lloyd George and Sir Winston Churchill, who knew his French viands and wines. Over the years, it became a rendezvous for show folk—Noël Coward, Gracie Fields, Dame Sybil Thorndike, Rex Harrison used to be habitués. The interior gleams with the luster of Paris—paneled walls with old paintings, bronze lamps, cut-plush chairs, art nouveau bronze figures set in window ledges. In the front drinking lounge you can wait for your table while making menu selections.

The Ivy had been getting a bit désuet, but with the arrival of Lord Lew Grade's wife, Kathleen, who now owns the Ivy, the old tradition of theatrical star-spotting is coming back. The paintings, paneling, and luxurious furnish-

ings remain, and the menu tends to be a little old-fashioned in its length and detail.

Sole is available with 13 different sauces and garnishes, but the table d'hôte luncheon or dinner is what you'll probably go for at £12 ($23.40). If you don't see anything you like, then order one of the lunchtime plats du jour, including a gigot of lamb or roast beef with the trimmings. These daily specials usually start at £6 ($11.70).

In the evening you can try a chateaubriand steak for two or duck in orange sauce among an array of dishes. Meals begin at £15 ($29.15) per person, but this is quite amusing for a night out among the celebrities. Tube: Tottenham Court Road.

Terrazza, 19 Romilly St., W.1 (tel. 437-8991), at one time was considered the most voguish restaurant in London. But the West End theater crowd and "society" are, alas, fickle. Whether in or out of fashion, Terrazza remains one of the best places in the capital for authentic Italian food. If you visit, you'll have a choice of three different dining rooms, both upstairs and down.

The food is classic, beginning with cocktail Amalfi, £2 ($3.90). House specialties include spaghetti with clams, £2 also; fritto misto mare (scampi, octopus, and other sea products deep-fried), £4.60 ($8.97); and rolled and stuffed breast of chicken, £4.20 ($8.19). You pay £1.20 ($2.34) for a smooth zabaglione. Lunch is served from noon to 3 p.m.; dinner from 6 p.m. to midnight. Tube: Tottenham Court Road.

Au Jardin des Gourmets, 5 Greek St., W.1 (tel. 437-1816), draws many a discriminating diner to some of the best French food in Soho. The restaurant has a Frenchman as its chef, and the traditional Gallic cuisine reflects the highest standards of his country. For appetizers, you can have such a treat as pâté maison. The soups are exceptionally good: vichyssoise and soupe à l'oignon gratinée. House specialties include carré d'agneau, red snapper with fennel sauce, roast duck with orange sauce, and a hot seafood dish in wine sauce. Vintage wines are available, but you can also order by the glass. The average price of a meal, including half a bottle of the house wine, is £15 ($29.25) per person. However, a set lunch or dinner is offered for just £7.50 ($14.63). The restaurant is open Monday to Friday from 12:30 to 2:15 p.m. and from 6:30 to 11:30 p.m. It is open on Saturday from 6:30 to 11 p.m. but closed on Sunday. Tube: Tottenham Court Road.

The Budget Range

Romano Santi, 50 Greek St., W.1 (tel. 437-5268), established in 1886, in the very heart of Soho, is one of the best values in this district, considering the grade of its cuisine. It's run by a friendly and polite international staff, under the direction of a distinguished and charming manager, Mr. Santi. The management has made it a duty to keep this building, which was erected in 1735, in its original condition. The continental restaurant features an excellent three-course luncheon for £3.65 ($7.12) to £4.95 ($9.65). A typical meal might include an assortment of hors d'oeuvres, followed by chicken chasseur, with a green vegetable, and peach Melba for dessert. The helpings are generous, and there are several main dishes from which to choose. Expect to spend at least £12 ($23.40) for an à la carte dinner. Main courses include tournedos Romano Santi, veal piccatine al Marsala, chicken Kiev, and trout San Remo (with prawns and tomatoes). You'll find the lack of elbow room either a plus or a minus, depending on the person you're elbowing at the next table. Romano Santi's is open from noon to 3 p.m. and from 6 to 11:45 p.m. It is also open Sunday and bank holidays. Tube: Tottenham Court Road.

The **Dumpling Inn,** 15a Gerrard St. (tel. 437-2567), in a small Chinese district of Soho, attracts a number of devoted regulars. Don't be fooled by the name or the Venetian murals—this is an elegant Chinese restaurant serving classical Mandarin dishes. The haute cuisine of China, Mandarin cooking dates back nearly 3000 years, and employs a number of unique cooking rituals, including the Mongolian hot pot. The fact that this restaurant serves somewhat small portions can be turned into an advantage because it gives you an opportunity to sample a variety of this delectable cuisine. You can savor the special tastes of Mandarin cooking in the sharkfin soup, the beef in oyster sauce, or the grilled pork or beef dumplings. Pancakes stuffed with discreetly flavored minced meat are a house specialty. Dinner reservations are recommended, and you should allow plenty of time for dining here since most dishes are prepared to your special order. The average meal will cost £8 ($15.60) per person, but just a large plate of grilled pork and dumplings will go for only £2.50 ($4.88). Tube: Tottenham Court Road.

Chuen Cheng Ku, 17 Wardour St., W.1 (tel. 437-1398), is one of the finest eateries in Soho's "New China." A large restaurant, Chuen Cheng Ku is noted for its Singapore noodles. Specialties are paper-wrapped prawns, rice in lotus leaves, steamed spare ribs in black bean sauce, shredded pork with cashew nuts, all served in generous portions. Dim sum (dumplings) are served from 11 a.m. to 6 p.m. The Singapore noodles, reflecting one of the Chinese-Malaysian inspirations, are thin rice noodles, sometimes mixed with curry and pork or else shrimp with red and green peppers. A set dinner costs £6 ($11.70) per person. Featured à la carte dishes include fried oysters with ginger and scallions, sliced duck with chili and black bean sauce, and steamed pork with plum sauce. The average à la carte meal costs £8 ($15.60), plus 10%. The restaurant is open daily until midnight. Tube: Tottenham Court Road.

NORTH SOHO: In this district we have one lone recommendation in:

The Upper Bracket

Lacy's, 26 Whitfield St., W.1 (tel. 636-2323 or 636-2411), is run by award-winning husband-and-wife team, William Lacy and Margaret Costa. He was the chef des cuisines at the Empress in Berkeley Street, and trained under the last living disciples of Escoffier. She is the author of *The Four Seasons Cookery Book* and *London at Table.* On the ground level is a small reception and cocktail area. Reached by going down a flight of stairs, the dining room is in the Moorish style, with tiled floors and white arches. Fresh food is prepared in unusual and imaginative ways. For hors d'oeuvres, I'd recommend the fish pâté with a yogurt sauce. A truly heavenly soup is the watercress, lettuce, and almond. I particularly enjoyed the seafood pancakes and the lamb kidneys flambéed with Dutch gin in a juniper berry-flavored sauce. A set dinner goes for £13.50 ($26.33); however, if you order à la carte, expect to spend from £16 ($31.20) up. Reservations are advisable. Meals are served from 12:30 to 2:30 p.m. and from 7:30 to 11 p.m. The luncheon menu is wonderful value for present-day London. It starts at about £12 ($23.40) for a three-course meal, including tax, cover charge, and coffee, but not service. The price of the main course is the price of the whole meal. In addition, they offer a wide range of excellent, low-priced wines. A half carafe of the house wine goes for £4 ($7.80). Tube: Tottenham Court Road.

BLOOMSBURY: Although the center of much sightseeing and a complex of hotels, Bloomsbury is relatively shy on really good restaurants. There are a few, of course, and one of the best is previewed below in—

The Budget Range

Tagore, 8 Brunswick Centre, off Russell Square, W.C.1 (tel. 837-9397), is one of the finest Indian restaurants in London. It has an unobtrusive and rather unattractive entrance in this modern complex of apartments and shops. Hardly what you'd expect if you're seeking delicate Indian cookery, including the best of tandoori dishes. Colored lights inside gently illuminate a display of art objects and paintings. Sitar music is provided nightly, and there is dancing as well, so it becomes somewhat like a nightclub.

Specialties include pan-fried herring, heavily spiced, lamb pasanda, and tandoori king prawn masalla. Tagore is an ideal center for vegetarians who will find a special menu of tempting dishes, including the special vegetable thali. Incidentally, if you're in the neighborhood, perhaps sightseeing at the British Museum, you might want to visit and sample the executive luncheon. Meals begin at £5 ($9.75), ranging upward. At the entrance is a large portrait of namesake Tagore, the Hindu poet and prose writer who died in 1941. The restaurant is open daily, including Sunday, from noon to 3 p.m. and from 6 p.m. till midnight. Tube: Russell Square.

HYDE PARK: If you crave greenery, this choice in the center of Hyde Park is welcome:

The Medium-Priced Range

The Serpentine, Hyde Park, W.2. (tel. 723-8783), is like a World's Fair exhibition center. It's in the center of Hyde Park, with an unobstructed view of the Serpentine Lake; the restaurant is a free-form glass structure built on different levels, with a separate area for drinks. The food is decidedly good, beginning with a selection of freshly prepared soups or a full range of fish and fruit appetizers. The menu features a full range of seafood and grilled meats. Main-course specialties include smoked and poached finnan haddock and roast beef and Yorkshire pudding. The average meal will cost about £10 ($19.50) per person. At lunch there's always a roast featured, going for £6 ($11.70), including a vegetable. For half a carafe of the house wine, expect to pay from £2.30 ($4.49). Meals are served daily from noon to 3 p.m. and from 6 to 11 p.m. It's best reached by taxi.

THE CITY: When the English talk about The City, they don't mean London. The City is the British version of Wall Street. Not only is it an important square mile of finance and business, but it contains many sights. Here are the buildings known the world over: the **Bank of England** on Threadneedle Street (entrance hall open to the public); the **Stock Exchange,** where you can watch transactions from a special gallery; **Lloyd's of London,** on Leadenhall, one of the world's great insurance centers. Lloyd's will insure anything from a stamp collection to a giraffe's neck.

Typical English food—shepherd's pie, mixed grills, roast beef—is dished up in dozens of the old pubs of The City. Here you can eat inexpensively along with the English, whether they be the man in the bowler worried about his

country's inflation, or a Cockney secretary anxious to get back to the sound of the Bow Bells.

The Budget Range

The **George & Vulture**, 3 Castle Court, Cornhill, E.C.3 (tel. 626-9710), is for the Dickens enthusiast, ye olde Pickwickian hostelrie, etc. This chophouse, founded in 1660, claims that it is "probably" the world's oldest tavern, and refers to an inn on this spot back in 1175. The George & Vulture no longer puts up overnight guests (although Dickens used to bed down here), but its three floors are still used for serving English meals. The Pickwick Club meets here now, by the way. Come here for lunch, Monday through Friday, noon to 2:45 p.m. No tables are booked after 1:20 p.m. Besides the daily specials, the George & Vulture features a mixed grill, a "loin chop, chump chop," or fried filets of Dover sole with tartar sauce. Potatoes and buttered cabbage are the standard vegetables. The apple tart is always reliable. The average meal will cost about £8 ($15.60). The system is to arrive and give your name, then retire to the Jamaica pub opposite for a drink. You are then fetched when your table is ready. The staff claims the wait is no more than 20 minutes. After lunch, explore the intricate nearby passageways, and discover the maze of shops, wine houses, pubs, and old buildings surrounding the tavern. Tube: Bank.

FLEET STREET: This street of ink, as it is called, is the gateway to The City. It is the center of London's newspaper and publishing world. The chances are that the person you're rubbing shoulders with in one of the old pubs is a writer or editor. Men and women of letters gather here, as they have for centuries.

The Budget Range

Cheshire Cheese, Wine Office Court, 145 Fleet Street, E.C.4 (tel. 353-6170), is one of the greatest of the old city chophouses, running since 1667. It is the place where Dr. Johnson dined with his friends and entertained them with his acerbic wit. This is quite possible, as the good doctor's house was practically within shouting distance of the Cheese. The two specialties of the house cost £3.75 ($7.31) each. The first is "ye famous pudding"—(steak, kidney, mushroom, and game)—and the other is Scottish roast beef, with Yorkshire pudding and horseradish sauce. The hot plate holds a giant joint of the roast beef, and the waiters will give you additional helpings (on your Wedgwood plate) warning you "not to waste it." For dessert, "ye famous pancake" is £1.20 ($2.34), and there is "toasted cheese" at £1.25 ($2.44). Lunch is served from noon to 2:30 p.m. (last orders), and dinners from 6 to 8:30 p.m. (last orders). Closed Saturday nights and all day Sunday. Tube: St. Paul's.

3. Other Locales

THE EAST END: You may want to plunge into the drab East End of London at least once. Much of it looks like slice-of-life background shots from countless films. But in restaurants it has a few potent drawing cards.

London's Most Famous Jewish Restaurant

Bloom's, 90 Whitechapel High St., E.1 (tel. 247-6835), is worth the crossover to the wrong side of the tracks. Although overcrowded, with frantic service, Bloom's continues to tempt with kosher delights. Sunday lunch, however, is completely impossible, so try to schedule your visit at some other time. Feast on a chicken blintz, followed by cabbage borscht. The main dishes are reasonably priced, with specialties such as sauerbraten and salt beef (corned). For dessert, you can order apple strudel. An average meal will cost £6 ($11.70). The restaurant is open 11:30 a.m. to 10 p.m., except on Friday when it closes at 3 p.m. (closed all day Saturday). Tube: Aldgate East.

Chinese Food in Limehouse

Remember "Limehouse Blues"? The limekilns, from which the East End parish takes its name, were abolished before the war, but the legend lives on. On the North Bank of the Thames, the district is unattractive, with lots of ugly buildings—but therein lies its charm. Populated by broken-down or retired seamen by day, Limehouse at night is often filled with fashionable West Enders on a slumming spree. The big attractions are the Chinese restaurants known as "The Friends" (a few originals and a host of imitators).

New Friends Chinese Restaurant, 53 West India Dock Rd., E.14 (tel. 987-1139), is so popular, it's adopted a reservations only policy. The pocketsize licensed restaurant, open from noon to midnight, doesn't concern itself with decoration—just food and a reputation for some of the best quality Cantonese dishes in England. Although the menu is filled with surprises (many diners call in advance to order special dishes), you will fare handsomely just by sticking to the routine listings: items such as beef fried with green peppers, £3.50 ($6.83); crunchy yet tender spare ribs for £3.50 also; sweet-and-sour pork for £3.30 ($6.44); and Kupar prawn for £5 ($9.75). If you want a truly special dinner, ask for Mr. Chung. West India Dock Road lies off Commercial Road and and Burdett Road.

Young Friends, 11 Penny Fields, Poplar, E.14 (tel. 987-4276). This is the domain of Raymond Low, and many West Enders cross the city to sample his gray mullet (on 24-hour notice). From the tiniest kitchen imaginable come excellent meals, served in a dining room that couldn't be more basic. Here are my suggestions for a memorable dinner: wonton soup, sharkfin soup, sweet-sour wonton, and stuffed chicken wings in oyster sauce. You can top your dinner with lichee nuts. A set meal goes for £5 ($9.75). Bring your own wine, as the restaurant is unlicensed. Penny Fields lies just off West India Dock Road. Lost? Call Raymond Low for directions.

READER'S RESTAURANT SELECTION: "Slender's Health Food Restaurant, 41 Cathedral Pl., E.C.4, is exactly in front of St. Paul's tube station. The menu at this fine eating place includes such items as tomato and watercress soup, lasagne verdi, and baked potato with butter. Herb teas and decaffeinated coffee are always served. They serve luscious desserts, such as apple-date pie, apricot meringues, and cheesecake, all at reasonable prices, from £3.50 ($6.83) for a full meal. The young people serving you are most pleasant, the food very well prepared and attractive. One may either eat in the restaurant or take food out. Beans, whole grains, and dried fruits are also sold. Hours are 8:30 a.m. to 6:15 p.m., Monday through Friday" (Jean See, Spokane, Wash.).

SOUTH OF THE THAMES: The **George Inn,** 77 Borough High St., S.E.1 (tel. 407-2056), across the bridge at Southwark, is a National Trust property, the only remaining London pub with an outside gallery. A touch of old England safely tucked away in an alley, the present building dates back some 300 years. Some claim that Shakespeare and his troupe performed in an old inn that stood on the same ground. Dickens not only frequented the George, but he also wrote about it in *Little Dorrit.* Recently the building next door was acquired by the owners and the pub has been enlarged to include a new wine bar.

You enter the George through a gateway into the "old bar," noteworthy for its functioning beer engines, which are nearly as old as the building itself, and a bar area complete with a fire for nippy days and the Act of Parliament clock. This bar offers a variety of hot snacks, while the newer wine bar has a large cold buffet counter. The remaining bar on the first floor is for more serious drinkers. Two original staircases lead to each of the two restaurants, where a traditional three-course English luncheon costs £5.50 ($10.73). Lunch is served Monday through Friday from noon to 2 p.m., and dinner Monday through Saturday from 6 to 9 p.m.

The **Royal Festival Hall Restaurant,** Belvedere Road, S.E.1 (tel. 928-2829), is on the third floor of this concert hall, with big picture windows overlooking the river and the floodlit buildings on the other side. In this dramatic setting, well-prepared food is served efficiently. Opening courses include french onion soup and prawn cocktail. Main dishes feature chicken suprême, although you may prefer the chateaubriand. There's always a trolley roast as well. For your dessert, you can make a selection from another trolley. A set lunch goes for £8.50 ($16.58), an à la carte dinner for about £15 ($29.25) per person. Lunch is offered Monday to Friday from noon to 3 p.m.; dinner, Monday to Saturday, from 6 to 11:30 p.m. Tube: Waterloo.

South of the Border, 8–10 Joan St., S.E.1 (tel. 928-6374). The name reflects the attitude a lot of people have toward London "South of the River" as the locals say, and it is rare to find a fashionable place to eat after a visit to the nearby Festival Hall, National Theatre, and Young Vic Theatre. Joan Street is at the junction of the Cut and Blackfriars, within easy reach of all. Once a mattress factory, the ground floor and gallery can seat more than 80 people and, in summer, there are also tables on the outdoor terrace.

The menu consists of a choice of various appetizers. There's always a homemade soup such as minestrone or white bean. Main dishes include a variety of chicken, lamb, beef, and fish dishes, such as chicken escalope, carbonnade of beef cooked in beer with potatoes and onions and served in its own pot, and fish pie stuffed with cod, shellfish, mullet, and crab. The price range is from £2.50 ($4.88) to £6 ($11.70). Desserts have such succulent names as Belvoir pudding steamed with fruits and custard. There is a good selection of wines and a choice from seven house wines beginning at £5 ($9.75) per bottle. The menu is frequently changed so a return visit can be recommended. The restaurant is open Monday to Saturday from 6 to 11:30 p.m. and from Monday to Friday from noon to 2:30.

555, 555 Battersea Park Rd., S.W.11 (tel. 228-7011), is a most unprepossessing café (in looks only) in a dreary commercial sector of London, south of the Thames. But surprise! The food is winning, the ingredients fresh. A gemütlich feeling prevails at night, and soon you're joining in the fun. The posters on the walls are more permissive than ever. You can get a number of good Baltic dishes here. Vera, the owner, oversees everything. By all means, try the homemade sausage. The pâté is also delicious, a bit crude but good. The suckling pig is highly recommended, and seems to be a house specialty. Vegetables come with everything; red cabbage is often featured. An entire meal will run about £9 ($17.55) to £10 ($19.50). Meals are served to a cosmopolitan crowd against a background of taped music. Vera says it's all in great fun, and we agree. It is closed Sunday and Monday, but open otherwise for dinner only from 7:30 p.m. till midnight. Take a taxi: you'll never find the place if you don't.

HAMPSTEAD: Keats, Downshire Hill, Hampstead, N.W.3 (tel. 435-1499), is a "small, serious restaurant for committed gourmets," just around the corner from Keats's house. The well-prepared food is the best in Hampstead. Considering the size of the restaurant—it has a capacity of only about 50 diners—the French menu is exceedingly ambitious, containing some 40 delectable dishes which are varied every five weeks. Proprietor Aron Misan's special pride is his wine cellar, which houses at least 100 varieties, including a collection of classified clarets in great vintages. An average dinner at Keats comes to about £15 ($29.15), not including wine. Keats is open every evening except Sunday. Reservations are a must. Tube: Hampstead.

Oslo Court, Prince Albert Road, N.W.8 (tel. 722-8795), is oddly situated for a restaurant, with an entrance on Charlbert Street, to the west of Regent's Park. But the food offered here, a combination Balkan and Scandinavian, is so good and so well prepared that it merits a taxi ride from Central London. I was there the night Richard Burton discovered the place, and he threatened to send all his friends. The waiters employed are highly skilled, and will even call you a cab at the end of the evening. Always reserve a table. It's easy to obtain space for lunch, more difficult in the evening.

The specialties are many and varied. I prefer for an appetizer the Kvarnerv fish soup or crab La Rochelie. Main-dish specialties include duck Bosnaka, veal cutlet trapiste, and sole Papa Augustine. Fresh vegetables are served, and nearly all the desserts are tempting. Expect to spend from £12 ($23.40) plus wine for dinner. In addition to the high standard of cooking, the wine list is also outstanding. The restaurant is open for lunch from 12:30 to 2 p.m. and for dinner from 6:30 to 10:30 p.m. It is closed all day on Monday and for lunch on Saturday.

Le Cellier du Midi, Church Row, N.W.3 (tel. 435-9998), is a basement French bistro, off Hampstead Heath Street. It's decorated with odd Victorian knickknacks, with bunches of garlic and onions hanging from the roof beams. Rough wooden tables are covered with red cloths. It's run by Henri Saux, who offers classical French cooking with the day's specialties shown on the blackboard. For £12 ($23.40), you're given a four-course meal with a choice of some 16 appetizers, including pâté and mussels marinière, then 20 main dishes such as pot au feu or boeuf Alaric. A tempting array of at least 15 desserts is offered nightly. It is wise to reserve, particularly on weekends. Le Cellier is well recommended for the quality of its cuisine and its general ambience. Tube: Hampstead.

Pippin, 83–84 Hampstead High Street, N.W.3 (tel. 435-6434), offers a fine array of strictly vegetarian dishes to tempt even the most skeptical nonvegetarian. Prices begin at £2 ($3.90). The freshly baked breads and cakes are prepared from Pippin's own organically grown wheat flour. The restaurant's Copella pure apple juice is the favorite beverage to accompany any dish. It's open daily from noon to midnight. Pippin offers morning coffee, lunch, afternoon tea, or dinner on its terrace restaurant. Tube: Hampstead.

NEAR OLYMPIA EXHIBITION HALL: Jonathan's Restaurant, 71 Blythe Rd., W.14 (tel. 602-2758), is in an almost suburban street, well away from the normal tourist haunts, behind Olympia Exhibition Hall. Once you have parked your car, paid off your taxi, or walked from the exhibition, ring the bell at no. 71, and you will be ushered into a small but well-stocked, picture-strewn bar. Raymond Clegg will pour your drinks or mix you one of his cocktails while his Danish wife, Hanne, will discuss the merits of the various dishes on the

extensive French menu. Downstairs, the restaurant is cozy with candles and fresh flowers on the linen tablecloths.

A hot avocat Jonathan, filled with seafood in a béchamel sauce, is £2.25 ($4.39), or perhaps you'll prefer escargot (snails) à la bourguignonne at £2 ($3.90) or frog legs sauteed in a tomato and onion sauce with garlic and herbs, also £2. Filet with Stilton cheese and a port wine sauce goes for £5.50 ($10.73). Venison, sauteed and served with red-currant sauce, is £5 ($9.75). Roast duckling flamed with brandy and offered in a cream and peppercorn sauce goes for £4.75 ($9.26). Most items on the menu can also be served plain grilled. There is an interesting selection of desserts, including crêpes suzette and cherries jubilee, cooked and flamed at your table. There is also an excellent wine list, with the house wine costing £3.75 ($7.31) a bottle. VAT is included but not the 10% service charge. In addition to an extensive à la carte menu, there are most attractively priced set luncheon and dinner menus from £4.95 ($9.65), including three courses, coffee, and VAT. The restaurant is open for lunch Monday through Friday from noon to 2:30 p.m. and for dinner Monday through Saturday from 7 to 11:30 p.m. It is also open for Sunday luncheon from noon to 3 p.m. at a set price of £5.95 ($11.60).

ISLINGTON: Frederick's Restaurant, Camden Passage, N.1 (tel. 359-2888). Originally, in 1789, the building was a pub called the Gun. Then in 1834 it was rebuilt and renamed "The Duke of Sussex" in honor of George III's sixth son, Prince Augustus Frederick. So when the restaurant opened in 1970, what more natural than to name it after the prince? As well as tables inside, you can eat in the Garden Room, designed like a Victorian glasshouse with a domed ceiling. It is air-conditioned and heated, with glass doors leading to a terrace and the large garden. There is much open brickwork and plants to create a pleasant, relaxed place in which to enjoy the delicacies of the excellent French cuisine.

Jean-Louis Pollet, chef de cuisine, changes the menu every fortnight, but there are so many delightful alternatives to each course that you would be hard put to work through it in two weeks. Appetizers include smoked salmon, French onion soup, snails, and fried camembert cheese. There are several fish dishes including turbot with buttered spinach, chicken, duck with orange, pork or lamb chops, peppersteaks, or, from the charcoal grill, a variety of steaks and cutlets served with garlic butter and béarnaise sauce.

Frederick's specialties include scampis St. Tropez and liver Berlinoise. Vegetables are always freshly prepared, and you can choose your own salad, specifying what you would like in it. Desserts are all homemade, and there is a good cheese board. A three-course meal with coffee will cost around £15 ($29.25), including VAT, but it is quite possible to dine for around £11 ($21.45) per person.

There is a long and excellent wine list and a very palatable French claret can be as little as £5.50 ($10.73), or the house wine is £3.75 ($7.31) a bottle. If you are in the area on Saturday, they do a set luncheon for £5.95 ($11.60). The set lunch on Saturday offers a choice of three appetizers, two main dishes with vegetable or salad, and a choice of three desserts, and coffee. VAT and service are included. This is the area for the antique hunter, so you may very well find yourself up there with time to enjoy a delicious meal. Tube: Angel.

4. Suggestions for Sunday

When much of the West End is closed on Sunday, you'll find more life—if you take a taxi, tube, or bus to Aldgate East and spend a hectic hour or so at **Petticoat Lane.** That's the street market where, even if you don't want to buy the goods, you can see the full wit and expertise of the Cockney street vendors. Look for the one who sells tea services, buy a toffee apple or a hot dog, and then go around the corner to **Club Row,** a street market for animals and birds.

Then a short walk will bring you down to the Tower of London and, right beside it, just below Tower Bridge, **St. Katharine's Dock** (nearest underground station, Tower Hill). This is a new development, created out of the old London dock area where the "breakfast ships," carrying bacon and eggs from Holland, used to tie up. It is gradually becoming a vast open-air pleasure area—but with a difference.

In the East Basin of the dock (behind the Dickens Inn) lie many old and famous vessels. This is the **Historic Ship Collection** of the Maritime Trust (the national charity responsible for saving Britain's historic ships). For an admission charge of £1.50 ($2.93) for adults and 50p (98¢) for children, you can go on board seven historic ships, from the Royal Research Ship *Discovery* (Captain Scott's ship which is currently being restored) to the Nore Light Vessel. There are also a three-masted topsail schooner, a Thames sailing barge, a steam herring drifter, a "dirty British coaster" of 1890 as described by John Masefield in his poem "Cargoes" and a steam tug. Other traditional sailing barges lie nearby, and in contrast to these, the elegant craft of visiting yachts people from all over the world.

By now you should be ready for a splurge luncheon at the **Carvery** of the Tower Hotel, St. Katharine's Way, E.1 (tel. 481-2575). For £9.50 ($18.53), you can retaliate by eating yourself silly on hot roast beef, lamb, and pork.

Or you can have a very English meal at the **Captain's Cabin,** St. Katharine-by-the-Tower, East Smithfield, E.1 (tel. 480-5907), opened in the Ivory House, where ivory was once stored upstairs, slaves in the cellar. The menu features game soup, venison, Captain Cook's Eastern Island chicken, and snacks such as the barge master's special. The average meal goes for £8 ($15.60). The cabin is decorated tavern style, with a flagstone floor and fishnets draped about. It is open daily from 11 a.m. to 11 p.m., including public holidays. Live music is featured every evening.

Perhaps the main attraction is the **Dickens Inn by the Tower,** St. Katharine's Way, E.1 (tel. 488-2208), a very carefully reconstructed 19th-century warehouse. Incorporating the original redwood beams, stock bricks, and ironworks, it is a balconied pub/restaurant on three levels. Sitting on a wooden chair and an old table, you can enjoy such bar snacks as cockles, mussels, rollmops, and a ploughman's lunch. Prices begin at £1 ($1.95) for one of the snacks, ranging upward to £2.50 ($4.88) for the hot dish of the day, accompanied by a vegetable.

For more elegant dining, go upstairs to the **Pickwick Room,** where old-fashioned English-style meals are available beginning at £12 ($23.40) per head. Specialties include a braised whole pigeon with onions and red wine sauce and sirloin of Scottish beef. Other selections include a rich house pâté in puff pastry, snails flavored with garlic and Pernod, a filet steak stuffed with oysters and marinated in champagne, and the classic roast beef with Yorkshire pudding. The inn's dessert specialty is Betsy Trotwood's tipsy cake. However, you can make other rich and fattening selections from the dessert trolley.

In the top-floor **Dickens Room** fish restaurant, you can order an unusual range of fish, making your selection from a slab at one end of the restaurant.

For a traditional cockney dish, try the jellied eels or perhaps the cockles and mussels. Fish dishes include whitebait, John Dory, salmon, and crayfish tails. An average fish dinner goes for £7 ($13.65).

The tavern keeps regular pub hours; otherwise, the Pickwick Room is open Monday to Friday from 12:30 to 2 p.m. and from 7:30 to 10 p.m., on Saturday from 7:30 to 10 p.m. only, and on Sunday from 12:30 to 2 p.m. The Dickens Room serves Monday to Saturday from noon to 3 p.m. and from 5 to 10 p.m. (Sunday, noon to 5 p.m.).

It's essential to book (tel. 488-2208).

EATING AFLOAT: An increasingly popular London activity is dinner aboard. On Wednesday, Saturday, and Sunday lunchtimes, **Catamaran Cruises** leave Westminster Pier, S.W.1 (tel. 839-2349). The cost is £8.80 ($17.16) per passenger. Evening floodlit supper cruises are also offered on Wednesday, Friday, and Sunday at 9 p.m. (you're back at 10:30 p.m.). Tours leave from Westminster Pier, and the cruise costs £2.70 ($5.27). If you purchase supper, the cost goes up to £7.50 ($14.63), including a basket containing french bread, cheese and butter, chicken, a lettuce and tomato salad, rice, sherry trifle, and a piece of fresh fruit. The boat is licensed to serve drinks, and there is a commentary on the historic buildings as you ply between Albert Bridge and Tower Bridge.

A showboat dinner cruise leaves every Sunday from May to December at 7 p.m., departing from Lambeth Pier. This showboat recaptures the atmosphere and gaiety of a Victorian music hall. A three-course English dinner, including wine, is served during the cruise for £18.50 ($36.08). You return at 11 p.m.

The Regents Canal which winds and twists through London is the home of **The Fair Lady,** departing from 250 Camden High St., N.W.1, two minutes from the Camden Town tube station. There are cruises most nights starting at 7:30 p.m. and costing £12.90 ($25.16) per person for a three-hour trip. Searchlights illuminate the banks and buildings, and there is live entertainment, a singer with a guitar. Dinner is a choice of three appetizers, then a selection of meat, poultry, or fish, dessert or cheese, and coffee. House wines go for £3.75 ($7.31) a bottle. The Sunday lunch is presented at 12:30 p.m. at a cost of about £8.50 ($16.58). Advance reservations are imperative (tel. 485-4433 or 485-6210).

The Dock Supper Club, Ladbroke Grove, W.10 (tel. 960-5456), offers a barbecue and disco cruise. Narrow boats depart from the dock at 8 and 10 p.m., cruising the Grand Union Canal, past Little Venice, through Maida Hill Tunnel, Regents Park, and the London Zoo. Guests order drinks on board, and there is music to entertain them. The barbecue, consisting of everything from chicken to a Texas burger, costs £7.50 ($14.63) per person, VAT included. Cruises leave at the junction of Kensal Road and Ladbroke Grove.

LUNCHTIME THEATER: There is a drama on the menu these days in many of the small theaters and pubs of London. The actors often include well-known names, and the plays the work of established writers, although this is an outlet for many a would-be Olivier, Ayckbourn, or Stoppard. With the play, which usually lasts about an hour, the audience can often enjoy a light, inexpensive meal, and prices are deliberately kept low so that the spectacle is available to all.

The **King's Head Theatre Club,** 115 Upper St., N.1 (tel. 226-1916), run by American-born Dan Crawford, charges £6.45 ($12.58) for a dinner and show. You pay a little extra for beer or wine and collect your meat and salad or steak-and-kidney pie on the way into the theater. Evening shows begin at 8 p.m., and dinner is served at 7. However, if you want to attend just the show, the charge is reduced to £2.50 ($4.88). The club's lunchtime theater is at 1:15 p.m., when tickets cost only £1 ($1.95).

The **Soho Poly Theatre Club,** 16 Riding House St., W.1 (tel. 636-9050), charges £1.50 ($2.93) for nonmenbers and £1.20 ($2.34) for members. Membership costs only £1 ($1.95) per year or else 30p (59¢) per day. Items on the food bar are individually priced and are not included in the cost of the ticket.

After your visit to the Changing of the Guard ceremony, the **Institute of Contemporary Arts,** Nash House, The Mall, S.W.1 (tel. 930-3647), charges £2.50 ($4.88), plus a 40p (78¢) membership fee, and is rapidly gaining a reputation for avant-garde productions.

At Richmond, the **Orange Tree Pub** (tel. 940-3633), just opposite Richmond Station, presents a mixture of new plays and classics. From September to May there are full-length evening productions, and tickets are £2 ($3.90). Productions are remarkably sophisticated in this 80-seat room over an attractive bar and restaurant. During the summer there's a season of one-act plays at lunchtime, performed by daylight, with admission under £1 ($1.95).

5. The Pubs of London

No activity is more typically British than to head for that venerated institution, the Public House, affectionately known as pub. Many are dreary Victorian monstrosities, patronized by the working men and women in the neighborhood. Others, particularly those in the West End, have glamor, basking in associations real (Charles Dickens, Samuel Johnson) or imagined (Sherlock Holmes). Pub crawling, as previewed in our introduction, is a real part of your English experience.

Many North American visitors who don't usually go to bars at home become rabid enthusiasts of the English pub. And most single women feel comfortable in pubs.

Licensing hours are unpopular in England—generally from 11 a.m. to 3 p.m. and from 5:30 to 11 p.m. On Sunday the hours are usually from noon to 2 p.m. and from 7 to 10:30 p.m. Persons under 16 are generally not allowed in pubs, and those under 18 aren't served alcoholic beverages.

The most noticeable change in English pubs, especially those in the West End, is in the improved standard of food served. However, many pubs still rely on snacks, as typified by the little meat pies, drab dough wrapped around last week's pork roast. Others serve superb sandwiches (fresh salmon stuffed between healthy slices of brown bread), even hot dishes, such as shepherd's pie. Some London pubs are pursuing a fine cuisine in a separate dining room on their premises—the fare ranging from lobster soup to river trout grilled in butter to roast Aylesbury duckling in orange sauce.

Our pub recommendations in all major tourist centers of the West End follow, the emphasis on those having historic interest (the Prospect of Whitby, Ye Olde Cock Tavern) or else those catering to special-interest groups, such as theater buffs and actors (Salisbury).

ST. JAMES'S: The **Red Lion,** 2 Duke of York St., St. James's Square, S.W.1 (tel. 930-2030), is only a short walk from Piccadilly Circus. Ian Nairn compared its spirit to that of Edouard Manet's painting *A Bar at the Folies-Bergère* (see the collection at the Courtauld Institute Galleries). Try to avoid peak hours, so that you'll be able to introduce yourself to the friendly owners, Roy and Corinne Hamlin, who pride themselves on the number of friends they have made. They offer pub luncheons at noon: steak pie with vegetables, £1.40 ($2.73), and a wide variety of sandwiches—all on healthy brown bread—at 52p ($1.01) a "cutting," as they say. All roasts are £1.80 ($3.51), vegetables included. Everything is washed down with Ind Coope's fine ales in this little Victorian pub, with its posh turn-of-the-century decorations—patterned glass, deep-mahogany curlicues—that recapture the gin-palace atmosphere. It is open six days a week from 11 a.m. to 3 p.m. and from 5:30 to 11 p.m. (on Sunday from noon to 2 p.m.). Mr. and Mrs. Hamlin rule their little kingdom in a way that would have pleased Queen Victoria—that is, with style and elegance. Single women can be at ease here. Tube: Piccadilly Circus.

The **Captain's Cabin,** 4 Norris St., S.W.1 (tel. 930-3979), just off Haymarket and close to Piccadilly Circus, is an old high London building on a narrow street with a narrow pavement—unremarkable from the outside. The ground floor and snackbar are busy at lunchtime. Here, try the Director's Bitter, which is pure English beer, and have cold meats and salads, hot sausages, steak-and-kidney pie, or a ploughman's lunch, at prices ranging from £1.20 ($2.34) to £3 ($5.85).

The **Dive Bar** in the basement is a small, paneled, quiet bar with a regular clientele. Dimly lit, it was famous during World War II as a rendezvous for airmen and servicemen on leave. Mementos from those days are still on the walls. Tube: Piccadilly Circus.

PICCADILLY CIRCUS: The **Cockney Pride,** at Piccadilly Circus, W.1 (tel. 930-5339), occupies the same spot as the formerly celebrated Criterion Restaurant. It is a clever reproduction, a latter-day tribute to the glory of Victoriana: tufted velvet banquettes, cut-glass mirrors, and converted brass oil lanterns. When ordering food, better take along a friend born within the sound of the Bow Bells; you'll need one for translations. For example, you can select such Cockney cuisine oddities as "bangers and mash" at £1.05 ($2.05) or cottage pie at £1.25 ($2.44). Tube: Piccadilly Circus.

LEICESTER SQUARE: The **Salisbury,** 90 St. Martin's Lane, W.C.2, is one of the most famous Victorian pubs of London, attracting today a largely gay patronage. Its glittering cut-glass mirrors reflect the faces of English stage stars (and would-be stars) sitting around the curved buffet-style bar, having a cold joint snack. A plate of the roast leg of pork on the buffet, plus a salad, costs from £2.20 ($4.29) to £3.50 ($6.83). If you want a less prominent place to dine or to nibble oysters, choose the old-fashioned wall banquette with its copper-topped tables, and art nouveau decor. The light fixtures, veiled bronze girls in flowing togas holding up clusters of electric lights concealed in bronze roses, are appropriate. In the saloon, you'll see and hear the Olivier of yesterday and tomorrow. Tube: Leicester Square.

TRAFALGAR SQUARE: The **Sherlock Holmes,** 10 Northumberland St., W.C.2 (tel. 930-2644), is for fans of the legendary English detective and his creator, Arthur Conan Doyle. You can order your mug of beer and then look at the recreation upstairs of 221B Baker Street's living room, where get-togethers of "The Baker Street Irregulars" are held. Such "Holmesiana" are included as the cobra of the *Speckled Band* and the head of the *Hound of the Basker-villes.* The food served upstairs reflects both an English and continental influence. Appetizers run from £1.05 ($2.05) to £1.50 ($2.93). Main-dish specialties include Dover sole at £7.50 ($12.68); trout, £4.60 ($8.97); and veal escalope Cordon Bleu, £5.50 ($10.73). Desserts from the trolley begin at £1.05 ($2.05). Downstairs you can order sandwiches for 75p ($1.46), salads from £1.50 ($2.93), and shepherd's pie at £1.25 ($2.48). Tube: Trafalgar Square.

SOHO: Maison Berlemont, 49 Dean St., W.1 (tel. 437-2799), is popularly known as the French House. Run by Monsieur G. R. Berlemont, it once was the unofficial headquarters of the French resistance in exile in London during the war. Nostalgic Frenchmen still come here, talking about the old days and purchasing outstanding *vins* by the glass. The pub has a plain exterior, and the decor is not remarkable. However, the hospitality of the patron is laudable, as are his bar-room snacks, especially the pâté and the excellent quiche Lorraine. A lot of authors, theater and film people are also attracted to "the French." Tube: Tottenham Court Road.

CHELSEA: King's Head & Eight Bells, 50 Cheyne Walk, S.W.2 (tel. 352-1820), is a historic Thames-side pub in a fashionable residential area of London, that has reopened after extensive redecoration and some reconstruction. It's popular with stage and TV personalities as well as writers. Many distinguished personalities once lived in this area. A short stroll in the neighborhood will take you to the former homes of such personages as Carlyle, Swinburne, and George Eliot. Press gangs used to roam these parts of Chelsea seeking lone travelers who were abducted for a life at sea. The snackbar has been upgraded to Cordon Bleu standards at pub prices. Tony and Veronica are in charge of catering, buying, preparing, and cooking everything. The best English beers are served here, as well as a goodly selection of wines and liquors. In season some specialties include sea trout, turkey coronation, and stuffed lamb cutlets. All year you can order such delights as lasagne, shepherd's pie, or steak-and-kidney pie. One English critic wrote of the "elegant pud" (meaning desserts) served here. Among them are chocolate roulade and fresh fruit soufflés. You can dine here for £5 ($9.75). It's best reached by taxi.

Trafalgar, 200 King's Rd., S.W.3 (tel. 352-1076), is a traditional pub with darts, dominoes, and pool tables right in the heart of Chelsea. It is especially popular with the young habitués of King's Road. Apart from DJ music on weekends, there's no dancing or entertainment. Its attraction is its clientele. Bar snacks run from 70p ($1.37) to £3 ($5.85), and hot and cold dishes are available during licensing hours at both lunchtime and in the evening. Tube: Sloane Square.

BELGRAVIA: The Grenadier, Wilton Row, S.W.1 (tel. 235-3400), is an old time pub on a cobblestoned street, sheltered by higher buildings, and protected from the noise of traffic. The Grenadier is one of the special pubs of London—associated with the Iron Duke. But today the smell is not of the horses of Wellington's officers. The scarlet front door of the one-time officers' mess is guarded by a scarlet sentrybox and shaded by a vine. The bar is nearly always crowded with blue-bloods and their thin, pale girlfriends. Very English meals are served in front of fireplaces in two of the small rooms behind the front bar. Luncheons and dinners are offered daily, including Sunday, from noon to 3 p.m. and from 7 to 11 p.m. A soup of the day is invariably featured. Main courses include such dishes as baked Virginia ham, followed by desserts including apple pie and cream. Lunch snacks at the bar range in price from £1 ($1.95) to £4 ($7.80) a plate. In the evenings, only hot sausages are available in the bar, going for 60p ($1.17). A lunch or dinner in the small restaurant will average around £6 ($11.70).

There is a gentle ghost, that of an officer who died after being flogged for cheating at cards. The decor is definitely Wellingtonian. At the entrance to Wilton Row (in the vicinity of Belgrave Square), a special guard ("good evening, guv'nor") is stationed to raise and lower a barrier for those arriving by "carriage." May British tradition never die. Pub enthusiasts are fanatic about the Grenadier. If anyone tries to tear it down, he may meet his Waterloo. Tube: Victoria Station.

The **Antelope,** 22 Eaton Terrace, S.W.1 (tel. 730-7781), on the fringe of Belgravia, at the gateway to Chelsea, caters to a hotchpotch of clients, aptly described as "people of all classes, colours and creeds who repair for interesting discussion on a whole gamut of subjects, ranging from sport to medieval history, wicker-work, bed-bug traps, and for both mental and physical refreshment." 'Nuff said? You can wine and dine upstairs, or else have lunch in a ground-floor chamber offering a cold buffet at prices ranging from £3.50 ($6.83). For openers, try the Antelope soup, followed by steak-and-kidney pie, and topped off by red-currant pie and cream. The trappings have long ago mellowed, as the history of the Antelope goes back to 1780. Tube: Sloane Square.

SHEPHERD MARKET (MAYFAIR): Shepherd's Tavern, 50 Hertford St., W.1 (tel. 499-3017), is a nugget, considered the pub of Mayfair. It attracts a congenial mixture of English, from those who read *The Times* every morning to a rather advanced set of young 'uns. There are many fine touches, including a collection of antique furniture. Attention is focused on the sedan chair which once belonged to the son of George III, the Duke of Cumberland (it's now fitted with a telephone for those very private "ring ups"). Many of the locals like to recall the tavern's associations with the pilots in the Battle of Britain. Bar snacks and hot dishes include shepherd's pie, curry or fish pie with vegetable, the prices beginning at £1.25 ($2.44) per serving. Upstairs, the restaurant has reopened, serving chicken and steak-and-kidney pie, as well as shepherd's and fish pies, along with a coterie of curry dishes and roast joints daily. A main dish will cost from £2.25 ($4.39) to £3 ($5.85). The tavern is popular with local business folk, and it's a good place for the visitor wanting to study local Mayfair life. Tube: Green Park.

BLOOMSBURY: The **Museum Tavern,** 49 Great Russell St., W.C.1 (tel. 242-8987), opposite the British Museum, is a turn-of-the-century pub, with all the trappings: velvet, oak paneling, and cut glass. It's right in the center of the London University area, and popular with writers and publishers. At lunch you can order real, good-tasting, low-cost English food. Such standard English fare is featured as shepherd's pie at £1.40 ($2.73) or beef in beer with two vegetables, £1.40 also. A fish pie with two vegetables costs £1.50 ($2.93). A cold buffet is offered, runing from £1 ($1.95), including herring, Scottish eggs, and veal and ham pies, as well as salads and cheese. Tube: Russell Square.

THE CITY: Old King Lud, 78 Ludgate Circus, E.C.4 (tel. 236-6610), is a Victorian pub built in 1855 on the site of the Old Fleet Prison. The former dungeons are now the cellars of this old-world pub, which bills itself as the home of the original Welsh rarebit. However, it no longer serves that specialty for which it became famous. Rather, it offers a selection of pâtés at 95p ($1.85) for which ranges from venison to duck with orange. Both hot and cold dishes are dispensed. One of the hot plates, such as beef curry with two vegetables, costs £1.70 ($3.32). Wine is sold by the glass, slections including claret at 72p ($1.40) or Anjou at 72p also. You can also order good Marlow Bitter here. The decor is in varying shades of green, including the tufted banquettes. Tube: Blackfriars.

Ye Olde Watling, 29 Watling St., E.C.4 (tel. 248-6235), is associated with Sir Christopher Wren; it was built after the Great Fire of London in 1666. On the ground level is a mellow pub, with an intimate restaurant upstairs which serves lunch from noon to 2:15 p.m., Monday through Friday. Under oak beams and on trestle tables, you can have a good choice of English food, with such traditional dishes as steak, kidney, and mushroom pudding, the house specialty. Steak and oyster pie is also good. On the ground floor, buffet bar salads, along with hot dishes, are in the £1.35 ($2.63) to £2.25 ($4.39) range. Upstairs, a small steak with vegetables or salad, plus a dessert, will run you about £5 ($9.75). Tube: Mansion House.

FLEET STREET: Ye Olde Cock Tavern, 22 Fleet St., E.C.4 (tel. 353-9706), boasts a long line of ghostly literary comrades, such as Dickens, who have favored this ancient pub. After having a half pint on the ground floor, diners go upstairs to have lunch in a former horse stall. "Ye fare" is served from 12:30 to 3 p.m. Of course, the food is traditionally English. A bowl of rich soup costs 70p ($1.37); a steak-and-kidney pie, £2.40 ($4.68); a delicious fruit trifle, 75p ($1.46). Tube: St. Paul's.

ALONG THE THAMES: The Prospect of Whitby, 47 Wapping Wall, E.1 (tel. 481-1095), is one of London's oldest riverside pubs, having been founded originally in the days of the Tudors. The Prospect has many associations—it was visited by Dickens, Turner, Whistler, in search of local "colour." Come here for a "tot," a "noggin," or whatever it is that you drink. The Pepys Room honors the diarist, who may—just may—have visited the Prospect back in its rowdier days, when the seamy side of London dock life held sway here. The pub is named after a ship, the *Prospect,* which sailed from its home port of Whitby and used to drop anchor outside the pub. Live music is heard every night from 8:30 to 11.

At the restaurant upstairs, you should reserve early and ask for the bow window table with fine views over the Thames. Apart from an à la carte menu, the restaurant offers two set menus at £9.50 ($18.53) and £11.50 ($22.43) per person, including VAT and service, plus half a bottle of wine. You're given a choice of several appetizers, along with a selection of four main dishes, as well as a dessert or cheese, then coffee. In the bar you can order snacks of various cold meats, salads, cheese, and your stuffing for a large chunk of french bread with butter.

Take the Metropolitan Line to Wapping Station. When you emerge onto Wapping High Street, turn right and head down the road along the river. Wapping Wall will be on your right, running parallel to the Thames. It's about a five-minute walk.

The City Barge, Strand-on-the-Green, Chiswick, W.4. Londoners head here for an outing and an evening pint of ale on a summer night. A little country pub, a nostalgic link with the past—it can be reached in 45 minutes from the center of London. Take the tube to Hammersmith, then change to bus 27 and get off at the beginning of Kew Bridge (during the day this can be combined with a visit to Kew Gardens). Then walk down a towpath (about a five-minute jaunt), past moored boats and a row of little Regency, Queen Anne, Georgian, and Dutch houses, till you reach the pub. Or you can go by boat from Westminster Pier to Kew Gardens, then visit the City Barge, and return to London by train. Regulars often bypass the little tables set outside (in summer) so as to have their pint while sitting on the embankment wall under a willow tree, and enjoying the boats chugging or gliding by.

The **Anchor**, 1 Bankside, Southward, S.E.1 (tel. 407-1577), is steeped in atmosphere, standing near what used to be the infamous debtors' prison, Clink (hence, the expression—"putting a man in the clink"). The original Anchor burned down in 1676 but was rebuilt and survived the bombs of World War II. Much of the present tavern, however, is aptly described by the management as "Elizabeth II." After getting off at the tube stop, you pass by Southwark Cathedral through a warehouse district that looks at night like Jack the Ripper country till you reach the riverside tavern. There's a viewing platform—especially popular during the day—right on the Thames. You'll find a number of bars named after the historical associations of the inn (Thrale Room, Dr. Johnson's Room, the Globe Bar, the Clink Bar, and the Boswell Bar). In addition, you can dine either upstairs or down in such "parlours" as the Boswell Grill or the Elizabethan Long Gallery Restaurant. The food is good, and meals begin at £6 ($11.70). The Anchor is open from noon to 2 p.m. for lunch and from 7 to 10 p.m. for dinner Monday through Saturday. On Sunday, lunch is from noon to 1 p.m.; dinner, 7 to 9 p.m. Tube: London Bridge.

ELEPHANT & CASTLE: South of the Thames, the following pub is easily reached by underground train to Elephant & Castle. From the station where you get off, it's a five-minute walk.

The **Goose and Ferkin**, 47–48 Borough Rd., S.E.1 (tel. 403-3590), is a pub which brews its own beer. The owner of this unique enterprise is David Bruce, who worked as a brewer for one of the big companies for many years until his chance came to buy the Goose and Ferkin. He obtained his own license to brew, and set about producing his own beers. A large mirror proclaims "Bruce's Brewery, established 1979." He brews three special strengths, Borough Bitter, 50p (98¢) for a half pint, Dog Bolter, 55p ($1.07) for a half, and, for special occasions, Earth Stopper, 80p ($1.56), and only served in halves. Be warned: This one is a real man's beer, and your 80p worth is the equivalent of three measures of whisky in strength.

Food is also available in this lovely old London pub. Each day there is a different hot dish costing from around £1.85 ($3.61). Or else you can order extra-large baps (bread buns) filled with your choice of meat and salad, costing from £1.10 ($2.15).

The whole operation is managed by the buxom Tint Watson and her husband Alistair. Son Neil is David's assistant brewer. From 8 p.m. onward, Crazy Jimmy plays the piano in the good old "knees up" style, and on Sunday at lunchtime the pub's group of dancers entertain, another traditional item.

HAMPSTEAD: The **Old Bull and Bush**, North End Way, N.W.3, is one of London's most famous pubs. Although built in this century, it traces its origins back to the mid-17th century. Hogarth's home was near the site (so it is believed) of the present pub. Florrie Forde's legendary song did much to fan its fame far and wide. The pub is in the center of the Heath, away from the commercial areas. It is a gathering spot for the young set of Hampstead, and weekend trippers from London. The drinking favorite is draft beer, and a fantastic number of mugs are consumed here. You can also get an assortment of sandwiches for around £1.05 ($2.05) and salads for around £1.60 ($3.12). It's not help yourself. You select and a waitress serves. A fire burns on nippy evenings. Tube: Hampstead.

6. The Wine Bars

For years, the stark, atmospheric, and ancient wine cellars of the old City have been patronized by businessmen in bowlers, and were almost a well-kept secret, as you never ran into a tourist or a woman there. However, that has changed now. Wine bars are the fashion, and the pub no longer completely dominates the drinking scene in the English capital.

With the coming of newer and trendier wine bars, London's drinking habits have undergone significant change. Wine bars are not only places at which to drink, but also to meet friends and enjoy good food. A few of the older, more established ones still offer only wine, but in today's terms a wine bar is likely to mean anything, including a disco!

The English taste for wine has increased, hence the number of wine bars springing up in all parts of the city. Nearly all the establishments recommended below sell wine by the glass, although if you're traveling in a party you may want to order by the bottle and share as it's less expensive that way.

We'll lead off with the most interesting collection of wine bars which still lie in the City and are best visited weekdays for lunch. In the other sections of town you can go for both lunch and dinner.

THE CITY: Olde Wine Shades, 6 Martin Lane, off Cannon Street, E.C.4 (tel. 626-6876), is the oldest wine house in the City, dating from 1663. It was the only City tavern to survive the Great Fire of 1666, not to mention the blitz of 1940. Only 100 yards from the Monument, the Olde Wine Shades used to attract Charles Dickens who enjoyed its fine wines. In the smoking room the old oil paintings have appropriately darkened with age, and the 19th-century satirical political cartoons remain enigmatic to most of today's generation. Some of the fine wines of Europe are served here, and port and sherry are drawn directly from an array of casks behind the counter. The owners, El Vino, the City wine merchants, boast that they can satisfy anyone's taste in sherry. A candlewick bar and restaurant is found downstairs, but upstairs, along with your wine, you can order french bread with ham off the bone at £1.40 ($2.73), Breton pâté at £1.10 ($2.15), and sandwiches beginning at 65p ($1.27). Jackets, collars, and ties are required for men. Jeans or cords are not permitted for women. Hours are from 11:30 a.m. to 3 p.m. and from 5 to 8 p.m. Closed Saturday, Sunday, and bank holidays. Tube: Monument.

Mother Bunch's Wine House, Arches F & G, Old Seacoal Lane, E.C.4 (tel. 236-5317), is a maze of vaults underneath the arches of Ludgate Circus. My favorite of all the wine houses, Mother Bunch's is one of the most atmospheric places for dining in the City, boasting a "well-stocked larder," with the best of hams and all manner of cheeses as well as game and other pies. Port wines of the most noted vintages are decanted daily "for gentlemen in the proper manner." In season, grouse, partridge, pheasant, and Scottish salmon are featured. Guests can dine in the mellow room downstairs or perhaps in the elegantly furnished upstairs room where many are seated around a large table and served family style. Sherry, port, and madeira "from the wood" begin at 85p ($1.66), and table wines by the glass start at £1 ($1.95). The favorite dish is a plate of smoked ham off the bone, although game pie is also praised. Strawberries and raspberries in season make fine dessert. Main lunchtime dishes cost around £2.25 ($4.39), and cheese and french bread go for £1.05 ($2.05). The wine house is open from 11:30 a.m. to 3 p.m. and from 5:30 to 8:30 p.m., Monday to Friday. Tube: Blackfriars.

Bow Wine Vaults, 10 Bow Churchyard, E.C.4 (tel. 248-1121), has existed long before the current wine bar fad. The atmosphere is staunchly masculine, and the vaults attract a loyal following of business and professional people who somehow manage to find their way back to their offices after a heavy eating and drinking session here. Sherries, port, and madeira are available by the glass, as are an assortment of table wines at prices ranging from 70p ($1.37) to £3.50 ($2.54), the latter price for a 1901 vintage madeira. A cold buffet with a salad will run you £2.65 ($5.18); there's a minimum charge of £4 ($7.80). The vaults are open from 11:30 a.m. to 3 p.m. and from 5 to 7 p.m. but closed weekends and bank holidays. Tube: Mansion House.

Jamaica Wine House, St. Michael's Alley, off Cornhill, E.C.3 (tel. 626-9496), lies in a tangle of City alleyways, and if you do manage to find it, you'll be at one of the first coffeehouses to be opened in England. In fact, the Jamaica Wine House is reputed to be the first coffeehouse in the Western world. Pepys used to visit it and mentioned the event in his Diary. The coffeehouse was destroyed in the Great Fire of 1666, rebuilt in 1674, and has remained, more or less, in its present form ever since. For years London merchants and daring sea captains came here to lace deals with rum and coffee. Nowadays, the two-level house dispenses beer, ale, lager, and fine wines to appreciative drinkers. The oak-paneled bar on the ground floor is more traditional, as the downstairs bar has been modernized. The Bank of England is only a stone's throw away. Tube: Bank.

NEAR LEICESTER SQUARE: Slatters, 3 Panton St., S.W.1 (tel. 839-4649), lies off Haymarket, a split-level wine bar convenient for theater-goers. It makes a good rendezvous for pretheater and after-theater suppers. A stylish informality reigns. Classical music plays in the background and the paintings on the wall are for sale. Some are originals; others are lithographs—all with theatrical and dance themes, executed and signed by Tome Merrifield and priced from £30 ($58.50). The house wine is from France. and you can drink it at 90p ($1.76) a glass, along with food offered by owner Kenneth Slatter. The smoked trout is a favorite opener, followed by the underdone pink roast beef. Try also the mackerel pâté served with french bread or perhaps baked ham or chicken. The cheese board is first class. The average three-course meal here will cost from £5 ($9.75). Closed on Sunday, Slatters is open for lunch or dinner until midnight. Happy hour is from 8 to 10 nightly. Tube: Leicester Square.

NEAR COVENT GARDEN: The Counter, 4 Great Queen St., W.C.2 (tel. 405-6598), is owned by K. C. Sulkin, J. Bryan, and D. Rudland— "KC," "Joe," and "David" to their regulars. Upstairs in this cream and blue restaurant, jitterbug, jazz, and beebop are the theme, evoking the eras of the '40s and '50s. Live music accompanies your meal, which might include, as a main dish, Dover sole, scallops and bacon, perhaps breast of chicken in puff pastry, followed by dessert, costing about £8.50 ($16.58), including the price of an appetizer as well. Downstairs in the fast-service Jazz Bar, snacks such as southern fried chicken, eggs Benedict, and spare ribs with jacket potatoes and salad, make up a meal for about £4.50 ($8.78). a bottle of wine is an extra £4.20 ($8.19). Finally, if you can remember how to dance in the '40s style, the floor is all yours. Tube: Holborn.

MAYFAIR: Downs Wine Bar, 5 Down St., W.1 (tel. 491-3810), attracts "the beautiful people" of Mayfair, who live in and around that square mile at the Hyde Park end of Piccadilly, near the Athenaeum Hotel. In fair weather, there are sidewalk tables. Every evening you can descend a spiral staircase to a simple, admission-free disco. Nearly 100 wines are available, each bottled in its country of origin. The food specialty is ham cooked in marmalade, costing £2.50 ($4.88) for a large platter with garnishes. On Sunday, a set lunch is featured for £5 ($9.75). The upstairs dining room is decorated in a modern style with chrome and cane chairs, along with banquettes. Hours are from 11:30 a.m. to 3 p.m. and from 5:30 to midnight daily, from noon to 3 p.m. and from 7 p.m. to 12:30 a.m. on Sunday. Tube: Green Park. .

IN BLOOMSBURY: Entrecôte, 124 Southampton Row, W.C.1 (tel. 405-1466), invites you to go downstairs to its Edwardian precincts. Attractive women students are the waitresses, and they will serve you the house specialty, an entrecôte with french fries. Selections from the cheese board are first rate. Other daily specials are offered as well—perhaps coq au vin or beef bourgignonne. In fact, the food is generally French inspired, and the wine list includes some Haut Médoc selections. The price of a meal ranges from about £5 ($9.75) to £8.50 ($16.58), with wine going for 80p ($1.56) a glass. A three-piece band plays nightly from 8 to 9; otherwise, there is disco music. The restaurant is open Monday to Saturday from 11:30 a.m. to 3:30 p.m. and from 3:30 p.m. to 1 a.m. On Sunday its hours are from 5:30 p.m. to midnight. Tube: Russell Square.

IN BELGRAVIA: Motcomb's, 26 Motcomb St., S.W.1 (tel. 235-6382), opposite Sotheby's Belgravia, is one of the handsomest and most charming wine bars in London. A small, friendly place above the main restaurant, it is run by Betty, Don, and Jani Phillips. The bar is decorated with old paintings and mementos and has a club-like atmosphere. A complete range of hot and cold homemade food is served for from £1 ($1.95), and there is a choice of wines available by the glass. In the restaurant there is a comprehensive à la carte menu with seasonal additions. Two can dine comfortably, with wine, in this oak-beamed old English restaurant for from £20 ($39). Specialties include Sloane salad, £2.75 ($5.36); game soup, £1.90 ($3.71); cold asparagus soup, £1.95 ($3.80); calf liver with bacon, £4.15 ($8.09); venison casserole, £4.75 ($9.26); and a magnificent dessert trolley, from £1.50 ($2.93). Motcomb's is open from noon to 3:30 p.m. and from 7 to 11 p.m. in the restaurant and from 11:30 a.m. to 3 p.m. and 5:30 to 11 p.m. in the bar, Monday to Friday. Tube: Knightsbridge.

Bill Bentley's, 31 Beauchamp Pl., S.W.3 (tel. 589-5080), stands on this restaurant- and boutique-lined street near Harrods. A small Georgian house, it offers many ground-floor rooms and a little sun-filled patio in back. Cozy and atmospheric, it presents a varied list of reasonably priced wines, including a fine selection of bordeaux. If you're in the neighborhood for lunch, you can enjoy a pub-style lunch, such as ham and salad, for £2.50 ($4.88). Hot main dishes are likely to include skate in black butter with capers for £4 ($7.80) and grilled lemon sole at £5 ($9.75). It's open daily from 11:30 a.m. to 3 p.m. and from

5:30 to 11 p.m., on Saturday from 6:30 to 11 p.m. Closed Sunday and bank holidays. Tube: Knightsbridge.

CHELSEA: Blushes, 52 King's Road, S.W.3 (tel. 589-6640), is the nearest you will get to a singles bar in London. This attractively decorated watering hole serves drinks and food all day from morning to midnight. The cuisine is excellent, and service is friendly. The average price for two for a meal with wine ranges from £8 ($15.60) to £12 ($23.40). At night, there is a busy cocktail bar in the basement. Be prepared to be kept waiting before you get in. They call the dress "smart" around here. Tube: Sloane Square

Charco's/Searcy's, 1 Bray Pl., S.W.3 (tel. 584-0765), has an entrance on two streets in Chelsea, lying right off King's Road. A very bright crowd patronizes this establishment, enjoying the reasonably priced wines and the good and inexpensive food, such as salads, cold meats on the buffet, and such hot dishes as moussaka. You can spend as little as 35p (68¢), although more likely £2.50 ($4.88). A slice of a roast joint and a salad is priced at £1.75 ($3.41). In summer you may dine at one of the sidewalk tables. The wine bar is open from 11 a.m. to 3 p.m. and from 5:30 to 11 p.m. daily (Sunday, noon to 2 p.m. and 7 to 10:30 p.m.). Tube: Sloane Square.

7. Country Dining Near London

The **Bell Inn,** Aston Clinton, Buckinghamshire (tel. Aylesbury 630252), is a coaching inn and believed to have been built at the end of the 18th century. Under the guidance of the Harris family, the inn has won extraordinary acclaim for its cuisine. Advertised by a large bell instead of an inn sign, it stands unobtrusively by the road, 40 miles from London and four miles from Aylesbury. It's a mossy brick structure, with crisp white windows and a Georgian portico. Inside, antiques are used liberally. The dining room in olive green is coolly elegant, with polished wood and sparkling glass and silver. You select your meal in a large stone-floored bar while having a drink. Lunch or dinner is a special event. The Bavarian chef, Jacques Dick, is a perfectionist. For a beginning, try his "smokies" or his pâté maison. Main dishes include poached salmon (in season only) and roast duck with apple sauce from the trolley, a specialty for two diners. We'd also recommend the tournedos Rossini, sea bass Provençal, and saddle of hare. The price of the average meal is about £20 ($39), including half a bottle of the house wine.

There are six bedrooms in the original inn, all with private baths, refrigerator, and mini-bar, and all tastefully decorated. Converted from a stable block are 15 more comfortable rooms, arranged around a courtyard across a narrow road from the inn. Such thoughtful touches have been added as bathrobes, bubble-bath powder, shampoo, whatever, all included in the luxuriously appointed baths. Room rates range from £40 ($78) to £60 ($117) for two persons, including a full English breakfast, VAT, and service. Some singles are available as well. A log fire in the lounge makes for a warm welcome to this old coaching inn.

LONDON: WHAT TO SEE AND DO

DR. JOHNSON SAID: "When a man is tired of London, he is tired of life, for there is in London all that life can afford." And that holds true today.

Come along with us as we survey only a fraction of that life: ancient monuments, boutiques, debates in Parliament, art galleries, Soho, dives, museums, theaters, flea markets, and castles. Some of what we're about to see was known to Johnson and Boswell, even Shakespeare, but much of it is new.

1. Getting Around Town

If you know the ropes, transportation within London can be unusually easy and cheap because London enjoys one of the best underground and bus systems in the world.

THE UNDERGROUND: The electric subways are, to begin with, comfortable—the trains have cushioned seats, no less. You purchase your ticket in advance either at a ticket booth or from an automatic ticket machine. Fares vary according to distance, from 20p (39¢) for short rides to a high of £1.60 ($3.12) to the outer extremities of Greater London. The fare from Heathrow to Piccadilly Circus is £1.10 ($2.15), and the average fare in central London is 20p (39¢). Be sure to keep your ticket: it must be presented at the end of the line. If you owe extra, you'll be billed then by an attendant.

Each subway line has its own distinctive color, and all you need follow is the clearly painted arrows. On every stairway, at every corridor turning, on every platform, are additional diagrams in color, giving the routes of the various trains. More diagrams are inside the trains themselves.

The Piccadilly line was recently extended to serve Heathrow Airport, giving London Transport the world's first connection between an airport and a major underground transportation system. Built with special consideration

for airline travelers, the Heathrow extension has trains with additional luggage space as well as moving walkways from the airport terminals to the underground station. The link enables incoming passengers to dash from Heathrow to Piccadilly Circus in only 40 minutes.

The Piccadilly line has increased its service to accommodate the demand created by the Heathrow extension, but be warned: if you're out on the town and are dependent on the underground, watch your time carefully—many of the subways stop running at midnight (11:30 p.m. on Sunday).

On Sunday and public holidays there is a maximum fare to anywhere (except Heathrow) on the network of 40p (78¢) for a single journey and 60p ($1.17) for a round trip. These are not Rover tickets and therefore each ticket can be used only once.

BUSES: The comparably priced bus system is almost as good. To find out about current routes, pick up a free bus map at the BTA, 64 St. James's St., Piccadilly, or at any London Transport Travel Information Centre.

After you have lined up (queued) for the bus, and picked a seat either downstairs or on the upper deck (where you can smoke, and where you'll see more of the city), a conductor will come by to whom you tell your destination. He or she then collects the fare and gives you a ticket. As with the subways, the fare varies according to the distance you travel. If you want to be warned when to get off, simply ask the conductor.

BARGAIN TRAVEL PASSES—SUBWAYS AND BUSES: London Transport, which operates one of the world's biggest urban transport systems, offers many special facilities for the visitor. Information on bus and underground services and sightseeing tours can be obtained by calling at London Transport's Travel Information Centre (at Heathrow Central, Victoria, Piccadilly Circus, Oxford Circus, St. James's Park. Euston, and King's Cross underground stations. These offices are open every day from 8:30 a.m. to 9:30 p.m. except Oxford Circus which closes at 6 p.m. on Sunday and St. James's Park which is open on Monday to Friday only, from 8:30 a.m. to 6:30 p.m. They sell Go-As-You-Please tourist tickets and take bookings for London Transport's guided coach tours.

Go-As-You-Please Tourist Tickets, very useful bargains for travelers to London. They give three or seven days of unlimited travel on London's red buses and most of the underground, and can be bought at underground stations or Travel Information Centres. They cost £14.50 ($27) for adults, £5.94 ($11) for children for three days; £17.30 ($32) for adults, £7.02 ($13) for children for four days; £25.94 ($48) for adults, £9.72 ($18) for children for seven days; and £42.16 ($78) for adults, £16.20 ($30) for children for 14 days.

Central London Rover. These are available for unlimited travel for one day on all London buses and underground trains throughout the central London area. They can be purchased from any underground station or Travel Information Centre in central London. They cost £1.60 ($3.12) for adults, 60p ($1.17) for children. **Red Bus Rovers.** These tickets give unlimited travel on London's red buses for one day and can be bought at any Travel Information Centre, most underground stations, bus garages, and agents of National Travel. They cost £1.20 ($2.34) for adults, 60p (59¢) for children.

TAXIS: You can get a cab in London either by heading for a cab stand, hailing one in the street, or telephoning 837-8800, 636-8771, 289-1133, 272-3030, or

286-4848. The minimum fare is 50p (98¢). On weekends and at night a surcharge of 10p (20¢) is added, these tariffs including VAT. It's recommended that you tip about 20% of the fare, and never less than 10p (20¢).

BOAT TRIPS: Touring boats operate on the Thames between April and September, taking you various places within London and also to nearby towns along the Thames. Main embarkation points are **Westminster Pier, Charing Cross Pier,** and **Tower Hill Pier**—a system that enables you, for instance, to take a "water taxi" from the Tower of London to Westminster Abbey. Not only are the boats energy-saving, bringing you painlessly to your destination, but they permit you to sit back in comfort as you see London from the river.

Several companies operate these boats, which vary from large launches to smaller speedboats. Many offer service every 20 minutes from 10:20 a.m. until dusk. Because of tides, however, no exact schedule is given; you simply go to the pier and take your chances. But the wait is usually short. From Westminster Pier to Tower Hill generally costs 90p ($1.76) one way, £1.30 ($2.54) round trip. There are deck chairs on board these water taxis, and beer is sold even during the hours when the pubs of London are closed. From Westminster Pier you can cruise down to Greenwich, paying £1.30 ($2.54) for a single ticket, £1.90 ($3.71) round trip. Also from Westminster Pier, you can board a boat to Kew and Richmond, costing £3.80 ($7.41) for a round-trip ticket.

For information about these boat trips, you can telephone **London Tourist Board's River Information Service** (tel. 730-4812) or the boat company (tel. 930-0970).

Capital Cruises of DCW House, 45a Heathfield Rd., S.W. 18 (tel. 615-7036), runs lunch and dinner cruises with buffet meals and disco. Prices range from £6 ($11.70) to £10 ($19.50) according to the menu.

OTHER VITAL DATA: Banking hours: In general, hours are from 9:30 a.m. to 3:30 p.m., Monday through Friday. Many exchange bureaus in the West End are open from 9 a.m. to 5:30 p.m. You get a better rate at exchange bureaus and banks than at your hotel. Selfridges and Harrods have banks open on Saturday and which keep longer hours than the banking houses.

Medical services: All medical treatment in the United Kingdom is free, except when you consult a physician privately. Hotels will get in touch with their house doctor should you need one.

Telephone services: In addition to being able to reach anywhere in the world, the telephone service offers the weather forecast (dial 246-8091); the time (dial 123); motoring conditions (dial 246-8021); daily information about main events in and around London (dial 246); activities concerning children's London (dial 246-8007); and the Financial Times Share Index and business news summaries (dial 246-8206).

To operate a telephone in London, pick up the receiver and dial your number. Have your money ready. When the person on the other end answers, insert 5p (10¢) for local calls. If you don't insert the coin, the party you are calling cannot hear your voice. You are granted two minutes per 5p coin. For long distance (known as a trunk call), you must insert 10p (20¢) when the call is answered. Coinboxes take only 5p and 10p coins, although many 50p (98¢) coinboxes are now being installed. Dialing codes are shown in the notice frame in telephone kiosks. After you dial your number, or code and number, you will either hear a regularly interrupted single tone, which means the line is busy, or a repeated brr-brr sound which means the exchange is trying to connect you.

When the call is answered, you will hear rapid pips. Immediately put a coin into the slot and speak. If you hear the pips again and wish to continue speaking, put another coin in the slot at once. Long-distance calls are cheaper between 6 p.m. and 8 a.m. Monday to Friday and all day Saturday and Sunday.

Note: Calls through a hotel switchboard will have a surcharge added to the normal post office cost of the call. Pay telephones are available in most hotel foyers.

The **Westminster International Telephone Bureau,** 1 Broadway, S.W.1, is open daily from 9 a.m. to 5:30 p.m., including Sunday. The bureau allows you to call all countries not available through call boxes (that is, outside Europe). There is a receptionist to help and to take your money once you've finished your call.

2. Seeing the Sights

London is not a city to visit hurriedly. It is so vast, so stocked with treasures that the visitor does himself or herself a disservice if he or she plans to "do" London in two or three days. Not only will a person miss many of the highlights, he or she will also fail to grasp the spirit of London and to absorb fully its special flavor, which is unique among cities. Still, faced with an infinite number of important places to visit and a time clock running out, the tourist will have to concentrate on a manageable group. I'll survey a personal list of the indispensable sights for those with a minimum of time, then follow in this section with "The Best of the Rest," But first, a digression.

BARGAIN TIP: The **Department of the Environment,** 25 Savile Row, W.1 (tel. 734-6010), offers a **Season Ticket to History** which allows the holder free and unlimited entry to all those places in England, Scotland, and Wales which are maintained by the British government. The cost of the ticket, payable only by international money order (sterling only) is £6 ($11.70) for adults, £3 ($5.85) for children under 16. Valid for one year, it can be purchased by mail only from Department of the Environment (St), AMHB Store, Room 32, Building 1, Victoria Road, South Ruislip, Middlesex HA4 0NZ, or at any of the Ancient Monuments which have custodians. A list of sights to be seen, including the Tower of London, Hampton Court Palace, Stonehenge, and Edinburgh Castle, giving opening times and available facilities is given free with each ticket order.

An **Open to View** ticket sells for $19 (U.S.) for adults, $9.50 for children, and includes free admission to more than 500 properties in Britain, including Edinburgh Castle, Churchill's Chartwell, Woburn Abbey, Hampton Court Palace, and Windsor Castle. It is good for one month after you first use it, and covers all properties in care of Britain's National Trust and those run by the Department of the Environment. It is estimated that anyone visiting as many as five of these sightseeing attractions will get back the initial outlay. In the U.S., inquire at **BritRail Travel International Inc.,** 630 Third Ave., New York, NY 10017; 333 North Michigan Ave., Chicago, IL 60601; or 510 West Sixth St., Los Angeles, CA 90014.

THE TOWER OF LONDON: This ancient fortress on the north bank of the Thames continues to pack 'em in because of its macabre associations with all the legendary figures who were either imprisoned or executed here, or both. James Street once wrote, ". . . there are more spooks to the square foot than in any other building in the whole of haunted Britain. Headless bodies, bodiless heads, phantom soldiers, icy blasts, clanking chains—you name them, the Tower's got them."

Back in the days of the axman, London was "swinging" long before *Time* magazine discovered that fact. Ranking in interest are the colorful attending Yeoman Warders, the so-called Beefeaters, in Tudor dress, who look as if they are on the payroll for gin advertisements (but don't like to be reminded of it).

Many visitors consider a visit to the Tower to be the highlight of their sightseeing in London—so schedule plenty of time for it. You don't have to stay as long as Sir Walter Raleigh (released after some 13 years), but give it an afternoon. Take either the Circle or District line to Tower Hill Station (the site is only a short walk away). You will be admitted March 1 to October 31 from 9:30 a.m. to 5 p.m. Admission prices vary according to the season, but count on spending around £3 ($5.85) for adults and £1.50 ($2.93) for children in July and August. In January, February, November, and December, it will be around £2 ($3.90) for adults and £1 ($1.95) for children, and in other months £2.50 ($4.88) and £1.20 ($2.34), respectively. In winter the hours are from 9:30 a.m. to 4 p.m. The Tower is also open on Sunday from March to October, in the afternoon only (2 to 5 p.m.), but these times tend to be overcrowded.

Don't expect to find only one tower. The fortress is actually a compound, in which the oldest and finest structure is the White Tower, begun by William the Conqueror. Here you can view the Armories, the present collection dating back to the reign of Henry VIII. A display of instruments of torture and execution will be spread before you, recalling some of the most ghastly moments in the history of the Tower. At the Bloody Tower, the Little Princes (Edward V and the Duke of York) were allegedly murdered by their uncle, Richard III.

The hospitality today far excels that of years ago, when many of the visitors left their cells only to walk to the headsman's block on Tower Hill. Through Traitors' Gate passed such ill-fated, but romantic, figures as Robert Devereux, a favorite of Elizabeth I, known as the second Earl of Essex. Elizabeth herself, then a princess, was once imprisoned briefly in Bell Tower. At Tower Green, Anne Boleyn and Katharine Howard, two wives of Henry VIII, lost their lives. The nine-day queen, Lady Jane Grey, and her husband, Dudley, also were executed, along with such figures as Sir Thomas More.

According to legend, the disappearance of the well-protected ravens at the Tower will presage the collapse of the British Empire (seen any around lately?)

For a well-spent 60p ($1.17) for adults, 30p (59¢) for children, you can see the Jewel House, where the Crown Jewels are kept, but go early in summer, as long lines usually form by late morning. Get a Beefeater to tell you how Colonel Blood almost made off with the crown and regalia in the late 17th century. Of the three English crowns, the Imperial State Crown is the most important—in fact, it's probably the most famous crown on earth. Made for Victoria for her coronation in 1838, it is today worn by Queen Elizabeth when she opens Parliament. Studded with some 3000 jewels (principally diamonds), it contains the Black Prince's Ruby, worn by Henry V at Agincourt, the battle in 1415 when the English defeated the French. In addition, feast your eyes on the 530-carat Star of Africa, a cut diamond on the Royal Sceptre with Cross. The Jewel House is closed for four to six weeks early in each year for the annual cleaning and overhaul.

The Tower of London has an evening ceremony called the **Ceremony of the Keys.** It begins with visitors who have tickets being admitted by a Beefeater around 9:35 p.m. It is, in fact, the changing of the guard and the ceremonial locking up of the Tower for yet another day in its 900 years. Nothing stops the ceremony. During World War II, a bomb fell within the castle walls during the ceremony, and nobody flinched—but the Tower was locked up two minutes late. Rumor has it that the guard that night was censured for tardiness, the pilot of the plane which dropped the bomb blamed as the culprit. The Beefeater will explain to guests the significance of the ceremony. For tickets, write to the Governor, Tower of London, London, E.C.3, England, requesting a specific date but also giving alternate dates you'd like to attend. One-week notice is preferred.

Although its outward appearance is so familiar to Londoners and visitors alike, one of the most exciting new sights London offers is the **Tower Bridge** (tel. 407-0922), the one that certain American thought he had bought when he purchased that other one farther up the river.

Tower Bridge was built during 1886 and 1894 with two towers 800 feet apart, joined by footbridges which provide glass-covered walkways for the public who can enter the north tower, take the elevator to the walkway, cross the river to the south tower, and return to street level. It's a photographer's dream, with interesting views of St. Paul's, the Tower of London, and in the distance, Big Ben and the Houses of Parliament. You can also visit the main engine room with its Victorian boiler and steam-pumping engines which raise and lower the roadway across the river.

There are models showing how the 1000-ton arms of the bridge can be raised in 1½ minutes to allow ships passage upstream. These days the bridge is only opened once or twice a week, and you'll be lucky to catch the real thing. You'll know if it is going to open, however, as a bell sounds throughout the bridge and road traffic is stopped. Admission is £2 ($3.90) with reductions for children. It is open daily in summer from 10 a.m. to 6:30 p.m. (to 4:45 p.m. in winter).

WESTMINSTER ABBEY: No less than such an illustrious figure as St. Peter is supposed to have left his calling card at the abbey. If it's true, we wouldn't be surprised—for nearly everybody else, at least nearly everybody in English history, has left his mark. But what is known for certain is that in 1065 the Saxon king, Edward the Confessor, rebuilt the old minster church on this spot, overlooking Parliament Square (tube to Westminster), and founded the Benedictine abbey.

The first English king crowned in the abbey was Harold in 1066, who was killed at the Battle of Hastings that same year. The man who defeated him, Edward's cousin, William the Conqueror, was also crowned at the abbey; the coronation tradition has continued to the present day, broken only twice (Edward V and Edward VIII). The essentially Early English Gothic structure existing today owes more to Henry III's plans than to any other sovereign, although many architects, including Wren, have contributed to the abbey.

Adults pay £1 ($1.95) and children pay 20p (39¢) to visit the Royal Chapel, the Royal Tombs, the Coronation Chair, and the Henry VII Chapel. Hours are Monday to Friday from 9:20 a.m. to 4:45 p.m.; Saturday from 9:20 a.m. to 2:45 p.m. and 3:45 to 5:45 p.m. On Wednesday, the abbey, including the Royal Chapels, are open with free admission from 6 to 8 p.m. This is the only time photography is allowed. On Sunday, the Royal Chapels are closed, but the rest of the church is open between services.

Built on the site of the ancient Lady Chapel, in the early 16th century, the Henry VII Chapel is one of the loveliest in Europe, with its fan vaulting, colorful Knights of Bath banners, and Torrigiani-designed tomb of the king himself over which is placed a 15th-centry Vivarini painting of *Madonna and Bambino.* The chapel represents the flowering of the Perpendicular Gothic style. Also buried here are those feuding sisters, Elizabeth I and Mary Tudor ("Bloody Mary"). Elizabeth I was always vain and adored jewelry. The effigy which lies on top of her tomb has been fitted out with a new set of jewelry, a gilded collar and pendant, a modern copy derived from a painting now at Hatfield House. The originals were stolen by souvenir hunters in the early 18th century. Her orb and sceptre were added earlier. In one end of the chapel you can stand on Cromwell's memorial stone and view the R.A.F. chapel containing the Battle of Britain memorial stained-glass window, unveiled in 1947 to honor the R.A.F.

You can also visit the most hallowed spot in the abbey, the shrine of Edward the Confessor (canonized in the 12th century). In the saint's chapel is the Coronation Chair, made at the command of Edward I in 1300 to contain the Stone of Scone. Scottish kings were once crowned on this stone (in 1950 the Scots stole it back, but it was later returned to its position in the abbey). Nearby are the sword and shield of Edward III.

Another noted spot in the abbey is Poets' Corner, to the right of the entrance to the Royal Chapel, with its monuments to everybody from Chaucer on down—the Brontë sisters, Shakespeare, Tennyson, Dickens, Kipling, Thackeray, Samuel Johnson, "O Rare Ben Johnson" (his name misspelled), even the American Longfellow. The most stylized and controversial monument is Sir Jacob Epstein's sculptured bust of William Blake. The latest tablet commemorates Dylan Thomas.

Statesmen and men of science—such as Disraeli, Newton, Charles Darwin —are also either interred in the abbey or honored by monuments. Near the west door is the 1965 memorial to Sir Winston Churchill. In the vicinity of this memorial is the tomb of the Unknown Soldier, symbol of British dead in World War I. Surprisingly, some of the most totally obscure personages are buried in the abbey, including an abbey plumber.

Many visitors overlook such sights as the 13th-century Chapter House, where Parliament used to meet (special shoes must be worn to walk across the 700-year-old floor). The Chapter House in the Great Cloister is open from 9:30 a.m. till 6 p.m. (closed on Sunday) from March through September. It shuts down at 3:30 p.m. off-season.

Even more fascinating are the treasures in the museum in the Norman undercroft (crypt), part of the monastic buildings erected between 1066 and 1100. The collection includes effigies—figures in wax, such as that of Nelson, and wood carvings of early English royalty. Along with the wax figures—the abbey's answer to Madame Tussaud—are ancient documents, seals, replicas of coronation regalia, old religious vestments (such as the cope worn at the coronation of Charles II), the sword of Henry V, and the famous Essex Ring that Elizabeth I is supposed to have given to her favorite earl. The museum, which charges 25p (49¢) for adults, 10p (20¢) for children, is open daily from 9:30 a.m. till 6 p.m., April 1 to September 30, 10:30 a.m. till 4 p.m. from October 1 to March 31. It is not open on Sunday during the winter.

For tours of the abbey with an expert guide, the cost is £2 ($3.90) per person. These tours operate Monday through Friday at 10:15 and 10:45 a.m., 2:15 and 2:45 p.m. On Saturday, the hours are 10:15 and 10:45 a.m. Inquire at the West Door for the meeting point.

For times of services and other information, telephone the Chapter Office, (tel. 222-5152).

Off the Cloisters, **College Garden** is the oldest garden in England, under cultivation for more than 900 years. Surrounded by high walls, flowering trees dot the lawns, and park benches provide comfort where you can hardly hear the roar of passing traffic. It is open on Thursday throughout the year, from 10 a.m. to 4 p.m. in winter, to 6 p.m. in summer. In August and September, band concerts are held at lunchtime from 12:30 to 2 p.m. Admission is free.

HOUSES OF PARLIAMENT: You may want to visit the Palace of Westminster at least twice. First, to see Western democracy at work (a debate in the House of Lords or the House of Commons), and again to explore the buildings. The first is difficult, the second relatively easy.

Although we can't assure you of the oratory of a Charles James Fox or a William Pitt the Elder, the debates are often lively and controversial (seats are at a premium during crises). The chances of getting into the House of Lords when it's in session are generally better than they are in the more popular House of Commons (even the Queen isn't allowed there). The old guard of the palace informs us that the peerage speak their minds more freely and are less likely to adhere to party line than their counterparts in the Commons.

The general public is admitted to the Strangers' Gallery in the House of Commons on "sitting days"—normally about 4:15 p.m. on Monday to Thursday (about 10 a.m. on Friday). Often there is considerable delay before the head of the public queue is admitted. You can speed up matters somewhat by applying at the American Embassy or the Canadian High Commission for a special pass—but this is too cumbersome for many. Besides, as reader Richard Grant put it, "The U.S. Embassy has only four tickets for daily distribution. Forget it and stand in line."

The head of the queue is normally admitted to the Strangers' Gallery in the House of Lords after 2:40 p.m. from Monday to Wednesday (often at 3 p.m. on Thursday). Line up at the St. Stephen's entrance. It is usually easier to get in after about 6 p.m.

The Houses of Parliament can also be visited when the members of Parliament are not meeting—that is, from 10 a.m. to 4:30 p.m. on Saturday (also on Easter Monday and Tuesday, spring and late summer bank holidays). You enter by the Norman Porch at Victoria Tower (when the Union Jack flies overhead, Parliament is in session). Guests can hook up with a guide who'll give them a running commentary, while escorting them through the handsomely decorated Robing Room and the Royal Gallery, with the sunburst theme on the ceiling, and the Princes' Chamber, with portraits of Henry VIII and his many wives. Incidentally, it was Henry VIII who packed up his linen and moved to Whitehall. From the days of Edward the Confessor to Henry VIII, the palace was a royal residence.

The House of Commons was destroyed by a German air attack on May 10, 1941, and was rebuilt by 1950. The Churchill Arch to the House of Commons remains in the damaged state in which it was found after the fire which destroyed the chamber. The stonework was cleaned but not restored in any way. The palace has been razed once before, in a fire in 1834.

Westminster Hall, scene of the trials of Guy Fawkes and of Charles I, is the oldest surviving structure in the complex. It is known for its hammerbeam roof built in the late 14th century by Richard II. Westminster Hall is open Monday to Thursday, and Saturday (unless the House of Commons is sitting) from 10 a.m. to 1:30 p.m. When both Houses are recessed, the time of opening is extended on Monday to Friday until 4 p.m. (until 5 p.m. on Saturday).

There is no charge for admission to the Palace of Westminster, but guides will expect remuneration; the usual tip is 50p (98¢). Further information about the work of the House of Commons is available by phoning 219-4272; House of Lords, 219-3107; or on the Post Office Prestel Viewdata system, frame 5000.

THE BRITISH MUSEUM: Within its imposing citadel on Great Russell Street in Bloomsbury (tube to Holborn or Tottenham Court Road), the British Museum shelters one of the most catholic collections of art and artifacts in the world, containing countless treasures of ancient civilizations. To storm this bastion in a day is a formidable task, but there are riches to see even on a cursory first visit. Basically, the overall storehouse splits into the National Museum of Antiquities and Ethnography and the Prints and Drawings division —each of which, in its own way, has much to offer.

As you enter the front hall, you may want to head first to the Assyrian Transept on the ground floor, where you'll find the winged and human-headed bulls and lions that once guarded the gateways to the palaces of Assyrian kings, along with a rare Black Obelisk from about 860 B.C. From here you can go into the angular hall of Egyptian sculpture to see the Rosetta Stone, whose discovery led to the deciphering of the mysterious hieroglyphics (on the opposite side of the stone is a booklet outlining the method).

Also on the ground floor is the Duveen Gallery, housing the Elgin Marbles, consisting chiefly of sculpture from a frieze on the Parthenon showing a ceremonial procession that took place in Athens every four years. Of the 92 metopes from the Parthenon, 15 are housed today in the British Museum. The metopes depict the to-the-death struggle between the handsome Lapiths and the grotesque, drunken Centaurs (see, in particular, the head of the horse from the chariot of Selene, goddess of the moon).

The classical sculpture galleries hold *The Caryatid* from the Erechtheum, a temple started in 421 B.C. and dedicated to Athena and Poseidon. Also displayed here is a statue of Mausolus, Prince of Caria in 353 B.C., whose tomb at Halicarnassus was listed among the seven wonders of the world. Look also for the blue and white Portland Vase, considered the finest example of ancient cameo carving, having been made between 27 B.C. and 14 A.D.

The department of Medieval and Later Antiquities has its galleries on the first floor, reached by the main staircase. Of its exhibitions, the Sutton Hoo funeral deposit, discovered at Ipswich, Suffolk, is, in the words of an expert, "the richest treasure ever dug from English soil"—containing gold jewelry, armor, weapons, bronze bowls and cauldrons, silverware, and the inevitable drinking horn of the Norse culture. No body was found, although the tomb is believed to be that of a king of East Anglia who died in the seventh century A.D. You'll also see the bulging-eyed Lewis Chessmen, Romanesque carvings by the Scandinavians of the 12th century, and the Ilbert collection of clocks and watches.

The featured attractions of the Upper Floor are the Egyptian Galleries, especially the mummies. The fourth Egyptian room is extraordinary, looking like the props for *Cleopatra,* with its cosmetics, domestic utensils, toys, tools, and other work. Some rare gems of Sumerian and Babylonian art—unearthed from the Royal Cemetary at Ur (southern Iraq)—lie in the room beyond: a bull-headed queen's harp (oldest ever discovered); a queen's sledge (oldest known example of a land vehicle); and a figure of a he-goat on its hind legs, crafted about 2500 B.C. In the Persian Landing rests "The Treasure of Oxus," a hoard of riches, probably from the fifth century B.C., containing a unique collection of goldsmith work, such as a nude youth, signet rings, a fish-shaped vase, and votive plaques.

One of the most popular attractions is a battered marble head which for years rested relatively forgotten in the gloomy basement of the museum. These days, dusted off, the one-foot-high head is displayed prominently, its identification by a U.S. scholar the subject of controversy. Dr. Iris Love of New York identified the head as that of the fourth century B.C. *Aphrodite* by Praxiteles. The head arrived at the British Museum in 1859 from an excavation site at Cnidus, in southwestern Turkey, on a peninsula overlooking the Aegean Sea. The Praxiteles *Aphrodite* had generally been regarded as lost. Some archeologists and scholars believe it still is—but not Iris Love and a host of believers.

The museum is open weekdays from 10 a.m. till 5 p.m. (on Sunday from 2:30 to 6 p.m.). It is closed Good Friday, Christmas Eve, Christmas Day, Boxing Day, New Year's Day, and the first Monday in May.

Incidentally, the Ethnography Department is housed at 6 Burlington Gardens, W.1, where the galleries are open to the public during the same hours as above. Seek out, in particular, the Benin bronze sculpture of Nigeria.

The British Library

In the east wing the galleries form part of the British Library (tel. 636-1544). In the Grenville Library you'll see the Benedictional (in Latin) of St. Ethelwold, Bishop of Winchester (A.D. 963–984), regarded as one of the most splendid medieval works of art in England. The library also contains the Manuscript Saloon, with its collection of autographs by such men as Cromwell, Disraeli, Sir Walter Raleigh, Newton, Pepys, Wren, Milton, Dr. Johnson, Pope, Fielding, and Swift.

There are also seven major exhibits (at least) of world interest: the Codex Sinaiticus (a Greek version of the Bible, written in the fourth century A.D.); the Lindisfarne Gospels (a masterpiece, viewed by experts as one of the important treasures from early Northumbria, written and illustrated about A.D. 698); Shakespeare's mortgage deed (with his signature, of course) to the Blackfriars Gate House: Capt. Robert Scott's journals telling of his attempt to reach the South Pole in the expedition of 1910–1912; a memorandum by Admiral Nelson explaining his plans for engaging the allied French and Spanish fleet, taken from the *Victory* logbook, and a letter to Lady Hamilton written two days before he died in the Battle of Trafalgar: and, finally, documents relating to the Magna Carta, including the Articles of the Barons, demands accepted by King John at Runnymede in June 1215, along with John's seal of white wax and two of the four surviving exemplifications of Magna Carta issued over his seal.

In the King's Library rests a First Folio (1623) of the comedies, histories, and tragedies of Shakespeare. In addition, don't miss the Gutenberg Bible, the first substantial book ever printed with movable type (of the copies known, the British Library possesses one printed on paper, another on vellum—circa 1455). There is also a display of priceless Oriental manuscripts and books.

Like the museum, the British Library often changes part of its permanent gallery displays to set up special exhibitions in rotation, for example, to mark a centenary. The opening times of the British Library's exhibition galleries are the same as those of the museum. Admission is free.

The Museum of Mankind

The Museum of Mankind, the Ethnography Department of the British Museum, is housed at 6 Burlington Gardens, W.1 (tel. 437-2224), where the galleries are open to the public during the same hours as those of the Bloomsbury museum. It has the world's largest collections of art and material culture from tribal societies. A dazzling selection of treasures from five continents is displayed, and a number of large exhibitions show the life, art, and technology of selected cultures. New exhibitions are mounted every year. Seek out, in particular, the pre-Columbian Mexican turquoise mosaics. Weekday hours are from 10 a.m. to 5 p.m.; on Sunday 2:30 to 6 p.m.; and there is no admission charged.

MADAME TUSSAUD'S: Strasbourg-born Marie Tussaud was to become world-famous as the madame of the macabre. She went to Paris at the age of six to join her uncle, Dr. Curtius. In 1770, he opened an exhibition of life-size wax figures. During the French Revolution, the head of almost every distinguished victim of the guillotine was molded by Madame Tussaud or her uncle.

After the death of Curtius, Madame Tussaud inherited the exhibition, and in 1802 she left France for England. For 33 years she toured the United Kingdom with her exhibition, and in 1835 she settled on Baker Street. The exhibition was such a success that it practically immortalized her in her day; she continued to make portraits until she was 81 (she died in 1850). The perennially popular waxworks (tel. 935-6861) are visited by some tourists even before they check out Westminster Abbey or the Tower of London.

Some of the works displayed came from molds cast by the incomparable Madame Tussaud herself. But to keep from becoming stilted the waxworks continue to make new figures, whoever is *au courant*. Of course, good old reliables, such as Sir Winston, can always be counted on to be there. Some of the figures—that of Voltaire, for example—were taken from life.

In the Chamber of Horrors, opened in 1980, you can have the vicarious thrill of meeting such types as Dr. Crippen, and walking through a Victorian London street where special effects include the shadow terror of Jack the Ripper. The instruments and victims of death penalties contrast with present-day criminals portrayed within the confines of prison.

An enlarged Grand Hall, as well as high-speed elevators and air conditioning, are welcome improvements. In "Heroes," with a sequence of sound, light, and projection, each hero is presented in turn, including Elton John, Humphrey Bogart, and Elvis Presley. On the ground floor, you can relive the Battle of Trafalgar, complete with Nelson's recreated flagship. Madame Tussaud's costs £2.75 ($5.36) for adults, £1.55 ($3.02) for children under 16. You can visit both Madame Tussaud's and the neighboring **Planetarium** for £3.85 ($7.51), £2.15 ($4.19) for children under 16. Take the tube to Baker Street (entrance on Marylebone Road). Madame Tussaud's is open daily from 10 a.m. till 6 p.m. (5:40 p.m. October to March), including Saturday and Sunday. It's closed only on Christmas Day.

TATE GALLERY: This building, beside the Thames on Millbank, houses the best grouping of British paintings from the 16th century on, as well as England's finest collection of modern art, from the French impressionists to pop. The Tate is open from 10 a.m. to 6 p.m. weekdays (on Sunday from 2 to 6 p.m.). To reach it, take the tube to Pimlico or bus 88 or 77. The number of paintings is staggering. If time permits, try to schedule at least two visits—the first to see the classic English works, the second to take in the modern collection (circa 1870 to the present). Since only a portion of the collections can be shown simultaneously, the works on display vary from time to time. However, the most time-pressed individual may not want to miss the following which are almost invariably on view:

The first giant among English painters, William Hogarth (1697–1764), is well represented, particularly by his satirical *O the Roast Beef of Old England, Calais Gate,* with its distorted figures, such as the gluttonous priest. The ruby-eyed *Satan, Sin, and Death* remains one of his most enigmatic works.

Two other famous British painters of the 18th century (exhibited in Galleries 4 and 17) are Sir Joshua Reynolds (1723–1792), and Thomas Gainsborough (1727–1788). Reynolds, the portrait painter, shines brightest when he's painting himself (two self-portraits hang side by side). Two other portraits, that of Francis and Suzanna Beckford, are typical of his work. His rival, Gainsborough, is noted for his portraits, too, and also landscapes ("my real love"). His landscapes with gypsies are subdued, mysterious; *The View of Dedham* is more representative. One of Gainsborough's most celebrated portraits is of Edward Richard Gardiner, a handsome boy in blue (the more famous *Blue Boy* is in California). Two extremely fine Gainsborough portraits have recently been acquired: *Giovanna Baccelli* (1782), who was well known both as a dancer and as the mistress of the third Earl of Dorset, and *Sir Benjamin Truman,* the notable brewer.

In the art of J. M. W. Turner (1775–1851), the Tate possesses its greatest collection of the works of a single artist. Most of the paintings and watercolors exhibited here were willed to the nation by Turner (collection divided among the Tate, the National Gallery, and the British Museum). Of his paintings of stormy seas, none is more horrifying than *Shipwreck* (1805). In the Petworth series, he broke from realism (see his *Interior at Petworth*). His delicate impressionism is best conveyed in his sunset and sunrise pictures, with their vivid reds and yellows. Turner's vortex paintings, inspired by theories of Goethe, are *Light and Color—the Morning After the Deluge,* and *Shade and Darkness—the Evening of the Deluge.*

In a nation of landscape painters, John Constable (1776–1837) stands out. Some of his finest works include *Vale of Dedham* and *Flatford Mill, on the River Stour,* painted in 1817, both scenes from East Anglia.

American-born Sir Jacob Epstein became one of England's greatest sculptors, and some of his bronzes are owned and occasionally displayed by the Tate. Augustus John, who painted everybody from G. B. Shaw to Tallulah Bankhead, is also represented here with portraits and sketches.

The Tate owns some of the finest works of the Pre-Raphaelite period of the late 19th century. One of the best of the English artists of the 20th century, Sir Stanley Spencer (1891–1959) is best represented by his two versions of *Resurrection* and a remarkable self-portrait (1913).

The Tate has many major paintings from both the 19th and 20th centuries, including Wyndham Lewis's portraits of Edith Sitwell and of Ezra Pound, and Paul Nash's *Voyages of the Moon.* But the sketches of William Blake (1757–1827) attract the most attention. Blake, of course, was the incomparable mystical poet and illustrator of such works as *The Book of Job, The Divine Comedy,* and *Paradise Lost.*

In the modern collections, the Tate contains Matisse's *L'Escargot* and *The Inattentive Reader,* along with works by Dali, Chagall, Modigliani, Munch, Ben Nicholson (large collection of his works), and Dubuffet. The different periods of Picasso bloom in *Woman in a Chemise* (1905), *Three Dancers* (1925), *Nude Woman in a Red Armchair* (1932), and *Goat's Skull, Bottle, and Candle* (1952).

Truly remarkable is the area devoted to the sculpture of Giacometti (1901–1966), and the paintings of two of England's best-known modern artists,

Francis Bacon (especially gruesome, *Three Studies for Figures at the Base of a Crucifixion*), and Graham Sutherland (see his portrait of W. Somerset Maugham).

Rodin's *The Kiss* and Marino Marini's *Cavaliere,* both world-famous pieces of sculpture, are on show. In addition, sculptures by Henry Moore and Barbara Hepworth are displayed.

Downstairs is a self-service cafeteria, offering tea, coffee, sandwiches, cakes, and ice cream.

Admission to the general gallery is free, but for special exhibitions, a charge of approximately £1 ($1.95) is made (half price for children).

For the **Tate Gallery Restaurant**, Millbank, S.W.1, telephone 834-6754 for reservations. The menus, at least the main dishes, are selected from a vast array of cosmopolitan dishes. Meals cost from £8.50 ($16.58) to £9 ($17.55). Wine by glass is available at 70p ($1.37). It is essential to reserve, as this place is very popular with Tate visitors as well as local business people. It's still the choice for taking a maiden aunt out to lunch, as the service, by pleasant young women, is good and polite, the dishes well prepared.

NATIONAL GALLERY: On the north side of Trafalgar Square, in an impressive neoclassic building, the National Gallery houses one of the most comprehensive collections of European paintings, representing all the major schools from the 13th to the early 20th centuries. The largest part of the collection is devoted to the Italians, including the Sienese, Venetian, and Florentine masters.

Of the early Gothic works, the *Wilton Diptych* in Room 1 (French school, late 14th century) is the rarest treasure. It stands in a niche by itself, and depicts Richard II being introduced to the Madonna and Child by such good contacts as John the Baptist and the Saxon king, Edward the Confessor.

A Florentine gem, a Virgin and grape-eating Bambino, by Masaccio (one of the founders of modern painting) is in Room 3. In Room 4 are notable works by Piero della Francesca, particularly his linear *The Baptism.*

In a specially lighted hall, Room 7, is the famous cartoon (in the fine arts sense) of *The Virgin and Child with Saint John and Saint Anne* by Leonardo da Vinci. Matter and spirit meet in the haunting nether world of the *Virgin of the Rocks,* a Leonardo painting, now hung in Room 8. Also in Room 8 are two other giants of the Renaissance—Michelangelo (represented by an unfinished painting, *The Entombment*), and Raphael (*The Ansidei Madonna,* among others).

The Venetian masters of the 16th century, to whom color was paramount, fill Room 9. The most notable works include a rare *Adoration of the Kings* by Giorgione; *Bacchus and Ariadne* by Titian; *The Beginning of the Milky Way* by Tintoretto (a lush galaxy, with light streaming from Juno's breasts); and *The Darius Family Kneeling Before Alexander the Great* by Veronese (one of the best paintings at the National). Surrounding are a number of satellite rooms, filled with works by major Italian masters of the 15th century—artists such as Andrea Mantegna of Padua (*Agony in the Garden*); his brother-in-law, Giovanni Bellini (his portrait of the Venetian doge, Leonardo Loredano, provided a change of pace from his many interpretations of Madonnas); finally, Botticelli, represented by *Mars and Venus, Adoration of the Magi,* and *Portrait of a Young Man* in Room 5.

The painters of northern Europe are well displayed. In Room 24, for example, is Jan van Eyck's portrait of G. Arnolfini and his bride, and Pieter Brueghel the Elder's Bosch-influenced *Adoration* (Room 25), with its unkingly kings and ghoul-like onlookers. In Room 28 the 17th-century pauper, Vermeer, is rich on canvas in a *Young Woman at a Virginal,* a favorite theme of his. Fellow Delft-ite Pieter de Hooch comes on sublimely in a *Patio in a House in Delft* (Room 28).

One of the big drawing cards of the National is its collection of Rembrandts in Rooms 15, 19, 26, and 27. Rembrandt, the son of a miller, became the greatest painter in the Netherlands in the 17th century. His *Self-Portrait at the Age of 34* shows him at the pinnacle of his life, his *Self-Portrait at the Age of 63* is more deeply moving and revealing. For another Rembrandt study in old age, see his *Portrait of Margaretha Trip* (Room 27). *The Woman Taken in Adultery* shows the artist's human sympathy. Rembrandt's portrait of his mistress, Hendrickje Stoffels, last displayed in public in the 1930s, has been bought and is now displayed by the National Gallery (Room 26). The picture is signed and dates from 1659. The purchase price has not been disclosed, but the market value is believed to be in the region of $2,000,000. Part of the prolific output of Peter Paul Rubens is to be seen in Room 20, notably his *Peace and War* and *The Rape of the Sabine Women.*

Five of the greatest of the home-grown artists—Constable, Turner, Reynolds, Gainsborough, and Hogarth—share their paintings with the Tate. But the National owns masterpieces by each of them. Constable's *Cornfield* is another scene of East Anglia, along with *Haywain,* perhaps his best known work, a harmony of light and atmosphere. Completely different from Constable is the work of Turner, including his dreamy *Fighting Téméraire* and *Rain, Steam, and Speed.* Room 34 is essentially a portrait gallery, hung with several works by Sir Joshua Reynolds, along with a Gainsborough masterpiece, *The Morning Walk,* an idealistic blending of portraiture with landscape. Finally, in a completely different brush stroke, Hogarth's *Marriage à la Mode* caricatures the marriages of convenience of the upper class of the 18th century.

The three giants of Spanish painting are represented in Room 41 by Velázquez's portrait of the sunken-faced Philip IV; El Greco's *Christ Driving the Traders from the Temple;* Goya's portrait of the Duke of Wellington (once stolen) and his mantilla-wearing *Dona Isabel de Porcel.*

Room 33 is devoted to 18th-century French painters such as Delacroix and Ingres; Room 44, 19th-century French impressionists such as Manet, Monet, Renoir, and Degas; and Room 45, 19th-century French postimpressionists such as Cezanne, Seurat, and Van Gogh.

The National Gallery (tube to Charing Cross) is open weekdays from 10 a.m. to 6 p.m.; on Sunday from 2 to 6 p.m. It is closed on January 1, Good Friday, Christmas Eve, Christmas Day, Boxing Day, and bank holidays. Admission is free.

KENSINGTON PALACE: Home of the State Apartments, some of which were used by Queen Victoria, this is another of the major attractions of the city, at the far western end of Kensington Gardens. The palace was acquired by asthma-suffering William III (William of Orange) in 1689, and was remodeled by Sir Christopher Wren. George II, who died in 1760, was the last king to use it as a royal residence.

The most interesting chamber to visit is Queen Victoria's bedroom. In this room, on the morning of June 20, 1837, she was aroused from her sleep with the news that she had ascended to the throne, following the death of her uncle, William IV. Thus, the woman who was to become the symbol of the British Empire and the Empress of India began the longest reign in the history of England. In the anteroom are memorabilia from Victoria's childhood—a dollhouse and a collection of her toys.

In Queen Mary's bedroom, you can see her mid-17th-century writing cabinet with its tortoise-shell surface. Incidentally, Mary II reigned with William III, and is not to be confused with the late Queen Mary (1867–1953), who also has many relics at Kensington. The late Queen Mary was born in Victoria's bedroom.

As you wander through the apartments, you can admire many fine paintings, most of which are from the Royal Collection. The State Apartments are open Monday through Saturday, 9 a.m. to 5 p.m; on Sunday, 1 to 5 p.m. Adults pay an admission of 40p (78¢), and children, 20p (39¢) January through March and October through December; 80p ($1.56) for adults and 40p (78¢) for children April through September. You enter from the Broad Walk, and you reach the building by taking the tube either to Queensway or Bayswater on the north side of the gardens, or High Street Kensington on the south side. You'll have to walk a bit from there, however. For more information, telephone 937-9561.

The palace gardens, originally the private park of royalty, are also open to the public for daily strolls around Round Pond, near the heart of Kensington Gardens. The gardens adjoin Hyde Park. Also in Kensington Gardens is the Albert Memorial to Queen Victoria's consort. Facing Albert Hall, it is a wart on the face of London, a statue that reflects all the opulent vulgarity of the Victorian era—it's fascinating, nonetheless.

ST. PAUL'S CATHEDRAL: During World War II, newsreel footage reaching America showed the dome of St. Paul's Cathedral lit by bombs exploding all around it. That it survived at all is miraculous, as it was hit badly twice in the early years of the Nazi bombardment of London. But St. Paul's is accustomed to calamity, having been burned down three times and destroyed once by invading Norsemen. It was in the Great Fire of 1666 that the old St. Paul's was razed, making way for a new Renaissance structure designed (after many mishaps and rejections) by Sir Christopher Wren.

The masterpiece of this great architect was erected between 1675 and 1710. Its classical dome dominates the City's square mile. Inside, the cathedral is laid out like a Latin cross, containing few art treasures (Grinling Gibbons's choir stalls are an exception) and many monuments, including one to the "Iron Duke" and a memorial chapel to American servicemen who lost their lives in the United Kingdom in World War II. Encircling the dome is the Whispering Gallery, where discretion in speech is advised. In the crypt lie not only Wren but the Duke of Wellington and Lord Nelson. A fascinating Diocesan Treasury was opened in 1981.

The cathedral (tube to St. Paul's) is open daily from 8 a.m. to 6 p.m. from mid-April to September. The crypt and galleries, including the Whispering Gallery, are open weekdays only from 10 a.m. to 4:15 p.m. in summer. The rest of the year the cathedral's hours are from 8 a.m. to 5 p.m. The crypt and galleries, on the other hand, are open only from 10 a.m. to 3:15 p.m. Guided tours lasting 1½ hours, and including the crypt and parts of St. Paul's not normally open to the public, take place daily at 11 a.m. and 2 p.m. when the cathedral is open and cost £2.50 ($4.88) for adults, £1.25 ($2.44) for children. For information, telephone 248-2705.

VICTORIA AND ALBERT MUSEUM: When Queen Victoria asked that this museum be named after herself and her consort, she could not have selected a more fitting memorial. The Victoria and Albert is one of the finest museums in the world, devoted to fine and applied art of many nations and periods, including the Orient. In many respects, it's one of the most difficult for viewing, as many of the most important exhibits are so small they can easily be over-looked. To reach the museum on Cromwell Road, take the tube to the South Kensington stop. The museum is open weekdays, except Friday, from 10 a.m. to 5:50 p.m., on Sunday from 2:30 till 5:50 p.m.

We have space only to suggest some of its finest art. The early medieval art in Room 43 includes many treasures, such as the Eltenberg Reliquary (Rhenish, second half of the 12th century). In the shape of a domed, copper-gilt church, it is enriched with champlevé enamel and set with walrus-ivory carv-ings of Christ and the Apostles. Other exhibits in this same salon include the Early English Gloucester Candlestick, and the Byzantine Veroli Casket, with its ivory panels based on Greek plays. Devoted to Islamic art, Room 42 con-tains the Ardabil carpet from 16th-century Persia (320 knots per square inch).

In the Gothic art exhibition (Rooms 22 through 25), there are some fine pieces—such as the Syon Cope, made in the early 14th century, an example of the highly valued embroidery produced in England at that time; a stained-glass window from Winchester College (circa 1400); a Limoges enameled triptych for Louis XII. The Gothic tapestries, including the Devonshire ones depicting hunting scenes, are in Room 38.

Renaissance art in Italy, Rooms 11 through 20, include such works as a Donatello marble relief, *The Ascension;* a small terracotta statue of the Madonna and Child by Antonio Rossellino; a marble group, *Samson and a Philistine.* by Giovanni Bologna; a wax model of a slave by Michelangelo. The highlight of the 16th-century art from the continent is the marble group *Neptune with Triton,* by Bernini (Room 21).

In Room 48 are displayed the cartoons by Raphael, which are owned by the Queen. These cartoons—conceived as designs for tapestries for the Sistine Chapel—include scenes such as *The Sacrifice of Lystra and Paul Preaching at Athens.*

Of the rooms devoted to English furniture and decorative art during the period from the 16th to the mid-18th century, the most outstanding exhibit is the Bed of Ware (Room 52), big enough for eight. In the galleries of portrait miniatures, two of the rarest ones are in Room 55—both by Hans Holbein the Younger (one of Anne of Cleves, another of a Mrs. Pemberton). In the painting galleries (8 and 9) are many works by Constable. His *Flatford Mill* represents a well-known scene from his native East Anglia. The museum's phone number is 589-6371.

THE BEST OF THE REST: Now, for those with more time to get acquainted with London, we'll continue our exploration of this sight-filled city.

Royal London

From Trafalgar Square, you can stroll down the wide, tree-flanked avenue known as **The Mall.** It leads to **Buckingham Palace,** the heart of Royal London (English kings and queens have lived here since the days of Victoria). Three parks—St. James's, Green, and the Buckingham Palace Gardens (pri-vate)—converge at the center of this area, where you'll find a memorial honor-ing Victoria.

London's most popular daily pageant, particularly with North American tourists, is the **Changing of the Queen's Guard** in the forecourt of Buckingham Palace. The regiments of the Guard's Division, in their bearskins and red tunics, actually are five regiments in one, including the Scots, Irish, and Welsh. The guards march to the palace from either the Wellington or Chelsea barracks, arriving around 11:30 a.m. for the half-hour ceremony. To get the full effect, go somewhat earlier. There is usually no ceremony when the weather is what the English call "inclement." But remember that your idea of inclement may not be a weather-toughened Londoner's idea of inclement. When in doubt, phone 222-1234 for information; tube to St. James's Park or Green Park. In winter the ceremony is on alternate days, so check by telephone.

You can't visit the palace, of course, without an invitation, but you can inspect the **Queen's Gallery** (entrance on Buckingham Palace Road). It may be visited from 11 a.m. to 5 p.m. Tuesday through Saturday (from 2 to 5 p.m. on Sunday) for an admission of 75p ($1.46) for adults, 30p (59¢) for children. As is known, all the royal families of Europe have art collections—some including acquisitions from centuries ago. The English sovereign has one of the finest, and has consented to share it with the public. I can't predict what exhibition you're likely to see, as they are changed yearly at the gallery. You may find a selection of incomparable works by old masters, and sometimes furniture and objets d'art.

You can get a close look at Queen Elizabeth's coronation carriage at the **Royal Mews,** on Buckingham Palace Road. Many other official carriages are housed here as well, including the Scottish and Irish state coaches. The Queen's horses are also housed here. The mews is open to the public on Wednesday and Thursday from 2 to 4 p.m. and charges an admission of 45p (88¢) for adults, 20p (39¢) for children. It is closed during Ascot week in June.

Official London

Whitehall, the seat of the British government, grew up on the grounds of Whitehall Palace, turned into a Royal residence by Henry VIII, who snatched it from its former occupant, Cardinal Wolsey. Beginning at Trafalgar Square, Whitehall extends southward to Parliament Square (Houses of Parliament and Westminster Abbey described earlier). On this street you'll find the Home Office, the Old Admiralty Building, and the Ministry of Defence.

At the **Cenotaph** (honoring the dead in two World Wars), turn down unpretentious Downing Street to the modest little town house at **No. 10,** flanked by two bobbies. Walpole was the first prime minister to live here; Churchill the most famous.

Nearby is the **Horse Guards Building,** where the changing of the Queen's Life Guard takes place daily at 11 a.m. and at 10 a.m. on Sunday. The ceremony lasts 20 minutes—a spectacle provided by the Life Guards and the Royal Horse Guards, combined to form the Household Cavalry. Mounted on their black horses, the guards in their white and red plumes, red and blue tunics, make for an exciting and dramatic show.

Across the street is Inigo Jones's **Banqueting House** (tel. 212-4785), site of the execution of Charles I. William and Mary accepted the crown of England here, but preferred to live at Kensington Palace. The Banqueting House was part of Whitehall Palace, which burned to the ground in 1698, although the ceremonial hall escaped razing. Its most notable feature today is an allegorical ceiling painted by Peter Paul Rubens. The Banqueting House may be visited weekdays from 10 a.m. to 5 p.m., except Monday, on Sunday, 2 to 5 p.m. Admission is 40p (78¢) for adults, 20p (39¢) for children.

Finally, you may want to stroll to Parliament Square for a view of **Big Ben,** the world's most famous timepiece.

Legal London

The smallest borough in London, bustling **Holborn** (pronounced Hoburn) is often referred to as Legal London, the home of the city's barristers, solicitors, and law clerks. It also embraces the university district of Bloomsbury. Holborn, which houses the ancient Inns of Court, was severely damaged in World War II bombing raids. The razed buildings were replaced with modern offices housing insurance brokers, realtors, whatever. But the borough still retains quadrangled pockets of its former days.

Turn south from busy Fleet Street down Middle Temple Lane, leading to the Embankment. You'll come to an area known as **The Temple,** named after the medieval order of the Knights Templar (originally formed by the Crusaders in Jerusalem in the 12th century). Here you'll find the Temple Church, one of four Norman "round churches" left in England. First completed in the 12th century, it has been restored. Look for the knightly effigies and the Norman door anytime from 10 a.m. to 5 p.m. (4 p.m. in winter). Readers Manly and Mary Johnson, from Tulsa, Oklahoma, were impressed with "a circle of grotesque carved portrait heads which have to be seen to be believed—a goat in a mortar board, characters making faces, rolling their eyes, lolling tongues, and even a couple of them with little fierce creatures biting their ears. There's also a 'dungeon' one flight up—ask the caretaker to show you."

The **Middle Temple** contains a Tudor hall completed in 1570 with a double hammer-beam roof. It is believed Shakespeare's troupe played *Twelfth Night* here in 1602. A table on view is said to have come from timber from Sir Francis Drake's *The Golden Hind.* The hall may be visited from 10 a.m. to noon and from 3 to 4:30 p.m. weekdays.

While in this district, you may also want to explore the area north of Fleet Street and the Temple. **Staple Inn,** near the Chancery Lane tube stop, is the last of the old Tudor fronts to be found in London. The inn, lined with shops, was constructed and reconstructed many times, originally having come into existence between 1545 and 1589. Dr. Johnson moved here in 1759, the year *Rasselas* was published.

On Chancery Lane you can visit the **Public Record Office** (see Other Museums), or else walk through a Tudor gateway into **Lincoln's Inn,** dating back to 1422. Another of the ancient Inns of Court, Lincoln's Inn forms an important link in the architectural maze of London. In the 17th century Inigo Jones erected a chapel here; Cromwell lived here at one time. To the east of Lincoln's Inn is the large square known as Lincoln's Inn Fields, with the Soane Museum (see Other Museums). Near the south of the fields on Kingsway is the **Old Curiosity Shop,** immortalized by Charles Dickens.

North of Lincoln's Inn in High Holborn stands the last of the four great Inns of Court—**Gray's,** restored after being heavily damaged by World War II bombings. Francis Bacon (not the modern artist) was the most eminent tenant to have resided here. Off Gray's Inn Road, it contains a rebuilt Tudor hall.

Other Museums

The present **Guildhall,** on King Street in Cheapside, The City, E.C.2 (tube to Bank; tel. 606-3030), was built in 1411. But the Civic Hall of the Corporation of London has had a rough time, notably in the Great Fire of 1666 and the 1940 blitz. The most famous tenants of the rebuilt Guildhall are *Gog and Magog,* two giants standing over nine feet high. The original effigies, burned in the London fire, were rebuilt only to be destroyed again in 1940. The present giants are third generation. Restoration has returned the Gothic grandeur to the hall—replete with a medieval porch entranceway; monuments to Wellington, Churchill, and Nelson; stained glass commemorating lord mayors and mayors; the standards of length; a 15th-century crypt; and colorful shields honoring fishmongers, haberdashers, merchant tailors, ironmongers, and skinners—some of the major Livery Companies. The Guildhall and Crypt may be visited Monday through Saturday from 10 a.m. to 5 p.m. (on Sunday, May to September only, from 10 a.m. to 5 p.m.).

The museum of the **Public Record Office,** on Chancery Lane, W.C.2 (tube to the Temple or Chancery Lane; tel. 405-0741), is one of the finest of the small museums of London, deserving far more attention than it gets. A mere recitation of some of its exhibits is all the selling it needs. To the left as you enter, you'll find two volumes of the *Domesday Book,* a general survey of England ordered by William the Conqueror in 1085. Here also are the navy log of the H.M.S. *Victory,* showing Nelson's dispatches relating to the Battle of Trafalgar; Elizabeth II's signed oath "to govern Great Britain"; exemplars of Magna Carta (Case VIII); John Bunyan's preaching license; one of the six authentic signatures known of Shakespeare, along with his Last Will and Testament, dated March 25, 1616; a letter from George Washington (Case XII) to his "great and good friend," King George III; letters from Maria Theresa, Frederick the Great, Catherine the Great, Marie Antoinette, and Metternich; the first confession of Guy Fawkes about the gunpowder plot to blow up the king, signed November 9, 1605; scads of royal autographs—Richard II, Edward IV, Catherine Parr, Anne Boleyn. The museum is open Monday through Friday from 1 to 4 p.m.

Sir John Soane's Museum, 13 Lincoln's Inn Fields, W.C.2 (tel. 405-2107), is the former home of a knight who lived from 1753 to 1837. Sir John, who rebuilt the Bank of England (not the present structure, however), was a "spaceman" in a different era. With his multilevels, fool-the-eye mirrors, flying arches, and domes, Soane was a master of perspective, a genius of interior space (his art gallery, for example, is filled with three times the number of paintings a room of similar dimensions would be likely to hold). That he could do all this—and still not prove a demon to claustrophobia victims—was proof of his remarkable talent. Even if you don't like Soane (he was reportedly a cranky fellow), you may still want to visit this museum to see William Hogarth's satirical series, *The Rake's Progress,* containing his much reproduced *Orgy,* and the less successful satire on politics in the mid-18th century, *The Election.* Soane also filled his house with paintings (Watteau's *Les Noces,* Canaletto's large *Venetian Scene*), and classical sculpture. Finally, be sure to see the Egyptian sarcophagus found in a burial chamber in the Valley of the Kings. Soane turned his house over to his country for use as a museum. It is open Tuesday through Saturday from 10 a.m. till 5 p.m. Take the tube to Chancery Lane or Holborn.

Just across the Thames in Lambeth Road, S.E.1, is the **Imperial War Museum** (tube to Lambeth North or Elephant and Castle; tel. 735-8922). This large domed building, built around 1815, the former Bethlehem Royal Hospital for the Insane, or Bedlam, houses the museum's collections relating to the two World Wars and other military operations involving the British and the Commonwealth since 1914.

A wide range of weapons and equipment is on display: aircraft, armored vehicles, field guns, small arms, and models, decorations, uniforms, posters, photographs, and paintings. You can see a Mark V tank, a Battle of Britain Spitfire, a German one-man submarine, and the rifle carried by Lawrence of Arabia, as well as the German surrender document, Hitler's political testament, and a German V2 rocket. There is an exhibition on trench warfare in the First

World War and a show of uniforms, medals, and accoutrements which belonged to the Duke of Gloucester. Paintings on display include works by well-known war artists such as William Orpen, Paul Nash, Stanley Spencer, and Jacob Epstein. There is also a collection of propaganda posters from the First and Second World Wars, plus Field Marshal Montgomery's three campaign caravans. The museum is open Monday to Saturday from 10 a.m. to 5:50 p.m., on Sunday from 2 to 5:50 p.m. It is closed on Good Friday, Christmas Eve, Christmas Day, Boxing Day, New Year's Day, and the first Monday in May. Admission is free.

The **National Army Museum,** Royal Hospital Road, S.W.3 (tel. 730-0717), in Chelsea (tube: Sloane Square), is one of London's newest museums. It traces the history of the British, Indian, and Colonial forces from 1485. (The Imperial War Museum above concerns itself with World Wars I and II.)

The National Army Museum stands next door to Wren's Royal Hospital. The museum backers agreed to begin the collection at the year 1485, because that was the date of the formation of the Yeomen of the Guard. The saga of the forces of the East India Company is traced, beginning in 1602 and going up to Indian independence in 1947. The gory and the glory—it's all here, everything from Florence Nightingale's lamp to the French Eagle captured in a cavalry charge at Waterloo, even the staff cloak wrapped round the dying Wolfe at Québec. Naturally, there are the "cases of the heroes," mementos of such outstanding men as the Dukes of Marlborough and Wellington. But the field soldier isn't neglected either. The museum is open weekdays from 10 a.m. to 5:30 p.m., on Sunday from 2 to 5:30 p.m. It is closed on New Year's Day, Good Friday, from December 24 to 26, and on the May bank holiday.

The **Wellington Museum,** at Apsley House, 149 Piccadilly, Hyde Park Corner, W.1 (tel. 499-5676), takes us into the former town house of the Iron Duke, the British general (1769–1852) who defeated Napoleon at the Battle of Waterloo. Wellington's London residence was opened as a public museum in 1952. Once Wellington had to retreat behind the walls of Apsley House—even securing it in fear of a possible attack from Englishmen, outraged by his autocratic opposition as prime minister to reform. In the vestibule you'll find a colossal statue in marble of Napoleon by Canova—ironic, to say the least. Completely idealized, it was presented to the duke by King George IV. In addition to three good paintings by Velázquez, the Wellington collection includes Correggio's *Agony in the Garden.* Jan Steen's *The Egg Dance,* and Pieter de Hooch's *A Musical Party.* You can see the gallery where Wellington used to invite his officers for the annual Waterloo banquet (the banquets were originally held in the dining room). The house also contains a large porcelain and china collection—plus many Wellington medals, of course. Also displayed is a magnificent Sèvres porcelain Egyptian service, made originally for Empress Josephine and given by Louis XVIII to Wellington. In addition, superb English silver and the extraordinary Portuguese centerpiece, a present from a grateful Portugal to its liberator, are exhibited. The residence was designed by Robert Adam and built in the late 18th century. The museum is open Tuesday, Wednesday, Thursday, and Saturday from 10 a.m. to 6 p.m., on Sunday from 2:30 to 6 p.m. Admission is free. Tube: Hyde Park Corner.

The **Commonwealth Institute,** Kensington High Street, W.8 (tube to Kensington High Street or no. 9 bus from Piccadilly Circus; tel. 602-3246), is a center of information on the 40 or so countries of the modern Commonwealth. There are continuous exhibitions on each country, and you can capture some of the atmosphere and flavor of places as different as Sri Lanka and Papua, New Guinea, Malaysia, and Trinidad. Admission is free, and there is an attractive and inexpensive restaurant called Flags, plus a shop selling Commonwealth crafts, gifts and books. The institute also has a free library and art gallery. It plays host to many cultural events, including dance, drama, music, and exotic food-tastings and festivals. Many, perhaps most, of these events are free. It's open Monday through Saturday from 10 a.m. to 5:30 p.m. and on Sunday from 2 to 5.

In London's Barbican district, E.C.2, in the bombed-out World War II area around St. Paul's Cathedral, the **Museum of London** at 150 London Wall (tel. 600-3699) allows visitors to trace the history of London from prehistoric times to the present—through relics, costumes, household effects, maps, and models. Exhibits are arranged so that visitors can begin and end their chronological stroll through 250,000 years at the main entrance to the museum. Of special interest to anglophiles is a large number of relics, possessions, and costumes of the monarchs of England, including such gruesome items as a vest supposedly worn by Charles I at his execution and the death mask of Oliver Cromwell. But the pièce de Résistance is the Lord Mayor's coach, built in 1757 and weighing in at three tons. This gilt and red, horse-drawn vehicle is like a fairytale coach. Visitors can also see the Great Fire of London in living color and sound; a Roman dinner, including the kitchen and utensils; a cell in Newgate Prison made famous by Charles Dickens; and, most amazing of all, a shop window with pre–World War II prices on the items.

The museum overlooks London's Roman and medieval walls and, in all, has something from every era before and after—including little Victorian shops and recreations of what life was like in London in the Iron Age. Anglo-Saxons, Vikings, Normans—they're all there, arranged on two-floors around a central garden. With quick labels for museum sprinters, more extensive ones for those who want to study, and still deeper details for scholars, this new museum, built at a cost of some $18 million, is an enriching experience for *everybody.*

A small coffeeshop helps sustain the visitor with various soft drinks, tea and coffee, plus sandwiches and other cold snacks. At least an hour should be allowed for a full (but still quick) visit to the museum, which will surely rank as one of the most worthwhile hours you'd spend in any museum in London. Free lectures on London's past are given during lunch hours. These aren't given daily, but it's worth inquiring at the entrance hall. In addition, the museum sponsors Dickens evenings five times a week. You can reach the museum by going up to the elevated pedestrian precinct at the corner of the London Wall and Aldersgate, five minutes from St. Paul's. It is open Tuesday through Saturday from 10 a.m. to 6 p.m., on Sunday from 2 to 6 p.m.; admission is free. Closed Sunday. Tube: St. Paul's, Barbican.

The **London Transport Museum,** Covent Garden, W.C.2 (tel. 379-6344), is in a splendidly restored Victorian building which formerly housed the flower market. Horse buses, motorbuses, trams, trolley buses, railway vehicles, models, maps, posters, photographs, and audio-visual displays illustrate the fascinating story of the evolution of London's transport systems and how this has affected the growth of London.

There are a number of unique working displays. You can "drive" a tube train, a tram, and a bus, and also operate full-size signaling equipment. The exhibits include a reconstruction of George Shillibeer's omnibus of 1829, a steam locomotive which ran on the world's first underground railway, and a coach from the first deep-level electric railway.

The museum is open every day of the year except Christmas and Boxing Day from 10 a.m. to 6 p.m. Admission charges are £1.60 ($3.12) for adults, 80p ($1.56) for children.

The **R.A.F. Museum,** Grahame Park Way, Hendon, N.W.9 (tel. 205-2266), shelters what must be the largest and most comprehensive collection of airplanes and equipment from every stage of British aviation. The aircraft are housed in a gigantic hangar, and there is also a special section, the Battle of Britain Museum, with souvenirs, photographs, and exhibits explaining and portraying those days when "so much was owed by so many, to so few." The museums are open Monday to Saturday from 10 a.m. to 6 p.m., on Sunday from 2 to 6 p.m. Admission is free to the R.A.F. Museum. For the Battle of Britain Museum, adults are charged £1 ($1.95); children, 50p (98¢). Facilities include a cinema, a licensed restaurant, a shop, and free car parking. Tube: Colindale.

The **National Postal Museum,** King Edward Building, King Edward Street, E.C.1 (tel. 432-3851), contains the post office's collection of British postage stamps, a worldwide stamp collection from 1878, and a philatelic correspondence archives covering postage stamps of 200 countries from 1855 onward. The museum is open Monday to Thursday from 10 a.m. to 4:30 p.m. and on Friday from 10 a.m. to 4 p.m.

A unique private museum in London, the home of **Dennis Severs,** 18 Folgate St., E.1 (tel. 247-4013), is a delight. Dennis is a young Californian who has lived in London since he was 16 years old and is utterly involved with England, the history and the culture of the place. He has restored a house on the edge of the City. Originally built in 1725, no. 18 was occupied by the Huguenot family Jervis, who were silk weavers.

Now the home belongs to Dennis and his black cat Whitechapel (who claims to have been born on the grounds of Buckingham Palace). The ten rooms of the house recreate with sound and vision the world of the 18th and 19th centuries. You walk into the kitchen of Beatrix Potter, with its blackened range holding simmering pots, the gleaming coppers and china glinting in the candlelight on the Welsh dresser. You explore the Dickens Room, the master bedroom (with Bob Cratchit's high desk in the corner). The withdrawing room with high-backed chairs and ornaments all add up to a fascinating picture of bygone times.

To visit the house and its charming occupants, telephone 247-4013 in the morning only. The three tours a week, evening only, last 2¼ hours. It is not practical for more than eight people to try to tour together, and this is only really suitable for historians, sensitive people, and those who wish to step back into the past world of candlelight, in a nonelectric, nongasoline age. The cost is £10 ($19.50) per person. The house is five minutes from Liverpool Street underground at the back of Spitalfields Market.

Another unique London museum is **Whitbread's Brewery,** Chiswell Street, E.C.1 (tel. 606-4455). Although beer is no longer brewed in Chiswell Street, the old brewery remains the headquarters of Whitbread's which has opened the magnificent old building to the public. The most impressive of the rooms is the Porter Tun Room, completed in 1784 and renowned for its massive unsupported King Post timber roof, the second largest of its kind in Europe. The lower part of this room is now renamed the Overlord Room and houses the remarkable Overlord embroidery, depicting the story of the invasion on June 6, 1944, of the Normandy beaches during World War II. The appliquéd embroidery, probably the largest of its kind—272 feet long and 3 feet high— was designed by Miss Sandra Lawrence and took 20 ladies of the Royal School of Needlework five years to complete. It is a remarkably complete record of the Allied Forces' progress into France. Admission to the embroidery is 75p ($1.46) for adults, 50p (98¢) for children, students, and senior citizens.

Also on display in the brewery is the Speaker's Coach. A magnificent affair of gold and finery, it was built in 1698 and is still used, drawn by dray horses, to convey the Speaker of the House of Commons on state occasions. The stables can be visited by appointment.

The coffeeshop is open Monday to Saturday from 8:30 a.m. to 5 p.m. and provides light snacks from or a three-course meal from £1 ($1.95).

Across the road on the north side of Chiswell Street, in the vaults below the Georgian terraces, is a cellar wine bar. The vaults are a honeycomb of tunnel-like rooms with curved brick ceilings, sawdust on the floor, and tables and benches set between old wine barrels. From the vast selection of wines a glass will cost about 75p ($1.46). Bottles start at £3.50 ($6.83). In one of the vaults, snacks are available. There is also a small restaurant area with tables and chairs and waitress service.

Other Galleries

National Portrait Gallery, Orange Street, W.C.2 (entrance around the corner from the National Gallery on Trafalgar Square; tel. 930-1552), gives you a chance to outstare the stiff-necked greats and not-so-greats of English history. In a gallery of remarkable and unremarkable portraits, a few paintings tower over the rest, including Sir Joshua Reynolds's first portrait of Samuel Johnson ("a man of most dreadful appearance"). Among the best are Nicholas Hilliard's miniature of a most handsome Sir Walter Raleigh (Room 1); a full-length Elizabeth I (painted to commemorate her visit to Sir Henry Lee Ditchley in 1592), along with the Holbein cartoon of Henry VIII (sketched for a family portrait that hung, before it was burned, in the Privy Chamber in Whitehall Palace)—both in Room 1. In Room 1, also, is a Portrait of William Shakespeare (with gold earring, no less). The artist is unknown, but the portrait bears the claim of being the most "authentic contemporary likeness" of its subject of any work yet known. The John Hayls portrait of Samuel Pepys adorns Room 4. Whistler could not only paint a portrait, he could also be the subject of one (Room 24). One of the most unusual portraits (Room 17) in the gallery—a group of the three Brontë sisters (Charlotte, Emily, Anne)—was painted by their brother, Branwell. An idealized portrait of Lord Byron by Thomas Phillips is pleased with itself in Room 13. For a finale, treat yourself to the likeness of the incomparable Aubrey Beardsley (Room 24). For sheer volume of portraiture, Queen Victoria reigns supreme. The admission-free gallery is open from 10 a.m. to 5 p.m. Monday to Friday, from 10 a.m. to 6 p.m. on Saturday, and from 2 to 6 p.m. on Sunday. Special exhibitions are held at the gallery from time to time.

The **Wallace Collection,** Manchester Square, W.1 (tel. 935-0687), off Wigmore Street, has an outstanding collection of works of art of all kinds bequeathed to the nation by Lady Wallace in 1897 and still displayed in the house of its founders. There are important pictures by artists of all European schools, including Titian, Rubens, Van Dyck, Rembrandt, Hals, Velázquez, Murillo, Reynolds, Gainsborough, and Delacroix. Representing the art of France in the 18th century are paintings by Watteau, Boucher, and Fragonard, and sculpture, furniture, goldsmiths' work, and Sèvres porcelain. Valuable collections also are found of majolica and European and Oriental arms and armor. Frans Hals's *Laughing Cavalier* is the most famous in the collection, but Pieter de Hooch's *A Boy Bringing Pomegranates* and Watteau's *The Music Party* are also well known. Other notable works include Canaletto's views of Venice (especially *Bacino di San Marco*); Rembrandt's *Titus;* and Gainsborough's *Mrs. Robinson (Perdita).* Worthy also is Boucher's portrait of the Marquise de Pompadour. The Wallace Collection may be viewed daily from 10 a.m. to 5 p.m., on Sunday from 2 to 5 p.m. Closed Christmas Eve, Christmas Day, Boxing Day, New Year's Day, Good Friday, and the first Monday in May. Tube: Bond Street.

The **Courtauld Institute Galleries,** Woburn Square, W.C.1 (tel. 935-9292), is the home of the art collection of London University—noted chiefly for its superb impressionist and postimpressionist works. It has eight works by Cézanne alone, including his *A Man with a Pipe.* Other notable art includes Seurat's *La Poudreuse,* Van Gogh's self-portrait (with ear bandaged), a nude by Modigliani, Gauguin's *Day-Dreaming,* Monet's *Fall at Argenteuil,* Toulouse-Lautrec's delicious *Tête-à-Tête,* and Manet's *Bar at the Folies Bergère.* The galleries have recently been enriched by the superb Princes Gate collection of old master paintings and drawings, including 32 oils by Rubens and outstanding works by Pieter Brueghel the Elder, Michelangelo, Rembrandt, Tiepolo, and Degas. The Lee of Fareham and Gambier-Parry collections feature classical works, including a *Virgin and Child* by Bernardino Luini, a Botticelli, a Giovanni Bellini, and a Veronese. The art works may be viewed Monday to Saturday from 10 a.m. to 5 p.m. and on Sunday from 2 to 5 p.m. Tube: Euston Square, Goodge Street, or Russell Square.

The **Hayward Gallery,** South Bank, S.E.1 (tel. 629-9495), presents a changing program of major exhibitions organized by the Arts Council of Great Britain. The gallery forms part of the South Banks Arts Centre, which also includes the Royal Festival Hall, the Queen Elizabeth Hall, the Purcell Room, the National Film Theatre, and the National Theatre. Admission to the gallery varies according to exhibitions, with cheaper entry on Monday and in the evening from 6 to 8 p.m. on Tuesday to Thursday. Hours are Monday to Thursday from 10 a.m. to 8 p.m.; Friday and Saturday, 10 a.m. to 6 p.m.; and Sunday, noon to 6 p.m. The gallery is closed between exhibitions, so check the listings before crossing the Thames.

The **Serpentine Gallery,** Kensington Gardens, W.1 (tel. 402-6075). The Old Teahouse, near the Albert Memorial, was an inspired choice for the Arts Council's London platform for professional artists whose work has not been seen in commercial galleries. Its four large rooms, spacious and adaptable, are well suited to the experimental, and large-scale works are often shown here. The fact that the gallery is in popular parkland not only means that there are excellent adjacent outdoor facilities for sculpture and events, but that it draws a crowd who generally would not think of going to a Bond Street exhibition. Usually a minimum of four artists is shown at a time and given freedom to use the space as they wish. The exhibitions are principally for those interested in the most outstanding contemporary trends and tendencies, and are carefully watched by the more far-sighted commercial gallery owners. The gallery now has a winter program as well, and stages some international shows, exhibitions by more established artists, and occasional retrospectives devoted to just one artist. The gallery is open daily from 10 a.m. to 7 p.m., April through October, and from 10 a.m. to 15 minutes before dusk during November through March. Admission is free. Closed Good Friday, Christmas Eve, Christmas Day, Boxing Day, and New Year's Day.

Homes of Famous Writers

Dr. Johnson's House: The Queen Anne house of the famed lexicographer is at 17 Gough Square (tel. 353-3745). It'll cost you 70p ($1.37), and it's well worth it. Students and children pay only 50p (98¢). It was there that Dr. Johnson and his copyists compiled his famous dictionary. The 17th-century building has been painstakingly restored (surely "Dear Tetty," if not Boswell, would approve). Although Johnson lived at Staple Inn in Holborn and at a number of other houses, the Gough Square house is the only one of his residences remaining in London. He occupied it from 1748 to 1759. It is open from

11 a.m. to 5:30 p.m., Monday through Saturday, May through September, closing half an hour earlier offseason. Take the tube to Blackfriars, then walk up New Bridge Street, turning left onto Fleet. Gough Square is a tiny, hidden square, north of the "street of ink."

Carlyle's House: 24 Cheyne Row (tel. 352-7087), in Chelsea (bus 11, 19, 22, or 39). For nearly half a century, from 1834 to 1881, the handsome author of *The French Revolution* and other works, along with his letter-writing wife, took up abode in this modest 1708 terraced house, about three-quarters of a block from the Thames, near the Chelsea Embankment. Still standing and furnished essentially as it was in Carlyle's day, the house was described by his wife as being "of most antique physiognomy, quite to our humour; all wainscotted, carved and queer-looking, roomy, substantial, commodious, with closets to satisfy any Bluebeard." Now who could improve on that? The second floor contains the drawing room of Mrs. Carlyle. But the most interesting chamber is the not-so-soundproof "soundproof" study in the skylit attic. Filled with Carlyle memorabilia—his books, a letter from Disraeli, a writing chair, even his death mask—this is the cell where the author labored over his *Frederick the Great* manuscript. The Cheyne (pronounced chainey) Row house may be visited weekdays, except Monday and Tuesday, from 11 a.m. to 5 p.m.; on Sunday from 2 to 5 p.m. Admission is £1 ($1.95) for adults, 50p (98¢) for children up to 16 years of age. Closed November through March.

Dickens's House: In Bloomsbury stands the house of the great English author Charles Dickens, accused in his time of "supping on the horrors" of Victoriana and read by Russians today to find out "what Britain is really like." Born in 1812 in what is now Portsmouth, Dickens is known to have lived at 48 Doughty St., W.C.1 (tube to Russell Square; tel. 405-2127) from 1837 to 1839. Unlike some of the London town houses of famous men (Wellington, Soane), the Bloomsbury house is simple, the embodiment of middle-class restraint.

The house contains an extensive library of Dickensiana, including manuscripts and letters second in importance only to the Forster Collection in the Victoria and Albert Museum. In his study are his desk and chair from the study at Gad's Hill Place, Rochester, on which he wrote his last two letters before he died (also the table from his Swiss chalet on which he wrote the last unfinished fragment of *The Mystery of Edwin Drood*). Dickens's drawing room on the first floor has been reconstructed, as have the still room, wash house, and wine cellar in the basement. The house is open daily, except Sunday and bank holidays, from 10 a.m. to 5 p.m. Admission is 75p ($1.46) for adults, 50p (98¢) for students, and 25p (49¢) for children.

Keats's House: The darling of romantics, John Keats lived for only two years at Wentworth Place, Keats Grove, Hampstead, N.W.3 (tel. 435-2062). Take the tube to Belsize Park or Hampstead or bus 24 from Trafalgar Square. But for the poet, that was something like two-fifths of his creative life, as he died in Rome of tuberculosis at the age of 25 (1821). In Hampstead, Keats wrote some of his most celebrated *Odes*—in praise of a Grecian Urn and to the Nightingale. In the garden stands an ancient mulberry tree which the poet must have known. His Regency house is well preserved, and contains the manuscripts of his last sonnet *("Bright star, would I were steadfast as thou art"),* a final letter to the mother of Fanny Brawne (his correspondence to his Hampstead neighbor, who nursed him while he was ill, forms part of his legend), and a portrait of him on his death bed in a little house on the Spanish Steps in Rome. Wentworth Place is open weekdays 10 a.m. to 1 p.m. and 2 to 6 p.m. On Sunday, Easter, and spring and summer bank holidays hours are from 2 to 5 p.m. Closed Christmas Day, Boxing Day, New Year's Day, Good Friday, Easter Eve, and May Day. Admission is free.

Churches

St. Martin-in-the-Fields, overlooking Trafalgar Square, is the Royal Parish Church, dear to the hearts of many an English person, and especially the homeless. The present classically inspired church, with its famous steeple, dates back to 1726. James Gibbs, a pupil of Wren's, is listed as its architect. The origins of the church go back to the 11th century. Among the congregation in years past was George I, who was actually a churchwarden, unique for an English sovereign. From St. Martin's vantage position in the theater district, it has drawn many actors to its door—none more notable than Nell Gwynne, the mistress of Charles II. On her death in 1687, she was buried here. Throughout the war, many Londoners rode out an uneasy night in the crypt, while blitz bombs rained down overhead. One, in 1940, blasted out all the windows.

Floating History

The Maritime Trust's **Historic Ship Collection** is at St. Katharine's Dock, E.1 (tel. 730-0096), which has been for some years the home of the old Nore lightship. That vessel has now been joined by the Thames sailing barge *Cambria,* a schooner, an East Coast herring drifter, a steam coaster the *Robin,* and now the H.M.S. *Discovery.* Captain Scott's ship which was removed from its berth at Victoria Embankment.

The Trust provides walk-around guide leaflets to help visitors interpret what they see, and souvenirs are sold aboard the *Cambria.* While the *Discovery* is in dock, it will be possible to see restoration work carried out on her massive timbers by traditional shipwrights and riggers. There are plenty of places for a snack lunch or a pint in a pub, and, of course, the Tower of London is just across the road. The ships are open daily from 10 a.m. to 5 p.m. (until dusk in winter), charging an admission of £1.50 ($2.93) for adults, 50p (98¢) for children.

A floating museum, H.M.S. *Belfast,* Symons Wharf, Vine Lane, S.E.1 (tel. 407-6434), is an 11,500-ton cruiser, the last of the great British warships. She's moored on the opposite bank of the Thames, looking out onto the Tower of London. The first shots were fired from her guns during the sinking of the *Scharnhorst,* and she saw distinguished service during the D-Day bombardment of Normandy. She also was in action in Korea. Exhibitions show the history not only of the H.M.S. *Belfast* but of cruisers in general. The huge engine and boiler rooms can be seen, together with many other working and living spaces. The price of admission is £1.80 ($3.51) for adults, half price for children. The hours are 11 a.m. to 5:50 p.m. daily. In winter the ship closes at sunset. Nearest tube stations: Tower Hill, Monument, and London Bridge. Boats run from Tower Pier in summer and on weekends in winter.

The Dungeon

The **London Dungeon,** 34 Tooley St., S.E.1 (tel. 403-0606), simulates a ghoulish atmosphere designed deliberately to chill the blood while reproducing faithfully the conditions which existed in the Middle Ages. Set under the arches of London Bridge Station, the dungeon is a series of tableaux, more grizzly than Madame Tussaud's, depicting life in Old London. The rumble of trains overhead adds to the spine-chilling horror of the place. Bells toll and there is constant melancholy chanting in the background. Dripping water and live rats make for even more atmosphere.

The heads of executed criminals were stuck on spikes for onlookers to observe through glasses hired for the occasion. The murder of Thomas à Becket in Canterbury Cathedral is also depicted. Naturally, there's a burning at the stake, as well as a torture chamber with racking, branding, and fingernail extraction.

If you survive, there is a souvenir shop selling certificates which testify that you have been through the works. The dungeon is open from 10 a.m. to 6 p.m. daily, charging £2.50 ($4.88) for adults, £1.25 ($2.44) for children.

A Royal Tournament

The **Royal Tournament** at Earl's Court, Warwick Road, S.W.5, is a military and athletic spectacular with a century-long history. The tournament is put on each summer by various branches of the British service. You'll see exhibitions by the King's Troop Royal Horse Artillery, the R.A.F., and the Household Cavalry with their skilled horsemanship. The Royal Navy Field Gun Competition is an audience favorite in which two teams struggle with heavy field artillery across a rough, obstacle-laden terrain.

The Massed Bands will perform throughout the tournament. Guests from foreign nations, such as the Carrousel de la Gendarmerie from Belgium, and the Oman Bank from South Arabia frequently make appearances. Performances are held daily, except Sunday, at 2:30 p.m. and 7:30 p.m. (no matinees on Monday). Seat prices range from £1.50 ($2.93) and up. For tickets or further information, write to: The Royal Tournament, Horse Guards, Whitehall, London, SW1A 2AX, U.K. (tel. 930-6000). Dates of the tournament for 1983 are July 13 through July 30.

Highgate Cemetery

This cemetery is the ideal setting for a collection of Victorian sculpture. Described as everything from "walled romantic rubble" to "an anthology of horror," the 20-acre cemetery in North London's old Highgate section attracts tombstone fanciers. The unkempt look of overgrown weeds combined with the clutter of obelisks and crosses give the graveyard a rare, Gothic kind of beauty. Several of the tombstones are masterpieces in themselves, including the full-size concrete grand piano, its top opened as if ready for a concert, marked only with the name Thornton and a poetic phrase by Puccini. Another grave, that of a sporting goods manufacturer, is decorated with crossed tennis rackets, cricket bats, and balls. The most tender marker is a life-like statue of a small boy with a ball, placed over the grave of a five-year-old boy. Highgate's most famous grave is that of Karl Marx, the founder of modern Communism, who died in Hampstead in 1883. On his tomb is a huge bust of Marx, inscribed with his quotation, "Workers of all lands, unite." The grave is seldom without a wreath or bouquet of red flowers, usually placed there by an Eastern embassy or a local Communist group. The cemetery adjoins Waterlow Park, a 29-acre landmark of Highgate. In the nearby community are also several historic houses, including the Cromwell House, dating from 1638, and the home of Samuel Taylor Coleridge.

Free Sights—London in Action

Those who have grown museum-weary might like to see workaday London engaged in its task of, say, trying to start a revolution at Speakers' Corner or sentencing a modern-day Jack the Ripper at Old Bailey. Here are a few of the action items available:

First, at the northwest extremity of Mayfair, head for **Marble Arch,** an enormous *faux pas* that the English didn't try to hide but turned into a monument. Originally it was built by John Nash as the entrance to Buckingham Palace, until it was discovered that it was too small for carriages to pass through. If you see a crowd of people nearby who look as if they are plotting revolution, you might be right. In this part of Hyde Park (tube to Marble Arch) is **Speakers' Corner,** where you will see English free speech in action. Everybody from Communists to Orgone theorists mounts the soapbox to speak his or her mind. The speeches reach their most violent pitch on Sunday, the best day to visit Marble Arch.

If you are intrigued with the operation of the courts, you may want to include a visit to the **Central Criminal Court** while you are in the area of St. Paul's. On the corner of Old Bailey and Newgate Street, E.C.4, the court was built on the site of the infamous Old Newgate Prison. Affectionately called Old Bailey, it has witnessed some great—and some dubious—moments in the history of British justice. The public is permitted to enter from 10:20 a.m. to 1 p.m. and from 1:50 to 4 p.m. Monday through Friday. Entry is strictly on a first arrival basis. Guests queue up outside (where, incidentally, the final public execution took place in the 1860s). Courts 1 to 4, 17, and 18 are entered from Newgate Street, and the balance from "Old Bailey." No persons under 14 are admitted, and teenagers from 14 to 17 must be accompanied by a responsible adult. No cameras or tape recorders are allowed. If you prefer civil cases to criminal ones, you can visit the **Law Courts** on The Strand, W.C.2 (tube to Temple), which are open Monday through Friday from 10 a.m. to 4 p.m.

The **Stock Exchange** has replaced New York as the world's leading money mart. On the trading floor of this money center, one of the most modern in the world, you can catch a glimpse of brokers and jobbers. Guides explain what the action means, and later you are shown a film in an adjoining cinema, giving you an insight into the world of high finance. The Visitors' Gallery entrance is in Old Broad Street, and the nearest underground station is Bank. Admission is free, and visiting hours are weekdays from 9:45 a.m. to 3:15 p.m. For more information, phone 588-2355.

London Zoo

One of the greatest zoos in the world, the London Zoo (tel. 722-3333) celebrated its 150th birthday in 1976. Among the thousands of animals, the most famous are the two giant pandas, Ching-Ching and Chia-Chia, a gift to Britain from the People's Republic of China. One of the most fascinating exhibits is the Snowdon Aviary. Many families budget almost an entire day to spend with the animals, watching the sea lions being fed or the elephants bathed on fine summer days. Also of interest is the Moonlight World, where animals of the night—the "nocturnal beasties"—wander in their special world, everything from Australian fruit bats to primitive echidnas.

The London Zoo occupies 36 acres of Regents Park, and is open every day except Christmas from 9 a.m. in summer and from 10 a.m. in winter, till 6 p.m. or dusk, whichever is earlier. You can go by underground to Baker Street or Camden Town and then take the no. 74 bus (Camden Town is nearer and an easy ten-minute walk). On the grounds are two fully licensed restaurants, one self-service, the other with waitresses. Admission is £3.50 ($6.83) for adults, £1.50 ($2.93) for children.

The Jewish Museum

The major communal building for English Jewry is **Woburn House,** Upper Woburn Place, W.C.1, near Euston Station. In these precincts you'll also come upon the hard-to-find Jewish Museum (tel. 387-3081), tucked away on a lovely square. Walk along Euston Road, and turn right onto Upper Woburn Place. When you reach Tavistock Square, turn right again, and there's the entrance. After entering, you're invited to sign a guest book, then you're guided up to the museum, a large salon filled with antiques relating to the history of the Jews. You'll come across many artifacts used in Jewish rituals. All the exhibits, in fact, are of interest to those concerned with Anglo-Judaica. It is open Monday to Thursday from 12:30 to 3 p.m. and on Sunday from 10:30 a.m. to 12:45 p.m. It is closed on Friday, Saturday, bank holidays, and Jewish holidays. The Jewish Historical Society runs the **Mocatta Library and Museum** at the neighboring University College on Gower Street.

LONDON INFORMATION: The **British Tourist Authority** operates a telephone tape which is changed daily, giving details of all sorts of things to do each day. On the day I tried it, the service reported there was a free jazz concert in Battersea Park, a flower show in Chelsea, and, in addition, it suggested that I visit the gallery at the National Maritime Museum at Greenwich. The tape gives prices and visiting hours and also tells you how to get there. For this information, telephone 499-9325.

There are several official information centers around The City and West End, providing particular data about a certain part of town. These centers know of exhibitions and places to visit which are seldom open to the public—the Livery Halls in The City, for example.

Centers include the **City of London Information Centre,** St. Paul's Churchyard, E.C.4 (tel. 606-3030), which is open Monday to Friday from 9:30 a.m. to 5 p.m. (Saturday and holidays from 10 a.m. to 6 p.m.). Others are operated by the London Tourist Board as follows: 26 Grosvenor Gardens, S.W.1, open during office hours for general advice and sale of tourist tickets, sightseeing tours, theater tickets, and guidebooks (this is the head LTB office to which mail inquiries should be sent); Victoria Station near platform 15, open daily from 9 a.m. to 8:40 p.m., a tourist information and accommodation center; Travel Information Centre, Heathrow Central Station, London Airport, open daily from 8 a.m. to 7:30 p.m., providing tourist information, hotel accommodations, and publications; Selfridges, Oxford Street, W.1; Harrods, Knightsbridge, S.W.3; Tower of London, E.C.3, by the main gate, tourist information, leaflets, and other publications, open from 9 a.m. to 5 p.m. Monday through Saturday and 2 to 5 p.m. on Sunday in summer; and telephone information service, 730-0791 from 9 a.m. to 6 p.m. Monday through Friday or call Teletourist, 246-8041, 24 hours a day for a selection of attractions and events.

Also providing information are the **British Tourist Authority,** 64 St. James's St., S.W.1 (tel. 629-9191), Easter to September 30, Monday through Friday from 9 a.m. to 6 p.m., on Saturday to 2:30 p.m.; October to Easter, Monday through Friday 9:15 a.m. to 5:30 p.m., on Saturday to 12:30 p.m.

3. Shopping for Value

In London, this "nation of shopkeepers" displays an enormous variety of wares. You can pick up bargains ranging from a still-functioning hurdy-gurdy to a replica of the crown jewels. For the best buys, search out new styles in clothing, as well as traditional and well-tailored men's and women's suits, small antiques and curios, woolens, tweeds, tartans, rare books, Liberty silks, Burberrys, English china, silver, even arms and armor, to name just a few.

Here is a brief survey of some of the more attractive merchandise offered:

ANTIQUE MARKETS—FOR CURIOS: Chelsea Antique Market, 245–253 King's Rd., S.W.3 (tel. 352-9695), is billed as the world's largest covered antique market. It's a gold mine where you can pan for some hidden little treasure. Sheltered inside a rambling old building, it offers endless browsing possibilities for the curio addict. In this ever-changing display you're likely to run across Staffordshire dogs, shaving mugs, Edwardian buckles and clasps, ivory-handled razors, old velours and lace gowns, wooden tea caddies, antique pocket watches, wormy Tudoresque chests, silver snuff boxes, grandfather clocks, and jewelry of all periods. The market is now owned by two of the stallholders, Peter and Adrian Harrington, dealers in rare books. It is open Monday through Saturday from 10 a.m. to 6 p.m. Closed Sunday. Tube: Sloane Square.

The **Antique Hypermarket,** 26–40 Kensington High St., W.8 (tel. 937-3727), is London's choicest antique mart, with more than 100 stalls owned by leading dealers. As a trading center of excellence, it is often called the Stock Exchange of the Antique World. Each stallkeeper is a specialist in his or her field. If you don't find what you want, chances are you'll be directed to someone who has it. You'll find rare books, bronzes from Tibet, Tudor (often Tudoresque) chests, inlaid boxes, rare china and jewelry, silver-tipped canes, old English clocks, model ships, tole tea caddies, and on the lower ground floor is a vast display of antique furniture and fabulous silver vaults. At the rear of the ground floor is an amusing place for a quick snack, the Pullman Train, a Victorian railroad dining car where you sit on plush seats and order sandwiches and salads. Tube: High Street Kensington.

Antiquarius, 15 Flood St., S.W.3 (tel. 351-1145), is the most varied of the indoor markets of London, with more than 200 stalls leased to collectors as a showcase for their wares—souvenir spoons, silver decanter labels, old books, authentic Tudor and Elizabethan furniture, rare helmets, antique guns and swords, silver pillboxes, snuff boxes, fine bone china, Roman glass, pocket watches, teapots, ornate wooden boxes, lead toy soldiers, military buttons, Oriental cannisters, dolls of every size, age, and character, mechanical toys, unusual walking sticks, and an amusing collection of art nouveau statuary. There's also a large selection of 1920s and 1930s fashion. Antiquarius is open from 10 a.m. till 6 p.m., Monday to Saturday. But it's closed Sunday.

Alfies Antique Market, 13–25 Church St., N.W.8 (tel. 723-6066), is one of the cheapest covered markets in London. The dealers come to buy here, inspecting more than 185 stalls, showrooms, and workshops.

Bond Street Antique Centre, 126 New Bond St., W.1, consists of 44 stands with more than 30 dealers selling antique jewelry, silver, watches, clocks, portrait miniatures, porcelain, glass, some small furniture, and Oriental antiques and antiquities. Prices are lower than those usually associated with Bond Street.

BEAUCHAMP PLACE: This is one of London's top shopping streets. Beauchamp Place (pronounced Beecham) is a block off Brompton Road, near Harrods Department Store. The *Herald Tribune* called it "a higgledy-piggledy of old-fashioned and trendy, quaint and with-it, expensive and cheap. It is

deliciously unspecialized." Whatever you're looking for—a pâté de marcassin to a carved pine mantelpiece—you are likely to find it here. Reject china, secondhand silver, old alligator bags, collages, custom-tailored men's shirts—whatever. It's pure fun even if you don't buy anything.

BOOKS: W. & G. Foyle, Ltd., 119–125 Charing Cross Rd., W.C.2 (tel. 437-5660), claims to be the world's largest bookstore, with an impressive array of hardcovers and paperbacks. The shop includes records, video tapes, and sheet music.

The **Children's Book Centre Ltd.,** 229 Kensington High St., W.8 (tel. 937-6314), is the best place to go for both children's books and toys. It is thought to be the largest children's book shop in the world and has thousands of titles, including volumes from both France and Germany. A feature of the book shop is that fiction, both hardback and paperback, is arranged according to age. The large toy department, which has been described as the most imaginative in London, offers a wide selection of toys, games, and stationery for all ages. The store is open from 9 a.m. to 7 p.m. Monday through Friday, 9 to 6 on Saturday. Tube: High Street Kensington.

THE BURLINGTON ARCADE: Opposite Fortnum and Mason on Piccadilly is the **Royal Academy of Arts** (tel. 734-9052), where there are remarkable art shows throughout the year. A door west of the Royal Academy is the **Burlington Arcade,** a glass-roofed passage from Piccadilly north for several hundred feet to the next street. It houses dozens of shops, all with tiny upper floors, devoted solely to the sale of luxuries almost beyond imagination. You can take a short stroll through, or spend a day wandering up and down, protected from the weather—no small item in rainy London. You will see some of the best that London has to offer in the way of jewelry, both antique and modern, clothing for both men and women, fine arts, linen, bric-a-brac, all in profusion. It is possibly the greatest single concentrated bit of luxury shopping in London. Pomp and ceremony may be departing, but if you linger in the arcade until 5:30, you can watch the beadles, those ever-present attendants, in their black and yellow livery and top hats, ceremoniously put in place the iron grills which block off the arcade until 9 the next morning, when they just as ceremoniously remove them, marking the start of the new business day. Tube: Piccadilly Circus.

CHINA: Lawleys, 154 Regent St., W.1 (tel. 610-141), offers a wide range of English bone china, as well as crystal and ovenware. The firm specializes in Royal Doulton, Minton, Royal Crown Derby, Wedgwood, Denby, Aynsley, and Webb Corbett, Stuart, Waterford, and Edinburgh, plus crystal and Lladro figures. Tube: Piccadilly Circus.

The **Reject China Shop,** 33–35 Beauchamp Pl. and at Beauchamp Corner, S.W.3 (tel. 584-9409), is really four shops at Knightsbridge, near Harrods Department Store. Offering a wide choice of china firsts and seconds, the shops were started almost on a whim by the Marquess of Queensberry and D'Arcy Conyers, a designer and film director, respectively. From a lowly basement dive, they have grown into a hit. They offer excellent china at prices at least 25% lower than most other stores. The merchandise changes constantly, and what you don't find today most likely will show up tomorrow. Offered are good buys in bone china dinner and coffee sets, earthenware, and ornamental china birds, flowers, and boxes. The shop is open from 9 a.m. to 7 p.m., seven days a week. Tube: Knightsbridge.

In addition, **Wedgwood** has a large shop at 249 Oxford St., W.1 (tel. 734-5656), at the corner of Regent Street. The staff there will explain their export plan to save you money on your souvenir buying. Besides selling tableware, the store offers inexpensive ashtrays in the traditional blue and white or in sage green and white. In any case, the store is like a miniature museum and well worth a visit. It also carries a collection of china, jewelry, pendants, earrings, and brooches. Tube: Bond Street. There are also Wedgwood shops at 158 Regent St. and 173 Piccadilly.

CHOCOLATES: Charbonnel et Walker Ltd., 28 Old Bond St., W.1 (tel. 629-4396), makes probably the best chocolates in the world and will send messages of thanks or love, spelled out on the chocolates themselves. Tony Sharp, who runs the bow-fronted shop on the corner of the Royal Arcade off Old Bond Street, will help you choose from the variety of centers. A quarter-pound selection will cost £1.50 ($2.93), and the box will be priced according to what you decide to put in it. They have ready-made presentation boxes as well. There is a City branch at 27b Throgmorton St., E.C.2 (tel. 588-1306). Tube: Bond Street.

CLOCKS: Strike One (Islington) Limited, 51 Camden Passage, N.1 (tel. 226-9709), sells clocks, watches, and barometers. It's in the heart of the Camden Passage Antiques Village in Islington (tube: Angel). Strike One clearly dates and prices each old clock, and every clock is guaranteed for a year against faulty workmanship. A wide selection of clocks is displayed, ranging from early English dial clocks to long-case clocks. Strike One specializes in Act of Parliament clocks. They issue a quarterly illustrated catalogue which is mailed internationally to all serious clock collectors. They also undertake to find any clock to a customer's requirement, if they do not have a suitable example in stock. The shop is owned by John Mighell, a former mining executive who loved clocks more than his job. He gave up his business more than a decade ago to found Strike One. The shop is open daily except Sunday from 9 a.m. to 5 p.m. (at other times by appointment).

CONTEMPORARY ART: Christie's Contemporary Art, 8 Dover St., W.1 (tel. 499-3701), offers original etchings, and lithographs, and screenprints by up-and-coming artists for around £30 ($58.50) to £60 ($117). You will certainly not end up with an absolute "pup," and your holiday purchase may turn out to be a first work of a second Picasso. The gallery also has the works of such masters as Henry Moore, David Hockney, Joan Miró, and John Piper. Each work is an authentic original, numbered and signed by the artist, then stamped with Christie's seal of authentication before delivery. You can send for a catalogue or just go along.

COVENT GARDEN ENTERPRISE: In the Central Market Building an impressive array of shops, pubs, and other attractions has opened. Judging from the already-existing enterprises in the area, the new Covent Garden will prove exciting for the visitor. After all, who would expect to find in central London a kite shop?

The **British Crafts Centre,** 43 Earlham St., Covent Garden, W.C.2 (tel. 836-6993), is a gallery and display center promoting the best of British crafts through exhibitions, information, and events. Many of the leading crafts people in Britain exhibit their work through the center, much of which is for sale. A program of changing exhibitions attempts to cover all the craft disciplines and their various applications, with the emphasis on contemporary original and professional work. The exhibition program is complemented by a second display area with a range of work changed each month. The ceramics, glass, jewelry, leather, metal, silver, textiles, and wood shown in the center have an appeal for the serious collector of fine crafts through to the person wanting an individual gift for a friend. Information is available about craft organizations, galleries, and studios throughout Britain. The center is open Tuesday to Friday 10 a.m. to 5:30 p.m., on Saturday from 10 a.m. to 4 p.m.

The following are places which have caught my interest.

The **Covent Garden General Store,** 111 Long Acre, W.C.2 (tel. 242-2721), offers a conglomeration of gifts and household items, ranging from pots, pans, glass and china, cups, mugs, money boxes, packing boxes, walking sticks, handbags, and shopping bags. It's ideal for browsing to find that odd souvenir which will have some use. Prices range from a few pence to several pounds, and they also sell herb teas, sea salt, spices and country jam, as well as natural soaps.

At 21 Neal St., W.C.2, the **Natural Shoes Store** sells all manner of footware from thong sandals to climbing boots made of natural leather.

The **Neal Street Shop,** 29 Neal St., W.C.2 (tel. 836-5254), sells herbal and traditional soaps, artificial flowers, cookery books, which jostle with pottery, baskets, glassware, chinoiserie, and Victoriana.

The **Warehouse,** 39 Neal St., W.C.2 (tel. 240-0136), specializes in beads and stones, providing the fittings, clasps, and strings to make necklaces and earrings.

Naturally British, 12 New Row, W.C.2 (tel. 240-0551), specializes in items made in Britain, including handmade pottery from Devon and Cornwall, tweed and knitwear from Scotland, leather goods, wrought-iron work, and carved woodwork. A perfectly carved rocking horse will cost upward of £350 ($682.50), but a three-dimensional jigsaw puzzle monkey, dog, or cat will go for only about £9 ($17.55).

The **Glasshouse,** 65 Long Acre, W.C.2 (tel. 836-8237), sells beautiful glass, and also invites vistors into the workshops to see the crafts people producing their wares.

Penhaligon's, 41 Wellington St. W.C.2, established in 1870 as a Victorian perfumery, holds a Royal Warrant to H.R.H. the Duke of Edinburgh. It offers a large selection of perfumes, aftershave, soap, and bath oils for men and women. Perfect gifts include antique silver perfume bottles. Prices range from £5 ($9.75) for soap to £500 ($975).

And **Robert White & Sons,** 25 Shelton St., W.C.2 (tel. 606-5558), will make you a full suit of armor to size for around £600 ($1170), or a miniature set with sword for about £80 ($156) on a stand three feet high. These are the people who make theatrical jewelry. In the workshop in Neal's Yard, they'll make you a fine copy of the crown jewels at a cost of £3500 ($6825).

Behind the Warehouse off Neal Street runs a narrow road leading to the already-mentioned **Neal's Yard,** a mews of warehouses which seem to retain some of the old London atmosphere. The open warehouses display such goods as vegetables, health foods, fresh-baked breads, cakes, sandwiches, and in an immaculate dairy, the largest variety of flavored cream cheeses you are likely to encounter.

At the top of Burleigh Street, off the Strand, beside the old Flower Market, is the **Covent Garden Flea Market.** This is a real browser's paradise, with its good, bad, and indifferent clothing, fruit, and vegetables—you name it. The stalls are mainly under cover, and stallholders range from the aristocratic through punk.

And **Coppershop,** 48 Neal St., W.C.2 (tel. 836-2984), is another one of the enthusiastic enterprises to blossom in the market, this one selling a wide range of English-manufactured copper goods. For the kitchen, you'll find jelly molds depicting rabbits, flowers, whatever, along with frying and omelet pans, plus more exotic sauté pans, pomme anna pans, and zabaglione pans. In addition to fish kettles, jardinières, and traditional coal scuttles, ideal as flower-pot holders, Coppershop has a wide range of other copper ornaments, lamps, miniatures, and watering cans. The shop is run by Sally and Michael Crosfield.

There are a multitude of tiny shops, mostly of a specialized nature, where artists and crafts people seem to have gathered to form a new community. In Bedfordbury, one of the tiny streets, Cherry Saltzer specializes in—not surprisingly—cats, in her shop called **Catz.** There are model cats, teapot cats, ashtray cats, cat calendars, cat badges, books, poster, and cat umbrellas. **Nubia,** 29 Bedfordbury, sells clothing and accessories from the '30s through the '60s. Elsewhere there are silversmiths, pewter, and copperware shops, and several small snackbars and restaurants. It's well worth making your own voyage of discovery and enjoy finding odd shops and souvenirs to take home.

DEPARTMENT STORES: Harrods, Brompton Road, at Knightsbridge, S.W.1 (tel. 730-1234), is the department store to end all department stores. As firmly entrenched in English life as Buckingham Palace and the Ascot Races, it is an elaborate emporium, at times as fascinating as a museum. In a magazine article about Harrods, a salesperson was quoted as saying: "It's more of a sort of way of life than a shop, really." Aside from the fashion department (including high-level tailoring and a "Way In" section for young people), you'll find such incongruous sections as a cathedral-ceilinged and arcaded meat market, even a funeral service. Harrods has everything: men's custom-tailored suits, tweed overcoats, cashmere or lambswool sweaters for both men and women, handstitched traveling bags, raincoats, mohair jackets, patterned ski sweaters, scarves of hand-woven Irish wool, pewter reproductions, a perfumery department, "lifetime" leather suitcases, pianos. Tube: Knightsbridge.

Much more economical, however, is **Selfridges,** on Oxford Street, W.1 (tel. 629-1234), one of the biggest department stores in Europe, with more than 550 divisions, selling everything from artificial flowers to groceries. The specialty shops are particularly enticing, with goods buys in Irish linen, Wedgwood, leather goods, silver-plated goblets, cashmere and woolen scarves. There's also the Miss Selfridge Boutique, for the young or those who'd like to be. To help you travel light, the Export Bureau will air freight your purchases to anywhere in the world, completely tax free. On the ground floor, the London Tourist Board will help you find your way around London's sights with plenty of maps, tips, and friendly advice. Tube: Bond Street.

Liberty & Company Limited, Regent Street (tel. 734-1234), celebrated its centenary in 1975. In 100 years the store became known worldwide for its exquisite fabrics. One whole floor of the department store is devoted to fabrics of all kinds from all over the world, including Liberty printed cottons, silks, and pure wool. Liberty printed Tana lawn costs approximately £4.25 ($8.29) a meter, and Liberty printed silk around £6.95 ($13.55) a meter. Liberty printed silk squares in all sizes and colors, for both men and women, can be found in the country's largest scarf department. Twenty-seven-inch squares cost approximately £14.95 ($29.15).

Other exciting departments include treasures from the Orient, a wide range of modern furniture, an extensive furnishing fabric department, including Liberty's own fabrics, plus the best china and glass from all over the world. Tube: Oxford Circus.

Marks & Spencer has several branches in London, attracting the thrifty British, who get fine buys, especially in woolen goods. The main department store is at 458 Oxford St., W.1 (tel. 486-6151), three short blocks from Marble Arch. Cashmere sweaters for women are in the £30 ($58.50) to £35 ($68.25) range, women's suits from £30 ($58.50) to £40 ($78). Cashmere sweaters for men cost from £35 ($68.25) to £40 ($78), and men's suits go for around £50 ($97.50) to £80 ($156).

In addition, you might visit **British Home Stores**, on Oxford Street, W.1, near the Oxford Circus tube station, between John Princes Street and Holles Street. Similar to Marks & Spencer, it is patronized almost exclusively by the English themselves, and is known for its buys in woolens. Look for bargains. British Home Stores also operates next to the Marks & Spencer building on Kensington High Street, just a few minutes from the tube station.

THE WORLD'S MOST ELEGANT GROCERY STORE: Fortnum and Mason Ltd., 181 Piccadilly, W.1 (tel. 734-8040), down the street from the Ritz, draws the carriage trade, the well-heeled dowager from Mayfair or Belgravia who comes seeking such tinned treasures as pâté de foie gras or a boar's head. She would never set foot in a regular grocery store, but Fortnum and Mason, with its swallow-tailed attendants, is no mere grocery store; it's a British tradition dating back to 1707. In fact, the establishment likes to think that Mr. Fortnum and Mr. Mason "created a union surpassed in its importance to the human race only by the meeting of Adam and Eve." In the Mezzanine Restaurant, you can mingle at lunch with the caviar and champagne shoppers. The "country cousin" (cheddar and cottage cheese blended with egg on brown bread) costs £2.80 ($5.46); a Danish pastry, 60p ($1.17). The pastries are calorie loaded, but divine. The chocolate and confectionery department is on the ground floor. The Fountain Restaurant has both store and street entrances (Jermyn Street), and is open from 9:30 a.m. until 11:30 p.m. from Monday to Saturday, for the benefit of theater-goers. The St. James's Room Restaurant on the fourth floor is open during normal store hours. Look for the Fortnum and Mason clock outside. Tube: Piccadilly Circus.

IRISH WARES: The Irish Shop, 11 Duke St., W.1 (tel. 935-1366), and 80 Buckingham Gate, S.W.1 (tel. 222-7132), unites northern and southern Ireland by stocking so much stuff in such a small area. Directed by Charles Bruton and Anthony Tarrant, it is a useful place for those who missed buying souvenirs in Ireland. All products are genuine. Prices are reportedly as close to those you'd pay in Ireland as possible. Merchandise ranges from china to woolens, from "tea-cosies" to Celtic-designed jewelry set with precious stones, to Irish linen. Waterford crystal comes in all styles and types. Belleek china and Gaelic coffee glasses—single or in a set—are also featured. You can purchase hand-woven tweed at about £5 ($9.75) a yard, a 45" by 45" Irish linen tablecloth, hand-embroidered, will be yours for £29 ($56.55). As the jerseys are all hand-knitted, you have to rummage to find the exact one to suit your particular shape and size. Women's skirts and dresses in fine wool are offered as well. Duke

Street is off Wigmore, a street running alongside Selfridges from Oxford Street. Tube: Oxford Circus.

Ireland House Shop Limited, 150–151 New Bond St., W.1 (tel. 493-6219), can eliminate a trip to Ireland, if you were planning to go just to pick up some of those wonderful Irish tweeds. Opened in conjunction with the Irish Tourism Bureau, this colorful shop provides hand-loomed tweeds, as well as handmade apparel and accessories for both men and women. Some quality merchandise here includes Aran sweaters from £55 ($107.25) to £70 ($136.50); all-wool dresses, around £45 ($87.75) to £85 ($165.75); as well as blouses at £6 ($11.70) to £10 ($19.50) and jumpers at £18 ($35.10) to £30 ($58.50). Tube: Bond Street.

JEWELRY: Gary Mark of London Ltd., 3 Station Approach Baker St., N.W.1 (tel. 935-3170), is a modern jewelry shop adjacent to Madame Tussaud's. Its owner, Gary M. Edel, sells the latest designs in gold and silver jewelry from Paris, Amsterdam, Rome, and London as well, with many exclusive styles at reasonable prices. The shop has an excellent reputation for design and value for money, and is so patronized by people worldwide when visiting London, and by Londoners themselves, that it is open every day. The shop also carries Swiss watches and a wide collection of gifts. Tube: Baker Street.

Another Gary Mark store is at the Mount Royal Hotel, Bryanston Street, W.1 (tel. 491-8502), inside the hotel, specializing in a complete range of Swiss and Japanese watches in the latest designs of gold and silver at reasonable prices. The latest store is at the luxurious Washington Hotel, Curzon Street, Mayfair, W.1, inside the hotel, selling jewelry, souvenirs, and electronic equipment at discount prices.

MEN'S CLOTHING—TRADITIONAL: Cassidy's, 114–116 King's Rd., S.W.3 (tel. 584-0397), presents the Old English look, but with a very up-to-date twist. Here for the young gentleman are velvet suits in almost every color under the sun, tweed jackets, ready-to-wear suits, sweaters, a wide choice of slacks, and a good collection of shirts. Cassidy's offers good variety at good prices. Tube: Sloane Square.

MILITARY MINIATURES: Tradition, 5a and 5b Shepherd St., W.1 (tel. 493-7452), sells a bewildering array of military miniatures—perfect in every detail. You name it, Tradition makes it. It has a vast stock of French cavalry figures, all sorts of British soldiers from the Napoleonic Wars, U.S. Cavalrymen from the War of 1812 and the Civil War, to name but a few. What more fitting souvenir of London than a British Grenadier, a Beefeater, or a Chelsea Pensioner? The range is enormous, and the shop will sell you figures painted or unpainted, marching, running, firing, kneeling, even dying. Tube: Green Park.

OLD MAPS: The Map House, 54 Beauchamp Pl., S.W.3 (tel. 589-4325), sells antique maps and engravings. The shop also has a vast selection of old prints of London and England, both in the original and in reproduction. It's an ideal place to find an offbeat souvenir of your visit. An original engraving, guaranteed genuinely more than 100 years old, can cost from as little as 75p ($1.46) to a massive £1800 ($3510). The Map House is open from 9:45 a.m. to 5:45 p.m.; Monday to Friday, and from 10:30 a.m. to 4 p.m. on Saturday. Directors are the Honorable and Mrs. C. A. Savile, the Earl and Countess of Mexborough; and S. N. P. Pointer. Tube: Knightsbridge.

County Hall (tel. 633-7193), headquarters of the Greater London Council, is just across Westminster Bridge on the south side of the Thames. It houses the Greater London History Library which contains an extensive collection of books on London history, and topography and maps, prints, and photographs of the Greater London area from the 16th century to the present day. The library is open to the public for reference purposes between 9:15 a.m. and 5 p.m. Monday to Friday, and photocopies or photographs of most documents can be ordered. More than 40 lithographic reproductions of maps and prints are on sale in Room B66, with prices ranging from 80p ($1.56) to £2.50 ($4.88). Incidentally, this shop contains the largest collection of books on London in London.

OLD SILVER AND PLATE: Stanley Leslie, 15 Beauchamp Pl., S.W.3 (tel. 589-2333), is a tiny shop stacked to the roof with a mass of mostly small old pieces of silver, plate, and pewter. It's just the place to spend hours ferreting around for a special present. It may look like junk, but the quality is very high—and it's amazing that Mr. Leslie knows what he's got there and how much is a fair price. He's a lovely London character, hovering ready to help in his glasses and jeweler's apron. Tube: Knightsbridge.

RAINCOATS: The word **Burberry** (store at 18 Haymarket, S.W.1, tel. 930-3343, near American Express, and at 165 Regent St., W.1), is synonymous with raincoats. Going far beyond the traditional designs that earned the firm a worldwide reputation, the store also features a wide range of apparel for both men and women. Don't think you'll get anything cheap. A Burberry trench coat will cost around £220 ($429) unless you're prepared to settle for a manufactured fiber one at around £175 ($341.25). Tube: Piccadilly Circus.

SAINT CHRISTOPHER'S PLACE: One of London's most interesting and little-known (to the foreign visitor) shopping streets is Saint Christopher's Place, W.1. It lies just off Oxford Street—walk down Oxford from Selfridges toward Oxford Circus, ducking north along Gees Court across Barrett Street. There you will be surrounded by antique markets, including **Under Two Flags** (at no. 4) for model soldiers, military prints, and books; and **M. McAlee** (no. 1A) for antique silver.

Fashion shops for men and women include **Chatters** (at no. 5), offering men's wear. Around the corner in James Street is **Anastasia**, displaying handmade children's clothing. Back on the Place, **Le Jardin** (no. 15) has classic women's wear, while **Pump** (no. 28) and **Mulberry** (no. 25) cater for footwear and accessories.

Jewelry is represented by **Trevor Lawrence** (at no. 11), offering a fine selection of exclusive pieces, and **Windsor Jewels** (no. 19), which stocks a vast variety of paste and counterfeit pieces which are hardly distinguishable from the real article.

The nearest tube is Bond Street.

SILVER: The **London Silver Vaults**, Chancery Lane, W.C.2 (tel. 242-3844), were established in Victoria's day (1882), and soon became the largest silver vaults in the world. You can actually go shopping in vault after vault for that special treasure. The vaults are open Monday to Friday from 9 a.m. to 5:30

p.m., on Saturday from 9 a.m. to 12:30 p.m. Closed on bank holiday weekends. Tube: Chancery Lane.

SOUVENIRS: The **Old Curiosity Shop**, 13–14 Portsmouth St., off Lincoln's Inn Fields, W.C.2 (tel. 405-9891), was used by Charles Dickens as the abode of Little Nell. One of the old Tudor buildings still remaining in London, dating from 1567, the shop crams every nook and cranny with general knickknackery, whatnots, china, silver, pewter, prints, and souvenirs—even Charles Dickens first editions. A popular item is an unframed silhouette of Little Nell's grandfather at 50p (98¢). Horse brasses go for £1.50 ($2.93), Old Curiosity Shop bookmarks cost 40p (78¢), and ashtrays with Dickensian engravings are £2.50 ($4.88). The shop is open every day of the week, including Sunday and holidays. Tube: Chancery Lane.

SPORTS GOODS: **Lillywhites Ltd.,** off Piccadilly Circus, S.W.1 (tel. 930-3181), has been around for more than a century, and some claim it's the most famous store in Europe. In times gone by, elegant Britishers came here for those tweedy things one wore on a fox hunt weekend. But Lillywhites has kept abreast of the times, and now offers everything for those ski weekends in Norway and Switzerland, as well as all types of athletic clothing, golf wear, country and sport shoes, not to mention tennis and scuba equipment. Tube: Piccadilly Circus.

STAFFORDSHIRE FIGURES: **Exhibition Galleries,** 4–12 Exhibition Rd., S.W.7 (tel. 589-3226), is an antique shop opposite the Contented Sole restaurant. It offers a mishmash of items—an unusually large collection of Staffordshire figures—at fair prices. The figures were once given by traveling peddlers as prizes. They were usually of well-known personalities of the period, and are items for serious collectors. The location is one minute from South Kensington Station.

STEAM ENGINE MINIATURES: **Steam Age,** 59 Cadogan St., S.W.3 (tel. 584-4357), is for steam engine buffs, and offers a rare selection of miniature, but accurately scaled, models of locomotives and stationary, marine, and traction engines permanently on display. They also stock a large range of steam fittings for model engineers. It's open Tuesday through Friday from 9:30 a.m. till 5:30 p.m., on Saturday from 9 a.m. till 1 p.m. Tube: Sloane Square.

STREET MARKETS: Street markets have played an important part in the life of London. They are recommended not only for bric-a-brac but as a low-cost adventure. In fact, you don't have to buy a thing. But be warned—some of the stallkeepers are mighty convincing. Here are the best ones:

Portobello Road Market: This Saturday market is one of the city's most popular flea markets. Take the tube to Ladbroke Grove Station, then walk east. Here you'll enter a hurly-burly world where stall after stall selling curios may tempt you. Items include everything from the military uniforms worn by the Third Bavarian Lancers to English soul food. Some of the stallholders are antiquarians, with shops in fashionable Kensington, Belgravia, and Chelsea—and they know the price of everything. Feel free to bargain, however. A pastime is dropping in for a pint of ale at one of the Portobello pubs. The best time to visit is on a Saturday between 9 a.m. and 6 p.m.

New Caledonian Market: Commonly known as the **Bermondsey Market** because of its location, it's on Long Lane, commencing on the west at the Borough underground station. At its extreme east end, it begins at Tower Bridge Road. It is also approachable by a longer walk from the tube stop at Elephant and Castle. The stalls are well known, and many dealers come into London from the country. The market gets under way at 5 a.m. This is even before the underground opens. Antiques and other items are generally lower in price than at Portobello Road and other street markets.

Petticoat Lane: On Sunday morning (go before noon), throngs of shoppers join the crowds on Petticoat Lane (also known as Middlesex Street, E.1; Tube to Aldgate East). The lanes begin at the Liverpool Street Station on the Bishopsgate side. Here you can buy clothing, food, antiques, and plenty of junk.

Camden Passage: This antique bric-a-brac market in Islington, N.1 (in back of the Angel), northeast of Bloomsbury, is open all week—but the best time to visit is on Saturday market day. On all days, the emphasis is on paintings, antiques, and similar hard items. Prices are not inexpensive, but there are bargains to be found if you look carefully through the more than 50 shops and 20 boutiques. Take the tube to the Angel stop.

Church Street: Along Church Street, N.W.8, you'll have to search through a wide assortment of junk, but you'll often come across a great buy. There's a lot of secondhand furniture that won't fit under your airplane seat, but you'll find smaller purchases as well. Business is conducted Tuesday through Saturday from 8 a.m. to 6 p.m. (mornings only on Thursday); on Saturday there is more merchandise from which to select. North of Marble Arch, Church Street crosses Edgware Road, one street beyond Harrow Road, and is reached by taking the tube to either Edgware Road or Marylebone.

READERS' MARKET SUGGESTIONS: "**Leather Lane** is a daily market. The best time to go to this bustling street market is at noon, as the vendors begin to pack up at 2 p.m. A great variety of things is sold: carts bearing fruits, vegetables, books, men's shirts and sweaters, and women's clothing. There are no try-ons (obviously, because this is an outdoor market), so there is a certain amount of risk involved in buying clothing. Even if you don't buy anything, it is interesting to have a look around" (Linda Aminoff, Kew Gardens, N.Y.). . . . "If you want to visit a London street market, but won't be in town for Saturday's Portobello Road or Sunday's Petticoat Lane, there are three everyday markets within or close to the West End: **Shepherd's Bush,** between the Shepherd's Bush and Goldhawk Road stations of the Metropolitan line (heavy on clothes and sundries); **The Cut,** behind Waterloo Station (small but fairly bustling in the morning); and **Berwick Street,** in the heart of Soho, which is heavy on fresh fruits and busiest around noon" (G. Berkowitz, DeKalb, Ill.).

STYLISH CLOTHING: **Carnaby Street,** just off Regent, is a legend, and legends take time to build. Often, by the time they are entrenched, fickle fashion has moved on elsewhere. Alas, Carnaby no longer dominates the world of pace-setting fashion. But the street is still visited by the curious, and some of its shops display lots of claptrap and quick quid merchandise. For value, style, and imagination in design, the **Chelsea** (King's Road) and **Kensington** boutiques have left Carnaby behind.

WELSH HANDICRAFTS: The **Welsh Craft Centre,** 36 Parliament St., S.W.1 (tel. 839-5056), is a gallery of things Welsh, ranging from hand-woven rugs, tapestries, and tweeds to Welsh lovespoons, brass miners' lamps, horse brasses, pottery, and stoneware. You can learn about the people and the history of the goods before buying at very geniune prices. Tube: Westminster.

WOOLENS: See Harrods, where the standards are high. But for a specialty shop, **D. & L. Estridge,** with stores at 61A Piccadilly, W.1 (tel. 493-7434), opposite the Ritz Hotel, and at 62 Regent St., W.1 (tel. 734-0195), next to the Café-Royal Grill Room, is a good choice (and it's not as expensive as one would judge from its location). Cashmere, camel's hair, shetlands, tartan kilts and skirts—Estridge is a virtual showcase of Scottish crafts. Good values are to be found in cashmere sweaters for around £35 ($68.25). Lambswool sweaters are around £18 ($35.10); shetland Fair Isle, £15 ($29.25). Authentic tartans cost £28 ($54.60). Cashmere and lambswool scarves sell for from £5 ($9.75). Tube: Piccadilly Circus.

READERS' SHOPPING SUGGESTIONS: "In London an outdoor (weather permitting) art show takes place on Saturday and Sunday on Piccadilly at Green Park (underground shop is Hyde Park or Green Park). The show extends for almost half a mile, and you can pick up good-quality drawings, watercolors, oils, and crafts" (Ray R. Conley). . . . "In London combine a Sunday afternoon outing at the Hyde Park Speakers' Corner with a stroll down Bayswater Road. Along the edge of the park, from Marble Arch for four blocks toward Lancaster Gate, stretches an outdoor art fair. Every possible type of art and craft is exhibited, from paintings on velvet to handmade pottery—and most at reasonable prices" (Phyllis and Steve Wilson, Chicago, Ill.). . . . "For those interested in posters, a visit to **London Transport Poster-Shop,** 55 Broadway, S.W.1, off St. James's Park, is recommended. Here you can choose out of hundreds of posters, at prices much lower than usual. As a special souvenir of London, for example, you might buy a map of the London Underground in its original size, as it is to be seen on every tube station. You can also buy books, souvenirs, and photos" (Rolf Hopke, Achen, West Germany).

"My husband and I want to add a suggestion about shopping for gifts that we found helpful on our trip to England. We restricted our buying to museum and cathedral shops. This is a good idea for several reasons. We found many wonderful people in these shops and learned a good deal about local history, their family backgrounds, and their historic ties. The items bought were well priced and quite lovely, e.g., note paper in the Jewish Museum in London; placemats and trivets in Warwick Castle; paperweights in the Ashmolean Museum at Oxford; and a facsimile of Wordsworth's 'Tintern Abbey' at the abbey. Also we felt that in making such purchases we contributed to the preservation of these sights and made it possible for other visitors to follow" (Henry and Gertrude Langsam, Malverne, N.Y.).

READER'S SUGGESTION: "The **London Brass Rubbing Centre** is at St. James's Church, Piccadilly, W.1 (tel. 437-6023), a two-minute walk from Piccadilly Circus. I visited it to discover a dozen or more young Americans who had walked by, seen the sign, and entered. For those parents who want to rest a bit while teenagers are vigorously occupied, and for those grownups who are interested in making their own brass rubbings at little expense, this center is ideal. Seventy exact copies of celebrated bronze portraits are ready for use. The center furnishes the paper, rubbing materials, and instruction on how to begin your own rubbing. There are also some books and pamphlets for sale on the subject. I did a bronze rubbing (gold on black) of a medieval knight about three feet high. The charges range from 50p (98¢) to £8 ($15.60). For those who become bitten by the bug, they also sell materials to take with you. There is a similar center in an annex to Westminster Abbey, with different bronzes. However, tourists flow through the large hall, and the general environment is much more distracting. I would strongly recommend the center at St. James's Church (in the basement) as an inexpensive way to pass several hours and obtain a personal work of art which would cost considerably more if purchased. Classical music plays all day for the 'rubbers.' Hours are from 10 a.m. to 6 p.m. Monday to Saturday; noon to 6 p.m. Sunday" (William A. Knowlton, West Springfield, N.H.).

Author's Note: During the summer, from May to October inclusive, the center runs a second brass-rubbing center at All Hallows Church by the Tower of London. It is open from 11 a.m. to 5:45 p.m. Monday to Saturday, and from 12:30 to 5:45 p.m. on Sunday. The church itself has the finest brasses in London, and a special feature of the center is that it includes the only facsimiles of these great brasses. All Hallows Church has a little-known museum beneath it which displays the Roman pavement of the villa on which the church was built, together with many artifacts of the church's early history and its connections with Roman times, the Great Fire of London, the executions at the Tower, World War II, and other historic events. It's well worth visiting.

4. London After Dark

London is crammed with nighttime entertainment. You'll have a wide choice of action—from the dives of Soho to elegant clubs. So much depends on your taste, pocketbook, and even the time of year. Nowhere else will you find such a panorama of legitimate theaters, operas, concerts, gambling clubs, discos, vaudeville at Victorian music halls, striptease joints, jazz clubs, folkmusic cafés, nightclubs, and ballrooms. For information about any of these events, ask a newsstand dealer for a copy of *What's on in London.*

THEATERS: The fame of the English theater has spread far and wide. In London, you'll have a chance to see it on its home ground. You may want to spend a classical evening with the National Theatre Company (formerly the Old Vic), or you may settle for a new play by Harold Pinter. You might even want to catch up on that Broadway musical you missed in New York, or else be an advance talent scout for next year's big Stateside hit.

You can either purchase your ticket from the theater's box office (the most recommended method), or else from a ticket agent, such as the one at the reservations desk of American Express (agent's fee charged, however). In a few theaters, you can reserve your spot in the gallery, the cheapest seats of all, but in some cases the inexpensive seats are sold only on the day of performance. This means that you'll have to buy your ticket earlier in the day, and—as you don't get a reserved seat—return about an hour before the performance and queue up for the best gallery seats. Occasionally you can enjoy a preshow staged by strolling performers called "buskers," next year's Chaplin—or last year's (the theater has its peaks and valleys).

If you want to see two shows in one day, you'll find that Wednesday, Thursday, and Saturday are always crammed with matinee performances. Many West End theaters begin their evening performances at 7:30.

Students and senior citzens get a break at most theaters (subject to availability) by being granted a discount at the local box offices. Currently, such discount tickets sell at a price beginning at £3.50 ($6.83) each.

The **Leicester Square Ticket Booth**, Leicester Square, W.C.2, sells theater tickets on the day of performance for half price, plus a 50p (98¢) service charge. Open from noon to 2 p.m. for matinee performances and from 2:30 to 6:30 p.m. for evening performances, they have a wide selection of seats available. Ask for the show you want to see, and they will offer alternatives if they fill your first choice. Tickets for "hits" are obviously not available often. There is frequently a long line, but it moves quickly and it is well worth the effort if you want to take in a lot of theater while you are in London—and save money. Many of the shows for which tickets are available are well displayed at the booth, so you can make up your mind on what to see as you wait in the queue.

Of London's many theaters, these are particularly outstanding:

The **National Theatre,** a concrete cubist fortress—a three-theater complex that stands as a $32-million landmark beside the Waterloo Bridge on the south bank of the Thames. It was first suggested in 1848, and it took Parliament 101 years to pass a bill vowing government support. Flaring out like a fan, the most thrilling theater in this complex is the **Olivier**, named after Lord Olivier, its first director when the company was born in 1962. (Olivier was succeeded in 1973 by Peter Hall, who created the Royal Shakespeare Company.) The Olivier Theater bears a resemblance in miniature to an ancient Greek theater. It's an open-stage, 1160-seat theater which is intended primarily for the classics. The **Cottesloe** is a simple box theater for 400 people, offering experimental plays. Finally, the 890-seat **Lyttelton** is a traditional proscenium arch house that doesn't have one bad seat for any theater-goer. In the foyers there are two bookshops, eight bars, a restaurant, and five self-service buffets (some open all day except Sunday), and many outside terraces with river views. For everyone, with or without tickets for a play, there is live foyer music, free, before evening performances and Saturday matinees, and free exhibitions. The foyers are open 10 a.m. to 11 p.m. except Sunday. Also guided theater tours are available daily, including backstage areas, for about £1.50 ($2.93).

Tickets range from £3.70 ($7.22) to £7.90 ($15.41), but midweek matinees are cheaper. Group bookings can be arranged in advance. Credit cards are accepted. You can book through a travel agent or with the theater in advance, and some tickets are available on the day of performance at £3.70 ($7.22).

For general information, telephone 733-0880. For ticket information, call the box office at 928-2252.

The National Theatre Restaurant will serve you a good meal for around £8.50 ($16.58), but at one of the coffee bars a snack will run around £2.50 ($4.88). If the weather is good, you can just sit and look out over the river and the London skyline spread before you. Tube: Waterloo Station.

The **Royal Shakespeare Company** has its famous theater in Stratford-upon-Avon and is also housed in the Barbican Theatre, Barbican Centre, E.C.2 (tube to Barbican or St. Paul's; tel. 628-8795 in London, or Stratford 292-271). A program of new plays and Shakespearean and other classics is performed here. Plays run in repertoire and are presented two or three times a week each. The company also has two smaller theaters where new and experimental plays are performed as well as classics: **The Other Place**, in Stratford, and **The Pit**, also in the Barbican Centre.

Royal Court Theatre, Sloane Square, S.W.1 (tel 730-1745; tube to Sloane Square). The English Stage Society has operated this theater for more than 25 years. The emphasis is on new playwrights (John Osborne got his start here with the 1956 production of *Look Back in Anger*). Also on the premises is the Theatre Upstairs, the studio theater also devoted to the work of new playwrights. Tickets in the main theater range in price from £2.50 ($4.88) to £5.50 ($10.73). At the Theatre Upstairs, the tickets go for £2.50 ($4.88) Monday through Thursday, £3 ($5.85) on Friday and Saturday.

The **Young Vic**, The Cut, Waterloo, S.E.1 (tel. 928-6363), aims primarily at the 15 to 25 age group, with some productions specifically for younger audiences. The Young Vic's repertoire includes such authors as Shakespeare, Ben Jonson, O'Casey, and Pinter, as well as specially written new plays. Performances begin normally at 7:30 p.m. Seats cost an average of £2.30 ($4.49).

Sadler's Wells Theatre is on Rosebery Avenue, E.C.1 (tel. 837-1672). Apart from its resident company Sadler's Wells Royal Ballet, it also plays host to other outstanding companies. Prices fluctuate from £1.50 ($2.93) to £10 ($19.50). Take the underground to Angel Station (Northern line). The theater is a three-minute walk. Or you can go by bus direct from Piccadilly (no. 19 or 38); from Holborn (no. 19, 38, or 172); to the Angel (no. 30, 43, 73, 104, 214, 277, or 279); and from Waterloo (no. 171 or 188), and change at Holborn.

Many theaters will accept bookings by telephone if you give your name and American Express card number when you ring. Then all you have to do is go along before the performance to collect your tickets which will be sold at the theater price. All theater booking agencies charge a fee. Once confirmed, the booking will be charged to your account even if you don't use the tickets. Only card holders can collect the tickets charged to their accounts.

THEATER CLUBS: Besides the productions in the regular theaters, several theater clubs have been established, originally to avoid the censorship of the Lord Chamberlain, although that is no longer necessary. These clubs are where the most experimental and avant-garde productions are staged. By stopping by at their box offices and paying a nominal fee, you can become a temporary member. The clubs include the **Mountview Arts Centre** and **Mountview Theatre School,** with two theaters, the Mountview Theatre and the Judi Dench Theatre, both at 104 Crouch Hill, N.8 (tel. 340-5885), and have been established for some 37 years. Sixty plays and musicals are presented annually, plus 30 films. Membership is free. Many courses are offered, mainly full time, although some evening part-time courses are also given. Affiliated theaters include the New Arts Theatre Club in London, the Hampstead Theatre Club, and the Traverse Theatre Club, Edinburgh. Performances on weekday evenings begin at 7:30 p.m. Matinees are at 3:30 p.m. There is no charge for seats, although donations are invited for the students' scholarship fund. Take the subway on the Piccadilly line to Finsbury Park and then a W2 or W7 bus (terminus). The theater is on the main road.

The **Holland Park Court Theatre** is a charming open-air stage in Holland Park, W.8, close to the Commonwealth Institute. It really has the air of a court theater in some Renaissance palace yard. There is a weekly program in June and July of opera and drama. Concerts and chamber music are presented on Sunday evenings. Tickets are £2 ($3.90) Tuesday through Saturday, £1.75 ($3.41) on Sunday. Shows begin at 7:30 nightly, at 2:30 p.m. for Saturday matinees. The Dutch Garden is floodlit until midnight, and the theater is closed on Monday. For program inquiries, telephone 633-1707. Tube: Kensington High Street.

The **Almost Free Theatre** has finally been forced to abandon its "pay what you can afford" policy, although it is still "almost free" in the sense that it provides a vehicle for young and established actors, writers, and directors to try new ideas without financial pressures. Admission is currently £1.50 ($2.93), inclusive of membership (which is reciprocal with most other London fringe theaters). The Almost Free is currently operating "in exile" while its home theater is being rebuilt. Details can be obtained from Inter-Action by telephoning 267-9421.

MUSIC HALLS: **Players,** Villiers Street (formerly the famous Gatti's "Under the Arches"), W.C.2 (tel. 839-1134). Nowadays, the Players is a Victorian music hall variety club. Top-notch entertainers often perform here. The presentation is professionally staged, with the appropriate settings and costumes. The master of ceremonies, the chairman, asks members to introduce their guests, who stand for a bow (and comments). Insults are exchanged in jest, especially if a guest is from one of the "colonies."

You can enjoy the entire show, having drinks only, although it's best to make an entire evening of it, order dinner, and stay for the dancing session after the show. To do that, you can have a generous dinner à la carte. Temporary membership is available for overseas members for £6 ($11.70) a week, £12 ($23.40) quarterly. It is essential that 48 hours elapse before a membership becomes valid. Incidentally, memberships must be paid in sterling. Application must be made in person. Dinner at £8 ($15.60) per head is served in the restaurant from 6:45 p.m. (reserve a table ahead). The show starts nightly at 8:30. Performances are given every night, except Sunday, but check in advance by calling the box office. Tube: Charing Cross Station. (Directly across the street from the Players, incidentally, is a house with a plaque commemorating the fact that Rudyard Kipling lived there between 1889 and 1891.)

Cockney Cabaret and Music Hall, 18 Charing Cross Rd., W.C.2 (tel. 408-1001), recaptures the atmosphere of a Victorian music hall. At the whisky and gin reception, you'll have the cockles of your heart warmed and learn about "mother's ruin" (large gins). The lively waiters and waitresses join the guests to sing along to the sounds of a honky-tonk piano. An East End meal, four courses of Cockney nosh, is served, along with unlimited beer and wine. Music to sing and dance marks the evening. The show is divided into two parts, featuring cabaret with both production numbers and solo performances. The hall is open daily in summer; however, in winter it is open only from Wednesday to Saturday. Admission is £18.50 ($36.08) per person Wednesday to Friday, rising to £20.50 ($39.98) on Saturday. The club is open from 8 p.m. Tube: Charing Cross.

Aba Daba, 328 Gray's Inn Rd., W.C.1 (tel. 722-5395), near King's Cross underground station, is not a club, like the Players' Theatre, and its admission charges are £3.50 ($6.83) per person. Charges must be paid 24 hours in advance. In winter the club is especially popular, and reservations are suggested. The place is more like a pub than a supper club, although in addition to drinks from its well-stocked bar you can also order typically British meals. Decorated in red, Aba Daba seats more than 100 guests at tiny tables. On show nights about half a dozen performers entertain, exchanging banter with members of the audience. This music hall presents shows on Thursday, Friday, and Saturday nights.

The **Pindar of Wakefield,** 328 Gray's Inn Rd., W.C.1 (tel. 722-5395 for reservations), perpetuates the convivial world of the Victorian music hall. Aided by tankards of foaming ale and authentic Cockney entertainment, the boisterous days of communal friendliness live on. As your chairman, the "garrulous glossarist" puts it, the Pindar is for "booze, ballads, and bonhomie," not to forget "bangers & mash and faggots." The admission charge is £3.50 ($6.83). In the pub you can order chicken, sausage, or scampi in the basket, at a cost ranging from £1.75 ($3.41) to £3.50 ($6.83). The show is billed as "a gargantuan garish gala gloriously gathered for your gracious gratifications." Usually six performers belt out tearjerkers, and you're given a song-sheet to help in the sing-alongs. Tube: King's Cross Station.

The **Rheingold Club,** Sedley Place at 361 Oxford St., W.1 (tel. 629-5343), has brought the old-world charm of an ancient Rhineland inn to the heart of Mayfair. Appropriately housed in a 100-year-old wine cellar, this nightspot provides a relaxed atmosphere where the strains of popular and Latin music are freely mingled with German drinking songs and Viennese waltzes. Wrought-iron lanterns cast a soft glow across Rhenish coats-of-arms, dark wooden beams, and historical copper etchings. Although celebrities frequently perform at the midnight cabaret, the patrons themselves are responsible for most of the entertainment.

The temporary membership you purchase at the entrance costs £5 ($9.75) for men and £4 ($7.80) for women, and entitles you to one free admission. The menu offers such wholesome German dishes as pickled knuckle of pork and sauerkraut served with pease pudding and boiled potatoes for £3.50 ($6.83). It also has a strong German draft beer at 60p ($1.17) for a half pint, and excellent German and French wines, from £4 ($7.80) for a simple qualitatswein to £7.50 ($14.63) for an Auslese. The Rheingold is open every night except Sunday from 7:30 p.m., closing at 1:30 a.m. on Monday and Tuesday, at 2 a.m. on Wednesday and Thursday, and remaining open until 2:30 a.m. on Friday and Saturday. Tube: Bond Street.

The luxury catamaran *Naticia* is a music hall showboat, leaving Lambeth Pier nightly at 7 p.m. for a four-hour cruise on the River Thames, returning at 11 p.m. There is a bar for a drink while you watch the landmarks slip by. Dinner is either a supper-basket with chicken, scampi, or some such, or a three-course meal with wine. At dinnertime a first-class, oldtime music hall program entertains you. Advance reservations are essential. Telephone **Catamaran Cruisers Ltd.**, Westminster Pier, S.W.1 (tel. 839-2349). The supper basket menu costs £13 ($25.35); the full dinner, £18.50 ($36.08).

NIGHTCLUBS: There are several kinds of nightclubs where you can eat or drink, be entertained, dance—even gamble. Most often these clubs are private—but don't turn away yet. To avoid the unpopular early closing hour of 11 p.m. for licensed public establishments, the private club has come into existence and may stay open till 3 and 4 a.m. In most cases, the clubs welcome overseas visitors showing passports, granting them a temporary membership—often for anywhere from £1 ($1.95) to £6 ($11.70) or more. The cost of a temporary membership may even be deducted from the price of dinner; however, there is no hard-and-fast rule. Many clubs offer dinner, a show, and dancing from £12 ($23.40) to £20 ($39) per person, including entertainment. No visitor to London should be afraid to ask about membership in a private club. After all, most of the clubs are in business to make money and welcome foreign patronage.

The Top Nightclubs

Eve, 189 Regent St., W.1 (tel. 734-0557), is London's longest established late-night club. Doyen of London's nightlife, owner Jimmy O'Brien launched it in 1953. Strip cabaret and erotic entertainment (at 1 a.m.) have replaced the floor shows previously presented. Dancing is to disco, alternating with live music of a high standard. Eve is open Monday to Friday from 10 p.m. to 3:30 a.m. Admittance is by membership only. There is an annual subscription of £5 ($9.75), but a special temporary membership for overseas visitors, valid for one night only, is granted for £1 ($1.95). Only one person in a party need be a member, and overseas visitors may be admitted on application without waiting the customary 48 hours. There is an entrance fee or cover charge of £5 ($9.75) for a member and each guest. An à la carte menu is available throughout the night and an All-In Champagne supper is offered until midnight. This includes the entrance fee, an apéritif, a three-course meal, a half bottle of champagne, brandy, and coffee, for £29.50 ($57.53). All prices include VAT. Charming girls, many of whom speak more than one language, are available as dining or dancing partners for unaccompanied men.

Royal Roof Restaurant, Royal Garden Hotel, Kensington High Street, W.8 (tel. 937-8000), lies on the top floor of the hotel, is elegant and refined, and overlooks Kensington Gardens and Hyde Park. From your table you will see the lights of Kensington and Knightsbridge, with a view of London's West End skyline. In a romantic candlelit aura, you can enjoy a three-course dinner for between £18 ($35.10) and £22 ($42.90), with a £2 ($3.90) entertainment charge. Joe Stein and his International Royal Roof Violins will serenade you at your table, and if you wish, you may dance the night away to the sounds of their quartet. The restaurant is open Monday to Saturday, 8 p.m. to 2 a.m. Reservations are necessary. Tube: High Street Kensington.

L'Hirondelle, Swallow Street, W.1 (tel. 734-6666), is a small but popular nightspot just off Regent Street. The spectacular hour-long stage shows put together by producer Chris Daniel are performed in what appears to be an all-gold environment, complete with golden-colored wallpaper, accessories, and sparkling chandeliers to reflect the entire scene. The company of glamorous showgirls go skillfully through their routines in colorful—and often scanty—costumes with overwhelming headdresses. Singers and dancers add their talents to the hour of variety and music. Two bands assure you of constant music for dancing throughout the rest of the evening.

You'll pay a minimum charge of £5.75 ($11.21) if you don't dine here, but L'Hirondelle offers a very good three-course méal package for about £12.50 ($24.38), which allows you to choose from a number of items in each course. There's also a more expensive à la carte menu. Wines are expensive, ranging from £12 ($23.40) for the house wine. A service charge and VAT are added to the tab. The entire staff of L'Hirondelle is courteous and efficient, assuring you of an enjoyable evening of dining, dancing, and entertainment. The club is open from 8 p.m. to 3:45 a.m., and dancing is from 9 p.m. to two live bands. The floor shows are at 11 p.m. and at 1:30 a.m. It's closed Sunday. Tube: Piccadilly.

Bouzouki and Plate Smashing

The **Elysse**, 13 Percy St., W.1 (tel. 636-4804), is for *Never on Sunday* devotees who like the reverberations of bouzouki and the smashing of plates. The domain of the Karegeorgis brothers—Michael, Ulysses, and the incomparable George—it offers hearty fun at moderate tabs. You can dance nightly, including Sunday, (until 3 a.m.) to music by Greeks. At two different intervals (last one at 1 a.m.) a cabaret is provided, highlighted by brother George's altogether amusing act of balancing wine glasses (I'd hate to pay his breakage bill). You can book a table either on the ground floor or the second floor, but the Roof Garden is a magnet in summer. The food is good, too, including the house specialty, the classic moussaka, and the kebabs from the charcoal grill. Expect to pay about £17 ($33.15) for a complete meal, including a bottle of wine. Tube: Goodge Street.

A Club with a Show

The **Talk of the Town,** hippodrome Corner of Leicester Square, W.C.2 (tel. 734-5051), is a popular nightspot choice, and has been since its opening in the autumn of 1958. The stage is big enough for the presentation of three big musicals—all at the same time. Pitched at those wanting to witness an extravaganza, with Rockette-type showgirls galore, it's a gimcrack theater-restaurant, sheltering about 750 on-the-towners who want a whole evening's entertainment for a comparatively low price. From Monday to Thursday, the cost per person is about £20 ($39), about £23 ($44.85) for Friday and Saturday splashes. Service is included. Tube: Leicester Square.

For this you get a three-course table d'hôte dinner (including coffee, but drink extra), followed by a floor show at 9:30 p.m. and later by dancing (three bands featured), plus the windup, the appearance at 11 p.m. of the headliner—often from the best of the international cabaret talent, but occasionally a local known exclusively within the British Isles.

A Theater Restaurant

The **London Room,** at the New London Centre, Parker Street, Drury Lane, W.1 (tel. 408-1001), is a theater restaurant set appropriately in the heart of London's theater district. The unique stage is fully automated—a horseshoe shape with two-tier dining. This, combined with the circular arrangement of the dining area, guarantees every guest a perfect view of all the action. The productions are all elaborately staged, with spectacular sets, colorful costumes, and glamorous showgirls. Emcees present revues often focusing on the musicals for which the Drury Lane district is so famous. Each evening there's a "star time," when international and British celebrities perform. A cabaret begins each night at 10:30 p.m., and you can dance right up to closing time at 1 a.m. The four-course dinner, consisting of seasonal specialties is superb. Admission is £14.50 ($28.28) Sunday to Friday, rising to £16.50 ($32.16) on Saturday. However, including drinks, the price goes up to £18.45 ($35.98) Sunday to Friday, to £20.45 ($39.88) on Saturday. Call in advance for reservations. Tube: Holborn.

From Madrigal to Modern

Tiddy Dols, 2 Hertford St., W.1 (tel. 499-2357), is a cluster of nine 18th-century houses in Mayfair's Shepherd Market. It's become one of London's hottest choices for dinner and entertainment, costing about £14.50 ($28.28) per head, including everything. The ground floor is restored and furnished in the Georgian manner, although the downstairs is more rustic, with exposed beams and all sorts of alcoves, nooks, and crannies. A young, friendly English staff serves you with a personal flair. Tiddy Dols is open seven nights a week for dinner and entertainment, serving from 6 p.m. to 1 a.m. The cuisine is old English, featuring such dishes as jugged hare, kipper mousse, roast pheasant, beef Wellington, many fruits and fools, and the famous gingerbread from which the establishment takes its name. Tiddy Dols is named after an eccentric seller of gingerbread who attended May Fair in the 18th century, singing, "Tid-dy Ti, Tid-dy ti-ti, Tid-y ti-dy, Doll!" as he sold the product of his special recipe, which the restaurant still makes today. Tiddy Dols also features such appropriate entertainers as Lord Julian Shepherd, the village town crier, Instant Sunshine, the Mayfair Syncopators, and two young men singing and playing madrigals to modern music on their extraordinary range of instruments. Finally, there is dancing every night from 11 p.m. until the restaurant closes at 2 a.m. There is a new budget menu at £1.60 ($3.12). For this you can eat, for example, quiche Lorraine with a mixed side salad. There are also light suppers at £5.75 ($11.21) and £7.25 ($14.14). The latter might cover Isabelle's emerald soup, aubergine (eggplant) delight, golden pancakes stuffed with hot bananas, a glass of wine, french bread and butter, and coffee and cream. All prices are inclusive of VAT and service. Tube: Green Park.

Mediaeval Feestes

Beefeater by the Tower of London, Ivory House, St. Katharine's Dock, E.C.3 (tel. 408-1001), is housed in the historic vaults alongside the Thames where ivory was stored in days of yore. During the Napoleonic wars, the vaults served as a prison for captured French soldiers.

In this historic setting, Merrie Olde England comes alive every night from 8 p.m. to midnight in the form of an enormous, rollicking, medieval feast. When you first arrive, you'll be led down into the vaults where you're greeted by no less a personage than Henry VIII, surrounded by serving wenches, jester, and madrigal singers. In no time at all you'll be caught up in the spirit of the celebration and forget that these are actors playing the parts of characters who lived 400 years ago.

Entertainment begins at the reception, where you sip honeyed wine to the tune of a few fa-la-lahs and hey-nonny-noes, and continues between courses ("removes") during the meal. Your party will be led in procession to the long trestle tables, where you'll dine in typical Tudor fashion, using no utensils except a knife. The leader of each procession becomes the "head boy" who is host for the table, filling all the plates and calling for more bread or wine as necessary. If you are lucky enough to be chosen, you'll be given a tall white hat to mark your distinguished position.

The dinner consists of a five-course sumptuous feast, topped off by all the wine and ale you can drink. During the meal, the entertainment, in the forms of magicians, acrobats, and musicians continues. There's even a very believable duel between two knights. Be sure to hiss the villain! Dinner is followed by dancing. The cost for the entire evening of food, entertainment, and dancing is £19 ($37.05) weekdays, rising to £21 ($40.95) on Saturday. In season, the Beefeater is open nightly. Otherwise it is open only Wednesday through Saturday. Tube: Tower.

1502 A.D. Tudor Rooms, 80–81 St. Martin's Lane, W.C.2 (tel. 240-3978). If you want to eat, drink, and be merry, then this is the place to be. A sumptuous banquet with a choice of many main courses in the atmosphere of the Tudor period. There is continuous entertainment throughout the evening, with actors impersonating King Henry VIII, Anne Boleyn, Jane Seymour, the court jester, minstrels, and a dancing bear, while guests are served by so-called wenches. The feast is made up of pâté, served with toast, a glass of Olde English mead, a choice of soups, Henry's tidbits, a selection of baby chicken, fresh river trout, beef casserole, roast pork, or roast lamb, followed by a medley of sherbets and then cheese and apple.

There's a star cabaret with a Turkish belly dancer, jugglers, and comedians, followed by disco dancing from midnight until 2 a.m. The cost is £14 ($27.30) per person for the evening or £18.50 ($36.08) with a bottle of wine, a jug of punch, or two jugs of ale per person; all rates include VAT.

Additionally, King Henry's luncheon is available Monday to Friday from noon to 3 p.m. At that time, for £8.50 ($16.58), including VAT, you can sample a choice of soups and main courses, followed by sherbet. From 3 to 5 p.m. the staff serves a traditional English tea with sandwiches and pastries in medieval surroundings. Tube: Trafalgar Square.

Eroticism in Soho

Raymond Revuebar Theatre, Walkers Court, Brewer Street, W.1 (tel. 734-1593), is a world center of erotic entertainment. The stage show, *Festival of Erotica,* is presented three times nightly, Sunday included, at 7, 9, and 11 p.m. There are licensed bars, and patrons can take their drinks into the theater. The price of admission is £7.50 ($14.63), and there is no membership fee. Whisky is around £1.25 ($2.44) per large measure. Tube: Piccadilly Circus.

The **Nell Gwynne,** 69–70 Dean St., W.1 (tel. 437-3278), entrance on Meard Street, is a showcase for some of the most interesting and novel striptease acts in London. The acts at the Nell Gwynne Club begin at 6 p.m. and run until 11 p.m. with shows at two-hour intervals. It is noted for the unique sensual routines and comedy striptease. Audience participation is also there, but the management likes to keep it subtle. The entrance fee of £5 ($9.75) includes VAT.

That admission fee also admits you to the **Comedy Store** on the same premises. Otherwise, you pay from £3 ($5.85) Wednesday through Friday and £4 ($7.80) on Saturday. There is dancing to disco music, with live shows by up-and-coming (and some arrived) comedians at 11 p.m. on Wednesday, Thursday, and Friday (also 8 p.m. on Friday and Saturday as well as midnight on Saturday). Drinks cost £2 ($3.90) for a double, and there are light snacks, pizzas, chicken in the basket, and scampi, with a meal priced at about £5 ($9.75) per person. Tube: Tottenham Court Road.

THE DISCOS: A firmly entrenched London institution, the disco is nevertheless as vulnerable as the Stone of Scone. Many of them open, enjoy a quick but fast-fading popularity, then close. Some possible favorites that may still be going strong upon your arrival are the following.

The **Marquee**, 90 Wardour St., W.1 (tel. 437-6603), is considered one of the best known centers for rock in Europe. Its reputation goes back to the '50s, but it remains forever young, in touch with the sounds of the future. Famous groups such as the Stones played at the Marquee long before their names spread beyond the shores of England. Fortunately, you don't have to be a member—you just pay at the door. If you have a Student Union Card from any country, it will cost you less to enter. The entrance fees vary, but usually fall in the £1 ($1.95) to £2.50 ($4.88) range, depending on who is appearing. There's a coffee and a Coke bar for light snacks; those 18 or older can order hard drinks. Many well-known musicians frequent the place regularly on their nights off. The quite small and very crowded club is one of the few which features live music. Hours are from 7 to 11 p.m. seven nights a week. Tube: Piccadilly Circus.

Music, 197 King's Rd., S.W.3 (tel. 352-9255), is one of the largest and most jam-packed of the disco-pubs of Chelsea. The DJ booth is a side pulpit. Entrance on Tuesday and Thursday is £1.50 ($2.93) before 10 p.m., then £3 ($5.85) thereafter. However, on Friday and Saturday night door charges are £4 ($7.80) all night. Beer goes for 80p ($1.56), a lager for 86p ($1.68). Bar snacks such as pies and pizzas are available in the 80p ($1.56) to £1.90 ($3.71) range. On Sunday admission is free, and the club is closed on Monday and Wednesday. The **Six Bells** pub is reached by a separate front entrance and provides a quiet drink in old-fashioned surroundings. In summer, any night of the week, you may want to take your mug of lager and stroll out into the garden where you'll seemingly meet half the young guys and gals of London. Tube: Sloane Square.

Valbonne, 62 Kingly St., off Regent Street, W.1 (tel. 439-7242), offers disco music noisy and heavy on the beat. The decor is now changed to modern, with mirrors and futuristic furniture. Masses of flashing and colored changing lights make a feature of the dance floor. There's a 100-inch video screen, showing a multitude of pictures. A light machine flashes words and sentences on the walls. Of the three bars, one is a quieter cocktail lounge, the others merely places to drink.

Admission to this fun palace of lights is £3 ($5.85) for women, £4 ($7.80) for men, Monday through Wednesday. Otherwise, both sexes pay the same: £4 ($7.80) for both men and women on Thursday and £5 ($9.75) on Friday and Saturday. There's an à la carte menu with a basic selection, offering meals that range from £7 ($13.65) to £8 ($15.60) per person, plus drinks. Tube: Piccadilly Circus.

Samantha's, 3 New Burlington St., W.1 (tel. 734-6249), just off Regent Street, has been one of London's most popular discos and nightspots since it opened about two decades ago. The central feature of the club is, of course, the disco, with its sound and light system controlled by a disc jockey who has taken up residence inside an E-type Jaguar. Flashing colored lights and curved mirrors create a surrealistic setting for the endless parade of youthful, energetic dancers. Besides the two bars which flank the disco, Samantha's offers several other facilities for those who require a momentary escape from the hectic vibrations of the main dance floor.

"Samantha's Playroom" is the favorite gathering spot for pinball or pool enthusiasts. A second area of bars and a smaller dance floor with quieter music are set apart from the disco so that even the highest decibels do not penetrate. Upstairs is one of Samantha's later creations, Sir Harry's Bar, where you can sip cocktails in a tropical atmosphere of cane furniture and animal skins. Admission to Samantha's is £4 ($7.80) per person or £7 ($13.65) per couple, which gives you access to any part of the club. Drinks average about £1.40 ($2.73), but you'll pay more for the "super cocktails" in Sir Harry's.

ROCK: **Rockgarden Restaurant & Dancehall,** 6–7 The Piazza, Old Covent Garden, W.C.2 (tel. 836-1929). Virtually every current major rock band in Britain has played at the Rockgarden in their infancy. The doors open every night at 7:30 p.m. and stay that way until 2 a.m. from Monday through Thursday. On Friday and Saturday, hours are until 3 a.m., and until midnight on Sunday. Set times are usually at 10 and 11 p.m. (on weekends, it's half an hour later). Admission is £1.50 ($2.93) or more, the more depending on the group. The restaurant is open Monday till Wednesday from 11:30 a.m. to 2 a.m. (Thursday, Friday, and Saturday from 11 a.m. till 6 in the morning of the next day; on Sunday from noon till midnight). Typical dishes include spare ribs at £3.45 ($6.73) and ratatouille at £1.50 ($2.93), although most diners prefer various burgers with toppings for about £2.30 ($4.49). Tube: Covent Garden.

JAZZ: **Ronnie Scott's,** 47 Frith St., W.1 (tel. 439-0747), has long been the citadel of modern jazz in Europe. Featured on almost every bill is an American band, often with a top-notch singer. The best English and American groups are booked. It's in the heart of Soho, a ten-minute walk from Piccadilly Circus via Shaftesbury Avenue, and worth an entire evening. You can not only saturate yourself in the best of jazz, but get reasonably priced drinks and dinners as well. There are three separate areas: the Main Room, the Upstairs Room, and the Downstairs Bar. You don't have to be a member, although you can join if you wish. The nightly entrance fee averages around £5 ($9.75) for members, £6.50 ($12.68) for nonmembers, depending on who is appearing. If you have a student ID you are granted considerable reductions on entrance fees, providing you come before 9:30 p.m., Monday through Thursday, without making a reservation beforehand. Drinks cost around 65p ($1.50) for whisky. The Main Room is open Monday through Saturday from 8:30 p.m. to 3 a.m. You can either stand at the bar to watch the show or sit at a table, where you can order a three-course dinner for around £8 ($15.60). The Downstairs Bar is more intimate, a quiet rendezvous where you can meet and talk with the regulars, usually some of the world's most talented musicians. The Upstairs Room is a disco, with unusual sculptured foam seating, where you can either dance or drink. On most nights a live band is featured. Incidentally, if you bypass the other two floors, you can get in here at a reduced entrance fee of around £3 ($5.85). Tube: Tottenham Court Road.

The **100 Club,** 100 Oxford St., W.1 (tel. 636-0933), is a serious contender for the title of London's finest jazz center. The emphasis here is strictly on the music, which begins each evening at 7:30 p.m. and lasts until midnight. Membership in the club costs £4 ($7.80) per year, and admission is usually between

£2 ($3.90) and £3 ($5.85). Without membership you'll pay an additional 50p (98¢). On Thursday nights, West Indian reggae is presented, but jazz—all kinds of jazz—is performed on the other six nights. The scheduled performers vary every night, so you'll have to phone ahead for that evening's program. However, you're sure to see the cream of jazz at the 100 Club, including such bands as Ken Colyer's All Star Jazzmen, Chris Barber's Band, and Mr. Acker Bilk and his Paramount Jazz Band. The club's menu features Creole cooking. There's also a fully licensed bar, serving liquor, wine, and beer. Tube: Tottenham Court Road.

A much cheaper way to hear jazz is at one of the many pubs in the West End offering it on certain nights of the week. Some charge admission; others allow you to listen for the price of your drink.

The **Bull's Head,** Barnes Bridge, S.W.13 (tel. 876-5241), offers live jazz all week, with musical happenings that sometimes get very lively indeed. The modern jazz is said by many to be the best in town. Weekdays it attracts shoppers and fashion designers to its old English snackbar, which is a fine place to meet for lunch.

Pubs offering music for the price of a drink include the following, but you should telephone first to make sure there is a performance on the night you wish to go: **The Angel,** 73 Lambeth Walk, S.E.11 (tel. 735-4309; tube to Lambeth North); **Moonlight Club,** at Railway Hotel, 100 West End Lane, N.W.6 (tel. 624-7611; tube to Kiburn Park); **New Golden Lion,** Fulham Road, S.W.6 (tel. 385-3942; tube to Fulham Broadway).

GAMBLING: London was a gambling metropolis long before anyone had ever heard of Monte Carlo and when Las Vegas was an anonymous sandpile in the desert. From the Regency period until halfway into the 19th century, Britain was more or less governed by gamblers. Lord Sandwich invented the snack named after him so he wouldn't have to leave the card table for a meal. Prime Minister Fox was so addicted that he frequently went to a cabinet meeting straight from the green baize table.

Queen Victoria's reign changed all that, as usual, by jumping to the other extreme. For more than a century, games of chance were so rigorously outlawed that no barmaid dared to keep a dice cup on the counter.

The pendulum swung again in 1960 when the present queen gave her Royal Assent to the new "Betting and Gaming Act." According to this legislation, gambling was again permitted in "bona fide clubs" by members and their guests.

Since London's definition of a "club" is as loose as a rusty screw in a cardboard wall, this immediately gave rise to the current situation, which continues to startle, amaze, and bewilder foreign visitors. For the fact is that you come across gambling devices in the most unlikely spots, such as discos, social clubs, and cabaret restaurants. All of which may, by the haziest definition, qualify as "clubs."

The more legitimate gambling clubs offer very pleasant trimmings in the shape of bars and restaurants, but their central theme is unequivocally the flirtation with Lady Luck. There are at least 25 of them in the West End alone, with many scattered through the suburbs. And the contrasts between them are much sharper than you find in the Nevada casinos.

Owing to a new law, casinos are not allowed to advertise, and if they do, they are likely to lose their licenses. Their appearance in a travel guide that doesn't accept advertising is still considered "advertising"—hence, I cannot recommend specific clubs as in the past.

However, most hall porters can tell you where you can gamble in London. It is not illegal to gamble, just to advertise it. You'll be required to become a member of your chosen club, and must wait 24 hours before you can play the tables, then strictly for cash. Most common games are roulette, blackjack, punto banco, and baccarat. Most casinos, as mentioned, have restaurants where you can expect a good standard of cuisine at a reasonable price.

CHESS: If you consider yourself a buff and wish to challenge the English or whomever, then Sunday from 10 a.m. to 7:30 p.m. is your time, and the venue is **Prompt Corner,** the Hampstead Restaurant, 1 South End Rd., N.W.3 (tel. 794-2846; tube to Hampstead).

FOLK MUSIC: The 20th-century troubadour makes his way to a smoke-gets-in-your-eyes candlelit haven called the **Troubadour Coffee House,** 265 Old Brompton Rd., S.W.5 (tel. 370-1434). The Troubadour is open to nonmembers. At one time, this club was young at heart, a pacesetter in a new kind of unpretentious, natural entertainment. It still offers many happy nights to an attractive, young crowd (if you can squeeze in).

You can dine upstairs, again if you can find a seat. From the ceiling hang musical instruments of every shape and size; the walls are covered with unusual trade signs of the Victorian era. Prices are quite reasonable, and the food consists of omelets, spaghetti bolognese, salads, and the like. The average one-course meal goes for £1.20 ($2.34), the price going up to £2.50 ($4.88) for two courses. Tube: Earl's Court.

FOR DANCING: Café de Paris, Coventry Street, off Piccadilly Circus, W.1 (tel. 437-2036), is a legend. Once Robert Graves considered it a worthy subject for a book; the Duke of Windsor went there to see Noël Coward perform. Now part of the Mecca chain, it is elaborately decorated with chandeliers. Changing lights set the mood. A band alternates with disco for dancing seven nights a week. According to the day and time (it's cheaper before 9:30 p.m.), admission prices range from £1.80 ($3.51) to £3 ($5.85). On Tuesday, women are admitted free. A three-course meal with a glass of wine and coffee comes to about £8 ($15.60). They do tea dances, with an admission costing £1.25 ($2.44). Another £1.85 ($3.61) gets you a pot of tea, a sandwich, and a piece of cake. Tube: Piccadilly Circus.

A CULTURAL COMPLEX: In the old **Riverside Studios,** Crisp Road, Hammersmith, W.6, an enterprising young group has developed a complex of theaters and exhibition rooms where, under the directorship of Peter Gill, unknown and not-so-unknown artists can demonstrate their skills. In the film theater seasons of movies demonstrate the producer's art or that of the camera person; visiting orchestras and dance teams perform nightly, and, in the restaurant, there is generally an exhibition of paintings or collages.

The restaurant is open from 11 a.m. to 11 p.m. Tuesday through Saturday, 12:30 to 11 p.m. on Sunday, and 11 a.m. to 6 p.m. on Monday, serving mostly homemade meals. A filling repast will cost about £3 ($5.85). The bar serves real ale among other beverages during licensing hours. Current programs are available throughout London, and the studios are well worth a visit, lying just a five-minute walk from Hammersmith underground station. Telephone the box office at 748-3354. Tickets for concerts, films, and plays cost about £3.50 ($6.83), but are increased on occasions when well-known performers appear.

VAUDEVILLE: This lives on in London on a grand scale.

Palladium, Argyle Street, W.1 (tel. 437-7373). World-famed for the best of vaudeville, it is equivalent to the former Palace in New York. Performers from America, the continent, and England can be seen here in acts that sometimes border on the spectacular. Seats normally range from around £2.50 ($4.88) to £8 ($15.60) for orchestra stalls, but it depends on who's appearing. Prices can go much higher. Tube: Oxford Circus.

Victoria Palace, Victoria Street, S.W.11 (tel. 834-1317), near Victoria Station, presents comedy, variety, and light entertainment, all at popular prices. Tube: Victoria Station.

GAY NIGHTLIFE: The most reliable source of information on all gay clubs and activities is the **Gay Switchboard** (tel. 837-7324). The staff there runs a 24-hour service of information on places and activities catering openly to homosexual men and women. The *Gay News,* available from some street news stalls, also carries advertisements. However, here are some suggestions: most are membership clubs which, nevertheless, welcome overseas visitors.

The Heaven, The Arches, Villiers Street, Charing Cross, W.C.2 (tel. 839-3852), is reckoned to be the largest and most sophisticated disco in all of Europe, with several bars and fantastic lighting and sounds from the nonstop disco. Once the Global Village, this is now the hottest gay spot in town. Membership is £20 ($39) for male and female gays only. Members are admitted free until 11 p.m.; after that, they pay a £1 ($1.95) entrance fee. Others pay an entrance fee of £3 ($5.85) at all times. The club is open Monday through Saturday. Tube: Charing Cross.

The Subway Club, 28 Leicester Square, W.C.2 (tel. 930-6986), is open from 10 p.m. to 3:30 a.m. Entrance is by membership only, which costs £10 ($19.50) per person, male or female. Dress is strict—denims, leather, or uniform. This is a heavy gay cruising club with pool, video, and wild U.S.-style disco. Food at the bar includes pizzas, hamburgers, and breakfast served in the early morning. Tube: Leicester Square.

The Copacabana, 180 Earls Court Rd., S.W.5 (tel. 373-3407), is a gay drinking place, with a £3 ($5.85) membership charge. There is free entrance to members until midnight; after that, a £1 ($1.95) fee. Others pay a £2 ($3.90) entrance fee at most times, more on weekends. Dress is optional, but no transvestites please. Drinks are half price until midnight, then you pay the whole whack. Tube: Earl's Court.

EAST END DRAG PUBS: In the East End is a series of pubs offering entertainment nightly. Drag acts (female impersonators) are the chief form of amusement. The English, especially the Cockneys of the East End, love to giggle and scream over the caricatures of men satirizing women. Many female impersonator acts find their way into the posh West End clubs which many of our readers will find too expensive. However, talent without all the fancy trappings appears almost nightly in some of these Victorian pubs. You pay no admission, no cover, no minimum—one of the bargain entertainment values in London.

One of the best is the **Union Tavern,** 146 Camberwell New Road, S.E.5 (tel. 735-3605)—Oval tube or bus 36 from Marble Arch. Some of London's top drag artists perform here. You should arrive earlier to get a comfortable seat. The "ladies" tend to make for a hysterical night. Two of the favorites (by now all the habitués know their acts) are bejeweled, begowned, bewigged, even breasted—a couple of sex sirens who do mime recordings of stars. Hopefully, you'll hear their rendition of Shirley Temple in *Animal Crackers* or Carol Channing in *Gentlemen Prefer Blondes.* A half pint of lager costs only 35p (68¢). Drag shows with gay disco or live groups are presented from 8 p.m. on Wednesday, Friday, and Saturday. There are also performances at 12:30 p.m. on Sunday and again at 8 p.m. The tavern closes nightly at 11 (at 10:30 on Sunday.

READER'S DRAG CLUB SUGGESTION: "I've often recommended two drag clubs to North American visitors. The **Black Cap,** 171 Camden High St., N.W.1 (tel. 485-1742), features a different drag act each night—some are hilarious, others grotesque, but it's excellent for a fun evening. The **Royal Vauxhall Tavern,** 372 Kennington Lane, S.E.11 (tel. 582-0833), lies on the south of the Thames, over the Vauxhall Bridge and near the Vauxhall tube station. It offers drag acts nightly—some of them original, some in pantomime to records. There's no cover charge—just the drinks you buy" (Howard Archer, London, England).

OPERA AND BALLET: London has treasures to offer the opera and ballet lover. The **Royal Opera House,** at Bow Street, is the center of the Royal Opera Company and the Royal Ballet. The Opera House advance box office, at 48 Floral St., is open from 10 a.m. to 7:30 p.m., Monday to Saturday (tel. 240-1066). A good seat can be had for £10 ($19.50), and sometimes one of the finest seats in the house will cost you no more than £16.50 ($32.16). Sixty-five rear amphitheater seats will be available for sale at 10 a.m. on the day of performance. Tube: Covent Garden.

English National Opera, London Coliseum, St. Martin's Lane, W.C.2 (tel. 836-3161 for reservations; 240-5258 for credit-card booking and inquiries), is the state-supported opera company that performs in English and draws many enthusiastic audiences. Light operas are often included in the repertory, and tickets can cost as little as £2.50 ($4.88). These cheap seats are in the balcony and may be reserved in advance, although a limited number are available on the day of the performance only. The average visitor may find the upper circle seats preferable, with prices ranging for most performances from £6.30 ($12.29). Tube: Trafalgar Square.

The **D'Oyly Carte Company** has no permanent home in London or elsewhere. Information can be obtained from the company's office address: Tabard House, 116 Southwark St., London SE1 0TA (tel. 928-7322). At **Gilbert's House,** which is now run as a hotel and restaurant, Gilbert and Sullivan concerts are given every Sunday night during dinner. It is called Grim's Dyke Country Hotel, Old Redding, Harrow Weald, Middlesex.

The **Barbican Centre,** The Barbican, E.C.2, is newly built and considered the largest art and exhibition center in Western Europe. It was created to make a perfect setting in which to enjoy good music and theater from comfortable, roomy seating.

The theater is now the home of the Royal Shakespeare Company which, of course, performs a wide range of works other than plays of the Bard. The Concert Hall is the permanent home of the London Symphony Orchestra and host to visiting performers.

There are often lunchtime concerts where the admission is £2.50 ($4.88) for the 45 minutes or so. Otherwise, seats are priced from £2.80 ($5.46) to £9 ($17.55) for evening performances. Matinees in the theater start at £1.75

($3.41), going upward to £7 ($13.65). In the evening, low-cost seats are still featured, although the best seats are likely to go for £9 ($17.55).

There are a number of bars and a self-service café and wine bar open from 9 a.m. to 10:30 p.m. Monday to Saturday, and from noon to 10:30 p.m. on Sunday. Called the Waterside Café, it has views over the artificial lake. In good weather patrons can sit on the terrace in the open air.

The main restaurant, the Cut Above, also overlooks the lake, a more formal place with a Carvery open from noon to 3 p.m. and from 6 p.m. until the last orders are taken half an hour after the end of the performance. The cost of a meal where you carve as much as you want from the succulent joints of meats is £8.50 ($16.58). Table reservations can be made by telephoning 588-3008.

The following numbers will be useful—628-8795 for the box office for seats for concerts and theatrical performances; 928-9760 for 24-hour information on performances of concerts; and 628-2295 for information about theatrical performances. Tube: Barbican.

CONCERTS: There are at least five major orchestras performing in London. They are: the London Philharmonic, the Royal Philharmonic, the BBC, the London Symphony, and the New Philharmonia.

These orchestras are to be heard mainly in the **Royal Festival Hall,** while in the adjoining **Queen Elizabeth Hall** and **Purcell Room** there are concerts of chamber music, lieder recitals, and poetry readings, among other presentations. In all, roughly 100 events take place each month in these three concert halls. Tube to Waterloo Station. Tickets are available from the Royal Festival Hall box office (tel. 928-3191), or the usual booking agents.

Royal Albert Hall, Kensington Gore, S.W.7 (tel. 589-8212). Acoustic improvements and other alterations have made this one of the world's finest auditoriums. The BBC Promenade Concerts are held here for eight weeks in summer. Throughout the year there are performances by top orchestras and artists, brass bands, and all manner of events ranging from covered court lawn tennis to the annual Royal British Legion Festival of Remembrance. Ticket prices vary according to the type of event.

Wigmore Hall, 36 Wigmore St., W.1 (tel. 935-2141). At this intimate auditorium, you'll hear excellent recitals and concerts. There are regular series, master concerts by chamber music groups and instrumentalists, song recital series, and concerts featuring special composers or themes throughout the year. In the summer, Wigmore Summer Nights and Sunday morning concerts are featured. Many good seats are in the £2 ($3.90) range. A free list of the month's concerts is available from the hall. Tube: Bond Street or Oxford Circus.

At **Victoria Embankment Gardens,** adjacent to Charing Cross underground station, bands from Her Majesty's Guards and Regiments as well as the London Police and Fire Brigade give twice-daily concerts from late May to early September. Special concerts by visiting bands from high schools in the United States, Canada, and Australia are occasionally arranged between the regular concerts. Details of concert times and programs are displayed in the gardens. A charge is only made when a deck chair is used.

City of Westminster Arts Council, Marylebone Library, Marylebone Road, N.W.1 (tel. 828-8070, ext. 4052), sponsors concerts, recitals, and exhibitions throughout the year. These are held in small and often little-known halls around the city. For current information, refer to the address above. The average entrance charge is around £2 ($3.90) and some promotions, such as exhibitions, are free. In most cases, payment is at the door, and no advance reservations are necessary. *What's On in Westminster* lists a wide range of such promotions. Free copies can be collected from the above address. Most of the shows are more of the amateur presentation.

5. Taking the Tours

In addition to the sights you can see in London by foot, or by using the tubes, there are numerous attractions that can be reached via several inexpensive coach tours. As an added bonus, there are dozens of fascinating trips that can be made on the Thames.

EASIEST WAY TO SEE LONDON: For the first-timer, the quickest and most economical way to bring the big city into focus is to take a two-hour, 20-mile circular tour of the West End and The City, the **'Round London Sightseeing Tour,** which is offered by London Transport, the city's official bus company. The cost is £2.60 ($5.07) for adults, £1.50 ($2.93) for children under 16. Some journeys are by open-top buses. Tours pass virtually all the major places of interest in Central London. There is no guide. Passengers are given an illustrated diagram of the route, showing points of interest.

The one drawback is that seats cannot be reserved, but the buses run with great frequency every day (except Christmas). From March to October, tours are at hourly intervals from 10 a.m. to 8 p.m. (9 a.m. to 4 p.m. in the winter). The starting points for the tour are Piccadilly Circus, Marble Arch, and Victoria.

LONDON'S WEST END AND THE CITY: If you prefer a more detailed look at the city's sights, then **London Transport** offers two highly regarded conducted coach tours.

For a look at the West End, a three-hour tour is offered, passing Westminster Abbey (guided tour), Houses of Parliament, Horse Guards, Trafalgar Square, and Piccadilly Circus, including the changing of the guard. The tour starts at 10 a.m. every day except Sunday from mid-March to mid-October, and the fare is £6 ($11.70) for adults £4.50 ($8.78) for children under 14.

London Transport's other popular three-hour tour is of The City, and includes guided trips to the Tower of London and St. Paul's Cathedral. The fare for this is £8 ($15.60) for adults, £5.50 ($10.73) for children. The tour is operated from March to October, leaving daily at 2 p.m. In summer the tour also leaves on Sunday.

These two tours are combined to form the London Day Tour, which costs £15 ($29.25) for adults, £11 ($21.45) for children under 14, including lunch. The tour leaves at 10 a.m.

The tours begin at Victoria Coach Station, at the corner of Buckingham Palace Road and Elizabeth Street. To reserve seats, go to the London Transport Travel Information Offices at: St. James's Park, Piccadilly Circus, King's Cross, Euston, Oxford Circus, or Victoria tube stations. Reservations cannot be made over the phone.

EVENING CRUISE TO GREENWICH: Thames Launches Limited offers a two-hour evening scenic cruise, leaving at 7:30 p.m. from Charing Cross pier on the Thames (tube to Embankment). The boat ride costs £2 ($3.90) round trip, and takes you on a cruise by the Houses of Parliament, Scott's *Discovery,* the Tower—all the way to Greenwich, where the last of the great clippers, *Cutty Sark,* is in drydock. The tour is operated May through September.

There's also a Disco Cruise, costing £7.25 ($14.14), including a free drink, a two-course buffet meal, and, of course, disco dancing while you drift past the sights. A dinner/theater cruise, with a traditional three-course meal and old-time music hall entertainment with top performers, costs £18.50 ($36.08). For reservations, telephone 839-2349, and for information on other boat trips, call 870-6158.

A CANAL BOAT IN LITTLE VENICE: When you get tired of fighting the London traffic, you might want to come here and take a peaceful trip (1½ hours) aboard the traditionally painted Narrow Boat *Jason* and her butty boat *Serpens.* Come for lunch along the most colorful part of the Regents Canal in the heart of London. The boat is moored in Blomfield Road, just off Edgware Road in Maida Vale. Little Venice is the junction of two canals and was given its name by Lord Byron.

To inquire about bookings, including the Boatman's Basket Luncheon Trip, get in touch with **Jason's Trip,** Opp. No. 60 Blomfield Rd., Little Venice, W.9 (tel. 286-3428). Advance booking is essential during high season. If you come by tube, take the Bakerloo line to Warwick Avenue. Face the church, turn left, and walk up Clifton Villas to the end and turn right (about two minutes). If you arrive early, you can browse around the shop which sells many brightly colored traditionally painted canal wares.

On the trip you'll pass through the long Maida Hill tunnel under Edgware Road, through Regents Park, the Mosque, the Zoo, Lord Snowdon's Aviary, past the Pirate's Castle to Camden Lock and return to Little Venice. The season begins Good Friday and lasts through September. During April and May, the boats run at 2 and 4 p.m. In June, July, August, and September, there is an additional morning trip as well as trips during the afternoon, but always telephone first. Refreshments are served on all trips, including a prebooked lunch on the 2 p.m. trip. The fare for a day trip is £1.75 ($3.41) for adults and 85p ($1.66) for children.

LONDON WALKS: J. W. **Travel,** 66 St. Michael's St., W.2 (tel. 262-9572). John Wittich, who owns J. W. Travel, started walking tours of London in 1960. He is a Freeman of the City of London and a member of two livery companies as well as having written six books on London walks. He is also director of the London History Fellowship. There is no better way to search out the unusual, the beautiful, and the historic, than to take a walking tour. The walks are conducted by guides who really know their business, and you don't need a reservation. Tours take place whatever the weather. The cost is 75p ($1.46) for adults, 50p (98¢) for students with ID cards, and free to children with adults. Some of the titles of the organized tours are "Steeple-chasing," "Dick Whittington," and "The Great Fire of London Walk."

You can hunt for ghosts or walk in the steps of Jack the Ripper, the infamous East End murderer of prostitutes in the 1880s. Relive Britain's monarchist past by wandering through the Royal Parks and Belgravia, or discovering the relics of Tudor London. Investigate the London of Dickens and Sherlock Holmes, or taste the delights of an evening's drinking in four historic pubs. These and many other walks (Roman London; 1660s: Great Plague and Great Fire; Ghosts) are included in the program of unusual and historical walks organized by **London Walks,** 139 Conway Rd., Southgate, London N14 7BH (tel. 882-2763). Walks take place on weekends all through the year and during the week throughout the summer. The cost is £1.30 ($2.54) for adults; children under 16 go free. No reservation is required. Get in touch with the above address for details.

Another small and enthusiastic company, a husband and wife team, offering a vast variety of London walks is **Discovering London.** It's operated by a Scot, Alex Cobban, a historian of some note whose guides are professionals. Mainly on Saturday and Sunday, but during the week as well, scheduled walks are planned, starting at easily found underground stations, to Dickens's London, Roman London, Ghosts of the City, the Inns of Court—Lawyers' London, Jack the Ripper. Mr. Cobban's knowledge of Sherlock Holmes is immense. No advance booking is necessary, and the walks cost £1.20 ($2.34), children under 16 go free, and students with ID cards are charged £1 ($1.95). Each walk takes about 1½ to 2 hours, except for the pub tours which usually are in the evening and allow time for drinking in interesting pubs. At these you pay for whatever you wish to drink, and enjoy the pleasure of jostling at the bar with the locals. Write, enclosing an international reply coupon, for a detailed schedule of the walks available during your stay in London. The address is Discovering London, 11 Pennyfields, Warley, Brentwood, Essex CM14 5JP, U.K. (tel. Brentwood 0277/213-704).

Theatreland Tours, 10 St. Martin's Ct., St. Martin's Lane, W.C.2 (tel. 836-0915), give you the exclusive opportunity to visit London's theaterland and to go backstage at a West End theater. After coffee at the Reception Centre at 10 St. Martin's Ct., off St. Martin's Lane, you leave in the company of an actor/guide on foot through Covent Garden and theaterland. You visit the city's oldest street, now the home of many of London's theatrical managers, as well as the Actors' Church with its many memorials to famous personages, including Ellen Terry.

The tour continues past many well-known theaters and pubs frequented by actors and theater managers, and also includes a visit to one of the theaters in the area, a behind-the-scenes preview. The tour finishes either with lunch at the Albery Theatre or with tea at the Waldorf Hotel. The cost is £7.50 ($14.63) per person, and the hours are from 10:30 a.m. to 2 p.m. The organizer is Josephine Burke. Tube: Trafalgar Square.

TOURS FOR CHILDREN: Junior Jaunts, 4A William St., S.W.1 (tel. 235-4750), is a responsible organization which will take children 5 to 15 years old off your hands for the entire day. The service provides tours for parties of no more than six children at a time to various points of interest in London. The small number in each group assures you that your child will be carefully supervised and that his or her interests will be taken into consideration. Tours range from a visit to the Regents Park Zoo to a trip to Buckingham Palace or the Tower of London to a museum tour which includes no less than six popular museums in London. Tours are flexible, and suggestions from the children are often incorporated into the activities. Tours cost from £15 ($29.25), and children are collected from their London hotel and returned to it. Tube: Knightsbridge.

6. One-Day Trips from London

It would be sad to leave England without ever having ventured into the countryside, at least for a day. The English are the greatest excursion travelers in the world, forever dipping into their own rural areas to discover ancient abbeys, 17th-century village lanes, shady woods for picnic lunches, and stately mansions. From London, it's possible to take advantage of countless tours—either by conducted coach, boat, or via a do-it-yourself method on bus or train. On many trips, you can combine two or more methods of transportation; for example, you can go to Windsor by boat and return by coach or train.

In this section, you'll find a sampling of what is available—but, first, some general tips.

DO-IT-YOURSELF: Many hidden sightseeing surprises are in store for the adventurous traveler who doesn't depend on guides and scheduled routes. And this is possible even if you don't rent a car. Several means of transportation are available: coach, train, or boat.

Highly recommended are the previously described Green Line Coaches, operated by London Country Bus Services. You can go to the Green Line Enquiry Office at Victoria (Eccleston Bridge) and pick up Green Line timetables giving specific details on routes.

For longer tours, say to Stratford-upon-Avon, you will find the trains much more convenient. Often you can take advantage of the many bargain tickets outlined in Chapter I. For further information about trains to a specific location, go to the British Rail offices at Lower Regent Street, off Piccadilly, S.W.1 (tube to Piccadilly Circus).

THE BRITAINSHRINKERS: This is a bonanza for travelers who want to make several quickie trips into the heart of England, without having to check out of their hotel room in London. Scheduled full-day tours are operated by Road 'n' Rail Tours Ltd. in cooperation with British Rail. You're whisked out of London by train to your destination, where you hop on a waiting bus to visit the various sights during the day. You have a light lunch in a local pub, and there is also free time to shop or explore. A guide accompanies the tour from London and back. Your return is in time for dinner or the theater. Included in the rates are entrance fees and VAT.

For more information, telephone 589-0156. It's possible to call this number, even on weekends, providing you do so before 4:30 p.m.

On one day trip, you can visit Warwick Castle, Stratford-upon-Avon, and Coventry Cathedral, at a cost of £22.20 ($43.29) for adults, £13.80 ($26.91) for children under 16, and a further reduction for Britrail Pass holders, making the cost £15.90 ($31.01) for adults, £10.70 ($20.87) for children. It's also possible to visit Scotland on an overnight trip, at a cost of £96.20 ($187.59) for adults, £62.40 ($121.68) for children, with substantial reductions for holders of Britrail Passes. One of the most heavily booked tours is to Bath and Stonehenge, taking in Salisbury Cathedral, costing £24.70 ($48.17) for adults, £15.20 ($29.64) for children under 16, again with additional reductions for Britrail Pass holders.

It's better to write **Britainshrinkers,** 22 Hans Pl., London, S.W.1, than to get in touch with British Rail.

London Transport Tours

The official bus company, **London Transport,** takes the lead in conducted coach tours to the places of interest in and around London. The coach tours are accompanied by an experienced guide, and they start from Victoria Coach Station. It is necessary to reserve seats; this is done at the London Transport Travel Information Centres at the St. James's Park, Piccadilly Circus, Oxford Circus, Victoria, King's Cross, and Euston underground stations.

An outstanding coach tour is offered to **Windsor Castle** and **Hampton Court Palace,** a half day's adventure that also includes Eton College, Runnymede, and the Kennedy Memorial. The tour departs daily at 10 a.m., getting back at 4:15 p.m. Adults pay £13 ($25.35); children under 14, £11 ($21.45). Rates include lunch and the admission charge to the State Apartments at Windsor. The tours are operated daily in summer and four times a week from October to March.

There is also a super tour to **Greenwich,** leaving London by ferry downstream to visit the old tea clipper, *Cutty Sark,* then the Royal Observatory and the National Maritime Museum at Greenwich, returning to central London by coach. Cost, including lunch and admissions, is £11 ($21.45) for adults, £8 ($15.60) for children. Both tours leave from Victoria Coach Station at 10 a.m., returning there about 5 p.m.

The London Transport Round London two-hour tour, unguided and nonstop, starts from Piccadilly Circus, Victoria Station, or Marble Arch. A free map of the 20-mile route is provided. The cost is £2.40 ($4.68) for adults, £1.50 ($2.93) for children, and you pay on board. Tours generally operate every hour on the hour, but check that. They also run a Panoramic Tour for £3 ($5.85) lasting two hours, starting from Victoria Station only.

HAMPTON COURT: On the Thames, 13 miles west of London, this 16th-century palace of Cardinal Wolsey can teach us a lesson. Don't try to outdo your boss—particularly if he happens to be Henry VIII. The rich cardinal did just that. But the king had a lean and hungry eye. Wolsey, who eventually lost his fortune, power, and prestige, ended up giving his lavish palace to the Tudor monarch. In a stroke of oneupmanship, Henry took over, even outdoing the Wolsey embellishments. The Tudor additions included the Anne Boleyn gateway, with its 16th-century astronomical clock that even tells the high water mark at London Bridge. From Clock Court, you can see one of Henry's major contributions, the aptly named Great Hall, with its hammer-beam ceiling.

To judge from the movie *A Man for All Seasons,* Hampton Court had quite a retinue to feed. Cooking was done in the Great Kitchens, which may be visited today for an admission of 40p (78¢) for adults, 20p (39¢) for children. Henry cavorted through the various apartments with his wives of the moment —everybody from Anne Boleyn to Catherine Parr (the latter reversed things and lived to bury her erstwhile spouse). Charles I was imprisoned at one time, and temporarily managed to escape his jailers.

Although the palace enjoyed prestige and pomp in Elizabethan days, it owes much of its present look to William and Mary of Orange—or rather to Sir Christopher Wren. You can parade through the apartments today, filled as they are with porcelain, furniture, paintings, and tapestries. The King's Dressing Room is graced with some of the best art. In Queen Mary's closet, you'll find Pieter Brueghel the Elder's macabre *Massacre of the Innocents.* Tintoretto and Titian deck the halls of the King's Drawing Room. Finally, be sure to inspect the Royal Chapel (Wolsey wouldn't recognize it). To confound yourself totally, you may want to get lost in the serpentine shrubbery Maze in the garden.

The State Apartments may be visited year round—April to September, weekdays from 9:30 a.m. to 6 p.m., on Sunday from 11 a.m. to 6 p.m.; October to March, weekdays from 9:30 a.m. to 5 p.m., on Sunday from 2 to 5 p.m. The admission is £1.50 ($2.93) for adults, 70p ($1.37) for children. The off-season admission is 80p ($1.56) for adults, 40p (78¢) for children. There is an extra charge for admission to any special exhibition held at the palace. Entrance to the maze is 10p (20¢).

Frequent trains run from Waterloo to Hampton Court Station. To come by boat, apply to Thames Passenger Services, Westminster Pier, S.W.1 (tel. 930-0921). Or take bus 201, 206, 216, or 264 weekdays; 267 on Saturday and Sunday only. Green Line Coaches 716, 716A, and 718 will deliver you to Hampton Court in about half an hour from London.

Where to Eat

After visiting the palace, lunch at **Bastians**, Hampton Court Road, in East Molesey, Surrey (tel. 977-6074), an attractive old building with a large stone-floored hall, roaring log fire, and comfortable chairs. Here you order an apéritif and select your meal. Then you go into the simple dining room or, in summer, into the tiny garden to eat al fresco.

The French menu includes such appetizers as moules marinières in season, an enormous platter, or trout mousse. Main dishes include filet steak, a whole small chicken, and lamb cutlets in a light mustard sauce. These courses are served with a delicious variety of sauces and well-cooked vegetables, depending on the season and availability. Desserts include crème brulée, sorbets, and chocolate mousse, and there is a good cheese board. A carafe of house wine is always available. Expect to spend from £8 ($15.60), plus wine. Prices include VAT but not the 12½% service charge. The restaurant is open Monday to Friday from 12:30 to 2:30 p.m. for lunch, Monday to Saturday from 7 to 10.45 p.m. for dinner (until 11:15 p.m. Saturday evenings).

KEW GARDENS: Nine miles southwest of central London at Kew, near Richmond, are the **Royal Botanic Gardens,** among the best known in Europe, containing thousands of varieties of plants. But Kew is no mere pleasure garden—rather, it is a vast scientific undertaking that happens to be beautiful. A pagoda, erected in 1761, represents the "flowering" of chinoiserie. One of the oddities of Kew is a Douglas fir flagstaff, more than 220 feet high. The Palm House, built in the heyday of Victoria by Decimus Burton, is replete with torrid temperatures and cannibalistic-looking vegetation—a sort of south of Pago Pago setting.

Much interest focuses on the red-brick **Kew Palace** (dubbed the Dutch House), a former residence of King George III and Queen Charlotte. It is reached by walking to the northern tip of the Broad Walk. Now a museum, it was built in 1631 and contains memorabilia of the reign of George III, along with a royal collection of furniture and paintings. It is open only April to October from 11 a.m. to 5:30 p.m. daily (on Sunday from 2 to 6 p.m.). Admission is 50p (98¢) for adults, 30p (59¢) for children over 10. The gardens may be visited from 10 a.m. to 8 p.m. in summer, to 4 p.m. in winter. Admission is 10p (20¢). Closed Christmas Day and New Year's Day.

At the gardens, **Queen Charlotte's Cottage** has been restored to its original splendor. Built in 1772, it is half-timbered and thatched. George III is believed to have been the architect. The house has been restored in great detail, including the original Hogarth prints which hung on the downstairs walls. The cottage is open on weekends and bank holidays. The least expensive and most convenient way to visit the gardens is to take the District line subway to Kew. The most romantic way to come in summer is via a steamer from Westminster Bridge to Kew Pier.

GREENWICH: Greenwich Mean Time, of course, is the basis of standard time throughout most of the world, the zero point used in the reckoning of terrestrial longitudes since 1884. But Greenwich is also home of the Royal Naval College, the National Maritime Museum, and the Old Royal Observatory. In drydock at Greenwich Pier is the clipper ship *Cutty Sark*, as well as Sir Francis Chichester's *Gipsy Moth IV*.

About four miles from The City, Greenwich is reached by a number of methods, and part of the fun of making the jaunt is getting there. Ideally, you'll arrive by boat, as Henry VIII preferred to do on one of his hunting expeditions. In summer, launches leave at regular intervals from either the Charing Cross or Westminster piers. Actually, Westminster is preferred, because the boats from Charing Cross are usually filled with tour group passengers. You can take the tube to New Cross, then bus 171a or 177. Buses 70 and 188 run from the Surrey Docks tube station. The boats leave daily to Greenwich every 20 minutes from 10 a.m. to 7 p.m., costing £2.10 ($4.10) for adults, £1.20 ($2.34) for children for a round-trip ticket.

Unquestionably, the *Cutty Sark*—last of the great clippers—holds the most interest, having been seen by millions. At the spot where the vessel is now berthed stood the Ship Inn of the 19th century (Victorians came here for whitebait dinners, as they did to the Trafalgar Tavern). Ordered built by Capt. Jock Willis ("Old White Hat"), the clipper was launched in 1869 to sail the China tea trade route. It was named after the Witch Nannie in Robert Burns's *Tam o'Shanter* (note the figurehead). Yielding to the more efficient steamers, the *Cutty Sark* later was converted to a wool-clipper, plying the route between Australia and England. Before her retirement, she knew many owners, even different names, eventually coming to drydock at Cutty Sark Gardens, Greenwich Pier, S.E.10 (tel. 858-3445), in 1954. For 80p ($1.56) for adults, 40p (78¢) for children, the vessel may be boarded weekdays from 11 a.m. to 6 p.m., on Sunday from 2:30 to 6 p.m. It closes at 5 p.m. in winter.

A neighbor to the *Cutty Sark*—and also in drydock—is Sir Francis Chichester's *Gipsy Moth IV* (also tel. 858-3445), in which he circumnavigated the world in 1967. He single-handedly fought the elements in his vessel for 119 days. For 20p (39¢) for adults, 10p (20¢) for children, you can go aboard (same hours as *Cutty Sark*). It's usually closed on Friday.

The **Royal Naval College** grew up on the site of the Tudor palace in which Henry VIII and Elizabeth I were born. William and Mary commissioned Wren to design the present buildings in 1695 to house naval pensioners, and these became the Royal Naval College in 1873. The buildings are a baroque masterpiece, in which the Painted Hall (by Thornhill 1708–1727) and the chapel are outstanding. It is normally open to visitors between 2:30 and 5 p.m. (latest time of admission 4:45 p.m.) daily, except Thursday and certain public holidays. These days are published in daily papers.

The **National Maritime Museum**, built around Inigo Jones's 17th-century Palladian Queen's House, portrays Britain's maritime heritage. Actual craft, marine paintings, ship models, and scientific instruments are displayed, including the full-dress uniform coat that Lord Nelson wore at the Battle of Trafalgar. Other curiosities include the chronometer (or sea watch) used by Captain Cook when he made his Pacific explorations in the 1770s. At the **Old Royal Observatory**, see the Greenwich Meridian Line, the internationally accepted 0 degrees longitude, and an exhibit of mariner's instruments, from astrolabes to an atomic clock. The museum is open Tuesday through Friday from 9 a.m. to 6 p.m. (on Sunday from 2 to 5:30 p.m.) in summer, and Tuesday through Friday from 10 a.m. to 5 p.m. (on Sunday from 2 to 5 p.m.) in winter. On Saturday all year, hours are from 10 a.m. to 6 p.m. It's closed Christmas Eve, Christmas Day,

Boxing Day, New Year's Day, Good Friday, May bank holiday, and every Monday. Admission is free. Just off the Navigation Room, in the west wing, is a licensed restaurant.

Eating In Greenwich

Trafalgar Tavern, Park Row, S.E.10 (tel. 858-2437), overlooks the Thames at Greenwich and is surrounded by many attractions. Directly opposite the tavern is the Royal Naval College, and nearby are the *Cutty Sark,* the National Maritime Museum, Greenwich Royal Observatory, and the *Gypsy Moth IV.*

Traditional English dishes and seafood specialties are featured. Many of the fish have never seen the Thames, and, consequently, dishes such as whitebait do not appear on table d'hôte menus, but only on the à la carte. To begin your meal, you can order deep-fried whitebait. You might follow with Dover sole or roast goose cooked in a cider sauce. Also good is English lamb roasted with rosemary and carved at your table. A three-course meal costs from £14 ($27.30) per person, plus wine and service.

In its most recent redecoration, the tavern retained all the original artist's designs, and it has many antique and historical pieces of naval equipment. All its rooms are named after famous sea admirals. For example, there is the Nelson Room, the Hardy and the Hawke and Howe Bars, the Duncan Room, also the Collingwood Room, and the Rodney and Hood Bars.

Lunch is served from noon to 2:30 p.m.; dinner, from 6:30 to 10:30 p.m. (only lunch is served on Sunday).

The **Cutty Sark Free House,** Ballast Quay, Lassell Street, S.E.10 (tel. 858-3146), has plenty of local color on its Thames-side perch. About a half mile from the railway station, this English riverside tavern will dispense drinks in an atmosphere in which you can eavesdrop on the conversation of oldtime salts (head to the second floor for the Captain's Bar). At lunch and dinner, traditional English fare, such as whitebait suppers and English roast beef, is featured. Dinner costs around £10 ($19.50), exclusive of wine and service charge, and lunches go for around £6.75 ($13.16).

RUNNYMEDE: Two miles outside Windsor is the meadow on the south side of the Thames, in Surrey, where King John put his seal on the Great Charter. John may have signed the document up the river on a little island, but that's being technical. Today, Runnymede is also the site of the John F. Kennedy Memorial, one acre of English ground given to the United States by the people of Britain.

In accommodations, the **Runnymede Hotel,** Egham (tel. Egham 6171), stands in ten acres of landscaped grounds on the Thames, bordering the Mede. The setting, near the spot where King John signed the Magna Carta, is just 17 miles from the heart of London (Waterloo can be reached by fast train in about half an hour). The water-view garden hotel is newly built, but not blatantly contemporary, providing a clean-cut freshness, open-view lounges, plus 90 well-equipped bedrooms, each with its own private bath or shower, renting for £29 ($56.55) nightly in a single, £37 ($72.15) in a double, a continental breakfast and VAT included.

English and continental cuisines are served in the River Room which is built on two levels, giving every table a view of the garden and river. A set lunch costs £6 ($11.70), a set dinner going for £7.25 ($14.14), plus £1 ($1.95) if you chose your meat course from the trolley of roast joints. Dancing is on Friday and Saturday nights. An à la carte meal will cost about £14 ($27.30), plus another £2.50 ($4.88) for a half bottle of wine. At night the Anglers Bar is one of the most attractive along the Thames.

SYON PARK: Just nine miles from Piccadilly Circus, on 55 acres of the Duke of Northumberland's Thames-side estate, is one of the most beautiful spots in all of Great Britain. There's always something in bloom. Called "The Showplace of the Nation in a Great English Garden," Syon Park was opened to the public in 1968. A nation of green-thumbed gardeners is dazzled here, and the park is also educational, showing amateurs how to get the most out of their small gardens. The vast flower- and plant-studded acreage betrays the influence of "Capability" Brown, who laid out the grounds in the 18th century.

Particular highlights include a six-acre rose garden and the Great Conservatory, one of the earliest and most famous buildings of its type, housing everything from cacti to fuchsias. In it is also housed a walk-through aviary full of exotic and brilliantly colored birds. In the old dairy you will find an interesting aquarium.

Operated by the Gardening Center Limited, Syon was the site of the first botanical garden in England, created by the father of English botany, Dr. William Turner. Trees include a 200-year-old Chinese juniper, an Afghan ash, an Indian bean tree, and a "Liquidambar." The gardens are open all the year (except for Christmas and Boxing Day). The gates open at 10 a.m. and close at 6 p.m. In winter, after October 31, gates close at 4 p.m. Admission is 70p ($1.37) for adults, 40p (78¢) for children.

On the grounds is **Syon House,** built in 1547, the original structure incorporated into the Duke of Northumberland's present home. The house was later remade to the specifications of the first Duke of Northumberland in 1766. The battlemented facade is that of the original Tudor mansion, but the interior is from the 18th century, the design of Robert Adam. Basil Taylor said of the interior feeling: "You're almost in the middle of a jewel box." In the Middle Ages, Syon was a monastery, later suppressed by Henry VIII. Katharine Howard, the king's fifth wife, later imprisoned in the house before her scheduled beheading in 1542. The house may be visited from noon to 5 p.m. from Good Friday until the end of September. (It is closed every other Friday but Good Friday, and every Saturday, because the duke is in residence during the summer. Adults can purchase a combined ticket to the gardens and house at a cost of £1.30 ($2.54), and children are charged 65p ($1.27). There is a restaurant for light meals and snacks. For more information, telephone 560-0881.

A DAY AT THE RACES: Within easy reach of central London, there are horse-racing tracks at Kempton Park, Sandown Park, and, the most famous of all, Epsom, where the Derby is the main feature of the summer meeting. Entrance to the courses for a day's racing can be as little as £1.50 ($2.93), but of course you pay more for a seat in a grandstand or on one of the most prestigious race days. Racing isn't conducted every weekend, so you should telephone **United Racecourses** at Epsom (tel. Epsom 26311) for information of the next meeting. You can drive yourself or, if you want to travel by rail, dial 928-5100 for details of train services.

WINDSOR, OXFORD, AND THE HOME COUNTIES

1. Windsor
2. Oxford
3. Hertfordshire
4. Buckinghamshire
5. Bedfordshire

WITHIN EASY REACH of London, the Thames Valley and the Chilterns are a history-rich part of England, and they lie so close to the capital they can be easily reached by automobile or Green Line coach. You can explore here during the day and return in time to see a show in the West End.

Here are some of the most-visited historic sites in England: the former homes of Disraeli and Elizabeth I, the estate of the Duke of Bedford, and, of course, Windsor Castle, 22 miles from London, one of the most famous castles in Europe and the most popular day trip for those visitors venturing out of London for the first time.

Of course, your principal reason for coming to Oxfordshire, our second goal, is to explore the university city of Oxford, about an hour's drive from London. But Oxford is not the only attraction in the county, as you'll soon discover as you make your way through Henley-on-Thames. The shire is a land of great mansions, old churches of widely varying architectural styles, and rolling farmland.

In a sense, Oxfordshire is a kind of buffer zone between the easy living in the southern towns and the industrialized cities of the heartland. In the southeast are the chalky Chilterns, and in the west you'll be moving toward the wool towns of the Cotswolds. In fact, Burford, an unspoiled medieval town, lying west of Oxford, is one of the traditional gateways of the Cotswolds (dealt with in a later chapter). The Upper Thames winds its way across the southern parts of the county.

The "Home Counties" are characterized by their river valleys and gentle hills. The beech-clad Chiltern Hills are at their most beautiful in spring and fall. This 40-mile chalk ridge extends in an arc from the Thames Valley to the old Roman city of St. Albans in Hertfordshire. The whole region is popular for boating holidays, as it contains a 200-mile network of canals.

1. Windsor

If you hop aboard a 701 or 704 Green Line coach at Victoria Station, you'll be delivered in little more than an hour to Windsor, site of England's greatest castle and its most famous boys' school.

You can also take an express nonstop bus (no. 700). Before 9 a.m., the single round-trip fare is £2.20 ($4.29), with half price for children. The same fare stands for the round trip to London from Windsor.

Windsor was originally called "Windlesore" by the ancient Britons who derived the name from winding shore—so noticeable as you walk along the Thames here.

THE SIGHTS: Your bus will drop you near the Town Guildhall, to which Wren applied the finishing touches. It's only a short walk up Castle Hill to the following sights:

Windsor Castle

It was William the Conqueror who founded a castle on this spot, beginning a legend and a link with English sovereignty that has known many vicissitudes. King John cooled his heels at Windsor while waiting to put his signature on the Magna Carta at nearby Runnymede; Charles I was imprisoned here before losing his head; Queen Bess did some renovations; Victoria mourned her beloved Albert, who died at the castle in 1861; the royal family rode out much of World War II behind its sheltering walls. When Queen Elizabeth II and her entourage are at Windsor, a Royal Standard flies, which means the State Apartments are off limits then. Otherwise, they may be visited weekdays from 10:30 a.m. to 5 p.m. from March to October; 10:30 a.m. to 3 p.m. November to February; also on Sunday from 1:30 to 5 p.m. The price of admission is £1 ($1.95) for adults, 50p (98¢) for children. The apartments are closed for about six weeks at Easter and for around three weeks in June when the Queen and Philip come here for the Ascot races. The apartments themselves contain many works of art, porcelain, armor, furniture, three Verrio ceilings, and several Gibbons carvings from the 17th century. The world of Rubens adorns the King's Drawing Room and in his relatively small dressing room is a Dürer, along with Rembrandt's portrait of his mother, and Van Dyck's triple look at Charles I. Of the apartments, the grand reception room, with its Gobelin tapestries, is the most spectacular.

The guard is changed daily at 10:30 a.m., except on Sunday. The Windsor changing of the guard is a much more exciting and moving experience, in my opinion, than the London exercises. In Windsor, the guard marches through the town, stopping the traffic as it wheels into the castle to the tune of a full regimental band when the court is in residence. When the Queen is not there, a drum and pipe band is mustered.

Old Master Drawings

The royal family possesses a rare collection at Windsor of drawings by old masters—notably Leonardo da Vinci. One Leonardo sketch, for example, shows a cat in 20 different positions; another is a study of a horse; still a third is that of Saint Matthew, a warmup for the head used in *The Last Supper*. In addition, you'll find sketches by William Blake, Thomas Rowlandson, and 12 Holbeins (don't miss his sketch of Sir John Godsalve). The drawing exhibition may be visited at the same time as the State Apartments for a 40p (78¢) for adults, 10p (20¢) for children admission. It remains open, unlike the State Apartments, when the Court is in residence.

Queen Mary's Dollhouse

Just about the greatest dollhouse in all the world is at Windsor. Presented to the late Queen Mary as a gift, and later used to raise money for charity, the dollhouse is a remarkable achievement and recreation of what a great royal mansion of the 1920s looked like—complete with a fleet of cars, including a Rolls-Royce. The house is perfect for Tom Thumb and family, and a retinue of servants. All is done with the most exacting detail—even the champagne bottles in the wine cellar contain vintage wine of that era. There's a toothbrush suitable for an ant. A minuscule electric iron really works. For late-night reading, you'll find volumes ranging from Hardy to Housman. In addition, you'll see a collection of dolls presented to the monarchy from nearly every nation of the Commonwealth. The dollhouse may be viewed for an admission of 40p (78¢) for adults, 10p (20¢) for children, even when the State Apartments are closed.

St. George's Chapel

A gem of the Perpendicular style, this chapel shares the distinction with Westminster Abbey of being a pantheon of English monarchs (Victoria is a notable exception). The present St. George's was founded in the late 15th century by Edward IV on the site of the original Chapel of the Order of the Garter (Edward III, 1348). You enter the nave first with its fan vaulting (a remarkable achievement in English architecture). The nave contains the tomb of George V and Queen Mary, designed by Sir William Reid Dick. Off the nave in the Urswick Chapel, the Princess Charlotte memorial provides an ironic touch. If she had survived childbirth in 1817, she—and not her cousin, Victoria —would have ruled the British Empire. The Edward IV "Quire," with its imaginatively carved 15th-century choir stalls (crowned by lacy canopies and colorful Knights of the Garter banners), evokes the pomp and pageantry of medieval days. In the center is a flat tomb, containing the vault of the beheaded Charles I, along with Henry VIII and one of his wives (no. 3, Jane Seymour). Henry's tomb has long been stripped of its former embellishments. Finally, you may want to inspect the Prince Albert Memorial Chapel, reflecting the opulent taste of the era of Victoria. The chapel is closed during services, and it's advisable to telephone to check opening hours at other times (tel. Windsor 65538). The chapel is usually open from 10:45 a.m. to 3:45 p.m. Monday to Saturday, and from 2 to 3:45 p.m. on Sunday. The price of admission is 80p ($1.56) for adults, 30p (59¢) for children.

Footnote: Queen Victoria died on January 22, 1901, and was buried beside her beloved Prince Albert in a mausoleum at **Frogmore** (a private estate), near Windsor (open only two days a year, in May). The Prince Consort died in December 1861.

Sunday Entertainment

There are often polo matches in **Windsor Great Park**—and at Ham Common—and you may see Prince Charles playing and Prince Philip serving as umpire. The Queen often watches. For more information, telephone Windsor 60633.

The Town Itself

Windsor is largely a Victorian town, with lots of brick buildings and a few remnants of Georgian architecture. In and around the castle are two cobblestoned streets—**Church** and **Market,** with their antique shops, silversmiths, and pubs. One shop on Church Street was supposedly occupied by Nell Gwynne who needed to be within call of Charles II's chambers. After lunch or tea, you may want to stroll along the three-mile, aptly named Long Walk.

STAYING OVER AT WINDSOR: If you don't have an engraved invitation to overnight at the castle, there's always room at one of the inns—except during Ascot Races and the Windsor Horse Show.

For those who decide to stay in Windsor and use it as a base for London sightseeing, trains run from Windsor Town Station and from Windsor and Eton Riverside Station to London. Trains leave London as late as 10:30 or 11 p.m., so it is quite easy to take in an early theater and dinner before returning to Windsor for overnight.

Alternatively, the **Windsor Theatre** (tel. Windsor 63444) has nightly performances of weekly productions. Run by John Counsell and his wife Mary Kerridge, this is one of the best repertory companies around London. Best seats are £6 ($11.70); the cheapest, £1.50 ($2.93).

The Upper Bracket

The **Old House Hotel** (tel. Windsor 61354) was designed and lived in by Christopher Wren in 1676. Between Eton and Windsor, the former town house occupies a prime position on the Thames, its gardens overlooking the swans and boats. The owners, Wren House Ltd., have maintained the beauty of the past, keeping the same architectural detail, furnishing the hotel with a collection of antiques. The central hall is impressive, with a Queen Anne black marble refectory table. Wren's former study is inviting; it's in apricot and white paneling, with his Empire desk, along with a fireplace and shield-back Hepplewhite chairs. Another area is a small apple-green salon, with linenfold walls, Tudor oak and chintz-covered chairs. The bay-windowed main drawing room, decorated with mirrors, sconces, and a formal marble fireplace, opens into a garden and a riverside flagstone terrace for after-dinner coffee and drinks. You can also drink in the Bamboo Room, ordering one of the specials, such as Planter's Punch.

All bedrooms have private baths. Singles range from £29.50 ($57.53) to £38 ($74.10); twins cost from £40 ($78) to £50 ($98). Most of the older and larger rooms have some select pieces of furniture. Some of the more recently built accommodations are compact, pleasantly decorated, and color coordinated. The food is among the best in Windsor (many nonresidents come in just to dine). Dinner is à la carte only, costing about £20 ($39) for two persons.

The Medium-Priced Range

Castle Hotel, High Street (tel. Windsor 51011), a small link in the Trusthouse Forte circuit, sits in a prominent position facing the Guildhall, across from the castle. Formerly a Georgian posting house, it enjoyed many prestigious visitors, such as second-string royal cousins, in its heyday in the 18th century. Nowadays, it's more likely to be patronized by parents visiting their sons at Eton. Its classic facade is a "parchment color." The interior may not contain the splendid furnishings of its former days, but the hotel is nevertheless comfortable and immaculate, with central heating throughout. A ballroom suite is its most attractive feature. All of the well-furnished rooms (new wing added) contain private baths, along with television and radio. A single room with bath rents for £30 ($58.50); it's £38 ($74.10) in a double with bath. Prices include tea- and coffee-making facilities, service charges, and VAT. Breakfast is extra.

Harte and Garter Hotel, High Street (tel. Windsor 63426), stands right opposite the castle, beside the Castle Hotel. Recently revamped, it is decidedly the best location for lovers of castles. It's very accessible to the Windsor Town Railway Station. All rooms have color TV, phone, radio, and tea- and coffee-making facilities. A single with bath goes for £23 ($44.85), rising to £37 ($72.15) in a double or twin, also with bath, these rates including VAT, service, and a full breakfast. Meals in the three grill rooms range in price from £4 ($7.80) to £7 ($13.65), and are likely to include rump steak or a mixed grill. Peas and jacket potatoes are always on the menu.

Royal Adelaide Hotel, Kings Road (tel. Windsor 63916), is opposite the famous Long Walk leading to Windsor Castle, five minutes away. An old Victorian hotel, it offers single rooms from £14.75 ($28.76) without bath to £22 ($42.90) with bath, and doubles or twins from £25 ($48.75) without bath to £32 ($62.40) with bath, including breakfast, VAT, and service. All units have radio, alarm, and tea-maker. There is good car parking at the rear for guests, and the hotel is warm and well furnished. The staff, used to a quick turnover of guests, may be a little offhand. A set lunch or dinner is available at £5.50 ($10.73) for a three-course meal.

Riverside Cottages

Riverbank Holiday Cottages, Clewer Court Road, Windsor, Berkshire SLH 5JH, are right down by the river on a Wind-in-the Willowy backwater. The compound is a collection of modern, comfortable, well-furnished cottages, with large living room, phone, color TV, and a private terrace opening onto the gardens with a view over the backwater to Millstream Island. Beyond the Willows you can see the River Thames. Each cottage has a well-equipped bath and two double bedrooms, renting for about £100 ($195) a week for four guests. Longer rentals are cheaper. The cottages are fully furnished, so all you need provide is your food. Send a list ahead (there's no reservations phone so you must write to the address above), and the kitchen will be stocked for you at your expense. They share the use of the island with a summer house and barbecue. Rowing dinghies are available free to more adventurous tenants. A car rental can be arranged, and it's worth noting that the daily rate in the cottages, including a daily ticket by express bus into London and back again, is only £6.50 ($12.68) per person. If there are four of you, you can enjoy the countryside, as well as take in the sights, go to a theater or two, for less than it costs you to live at home.

LUNCH AT WINDSOR: For lunch in Windsor, try the **William IV Hotel,** Thames Street, 100 yards from Eton Bridge (tel. Windsor 51004). This lovely old place (circa 1500) with its armor, beams, and log fire, invites visitors in with its friendly and local atmosphere. Just outside is the Chapter garden where the Windsor martyrs were burned at the stake in 1544 for their religious beliefs. It was from this inn that they received their last cups of strong ale "in gratification of their last wish." The house built by Sir Christopher Wren for his own use is opposite the William IV, and the great architect of St. Paul's was reputedly a regular visitor to the old tap room, as were diarists Evelyn and

Pepys. The present landlord is Ken Gardner, award-winning journalist and writer. Rub shoulders here with newspaper people and actors (nearby is the Theatre Royal), artists and rivermen, and drink traditional ale which is still pulled by old-fashioned beer engines.

The food is home-cooked, and the portions are guaranteed to satisfy gargantuan appetites. Scottish beef is served by two motherly locals, Lottie and Gert, who are quick and accurate. Try a steak or one of the house regional specials. A three-course luncheon costs £5 ($9.75), and might consist of soup, followed by a roast topside of beef with Yorkshire pudding, served with a selection of vegetables, and followed by a homemade apple pie with cream. In the evening you might prefer a sirloin steak with potatoes and peas or perhaps fried scampi. Bar lunches are also available, costing from £2.50 ($4.88). You can sit at sidewalk tables in a pedestrian area by the Eton Bridge, gazing up at the castle while enjoying lunch. The William IV lies at the bottom of Windsor Hill on the approach road to the bridge, which is now open to pedestrians only.

The house also rents out three double bedrooms, one with shower, charging from £21 ($40.95) for two persons, these tariffs including a good English breakfast.

For those to whom a town is not a town without its Chinese restaurant, Windsor offers **Windsor's Peking**, 14 High St. (tel. Windsor 66217). Downstairs is a small disco and bar. Upstairs, the restaurant specializes in Peking dishes. They have three set dinners at £6.50 ($12.68), £7 ($13.65), and £8.50 ($16.58) per person. Poultry and meat dishes include shredded beef with onion, grilled pork Peking style, and sliced duck with mushrooms. The specialty is barbecued Peking duck for £13 ($25.35). Peter Lam and his staff are very friendly and knowledgeable about the dishes. The restaurant is open daily from noon to 2:30 p.m. and from 6 to 11:30 p.m., on Sunday from noon until 11:30 p.m.

The **Ship Hotel**, Church Lane (tel. Windsor 64257), is a pub that is quite popular with the locals. Publican Geoff Holmberg looks after the lager, and Mrs. Holmberg is known in these parts for her farmhouse pie. Only pub lunches are served. For that main dish, plus soup, a salad, and vegetables, even homemade apple pie, the charge is £4 ($7.80) per head. Or you might try the more traditional roast beef with soup as an appetizer and apple pie for dessert. B&B terms are £10 ($19.50) per person, including morning tea or coffee. The Ship is well recommended for that "down home" feeling.

ETON: For our final sight, from Windsor Castle we must cross over a bridge spanning the Thames:

Eton College

Largest and best known of the public (private) schools of England, Eton College was founded by a teenage boy himself, Henry VI in 1440. Some of England's greatest men, notably the Duke of Wellington, have played on the fields of Eton. Twenty prime ministers were educated at Eton, as well as such literary figures as George Orwell and Aldous Huxley. Even the late Ian Fleming, creator of James Bond, attended. The traditions of the school have had plenty of time to become firmly entrenched (ask a young gentleman in his Victorian black tails to explain the difference between a "wet bob" and a "dry bob"). For 60p ($1.17) admission, the School Yard and Cloisters may be visited daily, 2 to 5 p.m., throughout the year, and also from 10:30 a.m. to 2 p.m. on school holidays, including most of July and all of August. If it's open, take a look at the Perpendicular chapel, with its 15th-century paintings and reconstructed fan vaulting.

Bernard Weintraub wrote, "Eton, the Gothic school on the Thames that has symbolized starched exclusiveness, is quietly lifting its cloak of privilege." In the future, along with the sons of diplomats and prime ministers, boys from poorer families will also be educated there, the tuition funded by scholarships. All of this represents the movement in England toward a classless society. One man put it this way, "The lifestyle of the young cuts across all classes—they're wearing the same clothes, listening to the same music, engaging in the same activities." However, the administration (at the moment) doesn't plan to go coed.

Lunch at Eton

The **Cock Pit**, 47 Eton High St. (tel. 95/60944), dates back to 1420, and it is a rendezvous for Eton students. The inn is owned by Italian Vittorio Bianchi and his English wife, Janet. Together they have considerably upgraded and internationalized the menu, although lunch still retains some fairly traditional English dishes. Light meals are served at lunch only in the upstairs bar where you can order sandwiches from £1.50 ($2.93) or pasta dishes such as cannelloni or lasagne at £2.20 ($4.29). At dinner a set menu is featured at £13 ($25.35), a three-course meal, or else you may prefer to select from an extensive à la carte menu, including roast beef. On nippy days, a fire burns in an old fireplace, but when the weather's warmer you'll be tempted to have lunch under an umbrella in the rear courtyard. Specialties include veal on the bone (cooked in butter and breadcrumbs) and saddle of lamb roasted with fennel, sage, rosemary, and cooked in white wine. A set afternoon tea here is served from 3:30 till 5:30 p.m., on Saturday and Sunday only. The restaurant is closed all day Monday. Dining hours are from 12:30 to 2:15 p.m. and from 7:30 to 10:30 p.m. Ask to be shown the knucklebone yard out back. Then you'll know why the restaurant is called the Cock Pit. The restaurant is licensed for alcohol, and has a varied wine list.

Eton Wine Bar (tel. Windsor 54921) is owned and run by William and Michael Gilbey of Gilbey's gin family, although no gin is served here. Just across the bridge from Windsor, it is a charming place set among the antique shops with pinewood tables and old church pews and chairs. There is a small garden out back. It is open seven days a week from 11:30 a.m. to 2:30 p.m. and from 6 to 10:30 p.m., but on Friday and Saturday they remain open until 11 p.m. Soups of the day are often imaginative and sophisticated (ever had watercress vichyssoise?). Another "starter" might be mussels marinated in a roquefort dressing. Main dishes include such treats as stuffed eggplant with a Provençal tomato sauce and rice. For a main dish and appetizer, expect to pay from £6.50 ($12.68). Each day two special dishes are featured, and desserts include pineapple and almond flan and damson crunch. Wine can be had by the glass or the bottle.

Antico, 42 High St. (tel. Windsor 63977), is an old building with beams spreading through several rooms. On your way to the tiny bar you cannot help but pass the magnificent cold table, displaying a vast array of hors d'oeuvres, fresh fish, and cold meats. Grilled fresh sardines are £2 ($3.90). There is a wide choice of fish dishes, such as sole grilled, colbert, or with mushrooms, capers, and prawns, each costing around £7 ($13.65). Beef filet goes for £6.20 ($12.09), and a kidney brochette for £4.70 ($9.17). Desserts from the trolley begin at £1.50 ($2.93). VAT and service are added to all bills, and there is a cover charge of 60p ($1.17). The restaurant is open for lunch daily, except Saturday, from noon to 2:30 p.m. Dinner is nightly from 7 to 11 p.m.

Eton Buttery, 73 High St. (tel. Windsor 54479), is just on the Eton side of the bridge from Windsor, a new building among the boathouses of the college with magnificent views over the river and up toward the town and the castle. Open seven days a week from 9:30 a.m. to 7 p.m., it is decorated with plain red brick walls, brown carpets and tables, caneback chairs, and a mass of potted plants. This is an up-market self-service buffet owned by Mrs. Ron Stanton, owner of the House on the Bridge restaurant, opposite.

Food is well displayed along spotless counters. There are waitresses to clear away and to bring you wine and drinks; otherwise, you help yourself to the variety of quiches, cold sliced meats, and specialty salads and pâtés. There is also a hot dish of the day. Expect to spend £5 ($9.75) for a meal.

SHOPPING IN WINDSOR: For those who have time to spare, Windsor offers a great variety of attractive shops for browsing or more serious souvenir hunting.

Scots Corner, High Street (tel. Windsor 51695), has Shetland sweaters for £6.50 ($12.68), women's Fair Isle jumpers for £12 ($23.40), and Cairngorm brooches, cufflinks, and necklaces from £5 ($9.75) to £15 ($29.25).

Woods of Windsor Ltd., at the Castle Perfumers, Queen Charlotte Street (tel. Windsor 55777), established in 1770, right beside the Guildhall, is a heady experience where you can buy a scented leaf of paper to slip between your hankies for 50p (98¢) or an elegant potpourrie for £12.50 ($24.38). In between are lavender and herb bags from £1.25 ($2.44) to £1.75 ($3.41), and oil to refresh potpourrie for £1.75 also.

Opposite, the **Token House** has one of the best selections of china and porcelain of all well-known makes, and further down the High Street, **Le Sac** has a wide selection of leather goods, handbags, wallets, scarves, and gloves.

A short walk down Peascod Street, opposite the Queen Victoria Statue, brings you to King Edward's Court. On the corner is **Hammick's Books,** 1 King Edward's Court (tel. Windsor 56456). Charles Hammick, ex-army, now runs a string of bookshops where you can get the latest paperbacks and guide-books, maps, and illustrated historical documentation on the town and the country.

At 34 King Edward's Court is **Le Pot,** a paradise of traditional cooking utensils, tableware, herbs, and spices. The large, once-bare shop is stuffed with cooking pots, garlic presses, earthenware casseroles, pepper mills, oven gloves, napkin rings, and egg cups. There is a large selection of kitchen knives, wooden spoons, and a gigantic stirring spoon. I counted 41 different herbs and spices, all small and easy to slip into a pocket, after being paid for, of course. Blue-and-white-striped butchers' aprons are also sold, and there is a mass of basket work and an excellent selection of cookbooks. Souvenirs can be purchased from under £1 ($1.95), although prices go up to £10 ($19.50), even £20 ($39). This is the domain and brainchild of Graham Cooper and actor friend Anthony Davidson. They are helped by several young women who are always willing to discuss the merits of various pots and utensils. It's a lovely place in which to buy souvenirs at prices lower than in Central London.

AROUND WINDSOR SIGHTSEEING TOUR: A 35-minute tour of Windsor and the surrounding countryside is offered in an open-top, double-deck bus with commentary. The ten-mile drive starts from Windsor Castle and passes the Royal Mews, the Long Walk, the Royal Farms, Albert Bridge, Eton College, and the Theatre Royal. The departure point is Castle Hill, near the King Henry VIII Gateway to Windsor Castle. Adults pay £1 ($1.95); senior citizens, 80p ($1.56); and children, 50p (98¢). The senior citizen fare is not valid on weekends, holidays, and in August. Tickets, along with information about dates of operation and departure times, are available from **Windsorian Coaches,** 17 Alma Rd. (tel. Windsor 56841).

GUIDED TOURS: Every day except Sunday a guided tour of Windsor Castle and the town leaves from the **Tourist Information Centre** in the Central Station, the one opposite the castle. The walking tour includes a look at the Long Walk, then the Guildhall and Market Cross House, along with the changing of the guard when possible. In the castle precincts, you'll visit St. George's Chapel, the Cloisters, and the Albert Memorial Chapel, finishing in the State Apartments. Subject to demand, the tour leaves at 10:15 a.m., costing adults £3 ($5.85) and children £1.50 ($2.93) for two hours. A one-hour tour is priced at £1.50 ($2.93) for adults and 75p ($1.46) for children. There are further departures during the day if demand merits it. All tours are accompanied by a licensed guide and include inside visits where possible.

NEARBY SIGHTS: Two attractions of interest are in the surrounding area.

One of England's Great Gardens

The **Savill Garden,** Wick Lane, Englefield Green (tel. Windsor 60222), is in Windsor Great Park and clearly signposted from Windsor, Egham, and Ascot. Started in 1932, the garden is now considered one of the finest of its type in the northern hemisphere. The display starts in spring with rhododendrons, camellias, and daffodils beneath the trees; then throughout the summer there are spectacular displays of flowers and shrubs all skillfully presented in a natural and wild state. It is open March 1 to December 24 from 10 a.m. to 6 or 7 p.m., and the admission is £1 ($1.95) for adults, and accompanied children under 16 are admitted free. There is also a licensed, self-service restaurant on the premises.

Adjoining the Savill Garden are the **Valley Gardens,** full of shrubs and trees in a series of wooded natural valleys running down to Virginia water. It is open daily, free, throughout the year.

Windsor Safari Park and Seaworld

In the safari craze sweeping the world, even the Royal Borough of Windsor hasn't been spared. The Safari Park and Seaworld, Winkfield Road (tel. Windsor 69841), is open just two miles from Windsor Castle on a site 23 miles from London. Take the M4 motorway and leave it at Junction 6. The park is on the B3022 road. There you can watch the performing dolphins and a killer whale, and drive through reserves of lions, tigers, baboons, giraffes, camels, and many other wild animals. It is open from 10 a.m. There are catering facilities, but you can picnic on acres of green. If you have a soft-top car or come on public transport from Windsor, take the safari bus through the reserves. Admission to Safari Park is £2.90 ($5.66) for adults, £2.30 ($4.49) for children. The dolphin and killer whale show, parrot show, and amusements are free.

THE WELLINGTON DUCAL ESTATE: If you'd like to make an interesting day trip in Berkshire, I'd suggest **Stratfield Saye** (tel. Basingstoke 882882), between the A4 and the A30, just west of the city of Reading. It has been the home of the Duke of Wellington since 1817 when the 17th-century house was bought for the Iron Duke to celebrate his victory over Napoleon at the Battle of Waterloo. Many memories of the first duke remain in the house, including his billiard table, battle spoils, and pictures. Recently, the funeral carriage which since 1860 had rested in St. Paul's Cathedral crypt was added to the ducal collection.

In the gardens is the grave of Copenhagen, the charger ridden to battle at Waterloo by the first duke. The lovely plain stone face of the house looks over a country park, with its lake, woods, and meadows.

There is a fascinating National Dairy Museum, with relics of 150 years of dairying. Other attractions include a riding school, nature trails, boating, and sailing on the lake. On summer weekends a miniature railway goes through the parklands.

The estate is open daily from March until the end of October from 10 a.m. to 5:30 p.m., charging an admission of £1.90 ($3.71) for adults, 95p ($1.85) for children. There are refreshments available and plenty of parking space.

INNS ALONG THE THAMES: For those who want to anchor into riverside villages with old inns along the Thames, I offer the following suggestions for the motorist.

Cookham-on-Thames

King's Arm Inn, Cookham-on-Thames in Berkshire (tel. Bourne End 20146), is a charming old inn in a riverside village where Stanley Spencer lived and painted for many years. The inn has an early 17th-century staircase, low beams, and plastered walls. In the gardens, which are floodlit at night, are the owner's three Pyrenees mountain dogs, great soft animals with thick white fur and a tendency to pose under the floodlights for the diners.

The small dining room is warm and softly lit, and the menu includes a very good chef's pâté, as well as the soup of the day made from fresh ingredients. Main dishes include roast duckling with orange and cherry sauce, chicken poached in wine, and sliced filet of beef with mushrooms cooked in beer. There are also T-bone steaks, entrecôte, and grilled sole. Desserts include fruit pies and tarts. A meal will cost around £8 ($15.60), including VAT and service. A very good light red wine goes for £5 ($9.75) a bottle.

On Sunday, there is a traditional English lunch with roast joint and all the trimmings. The inn serves food from noon to 1:45 p.m. and from 7 to 10 p.m. Closed Sunday evening.

The landlord, Martin Cummings, and his wife Joy, also have rooms in the hotel which go for £15 ($29.25) in a single, £25 ($48.75) in a double or twin. Some units are in the main building, and some in the Cumming's own house just across the narrow street, beside another inn. The place is comfortably furnished, with many antiques and good beds, but none of the rooms has a private bath, however. The nightly rate includes VAT, service, and a breakfast of almost whatever you wish to have in the traditional English style.

Streatley-on-Thames:

This Thameside village has some old buildings and a fine Priory church. And it has the **Swan Hotel,** Streatley-on-Thames, Berkshire (tel. Goring

873737), a pleasant riverside inn. The hotel Swan has now been much enlarged, but still it retains much of its old charm. It would take a lot to ruin the tranquility and eternity of the River Thames. Gardens slope down to the water, and your hire-cruiser will nestle happily alongside while you have dinner. The menu is unstartling, mainly grills, steaks, roast chicken, and desserts from the trolley. A set luncheon goes for £5.50 ($10.73), rising to £6.50 ($12.68) on Sunday. An à la carte lunch or dinner will cost from £10 ($19.50).

If you are touring, or spending a last night before Heathrow Airport and departure, single rooms go from £24 ($46.80), with or without bath; doubles from £30 ($58.50) to £36 ($70.20). All prices are subject to a service charge, and breakfast is extra.

Bray-on-Thames

Twenty-eight miles from London, you come upon this attractive Thames-side village, with its beautiful old almshouses, timbered cottages, and small period houses. Windsor Castle is but just a short jaunt away. The town was once famous for its 16th-century "Vicar of Bray" who couldn't make up his mind about his religious or political affiliations.

Into such a town, with its gliding swans and willows bordering the Thames, the Roux brothers of Le Gavroche fame have opened the **Waterside Inn**, with its impeccable cooking but astronomical prices. Those who cannot afford such a place will be amply rewarded at the following, more modestly priced recommendation.

The **Hinds Head Hotel**, Bray-on-Thames, Berkshire (tel. Maidenhead 26151), lies on the bend of a very busy, narrow road, but there's ample parking in front of the restaurant. Although calling itself a hotel, the Hinds has no rooms to rent. There is a bar and you can take your pint in with you if you wish, as the wine list is expensive. A three-course lunch costs £11.50 ($22.43) and a four-course lunch is £12.50 ($24.38), plus VAT and service. A three-course dinner goes for £12.50 also; a four-course dinner, £13.50 ($26.33). There is a fish course before the roast beef, pork, or lamb, with all the trimmings. Be warned, the friendly waitresses bring around three sorts of potatoes and then about four different green vegetables. A bottle of the house wine is £6.80 ($13.26). Hours are from 12:30 to 2 p.m. and from 7:30 to 10 p.m. This is the sort of place to come to on a nice Sunday for a good old English "blow-out" lunch. The portions are large, and the standard of cuisine pretty high on the plainer dishes.

Henley-on-Thames

At the eastern edge of Oxfordshire, only 35 miles from London, Henley-on-Thames is a small town and resort on the river. At the foothills of the Chilterns, it is the headquarters of the Royal Regatta held annually in July, the Number One event among European oarsmen. The regatta dates back to the first years of the reign of Victoria.

The Elizabethan buildings, the tearooms, and inns along the town's High Street live up to one's conception of what an English country town looks like—or should look like.

The life here is serene, and Henley-on-Thames makes for an excellent stopover en route to Oxford. Warning: During the Royal Regatta, rooms are virtually impossible to get at the fashionable inns of Henley, unless you've made reservations months in advance.

The **Red Lion,** Henley Bridge (tel. Henley-on-Thames 2161), is a former coaching inn, dating from the 16th century. A bedchamber used to be kept ready for the Duke of Marlborough, who would stop over on his way to his palace at Blenheim. The guest list reads like a hall of fame, including such notables as Johnson and Boswell, even George IV who, it is said, downed more than a dozen lamb chops one night. The red brick facade, with its climbing wisteria, remains untouched, but most of the interior has been renovated and modernized. Nowadays, wayfarers enjoy central heating and private baths in most of the rooms, some of which are named after famous personages who have stopped over. The decor in most of the bedrooms has been brightened with contemporary furnishings and color-coordinated pieces. A bathless single costs £20 ($39), rising to £30 ($58.50) with bath, and bathless doubles go for £30 ($58.50) increasing to £35 ($68.25) with bath, these tariffs including an English breakfast and VAT. Guests congregate in the low-beamed lounge. Opening onto views of the Thames, the Riverside Restaurant is cozy in green and gold. A three-course lunch goes for £5 ($9.75). On Saturday nights, a pianist plays, and a four-course set meal is priced at £7.50 ($14.63). Otherwise, an à la carte dinner will average £8.50 ($16.58).

EN ROUTE TO MAIDENHEAD: On the river road from Windsor to Maidenhead, the motorist comes across the **Oakley Court Hotel,** Windsor Road, Water Oakley, Windsor (tel. Maindenhead 74141). This old house, once owned by the Avery family of weighing scales fame, has emerged from a semiretirement and blossoms as a most attractive riverside hotel. The house with its turrets and chimneys contains the reception and the living rooms, and the restaurant. One new wing of bedrooms extends from the old house, another, built beside the river, is a 30-foot walk from the main building. This is, in my opinion, the best place to be, with lovely views of the river and the garden, but some may wish to be within closer walking distance of the main building.

Of the 75 rooms, those in the old house have high ceilings, interesting shapes, and one still contains the original paneling. The bookshelves are stocked with ancient tomes. In the two modern wings, the rooms are of generous size and have modern bathrooms en suite. All have color TV and radio with remote control and phone. There is full room service. Units go for £40 ($78) to £50 ($97.50) for two, including an English breakfast, VAT, and service.

The restaurant serves a set luncheon for £7.50 ($14.63), including such fare as roast stuffed breast of veal with spinach and ham, royal jugged hare, and lamb cutlets. The set dinner is more elaborate—perhaps a leg of lamb, filet of trout, or noisettes of lamb—all for £12.50 ($24.38). The à la carte menu is priced according to availability but includes a wide variety of hors d'oeuvres, soups, fish, and poultry. The chef's specialties include tournedos de boeuf Princesse and mignonettes de boeuf exotiques. A well-chosen meal will cost about £20 ($39) per person, including a bottle of wine for two diners.

Geoffrey Tucker, the general manager, lived for many years in Barbados and was the general manager of the Colony Club. He has brought his vast experience into good use in providing nice international touches—iced water on the tables as a matter of course, gentle piano music most evenings in the restaurant, linen napkins, and ever-clean tablecloths.

This is a very convenient first or last night's stop for Heathrow Airport, just half an hour away—avoiding the harsh commercialism of the airport hotels. The hotel is planning a river-bus service to Windsor town down one of the most colorful reaches of the river.

EN ROUTE TO OXFORD: Between Henley-on-Thames and Oxford (a 24-mile drive) lies the following recommendation.

The **Swan Inn,** Tetsworth, Oxfordshire (tel. Tetsworth 281), is an old inn which has been in business for at least 700 years. Over the centuries it has been added to, and examples of the various architectural styles can be seen around the house. Elizabeth I and then Queen Victoria stayed here. It is reputed to be haunted and could very well be, as it has had many occupants since the monks who ran the first hostelry left in the 14th century. Singles go for £16 ($31.20); doubles, from £28 ($54.60)—including a full breakfast and VAT. Lunch can be ordered for £6.50 ($12.68), and a set dinner begins at £7 ($13.65), depending on your choice from a selection of well-cooked roasts, grills, and salads. If you're ordering à la carte, expect to pay from £11 ($21.45). The Swan makes an ideal last-night stopover on the way back to Heathrow or for someone leaving the Cotswolds and Oxford and wanting to stop over before plunging into London.

2. Oxford

A walk down the long sweep of The High, one of the most striking streets in England; a mug of cider in one of the old student pubs; the sound of a May Day dawn when choristers sing in Latin from Magdalen Tower; the Great Tom bell from Tom Tower, whose 101 peals traditionally signal the closing of the college gates; towers and spires rising majestically; the barges on the upper reaches of the Thames; nude swimming at Parson's Pleasure; the roar of a cannon launching the bumping races; a tiny, dusty bookstall where you can pick up a valuable first edition. All that is Oxford—57 miles from London and home of one of the greatest universities in the world. An industrial city, the center of a large automobile business, as well as a university town, Oxford is better for sightseeing in summer. The students are wherever Oxford scholars go in the summer (allegedly they study more than they do at term time), and the many bed-and-breakfast houses—vacated by their gown-wearing boarders—will be happy to offer you an accommodation. But you'll be missing a great deal if you view Oxford without glimpsing its life blood.

However, at any time of the year, you can enjoy a tour of the colleges, many of them representing a peak in England's architectural kingdom, as well as a valley of Victorian eyesores. Just don't mention the other place (Cambridge) and you shouldn't have any trouble.

The city predates the university—in fact, it was a Saxon town in the early part of the tenth century. And by the 12th century, Oxford was growing in reputation as a seat of learning—at the expense of Paris. The first colleges were founded in the 13th century. The story of Oxford is filled with conflicts too complex and detailed to elaborate here. Suffice it to say, the relationship between town and gown wasn't as peaceful as it is today. Riots often flared, and both sides were guilty of abuses.

Nowadays, the young people of Oxford take out their aggressiveness in sporting competitions, with the different colleges zealously competing in such games as cricket and soccer. However, all colleges unite into a powerful university when they face matches with their traditional rival, Cambridge.

Ultimately, the test of a great university lies in the men it turns out. Oxford can name-drop a mouthful: Roger Bacon, Samuel Johnson, William Penn, John Wesley, Sir Walter Raleigh, Edward Gibbon, T. E. Lawrence, Sir Christopher Wren, John Donne, William Pitt, Matthew Arnold, Arnold Toynbee, Harold Macmillan, Graham Greene, A. E. Housman, Lewis Carroll, and even Dean Rusk.

OXFORD

N

POLSTEAD RD.

NORHAM RD.

BRADMORE RD.

PLANTATION ST.

WALTON ST.

TO

ST. GILES ST.

PARKS

SOUTH PARKS RD.

ST. CROSS RD.

MANSFIELD RD.

CHERWELL RIVER

MARSTON RD.

TO

BEAUMONT ST.

HOLYWELL

HEADINGTON RD.

STATION

GEORGE ST.

CORNMARKET ST.

RD.

ST.

New College

Magdalen College

University College

Merton College

NEW RD.

HIGH ST.

Christ Church College

ST. ALDATE'S

MORRELL AVE.

IFFLEY RD.

COWLEY RD.

THAMES RIVER

TO

MAGDALEN RD.

Many Americans arriving in Oxford ask, "Where's the campus?" If an Oxonian shows amusement when answering, it's understandable. Oxford University is, in fact, made up of 28 colleges, including five just for women (scholars in skirts in years past staged, and won, the battle for equal rights). To tour all of these would be a formidable task. Besides, a few are of such interest they overshadow the rest.

In season (from Easter through October), the best way to get a running commentary on the important sightseeing attractions is to go to the **Oxford Information Centre**, St. Aldate's Street, opposite the Town Hall, near Carfax (tel. Oxford 726871). Walking tours through the major colleges leave daily from Easter to mid-November at 10:45 a.m. and 2:15 p.m., last two hours, and cost £1.25 ($2.44). The tour does not include New College or Christ Church, which charge 50p (98¢).

At **Punt Station**, Cherwell Boathouse, Bardwell Road (tel. Oxford 55978), you can rent a punt at a cost of £2 ($3.90) on weekdays, £2.40 ($4.68) on weekends, per hour, plus a £10 ($19.50) deposit which must be posted. Similar charges are made on rentals at Magdalen Bridge Boathouse and at the Folly Bridge Boathouse.

WHAT TO SEE: Of the many well-known buildings in Oxford—Radcliffe Camera, whose dome competes in a city of spires; Sheldonian Theatre, an early work of Wren's; the Bodleian Library, one of the most important in the world —I have narrowed down the sights to a representative list of a few colleges.

A Word of Warning

The main business of a university, is, of course, to educate—and unfortunately this function at Oxford has been severely interfered with by the number of visitors who have been disturbing the academic work of the university. So, with deep regret, visiting is now restricted to certain hours and small groups of six or fewer. In addition, there are areas where visitors are not allowed at all, but your tourist office will be happy to advise you when and where you may "take in" the sights of this great institution.

Christ Church

Begun by Cardinal Wolsey as Cardinal College in 1525, Christ Church, known as The House, was founded by Henry VIII in 1546. Facing St. Aldate's Street, Christ Church has the largest quadrangle of any college in Oxford.

Tom Tower houses Great Tom, the 18,000-pound bell referred to earlier. It rings at 9:05 nightly, signaling the closing of the college gates. The 101 times it peals originally signified the number of students at the time of the founding of the college. The student body number changed, but Oxford traditions live on forever.

In the 16th-century Great Hall, with its hammer-beam ceiling, are some interesting portraits, including works by those old reliables, Gainsborough and Reynolds. Prime ministers are pictured, as Christ Church was the training ground for 13 prime ministers: men such as Gladstone and George Canning. There is a separate picture gallery.

The cathedral, dating from the 12th century, was built over a period of centuries. (Incidentally, it is not only the college chapel, but the cathedral of the diocese of Oxford.) The cathedral's most distinguishing features are its Norman pillars and the vaulting of the choir, dating from the 15th century. In the center of the Great Quadrangle is a statue of Mercury mounted in the center of a fish pond. The college and cathedral can be visited between 9:30 a.m. and noon and from 2 to 4:30 p.m. Entrance fee is 50p (98¢).

Magdalen College

Pronounced "maud-len," this college was founded in 1458 by William of Waynflete, bishop of Winchester and later chancellor of England. Its alumni range all the way from Wolsey to Wilde. Opposite the botanic garden, the oldest in England, is the bell tower, where the choristers sing in Latin at dawn on May Day. The reflection of the 15th-century tower is cast in the waters of the Cherwell below. On a not-so-happy day, Charles I—his days numbered—watched the oncoming Roundheads. But the most celebrated incident in Magdalen's history was when some brave Fellows defied James II. Visit the 15th-century chapel, in spite of many of its latter-day trappings. The hall and other places of special interest are open when possible.

A favorite pastime is to take Addison's Walk through the water meadows. The stroll is so named after a former alumnus, Joseph Addison, the 18th-century writer and poet noted for his contributions to *The Spectator* and *The Tatler.* The grounds of Magdalen are the most extensive of any Oxford college, even containing a deer park. You can visit Magdalen each day from 2 to 6:15 p.m.

Merton College

Founded in 1264, this college is among the trio of the most ancient at the university. It stands near Corpus Christi College on Merton Street, the sole survivor of Oxford's medieval cobbled streets. Merton College is noted for its library, said to be the oldest in England, having been built between 1371 and 1379. In keeping with tradition, some of its most valuable books were chained. Now only one book is so secured, to show what the custom was like. One of the treasures of the library is an astrolabe (astronomical instrument used for measuring the altitude of the sun and stars), thought to have belonged to Chaucer. You pay only 30p (59¢) to visit the ancient library, as well as the Max Beerbohm Room (the satirical English caricaturist who died in 1956). Both are open from 2 to 4 p.m. (4:30 p.m. March 2 to October 1) daily, and, in addition, from 10 a.m. to noon on Saturday and Sunday only. You can also visit the chapel, dating from the 13th century, at these times.

University College

On The High, University College is the oldest one found at Oxford, tracing its history back to 1249 when money was donated by an ecclesiastic called William of Durham. More fanciful is the old claim that the real founder was Alfred the Great. Don't jump to any conclusions about the age of the buildings when you see the present Gothic-esque look. The original structures have all disappeared, and what remains today represents essentially the architecture of the 17th century, with subsequent additions in Victoria's day, as well as in more recent times. For example, the Goodhart Quadrangle was added as late as 1962. Its most famous alumnus, Shelley, was "sent down" for his part in collaborating on a pamphlet on atheism. However, all is forgiven today, as the romantic poet is honored by a memorial erected in 1894. The hall and chapel of the University College can be visited during vacations from 10 a.m. to noon and from 2 to 4 p.m. (otherwise, from 2 to 4 p.m.).

New College

New College was founded in 1379 by William of Wykeham, bishop of Winchester and later lord chancellor of England. The college at Winchester supplied a constant stream of candidates. The first quadrangle, dating from before the end of the 14th century, was the initial quadrangle to be built in Oxford, forming the architectural design for the other colleges. In the antechapel is Sir Jacob Epstein's remarkable modern sculpture of *Lazarus,* and a fine El Greco painting of St. James. One of the treasures of the college is a crosier (pastoral staff of a bishop), belonging to the founding father. In the garden, you can see the remains of the old city wall and the mound. The college (entered at New College Lane) can be visited from 2 to 5 p.m. weekdays at term time (otherwise, from 11 a.m. to 6 p.m.). On weekends, it is open from noon to 6 p.m.

WHERE TO STAY: The accommodations in Oxford are limited, although the addition motels on the outskirts has aided the plight of those who require modern amenities. Recently, some of the more stalwart candidates in the city center have been refurbished as well. In addition, motorists may want to consider two grand old country houses on the outskirts, which offer the best living in Oxford if you don't mind commuting.

When the tourist rush is on, why tire yourself further? The **Oxford Association of Hotels and Guest Houses** has provided an efficient accommodation secretary, Mr. J. O'Kane, who also operates the Earlmount Guest House at 322/4 Cowley Rd. (tel. Oxford 40236). If Mr. O'Kane cannot accommodate you himself, he will spare no effort in helping you to find the kind of accommodation you require. Advance single or party bookings can also be made, long or short term, single person or party booking. No fees are charged. B&B prices begin at £7 ($13.65) per person.

The **Oxford Information Centre** (tel. Oxford 762871) operates a room-booking service for personal callers for a fee of 50p (98¢) from Easter to September. If you'd like to seek out lodgings on your own, the staff at the center will provide a list of accommodations, or you may try one of the following recommendations:

The Upper Bracket

Randolph Hotel, Beaumont Street (tel. Oxford 47481), is a recently refurbished Gothic-Victorian monument, dating back to 1864. For more than a century, it has been Oxford's prestige hotel, centrally situated and commanding an impressive vantage point overlooking St. Giles, the Ashmolean Museum, and the Cornmarket. The lounges, although modernized, are still cavernous enough for dozens of separate conversational groupings; and the furnishings are bright and contemporary. Run as a member of Trusthouse Forte Ltd., the hotel contains 111 rooms, all with private bath, telephone, radio and color TV. The price for a single is from £30 ($58.50), from £38 ($74.10) for a double. The Randolph Restaurant boasts a high standard of cuisine, and specializes in flambé dishes. A set lunch goes for £6 ($11.70), a set dinner for £8 ($15.60), and there's a very good à la carte menu as well. A wide selection of wines is also available. The restaurant is open from 12:30 to 2:30 p.m. and from 7 to 9:45 p.m. Service charge and VAT are included in the tariffs. There is also a popular coffeeshop with an entrance off the street.

The Medium-Priced Range

The **TraveLodge**, Peartree Roundabout, Woodstock Road (tel. Oxford 54301), is ideal for motorists who want to be within easy reach of the university and shopping districts of Oxford, yet set apart at the city edge for a quiet night's sleep. Easy to spot, near a large bus stop, the lodge invites with international flags fluttering in the breezes. Its lower-level bedrooms open onto private terraces. The furnishings are in the typical motel style, with compact, built-in necessities. Each of the rooms has a picture-window wall, a private bath with shower, a television and radio, individually controlled heating and tea-making facilities. Room rates in a single are £22 ($42.90), £29 ($56.55) for a double. Some family rooms for three or four persons cost the double rate, plus £3 ($5.85) per extra bed. In the Autogrill (open at 7:30 a.m.), you can order an English breakfast. Otherwise, a continental breakfast is included in the room rates, as are service and VAT. On the grounds are a swimming pool, the fully licensed Blenheim Bar, a 24-hour cafeteria, and a garage.

The **Oxford Europa Hotel,** Godstow Road, Wolvercote Roundabout (tel. Oxford 59933), one of the Grand Metropolitan chain members, incorporates the principles of advanced motel design, with an emphasis on spacious, glassed-in areas and streamlined bedrooms. Its position is ideal, hidden from the traffic at the northern edge of Oxford, two miles away, at the junction of the A40 and the A34. Although generally patronized by motorists, it can also be reached by bus. In a double or twin, with a full breakfast, you pay £37 ($72.15) for two, £25 ($48.75) in a single. On the second floor is a restaurant, and there are drinking bars as well, with traditional entertainment on most nights.

Eastgate Hotel, Merton Street, off The High (tel. Oxford 48244), is a hotel of character, exquisitely placed opposite Merton College and on The High. It's smallish—in fact, it is a group of older buildings joined together and modernized. The bedrooms are clean-cut, borrowing their inspiration from the compact, serviceable designs of Scandinavia. Singles without bath cost from £18.50 ($36.08) nightly, rising to £29 ($56.55) with bath; and doubles without bath rent from £31 ($60.45), going up to £37 ($72.15) with bath. All units have color TV sets, and tariffs quoted include a full English breakfast, although VAT is extra. The lounge opening onto The High is pleasantly furnished; the dining room is airy and comfortable.

Royal Oxford Hotel, Park End Street (tel. Oxford 48432), is an oldish establishment given a new lease on life by a drastic renovation of its interior. Near Oxford Station, about a ten-minute walk from the center of the city, it is a comfortable and convenient place at which to stay. Of its 25 bedrooms, 12 have private baths, and all have color TV, phone, and radio. A bathless single goes for £18.50 ($36.08); with bath, £25 ($48.75). A bathless twin or double rents for £28 ($54.60), increasing to £32 ($62.40) with bath. Prices include service, VAT, and breakfast. The bedrooms are well kept, with modern, compact furnishings, and all have television.

The Budget Range

The **Old Parsonage Hotel,** 3 Banbury Rd. (tel. Oxford 54843), is so old it looks like an extension of one of the ancient colleges. Originally a 13th-century hospital named Bethleen, it was restored in the early 17th century. Today, it's slated for designation as an ancient monument. Near St. Giles Church, it is set back from the street behind a low stone wall and sheltered by surrounding trees and shrubbery. However, most of the rooms are in a modern wing which is more institutional in character. The owners charge from £13 ($25.35) per person nightly for bed and breakfast in a single, from £23 ($44.85) in a twin or double. Should you want a private shower, the price is increased to £24 ($46.80) for two persons. Twenty rooms have been added to the accommodations. Some of the large front rooms, with leaded-glass windows, are set aside for travelers. Many rooms are big enough to have a living-room area, armchairs, antique chests, and soft beds. You have breakfast in a pleasant Swedish-style dining room, overlooking the garden. A licensed restaurant and bar are on the premises.

Ascot Guest House, 283 Iffley Rd. (tel. Oxford 240259), is ideally located in the quiet outskirts of Oxford, yet only minutes away by bus or car from the city center. The owner, Mrs. Elizabeth Neville, has performed the difficult task of combining friendliness, high standards, and reasonable prices in her recently refurbished home. All rooms have wall-to-wall carpeting, telephones, and hot and cold running water. The per-person charge of £7 ($13.65) per night includes breakfast and VAT. Parking facilities are plentiful here, and it's usually less expensive and more convenient to leave your car at the guest house and take the frequent buses into the city. When Mrs. Neville is unable to accommodate any more guests, she will cheerfully recommend other guest houses in the area.

Belmont Guest House, 182 Woodstock Rd. (tel. Oxford 53698), is on a tree-lined avenue in the residential part of Oxford, about one mile from the city center. It's on the main road and close to Blenheim Palace, Stratford-upon-Avon, the Midlands, and the Lake District. All rooms have central heating and hot and cold running water. Bath, showers, and a good English breakfast are supplied. Most rooms can be used as either doubles, twins, or family rooms. The charge is £7 ($13.65) per person for B&B.

LIVING ON THE OUTSKIRTS: Weston Manor, Weston-on-the-Green (tel. Bletchington 50621), is a moated stone manor house, only eight miles from Oxford (on the A43 Oxford-Northampton road)—ideal as a center for touring the district (Blenheim Palace is only five miles away). The manor, owned and run by the Price family, is rooted in the 11th century; portions of the present building date back to the 14th and 16th centuries, with later additions in Victoria's day. Although long owned by noblemen, the estate was an abbey until they were abolished by Henry VIII. Of course, there are ghosts, such as Mad Maude, the naughty nun who was burned at the stake for her "indecent and immoral" behavior. She returns to haunt the Oak Bedrooms. Prince Rupert, son of Charles II, hid from Cromwell's soldiers in one of the fireplaces, eventually escaping in drag as the "maiden of the milk bucket."

As you enter the driveway, you pass two elm trees, dating back to 1672, and proceed into a formal car-park area. The reception lounge is furnished with antiques, dominated by a Tudor fireplace and a long refectory table, the latter glowing from centuries of polishing. The various lounges have fine old pieces. Most of the bedrooms are spacious, furnished with antiques (often four-posters), old dressing tables, and chests. The cost of staying here is £25 ($48.75) in a single without bath. Doubles without bath go for £37 ($72.15), increasing to £46 ($89.70) with bath. All these tariffs include an English breakfast, VAT, and service. Breakfast is served in the yellow morning room, with your table set in front of the stone-mullioned and leaded windows. The view is of the formal garden, edged with animal and bird figures trimmed out of the old yew hedges.

In the Great Hall, one of the most beautiful dining rooms in England, you'll be served your lunch and dinner. It's like a chapel, with an open raftered and beamed ceiling, the lower portion solidly paneled with a rare example of linenfold. There's a minstrels' gallery and a large wrought-iron chandelier. The food is first rate. A cold buffet is featured in the bar for £3.50 ($6.83). On any given dinner menu, you're likely to find roast Aylesbury duckling, spring chicken, sirloin steak, Scottish salmon, or rainbow trout. Dinner ranges in price from £9 ($17.55) to £15 ($29.25), depending on your choice of a main course, and the big Sunday lunch costs £9 ($17.55). In warm weather, you can enjoy the open-air swimming pool, surrounded by its gardens.

Studley Priory Hotel, Horton-cum-Studley (tel. Stanton St. John 203), may be remembered by those who saw *A Man for All Seasons*. The former Benedictine priory, now a hotel, was used for background shots for the private residence of Sir Thomas More. It is a stunning example of Elizabethan architecture, although it originally dates from the 12th century. Lived in for around 300 years by the Croke family, it was brought by Mr. and Mrs. E. E. Parke in 1961. They receive guests for £28 ($54.60) in a single, from £32.50 ($63.38) to £50 ($98) in a double. All of the rooms have private baths.

Only seven miles from Oxford, the manor is protected from noise by its gardens and lawns. Stone built, in the manorial style with large halls and long bedroom wings, Studley is gabled with mullioned windows. The rooms are large, the beds soft, and the furnishings tasteful. Even if you're not staying over, you may want to drop in for lunch or dinner, with a four-course meal averaging around £10.50 ($20.48). Getting here is a bit complicated—so be armed with a good map when you strike out from Oxford.

WHERE TO EAT: **Restaurant Elizabeth,** 84 St. Aldate's (tel. Oxford 42230), in an intimate and special restaurant that (in spite of its name) owes the inspiration of its cuisine to the continent, notably Spain, France, and Greece. Under the watchful eye of Antonio Lopez, it attracts Oxonians who appreciate good food served in a friendly, inviting atmosphere. For appetizers, try either the ttoro (a Basque fish soup served with aïoli), or avgolemono (the Greek national soup—chicken bouillon laced with a beaten egg and lemon juice). Favorite main dishes which I highly recommend include juicy, light quenelles, duck with orange sauce, moussaka, charcoaled prawns with aïoli, and coq au vin. For dessert, the syllabub is a winner. Including wine and coffee, plus all the extras, the cost of a dinner is about £20 ($39) per person. Wine by the liter, both bourgogne and bordeaux, is available. The restaurant is open for dinner from 6:30 to 11 p.m. every day, except Monday. Sunday lunch is from 12:30 to 2:30 p.m. and dinner from 7 to 10:30 p.m.

La Sorbonne, 130A The High (tel. Oxford 41320), in a 17th-century building, is tucked away on a narrow lane off The High. True to its name, it provides typically French meals from time-tested recipes. A good beginning is the chef's special, moules marinières, offered from October to March only. An alternative suggestion is escargots bourguignonnes or perhaps a fresh herb and vegetable soup. Mr. Chavagnon, the chef de cuisine and proprietor, offers not only the usual French dishes, but the following specialties as well: jugged hare, wild duck, and suprême de volaille estragon. A soufflé for two is a specialty. Mr. Chavagnon says: "We charge a lot for soufflés because they require a lot of care and attention. When we tried to charge less, everybody wanted one and we couldn't cope." Expect to pay, on an average, about £16 ($31.20) per head. The restaurant is open from noon to 2:30 p.m. and from 7 to 10:30 p.m. It's closed on Sunday.

The **Cherwell Boathouse Restaurant,** Bardwell Road (tel. Oxford 52746), is owned by the people who rent out the punts, and it's run by a cheerful committee of amateurs who cater to improverished undergraduates. The menu contains items which have obviously come from friends (Di's pork with mushrooms, for example). Two fixed menus which are rarely repeated are offered at each meal, and the cooks admit they try out new dishes all the time. Appetizers include soups or fish or meat pâtés, followed by casseroles, pies, and hot pots, then some exotic dessert—cikolatak pasta, rum soufflé, or fruit fool.

There is a very reasonable wine list, including brandy after dinner. The restaurant is open every evening from 8 to 10:30 p.m. and for Sunday lunch. For a regular dinner, the charge is £7.90 ($15.41), although Sunday lunch is only £7.40 ($14.43), including VAT. It's recommended that you make a reservation. Children, if they don't order a full meal, are granted half price. In summer the restaurant also does an all-day cold buffet in the Marquee for thirsty punters. This place surely must be one of the most English, most attractive, and least known of the eating establishments of Oxford. It also provides an opportunity to observe a most important aspect of Oxford undergraduate life.

Saraceno, Magdalen Street (tel. Oxford 49171), is rather unobtrusive, hidden around the corner from the Randolph Hotel and opposite St. Mary Magdalen Church. It's in the basement so only the door and a small sign announce its presence. The kitchen is separated from the dining room by vast red glass panes, behind which a puppet show of figures dance and weave among the pots and pans.

Saraceno is, after all, an Italian restaurant, and all the usual pasta dishes are available with just the right sauces. After ordering one, you might settle later for scaloppine with sage and olives, baron of lamb with marsala, Dover sole Colbert, or rainbow trout with almonds. Appetizers include scrambled eggs with caviar, smoked mackerel, and prosciutto with melon. They have a very special dish of quail served in a rich wine sauce with plain cooked vegetables or salad. With ample portions of the Italian house wine, a meal will cost about £12 ($23.40) per person, including a creamy dessert from the trolley, perhaps a syllabub or Bavarian cream with liqueur.

THE SPECIAL PUBS OF OXFORD: The **Bear Inn,** Alfred Street, is an Oxford tradition, a short block from The High overlooking the north side of Christ Church College. It's the village pub. Its swinging inn sign depicts the bear and ragged staff, old insignia of the Earls of Warwick, who were among the early patrons. Built in the 13th century, the inn has been known to many famous people who have lived and studied at Oxford. Over the years, it's been mentioned time and time again in English literature.

The Bear has served a useful purpose in breaking down social barriers, bringing a wide variety of people together in a relaxed and friendly way. You might talk with a rajah from India, a university don, a titled gentleman—and Dave and Des Beeson, who are the latest in a line of owners that goes back more than 700 years.

They may explain to you their astonishing hobby: collecting ties! Around the lounge bar you'll see thousands of snipped portions of neckties, which have been labeled with their owners' names. For those of you who want to leave a bit of yourself, a thin strip of the bottom of your tie will be cut off (with your permission, of course) with a huge pair of ceremonial scissors. Then you, as the donor, will be given a free drink on the house. After this initiation, you may want to join in some of the informal songfests of the undergraduates.

The shelves behind the bar are stacked and piled with delicious items to nibble on: cheese, crisp rolls, cold meats, flans. Homemade pie with french fries and beans costs £1.50 ($2.93); a ploughman's lunch, £1 ($1.95); and many salads are offered, from £1.30 ($2.54).

The **Trout Inn,** 195 Godstow Rd., near Wolvercote (tel. Oxford 54485), lies on the outskirts of Oxford. Ask any former or present student of Oxford to name his most treasured pub, and his answer is likely to be the Trout. Hidden away from visitors and townspeople, the Trout is a private world where you can get ale and beer—and top-notch meals. Have your drink in one of the historic rooms, with their settles, brass, and old prints, or go out in sunny weather to sit on a stone wall, where you can feed crumbs to the swans that swim in the adjoining weir pool. Take an arched stone bridge, stone terraces, architecture that has wildly pitched roofs and gables, throw in the Thames River, and you have the Trout. If you don't have a car, take bus 520 or 521 to Wolvercote, then walk.

Daily specials are featured for lunch. The seafood platter's popular, as is a tempting seven-ounce entrecôte. For dessert, try the fruit tart with cream. The pub is open from noon to 2 p.m. and from 7 to 10 p.m. Salads are served during the summer and grills in winter. Expect to pay about £7 ($15.65) for a meal, unless you settle for just a plate of smoked trout or salmon with brown bread and butter. If so, you're likely to pay £2.60 ($5.07).

On your way there and back, look for the view of Oxford from the bridge. And go ahead and talk with the undergraduates, who usually like telling about their university. They may even ask you to have tea at one of their colleges, where the average visitor rarely penetrates.

EATING AND DRINKING NEAR TO OXFORD: White Hart, Fyfield, seven miles along the A420 Oxford/Swindon/West Country road (tel. Frilford Heath 390585), is high on the list of Oxford students who want to celebrate by taking their friends to a romantic inn—once the Fyfield Chantry—for a superb dinner. It's a public house, dating from the early 15th century, and owned since 1580 by St. John's College (although the present building is leased). In the 1960s the college renovated the inn, successfully restoring its old-world charm. It was once the home of a chantry priest and five almsmen until it was dissolved under Henry VIII. What was the lower chamber for the priest has now been transformed into a raftered dining room; and the ancient kitchen is the beamed lounge bar. The menu consists of house specialties, plus the dishes of the day. A lunch costs £4.75 ($9.26); a three-course dinner, from £6.50 ($12.68) to £11 ($21.45), including VAT, the difference in price depending on your selection of a main dish. The wines, an excellent selection, are extra. Specialties of the White Hart include traditional English food, with emphasis on game. The restaurant is open daily, and reservations are advised.

BLENHEIM PALACE: This extravagant baroque palace regards itself as England's answer to Versailles. Blenheim is the home of the 11th Duke of Marlborough, a descendant of the first Duke of Marlborough (John Churchill), an on-again, off-again favorite of Queen Anne. In his day (1650–1722), the first duke became the supreme military figure in Europe. Fighting on the Danube near a village named Blenheim, Churchill defeated the forces of Louis XIV. The lavish palace of Blenheim was built for the duke as a gift from the queen. It was designed by Sir John Vanbrugh, who was also the architect of Castle Howard. Landscaping was carried out by Capability Brown.

The palace is loaded with riches; antiques, porcelain, oil paintings, tapestries, and chinoiserie. But more North Americans know Blenheim as the birthplace of Sir Winston. Today, the former prime minister lies buried in Bladon Churchyard, near the palace.

Blenheim Palace is open every day from mid-March to October, inclusive, from 11:30 a.m. to 5 p.m. The last tour is at 5 p.m., and the last admittance to the palace is at 4:45 p.m. On spring bank holidays, Sunday, and Monday, charity events take place in the park, when different prices and times apply. The admission fee is £2.25 ($4.39) for adults, £1.10 ($2.15) for children.

In the park is the Bleinheim Model Railway, second largest in Britain, which you can usually ride on weekends in season. The palace is at Woodstock, eight miles north of Oxford on the A34 road to Stratford-upon-Avon. From Oxford, do-it-your-selfers take bus 44 from the Gloucester Green Bus Station, which make the run to Woodstock. For information, telephone Woodstock 811325.

3. Hertfordshire

Like a giant jellyfish, the frontier of Greater London spills over into this county, once described by Charles Lamb as "hearty, homely, loving Hertford-shire." This fertile land lies northwest of London and supplies much of that city's food, although industry has crept in. Hertfordshire is sometimes called "the market basket of England."

Its most important tourist attraction, which is usually visited on a day trip from London, follows.

HATFIELD HOUSE: One of the chief attractions of Hertfordshire, and one of the greatest of all English country houses, Hatfield House is just 21 miles north of London on the A1. To build what is now the E-shaped Hatfield House, the old Tudor palace at Hatfield was mostly demolished. The Banqueting Hall, however, remains.

Hatfield was much a part of the lives of both Henry VIII and his daughter Elizabeth I. In the old palace, built in the 15th century, Elizabeth romped and played as a child. Although Henry was married to her mother, Anne Boleyn, at the time of Elizabeth's birth, the marriage was later nullified (Anne lost her head and Elizabeth her legitimacy). Henry also used to stash away his oldest daughter, Mary Tudor, at Hatfield. But when Mary became Queen of England, and set about earning the dubious distinction of "Bloody Mary," she found Elizabeth a problem. For a while she kept her in the Tower of London, but she eventually let her return to Hatfield (Elizabeth's loyalty to Catholicism was seriously doubted). In 1558, while at Hatfield, Elizabeth learned of her ascension to the throne of England.

The Jacobean house that exists today contains much antique furniture, tapestries, and paintings as well as three much-reproduced portraits, including the ermine and rainbow portraits of Elizabeth I. The Great Hall is suitably medieval, complete with a minstrel's gallery. One of the rarest exhibits is a pair of silk stockings, said to have been worn by Elizabeth herself, the first lady in England to don such apparel. The park and the gardens are also worth explor-ing. The Riding School and Palace Stables contain a number of interesting historical and costume exhibitions.

Hatfield is usually open from March 25 through October 7 daily, except on Monday and Good Friday, from noon to 5 p.m. (on Sunday, from 2 to 5:30 p.m., and on bank holiday Mondays from 11 a.m. to 5 p.m.). Admission is £1.65 ($3.22). The house is across from the station in Hatfield. From London, take Green Line coach 724 or 732, or the fast trains from King's Cross.

Luncheons and teas are available in the converted coach house in the Old Palace yard.

Elizabethan banquets are staged Tuesday, Thursday, Friday, and Saturday, with much gaiety and music. Guests are invited to drink in an anteroom, then join the long tables for a feast consisting of typical English food, ending with the classic syllabub. Wine is included in the cost of the meal, but you're expected to pay for your predinner drinks yourself. The best way to get there from London is to book a coach tour for an inclusive fee from £16.50 ($32.16). The Evan Evans agency has tours leaving from Russell Square or even from 41 Tottenham Court Rd. The coach returns to London after midnight. If you get there under your own steam, the cost is £12 ($23.70) on Tuesday and Thursday, £14 ($27.30) on Friday and Saturday. For reservations, telephone Hatfield 62055.

In Old Hatfield, a fine place for light lunches and good lager is **Eight Bells,** a pub on Park Street. For Dickens fans, it was the inn where Bill Sikes and his dog found temporary refuge after the brutal murder of Nancy. It's a rickety old corner inn with a central bar for drinks and dining nooks—in all, a forest of time-blackened beams, settles, and pewter tankards. A bowl of homemade soup costs 35p (68¢), and the cook's specialty is smoked mackerel filet at £1.35 ($2.63).

HERTFORD: This old Saxon city is the county town, containing many fine examples of domestic architecture, some of which date back to the 16th century. Hertford is reached via the A1 or A10 from London. Samuel Stone, founder of Hartford, Connecticut, was born here. The town's Norman castle has long been in ruins, although part of the still-standing keep dates from the 16th century.

For food and lodgings, try the **Salisbury Arms Hotel,** Fore Street (tel. Hertford 53091), which has been called "always Hertford's principal inn." For 400 years it's been feeding and providing lodgings to wayfarers, or giving a hot grog to the coachman, a stable for his horses. Although the stables have long given way to a car park, a sense of history still prevails. In the cellar is medieval masonry predating the 16th-century structure around it. Cromwell is said to have lodged here, and both Royalists and Roundheads have mounted the Jacobean staircase. Bedrooms now spill over into a modern extension, a total of 22 functionally furnished rooms added to the 10 more antiquated original ones. Rates depend on the room occupied—single, double, or twin. Singles start at £15 ($29.25), going up to £17.50 ($34.13) for those requiring a private bath. Two persons pay from £22.50 ($43.88) to £25 ($48.75). Good, wholesome English "fayre" is provided. At lunch, when most visitors stop by, a cut from the roast of the day goes for £3.50 ($6.83) with vegetables. The dining room is paneled and intimately partitioned. There is, as well, a well-stocked cellar. Dinners are from £8 ($15.60).

ST. ALBANS: This cathedral city, just 21 miles northeast of London, dates back 2000 years. It was named after a Roman soldier, the first Christian martyr in England. Don't ask a resident to show you to the **Cathedral of St. Albans.** Here it's still known as "The Abbey," even though Henry VIII dissolved it as such in 1539. Construction on the cathedral was launched in 1077, making it one of the early Norman churches of England. The bricks, especially visible in the tower, came from the old Roman city of Verulamium at the foot of the hill. The nave and west front date from 1235.

The **Verulamium Museum** at St. Michael's stands on the site of the Roman city. Here you'll view some of the finest Roman mosaics in Britain. Part of the Roman town wall, a hypocaust, and a theater and its adjoining houses and shops are still visible. Visit in summer from 10 a.m. to 5:30 p.m. weekdays (on Sunday from 2 to 5:30 p.m.), and in winter from 10 to 4 weekdays, 2 to 4 on Sunday, paying 50p (98¢) for adults, 30p (59¢) for children and students.

The **Clock Tower** at Market Place was built in 1402, standing 77 feet high, a total of five floors.

From St. Albans you can visit **Gorhambury House,** a classic-style mansion built in 1777, containing 16th-century enameled glass and historic portraits. It's open, May to September, only on Thursday (2 to 5 p.m.), charging adults £1 ($1.95) for admission; children 60p ($1.17). The location is 2½ miles north of St. Albans near the A5.

Salisbury Hall (tel. Bowmans Green 23274), a 17th-century house surrounded by a Norman moat, lies five miles south of St. Albans on the A6. Nell Gwynne, Charles II, even Jenny Churchill and her son Winston, have all stayed here. Inside, the fireplaces are of exceptional beauty. Also displayed is the prototype of the de Havilland "Mosquito" aircraft which was designed and built at Salisbury Hall in World War II. Visits are possible from Easter Sunday to October 1 on Sunday from 2 to 6 p.m. It is also open on Thursday from 2 to 6, from July 6 till around the end of September. Admission is £1.40 ($2.73) for adults, 70p ($1.37) for children.

Back in St. Albans, I offer the following recommendations for food and lodgings:

Food and Lodging

St. Michael's Manor Hotel, Fishpool Street (tel. St. Albans 64444), stands on five acres of landscaped gardens, with a private reflection lake, about a ten-minute walk from the heart of St. Albans. At its core is an original manor house dating from the 16th century. The dedicated Newling Ward family run the hotel with flair and grace. To the original structure a William and Mary bow-fronted center section has been added, along with a Georgian-style extension.

The grounds of the hotel contain such trees as cedars of Lebanon and hornbeam, and all the attractively furnished bedrooms are named after the trees in the garden. Bathless singles cost £20 ($39) nightly, bathless twins going for £30 ($58.50). A twin room with a private bath and shower costs £34 ($66.30), including a full English breakfast. The Lilac Honeymoon Suite is most impressive, with its four-poster bed and lilac-colored decor.

In the Georgian-style dining room, lit by candlelight, a well-prepared international menu is presented nightly to both residents and nonresidents. At lunchtime, the chef serves a table d'hôte menu with coffee at £6 ($11.70) per head. For dinner, a three-course meal is offered at £9 ($17.55) per head, but the restaurant also has a reasonable à la carte menu at around £14 ($27.30) per person.

The **White Hart Hotel,** Holywell Hill (tel. St. Albans 53624), is a timbered inn of uncertain origin. It may have been a 13th-century coaching inn. At the White Hart, formerly called the Hartshorn, Hogarth painted the picture of himself which hangs in London's National Portrait Gallery. Of architectural interest is a lounge with a minstrels' gallery, oak timbering, and a collection of copper and antiques. The old-world dining room has Windsor chairs and paneled walls, and there are two lounge bars, all in the old English style. Bedrooms come with hot and cold running water, but none of the ten units has a private bath. Singles are expensive—£18 ($35.10) for B&B, although doubles or twins go for a more moderate £22 ($42.90) nightly, these tariffs including VAT, service, and a full English breakfast. In the dining room you can order from a table d'hôte menu and an à la carte selection. The White Hart stands opposite the cathedral and a short walk through the abbey grounds leads to the ruins of Roman Verulamium.

For dining, **Zorbas Greek Restaurant,** 3 French Row (tel. St. Albans 60609), seems an incongruous choice in such an historic English town, but it is a good and fairly inexpensive eating place. Right in the old part of town, it is reached by going along a pedestrian mall. The Theocharides family welcome you if you've come to dine, although I've seen them politely turn away English ladies who drop in just for afternoon tea, which they don't serve, incidentally. The house specialty, served with rice, is a kebab. You might prefer to begin with a Greek salad or hummus (ground chick peas with garlic). Pita bread is also served, as is the classic Greek moussaka. Another house specialty is stuffed vine leaves. Meals, excluding your drink, begin at £7 ($13.65). Although closed for lunch on Sunday and holidays, the restaurant is open otherwise until 3 p.m., and for dinner from 6 to 11 p.m.

SHAW'S CORNER: Just southwest of Ayot St. Lawrence, three miles northwest of Welwyn, stands the home where George Bernard Shaw lived from 1906 to 1950. The house is practically as he left it at his death. In the hall, for example, his hats are still hanging, as if ready for him to don one. His personal mementos are in his study, drawing room, dining room, and writing hut, which can be visited in March and November on Saturday and Sunday, and from April 1 to October 31 on Wednesday through Sunday from 11 a.m. to 1 p.m. and from 2 to 6 p.m. (or sunset if it comes before 6). Admission is £1.10 ($2.15) for adults, half price for children.

4. Buckinghamshire

This is a leafy county, lying north of the Thames and somewhat to the west of London. Its identifying marks are the wide Vale of Aylesbury, with its sprawling fields and tiny villages, and the long chalk range of the Chilterns. Going south from the range, you'll find what is left of a once-great beech forest.

A good center for touring the Chilterns is—

AYLESBURY: Gourmets still speak of its succulent ducks, a prize-winning dish on any table, although ducks bearing that name are usually raised elsewhere these days. The county town, Aylesbury has a number of timbered inns, old houses, and a wide Market Square. Although less than 40 miles from London, it remains cozily old world.

Six miles northwest of Aylesbury, **Waddeson Manor** (tel. Aylesbury 651211) contains an outstanding collection of decorative art of the 17th and 18th centuries. Among the paintings are portraits by Reynolds, Gainsborough, and Romney. Visiting times are from March 24 to October 31, Wednesday to Sunday, from 2 to 6 p.m. Admission to the grounds, aviary, and house is £1.50 ($2.93), £2 ($3.90) on Friday when extra rooms are shown. The manor was built in the late 19th century for the Baron Ferdinand de Rothschild.

Back in Aylesbury, you can find food and lodgings at the **Kings Head,** Market Square (tel. Aylesbury 5158), a half-timbered hotel that was once a 15th-century coaching inn. It is one of the finest examples of Tudor architecture in Buckinghamshire. Its 15 bedrooms overlook a cobbled courtyard. Because of its heavy patronage by business people on weekdays, I've never been able to get a room unless reserved well in advance. Rooms, incidentally, cost from £25 ($48.75) in a double, plus VAT, and from £16 ($31.20) in a single, plus VAT. No unit has a private bath. Lunch is served from noon to 2 p.m. and dinner from 7 to 9 p.m. (from 7:30 to 10 p.m. on Saturday). Try to have a predinner drink in the cozy pub in back, with its collection of weapons. Bar lunches start at £1.40 ($2.73), going up to £3 ($5.85). A set dinner is offered for £7 ($13.65), although there is an à la carte menu as well. The inn was much frequented by Cromwell, and his chair is still on view in the lounge bar. He slept in the Cromwell Room upstairs with its extra-large bed.

BUCKINGHAM: This old market town on the River Ouse was once the county town of Buckingham. It has a fine 13th-century Chantry Chapel and some 18th-century houses.

If you're motoring through, try to plan a luncheon or dinner stopover at **Old Market House,** Market Hill (tel. Buckingham 2385), housed in one of the town's most interesting buildings, a black-and-white timbered structure with leaded-glass windows. A three-course set luncheon is offered at £5 ($9.75) from noon to 2:15 p.m. If you arrive earlier, you can order morning coffee from 9:30 to 11 a.m. Dinner is à la carte, beginning at £8 ($15.60) and features the chef's specialty—chicken chasseur. Dinner is served every evening from 7 to 9:15 p.m. except Sunday and Monday. Wine is sold by the glass at 75p ($1.46).

Food and Lodging

White Hart, Market Square (tel. Buckingham 2131), is an oldish market-town hotel, with 18th-century origins, although the plaster facade and portico are Victorian additions. In recent years the hotel has been remodeled and equipped for modern comfort, its renovation bringing simplicity to the interior. All of the hotel's 20 bedrooms have private baths, television sets, and coffee-making facilities. Singles rent for £24 ($46.80) and doubles cost £32 ($62.40) with private bath. The hotel's dining room, called the Georgian Room, has its own small dance floor, and there is a lounge bar as well. They also have a Country Kitchen, serving steaks, trout, seafood pancakes, all with fresh salads and granary bread. Meals cost from £5 ($9.75) to £8.50 ($16.58).

JORDANS VILLAGE: Old Jordans, Jordans Lane, in Jordans Village (tel. Chalfont St. Giles 4586), is a farm dating back to the Middle Ages. But its recorded history starts in the early 17th century when one Thomas Russell, sitting tenant, bought the freehold, signing the deed with his thumbprint. The house was added to over the years, and in the mid-17th century William Penn, founder of Pennsylvania, and other well-known Dissenters stayed here and worshipped.

Now the property of the Quakers, the house is run as a conference center, but they have several simply furnished rooms available for overnight guests at £10.25 ($19.99) in a single, £16.75 ($32.66) in a double, including breakfast.

On the grounds is the Mayflower Barn, built almost undisputably from timbers from the ship *Mayflower* in which the first Pilgrims sailed to the New World. These days the beams ring to the strains of concert music and recitals performed by top-notch artists.

Morning tea or coffee with crackers goes for 40p (78¢), and an afternoon tea of scones and jam for 75p ($1.46). These are served in the great kitchen/

dining room of the hall. Supper at £2.50 ($4.88) is served at 7 p.m.; and reservations are a must.

It's a very peaceful place, full of history, and perhaps a little isolated from today's bustle.

MILTON'S COTTAGE: The modern residential town of Gerrards Cross is often called the Beverly Hills of England, as it attracts the wealthy-chic who settle here in many beautiful homes. Surrounding this plush section are several tucked-away hamlets, including **Chalfont St. Giles,** where the poet Milton lived during the Great Plague in 1665. He completed *Paradise Lost* here. In this 16th-century cottage are two museum rooms containing 93 rare books, including first editions of *Paradise Lost* and *Paradise Regained* and other Miltoniana, with exhibits of interest to young and old. A beautiful cottage garden is a further attraction. The house is open daily, except Monday, from February 1 to October 31 (on spring and summer bank holiday Monday from 10 a.m. to 1 p.m. and 2 to 6 p.m.; on Sunday from 2 to 6 p.m.). Charges are 60p ($1.17) for adults and 20p (39¢) for children. It is closed November, December, and January. For information, write to Milton's Cottage, Dean Way, Chalfont St. Giles, Bucks, HP8 4JH, U.K. (tel. Chalfont St. Giles 2313).

West of Gerrards Cross, the town of Beaconsfield, with its broad, tree-lined High Street, enjoys many associations with Disraeli. Visitors pass through here en route to—

HUGHENDEN MANOR: Outside High Wycombe, in Buckinghamshire, sits a country manor that gives us not only an insight into the age of Victoria, but acquaints us with a remarkable man. In Benjamin Disraeli we meet one of the most enigmatic figures of 19th-century England. At age 21, Dizzy published anonymously his five-volume novel *Vivian Grey.* But it wasn't his shining hour. He went on to other things, marrying an older widow for her money, although they developed, apparently, a most successful relationship. He entered politics and continued writing novels, his later ones meeting with more acclaim.

In 1848 Disraeli acquired Hughenden Manor, a country house that befitted his fast-rising political and social position. He served briefly as prime minister in 1868, but his political fame rests on his stewardship as prime minister during 1874–1880. He became Queen Victoria's friend, and in 1877 she paid him a rare honor by visiting him at Hughenden.

In 1876 Disraeli became the Earl of Beaconsfield: he had arrived. Only his wife was dead, and he was to die in 1881. Instead of being buried at Westminster Abbey, he preferred the simple little graveyard of Hughenden Church.

His library is preserved much as he left it. In fact, Hughenden contains an odd assortment of memorabilia, including a lock of Disraeli's hair. The letters from Victoria, the autographed books, and especially a portrait of Lord Byron, known to Disraeli's father.

If you're driving to Hughenden Manor on the way to Oxford, continue north of High Wycombe on the A4128 for about 1½ miles. If you're relying on public transportation from London, take coach 711 to High Wycombe, then board an Alder Valley bus (323, 324, 333, or 334). The manor house and garden are open daily except Monday and Tuesday from April to October, from 2 to 6 p.m. (from 12:30 to 6 p.m. on Sunday and bank holidays). In March and November, they're open on Saturday and Sunday only from 2 to 5 p.m. (or sunset if earlier). Admission for adults is £1.30 ($2.54), half price for children.

It is closed all December, January, and February, and on Good Friday. For more information, telephone High Wycombe 28051.

WEST WYCOMBE: Snuggled in the Chiltern Hills 30 miles west of London, the village of West Wycombe still has an atmosphere of the early 18th century. The thatched roofs have been replaced with tiles, and some of the buildings have been removed or replaced, but the village is still two centuries removed from the present day.

In the mid-18th century, Sir Francis Dashwood began an ambitious building program at West Wycombe. His strong interest in architecture and design led Sir Francis to undertake a series of monuments and parks which are still among the finest in the country today. He also sponsored the building of a road using the chalk quarries on the hill to aid in the support of the poverty-stricken villagers. The resulting caves became the meeting place of "The Knights of St. Francis of Wycombe," later known as **The Hellfire Club.** The knights consisted of a number of illustrious men drawn from the social circle surrounding the Prince of Wales. Its members "gourmandized," swilling claret and enjoying the company of women "of a cheerful, lively disposition . . . who considered themselves lawful wives of the brethren during their stay."

You can tour the caves, wandering through a quarter mile of winding passages, past colorful waxwork scenes brought to life by sound and light effects. The caves are open from 11 a.m. to 6 p.m. daily from March through September, and from noon to 4 p.m. on weekends only during the rest of the year. Admission is £1.50 ($2.93) for adults, 75p ($1.46) for children.

Other sights at West Wycombe include the **Church of St. Lawrence,** perched atop West Wycombe Hill and topped by a huge golden ball. Parts of the church date from the 13th century; its richly decorated interior was copied from a third-century Syrian sun temple. The view from the hill is worth the trek up. Near the church stands the **Dashwood Mausoleum,** built in a style derived from Constantine's Arch in Rome.

A visit to **West Wycombe House,** home of the Dashwoods, is of both historical and architectural interest. Both George III and Ben Franklin stayed here, although not at the same time. The house is one of the best examples of Palladian-style architecture in England. The interior is lavishly decorated with paintings and antiques from the 18th century.

During your tour, you may also wander freely through the village, stopping for lunch at one of the public houses, or browsing through the gift shop. Four miles of nature trails also meander about the village, through forests and farmlands.

Although the Dashwood house is open only from June 1 to August 30, the rest of the village may, of course, be visited all year. The house is open Monday to Friday from 2:15 to 6 p.m. and charges an admission of £1.60 ($3.12) for adults and 80p ($1.56) for children. If you just want to visit the grounds, the cost is reduced to 80p ($1.56).

The telephone number of the West Wycombe Park Office is High Wycombe 24411.

5. Bedfordshire

This county contains the fertile, rich Vale of Bedford, crossed by the River Ouse. Most visitors from London head here on a day trip to visit historic Woburn Abbey (previewed below). Others know of its county town—

BEDFORD: On the Ouse, Bedford contains many riverside parks and gardens, but is better known for its associations with Bunyan. In Mill Street stands the 1850 **Bunyan Meeting House,** erected on the site of a barn where Bunyan used to preach. The bronze doors, considered to be artistically outstanding, illustrate ten scenes from *Pilgrim's Progress.* The Bunyan Meeting House contains the surviving relics of Bunyan and a famous collection of the *Pilgrim's Progress* in 165 languages. Open Tuesday to Saturday from 2 to 4 p.m., it charges 30p (59¢) for admission.

About 1½ miles south of Bedford lies Elstow, Bunyan's reputed birthplace. Here you can visit **Elstow Moot Hall,** a medieval market hall containing exhibits depicting the life and times of John Bunyan. It is open Tuesday through Saturday, 10 a.m. to 1 p.m. and 2 to 5 p.m. (on Sunday from 2 to 5:30 p.m., or dusk in winter), charging 20p (39¢) for adults, 10p (20¢) for children. For more information, telephone Bedford 66889.

The **Swiss Garden,** Old Warden, near Biggleswade, is an unusual romantic site dating from the early 19th century. It contains the original buildings and features, together with many interesting plants and trees, some of great rarity. A lakeside picnic area in adjoining woodlands is open at all times. Hours for the garden are from 2 to 6 p.m. (last admission at 5:15 p.m.) on Wednesday, Saturday, Sunday, bank holiday Mondays, and Good Friday from March 27 to October 24. The garden lies approximately 2½ miles west of Biggleswade adjoining the Biggleswade–Old Warden road about two miles west of the A1. For more information, telephone Bedford 63222, ext. 30.

Stevington Windmill, dating from about 1770, is a particularly fine example of a post mill, fully restored in 1921. The Bedfordshire County Council acquired the mill in 1951, when further extensive restoration work was carried out. Stevington Mill was probably the last windmill in the country working with four common (i.e., cloth-covered) sails. Visitors to the mill may borrow the keys between the hours of 10 a.m. and 7 p.m. (dusk in winter) from the Landlord, Royal George, Silver Stevington. The location is a half mile southeast of Stevington. For more information, telephone Bedford 63222, ext. 30.

WOBURN ABBEY: Few tourists visiting Bedfordshire miss the Georgian mansion of **Woburn Abbey,** the seat of the Dukes of Bedford for more than three centuries. The much-publicized 18th-century estate is about 42 miles from London outside Woburn. Its State Apartments are rich in furniture, porcelain, tapestries, silver, and a valuable art collection, including paintings by Van Dyck, Holbein, Rembrandt, Gainsborough, and Reynolds. A series of paintings by Canaletto, showing his continuing views of Venice, grace the walls of the dining room in the Private Apartments (Prince Philip said the duke's collection was superior to the Canalettos at Windsor—but Her Royal Highness quickly corrected him). Of all the paintings, one of the most notable from an historical point of view is the *Armada Portrait* of Elizabeth I. Her hand rests on the globe, as Philip's invincible armada perishes in the background.

Queen Victoria and Prince Albert visited Woburn Abbey in 1841. Victoria slept in an opulently decorated bedroom (her night dress is still there). In 1954, another queen—this one of the cinema, Marilyn Monroe—slept in the same bed as a publicity stunt. Victoria's Dressing Room contains a fine collection of 17th-century paintings from the Netherlands. Among the oddities and treasures at Woburn Abbey are a Grotto of Shells, a Sèvres dinner service (gift of Louis XV), a China Salon, and a chamber devoted to memorabilia of "The Flying Duchess." Wife of the 11th Duke of Bedford, she was a remarkable woman, who disappeared on a solo flight in 1937 (the same year as Amelia Earhart). The duchess, however, was 72 years old at the time.

In the 1950s, the present Duke of Bedford opened Woburn Abbey to the public to pay off some $15 million in inheritance taxes. In 1974 he turned the estate over to his son and daughter-in-law, the Marquess and Marchioness of Tavistock, who reluctantly took on the business of running the 75-room mansion. And what a business it is, drawing more than a million visitors a year and employing more than 300 persons to staff the shops and grounds.

Today, Woburn Abbey is surrounded by a 3000-acre park containing many rare and exotic animals (ten varieties of deer). Some people visit just to see the animals. While seated in one of 57 gondolas on the two-mile cable lift, you pass over lions, elephants, and giraffes. What would Humphry Repton, the designer of the estate's park in the 18th century, say?

Woburn Abbey is outside Woburn, near Dunstable. It is hard to reach by public transportation from London, so you may prefer to take one of the organized tours.

From January to Easter the park is open from noon to 3:45 p.m., the house from 1 to 4 p.m. From Easter on, the park is open from 10 a.m. to 4:45 p.m., the house from 11 a.m. to 5 p.m. The abbey is closed throughout January and December, with the exception of New Year's Day. To visit Woburn Abbey, the charge is £2 ($3.90) for adults and £1 ($1.95) for children and senior citizens. To economize if it fits your needs, I'd suggest a family ticket, going for £5.25 ($10.24) and admitting two adults and up to four children. When not in use by the family, visitors may see the private apartments at an additional charge of 30p (59¢) for adults, 10p (20¢) for children and senior citizens.

To visit the Deer Park by car, the fee is £1.50 ($2.93), inclusive of passengers. The Deer Park entrance charge doesn't apply to visitors who purchase their abbey ticket as they enter the park. To visit the Animal Kingdom as a coach passenger costs £1.30 ($2.54) for adults and 65p ($1.27) for children. However, if you're driving, a car with occupants is admitted for £5 ($9.75). For more information, telephone Woburn 666.

After visiting the abbey, a good spot for both food and lodgings is the **Bedford Arms,** George Street (tel. Woburn 441). This is a Georgian coaching inn with a checkered history which blends the old and new at the gates of the estate of the Duke of Bedford. Tastefully modernized, it still preserves a mellow charm. Its 75-seat Gerogian dining room, Hollands, was designed by Henry Holland, architect of Woburn Abbey. Guests are housed in one of the pleasantly furnished bedrooms, more than half of which contain private baths or showers. Bathless singles rent for £27 ($52.65), going up to £33 ($64.35) with private bath. Bathless twins cost from £38 ($74.10), £41 ($79.95) with private bath, each unit containing coffee-making facilities, radio, phone, automatic alarm system, and color TV. A new block provides 20 executive-style bedrooms furnished and decorated to extremely high standards. All these rooms have private baths, color TV, radio, and drinks facilities. This block brings the hotel's complement of bedrooms to 60. The Tavern adjoining the hotel's main restaurant has been restored, its old beams exposed as well as its inglenook fireplaces. By contrast, a cocktail bar has been designed as an ideal place for a predinner drink or cocktail. The bar, with its gray suede-covered walls and soft-pink draperies, creates an atmosphere of luxury.

KENT, SURREY, AND THE SUSSEXES

LYING TO THE SOUTH and southeast of London are the shires (counties) of Kent, Surrey, and the Sussexes. Combined, they form a most fascinating part of England to explore, and are easy to reach, within commuting distance of the capital.

Of all the centers, **Canterbury** in Kent is of foremost interest, but the old Cinque ports of **Rye** and **Winchelsea** in East Sussex are equally exciting, as is **Brighton** in its own distinctive way. In and around these major meccas are dozens of castles and vast estates, monuments, homes of celebrated men, cathedrals, yachting harbors, and little villages of thatched cottages.

The range of accommodations varies from an old-world smugglers' inn at the ancient seaport of Rye to a 16th-century house in Canterbury featured in *David Copperfield*. Throughout the counties of the south coast, you'll discover some superb bargains, as the English themselves come to these coastal shires for the sun and are accustomed to paying reasonable rates.

In the fog-choked cities of northern England, the great dream for retirement is to find a little rose-covered cottage in the south, where the living's easier.

SURREY, THE SUSSEXES AND KENT

KENT

Fresh from his cherry orchard, the Kentish farmer heads for his snug spot by an inglenook, with its bright-burning fire, for his glass of cherry brandy. The day's work is done. All's right with the world.

We're in what was once the ancient Anglo-Saxon kingdom of Kent, on the fringes of London yet far removed in spirit and scenery. Since the days of the Tudors, cherry blossoms have pinkened the fertile landscape. Not only orchards, but hop fields abound. The conically shaped oasthouses with kilns for drying the hops dot the rolling countryside. Both the hops and orchards have earned for Kent the title of the garden of England. And in England the competition's rough for that distinction.

The country is also rich in Dickensian associations—in fact, Kent is sometimes known as Dickens Country. His family once lived near the naval dockyard at Chatham. At **Rochester**, 30 miles from London, you'll find his home, Gad's Hill, at the edge of town (in *Pickwick Papers* is a description of the Bull Inn).

Charles Dickens Centre, Eastgate, High Street, in Rochester, is open seven days a week, from 10 a.m. to 12:30 p.m. and 2 to 5:30 p.m. Admission is £1 ($1.95) for adults, 50p (98¢) for children. The museum has tableaux depicting various scenes from Dickens's novels, including a Pickwickian Christmas scene, then the fever-ridden graveyard of *Bleak House,* scenes from *The Old Curiosity Shop* and *Great Expectations, Oliver Twist,* and *David Copperfield.* There is clever use of sound and light. Information is also available at the centre on various other sights in Rochester associated with Dickens, including Eastgate House and, in the garden, the chalet transported from Gad's Hill Place, where Dickens died, as well as the Guildhall Museum, Rochester Cathedral, and the mysterious "6 Poor Travellers' House." Pick up a brochure which includes a map featuring the various places and the novels with which each is associated. For further information, telephone Rochester 44176.

Canterbury, the road to Dover, the byways of Kent, were all known to the Victorian novelist. At Broadstairs, his favorite seaside resort, what is now **Dickens House Museum** (tel. Broadstairs 62853), on the main seafront, was once the home of Mary Pearson Strong, on whom he based much of the character of Betsey Trotwood, David Copperfield's aunt. It is open daily from 2:30 to 5:30 p.m. from April to October, charging 35p (68¢) admission for adults, 15p (29¢) for children. On Tuesday, Wednesday, and Thursday, from June to September, it is also open from 7 to 9 in the evening.

An attraction for Canadian readers is the square, red brick, gabled home where James Wolfe, the English general who defeated the French in the battle for Québec, lived until he was 11 years old. Called **Québec House,** a National Trust property, it contains memorabilia associated with the military hero, who was born in Westerham (Kent) on January 2, 1727. The house which Wolfe's parents rented may be visited March to October—daily except Thursday and Saturday, 2 to 6 p.m., for an admission charge of £1 ($1.95), 50p (98¢) for children.

Kent suffered severe destruction in World War II, as it was the virtual alley over which the Luftwaffe flew in its infamous blitz of London. After the fall of France, a German invasion was feared. Shortly after becoming prime minister in 1940, Churchill sped to Dover, with his bowler, stogie, walking cane, and pin-striped suit. Once there, he inspected the coastal defense and gave encouragement to the men digging in to fight off the attack. But Hitler's "Sea Lion" (code name for the invasion) turned out to be a paper tiger.

In spite of much devastation, Kent is filled with interesting old towns and stately homes.

1. Kent's Country Houses and Castles

CHURCHILL'S HOME: For many years, Sir Winston lived at **Chartwell** (tel. Crockham Hill 368), which lies 1½ miles south of Westerham in Kent. Churchill, a descedant of the first Duke of Marlborough, was born in grand style at Blenheim Palace on November 30, 1874. Chartwell doesn't pretend to be as grand a place as Blenheim, but it's been preserved as a memorial, administered by the National Trust. The rooms remain as Churchill left them, including maps, documents, photographs, pictures, and other personal mementos. In two rooms are displayed a selection of gifts that the prime minister received from people all over the world. There is also a selection of many of his well-known uniforms. Terraced gardens descend toward the lake with its celebrated black swans. In a garden studio are many of Churchill's painting. Go if you want to see where a giant of a man lived and worked. The house is open from March 1 to November 30 on Tuesday, Wednesday, and Thursday from 2 to 6 p.m.; Saturday and Sunday from 11 a.m. to 6 p.m. Entrance to the house and gardens costs £1.70 ($3.32) for adults, 80p ($1.56) for children. There's a restaurant, serving snacks, tea, and coffee.

KNOLE: Begun in the mid-15th century by Thomas Bourchier, archbishop of Canterbury, Knole (tel. Seven Oaks 53006) is one of the largest private houses in England, and is considered one of the finest examples of the purely British Tudor style of architecture.

Henry VIII confiscated it along with other church property in 1537, and it was later granted to Thomas Sackville, Earl of Dorset, by Queen Elizabeth I. Sackville, whose descendants reside in Knole to the present day (although the building was donated to the National Trust in 1946), extended the mansion by adding long gabled wings and the great hall.

The completed house is huge, with 365 rooms, seven courts, and more than 50 staircases. The elaborate paneling and friezework provide a background for the 17th- and 18th-century tapestries and rugs, the Jacobean furniture, and the collection of family portraits.

Knole, in the village of Seven Oaks, about five miles north of Tonbridge, is open April to September, Wednesday to Saturday, bank holiday Mondays, and Good Friday from 11 a.m. to 5 p.m. (on Sunday from 2 to 5 p.m.). In October and November, it is open Wednesday to Saturday from 11 a.m. to 4 p.m. (on Sunday from 2 to 4 p.m.). It is closed from December to March. Admission is £1.70 ($3.32) for adults, 80p ($1.56) for children.

HEVER CASTLE: The 13th-century moated castle (tel. Edenbridge 865224) just three miles southeast of Edenbridge has the distinction of having been the residence of two of the wives of Henry VIII. The family home of Anne Boleyn, it was forfeited by Henry's second wife—along with her head. Later, Henry gave Hever Castle to his proxy wife, the "great Flanders mare," Anne of Cleves when he discovered that this mail-order bride did not live up to her Holbein portrait. Anne did not mind, however, since she was perfectly happy to settle into a comfortable castle with plenty of money. It was certainly better than the king's usual alternative.

The forecourt of the castle and the gardens were used during the filming of *Anne of a Thousand Days* in 1969. The fortress-like Hever Castle is open to the public from April through October. Hours are from noon to 5:15 p.m. (last entry) daily except Monday and Thursday (not open on Good Friday or the fourth Sunday in May; open bank holidays). Admission is £1.50 ($2.93) for adults and 80p ($1.56) for children.

The estate, now the home of Lord and Lady Astor of Hever, was redesigned around the turn of the century to include a formal Italian garden, complete with fountains, classical statuary, and shrubbery trimmed into fantastic shapes. The grounds also include a 35-acre lake through which the Eden River flows. The gardens are open from 11:30 a.m. to 5 p.m. (last entry) on the same days as the castle. Admission is £1 ($1.95) for adults, 50p (98¢) for children. Admission to the castle grounds is required before you can purchase your additional ticket to the castle. A fully licensed restaurant is open near the lake.

Lord Astor now rents his castle—lock, stock, moat, and drawbridge—at a cost of £220 ($429) per person for 24 hours, including food, drink, cigars, butler, and staff. If you take it, let me know how you like it!

CHILHAM CASTLE GARDENS: This former royal property can be reached from the M2 Faversham turnoff, the A252 Canterbury-Maidstone road, or the A28 Ashford-Canterbury road. It was used as a hunting lodge by more than one royal personage until King Henry VIII sold it. The castle gardens are closed on Monday and Friday. From April 1 to May 2 and September 28 to October 31, hours are from 2 to 6 p.m., and admission is £1.40 ($2.73) for adults, 70p ($1.37) for children, going up to £1.50 ($2.93) for adults and 75p ($1.46) for children from May 4 to September 26, when the gardens are open from noon to 7 p.m.

Falconry displays are given hourly. On Sunday, jousting is staged, and the charge is £1.75 ($3.41) for adults, 90p ($1.76) for children. If the jousting is canceled because of weather, the weekday rates apply. On a holiday Sunday and Monday when there are medieval jousting tournaments, the cost for an adult is £2.50 ($4.88); for children, £1 ($1.95). For information, telephone Chilham 319.

PENSHURST PLACE: This magnificent English Gothic-style mansion, one of the outstanding country houses in Britain, lies 33 miles from London and 3½ miles west of Tonbridge on the Tunbridge Wells Road. Sir John de Pulteney, four times mayor of London, built the stone house whose Great Hall forms the heart of Penshurst, even after more than 600 years. The boy king, Edward VI, presented the house to Sir William Sidney, and it has remained in this family ever since, becoming, in 1554, the birthplace of the soldier-poet, Sir Philip Sidney. In the first half of the 17th century, Penshurst was known as a center of literature, attracting such personages as Ben Jonson.

Visitors are shown through the premises, including the splendid State Dining Room and Queen Elizabeth's Room. In the Stable Wing is an interesting Toy Museum. The ten-acre walled garden is divided into hedged enclosures, a legacy from the Tudor era. The home park is grazed by rare sheep and the lake is the home of many wildfowl. The site is open daily except Monday from April 1 to October 3 and each bank holiday. The gardens and home park hours are from 12:30 to 6 p.m. and the house from 1 to 5:30 p.m. Admission is £2 ($3.90) for adults, £1 ($1.95) for children.

LEEDS CASTLE: This castle at Maidstone, dating from A.D. 857, was once described by Lord Conway as the loveliest castle in the world. Originally built of wood, it was rebuilt in 1119 in its present stone structure. It is surrounded by a moat and is an almost impregnable fortress.

The castle has strong links with America through the sixth Lord Fairfax who, as well as owning the castle, owned five million acres in Virginia and was a close friend and mentor of the young George Washington.

Within the surrounding parkland, there is a wild wood garden and duckery where rare swans, geese, and ducks can be seen, and the aviaries contains a superb collection of birds, including parakeets and cockatoos. Dogs are not allowed here, but dog lovers will enjoy the Great Danes of the castle and the unique collection of dog collars dating from the Middle Ages. A nine-hole and an 18-tee golf course are open to the public daily.

The castle is open from April 1 to October 30 on Tuesday, Wednesday, Thursday, and Sunday (every day during August) from noon to 5 p.m. Admission is £2.75 ($5.36) to the castle and grounds.

From November 1 to the end of March, Sunday lunch is offered. A sherry reception is followed by a four-course lunch with wine and then a tour of the castle. The all-inclusive rate is £8.50 ($16.58) for adults, £7.50 ($14.63) for children. Advance reservations are essential.

Every Saturday from 7:15 to 11 p.m., a Kentish evening takes place in the Jacobean Tithe Barn, the Fairfax Hall, when a six-course meal is served with wine and musical entertainment for £16 ($31.20) per person. Advance booking is also essential. Telephone Maidstone 65400 for reservations.

Postscript: **Violet Bourne,** 70 High St., Milton Regis, near Sittingbourne (tel. Sittingbourne 23762 in the evenings), owns the Elizabethan house in which she lives and has filled it with Victoriana. Each room has been furnished absolutely to period down to the last ornament and trinket—a tiny purse made of shells, polished and lacquered musical boxes, and chiming clocks. She is delighted to take visitors around, charging 50p (98¢) to see her lovely collection. She prefers afternoon visitors, and receives guests from April to October only. Please telephone before arriving.

2. Canterbury

Under the arch of the ancient West Gate journeyed Chaucer's knight, solicitor, nun, squire, parson, merchant, miller, and cook—spinning racy tales. They were bound for the shrine of Thomas à Becket, archbishop of Canterbury, who was slain by four knights of Henry II on December 29, 1170. (The king later walked barefoot from Harbledown to the tomb of his former friend, where he allowed himself to be flogged in penance.) The shrine was finally torn down in 1538 by Henry VIII, as part of his campaign to destroy the monasteries and graven images. Canterbury, then, had already been an attraction of long standing.

The medieval Kentish city, on the Stour River, is the mother city of England, its ecclesiastical capital. Mother city is an apt title, as Canterbury was known to have been inhabited centuries before the birth of Jesus Christ. Julius Caesar once went on a rampage near it. Although its most famous incident was the murder of Becket, the medieval city witnessed other major moments in English history—including Bloody Mary's ordering of nearly 40 victims to be burned at the stake. Richard the Lionhearted came back this way from crusading, and Charles II passed through on the way to claim his crown.

Canterbury was once completely walled, and many traces of its old fortifications remain. In the 16th century, weavers, mostly Huguenots from northern

France and the Low Countries, fled to Canterbury to escape religious persecution. They started a weaving industry that flourished until the expanding silk trade with India ruined it.

The old city is much easier to reach today than it was in Chaucer's time. As it lies 56 miles from London, it is within a 1½-hour train ride from Victoria Station.

During summer, guided lecture tours of the city are arranged by the **Tourist Information Office,** 22 St. Peter's St. (tel. Canterbury 66567). The tours leave from the lottery kiosk at Long Market at 2:15 p.m. from Monday to Friday. The fee is 60p ($1.17) per person.

Now, as in the Middle Ages, the goal of the pilgrim remains:

CANTERBURY CATHEDRAL: The present Gothic structure, erected on the site of an even earlier church, dates back 100 years (1070) before the murder of Becket. From the outside, the Perpendicular tower in the center (known locally as Bell Harry) comes into view first. Inside, the Perpendicular Gothic nave was built in the 14th century with a fan-vaulted ceiling. It soars. The early Gothic 12th-century choir, considered revolutionary in the history of English architecture, represents mainly the guiding talent of William of Sens (the building of the choir cost the master mason his life, as he suffered a fall that eventually caused his death).

As mentioned before, Becket's shrine was destroyed by the Tudor king, but the site of that tomb is in Trinity Chapel, near the High Altar. The saint is said to have worked miracles, and the cathedral contains some rare stained glass depicting those feats. Perhaps the most miraculous thing is that the windows escaped Henry VIII's agents of destruction and Hitler's bombs as well (part of the cathedral was hit in World II).

Near Becket's shrine is an effigy marking the grave of Edward, "The Black Prince," who died in 1376 and is famed chiefly for his role in the Battle of Poitiers when he netted the French king, John II. Also in the area is the tomb of Henry IV (who died in 1413), and that of his queen, Joan of Navarre. East of the Trinity Chapel is "Becket's Crown," in which is a chapel dedicated to "Martyrs and Saints of Our Own Time." St. Augustine's Chair, one of the symbols of the authority of the archbishop of Canterbury, stands behind the high altar.

A SEARCH FOR ROOTS: Know Your Ancestors, Northgate (tel. Canterbury 68664), specializes in compiling family trees, establishing rights to coats-of-arms, and searching for ancestral British roots. The cost depends on the nature and complexity of the task, and the availability of records to be searched. A £50 ($97.50) retainer is required, but you will end up with your "roots" discovered and documented. If you have to return home before the task is completed, they will send the finished article to you.

WHERE TO STAY: Before you can begin any serious exploring, you'll need to find a hotel. You have several possibilities, both in the city and on the outskirts, ranging from craggy Elizabethan houses of historic interest to modern studio-type bedrooms with private baths. I'll proceed in descending order of cost.

The Upper Bracket

Slatters, St. Margaret's Street (tel. Canterbury 63271), is a record of the city's changing past. Originally, its Jolly Miller Restaurant was built in the 17th century, and many of its old beams and stones are intact. But today the hotel has branched out, erecting a new structure on ground once occupied by buildings bombed in World War II. Slatters, as a result, has emerged as one of the most up-to-date establishments in the shire. The contemporary bedrooms, most with private baths, are motel-like in their efficiency. Most of the rooms convert into sitting areas during the day, with armchairs, a radio, and television. All rates include breakfast. A bathless single rents for £19.55 ($38.12), going up to £27.60 ($53.82) with bath. A bathless double is tabbed at £28.75 ($56.06), rising to £36.80 ($71.76) with bath, these tariffs including an English breakfast, service, and VAT. A set lunch costs around £5 ($9.75); a table d'hôte dinner, about £7 ($13.65); depending on your choice of a main dish. Parking is available even though you're in the heart of congested Canterbury, a five-minute stroll from the cathedral. The fully licensed Jolly Miller Restaurant serves lunch and dinner.

Chaucer, Ivy Lane (tel. Canterbury 64427), harmonizes modern features with its original Regency character. It's within strolling distance of the cathedral in the old part of the city. The bedrooms are well furnished, with good central heating, adequate storage space, and comfortable beds. The hotel has 51 bedrooms, 31 with private bathrooms. Facilities for making your own morning coffee or tea are available in the rooms, as well as color TV, radio, and telephone. A bathless single rents for £20 ($39) nightly, increasing to £23 ($44.85) with private bath. Bathless doubles go for £26 ($50.70), rising to £32 ($62.40) with bath. The Pilgrim's Bar is comfortable and tastefully decorated and offers a variety of bar snacks. The Dickensian restaurant is known for its local specialties, such as filet of beef Chaucer and Pilgrim's lamb. Service and VAT are included in the tariffs. A set lunch costs £4.50 ($8.78) for three courses, a set dinner going for £6.50 ($12.68) for four courses.

The Medium-Priced Range

The **County Hotel,** High Street (tel. Canterbury 66266), has been a hotel since the closing years of the reign of Victoria. But its recorded history goes back to the end of the 12th century, when Jacob the Jew built a private town house on the spot. Over the years, it has undergone many changes and alterations, in both its structure and its name. It was first licensed in 1629. Today, it offers 73 luxury bedrooms fully equipped with private bathrooms and showers, color TV, tea- and coffee-making facilities, radios, telephones, and a bowl of fruit. The intimate restaurant offers a full à la carte menu, or for a more informal meal the coffeeshop is open from 11 a.m. to 11 p.m. The rate for a single room is £28 ($54.60) and for a twin or double room, £37 ($72.15). All prices include a full English breakfast and VAT. The service charge is left to the customer's discretion. The average cost of a meal in the restaurant is £6.50 ($12.68) for lunch and £7.50 ($14.63) for a four-course set dinner. The coffeeshop is open for quick grills and omelets.

The **Falstaff Hotel,** St. Dunstan's Street (tel. Canterbury 62138), is a restored coaching inn (you drive in where coaches from London to Dover used to unload their passengers). Just outside Westgate, near the River Stour, it is easy to spot, with its black-and-white timbered gables. Its street floor is devoted to pub-style lounges, the soul of Falstaff even after 500 years. On the floors above are a dining room, with its collection of antique clocks and framed Dutch tiles, and the well-kept bedrooms. Each of the rooms has hot and cold running water, and at least ten are fitted with private baths or showers. The rate in a single is £16 ($31.20). Twins range from £30 ($58.50) to £33 ($64.35), depending on the plumbing. Tariffs include an English breakfast. A three-course lunch or dinner costs from £6 ($11.70).

The Budget Range

Cathedral Gate Hotel and Restaurant, 37 Burgate (tel. Canterbury 64381), is for modern-day pilgrims who want to rest their bones at an inn shouldering up to the cathedral's gateway. In 1620 this former hospice became one of the earliest of the fashionable coffee and tea houses of England. Its facade was added in the 19th century, however. The interior reveals many architectural features of the 17th century. Ms. Adsett is devoted to the hotel, and has done much to furnish it as authentically as possible. Two curved bay windows in the living room overlook the little square in front of the gateway. On chilly nights, log fires burn in an old fireplace, although the bedrooms are heated electrically. Each of the 33 bedrooms has hot and cold running water. Some contain private baths. Single rooms start at £9 ($17.55) for a top-floor unit (be warned, there's no elevator). A single with bath on the second floor costs £11.50 ($22.43). Doubles begin at £13 ($25.35), rising to £19.50 ($38.03) with bath, tariffs including VAT, service, and a continental breakfast. The ground-floor restaurant serves morning coffee, luncheon, afternoon teas, and evening snacks, and is licensed. A good meal in the restaurant will come to about £4.50 ($8.78).

The **House of Agnes Hotel,** 71 Saint Dunstan's St. (tel. Canterbury 65077), remains much as Dickens described it in *David Copperfield,* as the home of Agnes Wickfield, heroine of the novel. Built in the 16th century, the House of Agnes is an authentic, Tudor black-and-white timbered building—historic surroundings at budget prices. The Frost family, who run it, quote B & B terms (depending on the room and the time of year) ranging from £10 ($19.50) inclusive. Some of the bedrooms are handsome and cozy; all ye olde chambers have hot and cold running water and free color TV. The hotel has its own car park and full central heating.

WHERE TO EAT: The **Castle Restaurant,** 71 Castle St. (tel. Canterbury 65658), is frequented by in-the-know "Canterburians" as the choicest dining spot in the medieval city (the building dates back to 1485)—choice not only because of its refined cuisine, but because of economy, too. It is directed by Mr. and Mrs. Benjamin, who keep it unpretentious and unspoiled. For suggestions: The soups have rarely been found disappointing—a choice of two is offered daily. The specialties run to grills and fish dishes (prices include chips and garden peas), with such favorites as large Dover sole and rainbow trout. Two grilled lamb cutlets are another favorite. The desserts are especially good and widely varied, often featuring a gooseberry tart with fresh cream. Meals, not including your drink, begin at £7.50 ($14.63). The restaurant is open from 10 a.m. to 10 p.m. On Saturday, it's imperative to reserve before 4 p.m.

Adelaide Silver Grill, Adelaide Place (tel. Canterbury 65658), is part of the Castle Restaurant recommended above. It, too, is run by the Benjamins. Mr. Benjamin flits between one restaurant and the other via the "coalhole." The grill room has a slower turnover and higher prices. The food is good, and the place has a fine reputation among locals. Both restaurants are joined by a common kitchen, although much of the cooking in the Adelaide is on a grille in the dining room. The average price of a meal is £9 ($17.55), including drinks. For appetizers, try a selection of hors d'oeuvres from the trolley, which holds

18 different varieties. Grilled fish is a main dish specialty, and a meat specialty is grilled Barnsley chop with mint sauce (a double loin lamb chop). Incidentally, steaks and chops are on display, and you can select your own if you wish. A choice from the sweets trolley will cost you an additional £1.50 ($2.44). With its reds and browns, the dining room is inclined to give one the feeling of a nightclubbish place. You need to reserve for Saturday luncheons.

On the Outskirts

The **Abbot's Fireside**, Elham (tel. Elham 265), has been a well-known restaurant for many years. The Prebble family has owned the inn for the past decade or so, although the family's roots in the village go back to the 14th century. The building is circa 1480, an example of pre-Renaissance architecture. Its wooden mullions and transoms have been well preserved. The whole structure leans forward, as if it's been standing too long. Latticed windows and grotesquely carved wooden brackets give an old-world aura. In one room is a great old fireplace, carved by a monk, from which the establishment takes its name. The Duke of Wellington made this his garrison headquarters when he was mustering his army for battle against Napoleon. Charles II and the Duke of Richmond are reported to have hidden in the chimney while pursued by Roundheads. The inn also has a rare Parliament Clock, thought to be 16th century, and in the restaurant a "coat of chain mail" from the 14th century, reputedly worn by the Black Prince.

Try to schedule at least a luncheon visit, enjoying a three-course meal for £4 ($7.80), featuring standard English fare. If you fall in love with the place, you can stay over. For your bed, breakfast, and evening meal, you're charged £16 ($31.20) nightly. B&B only is £11 ($21.45). All prices include VAT.

In the area is the **Romney, Hythe & Dymchurch Light Railway Co.**, the world's smallest public railway. The engines are all steam driven, the carriages covered so there is no fear of getting wet. The line is 13½ miles long from Hythe (Kent) to New Romney and Dungeness, and the trains are one-third-size miniature versions of the kind of trains that ran on English or North American mainline railways in the 1920s. The line has a complicated rail fare, depending on the distance traveled. Otherwise, you can purchase a runabout ticket valid for unlimited travel, costing about £7 ($13.65) per day. Children travel for one-quarter of the adult fare. It operates daily from Easter to the end of September (on Sunday throughout the year). The railway is reached by road along the A259. The ride takes about half an hour. Naturally, the ticket includes freedom to travel for a whole day as services permit on the R.H.&D. Railway. Telephone New Romney 2353 for train times. The terminal of the railway, Hythe, is near Folkestone, which can be reached by frequent trains from London.

To go to Elham, leave Canterbury on the Dover road, five miles out turn right and Elham's five miles farther. A right turn and another five miles will take you to Hythe.

3. Dover

Dover, one of the ancient Cinque ports, is famed for its white cliffs. In Victoria's day, it basked in popularity as a seaside resort. Today it is of importance mainly because it is a port for major cross-Channel car and passenger traffic between England and France (usually Calais). Sitting in the open jaws of the white cliffs, Dover was one of England's most vulnerable and easy-to-hit targets in World War II and suffered repeated bombings that destroyed much of its harbor.

Hovering nearly 400 feet above the port is **Dover Castle,** one of the oldest and best known in England. Its keep was built at the command of Becket's fair-weather friend, Henry II, in the 12th century. You can visit the keep year round, generally from 9:30 a.m. to 5:30 p.m. in summer (it closes earlier off-season), for an admission of 75p ($1.46); children and senior citizens pay 30p (59¢). Admission to the underground works is 40p (78¢) for children and senior citizens. Admission to the castle grounds is free. The ancient castle was called back to active duty as late as World War II. The "Pharos" on the grounds is a lighthouse built by the Romans in the first half of the first century. The Romans landed at nearby Deal in 55 B.C. and 54 B.C. The first landing was not successful. The second in 54 B.C. was more so, but after six months they departed, and did not return until nearly 100 years later, 43 A.D., when they occupied the country and stayed 400 years.

WHERE TO STAY: The **White Cliffs Hotel,** Sea Front (tel. Dover 203633), is the traditional choice, with many of its bedrooms facing the Channel. Clinging tenaciously to the past, its facade is impressive, built like a string of attached town houses, with an unbroken seafront balcony and a glass-enclosed front veranda. The bedrooms are comfortable and tranquil. The rooms facing the sea carry the higher price tag, of course. A waterfront double with private bath rents for £31.50 ($61.43). A bathless double costs £28.50 ($55.58). A single without bath is £16.50 ($32.16), rising to £19 ($37.05) with bath. Tariffs include a full English breakfast and VAT. Late-supper service and a covered garage are available. The hotel is close to the eastern and western docks and the hoverport for travel to and from France and Belgium.

The **Dover Stage Coachotel,** Sea Front (tel. Dover 201001), is for those who desire streamlined motel efficiency. Set back from the sea, it opens onto its own miniature plaza with flowers and fountain. Six floors of the most up-to-date bedrooms attract cross-Channel overnighters. The entire waterfront facade zig-zags, with angular bayview bedrooms and individual balconies. The studio-style rooms have built-in furnishings, and hot and cold running water—but no private baths. Price for B&B is £17.25 ($33.64) in a single, £26 ($50.70) in a twin, including breakfast, service, and VAT. On the ground floor are a breakfast room and a drinking lounge. In addition, appetizing meals are served, featuring a three-course luncheon for £6.50 ($12.68). Dinner is à la carte.

East Cliff Hotel, Marine Parade, Eastern Docks (tel. Dover 202299), stands serenely on the promenade under the White Cliffs of Dover, at the entrance to the leading line of the ferry and hovercraft to Calais. It's a well-kept establishment. Some of the rooms have a dramatic view of the harbor, and all come well equipped although without private baths. The B&B rate is £12.50 ($24.38) per person, inclusive of service and VAT. Bar meals include a T-bone steak, served with salad and french fries, for £6 ($11.70), and it's available at both lunch and dinner.

The **Holiday Inn,** Townwall Street (tel. Dover 203270), stands in the center of town, just a few minutes away from the railway station, the seafront, and the international ferry and hoverport terminals. Small as Holiday Inns go in England, it offers 83 rooms, designed in the typical utilitarian chain motif, each with a private bath, color TV, radio, in-house movies, direct-dial phones, plus individually controlled air conditioning and heating. Singles rent for £28 ($54.60) nightly, the tariff increasing to anywhere from £35 ($68.25) to £38.50 ($75.08) in a double. VAT and breakfast are extra. On the premises is an attractive heated indoor swimming pool, along with a fitness center. You can dine in a modern restaurant at the inn or order a snack in the coffeeshop, perhaps a drink in the Lord Warden bar.

WHERE TO EAT: **Britannia,** Townwall Street (tel. Dover 203248), across from the Dover Stage Coachotel, near the seafront, brings imagination and flair to an otherwise dull restaurant town. In a modern pub setting, you can sample good English food: Canterbury lamb cutlets, grilled Dover sole. But the chef reaches out to France and Spain as well for inspiration. On my latest rounds, I spotted six Spanish specialties on the menu, including such treats as Valencian paella. The appetizers are tempting as well, including pâté maison and lobster soup with brandy. Among the desserts, I prefer the Tia Maria walnut parfait. A three-course lunch is offered for £5.50 ($10.73), a set three-course dinner for around £7 ($13.65). However, to sample the specialties, you'll have to order from the à la carte menu, with main dishes priced from £4 ($7.80) to £8.50 ($16.58). An average meal will cost about £11 ($21.45), including half a carafe of wine.

For our next and final stopover in Kent, we go inland, 37 miles from London, to a once-fashionable resort.

4. Tunbridge Wells

Dudley, Lord North, courtier to James I, is credited with the discovery in 1606 of the mineral spring that started it all. His accidental find led to the creation of a fashionable resort that reached its peak in the mid-18th century under the foppish leadership of "Beau" Nash. Beau or Richard Nash (1674–1761) was a dandy in his day, the final arbiter of what to wear and what to say—even how to act (for example, he got men to take off their boots and put on stockings). But, of course, most of his time was devoted to Bath. Even so, Tunbridge Wells enjoyed a prime spa reputation from the days of Charles II through Victoria. Because so many monarchs visited it, Edward VII named it Royal Tunbridge Wells in 1919. Over the years the cure was considered the answer for everything from too many days of wine and roses to failing sexual prowess.

The most remarkable feature of Tunbridge Wells is its Pantiles, a colonaded walkway for shoppers, tea-drinkers, and diners, built near the wells. At the Assembly Hall, entertainment such as opera or vaudeville is presented.

Alas, there's nothing sadder in tourism than a resort that's seen its day. Still, it's worth a visit—just for a fleeting glimpse of the 18th century.

Canadians touring in the area may want to seek out the grave of the founder of their country's capital. Lt. Col. John By of the Royal Engineers (1779–1836) died at Shernfold Park in Frant East Sussex, near Tunbridge Wells, and is buried in the churchyard there. His principal claim to fame is that he built the Rideau Canal in Upper Canada and established what was later to be the capital of the Dominion of Canada—the city of Ottawa.

The Rideau Canal, some 124 miles long, links the city of Kingston on the St. Lawrence River with the city of Ottawa on the Ottawa River. Between 1826 and 1832 John By successfully constructed this canal through an unexplored wilderness for the British government. At the northern end of the canal he laid out "Bytown." Twenty years later this was renamed Ottawa, and it became the capital of a united Canada. His grave near Tunbridge Wells is marked with a plaque erected by the Historical Society of Ottawa in 1979.

Food and Lodging

Calverley Hotel, Crescent Road (tel. Tunbridge Wells 26455), is an old stone hotel facing Calverley Park, gardens of special interest in themselves. The hotel's enormous lounge, furnished with comfortable chairs and decorated in relaxing colors, opens onto the terrace and gardens. The dining room also overlooks the gardens. The bedrooms, on the upper floors, are reached by elevator. Each room has central heating, telephone, radio, and many have private bath or shower. Guests frequently meet in the warm and friendly cocktail bar for drinks before dinner. Overnight rates at the Calverley range from £16 ($31.20) for a bathless single to £32 ($62.40) for a double with private bath. Breakfast is included, but you'll pay an additional £5 ($9.75) for the table d'hôte luncheon, and about £7.50 ($14.63) for dinner. VAT is added to all charges.

The **Spa Hotel,** Mount Ephraim Road (tel. Tunbridge Wells 20331), is for those who insist on gracious living. Far superior to any other in the vicinity, the Spa is like a sprawling manor house successfully converted to receive guests. The interior has been updated, with comfortable furnishings. The great drawing rooms, as well as the cathedral high-ceilinged dining room, open onto the rear gardens, with their spreading lawns, groves of trees, and beds of flowers. It's a peaceful oasis, only 30 miles from London, but miles away from London prices. The Spa was built in 1766 as a private house.

Throughout the hotel are more than 70 well-furnished and centrally heated bedrooms, reached by elevator, containing private bathrooms, TV, and radio. You pay around £25 ($48.75) per person in a room with bath. The terms include breakfast, service, and taxes. To be quoted boarding-plan terms, you must stay a minimum of four days or more. Otherwise, you can order meals separately, with a table d'hôte luncheon going for £7 ($13.65), a set dinner for £9 ($17.55). Garage facilities are available.

Wellington Hotel, Mount Ephraim Road (tel. Tunbridge Wells 20286), enjoys a regal position, with a grassy Common as its front domain. From every side, there is a view of the sprawling countryside. The old hotel suggests a Charles Addams drawing, with a mansard roof, rows of dormers, and Regency balconies. Catering mostly to families and business people, it also attracts motorists passing through Tunbridge Wells. For a superior double room with private bath, the charge is from £36 ($70.20) nightly, including breakfast, VAT, and service. Less expensive doubles go for only £32 ($62.40). A four-course dinner will cost from £6 ($11.70).

Instead of leaving London for Kent, you might head directly south of the capital to inviting Surrey.

SURREY

This tiny county has for some time been in danger of being gobbled up by the growing boundaries of London and turned into a sprawling suburb. Already some of the densely populated area in Surrey is now part of Greater London. But Surrey still retains much unspoiled countryside, largely because its many heaths and commons do not make good land for postwar suburbanite houses. Essentially, Surrey is a county of commuters (Alfred, Lord Tennyson was among the first), since a worker in the city can practically travel to the remotest corner of Surrey from London in anywhere from 45 minutes to an hour.

Long before William the Conqueror marched his pillaging Normans across its chalky North Downs, Surrey was important to the Saxons. In fact, early Saxon kings were once crowned at what is now **Kingston-on-Thames** (their Coronation Stone is still preserved near the Guildhall).

LIVING IN TUDOR SPLENDOR: The best of England—the best living accommodations, in particular—are to be found in the countryside. There you can sometimes live like a duke or duchess for the same amount you'd pay for only a fairly good room in London. Transportation facilities are often so good that you can enjoy the best of two worlds, darting into London for all its attractions, while enjoying the lower costs and better surroundings of rural England. For those who want to be in the vicinity of Heathrow Airport, yet within easy access of central London, I have the following recommendation in the upper bracket:

Great Fosters, Egham (tel. Egham 33822), is one of the most impressive old manor houses of England. It was built in 1550 and in its day belonged to Elizabeth I and was a hunting lodge in Windsor's Royal Forest. Although only 18 miles from London, it still preserves the link to its past. A red brick Tudor building, with stone-mullioned windows, many gables, and towering chimneys, it is placed in a private garden, where paths cut through formal grounds of clipped yew hedges, roses, and rhododendrons—and a swimming pool. The architectural features of the interior are in the grand style, as witness the main hall with its carved black oak Jacobean fireplace. In the 15th-century Tithe Barn, with its high-vaulted and raftered oak beams, excellent English meals are served and an orchestra plays for dancing on Saturday nights. Some of the master bedrooms are worthy of royalty. For example, the gilt-paneled Italian bedroom contains an overscale bed with hand-carved cherubs on the posts. Period twins or doubles rent from £54 ($105.30) per night, dropping to £45 ($87.75) in a single. Period and second-floor singles cost from £26 ($50.70) per night, increasing to £42.50 ($82.88) in second-floor twins or doubles. These room rates include a full English breakfast, service, and VAT. Great Fosters is only a half mile from Runnymede and the Kennedy Memorial, and only seven miles in different directions from Windsor Castle and Hampton Court Palace.

5. Richmond

Want to spend an afternoon in a Thames river town? Richmond in Surrey is only a 30-minute ride from London, and can be easily reached by the underground trains, or else Green Line coaches 716 or 716a from Hyde Park Corner. The old town, popular in Victorian times, has good public rail links with London, and it offers the escape many seek from the rush and bustle of the metropolis. If you're feeling lighthearted, take the boat trip down the Thames. Turner himself, art materials in hand, came here for inspiration.

Richmond is only one mile from Kew and its botanical gardens. You may prefer a combined excursion to Kew Gardens and Richmond on the same day. One of the attractions of the Thames town is the 2500-acre **Richmond Park,** first staked out by Charles I in 1637. It is filled with photogenic deer and waterfowl. Richmond has long enjoyed associations with royalty, as Henry VII's Richmond Palace stood there (an even earlier manor was razed). Queen Elizabeth I died in the old palace in 1603. Somebody's short-sightedness led to the palace's being carted away, and only a carriageway remains.

If you want to be like the English, you'll climb **Richmond Hill** for a view of the Thames considered by some to be one of the ten best views in the world. The scene reminded William Byrd of a similar view near his home on the James

River in Virginia, inspiring him to name the city founded there in 1737 Richmond.

There are good shops and an excellent theater facing the green on which, in summertime, cricket matches are played. Boating happens on the river. Richmond Park has a public golf course, and you can rent a horse from the local stables. The Richmond Ice Skating Rink has been the nursery of many of England's skating champions. Wimbledon and the Tennis Championships are within easy reach, as is Hampton Court Palace.

At Petersham, the 13th-century St. Peter's Church is the burial place of Capt. George Vancouver. The Queen Mother's parents, Lord and Lady Glamis, were married there. It also has some very old wooden box pews. At St. Anne's Church at Kew Green, the painters Gainsborough and Zoffany were buried.

WHERE TO EAT: Londoners often go down to Richmond for the day, browse through its art galleries, and then dine out—which must account for the town's number of good restaurants. Our recommendation follows:

Richmond Rendezvous, 1 Paradise Rd. (tel. 940-5114), bills itself with some justification as "the leading Peking-style restaurant in the United Kingdom." You would never suspect it, however, to judge from the unprepossessing decor. The food is superb, especially if you stick to the chef's specialties and avoid the routine Chinese restaurant fare. Three dishes, designed to delight, include barbecued Peking duck, steamed and deep fried, or a variety of meats in a chafing dish. Also recommended are hot-and-sour Peking soup, scampi Peking style, sliced beef in oyster sauce, and diced chicken in yellow bean sauce. If there are six persons in your party, you can forego the above and leave it to the chef, who will prepare you a Peking dinner at £7 ($13.65) per head. The restaurant has overflowed to an annex at 1 Wakefield Rd. (tel. 940-6869). In London, the chain runs two more restaurants, one the **Soho Rendezvous,** 21 Romilly St., W.1 (tel. 437-1486), specializing in a Peking-style cuisine, and another, the **Chiu Chow Inn,** 21 Lisle St., W.C.2 (tel. 437-8919), also specializing in Peking-style cooking. Both of these establishments are in the moderately priced bracket. The chain is owned and run by T. H. Yung, who supervises the Richmond branch.

WHERE TO STAY: The **Richmond Gate,** Richmond Hill (tel. 940-0061), and the **Petersham,** Richmond Hill (tel. 940-7471), are two privately owned hotels, 200 yards apart, which are operated and managed as one. From the top of Richmond Hill, both hotels enjoy a view of the Thames that has attracted famous artists for centuries, and both hotels have interesting historical features. The Richmond Gate comprises two adjoining Georgian buildings, one originally occupied by a member of the Penn family. The Petersham, built as a hotel in 1864, has a remarkable spiral stone staircase dominated by ceiling murals of well-known Renaissance painters. Bedrooms are a careful blend of old and new, all with private bathroom, color TV, radio, and telephone. Room service is offered until 10 p.m., and two restaurants are available. Nightingales restaurant at the Petersham enjoys a panoramic view of the river, and the à la carte menu offers a wide choice of international dishes. A three-course set menu is available at lunchtime for £8 ($15.60). Gates bar-restaurant at the Richmond Gate is an informal facility specializing in fresh seasonal produce. Snacks in the bar or an à la carte menu can be yours at lunchtime, and in the evenings a three-course menu is offered at £9 ($17.55). Single rooms cost £32 ($62.40). An extra bed in the room is £10 ($19.50). Specially reduced rates based on two- or three-night stays will be quoted. All tariffs include a full English breakfast and VAT.

6. Haslemere

A quiet, sleepy town, Haslemere attracts because early English musical instruments are made by hand there. Ever hear a harpsichord concert? An annual music festival (see below) is the town's main drawing card. Over the years, the Dolmetsch family has been responsible for the acclaim that has come to this otherwise unheralded little Surrey town, which lies in the midst of some of the shire's finest scenery. Haslemere is only an hour's train ride from Waterloo Station in London, about 42 miles away.

THE FESTIVAL: It isn't often that one can hear such exquisite music played so skillfully on the harpsichord, the recorder, the lute, or any of the instruments designed so painstakingly to interpret the music of earlier centuries. Throughout the year, the Dolmetsch family makes and repairs these instruments, welcoming visitors to their place on the edge of Haslemere. They rehearse constantly, preparing for the concerts that are held in July, and last nine days.

You can get specific information by writing to the **Haslemere Festival Office**, Jesses, Grayswood Road, Haslemere (or telephone Haslemere 2161 between 9 a.m. and 12:30 p.m. daily). During the festival, matinees begin at 3:15 p.m., evening performances 7:30 p.m. For seats in the balcony, prices range from £1.60 ($3.12) to £2.80 ($5.46), with stall seats going from 80p ($1.56) to £2.20 ($4.29).

WHERE TO STAY: The **Georgian Hotel**, High Street (tel. Haslemere 51555), is in the middle of the town, within walking distance of the Dolmetsch Center. Antiques and period accessories are well placed throughout. The B&B rate per person ranges from £14.55 ($28.37) to £16.80 ($32.76) nightly, the latter for a single with private bath. (Of the hotel's 22 pleasingly furnished bedrooms, 13 have private baths.) The hotel, although Georgian, is actually named after the U.S. State of Georgia. James Edward Oglethorpe, a member of Parliament in the 18th century, who owned the hotel, founded the state of Georgia. The establishment is licensed, and you can have healthy-size drinks before dinner. The garden is a favorite spot for afternoon tea.

A Hotel on the Outskirts

Lythe Hill Hotel, Petworth Road, near Haslemere (tel. Haslemere 51251), is a 14th-century farmhouse of historic interest set in 14 acres of beautiful parkland overlooking National Trust woodlands and just one hour from London, Heathrow, and Gatwick. Across the courtyard is the newer part of the hotel in converted 16th-century farm buildings which offer a luxurious accommodation, 28 rooms and suites, handsomely decorated public rooms, and a restaurant serving international and English dishes, both table d'hôte and à la carte. In the Italian garden, a dinner dance is staged on Saturday evenings.

The black-and-white timbered farmhouse has six period bedrooms with all modern comforts, and in the Tudor room stands a four-poster bed dated 1614. Downstairs in the oak-beamed and paneled dining room is the renowned **Auberge de France** restaurant, offering a fine French cuisine at candlelit, polished oak tables. Specialties include escalope de veau Jeanette, suprême de volaille

Souvaroff, crêpes suzette, and a cellar of fine wines. Dinner for two in the auberge costs around £27 ($52.65).

The table d'hôte menu in the main hotel restaurant is around £8.50 ($16.58) to £12 ($23.40); and a twin room with private bath for two, including a continental breakfast and VAT, plus the service charge, is £52 ($101.40).

Madame Colonna, the patronne of the Lythe Hill Hotel, started with a farmhouse and now owns what is really a French hamlet in Surrey, offering peace and comfort as well as a genuine French cuisine. The auberge is closed for lunch on Tuesday and all day on Monday.

READER'S HOTEL SELECTION: "**Trumble's Hotel and Restaurant** on Stanhill (the road to Newdigate), Charlwood, Surrey (tel. Crawley 862212), is a wonderful place to stay overnight, or just to dine, if your plane comes in at Gatwick Airport. The hotel is only ten minutes by car from there, in lovely rolling country. Its rooms are large and beautiful, some furnished with fine antiques (two bedrooms have canopied four-poster beds). All bedrooms have private bathrooms, radio, and color TV. In a double room, the cost of B&B is £30 ($58.50) for two. There's nothing gloomy—everything's airy and cheerful and comfortable, and the 'full' heat is really that. Proprietors Sue and Peter Trumble will advise on touring and car rental, and often have maps you can borrow. Dinner here averages about £11 ($21.45) per person and is of gourmet quality. We had black currant pie that was the best pie we had ever tasted. House specialties are traditional roast beef for Sunday lunch, roast duckling with orange sauce and fresh wheels of orange, very tender steaks, and plenty of fresh English fish. Also try the homemade lemon meringue pie. Excellent wines and liqueurs are available. There's a small Victorian bar. Trumble's would be a splendid place to spend a week or two. With a car, you could travel to Canterbury, Oxford, the South Coast, or Winchester, to name a few good spots, and get back in time for a memorable dinner. Also you can drive to Gatwick Airport, leave your car, and take the short train ride to London for the day. Trains run every 15 minutes during the day, every hour at night. Charlwood village is full of historic houses, some more than 300 years old. The church has a wall pre-William the Conqueror and 1066. My husband and I thought this the nicest place and the best buy on our 1000-mile tour of England. It is advisable to reserve ahead by telephone. The international telephone number is +44-293-862212" (Mrs. Janet Kay, Rochester, N.Y.).

GUILDFORD: The old and new meet in the county town on the Wey River, 40 minutes by train from Waterloo Station in London. Charles Dickens believed that its High Street, which slopes to the river, was one of the most beautiful in England. The Guildhall has an ornamental projecting clock which dates back to 1683.

Lying 2½ miles southwest of the city, **Loseley House** (tel. Guildford 71881), a beautiful and historic Elizabethan mansion visited by Queen Elizabeth I, James I, and Queen Mary, has been featured on TV and in five films. Its works of art include paneling from Henry VIII's Nonsuch Palace, period furniture, a unique carved chalk chimneypiece, magnificent ceilings, and cushions made by the first Queen Elizabeth. The mansion is open from the end of May to September 25 on Wednesday, Thursday, Friday, and Saturday from 2 to 5 p.m., charging £1 ($1.95) for adults, 60p ($1.17) for children.

Food and Lodging

Angel Hotel, High Street (tel. Guildford 64555), is an old coaching inn in the middle of the steep main street of town. Its entrance and part of its courtyard are Tudor, and many other original features of this once-busy hostelry have been maintained. Inside, there is lavish paneling, plus a huge, open fireplace as well as exposed beams. Great oak timbers from old ships at Portsmouth were used to support the gallery.

Most of the two dozen bedrooms, including two family rooms, are simply furnished, although some are quite attractively decorated (these disappear first to those who reserve ahead). Each has a private bath, as well as a phone, radio, TV, and coffee-maker. Rates begin at £24 ($46.80) in a single, going up to £32 ($62.40) in a double, including VAT and service. In addition to a well-decorated bar, the hotel has a quick-service Buttery as well as a unique 13th-century restaurant in the crypt, with medieval architecture making for cozy surroundings. The restaurant offers a wide range of dishes, including English roasts, at an average price of £7 ($13.65) per person, plus 72p ($1.40) for a glass of wine.

DORKING: This country town lies on the Mole River, at the foot of the North Downs. Within easy reach are some of the most scenic spots in the shire, including Silent Pool, Box Hill, and Leith Hill. Three miles to the northwest stands **Polesden Lacey** (tel. Bookham 53401), a former Regency villa containing the Greville collection of antiques, paintings, and tapestries. In the early part of this century, it was enlarged to become a comfortable Edwardian country house when it was the home of a celebrated hostess, who frequently entertained royalty there. The 18th-century garden is filled with herbaceous borders, a rose garden, and beech walks, and in all the estate consists of 1000 acres. The house is open in March and November on Saturday and Sunday only from 2 to 5 p.m.; April to the end of October, daily, except Monday and Friday, from 2 to 6 p.m. (closed Good Friday but open bank holiday Mondays). The charge to visit both the house and garden is £1.40 ($2.73) for adults, 70p ($1.37) for children. The garden is open daily all year from 11 a.m. to sunset. To visit just the garden, adults are charged 60p ($1.17) and children pay 30p (59¢). A licensed restaurant on the grounds is open from 11 a.m. on the days the house can be visited.

Back in Dorking, you can find accommodations at the following:

Burford Bridge Hotel, Box Hill (tel. Dorking 884561), offers stylish living in a rural town from which a train will zip you into London in less than half an hour. At the foot of the beauty spot of Box Hill, the hotel has a lot of historical associations. Lord Nelson was a frequent patron, and Keats completed *Endymion* here in 1817. Everyone from Wordsworth to Robert Louis Stevenson also frequented the place. You get the best of both the old and the new here, including a tithe barn (circa 1600) as well as 52 large, colorfully decorated bedrooms, renting for £29.50 ($57.53) in a single, from £39.50 ($77.03) to £43.50 ($84.83) in a double. Each room has its own bath or shower, plus a phone and color TV. The restaurant serves good English food, and a bar opens onto a flowered patio with a fountain. Pub snacks are served in the Nelson Bar. Concerts are held regularly in winter, and in summer you can enjoy the hotel's own swimming pool.

White Horse Hotel, High Street (tel. Dorking 881138). Just ten miles from Gatwick Airport, you can dine or lodge at a hotel which dates in part from 1500. Once the vicarage of Dorking, the White Horse by tradition was supposed to have been the "Marquis of Granby" in the *Pickwick Papers.* At least Dickens was known to have frequented the bar parlor.

An atmospheric place of creaking timbers and low beamed ceilings, the inn offers 70 bedrooms, including 18 family units, each with private baths or showers, plus phones, radios, TV sets, and coffee makers. A single with bath costs from £26 ($50.70), a double renting for £36 ($70.20). Often called "the most interesting house in Dorking," the inn has a restaurant as well as a Pickwick bar offering hot and cold snacks.

After visiting Surrey, you can head south toward the English Channel and the sprawling shires of Sussex.

THE SUSSEXES

If King Harold hadn't loved Sussex so much, the course of English history might have been changed forever. Had the brave Saxon waited longer in the north, he could have marshaled more adequate reinforcements before striking south to meet the Normans. But Duke William's soldiers were ravaging the countryside he knew so well, and Harold rushed down to counter them.

Harold's enthusiasm for Sussex is understandable. The landscape rises and falls like waves. The country is known for its Downlands and tree-thickened Weald, from which came the timbers to build England's mighty fleet in days gone by. The shires lie south of London and Surrey, bordering Kent in the east, Hampshire in the west, and opening directly onto the sometimes sunny, resort-dotted English Channel.

Like the other sections in the vulnerable south of England, the Sussexes witnessed some of the most dramatic moments in the country's history. Apart from the Norman landings at Hastings, the most life-changing transfusion of plasma occurred in the 19th century, as middle-class Victorians flocked to the seashore, pumping new spirit into Eastbourne, Worthing, Brighton, even old Hastings. The cult of the saltwater worshippers flourished, and has to this day. Although **Eastbourne** and **Worthing** are much frequented by the English, I'd place them several fathoms below **Brighton** and **Hastings,** which are much more suitable if you're seeking a holiday by the sea.

Far more than the resorts, the old towns and villages of the Sussexes are intriguing, particularly **Rye** and **Winchelsea,** the ancient towns of the Cinque Port Confederation. No Sussex village is lovelier than **Alfriston** (and the innkeepers know it, too); **Arundel** is noted for its castle; the cathedral city of **Chichester** is a mecca for theater buffs. Traditionally, and for purposes of government, Sussex is divided into East Sussex and West Sussex. I've adhered to that convenient dichotomy.

I'll begin in East Sussex, where you'll find many of the inns and hotels within commuting distance of London.

7. Rye

"Nothing more recent than a Cavalier's Cloak, Hat and Ruffles should be seen in the streets of Rye," said Louis Jennings. He's so right. This ancient town, formerly an island, was chartered back in 1229. Rye, 65 miles below London, near the English Channel, and neighboring Winchelsea were once part of the ancient Cinque Ports Confederation. Rye flourished as a smuggling center, its denizens sneaking in contraband from the marshes to stash away in little nooks (even John Wesley's firm chastisements couldn't stop what was a strongly entrenched tradition).

But the sea receded from Rye, leaving it perched like a giant whale out of water. Its narrow, cobblestoned streets twist and turn like a labyrinth. It has long been considered a special place, having attracted any number of famous men, including Henry James, who once lived in the Lamb House on Mermaid Street.

Attacked several times by French fleets, Rye was practically razed in 1377. But it rebuilt sufficiently, decking itself out in the Elizabethan style so that Queen Elizabeth I, during her visit in 1573, bestowed upon the town the distinction of Royal Rye.

Today the city has any number of specific buildings and sites of architectural interest, notably the 13th-century **Ypres Tower** (sheltering the Rye Museum), and the 15th-century **St. Mary's Parish Church,** with its unusual clock.

WHERE TO STAY: The **Mermaid Inn,** Mermaid Street (tel. Rye 3065), is one of the most famous of the old smugglers inns of England, known to that band of cutthroats, the real-life Hawkhurst Gang, as well as to Russell Thorndike's fictional character, Dr. Syn. One of the present rooms, in fact, is called Dr. Syn's Bedchamber, and is connected by a secret staircase—set in the thickness of the wall—to the bar. That room, with a private bath, rents for £18.50 ($56.08) per person nightly, as does the Elizabethan Chamber (with four-poster and private bath). Two other special rooms—the Fleur-de-Lys Chamber and the Tudor Rose Chamber—contain private baths and twin beds, and cost £15.60 ($30.42) per person. Terms include breakfast, and a 10% service charge is added. Other less expensive rooms are equipped with hot and cold running water, some with baths, attractive furnishings, and are available in single, double, or twin. The charge is from £14.50 ($28.28) per person, including breakfast. The Mermaid has sheltered everybody from Queen Elizabeth I to George Arliss. When Elizabeth came to Rye in 1573, the inn had already been operating nearly 150 years. A covered carriageway leads to the car park. In the center of the hotel is a courtyard, where you'll see a pedestal fountain with water flowing down on the heads of water lilies. The Mermaid has also taken over the 16th-century Ship Inn at the foot of Mermaid Street which, with its 12 bedrooms and restaurant on the first floor, complements the Mermaid very well. The Mermaid also makes a good dining and pub choice (see below).

Monastery Hotel, 6 High St. (tel. Rye 3272), is an early 17th-century building that grew up over the ruins of a 13th-century friary of the Augustinian order. Its own monastic garden backs up against the walls of the old friary. Nowadays, the house offers seven modernized double- and twin-bedded rooms (with hot and cold running water, private showers, central heating, and razor points), renting at £10.50 ($20.48) per person for B&B. There is a comfortable lounge, with color television, and a restaurant installed in an attractive room overlooks the Old Friary Chapel. For nearly 50 years, the Monastery has been receiving guests, the welcome today provided by the resident manager, Mr. Jon Culverhouse.

WHERE TO EAT: The **Mermaid Inn,** Mermaid Street (tel. Rye 3065), doesn't depend totally on its Elizabethan atmosphere and smuggling associations—it also serves good food, and has the most charming tavern in Rye. The cooking is English with frills. For £5.50 ($10.73) you can have a table d'hôte luncheon such as this typical one: a rich kidney soup, followed by poached salmon with hollandaise (superb), accompanied by three vegetables, including beans. Imported cheese or fruit pies such as black currant and apple round out the meal. Lunch is served from 12:45 to 2 p.m. At the dinner, from 7:30 to 9:30 p.m., your tab will average £7 ($13.65). The dining room itself, with its linenfold paneling, Caen stone fireplaces, and oak-beamed ceiling, makes for an ideal setting. Even if you're not dining at the Mermaid, drop in to the old Tudor pub, with its 16-foot-wide fireplace (look for a priest's hiding hole).

The **Flushing Inn,** Market Street (tel. Rye 3292), is in a 16th-century inn on a cobblestoned street. It has preserved the best of the past, including a wall-size fresco in the restaurant dating from 1544 and depicting a menagerie of birds and heraldic beasts. A rear dining room overlooks a carefully tended flower garden. A special feature is the Sea Food Lounge Bar, where sandwiches and plates of seafood are available from £1.80 ($3.51) to £5 ($9.75). In the main restaurant, luncheons are offered for from £6 ($11.70); dinners run from £8 ($15.60). Besides these lunches and dinners, gastronomic evenings are held at regular intervals between October and April. For one of these specially prepared meals, including your apéritif, wine, and after-dinner brandy, you pay £18 ($35.10) per person. Fine Wine evenings cost £19 ($37.05) per person. The inn is closed Monday night, all day on Tuesday, and two weeks after Christmas.

8. Winchelsea

The sister Cinque Federation port to Rye, Winchelsea has also witnessed the water's ebb. It traces its history back to Edward I, and has experienced many dramatic moments, such as sacking by the French. Today it is a dignified residential town (Ellen Terry's former cottage can be seen huddling up to Strandgate, on the road to Rye). In the words of one 19th-century writer, Winchelsea is "a sunny cream of centuries ago." Its finest sight is a badly damaged 14th-century church, containing a number of remarkable tombs.

WHERE TO STAY: The **New Inn** (tel. Winchelsea 252) is an old hostelry in the middle of this picture-postcard village, across the road from the 14th-century church. It has all the mellow associations of a country inn of England —pleasant, comfortable rooms, a tavern, good food, a garden in the rear, a fireplace, old settles (high enough to keep the draft off), plenty of battered, but polished, brass and copper steins hanging from the ceiling, even a dart game going. Run by John Wood, the New Inn rents its well-furnished (many quite large) doubles for £25 ($48.75) per night (innerspring mattresses) including a big English breakfast and VAT, plus 10% for service. All the rooms have hot and cold water. A three-course dinner is served for around £10 ($19.50).

On the Outskirts

Justins Hotel, Bodiam, near Robertsbridge (tel. Staplecross 372), is a Tudor-style estate set in a well-tended two-acre garden, surrounded by tall trees and a view of the Sussex Downs. Only 12 miles from Rye and Winchelsea, it is very close to Bodiam Castle, built in 1386 and considered one of the most magnificent castles of its kind in England.

Your resident owners are Thalia and Bob Turner, who have installed private baths in eight of their ten attractively furnished bedrooms, charging from £11.20 ($21.84) per person nightly for B&B, or £16.70 ($32.57) per person for half board. After enjoying a drink and friendly conversation in the cocktail bar, guests can order good cookery served in the oak-paneled dining room. Personal service is a hallmark of the establishment.

9. Hastings and St. Leonard's

The world has seen bigger battles, but few are as well remembered as the Battle of Hastings in 1066. When William, Duke of Normandy, landed on the Sussex coast and lured King Harold (already fighting Vikings in Yorkshire) southward to defeat, the destiny of the English-speaking people was changed forever. It was D-Day in reverse. The actual battle occurred at what is now Battle Abbey (nine miles away), but the Norman duke used Hastings as his base of operation.

Hastings suffered other invasions—it was razed by the French in the 14th century. But after that blow a Tudor town grew up in the eastern sector, and it makes for a good stroll today. The more recent invasion threat, that of Hitler's armies, never came to pass, although the dragons' dentures put up across the countryside stood waiting to bite into Nazi tanks.

Linked by a three-mile promenade along the sea, Hastings and St. Leonard's were given a considerable boost in the 19th century by that eminent tripper Queen Victoria, who visited several times. Both towns no longer enjoy such royal patronage; rather, they do a thriving business with Midlanders on vacation. Hastings and St. Leonard's have the usual shops and English sea-resort amusements. Only 63 miles from London, they are serviced by fast trains from Victoria Station.

The two chief attractions are:

HASTINGS CASTLE: In ruins now, the first of the Norman castles to be built in England sprouted up on a western hill overlooking Hastings, circa 1067. Precious little is left to remind us of the days when proud knights, imbued with a spirit of pomp and spectacle, wore bonnets and girdles. The fortress was ordered torn down by King John in 1216, and later served as a church and monastery until it felt Henry VIII's ire. Owned by the Pelham dynasty from the latter 16th century to modern times, the ruins have been turned over to Hastings. It is open from 10 a.m. to 5 p.m. daily from Easter to September, charging an admission of 40p (78¢) for adults, 25p (49¢) for children. From the mount, you'll have a good view of the coast and promenade.

THE HASTINGS EMBROIDERY: A commemorative work, the Hastings Embroidery was first exhibited in 1966. It is a remarkable achievement that traces 900 years of English history through needlework. Depicted are some of the nation's greatest moments (the Battle of Hastings, the coronation of William the Conqueror) and its legends (Robin Hood). In all, 27 panels, 243 feet in length, depicting 81 historic scenes, are exhibited at the Town Hall (tel. Hastings 424182). The history of Britain comes alive—the murder of Thomas à Becket, King John signing the Magna Carta, the Black Plague, Chaucer's pilgrims going to Canterbury, the Battle of Agincourt with the victorious Henry V, the War of the Roses, the Little Princes in the Tower, Bloody Mary's reign, Drake's *Golden Hind,* the arrival of Philip's ill-fated Armada, Guy Fawkes's gunpowder plot, the sailing of the *Mayflower,* the disastrous plague of 1665 and the great London fire of the following year, Nelson at Trafalgar, the Battle of Waterloo, the Empress of India, Victoria, the Battle of Britain, and the D-Day landings at Normandy. Also exhibited is a scale model of the battlefield at Battle, depicting William's one-inch men doing in Harold's mini-soldiers. Also displayed is a collection of dolls in period costumes. Admission is 60p ($1.17).

WHERE TO STAY: Royal Victoria Hotel, Marina (tel. Hastings 433300), is peacock-proud of its seafront prominence. It owes its fame to Queen Victoria, who visited here several times. Most of its bedrooms face the sea, but others look onto St. Leonard's Gardens. Inside, the furnishings are fairly modern, although many of the grandest architectural features are still intact. It offers nearly 90 bedrooms, only 14 of which have private baths, although another 11 units contain private showers. Many of the rooms are quite large—good beds, sound comfort. The highest prices are charged from June 1 to September 30.

A bathless single rents for £12.50 ($24.38), going up to £15.50 ($30.23) with bath. A bathless double is £25 ($48.75) rising to £30 ($58.50) with complete bath. These prices include breakfast, service charge, and VAT. Special rates for stays of more than three days are offered. Guests gather evenings in the Crown Bar, which has many fine old touches. Lunch is £5 ($9.75); dinner, £6.50 ($12.68). The chef's specialty is the local sole.

Beauport Park Hotel, Route A2100 (tel. Hastings 51222), is one of the best places to stay in the Hastings–Battle district. It looks much older than it is. It was originally erected as the private estate of General Murray, once the governor of Quebec (he had previously served under General Wolfe). However, a fire in 1923 swept over it, and it was later reconstructed in the old style. Now run as a hotel accommodating 30 guests, it is surrounded by beautiful gardens (the Italian-style grounds in the rear contain statuary and vivid flowering shrubbery). The living room and drinking lounge are tastefully furnished, and the French windows in the dining room open onto the park-like rear. The B&B rate ranges from £15 ($29.25) to £17.50 ($34.13) per person daily. All first-floor rooms have private bathrooms with shower, direct-dial telephone, and TV.

The hotel offers an ambitious cuisine, well prepared and handsomely served. Some of the produce comes from the hotel's own gardens. A set lunch is featured for £5.50 ($10.73) at which a varied choice is available. The set dinner is £7.50 ($14.63), and again the choice is wide. The à la carte menu offers such tempting dishes as a half dozen escargots, real turtle soup, chateaubriand for two. A rich and creamy dessert is the zabaglione.

10. Battle

Nine miles from Hastings is the old market town, famed in history as the site of the Battle of Hastings in 1066. William the Conqueror founded Battle Abbey (some of the stone was shipped from Caen) to commemorate his victory over Harold, the last of the kings of the English. The town grew up around the abbey. Regrettably, stucco has been plastered over many of Battle's half-timbered buildings, a notable exception being the Pilgrim's Restaurant (see below). Even the church was torn down as part of the act approved by Henry VIII in 1537 to dissolve the monasteries.

But some buildings and ruins remain in what Tennyson called: "O Garden, blossoming out of English blood." The principal building is the Abbots' House, at present rented to a public (private) school for girls (not open to visitors). Of architectural interest is the Gatehouse, with its octagonal towers, standing at the top of the Market Square. All of the north precinct wall still stands, and one of the most interesting sights of the ruins is the ancient Dorter Range, where the monks once slept.

Harold was killed and dismembered by William, Duke of Normandy. Encircled by his house-carls, Harold battled bravely not only for his kingdom but his life. The abbey is open year round—from 9:30 a.m. to 5:30 p.m. (on Sunday from 2 to 5:30 p.m.) in summer; from 9:40 a.m. to 4 p.m. in winter (on Sunday from 2 to 4). Admission charges are £1 ($1.95) for adults in summer, 50p (98¢) for children and senior citizens. In winter, charges are lowered to 50p (98¢) for adults and 25p (49¢) for children and senior citizens.

WHERE TO STAY: George Hotel, High Street (tel. Battle 4466), has been purchased by an ex-Californian, David M. Crum, who has brought modern standards to this old coaching inn, dating from 1699. All bedrooms now have private bathrooms and are beautifully decorated, featuring different Sanderson and Laura Ashley wallpaper prints and color schemes throughout. There is central heating in the entire hotel, open log fireplaces in the lounge and saloon bar, and the hotel has its own private car park. Prices, including a continental breakfast, are £16.50 ($32.16) in singles, £25 ($48.75) in a double or a twin, including free coffee- or tea-making facilities. Family rooms with a double bed and two single beds rent for £29 ($56.55). All prices include service and tax. Lunch is from £2.25 ($4.39), and dinner, featuring steak-and-kidney pie and local dishes, costs from £4.50 ($8.78). Special bargain terms are offered, for couples staying two nights or more, at a rate beginning at £15 ($29.25) per person, including dinner, bed, and a continental breakfast.

WHERE TO DINE: The **Gateway Restaurant,** 78 High St. (tel. Battle 2856), is owned and run by John and Moira Gregson. He did his training as a chef on the Orient Line ships, was torpedoed in the war, and then became head chef at the BBC—for radio and then TV. Moira was in service to members of the Mountbatten family, and their son and wife are also in the catering business. And that is only a small part of the family's accomplishments.

The meals offered show their skills; everything that can be is homemade. The steak-and-kidney pie is superb, and there is always a joint roasted to perfection and served with fresh vegetables. Follow this with, perhaps, black currant pie or melt-in-the-mouth suet pudding (the old-fashioned kind) with syrup. Your meal is likely to cost only £3 ($5.85). The accent is on English dishes, and the menu changes according to season. They are open at 10 a.m. for coffee, closing after the last tea is served around 5 p.m. In mild weather you can sit out on the smooth lawn, smell the roses, and enjoy the view of the abbey across the road. The restaurant is closed on Sunday and also on Monday in winter.

Pilgrim's Restaurant, Battle Village Green, High Street (tel. Battle 2314), adjacent to Battle Abbey, is an early 14th-century, black-and-white timbered house—the preferred place for lunch or afternoon tea while in town. You'll not only receive good portions of homemade food, but you'll encounter an authentic atmosphere. Recommended is the set lunch for £5 ($9.75), which is likely to include the soup of the day, hot roast shoulder of lamb with vegetables, and a special English dessert. A 10% service charge is added. An afternoon tea costs £1.60 ($3.12), and features toasted buttered scones (biscuits) and assorted cakes. The more elaborate Sunday lunch costs £5.50 ($10.73).

Owned by Mr. and Mrs. Peter and Heather Randall-Nason, the Pilgrim is a treasure house of antiquity. Peter and Heather gave up the pressure of commercial life for the pleasure of restaurant life. They both enjoy preparing and serving food—Peter had his first job at the age of six working on Saturday for his grandfather, a master confectioner. There is also a separate light meal restaurant where the choice is wide and varied. You may have lunch in the two-story, high-pitched main room with its open brick hearth, exposed beams, and collection of antiques, or you may prefer the smaller adjoining room where the tables are placed in front of an old open fireplace. The licensed restaurant is open seven days a week from 10:30 a.m. until 5:30 p.m.

11. Alfriston and Lewes

Nestled on the Cuckmere River, **Alfriston** is one of the most beautiful villages of England. Its High Street, with its old market cross, looks like one's fantasy of what an English village should be. Some of the old houses still have hidden chambers where smugglers stored their loot. Alfriston has several old inns, the best known of which is the Star, now a Trusthouses Forte hotel with its heraldic carvings outside.

During the day, Alfriston is likely to be overrun by coach tours (it's that lovely, and that popular). The village lies about 60 miles from London, northeast of Seaford on the English Channel, in the general vicinity of the resort of Eastbourne and the modern port of Newhaven.

Only about a dozen miles along the A27 toward Brighton lies **Lewes,** an ancient Sussex town, worth exploring. Centered in the South Downs, Lewes lies 51 miles from London. Since the home of the Glyndebourne Opera is only five miles to the east, the accommodations of Lewes are often frequented by cultured guests.

The county town has many historical associations, listing such residents as Thomas Paine who lived at Bull House, High Street, now a restaurant. The half-timbered **Anne of Cleves House,** so named because it formed part of that queen's divorce settlement from Henry VIII, is now a Museum of Local History and is cared for by the Sussex Archaeological Society. (Anne of Cleves never lived in the Anne of Cleves House, and there is no proof that she ever visited Lewes.) The museum has a furnished bedroom and kitchen and displays of furniture, local history, the Wealden iron industry, and other local crafts. It is found on Southover High Street and is open weekdays from mid-February to November from 10 a.m. to 5 p.m.; on Sunday from April to October from 2 to 5 p.m. Admission is 60p ($1.17) for adults, 30p (59¢) for children. Lewes, of course, grew up around its Norman castle. From the tower you can obtain a fine view of the countryside. To visit **Lewes Castle and Museum,** a joint ticket costs adults 80p ($1.56); children, 40p (78¢). To visit the castle only costs 60p ($1.17) for adults, 30p (59¢) for children. The castle and museum are open all year from 10 a.m. to 5:30 p.m., Monday through Saturday (also on Sunday from April to October, from 2 to 5:30 p.m.). Accommodations are impossible during the Glyndebourne Opera festival, but adequate at other times.

WHERE TO STAY IN ALFRISTON: If you're spending the night, try to get a room at one of the old inns.

The **Star Inn** (tel. Alfriston 870495) answers the craving of those who want all the charm of Tudor living without having to sacrifice 20th-century comfort. The present building dates from 1450, although it was originally founded in the 1200s, perhaps to house pilgrims en route to Chichester and the shrine of St. Richard. The timbered inn is a gem. In the center of the village, its carved front still unchanged, it boasts an overhanging second story of black and white timbers and bay windows. The lounges are on several levels, a veritable forest of old timbers, seasoned by the centuries. The furnishings and decorations blend well, with a Tudor refectory table, a bowl of English garden flowers, Windsor armchair, wrought-iron ceiling lights, old engravings, and several fireplaces.

Out back is a motel-type wing, with every studio-style room offering a private bath. Each is simply furnished in a tasteful style, well designed, with radio and telephone, heating, and built-in wardrobes. In rooms with bath, the rate in a single is £25 ($48.75), £33 ($64.35) in a double or twin. Tariffs include service and VAT. A set luncheon goes for £6 ($11.70), a set dinner for £8.50 ($16.58).

Deans Place Hotel (tel. Alfriston 870248) is a vine-covered country house, dating from the early 18th century and sitting under great old shady trees in its own gardens bounded by the Cuckmere River. At the edge of the village of Alfriston, it is a good introduction to gracious English life. You can play croquet, knocking those wooden balls around the green lawns, or you can relax by the heated (in summer only) outdoor swimming pool. A single with bath is £11.70 ($22.82); a double or twin with bath, £20 ($39). A continental breakfast, service, and VAT are included.

The meals are excellent, with a regular table d'hôte lunch going for £5 ($9.75), a three-course dinner for £6.50 ($12.68). Deans Place is open from February to December.

WHERE TO STAY IN LEWES: White Hart Hotel, High Street (tel. Lewes 3794), was labeled by Thomas Paine as "the cradle of American Independence," owing to his founding of the volatile and aptly named Headstrong Club there in 1761. Originally, it was the town house of the Pelhams, a kind of first family of Lewes. Later, it became a coaching inn, although the facade today dates from the 19th century. In yet another century, the representative of the Soviet Union met here with the British foreign secretary as a prelude to the resumption of diplomatic relations between the two countries.

A single with bath costs from £24 ($46.80) to £32 ($62.40); a double or twin with bath, £36 ($70.20) to £39 ($76.05); including an English breakfast, service, and VAT. Units in the annex have individual color TV sets, but if you're in the main building you have to watch TV in the lounge. All the tidily kept bedrooms have hot and cold running water and are comfortably furnished. The Sheriff's Room on the second floor is like a private club, with 16th-century timbers and cozy armchairs for quiet talks and drinks. The wine cellars once whispered with the sighs of 16th-century Protestant martyrs (many were buried there).

The dining room, with its view of the Downs, is warmly decorated with paneling and a hand-carved formal fireplace. Here, while sitting on red banquettes, you can order some of the finest viands in Lewes. A table d'hôte lunch costs £5.50 ($10.73), a set dinner going for £7 ($15.65).

The **Shelleys Hotel** (tel. Lewes 2361) is a manor house dating back to 1526. In its day, it was owned by the Earl of Dorset, before it was sold to the Shelley family, distant relatives of the poet. Radical changes were made to the architecture in the 18th century. Nowadays, the standards of the management are reflected in the fine antiques, the bowls of flowers, the paintings and prints, the well-kept garden, and, most important, the staff. In the rear is a sun terrace and lawn for tea and drinks. Horse chestnuts and copper beech shade the grounds.

The central hall is characterized by Ionic columns, a Welsh cupboard, a domed ceiling, and the coat-of-arms of the Shelley family. The bay windows of the front drawing room open onto the rear gardens, and the drinking lounge is paneled. The bedrooms are personal, individually furnished, usually spacious and most comfortable. Singles with shower cost from £26.50 ($51.68); doubles with bath/shower, from £43.50 ($84.83). Service and VAT are included in all charges. Room 11 has a 16th-century frieze of Bacchanalian figures and a design of entwining grapes and flowers. You can, by the way, order meals at Shelleys. Lunch costs from £5 ($9.75); dinner is from £7.50 ($14.63).

12. East Grinstead

Twenty-four miles from Lewes and you're at East Grinstead on the A22 Eastbourne road, 30 miles south from London. It has much charm, especially in its well-preserved, half-timbered buildings, Jacobean almshouses, and the Church of St. Swithin, built in the Perpendicular style. As a base for exploring the North Downs and Ashdown Forest, it attracts many English visitors. I prefer it, however, because of Gravetye Manor (see below), one of the finest accommodations in the south of England. East Grinstead can be reached by the Green Bus Line from London.

WHERE TO STAY: Gravetye Manor (tel. Sharpthorne 810567). Your own room is in an Elizabethan manor, part of an estate set in the hills, standing in its own 30 acres of woods, orchards, and a trout lake. It's approached by a mile-long winding driveway leading into an entrance courtyard. Later, you can discover the restored formal gardens, the lifetime creation of one of England's leading horticulturists, William Robinson.

The spacious drawing room has tasteful furnishings, with many antiques. The bedchambers are individual, each one named after trees on the estate: ash, bay, beech, whatever. Mediium-size and large double- or twin-bedded rooms range in price from £55 ($107.25) to £73 ($142.35) nightly. One is the former master bedroom, with a massive carved four-poster, as well as wood-carved portraits of the original owners over the fireplace (Richard and Katherine Infield in 1598). Other smaller doubles with private showers go for £47 ($91.65). The rates in a single with private bath are from £38 ($74.10). These prices are inclusive of a continental breakfast. Service is also included, but VAT is added to the entire account. Write well in advance for reservations in high season.

Dinner is to be savored, not rushed. Jacketed waiters are trained by the restaurant manager, Helmut Kircher. He supervises what some wine experts claim to be the best cellar in England, some 500 listings. The kitchen is the domain of a true Englishman, Allan Garth. He delights not only with his British dishes, but also he has been trained in imaginative French cuisine—a happy combination.

13. Brighton

Back in 1753, when Dr. Russell propounded the seawater cure—even to the point of advocating the drinking of an "oceanic cocktail"—he launched a movement that was to change the life of the average English person, at least his or her vacation plans. Brighton was one of the first of the great seaside resorts of Europe.

The original swinger who was to shape so much of its destiny arrived in 1783, after just turning voting age; he was the then Prince of Wales, whose presence and patronage gave immediate status to the seaside town.

Fashionable dandies from London, such as Beau Brummell, began turning up. The construction business boomed, as Brighton blossomed with charming and attractive town houses, well-planned squares and crescents. From the Prince Regent's title came the voguish word "Regency," which was to characterize an era, but more specifically refers to the period between 1811 and 1820. Under Victoria, and in spite of her cutting off the patronage of her presence, Brighton continued to flourish.

Alas, in this century, as the English began to discover more glamorous spots on the continent, Brighton lost much of its old joie de vivre. It became more aptly tabbed as tatty, featuring the usual run of fun-fair-type English seaside amusements ("let's go down to Brighton, ducky"). Happily, that state of affairs is today changing rapidly, owing largely to the huge numbers of Londoners moving in (some of whom have taken to commuting, as Brighton lies only one hour—frequent train service—from Victoria Station). The invasion is making Brighton increasingly lighthearted and sophisticated.

The Lanes, a closely knit section of alleyways off North Street in Brighton (many of the present shops were formerly fisherman's cottages) were frequented in Victoria's day by style-setting curio and antique collectors. Many are still there, although sharing space with boutiques.

THE ROYAL PAVILION: Among the royal residences of Europe, the Pavilion at Brighton—a John Nash version of an Indian mogul's palace—is unique. Ornate and exotic, it has been subjected over the years to the most devastating wit of English satirists and pundits. But today we can examine it more objectively as one of the outstanding examples of the orientalizing tendencies of the romantic movement in England.

Originally, the pavilion was built in 1787 by Henry Holland. But it no more resembled its present look than a caterpillar does a butterfly. By the time Nash had transformed it from a simple classical villa into an Oriental fantasy, the Prince Regent had become King George IV. He and one of his mistresses, Lady Conyngham, lived in the palace until 1827.

A decade passed before Victoria, then queen, arrived in Brighton. Although she was to bring Albert and the children on a number of occasions, the monarch and Brighton just didn't mix. The very air of the resort seemed too flippant for her—and the latter-day sea-bathing disciples of Dr. Russell trailed Victoria as if she were a stage actress. Further, the chinoiseries of the interior and the mogul domes and cupolas on the exterior didn't sit too well with her firm tastes—even though the pavilion would have been a fitting abode for a woman who was to bear the title Empress of India.

By 1845 Victoria and Brighton had had it. She began packing, and the royal furniture was carted off. Its tenants gone, the pavilion was in serious peril of being torn down. By a narrow vote, Brightonians agreed to purchase it. Gradually, it has been restored to its former splendor, enhanced in no small part by the return of much of its original furniture on loan by the present tenant at Buckingham Palace.

The caretakers put out the silverware, gold plate, and porcelain during the annual Regency Exhibition from June to September. But at any time you can walk through the world of crustacean ceilings, winged dragons, silk draperies, lacquered furniture, water-lily chandeliers, gilt dolphins, Chinese mythological figures, and serpents who hold everything up.

Of exceptional interest is the domed **Banqueting Hall,** with a chandelier of bronze dragons supporting lily-like glass globes. In the Great Kitchen, with its old revolving spits, is a collection of Wellington pots and pans, his *batterie de cuisine,* from his town house at Hyde Park Corner. In the State Apartments, particularly the domed Salon, dragons wink at you, serpents entwine, lacquered doors shine. The Music Room, with its scalloped ceiling, is a salon of water lilies, flying dragons, sunflowers, reptilian paintings, bamboo, silk, and satin. Currently this room is being painstakingly restored, and the fascinating work can be seen in progress. In the second-floor gallery, look for Nash's views of the pavilion in its elegant heyday. Finally, don't miss the sitting room of the king's "wife," Mrs. Fitzherbert, with some of her former furniture.

From June to early October the pavilion is open daily from 10 a.m. to 6 p.m. It closes at 5 p.m. off-season. The admission charges are: June to October (Regency Exhibition), adults, £1.60 ($3.12); children 70p ($1.37). For the rest of the year, adults pay £1.30 ($2.54); children 55p ($1.07). The Royal Pavilion is in central Brighton. Telephone Brighton 603005 for information.

READER'S TOUR SUGGESTION: "**Mr. Cliff Edwards** conducts a walk-around tour of the old landmarks and points of interest in Brighton. He leads this most informative and entertaining tour, quoting poetry, historical facts, and even a bit of song, each Tuesday at 2:30 p.m., Wednesday at 10:30 a.m., and Thursday at 7:30 p.m. All tours start from the Marlborough House, which is also the Tourist Information Centre. The walk takes about 1½ hours, costing 50p (98¢). The tour is sponsored by Watneys Red Lion and is quite a bargain. Mr. Edwards finishes up at the local cemetery, describing some of the people buried there, and their exploits. This takes an extra half hour and is optional" (Paul Engel, Palo Alto, Calif.).

WHERE TO STAY: Hundreds of accommodations are to be found in all price ranges. Regrettably, many are establishments, to quote Norman Mailer, "where elderly retired India colonels brood through dinner. . . ." However, that situation is changing now, as the most celebrated relics of yesteryear are experiencing (or have experienced) extensive overhauling. We'll survey the leading hotels, then proceed to a representative sampling of the accommodations awaiting those who must keep expenses trimmed.

The Upper Bracket

Grand Hotel, Kings's Road (tel. Brighton 26301), unquestionably has grandeur. Built in 1864, it is listed as a building of architectural and historical importance by the Department of Environment. The interior is impressive, the outstanding features being the wrought-iron staircase and the dome. The Victorian era has been skillfully recreated on the ground floor, but the bedrooms, all with private bath, radio, and TV, are modern. There are 166 bedrooms, plus seven luxury suites for VIPs.

Singles range from £32 ($62.40). Doubles go from £62 ($120.90) facing the sea. Terms include an English breakfast and VAT. En pension terms are quoted as well. The Grand also offers a table d'hôte luncheon for £10 ($19.50) and a dinner for £12 ($23.40), both inclusive. There are special weekend rates available throughout the year, excluding public holidays.

The Medium-Priced Range

Royal Albion Hotel, Old Steine (tel. Brighton 29202), stands right on the seafront, opposite the Palace Pier. As a hotel, it is one of the traditional choices of Brighton, with lots of Regency character and history, dating back to 1826. Inside, the hotel has been luxuriously decorated and furnished to a very high standard. All rooms have private bath/shower, color television, radio, telephone, and a tea- and coffee-making machine. The majority of the rooms have a superb sea view. Sir Harry's Bar, with a nautical theme, is named after the late Sir Harry Preston, who owned the hotel in the early 1900s. There is also a spacious lounge with magnificent views onto the seafront and a large Regency-style restaurant. The rates are £33 ($64.35) for a single and £48 ($93.60) for a twin or double room, inclusive of VAT and service. Table d'hôte menus range from £7.50 ($14.63) per person.

Courtlands Hotel, The Drive, Hove (tel. Brighton 731055), lies 400 yards from the sea, opening onto the wide thoroughfare known as "The Drive," about a mile from the center of Brighton. It is a comfortable Victorian building, recently modernized, with 65 rooms, of which 60 contain private baths or showers en suite and color TV. This includes units in the Courtlands complex —five particularly agreeable rooms in the cottage and coach house annex, which possess mini-bars and tea- and coffee-making facilities. Bedrooms are spacious and harmonious, with prices set according to plumbing. Per-person rates include a full English breakfast, service, and **VAT**. Bathless singles cost £20 ($39), rising to £28 ($54.60) with bath. Doubles with bath rent for £25 ($48.75) per person. This traditional hotel has more than adequate facilities, including the Golden Dolphin lounge bar and a dining room opening onto gardens. A good cuisine, both international and English, is assured. The hotel has a small children's playground, as well as a games room, and adequate parking is provided.

The Budget Range

Kennedy Palace Hotel, 11/12 Marine Parade (tel. Brighton 604928), honors the assassinated American president, and is also a good place for B&B or full board. The proprietors, A. and Y. Stylianou, charge £11 ($21.45) in a single, £20 ($39) in a double. Their fully licensed restaurant and bar is open to nonresidents as well. Their house, a Regency treasure, with an authentic bow front and an encircling balcony, has tables out on the patio so that guests may enjoy the view of the sea. The service is personal, the welcome friendly at the family-run establishment.

The **Regency Hotel,** 28 Regency Sq. (tel. Brighton 202690), is a charming Regency building with bow windows, carved doors, and a canopied balcony facing south across the square toward the pier and the sea. It was recently refurbished in a traditional style, yet incorporating modern comforts such as central heating and baths. Most units face the sea. For that romantic splurge night, you can reserve the Regency Suite, overlooking the water. This is an enormous room with a canopied bed, private sun balcony, and tented bathroom "just like something out of the Royal Pavilion." The rest of the hotel is comfortably furnished. The chandeliers are pure sparkling Waterford crystal. The hotel has a coal fire burning throughout the winter months in the original fireplace in the lounge. Overnight will cost from £14 ($27.30) per person, including a full English breakfast.

Ryford Private Hotel, 6 and 7 New Steine (tel. Brighton 681576), on a Regency square adjacent to the Marine Parade, is within minutes of the seafront, the Palace Pier and the Aquarium. The comfortable lounge and some of the guest rooms offer views of the sea. All 25 rooms are carpeted and immaculate, complete with hot and cold running water. B&B rates per person per night are about £9.50 ($18.53). Dinner is also available in the spacious dining room where excellent cuisine is prepared and served under the personal supervision of the resident proprietors.

DINING OUT IN BRIGHTON: English's Oyster Bar and Seafoods Restaurant, 29/31 East St. (tel. Brighton 27980), is my leading choice for superbly cooked fish, served in a well-preserved, 19th-century building conveniently opening onto "The Lanes." It combines a romantic setting with good food. For years, diners have been making such wise selections as a half dozen Colchester oysters for £4.45 ($8.68), or a hot lobster pâté at £3 ($5.85) per serving. The chef is known for such specialties as Dover sole (plate-size) for £6.65 ($12.97) and fresh locally caught plaice, £4 ($7.80). The pièce de résistance is the bouillabaisse at £4 also per person. The chef also offers a set two-course table d'hôte menu at £4.95 ($9.65), which is available for luncheon and dinner every day. You're given a selection of appetizers, plus a choice of five main courses. The restaurant is open for lunch every day, including Sunday, from noon to 2:20 p.m., and for dinner from 6 to 10:20 p.m. every day except Sunday.

The **French Connection Restaurant,** 11 Little East St. (tel. Brighton 24454), occupies a Georgian fisherman's cottage. Lionel Roberts and Bernard Brick run this elegant and comfortable little place, which is considered among the best restaurants in Brighton. All vegetables are purchased fresh daily, and the fish is caught locally. The restaurant is open Monday to Saturday for lunch and dinner, featuring an extensive table d'hôte menu for around $12 (U.S.), excluding wine, or else a full à la carte menu from around $22, exclusive of wine. The restaurant is frequented by many show business and political personalities, and is very popular with American tourists and business people. All major credit cards are accepted. Reservations are suggested.

Christopher's, 24 Western St. (tel. Brighton 775048), is a favorite bistro in Brighton. Operated by a former chef at London's Carlton Tower and his banker partner, the restaurant is a champion of creative cookery. Given sufficient notice, the chef will endeavor to prepare any dish you request. Appetizers include a homemade pâté for £1.25 ($2.44). Main dishes are à la carte, and are likely to feature filet maison, a steak with wine and mushroom sauce served in a light puff pastry, for £5.90 ($11.51), or côte de pork Julietta, pork chops cooked with prawns and asparagus and served in a cherry brandy sauce, for £4.60 ($8.97). Vegetables are served separately and cost about 55p ($1.07) per portion. All desserts are homemade and average about £1.30 ($2.54). Dinner is served from 7 to 10:45 p.m. daily except Wednesday. Reservations are recommended.

The **Swiss Restaurant** (also called the William Tell), 11–12 Queen's Rd. (tel. Brighton 26865), is a miniature Alpine world, tucked away in a building a block north of the clock tower. In this pine-paneled room, run by John and Heather Winslow, you'll be served top-notch Swiss dishes, along with French fare. The national dish of Switzerland, fondue Neuchatelloise, costs £9 ($17.55) for two persons. For more elaborate dining, you can order the fondue bourguignonne for two persons at £12 ($23.40). Other specialties include rösti, a Swiss potato dish, at £1 ($1.95). For dessert, try the pineapple with kirsch at £1.75 ($3.41). The place is open daily, except Sunday, from noon to 2 p.m. and from 6 to 10 p.m.

Henekeys, 4–6 Ship St. (tel. Brighton 27492), is the leading pub (established in 1695), which makes it big on atmosphere. Even if it didn't serve good food and drinks (which it does), it'd make an interesting stopover, inviting with its old timbers, bricks, stones, and leaded-glass windows. In the center is a beer garden (open in summer only), and there's a lounge bar upstairs. Behind the Old Ship Hotel, it's especially popular at lunch. The fare is very English, and includes locally caught plaice, a grilled sirloin, and scampi. A completely satisfying meal can be ordered here for about £6.50 ($12.68). These main dishes, all served in the Steak Bar, come with pie or cheese. Henekeys keeps regular pub hours.

Tureen, 31 Upper North St. (tel. Brighton 28939), is one of my favorite Brighton bistros, a rare one that makes available (see the blackboard for daily specials) some of the best of the English and continental dishes at low prices— including an always-good soup "from the tureen" for 95p ($1.85). Main courses include such delectable fare as a whole pigeon and walnut casserole, filet steak wrapped in pastry, mushrooms, and onion, and lamb sweetbreads in a mushroom and white wine sauce. A three-course set luncheon is served from Tuesday to Saturday for the low cost of £3.25 ($6.34). Otherwise, if ordering à la carte at dinner, expect to pay from £8 ($15.60). Three fresh vegetables are included in the price of the main course. In addition, the restaurant does a budget Sunday traditional family lunch at £5.50 ($10.73), including three courses, plus coffee. The Tureen is hot from noon to 2 p.m. Tuesday to Sunday, and from 7 p.m. to midnight (last orders at 9:30) Tuesday to Saturday.

Browns Restaurant and Coffee House, 3–4 Duke St. (tel. Brighton 23501), is a charming, rather 1930s place with plain tables and hoop-backed chairs. There is no bar so the staff prefers diners to wait in the Victory Inn at 7 Duke St. where they collect eaters when tables become available. Dishes have imaginative accompaniments. For example, spaghetti dishes are served with hot cheese bread and a salad; pies, including chicken and chestnut, pork, apple, and cider, come with cottage fried potatoes (sauteed) rather than the ubiquitous chips. American-style sandwiches are featured as well, along with spare ribs, chili, stuffed trout, and invariably a special of the day such as braised oxtail (game in season). Salads and grills make up the small but tasty menu. Followed by thick dark-chocolate cake and coffee, a meal will cost around £5 ($9.75) a person.

14. Arundel

This small and beautiful town in West Sussex, only 58 miles from London, four miles from the English Channel, nestles at the foot of one of England's most spectacular castles. The town was once an Arun River port, its denizens enjoying the prosperity of considerable trade and commerce. The harbor traffic is gone, replaced by coaches filled with visitors who come to visit Le Castle.

ARUNDEL CASTLE: The ancestral home of the Dukes of Norfolk, this baronial estate (tel. Arundel 883136) is a much-restored mansion of considerable importance. Its legend is associated with some of the great families of England—the Fitzalans and the powerful Howards of Norfolk. Arundel Castle traces its history back to King Alfred; its keep goes back to around the Conquest.

Over the years, Arundel Castle suffered destruction, particularly during the Civil War when Cromwell's troops stormed its walls, perhaps in retaliation for the 14th Earl of Arundel's (Thomas Howard) sizable contribution to Charles I. In the early 18th century, the castle virtually had to be rebuilt. In late Victorian times, it was remodeled and extensively restored again. Today it is filled, as you'd expect, with a good collection of antiques, along with an assortment of paintings by old masters such as Van Dyck and Gainsborough.

The castle is open from April 1 until the last Friday in October, Monday to Friday inclusive, from 1 to 5 p.m. It is open at noon during June, July, and August, and all bank holidays. The last admission time any day is 4 p.m. (the castle is not open on Saturday). Admission charges are £1.70 ($3.32) for adults, £1 ($1.95) for children 5 to 15 years of age. Surrounding the castle is an 1100-acre park (scenic highlight: Swanbourne Lake).

READER'S SIGHTSEEING TIP: "The little **Museum of Curiosity,** 6 High St., will delight children (and their parents) with its displays of small animals in storybook tableaux. It is open daily Easter through October. Admission is 20p (39¢) for children, 40p (78¢) for adults" (Ralph Williams, Falls Church, Va.).

WHERE TO STAY: Norfolk Arms, High Street (tel. Arundel 882101), is a former Georgian coaching inn set in the center of the town, just a short walk from the castle. The lounges and dining room are in the typically English country-inn style—that is, unostentatious but unquestionably comfortable. The hotel has been restored with many modern amenities blending with the old architecture. The bedrooms are handsomely maintained and furnished, each with personal touches. Most rooms have private bathrooms, and all have color television. It is a medium-priced place. The B&B rate is £17 ($33.15) per person without bath, £18 ($35.10) per person with bath, VAT included. No service is charged.

In the restaurant you can order good English cooking with Host's Luncheon for £5 ($9.75). When available, fresh local produce is offered. You can also dine on a specialty menu for £7 ($13.65), which includes many traditional English dishes.

Bridge Hotel, Queen Street (tel. Arundel 882242), is a substantial inn on the banks of the Arun River run by a Portuguese man, Orlando Simoes. The bedrooms have views of the castle, and the location's only a minute or two from the town center. In all, the Bridge rents out 13 well-maintained bedrooms, with hot and cold running water and soft beds. The B&B rate is from £13 ($25.35) per person, including VAT and service. The lounges and bedrooms are comfortable and roomy. Ask for a breakfast table opening toward the river view. Snacks begin at £1 ($1.95), complete meals at £6 ($11.70). You'll find a car park and a lock-up garage.

15. Chichester

According to one newspaper, Chichester might have been just a market town if the Chichester Festival Theater had not been established in its midst. One of the oldest Roman cities in England, Chichester is in vogue, drawing a chic crowd from all over the world who come to see its theater's presentations.

Only a five-minute walk from the Chichester Cathedral and the old Market Cross, the 1400-seat theater, with its apron stage, stands on the edge of Oaklands Park. It opened in 1962 (first director: Lord Laurence Olivier), and its reputation has grown steadily, pumping new vigor and life into the former walled city. Of course, in some quarters there is still resentment, and occasionally you hear suggestions that the pounds could have been better spent on a municipal swimming pool. But others point to the success of the Chichester theater in having given fresh stimulus to the living theater in England.

THE FESTIVAL THEATER: Booking generally opens in the middle of March, although the season might not start till the middle of May (it continues until late September). The price of seats ranges from £1 ($1.95) to £6.50 ($12.68) for the finest tickets in the house. A limited number of £1 ($1.95) seats go on sale at the box office on the day of each performance, and are sold on a first-come, first-served basis. Reservations made over the telephone will be held for a maximum of four days (call Chichester 781312). It's better to mail inquiries and checks to the box office, **Chichester Festival Theatre,** Oaklands Park, Chichester. Matinee performances begin at 2:30 p.m., evening shows Monday to Thursday at 7 p.m. and Friday and Saturday at 7:30 p.m.

How to get there: If you would like to come down from London, 62 miles away, for a matinee, then catch the 11:28 train from Victoria Station which will deliver you to Chichester by 1:05 p.m., in plenty of time. For an evening performance, board the 4:28 p.m. train from Victoria Station, arriving at 6:07 p.m. Regrettably, there is no direct late train back to London after the show. Visitors who must return can make a connection via Brighton, arriving at Victoria station shortly after midnight.

WHERE TO STAY: In Chichester, you have a choice of living either at one of the old inns inside the city, or at a motel on the outskirts.

The **Ship Hotel**, North Street (tel. Chichester 782028), is one of the classic Georgian buildings of the city, only a few minutes walk from the cathedral, the Chichester Festival Theatre, and many fine antique shops.

The Ship was built as a private house in 1790 for Admiral Sir George Murray (one of Nelson's commanders) and still retains an air of elegance and comfort. A grand Adam staircase leads from the main entrance to the bedrooms (most with private bathrooms) which are all named after historic ships. Single room prices are around £15 ($29.25) and doubles go from £28 ($54.60). A full English breakfast is included. Good pub lunches are offered at around £2 ($3.90). The Victory Bar is one of Chichester's most popular meeting places. The welcoming restaurant offers excellent value for money with its à la carte and special four-course dinner menus each evening from £6.50 ($12.68).

Dolphin & Anchor, West Street (tel. Chichester 785121), is two old inns joined together and run as a Trusthouses Forte. The situation is prime, right at the historic 15th-century Market Cross and opposite the Chichester Cathedral a ten-minute walk from the Festival Theatre. The tradition of good inn-keeping is honored here, in a setting that blends 19th-century architectural features with 20th-century comforts, including an old coaching entrance, but a new wing of handsomely furnished bedrooms as well. The two-in-one inn has 54 bedrooms, all with baths, TV, radio, and telephone. A single with bath is £26 ($50.70), increasing to £34 ($66.30) in a twin with bath, these tariffs including service and VAT. There are lounges, bars, the Whig and Tory Restaurant, and the Roussillon Coffee Shop, which serves light meals and grills until 10 p.m.

Chichester Lodge Hotel, Westhampnett, Chichester (tel. Chichester 786351), is a boon to motorists because it's a mile from the city center on the main A27 with large car-parking facilities. A covered passageway connects it to the older White Swan Inn nearby. The attractively styled hotel offers 43 modern bedrooms tastefully furnished, containing private bathrooms, telephone, radio, tea-making facilities, and color TV. The rate is £37 ($72.15) for a double and £27 ($52.65) for a single, including VAT service, and a full English breakfast. The hotel has an attractive cocktail bar and restaurant serving a set lunch for £6 ($11.70), a table d'hôte dinner for £8 ($15.60), including VAT and service.

WHERE TO EAT: Unlike its limited number of accommodations, Chichester abounds with good restaurants. We find the following establishments superior, both for food and value.

Little London Restaurant, Little London, off East Street (tel. Chichester 784899), nestles in a charming little building. The fully licensed restaurant serves a fine cuisine, each dish prepared individually. The service and reception are friendly as well. In an atmosphere of subdued taste, you can order from one of the small, but very select, menus, while seated on an upholstered chair at a pink-clothed table. At lunch, a three-course table d'hôte meal is served for £6 ($11.70), including, for example, pears with tarragon mayonnaise, roast rolled rib of beef, and profiteroles in chocolate sauce. In the evening, there is a small à la carte menu which varies during the year, serving such delicacies as caviar cream, nut cutlets, sweetbread pie, or guinea fowl in red wine and herbs. Coffee is an additional 60p ($1.17), and there is a cover charge of 40p (78¢). The vegetables of the day are included in the price of the main dishes. The desserts are homemade and mouthwatering. You must reserve. The restaurant is closed all day Sunday and Monday, but open otherwise from noon to 2 p.m. and from 7 to 10 p.m. On Saturday nights and also during the May to September Festival Theatre season, there are two sittings, at 7:30 and 9:45 p.m. The place is usually closed for one week in February.

Also on the premises is the fully licensed, self-service **Savourie,** offering a variety of soups, pâtés, and hot pies. Salads and jacket potatoes are also good. Such desserts as chocolate gâteau are offered. Meals begin at £4 ($7.80). This place is well worth recommending for its good service and the high standard of its food. Wicker chairs are placed before clean white tables. As East Street is a pedestrian way, you must be prepared to walk to the restaurant, only a short distance.

The **Roussillon Coffee Shop,** Dolphin Anchor, West Street (tel. Chichester 785121), serves snacks and light meals from 10 a.m. to 10 p.m. daily. Those on the sightseeing run might settle happily for a cheese and bacon burger at £2.85 ($5.56), although fish dishes and sirloin steak (ten ounces uncooked weight, served with french fries) are also featured. A complete hot meal is likely to cost from £7 ($13.65). Children under 14 may choose from the main menu at half price.

The **Coffee House,** West Street (tel. Chichester 784799), stands right beside the Dolphin & Anchor, opposite the cathedral. It has a good reputation for satisfying food at low prices. A small place, it provides plats du jour including a shrimp salad at £2.25 ($4.39). Hot snacks, such as Welsh rarebit with bacon at £1 ($1.95), are offered from 10 a.m. to closing. A soup of the day goes for 40p (78¢). In the licensed restaurant you can order good-tasting omelets beginning at £1.10 ($2.15), or a selection from the cold buffet, costing from £1.90 ($3.71).

THE LOCAL PUB: The **Royal Arms,** East Street, near the Market Cross, is a pub built in 1576 and known locally as the Punch House, as it became famous in the early 19th century for the making and sale of Chichester milk punch. Hosts Tim and Val Biggs offer a full range of hot and cold bar snacks lunchtime and evenings. Prices range from 75p ($1.46) to £2 ($3.90).

THE OPEN AIR MUSEUM: On a 40-acre site at Singleton, six miles north of Chichester on the A286 (London Road), Old England is being recreated. In a natural setting of mature woodland and meadows, buildings in which men and women lived and worked from the Middle Ages to the 19th century are being assembled. It's part of the **Weald & Downland Open Air Museum** (tel. Singleton 63348), open every day except Monday from April through October (but including Monday in June, July, and August, and all bank holidays) from 11 a.m. to 5 p.m. Admission for adults is £1.24 ($2.44); children, senior citizens, and students pay 75p ($1.46). Although still in the growing stage, the museum includes the 17th-century Market Hall from Titchfield in Hampshire, three 15th-century farmhouses, a 1731 granary, a timber-framed medieval house with wattle and daub walls, a treadwheel of 1600, a reconstruction of a Saxon weaver's hut considered to date from A.D. 500, a charcoal burner's hut, a weather-boarded toll cottage from Sussex, a working 18th-century watermill producing stone-ground flour, and two 18th-century barns containing exhibitions.

FISHBOURNE: A worthwhile visit only two miles from Chichester is the **Roman Palace** (tel. Chichester 785859), the largest Roman residence yet discovered in Britain. Built around A.D. 75 in Italianate style, it has many mosaic-floored rooms and even an underfloor heating system. The gardens have been restored to their original first-century plan. The story of the site is told both by an audio-visual program and by text in the museum. There is free parking and a cafeteria. The museum is open from March through November. Admission for adults is £1 ($1.95). Students and senior citizens pay 60p ($1.17), and children are charged 30p (59¢).

LIVING ON THE OUTSKIRTS: One of the most interesting ways to attend the theater in Chichester is from a base on the outskirts. That way, you get to enjoy the best of English village life, but can conveniently go into the city whenever you want. Some recommendations follow.

Old Bosham

One of the most charming little villages of West Sussex, Bosham was a Saxon hamlet (King Harold lived near here in a now disappeared palace). Its little church was depicted in the Bayeux Tapestry. Near the harbor, it is reached by a narrow lane. Its graveyard overlooks the boats (a daughter of King Canute is buried inside). The church is filled with ship models and relics, showing the villagers' link to the sea. Bosham is principally a sailing resort, linked by good bus service to Chichester.

The **Millstream Hotel,** Bosham (tel. Bosham 573234), is set on the road to the village of Bosham and its harbor, off the A27. Completely redecorated, the rooms have different colors, but all are outfitted with floral-patterned wallpaper. The decor is in keeping with the country cottage-type hotel. Beds are new and comfortable. Of the 22 rooms, 19 have baths, costing couples £38 ($74) nightly. However, two persons in a bathless room pay £34 ($66.30). Singles in bathless rooms are charged £18 ($35.10). The cocktail bar at the entrance to the restaurant is tastefully furnished with white bamboo chairs and tables, plus green carpeting. At the adjoining restaurant, you can order such à la carte dishes as moules marinières, roast duck braised with petits pois, £4.80 ($9.36), and desserts for around £1.50 ($2.93). A set luncheon is £7 ($13.65).

Incidentally, Mr. Goodman, of the Bosham Sea School, next to the Millstream Hotel, hires out sailing dinghies of the Wayfarer type. Of course, you should be experienced before taking a boat out. Those who aren't can generally get a local person to go with them if they'd like to go sailing for the day.

Midhurst

The **Spread Eagle Hotel** at Midhurst (tel. Midhurst 2211) started life as a 15th-century coaching inn, and has been much lived in, altered, and loved ever since. The inn and the market town of Midhurst are so steeped in history that the room you sleep in, the pavement you walk have a thousand tales to tell. The rooms have beams, small mullioned windows, and unexpected corners, although most units have been modernized with bathrooms en suite, along with radio, color TV, and phone. The Queen's Suite with a four-poster bed goes for £65 ($126.75) a night. However, you can rent a double or twin room from £36.50 ($71.18) or a single from £25 ($48.75), including VAT, service, and a large English breakfast.

Dinner is served in the dining hall, lit by candles which flicker on the gleaming tables. In the winter, huge log fires blaze to greet travelers. The lounge with its timbered ceiling is where Queen Elizabeth I and her court might have sat to watch festivities in the Market Square outside. The eagle in the lounge is the actual one which decorated the back of Hermann Goering's chair in the Reichstag. It was acquired for its aptness in the "Spread Eagle."

There are several bars where you can sit and watch the locals and sip a glass of sherry after a day of exploration. Midhurst lies only 12 miles from Chichester, only a bit farther from Arundel and Bosham; Brighton is just 36 miles down the road. It's also quite a good place for a first or last night for those boarding a flight at Gatwick Airport.

AT HOME WITH AN AMERICAN COUPLE: At Home, Arundel Holt Court, Bedham, Fittleworth, Pulborough (tel. Fittleworth 221). Bill and Gretchen Stevens, an American couple, live at Arundel Holt Court and offer two private bedrooms in their own house. The guest suite has a library lounge and tea- and coffee-making equipment. There is another bedroom under the roof, with a comfortable sitting area and drinks cupboard. Both have private bathrooms. The Stevenses will provide breakfast and evening meals either in your own suite or en famille in their own charming dining room. They are both good cooks and feature traditional American farmhouse, Italian, and Mexican dishes, with barbecues for hot summer evenings.

They will gladly give information on the various local sights and arrange for excursions to the coast, to Brighton, or Chichester for the theater, Goodwood for racing, or to Glyndebourne for the opera.

They are able to book you into some 50 private houses around England, Scotland, and Wales, apart from their own. The price for one night is £35 ($69.23) per person for a bed, private bath, use of a private sitting room, and breakfast. Lunch is served for £4 ($7.80), dinner for £9 ($17.55). However, if you order dinner with wine, expect to spend from £12 ($23.40). B&B for two persons is from £55 ($107.25); for four persons, from £80 ($156). Weekly rates are also available, and according to these terms you pay for six nights, getting the seventh one free.

Bill and Gretchen were traveling by ship from the United States to France. On board they met some English people and decided to stop over in England first. They've never left. Bill worked among the youth of Puerto Rico for many years.

You can write for a list of the other properties they represent in the area of England you intend to visit.

Chapter VII

HAMPSHIRE AND DORSET

STONE FARMHOUSES—Burke's Landed Gentry—all this belongs to the countryside of the 17th century. Fireplaces where stacks of logs burn gaily. Wicker baskets of apples freshly brought in from the orchard (ever had home-made apple butter?). Chickens stuffed with dressing and roasted with strips of bacon on top to keep them tender and juicy. Milk that doesn't come from bottles. Old village houses, now run as hotels, possessing quality and charm. Beyond the pear trees, on the crest of a hill, the ruins of a Roman camp. A village pub, with two rows of kegs filled with varieties of cider, where the hunt gathers.

You're in Hampshire and Dorset, two shires guarded zealously by the English, who protect their special rural treasures. Everybody knows of South-ampton and Bournemouth, but less known is the undulating countryside lying inland. Your car will take you through endless lanes, revealing tiny villages and thatched cottages untouched by the industria' invasion.

SOUTHERN COUNTIES

HAMPSHIRE

This is Jane Austen country—firmly middle class, largely agricultural, its inhabitants doggedly convinced that Hampshire is the greatest spot on earth. Austen wrote six novels of manners, including *Pride and Prejudice* and *Sense and Sensibility,* that earned her a room at the top among 19th-century writers. Her books provided a keen insight into the solid middle-class English who were to build such a powerful Empire. Although the details of the life she described have now largely faded ("At five o'clock the two ladies retired to dress, and at half-past six Elizabeth was summoned to dinner"), much of the mood and spirit of Hampshire depicted in her books remains.

Born in 1775, Jane Austen was the daughter of the rector of Steventon. Although she lived in Bath for a while, and for a troubled time in Southampton, she spent most of her life at **Chawton,** (tel. Alton 83263), near Alton, where her home may be visited today. You can see the writing desk on which she penned such memorable novels as *Emma* (her "handsome, clever, and rich" heroine, Emma Woodhouse). There is an attractive garden in which visitors are invited to have picnics, and an old bakehouse with Miss Austen's donkey cart. About a mile from the station, the home is open daily, including Sunday from 11 a.m. to 4:30 p.m. for 60p ($1.17) admission; children under 14, 10p (20¢). It is closed Monday and Tuesday from November 1 to March 31.

Hampshire embraces the **New Forest** (don't expect anything in England labeled "new" to be new), the **South Downs,** the **Isle of Wight** (Victoria's favorite retreat), the passenger port and gateway city of **Southampton,** and the naval city of **Portsmouth.**

Going west from Southampton, you'll come to the New Forest, more than 90,000 acres selfishly preserved by William the Conqueror as a private hunting ground (poachers met with the death penalty). William lost two of his sons in the New Forest—one killed by an animal, the other by an arrow. Today, it is a vast and unspoiled woodland and heath, ideal for walking and exploring.

Although Hampshire is filled with many places of interest, for our purposes I've concentrated on two major areas that seem to hold the most appeal for visitors: Southampton for convenience and Winchester for history.

LUNCHEON STOPOVERS ON THE WAY: For those driving down to Winchester and the New Forest, there is a good lunch stop at **Selborne.** After taking the A31 from London to Chawton to see Jane Austen's home, take the signposted B3006 to Selborne, five miles away. In the 18th century, Gilbert White, the author of the *Natural History of Selborne* and a pioneering botanist, lived here.

At the **Queens Hotel** (tel. Selborne 272) you can order a pub lunch of homemade soup, Queensburger, and Welsh rarebit for £1.50 ($2.93). The daily traditional dish from the restaurant is available in the bars for about £1.75 ($3.41). Or else eat in the fantastically decorated dining room under a canopy of brass jugs, bits of farm equipment, corncobs, and "god-whattery" hanging from the old oak beams. David, son of the owner, Blake Paton, ladles out the special Peggy Paton's homemade soup (his mother's recipe), plus large portions of freshly roasted beef with all the trimmings, such as Yorkshire pudding, roast potatoes, and properly cooked cabbage (that is, al dente with a little butter and some pepper). On other days there is lamb with mint sauce and red currant jelly. Desserts are homemade, and the fruit pies and cream are especially good. The bill, including VAT, will come to around £4.50 ($8.78) per person. If you can drive after leaving the place, Winchester is not too far away if you retrace your steps on the A31. The hotel is open for lunches from 12:30 to 1:45 p.m.

and for dinners from 7:30 to 8:45 p.m. Accommodation with a full English breakfast is available from £9 ($17.55) per night. Six of the nine bedrooms have private bath or shower and toilets.

Similarly at Hurstbourne Priors, between Andover and Whitchurch, on the B3400, stands the **Portsmouth Arms** (tel. Whitchurch 2000), another country pub serving good food. The range of hot dishes isn't large, but there are usually two choices as appetizers—smoked mackerel, soup, pâté—followed by pork chops, ham steaks, or lamb, all served with freshly picked and freshly cooked vegetables in season. Cheese, homemade pie, or trifle finishes the meals which, with coffee, comes to about £4.50 ($8.78) per person. The "Arms" is open for lunch from noon to 2:30 p.m. and for dinner from 7 to 10:30 p.m.

1. Portsmouth

Virginia, New Hampshire, even Ohio, may have their Portsmouths, but the daddy of them all is the old port and naval base on the Hampshire coast, 70 miles south of London. German bombers in World War II virtually leveled the city, hitting about nine-tenths of its buildings. But the seaport has recovered admirably.

Its maritime associations are known around the world. From Sally Port, the most interesting district in the Old Town, "Naval heroes innumerable have embarked to fight their country's battles." That was certainly true on June 6, 1944, when Allied troops set sail to invade occupied France.

Of chief interest is Lord Nelson's flagship, H.M.S. *Victory,* a 104-gun, first-rate ship of the line, now at No. 2 Dry Dock in Portsmouth Naval Base, (tel. Portsmouth 22351). Although she first saw action in 1778, her fame was earned on October 21, 1805, in the Battle of Trafalgar when the English scored a victory over the combined Spanish and French fleets. It was in this battle that Lord Nelson lost his life. The flagship, after being taken to Gibraltar for repairs, returned to Portsmouth with Nelson's body on board (he was later buried at St. Paul's in London). It is open March 1 to November 1, weekdays, 10:30 a.m. to 5:30 p.m.; on Sunday from 1 to 5 p.m. From November 1 to March 1, weekdays, 10:30 a.m. to 4:30 p.m. and on Sunday from 1 to 4:30 p.m. There is no admission charge.

The **Royal Naval Museum** (tel. Portsmouth 22351, ext. 23868) stands opposite H.M.S. *Victory,* in her unique setting in the old naval dockyard, and houses many naval relics that are complementary to the ship. These include personal items which belonged to Lord Nelson and his officers, fine collections of figureheads, paintings, and ship models, and a special display of Nelson memorabilia given by Mrs. Lily McCarthy, CBA, an American citizen. Other galleries are devoted to the fascinating Victorian era with the great changeover from sail to steam, the Second World War, and the navy of today.

The museum is open daily from 10:30 a.m. to 5 p.m. (on Sunday from 1 to 5 p.m.) in summer, closing at 4:30 p.m. in winter. There is a 50p (98¢) admission charge. The museum complex also includes a buffet and a well-stocked souvenir shop.

Portsmouth was the birthplace of Charles Dickens, and the small terrace house of 1805 in which the famous novelist made his appearance on February 7, 1812, and lived for a short time, has now been restored and furnished to illustrate the middle-class taste of the early 19th century. Called **Charles Dickens' Birthplace Museum,** it is at 393 Old Commercial Rd., Mile End (tel. Portsmouth 827261). It is open daily from 10:30 a.m. to 5:30 p.m., except Christmas Day and Boxing Day. Admission is 30p (59¢) for adults, 12p (23¢)

for students and children. Family tickets (four persons) are available for 60p ($1.17). Last tickets are sold at 5 p.m.

Jutting out into the harbor, **Portchester Castle** has one of the finest examples of early Saxon timber work in all of England. It was here that Henry V assembled his men for the assault on Agincourt in 1415. In addition, Portsmouth also has one of the best surviving Roman forts in England.

WHERE TO STAY: Overnighting in Portsmouth? If so, try the following:

Keppel's Head Hotel, The Hard (tel. Portsmouth 21954), is an impressive Victorian brick monument facing the train ferry pier. A prestigious hotel for generations, the inn preserves its traditional niceties, with good old-style bedrooms, some with private baths. Singles rent for £27 ($52.65), with doubles going for £35 ($68.35), including a full English breakfast and VAT. Some travelers to the Isle of Wight stop off here to dine at the Captain's Table. The cuisine is English, including such dishes as thick slices of ribs of beef with Yorkshire pudding, or roast loin of pork with apple sauce. Various à la carte dishes are served.

WHERE TO EAT: The **Lone Yachtsman** at the Point (head up Broad Street; tel. Portsmouth 24293) is a revamped pub that is the center of the local life of old Portsmouth. Decorated in a nautical theme, it commands a view of the harbor from its perch on the end of a promontory. You can drink in the Sir Alec Rose bar (popular with yachting people) or else dine at the Lively Lady (hot luncheons Monday to Friday from noon to 2:30 p.m.). Among the usual entrees are such tempting items as the soup of the day and steak, kidney, and mushroom pie. A tradition is the hot fruit pie, served with thick cream. A snack meal will cost around £1 ($1.95) to £3.50 ($6.83), with a set lunch going for £3.60 ($7.02).

The Hungry One, 15 Arundel Way, Arundel Street (tel. Portsmouth 817114), is a simple, clean snackbar, offering a wide range of salads from plain cheese to fresh salmon from about £1.60 ($3.12) to £2.20 ($4.29), plus well-cooked chickens and chips, plaice and chips, scampi and chips for about the same prices. Desserts are about 65p ($1.27) It is noted for its coffee served with fresh creams.

IN THE ENVIRONS: The **Old House,** The Square, Wickham, near Fareham (tel. Wickham 833049), is a tiny village-square hotel built in 1702, in the time of Queen Anne. It is personally run by its owners, Mr. and Mrs. Skipwith. The hotel stands in a preserved Georgian square of Wickham, and is noted for its good restaurant, which is closed at lunchtime on Monday and Saturday (all day on Sunday).

The hotel's bedrooms, each with private bath, are not rented on Saturday and Sunday, and therefore it is open on weekdays only. Prices are from £27 ($52.65) in a single, from £39 ($76.05) in a double, these tariffs including a full English breakfast, service charge, and VAT.

The garden overlooks the Meon River, and the restaurant specializes in a French provincial cuisine, a complete meal costing from £16 ($31.20). The menu changes frequently, and care goes in to the selection of the vegetables as well. On one occasion, local spring greens, with butter and black pepper, were excellent. Lunch is served from 12:30 to 2 p.m. and dinner from 7:30 to 9:30 p.m. Always reserve well in advance. The restaurant is closed all day on Sunday and at lunch on Monday.

Off the Portsmouth-Southhampton road, follow the signs to Hamble. You will soon come to **Beth's Restaurant,** The Quay, in Hamble (tel. Hamble 4314). Even in a village of ancient shops and houses, the Queen Anne house stands out with its typical plain front, large windows, and welcoming front door. Inside, the bar with its roaring log fire and antique furniture is more a drawing room, and you might be excused for thinking you've come to the wrong place.

Never fear. Beth Cockburn has specially created the family home atmosphere, and you can relax in a deep armchair with an apéritif while deciding on your meal. Upstairs, the restaurant has lovely views over the Hamble River, one of the best-known yachting centers in the country.

The menu is changed frequently, along with the seasons and the availability of fresh produce. Mostly French dishes are offered, but there are some rather elaborate English ones as well. Appetizers include homemade pâté with a celery and orange salad, a hot fish pâté with a herb sauce, and gravad lax, home-cured salmon not often found outside Norway. Main dishes include guinea fowl baked with limes and cream cheese, fresh local fish, lamb kidneys with port Dijon mustard, and sirloin steak served with special butters—herb, garlic, or "alcoholic." Your meal is rounded off with a light homemade dessert or cheese. The average price is £8.50 ($16.58), including vegetables and VAT but not wine.

They also do a special menu for £7.50 ($14.63), including an appetizer, a main dish, and dessert, but not service. The restaurant is open for lunch from 12:30 to 2:30 p.m. and for dinner from 7:30 until the last orders are taken at 9:30 p.m. They are closed from Sunday night to Tuesday night, and also in January and February. They make sure that you're not hurried from your table and have time to enjoy a relaxing meal. Telephone to reserve a table, as they are very popular.

They also do breakfast from 9 a.m. if you happen to be touring in the area. In summer, they open the garden behind the house, weather premitting, and lunches and dinners are served there. The fare consists of various barbecues—steaks, hamburgers, chicken, local mackerel, and bass, all served with baked jacket potatoes and salads, ranging in price from £2 ($3.90) to £5 ($9.75). Fresh lobster with lemon mayonnaise is a summer special.

2. Southampton

To many North Americans, England's No. 1 passenger port, home base for the *Queen Elizabeth 2,* is the gateway to Britain. Southampton is a city of wide boulevards, parks, and shopping centers. It was rebuilt after German bomb damage, which destroyed hundreds of its old buildings.

In World War II, Some 3½ million men embarked from here (in the First World War, more than twice that number passed through Southampton). Its supremacy as a port has long been recognized and dates from Saxon times when the Danish conqueror, Canute, was proclaimed king here in 1017.

Southampton was especially important to the Normans and kept them in touch with their homeland. It shares the dubious distinction of having imported the bubonic plague in the mid-14th century that wiped out a quarter of the English population. Near the docks is a memorial tower to the Pilgrims, who set out on their voyage to the New World from Southampton on August 15, 1620.

If you're waiting in Southampton between boats, you may want to use the time to explore some of the major sights of Hampshire that lie on the periphery of the port—the New Forest, Winchester, the Isle of Wight, and Bournemouth in neighboring Dorset.

WHERE TO STAY: The **Post House,** Herbert Walker Avenue (tel. South-ampton 28081), is a Trusthouses Forte oasis of style and taste, the pacesetter of modern hotels on the south coast. Ten floors tall, it was built near the New Docks to overlook the harbor, but is only five minutes away from the city center. You can unload your luggage under a sheltered drive, and walk straight into the reception area. The rooms, 132 in all (nine studio and eight syndicate accommodations), are handsome and spacious, decorated in strong bold colors, with fine built-in pieces, picture-window walls, private baths, telephones, radio, and television. Twin or double rooms cost £28 ($54.60) per person; a single, £34 ($66.30). Your breakfast is extra, but all rates include service and VAT. The facilities of the hotel are exceptional, especially the heated open-air swim-ming pool. The residents' lounge has a color television. The Harbour Bar adjacent to the restaurant has an intimate atmosphere. For dining in the Solent Room see my restaurant recommendations.

Dolphin Hotel, High Street (tel. Southampton 26178), which dates back to the 13th century, was Jane Austen's choice, even Thackeray's when he was writing *Pendennis.* In time, Queen Victoria arrived in a horse-drawn carriage at this Georgian inn and coaching house. A classic brick building, with a pair of bow windows, it is in the center of the city, and is approached through an arched entrance, over which rests a coat-of-arms of William IV and Queen Adelaide. The 73 bedrooms vary widely in size, but are generally spacious and well furnished. All have baths. Singles cost £27 ($52.65); doubles and twins, £36 ($70.20). The lounge is dignified, nicely paneled, and tidily kept. The open staircase holds a rare collection of naval uniform prints. Meals at the Dolphin are quite good, with a table d'hôte dinner beginning at £7 ($13.65). Drinks are served in the Nelson Bar.

Polygon Hotel, Cumberland Place (tel. Southampton 26401), 15 minutes to the Ocean Terminal, is the ideal hotel for transatlantic passengers just off the *Queen Elizabeth 2.* Set quietly back overlooking West Park and the Civic Centre, it is run as a member of Trusthouses Forte Hotels Ltd. It offers 119 well-furnished bedrooms, all with private baths, telephones, radios, and color TV sets. A single is £28 ($54.60), and a twin is £36 ($68.25), including service and VAT. A bar and restaurant are on the premises; there is ample parking space, plus near-instant taxi service.

Cotswold Hotel, Highfield Lane (tel. Southampton 559555), is a modern hotel, offering plain, comfortable overnight accommodations. All rooms have telephone, radio, color TV, tea- and coffee-making equipment, and most have bathrooms or showers. There is a good car park and a night porter. A good feature is that a supper menu takes over from dinner at 9 p.m. and goes on until last orders are given at 11 p.m. Gilley's restaurant is open daily, virtually all day—a coffeeshop-type place with bench seats around "stall" tables. At lunch-time, including Sunday, roast ribs of beef, served from a majestic trolley sal-vaged from the transatlantic liner R.M.S. *Queen Mary,* are the specialty, accompanied by horseradish sauce and Yorkshire pudding. In season fresh local salmon is an added attraction. Lunch or dinner will cost you around £6 ($11.70) to £8 ($15.60) a person for three courses. Supper includes kebabs, barbecued chicken, beefburgers, and mixed grill. Most Saturday nights they have a dinner dance. Rooms go for £20.50 ($39.98) to £26 ($50.70) in a single, from £33.20 ($64.74) to £37.60 ($73.32) in a double, including an English breakfast, VAT, and service.

WHERE TO DINE: The **Solent Room,** Post House, Herbert Walker Avenue (tel. Southampton 28081), is a distinguished restaurant in a colorful setting. On the ground floor of this ten-story modern hotel, top-notch meals are served against a background of bright-red floors and walls. The service is friendly and attentive and the cuisine is international. A three-course lunch is £7.50 ($14.63), and a three-course dinner begins at £9 ($17.55) to £11 ($21.45). All charges are inclusive of service and VAT. The headwaiter will present you with a comprehensive list of wines.

Cobbett's Restaurant, The Square, Botley (tel. Botley 2068), is run with flair by Mr. and Mrs. Charles Skipwith, who prepare French dishes with skill, using fresh ingredients whenever possible. Even the vegetables—too often neglected in restaurants in England—are well prepared, tender and crisp. Mr. Skipwith's wife, Lucie, comes from Bordeaux, France, and she does the cooking, taking pride in selecting original and unusual dishes. To her the words "deep freeze" are dirty words. Seating 40, the snug restaurant has a 16th-century beamed bar where pre- and postdinner drinks are served. The menus and prices change seasonally, so I can't recommend particular specialties. However, recent main courses included tournedos Curnonsky and a regional cassoulet. Fresh vegetables in season are always offered. The hors d'oeuvres are good, especially the salade des crudités. Although the list varies, depending on what's available at the market, a recent plate featured celery, tomatoes, fennel, watercress, chicory, cucumber, egg, artichoke hearts, and other vegetables. Expect to pay about £12 ($23.40) to £15 ($29.25) per head, including VAT. A three-course lunch at £7.50 ($14.63) is served from 12:30 to 2 p.m.; dinner, 7:30 to 10 p.m. Closed Sunday and for a two-week summer vacation.

The Best Pub in Town

The **Red Lion,** High Street, is one of the few architectural jewels that survived World War II. The pub is rooted in the 12th century (a Norman cellar), but its high-ceilinged and raftered Henry V Court Room is in a later style. The room was the scene of the trial of the Earl of Cambridge and his accomplices, Thomas Grey and Lord Scrope, who were condemned to death for treason in plotting against the life of the king in 1415. The Court Room is adorned with coats-of-arms of the noblemen who served as peers of the trio. All this bloody history needn't deter you. The Red Lion is a friendly, fascinating place at which to stop in for a drink, a good old English pub lunch, and a chat.

SIDE TRIPS FROM SOUTHAMPTON: If postwar Southampton is too modern for your taste, and you want to capture the flavor of old England, then strike out for the **Fox and Hounds Inn,** Hungerford Bottom, Old Bursledon (tel. Bursledon 2784), between Southampton and Portsmouth—not far from the ferry to the Isle of Wight, and close to the Bursledon Railroad Station. It would take the writing ability of Dickens and the visual techniques of Hogarth to capture the spirited image of this inn, which dates back to 1338. You can have your wine-tasting experience in either the Hunter's Bar or the Farmer's Kitchen. Against a backdrop of horse brasses, a heavily beamed ceiling, and an open fireplace, the legendary mead—known to both the English and the Vikings—is dispensed. The Saxons considered it an elixir, and it is believed that the honey-based drink was the customary toast following a wedding—hence, the term honeymoon. Between lifting your maple and silver "mazer," you can sample Hampshire farm cheese served with good-tasting cottage bread. The Fox and Hounds, run by Bill and Joy Rout, is also noted for its English wines, which can be ordered on draft. If you've tasted cowslip before, you surely haven't sampled damson dandelion! From your beer-barrel seat, you can also take your chance on some sloe gin. English wines cost 55p ($1.07) per glass; a half pint of draft cider or beer, 35p (68¢). At the rear of the inn is a timbered barn serving as both a museum of farming artifacts (old farm wagons, carts, and smithy tools) and a self-service dining room. Here you dine on benches at one of the longest, oldest tables in England. During winter, the table nearest the ten-foot-wide fireplace is favored. Summertime, tables are also available in the courtyard beside an ancient wine press, under a rose arbor. Soups are 55p ($1.07); sandwiches, £1.20 ($2.34) and up. Helpings of fresh fruit salad cost 75p ($1.46).

Directions: Go on road A27 from Southampton, toward Portsmouth. After passing Lowford, turn right onto Long Lane, pass the school on School Road, and you'll reach a road called Hungerford Bottom. The Fox and Hounds is on your right.

BROADLANDS: At Romsey (tel. 516878), Earl Mountbatten of Burma lived until his assassination in 1979. On their honeymoon, he lent his mid-16th-century house to H.M. the Queen when, as Princess Elizabeth, she married Prince Philip. More recently, Prince Charles and Princess Diana spent the first nights of their honeymoon there. Now a shrine to Britain's last war hero, the 40-room Georgian mansion lies 87 miles southwest of London. Originally constructed as an adjunct to Romsey Abbey, the house was purchased by Lord Palmerston in 1736 and later decorated in a fine Palladian style. Capability Brown landscaped the gardens, and Broadlands today still retains some 6000 acres of park and farmland. There is a fine exhibition and show depicting the highlights of Lord Mountbatten's brilliant career as a sailor and diplomat until his partial retirement from public life. In the dining room you'll find four Van Dyck oil paintings, plus grilles by Whistler. The house is open daily, except Monday (daily including Monday in August and September), April to September, from 10 a.m. to 6 p.m. Admission is $4 (U.S.) for adults, $2.75 for students, and $2.10 for children, the elderly, and the disabled.

3. New Forest

The New Forest came into the limelight in the times of Henry VIII, who loved to hunt here, as venison abounded. Also with his enthusiasm for building up the British naval fleet, he saw his opportunity to supply oak and other hard timbers to the boatyards at Buckler's Hard on the Beaulieu River for the building of stout-hearted men-o'-war. Today you can visit the old shipyards, the museum with its fine models of men-o'-war, pictures of the old yard, and dioramas showing the building of these ships, their construction, and their launching. It took 2000 trees to build one man-o'-war.

Stretching for about 92,000 acres, New Forest is a large tract 14 miles wide and 20 miles long. William the Conqueror laid out the limits of this then-private hunting preserve. Those who hunted without a license faced the executioner if they were caught, and those who hunted but missed had their hands severed.

Nowadays, New Forest is one of those places traversed by a motorway by those motorists bound for the southwest. However, I'd suggest you stop a moment and relax.

This used to be a forest, but now the groves of oak trees are separated by wide tracts of common land which is grazed by ponies and cows, hummocked with heather and gorse, and frequented by rabbits. Away from the main arterial roads, where signs warn of wild ponies and deer, there is a private world of peace and quiet.

FOOD AND LODGING: My recommendations for food and lodging follow, beginning with the finest establishment in the entire area.

New Milton

Chewton Glen Hotel, New Milton, Hampshire (tel. Highcliffe 5341), is a gracious old country house on the fringe of the New Forest. It's within easy reach of Southampton and Bournemouth for those who want to escape from the bustle of the 20th century. Follow the signpost off the B3055, New Milton–Christchurch road, through well-kept parkland to a private car park. The staff will arrange for you to be met if you intend to arrive by ship or train at Southampton.

Rooms are either in the old house or else in the new wing. In your bedroom you'll find "a tot" of sherry along with a bowl of fresh flowers to greet you. In the old house, you will either take the magnificent staircase to one of the well-furnished chambers, decorated with chintz armchairs, good beds, and lovely views over the spacious grounds, or find yourself on the ground level with French doors opening onto your own private patio. Here the decor is in muted colors, the rooms named for the heroes of novels written by Captain Marryat (he was the author of *The Children of the New Forest*). There is full room service so you can retire fully from the world if that is your wish. In the old part, the rooms have eaves and dormer windows, and some have been combined to provide family accommodations.

Settle in and wander downstairs to explore the many lounges, arranged so that you can join the small crowd in the bar, or sit and talk in the big drawing room. Everywhere log fires burn and fresh flowers add fragrance. In the hall an information office provides details of local excursions, golf, sailing, and horse-riding. Guests can also swim in an open-air heated swimming pool. The garden sweeps down to a stream and then to rhododendron woods. In addition there are tennis courts and a croquet and putting green.

In the dining room, the standard of cooking and the presentation of the food is high. Particular emphasis is placed on fresh ingredients. The chef de cuisine, Pierre Chevillard, places an emphasis on nouvelle cuisine, complemented by excellent sauces and velvety-smooth desserts. Toni Ferrario is one of the most efficient restaurant managers in the country. Your dinner will be a treat. The set meal of three magnificent courses is changed daily. A set lunch is £8 ($15.60), going up to £9.50 ($18.53) on Sunday. A set dinner costs £13.50 ($26.33), rising to £14.50 ($28.28) on Saturday. The à la carte menu includes such delicacies as sweetbreads and Scottish salmon, and such daily specialties as lobster in season. An à la carte dinner will cost about £40 ($78) for two persons. But you will probably find the set meal delicious and adequate for the best of trenchermen. A simpler but equally excellent luncheon is provided, and the kitchen will also prepare a succulent picnic for you to take on an excursion. The wine cellar contains a choice of well-chosen French and German wines— and some Italian ones, too.

The price for all this begins at £68 ($132.60) for two persons, including VAT, service, and a continental breakfast. The Marryat suite is priced at £117 ($228.15) for two, and the recently converted coach houses are delightful duplexes, with two bathrooms each, costing £100 ($195) for two.

The hotel is owned by Martin Skan and his family, and their influence and that of their general manager, David Brockett, can be seen in the many thoughtful touches, the friendly attitude of the efficient staff, and the spotless condition of the hotel and grounds.

This hotel is my choice for the best in England.

Buckler's Hard

The **Master Builders House Hotel**, Buckler's Hard (tel. Buckler's Hard 253), is a lovely 18th-century main house which was once the home of master shipbuilder Henry Adams, who was responsible for many of the wooden walls which dominate the seaways of the world. Today there is a new wing which accommodates guests in pleasant double rooms with bath, color TV, and tea- and coffee-making facilities. The main house has only four rooms available to guests.

The space in the main building is devoted to the Yachtsman Buffet Bar, which provides good, ample snack meals and the restaurant with its wide windows overlooking the busy river. Doubles and twins are rented to just one person for £18.50 ($36.08), but only £15.50 ($30.23), per person based on double occupancy. However, there are some small singles going for only £13.50 ($26.33) nightly. All rates include an English breakfast, VAT, and service. Lunch or dinner from the reasonable à la carte menu costs about £7 ($13.65) per person.

This is an ideal center from which to explore New Forest and the coastline. The **Maritime Museum** in the village contains models of the famous ships built here, including the *Agamemnon*, Nelson's favorite, and the *Euryalus* and the *Swiftsure*, which fought at the Battle of Trafalgar. Also on display are the tools used to build the ships. The way of life on board in the 19th century is displayed in pictures and with models, and there are charts and information about modern sailors, Sir Francis Chichester among them.

The museum is open daily from 10 a.m. to 9 p.m. in summer, closing earlier during the rest of the year. The walk back to Beaulieu, 2½ miles, along the riverbank is well signposted through the woodlands. In summer, cruises operate from the riverfront to the Isle of Wight, and on most days also to Southampton up the busy channel past Fawley's oil refinery and the Hamble River with its yachts and weekend dinghy sailors.

Ashurst

Beaulieu Road Hotel, Ashurst (tel. Ashurst 2141), stands on the B3056 from Lyndhurst to Beaulieu. It was said to have been built by the grandfather of the present Lord Montagu close to the Beaulieu Road Railway Station to accommodate the overflow of guests arriving from London to shoot on the estate.

Nowadays the red brick building, surrounded by pine trees, has comfort- able bedrooms, some with bath, which rent for £10 ($19.50) per person nightly, including a large English breakfast.

Dinners are mainly grills and roasts, particularly New Forest venison, a large meal costing around £6 ($11.70). They also have a snackbar at lunchtime with quiches, sandwiches, and several homemade hot dishes, ranging in price from 75p ($1.46) to £2.50 ($4.88) a portion.

Every autumn, the highlight of the year is the Beaulieu Road New Forest Pony Sales in the stockyards of the local railway station, when ponies newly rounded up from the forest are sold. The hotel's drinking license is extended to cover the whole day.

Mrs. McGrath is the owner and manager of the hotel, and she'll see that you're well provided for. As an additional bonus, the hotel has a swimming pool and tennis court—and your horse can be stabled at very low cost. The sur- rounding area is gentle walking country, as there are no startling or steep hills and dales to negotiate. It's also marvelous for horseback riding.

Lyndhurst

Lyndhurst Park Hotel, High Street (tel. Lyndhurst 2824), is a large old country house with trees and lawns, plus a swimming pool and golf practice net. Bedrooms are equipped with TV, radio, phone, and tea- or coffee-makers, costing from £13 ($25.35) per person without bath, from £16 ($31.20) with bath, including VAT and an English breakfast.

There are two bars with beams, high-backed settles, and harnesses decorating the brick walls and the high-ceilinged, woodpaneled dining room. A surprisingly wide selection of dishes is offered, both at lunch and dinner. Appetizers are likely to include scallops with lobster and cheese sauce or fried camembert cheese in breadcrumbs. Main dishes include grilled Lymington plaice (a local fish), pot-roasted local pheasant, and sirloin steaks. A three-course meal with coffee will cost about £6 ($11.70), except on Saturday night when they have dancing at dinnertime. Then the cost of the evening will be from £8.50 ($16.58). It's very pleasant and comfortable.

The **Crown Hotel,** High Street (tel. Lyndhurst 2722), stands on a spot where there has been a hostelry for centuries, on the main street of the village opposite the church with its tall spire. The present building is a mere 100 years old, and the bedrooms are snug with color TV, radio, phone, and a drink cabinet. All units rent for £14 ($27.30) per person in a double, including VAT and a full English breakfast.

Much local produce is used in the dining room, including venison Walter Tyrrell, commemorating the hunter who missed the deer and loosed the arrow which pierced the heart of William Rufus, king of England. This specialty is a rich concoction of meat, mushrooms, and onions cooked in red wine and cream with red currants and brandy. Steak Agamemnon is named for one of the wooden warships built at nearby Buckler's Hard.

A meal will cost around £7 ($13.65), and there are also simple dishes such as grills and salads available. Sunday lunch at £5.50 ($10.73) is well patronized by the local people. They also do substantial bar snacks with at least one hot dish of the day with vegetables, such a meal costing about £1.50 ($2.93) for a large helping.

Brockenhurst

New Park Manor, Lyndhurst Road, Brockenhurst, New Forest (tel. Brockenhurst 3467), is a former royal hunting lodge dating from the days of William the Conqueror. It is the only hotel in the New Forest itself. In 1666 King Charles made New Park his favorite hunting lodge on his return from exile in France, and came here accompanied by Nell Gwynne.

Now a modern country hotel, the manor has some 20 bedrooms which were opened to the public in 1970. The original rooms have been preserved, including such features as beams and open log fires. The owners have installed central heating throughout, and the bedrooms contain TV sets and many amenities, such as electric razor points. Most of the chambers have private bathrooms. I prefer the second-floor bedrooms, with exposed beams and sloping ceilings. A room and a full English breakfast costs from £18 ($35.10) per person daily. Included in the tariff is the use of a swimming pool, in a sheltered corner of the garden (heated in summer), and a hard tennis court. Riding from the hotel's stables is available at a reduced rate for guests.

The candlelit restaurant, with its log fire, specializes in flambé cookery. Backed up by a good wine list, the chef often uses fresh garden produce and the hotel's own bacon and pork from its pig farm. Saturday dinner-dances are increasingly popular. The hotel lies half a mile off the A337 Lyndhurst-Brockenhurst road past the 500-year-old thatched lodge to the manor.

Balmer Lawn Hotel, Brockenhurst (tel. Lymington 23116), is a sophisticated place, with grounds blending with those of New Forest, a heated swimming pool, and pleasant comfortable lounges in which to relax. Lunch costs from £5.50 ($10.73); dinner, from £7 ($13.65). The menu offers many interesting selections. After a local fish or venison, you might try, for example, a date-and-ginger pie. Rooms without bath go for £16 ($31.20) per person, rising to £19 ($37.05) per person with bath, including VAT and a full breakfast. Ideal for the visitor, the hotel lies on the A337, the Lyndhurst-Lymington road, about a mile outside of Brockenhurst. Opposite the hotel is the village cricket field, where on summer weekends guests can stroll out to watch the game played as it should be—by local enthusiasts.

Lymington

The **Angel Hotel**, 108 High St. (tel. Lymington 72050), is a 13th-century inn right on the main street with a large car park behind it in the courtyard. The plain bedrooms have TV, radio, and tea- and coffee-making facilities, costing £12.40 ($24.18) per person in a double. They also rent out family rooms at a rate of £11 ($21.45) per person for up to four guests per unit. A full English breakfast is served and included in the tariff. A set lunch for £4.50 ($8.78) includes a soup of the day or appetizer, followed by a grill or roast, then a dessert from the trolley. There's also a wide à la carte menu, but they warn there is a delay of 30 minutes or so on any order.

Smuggler's Cave Restaurant, 6 Queen St. (tel. Lymington 72603), is a simple place with clean bare tables where the food and the size of the portions are what matter. It has real "home away from home" qualities and quantities. A lunch of the day is likely to include homemade soup, steak-and-kidney pie with fresh vegetables, or fish and chips, perhaps a seafood platter. Everything is fresh. A dish will cost around £2 ($3.90). It's run by "Gil," who used to work at the Lansdowne Club in London's Berkeley Square before going on to the Café Royal. Mary Hamilton waits on tables and generally keeps everyone content. Their place is open seven days a week, and they do a four-course Sunday lunch for £3.50 ($6.83). In the evenings they do simple appetizers, followed by duck with orange sauce, coq au vin, or perhaps venison with black cherries. A meal, including VAT, costs about £6 ($11.70).

Marlo's Barge Restaurant, Bridge Yard (tel. Lymington 72237). An old steel Humber barge, *Maria II* has been converted into a restaurant open Wednesday to Sunday from 7 p.m. You're advised to reserve a table, as there's not much room. Appetizers range from the soup of the day at 95p ($1.85) to fresh trout at £1.80 ($3.51). Main dishes include chicken with tarragon, noisettes of lamb, sweetbreads, fresh local fish such as plaice or monkfish, and especially crab, depending on availability. These platters go for about £4.50 ($8.78), including vegetables and a salad. It's a fun place with a cheerful atmosphere and good food, and it's also easy to find—right beside the railway station in this little town.

The **Old Bankhouse Bistro**, 68 High St. (tel. Lymington 78888), is a basement place with a wooden floor and an old brick wall behind the bar which is long and narrow. It's very popular with the locals who like its friendly atmosphere and excellent value meals. It's open daily except Monday from noon to 3 p.m. and from 6 to 11 p.m. You lunch off chicken pâté or taramasalata, perhaps soup of the day, for 60p ($1.17). For anywhere from £1.50 ($2.93) to £2 ($3.90), you can order seafood, lasagne, spicy chicken with rice, or lamb casserole with jacket potato and salad. If you're really hungry, then I'd suggest the sirloin steak with potato and salad for £4 ($7.80).

Fagin's Restaurant, 135 High St., is a real Dickensian-type, low-ceilinged restaurant, with oak beams, high-backed chairs, and dining alcoves with stools. Try the Fagin's cocktail of prawns, celery, apple, and walnuts in Marie-Rose sauce, or the homemade sardine and anchovy pâté with brown bread. I also enjoy the crudités (fresh raw vegetables) with a cheese dip. Perhaps you'll follow with a whole grilled local plaice, chicken casserole, or an entrecôte steak with mushrooms and brown sauce. Desserts from the trolley finish off the meal, and fresh vegetables cost extra. Expect to spend from £7.50 ($14.63).

The Buttery, 20 High St., is an ideal place for morning coffee or a quick snack lunch. Salads and omelets are good, costing from £1.50 ($2.93), and sandwiches start at 35p (68¢). It's a busy, cheerful place with quick service.

For those who just want "pub-grub," Mr. Keen at **King's Head,** at the bottom of High Street, offers a wide range of bar snacks from noon to 2 p.m. and also in the evenings. Perhaps you'll sample his cannelloni with a meat and tomato sauce, or else chicken in the basket with straw potatoes. Portions go for about £2 ($3.90). On Sunday, he does only a ploughman's lunch.

BEAULIEU ABBEY: This stately home in the New Forest draws more visitors than Woburn Abbey. The abbey and palace house, as well as the National Motor Museum, are on the property of Lord Montagu of Beaulieu, at Beaulieu, five miles southeast of Lyndhurst and 14 miles south of Southampton. Originally, a Cistercian Abbey was founded on this spot in 1204, and the ruins can be explored today. The palace house was the gate house of the abbey before it was converted into a private residence in 1538. The house is surrounded by gardens. On the grounds, one of the best and most comprehensive motor museums in the world, with more than 200 vehicles, is open to the public. It traces the story of motoring from 1895 to the present day. Famous autos include four land-speed record holders, among them Donald Campbell's "Blue Bird." The museum was based on the Montagu family's collection of vintage cars. All the facilities are open every day from 10 a.m. to 6 p.m. (till 5 p.m., November to March). Inclusive admission to the museum, house, abbey ruins, and gardens is £2.50 ($4.88) for adults, £1.25 ($2.44) for children.

Food and Lodging

Montagu Arms, in Beaulieu (tel. Beaulieu 612324), was built with locally made bricks and tiles as well as timbers from the New Forest. This time-tested favorite combines the comfort of a country manor house with the cozy hospitality of a mellow wayside inn. The hotel staff keeps up an old English garden which is well sheltered and filled with some rare plants. The main lounge overlooks this garden, and the dining room, serving good food and wine, is oak beamed and paneled. In one of the three bars, the counter was fashioned from an old wine press.

The bedrooms are immaculately kept and modernized, most of them containing private baths and wall-to-wall carpeting. Singles rent from £20 ($39), and doubles range from £30 ($58.50) to £38 ($74.10), including a full English breakfast.

4. Isle of Wight

Four miles across the Solent from the South Coast towns of Southampton, Lymington, and Portsmouth, the Isle of Wight is known for its sandy beaches and its ports, favored by the yachting set. The island, which long attracted such literary figures as Alfred Tennyson and Charles Dickens, is compact in size, measuring 23 miles from east to west, 13 miles from north to south. You can take regular ferryboats over, although hydrofoils cross the Solent in just 20 minutes from Southampton.

Long a favorite of British royalty, the island has as its major attraction **Osborne House,** Queen Victoria's most cherished residence, lying a mile southeast of East Cowes. Prince Albert himself designed the Italian-inspired mansion which stands in lush gardens, right outside the village of Padmore. The rooms have remained as Victoria knew them, right down to the French piano she used to play and with all the cozy clutter of her sitting room. Grief-stricken at the death of Albert in 1861, she asked that Osborne House remain as it was, and so it has been. Even the turquoise scent bottles he gave her, decorated with cupids and cherubs, are still in place. It was at her bedroom in Osborne House that the queen died on January 22, 1901. Times of admission are April 5 to June 26 from 11 a.m. to 5 p.m. (same hours from September 6 to October 9). From June 28 to September 4, hours are 10 a.m. to 5 p.m. The house is closed on Sunday. Price of admission is £1.80 ($3.51) for adults, 90p ($1.76) for children.

A completely different attraction, **Carisbrooke Castle** is where Charles I was imprisoned by the Roundheads in 1647. This fine medieval castle is in the center of the island, 1½ miles southwest of Newport. Everybody heads for the Well House, concealed inside a 16th-century stone building. Donkeys take turns treading a large wooden wheel connected to a rope which hauls up buckets of water. The castle is open from mid-March to mid-October, weekdays from 9:30 a.m. to 6:30 p.m. In winter it closes at 4 p.m. On Sunday in season its hours are from 9:30 a.m. to 6:30 p.m., but from 2 to 4 p.m. in the other months. Admission is £1.20 ($2.34) for adults, half price for children. Charges drop to 60p ($1.75) for adults (half price for children) in winter.

You have a choice of several bases on the Isle of Wight unless you're what the English call a "day-tripper."

Cowes is the premier port for yachting in Britain. Henry VIII ordered the castle built there, but it is now the headquarters of the Royal Yacht Squadron. The seafront, the Prince's Green, and the high cliff road are worth exploring. Hovercraft are built in the town, and it's also the home and birthplace of the well-known maritime photographer, Beken of Cowes. It's almost *de rigueur* to wear oilskins and wellies, leaving a wet trail behind you.

Along the southeast coast are the twin resorts of **Sandown,** with its new pier complex and theater, and **Shanklin,** at the southern end of Sandown Bay which has held the British annual sunshine record more times than any other resort. Keats once lived in Shanklin's Old Village.

Farther along the coast, **Ventnor** is called the "Madeira of England," because it rises from the sea in a series of steep hills.

On the west coast, the sand cliffs of **Alum Bay** are a blend of many different colors, a total of 21 claimed. The Needles, three giant chalk rocks, and the Needles Lighthouse, are further features of interest at this end of the island. If you want to stay at the western end of Wight, refer to my recommendations under **Totland Bay, Ullcase,** and **Freshwater Bay.**

Newport is the capital, a bustling market town lying in the heart of the island.

Visitors who'd like to explore the Isle of Wight just for the day can take an **"Around the Island"** six-hour bus tour which leaves from the Cowes Coach Park at 11:40 a.m. daily from May to October. The price is £3 ($5.85) for adults, £2 ($3.90) for children. For further information, telephone Cowes 524221.

The ferry from Southampton to the Isle of Wight costs £2.55 ($4.97) for a round-trip ticket, or else you can take a ferry/hydrofoil combination, a round-trip ticket going for £3.75 ($7.31).

The Lymington/Yarmouth (Isle of Wight) ferry charges £14 ($27.30) for a medium-size car and £2.75 ($5.36) for each passenger on a day round-trip ticket. The more usual way of reaching the island is by ferry from Portsmouth Harbour or by hovercraft from Southsea, both of which take you to Ryde, a busy seaside town in summer, the railhead for the island's communications system. Arriving in Yarmouth, however, is something else. It's a yacht harbor, with pubs cluttering the wall.

VENTNOR: Madeira Hall, Trinity Road (tel. Ventnor 852624), is perhaps one of the nicest places to stay on the Isle of Wight. In an estate garden of lawns, tall trees, and flowering shrubs stands this stone manor house, with mullioned windows, gables, and bay windows. It has housed interesting people, such as Lord Macaulay, who wrote some of his well-known essays here. And there are associations with Charles Dickens and some of his characters. On the grounds is a heated swimming pool and an 18-hole putting course. All bedrooms are fitted with bed lights and wash basins. There are ample baths and toilets in the corridors. Three rooms have been equipped with private baths, one with a private shower. Half-board terms are from £13.50 ($26.33) per person in a double or twin without bath, rising to £17 ($33.15) per person with private bath, including service and VAT. Mr. and Mrs. Waring are the resident hosts.

SANDOWN: St. Catherine's Hotel, 1 Winchester Park Rd. (tel. Ventnor 402392), stands in its own garden a few minutes' walk from Sandown's sandy beach and pier complex, with its sun lounges and theater. St. Catherine's was built in 1860 of creamy Purbeck stone and white trim, for the dean of Winchester College; a modern extension was added for streamlined and sunny bedrooms. Bright colors have been used generously in the interior—the living room has a cherry-red carpet and draperies to match at the wide bay windows. The walls are soft sage green, and the dining room is done in rose pink and olive. Bedrooms have bright bedspreads, white furniture, and built-in headboards. Most of the bedrooms face the sun and are centrally heated. Tucked away in your bedroom are tea- and coffee-making facilities. Many of the rooms contain private baths or showers en suite. Jim and Maureen Hitchcock welcome you, charging a peak rate of £20 ($39) per person for room with bath or shower, breakfast, and dinner, including VAT and service. Bathless rooms are cheaper, costing only £14.50 ($28.28) per person, and including only breakfast.

FRESHWATER BAY: Farringford Hotel, Bedbury Lane, Freshwater (tel. Freshwater 752500), once the home of Lord Tennyson, has a pleasant, old-fashioned country ambience. A holiday, recreational estate, it has at its core a fine stone manor house and is surrounded by cottages on attractively landscaped grounds. It's adapted to the taste of the English who are accepted from April until the end of October. Depending on the season, the B&B rate ranges from £13.20 ($25.74) to £17.60 ($34.32) per person. Half board goes from £18.70 ($36.47) to £23.10 ($45.05) per person, including VAT and service. Dinner is four courses of well-cooked simple dishes, and lunch can be a snack in the bar lounge. There is a nine-hole golf course free to hotel guests, as well as tennis courts, a swimming pool, a croquet lawn, and a sports pavilion.

In addition, the hotel also rents out self-catering suites available in cottages on the grounds. Four guests can live comfortably for anywhere from £20 ($39) to £42.50 ($82.88) per day. They can take their meals at the hotel where a dinner costs from £7 ($13.65), and a Sunday lunch, £5 ($9.75). These units have color TV and a fully equipped kitchen, where guests can hire the services of a maid for £3 ($5.85) a day if they don't want to do cleaning.

CHALE: Clarendon Hotel, Newport Road (tel. Niton 730431), lies on the most southerly part of the island, where the vegetation is almost tropical. From here, you have views over the Channel to the mainland coast. The Clarendon is a cheerful, friendly place at which to spend the night. The rooms are simple and comfortable, with tea- and coffee-making equipment. Breakfasts are included in the rate of £9.50 ($18.53) per person without bath, £12.50 ($24.38) with bath. They also offer a half-board rate of £15.50 ($30.23) per person daily. The meals are ample, with many fresh ingredients. In the Wight Mouse Inn, the pub of this old hostelry, they serve a large selection of beers, including real ales and malt whiskies, in addition to the more usual drinks. "Mine host," John and his wife Jean keep a tight rein on the place, seeing that everything is spotless and shining bright.

5. Winchester

The most historical city in all of Hampshire, Winchester is big on legends —it's even associated with King Arthur and the Knights of the Round Table. In the Great Hall, all that remains of Winchester Castle, a round oak table, with space for King Arthur and his 24 knights, hangs on the wall. But all that spells undocumented romance. What is known, however, is that when the Saxons ruled the ancient kingdom of Wessex, Winchester was the capital.

The city is also linked with King Alfred, who is honored today by a statue, and is believed to have been crowned here. The Danish conqueror, Canute, came this way, too, as did the king he ousted, Ethelred the Unready (Canute got his wife Emma in the bargain). The city is the seat of the well-known Winchester College, whose founding father was the bishop of Winchester, William of Wykeham. Established in 1382, it lays claim to being the oldest public (private) school in England.

Traditions are strong in Winchester. It is said (although I've never confirmed the assertion) that if you go to St. Cross Hospital, now an almshouse, dating from the 12th century, you'll get ye olde pilgrim's dole of ale and bread (and if there's no bread, you can eat cake!). Winchester, 65 miles from London, is essentially a market town, on the Downs on the Itchen River.

WINCHESTER CATHEDRAL: For centuries Winchester Cathedral has been one of the great mother churches of England. The present building, the longest cathedral in Britain, dates from 1079, and its Norman heritage is still in evidence. When a Saxon church stood on this spot, St. Swithun, bishop of Winchester and tutor to young King Alfred, suggested modestly that he be buried outside. When he was later buried inside, it rained for 40 days. The legend lives on: just ask a resident of Winchester what will happen if it rains on St. Swithun's Day, July 15.

Of the present building, the nave with its two aisles is most impressive, as are the chantries, the reredos (late 15th century), and the elaborately carved choir stalls. Of the chantries, that of William of Wykeham, founder of Winchester College, is perhaps the most visited (it's found in the south aisle of the nave).

The cathedral also contains a number of other tombs, notably those of Jane Austen and Izaak Walton (exponent of the merits of the pastoral life—*The Compleat Angler*). The latter's tomb is to be found in the Prior Silkestede's Chapel in the South Transept. Jane Austen's grave is marked with a commemorative plaque. Winchester Cathedral contains in chests the bones of many of the Saxon kings and the remains of the Viking conqueror, Canute, and his wife, Emma, in the presbytery. The son of William the Conqueror, William Rufus (who reigned as William II), is also believed to have been buried at the cathedral.

The Crypt is flooded for a large part of the year, and at such times is closed to the public. When it's not flooded, there are regular tours at 10:30 a.m. and 2:30 p.m. The Library, in which is displayed the Winchester Bible and other ancient manuscripts, is open for limited hours throughout the summer season (except Monday mornings and Sunday, and on Wednesday and Saturday for the rest of the year). In January the library is open on Saturday only. The Treasury is open during the summer season from 11 a.m. to 5 p.m. It is small and does not require a guide.

WHERE TO STAY: Accommodations are limited, but adequate. I'll survey the most expensive recommendations first.

The Upper Bracket

Wessex Hotel, Paternoster Row (tel. Winchester 61611), has won over critics who protested such a modern structure adjacent to the grounds of Winchester Cathedral. Three stories high, built of natural brick, it turns most of its walls of windows toward a view of the Norman Tower. The lounges and reception areas are built on several open levels, using such elements as colored tiles, plastic and wood paneling, and simple hand-woven fabrics. The bedrooms —93 in all, each with private bath—are warmed by soft materials and Scandinavian-style furnishings, with such amenities as telephones and bedlamps. A single rents from £32 ($62.40), a double from £38 ($74.10). The coffeeshop is open from 10 a.m. until 10 p.m. daily, and the hotel's main restaurant has large picture windows overlooking the cathedral and its grounds.

The Medium-Priced Range

Royal Hotel, St. Peter Street (tel. Winchester 3468), is a fine, old hotel, built at the end of the 17th century as a private house. For 50 years, it was used by nuns from Brussels as a convent before being turned into a hotel. As a hotel, however, it soon became the center of the city's social life. It's only a few minutes' walk to the cathedral, yet still enjoys a secluded position. Best of all is the garden hidden behind high walls. If you like a hotel where old-fashioned values and comfort predominate, you'll appreciate the Royal. Bathless singles go for £18 ($35.10), doubles for £27 ($52.65). With bath, a single is £20 ($39); a double, £32 ($62.40). For a double room with a four-poster and private bath, the charge is £37 ($72.15) a night. These prices include a traditional English breakfast, VAT, and service. Meals are served in a small, formal dining room, with a view of the private garden.

The Budget Range

Southgate Hotel, Southgate Street (tel. Winchester 51243), is a brick house in the center of Winchester. It opens onto a rear garden with flowerbeds and an old walnut tree. Christopher Wren designed and built Southgate in 1715, and many of the original architectural details remain (note the front entry with the glass lights over the doorway). All the bedrooms are equipped with hot and cold running water. The B&B rate is £12.50 ($24.38) per person, including VAT, service, and a full English breakfast. A set luncheon goes for £5 ($9.75), a dinner for £6 ($11.70). However, bar snacks cost from 75p ($1.46) to £1.50 ($2.93).

WHERE TO EAT: The Elizabethan, 18–19 Jewry St. (tel. Winchester 3566). In an atmosphere of another century, under hand-hewn timbers, you dine by candlelight, on sparkling white linen. You have a choice of cozy nooks or a galleried main dining room. Well run under the personal supervision of the Harrison family, the kitchen offers an excellent Anglo-French cuisine. The licensed restaurant serves table d'hôte lunches at around £5 ($9.75) and a full à la carte menu. The extensive choice of dishes provides for an interesting lunch or dinner at about £10 ($19.50) per person. Flambé dishes are a specialty. Light refreshments are served at lunchtime in the fully licensed modern bar. The restaurant is open from noon to 2 p.m., and from 7 to 10 p.m. On Sunday, only lunch is served. Closed Monday.

The **Old Chesil Rectory Restaurant,** Chesil Street (tel. Winchester 3177), is just a short walk from the cathedral. Once a rectory, the unusual timber-and-stucco building dates from the 15th century. Inside and out the Old Chesil exudes an air of merrie Old England, but the food served in the heavily beamed dining room is the finest quality northern Italian cuisine. The menu is a wonderful mélange of creative and classical dishes, including pollo sorpresa (chicken surprise), rolled, stuffed chicken breasts flavored with garlic and herbs, costing £4.25 ($8.29), or scaloppa alla Boccaccio, a delightful combination of veal, lobster, and cheese cooked with Orvieto wine, at £4.95 ($5.65). Appetizers include a prawn and melon cocktail at £1.95 ($3.80) or seafood hors d'oeuvres at £2.55 ($4.97). The tasty Italian desserts cost about £1.50 ($2.93). Menus change quite frequently, depending on what is in season. The Old Chesil is open daily except Sunday evenings and Monday. Otherwise, it serves lunch from noon to 2:30 p.m. and dinner from 7 to 10:30 p.m.

Splinters, 9 Great Minster St. (tel. Winchester 64004). Downstairs in the Edwardian bar, soup of the day with roll and butter is 85p ($1.66), and there are several hot dishes, such as quiche with salad, moussaka, or cottage pie at around £1.85 ($3.61). Desserts are about 85p ($1.66). Upstairs, the elegant plushy restaurant serves à la carte meals, including coq au vin and other French stalwarts or grills. A meal will cost around £9 ($17.55) a person, or you can just have a light meal from the same sort of things as are available downstairs. A glass of wine costs 75p ($1.46), and there is a very good selection of more expensive French and German wines available by the bottle. Mike Sherret and his wife, Fiona, are the owners. It is open for lunch from 11 a.m. to 2:30 p.m. and dinner from 6:30 to 10:30 p.m. Monday to Saturday.

A Pub Crawl

Instead of lunching at one of the above restaurants, you may want to drop in at the **Royal Oak Pub,** which is to be found in a passageway leading from the High Street and next door to the God Begot House. The Royal Oak serves lunches at the bar from noon to 2 p.m. daily, Monday through Saturday. Various hot and cold snacks, hot meals, and an extensive serve-yourself cold buffet are available. The pub also contains the oldest bar in England, which is worth a visit, as indeed is the pub itself—a busy, friendly hostelry with lots of atmosphere. For those with a liking for live traditional or New Orleans jazz, this can be enjoyed in the bar on Monday and Thursday from 8:30 to 10:30 p.m. at no extra charge apart from the cost of your drinks.

The **Old Market Pub,** The Square, is ideal for those who enjoy a local. It offers a relaxed, friendly, unself-conscious atmosphere, a proper background in which to enjoy a pint. The corner pub sits opposite the cathedral in the oldest and most historic district of Winchester. It's mellowed enough to have timbers galore, cozy nooks, and a collection of oddments. The owners are always pleased to see travelers who wish to sample traditional ales drawn by hand pumps, and sample snacks either from the cold buffet or hot snacks menu.

DORSET

This is Thomas Hardy country. By now, you've probably seen *Far from the Madding Crowd* or *Tess*, and know Dorset is the Wessex of Hardy novels. Some of the towns and villages, although altered considerably, are still recognizable from his descriptions. However, he changed the names to protect the innocent. Bournemouth, for example, became Havenpool, Weymouth converted to Budmouth. "The last of the great Victorians," as he was called, died in 1928 at the age of 88. While his tomb rests in a position of honor in Westminster Abbey, his heart was cut out and buried in his beloved Dorsetshire.

One of England's smallest shires, Dorset stretches all the way from the old seaport of **Poole** in the east to **Lyme Regis** in the west (known to Jane Austen). Dorset is a southwestern county, bordering the English Channel. It's big on cows, and Dorset butter is served at many an afternoon tea. Mainly, it is a land of farms and pastures, with plenty of sandy heaths and chalky downs.

The most prominent tourist center of Dorset is the Victorian seaside resort of Bournemouth. If you don't anchor there, you might also try a number of Dorset's other seaports, villages, and country towns. For the most part, we've hugged closely to the impressive coastline.

Incidentally, Dorset, as the vacation-wise English might tell you if they wanted to divulge a secret, is a friend of the budget traveler.

6. Bournemouth

The south coast resort at the doorstep of the New Forest didn't just happen: it was carefully planned and manicured, a true city in a garden. Flower-filled, park-dotted, Bournemouth contains great globs of architecture inherited from those arbiters of taste, Victoria and her son Edward. Its most distinguished feature is its Chines (shrub-filled, narrow steep-sided ravines) along the zig-zag coastline. The real walking English strike out at, say, Hengistbury Head, making their way past sandy beaches, both the Boscombe and Bournemouth Piers, to Alum Chine, a distance of six miles, and a traffic-free walk to remember.

It is estimated that of the nearly 12,000 acres which Bournemouth claims for its own, about one-sixth is turned over to green parks and flowerbeds, such as the Pavilion Rock Garden, through which amblers pass both day and night. The total effect, especially in spring is dramatic, and helps explain Bournemouth's long-established popularity with the garden-loving English. Bournemouth was discovered back in Victoria's day, when seabathing became a firmly entrenched institution, often practiced with great ritual. Many of the comparatively elegant villas that exist today (now largely bed-and-breakfast houses and hotels) were once private homes.

Bournemouth, which along with Poole and Christchurch, forms the largest urban area in the south of England, is not as sophisticated as Brighton. Increasingly, it is becoming a retirement place for widowed or single English ladies. But Bournemouth and its neighbors also have some 20,000 students attending the various schools or colleges, who explore, in their off-hours, places written about or painted by such poets and artists as Shelley, Beardsley, and Turner.

The resort's amusements are wide and varied. At the Pavilion Theatre, for example, you can see West End-type productions from London. The Bournemouth Symphony Orchestra is justly famous in Europe. And there's the usual run of golf courses, band concerts, variety shows, and dancing.

Bournemouth is about 104 miles from London, easily reached in about one hour 40 minutes on an express train from Waterloo Station. It makes a good base for exploring a historically rich part of England. On its outskirts are the New Forest, Salisbury, and Winchester, and the Isle of Wight (15 miles away, the former seaside retreat of Victoria).

WHERE TO STAY: Bournemouth offers accommodation choices in all price ranges. I'll begin with—

The Upper Bracket

Royal Bath Hotel, Bath Road (tel. Bournemouth 25555), was built in the Victorian era to simulate a French château, with towers and bay windows looking out over the bay and Purbeck Hills. In its own three acres of cliff-top gardens is a heated swimming pool. The rate is £35 ($68.25) per person per day, inclusive of service and taxes. The table d'hôte lunch and dinner prices start at £9 ($17.55). The resident band plays for a dinner-dance Saturday evenings. For health enthusiasts, there is a sauna bath, as well as Swedish massages and special diets. Every bedroom, 135 in all, has a private bath and television (the large accommodations contain sitting areas as well).

The Medium-Priced Range

Norfolk Hotel, Richmond Hill (tel. Bournemouth 21-521), is one of the oldest prestige hotels of the resort, built a few blocks from the seafront and the shopping area in the center of town. Disregarding what lies on its periphery, it is like a country estate, with a formal entrance and a rear garden and fountain shaded by trees. The public rooms are geared to holiday guests, with two drinking bars. The bedrooms—more than half with private baths—are furnished with traditional, serviceable pieces, comfortable and satisfactory. The Norfolk charges its highest rates from April 1 to the end of October.

In a room without bath, the rate is £20 ($39) per person nightly, rising to £23 ($44.85) in a unit with bath, these tariffs including an English breakfast, dinner that evening, VAT, and service. The set dinner-dance on Saturday is included in the above rates. However, if you're a nonresident and wish to attend, expect to pay from £8 ($15.60) for dinner and nothing extra on Saturday when you can dance.

Langtry Manor Hotel, 26 Derby Rd., East Cliff (tel. Bournemouth 23887), originally called the Red House, was built in 1877 for Lillie Langtry, the famous Jersey Lily, as a gift from Edward VII to his favorite mistress. The house contains all sorts of reminders of its illustrious inhabitants, including initials scratched on a windowpane and carvings on a beam of the entrance hall. On the half-landing is the peephole through which the prince could scrutinize the assembled company before coming down to dine, and one of the fireplaces bears his initials.

Mrs. Pamela Hamilton Howard, the present owner, has carefully furnished the hotel in the Edwardian style, and on Saturday she has six-course Edwardian dinner parties. There is no menu; the dishes are just produced for inspection. Other evenings dinner is a more usual four-course affair at £8 ($15.60).

Bedrooms range from ordinary twins with bathroom from £15.75 ($30.71) per person, including breakfast. The Lillie Langtry suite, Lillie's own room, with a four-poster bed draped in Nottingham lace and a double heart-shaped bathtub (not to mention the more modern refinements of color TV, refrigerated bar, and toilet), goes from £25.75 ($50.21), or you can rent the Edward VII suite, furnished as it was when His Royal Highness lived in this spacious room. The huge carved oak fireplace has hand-painted tiles showing scenes from Shakespeare. The four-poster bed can be made up as either twins or a large double bed, and you have a bathroom en suite, color TV, a refrigerated room bar, and a telephone. The cost is £35 ($68.25) per person nightly. All rates are subject to VAT.

The Budget Range

Belgravia Hotel, 56 Christchurch Rd., East Cliff (tel. Bournemouth 20857), is a gracious brick mansion in a smart section of the resort, set in 1½ acres of ground. Terms are from £8.50 ($16.58) per person per day, according to the season, for bed and a full English breakfast. Dinner is available on request, costing from £5 ($9.75) per person. The Belgravia is a five-minute walk along a zig-zag path to the beach. It is a pleasant house with a mansard roof, and all rooms are bright and sunny. Reservations of only one or two nights are almost impossible during high season, when one-weekers are given priority, of course.

Apartments by the Week

Miami Court, 27a Surrey Rd., Westbourne, Bournemouth (tel. Bournemouth 764329), will intrigue travelers tired of hotels and guest houses. Here, at these holiday flats, guests can enjoy a private life, preparing their own kind of food. This, of course, is an increasingly popular way of traveling in Europe. The apartments or "flats" are ideally situated, allowing you to explore the coast, inland country villages, and stately homes.

The new block of eight apartments has its own garden; and, best of all, there is a woods in the rear with a stream, as well as a pathway leading to the seafront and Bournemouth Square.

Owners Howard Archer and Michael Marshall used to run the Camelot Hotel in London, where they made many friends among American travelers and, incidentally, won an award as the best small hotel of the year. To the Miami Court in Bournemouth, they bring the same personal flair that distinguished them in London.

At their new location, they provide one-, two-, and three-bedroom apartments which are completely furnished. The flats are centrally heated as well and contain TV sets and refrigerators. The highest tariffs are charged from June to September, £45 ($87.75) per person weekly. Between October and April, the rates are slashed in half. Then the flats rent for only £22 ($42.90) per person weekly.

Write to them for a reservation and the amount of deposit required.

WHERE TO DINE: Trattoria San Marco, 148 Holdenhurst Rd. (tel. Bournemouth 21132), has a small and intimate atmosphere, and is run by Angie and Ettore Longi. He is an English-born Italian, and she is from Parma, where the best salami and Parmesan cheese come from. The cost of the menu varies with the season and availability of certain produce. Specialties include minestrone, suckling pig, stracciatella, salami, prosciutto con melone, piccatini (veal pieces), saltimbocca, and pasta. Try quail eggs, followed by escalope of veal Sofia Loren, with a walnut meringue to finish. In other words, there's something for everybody at a cost of about £11 ($21.45) per person for a three-course meal, plus wine, which begins at £3.20 ($6.24) per bottle. They won't serve cheap wines—"it should be used for cooking." The restaurant is open daily, except Monday and bank holidays, from noon to 2:30 p.m. and from 6:30 p.m. to midnight.

Fisherman's Haunt Hotel, Salisbury Road, Route B3347, Winkton, near Christchurch (tel. Christchurch 484071), is an ancient inn (built in 1673) just two miles from the English Channel. Authentic regional British dishes are the fare in the dining room which overlooks the River Avon. Open from 12:30 p.m., Fisherman's Haunt offers a set luncheon for £4.50 ($8.78). Weeknight dinners are served from 7 to 10 p.m., costing from £7 ($13.65). A special feature of the restaurant is the traditional family-style Sunday midday meal. If you decide to bed down here for the night, your breakfast on the following morning is the classic, full English one. Most rooms contain private bath facilities.

7. Shaftesbury

The origins of this typical Dorsetshire market town date back to the ninth century when King Alfred founded the abbey and made his daughter the first abbess. King Edward the Martyr was buried there, and King Canute died in the abbey but was buried in Winchester. Little now remains of the abbey, but the ruins are beautifully laid out. The museum adjoining St. Peter's Church at the top of Gold Hill give a good idea of what the ancient Saxon hilltop town was like.

Today, ancient cottages and hostelries cling to the steep cobbled streets, thatched roofs frown above tiny paned windows, and modern stores vie with the street market in the High Street and the cattle market off Christy's Lane.

The town, right on the A30 from London, is an excellent center from which to visit the Hardy Country (it appears as Chaston in *Jude the Obscure*), Stourhead Gardens, and Longleat House.

FOOD AND LODGING: The Royal Chase Hotel (tel. Shaftesbury 3355) is a Georgian house with Victorian additions, and as such has had varied occupants. Once a button-making factory and then a monastery, it is now a delightfully informal hotel run by George and Rosemary Hunt with their assistant, Liz Thomas. Most rooms have baths and go for £21 ($40.95) per person per night, including a full breakfast, early-morning tea, newspaper, service, and VAT. A meal in the Country Kitchen Restaurant, with its gingham cloths and hoop-backed chairs, will cost around £8 ($15.60) and includes several local dishes—pork filet cooked in cider or bluevinney cheese and Dorset knobs. House wine is £4.50 ($8.78) a bottle.

From November to March they also offer bargain rates, among which is the Real Ale Break at around £30 ($58.50) per person for two nights, including accommodation, a full English breakfast, five pints of traditional ale; plus a free bottle of Thomas Hardy's Ale, featured in the *Guinness Book of Records* as the strongest beer brewed in a bottle. Even for less fanatical drinkers, the bar, dominated by an open-kitchen range and decorated with Dorsetshire bygones, is an attraction. There are traditional bar games, shove ha'penny, and table skittles at which to pitch your skill. On weekends, the Cellar Bar also offers snacks and a wide selection of wines at lunchtime, and in the evenings if you don't want a full meal in the restaurant.

Milestones, at Compton Abbas, lies between the church and the village post office, 2½ miles south of Shaftesbury on the A350. Just the telephone exchange of this ideal English tearoom is enough to make one curious about it (tel. Fontmell Magna 811360). Two delightful old ladies, Mrs. Smith, the owner, and her friend, preside over the spotless, beamy little place with views over the Dorset hills. Their farmhouse teas, with boiled eggs, fresh sandwiches, homemade scones, and cakes are accompanied by tea or coffee. Expect to pay from £1.40 ($2.73) per person. Morning coffee is served from 10 a.m. to 1 p.m. and afternoon tea from 2:30 to 5:30 p.m.

8. Wool

Set in the midst of pastoral scenery, known to readers of Hardy, the sleepy hamlet of Wool is one of the most charming in East Dorset. On the Frome River, it has thatched cottages on either side of the road. The stream that winds its way through the maze of streets and lanes lures waders.

The district was also known to T. E. Lawrence, Lawrence of Arabia, who died in a motorcycle crash in 1935. His former home, **Clouds Hill,** lies four miles to the northwest (one mile north of Bovington Camp). It is open Wednesday to Friday (also Sunday) from April until the end of September, from 2 to 5 p.m. (from October until the end of March, it is open only on Sunday, from 1 to 4 p.m.), charging an admission of 80p ($1.56).

WHERE TO STAY AND EAT: Woolbridge Manor Hotel (tel. Bindon Abbey 462313) is a small manor house edging up to the village. It owes its present fame to its Thomas Hardy associations, having been a setting in *Tess of the D'Urbervilles.* The owners, Mr. and Mrs. Peter Maddocks, have furnished the place attractively. The manor, which dates from medieval times, is a good backdrop for all the copper, brass, and oak. Most of the basic food cooked here comes from the manor farm, and you know what that means— fresh berries, thick cream, pears, apples, pheasant, local venison, and salmon from the river. You can enjoy a dinner starting at £8 ($15.60). A single rents for £19 ($37.05) per night, the tariff increasing to £25 ($48.75) in a double, including VAT and breakfast.

9. Wareham

This historic little town on the Frome River is about a mile west of Poole Harbor. Many find it a good center for touring the south Dorset coast and the Purbeck Hills. It contains remains of early Anglo-Saxon and Roman town walls, plus the Saxon church of St. Martin with its effigy of Lawrence of Arabia.

FOOD AND LODGING: The Old Granary, The Quay (tel. Wareham 2010), is a riverside country pub, where you dine either inside or on a terrace overlooking the boats and swans. The interior dining room has a charm of its own, with bentwood chairs, a wine rack, a natural wood sideboard, and white walls displaying a collection of locally painted watercolors. A gracious and informal atmosphere prevails. The secret behind the success of the Old Granary is its fine cuisine; the owners, Mr. and Mrs. Michael Hipwell, try hard to stick to natural country foods. Homemade soups go for 65p ($1.27); pâté for £1.20 ($2.34); a filet of pork in a barbecue sauce, £5 ($9.75); Dorset lamb chops with cheese and onion, also £5. A hefty portion of homemade fruit pie with cream is 75p ($1.46). The restaurant is open every day. If you wish to overnight here, the charge is £22 ($42.90) per person, including a full English breakfast, dinner, and taxes.

A COUNTRY MANOR: At Culeaze, near Wareham, **Col. and Mrs. Anthony Barne** (tel. Wareham 7209), along with two Labrador retrievers, welcome you to this manor house, standing in the center of the estate known as Culeaze. They offer two double rooms and two single rooms, with private baths, charging £25 ($48.75) per person per night, including everything except lunch. Drinks are served before dinner and wine is offered at dinner. As their pillared manor house lies off the beaten track, a car is essential. For their own reasons, they don't encourage first-time visitors to stay more than three days, but they have friends in Somerset, Wiltshire, and Norfolk who would be pleased to welcome you. During the day you can visit Salisbury Cathedral, Wilton House, Abbotsbury, and Portland Bill, along with Stonehenge. Here is a rare chance to experience a fast-fading English way of life. For more information or reservations, write to Col. A. M. Barne, O.B.E., Culeaze, Wareham, Dorsetshire, BH20 7NR, England.

10. Dorchester

Thomas Hardy, in his 1886 novel *The Mayor of Casterbridge,* gave Dorchester literary fame. But it was known to the Romans; in fact, its Maumbury Rings, south of the town, is considered the best Roman amphitheater in Britain, having once resounded with the shouts of 12,000 spectators screaming for gladiator blood. Dorchester, a country town, was the setting of another bloodletting, the "Bloody Assize" of 1685, when Judge Jeffreys condemned to death the supporters of the Duke of Monmouth's rebellion against James II.

But it is mostly through Hardy that the world knows Dorchester. Many of his major scenes of love and intrigue took place on the periphery of Dorchester. The land was best known to Hardy, since he was born in 1840 at **Higher Bockhampton,** three miles northeast of Dorchester. His home, now a National Trust property, may be visited by the public from March to October, from 11 a.m. to 6 p.m. or dusk, whichever is earlier. But to go inside, you must make an appointment with the tenant. You may write in advance to **Hardy's Cottage,** Higher Bockhampton, Dorchester, Dorset, England, or telephone Dorchester 2366. You approach the cottage on foot, a ten-minute walk after parking your vehicle in the space provided in the wood. The admission is 80p ($1.56).

You may also want to browse around the **Dorset County Museum** on High West Street (next to St. Peter's Church), with its gallery devoted to memorabilia of Thomas Hardy. In addition, you'll find prehistoric and Roman relics, plus natural history exhibits and others pertaining to the geology of the region. The museum is open weekdays from 10 a.m. to 1 p.m. and from 2 to

5 p.m.; admission is 50p (98¢) for adults, 25p (49¢) for children 5 to 16 years of age (children under 4, free).

WHERE TO STAY: The **Wessex Hotel,** High West Street (tel. Dorchester 62660), is an architecturally interesting Georgian structure built on medieval foundations. In the town center, the quiet hotel offers 17 bedrooms with full residential services. Room rates range from £10.12 ($19.73) for a single room to £18.22 ($35.53) for a double or twin. Prices include a full English breakfast, service, and VAT. The Wessex also offers a small cozy bar for guests as well as a public restaurant. Lunch or dinner of two courses costs from £2.50 ($4.88) to £5 ($9.75).

The **Antelope Hotel,** South Street, Cornhill (tel. Dorchester 63001), was known in medieval times. Subsequently, it has received a Victorian overlay. The high point (or low) in its history was when Judge Jeffreys held his Bloody Assize here. Old and traditional, it's been the wayfarer's choice for generations.

It charges £23 ($44.85) nightly for a double, including breakfast. It's £15 ($29.25) for singles, these tariffs including an English breakfast, VAT, and service. A table d'hôte dinner costs from £6 ($11.70).

WHERE TO EAT: **Judge Jeffreys' Restaurant,** High West Street (tel. Dorchester 64369), opposite the County Museum, is an attractive stop on your cross-country jaunt. Dating back to the 14th century, it had the dubious distinction of lodging that "cantankerous alcoholic," Judge Jeffreys, during the Bloody Assize. The restaurant today offers different services in each room. In the Judge's Room, a traditional three-course lunch is served. In the Tudor Room, an à la carte steak and trout menu is offered, and a roast joint is prepared daily. Try also the scallops, plaice, haddock, eggs, even their hamburgers. A set luncheon or dinner costs from £5 ($9.75) to £7 ($13.65). In the bar and lounge, snacks and salads can be ordered. Evening meals are served from mid-June to mid-October on Wednesday, Friday, and Saturday, the final orders taken at 10 p.m. The proprietor, Brian Bean, takes pride in the old English atmosphere of massive oak beams, an oak spiral staircase, stone-mullioned windows, paneled rooms, Tudor fireplaces. Most important, the restaurant's haunted. During its restoration in 1928, parts of a human skeleton were discovered in a bricked-up part of the east wall.

INNS ON THE OUTSKIRTS: **Brace of Pheasants,** Plush (tel. Piddletrenthide 357). Joan Chandler has transformed this row of two adjoining thatched cottages and a village forge, dating from the 16th century, although rebuilt in the old style after a fire. Formerly the owner of a toy factory, she sought and found a new way of life in this tiny hamlet, 15 miles from the coast. The major activity takes place in the all-purpose living, dining, and drinking room—a cozy setting with inglenooks, antiques, comfortable armchairs, and old decorative objects. Mrs. Chandler is an informal hostess, well known in the area for her Cordon Bleu meals. She offers a four-course meal for a set price of £8.50 ($16.58), with such dishes as fruits de mer, good-tasting soups and pâtés, quenelles de brochet, and main courses such as wild duck with orange sauce, venison (in season), and homemade cakes and desserts. In the restaurant upstairs, beautiful views can be enjoyed from the little dormer windows, and many guests prefer to dine "under the thatch." She accepts 50 guests per meal (reservations are imperative), and the table is yours for the evening. There is only one sitting per evening, at 8:30. Varied bar snacks are available midday and evenings, and you can enjoy them in a beautiful old room with a log fire and a bar serving counter. This is separate from the main bar which means you can bring in children. In summer you can also enjoy a lovely big garden. How to get there: Take the B3143 out of Dorchester to Piddletrenthide, turning off at the sign to Plush. The inn will be on your left. It is open seven days a week for both lunch and dinner.

Summer Lodge, Evershot (tel. Evershot 424), is a country-house hotel 12 miles north of Dorchester, where its resident owners, Nigel and Margaret Corbett, provide care, courtesy, and comfort. Once the home to the heirs of the Earls of Ilchester, the country house, in the attractive village of Evershot, stands on four acres of secluded gardens. Evershot appears as Evershed in *Tess of the D'Urbervilles,* and author Thomas Hardy designed a wing of the house.

In this relaxed, informal atmosphere, guests rent rooms with views either of the garden or over the village rooftops to the fields beyond. Although centrally heated, the hotel offers log fires in winter. Guests sit around the fire getting to know each other in a convivial atmosphere. All rooms have a private bathroom en suite. Rates range from £24 ($46.80) to £27.50 ($53.63) per person, including a full English breakfast, a five-course dinner with after-dinner coffee, and VAT. There is a 25% supplement for single occupancy of a double room.

Mrs. Corbett, who does the cooking, specializes in traditional English dishes the way they should be done, placing the emphasis on home-grown and local produce. In addition to the dining room with its French windows opening onto a terrace, the Corbetts have a bar and a TV room. They will direct you to places of local interest, including National Trust houses.

READER'S HOTEL SELECTION AT FRAMPTON: "Our very favorite place on our entire trip was **The Court** (tel. Maiden Newton 20242) at Frampton, a tiny village in Dorset, near Dorchester in the Thomas Hardy country. The Court is a beautiful manor house, elegantly furnished, run by two lovely women. It's on a secluded lane and contains 60 acres of woods and fields, a pond, and a charming menagerie of ducks, chickens, a golden retriever, a Siamese cat, and peacocks. There are ample bathrooms and a shower room. Our breakfast, served in their first-floor dining room overlooking the garden and pond, included hot homemade rolls, fresh milk and homemade butter from their Jersey cows, and generous servings of sausage, bacon, and eggs, with, of course, marmalade and tea. We had electric kettles in our rooms, and Mrs. Goddard brought us a doily-lined tray with a bone china cup and saucer and teapot for our early morning tea. There was also a small covered pitcher of cream, sugar, and tea bags. Dinner, bed, and breakfast (no children) in the best English manor tradition are £16 ($31.20) per person" (Alice L. Jones, Au Sable Forks, N.Y.).

11. Bridport

On Thomas Hardy's fictional Wessex terrain, Bridport was "Port Bredy." The town lies inland, although there is a harbor one mile away at the holiday resort of West Bay, near the end of Chesil Beach. Ropes and fishing nets are Bridport specialties. Many a man dangled from the end of a "Bridport dagger" —that is, a rope—especially when Hanging Judge Jeffreys was around.

WHERE TO STAY AND EAT: The **Bull Hotel,** East Street (tel. Bridport 22878), a 16th-century coaching inn, now houses modern wayfarers in its 22 bedrooms, all with hot and cold running water, many overlooking the old courtyard. Rates range from £10 ($19.50) per person nightly, including an English breakfast and VAT. The atmosphere is old-worldish, complete with a minstrels' gallery and enough bars to satisfy anybody. The bedrooms are simply, but comfortably, furnished. In 1939, George VI stopped off at the Bull. The hotel remains open all year and is run under the close personal supervision of the Terleski family. Fresh local food and fish dishes are a specialty. Luncheons range from £3.50 ($6.83) and dinners from £6 ($11.70).

Eype's Mouth Hotel, Eype, 1½ miles west of Bridport and one mile south of the A35 Bridport/Lyme Regis road (tel. Bridport 23300), is a gracious country house, right on the sea, surrounded by its own grounds, a five-minute walk from the beach. Most of the public rooms and bedrooms open south toward the water. At times, Eype's Mouth seems like an English version of a villa on the Riviera, with a sea-view front terrace, where you can relax and have drinks or tea. The hotel's managed by Mrs. Ian Forbes, who also provides meals for nonresidents. The rooms are centrally heated, containing hot and cold water basins. There are convenient corridor toilets and baths, plus nine private bathrooms. Generally a guest stays here on what is called inclusive terms, meaning bed, breakfast, luncheon (perhaps a packed picnic variety), and dinner. The rate (minimum of three days) is from £19.48 ($37.99) per person daily, going slightly higher in June, July, August, and September. For straight B&B, you pay from £13.15 ($25.64) to £15.32 ($29.87) per person nightly, the latter in a room with private bath. The rooms are plain, but comfortable. There is a lounge bar and cellar bar with live entertainment, along with a dinner-dance every Saturday night.

12. Chideock

Chideock is a charming village one mile west of Bridport. It's a hamlet of thatched houses, with a dairy farm found in the center. About a mile away from the coast, it's a gem of a place for overnight stopovers, or especially longer stays. The countryside, with its rolling hills, makes excursions a temptation.

WHERE TO STAY: Chideock House Hotel (tel. Chideock 242) is perhaps the prettiest thatched house in Chideock, a village of winners. Set near the road, with a protective stone wall, the house opens onto a rear garden of flowers, shrubs, and fruit trees. A driveway through the gardens leads to a large car park (wood-burning fires on cool days). You can stay here on a B&B basis at a cost beginning at £14 ($27.30) per person nightly. The hotel has been extended, and most of its bedrooms have baths en suite. The cuisine reflects the skill of a Swiss chef. In addition to the à la carte restaurant, a Copper Grill has opened, decorated with antique pieces of copper and featuring large steaks and fish dishes. Especially interesting is the Tudor part of the house, and the Adam fireplace in the lounge. The house quartered the Roundheads in 1645, and the ghosts of the village martyrs still haunt, as their trial was held at the hotel. Resident owners are Alf and Barbara Way and Kevin and Alison Davies.

The **Thatch Cottage** (tel. Chideock 473). You'd never suspect that under the thatch of this 17th-century cottage are the comforts of home. The owner, Reena O'Rourke, accepts paying guests year round. While this is essentially a summer resort, there are those who welcome the idea of staying winter weekends, snugly sitting in front of the fireplace after enjoying good home cooking. Fresh local produce is a specialty. Most of the year, the charge is £8.50 ($16.58) per person for B&B. If you want to walk to the beach, you can ask your hostess to pack a picnic lunch. It's best to make Chideock your center for a week, exploring the many sights in the area on day trips. Weekly costs for B&B range from £52 ($101.40). Reservations are necessary from June to September.

13. Charmouth

On Lyme Bay, Charmouth is another winner. A village of Georgian houses and thatched cottages, Charmouth contains some of the most dramatic coastal scenery in West Dorset. The village lies to the west of Golden Cap, which is—according to the adventurers who measure such things—the highest cliff along the coast of southern England.

WHERE TO STAY: The **Queens Armes Hotel** (tel. Charmouth 60339). Catherine of Aragon, the first of Henry VIII's six wives and the daughter of Ferdinand and Isabella of Spain, is believed to have stayed in this hotel near the sea. It also figured in the flight of King Charles II, who spent the night here, with the Roundheads in hot pursuit. Since the Queens Armes is right on the road, you may not suspect its inner charm: a rear flower garden, oak beams, pewter, old doors with creaky hardware, a dining room with dark oak tables and Windsor chairs, the living room with its Regency armchairs and antiques. Records don't reveal what the hotel charged for housing royalty. But you can stay here in one of the simply furnished rooms for £14 ($27.30) per person for B&B. If you wish, you can also take all your meals. Lunch costs depend on your choice; a dinner goes from £6.50 ($12.68). The hotel specializes in well-prepared, delicious English fare, such as succulent roast beef. The owners, Mrs. and Mrs. Rolfe, have pleasantly added their own touches to the house.

13. Lyme Regis

On Lyme Bay near the Devonshire border, the resort of Lyme Regis is one of the most attractive centers along the south coast. For those who shun such big, commercial holiday centers as Torquay or Bournemouth, Lyme Regis is ideal—the true English coastal town, with a highly praised mild climate. Sea gulls fly overhead; the streets are steep and winding; walks along Cobb Beach brisk and stimulating; the views, particularly of the craft in the harbor, photogenic. Following Lyme Regis's career as a major seaport (the Duke of Monmouth landed here to begin his unsuccessful attempt to become king), one finds it was a small spa for a while, catering to such visitors as Jane Austen.

The seaside town was the location of the film *The French Lieutenant's Woman,* and the actors stayed in the town's two main hotels.

The town also boasts the 1979–1980 world champion and best-dressed town crier. Richard Fox is just maintaining a tradition which has been handed down for 1000 years in Lyme Regis when he announces the local news. He'll also take visitors on a two-hour tour of the resort on Tuesday and Thursday at 2:30 p.m. to see the Cobb, the harbor from which ships sailed to fight the Spanish Armada. The walk heads up old Broad Street. Mr. Fox can be reached at the Witchcraft Gallery, Broad Street (tel. Lyme Regis 3803).

The surrounding area is a fascinating place for fossilism. Mary Anning discovered in 1810 at the age of 11 one of the first articulated ichthyosaur skeletons. She went on to become one of the first professional fossilists in the country. Books telling of walks in the area and the regions where fossils can be seen are available at the local Information Bureau in the Guildhall on Bridge Street.

WHERE TO LODGE AND EAT: The **High Cliff Hotel**, Sidmouth Road (tel. Lyme Regis 2300), is an impressive Regency house, placed in the midst of surrounding gardens on the edge of a cliff, providing views of the coast. Formerly the home of Lord Lister, the doctor who pioneered antiseptic surgery, it now accepts paying guests. The present manager and director is Patricia Webb. High Cliff was opened by her parents in 1935, and has continued to be personally owned and managed by her family ever since, with no changes of ownership contemplated in the foreseeable future. Inside, the central formal hallway, lounges, and dining room are tastefully decorated, with a sprinkling of good antiques. Bedrooms are appropriately homelike, with good beds, hot and cold running water, and comfortable furnishings. The charge is from £16.50 ($32.16) per person for B&B. A three-course dinner goes for £6.50 ($12.68), or four courses for £7.50 ($14.63).

The **Mariners Hotel,** Silver Street (tel. Lyme Regis 2753), has been a coaching inn since 1641, and now it's owned by Brian and Joan Lambert. They are proud, and rightly so, of the view from their lounge of the Dorset coastline —all the way around to the lighthouse at Portland Bill. This view of approximately 25 miles is considered the best in Lyme Regis. Modern plumbing has been installed, including hot and cold running water in all 16 bedrooms (12 with private bath or shower). Of course, the 17th-century rooms retain their special charm, crooked and irregular. Full fire precautions have been implemented.

In the low-ceilinged dining room, you are served excellent food. For bed, breakfast, and a four-course evening meal, the daily rate ranges from £19.50 ($38.03) to £23.50 ($45.83) per person, including VAT.

The building was immortalized by Beatrix Potter in her painting of "Susan the Cat and Stumpy the Dog," in *The Tale of Little Pig Robinson,* published in 1902. The tulip tree in the garden is one of the five oldest in England, more than 300 years old.

Kersbrook, Pound Road (tel. Lyme Regis 2596), lives up to its boast of being the "dream house of the Dorset Riviera." Stone built in 1790, Kersbrook is crowned by a thatched roof and sits on a ledge above the village, which provides a panoramic view of the coast. Mr. and Mrs. James Robshaw are the proprietors of Kersbrook, charging from £12 ($23.40) for B&B, £17 ($33.15) for half board. Many of the rooms have private baths and showers available at a small extra cost.

Bell Cliff, Broad Street (tel. Lyme Regis 2459), is a miniature white house set like a jewel upon a cliff edge, overlooking the sea and near the bottom of the main street. It was part of the film set for the *The French Lieutenant's Woman.* Whether for morning coffee, lunch, afternoon tea, or dinner, it's a good choice, specializing in good home cooking. A complete meal at noon costs from £3.50 ($6.83) to £4 ($7.80), increasing to about £6 ($11.70) at dinner. Lunch specialties include homemade steak-and-kidney pie, plus apple tart and clotted cream. Dinner might be scampi or steak. Fish dishes are recommended heartily, and the french-fried potatoes accompanying them are crisp and done to order. In the afternoon, order the Dorset cream tea at £1.30 ($2.54). Bell Cliff is open throughout the year seven days a week. Reservations are advisable in summer.

The **Cobb Arms,** down by the Cobb, is a blue-painted pub right on the harborside where you can order bar snacks such as braised beef with vegetables for £1.75 ($3.41). Or else you can dine in the restaurant on fresh Lyme Bay plaice with a salad and vegetable at £4.20 ($8.19), or local Dover sole at £6.50 ($12.68). Fresh local scallops are often sauteed in herb butter and served with a salad and brown bread and butter for £7 ($13.65). Appetizers include soups, pâtés, and smoked fish, ranging from 75p ($1.46) to £3.20 ($6.24). There are also mixed grills, rump or T-bone steaks, served with jacket potatoes and salads, costing from £4.50 ($8.78) to £6.50 ($12.68).

As you eat, you can look out over the harbor in very much the same way as the French lieutenant's woman did. It was in this pub that the members of the cast and the stars were dressed and made up for their parts in the film.

Next to the inn is the Lifeboat Station, with its lifeboat ever ready to put to sea to rescue sailors in distress.

The **Royal Lion,** Broad Street (tel. Lyme Regis 2768), is an old coaching inn, once known as the White Lion. On the side of a hill, it climbs up from the sea, with country-style furnishings in the oak-beamed bar and lounge. The bedrooms are also country style, including one with a canopied bed used regularly by Edward VII when he was Prince of Wales (his mistress, Lillie Langtry, was born in Lyme Regis). A room and a large breakfast costs £12.50 ($24.38) per person, including VAT and an early-morning cup of tea brought up with the daily papers. They also quote a half-board rate of £18.20 ($35.49) per person for those staying three days or more. Ordered separately, a dinner will cost around £6.50 ($12.68), and you're given a choice of fresh local fish along with grilled meat dishes.

The **Three Cups Hotel,** Broad Street (tel. Lyme Regis 2732). Although this hotel is up the hill from the seashore, most of its rooms have views overlooking the Cobb. A building more than 200 years old, it has handsome bow windows over the main entrance which was featured in the film. Window boxes brighten the stone exterior, and inside the rooms are light and airy with comfortable beds. All units contain hot and cold running water, as well as tea- and coffee-making equipment. TV can be provided, and each room already has a phone and radio. Corridors are narrow and the floors may creak, but no expense is spared to offer a friendly welcome to the traveler. Rooms go for £12.50 ($24.38) per person, including VAT and a full breakfast. A set dinner costs from £6.50 ($12.68), or else you can enjoy some enterprising snacks in the bar, including crab salad at £2.55 ($4.97) or else fresh soup and french bread at 75p ($1.46). Grills range from £4.50 ($8.78) to £5.25 ($10.24).

15. Donyatt

After Lyme Regis, you may want to journey to Donyatt, a village near Ilminster. Just outside the village of Donyatt, between the A303 and the A30 London/West Country roads, stands the following recommendation:

Thatchers Pond, Donyatt, near Ilminster (tel. Ilminster 3210), is a 15th-century thatched limestone farmhouse where Michael and Pamela Smith, both experienced caterers, offer a vast cold table for lunch and dinner daily except Monday. The house is warm and welcoming, with old clocks, guns, and swords adorning the walls of the flagstoned hall and dining room. Meals are served from a vast table laden with fresh lobster, salmon, crab, and prawns, cold roast beef, ham, tongue, homemade pâté, quiches, and mousse. You're offered a choice of any two meats and then are allowed to help yourself from a selection of 25 different salads. The dessert trolley is laden with succulent sweets, and there is cheese if you prefer it. The bar offers beers and wines, and coffee is available, but no tea. The main course is large enough, but if you're a good trencher person an appetizer can be provided at an extra £1.75 ($3.22). Lunch from the buffet costs £6.50 ($12.68); dinner, £7.50 ($14.63). Thatchers is open from noon to 2 p.m. for lunch. There are two sittings for dinner, one at 7:30, another at 9 p.m.

DEVON AND CORNWALL

THE GREAT PATCHWORK QUILT area of the southwest of England, part of the "West Countree," abounds with cliffside farms, rolling hills, foreboding moors, semitropical plants, and fishing villages—all of which combine to provide some of the finest scenery in England. The British approach the sunny countries of Devon and Cornwall with the same kind of excitement one would normally reserve for hopping over to the continent. Especially along the coastline, the British Riviera, many of the names of the little seaports, villages, and resorts have been synonymous with holidays in the sun: Penzance, Looe, Polperro.

Many small towns and fishing villages do not allow cars to enter. These towns provide car parks on their outskirts, but this can involve a long walk to reach the center or the harbor. In high season, from mid-July to mid-September, the more popular villages get quite crowded, and one needs reservations in the limited number of hotels available.

It's easy to involve yourself in the West Country life, as lived by the British vacationers. Perhaps you'll go pony trekking across moor and woodland, past streams and sheep-dotted fields, stopping at local pubs to soak up atmosphere and ale. Chances are your oddly shaped bedroom will be in a barton (farm) mentioned in the Domesday Book or in a thatched cottage neither straight, level, nor true.

Fishermen can catch their lunch (salmon and trout in such rivers as the Dart), then take it back to the kitchen of their guest house to be grilled. Life is usually very informal. The hosts here, many of farming stock, don't like to "muck about" putting on airs for tourists. In the morning, your landlady might be out picking runner (string) beans for your dinner. Later, she'll bring up pails from the milk house, and you can watch her create her own version of clotted Devonshire cream—cooked on the back of the stove. For dessert that night, you'll get a country portion heaped on your freshly picked gooseberries.

When a Devonian invites you to walk down the primrose path, he or she means just that. The primrose is practically the shire flower of this most beautiful of counties. Devon is a land of jagged coasts—the red cliffs in the south facing the English Channel, the gray cliffs in the north opening onto the Bristol Channel.

Aside from the shores, a great many of the scenic highlights appear in the two national parks, **Dartmoor** in the south, **Exmoor** in the north. First, we'll explore:

SOUTH DEVON

It's the lazy life in South Devon, as you sit in the orchard, enjoying the view of the coast from which Raleigh and Drake set sail. Almost every little hamlet, on some level, is geared to accommodate tourists, who flock here in great numbers from early spring to late fall. There is much to see and explore (although a minimum of historical sights), but mainly the tranquil life prevails.

1. Beer

Only seven miles from the last stopover in Dorset (Lyme Regis), is the town of Beer, no longer a center for smugglers, but still colorful with its small fleet of fishing craft, sandy beach, white cliffs, and pebbly cove. I can think of no better way to acquaint you with the fine accommodations of Devon than to introduce:

Bovey House, Beer, near Seaton (tel. Branscombe 241), on the edge of the village, about 1½ miles away. Picture the sort of dreams you're likely to have at Bovey House, sleeping in the Charles II room, with its designed ceiling which tells the story of how the king finally escaped the Roundheads by hiding in an oak tree. After poking about, knocking, and old-fashioned snooping, you're likely to find a concealed door leading to an underground passageway to the sea, a mile and a half away.

A 12th-century manor with an avenue of trees leading to the village road, Bovey was presented to Queen Catherine Parr by King Henry VIII as part of her dowry following the dissolution of the monasteries. It is the favorite property of its present owner, Lord Clinton. In one of his off-moments, he was

CORNWALL AND DEVON

persuaded to let his tenants, Mr. and Mrs. Alan Roberts, accept paying guests under the guise of house parties.

When you see the antique furnishings in the drawing room, you'll want to whisk them away into the night. Adam, Chippendale, Georgian—all the important furniture periods are represented here. The linenfold paneling in the dining room is museum caliber. There are collections of old china, silver, paintings, and sculpture. The spacious bedrooms contain antiques and beds that blend in with the atmosphere. A famous playwright once used the house as the model for the setting in one of his plays. In the drawing room you'll occasionally meet political leaders of England, perhaps stage stars—those who love this way of life.

Tea- and coffee-making facilities are provided in the bedrooms. You can also arrange to have a lunch packed for a later meal near the shore or on a picnic walk. Be sure to find a secluded, protected spot—this is hunting country, and one often sees a pack of hounds and hunters chasing a fox.

I've deliberately held off telling you the price till last. It's the nicest surprise of all! For your bed, breakfast, and evening dinner, you are charged from £12.22 ($23.83) per person, depending on the location of the room, plus a small service charge and VAT. Bovey House is open mid-March to mid-November. This is one of the best values in England.

2. Exeter

The county town of Devonshire, on the banks of the Exe River, Exeter was a Roman city founded in the first century A.D. Two centuries later, it was encircled by a mighty stone wall, traces of which remain today. Conquerors and would-be conquerors, especially the Vikings, stormed the fortress in the centuries to come. None was more notable than William the Conqueror. Irked at Exeter's refusal to capitulate (perhaps also at the sheltering of Gytha, mother of the slain Harold), the Norman duke brought Exeter to its knees on short notice.

Under the Tudors, the city grew and prospered. The cocky Sir Walter Raleigh and Sir Francis Drake cut striking figures strolling through Exeter's streets. In May 1942, the Germans bombed Exeter, destroying many of the city's architectural treasures. Exeter was rebuilt, but the new, impersonal-looking shops and offices couldn't replace the Georgian crescents and the black-and-white timbered buildings with their plastered walls. Thankfully, much was spared, including the major architectural treasure—

EXETER CATHEDRAL: Owing its present look to the Decorated style of the 13th and 14th centuries, the Exeter Cathedral of St. Peter actually goes back to Saxon times. Even Canute, the Viking conqueror, got in on the act of rebuilding around 1017. The cathedral of Bishop Warelwast came into being in the early 12th century, and the north and south towers serve as reminders of the Norman period. The remarkable feature of the present Gothic building is the nave, with its tierceron vaulting, stretching out for some 300 feet, broken only by an organ. The cathedral did suffer damage in the 1942 German bombings, losing its St. James's Chapel, which subsequently has been restored. But most of the treasures remained intact, including the rows of sculpture along the west front; the 14th-century Minstrels' Gallery, its angelic figures with Early English musical instruments in hand; and the carved oak 14th-century bishop's throne.

EXETER MARITIME MUSEUM: At The Quay (tel. Exeter 58075), the maritime museum has a collection of more than 100 small craft and shelters the world's largest collection of English and foreign craft, ranging from the Congo to Corfu. This is an "active museum." You can sail sampans, paddle canoes, or row ocean rowers. They even "quant" here, but you've got to inquire about that one! They still steam their steamers, including the oldest one in the world still steaming. Five colorful Portuguese chatas are available for rent at the museum from May to September, carrying a maximum of six passengers. The boats are rowed along the three miles of navigable water on the River Exe and the canal, the oldest in Britain, at a charge of 80p ($1.56) per hour. The museum is open every day of the year, except Christmas and Boxing Day, from 10 a.m. to 5 p.m. (October to May) and from 10 a.m. to 6 p.m. (June to September). Adults pay an admission of £1.70 ($3.32); children, 85p ($1.66).

OTHER MONUMENTS: Much of the old remains. The **Exeter Guildhall,** a colonnade building on The High, is regarded as the oldest municipal building in the kingdom. The earliest reference to the Guildhall is contained in a deed of 1160. The Tudor front which straddles the pavement was added in 1593. Inside is a fine display of silver in the gallery. It contains a number of paintings as well, including one of Henrietta Anne, daughter of Charles I (she was born in Exeter in 1644). The ancient hall is paneled in oak. The Guildhall is open throughout the year, Monday to Saturday, from 10 a.m. to 5:30 p.m., and admission is free.

Rougemont Castle, with its Norman gateway, is now largely a memory. Rougemont was created for William the Conqueror. Over the centuries the castle fell into ruins. Now there has been some consolidation of masonry, and it is pleasant to stroll through Rougemont Gardens.

If time remains, see also **St. Nicholas Priory, The Mint,** lying off Fore Street, a 15th-century craft building; and the underground passageways at **Princesshay,** off The High (the subterranean water supply channels of medieval times).

WHERE TO STAY: In accommodations, Exeter has a number of comfortable choices.

Rougemont Hotel, Queen Street (tel. Exeter 54982), is imbued with a stylish flair that none of its competitors provides. Fairly recently, this great, old-fashioned hotel, opposite the Central Railway Station, underwent a metamorphosis, emerging as a solid place at which to stay. Its neoclassic architecture is a background for the contemporary furnishings. The bone-white walls in the reception lounge are a foil to the golds and oranges. Much of the comfort and tasteful decor are found in the bedrooms. Singles rent from £22 ($42.90); doubles, from £32 ($62.40)—including VAT and an English breakfast. Amenities include telephones, radios, TV, and private baths.

Dinner is à la carte, beginning at £9 ($17.55). Guests gather in the Adam-style Cavendish Bar for drinks—sparkling with crystal and vibrant in gold and white. An excellent stock of wines comes from the cellar, which, incidentally, was once used as a debtor's prison.

Royal Clarence Hotel, Cathedral Yard (tel. Exeter 58464), a Georgian-style building, miraculously escaped destruction during the war. A hotel full of history, it possesses modern amenities: all of the 63 bedrooms have private bathrooms, and many overlook the Cathedral Green. Comfortable lounges display a mixture of antiques, gilt mirrors, and modern pieces. The restyled restaurant is open to the public, and a table d'hôte luncheon costs from £5.45 ($10.63), and a table d'hôte dinner from £6.55 ($12.77). A single room with bath rents from £22 ($42.90), a double with bath from £36 ($70.20). Prices include all taxes. The general manager is Arthur E. Barnes.

The **Devon Motel,** Exeter Bypass, Matford (tel. Exeter 59268), lies on the outskirts of the city at the western sector of the bypass on the A38. Convenient to the airport and as a stopping-off point for those headed for the West Country, it is one of the Watney Lyons properties, built in a style familiar to most North Americans. You drive your car into your own open garage, and your bedroom and private bath are directly overhead. Singles pay £20 ($39); doubles, £30 ($58.50)—including breakfast, service, and VAT. Some cheaper singles are in the old part of the hotel and are without bath, costing from £18 ($35.10) nightly. However, all doubles and units in the new wing have private baths. Inside, all is compact and built-in, with a picture window overlooking the meadows beyond. On the premises are a restaurant and drinking bars, serving a set lunch for £3 ($5.85) and dinner from £6 ($11.70).

The **White Hart Hotel,** South Street (tel. Exeter 37511), is one of the oldest inns of Exeter, with a mass of polished slate floors, oak beams, and gleaming brass and copper adorning the walls and mantels. The lounges are chintzy and comfortable. Bedrooms have character; however, those in the modern extension are functional and efficient. Most units have TV, phone, bath, or shower, renting from £25 ($48.75) to £35 ($68.25) per night for two persons, including VAT, service, and an English breakfast. The hotel's wine bar, the well-known Bottlescrew Bill's, offers pâtés, cheese, salads, omelets, pastries, sandwiches, and a hot dish of the day, perhaps ham and turkey vol-au-vents or beefsteak and oyster pie with a jacket potato and asparagus. A good snack meal is under £3 ($5.85).

WHERE TO EAT: The **Ship Inn,** Martin's Lane (tel. Exeter 72040), a short walk from the cathedral, was often visited by Sir Francis Drake, Sir Walter Raleigh, and Sir John Hawkins. Of it Drake wrote: "Next to mine own shippe, I do most love that old 'Shippe' in Exon, a tavern in Fyssh Street, as the people call it, or as the clergie will have it, St. Martin's Lane." The pub still provides tankards of stout and lager and is still loved by both young and old. The reconstructed dining room on the second floor also retains the early English atmosphere: settles, red leather and oak chairs. The fare is hearty English, the service friendly. At either lunch or dinner, you can order such temptations as onion soup, grilled rainbow trout, or grilled rump steak. The price of the main courses includes vegetables, roll and butter. The portions, as in Elizabethan days, are large. A two-course meal ranges in price from £3 ($5.85) to £6.50 ($12.68). The restaurant is open from noon to 2 p.m. and from 6:30 to 10:30 p.m., Monday through Saturday. Closed Sunday, and all bank holidays. The bars are open from 10:30 a.m. to 2 p.m. and 5 to 10:30 p.m. weekdays.

Coolings Wine Bar, 11 Gandy St. (tel. Exeter 34183). In one of the older and more interesting little streets of the city, this is a friendly place with beams above the checked cloths of the tables. Some of the dining space is in the cellars of the old building. All the food is prepared on the premises, and that includes a good selection of cold meats, pies, and quiches, as well as chicken Waldorf, sugar-baked ham, each served with a variety of salads, then two or three daily hot dishes, chalked up on the blackboard. A plateful, either hot or cold, will cost about £1.75 ($3.41). Desserts are available at 55p ($1.07) to 75p ($1.46). House wine is 55p ($1.07) a glass. It is open daily except Sunday from noon to 2:15 p.m. and from 5:30 to 11:30 p.m.

WHERE TO STAY AND EAT OUTSIDE EXETER: In the Exe Valley, four miles south of Tiverton and ten miles north of Exeter, lies **Bickleigh**, a hamlet with a river, an arched stone bridge, a mill pond, and thatched-roof cottages—a cliché of English charm, one of the finest spots in all of Devon. In this village, I have a recommendation in the medium-priced range:

The **Fishermen's Cot Hotel** (tel. Bickleigh 237) sits like a picture postcard across the way from Bickleigh Bridge. Even though it's thatched and blends beautifully into the local setting, it is newer than most of the houses here, and has all the heating and plumbing necessary. In a single, the rate ranges from £10.50 ($20.48) to £14 ($27.30), with doubles costing from £18 ($35.10) to £22 ($42.90). Tariffs depend on whether or not you have a private bath. Chances are you'll be served some of the best food in Devon. Ask if the cook will make you a chocolate mousse—light and airy, of country-fresh eggs. The Cot serves excellent trout dishes. Bar snacks are available at lunchtime, ranging from a soup with roll and butter up to a sirloin steak and priced from 65p ($1.27) to £5.20 ($10.14). A table d'hôte dinner costs from £5.50 ($10.73). Fishermen particularly like the place, because they can catch salmon and trout right in front of the hotel on the banks of the Exe. The hotel is fully licensed. There are dinner-dances on Saturday.

Trout, on the main Tiverton/Exeter Road, A396, four miles south of Tiverton (tel. Bickleigh 339), is a former 17th-century coaching inn, transformed skillfully into three pubs and a gourmet restaurant. The long, low thatched roof with tiny leaded windows encloses the former stables, converted into a spacious and dramatic restaurant, with heavy dark beams and oak furniture. A collection of copper and glittering horse brasses, turkey-red table linens, and ladderback chairs provide a warm atmosphere for dining. Pre-dinner drinks are provided in one of the pubs, the most popular one containing an old open fireplace, made from the original bridge stone. A sign indicates that the inn was built in 1630 as a trout hatchery.

A buffet lunch and evening snacks are available in the bar seven days a week. A meal includes smoked trout, Austrian cheese, chicken or pâté, with a salad, and homemade desserts. The restaurant does only à la carte dinners. Appetizers might include pâté and a Cumberland sauce or whitebait, perhaps a homemade soup. Main-dish specialties are beef Stroganoff, veal Marsala, chicken mornay, and lamb cutlets. A hot cooked meal costs from £3.50 ($6.83) to £5 ($9.75), and a buffet is offered daily, two courses going from £3 ($5.85).

An Old Manor at Ottery St. Mary

The sleepy little market town, where the incomparable Coleridge *(The Rime of the Ancient Mariner, Kubla Khan)* was born, lies in the Otter River Valley, only ten miles east of Exeter. See the almost perfectly preserved church from the 14th century. The old cloth town makes a good base for exploring the South Devon coastline, particularly if you center at the following medium-priced recommendation.

Salston Hotel (tel. Ottery St. Mary 2310), an old manor house, lies 1½ miles off the main A30 London road, and a mile from Ottery St. Mary. The hotel is officially listed as a building of historical and architectural interest. Even though it's lost most of its acreage and original furnishings, the exterior is intact—a rambling three-story brick hotel with dozens of chimneys and gables. The lounge is large, with a bay window opening onto the gardens. A ballroom, built for the visit of Princess Alexandra of Teck (that name will send you rushing to your history books), has a Tudor fireplace. The Salston has just built a new 12-bedroom extension, with luxury rooms, each with shower, hairdryer, refrigerated mini-bar, and a double and single bed. Charges are £24 ($46.80) in a single with private bath in one of the new luxury rooms, or else £22 ($42.90) in a single in one of the traditional rooms. B&B in a double luxury room is £34 ($66.30) for two persons, or £32 ($62.40) for two in one of the traditional rooms. Spa fans will find a health studio run in conjunction with the Salston, and two squash courts have been completed. There is a 20- by 48-foot swimming pool, plus an adjoining Norwegian pine cabin with sauna, solarium, and a massage and relaxing room, available at an extra charge. There is also a swimming instructor. Most Friday evenings, the years roll back to 1530. In front of the Henry VIII fireplace, a medieval banquet is spread, complete with costumed serving "wenches," minstrel singers, and a jester. Featured at a "six-remove" banquet are such items as game soup based on a 16th-century recipe, Tudor-style pâté, ribs of oxen, and lots of mead and ale. The latest innovation of the hotel is a French Cellar Restaurant in the original vaulted wine cellars which is open Tuesday through Saturday until 10:30 p.m.

READER'S HOTEL SELECTION: "Louisiana-born James Henry and his English wife own one of the oldest (1487) continuously licensed pubs in England, the **Oxenham Arms,** South Zeal, Devon (tel. Sticklepath 244). The carefully preserved inn was originally built in the 12th century and used as a monastery. A cob-walled double room is £12.50 ($24.38) per person, tax included, with a choice of breakfast menus. Seventeen miles west of Exeter, the inn is just a short hike into the bracken and gorse-covered hills of Dartmoor National Park" (A. Emerson Smith, Columbia, S.C.)

3. Dartmoor

Antiquity-rich Dartmoor lies in the southern part of the shire. The Tors (huge rock formations) of this granite mass sometimes soar to a height of 2000 feet. The national park is a patchwork quilt of mood changes: gorse and purple heather, Dartmoor ponies, a foreboding landscape for the experienced walker only, gorges with rushing water.

Some 13 miles west from Exeter, the peaceful little town of **Moreton Hampstead,** perched on the edge of Dartmoor, makes a good center. The heavily visited Dartmoor village of **Widecombe-in-the-Moor** is only seven miles from the town. Moreton Hampstead contains much that is old, including a market cross and several 17th-century colonnaded almshouses.

WHERE TO STAY AND EAT: Manor House Hotel (tel. Moreton Hampstead 355), at the edge of Dartmoor, is a converted, gabled, Jacobean manor. It is in the midst of 200 acres of parkland, much of which has been cultivated for the pleasure of guests. This upper-bracket hotel is a favorite with fishermen (trout in the Bovey and Bowden Rivers, salmon in the Teign), and with golfers as well who are drawn to the 18-hole course which hotel guests can use free of charge. Built for a distinguished family, the manor has lost its old grandeur, but added the new lure of modern amenities. The halls, reception lounge, drawing and dining rooms are for life on a large scale; the bedrooms are often outsize (some suitable for a diplomatic reception); the furnishings are comfortable, with good beds, and all the rooms have private baths. Expect to pay from £29 ($56.55) to £35 ($68.25) for B&B in a single room. In a double or twin, two persons are charged anywhere from £43 ($83.85) to £78 ($152.10). VAT and service are included in all tariffs. The cuisine blends some of the best English dishes with fine continental fare. An à la carte lunch costs about £8 ($15.60) for two courses and coffee, with a set dinner going for £10 ($19.50).

Gidleigh Park Hotel, Chagford (tel. Chagford 2225), is set one mile from the edge of Dartmoor in beautiful countryside. A visit to this hotel is highly recommended, if you can find it. Its owners, Kay and Paul Henderson, have renovated and refurnished the house with flair and imagination.

In a park of 30 acres, the mansion is Tudor style, lying just two miles from Chagford. Large beech and oak trees abound. Inside, the oak-paneled public rooms and the open log fires invite a return to yesterday. The windows open onto views of the garden and the Teign Valley, with Dartmoor lying beyond.

Most of the bedrooms, 11 in all, are on the second floor and are approached by a grand staircase. All rooms contain private bath, color TV set, and phone. Half board ranges from £40 ($78) per person nightly, plus VAT.

Good-tasting meals are served in an oak-paneled dining room. The menu is changed daily, and only the best and freshest products are used. Cheeses are supplied by Paxton & Whitfield of London, and the wine cellar is one of the most extensive and reasonably priced in England. Kay Henderson trained at Cordon Bleu in London and Paris. She believes it is better to make up a meal from the freshest produce available each day from local farmers, fishermen, and the hotel's own garden, than to offer a large choice of indifferently prepared à la carte dishes.

How to get there: From Chagford Square turn right into Mill Street at Lloyds Bank. After 200 yards, fork right and down the hill to the crossroads. Cross straight over into Holy Street, following the lane passing Holy Street Manor on your right and shifting into low gear to negotiate two sharp bends on a steep hill. Over Leigh Bridge turn a sharp right into Gidleigh Park. A half-mile drive will bring you to the hotel.

The **Great Tree Hotel,** Sandypark, near Chagford (tel. Chagford 2491), is a comfortable country house set in 18 acres of private gardens and woodland. There in the early morning the only sounds you are likely to hear are the calls of birds, the noise of white water running through the wood, and the occasional moo of a cow. All bedrooms have bath or shower, color TV, radio, and tea- and coffee-making facilities. Many of them are on ground level, with lovely views over the gardens. A single room with bath or shower costs £19.50 ($38.03) in low season, rising to £25 ($48.75) in summer. A double with bath or shower goes for £37 ($72.15) in low season, £48 ($93.60) in high, including a large breakfast, a table d'hôte dinner, and early-morning tea or coffee.

There's a cozy lounge with high beams. A roaring log fire burns on cold days. In the snug cocktail lounge, bar snacks are served at lunch, including homemade soup, toasted sandwiches, a ploughman's lunch, cold meats, salads, and fresh scampi. Mr. and Mrs. Manchester came from the north some years ago, bringing with them John, the chef, and his wife Maureen who runs the dining room.

The standard of food is high, and there's a good à la carte menu as well as a set dinner. Much of the fruit and vegetables come from the hotel's own gardens, and they pride themselves on providing fresh fish and local meat. A set lunch costs about £5.50 ($10.73), and picnic lunches can be packed if you ask the evening before. Cream teas are served on the terrace in summer and by the fire in winter at a cost of £1.75 ($3.41).

Moor Park Hotel, Chagford (tel. Chagford 2202), is another charming place in the heart of Dartmoor, where B&B costs £13 ($25.35) in a single without bath, £14.50 ($28.28) with bath. Doubles without bath rent for £12.50 ($24.38) per person, going up to £15.50 ($30.23) with bath, all plus VAT. Bedrooms are simply furnished but comfortable, and the lounges are cozy with deep armchairs, wood fires, and highly polished furniture. Meals consist of simple dishes, such as leek-and-potato soup, smoked fish pâté, and roast joints, accompanied by fresh seasonal vegetables and followed by such desserts as grilled bananas with honey or trifle with clotted cream. Expect to spend from £7.50 ($14.63) for the set menu.

An à la carte bill of fare provides steaks, tournedos Rossini, escalope Cordon Bleu, and trout with almonds. If you want to branch out and order an exotic dessert, I'd recommend the crêpes suzette or the peach and cherry flambé. An average meal without one of these exotic concoctions will cost from £10 ($19.50). The place has a friendly atmosphere, extending a hearty welcome to passersby.

Moorwood Cottage Restaurant, Lustleigh, near Newton Abbot (tel. Lustleigh 341). It's easy to drive past the small 17th-century cottage with beetling thatch and leaded windows on the A383 highway between Moretonhamstead and Bovey Tracey. Take it easy and stop for lunch in this tiny dining room, furnished with antiques, a log fire burning on nippy days, and fresh flowers on the tables. Michael Harris is the inspired chef, and his wife Claudia is the self-styled wine waitress, barmaid, and reception committee.

You're given a warm greeting, then asked to make your selection from six or so appetizers, likely to include a homemade soup, spinach-and-bacon pâté, or a Moorwood cocktail of prawns, corn, apple, and fresh celery with dressing. The main courses include veal with spices, herbs, onions, and tomatoes; roast duckling in wine with pineapple and ginger; poached Devon salmon with sorrel mayonnaise; or filet of beef in cream, madeira, and green peppercorns. All dishes are accompanied by potatoes and fresh vegetables or a salad on the side.

The homemade desserts are luscious, particularly a chocolate and brandy mousse with Devonshire cream, or black currant sorbet with Kirsch and cream. Coffee ad infinitum is served in the lounge with liqueurs. A three-course meal will cost around £8 ($15.60), but you can dine majestically for £6.50 ($12.68). There's a good wine list, including some Californian and South African vintages, with a bottle costing as little as £4.50 ($8.78). The French house wine is £3.95 ($7.70) a bottle, 70p ($1.37) a glass.

Teignworthy Hotel, Frenchbeer, near Chagford (tel. Chagford 3355), is an attractive granite and slate country house where John and Gillian Newell and their family welcome you as guests. All bedrooms have baths, color TVs, and phones, and there is room to relax in privacy. They have a drawing room with an open log fire and a small bar for predinner drinks.

John does most of the cooking, aided by the Newells' daughters, Debbie and Rebecca, plus various local girls. His individual style is becoming very popular in the area, and dinner can include poached brill with dill hollandaise, trout with Pernod, or filet of pork with date and red wine sauce. Wherever possible, local fresh produce is used. A liter of house wine is £4.50 ($8.78) and up. There is also a good, well-thought-out wine list.

Overnight stays, including an English breakfast and dinner, will cost £30 ($58.50) per person, including VAT.

Lydford House Hotel, Lydford, near Okehampton (tel. Lydford 347), is a family-run country house hotel, peacefully set in more than three acres of grounds, just on the edge of Dartmoor. It was built in 1880 by the well-known Dartmoor artist, William Widgery. Several of his paintings hang in the residents' lounge. The hotel is particularly known for its food and features homecooking, using fresh and local produce wherever possible. Owners Ron and Ann Boulter have set the following rates: £10 ($19.50) per person nightly for room and English breakfast; £11.25 ($21.94) for a room with private bath. For room, breakfast, and table d'hôte dinner, the charge is £15 ($29.25), £16.25 ($31.69) with private bath. Weekly terms are available, and all prices include service and taxes. Lydford House has its own riding stables in the grounds.

Superb riding on Dartmoor is available by the hour, or you can enjoy inclusive riding holidays. Beginners are welcome, and expert tuition is offered. The stables are under the personal supervision of Claire Boulter, BHSAI.

The **Castle Inn**, Lydford, near Okehampton (tel. Lydford 242), is a 16th-century inn next to Lydford Castle. The low inn, with its pink facade and row of rose trellises, is the hub of the village, along with the all-purpose grocery store and post office. The inn's owners, Mr. and Mrs. Red, have maintained the character of the commodious rustic lounge, with its valuable collection of old furniture and accessories, including wing chairs, a grandfather's clock, and antique prints. One room is called the "Snuggery," containing a group of high-backed oak settles arranged in a circle. Meals are served buffet style, from noon to 2 p.m., a great spread set out on a long table. The cost depends on your selection of a main course. The salads are on a help-yourself basis. Buffet salads at lunch cost about £2.50 ($4.88) with a main course. Snacks are available as well, and you can take your plate, along with a lager, and sneak off to an inviting nook. A three-course dinner will run about £7 ($13.65). For a bed and a large country-style breakfast, the charge is £11 ($21.45) in a single, £19 ($37.05) in a double. The bedrooms, although not large, are well planned and attractively furnished, often with mahogany and marble Victorian pieces, each room with its own color scheme.

Holne Chase Hotel (tel. Poundsgate 471) is a white-gabled country house, within sight of trout and salmon fishing waters. You can catch your lunch and take it back to the kitchen to be cooked. Although the mood of the moor predominates, Holne Chase is surrounded by trees, lawns, and pastures, a perfect setting for walks along the Dart. It's off the main Ashburton-Princetown road, between Holne Bridge and New Bridge. Holne Chase is run by Mary and Kenneth Bromage, who returned to their native Devon to preserve the house "as a sanctuary of peace and hospitality." Every bedroom in the house is named after a tributary of the River Dart. The best way to stay here is to take the half-board rate, which ranges from £21.50 ($41.93) to £29.50 ($57.53) in a single, from £43 ($83.85) to £48 ($93.60) in a double or twin. The more expensive tariffs are for units with private baths.

The house is furnished in period style, with a fine English 18th-century oak dresser base serving as the bar. The cooking combines the best of English fare with specialty dishes that are made all the better whenever produce from the gardens is used or fresh fish from the Dart River and Torbay. Devon beef and lamb are also featured. The old cellars hold a good selection of wines.

Leusdon Lodge Guest House, Poundsgate (tel. Poundsgate 304), is a 150-year-old stone country house, with gables, chimneys, and beyond the garden, views of Dartmoor National Park. Its owners are Neelia and Denis Hutchins, who probably know more about this area than anyone else. Denis was once the chairman of the Dartmoor Tourist Association, and likes to help guide you to the best local sights, to a picnic beside a crystal-clear brook, or to tell the history of the moor and its mystical folklore. On cool nights he lights a log fire in the living room, joining guests in talks. There are seven rooms with soft beds and hot and cold water basins. Your breakfast will be abundant and varied. Dinners are English at their traditional best. The charge is £16 ($31.20) per person for half board, the only terms offered. However, you'll be charged an extra £1.50 ($2.93) per person for a room with private bath. Meals are served in the dining room with its hand-carved paneled walls and an ornate fireplace. Specialties include steak-and-kidney pudding, Dartmoor rabbit in cider, and beefsteak casserole with dumplings. In winter there is full central heating, even a festive Christmas house party, as well as medieval banquets.

Old Walls Farm, Ponsworthy, near Ashburton (tel. Poundsgate 222), is a substantial, stone-colored plastered country home set remotely on a working farm and reached by very narrow lanes. Here you are comfortably in the heart of the moors, and in the safe, knowing hands of owner Bill Fursdon, an expert on the area. He is a genial, handsome, white-haired gentleman with a gracious smile who is by avocation a naturalist. He'll take you on a short walk around his farm, showing you his collection of cows, mongrel dogs, ducks, a pet goat (its milk is served at breakfast, but it's strictly optional), and a beautiful little river, lying a short distance from the house. He'll make handmade maps, pinpointing the places of interest within driving distance.

His house is a living tribute to a fast-disappearing era. He is assisted by his wife, Elizabeth, who plays the organ on Sunday at the village church, and their son who lives in a separate home close by. Guests relax around a stone fireplace in the drawing room, or else on a sunny day enjoy a crescent-shaped, all-glass sun room. From the latter, the view of the moorland is exceptional. The living room has an old grand piano, a Victorian card table, a soft arm sofa, and armchairs placed in a curving bay recess.

The B&B rate is about £9 ($17.55) per person. Breakfast is a special event in the dining room, and you can have as much food as you want, including mouslie, a concoction of oats, bran, wheat germ, raisins or dates, served with brown sugar, goat's milk, and a glob of clotted Devonshire cream.

Old Walls Farm is reached from the A38 dual carriageway which runs between Exeter and Plymouth. Turn onto the B3357 (signposted Dartmoor) at Ashburton, then right at Poundsgate onto 984, going through the hamlet of Ponsworthy, passing the all-purpose post office and store.

A VISIT TO AN ABBEY: Sir Francis Drake's House, Buckland Abbey, Yelverton, was originally a Cistercian monastery in 1278. It was dissolved in 1539 and became the country seat of Sir Richard Grenville and later Sir Francis Drake (two great sailors). It remained in the Drake family until 1946 when the abbey and grounds were handed over to the National Trust. The abbey is now a museum, housing portraits, mementos, including Drake's drum, banners, and a superb collection of model ships. The abbey lies three miles west of Yelverton off the A386. It is open Monday to Saturday from 11 a.m. to 6 p.m. (on Sunday from 2 to 6 p.m.). In winter it is open only on Wednesday, Saturday, and Sunday from 2 to 5 p.m. Admission is £1.20 ($2.34) for adults, 60p ($1.17) for children.

4. Torbay

In April 1968, the towns of Torquay, Paignton, and Brixham combined to form the "County Borough of Torbay," as part of a plan to turn the area into one of the super three-in-one resorts of Europe. Vacationers from the factories of the Midlands find it easier to bask in the home-grown Devonshire sunshine than to make the pilgrimage to Rimini or the Costa del Sol.

Torquay, set against a backdrop of the red cliffs of Devon, contains 11 miles of coastline, with many sheltered pebbly coves and sandy beaches. With its parks and gardens (including numerous subtropical plants and palm trees), it isn't hard to envision it as a Mediterranean-type resort (and its retired residents are fond of making this comparison, especially in postcards sent back to their cousins in Manchester). At night, concerts, productions from the West End (the D'Oyly Carte Opera appears occasionally at the new Princess

Theatre), vaudeville shows, and ballroom dancing keep the holiday-makers—and many honeymooners—regally entertained.

If you suddenly long for an old Devonshire village, you can always ride the short distance to **Cockington,** still in the same borough, which contains thatched cottages, an old mill, a forge, and a 12th-century church. Furthermore, if you want to visit one of the great homes of England, you can call on **Oldway,** in the heart of Paignton. Started by the founder of the Singer sewing-machine dynasty, Isaac Merritt Singer, and completed the year after he died (1875), the neoclassic mansion is surrounded by about 20 acres of grounds and Italian-style gardens. Inside, if you get the feeling you're at Versailles, you're almost right, as many of the rooms were copied. Open all year, Oldway may be visited weekdays from 9 a.m. to 1 p.m. and from 2 to 5:15 p.m. (on Saturday and Sunday from 2:30 to 5 p.m., May to September only). Admission is free. The gardens are always open.

WHERE TO STAY AND EAT: Rainbow House, Belgrave Road (tel. Torquay 211161), is like a complete resort, having been enlarged and integrated with the adjoining San Remo Hotel. Facing south and open throughout the year, the hotel has been in the Marshall family for about two decades. Once a large and stately house, the hotel has expanded until now it has more than 100 bedrooms, each with bath en suite, plus a number of self-catering apartments. The peak B&B rate charged is £20.50 ($39.98), although half-board terms are £24.50 ($47.78) per person. Singles pay a £2 ($3.90) supplement.

Facilities include a heated pool and sun terraces, a Caribbean coffeeshop, an apéritif bar, plus a sauna and solarium. Public rooms are furnished in bright, modern colors. In the hotel's nightclub, you can dance to a first-class band and often enjoy cabaret entertainment. The hotel's à la carte specialty restaurant, the Pot of Gold, serves an international menu, or you can patronize the grill for late-night dining. In addition to that, the hotel also offers a main restaurant, serving some local specialties among its traditional repertoire. If you're not booked on half-board terms, expect to pay from £7.50 ($14.63) for dinner.

Palm Court Hotel, Sea Front (tel. Torquay 24881), is a Victorian crescent built facing south onto the esplanade overlooking Torbay, and offers style and good living. Two lounges are wood paneled with leaded-glass windows. In the dining room is a minstrels' gallery. There are two up-to-date bars and a coffeeshop, open all day. All rooms have been modernized and have color TV, tea- and coffee-making facilities, central heating, telephone, and radio. Of the bedrooms, 42 have private bathrooms. There is an elevator to two floors. From June through September, B&B rates are from £12.85 ($25.08) to £17.25 ($33.64), including service. With garden chairs and tables on the sun terrace outside the coffeeshop, the Palm Court becomes a social center. At night the colored floodlighting around the bay evokes a Riviera atmosphere outside the hotel.

The **Alpine Hotel,** Warren Road (tel. Torquay 27612), is a remake of one of the old homes of Torquay, on the top of the city's Rock Walk. This one was the creation of Lady Singer, of the sewing machines. (Perhaps she could see Oldway from here, where her husband had extended an invitation to Isadora Duncan.) A cliff-hanging hotel, the Alpine overlooks the marina harbor. The bedrooms are pleasantly equipped with modern furnishings and are light and airy. Depending on the room, its view, its balcony, or its plumbing, the half-board rates range from £18 ($35.10) to £22 ($42.90) per person. A service charge and VAT are included.

Lanscombe House, Cockington Village (tel. Torquay 607556), is a 250-year-old Georgian "Dower" house, with its own trout pond. It's the only hotel in this village, famous throughout England for its thatched cottages, old forge, riding stables, and country walks. The considerate hosts are Mr. and Mrs. Malcolm Goldby, who do much to see that your stay is an enjoyable one. Set in a two-acre garden, the house resembles a church rectory, with large lounges and dining rooms opening onto views. The owners rent out about ten bedrooms at prices ranging from £9.50 ($18.53) to £12.50 ($24.38) per person, depending on the accommodation and time of year. However, it's best to take the half-board rate, costing from £15 ($29.25) to £18 ($35.10) per person nightly, including VAT and service. The dinner is home-cooked, typically English fare. The eggs served here, for example, are called "free range" in England, meaning the chickens are allowed to roam the estate. Everything is backed by a good wine cellar, and before dinner you can enjoy a drink in the wood-beamed and thatched bar.

Colindale, Rathmore Road (tel. Torquay 23947), is a good choice. And it's about as central as you'd want, opening onto King's Garden, as well as lying within a five-minute walk of Corbyn Beach, and three minutes from the railway station. The B&B rate, set by Messrs. Spencer and Gold, is £8.95 ($17.45) per person in high season. But the best arrangement in one of their nine well-kept double rooms is to take the partial board weekly rate—£80 ($156) per person. Colindale is one of a row of attached brick-built Edwardian houses, with gables and chimneys. It's set back from the road, with a tiny parking court in front. Messrs. Spencer and Gold have a wine list far superior to most large hotels and an attractive cocktail bar.

A Gourmet Cooking School (off-season only)

South Devon Technical College, Newton Road (tel. Torquay 35711), is a cooking school that serves inexpensive—but gourmet-level—lunches during the school terms (closed July, August, and the first two weeks in September, as well as on weekends). You pay a set £5 ($9.75) including coffee—and are offered the results of the day's lesson. Supervised by expert teachers, the young chefs turn out excellent meals. Lunch is served at 12:30 p.m. (you must reserve no more than seven days in advance; telephone between 10:30 a.m. and 4:30 p.m.). You leave tips at your discretion. It's pointless to give menu suggestions, as the bill of fare changes daily. It's usually in French, beginning with hors d'oeuvres and following with soup, then fish, such as filet of sole, the main course, perhaps entrecôte tyrolienne, accompanied by vegetables, and, finally dessert. The modern-looking restaurant is licensed, and offers a selection of table wines, apéritifs, and liqueurs. The linen is starched stiff white, the silver sparkling, and the copper chafing dishes shining.

5. Totnes

One of the oldest towns in the West Country, the ancient borough of Totnes rests quietly in the past, seemingly content to let the Torbay area remain in the vanguard of the building boom. On the Dart River, 12 miles upstream from Dartmouth, Totnes is so totally removed in character from Torquay that the two towns could be in different countries. Totnes has several old historic buildings, notably the ruins of a Norman castle, an ancient guildhall, and the 15th-century church of St. Mary, made of red sandstone. In the Middle Ages, the old cloth town was encircled by walls, and the North Gate serves as a reminder of that period.

WHERE TO STAY: Royal Seven Stars Hotel (tel. Totnes 862125) is a coaching inn, rebuilt in 1660 although tracing its origins back 500 years before that. Whitewashed and severe, it stands on a street not far from the Dart at the bottom of Fore Street. The interior courtyard, built for horses and carriages, has been enclosed in glass, with an oak staircase leading to the second-floor bedrooms, which have been upgraded with built-in furniture. In the courtyard are interesting antiques, such as a heraldic shield, hand-carved chests, and an inlaid grandfather's clock, forming the most inviting part of the inn. The rooms are in the old style—nothing fancy, but heartily recommendable for their comfortable beds, soft eiderdowns. There's hot and cold running water; half of the rooms have private baths. You pay £23 ($44.85) to £28 ($54.60) in a double room, from £14.75 ($28.76) to £18 ($35.10) in a single, inclusive of VAT and breakfast. A modern restaurant has replaced the old dining room. Open until 9:15 p.m., it offers a lunch from £3.95 ($7.70), dinner from £6.50 ($12.68), plus a choice of à la carte dishes. Olde Tyme Music Hall, dinner, dance, and cabaret are offered in the Star-lite Room every Saturday night. Reservations are necessary.

Broombrough House Farm, on the outskirts of Totnes (tel. Totnes 863134), is a gracious 100-year-old, many-gabled stone manor house set on a hill about a ten-minute walk from Totnes. Owner Joan Veale loves to show guests around the farm, which was designed by Sir George Gilbert Scott. Four spacious and well-furnished bedrooms are on the first floor (two shower rooms and one bathroom are shared). They are centrally heated, each containing twin beds, innerspring mattresses, and hot and cold running water. The daily charge is £8 ($15.60) for bed and a farm-style breakfast, plus another £5 ($9.75) for dinner. Guest lounges are spacious and comfortable. This place is highly recommended, especially to those who have never experienced life on a farm.

WHERE TO EAT: The Elbow Room, 6 North St. (tel. Totnes 863480), is a one-time cider press and adjoining cottage converted into an intimate rendezvous for diners. The original 300-year-old stone walls have been retained and decor matched to them to give a unique atmosphere. Mr. and Mrs. B. J. Sellick provide a standard of food and service which attracts gourmets. Mrs. Sellick combines technical skill with inspiration and a flair for the unusual in the selection, preparation, and presentation of her appetizers, main courses, and homemade desserts. Main courses are accompanied by, and inclusive of, fresh vegetables. The menu is restricted to a maximum of ten international dishes, ranging from truite farci de Georges Bernard (trout, boned and stuffed with salpicon of shellfish, wrapped in a pancake, and baked) to escalope de veau Maître Martino, an original of scalloped veal filled with cream cheese, chives, gherkins, mushrooms with cream and white wine. The price of a complete meal, including half a bottle of wine, is from £12 ($23.40) per person. Mr. Sellick presides over the restaurant with charm and unobtrusive expertise, and offers a wine list to match the food. The Elbow Room extends a warm welcome.

ffoulkes Restaurant and Wine Bar, 30 High St. (tel. 863853), hides behind a Tudor facade on the main street of Totnes. Enjoy an inexpensive meal or a snack in the wine bar or indulge yourself in the à la carte restaurant. The wine bar menu offers a range of foods which average about £4.95 ($9.65) per person and includes a glass of wine and unlimited coffee. In the restaurant, the food is cooked to order, and the service is polite and skilled. Choose from the extensive menu such dishes as venison Diane, duck Marco Polo, and sole caprice. Main-course dishes start at £4.25 ($8.29) and average about £6 ($11.70). Desserts are priced from £1.40 ($2.73). The wine bar is open every day for both lunch and evening drinking and eating, while the restaurant serves dinner only, from 7:30 p.m. daily Monday through Saturday.

WHERE TO STAY AND EAT ON THE OUTSKIRTS: In and around this area is some of South Devon's finest scenery. The hamlets, such as **Dartington**, are especially pleasing. Here, a Yorkshireman and his American-born wife (one of the Whitneys) poured energy, courage, imagination, and money into the theory that such a village could be self-sufficient. They used historic **Dartington Hall**, built in the late 14th century and restored by them after 1925, as their center. In the surrounding acres of undulating hills and streams, several village industries were created—housing construction, advanced farming, cloth milling, and an experimental school. During the day, visitors are welcome to tour the extensive grounds and can make purchases of handmade crafts in the community store. My food and lodgings recommendations in the village follow.

The **Cott Inn** (tel. Totnes 863777), on the old Ashburton-Totnes turnpike, is the second-oldest inn in England, built in 1320. It is a low, rambling, two-story building of stone, cob, and plaster, with a thatched roof and walls three feet thick. The owner, Nigel Shortman, charges £13.25 ($25.84) per person, plus service and VAT, for a full English or a continental breakfast and occupancy of one of their low-ceilinged old beamed rooms upstairs, where modern conveniences, including hot and cold running water, have been skillfully installed.

The inn is a gathering place for the people of Dartington, and here you'll feel the pulse of English country life. Even though it is a lowly pub, it is sophisticated—and you'll hear good talk here. In winter, log fires keep the lounge and bar snug. You'll surely be intrigued with the tavern, perhaps wanting to take a light meal there. Eating out in restaurants today is an expensive proposition, so Mr. Shortman offers his customers a superb hot and cold buffet where prices for the numerous dishes vary between £1 ($1.95) and £4.50 ($8.78). Even if you're not staying over, at least drop in at the pub.

Stoke Gabriel

About four miles southeast of Totnes sits the little village of Stoke Gabriel, one of the loveliest in Devon. Famous as a fishing hamlet, it lies on a creek of the Dart River. Dartmouth is only six miles south of the village (equidistant to Torquay). Desirable as a base is:

The **Gabriel Court Hotel** (tel. Stoke Gabriel 428206), is a manor house which until recently had been owned by one family since 1485. What must the ghosts have thought when Michael and Eryl Beacom acquired it and guests started to fill up the rooms, chasing away the cobwebs of the past? The gleaming white house is surrounded by gardens, hedges, and magnolia trees. A heated swimming pool has been added. B&B rates are from £15 ($29.25) per person. You might get a room in the new wing, containing eight bedrooms, all with private baths. The majority of the other comfortable rooms also have private baths or shower and toilet facilities, and the remaining few feature hot and cold running water only. Gabriel Court enjoys a reputation for its well-cooked English food, enhanced all the more by fruit and vegetables from the garden, as well as trout and salmon from the Dart and poultry from nearby farms. The hotel has a bar offering moderately priced wines. It remains open all year.

6. Dartmouth

At the mouth of the Dart River, this ancient seaport is the home of the Royal Naval College. Traditionally linked to England's maritime greatness, Dartmouth sent out the young midshipmen who ensured that Britannia ruled the waves. You can take a river steamer up the Dart to Totnes (book at the kiosk at the harbor). The view along the way is of Devon's most beautiful river.

Dartmouth's 15th-century castle was built during the reign of Edward IV. The town's most noted architectural feature is the Butterwalk, lying below Tudor houses. The Flemish influence in some of the houses is pronounced.

WHERE TO STAY: The **Royal Castle Hotel,** The Quay (tel. Dartmouth 2397), has been a coaching inn since 1639, having slept a host of visitors, including Sir Francis Drake, Queen Victoria, Charles II, and Edward VII (bedrooms named after them commemorate their visits). Horse-drawn carriages (as late as 1910) would dispatch their passengers in a carriageway, now enclosed to make the reception hall. Everywhere you look, you see reminders of the inn's rich past. The glassed-in courtyard, with its winding wooden staircase, has the original coaching horn and a set of 20 antique spring bells connected to the bedrooms. Many of the rooms opening off the covered courtyard and the rambling corridors have antiques, and the beds are soft.

A single without bath costs £18 ($35.10), rising to £25 ($48.75) with bath. A double without bath is £29 ($56.55), going up to £35 ($68.25) with bath. These tariffs include breakfast and VAT. The meals are excellent, in the best of the English tradition. A set lunch goes for £4.50 ($8.78), a set dinner for £6 ($11.70). A favorite place to settle in is the Galleon Bar, once two old kitchens, with double fireplaces and large hand-hewn beams said to have been rescued from Armada ships. There are two other pub-style bars, with settles, popular with the locals. Guests lounge on the second floor in a room with a bay window overlooking the harbor.

The **Victoria Hotel,** Duke Street (tel. Dartmouth 2572), is an unheralded little hotel, just 150 yards from the harbor. However, it is a sophisticated oasis, showing excellent taste in both the hotel and restaurant. The Victoria is a favorite retreat of the officers of the Naval College (at times, you feel that Gilbert and Sullivan wrote their operettas there). For B&B guests pay £26 ($50.70) in a twin, £13 ($25.35) in a single. A favorite place for before-dinner drinks is one of the Victorian slipper chairs in front of the lounge fireplace. The bedrooms are immaculate, tidy, and personal, the beds fresh and restful. Recommended on the à la carte menu are the chef's own pâté, T-bone steak, and locally caught fish. Try Ushers Best real ale or the local cider.

WHERE TO DINE: Taylors, The Quay (tel. Dartmouth 2748). Almost out of place in a peaceful south coast river town, Taylors's decor is straight out of Arabia, a huge black tent decorated with goatskins and brilliantly colored tassels. A camel comes at you through a mirage on one wall. Diana Taylor was an assistant master of horses for the film *Khartoum* and was in charge of the boats used in *A Man for All Seasons.* Her theatrical flair for the dramatic shows now that she has settled in rural England, and is reflected in the black chairs and tables as well as the dim lights.

Diana excels in buying fresh ingredients for the dishes, which feature plenty of fresh fish and seafood. One of the charming young women on the staff will lead you to the bar where an open fire burns, provide your apéritif, and help you to choose your meal. Dartmouth is the biggest crabbing port in

Europe, so the kitchen does some interesting crab dishes. Plaice is served stuffed with crabmeat, and filets of lemon sole are stuffed with mushrooms and fennel. Plaice is also served in a sauce of mustard-flavored mussels and brandy. These dishes range in price from £6 ($11.70) to £7 ($13.65). Other specialties in the same price range include steak au poivre, chicken with horseradish cream and walnuts, sweet-and-sour chicken with water chestnuts, liver with Dubonnet and fresh orange juice, and chicken curry with poppadoms, along with Bombay duck. Fresh vegetables are always featured, and rice or a salad accompanies all main dishes.

Appetizers include Taylor's pâté, moules (mussels) marinières in season, and grilled crabmeat with parmesan. These range from £1.10 ($2.15) to £2.30 ($4.49). Vegetarians are catered for with vegetable curry, risotto, and fresh vegetables simmered in cream, with nuts and herbs, all for just under £6 ($11.70) a dish. There's also a set three-course luncheon offered for £8 ($15.60). There are lovely views from the bow window down the River Dart to the sea.

The restaurant is open daily from noon to 2 p.m. and from 7 to 10:30 p.m. It is closed for a month from mid-January to mid-February.

The **Cherub**, Higher Street (tel. Dartmouth 2571), was built around 1380 and maintains much of its original decor, the uniqueness of the old timbered building an attraction to North Americans. The owners of this very attractive and friendly pub, Roy and Lois Thwaites, serve bars meals at lunch for from 60p ($1.17) to £1.65 ($3.22) each. In the evenings they offer a popular, although intimate, candlelight restaurant, seating just 20 persons. The average meal there costs about £10 ($19.50) with drinks. Every item is home-cooked, and the chef specializes in local crab and seafood dishes such as Dover sole and turbot in a Devonshire cream sauce. It's open seven days a week.

Bay Tree Restaurant, Fairfax Place (tel. Dartmouth 3167), is a typical English tea shop with cakes for sale in the windows. Inside it has wheelback chairs placed around dark mahogany tables. Cheerful local women hover about to serve. A Devon cream tea for two costs 90p ($1.76), and they have a mouthwatering selection of toasted scones and teacakes, along with sandwiches and toasted buns, all served from 3:15 to 5:30 p.m. Light meals include poached eggs, fried fish and chips, and beans on toast, served from noon to 2 p.m. and again from 6:30 p.m. when a dish will cost around £2 ($3.90). A set lunch is featured for £2.25 ($4.39), including such items as a homemade vegetable soup, roast chicken or beef, lamb curry, and steak-and-kidney pudding (the sort with the crust rather than the pie), followed by, say, lemon meringue or apple pie.

7. Plymouth

The historic seaport of Plymouth is more romantic in legend than in reality. But this was not always so. In World War II, the blitzed area of greater Plymouth lost at least 75,000 buildings. The heart of present-day Plymouth, including the municipal civic center on the Royal Parade, has been entirely rebuilt—the way that it was done the subject of much controversy.

For the old you must go to the Elizabethan section, known as the **Barbican,** and walk along the quay in the footsteps of Sir Francis Drake (once the mayor of Plymouth), and other Elizabethan seafarers, such as Sir John Hawkins, English naval commander and slave trader. It was from here in 1577 that Drake set sail on his round-the-world voyage. An even more famous sailing took place in 1620 when the Pilgrim Fathers left their final port in England for the New World. That fact is commemorated by a plaque at the harbor.

While playing bowls on Plymouth Hoe, Drake was told that the Spanish Armada had entered the Sound. In what must surely rank as one of the greatest displays of confidence of all time, he finished the game before taking off.

Apart from the Hoe, the most interesting part of the city is the area around the departure point of the Pilgrim Fathers in 1620, the already-mentioned Barbican. Here you'll find the Memorial Gateway to the Waterside whence, as tradition has it, they embarked on the *Mayflower*. Here, too, is the Blackfriars Refectory Room, dating from 1536, in Southside Street. The building is a national monument and one of Plymouth's oldest surviving buildings. It's now owned by Plymouth Gin Distillery, which welcomes visitors Monday to Friday to see the small exhibition of the history of the building. It was here that the Pilgrims finally met prior to setting sail for the New World.

The Barbican is a mass of narrow streets, old houses, and quayside shops selling antiques, brasswork, old prints, and books. Fishing boats still unload their catch at the wharves, and passenger-carrying ferry boats run short harbor cruises. A one-hour trip includes a visit to Drake's Island in the Sound, the dockyards, and naval vessels, plus a view of the Hoe from seaside. The cost is £2.60 ($5.07) per person. For other cruises, get in touch with **Millbrook Steamboat and Trading Co.**, Cremyll Quay (tel. Plymouth 822202).

The **Barbican Craft Centre**, White Lane, in the Barbican, has workshops and showrooms where you can watch and talk to the people engaged in crafts. You'll see such sights as a potter throwing a special design or a glass-blower fashioning a particular glass. Woodcarvers, leather workers, and weavers are also busy, and you can buy their products at reasonable prices, even commissioning your own design if you're lucky. Prices range from a few pounds for a hand-tooled belt to £20 ($39) for a hand-woven blanket rug.

WHERE TO STAY: Still a major base for the British navy, Plymouth makes for an interesting stopover. The pick of the lot in accommodations follows.

Duke of Cornwall, Millbay Road (tel. Plymouth 266256), is a Gothic-Victorian monument. Spared from World War II bombings, it looms like a château. Many of its bedrooms open onto balconies with views of the harbor. Considerable modernization has enlivened the interior. The bedrooms have been successfully upgraded, with compact, streamlined furnishings. A single with bath rents for £22 ($42.90) nightly, the cost rising to £34 ($66.30) in a double, these tariffs including an English breakfast and VAT. In the paneled Clan Bar, you can order good drinks in a setting of tartan floors and country-keg stools. The dining room is contemporary, with draped walls, a circular ceiling, and banquettes for cozy dining. A set lunch costs £5.50 ($10.73); a set dinner, £8 ($15.60). Latecomers are drawn into the Spider's Web in the cellar.

Holiday Inn, Armada Way (tel. Plymouth 662866), would probably have upset the departure plans of our forefathers. If they'd known how luxurious the new Holiday Inn would be, they might never have sailed. It's one of the most distinguished hotels in the West Country, set beside a park, overlooking the harbor and the Hoe. Rising like a midget skyscraper, it contains 222 good-size bedrooms with long double beds. Singles go from £29.50 ($57.53), doubles from £32.50 ($63.38), plus VAT. The rooms are fashionable, with air conditioning, wide picture windows, TV, radios, telephones, and private baths. Babysitting is available. A covered swimming pool is on the grounds, and there's a sauna and sun terrace as well, with garden tables set up for poolside refreshments. On the top floor is the Penthouse, with superb views across Plymouth Sound, and on the ground floor there's a specialty fish and meat restaurant, Mongers.

Blackfriars Restaurant and Hotel, 58 Southside St. (tel. Plymouth 668827), owned and run by David King, lies at the top of a paved courtyard and built on the site of an old malthouse which probably belonged to the Blackfriars Monastery. This is the only hotel within the historic Barbican area of the city. You can almost believe yourself back two or three centuries as you arrive at this small hotel.

Family run, it offers a bed and a continental breakfast for £13 ($25.35) in a single, from £22 ($42.90) in a double. All the smallish Swedish pine-paneled units have showers and toilets en suite, as well as coffee- and tea-making facilities (TV is also available on request).

The restaurant is open from 10:30 a.m. to 6 p.m. Monday to Friday and from 10:30 a.m. to 5 p.m. on Saturday. It's run by Sally, daughter of David King. It serves mainly whole foods, using local produce. I recently enjoyed the lettuce soup. There's a wide range of salads, at least 20 in all, and you can take your choice of any four with a sunflower oil dressing. Also offered are savory flans, hot dishes such as beef stew with a jacket potato, the queen of bread puddings, junket, an Elizabethan sorbet, and a large selection of homemade cakes, cookies, baps, rolls, and sandwiches which are available to take away if you don't want to eat in.

Mayflower Post House, The Hoe (tel. Plymouth 62828), was built in 1970 to celebrate the 350th anniversary of the Pilgrims' voyage. It's a white, nine-story building, standing high on a hill above Plymouth Hoe, commanding a view over the wide sweep of Plymouth Sound. The hotel has a resort character, with a heated outdoor swimming pool, three bars, a restaurant, and a buttery with a naval flag decor. Each of the 104 bedrooms is decorated as a bed-sitting room, with wall-wide windows, desks, armchairs, TV, telephone, and private bath, even facilities for making your own tea or coffee. Higher rates are in effect from May 25 till October, with singles costing approximately £28 ($54.60); doubles or twins, £40 ($78). Breakfast is extra, but VAT and service are included.

The **Anchorage,** Grand Parade, West Hoe (tel. Plymouth 668645), boasts a choice location, on the Grand Parade by the sea, overlooking Plymouth Sound. Owned by Mr. and Mrs. Willmott, the hotel is simply furnished in a modified modern style. Without flair or frills, it provides its own drama. The rooms have innerspring mattresses, hot and cold running water, and electric heaters. The rate for B&B is from £7.50 ($14.63) to £8.50 ($16.58) per night. An evening meal is available for about £3 ($5.85).

The **Imperial Hotel,** 3 Windsor Villas, Lockyer Street (tel. Plymouth 27311), is for anyone who prefers a small, friendly place, rather than a commercial hotel. The proprietors are great characters who enjoy making guests feel at home. Mr. Brooks was a rubber planter in Malaya, but retired here and he and Mrs. Brooks bought this attractive Victorian house. The hotel is tastefully furnished, indicating the experienced travel background of its owners. The rate is £10 ($19.50) in a single, rising to £22 ($42.90) in a double, including breakfast and service. VAT is extra. Some ground-floor rooms are offered to those who have difficulty with stairs. The cocktail bar is well stocked, and a four-course evening meal with coffee is £5 ($9.75).

WHERE TO EAT: If you're pressed for time and are only passing through, try at least to visit the Barbican—perhaps for a meal. My dining choice is **Green Lanterns,** 31 New St. in the Barbican (tel. Plymouth 660852). A 16th-century eating house, on a Tudor street, the Green Lanterns lies 200 yards from the Mayflower Steps—about as close to the Pilgrim Fathers as you can get.

Even to this day, it's a good restaurant. At lunchtime only, an extensive menu of reasonably priced dishes is served from £3.50 ($6.83).

At dinner all main course dishes are served with the fresh vegetables of the day. Some very unusual dishes are offered, including Barbican brill, pigeon in Pimlico (a whole baby pigeon, stuffed with herb-flavored forcemeat, wrapped in bacon, roasted and served with sauce and little pastry cases), pheasant Gitana, Widdicombe duck (an old Devonshire dish), and Harriet steak. Expect to spend from £10 ($19.50) for dinner. Old English mead is sold by the bottle here for £5.50 ($10.73). All the desserts are served with Devonshire cream. Family owned, the Green Lanterns is run by Sally M. Russell and Kenneth Pappin, who are fully aware that voyaging strangers like the Elizabethan atmosphere, traditional English fare, and personal service. The restaurant is near the municipally owned Elizabethan House. It's licensed until 11:30 p.m. and closed Sunday. Reservations for dinner are advisable.

Oysters Restaurant and Wine Bar, 48 Southside St. in the Barbican (tel. Plymouth 25656). A glass-fronted hallway leads to a rather pleasant wine bar, dimly lit yet welcoming with a crackling log fire and lights dancing off stone walls. Sit at the bar or in one of the snug alcoves to imbibe the house wine, tempered by a bar snack, such as soup, sandwiches, omelets, or the more enterprising chicken-and-mushroom pie, curry, mussels marinière, or half a dozen oysters. Prices range from 55p ($1.07) to £2.55 ($4.97) per portion. Try french bread toasted with a filling of onion, mushrooms, tomato, pepper, and mixed herbs at 70p ($1.37). A glass of wine is an extra 62p ($1.21).

Behind the bar, the Restaurant at the Back, managed by Richard Odgers, is open at the same hours as the bar. The cook features many fish dishes, such as crab, whitebait, clams, herring, oysters, prawns, mullet, sole, and skate, along with some meat and poultry specialties. The steak and pot-roast pigeon is to be eaten in the fingers with a rich bilberry sauce, rather tasty at £4.75 ($9.26) a portion. The average three-course meal costs £12 ($23.40).

The Barbican Wine Lodge, Quay Road in the Barbican (tel. Plymouth 660875), lies right on the quayside, across the water from the Customs House. The lodge is an old building with wooden floors softened by sawdust. Vintage wines are stacked in racks behind the bar under an oak-beamed ceiling. Parking is possible directly outside if you can find a space among the local cars, as this is a popular place, owned and run by Alastair Orr Ewing. It is open from 11 a.m. to 2:30 p.m. and from 6 to 10:30 p.m. Monday to Saturday (closed on Sunday).

This is an ideal place to stop during your exploration of Plymouth. There is a good ambience, plus a wide range of snacks to sate the appetite, including avocado vinaigrette, pâtés, hot soups, quiches, salads, and cold plates of meat—ham, beef, pork, or lamb. They also feature fresh crab, Dunster chicken, and Barbican vol-au-vents, as well as steaks. No main dish costs more than £3 ($5.85), and a meal will only set you back an average of £2.75 ($5.36). A glass of wine is 65p ($1.27), or perhaps a mulled wine in winter at 70p ($1.37).

The **Queen Anne Tea and Coffee House,** White Lane, in the Barbican (tel. Plymouth 262101), stands next to the previously recommended Barbican Craft Centre. It's a bow-fronted, white-painted tea shop where from 11 a.m. to 1 p.m. you can order fresh coffee, tea, savories, cakes, delicacies, and sandwiches which, as the menu says, titillate the tastebuds. White wood tables and chairs, along with white-paneled walls, make for a bright and cheerful place. It's ideal for a quick snack or a Devonshire cream tea, costing 90p ($1.76). You can also drop in, ordering just a large mug of coffee for 50p (98¢). Leslie and Joan Killick also offer B&B for £10.50 ($20.48) in a single, from £15 ($29.25) in a double. This is one of the very few places I've found in the heart of Plymouth, within a moment's walk of the spot where the Pilgrim Fathers set sail.

NORTH DEVON

"Lorna, Lorna . . . Lorna Doone, my lifelong darling," is the wailing cry you'll think of as you lie abed in your North Devon farmhouse. A wildness seems to enter the air at night on the edge of the moody Doone Valley. Much of the district is already known to those who have read Victorian novelist R. D. Blackmore's romance of the West Country, *Lorna Doone*.

The bay-studded coastline is mysterious. Pirates and smugglers used to find havens in crooked creeks and rocky coves. The ocean crashes against the rocks, and the meadows approach so close to the cliff's edge that you wonder why they don't go spilling into the sea, sheep and all. The heather-clad uplands of Exmoor, with its red deer, extend into North Devon from Somerset, a perfect setting for an English mystery thriller. Favorite bases are Clovelly and the twin resorts of Lynton and Lynmouth. Our first stopover is the best:

8. Clovelly

This most charming of all Devon villages is overpopular in summer. Still, it remains one of the main attractions of the West Country. Starting at a great height, the village cascades down the mountainside, with its narrow, cobblestoned High which makes travel by car impossible. (You park your car at the top and make the trip by foot.) Supplies are carried down by donkeys. Every yard of the way provides views of tiny cottages, with their terraces of flowers lining the main street. The village fleet is sheltered at the stone quay at the bottom.

To avoid the climb back up the slippery, cobblestoned incline, go to the rear of the Red Lion Inn and "queue up" for a Land Rover. In summer, the line is often long, but considering the alternative, it's worth the wait. Two Land Rovers make continuous round trips, costing 25p (49¢) per person.

WHERE TO STAY: A warning: It's hard to get a room in Clovelly. Advance reservations, with a deposit, are imperative during the peak summer months, although you can always telephone in advance and just possibly get a bed.

A tip: To avoid the flock of tourists, stay out of Clovelly from around 11 in the morning till teatime. After tea, settle in your room, and have dinner—perhaps spend the night in peace and contentment. The next morning after breakfast, you can walk around the village or go for a swim in the harbor, then visit the nearby villages during the middle of the day when the congestion sets in. Bideford, incidentally, is 11 miles away.

The **New Inn** (tel. Clovelly 303), about halfway down the High Street, is the village pub, a good meeting place at sundown. It offers the best lodgings in the village, in two buildings on opposite sides of the steep street (but only a 12-foot leap between their balconies). B&B ranges from £10 ($19.50) to £12 ($23.40) per person, inclusive. If you're only stopping over, then this little country inn is recommended for meals. A wide choice of moderately priced à la carte meals is offered in the oak-beamed dining room. The local fare, including genuine Devonshire cream, is featured whenever possible. Locally caught lobsters are prepared by a skilled chef exactly as you want them. The hotel is open most of the year. Motorists can park in the car park or in the garage at the top of the street. It is advisable to pack an overnight case, as the luggage has to be carried down (but is returned to the top by donkey).

Red Lion, The Pier (tel. Clovelly 237), may well have the best location in the village—at the bottom of the steep cobbled street, right on the stone seawall of the little harbor. Rising three stories, it is an unspoiled country inn, the life centering on an antique pub where the villagers gather to satisfy their thirsts over pints of ale. Most of the bedrooms look directly onto the sea. All have hot and cold running water and adequate furnishings. The cost is £9.50 ($18.53) per person nightly, including breakfast. Other meals are available in the seaview dining room. The manager can arrange for boating in the bay, and suggests that the Red Lion is not suitable for children under 7 years of age.

On the Outskirts

Foxdown Manor, (tel. Horns Cross 221), is only five miles from Bideford, six from Clovelly. In a setting of valleys and wooded hills just a mile from the sea, this splendid Victorian house is reached by a serpentine maze of narrow lanes. Its owners and proprietors, Bruce and Belinda Ross, have worked to restore the manor to its original state, with suitably modern conveniences added, of course. One bedroom has a four-poster bed dating from 1760. All of the rooms are equipped with private baths or showers.

The old stone stables adjoining the main house have been converted into fully equipped cottages with two to three bedrooms in each. After a good night's sleep, guests are free to wander the ten acres of fields and woodlands or to take advantage of the manor's many facilities, including a sauna, whirlpool bath, heated pool, miniature golf course, croquet lawn, solarium, indoor game room, and tennis court. Other activities, such as riding, golfing, and hunting are also available in the area.

The six-course dinner menu served in the Victorian candlelit dining room is a special treat prepared by Cordon Bleu chef Mrs. Ross. The vegetables are home-grown, and the dairy products are obtained from the manor's own Jersey cow. Rates per person for a bed, full English breakfast, and the six-course dinner are about £20 ($39) per day. Special weekly rates are available for the cottages or rooms as well.

Foxdown Manor makes a particularly good center for exploring North Devon—Clovelly, Exmoor, Dartmoor, the North Cornish coastline. If you don't feel like driving, then you can enjoy rambles and walks, as Devon has miles and miles of cool, shady primrose paths. All of a sudden you'll come across masses of wildflowers, and your spirit will soar.

Foxdown lies off the A39 road. Take the first left turn after Horns Cross village or the first right after Hoops Inn.

Beaconside, Monkleigh, near Bideford (tel. Bideford 77205), was built around 1860 and still retains its high ceilings and the large rooms typical of that era. Your hosts, Thea and Andrew Brand, have brought their own personal style and a dash of humor to the running of this place which they like to think of as typical of "visiting friends in the country." They offer only nine pleasantly furnished bedrooms, each with private bath or shower, plus color TV. The daily rate peaks at £30 ($58.50) per person, which includes an imaginatively prepared, four-course dinner often featuring beef Wellington and baked sea bass with fresh fennel. VAT and service are included. The place is secluded. When you're not using the swimming pool, you might select a volume from the massive collection of books, or perhaps you'll do no more than contemplate the view from the drawing room.

READER'S HOTEL SELECTION AT BIDEFORD: "The **Royal Hotel** (tel. Bideford 2005) was a pleasant surprise. We found the staff very helpful, and the meals excellent with large portions. Kingsley wrote *Westward Ho!* here, and the staff will gladly show you the Kingsley Room with many antiques and a beautiful Italian ceiling. A bathless single costs £13 ($25.35), increasing to £16 ($31.20) with bath. A double room without bath goes for £21 ($40.95), rising to £24 ($46.80) with bath. These tariffs include breakfast. A four-course dinner costs £6.75 ($13.16)" (Mrs. Robert Davison, Delta, B.C., Canada).

9. Lynton-Lynmouth

The north coast of Devon is set off most dramatically in Lynton, a village some 500 feet high. It is a good center for exploring the Doone Valley and that part of Exmoor that spills into the shire from neighboring Somerset. The Valley of Rocks, west of Lynton, offers the most spectacular scenery.

The town is joined by a cliff railway to its sister, Lynmouth, about 500 feet lower. The rivers of East and West Lyn meet in Lynmouth, a popular resort with the English. For a panoramic view of the rugged coastline, you can walk on a path halfway between the two towns that runs along the cliff. From Lynton, or rather from Hollerday Hill, you can look out onto Lynmouth Bay, Countisbury Foreland, and Woody Bays in the west.

FOOD AND LODGING: The **Tors Hotel** (tel. Lynton 3236), set high on a cliff, opens onto a view of the coastline and the bay of Lynmouth. It was built in the fashion of a Swiss château, with more than 40 gables, Tyrolean balconies jutting out to capture the sun (or the moon), black-and-white timbered wings, and some 30 chimneys. Surrounding the hotel are a terrace and a heated swimming pool. The interior has been modernized, and much attention has been paid to the comfortable bedrooms. A single without bath is £14 ($27.30), rising to £18 ($35.10) with bath. A bathless double costs £28 ($54.60), going up to £35 ($68.25) with bath, including breakfast and VAT. A three-course luncheon costs £3.50 ($6.83), and a set dinner is offered for £6.35 ($12.38). The hotel is closed from November to March.

The **Rising Sun Hotel** (tel. Lynton 3223) is perhaps one of the most colorful thatched inns in England—especially as it's right at the end of the quay at the mouth of the Lyn River. Not only is the harbor life spread before you, but you can bask in the wonder and warmth of an inn in business for more than 600 years. In bedroom after bedroom, with crazy levels and sloping ceilings, you'll have views of the water, the changing tides, and bobbing boats. The place is owned by hoteliers Mr. Wade and Mr. Jeune. The inn is closed in January; otherwise, they make sure that either one or the other of them is there to supervise things. They charge from £11.50 ($22.43) per person for an overnight stay, including an English breakfast, service, and VAT. Even if you're not staying over, you may want to sample the English cuisine: dinners from £7 ($13.65). It's a delight dining at the Rising Sun, as everything is 101% British in the dining room, with its deeply set window and fireplace. See the original 14th-century fireplace in the bar.

Rock House, Lynmouth (tel. Lynton 3508), stands in the Manor Grounds between the Lyn River and the shore overlooking the Bristol Channel as well as Lynmouth Harbour. Run by Paddy and Paul Green, it is reached by a bridge and occupies one of the most dramatic positions in the village. The bedrooms, each with hot and cold running water and much homelike comfort, rent for £10 ($19.50) per person nightly, including breakfast, VAT, and service. Meals, served in a Regency dining room with its original ceiling moldings, include fresh vegetables and homemade desserts such as puddings. The fare is typically English. Full central heating has been installed, and if guests visit in the spring and autumn, rates are reduced. Children under 12 sharing their parents' room also get a reduction of 10%. The half-board tariff is from £16 ($31.20) per person daily. Dinner is also served to nonresidents, costing from £7 ($13.65); however, you should telephone for a reservation. Outside is a large, sheltered garden with parking available.

Ye Olde Cottage (Spinning Wheel Restaurant) (tel. Lynton 3297) is a miniature, quayside inn, centered in this tiny resort with an unspoiled view of the harbor. Here you can get inexpensive teas and meals. For five generations, the Wakeham family has been operating the inn. Chef Peter Wakeham and his wife Heather are always to be found at the place—either in the kitchen or in the dining room looking after their guests. Peter's mother and father are called in when things get hectic. It's a favored spot for a thoroughly English Devonshire cream tea with all the trimmings. At mealtime you can order a two- or three-course meal based on such traditional English "fayre" as roast beef or West Country chicken and homemade pies and tarts. From the à la carte menu you can select such delights as rainbow trout, Lyn salmon, and a full range of steaks. Expect to pay from £5 ($9.75) to £9 ($17.55) for an à la carte dinner. Peter has also introduced a line of dishes cooked in wine and cider, to his own recipes. The restaurant is open daily from 10:30 a.m. to 9:30 p.m. from March to November.

READERS' HOTEL SELECTION: "The **Bonnicott Hotel,** on Watersmeet Road (tel. Lynton 3346), is the former vicarage of Lynmouth's Anglican church. Resting slightly back and above the sea, the Bonnicott has a beautiful dining room with large picture windows providing a wonderful view of the water. Ten cozy rooms have an equally good sea view, and the downstairs bar, with an open-hearth fire, is well stocked. The owners, Pam and George, are a husband and wife who personally execute every detail of the running of the hotel. George gives most attentive service to his guests at breakfast, dinner, and at night when he tends the bar until whatever time his guests choose to retire. Pam, who prepares all the food for breakfast and dinner, is truly a gourmet cook. Each of the five four-course dinners we were served during our stay was English cuisine at its finest, and much of it was local to Devon. From the thick clotted cream which graced the fresh homemade berry pies to the stuffed brook trout pulled from the neighboring streams, each course was different and delicious on each of our five nights there. The service did not stop with fine food and spirits, however. Pam and George were available for our every need, providing invaluable information about the best hikes, best local shopping, and best of all, local color and history, including, of course, the real-life locations of the scenes from the novel *Lorna Doone.* The cost is £9.50 ($18.53) per person for B&B, £13 ($25.35) per person for half board" (Tom and Laura Groce, Austin, Texas).

10. Combe Martin

Noted for its strawberry fields and mild climate, Combe Martin is surrounded by magnificent scenery: high, rugged cliffs, wild moors, and rocky shorelines. Among the rocks are some of Britain's favorite beaches, and local boatmen can take you to spots, impossible to reach on foot, where the scenery is breathtaking. The village is small, with the High Street as its shopping district. An old English church built in the Perpendicular style of architecture is the main historical structure in the town. Just six miles from Ilfracombe, Combe Martin is a good base for excursions into Exmoor.

WHERE TO STAY: **Saffron House,** King Street (tel. Combe Martin 3521), is an old farmhouse successfully adapted into a popular small hotel. Just a short walk from the village harbor, the house is set back from the road where it overlooks the village and surrounding countryside. The owners, Mr. and Mrs. Chantler, are sincerely interested in your comfort, and from the moment of your friendly reception, you know you're going to enjoy your stay. The guest rooms are clean and comfortable, with the benefit of full central heating. There are also two lounges, one with color TV, the other with a well-stocked bar. B&B rates are about £8 ($15.60) per person per night, including VAT. Guests have use of a heated swimming pool, and the property has been recently extended to improve dining room and lounge facilities. The Chantlers are only too happy to point out local areas of interest, and, if they aren't too busy, they may just accompany you on a walk through the cliff paths.

CORNWALL

The ancient Duchy of Cornwall is the extreme southwestern part of England, often called "the toe." But Cornwall is one toe that's always wanted to dance away from the foot. Although a peninsula, it is a virtual island—if not geographically, then spiritually. Encircled by coastline, it abounds with rugged cliffs, hidden bays, fishing villages, sandy beaches, and sheltered coves where smuggling was once practiced with consummate skill. Many of the little seaports with their hillside-clinging cottages resemble towns along the Mediterranean, although Cornwall retains its own distinctive flavor.

The true Cornish people are generally darker and shorter than the English. Their Celtic origin still lives on in superstition, folklore, and fairy tales. King Arthur, of course, is the most vital legend of all. When Cornish men speak of King Arthur and his Knights of the Round Table, they're not just handing out a line to tourists. To them, Arthur and his knights really existed, romping around Tintagel Castle, now in ruins—Norman ruins, that is—lying 300 feet above the sea, 19 miles from Bude.

The ancient land had its own language up until about 250 years ago, and some of the old words ("pol" for pool, "tre" for house) still survive. The Cornish dialect is more easily understood by the Welsh than by those who speak the Queen's English.

The Cornish men, like the Welsh, are great miners (tin and copper), and they're fond of the tall tale. Sometimes it's difficult to tell when they're serious. One resident, for example, told me that he and his wife had been walking in the woods at twilight, but had lost their way. He claimed that the former owner of the estate (in Victoria's day) appeared suddenly in a dog-carriage and guided them back to where they'd taken the wrong turn. If this really had happened, I wouldn't be surprised—at least not in Cornwall.

The English come here for their holidays in the sun. But some of the places where everybody goes, I'd recommend that you avoid. For example, there's little point in going to Land's End, the westernmost tip of England, a narrowing hunk of bleakness and crude cottages set up to peddle ice cream and souvenirs.

In lieu of such a trip, I'd suggest berthing at one of the smaller fishing villages, such as East and West Looe, Polperro, Mousehole, or Portloe—where you'll experience the true charm of the duchy. Many of the villages, such as St. Ives, have now become artists' colonies. In some of the pubs and restaurants frequented by painters, a camaraderie prevails, especially in the nontourist months. Recently, for instance, at one of the artists' hangouts (bleached wooden tables, handmade stools), three young men who had finished dining brought out guitars and spontaneously launched into folk songs for the rest of the evening. Detecting the accent of some visiting Americans, they sang (with appallingly perfect accents) several country music favorites, although it was their repertoire from Ireland and Wales that cast the greater spell.

Except for St. Ives and Port Isaac, most of my recommendations lie on the southern coast, the so-called Cornish Riviera, which strikes many foreign visitors as being the most intriguing. However, the north coast has its own peculiar charm.

A SIDE TRIP TO LIZARD: The most southerly point of England is the Lizard, an unremarkable spot with jagged rocks reaching out into the sea where cormorants and gulls fish.

Right on the point, beneath the lighthouse, is the workshop of a man who must surely be one of the most perfect one-man cottage industries in the country. Mr. Casley runs **Lizard Point Serpentine Works** in one of the small shacks by the car park. There he turns, polishes, and fashions into pots, vases, ashtrays, and dishes, the serpentine stone found only in this part of the country. The veins in the stone can be green, gray, or sometimes red. A small vase will cost about £4 ($7.80); a larger one, £6 ($11.70).

Ornamental barometers and clocks are a lot more, but these are absolutely genuine souvenirs made by a man who is entirely at peace with himself and the country he lives in. The family, his son, and his brother assist with the quarrying of the stone which comes from under Coonhilly Down close by, the site of the country's largest radio receiving and space-tracking station. Mr. Casley's son, another blue-eyed Cornishman, is fast learning the trade so there is every hope that still in 50 years there will be someone whistling happily in the tiny workshop on the tip of the Lizard.

POLDARK MINING CO. LTD.: Wendron Forge (tel. Helston 3173), stands three miles north of Helston on the B3297 road. As you have driven around Cornwall, the old workings of the tin mines will have been evident everywhere. Here you have the chance of visiting a mine and walking through the old workings which extend for several miles beneath the surface. They have just discovered yet another cavern, and the tour of the mine will soon take longer than the present three-quarters of an hour. Above ground is a museum of mining artifacts, mining equipment, steam engines, drills, and a history of mining. There is a souvenir shop and another selling good-quality local products, a snackbar, and a children's play area if they don't want to see the exhibits. Admission is £1.50 ($2.93) for adults, 80p ($1.56) for children. The mines are open seven days a week from 10 a.m. to 6 p.m.

TALL TREES RIDING CENTRE: At Davidstow, near Camelford (tel. Otterham Station 249), Mrs. Margaret Harrison, with her two daughters and various other assistants and working pupils, runs stables of 23 horses and ponies. They offer weekly courses when days are spent on long rides over majestic Bodmin Moor, through forests, and along bridle paths and country lanes. Accommodation, including breakfast and supper, is £50 ($97.50) per week for adults, £42 ($81.90) for children, plus VAT. If you cannot spare the time for a week, a day's riding, including lunch, is £12 ($23.40).

11. Looe

After your visit to Plymouth, about 15 miles away, you can either take the Tamar Suspension Bridge to Cornwall, or else cross by ferry from Plymouth. You'll soon arrive in the ancient twin towns of East and West Looe, connected by a seven-arched stone bridge which spans the river. In the jaws of shrub-dotted cliffs, the fishing villages present a stark contrast to Plymouth. Houses scale the hills, stacked one on top of the other in terrace fashion.

In both fishing villages you can find good accommodations and interesting people. Fishing and sailing are two of the major sports, and the sandy coves, as well as East Looe Beach, make choice spots for seabathing. Beyond the towns are cliff paths and downs worth a ramble. In these villages you'll find varied lifestyles: the traditional Cornish fishermen landing pilchard; the sophisticates enjoying the unspoiled atmosphere; summer visitors down for a week or so; and the artists and artisans who live and work here.

Looe is noted for its shark-angling, but you may prefer simply walking the narrow, crooked medieval streets of East Looe, with its old harbor and 17th-century guildhall.

WHERE TO STAY: Space and prices are at a premium in July and August. Some hotels are so heavily booked that they can demand Saturday-to-Saturday clients only. I have not recommended such establishments, as I feel that their managers aren't interested in patronage by international visitors.

Hannafore Point Hotel, West Looe (tel. Looe 3273), is a rambling, many-gabled structure commanding an advantageous view of the harbor, overlooking miles of Cornish coastline and one of the most beautiful bays in Cornwall. In addition to the older bay-windowed chambers, newer sections of the hotel have been built with walls of glass for viewing the harbor and St. George's Island. The entrance opens onto several levels of comfortable lounges and bars, with cantilevered stairs, balconies, and birch paneling. The modern bedrooms all include either private baths or showers, and most of the front rooms have their own balconies. B&B rates vary depending on the view, location of the room, and the time of year. From May to October, a single or double room rents for about £36 ($70.20). The panoramic view adds to the pleasure of dining in the St. George's Restaurant, where fresh, first-class ingredients are used in the fine Cornish and French cuisine.

Hannafore Point is in the main center for shark and deep-sea fishing, and is ideal for exploring either Cornwall or parts of Devon.

The **Boscarn Hotel,** The Seafront.(tel. Looe 2923). This hotel has 22 bedrooms and sits right on the beach of East Looe, the safest bathing beach in Cornwall. Built more than half a century ago, it is a beautiful old building that provides modern facilities. There are two nicely decorated large bars, one available as a function room and providing entertainment and disco action. There is a cozy residents' bar as well. A large family room provides plenty of free games for children of all ages, and swings and slides are found in the garden overlooking the beach. An excellent English breakfast is served, as is lunch, although dinners aren't offered. Prices, inclusive of VAT, are from £9.50 ($18.53) per person or £55 ($107.25) for a week, breakfast included. Families are welcome. The Boscarn is a comfortable and well-recommended hotel for a relaxed holiday.

Klymiarven Hotel, Barbican Hill, in East Looe (tel. Looe 2333), is a 180-year-old manor house, standing in its own wooded and terraced gardens above the harbor. The cellars are even older, and it is believed that smugglers made use of their dank, underground passages. The hotel is small, containing only eight bedrooms in the older part of the house plus six modern accommodations, each with a private bath and balcony. The rooms are comfortable and well appointed, costing from £12 ($23.40) to £15 ($29.25) per person for a bathless double or single, from £14 ($27.30) to £20 ($39) for a double with shower or bath. Prices include VAT and a full English breakfast. The immaculately kept house is owned by its resident proprietors Bruce and Daphne Henderson, who are known locally for their good food, served in a Regency dining room. Hot and cold bar lunches are available, served around the attractive swimming pool, weather permitting. A set dinner costs £8 ($15.60), but you get better value if you ask for half-board terms, when the inclusive dinner costs approximately £7 ($13.65). Guests gather in the hotel's attractively furnished lounge with French windows opening onto the garden. In addition, the hotel has a sun lounge bar and terrace, plus a second bar in the cellar.

The **Smugglers House,** Middle Market, near the old Guildhall (tel. Looe 2397), built in the 15th and 17th centuries, was once the headquarters of smugglers. The hotel is tucked away right in the center of the village, a few minutes' walk from the quay, the seafront, and the shops. The hotel has an original Cornish granite fireplace, and the beams in the restaurant and bar are believed to be from the ships of the Spanish Armada. There is reputed to be a tunnel in the restaurant which was used by the ancient smugglers, but attempts to find the entrance have been unsuccessful. Rooms without bath rent for £11 ($21.45) per person nightly, increasing to £13.50 ($26.33) per person with private bath, plus VAT. The breakfasts are super, with bacon, eggs, sausage, and tomato, all the trimmings. Your room will be immaculate, and the beds will be fresh and soft. There is also a Dungeon Restaurant (open to both residents and nonresidents), an authentic smugglers' haunt, known for its fresh English steaks and a large choice of food and wine.

The **Fisherman's Arms,** Higher Market Street (tel. Looe 2215), the main street in East Looe, is housed in a building dating from 1611. It is about 70 yards from the beach. Mr. and Mrs. Cobbing provide an array of sandwiches and locally caught crabs and shellfish. The average price for a "cutting" is from 85p ($1.66) to £1.20 ($2.34). The decor is provided by antique guns, spears, brass, and copper. B&B is available from £7 ($13.65) nightly. Only double rooms are offered.

If you wish, you can strike out from Looe on the cliff walk, a distance of 4½ miles, to Polperro. The less adventurous will drive.

WHERE TO STAY AND EAT OUTSIDE LOOE: Just three miles north of East Looe on Route B3254 is the quiet country village of **Duloe,** a perfect spot for a drowsy holiday or an ideal center from which to explore Cornwall and parts of Devon. Nearby is the complete seclusion of the Bodmin Moor, while the cliffs and fishing villages of the south coast are just a short drive away. Half a mile south of the village on the road to Looe is the **Duloe Manor Hotel,** Duloe, near Liskeard (tel. Looe 2795), a lovely old Cornish house dating from around 1700. The owners, Mr. and Mrs. Hayter, like to refer to the hotel as having a "visiting friends in the country" kind of atmosphere. Indeed, the house is rich in character and warmth, from the tastefully decorated bedrooms and sitting rooms to the Victorian lounge with its carved mahogany bar and open fireplace. Guests are welcome to wander the nine acres of grounds surrounding the hotel or stroll through the 250-year-old lime tree avenue. A tennis court and heated swimming pool round out the list of amenities.

The dining room, once the kitchen of the old house, retains the cozy character of the former room with the old meat hooks and the open-hearth fireplace. Here five-course table d'hôte dinners are served daily, all prepared almost entirely from local produce. Rates at the Duloe Manor for dinner, bed, and breakfast range from £23 ($44.85) per person for rooms without private bath to £25 ($48.75) for rooms with bath. Prices include service charges and VAT.

Shutta, Stoke Climsland, near Callington (tel. Stoke Climsland 389), is a guest house par excellence. Peter and Joan Davis welcome guests to their lovely

16th-century home where breakfast is served in the ancient beamed cider house of the old structure. They only have two rooms, one with two beds, the other a large double bed. Both have private bathrooms and television. They charge £8 ($15.60) per person for bed and a massive breakfast. To get there, drive on the A388 from Callington toward Bodmin Moor and, at the Swingle Tree, bear right toward Stoke Climsland. Shutta is on the right.

12. Polperro

This ancient fishing village is reached by a steep descent from the top of a hill. Motorists in summer are forbidden to take their cars down unless they are booked in a hotel. Why? Because otherwise they'd create too much of a traffic bottleneck in July and August. At one time, it was estimated that nearly every man, woman, and child in the village spent time salting down pilchards for the winter, or smuggling. Today, tourists have replaced the contraband.

You'd have to search every cove and bay in Cornwall to turn up with a village as handsome as Polperro, which looks almost as if it had been removed intact from the 17th century. The village is tucked in between some cliffs. Its houses—really no more than fishermen's cottages—are bathed in pastel-wash. A small river, actually a stream called the Pol, cuts its way through Polperro. The heart of the village is its much photographed, much painted fishing harbor, where the pilchard boats, loaded to the gunnels, used to dock.

There's a large car park, the price based according to the length of your stay. For those unable to walk, a horse-drawn bus carries visitors to the town center for 40p (78¢).

WHERE TO STAY: Noughts and Crosses Hotel (tel. Polperro 72239). One side of this 16th-century pub-hotel faces a narrow street, and the other a five-foot-wide "river" which goes through the center of the village. The Noughts and Crosses charges £10 ($19.50) per person nightly for B&B. Children are not accepted, and booking in season must be for at least three nights. Its name came from the bookkeeping habits of a baker, its one-time owner. She made a small "o" whenever she sold a small loaf of bread and a large "O" when she sold a large loaf. When the loaves were paid for, she would cross them off with an "X." The hotel has windows opening by the Pol. You may remember the crooked stairway, the time-aged beams. The quite-good bedrooms are pleasingly furnished, with hot and cold running water and beds with inner-spring mattresses. Basket meals, snacks, and chilled beer are served in the two well-equipped bars. Steaks, scampi in a basket, and fried chicken are served with fried potatoes. There is a dining room upstairs in which residents of the hotel can eat their bar snacks. Expect to spend from £5 ($9.75) for a complete meal. No accommodations are offered from November through January.

WHERE TO EAT: The Captain's Cabin, Lansallos Street (tel. Polperro 72292), is owned by Victor S. Moore, his wife Hazel, and their son Anthony. They are pleased when Americans come by. While they don't have bedrooms for overnight guests, they have been known to give travelers tips about where to find a room. You'll surely want to dine with the Moores, among the antique furniture in their low-beamed dining room. The cuisine is very comprehensive, and Mr. Moore and his son enjoy a fine reputation for their fish dishes, from among which you may order crab mornay, trout à la Bretonne, grilled sole, plus many other choices. The Moores have a table d'hôte lunch at £7 ($13.65), and a choice of six snack lunches, which include a glass of beer, tea, or coffee. For dinner there is also a four-course table d'hôte menu for £9 ($17.55), as well as a full à la carte menu costing from £12 ($13.40), excluding wine.

The **Pengelly,** near the harbor, is where locals and visitors go for their evening pints of beer and social activity; it is a large L-shaped room with a fireplace that burns brightly at night. Why don't you sit in the window seat and listen to the talk of the villagers? That isn't really as rude as it sounds—since you probably won't be able to understand a word of their thick Cornish dialect. You may like the absence of quaint bits of decor in this honest pub, the center of life in Polperro.

WHERE TO STAY AND EAT ON THE OUTSKIRTS:

If you find the busy activity of the two little harbors of Looe and Polperro too much for you, then you can live in far greater style at two of England's outstanding inns, just outside. **Pelynt,** about three miles north of Polperro, is a small, sleepy village; and **Lanreath,** lying off the road to West Looe, is another peaceful, pleasant community.

The **Jubilee Inn,** Pelynt (tel. Lanreath 20312), was restored as part of a scheme to honor Queen Victoria's Jubilee, by using only the best handmade Victorian furnishings, even in the bedrooms. Today, the rate for a handsomely decorated room and big English breakfast is £14 ($27.30) in a single without bath, £23 ($44.85) in a double. A room with bath is £2.50 ($4.88) per person extra. These tariffs include breakfast, VAT, and service. The food is good, with the vegetables coming fresh from the inn's own garden. A set three-course lunch goes for £6.50 ($12.68), increasing to £7 ($13.65) for dinner. The inn is a comment on, rather than monument to the past. The lounge has a hooded fireplace, with a raised hearth, Windsor armchairs, antique porcelain, and copper bowls filled with flowers cut from the garden behind the building. The dining room is elegantly Victorian, with mahogany chairs and tables. The only sound you hear is the rustling of the starched aprons of the maids. A fairly sophisticated crowd of people come here to eat and drink at the public bar. A circular, glass-enclosed staircase takes you to the bedrooms. Fitting onto the outside, the winding stairway has been built to serve as a combined tower and hothouse. The stone steps are covered with carpeting, and vines and plants grow happily in the sunlight streaming in through the glass walls.

The **Punch Bowl Inn,** at Lanreath (tel. Lanreath 20218), has had a checkered past, serving in turn as a courthouse, coaching inn, and rendezvous for smugglers. Now its old fireplaces and high-backed settles, and its bedrooms with their four-posters, provide hospitality to travelers from abroad, as well as to the discriminating English. For stays of only one night, the B&B rate in high season, June through September, is £16 ($31.20) per person. A much better course is to take the partial-board rate of £21 ($40.95) per person, inclusive. Even if you're only stopping over, you may want to sample the fare or drinks in one of the kitchens (really bars, among the few "kitchens" licensed in Britain as "bars"). In the Stable Restaurant, with its Tudor beams and fireplace, you'll be served lunches from the grill menu, dinner from £7.50 ($14.63). There is a modern lounge, TV room, air-conditioned cocktail bar, and an additional bedroom wing. Many rooms have their own private bathrooms. Advance bookings of less than three nights are not accepted during the high season.

13. Fowey

Called the Dartmouth of Cornwall, Fowey is a town of historical interest (one of the most ancient seaports in the West Country). Once the Fowey

Gallants sailed the seas and were considered invincible when raiding French coastal towns. However, occasional retaliation was inevitable. At the time of the Armada, Fowey sent more ships than London. With its narrow streets and whitewashed houses, it has remained unspoiled over the years, enjoying a sheltered position on a deep-water channel. Its creeks and estuary attract sailors and fishermen. If you climb to St. Catherine's Point, you'll be rewarded with a view of the harbor. Sandy beaches and coves are there to explore as well (there's also an 18-hole golf course within easy reach of Carlyon Bay).

WHERE TO STAY: Riverside, Passage Street (tel. Fowey 2275), is the all-purpose ferry-landing hotel of Fowey. Directly on the water, the hotel is at the little car-ferry station where regular crossings leave for Bodinnick. Paintings by Mrs. Featherstone, wife of the owner, decorate the walls of the hotel, and glass and china ornaments, as well as potted plants, make the place extremely warm and inviting. The 14 bedrooms are handsomely decorated in a bright, cozy, comfortable manner. Six have private bath or shower, although all have hot and cold running water..From the rooms there are views of the river, where a variety of scenery is created by the passing river craft and ferries. Rates are based on the time of the year and the view. Bed and a full English breakfast costs from £13 ($25.35) to £16 ($31.20) per person daily, plus VAT and service. Half board ranges from £20 ($39) to £24 ($46.80) per person, the latter including private bath. The chef specializes in hot and cold salmon and lobster dishes; the produce bought locally is fresh. The hotel also offers an excellent wine list with a comprehensive choice of both English and continental wines. The menu is changed daily to ensure that variety is a key factor. If you're visiting just for dinner, the set meal goes for about £9 ($17.55).

14. Truro

This ancient town on the Truro River is the only cathedral city in Cornwall. As such, it is the ecclesiastical center of Cornwall. The cathedral church of St. Mary was begun in 1880 in the Early English style (the spires are in the Norman Gothic design). The town is within 8 to 20 miles of the Cornish beaches. It can be used as a base to explore the countryside, which ranges from bleak Bodmin Moor to fertile farmland and the Winter Roseland of the Falmouth Estuary.

WHERE TO STAY: Pencowl, 12 Ferris Town (tel. Truro 4946), is a centrally positioned corner house owned by the Endacotts, who take the business of entertaining overseas guests very seriously. They have no public rooms, but each room has its own color TV, table and chairs, refrigerator, toaster, and kettle, as well as cutlery and crockery—in addition to the normal bedroom furniture. There are four kitchens for the use of guests who wish to prepare their own meals, and they provide a continental breakfast in the rooms for those who prefer it. All linen is provided, and the units are serviced daily except Sunday. Charges range from £5.50 ($10.73) to £7 ($13.65) per person nightly, dropping by stages to £26 ($50.70) to £37 ($72.15) per person weekly. The rate depends on the time of year, the length of the stay, and is for the accommodation only. The Endacotts also have a two-bedroom, fully self-contained apartment available for a rental on a weekly basis, costing from £70 ($136.50). to £110 ($214.50) per week, depending on the time of year. Free golf at the Truro Golf Club is available to all guests. Mrs. Endacott is a member of the local

Family History Society, and will be happy to direct those seeking out their Cornish Family history to the nearby County Record Office and the museum.

15. Portloe

If you really want to get away from it all and go to that hidden-away Cornish fishing village, then Portloe is for you. On the slope of a hill, opening onto Veryan Bay, it is reached by a road suitable for cars—but chances are you may get sidetracked and spend the rest of the afternoon on byways, opening and closing gates to keep the cattle from straying.

Portloe is an ideal stopover on the south Cornish coast if you're traveling in July and August, when the popular tourist centers, such as Looe and St. Ives, are overrun with sightseers.

WHERE TO STAY: The **Lugger,** Portloe (tel. Veryan 322), is a prestigious inn, yet the narrow lane that leads the way to the establishment was obviously created by a goat. You'll find the inn fresh, sparkling clean—a good spot at the top of the harbor slip, with a bay and boats at hand. The whole picture—water dashing and pounding the nearby rocks, the sunsets, the beach, the stone walls, the crazy roofs of the houses of the fishermen—all requires that you take dozens of rolls of film with you . . . or none at all. The 17th-century establishment is managed by the Powell family. They'll put you up for from £20 ($39) to £25 ($48.75) per person per night for bed, an English breakfast, and a four-course dinner. The charge for an excellent bar lunch will average around £4 ($7.80). All prices are inclusive of tax. The inn, open late February to early November, is believed to have been a smugglers' hideaway, on the coast between St. Austell and St. Mawes. Guests at the Lugger can also dine at the Idle Rocks Hotel at St. Mawes, just eight miles away, on a reciprocal arrangement.

The **Rising Sun** (tel. St. Mawes 270233) is a colorful inn on the seafront—made of a row of white fishermen's cottages, with a slate roof, and a flagstone terrace out front. Inside, every square inch oozes with tasteful charm. The locals gather in the pub, with its Windsor chairs grouped around the fireplace. The dining room has lush gold walls with paintings by Michael Oelman in the form of two poems, *Kubla Khan* and *Jacob's Ladder*. English gentility reigns here. The proprietor, Mrs. Campbell Marshall, sets the gracious pace, and is known for her cuisine. You can stay here for anywhere from £26 ($50.70) to £30 ($58.50) per person in rooms with bath, including an English breakfast, service, and VAT. Lunch and dinner are both à la carte, and you can expect to pay from £12 ($23.40), with wine extra. The dining room has become very popular, with its changing menu of imaginative dishes using local produce whenever possible. Lunch is from 1 to 1:45 p.m., dinner from 7:30 to 8:45 p.m. Closed November and December.

16. St. Mawes

Overlooking the mouth of the Fal River, St. Mawes is often compared to a port on the Riviera. Because it's sheltered from northern winds, subtropical plants grow here. From the town quay, you can take a boat to Frenchman's Creek, Helford River, and other places. St. Mawes is noted for its sailing, boating, fishing, and yachting. Half a dozen sandy coves lie within 15 minutes by car from the port. The town, built on the Roseland Peninsula, makes for interesting walks, with its color-washed cottages and sheltered harbor. On Castle Point, Henry VIII ordered the construction of St. Mawes Castle. Falmouth, across the water, is only two miles away.

WHERE TO STAY: Tresanton (tel. St. Mawes 270544), is a member of the Relais de Campagne. It is really three buildings, the oldest one dating from the 18th century. One is on the roadside, another halfway up, and the third—the main part of the hotel—on top of the hill and away from the traffic noise. In the middle is an attractive cocktail lounge, with a veranda overlooking the sea. The upper level also has spacious veranda terraces—so there are a lot of places to sit outside among the flowers, looking across the bay. The bedrooms are nice and bright, furnished for the most part in the French country-house manner. In high season, May through October, singles range from £28 ($54.60) to £34 ($66.30), doubles or twins from £31 ($60.45) to £44 ($85.80) per person. The latter have private baths en suite. All the accommodations face the sea. Service and VAT are extra. The lounge has an open fireplace and comfortable chairs. The dining room, also overlooking the sea, has attractive murals and a verdant decor that is designed to carry the eye from the house to the sun terraces, the subtropical gardens, and the sea beyond. The menu is limited but good, including such dishes as caneton (duckling) à l'orange and grilled Dover sole.

The **Idle Rocks** (tel. St. Mawes 270771) proudly stands on a terrace above St. Mawes Harbor, commanding views of the open sea and the mouth of the River Fal. The building is a bit of old Cornwall, with its mansard roof and white stucco walls. Diners at the excellent restaurant can view the sea from any table as they enjoy a blend of English and continental cuisine. The cocktail bar opens onto the 145-foot promenade where you may sip an apéritif while you take in the warm and sparkling scene.

The hotel has a total of 22 guest rooms, 15 in the main building and the remaining 7 in the annex, 50 yards away. All have private baths, and both buildings offer the comfort of central heating. Daily rates per person range from £20 ($39) for a double or single in the annex to £26 ($50.70) for a double or single in the main building overlooking the sea. Rates include bed, full English breakfast, morning and afternoon teas, and the table d'hôte dinner, as well as tax. For an evening out at no extra cost, guests at the Idle Rocks can dine at the Lugger Hotel at Portloe, just eight miles away, on a reciprocal agreement.

Braganza, Grove Hill (opposite the Catholic church), St. Mawes (tel. St. Mawes 270281), is a Regency house, furnished with antiques and furniture of the period. You will be warmly welcomed by Polish-born Mrs. Zofia Moseley, now a confirmed Cornish woman, who loves meeting people and speaks several languages. The house offers five twin-bedded rooms, three of which have private baths. All are centrally heated. Visitors gather in the lounge to watch television. The staircase is a perfect Regency one. The charge is £9.50 ($18.53) per person per night for rooms with a private bathroom, £8.50 ($16.58) per night without bath. These tariffs include an English breakfast which can be served in your room at no extra cost. The house has an extensive garden overlooking the harbor of St. Mawes where the racing of yachts takes place each Sunday and Thursday in season. Lord Byron, who stayed in Falmouth in 1809, may have visited this house, for he mentions its name in one of his poems. It's said that his limping step can be heard at Braganza.

17. Falmouth

A lot of cutthroat ship wreckers used to live in the area. In fact, when John Killigrew, a leading citizen, started to build a lighthouse on Lizard Head, they protested that the beacon in the night would deprive them of their livelihood and "take awaye God's Grace from us." Falmouth, 26 miles Penzance, is today a favorite base for the yachting set, who consider it one of the most beautiful harbors in Europe. On a small peninsula, Falmouth's old section overlooks the land-locked inner harbor. The newer part, center for most of the hotels, faces the bay and commands a panorama from St. Anthony's Lighthouse to Pendennis Castle. Warmed in winter by the Gulf Stream, Falmouth has become a year-round resort. Built on a promontory overlooking the estuary of the Fal, it was once occupied in part by the captains of old mail-carrying packet ships. Many find it a good center for touring the rugged Cornish coastline. It's possible, for example, to take a ferry from Falmouth to St. Mawes, a 20-minute ride.

WHERE TO STAY: **Green Bank Hotel,** Green Bank (tel. Falmouth 312440), hangs tenaciously to the old days of the Post Office Packet Services (1688–1850). Beside the shore road, this medium-priced hotel overlooks the water with its own landing pier. Over the years, it has been expanded, but it remains traditional in every sense. The spacious lounges have views of the harbor, and the rooms are comfortably furnished. In a single, the rate ranges from £22.50 ($43.88) to £24.50 ($47.78), increasing to anywhere from £36 ($70.20) to £40 ($78) in a double or twin. The higher tariffs are for harbor-view units. Stays of three nights get a half-board quotation which is always advantageous. Even if you don't stay here, consider an old-fashioned English meal in the water-view dining room favored by local yachting people. Set lunches go for £5 ($9.75), dinners for £9.50 ($18.53).

The **Tudor Court,** Melville Road (tel. Falmouth 312807), once part of the local manor house, is within 200 yards of the sea and offers a variety of rooms, some with private bath and a view of the bay. The hotel has a licensed bar and a comfortable lounge with color TV. All meals are prepared and cooked on the premises by the resident proprietress, Mrs. Edna Jefferys. Fresh local produce is used whenever possible. The court is open throughout the year, including Christmas. Higher rates are charged from June to the end of August, when half board costs from £14 ($27.30) per person, plus VAT.

On the Outskirts

Budock Vean Hotel, Golf and Country Club, near Falmouth (tel. Mawnan Smith 250288). Since this place lies a few miles from Falmouth, a cab will be sent to meet you at the railway station. Or else you can drive there yourself, among the pines and subtropical vegetation sloping sharply to the Helford River. You come to an old stone house with a stout front door and bright welcoming hall. There Peter, the porter, will grab your bags and hurry them to your room.

Afternoon tea is laid out on the polished table for you to help yourself; tea comes in large pots to be drunk in the depths of a chintzy armchair in the drawing room. Some bedrooms are in the old house, others in the new wing, and all have bathroom and toilet. A few units have magnificent views over the gardens and down to the distant river, and others overlook the private golf course.

The chef, John Trout, is a local man of great skill, and meals are a selection of international and English dishes. Portions are large. Included in the cost of your room is the free use of the indoor, heated swimming pool. The glass walls roll back in summer to join it to the garden, and in winter an enormous log fire burns on the open grate for additional heating. The main attraction for many is the 18-hole golf course with greens fees of £2.50 ($4.88) a day, £12 ($23.40) a week. But for those who just want to walk, the gardens slope down to a private cove where sailboats lie at anchor and gulls wheel raucously above the water.

Peter Whiteside, a Canadian, owns and runs the place with the help of his son, Justin. Their boast is that a Whiteside is always on duty, and they certainly have an excellent staff to back up their efforts. Dinner, bed, and a full breakfast costs £25 ($48.75) per person, rising to £35 ($68.25) from mid-June until the end of September. VAT and service are extra. A buffet lunch of soup, cold meats, and a salad costs £3.50 ($6.83); a full lunch £7 ($13.65).

18. Penzance

This little Gilbert and Sullivan harbor town is the end of the line for the Cornish Riviera Express. A full 280 miles southwest from London, it is noted for its equable climate (it's one of the first towns in England to blossom out with spring flowers), and summer throngs descend for fishing, sailing, and swimming. Overlooking Mount's Bay, Penzance is graced in places with subtropical plants, as well as palm trees.

The harbor is used to activity of one sort or another. *The Pirates of Penzance* were not entirely fictional. The town was raided by Barbary pirates, destroyed in part by Cromwell's troops, sacked and burnt by the Spaniards, and bombed by the Germans. In spite of its turbulent past, it offers tranquil resort living today.

The most westerly town in England, Penzance makes a good base for exploring Land's End, the Lizard Peninsula, St. Michael's Mount, the old fishing ports and artists' colonies of St. Ives, Newlyn, and Mousehole—even the Scilly Isles.

THE SIGHTS: St. Michael's Mount is reached at low tide by a causeway three miles east of Penzance. Rising about 250 feet from the sea, St. Michael's Mount is topped by a partially medieval, partially 17th-century castle. At high tide, the mount becomes an island, reached only by motor launch from Marazion. A Benedictine monastery, the gift of Edward the Confessor, stood on this spot in the 11th century. The castle, with its collections of armor and antique furniture, is open, weather and tide permitting, April to October on Monday, Tuesday, Wednesday, and Friday from 10:30 a.m. to 4:45 p.m. (November to March, on Monday, Wednesday, and Friday when possible). It charges £1.75 ($3.41) for adults, £1 ($1.95) for children. There are conducted tours at 11 a.m. and noon, then at 2 and 3 p.m., weather permitting. You can only go over when the causeway is dry. If you mistime it, they won't send a boat over to pick you up and rescue you from the island. There is, however, a tea garden and a café on the island, both of which are open in summer so you probably won't starve to death.

From Penzance, take bus 20, 21, or 22, then get off at Marazion, the town opposite St. Michael's Mount. To avoid disappointment, it is a good idea to telephone the office of St. Michael's Mount (tel. Penzance 710507) to learn the state of the tides, especially during the winter months when a regular ferry service does not operate.

Craggy **Land's End** is where England comes to an end. Here you'll find the last of everything. Land's End, lying nine miles west of Penzance, is reached by bus 1 or 1B.

The **Minack Theatre** in Porthcurno, nine miles from Penzance, is unique. It's carved out of the Cornish cliff-face with the Atlantic as its impressive backdrop. In tiered seating, similar to that of the theaters of Ancient Greece, 550 persons can watch the show and the rocky coast beyond the stage. The theater is generally open to visitors who come sometimes just for sightseeing, although you may want to attend an evening performance. To reach Minack, leave Penzance on the A30 heading toward Land's End. After three miles, bear left onto the B3283 and follow the signposts to Porthcurno. Or you can take bus 4 or 4A from Penzance. For details, telephone St. Buryan 471 during the season, lasting from the end of June to mid-September. Seats cost around £1.50 ($2.93) at the box office.

WHERE TO STAY: Back in Penzance, it is time to find a room.

The **Abbey Hotel,** Abbey Street (tel. Penzance 66906), is a well-preserved old place that is frequented by discerning guests. The bonus is its situation (on a narrow sidestreet, on several terraces, directly overlooking Penzance Harbor). You can stay at the Abbey, having only your room and breakfast, or all of your meals in the restaurant downstairs (see dining recommendations below). The B&B rate per person averages around £14 ($27.30), plus VAT. Some of the larger and better appointed rooms may run higher. Behind the hotel is a tiny formal garden on two tiers, each with a view of the water. Here the herbs are grown that are used to spice the delicately flavored meats in the restaurant downstairs. The owners, the Cox family, have brought their vitality, style, and charm into the hotel business.

Richmond Lodge, 61 Morrab Rd. (tel. Penzance 5560), is one of the friendliest guest houses in Cornwall, in a convenient position making it an ideal center from which to explore the whole of the Land's End peninsula. An informal atmosphere prevails. The owners, Jean and Pat Eady, possess a wealth of local knowledge and are always at hand to attend to your needs. Good home-style cooking is served in an attractively furnished Delft blue and white dining room. You have the opportunity to experience living in a delightful early (1790) Victorian town house on the B&B plan for £42 ($81.90) per week. Dinner costs an additional £3 ($5.85) per night.

READER'S HOTEL SELECTION: "The **Georgian House,** Chapel Street (tel. Penzance 5664), once the home of the mayors of Penzance, has been completely renovated into a cozy, intimate hotel. The proprietors, Derek and Brenda Gibbard, with their friendly manner made us feel right at home and attended to all our needs promptly and cheerfully. The relaxed atmosphere of the dining room with its sea motif goes well with the excellent Cornish menu. The hotel is centrally heated and carpeted throughout. Our room was newly furnished, well-lighted, and had a full bath. The rate in a room without a private bath is £6.50 ($12.68) per person per night, rising to £8.50 ($16.58) per person with bath, plus VAT. The location is a plus in that it is directly across the street from the Admiral Benbow Restaurant, and only two blocks from the town center in one direction and the harbor and Promenade in the other" (Ben N. Cox, Wabash, Ind.).

WHERE TO EAT: Bistro One, 46 New St. (tel. Penzance 4408), is owned and run by a husband-and-wife team, the Harrises. It's a pleasant, warm, and candlelit place with a relaxed atmosphere. Ron Harris cooks tempting dishes such as sauteed kidneys with fresh vegetables, grilled liver and bacon with tomatoes. His appetizers are likely to include a homemade soup, freshly made pâté, and smoked fish. Tempting desserts include a selection of mousse and fruit pies, among other offerings. The bistro is open Monday to Saturday from 7 to 10 p.m. (closed Monday in winter). Expect to pay from £12 ($23.40) for three courses.

Le Tarot, 19 Quay St. (tel. Penzance 3118), brings sophistication and intimate ambience with flair to the cuisine offered in Penzance. Classic French dishes and local specialties are prepared by expert chefs under the watchful eye of the proprietors, Keith and Moira Kennedy. He was in industry, and she was a Cordon Bleu–trained chef. When they moved in, they brought along their chef from the Savoy in London.

Each dish is cooked to order, so plan a leisurely meal on such dishes as bonne femme turbot Nelson, lobster Américaine, steak au poivre, to name but a few. All ingredients are the freshest possible. A three-course meal goes for £8 ($15.60), plus another £2.50 ($4.88) for half a carafe of the French house wine. A three-course traditional Sunday lunch is offered for £5 ($9.75). In summer the restaurant is open seven nights a week. It is completely closed, however, from January to mid-February. The wine list contains a choice of 50 different kinds, carefully selected.

The **Admiral Benbow,** Chapel Street (tel. Penzance 3448), is a restaurant-cum-museum dedicated to the sea, that has to be experienced to be believed. What started out as a simple two-story timbered inn has grown into a showcase of nautical objects. Open every day of the week for morning coffee, lunch, and dinner, it serves meals on the lower floor with its nooks and crannies, benches and booths. On the upper level there's a lounge bar (you wait here for a table if Admiral Benbow can't take any more on board downstairs). If you prefer to eat in the bar, a hot and cold buffet luncheon is served, where for £2.50 ($4.88) you may choose from a wide selection of cold meats, pâtés, and quiches, all served with fresh salad. The inn is owned by Roland Morris, a professional diver who has been discovering treasures for years on old wrecks around Cornwall and Scilly Isles.

When you get a table, consult the "Tavern Vittals Chart and Grog Log," the latter studded with everything from fine French bottled clarets to Hungarian Bull's Blood. You'll find the Cornish crab soup as an appetizer. Among the principal à la carte selections are chicken Kiev, fresh rainbow trout, and entrecôte tyrolienne. For dessert try one of the old English standbys, such as home-cooked fruit tart, although an order of Cornish cream would make it sparkle. Expect to spend from £7 ($13.65) for a complete meal.

Attached to the inn is a nightclub, open from 9 p.m. till 1 a.m. It charges half-price admission to the patrons of the restaurant.

On the Outskirts

Lesceave Cliff Hotel, Praa Sands, near Penzance (tel. Germoe 2325), is reached down a tiny lane, well marked off the A394 from Helston to Penzance. You drive down between high banks with nary a view of anything until you suddenly emerge with the spread of Praa Sands lying below you. The hotel owns much of the land between it and the sea, and the uninterrupted views are magnificent. A typical seaside hotel with much white paint, chintzy chairs, and bright furnishings, it charges from £15 ($29.25) per person for room and breakfast, including VAT. The whole of the Cornish peninsula is close at hand.

19. The Scilly Isles

Perhaps the most important and scenic excursion from Penzance is a day trip to the Scilly Isles, lying off the Cornish coast, about 27 miles southwest of Land's End. The granite isles are noted for their sandy beaches, palm trees, and warm climate (Gulf Stream–protected flowers bloom in December). One looks at flowers and gardens a lot in the Scillies, but the islands also have bird sanctuaries and seal colonies. **St. Mary's** is the largest inhabited island, and the site of most tourist facilities. From there, you can take a motor launch to the major sightseeing attration—the **Tresco Abbey Gardens,** on the **Isle of Tresco.** Not only can you explore terraced gardens, but you can also duck inside the **Valhalla Ship Museum** (collection of figureheads—gleaned from wrecks in the islands). The gardens are open all year, weekdays only, including Saturday, from 10 a.m. to 4 p.m. Admission is £1.50 ($2.93).

From Penzance, the Scilly Isles may be visited by helicopter or by sea. A ship, *Scillonian III,* maintains year-round connections to St. Mary's. For details of sailings and fares, apply to **Isles of Scilly Steamship Co. Ltd.,** Quay Street (tel. Penzance 2009). **British Airways Helicopters** at the Heliport in Penzance (tel. Penzance 3871) operates daily except Sunday throughout the year to the Isles of Scilly, the one-way flight taking only 20 minutes. A round-trip day excursion fare is available for travel any day (except Saturday during May, June, July, August, and September). The round-trip day fare is £22 ($42.90) per adult.

Incidentally, the already-mentioned Isles of Scilly Steamship Company, Quay Street, in Penzance, not only operates the regular service to the Scilly Islands, but also runs in-season daily cruises along the Cornish coast and to the islands, allowing four hours ashore before returning to Penzance.

Hanjague Guest House, St. Mary's (tel. Scillonia 22531), is a modern bungalow near the center of the island, offering good views stretching from the heliport in the southeast across Old Town Bay and Peninnis Headland to Buzza Mill in the southwest. Owners Dorothy and David Oxford will meet arriving guests at the heliport or quay if notified in advance. For bed, breakfast, and dinner, the Oxfords charge £19 ($37.05) per person all year. Rooms are comfortably furnished and centrally heated, containing hot and cold running water. In the studio lounge is a fine display of wildlife prints by the artist William Timym.

Tremellyn Private Hotel, St. Mary's (tel. Scillonia 22656), is a complex on one of the higher parts of St. Mary's, with views of the harbor, Tresco, Samson, and the other islands, yet it lies only a short walk from Porthcressa Beach, the old town, and the quay. The "mother house," Tremellyn, contains the dining room, lounge, TV room, and some bedrooms. Otherwise, guests are housed in private bungalows owned and looked after by Scillonian families, all lying within 100 yards of Tremellyn. All units rented out contain hot and cold running water. The B&B rate, including VAT, is £12.50 ($24.38) per person, increasing to £17 ($33.15) per person for half board. Although advance reservations are for a period of one week, they will always offer accommodations if they have a room available on the night you arrive.

LODGINGS AT LAND'S END: Old Success Inn, Sennen Cove, Land's End (tel. Sennen 232). Just before you reach Land's End, turn right and follow the road down to Sennen Cove. The Old Success lies at the bottom, facing the sea and wide sandy beaches. Surfing rollers come in from the Atlantic almost to the foot of the sea wall beneath the 17th-century fishermen's inn. Over the years it has been extended and modernized, now offering bright, clean rooms, many with private bath, all with radio, tea and coffee maker, electric heater, and wash basin.

Downstairs there is a lounge with color TV and fantastic panoramic views over the Atlantic, a cozy lounge bar, and Charlie's Bar where the locals and the fishermen join the residents of an evening. The chef, Don Woodward, provides bar snacks at lunch and a set three-course meal for £6.50 ($12.68). Fresh local fish with fresh vegetables are featured. Try the grilled river trout or the fresh Cornish crab and salad.

For those who seek more energetic exercise than an evening walk along the sand, there is the Surf Bar by the beach which is separated from the inn by a large car park. Disco music is played on summer evenings. Gillian and Tony Webster have run the inn for the past few years. B&B is £9 ($17.55) in low season, rising to £12 ($23.40) from May to September. Packed lunches can be provided. All rates include VAT.

20. St. Hilary, Newlyn, and Mousehole

For even more interesting living than that described above, we turn to the outlying district of Penzance, beginning first on the eastern side of the bay at St. Hilary, then heading south to Newlyn and Mousehole.

ST. HILARY: The **Old Vicarage Country Hotel**, St. Hilary, a short drive east from Marazion (tel. Marazion 710572), is a secluded retreat of much charm. It will please those who respond to quiet, gentle hours spent in an old house, surrounded by woods and gardens. Once a vicarage, it is owned by Mr. and Mrs. Stoten, who accept guests for a low charge of £11 ($21.45) per person nightly for B&B. The dinner, bed, and breakfast rate is £14 ($27.30) per person. Each room is individually decorated—casual, but comfortable. The beds have innersprings, and there is adequate hot and cold running water. The living room is spacious, and just right for fireside chats. Home cooking is a feature of the place. On Saturday a five-course evening dinner for nonresidents goes for £6 ($11.70). The hotel receives only from May to September. The house, the subject of a book entitled *Twenty Years at St. Hilary,* is about a 15-minute walk from Perranuthnoe Beach and within sight of St. Michael's Mount.

NEWLYN: From Penzance, a promenade leads to Newlyn, a mile away, another fishing village of charm on Mount's Bay. Stanhope Forbes, now dead, founded an art school in Newlyn. The village has an artists' colony, attracting both the serious painter and the amateur sketcher. From Penzance, Newlyn is reached by taking bus 1 or 1B. For a dining or overnighting recommendation, try the following.

The **Smugglers Hotel and Restaurant**, Fore Street (tel. Penzance 4207), is the central mecca for those who create in clay and paint. An artist's dream come true, this little two-story inn lies right on the roadside, across from the Newlyn Harbor. You pay £12 ($23.40) in a single, £20 ($39) in a double for a good bed and a big Cornish breakfast. The rooms are bright and sparkling clean, with innerspring mattresses and water basins. With a bath en suite, a room costs an extra £2 ($3.90) per day. Good shore dinners are served till around 10 p.m. Conversation in the lounge or in the dining room is often most rewarding. The bar is found in the granite-walled cellars, with tables and benches made from local driftwood. The original tunnel used by smugglers, although now blocked, can still be seen.

MOUSEHOLE: Still another Cornish fishing village, Mousehole lies three miles south of Penzance (take bus 9). The hordes of tourists who flock here haven't changed it drastically: the gulls still squawk, the cottages still huddle close to the harbor wall (although they look as if they were built more to be photographed than lived in), the fishermen still bring in the day's catch, the salts sit around with their pipes talking about the good old days, and the lanes are as narrow as ever. About the most exciting thing that's occurred around here was the arrival in the late 16th century of Spanish galleons, whose sailors sacked and burnt the village. In a sheltered cove, off Mount's Bay, Mousehole (pronounced mou-sel) has developed an artists' colony, which is home to both painters and potters. For rooms and meals, try the following recommendations in the village.

Old Coastguard Hotel, The Parade (tel. Mousehole 222), is a 19th-century structure, on the edge of Mousehole, with a private, unspoiled view of the bay. Open all year, it's a center for artists and others who enjoy such an atmosphere. The old inn has stairways and halls leading directly to the oddly shaped bedrooms. For a bathless double, the owners, Mrs. O. Sidoryk and Mr. S. Donnelly, charge from £12.35 ($24.08) per person nightly. This rate includes a full breakfast with, if you wish, mackerel, fresh Newlyn sole or kippers, or perhaps sausage, egg, and bacon, served with fruit juice, tea, or coffee. Dinners, served from 7 to 9:30 p.m., are exceptional, too. Every night you can select from the à la carte menu which has a wide range of seafoods, for a minimum charge of £7 ($13.65) per person. They also have two special menus which offer a three-course meal for residents only. Also served between 6 and 9:30 p.m. is an extensive range of hot and cold bar meals. All prices are inclusive of service and VAT.

On the Outskirts

Lamorna Cove Hotel, at Lamorna Cove, near Penzance (tel. Mousehole 411). This is one of the most perfect Cornish coves, seemingly inaccessible down a winding, narrow road, dropping always toward the sea until you suddenly emerge onto the sea wall of the tiny cove.

Above the cove, signposted off the approach lane, lies the Lamorna Cove Hotel. The present owners, Mr. and Mrs. Stewart Bolton, have carefully added to the old stone building, once a tiny chapel with a bell tower. They once even blasted several tons of rock from the cliff face to provide more room, a peaceful haven with views over the sea and the cove. The bar is in the chapel. A large dining room runs the length of the building, and there are several lounges full of comfortable chairs, with a roaring log fire against the southwesterly gales.

Accommodations are in the main hotel with bath or shower, some with balcony. There are also two cottages, one suitable for four, the other for five persons. A rocky garden clings to the cliffside and then surrounds a small swimming pool with a sun-trap terrace overlooking the sea. B&B ranges from £26 ($50.70) per person to £32 ($62.40) per person in high season in double accommodation. There is also a suite available and a deluxe double room, costing £36 ($70.20) and £41 ($79.95) per person per night. From October until the end of May, prices are substantially reduced.

If you do not have the time to stay at the hotel, their bar lunches can be well recommended. On Sunday, a traditional luncheon of sirloin of beef, filet of sole, or pork chops, buttered cabbage, rutabagas, roast potatoes (fresh vegetables in season), followed by pie with Cornish cream, brandy snaps, or cheese costs around £7 ($13.65). Dinners at £10 ($19.50) are quite a feast.

21. St. Ives

This north coast fishing village, with its sandy beaches, is England's most famous art colony. Only 20 miles from Land's End, 10 from Penzance, it is a village of narrow streets and well-kept cottages. The artists settled in many years ago and have integrated with the fishermen and their families.

The art colony was established long enough ago to have developed several schools or "splits," and they almost never overlap—except in a pub where the artists hang out, or where classes are held. The old battle continues between the followers of the representational and the devotees of the abstract in art, with each group recruiting young artists all the time. In addition, there are the potters, weavers, and other crafts people—all working, exhibiting, and selling in this area. There are several galleries to visit, with such names as the Sail Loft.

A word of warning: St. Ives becomes virtually impossible to visit in August, when you're likely to be trampled underfoot by busloads of tourists, mostly the English themselves. However, in spring and early fall, the pace is much more relaxed, and a visitor can have the true experience of the art colony.

BARBARA HEPWORTH MUSEUM: At Trewyn Studio and Garden, on Barnoon Hill (tel. St. Ives 796226), the former home of Dame Barbara Hepworth contains a museum of sculpture by the artist from 1929 until her death in 1975 together with photographs, letters, and other papers documenting her life and background. The garden, too, contains sculpture and is well worth a visit. The museum is open year round from 10 a.m. to 5:30 p.m., Monday to Saturday. Closed on Sunday. Admission is 50p (98¢) for adults, 25p (49¢) for children and students. There is limited parking some 200 yards away, but visitors may like to leave their cars at Lelant Station some three miles away and use the park-and-ride service into St. Ives.

WHERE TO STAY: Tregenna Castle Hotel (tel. St. Ives 5254), standing on its own 100 acres, was once a castle. It was optimistically earmarked by Von Ribbentrop to be Hitler's British Berchtesgaden. Approached by a long driveway, it crowns a hill high above the fishing village of St. Ives. While the interior is spacious and a good background for gracious living, the grounds contain gardens and lawns, an open-air, heated swimming pool with a flagstone edging for sunbathers, three lawn tennis courts, three hard courts, a croquet lawn, a putting green, a squash court, a badminton court, and a nine-hole golf course. There is also a health room complete with Turkish baths, a Relaxatron bed, and a Vibro belt. There are riding stables situated within the grounds and arrangements can be made for shark, mackerel, and fly fishing. The bedrooms usually are of good size, handsomely maintained with contemporary furniture, and more than 80% have private bathrooms. The rates vary according to the season and the location of the room. From June 16 to September 15, the B&B rate, inclusive of service charge and VAT, is from £26 ($50.70) in a bathless single, £38 ($74.10) in a single with bath. A bathless double costs from £43 ($83.85), from £67 ($130.65) with bath. Tregenna has its own vegetable garden and trout pool. A set lunch goes for £7 ($13.65) and a set dinner for £11 ($21.45), inclusive of service and VAT. In addition, there is a well-stocked cellar, and an orchestra plays for dancing two nights a week in season.

Garrack Hotel, Higher Ayr (tel. Penzance 796199), from its two-acre cliff knoll, commands a panoramic view of St. Ives and Portmeor Beach. The vine-covered little hotel, once a private home, is reached by heading up a narrow lane. It's one of the friendliest and most efficiently run small medium-priced hotels on the entire coast, with every room furnished in a warm, homey manner. The atmosphere in the living room is inviting, with a log-burning fireplace, antiques, and comfortable chairs. The Garrack belongs to Mr. and Mrs. Kilby, who are proud of their meals (see my dining recommendations). Each bedroom has an innerspring mattress and hot and cold running water (most with private baths). Prices vary because of the view, the size of the room, and the season. B&B costs from £8.80 ($17.16) to £12 ($23.40) per person for a room without bath and from £11 ($21.45) to £17.50 ($34.13) per person for rooms with bath or shower, plus VAT.

The **Trecarrell Hotel**, Carthew Terrace (tel. Penzance 795707), is housed in a 140-year-old building in a quiet quarter of St. Ives. The restaurant, bar, and kitchen are under the close personal supervision of the proprietors, Don and Liz Fraser, who take pride in their table. The best local produce and meats are used, along with fish caught fresh from the Atlantic Ocean. They make many "Olde English" dishes and offer specialties, such as a citrus and ginger trifle made with fresh oranges, lemons, eggs, and Cornish cream. Continental dishes are also available. The hotel is centrally heated throughout and is small, with 16 guest rooms in all. But each room is individually decorated, and many have private bathrooms or showers.

Rents per week in high season are from £101.43 ($197.79) to £113.62 ($221.60) per person, and the daily half-board rates are from £16.79 ($32.74) to £18.79 ($36.64) additional per person. These figures are inclusive of VAT and a full English breakfast, plus a four-course table d'hôte evening meal. The bar is well stocked with beers, liqueurs, and liquors, and a wide range of table wines is available. The Trecarrell is a friendly, spotlessly clean hotel, with excellent service and good food.

WHERE TO EAT: The **Chef's Kitchen**, Halsetown (tel. Penzance 796218), stands on a point above St. Ives on a back road to Penzance. It's in an old granite post office, very unobtrusive among the cottages. It's on the left as you come up the main street from St. Ives. Since it's so easy to miss, go slowly. The old post office has been converted into a bar lounge, plus an adjoining cottage which is the restaurant, seating 32 guests. When you reserve a table (and reservations are imperative), you have it for the evening. Orders are taken between 7 and 11 p.m. Mr. and Mrs. Wright are joint owners, with Mr. Wright supervising the kitchen. As a chef and chef lecturer, he has had some 20 years of experience, mainly in Oslo and Geneva. Menus are changed every two weeks and range in price from £7.50 ($14.63) to £15 ($29.25) for a three-course dinner with four vegetables and a full seasonal side salad. VAT is included, and there is no service charge.

On my latest rounds, such outstanding dishes were offered as crab claws in almond with prawn sauce, seafood pancakes Cardinal, roast grouse à la anglaise, a ballontine of chicken with a truffle sauce, and salmis of pheasant forestière.

Reservations are recommended, and the last orders are taken at 10:30 p.m. A diner seeking a high-class cuisine will not be disappointed here.

The **Garrack Hotel**, Higher Ayr (tel. Penzance 796199), the domain of Mr. and Mrs. Kilby, is outstanding, producing an excellent cuisine—using, when possible, fresh vegetables from their own garden. The hotel dining room, open to nonresidents, offers regular à la carte listings, plus cold buffet or snacks at the bar, and a £6.75 ($13.16) dinner from 7 to 8:30 p.m. The menu reflects some of the finest of English dishes, such as roast shoulder of lamb with mint sauce, fried filet of plaice, and a wide sampling of continental fare, such as filet

of bass meunière and escalopes de veau Cordon Bleu. A 10% service charge
and VAT are added. The Kilbys' son Michael has joined his parents in the
operation of the hotel and restaurant after completing a training period with
Claridges in London.

The Sloop is right on The Quay, next to the art colony on the hill. The
pub has old charm, tracing its history back to 1644, but it's the life here that's
important. The Lounge Bar is for daintier types, the Cellar Bar for intimate
rendezvousing. But in the Public Bar, you're likely to find artists and old sea
dogs mixing congenially. The local fishermen come in for their evening game
of darts and to talk to the owner-bartender. Apparently, the success of the pub
depends a great deal on the gift of gab of the bartender. A recent visit was
memorable. Six rugged Breton sailors made room at their long table for me.
Their words were unfathomable, but not their friendliness. They were in port
overnight and were sampling the English beer. The youngest, the cabin boy,
was tagging along, trying to imitate his older companions. The walls of the
interior are covered almost entirely by the works of a master who exchanged
them for his nightly ration of good English ale.

In the restaurant you can order such traditional English food as roast
joints for £12 ($23.40) per person. In the newer cellar bistro, an array of food
such as steaks, salads. and quiches is offered, with quick service, ranging in
price from £3.50 ($6.83) to £5 ($9.75). The Sloop will also provide overnight
accommodations at a rate of £12.50 ($24.38) per person, including VAT,
service, and an English breakfast.

22. Port Isaac

The most unspoiled fishing village on the north Cornish coastline is Port
Isaac, nine miles from Wadebridge. This Atlantic coastal resort retains its
original character, in spite of the intrusions of large numbers of summer visitors. By all means wander through its winding, narrow lanes, gazing at the
whitewashed fishermen's cottages with their rainbow trims.

WHERE TO DRINK AND SNACK: The **Golden Lion**, Fore Street (tel. Port
Isaac 336), is perhaps the most handsomely positioned pub in the old fishing
harbor. Owned by Mr. and Mrs. Spry, it offers good drinks, snacks, and crab
sandwiches.

For meals, try the **Harbour Café**, Fore Street (tel. Port Isaac 237), in the
center of the village. It has a special fame, featured several times on British
television and once in scenes from the Sherlock Holmes thriller, *The Devil's
Foot*. The unique café is designated as a building or architectural and historic
interest, and is one of several buildings on this treacherous stretch of coast that
used the timber of wrecked galleons in construction. The owners, Messrs.
Wooding and Muller, offer complete meals as well as snacks. On the menu are
such local dishes as crab and mackerel salads, plus a number of other specialties, with selected table wines. Meals begin at around £6 ($11.70). Perhaps you
will arrive in the afternoon, when you can have a real Cornish cream tea, and
if your appetite is still unsatisfied, you may care to try some homemade gâteau
topped with a portion of clotted cream.

READERS' HOTEL SELECTIONS: "The **Tre-Pol-Pen Hotel** (Tel. Port Isaac 232) is in
the newer part of the village, just before the steep descent down into the cove and the
old section. Charges are £8.50 ($16.58) per person during the main season for clean,
bright rooms, a substantial breakfast (several choices), use of a lounge with color TV,
and free baths. There is a large dining area where breakfast is served, and Cornish cream

teas can be ordered during the afternoon. A meal at night costs from £4 ($7.80) per person. Some of the rooms have beautiful views of the coast. There is a car park, which is necessary, as to drive down into the village is difficult in winter and virtually impossible in summer. All rooms have hot and cold water and are centrally heated. Bookings are necessary in summer" (Mr. and Mrs. David Peters, Highgate, Australia). . . . "The **Hathaway Guest House** (tel. Port Isaac 888416), is beautifully situated on the cliff on the western side of Port Isaac harbor. The house overlooks not only the village and harbor, but also the coastline and beyond. Resident proprietor Enid Andrews offers colorfully decorated rooms with breakfast at £8 ($15.60) per person in April, May, and June, and £9 ($17.55) in July, August, and September. Dinner is available for £5 ($9.75). It is less than a five-minute walk to the pub and shops, and a two-mile cliff walk begins at the door. There's a car park, and children are welcome" (A. Emerson Smith, Columbia, S.C.).

23. Tintagel

On a wild stretch of the Atlantic coast, Tintagel is forever linked with the legends of King Arthur, Lancelot, and Merlin. The Norman ruins, popularly known as "King Arthur's Castle," stand 300 feet above the sea on a rocky promontory. The colorful writing of Lord Tennyson in *Idylls of the King* greatly increased the interest in Tintagel, as did the writings of Geoffrey of Monmouth. The ruins, which date from Geoffrey's time, are what remains of a castle built on the foundations of a Celtic monastery from the sixth century.

In summer, many visitors make the ascent to Arthur's lair, 100 rock-cut steps. You can also visit Merlin's Cave and the "Old Post Office," a miniature 14th century manor in the center of the village (open May to September, weekdays, 10 a.m. to 8 p.m., and on Sunday from 1 to 5 p.m.).

If you become excited by legends of Knights of the Round Table, you can go to **Camelford,** five miles inland from Tintagel. The market hall there dates from 1790, but, more interestingly, the town claims to be Camelot.

The **Old Post Office** (tel. Bodmin 4281) at Tintagel is a National Trust property. It was once a 14th-century manor, but since the 19th century it has had connections with the post office. In the village center, it has a genuine Victorian post room which is open, April to October, daily from 11 a.m. to 6 p.m., or sunset if earlier. Admission is 60p ($1.17), including a guidebook.

Trebrea Lodge, Trenale, near Tintagel (tel. Camelford 770410), may appear as a dignified stately home, but in truth it looks and feels inside like an old Cornish farmhouse, although it is centrally heated. It dates back to 1315, and was lived in by the same family for more than 600 years. The house, now owned by Ann and Guy Murray, looks straight out across fields to the sea, and each bedroom has a good view. Rooms are available in many sizes, and each has hot and cold water, color TV, radio, intercom (and even a baby-listening service). Some of the units now have private bathrooms. Evenings are cozy in the drawing room around an open fire. You can have drinks in the bar which is installed in an old fireplace. There is a Victorian smoking room as well. Dining is most informal, and all food is homemade by Mrs. Murray, who has mastered true English recipes. The cost is £14.50 ($28.28) per person for half board.

READER'S HOTEL SELECTION: "I most sincerely recommend the **Bossiney House Hotel,** just outside Tintagel as you approach from Boscastle (tel. Camelford 770240). The hotel is owned by brothers John and Reg Wrightam and their families. The hotel is extremely comfortable, with a TV lounge and a well-stocked bar/lounge, and a wide expanse of lawn with a putting green. Our rooms were comfortably furnished, with full bath and central heating. The meals are family prepared and good tasting. The price is £18.50 ($36.08) per person per night, which includes a room with dinner, breakfast, and morning tea brought to the room" (Kathleen Martin, Englishtown, N.J.).

WILTSHIRE, SOMERSET, AND AVON

FOR OUR FINAL LOOK at the West Countree, we move now into Wiltshire, Somerset, and Avon, the most antiquity-rich shires of England. When we reach this area of woodland and pastoral scenes, London seems far removed—even divorced from the bucolic life here.

On cold, windswept nights in unrecorded times, the Druids used to steal across these plains, armed with twigs. Sheltered by boulders, they'd burn their sloe with rosemary to ward off the danger of witchcraft.

Most people seem to agree that the West Country, a loose geographical term, begins at Salisbury, with its Early English cathedral. Nearby is Stonehenge, England's oldest prehistoric monument. Both Stonehenge and Salisbury are in Wiltshire.

Somerset is even more varied—the diet richer not only in historical cities, but in wild scenic grandeur, especially in Exmoor, the home of the red deer. The legendary burial place of King Arthur at Glastonbury, and the cathedral city of Wells, also await you on your visit to Somerset. The old Roman city of Bath is the main target in the county of Avon.

WILTSHIRE

When you cross into Wiltshire, you'll be entering a county of chalky, grassy uplands and rolling plains. Most of the shire is agricultural, and a large part is devoted to pastureland. Wiltshire produces an abundance of England's dairy products, and is noted for its sheep raising. In this western shire, you'll traverse the Salisbury Plain, the Vale of Pewsey, and the Marlborough Downs (the last gobbling up the greater part of the land mass). Unquestionably, the crowning achievement of Wiltshire is:

1. Salisbury

Long before you've made the 83-mile trek from London, the spire of Salisbury Cathedral comes into view—just as John Constable painted it so many times. The 404-foot pinnacle of the Early English and Gothic cathedral is the tallest in England. But Salisbury is also a fine base for touring such sights as Stonehenge.

Salisbury, or New Sarum, lies in the valley of the Avon River. Filled with Tudor inns and tearooms, it is known to readers of Thomas Hardy as Melchester and to the Victorian fans of Anthony Trollope as Barchester.

SALISBURY CATHEDRAL: You can search all of England, but you'll find no purer example of the Early English, or pointed, style than Salisbury Cathedral. Its graceful spire has already been mentioned, but the ecclesiastical building doesn't depend totally on the tower for its appeal.

Construction began as early as 1220, then took 38 years to complete, which was jet-age speed in those days (it was customary to drag out cathedral building for three centuries at least). The spire began soaring at the end of the 13th century. Despite an ill-conceived attempt at revamping in the 18th century, the architectural harmony of the cathedral was retained.

The cathedral's octagonal Chapter House (note the fine sculpture) is especially attractive, dating from the 13th century. The Library contains one of the four copies of the Magna Carta. The cloisters enhance the beauty of the cathedral. The Close, with at least 75 buildings in its compound (some from the early 18th century, although others predate that), is exceptionally large, setting off the cathedral most fittingly. The cathedral now charges an admission of 50p (98¢) per person, although strong objectors are still admitted free.

TOURS: Wessexplore runs leisurely guided walks through the city and the surrounding countryside. Telephone Don Cross at Shrewton 620385 for further information.

There are also regular guided walks of about 1½ hours' duration through the city, visiting St. Thomas's Church and the Cathedral Close. The starting point is the noticeboard on the side of the Guildhall facing Queen Street. Departure is daily at 6:30 p.m. in summer and also at 2:30 p.m. on Wednesday. The cost is 50p (98¢) for adults, 30p (59¢) for children. An entire family can go on the walk for £1.50 ($2.93). Tours are operated from the **Tourist Information Office,** 10 Endless St. (tel. Salisbury 4956).

WHERE TO STAY: The **Rose and Crown,** East Harnham (tel. Salisbury 27908), is an inn-collector's gem. An unspoiled, half-timbered, 13th-century hostelry, it lies at the edge of Salisbury. The Avon River winds its way within a few feet of the Rose and Crown, and beyond the water you can see the tall spire of the cathedral. The lawns and gardens between the inn and the river are shaded by old trees, and chairs are set out so you can enjoy the view and count the swans. The inn, part of the Grand Metropolitan Hotels chain, contains both a new and an old wing. The new wing is modern, but, to me, the old wing is more appealing, with its sloping ceilings, antique fireplaces, and furniture. A single rents for £30 ($58.50), a double with bath going for £40

SALISBURY

AVON RIVER

DEVIZES RD.

Wilton House

WILTON RD.

ST. PAUL'S RD.

NELSON RD.

CASTLE RD.

To Stonehenge →

WYNDHAM RD.

ST. MARKS AVE.

LONDON RD.

RD.

CASTLE ST.

BEDWIN ST.

P.O.

WINCHESTER ST.

STATION

STATION

FISHERTON

CRANE ST.

HIGH ST.

NEW CANAL

NEW ST.

MILFORD ST.

BROWN ST.

ST. JOHN ST.

RAMPART RD.

ST. ANNE ST.

SOUTHAMPTON RD.

NADDER RIVER

EXETER ST.

CATH.

AVON RIVER

HARNHAM RD.

NEW BRIDGE

SALISBURY CATHEDRAL

($78), including an English breakfast, service, and VAT. You can have lunch overlooking the river. The fare is English. A set luncheon goes for £5 ($9.75), a dinner from £8 ($15.60). Across the countyard (where there's free parking) are two taverns. You can easily walk over the arched stone bridge to the center of Salisbury from here in ten minutes or so.

White Hart, St. John Street (tel. Salisbury 27476), combines the best of the old and the new worlds. The White Hart has been a Salisbury landmark since Georgian times. Its classic facade is intact, with tall columns crowning a life-size effigy of a hart. The older accommodations are traditional, but a new part has been added with skill, making for a total of 73 bedrooms. It's in the rear, opening onto a large car park—like a motel. New-wing units are tastefully conceived and attractively decorated. The highest prices are charged from April 1 to October 31, when singles range from £21 ($40.95) to £24 ($46.80), doubles from £29.50 ($57.53) to £34.50 ($67.28). The higher prices are for rooms with private baths. The service charge and VAT are included. You can have your before-dinner drink in the Elizabethan Bar.

The **King's Arms Hotel,** St. John Street (tel. Salisbury 27629), is a former coaching inn, in black-and-white Tudor style, with leaded-glass windows, an old pub sign out front, and a covered entranceway. It is unsophisticated without being self-consciously so. The King's Arms charges from £14.61 ($28.49) in a single without bath to anywhere from £22.62 ($44.11) to £27.95 ($54.50) in a double or twin, the more expensive tariffs including a private bath or shower. A special feature of the King's Arms is its attractively styled chamber with a four-poster bed, this one carrying a price tag of £38.72 ($75.50). Families might want to book the family suite, suitable for four persons, at a cost of £41.26 ($80.46). Rates include breakfast, service, and VAT. The rooms are good, with wash basins, radios, heating, and soft beds.

No one seems to know the age of the inn, although it's generally assumed it was built around the time of the completion of the cathedral. Conspirators helping Charles II flee to France were thought to have met here in the mid-17th century. The hotel contains fine old oak beams, the original ironwork, a priest's hiding hole, the Elizabethan fireplace. Have a pint of ale in the oak-beamed pub, sitting in a high-backed settle, warming yourself in front of the flames.

The **Grange Hotel,** St. Marks Avenue, off London Road Roundabout (tel. Salisbury 25321), stands in the highest part of Salisbury, on 1½ acres of pleasant gardens. Its architecture is an example of "Victorian Mock Tudor." When constructed, the hotel incorporated the space and comforts required by wealthy Victorians. It is built of brick, with many bay windows, gables, carved fireplaces, and a dark oak central hall with an open winding staircase. The furnishings and decor are in keeping with the style of the building. Most of the bedrooms have private baths and are individually decorated, each bearing the name of a cathedral. Depending on the plumbing, rates in a single range from £12.50 ($24.38) to £15 ($29.25), in a double from £23 ($44.85) to £28 ($54.60). A three-bedded accommodation costs £35 ($68.25) with bath. All these tariffs include an English breakfast, VAT, and service, and most rooms contain TV and telephones. Good food is served in the restaurant, a set dinner costing from £5.50 ($10.73), although if you order à la carte at either lunch or dinner expect to pay from £7 ($13.65).

WHERE TO EAT: Provençal, 14 Ox Row, Market Place (tel. Salisbury 28923), provides the most sophisticated setting of any dining place in Salisbury, and has the most ambitious French cuisine as well. This second-story restaurant overlooks the Market Place, has a sedate bistro setting, and a friendly staff to serve you. The menu is changed frequently, depending on the availability of produce and the season. Edward Moss, the owner, is in the kitchen. He offers a table d'hôte luncheon for around £5 ($9.75), a set dinner for £8.50 ($16.58). If you order à la carte, expect to pay from £8 ($15.60) at lunch, from £12 ($23.40) at dinner. The restaurant is open from noon to 1:30 p.m. and from 6 to 10:30 p.m. (except for Saturday lunch and all day Sunday). The wine list contains a number of really good French-bottled wines, as well as an excellent carafe.

The **Haunch of Vension,** Minster Street (tel. Salisbury 22024), deserves its popularity. Right in the heart of Salisbury, this creaky-timbered, 14th-century chophouse serves some excellent dishes, especially English roasts and grills. Stick to its specialties, and you'll rarely go wrong. Diners with more adventurous palates will sample a bowl of game soup. The pièce de résistance of the inn is its roast haunch of vension, with chestnut purée and red currant jelly. All this good food and hospitality is offered in a treasured building, dating back to 1320. The centuries have given a gleam to the oak furnishings, and years of polishing have worn down the brass. Twisting steps lead to tiny, cozy rooms (there is one small room with space for about four to sit where you can saturate yourself in the best of England's yesterdays and todays). Two windows of the barroom overlook St. Thomas's cloisters (naturally, it's called the Cloisters Chamber). Dancing fires are kept burning in the old fireplace; heavy beams are overhead; antique chairs encircle the tables. An average meal will cost from £10.50 ($20.48), including wine, VAT, and service. Hours are from noon to 2 p.m. and from 7 to 9:30 p.m. The restaurant is closed on Sunday and Monday.

Claire's Restaurant, 7–9 Market Pl. (tel. Salisbury 3118), is open daily except Sunday from noon to 2:30 p.m. and from 6:30 to 10:30 p.m. Right in the middle of the city, it is convenient as a lunch or dinner stop for the traveler. Homemade steak-and-kidney pie; cottage, fish, and other pies; deep-fried scampi; whole fresh plaice; barbecued chicken; and beef cooked in beer are featured. Daily specialties are on the blackboards. Prices go from £2.10 ($4.10) to £4.50 ($8.78). All main dishes are served with fresh vegetables and trimmings, including a dessert such as a traditional hot homemade crumble or pie. Your meal will cost under £6 ($11.70), and house wine goes for 65p ($1.27) a glass.

The Local Pub

The **New Inn,** 43 New St. (tel. Salisbury 27679), isn't new at all. Backing up to the cathedral Close wall, it's definitely part of old England. The center of the inn is the serving bar, which is a common counter for three outer rooms—one is a tiny sitting area, another a tavern with high-backed settles and a fireplace, the third a lounge with a dart board. You'll find stacks of little pork pies, to be eaten cold and washed down with pints of ale. Prices range from 45p (88¢) to £1.50 ($2.93). A half-pint of draft cider costs 60p ($1.17). The Historical Society, incidentally, once discovered several human bones in an oven behind an old doorway.

ON THE OUTSKIRTS: The **Silver Plough,** Pitton, near Salisbury (tel. Farley 266), lies just off the A30 road from London to Salisbury. It's a pretty country pub with a skillfully added restaurant. The pub has a reputation for country wines and English cheeses. You can sup at least 17 varieties and eat home-baked cottage loaves with a wide selection of cheese for your lunch, in the beamed lounge bar, hung with tankards, coachhorns, and other country memorabilia. In addition to the cheese served for lunch, the restaurant is also open. The bar, incidentally, serves a full snack menu of homemade dishes, featuring steak-and-kidney pie, grilled steak, and various pastas.

There is also a dining room, where the chef does succulent grills and roasts for the set meals or else provides you with an à la carte dinner. The owners pride themselves on providing everything from a simple ploughman's lunch at £1.30 ($2.54) to a full meal, a set dinner going for £10 ($19.50). On the table d'hôte are featured such tempting items as roast duckling with orange and brandy sauce, chicken cooked in red wine and mushrooms, trout poached in white wine with shrimp and mushrooms. The Silver Plough has known many famous visitors, but, apart from displaying a signed letter from Queen Victoria, the management prefers to stick to its quiet country atmosphere and to concentrate on making its guests feel at home.

READER'S HOTEL SELECTION AT AMESBURY: "The **Fairlawn Hotel** (tel. Amesbury 2103) is ideally located for an in-depth visit to the archeological sites on Salisbury Plain. It is only two miles from Stonehenge and one mile from Woodhenge and Durrington Walls. The hotel is a Georgian building well into its third century. Bed and breakfast cost is £10 ($19.50) in a single, £18.50 ($36.08) in a double without bath, £22 ($42.90) in a double with bath, and from £26 ($50.70) to £32 ($62.40) in family rooms for three to four persons, these tariffs including VAT. The rooms are immaculate and sunny. The hotel also has a cocktail lounge and restaurant, serving a three-course evening meal for about £8 ($15.60). Gerald Hawkins, author of *Stonehenge Decoded,* stayed at the Fairlawn when he visited the area. The Tourist Information Centre in Salisbury will gladly make your reservations to assure the availability of a room before you start for Amesbury" (Edward Pasahow, San Diego, Calif.).

SIDE TRIPS FROM SALISBURY:

Less than two miles north of Salisbury is **Old Sarum,** the remains of what is believed to have been an Iron Age fortification. The earthworks were known to the Romans as Sorbiodunum, and later to the Saxons. The Normans, in fact, built a cathedral and a castle in what was then a walled town of the Middle Ages. Parts of the old cathedral were disassembled to erect the cathedral at New Sarum.

Wilton House

In the small borough of Wilton, less than three miles to the west of Salisbury, is one of England's great country estates, Wilton House (tel. Wilton 3115), the home of the Earl of Pembroke. The stately house dates from the 16th century, but has seen modifications over the years, as late as Victoria's day. It is noted for its 17th-century state rooms by Inigo Jones. Many famous personages have either lived at or visited Wilton. It is believed that Shakespeare's troupe entertained here. Plans for the D-Day landings at Normandy were laid out here by Eisenhower and his advisers, in the utmost secrecy, with only the silent Van Dycks in the Double Cube room as witnesses. The house is filled with beautifully maintained furnishings, especially a collection of Chippendale. Wilton House displays some of the finest paintings in England, including works by Rembrandt, Rubens, Reynolds, and the already-mentioned Van Dycks. An exhibition of 7000 model soldiers and the "Pembroke Palace" dollhouse are also to be seen.

The estate lies in the midst of 20 acres of grounds, with cedars of Lebanon, the oldest of which were planted in 1630. The Palladian Bridge was built in 1737. Wilton House may be visited from Tuesday through Saturday from 11 a.m. to 6 p.m., April through September. Admission is £1.50 ($2.93) for adults, 60p ($1.17) for children under 16. On Sunday, April through September, the historic house is open from 1 to 6 p.m. The licensed, self-service restaurant is open all day, and offers hot and cold lunches and afternoon teas. There is an adventure playground for children.

Stonehenge

Two miles west of Amesbury and about nine miles north of Salisbury is the renowned Stonehenge, believed to be anywhere from 3500 to 4000 years old. This huge oval of lintels and megalithic pillars is the most important prehistoric monument in Britain.

Some Americans have expressed their disappointment after seeing the concentric circles of stones. Admittedly, they are not the pyramids, and some imagination has to be brought to bear on them. Pyramids or not, they represent an amazing engineering feat. Many of the boulders, the bluestones in particular, were moved dozens of miles (perhaps from southern Wales) to this site by the ancients. If you're more fanciful, you can always credit Merlin with delivering them on clouds from·Ireland.

The widely held view of the 18th- and 19th-century romantics that Stonehenge was the work of the Druids is without foundation. The boulders, many weighing several tons, are believed to have predated the arrival in Britain of the Celtic cult. Recent excavations continue to bring new evidence to bear on the origin and purpose of Stonehenge. Controversy surrounds the prehistoric site especially since the publication of *Stonehenge Decoded* by Gerald S. Hawkins and John B. White, which maintains that Stonehenge was an astronomical observatory. That is, a Neolithic "computing machine" capable of predicting eclipses.

Others who discount this theory adopt Henry James's approach to Stonehenge, which regards it as "lonely in history," its origins and purposes (burial ground? sun-worshipping site? human sacrificial temple?) the secret of the silent, mysterious Salisbury Plain.

If you don't have a car, getting to Stonehenge can be difficult unless you're athletic. First take the bus to Amesbury, then walk about 2½ miles to Stonehenge. The British do this all the time, and they don't complain. But if that is too strenuous, you'd better take one of the organized coach tours out of Salisbury.

To protect these ancient stones, Stonehenge has been fenced off.

Longleat House

Between Bath and Salisbury, Longleat House (tel. Maiden Bradley 551), owned by the sixth Marquess of Bath, lies four miles southwest of Warminster, 4½ miles southeast of Frome on the A362. The first view of this magnificent Elizabethan house, built in the early Renaissance style, is romantic enough, but the wealth of paintings and furnishings within its lofty rooms is enough to dazzle.

A tour of the house, from the Elizabethan Great Hall, through Libraries, the State Rooms, and the Grand Staircase, is awe inspiring in its variety and splendor. The State Dining Room is full of silver and plate, and fine tapestries and paintings adorn the walls in rich profusion. The Library represents the finest private collection in the country. The Victorian kitchens are open during the summer months, offering a glimpse of life below the stairs in a well-ordered country home. Various exhibitions are mounted in the Stable Yard. Events are staged frequently in the grounds, and the Safari Park contains a vast array of animals in open parklands.

The house is open daily, except Christmas, from 10 a.m., at an admission of £1.50 ($2.93) for adults and 60p ($1.17) for children and senior citizens. To enter the Safari Park in a hard-topped car or minibus is £1.50 ($2.93) for adults and £1 ($1.95) for children and senior citizens. Visitors not wanting to use their own vehicle can take one of the safari buses at £1.80 ($3.51) for adults or £1.20 ($2.34) for children and senior citizens. In addition, there's a "smashing" 15-inch gauge railway, costing 60p ($1.17) for adults, 30p (59¢) for children and senior citizens.

A maze, believed to be the largest in the world, has been added to the attractions by Lord Weymouth, son of the marquess. It has more than 1½ miles of paths among yew trees. The first part is comparatively easy, but the second part is very complicated, with bridges adding to the confusion. It knocks the Hampton Court maze into a cocked hat, as the British say. A visit to the maze costs adults 25p (49¢) and children and senior citizens only 15p (29¢).

Stourhead

After Longleat, you can drive six miles down route 3092 to Stourton, a village just off the B3092, three miles northwest of Mere (A303). Stourhead, a Palladian house, was created in the 18th century by the banking family of Hoare. The magnificent gardens became known as *le jardin anglais* in that they blended art and nature. Set around an artificial lake, the grounds are decorated with temples, bridges, islands, and grottos, as well as statuary. The gardens are open all year, daily from 8 a.m. to 7 p.m. (or until dusk if earlier). The house is open April, September, and October on Monday, Wednesday, Saturday, and Sunday, from 2 to 6 p.m. In May, June, July, and August it can be visited daily, except Friday, from 2 to 6. Picnicking in the gardens is welcomed. Admission to the house is £1.40 ($2.73) for adults, 70p ($1.37) for children; to the gardens, £1 ($1.95) for adults, 50p (98¢) for children. For more information, telephone Bourton 0348.

Avebury

One of the largest prehistoric sites in Europe, Avebury lies about six miles west of Marlborough, on the Kennet River. It is gaining in popularity with visitors now that the British have had to rope off the sarsén circle at Stonehenge (see above). Explorers are able to walk the 28-acre site at Avebury, winding in and out of the circle of more than 100 stones, some weighing up to 50 tons. They are made of sarsén, a sandstone found in Wiltshire. Inside this large circle are two smaller ones, each with about 30 stones standing upright. Native Neolithic tribes are believed to have built these circles.

The village of Avebury, taken over by the National Trust, has been called the Ancient Capital of England. Standing beside one of the greatest megalithic stone circles of Europe is **Avebury Manor** (tel. Avebury 23203), a fine Elizabethan house, which is noted for its beautiful plasterwork ceilings, oak paneling, and early English furniture, as well as its herb gardens and topiary. Although lived in by its owners, D. and S. Nevill-Gliddon, it is open to the public daily throughout the year by appointment, charging £1 ($1.95) for admission, half price for children. The manor lies one mile north of the London-Bath road, the A4, on the A361.

The **Alexander Keiller Museum** (formerly the manor coach house) and the **Wiltshire Folk Society Great Barn** are within the Avebury complex. Refreshments are available. In addition, there is limited guest accommodation by appointment only.

After sightseeing—and still in the same vicinity—you may be ready for a "cuppa."

2. Castle Combe

Once voted Britain's prettiest village, Castle Combe was used for location shots for *Dr. Doolittle*. About 9½ miles from Bath, this little Cotswold village is filled with shops selling souvenirs and antiques. The village cottages are often set beside a trout stream, and are made of stone with roofs laden with moss. The church is unremarkable except for its 15th-century tower. An old market cross and a triple-arched bridge are much photographed.

FOOD AND LODGING: The **Manor House Hotel**, Castle Combe (tel. Castle Combe 782206), is a country estate whose original manor was a 14th-century baronial seat. Set in 26 acres of gardens and parkland, it is a family-run hotel. Mr. and Mrs. Oliver Clegg are the hosts. To the south, the lawns sweep down to the trout-stocked Bybrook River where fishing is permitted for a fee. Thirty-four rooms, 29 with bath, three with shower, are offered overlooking the garden. A double with shared bath is £36 ($70.20) per night, rising to £45 ($87.75) with private bathroom. A bathless single costs £16 ($31.20), going up to £20.50 ($39.98) with private bath. A 12½¢ service charge is added, plus VAT. The bedrooms are clean and well decorated, furnished mostly with sunny yellow carpeting and light wallpaper. Some contain antiques, and two have four-posters. The garden wing annex consists of a row of genuine Cotswold stone cottages at the entrance to the grounds. These were gutted and rebuilt to provide good-size rooms with baths.

From the à la carte menu, you can order such dishes as roasts from the trolley, £6.50 ($12.68). At Sunday lunch, a table d'hôte is featured for £7 ($13.65) and on summer evenings, a cold buffet is offered. It's self-service, and you can eat as much as you like. Although casual informality prevails during the day, men in the evening should wear a jacket and tie. Jeans and denims are not acceptable. The hotel has an outdoor swimming pool for summer use only, and an all-year tennis court.

The **White Hart Inn**, at Ford, near Castle Combe (tel. Castle Combe 782213), is run by Ken Gardner and his wife, Lily, who cater to the local population swelled during the summer months by passing tourists. The inn is a lovely old 16th-century building with gardens running down to the river. They have added a heated swimming pool to the amenities, but the bars remain low-ceilinged with blackened beams and open fires. Various local souls help in the bars and in the dining room, where residents can dine for £9 ($17.55) from a menu including braised venison (caught, matured, and marinated locally in port wine). If this is not enough, bar food offered can be anything from chicken casserole in cider to home-cooked ham. And the cost is for as little as around £2.75 ($5.36).

Bedrooms, some with four-poster beds, contain private baths, renting from £27 ($52.54) a night, including an enormous breakfast with lashings of real coffee. The honeymoon suite which includes a dressing room is £32 ($62.40) a night. Ken, who claims that his American-bred boxer dog is better looking than he is, reckons he must have a sense of the ludicrous. Otherwise, how would he, an award-winning newspaperman who has traveled the world, exist in a place like this? He enjoys the constantly changing stream of folk who while away the hours in the bar and has a marvelous store of tall stories with which to regale them when conversation falters.

The Local Pub

No accommodation but plenty of local color is offered at the **White Hart,** (tel. Castle Combe 782295), on the main road through the village. It's a pub painted white and built of Cotswold stone with a stone tile roof. Dating from either the 13th or 14th century, it has low ceilings (in the cellars are Norman arches). The main bar is divided into two friendly parts, with a cold buffet counter for meals. The garden is also open to visitors, and the parlor bar admits children. This is the first venture of Dennis and Cath Wheeler (she calls it "my husband's indulgence"). Den, as he is known, works in London, commuting daily, and Cath is helped by her attractive daughters. Den's specialty is a landlord's pâté, and he claims the ingredients aren't poached. Home-cooked ham or beef, with coleslaw, bread, and butter, is offered at £2.40 ($4.68). In winter, hot soups, chili, and toasted sandwiches are available. Traditional bitter beer from wooden barrels is popular with the locals. They have a black cat, Pussy Galore, who drinks milk with her paw from a wine glass, and a King Charles spaniel known as Jack the Ripper. This is one of the few traditional English pubs in the Cotswolds recommended for evening visits.

3. Lacock

This is a National Trust village, with a 13th-century abbey in ruins and adjoining 16th-century houses and gardens. Within an easy drive of Bath, it contains a delightful 14th-century inn, **Sign of the Angel,** Church Street (tel. Lacock 230), ideal for a meal. Mr. and Mrs. Levis run this small inn, offering gourmet meals in an atmosphere that makes one feel he or she has stepped back into Shakespeare's time, maybe even earlier. Before an open fire on nippy days, food is served under a heavily beamed ceiling. Roasts are often featured on the menu. A set luncheon or dinner runs around £15 ($29.25) per person, and a reservation is essential. Lunch is served from 1 to 1:30 and dinner from 7:30 to 8 (one sitting only). The Sign of the Angel is closed for luncheon on Saturday and for dinner on Sunday (also it shuts down for Christmas holidays).

In addition, you'll find six "quaint" rooms, some with patchwork quilts and all with private bathrooms. Bed and full English breakfast ranges from £35 ($68.25) to £40 ($78) in a double room, including VAT and service. In all, it's an overnight stop that can be one of lasting memories (no guests under 12 are permitted, however).

SOMERSET

When writing about Somerset, it's difficult to avoid sounding like the editor of *The Countryside Companion,* waxing poetic over hills and valleys, dale and field. The shire embraces some of nature's most masterly scenic touches in England. Mendip's limestone hills undulate across the countryside (ever had a pot-holing holiday?). The irresistible Quantocks are the pride of the west, especially lovely in spring and fall. Here, too, is the heather-clad **Exmoor National Park,** a wooded area abounding in red deer and wild ponies, much of its moorland 1200 feet above sea level. Somerset opens onto the Bristol Channel, with Minehead the chief resort, catering primarily to the English.

Somerset is rich in legend and history, and is particularly fanciful about its associations with King Arthur and Queen Guinevere, along with Camelot and Alfred the Great. Its villages are noted for the tall towers of their parish churches. Of the many Norman castles erected in the country, the most important one remaining is **Dunster Castle,** three miles southeast of Minehead in the village of Dunster, just off the A39 (tel. Dunster 314). The National Trust owns the property and 30 acres of surrounding parkland. Terraced walks and gardens command good views of Exmoor, the Quantock Hills, and the Bristol Channel. Outstanding among the contents within are the 17th-century panels of embossed painted and gilded leather depicting the story of Antony and Cleopatra, and a remarkable 16th-century portrait of Sir John Luttrell shown wading naked through the sea with a female figure of peace and a wrecked ship in the background. The 17th-century plasterwork ceilings of the dining room and staircase and the finely carved staircase balustrade of cavorting huntsmen, hounds, and stags are also particularly noteworthy. The castle may be visited from April until the end of September every day except Friday and Saturday from 11 a.m. to 5 p.m. (last admission 4:30). In October it is open on Tuesday, Wednesday, and Sunday from 2 to 4 p.m. Admission is £1.70 ($3.32) for adults, 85p ($1.66) for children.

A quiet, unspoiled life characterizes Somerset. You're likely to end up in an ivy-covered old inn, talking with the regulars, and being served broiled salmon that night by the fireside. Or you may stop at a large estate that stands in a woodland setting, surrounded by bridle paths and sheep walks (Somerset was once a great wool center). Maybe you'll settle down in a 16th-century thatched stone farmhouse, set in the midst or orchards in a vale. Somerset is reputed (and I heartily concur) to have the best cider anywhere. When you lounge under a shady Somerset apple tree, downing a tankard of refreshingly chilled golden cider, all the types you've drunk in the past taste like apple juice.

My notes on Somerset, accumulated over many a year, would easily fill a book. But because space is limited I've confined myself in the main to the shire's two most interesting towns—Wells and **Glastonbury.**

4. Wells

At the south of the Mendip Hills, the cathedral town of Wells is a medieval gem. It lies only 21 miles from Bath, 123 from London. Wells was a vital link in the Saxon kingdom of Wessex—that is, important in England long before the arrival of William the Conqueror. Once the seat of a bishopric, it was eventually toppled from its ecclesiastical hegemony by the rival city of Bath. But the subsequent loss of prestige has paid off handsomely in Wells today. After experiencing the pinnacle of prestige, it fell into a slumber—hence, much of its old look remains. Wells was named after wells in the town, which were often visited by pilgrims to Glastonbury in the hope that their gout could be eased by its supposedly curative waters. The crowning achievement of the town is: ·

WELLS CATHEDRAL: Dating from the 12th century, Wells Cathedral is a well-preserved example of the Early English style of architecture. The medieval sculpture (six tiers of hundreds of statues now in process of conservation) of its west front is without peer in England. The western facade was completed in and around the mid-13th century. The landmark central tower was erected in the 14th century, with its attractive fan vaulting attached later. The inverted arches were added to correct the sinking of the top-heavy structure.

Much of the stained glass dates from the 14th century. The star-vaulted Lady Chapel, also from the 14th century, is in the Decorated style. To the north is the vaulted Chapter House, built in the latter 13th century. Look also for a medieval astronomical clock (knights in armor jousting).

After a visit to the cathedral, walk along its cloisters to the moated Bishop's Palace. The swans in the moat ring a bell when summoned to eat at 11 a.m. and 4 p.m. Its former Great Hall, built in the 13th century, is in ruins. Finally, the small lane known as the Vicars' Close is one of the most beautifully preserved streets in Europe.

FOOD AND LODGING: The **Star Hotel** (tel. Wells 73055) had its origins somewhere in the 16th century, but is best associated with the great coaching era. The cobbled carriageway is still a feature and leads to the dining room— once the stables. The hotel has been modernized, yet retains its old charm and unhurried pace. Copper and brass are used extensively for decoration, and several original stone walls and timbers have been exposed. The hotel front was restored in the Georgian period. A single ranges from £12.50 ($24.38) if bathless to £15 ($29.25) with bath, a double without bath costing £21 ($40.95), going up to £23 ($44.85) with bath, including VAT and an English breakfast. Tariffs are reduced in the off-season, so inquire when reserving a room. Five rooms have four-poster beds. Under the resident proprietor, Mark Nandi, the inn is fast gaining a reputation for good food. A set menu at lunchtime goes for £5 ($9.75), increasing to £9 ($17.55) for an à la carte dinner. Bar snacks range from 65p ($1.27) to £3.50 ($6.83), including salads, steaks, and the day's specials. They have real ale.

The **Crown Hotel**, Market Place (tel. Wells 73457), was built in the 15th century as a coaching inn. In Elizabethan times, it witnessed a number of additions. You'll find open beams in at least one of the bedrooms. A bathless single rents for £15 ($29.25); with bath, £18.50 ($36.08). Doubles without bath cost £26 ($50.70); with bath, £28 ($54.60). However, a few with four-poster beds cost from £30 ($58.50) per night. These terms include a full English breakfast and VAT. Tea- or coffee-making facilities and color TV are in all the rooms. Lunch or dinner in the restaurant begins at £7 ($13.65) for three courses. They also have the Pen Coffee Shop, serving light snacks. The Crown, just two minutes from Wells Cathedral, offers a pleasant "home away from home" to visitors.

The **Red Lion**, Market Place (tel. 72616), is owned by Mr. Chapman who also directs the Swan. The Red Lion is also an attractive old inn, with a wider availability of rooms in case the smaller Swan is full. Here a single with bath goes for £18 ($35.10), but only £15 ($29.25) without bath. A bathless double rents for £27 ($52.65), increasing to £31 ($60.45) with bath. The dining room serves a good meal for £7.50 ($14.63), with such English specialties as home-baked ham and steak-and kidney pie. There is a pretty courtyard with tables and chairs for a pleasant drink in the evening.

Regency Hotel, New Street (tel. Wells 75471), is an informal, family-run, licensed hotel in a charming 235-year-old Georgian house, reputedly designed by Sir Christopher Wren. In the center of Wells, it is listed as a building of architectural merit. The hotel is under the personal supervision of its resident owners, Mr. and Mrs. Hall, who maintain a friendly atmosphere and offer good food and accommodation. All their bedrooms have full central heating, hot and cold running water, electric shaver points, and some are equipped with shower cabinets and color TV. There is a residents' lounge with color TV and a cocktail lounge. With breakfast included, doubles rent for £23 ($44.85), and singles go for £14 ($27.30), including VAT and service. In the licensed restaurant, à la carte meals cost around £7 ($13.65), plus VAT, although you can order a table d'hôte menu at £5.50 ($10.73). Outside you'll find a large free car park.

The **Ancient Gate House,** across from the cathedral (tel. Wells 72029), is ideal all year for good English or Italian meals or slumber, Tudor style. Part of the Great West Gate, called Browne's Gate, it overlooks the stunning west front of the cathedral. In fact, it is part of the ecclesiastical precincts. Three of its rather worn-looking bedrooms have intricately carved four-poster beds. One, for example, was carved by a craftsman who specialized in Tudor roses and monstrous dream-haunting figures which appear on the headboard. The oak-beamed rooms have lovely furniture. Modern facilities, such as electric heaters and water basins, have been installed without wrecking the spirit of the building.

The hosts, Mr. and Mrs. Rossi, charge from £14 ($27.30) per person for B&B. The price for bed, breakfast, and evening dinner is from £18.50 ($36.08), plus VAT.

If you can't stay here, at least stop in for lunch, noon to 2 p.m. For a luncheon of three courses you'll pay for £5 ($9.75). It is a mystic and moving experience to sit on the lawn, 60 feet of frontage on the cathedral green, and take afternoon tea in the shade of the limes.

The **City Arms,** 69 High St. (tel. Wells 73916), is the former city jail, but now it's been converted into a local pub and restaurant. It has a high beamed ceiling, and around the dining tables are dark-oak Windsor chairs. On the ground floor is a pub, with an open-air courtyard and umbrella-crowned tables, a popular gathering place for the youth of Wells, who order cold bar snacks from 70p ($1.37) to £1.80 ($3.51). The restaurant upstairs offers mainly grills, homemade soups, and desserts. A grilled sirloin and salad will cost about £3.50 ($6.83). Fish and chips, steak-and kidney pie, and soups are also offered. Even if you're not hungry, drop in for a pint and soak up the atmosphere.

5. Bleadney

The unspoiled character of the West Country has been preserved in the quiet rural village of Bleadney, just four miles west of Wells on the B3139. Overlooking the moors toward the Cheddar Valley and Mendip Hills, the village is a convenient center for the exploration of the beauty and history of Somerset with its medieval castles and cathedrals as well as its serene country-side and miles of coastline.

WHERE TO STAY: **Threeways Country Hotel and Restaurant** (tel. Wells 78870) stands on five acres of garden and paddock through which flows the **Axe River.** Guests can waken to a refreshing view of the moors and valleys surrounding the village. The inn provides clean, comfortable double or twin-bedded rooms with hot and cold running water and central heating. A double costs about £6.50 ($12.68) per person, going up to £9.50 ($18.53) per person for a room with a private shower. Prices include a continental breakfast, but you can have a full English breakfast for another £1.25 ($2.44). VAT is added to all charges.

In summer, the restaurant at Threeways is open six days a week, serving snacks from £1 ($1.95), although the more adventurous may prefer trout or one of the inn's succulent filet steaks.

6. Glastonbury

The goal of the medieval pilgrim, **Glastonbury Abbey**, once one of the wealthiest and most prestigious monasteries in England, is no more than a ruined sanctuary today. But it provides Glastonbury's claim to historical greatness, an assertion augmented by legendary links to such figures as Joseph of Arimathea, King Arthur, Queen Guinevere, and St. Patrick.

It is said that Joseph of Arimathea journeyed to what was then the Isle of Avalon, with the Holy Grail in his possession. According to tradition, he buried the chalice at the foot of the conically shaped Glastonbury Tor, and a stream of blood burst forth. (You can scale this more than 500-foot-high hill today, on which rests a 15th-century tower.)

At one point, the saint is said to have leaned against his staff, which immediately was transformed into a fully blossoming tree. A cutting alleged to have survived from the Holy Thorn can be seen on the abbey grounds today. It blooms at Christmastime. Some historians have traced this particular story back to Tudor times.

Joseph, so it goes, erected a church of wattle in Glastonbury. The town, in fact, may have had the oldest church in England, as excavations have shown.

The most famous link—popularized for Arthurian fans in the Victorian era by Tennyson—concerns the burial of King Arthur and Queen Guinevere on the abbey grounds. In 1191, the monks dug up the skeletons of two bodies on the south side of the Lady Chapel, said to be those of the king and queen. In 1278, in the presence of Edward I, the bodies were removed and transferred to a black marble tomb in the choir. Both the burial spot and the shrine are marked today.

A large Benedictine Abbey of St. Mary grew out of the early wattle church. St. Dunstan, who was born nearby, was the abbot in the tenth century, later becoming archbishop of Canterbury. Edmund, Edgar, and Edmund "Ironside," three early English kings, were buried at the abbey.

In 1184 a fire destroyed most of the abbey and its vast treasures. It was eventually rebuilt after much difficulty, only to be dissolved by Henry VIII. Its last abbot, Richard Whiting, was hanged by the neck at Glastonbury Tor. Like the Roman forum, the abbey for years later was used as a stone quarry.

The modern-day pilgrim to Glastonbury can visit the ruins of the Lady Chapel, linked by an Early English "Galilee" to the nave of the abbey. The best preserved building on the grounds is a 14th-century octagonal Abbot's Kitchen, where oxen were once roasted whole to feed the wealthier of the pilgrims (that is, the biggest donors). You can visit the ruins and museum from 9:30 a.m. till dusk for 50p (98¢) for adults, 25p (49¢) for children under 16.

Glastonbury may be one of the oldest inhabited sites in Britain. Excavations have revealed Iron Age lakeside villages on its periphery. Some of the discoveries dug up may be viewed in a little museum in the High Street.

After the destruction of its once-great abbey, the town lost prestige. It is a market town today. The ancient gatehouse entry to the abbey, by the way, is a museum, its principal exhibit a scale model of the abbey and its community buildings as they stood in 1539, at the time of the dissolution.

SOMERSET RURAL LIFE MUSEUM: Abbey Farm, Chilkwell Street (tel. Glastonbury 32903). The main part of the exhibition is Abbey Barn, the home barn of the abbey, built in 1370. The magnificent timbered roof, the stone tiles, and the sculptures outside, including the head of Edward III, make it special. There are also a Victorian farmhouse and various other exhibits illustrating farming in Somerset during the "horse age" and domestic and social life in

Victorian times. In summer they have demonstrations of butter making, weaving, basketwork—anything which has reference to the rural life of the country, now rapidly disappearing with the invention of the engine, the freezer, and the instant meal. The museum is open daily from 10 a.m. to around sunset (on Sunday from around 2 p.m. to sunset). Admission is 50p (98¢) for adults, (39¢) for children. There is a snackbar for light meals and soft drinks.

WHERE TO STAY: If you're one of the lucky few who can stay over in this town rich in history, you can lodge where the wealthy pilgrim of yore did.

The **George & Pilgrims Inn,** High Street (tel. Glastonbury 31146), is one of the few pre-Reformation hostelries still left in England. Once it offered hospitality to Glastonbury pilgrims; now it accepts modern travelers. In the center of town, the inn has a facade that looks like a medieval castle, with stone-mullioned windows with leaded glass. Some of the bedrooms are former monk cells, others have four-posters, carved monuments of oak. You may be given the Henry VIII Room, where the king watched the burning of the abbey in 1539. Prices start at £13 ($25.35) for a single room, £16 ($31.20) per person in a double, VAT and an English breakfast included. A well-worn spiral staircase was in use by the monks for centuries, and if your dressing robe looks anything like a monk's robe, you may stir up the ghosts of the past as you walk along the corridors. You could be drawn to the old kitchen which is now the Pilgrim's Bar with its old oak beams. Even if you don't stay over, you may want to stop in for lunch or dinner in the Regency Restaurant to enjoy the excellent à la carte or table d'hôte menus, both of which feature traditional local dishes, or homemade fare in the snackbar. A set luncheon goes for £5 ($9.75), a dinner for £7.50 ($14.63).

LIVING IN THE ENVIRONS: Hayvatt Manor Guest House, Hayvatt (tel. Glastonbury 32330), is an attractive stone house, set back from the road, with true English gardens, even a hothouse where grapes are grown for making wine. The manor house is three miles from Glastonbury via Shepton Mallet Road. The owners, Mr. and Mrs. E. N. Collins, quickly become Norman and Molly, they are so down-to-earth and hospitable. They have three double, and one single room, for which they charge £7.50 ($14.63) per person for B&B, plus £6 ($11.70) for an evening dinner of three courses and coffee. They grow their own vegetables and fruits for their meals. Families may want to inquire about one of their attached apartments, where you can cook meals for yourself. These go for a weekly rate of £65 ($126.75), and for that you get a sitting room, two bedrooms, and bath, plus a folding bed and cot. Besides making his own wine, Norman has many hobbies, including playing a Hammond organ in the living room and doing special woodwork on boats. The Collinses are justly proud of their house, which has been designated by the government as worth preserving.

7. The Caves of Mendip

The Caves of Mendip are two exciting natural sightseeing attractions in Somerset—the great caves of Cheddar and Wookey Hole, both easily reached by heading west out of Wells. After leaving Wells, you'll first come to **Wookey Hole** (tel. Wells 72243), less than two miles away, the source of the Ax River. In the first chamber of the caves, you can see, as legend has it, the Witch of Wookey turned to stone. These caves were believed to have been inhabited by prehistoric people at least 60,000 years ago. Even in those days there was a housing problem, with hyenas moving in and upsetting real-estate values. A museum nearby exhibits prehistoric relics.

In 1973 Madame Tussaud's bought the ravine and a mill where paper has been made since the 17th century. In Madame Tussaud's storage room, more than 2000 molds of the famous and the infamous have been brought to Wookey Hole for safekeeping. Adults pay £1.95 ($3.80); children under 16, £1.15 ($2.24). Wookey Hole is open every day from 10 a.m. The last visitors are admitted at 6 p.m. from April to September, and at 4:30 p.m. from October to March.

At **Cheddar,** eight miles from Wells, you'll find an attractive village, famous for its cheese and an underground river (the Yeo), powerful enough to hollow out the spectacular Cheddar Gorge, a two-mile-long pass through 450-foot-high limestone cliffs. It's unlawful to try to mount the cliffs, except by way of Jacob's Ladder, an exhausting 322 steps to the top. Your "heavenly" reward will be panoramic views of the Mendip Hills and the Somerset moors. The cost of the climb is 30p (59¢) for adults, 20p (39¢) for children. The main attractions of the gorge, however, are below the limestone cliffs, in **Gough's Cave** and **Cox's Cave,** with their stalactites and unique rock formations. The museum contains exhibits of prehistoric man taken from the caves and dating as far back as 8000 B.C. Gough's Cave, with an admission price of £1 ($1.95), is open year round, every day, from 10 a.m. to 6 p.m. Cox's Cave, with an admission price of 75p ($1.46), is open all year from 10 a.m. to 6 p.m. Parking is free.

WHERE TO STAY: In and around this area, you'll find some interesting accommodations, as typified by the **George Hotel** (tel. Wedmore 712124), which lies three miles south of the Cheddar Gorge in the modest village of Wedmore. Here, King Alfred made peace with the Danes, and their ruler Guthrum in A.D. 878, forcing him to be baptized. Faced with such antiquity, nothing but an old-world coaching inn will do. The George, part of which dates back to the 1350s, has for centuries been giving strangers a refreshing pint of ale and a restful night's sleep in one of the 12 upstairs bedrooms. The B&B rate is £11 ($21.45) per person nightly. Bar lunches are available for £1.25 ($2.44) to £1.75 ($3.41), dinner from £5 ($9.75).

Behind the cellar bar are barrels of ales and beer, and rows of mugs hang from an overhead, time-blackened beam. Everywhere there is a sense of living in the past. It was in 1926 that the custom of holding "court leet of Wedmore" (a special type of manorial court) was abandoned, but the inn still functions as the center of village life. Today it is owned and run by the Hendersons.

THE CHEESE TOUR: Chewton Cheese Dairy, Priory Farm, Chewton Mendip (tel. Chewton Mendip 560), is one of the six remaining dairies in England still making cheddar in the traditional way. Visitors are welcome to watch the cheesemaking process, which takes place every morning. Mid-morning is the best time to arrive. After the tour, you may wish to purchase a "truckle" (or wheel) of mature cheddar to send home. A six-pound wheel costs about £16 ($31.20), including shipping. The knowledge that Prince Charles is also a customer adds even more flavor to one of England's unique products.

AN INN NEAR MINEHEAD: The **Ship Inn,** Porlock Weir, near Minehead (tel. Porlock 862753). As you drive along the A39 road from Bridgewater, through the Quantock Hills and toward North Devon and Exmoor, signs on your right will lead you down from Porlock to Porlock Weir, a tiny little port on the Bristol Channel backed by the Exmoor foothills. The Ship Inn is very old—almost 1000 years of history may have swept past it. Typical of many hard-working seaside harbors, timbers dragged from the sea have been used in the construction of the inn. Ceilings are low and windows are small.

All rooms but one have private bathrooms. Overnight, including a large English breakfast, will cost you around £16 ($31.20), plus VAT and service. Dinner is priced from £7 ($13.65) per person, and lunches are somewhat cheaper, about £5 ($9.75) for three courses.

The Sechiari family, who have run the hotel for many years, will do all they can to make you welcome, although they do not cater to small children.

AVON

Avon is the name that has been given to the area around the old port of Bristol—an area that used to be in Somerset.

8. Bath

Victoria didn't start everything. In 1702, Queen Anne made the 115-mile trek from London to the mineral springs of Bath, thereby launching a fad that was to make the city the most celebrated spa in England. Of course, Victoria-come-lately eventually hiked up, too, to sample a medicinal cocktail (which you can still do today), but Bath by then had passed its zenith.

The most famous personage connected with Bath's scaling the pinnacle of fashion was the 18th-century dandy, Beau Nash. He was the final arbiter of taste and manners (one example: he made dueling déclassé). The master of ceremonies of Bath, he cut a striking figure as he made his way across the city, with all the plumage of a bird of paradise. While dispensing (at a price) trinkets to the courtiers and aspirant gentlemen of his day, Beau was carted around in a liveried carriage.

The gambler was given the proper setting for his considerable social talents by the 18th-century architects John Wood the Elder and his son. These architects designed a city of stone from the nearby hills, a feat so substantial and lasting that Bath today is the most harmoniously laid out city in England.

Their work done, the Georgian city on a bend of the Avon River was to attract a following among leading political and literary figures—Dickens, Thackeray, Nelson, Pitt. Canadians may already know that General Wolfe lived on Trim Street, and Australians may want to visit the house at 19 Bennett St. where their founding father, Admiral Philip, lived. Even Henry Fielding came this way, observing in *Tom Jones* that the ladies of Bath "endeavour to appear as ugly as possible in the morning, in order to set off that beauty which they intend to show you in the evening."

Bath has had two lives. Long before its Queen Anne, Georgian, and Victorian popularity, it was known to the Romans as Aquae Sulis. The foreign legions founded their baths here (which may be visited today), so they might ease rheumatism in the curative mineral springs.

Remarkable restoration and careful planning have ensured that Bath retains its handsome look today. The city suffered devastating destruction from the infamous Baedeker air raids of 1942, when Luftwaffe pilots seemed more bent on bombing historical buildings, such as the Assembly Rooms, than in hitting any military target.

The major sights today are the rebuilt Assembly Rooms, the abbey, and the Pump Room and Roman Baths. But if you're intrigued by architecture and city planning, you may want to visit some of the buildings, crescents, and squares. The North Parade, where Goldsmith lived, and the South Parade where Fanny Burney (English novelist and diarist) once resided, represent harmony, the work of John Wood the Elder. The younger Wood, on the other hand, designed the Royal Crescent, an elegant half-moon row of town houses copied by Astor architects for their colonnade in New York City in the 1830s. Queen Square is one of the most beautiful (Jane Austen and Wordsworth used to live here—but hardly together), showing off quite well the work of Wood the Elder. And don't miss his Circus, built in 1754, as well as the shop-flanked Pulteney Bridge, designed by Robert Adam and compared aptly to the Ponte Vecchio of Florence.

BATH ABBEY: Built on the site of a much larger Norman cathedral, the present-day abbey is a fine example of the late Perpendicular style. When Queen Elizabeth I came to Bath in 1574, she ordered that a national fund be set up to restore the abbey. The west front is the sculptural embodiment of a Jacob's Ladder dream of a 15th-century bishop. When you go inside and see its many windows, you'll understand why the abbey is called the "Lantern of the West." Note the superb fan vaulting, achieving at times a scalloped effect. Beau Nash was buried in the nave and is honored by a simple monument totally out of keeping with his flamboyant character.

PUMP ROOM AND ROMAN BATHS: Founded in A.D. 75 by the Romans, the baths were dedicated to the goddess Sul Minerva. In their day they were an engineering feat, and even today are considered among the finest Roman remains in the country. They are still fed by the only hot spring water in Britain. After centuries of decay, the baths were rediscovered in Victoria's reign. Further major excavations are now taking place (under cover) to locate the temple of Sul Minerva and these excavations are open to the public. The museum connected to the baths contains many interesting objects from Victorian and recent digs (look for the head of Minerva). Coffee, with music, can be enjoyed in the 18th-century Pump Room, or you can have a drink at the licensed restaurant on the terrace. The Pump Room, Roman Baths, excavations, and museum are open daily in summer from 9 a.m. to 6 p.m. In winter, weekday hours are from 9 a.m. to 5 p.m., on Sunday from 11 a.m. to 5 p.m. Admission is £1.20 ($2.34). Telephone Bath 61111 for more information.

THE ASSEMBLY ROOMS: Lying right off the Circus, the Assembly Rooms were originally designed by John Wood the Younger in 1769. Partly destroyed by 1942 air raids, the rooms have been restored to the height of their 18th-century elegance, when the fashionable dandies and their ladies paraded about. Today they house a Costume Museum (tel. Bath 61111), founded on the collection of Mrs. Doris Langley Moore, and greatly enlarged and enriched by donations from many sources. The display of clothes covers more than 300 years of fashion history—Madame Recamier's lounging ladies, Jane Austen's upper-middle-class look, styles right out of Watteau paintings, the Alice B. Toklas post–World War I garb, up to Dior Haute couture and a '60s mini by Mary Quant.

Men's apparel isn't neglected in the exhibition, and there are embroidered silk suits of the 18th century, tailored coats worn by Victorian gentlemen, and outfits brought up to the present day by some of the world's leading fashion designers. There are also several dresses belonging to the British royal family, children's clothes, underwear, jewelry, and dolls. Head first for the Card Room, known to Dickens readers from the descriptions in *Pickwick Papers*. The museum is open weekdays in summer from 9:30 a.m. to 6 p.m., on Sunday from 10 a.m. to 6 p.m. Winter hours are 10 a.m. to 5 p.m. weekdays, 11 a.m. to 5 p.m. on Sunday. Admission is £1.50 ($2.93) for adults, 50p (98¢) for children.

BATH FESTIVAL: This annual festival of the performing arts lasts 17 days and takes place at the end of May and beginning of June. Essentially it's a festival of music under the artistic direction of Sir William Glock. Concerts are held in the Assembly Rooms, the Guildhall, the abbey, Wells Cathedral, and many other historic houses and churches in the area. The varied program includes concerts by the major British choirs and chamber orchestras, an international line-up of soloists and chamber groups, exhibitions, lectures, garden and church tours. All information can be obtained from the Bath Festival Office, 1 Pierrepont Pl., Bath, BA1 1JY (tel. Bath 62231). Finally, on the outskirts of Bath stands this leading attraction:

A GEORGIAN HOUSE: No. 1 Royal Crescent (tel. Bath 28126), is a Georgian House as it was. By the generosity of Major Cayzer, the house was bought and handed over to the Bath Preservation Trust in 1968 for the fulfillment of a long-cherished idea—the creation of an authentic Georgian interior—so that people could see what the inside of a Bath house looked like in its heyday. It is open from March to October inclusive, Tuesday to Saturday from 11 a.m. to 5 p.m., on Sunday from 2 to 5 p.m. Last visitors are admitted at 4:40 p.m. Admission is 50p (98¢) for adults and 35p (68¢) for children and students.

CLAVERTON MANOR: Some 2½ miles outside Bath, you get a glimpse of life as lived by a diversified segment of American settlers until Lincoln's day. It was the first American museum established outside the United States. A Greek Revival house, designed by a Georgian architect, Claverton Manor sits proudly in its own extensive grounds high above the Avon valley. Among the authentic exhibits—shipped over from the States—are a New Mexico room, a Conestoga wagon, an early American beehive oven (ever had gingerbread baked from the recipe of George Washington's mother?), the dining room of a New York town house of the early 19th century, and (on the grounds) a copy of Washington's flower garden at Mount Vernon. You can visit the museum from the end of March to the end of October, daily except Monday from 2 to 5 p.m. Entrance charge is £1.50 ($2.93).

READER'S SIGHTSEEING TIP: "The mayor's **Corps of Honorary Guides** conducts free walking tours of the City of Bath every day during the summer (end of May to end of September), bank holidays and every Sunday and Wednesday from October to May. Guides are also available for private parties at other times if required. These guides are unpaid and act in a purely honorary capacity: they do not accept gratuities. A tour lasts approximately 1¾ hours and visitors see the main points of historical and architectural interest within the city. For further information, write to Mr. J. Clifton, Assistant Director, Department of Leisure and Tourist Services, Pump Room, Bath, BA1 1LZ, Avon" (R. Alter, Lexington, Ky.).

WHERE TO STAY: In accommodations, Bath offers a wide choice—some in architectural landmarks.

　　Landsdown Grove Hotel, Landsdown Road (tel. Bath 315891), is a well-run hotel outside the center of the city, set on the northern slopes with magnificent views, 600 feet above sea level. Its drawing room is informal, with flowering chintz draperies, a large gilt and marble console, and comfortable armchairs. A modernization program has produced not only carpeting and fresh paint, but full central heating throughout and private bathrooms and showers and color TV in all the cheerful, comfortable bedrooms. Single rooms with bath cost from £27 ($52.65); doubles with bath, from £41 ($79.95). All rates include VAT and a full English breakfast. It's a pleasure to eat in the sunny dining room, with its bay window that opens onto the garden. Before-dinner drinks are available in the cocktail bar, which is decorated with delightful murals of Edwardian fairground scenes, while a bar annex is adorned with illustrations of oldtime music halls, bringing a uniquely charming atmosphere. Bathonians as well as visitors to the hotel patronize this place. There is an area for parking your car, as well as a covered garage.

Royal York Hotel, George Street (tel. Bath 61541), was a coaching inn in Georgian days, and now provides moderate comfort at a location within easy walking distance of the abbey. Every room is centrally heated, and there are elevators to all floors. Each unit contains a radio, telephone, and razor outlet—and is furnished with tasteful, traditional pieces, appropriate to the genteel character of the hotel. Some rooms have private baths. In high season (April to October), the rate in a single ranges from £18 ($35.10) to £25 ($48.75), the latter with private bath. Doubles or twins range from £28 ($54.60) to £37 ($72.15). Tariffs include VAT, service, and a full English breakfast. Try to get an accommodation in the rear, as these rooms are much quieter.

Royal Crescent Hotel, 15–16 Royal Crescent (tel. Bath 319090), is a special place for special people. It stands proudly in the center of the famed Royal Crescent, a Georgian colonnade of town houses designed by John Wood the Younger in 1767. The owners are continuing the tradition that has made this hotel a comfortable and pleasant place to stay. The 29 bedrooms—all with private bath, telephone, color TV, and radio—vary greatly in size, but all are nicely furnished and well equipped. The hall, lounges, and main staircases are said by eminent architects to represent the 18th century at its peak. Everything is furnished with a high standard of luxury and comfort. Central heating runs throughout.

An excellent cuisine is provided by the chef and his staff. The hotel has a good wine cellar and attractive bar. An elevator runs to all floors. In addition to the facilities, the hotel has a courteous and friendly staff. Attractive gardens lead to garages. The B&B rate is £36 ($70.20) in a single, £27.75 ($54.11) to £42 ($81.90) per person in a double. These prices include a continental breakfast, service, and VAT. Dinner is from £13.50 ($26.33) per person.

Jane's Hotel, Manvers Street (tel. Bath 65966), is central, a short walk from the main railroad and bus stations and near the abbey and the Roman Baths. Ample parking space is available in the multistory car park behind the hotel. The hotel is a Victorian building created from a row of terraced houses. It provides clean, comfortable bedrooms, with plenty of hot water, tea-and-coffee-making facilities, and color TV, at a cost ranging between £15 ($29.25) and £17 ($33.15) per person, including tax. Jane's is managed by Adrian Leonards, a Cornishman, who, along with his staff, has spent the last few years refurbishing, repainting, and improving the hotel.

Recently opened is the French-style Crêperie and Wine Bar, created in a separate section of the hotel. This is the innovation of Christopher Bradshaw, son of the proprietor. Open from 11 a.m. to 11 p.m., it offers excellent value for money, along with good music. One of the West Country's most popular nightclubs is beneath the hotel. It's the Beau Nash Disco, which opens at 8 p.m.

and closes late. Entrance is free to hotel guests. Otherwise, visitors pay £2 ($3.90) per person.

Villa Magdala, Henrietta Road (tel. Bath 25836), is a "country" guest house just a five-minute walk from the center of Bath. In a quiet residential area across the Avon from the Parade Gardens and overlooking Henrietta Park, the villa was completed in 1868 and named after the Battle of Magdala which was fought the same year. The stone and gabled structure offers many features of a residential hotel, including refrigerators, baths or showers, color TVs, hotplates, central heating, and baby-listening services. A few of the rooms are even furnished with deluxe four-poster beds. Rates range from approximately £16 ($31.20) for a single room with private shower to £25 ($48.75) for a double room with four-poster and bath. Price per night includes VAT and a full English breakfast. Ample car parking is provided on the grounds. You get real personal attention from the hosts, Len and Beryl Willis. Their breakfast menu is most comprehensive. The ham is home-cooked, simmered in stock, and eggs are done the way you want them. Mrs. Willis takes care to see that the prunes are just right, as she soaks and then simmers them with lemon.

Christopher Hotel, High Street (tel. Bath 60029), is an attractive, well-run hotel, with an 18th-century facade, one of Bath's oldest coaching inns. Opposite a side of the abbey and overlooking the Grand Parade, it is only a one-minute walk from the Roman Baths. The residents' lounge combines traditional and modern elements. The bedrooms are pleasantly furnished and well kept; a double with bath costs £27.50 ($53.63) nightly. The rates include an English breakfast. You can order good food in the restaurant, which has both a table d'hôte and an à la carte menu. The hotel has two bars but no elevator. A multistory car park is nearby.

The **Old Mill,** Toll Bridge Road (tel. Bath 858476), is a small, family-run hotel right on the Avon, beside a stone bridge in Batheaston, about 2½ miles from Bath on the A4 to Chippenham. Nearly every bedroom has a view of the river, with its willows, punting boats, and towering trees. Rooms are being modernized, especially with the addition of radios, intercoms, and baby-listening devices. Two lovely four-poster beds have been added as well. In the main hotel, a double room with private bath costs from £32 ($62.40), dropping to £28 ($54.60) without facilities. Incidentally, this latter price is the tariff for a double room with private bath in the annex. Some rooms in the annex without private plumbing are rented slightly cheaper. Tariffs include VAT, service, and an English or continental breakfast. Honeymooners can ask about the bridal suite.

For such a small establishment (only 16 bedrooms), the hotel has a large restaurant, and in fact that is the basis of its local renown. Vincent Cimatti, since taking over the establishment in the early '70s, still does a lot of the cooking himself, although he hires an excellent chef. Fresh foods are prepared to traditional English and French recipes and served in the relaxed atmosphere of the inn's Riverside Restaurant.

The menu changes as the seasons do, so I hesitate to recommend specific dishes. Although you can usually find a good steak and most often salmon, try, if possible, one of the inn's specialties such as "quails dressed in their nightshirts"—that is, filled with a chestnut dressing and cooked in pastry, with a raspberry sauce to cover. Vegetables are often unusual, including marrow flowers. Mr. Cimatti often grows many of his own vegetables. For dessert, I'd suggest one of his velvety mousses. A chef's menu offers a three-course meal for £8.50 ($16.58) per diner, a very good value. However, if you prefer a wider selection from the à la carte menu, expect to spend from £12 ($23.40) per head, plus the cost of your wine.

Lunch is offered from 12:30 to 2 p.m. and dinner from 7:30 to 9:30 p.m. (till 8:30 p.m. on Sunday).

Living on the Outskirts

Homewood Park, Hinton Charterhouse (tel. Limpley Stoke 2643), is set in ten acres of garden, just five miles south of Bath on the A36 Bath-Warminster road. Stephen and Penny Ross, who ran the successful Popjoys restaurant in Bath, have converted the property and now offer eight bedrooms with private baths. This small, family-run hotel was built in the 18th century, then subsequently enlarged in the 19th century. Overlooking the Limpley Stoke Valley, it is a large Victorian house, its grounds adjoining the 13th-century ruin of Hinton Priory.

The B&B rate is from £14 ($27.30) per person nightly. Of course, most visitors come here for the cuisine, served in a dining room facing south, overlooking the gardens. The French and English cooking is prepared with skill and flair, and expect to spend from £12 ($23.40) for a meal. The service is friendly and efficient.

On the grounds is a tennis court, and riding can be arranged with the stables next door.

Robins Close Country House Hotel, Middle Green Road, Wellington (tel. Wellington 2032), stands on 17 acres of secluded grounds in the Somerset countryside. At the turn of the century, this was built as a large family house, and it's still very much a family affair, tastefully run by two brothers and their families. The Fairbrass clan sees to your comfort and well-being.

If you're driving to the manor house (the only way I'd recommend), Wellington lies on the A38 between Taunton and Exeter. The M5 runs near the town (take the exit at no. 26).

A total of 12 bedrooms is rented, each modernized and pleasingly decorated. Some have bathrooms en suite. It's best to stay here on half-board rates, costing from £17 ($33.15) in a single and £32 ($62.40) for two persons. Children, sharing a room with two adults, are granted reductions.

In the restaurant, where a dinner costs from £7.50 ($14.63), English fare is featured, along with some continental selections. From the well-stocked cellar comes a wide variety of fine wines, all reasonably priced.

WHERE TO DINE: Bath is increasingly gaining a reputation as a gourmet citadel. If you have a car, consider a meal on the outskirts of town at the previously recommended Old Mill.

Popjoy's, Beau Nash House, Sawclose (tel. Bath 60494), is housed in a 1720 Regency building which was once the home of the notorious Beau Nash, the "King of Bath." The restaurant is named after Julianna Popjoy, Nash's last mistress. Her ghost is said to haunt the drawing room. When Nash died in 1761, Julianna vowed never again to sleep in a bed, and spent the rest of her life gathering herbs and living in a hollow tree in Wiltshire.

With such a background, Popjoy's is certain to be something more than the run-of-the-mill restaurant. Its food, decor, and service all add up to making this one of the best restaurants in the West Country. You'll be greeted at the door and led up the sweeping stairs to the elegant drawing room with blazing fire and discreet bar. There you sip your apéritif while studying the menu full of original dishes. When you have made your choice, it is cooked to order. Nothing is frozen, prepacked, or partially cooked here. Fresh meat is accompanied by sauces cooked with each order using fresh herbs and vegetables fresh from the market. Your choice of fish depends entirely on yesterday's catch. But be warned—take a pause before ordering your dessert, which will be a rich treat from the kitchens at Popjoy's. The Beau's Delight, a hot chocolate soufflé, needs a few moments' respite before you indulge. This is one of the specialties of Popjoy's.

This eating experience costs approximately £14 ($27.30) per person, inclusive. Dinner is served Monday through Saturday. Lunch is offered from April to October.

The Hole in the Wall, 16 George St. (tel. Bath 25242), may give you one of your finest gourmet experiences in Avon. Tim Cumming in the kitchen has recovered the restaurant from a rather low ebb. You enter what looks like the living room of a Georgian town house, where a hostess greets you, takes your name and order for a drink, and presents you with the impressive menu. She'll even help you plan your meal if you prefer. All the selections are especially prepared for you. When your table is ready, you descend into a colorful, old-world dining room, with an attractive decor that includes a great "dungeon" fireplace. The benches, tables, and chairs are antiques.

To start the meal, you face a choice of both "cold and hot beginnings," which are likely to include fish soup with wine, saffron, and herbs. Main courses include the fish specialty of the day, depending on what the market has to offer. The menu is changed frequently, but you may be lucky enough to find such items as baked ham with mead and spiced peaches, civet of venison, and chicken braised with eggplant in wine. For dessert, the homemade fruit sorbets are smooth, as is the creamy syllabub. Count on spending at least £18 ($35.10) for dinner, including the house wine.

The restaurant has a selection of more than 120 wines, including a number of "bin ends," usually older vintages, which are offered at reasonable prices. The Hole in the Wall is open daily, except Sunday, for lunch from noon to 2 p.m., and for dinner from 7 to 10:30 p.m.

The Hole in the Wall is really what the French call a restaurant *avec chambres.* The upper floors of this splendid Georgian town house have been converted to provide eight double bedrooms, pleasantly and comfortably furnished, with private bath, TV, and phone. Although primarily a restaurant, the establishment nevertheless offers all the amenities of a hotel. A double or twin-bedded room ranges in price from £34.50 ($67.28) to £46 ($89.70). There are no singles as such; however, sole occupancy of a double room costs £23 ($44.85). Tariffs quoted include a continental breakfast, service, and VAT.

Beaujolais, 5 Chapel Row (tel. Bath 23417), is run by French proprietors, Jean-Pierre Auge and Philippe Wall, on true bistro lines. You enter through the undistinguished front door and find a seat in one of the three rooms of brightly clad tables. Then you're greeted by a member of the friendly and knowledgeable staff. Call in advance for a reservation, as this cheerful place has become very popular. You'll definitely need to give notice if you want one of the more private tables for four with settles. Fresh materials are used in the dishes served. Appetizers cost around £1.50 ($2.93), and main courses begin at £5 ($9.75). However, there is rarely a main course costing more than £8 ($15.60), which is what you are likely to pay for specialties like sea bass, half a roast pheasant, or venison. A new menu is offered every day, and it attaches importance to fish. Among the most popular appetizers are crêpe au camembert, fish soup, and piperade, to be followed by poulet en croûte Napoléon, coquilles St. Jacques à la Provencale, and entrecôte steak moscovite. The Beaujolais is open from 12:30 to 2:30 p.m. for lunch on Friday and Saturday and from 7:30 to 11:30 p.m. for dinner Monday to Saturday. Faint music plays in the background, and the atmosphere is informal, the value excellent.

Clarets Wine Bar, Kingsmead Square (tel. Bath 66688), is a cellar with whitewashed walls beneath one of Bath's Georgian houses. Simple slate floors and mahogany tables and benches and a plain decor show that David Tearle is an experienced restaurateur who offers simple surroundings and high-quality food. Casseroles of lamb and eggplant, pork and cucumber, or meatless vegetables and cheese are around £2.75 ($5.36). Interesting salads, cottage cheese and green figs, and homemade terrine go for £1.75 ($3.41) to £2.25 ($4.39). There is soup served with granary bread and homemade desserts. Try the St. Emilion au chocolat. A good meal will cost about £4 ($7.80) to £5 ($9.75), washed down with wine by the glass at 75p ($1.46) or from £4 ($7.80) a bottle. In summer they go really "bistro" and have tables outside for al fresco eating. It is open from 10 a.m. to 12:30 p.m. and from 6:30 to 11 P.m., Monday to Saturday; on Sunday from 7 to 10:30 p.m. only.

Sally Lunns House, North Parade Passage (tel. Bath 61634), is a tiny gabled stone coffeeshop, with a Georgian bay window, original early Tudor fireplaces, and "bow and arrow" cupboards. The house is a landmark in Bath, built in 1482 and considered the oldest structure in the city. Sally Lunn was known by legend to all Bathonians for her buns baked in the cellars here in 1680. The same tradition of good cakes is carried on today (also salads and light meals are served all day). Take your coffee, tea, or hot chocolate at a natural wood tavern table, or while seated in a settle. Coffee with a Sally Lunn bun costs only 55p ($1.07). You can have toasted sandwiches at £1.20 ($2.34), chocolate gâteau at 85p ($1.66). In addition, the owner has opened a Salad Bowl on the first floor which serves from Easter until Christmas, between noon and 2 p.m. This is a help-yourself plate which costs from £2.50 ($4.88), depending on which salads or dishes you select. You can eat as much as you like, although soups, coffee, and desserts are extra.

In addition, the owner, Keith S. Reynolds, has opened an evening restaurant, where the service is as charming as the setting. The restaurant is licensed, and meals are by candlelight. Added to the list of French and German wines is an assortment of English country wines, including gooseberry and dandelion. At a cost of about £8 ($15.60) per head, you are faced with a choice of seven appetizers, 12 main dishes, and an assortment of desserts (or cheese if you prefer). This set price is inclusive of wine and VAT, but not service, which is left to the discretion of the customers. The restaurant seats only 32 diners, so reservations are important. The owner has also opened a small bar in the ancient cellars. The house is easy to spot—near the abbey, off Church Street.

9. Bristol

Bristol, the largest city in the West Country, is a good center for touring western Britain. Its location is 10 miles west of Bath, just across the Bristol Channel from Wales, 20 miles from the Cotswolds, and 30 miles from Stonehenge. This historic inland port is linked to the sea by seven miles of the navigable Avon River. Bristol has long been rich in seafaring traditions and has many links with the early colonization of America. In fact, some claim that the new continent was named after a Bristol town clerk, Richard Ameryke. In 1497 John Cabot sailed from Bristol, which led to the discovery of the northern half of the New World.

In Bristol, the world's first iron steamship and luxury liner has been restored to her 1840 glory. She's the 3000-ton S.S. *Great Britain,* and was created by Isambard Brunel, a Victorian engineer. Visitors can go aboard this "floating palace" between 10 a.m. and 5 p.m. for an admission of $2 (half price for children), telephone Bristol 28157.

At the age of 25 in 1831, Brunel began a Bristol landmark, a suspension bridge over the 250-foot-deep Avon Gorge at Clifton.

The best way to discover the sights of Bristol, both obvious and hidden, is to take one of the guided walking tours operated by the city, costing 80p ($1.56) per person (children and senior citizens are granted half-price tickets). Lasting an hour and a half, these walks leave from the Exchange on Corn Street at 11 a.m. on Monday and Tuesday and on other days at 2:30 in the afternoon. On Sunday, guided tours cover the suburb of Clifton, where the visitor finds the biggest concentration of Georgian buildings, particularly the Royal York Crescent, overlooking Avon Gorge. Visitors are often astonished to find that Bristol has more Georgian buildings than its neighbor, Bath.

The city's floating harbor was formed by damming up the Avon River in 1809. A tour boat leaves from the harbor, daily at noon and again at 2, 3, and 4 p.m., costing £1 ($1.95) for adults, 50p (98¢) for children. For more information about these tours, telephone Bristol 28157.

Bristol Cathedral was begun in the 14th century on the site of a Norman abbey. The central tower was added in 1466. The Chapter House and Gatehouse are good examples of late Norman architecture, and the choir is magnificent.

Another church, **St. Mary Redcliffe,** was called "the fairest, goodliest, and most famous parish church in England" by such an authority as Elizabeth I. Built in the 14th century, it has been carefully restored.

Cobbled King Street is known for its Theatre Royal, the smallest English playhouse and the oldest in continuous operation. Many old taverns line this quayside area, principally the 17th-century **Llandoger Trow,** once the haunt of pirates. A few blocks up King Street from the Lightship, Llandoger Trow is reputed to have figured in *Treasure Island* by Robert Louis Stevenson. Guests drop in for a drink at the Smuggler's Bar or the Old Vic Bar, later perhaps enjoying a plaice or a steak dinner in an atmosphere of time-worn beams and old fireplaces.

This is also the home of the **Bristol Old Vic,** the city's repertory company. For information about tickets or its current presentation, telephone the box office at Bristol 27466.

FOOD AND LODGING: **Holiday Inn,** Lower Castle Street (tel. Bristol 294281), is a modern city-center hotel, ideal for the business traveler, but also suitable to the tourist who makes it to this part of the West Country. The heated swimming pool is impressive, and the foyer is spacious. Public areas are well groomed, comfortable, and stylish, in the tradition of this popular chain. You have a choice of two bars, and the Restaurant Panache serves an à la carte menu as well as snacks. Bedrooms are uniformly furnished, bright, and cheerful, with double beds (doubles have two) and good tiled bathrooms. Singles cost £29.50 ($57.53) nightly, and the double tariff ranges from £32.50 ($63.38) to £39 ($76.05).

Instead of finding lodgings in Bristol, many visitors prefer to seek out the accommodations in the leafy Georgian suburb of Clifton, near the famous suspension bridge.

There you'll find **Oakfield,** Oakfield Road, off Whiteladies Road (tel. Bristol 35556), an impressive guest house that would be called a town house in New York, with an Italian facade. It's on a quiet street, and everything is kept spic and span under the watchful eye of Mrs. D. L. Hurley. Every pleasantly furnished bedroom has hot and cold running water and central heating. The charge is £10.50 ($20.48) daily in a single, from £9.50 ($18.53) per person, based on double occupancy, these tariffs including breakfast. For another £5 ($9.75) you can enjoy a good, home-cooked dinner.

Alandale Hotel, Tyndall's Park Road, Clifton (tel. Bristol 35407), is an elegant early Victorian house that retains a wealth of its original features, including a marble fireplace and ornate plasterwork. The hotel is under the supervision of Mr. Johnson, who still observes the old traditions of personal service. For example, afternoon tea is served, as are sandwiches, drinks, and snacks in the lounge (up until midnight). A continental breakfast is available in your room until 10 a.m., unless you'd prefer a full English breakfast in the dining room. Terms are from £9 ($17.55) per person nightly in a twin-bedded unit, plus VAT

Among the restaurants, the most creative cookery is found at **Michael's** 129 Hotwell Rd. (tel. Bristol 26190), run by Michael McGowen. His charming and well-patronized restaurant is near Clifton, on a highway leading toward the piers. In his pleasant bar, decorated like an Edwardian parlor, an open fire burns. The dining room is also bright and inviting. Michael's menu is imaginative, and he likes to change it, depending on the availability of seasonal produce. Service is informal and enthusiastic. Lunch is offered from £8.25 ($16.09). Dinner is served until midnight (on Saturday till 1 a.m.). Expect to pay about £14 ($27.30) per person, including the wine of the house. Always call for a table. The restaurant is closed for part of August. There's no smoking in the dining room. If you want a cigarette, stick to the bar.

For more casual dining, **Flipper,** at 6 St. James Barton, at the edge of Breadmead, is said to serve the best fish 'n' chips in town. If you want to take out your dinner, it'll cost only about £1.25 ($2.44), a little more if you prefer to sit down and eat it on the premises. Good-tasting cod or halibut, served with crisp chips, is freshly prepared daily.

Behind a Georgian facade lies **Parks Restaurant and Coffee House, 51** Park St., a favorite hangout for university students. Here you can sample red mullet (Leghorn style), or steak-and-kidney pie for around £5 ($9.75) per main dish with vegetables.

Chapter X

THE COTSWOLDS

THE COTSWOLDS, the once-great wool center of the 13th century, lie mainly in the county of Gloucestershire, although parts dip into Oxfordshire, Warwickshire, and Worcestershire. If possible, try to explore the area by car. That way, you can spend hours surveying the land of winding goat paths, rolling hills, and sleepy hamlets, with names such as Stow-on-the-Wold, Wotton-under-Edge, Moreton-in-Marsh, Old Sodbury, Chipping Campden, Shipton-under-Wychwood, Upper and Lower Swell, and Upper and Lower Slaughter, often called "The Slaughters." These most beautiful of English villages keep popping up on book jackets and calendars.

Cotswold lambs used to produce so much wool they made their owners very rich—wealth they invested in some of the finest domestic architecture in Europe, made out of the honeybrown Cotswold stone. The wool-rich gentry didn't neglect their church contributions either. Often the simplest of villages will have a church that in style and architectural detail seems to rank far beyond the means of the hamlet.

Picture yourself as part of the life of these hills:

"Come on in through the kitchen" is all you need hear to know that you've found a homelike place where naturalness and friendliness prevail. Many readers will want to seek out comfortable (although decidedly unchic) accommodations in little stone inns that survive among the well-known and sophisticated hotels that advertise heavily. Perhaps you'll be served tea in front of a two-way fireplace, its walls made of natural Cotswold stone. Taking your long pieces of thick toasted bread, saturated with fresh butter, you'll find the flavor so good you won't resist putting on more chunky cherry jam.

Or maybe you'll go down a narrow lane to a stately Elizabethan stone manor, with thick walls and a moss-covered slate roof. Perhaps you'll arrive at haying time and watch the men at work in the fields beyond, as well as the cows and goats milked to produce the rich "double cheese" you'll be served later. Your dinner that night? Naturally, a roast leg of Cotswold lamb.

Or you may want to settle down in and around Cheltenham, where the view from your bedroom window of the Severn Valley to the Malvern Hills to the Welsh mountains is so spectacular that old King George III came for a look. The open stretches of common, woodlands, fields, and country lanes provide the right setting for picnics. Life inside your guest house may be devoted to comfort and good eating—baskets of fresh eggs, Guernsey milk, cream, poultry, and a variety of vegetables from the garden.

If your tastes are slightly more expensive, you may seek out a classical Cotswold manor (and there are dozens of them), with creamy field stone, high-pitched roofs, large and small gables, towering chimneys, stone-mullioned windows, a drawing room with antique furnishings, a great lounge hall, and ancient staircase, flagstone floors. Such Cotswold estates represent England at its best, with clipped hedges, rose gardens, terraces, stone steps, sweeping lawns, old trees, and spring flowers. Here you can revel in a fast-disappearing English country life.

The adventure begins in:

1. Burford

In Oxfordshire, Burford is the gateway to the Cotswolds. This unspoiled medieval town, built of Cotswold stone, is 19 miles to the west of Oxford, 31 miles from Stratford-upon-Avon, 14 miles from Blenheim Palace, and 75 miles from London. Its fame rests largely on its early Norman church (c. 1116) and its High Street, lined with coaching inns. Oliver Cromwell passed this way, as did Charles II and Nell Gwynne. Burford was one of the last of the great wool centers, the industry surviving into Victoria's reign. You may want to photograph the bridge across the Windrush River, where Queen Elizabeth I once stood. Burford is definitely equipped for tourists, as the antique shops along The High will testify.

WHERE TO STAY: Whether you're staying over or simply stopping off for lunch, there's a choice of some romantic old inns.

The **Bay Tree Hotel**, Sheep Street (tel. Burford 3137), would astonish the former owner of this 400-year-old, stone-gabled home. Surely Sir Lawrence Tanfield would never have predicted that this stately old house would become a quiet and peaceful setting for retreat-seekers. In his time, he was the unpopular Lord Chief Baron of the Exchequer to Elizabeth I—and was not noted for his hospitality. But time has erased the bad memory, and the splendor of this Cotswold manor house remains.

For a stay of three days (the minimum full-board requirement), you are charged £20 ($39) per person daily in a bathless double. If you prefer B&B only, the rate is from £14 ($27.30) per person (higher in a room with bath).

This is one of the showplaces of England. The house has oak-paneled rooms with huge stone fireplaces, where logs burn in chilly weather. There is a high-beamed hall with a minstrel's gallery. Room after room is furnished tastefully with antiques. The 20th-century comforts, such as central heating and a large number of bathrooms, have been discreetly installed. And the beds are a far cry from the old rope-bottom contraptions of the days of Queen Elizabeth I. You will sleep peacefully on soft mattresses.

Try to get one of the rooms overlooking the terraced gardens at the rear of the house. As the season changes, new flowers come into bloom against the old stone walls. Flagstone walks, tidy lawns, and comfortable garden furniture will lure you into a lazy afternoon. A servant will bring you a tray at teatime.

You dine at night by candlelight: the meals are first class, some of the finest you'll be served in Cotswolds. A recent lunch for £4 ($7.80) consisted of a smoked salmon omelet, served with string beans and potatoes, and a spicy hot mince pie with brandy butter for dessert. Dinner is £6 ($11.70), and the big Sunday lunch costs the same.

Have after-dinner coffee on the terrace and experience twilight. Slowly the soft shadows grow darker and longer: this is the moment of enchantment in England. You may even hear a meadow lark.

The **Lamb Inn**, Sheep Street (tel. Burford 3155), is a thoroughbred Cotswold house, built solidly in 1430 of thick stones, with mullioned and leaded windows, many chimneys and gables, and a slate roof mossy with age. On a quiet street, it opens onto a stone-paved rear garden, with a rose-lined walk and a shaded lawn. Mrs. Nancy North Lewis is the owner; a most gracious hostess, she is joined by three of her sons. Some members of their staff have been with the inn for 20 years. The chef is Cordon Bleu oriented, and the meals, served in the beamed dining room with a garden view, attract nonresidents, who pay £4 ($7.80) for a set luncheon, £6 ($11.70) on Sunday. A set dinner goes for £6 also. If you're dining in the right season, you can feast on treats of the river or forest, such as salmon, venison, trout, game, roast capon.

While there is a per-person B&B rate of £15.50 ($30.23) to £18.50 ($36.08) —the latter with a private bath—most dollarwise visitors stay for at least three days so they can take advantage of the half-board rates, ranging from £21 ($40.95) to £23 ($44.85) per person daily. The bedrooms are a mixture of today's comforts, such as soft beds and plentiful hot water, and yesterday's antiques. The public living rooms contain heavy oak beams, stone floors, window seats, Oriental rugs, and fine antiques (Chippendale, Tudor, Adam, Georgian, Jacobean). In the drinking lounge, a special beer, made in an adjoining brewery, is served. In addition, a four o'clock tea is offered in front of the fireplaces, or else, weather permitting, out on the flagstoned courtyard.

2. Clanfield

Clanfield lies at the foot of the Cotswolds, near the upper reaches of the Thames. In the heart of "hunting country," it is convenient to Cheltenham and the Newbury race courses. Golf and fishing are available nearby. Clanfield lies 20 miles from Oxford, eight miles from our last stopover in Burford, and 16 miles from Swindon, and also makes a center for visits to Blenheim Palace,

Stratford-upon-Avon, Henley-on-Thames, and the Cotswold Wild Life Park, only a ten-minute drive from the following recommendation.

WHERE TO STAY: The **Plough Hotel and Restaurant,** Clanfield (tel. Clanfield 222), is a perfect example of a mid-16th-century Elizabethan manor house. Throughout the summer, climbing roses cover the honey-colored Cotswold stone walls. Its attractive gardens just opposite the village green offer a peaceful spot for meditation. Under protection as a landmark building, the Plough maintains an air of authenticity inside as well, with cloistered halls, massive fireplaces, and fine antiques and tapestries.

The restaurant has become internationally recognized, having won various awards for its cuisine every year since 1970. Dinners are served in the Knights' and Tapestry Rooms with their authentic period furnishings. During the summer months, luncheon is frequently served in the small walled garden. Drinks are available in the beamed lounge with its magnificent Elizabethan fireplace. The Plough is open seven days a week, with luncheon prices beginning at £8 ($15.60) and the à la carte dinner from £12 ($23.40). VAT is added to the tab.

For those desiring overnight accommodations, the Plough offers several small but attractively furnished rooms. A double room with bath goes for £35 ($68.25). For this same price, you might also be assigned a double room with a four-poster bed. A single without bath goes for £20 ($39), the price rising to £25 ($48.75) with bath. VAT is included, but a service charge is added.

3. Minster Lovell

From Oxford along the A40, you pass through Witney. Soon after, you turn right at the Minster Lovell signpost, about half a mile off the highway between Witney and Burford. The village's main attraction is **Minster Lovell Hall,** the remains of a moated house where an early Lovell supposedly hid out and starved to death after a battle in the area.

By the Windrush River, Minster Lovell is mainly built of Cotswold stone, with thatch or stone-slate roofs. It's rather a pity there is a forest of TV aerials, but the place is still attractive to photographers.

The **Old Swan Hotel,** Minster Lovell (tel. Asthall Leigh 614), was built in the 14th century and visited by Richard III in the 15th. It is still run in the traditional English manner. The lawns and gardens are dominated by centuries-old horse chestnuts. In winter a warm, relaxed atmosphere is created by the chintz-covered armchairs and the log fires in the inglenooks. The hotel's unusual sign is that of a flying swan. The food is good, and the restaurant offers both continental and traditional English dishes prepared by a team of enthusiastic young chefs. The headwaiter has served the hotel for more than 30 years. A timbered ceiling, candlelight, and real oil lamps make for a memorable dinner. A table d'hôte luncheon costs from £6 ($11.70) on weekdays, £7 ($13.65) on Sunday. Dinner tabs are, of course, more expensive. Garlic mushrooms followed by chicken Cotswold or tournedos Stilton, with fresh vegetables and a light gâteau from the trolley, will be about £2 ($23.40). The five bedrooms are centrally heated and double- or twin-bedded accommodations, costing £32 ($62.40) for two persons per night. This includes a full English breakfast, VAT, and service.

4. Bibury

On the road from Burford to Cirencester, Bibury is one of the loveliest spots in the Cotswolds. In fact, the utopian romancer of Victoria's day, poet

William Morris, called it England's most beautiful village. On the banks of the tiny Coln River, Bibury is noted for **Arlington Row,** a gabled group of 15th-century cottages, its biggest and most-photographed drawing card. The row is protected by the National Trust.

Arlington Mill dates from the 17th century and was in use until the outbreak of World War I. It contains a collection of 19th-century mill machinery, along with Peter Waals furniture, Victorian costumes and furniture, and Staffordshire china. The mill is open March to October and most winter weekends from 11 a.m. to 7 p.m., and charges 70p ($1.37) admission for adults, 35p (68¢) for children. They also have pottery for sale.

WHERE TO STAY: Bibury is a good base for touring the old wool towns of the North Cotswolds. For those who prefer a secluded roadside oasis, I have the following recommendations:

Bibury Court Hotel (tel. Bibury 337) is a Jacobean manor house built by Sir Thomas Sackville in 1633 (parts of it date from Tudor times). Its eight acres of grounds are approached through a large gateway, the lawn extending to the encircling Coln River. The house was privately owned until it was turned into a medium-priced hotel in 1968. The structure is built of Cotswold stone, with many gables, huge chimneys, leaded-glass stone-mullioned windows, and a formal graveled entryway. Inside there are many country manor furnishings, and antiques, as well as an open stone log-burning fireplace. In a double, the inclusive B&B rate is £25 ($48.75), dropping to £14.50 ($28.28) in a single. Many of the rooms have four-poster beds, original oak paneling, and antiques. Meals are an event in the stately dining room, where lunches and dinners start at £7 ($13.65). After tea and biscuits in the drawing room, walk across the lawn along the river where you find a doorway leading to a little church. On your return, head for one of the coaching houses which has been converted into a drinking lounge, a restful place for a glass of stout.

The **Swan Hotel** (tel. Bibury 204) is a scene-stealer. Before you cross over the arched stone bridge spanning the Coln, pause and look at the vine-covered facade. Yes, it's the same view that has appeared on many a calendar. The former coaching inn will bed you down for the night in one of its handsomely appointed chambers, all with bath or shower, charging £17.75 ($34.61) per person nightly. A traditional English breakfast and VAT are included. All of the rooms have been modernized, and there are many comforts. The special feature of the Swan is the small stretch of trout stream reserved for guests. If you're just passing through for the day, you may want to stop over and order the £6.75 ($13.16) lunch or the £9.50 ($18.53) dinner.

When you see the gardens at the Swan, your exploring days may be over.

5. Cirencester

Don't worry about how to pronounce the name of the town. Even the English are in disagreement. Just say "siren-sess-ter" and you won't go too far wrong. Cirencester is often considered the unofficial capital of the Cotswolds, probably a throwback to its reputation in the Middle Ages when it flourished as the center of the great wool industry.

But even in Roman Britain, five roads converged on Cirencester, which was called Corinium in those days. In size, it ranked second only to London. Today, it is chiefly a market town, a good base for touring, as it lies 34 miles from Bath, 16 from the former Regency spa at Cheltenham, 17 from Gloucester, 36 from Oxford, and 38 from Stratford-upon-Avon. The trip from London is 89 miles. In the heart of the town itself are two important sights:

Corinium Museum on Park Street(tel. Cirencester 5611) houses archeological remains left from the Roman occupation of Cirencester. The mosaic pavements found on Dyer Street in Cirencester in 1849 are the most important exhibit. And the provincial Roman sculpture (Minerva, Mercury), the pottery, the bits and pieces salvaged from long-decayed buildings, provide a remote link with the civilization that once flourished here. The museum has been completely redeveloped and modernized. It's open from 10 a.m. to 6 p.m. weekdays, 2 to 6 p.m. on Sunday. Admission is 40p (78¢) for adults, 20p (39¢) for senior citizens and children. The museum is closed on Monday from October to April.

Cirencester Parish Church, dating back to Norman times and Henry I, is the Church of John the Baptist, overlooking the Market Square. (Actually, a church may have stood on this spot in Saxon times.) In size, the Cirencester church appears to be a cathedral—not a mere parish church. The present building represents a variety of styles, largely Perpendicular, as in the early 15th-century tower. Among the treasures inside are a 15th-century pulpit and a silver-gilt cup given to Queen Anne Boleyn two years before her execution.

WHERE TO STAY: Stratton House Hotel, Gloucester Road (tel. Cirencester 61761), on the outskirts of town, has a delightful country-house atmosphere in a building that is part Jacobean and part Georgian. This mellow old house, which stands in its own beautiful grounds with a walled garden and herbaceous borders, is inviting and extremely comfortable. The bedrooms are large and most have bathrooms en suite. In the dining and drawing rooms, some fine antique furniture and oil paintings may be seen. The half-board rates range from £24.25 ($47.29) to £26.50 ($51.68) per person. These tariffs include an English breakfast and a well-served dinner with a wide choice of British dishes. There is a timbered-beam bar, and in winter log fires blaze in this bar and in the main hall.

If you don't want to stay at a hotel, you might try **La Ronde Guest House/Restaurant,** 52–54 Ashcroft Rd. (tel. Cirencester 4611), run by Mr. and Mrs. N. E. Shales, who charge approximately £12 ($23.40) per person for B&B. They have family rooms, as well as doubles and twins. In the town center, within walking distance of Cirencester Park, the Abbey Grounds, and the museum and parish church, the small hotel is licensed and is a good center for exploring all the Cotswolds. The dining room offers a varied menu and an extensive wine list. Dinner is from £7.50 ($14.63). The hotel offers central heating, hot and cold running water in all the rooms, and has a color TV lounge as well.

WHERE TO DINE: The **Crown,** West Market Place (tel. Cirencester 3811), has been a coaching inn since the 14th century. Its position is perfect, opposite the lovely old parish church. Many of the Crown's original architectural features have been preserved, and the old beams tell a story of long ago. The Crown operates both a bar and the Old Swan Restaurant, where hot and cold buffets are served. In addition, it has a medieval ballroom, where medieval-style banquets are occasionally held.

The menu is changed daily, and the food is the usual traditional English dishes. By that, I mean homemade soup with crusty bread, cottage pie, pork in cider and rosemary, and chicken, leek, and cheese hot pie. A homemade fruit pie with fresh cream is the favorite dessert. Meals begin at £4 ($7.80), plus the cost of your beverage.

6. Painswick

The sleepy little town of Painswick, four miles northeast of Stroud, is considered a model village. All of its houses, while erected at different periods, blend harmoniously, as the villagers used only Cotswold stone as their building material. The one distinctive feature on the Painswick skyline is the spire of its 15th-century parish church. The church is linked with the legend of 99 yew trees, as well as its annual Clipping Feast (not the yew trees—rather, the congregation joins hands and circles around the church as if it were a Maypole, singing hymns as they do). Ancient tombstones dot the churchyard. Finally, you may want to visit **Court House**, a private Cotswold manor (see the court room of Charles I), open to the public for 20p (39¢) on Thursday only, June to mid-September, from 2 to 5 p.m. It is also open by special appointment (tel. Painswick 813689).

WHERE TO STAY: The **Painswick Hotel** (formerly the Cranham Wood Hotel), Kemps Lane, stands at the rear of the church (tel. Painswick 812160). Completely refurnished, this beautiful Georgian house was once a royal vicarage and is encircled by terraces of formal gardens. The hotel reception area was once the private chapel. For the upcoming season, I think this hotel offers exceptional value. Many readers have reported it to be the highlight of their Cotswold tour. In rooms, cuisine, and service, it merits consideration enough to rate a major detour from wherever else you were going. There are rooms both with and without private bathrooms, and the rates for bed and an English breakfast start at £14 ($27.30) per person, including VAT. The hotel has high standards of cuisine and service. It is managed by resident proprietors, who give particular attention to their North American guests.

WHERE TO DINE: The **Country Elephant** (tel. Painswick 813564) is an excellent restaurant serving fine, English country-style cuisine. Owned and operated by Michael and Jane Medforth, the restaurant has a distinct personal touch. Mrs. Medforth does the cooking, keeping the menu limited so that only the freshest ingredients are used. In the simple dining room done in modern style, you can enjoy steak-and-mushroom pie with bacon and red wine, pork chops stuffed with apricots, almonds, and raisins and baked in cider with herbs, or a fresh grilled trout with cream and chives. Appetizers may include a homemade cream of watercress soup or an individual prawn and cheese quiche. The menu changes twice a week and sometimes even more often depending on what is available at the local markets. A meal will cost about £11 ($21.45) per person, plus 10% for service. Although they offer the finest California wines in their cellar, an inexpensive French wine will cost from £5.50 ($10.73) a bottle. The restaurant is open Tuesday through Saturday from 7 to 11 p.m., and also for Sunday lunch from 12:30 to 2:30 p.m.

ON THE OUTSKIRTS: Edge Farm Cottage, Edge, near Stroud in Gloucestershire (tel. Painswick 812476), is a carter's dwelling dating from 1800, nestled in what has been called "a secret part of the Cotswolds." Aside from the charm of the house, what makes Edge Farm Cottage special is its owner, Barbara

Blatchley, who, along with her doctor husband, welcomes guests. They've modernized their spacious house and have centrally heated it. Available are two guest bedrooms, each with twin beds, basin, and shower. Parties of two, three, or four persons are preferred.

The cost is £24 ($46.80) per person per day, including not only the bed and a full breakfast, but a good dinner with wine. Mrs. Blatchley offers personalized home cooking, well-prepared British food, including roasts, game such as pheasant and venison, and salmon when in season. Guests eat together in a dining room with an old bread oven, enjoying the conversation.

As a qualified guide for the Heart of England Tourist Board, Mrs. Blatchley will also offer her services with a car, charging about £50 ($97.50) for a full day's tour.

7. Cheltenham

In a sheltered area between the Cotswolds and the Severn Vale, a mineral spring was discovered by chance. Legend has it that the Cheltenham villagers noticed pigeons drinking from a spring, and observed how healthy they were. The pigeon has therefore been incorporated into the town's crest.

Always seeking a new spa, George III arrived in 1788 and launched the town. The Duke of Wellington also came to ease his liver disorder. Even Lord Byron came this way, too, proposing marriage to Miss Millbanke.

Some 100 miles from London, Cheltenham is one of England's most fashionable spas. Its architecture is mainly Regency, with lots of ironwork, balconies, and verandas. Attractive parks and open spaces of greenery make the town especially inviting.

The main street, the Promenade, has been called "the most beautiful thoroughfare in Britain." Rather similar are such thoroughfares as Lansdowne Place and Montpelier Parade. The design for the dome of the Rotunda was based on the Pantheon in Rome. Montpelier Walk, with its shops separated by caryatids, is one of the most interesting shopping centers in England.

You can take guided tours of Cheltenham on foot by checking in at the Tourist Information Centre on the Promenade. A one-hour tour costs about £2 ($3.90) and is well worth it, especially if you're interested in Regency architecture. However, an advance notice of at least two days is required.

WHERE TO STAY: Queens Hotel, Promenade (tel. Cheltenham 514724), can be safely considered the best hotel at the spa. At the head of the Regency Promenade, this upper-bracket hotel looks down on the gardens. Architecturally, it is imposing, built in 1838 in the style of the Roman temple of Jupiter. This distinguished hotel has a Regency decor and an unusually fine staircase. There are 77 bedrooms, all with private baths, radios, and color televisions. Accommodations at the back are quieter. Everything is well furnished, although decidedly old-fashioned. A single rents for £28 ($54.60), a double for £40($78), including service and VAT. The restaurant serves a business person's luncheon at £3.50 ($6.83) for two courses. The budget-conscious can enjoy a Queen's Table lunch from £2.40 ($4.68). A complete set dinner is £6.25 ($12.19).

Malvern View Hotel, Cleeve Hill (tel. Bishops Cleeve 2017), thinks of itself justifiably as a restaurant *avec chambres*. It offers only seven double bedrooms, with central heating, color TV, and private baths or showers (one chamber has a four-poster bed). These rent for £17 ($33.15) per person, with an extra £12 ($23.40) charged for dinner. The hotel's reputation for food is the finest for 20 miles around. Commanding views over Severn Vale to the Malvern

ENGLAND

LONDON

KENILWORTH

WARWICK

WARWICK

A46

A41

STRATFORD-UPON-AVON

WORCESTER

WORCESTEP

A34

EVESHAM

CHIPPING CAMPDEN

A38

BROADWAY

MORETON-IN-MARSH

Royal Sudeley Castle

WINCHCOMB

STOW-ON-THE-WOLD

LOWER SWELL

UPPER AND LOWER SLAUGHTER

CHIPPING NORTON

CHELTENHAM

BOURTON-ON-THE-WATER

GLOUCESTER

SHIPTON-UNDER-WYCHWOOD

OXFORD

PAINSWICK

GLOUCESTER

A40

BURFORD

A46

A417

CLANFIELD

BIBURY

N

GLOUCESTER, WORCESTER AND WARWICK

NAILSWORTH

CIRENCESTER

WOTTON-UNDER-EDGE

TETBURY

MALMESBURY

Hills and the Welsh mountains beyond, the hotel is five miles north of Cheltenham, on the A46 to Broadway. It's a long, low, stone structure, with white shutters and a surrounding garden. The country-style dining room is furnished with antiques, including wheelback chairs. The silverware is real silver and the glassware cut glass. The menu is wide, including various good French dishes. On my most recent rounds, I ordered ratatouille. This appetizer was followed by a giant quail stuffed with pâté in brandy. The vegetables of the day were fresh, a luxury these days. No lunch is served, and the restaurant is closed Sunday to nonresidents. Otherwise, dinner is offered from 7:30 to 9:30 p.m. If you're driving out from Cheltenham, you should telephone first.

Lilleybrook Hotel, Cirencester Road, Charlton Kings (tel. Charlton Kings 25861), is set on the outskirts of Cheltenham, providing a base for touring. The hotel is privately owned and has a policy of personal and friendly service. The decor enhances the image of the typical English country house. The bedrooms are equipped with central heating, a private bath or shower, and a color TV. Other facilities include a first-class à la carte restaurant, the Clock Tower Bar and Bistro (specializing in crêpes), a sauna, a solarium fit-and-trim room, and a private nightclub called Brooks, which provides live entertainment and specialty evenings. The clubhouse of the Lilleybrook Golf Course is five minutes' walk from the hotel. There are parking facilities for 200 cars. Their special weekend bargain rate is £19 ($37.05) per person per night, including dinner, bed, breakfast, service, and VAT.

WHERE TO EAT: Aubergine, Belgrave House, Imperial Square (tel. Cheltenham 31402), provides a creative English and French cuisine in a semibasement bistro setting. The cooking is by the owner and his wife, Iñaki and Sue Beguiristain (she's responsible mainly for the desserts). The atmosphere ranks high. Coconut matting is placed on the plain floors, the wood chairs and tables; and the walls are red—an overall effect that is cheerful. Mr. Beguiristain speaks almost no English, but his friendly staff does. The French onion soup and gazpacho are good. Main dishes include steak au poivre, trout with almonds, tongue in madeira sauce, and veal in brandy cream. There is always fresh fish and game in season. All the dishes are cooked to order, so patience is required. You can eat here for as little as £9 ($17.55) for two courses. Or if you finish with one of the desserts, such as chocolat à la crème, and have a bottle of Rioja wine, the bill is more likely to come to £16 ($31.20) a head, plus service. It's open for lunch from noon to 1:45 p.m. and for dinner from 7 to 10 p.m. The restaurant is closed for lunch on Monday and all day on Sunday. They also close for a summer holiday.

Montpelier Wine Bar and Bistro, Bayshill Lodge, Montpelier Street (tel. Cheltenham 27774), is an imposing Regency building converted from an old established shop to a cellar bistro and first-floor wine bar. Very busy at lunchtime, but worth the effort to get in, it offers a choice of some 12 wines by the glass at around 75p ($1.46). Then you can select a hot meal from the blackboard menu. A soup is always featured among the various appetizers, then cold meats, homemade quiche, prawns, smoked fish, lasagne, interesting salads, and a good selection of desserts. Pay around £3.50 ($6.83) for a satisfying meal either in the cellar or, in good weather, on the terrace. It is open from Monday to Saturday, noon to 2:30 p.m. and 6 to 10:30 p.m.

That Sandwich Place, Regent Street (tel. Cheltenham 29575), is a good luncheon choice, located in back of Cavendish House, a department store. Mr. Whittaker is the owner, and he is assisted by several very helpful local women who know how to make at least 200 different kinds of sandwiches, costing from

30p (59¢) to £1 ($1.95), plus an additional 25p (49¢) if you request salad garnishes such as lettuce and tomato. The repertoire uses such ingredients as peanut butter, cheese, prawns, pâté, beef, even bananas. Milkshakes, tea, and coffee are sold as well at 25p (49¢) to 35p (68¢) a drink. You have a choice of eating on the premises or else ordering from the take-away service.

Forrests Wine House, Imperial Lane (tel. Cheltenham 38001), is an extraordinarily economical place to eat. It's a small wine bar in an old bakery with tables given some intimacy by stall seats which divide the room. Presiding is Mrs. Henry Forrest-Hamdon (a true Cheltenham name if ever there was one). She provides a super menu with a daily homemade soup. There is a selection of homemade pâtés served with french bread and Middle Eastern dips with pita bread for £1 ($1.95). Also available is a different hot dish daily, £1 also, including homemade quiche, pizza, or pancakes with a cheese and spinach filling. For £2 ($3.90), you could have such dishes as spicy Mexican tacos with salad, lasagne with salad, chili con carne, or spaghetti Bolognese. For £3 ($5.85), continental dishes are prepared, including roast lamb flavored with rosemary and coriander or beef roulade with red cabbage Alsacienne and sauté potatoes. Upward of 20 different wines are available by the glass, so you can conduct your own tasting if you don't have to drive farther. Prices range from about 60p ($1.17). The house is open daily except Sunday from 10:30 a.m. to 2:30 p.m. and 7 to 10 p.m. (to 11 p.m. on Friday and Saturday).

On the Outskirts

The Mill Inn and the **Mill House Restaurant,** Withington, near Cheltenham (tel. Withington 204), have charm and hearthside comfort. The inn, until fairly recently a corn or grist mill, has a small number of pleasantly decorated bedrooms, some of which have private baths, renting anywhere from £20 ($39) to £24 ($46.80) per person nightly, including sherry and a fruit bowl upon arrival, a full English breakfast, and the service charge, but not VAT. The units open onto the river and a lake beyond. In winter guests enjoy the log fires, and, in summer they retreat to the riverside garden.

The village of Withington lies at the head of the Coln Valley, one of the most attractive spots in the Cotswolds.

8. Royal Sudeley Castle

In 1962 Elizabeth Chipps of Lexington, Kentucky, met and married Mark Dent-Brocklehurst, the wedding taking place in the 16th-century chapel of Royal Sudeley Castle (tel. Winchcombe 602308). In 1970 her husband died, and Elizabeth inherited the 15th-century castle in the Cotswold village of Winchcombe, six miles northeast of Cheltenham. The history of the castle dates back to Saxon times, when the village was the capital of the Mercian kings.

Elizabeth Dent-Brocklehurst, now Lady Ashcombe, first opened the castle to visitors shortly after her husband's death, to enable people to share the treasures of royal relics, stained glass, tapestries, and paneling. The gardens are formal and surrounded by rolling farm and parkland. The herb garden dates from the time when Catherine Parr, sixth wife of Henry VIII, lived and died at Sudeley. There are several permanent exhibitions, some magnificent pictures and furniture, and peacocks that strut on the grounds.

There is now a permanent exhibition of toys and dolls, with more than 9000 items, the best known of which is the rocking horse said to have belonged to King Charles I in the early 1600s. The collection belongs to Mrs. Kay Desmonde, who has at last found a place where the public can see what is said to be the largest assembly of toys in Europe. No extra admission is charged to the exhibition, which lies to the right of the keep as you enter the castle.

The castle also has a restaurant good enough to participate in the "Taste of Britain" scheme, offering particularly good local recipes of an international standard. Lunch can be a ploughman's variety or else a hot dish of the day or cold local ham.

The castle is open daily from noon to 5:30 p.m., March 1 to October 31. The grounds are open from 11 a.m. Admission prices are £2.25 ($4.39) for adults, £1 ($1.95) for children.

9. Malmesbury

At the southern tip of the Cotswolds, the old hill town of Malmesbury is encircled by the Avon River. In the center of England's "Middle West," it makes a good base for touring the Cotswolds. Cirencester is just 12 miles away; Bibury, 19 miles; and Cheltenham, 28 miles. Malmesbury is a market town, with a fine market cross. Its historical fame is reflected by the Norman abbey built there on the site of King Athelstan's grave.

Malmesbury is considered the oldest "borough" in England, as it was granted its charter by Alfred the Great in 880. In 1980 it celebrated its 1300th anniversary. Some 400 years ago the Washington family lived there, leaving their star-and-stripe coat-of-arms on the church wall. In addition, Nancy Hanks, Abraham Lincoln's mother, came from Malmesbury. The town still has members of the family, noted for their lean features and tallness. The Penns of Pennsylvania also originally came from Malmesbury.

WHERE TO STAY: The Old Bell, Abbey Row (tel. Malmesbury 2344), is an unusual place—once a monastic retreat—to use as a touring center. It sits in the heart of the town, adjoining the Norman abbey. Its facade is wisteria-covered stone, with six gables and two towering chimneys; an iron picket fence guards the flowers and shrubbery. The inn opens onto a formal garden, with graveled monks' walks leading to the rear back wall, with its little stone gazebo bordering the Avon below. Architecturally, much remains of the original building, including a 13th-century window and a medieval spiral staircase. There are 19 centrally heated bedrooms, nine of them with private baths (otherwise hot and cold running water). Singles range from £18.50 ($36.08) to £27 ($52.65), and doubles range from £31 ($60.45) to £37 ($72.15), including VAT. Open year round, the inn is often used by sportsmen, especially during Saturday hunts. Guests congregate in the dining room and the informal lounges and bars. The dining room is more modern (Regency), serving lunch for £6 ($11.70); dinner, £8 ($15.60).

WHERE TO DINE: Apostle Spoon, 6 Malmesbury Cross (tel. Malmesbury 3129), is run by Mr. and Mrs. Smalley, who serve tasty food. The restaurant stands facing the octagonal market cross, adjoining the abbey. A two-course meal is featured for anywhere from £6 ($11.70) to £8.50 ($16.58). Included in this à la carte meal are such main dishes as sirloin on the bone, kidneys in wine, pepper steak, salmon steak, chicken Wellington, and grilled ham. Appetizers begin at £1.25 ($2.44). The restaurant is open daily in summer; in winter it is closed on Sunday and Monday.

10. Tetbury

Tetbury, in South Gloucestershire, is a sleepy Cotswold town, with old stone houses, some fine medium-priced inns, and an antique market hall. It is here that Prince Charles and Princess Diana live at Highgrove. Although the house is not open to the public, and you cannot see it from the road, you may catch a glimpse of the princess shopping in the village.

WHERE TO STAY: The **Close,** Long Street (tel. Tetbury 52272), dates from 1695 and takes its name from a Cistercian monastery to which it was linked. It was once the home of a wealthy Cotswold wool merchant. Architecturally, it is built of warm honey-brown Cotswold stone, with gables and stone-mullioned windows. The ecclesiastical-type windows in the rear overlook a garden with a reflection pool, a haven for doves. Inside, you'll find a Georgian room with a domed ceiling (once it was an open courtyard), where predinner drinks are served and you can peruse the menu. Dining is in one of two rooms. Owners Jean-Marie and Sue Lauzier have spared none of their attractive antiques and silver, proudly sharing their treasures with guests. Candlelight on winter evenings, floral arrangements, sparkling silver and glass are just the background for the fine food.

The cooking is superb, and an à la carte menu offers specialty dishes. At lunch or dinner appetizers might include homemade soup. Main dishes feature chicken cooked in champagne and encased in light pastry; steaks, beef, and fish; even an exotic guinea fowl for two persons. Desserts from the trolley are always tempting. A dinner costs from £12 ($23.40) per person. Fixed menus are also offered for lunch from £6 ($11.70) to £8 ($15.60), and a full afternoon tea is available at £1.85 ($3.61).

Most of the 12 bedrooms (all contain private baths) are spacious and handsomely furnished with antiques. A single room ranges in price from £18 ($35.10) to £26 ($50.70), a double from £16.50 ($32.16) to £27 ($52.65) per person. A child sharing a room with parents is granted a reduction. A continental breakfast, service, and VAT are included.

The **White Hart Hotel,** Market Place (tel. Tetbury 52436), is a 16th-century inn in the village center. Sympathetically modernized, the hotel now has lovely bedrooms with private baths, while downstairs it retains its old-world charm. Log fires, stone walls, and lots of copper antiques adorn this privately owned hotel. Sunday lunch costs £5.95 ($11.60), and bar snacks range from 65p ($1.27) to £1.50 ($2.94). Bedrooms are from £17 ($33.15), including a full breakfast and VAT. Rooms are fully equipped with color TV, telephone, central heating, and double glazing.

11. Wotton-under-Edge

At the western edge of the Cotswolds, in Gloucestershire, Wotton-under-Edge is in the rural triangle of Bath (23 miles), Bristol (20 miles), and Gloucester (20 miles). Many of its old buildings indicate its former prosperity as a wool town. One of its obscure claims to fame is that it was the home of Sir Isaac Pitman, who invented shorthand. Its grammar school is one of the oldest in England, founded in 1834 and once attended by Dr. Edward Jenner, discoverer of the smallpox vaccine.

WHERE TO STAY: The **Swan Hotel,** Market Street (tel. Wotton-under-Edge 2329), lures with its Georgian facade, painted a distinctive blue. It offers comfortable rooms with and without private bath, but it is the fine French cuisine that attracts locals and visitors alike. Premeal drinks are taken in the Lounge Bar with an open fireplace. Meals are served in the restaurant, with its heavy beams, Windsor chairs, polished tables, and fireplace. In the Cotswold Restaurant, you can order either table d'hôte or à la carte. A three-course meal costs from £10.50 ($20.48). Specialties include beef Stroganoff and steak Diane maison. The Grill Restaurant is open for light meals starting from £3.50 ($6.83). A three-course meal goes for £6.50 ($12.68). On Saturday night, there's a dinner-dance with the resident band. Bathless singles cost £21 ($40.95), £25 ($48.75) with bath. A double room without bath is £27.50 ($53.63); with bath, £32 ($62.40). Tariffs are inclusive of VAT and breakfast.

12. Shipton-under-Wychwood

Taking the A361 road, en route from Burford to Chipping Norton, you arrive after a turn-off at the little village of Shipton-under-Wychwood in Oxfordshire. It's about four miles north of Burford; but don't blink—or you'll pass it right by. The monks of Bruern Abbey used to run a hospice in the village. That hospice is now an inn, and even it has some serious competition today.

WHERE TO STAY: The **Shaven Crown,** High Street (tel. Shipton-under-Wychwood 830330), was originally a hospice operated by monks as part of Bruern Abbey. In the 13th century, it served as a center for dispensing aid to the poor. Built of rugged Cotswold stone during the reign of Queen Elizabeth I, it is on the main village road, and opens onto a triangular village green in the shadow of a church. Most of the rooms overlook a cobblestoned courtyard and garden, and have attractive antiques. Hot and cold running water have been installed in every bedroom, and there are adequate hallway baths and toilets, and two of the bedrooms have private baths. The charge is £36 ($70.20) nightly for B&B in a double room with private bath, although this is lowered to £34 ($66.30) in a bathless double. Tariffs include a full English breakfast. Singles are charged £15 ($29.25) nightly on the B&B arrangement.

The **Lamb Inn,** High Street (tel. Shipton-under-Wychwood 830465), is a small stone Cotswold inn and perfect if you're seeking a simple village stopover serving a superior cuisine. It's owned by Hugh and Lynne Wainwright, who gives a cordial welcome. Twins and doubles with bath cost £23 ($44.85) per night, including a continental breakfast and VAT. Each room in the inn is country style.

A five-course dinner goes for around £12 ($23.40). Main dishes are based on the season and the day's buying, but are likely to include roast pheasant, grilled trout with almonds, and coq au vin. The house specialty is filet Wychwood, filet steak in a cream sauce. At Sunday lunch the traditional roast beef or lamb is offered, with all the trimmings, £6 ($11.70). At lunch a hot and cold buffet is available in the bar and you eat very well for around £5 ($9.75), or you can get something for as little as £1.50 ($2.93). The restaurant is closed on Sunday evening.

On the Outskirts

The **Wychwood Arms Hotel,** Ascott-under-Wychwood (tel. Shipton-under-Wychwood 830271). Until recently the Wychwood Arms was a local pub, a Cotswold-stone building among many. But Tim Randall and his wife Miranda have converted the upper floor to provide five comfortable double bedrooms, all with private bathroom, telephone, and color TV. The rate for a room and continental breakfast, including VAT and service, is £30 ($58.50) in a double,

£22 ($42.90) in a single. The furnishings are those of a country pub, and the pictures and prints which adorn the walls follow a sport theme. There is central heating throughout, and the atmosphere is friendly.

At lunch, apart from a thriving bar trade, they provide a simple menu of ploughman's lunch at £1.20 ($2.34), or a rump steak, £6 ($11.70). In the evening, all items on the dinner menu are cooked to order, so you must expect a small delay before tucking into French onion or oxtail soup or local game pâté. Main dishes include local roast pheasant and baked trout. Vegetables accompanying each dish are fresh and tasty. The meal, costing £8 ($15.60), is rounded off with a light dessert and coffee. The location is good, only 18 miles from Oxford, 26 miles from Stratford-upon-Avon.

13. Chipping Norton

Just inside the Oxfordshire border is Chipping Norton, another gateway town to the Cotswolds. Since the days of Henry IV, it has been an important market town, and its main street is a curiosity as it's built on a slope, making one side higher than the other.

Chipping Norton has long been noted for its tweed mills; also seek out its Guildhall, its church, and its handsome almshouses. If you're touring, you can search for the nearby prehistoric Rollright Stones, more than 75 stones forming a circle 100 feet in diameter—the "Stonehenge of the Cotswolds." Chipping Norton lies 11 miles from Burford, 20 miles from Oxford, and 21 miles from Stratford-upon-Avon.

WHERE TO STAY: The **Crown and Cushion Hotel,** The High (tel. Chipping Norton 2533), dates back to 1497 and was originally a coaching inn. Half of the bedrooms are equipped with private shower baths, phones, and television sets, and all are centrally heated. Rates are £13.50 ($26.33) per person in a room without bath, rising to £19.50 ($38.03) per person with bath, these tariffs including breakfast and VAT. Off-season bargain breaks are offered. The bar can provide hot and cold snacks morning and evening. The restaurant is à la carte. There's a color TV lounge, plus a residents' reading room. This is an ideal center for touring the Cotswolds, and it's close to Oxford, Stratford-upon-Avon, Cheltenham, and Silverstone. Resident proprietors are Jim and Margaret Fraser, who come from Limerick in Ireland, and visitors find it amusing when they discover this couple running an "old English coaching inn." The Frasers are helpful in finding accommodations elsewhere in the Cotswolds when their hotel is full.

An Old Mill on the Outskirts

The **Mill Hotel,** Kingham, Oxfordshire (tel. Kingham 255), five miles south of Chipping Norton, provides an up-to-date budget-range accommodation in an old stone mill, with its original bakehouse and open stone fireplaces. The stone water ducts at the rear have been converted into a formal garden, and in the front there is a rose arbor and a lawn with benches for those who want to enjoy the views and the sun. The Mill is owned by Mr. and Mrs. Barnett. All of the bedrooms have hot and cold running water (most contain private baths), and the furnishings are modern and streamlined. The B&B rate in a single is £19.50 ($38.03), £26 ($50.70) in a double. A double with private bath is £30 ($58.50). Specialties include rainbow trout and roast duckling. There are several lounges, one opening onto another; all have their original beams. Guests congregate in either the sitting room, with its inglenook and wood-burning fireplace, or in the tavern with its Windsor chairs and wine-barrel bar.

FOOD AT AN OLD INN: On the B4450 across country from Chipping Norton to Stow-on-the-Wold, right on the village green at Bledington, lies the **King's Head,** Bledington, Oxfordshire (tel. Kingham 365). This lovely 16th-century inn has been catering to travelers for more years than it's possible to remember. Nowadays, Joan Powell provides real ale to be quaffed in the beer garden or in the low-ceilinged bars. Lunchtime and in the evenings a buffet provides an ample meal of smoked mackerel, scotch eggs, steak-and-wine pie, and pâtés which complement the usual bar snacks. There is always a steaming pot of soup going, and chocolate and cream cakes are there if you don't want cheese. You can eat for as little as £1 ($1.95), or the most extravagant dish will cost around £5 ($9.75). She also offers three pleasantly furnished bedrooms, for which she charges £18 ($35.10) for two persons sharing a double, this tariff including breakfast.

14. Bourton-on-the-Water

In this most scenic Cotswold village, you can be like Gulliver, voyaging first to Brobdingnag, then to Lilliput. Brobdingnag is Bourton-on-the-Water, lying 85 miles from London, on the banks of the tiny Windrush River.

To see Lilliput, you have to visit the Old New Inn. In the garden is a near-perfect and most realistic model village. It is open daily from 8:30 a.m. till dusk, and costs 50p (98¢) for adults, 30p (59¢) for children.

If you're coming to the Cotswolds by train from London, you'll find the nearest rail station is in Moreton-on-Marsh, eight miles away. Buses make connections with the trains, however.

READERS' SIGHTSEEING SUGGESTION: "Tourists should visit **Birdland** (tel. Bourton-on-the-Water 20689) nearby. It consists of a beautifully designed garden of 4½ acres, a veritable paradise for some 600 birds of 158 different species. The macaws (each named) are particularly interesting and colorful—they love entertaining visitors with their antics and chatter. There is an exquisite group of flamingoes and a large collection of penguins with an eye-level pool so that they can be seen feeding, which is a rare sight. Also there are hummingbirds and others in a tropical house. A wildlife art gallery, opened by Sir Peter Scott, is part of the attraction. Admission is £1 ($1.95) for adults, 50p (98¢) for children, and 70p ($1.37) for senior citizens" (D. and R. Hosie, Balwyn, Victoria, Australia).

WHERE TO STAY: Bourton-on-the-Water offers a handful of quite-good accommodations, all of them inexpensive in spite of its reputation as a tourist attraction.

The **Old New Inn** (tel. Bourton-on-the-Water 20467) can lay claim to being the leading hostelry in the village. Right in the center, overlooking the river, it's a good example of Queen Anne design. But it is mostly visited because of the miniature model village in its garden (referred to earlier). Hungry or tired travelers are drawn to the old-fashioned comforts and cuisine of this most English inn. The B&B rate is £14 ($27.30) per person nightly, including service charge and VAT. The rooms are comfortable, with homey furnishings, soft beds, and hot and cold running water. Packed lunches at £2 ($3.90) will be provided for your excursion jaunts. You may want to spend evenings in the pub lounge, playing darts or chatting with the villagers. Non-residents may also want to stop in for a meal, with lunches at £3 ($5.85), dinners from £8 ($15.60).

The **Old Manse Hotel** (tel. Bourton-on-the-Water 20642) is reminiscent of the setting of Nathaniel Hawthorne's *Mosses from an Old Manse.* A gem architecturally, the hotel is by the slow-moving river that wanders through the village green. Built of ivy-covered Cotswold stone, with chimneys, dormers, and small-paned windows, it has been modernized inside, and all rooms have radio, color TV, and central heating. The proprietor, Mrs. Wendy Parkes, charges from £37 ($72.15) for two persons in a twin with private bath, a continental breakfast included. Rates are lowered off-season. The inn's best feature is the stone fireplace in the dining room, as well as the wood-paneled bar. Dining is a treat here. A three-course lunch or dinner costs about £6.50 ($12.68), but you can order from an à la carte menu as well. The manse is closed during the first week in January.

Chester House Hotel & Motel (tel. Bourton-on-the-Water 20286) is a weathered, 300-year-old Cotswold stone house, built on the banks of the Windrush River. Owned and managed by Mr. and Mrs. J. Davies, the hotel is an ideal center for touring. A double room without bath rents for £26 ($50.70), increasing to £30 ($58.50) with bath and TV.

15. Lower Swell

Near Stow-on-the-Wold, Lower Swell is a twin. Both it and Upper Swell, its sister, are small villages of the Cotswolds. The hamlets are not to be confused with Upper and Lower Slaughter.

WHERE TO STAY: You may want to anchor in for the night or stop for a meal at the following recommendation:

Old Farmhouse Hotel (tel. Stow-on-the-Wold 30232) is a small, intimate, 16th-century hotel in the heart of the Cotswolds. It is owned by David and Ann Gladstone, who have built up a reputation for excellent food and a warm, friendly atmosphere. The hotel is pleasantly furnished, and the cocktail bar (which only has a restaurant-and-residential license) and restaurant are popular with locals and visitors alike.

The bedrooms are comfortable and have central heating. A single rents for £15.30 ($29.84), increasing to anywhere from £25 ($48.75) to £29 ($56.55) in a double or twin, including VAT, service, and an English breakfast. Light lunches (soup, smoked salmon, chicken-in-the-basket, sandwiches, ice cream, etc.) are served à la carte Monday to Saturday from 12:15 to 2:15 p.m., while on Sunday a traditional English lunch is featured. A four-course dinner with coffee is served from 7:30 p.m. Monday through Saturday, and is likely to be a mouthwatering, filling repast from around £9 ($17.55) per person. The farmhouse is closed from Christmas Eve to the third week in January.

16. Upper and Lower Slaughter

Midway between Bourton-on-the-Water and Stow-on-the-Wold are the twin villages of Upper and Lower Slaughter. Don't be put off by the name because these are two of the prettiest villages in the Cotswolds. Actually the name "Slaughter" was a corruption of "de Sclotre," the original Norman landowner. The houses are constructed of honey-colored Cotswold stone, and a stream meanders right through the street, providing a home for the ducks which wander freely about, begging scraps from kindly visitors. In Upper Slaughter you can visit a fine example of a 17th-century Cotswold manor house.

WHERE TO STAY: Lords of the Manor Hotel, in Upper Slaughter (tel. Bourton-on-the-Water 20243), is a rambling 17th-century house standing on several acres of rolling fields and gardens which include a stream flowing through the grounds in which guests fish for brown trout. Completely modernized in its amenities, the hotel has still been successful in maintaining the quiet country-house atmosphere of 300 years ago.

The 15 guest rooms are equipped with private bath, and many rooms have pleasant views of the Cotswold hills. The walls in the lounge bar are hung with family portraits of the original Lords of the Manor. Another bar overlooks the garden, and chintz and antiques are everywhere.

The country atmosphere is carried into the dining room as well, with its antiques and mullioned windows. All the well-prepared dishes are fresh and home-cooked. You'll pay an average of about £11 ($21.45) for a meal which may consist of leek and potato soup or broiled scallops wrapped in bacon for an appetizer, grilled rainbow trout with almonds, or chicken Kiev for the main course, and a selection of rich homemade desserts from the trolley. Room rates, which include breakfast, VAT, and service charge, range from £36 ($70.20) to £52 ($101.40) for a double room, depending on facilities. Singles go from £23 ($44.85) to £32 ($62.40) a night.

17. Stow-on-the-Wold

This is an unspoiled Cotswold market town, in spite of the busloads of tourists who stop off en route to Broadway and Chipping Campden, about ten miles away. The town is the highest in the Cotswolds, built on a wold about 800 feet above sea level. In its open market square, you can still see the stocks where offenders in days gone by were jeered at and punished by the townspeople with a rotten egg in the face. The final battle between the Roundheads and the Royalists took place in Stow-on-the-Wold. The town, which is really like a village, is used by many not only for exploring the Cotswold wool towns but Stratford-upon-Avon, 21 miles away. The nearest rail station is at Moreton-in-Marsh, four miles away.

WHERE TO STAY: A wealth of old inns is to be found here.

Stow Lodge Hotel (tel. Stow-on-the-Wold 30485) dominates the Market Place, but is set back far enough to maintain its aloofness. Its gardens, honeysuckle growing over the stone walls, diamond-shaped windows, gables, and many chimneys, capture the best of country living, while letting you anchor right into the heart of town. Mr. and Mrs. Jux, the owners, who are partners with their daughter and son-in-law, Mr. and Mrs. Hartley, offer 22 ample, well-furnished bedrooms, all with private baths, radio, TV, B&B, central heating, and tea-and coffee-making facilities. The B&B rate ranges from £15 ($29.25). Arrange to have your afternoon tea out back by the flower garden. The owners discovered an old (approximately 1770) open stone fireplace in their lounge, so they now offer log fires as an added attraction.

Unicorn Hotel (tel. Stow-on-the-Wold 30257) was a posting house and staging inn, putting up wayfarers on the old Fosse Way. Nowadays run as a hotel, it is built of the local stone—low and sprawling with miniature dormers. While there is a nicely furnished residents' lounge, even two pubs, the emphasis is placed on the dining room and the bedrooms overhead. They offer 20 rooms, all with private bath or shower and toilet, color TV, radio, telephone, trouser presser, and tea- and coffee-making facilities. The rate for a double- or twin-bedded room is £37.50 ($73.13), including service charge, a full English breakfast, and VAT. The rooms are pleasant, excellent for sleeping, especially the chambers away from the road. The dining room provides table d'hôte and à la carte menus specializing in old English cooking with dishes of local origin. Summer season luncheon is available from the chef's table. There is an excellent choice of table wines. This heart of England hotel offers walks and historic places of interest within easy reach.

The **Kings Arms Hotel** (tel. Stow-on-the-Wold 30364) is a 500-year-old posting house, opening onto the Market Square. The much-traveled Charles I slept here, on May 8, 1645. You can, too, surrounded by some fine old antiques, for £11.50 ($22.43) per person nightly for B&B or £18 ($35.10) nightly for bed, breakfast, and a three-course dinner, plus VAT. The lucky ones get the King Charles room itself, with its carved bed and open fireplace. The other bedrooms are all comfortably furnished with all modern comforts—innerspring mattress, bedside lamp, TV, and wash basin. In the dining room, dinner averages £7.50 ($14.63). Hot and cold snacks are served in the new lounge-bar at lunchtime and in the evening, from as little as £1.20 ($2.43). The family-run hotel gives you personal service at all times and is fully centrally heated.

The **Talbot Hotel,** The Square (tel. Stow-on-the-Wold 30631), is an old house on the main square overlooking the church, the village stocks, and the bustling life of the small country town. The hotel has a lot of very comfortable bedrooms, mostly with bath or shower, in the main building and in the annex across the road. A single without bath goes for £12 ($23.40), increasing to £18 ($35.10) with bath. Doubles or twins are priced from £22.50 ($43.88) to £32 ($62.40), depending on the plumbing. Family rooms with bath go for £29 ($56.55) for three persons or else £34 ($66.30) with shower for four occupants. However, it is perhaps more for the excellence of the bar snacks that I include the Talbot here.

The lounges and bars are warm and cheerful, with open log fires burning, fresh flowers, and cozy chairs. Snack lunches are served daily and include such things as prawns in cheese sauce, jacket potatoes filled with cheese and onions, Welsh rarebit, cottage pie, and chicken and ham vol-au-vent. These hot or cold snacks cost from £1 ($1.95) to £3 ($5.85).

For those who stay at the hotel or passersby who require a more substantial and leisurely meal, the dining room specializes in many traditional dishes made from fresh local ingredients and accompanied by fresh vegetables. The manager, Mr. Curwen-Reed, has run the place for several years and takes great pride in the excellence of his menus. A set luncheon goes for £5.50 ($10.73), a set dinner for £6.50 ($12.68).

18. Moreton-in-Marsh

As it's connected by rail to Paddington Station in London (83 miles away), Moreton-in-Marsh is an important center for train passengers headed for the Cotswolds. It is very near many of the villages of interest—Bourton-on-the-Water, 8 miles; Stow-on-the-Wold, 4 miles; Broadway, 8 miles; Chipping Campden, 7 miles; Stratford-upon-Avon, 17 miles away.

Each of the Cotswold towns has its distinctive characteristics. In Moreton-in-Marsh, look for the 17th-century Market Hall and its old Curfew Tower, and then walk down its High, where Roman legions trudged centuries ago (the town once lay on the ancient Fosse Way). Incidentally, if you base here, don't take the name Moreton-in-Marsh too literally. Marsh derives from an old word meaning border.

WHERE TO STAY: For accommodations, seek out the following:

Manor House Hotel (tel. Moreton-in-Marsh 50501) is a 300-year-old stone manor, complete with its own ghost, a priest's hiding hole, a secret passage, and a Moot Room used centuries ago by local merchants to settle arguments over wool exchanges. Placed prominently on the main village street, it is formal, yet gracious, and its rear portions reveal varying architectural periods of design. Here, the vine-covered walls protect the garden, a tranquil retreat. Inside are many living rooms, one especially intimate with leather chairs and a fireplace-within-a-fireplace—ideal for drinks and the exchange of "bump-in-the-night" stories. Servants are instructed to keep the log fires burning—"never spare the woodpile."

You can't miss on most of the bedrooms, as they are tastefully furnished, often with antiques or fine reproductions. Many have fine old desks set in front of window ledges, with a view of the garden and ornamental pond. The centrally heated rooms have hot and cold running water or else private baths. All contain color TV sets. A single without bath costs £18.50 ($36.08), increasing to £25 ($48.75) with bath. In a bathless double, the tariff is £33 ($64.35), going up to £45 ($87.75) with bath, including breakfast, VAT, and service. In addition, Apple House, between the garden and the hotel orchard, contains three double bedrooms, each with shower, toilet, and basin en suite. Centrally heated, it has proven very popular with visitors. The cost is £29.50 ($57.53) per room, with breakfast, service, and VAT included.

A favorite nook is the bar-lounge, with its garden view through leaded Gothic windows. Evening meals in the two-level dining room are candlelit. A table d'hôte lunch goes for £5.50 ($10.73), dinner for £8.50 ($16.58).

The **Redesdale Arms** (tel. Moreton-in-Marsh 50308) is an old coaching inn, on the main village street, its original Cotswold stone features intact. Guests gravitate to the bar-lounge, where drinks are served in front of a six-foot-high stone fireplace. In warmer months, the rear paved terrace is the focal point, with tables set out for refreshments. The bedrooms are simply furnished, with soft beds, dressing tables with three-way mirrors, and hot and cold running water. A single without bath costs £15 ($29.25); a double or twin without bath goes for £28 ($54.60), and a double or twin with bath, £32 ($62.40). These charges include service and VAT. The inn is also well known for its meals. A three-course dinner goes for £8 ($15.60), although a full à la carte menu is available as well. Bar snacks are available at lunchtime, and on Sunday you can enjoy the classic English roast luncheon for £7.50 ($14.63).

White Hart Royal Hotel, High Street (tel. Moreton-in-Marsh 50731), is one of the Trusthouses Forte hotels. It's also another one of the hostelries graced by Charles I (in 1644), who did a lot of sleeping around. The inn provides the amenities of today without compromising the personality of yesteryear. There are two dozen well-furnished bedrooms, with hot and cold running water (some with private bath), innerspring mattresses, and a few antiques intermixed with basic 20th-century pieces. A single goes for £19 ($37.05) without bath, £24 ($46.80) with bath. A bathless double or twin is £26 ($50.70), increasing to £32 ($62.40) with bath. All rates include service and VAT. The old hallway is romantic, as is the bar lounge, built of irregular Cotswold stone. You can have drinks in front of the ten-foot open fireplace. Over the bar and on the walls is a good collection of swords, pewter, and copper warming pans.

19. Broadway

This is the best known Cotswold village. Its wide and beautiful High Street is flanked with honey-colored stone buildings with mullioned windows remarkable for the harmony of their style and design. Overlooking the Vale of Evesham, Broadway is virtually mobbed with tourists in summer, a major stopover for bus tours. That it retains its charm in spite of the invasion is a credit to its character.

Broadway lies near Evesham at the southern tip of Worcestershire, more than just a sauce familiar to steak lovers. Many of the prime attractions of the Cotswolds as well as Shakespeare Country lie within easy reach of Broadway. Stratford-upon-Avon is only 15 miles away. The nearest rail stations are at Evesham and Moreton-in-Marsh.

WHERE TO STAY: For lodgings, Broadway has the dubious distinction of sheltering the most expensive inn in the Cotswolds. Even the guest houses can command a good price—and get it.

The Upper Bracket

The **Lygon Arms** (tel. Broadway 852255) basks in its well-deserved reputation as one of the greatest old English inns. Sitting sedately in the center of the village, it opens onto a private garden in the rear, with three acres of lawns, trees, and borders of flowers, stone walls with roses, and nooks for tea or sherry. The oldest portions, built of fieldstone with a mossy slate roof, date from the 16th century. But builders in each century have made their additions. There seems to be some basis to the claim that Oliver Cromwell slept here on the night before the Battle of Worcester.

The Lygon Arms is now under the personal supervision of its owner, Douglas Barrington. The various lounges are appropriately decorated; there are smaller ones with tall and wide fireplaces where logs burn on chilly days. For example, an inglenook lounge, made from the original kitchen, has a 12-foot-wide fireplace, with a carved beam, a collection of wood, copper, and pewter artifacts.

The bedrooms vary in size and importance, their prices including a full English breakfast, early-morning tea brought to your room, and an English newspaper. You'll find a welcoming glass of sherry upon entering your private chamber. A single rents for £30 ($58.50); a double or twin, from £57.50 ($112.13) to £66 ($128.70), the latter with a four-poster bed. All rooms have private bath and toilet, along with TV. In the carpeted baths are such extras as tissues and bubble-bath solutions. There are a few private sitting rooms such as the one used by Cromwell, with its ornate plaster ceiling frieze, Tudor fireplace, and Cromwellian chairs.

You dine by candlelight in the oak-paneled Great Hall, with a Tudor fireplace, a cove ceiling, and a Minstrels' Gallery. The cuisine is international (even American specialties). A fixed-price luncheon begins at £7 ($13.65), £8 ($15.60) on Sunday. A fixed-price dinner starts at £12 ($23.40) and goes up.

Even if you aren't spending the night, a meal or afternoon tea in the lounge beside a log fire is a way to savor the fine flavor of this historic inn.

The Medium-Priced Range

The **Broadway Hotel**, The Green (tel. Broadway 852401), is right on the village green, perhaps one of the most colorful houses in Broadway. It is a converted 15th-century house, formerly used by the abbots of Pershore, combining the half-timbered look of the Vale of Evesham with the stone of the Cotswolds. While keeping its old-world charm, the hotel has been modernized and converted to provide comforts. It recently was refurbished, with more private baths being added. There is hot and cold running water in the bedrooms, as well as central heating and bedside telephones. A bathless single costs £20 ($39), rising to £23 ($44.85) with bath; and bathless doubles go for £34 ($66.30), increasing to £39 ($76.05) with bath. All these tariffs include a full English breakfast, service, and VAT. A few of the rooms contain four-poster beds. The cooking is fine, the service personal, the dining room attractive, the bedrooms pleasantly furnished. The attractive, comfortable cocktail bar is well stocked.

The **Dormy House Hotel,** Willersey Hill, near Broadway (tel. Broadway 852711), is a manor farmhouse, standing high on a hill above the village of Broadway, with views in all directions. Its spectacular position has made it a favorite place for those who desire either a meal, afternoon tea, or lodgings. Halfway between Broadway and Chipping Campden, it was created from a sheep farm. The owners have transformed it, remaking an old adjoining timbered barn into studio-style rooms, with open-beamed ceilings, window seats, a few antiques, good soft beds, and full central heating. Singles start at £19 ($37.05), rising to £28 ($54.60) in a luxury suite. Twins or doubles begin at £40 ($78), going up to £60 ($117) in a suite. There's also a private cottage with two twin bedrooms and a lounge bathroom priced at £100 ($195) for four persons. Rates include VAT and a continental breakfast.

The tavern meals in the bar have become popular, as the word is out that you get the most for your money here. Only fresh foods—nothing canned—are used. The breads and cakes are baked right on the premises in the farm kitchen. The dining room is gaining a reputation for haute cuisine second to none in the Cotswolds. Expect to spend from £9 ($17.55) for an à la carte dinner. There is also a fine cellar. In the lounge is a pleasant mixture of old pieces, comfortable armchairs, and a cozy fireplace. A feature of Dormy is the ingeniously decorated tavern lounge.

The Budget Range

Bankside House, 140 High St. (tel. Broadway 852450), is in the exclusive residential area of Broadway—and isn't allowed to put out a sign—but it accepts B&B guests who want to live in the atmosphere of a private home. Its owner, Elizabeth B. Oldham, tells the story quite aptly: "My bacon is crisp and my toast is hot! And I'm an American doing bed and breakfast in Broadway." Double rooms go for £9.50 ($18.53) per person nightly, with extra-wide twin beds and a large breakfast. The house dates from the 15th and 16th centuries, and is said to have belonged to Catherine Parr, one of the wives of Henry VIII. It is a honey, with its low beams, huge fireplaces, and garden. But it is the geniality and helpfulness of Mrs. Oldham that makes a stopover here a highlight of your Cotswold jaunt.

WHERE TO DINE: **Hunter's Lodge Restaurant** (tel. Broadway 853247) is set back quietly from the long High Street, surrounded by its own lawns, flower beds, shady trees, and flowering shrubs. The stone gables are partially covered with ivy, and the windows are deep-set with mullions and leaded panes. There is a formal entrance, with a circular drive and a small foyer furnished with antiques. The restaurant serves outstanding food, prepared by its Swiss chef-patron of international reputation. The menu, which is changed every month, features high-quality seasonal food and fresh vegetables. Try, if featured, the rabbit casserole or guinea fowl with ginger and lemon. The vegetables are crisp, the meats tender. Also, homemade desserts and chocolates are available. The cost is about £35 ($68.25) for two persons at dinner. Lunches are served from 12:30 to 2 p.m., and dinners from 7:30 to 10 p.m. The Lodge is closed on Sunday nights and all day Monday.

20. Chipping Campden

The English themselves, regardless of how often they visit the Cotswolds, are attracted in great numbers to this town. It's neither too large nor too small. Off the main road, it's easily accessible to major points of interest, and double-decker buses frequently run through here on their way to Oxford (36 miles away) or Stratford-upon-Avon (12 miles away).

Chipping Campden is the winner of the "Best Kept Village Award" in the Bledisloe Cup competition. Rich merchants built homes of Cotswold stone along its model High Street. They have been so well preserved that Chipping Campden to this day remains a gem of the Middle Ages. Its church dates from the 15th century, and its old Market Hall is the loveliest of the Cotswolds. Look also for its almshouses.

WHERE TO STAY: Here are several good choices, all in the medium-priced range:

The **Noel Arms,** High Street (tel. Evesham 840317), may make you a snob. You just may assume a title for the night, dreaming that this is your personal manor house, with its staff of servants. Dating back to the 14th century, the Noel Arms is a famous establishment. It charges £17.60 ($34.32) for a bathless single, £18.90 ($36.86) for a single with shower. Bathless doubles go for £25.70 ($50.12), doubles with bath for £30 ($58.50), plus VAT, for a bed and a full English breakfast. You can drive your car under the covered archway and into the old posting yard, where parking is private.

Mr. and Mrs. R. P. Sargent, the owners, have had much experience in running hotels, and they offer a warm welcome to their visitors from overseas. Their food always draws praise. Lunch averages £5 ($9.75), and a dinner costs as little as £7 ($13.65), if you order from the à la carte menus. The food is traditional English: poached salmon, roast sirloin of beef with Yorkshire pudding, roast leg of lamb with onion sauce, steak hollandaise, apple and loganberry pie.

There's a private sitting room for residents, but you may prefer the lounge, with its 12-foot-wide fireplace. The adjoining room is the public tavern—public in the sense that it's frequented by the locals. It's almost too quaint: old worn curved settles where you can drink beer from mugs of pewter, and soak up an atmosphere enhanced by racks of copper, brass pans, medallions, and oak chairs worn from centuries of use.

The **Cotswold House Hotel** (tel. Evesham 840330) is a stately, formal Regency house, dating from 1800. Right in the heart of the village, opposite the old wool market, it is run by two gentlemen partners, Graeme Black and Geoffrey Douglass. They have teamed up to bring a high taste level to this handsome old house, and are rightfully proud of the winding Regency staircase in the reception hall. All of the bedrooms have been renovated and two medieval cottages in the garden have been turned into very comfortable bedrooms with bathrooms. Each bedroom has its own personality, enhanced in some cases by antiques. A bathless single goes for £18.50 ($36.08), a double for £30.50 ($59.48). A double with private bath rents for £38 ($74.10). VAT is extra.

Taking your meals in the elegant Adam dining room is one of the pleasures of stopping over. The food is prepared with imagination and skill, a set dinner going for £7.50 ($14.63). A typical meal might include cream of celery soup, baked rainbow trout with almonds or roast leg of pork with apple sauce, along with fresh vegetables, followed by a wide selection of desserts. Set lunches are served in the dining room on Sunday. They begin with the largest table of hors d'oeuvres outside Claridge's. Otherwise bar lunches, snacks, salads, sandwiches, and soups fill the public need, judging by their popularity. Both guests and nonresidents are welcomed in this elegant background of fluted columns, an ornate ceiling, and three arched windows opening onto the garden in the rear. The front drawing room is homelike and informal, with a fine collection of framed needlework. Fires burn during the winter months, and the drinking lounge is a cozy spot on a cold day. The friendly management will do much to try to provide tickets for the Shakespeare performances and will offer after-theater suppers if you arrange them in advance.

Kings Arm Hotel, Chipping Campden (tel. Evesham 840256), stands right by the Market Square. It is partly Georgian, partly much older, a pretty house with a large garden in which you can wander and whence come the fresh vegetables for your well-prepared dinner. Bathless singles rent for £15.18 ($29.60); bathless doubles, £30.36 ($59.20); doubles with bath, £37.95 ($74). Tariffs include breakfast, service, and VAT. All the accommodations are well furnished and spotlessly clean. Snacks for lunch start at £1.50 ($2.93), and a Sunday lunch in the traditional English style is served for about £8.50 ($16.58). A table d'hôte dinner is a good meal with interesting dishes, costing about £10 ($19.50).

TIME OUT FOR TEA: Bantam Tea Rooms, High Street (tel. Evesham 840386). Real old-fashioned English afternoon teas are served in this lovely bay-windowed 17th-century stone house. You can almost feel the warmth from the much-used oven when you enter to be greeted by Judith McKay and her staff of cheerful local women. Tea can be just a pot of tea and a teacake for 80p ($1.56), or you can indulge in homemade scones, crumpets, sandwiches, and homemade pastries and cakes. Tea is served from 2 to 5:15 p.m. Tuesday through Sunday. It is almost an anticlimax to say that they also serve lunches Tuesday through Saturday with a selection of quiches and salad, cold game pie, pâtés, omelets, and salads (apple, date and nut?) for around £2 ($3.90). This is the brainchild of a cookery writer and her husband, but you can rely on Judith McKay to see that everything is in "apple pie order."

Chapter XI

STRATFORD AND THE HEART OF ENGLAND

1. Stratford-upon-Avon
2. Warwick
3. Kenilworth Castle
4. Coventry
5. Hereford and Worcester
6. Salop (Shropshire)
7. Staffordshire

SO CLOSE TO LONDON, so rich in fascination, the Shakespeare Country in the heart of England is that district most visited by North Americans (other than London, of course). Many who don't recognize the county name, Warwickshire, know its foremost tourist town, Stratford-upon-Avon, the birthplace of England's greatest writer.

The county and its neighboring shires form a land of industrial cities, green fields, and sleepy market towns—dotted with buildings, some of which have changed little since Shakespeare's time. Here are many of the places that have magic for overseas visitors, not only Stratford-upon-Avon, but also Warwick and Kenilworth Castles, as well as Coventry Cathedral.

Those who have time to penetrate deeper into the chapter will find elegant spa towns, such as Great Malvern, historic cathedral cities such as Hereford and Worcester, and industrial archeology at Stoke-on-Trent (the famous potteries). Scenery in Salop ranges from untamed borderlands to gentle plains which give way in the north to wooded areas and meres.

AN ENGLISH JOURNEY: These tours, booked at Woodbury Old Farm, Shelsley Beauchamp, Worcestershire WR6 6RL (tel. 08865-252), were started by Caroline Clist and her partner, Jane Moyle. The venture began as a hobby and is now an international concern. Caroline and Jane invite visitors to take a journey through the familiar sights of the Cotswolds and Stratford-upon-Avon, as well as the little-known countryside of Hereford and Worcester, Salop, and the Welsh Borders, lunching and staying overnight in private homes or country inns.

If you opt for a tour, your charming guide will meet you at the railway station and look after you throughout your trip. Lunch will vary from a quick snack in a historic pub to a Sunday meal en famille in a Georgian manor house. Overnight may be spent in a restored 17th-century water mill or a 12th-century castle, but everywhere you will be treated as an honored family guest instead of being just a "room number."

Overnight stays—including drinks, bed, breakfast, and your own bathroom in a private house, inclusive of all reasonable private comforts—cost about £70 ($136.50) for two people. Lunch in private houses (you can opt for just this if you are touring self-drive) is £8.50 ($16.58) per person, including wine. Add £59 ($115.05) a day for two people, plus £15 ($29.25) a day per person over two to cover the cost of your guide, transportation, and afternoon tea.

1. Stratford-upon-Avon

This town has a phenomenal tourist trade. Actor David Garrick really got it launched in 1769 when he organized the first of the Bard's birthday celebrations. It is no secret by now, of course, that William Shakespeare was born in Stratford-upon-Avon on April 23, 1564.

Surprisingly little is known about his early life, as the frankest of his biographers concede. Perhaps because documentation is so lacking about the writer, much useless conjecture has arisen (did Elizabeth I really write the plays?). But the view that Francis Bacon wrote all of Shakespeare's work would certainly stir up *The Tempest,* if suggested to the innkeepers of Stratford-upon-Avon. Admittedly, however, some of the stories and legends connected with Shakespeare's days in Stratford are largely fanciful, invented belatedly to amuse and entertain the vast number of literary fans making the pilgrimage.

Today's magnet, in addition to Shakespeare's birthplace, is the Royal Shakespeare Theatre, where Britain's foremost actors perform during a long season that lasts from Easter until January. Stratford-upon-Avon is also a good center for trips to Warwick Castle, Kenilworth Castle, Sulgrave Manor (ancestral home of George Washington), Compton Wynyates, and Coventry Cathedral. The market town lies 92 miles from London, 40 from Oxford, and 8 from Warwick.

THE SIGHTS: Besides the attractions on the periphery of Stratford, there are many Elizabethan and Jacobean buildings in this colorful town—many of them administered by the Shakespeare Birthplace Trust. One ticket—costing £2.20 ($4.29) for adults, 90p ($1.76) for children—will permit you to visit the five most important sights. You should pick up the ticket if you're planning to do much sightseeing (obtainable at your first stopover at any one of the Trust properties). The houses are open from 9 a.m. to 6 p.m. weekdays (on Sunday from 2 to 6 p.m.), from April through October; Shakespeare's birthplace and Anne Hathaway's Cottage open at 10 a.m. on Sunday during the summer. Off-season, the houses are open from 9 a.m. to 4 p.m. On winter Sundays, only Shakespeare's birthplace and Anne Hathaway's Cottage are open, from 1:30 to 4:30 p.m. On weekdays in summer, both remain open until 7 p.m.

Shakespeare's Birthplace

On Henley Street, the son of a glover and whittawer was born on St. George's day (April 23) in 1564, and died 52 years later on the same day. Filled with Shakespeare memorabilia, including a portrait, and furnishings of the writer's time, the Trust property is a half-timbered structure, dating from the early years of the 16th century. The house was bought by public donors in 1847 and preserved as a national shrine. You can visit the oak-beamed living room, the bedroom where Shakespeare was born, a fully equipped kitchen of the period (look for the "baby-minder"), and a Shakespeare Museum, illustrating his life and times. Later, you can walk through the garden out back. It is estimated that some 660,000 visitors pass through the house annually. If visited separately, admission is 90p ($1.76) for adults, 30p (59¢) for children. Next door to the birthplace is the modern Shakespeare Centre, built to commemorate the 400th anniversary of the Bard's birth. It serves both as the administrative headquarters of the Birthplace Trust and as a library and study center. An extension to the original center, opened in 1981, includes a Visitors' Centre providing reception facilities for all those coming to the Birthplace.

Anne Hathaway's Cottage

One mile from Stratford in the hamlet of Shottery is the thatched, wattle-and-daub cottage where Anne Hathaway lived before her marriage to the poet. In sheer charm, it is the most interesting and most photographed, it would seem, of the Trust properties. The Hathaways were yeoman farmers, and—aside from its historical interest—the cottage provides a rare insight into the life of a family of Shakespeare's day. If the poet came a-courtin', he must have been treated as a mere teenager, as he married Miss Hathaway when he was only 18 years old and she much older. Much of the original furnishings, including the courting settle, and utensils are preserved inside the house, which was occupied by descendants of Shakespeare's wife until 1892. After a visit through the house, you'll surely want to linger in the garden and orchard. You can either walk across the meadow to Shottery from Evesham Place in Stratford (pathway marked), or else take a bus from Bridge Street. The admission is 80p ($1.56) for adults, 30p (59¢) for children.

New Place

This site is on Chapel Street, where Shakespeare retired in 1610, a prosperous man to judge from the standards of his day. He died there six years later, at the age of 52. Regrettably, only the site of his former home remains today, as the house was torn down. You enter the gardens through Nash's House (Thomas Nash married Elizabeth Hall, a granddaughter of the poet). Nash's House has 16th-century period rooms and an exhibition illustrating the archeology and history of Stratford. The heavily visited Knott Garden adjoins the site, and represents the style of a fashionable Elizabethan garden. New Place itself has its own Great Garden, which once belonged to Shakespeare. Here, the Bard planted a mulberry tree, so popular with latter-day visitors to Stratford that the cantankerous owner of the garden chopped it down. The mulberry tree that grows there today is said to have been planted from a cutting of the original tree. The admission is 50p (98¢) for adults, 20p (39¢) for children.

Mary Arden's House

A timbered Tudor farm, this is the house where Shakespeare's mother, the daughter of a yeoman farmer, lived. The farmstead lies in the village of Wilmcote, three miles from Stratford-upon-Avon. Look for the stone dovecote out back, and the farming museum in the barns. The admission is 50p (98¢) for adults, 20p (39¢) for children.

By now, you will have seen the Trust properties, except for Hall's Croft (see "Where to Eat" further on). Other interesting sights not administered by the Trust foundation include the following:

Harvard House

Not just of interest to Harvard men, Harvard House on High Street is a fine example of an Elizabethan town house. Rebuilt in 1596, it was once the home of Katherine Rogers, mother of John Harvard, founder of Harvard University. In 1909, the house was purchased by a Chicago millionaire, Edward Morris, who presented it as a gift to the American university. Its present furnishings are not original, although they are of the period when Miss Rogers lived in the house. But the floors, made of the local flagstone, are authentic. Look for the Bible Chair, used for hiding the Bible during the days of Tudor persecution. Harvard House, charging admission of 40p (78¢) for adults, 20p (39¢) for children, is open April through September from 9 a.m. to 1 p.m. and from 2 to 6 p.m. weekdays, from 2 to 6 p.m. on Sunday; October through March from 10 a.m. to 1 p.m. and 2 to 4 p.m. weekdays, closed Sunday. Finally, you may want to visit the:

Holy Trinity Church

In an attractive setting near the Avon, the parish church of Stratford-upon-Avon is distinguished mainly because Shakespeare was buried in the chancel ("and curst be he who moves my bones"). The Parish Register records his birth and death (copies of the original, of course). No charge is made for entry into the church, described as "one of the most beautiful parish churches in the world," but visitors wishing to view Shakespeare's tomb are asked to donate a small sum, at present 15p (29¢) for students, 20p (39¢) for adults, toward the restoration fund.

A Wax Museum

Louis Tussaud's Waxworks, 60 Henley St. (tel. Stratford-upon-Avon 5880), illustrates the comedies, tragedies, and histories of Shakespeare, including scenes from *Romeo and Juliet* and *A Midsummer Night's Dream.* The location is near Shakespeare's Birthplace, and hours are daily from 9:30 a.m. to 5:30 p.m., including Sunday. Adults pay 85p ($1.66) admission, and children are charged 45p (88¢). The best buy is the family ticket, admitting two adults and two children at a cost of £2 ($3.90).

AN ELIZABETHAN SHOW: The new **Heritage Theatre,** Waterside (tel. Stratford-upon-Avon 69190), presents a full-time show, an Elizabethan pageant which tries to recreate the time of Shakespeare. The theater stands near the Royal Shakespeare Theatre. Its presentation tells the story of the great pageant which Lord Leicester scheduled for Queen Elizabeth in the summer of 1575. After a Royal Progress across the country, it culminated in several days of dances, songs, plays, and pomp at Kenilworth Castle. As a young man, Shakespeare is believed to have witnessed and been influenced by this pageant. The Heritage uses music, an eight-track sound tape, lights, costumes, and scenery, and dialogue is spoken by members of the Royal Shakespeare Theatre. Shows are on the hour and half hour daily from 9:30 a.m. to 8:30 p.m., April to September; 9:30 a.m. to 5 p.m., October to March. Admission is £1.60 ($3.12) for adults, £1.20 ($2.34) for students, senior citizens, and children over

6 (no charge for children under 6). A special family ticket (two adults and up to four children) costs £4 ($7.80).

TOURS: **Guide Friday,** 13 Waterside (tel. Stratford-upon-Avon 294466), has a central location near the theater and opposite the canal basin. They have opened a large information office which will give out free town maps and brochures, as well as information on the area. Hotel and guest-house reservations will be made from 9 a.m. to 9 p.m. at a cost of £1 ($1.95) per reservation. Tickets for tours and the theater can also be purchased here.

Tour prices include the Shakespeare Lecture Tour at £3.50 ($6.83), Warwick and Kenilworth Castles at £4 ($7.80), and the Cotswolds and villages at £4.50 ($8.78). The Quick Town Tour includes Mary Arden's House and Anne Hathaway's Cottage at £2 ($3.90), and the Cotswold pub tour goes for £3.50 ($6.83). On the latter, you pay for your own drinks.

The Shakespeare Connection is a service operated by British Rail and Guide Friday Ltd., a combined road/rail ticket from London Euston Station to Stratford-upon-Avon. The cost is about £11 ($21.45) per person, second class, for the round trip which drops you right outside Shakespeare's Birthplace. It's now possible to be standing by the Bard's bed in Stratford in less than two hours from the time you leave London. You can leave Euston at 8:35 a.m. and arrive in Stratford at 10:30 a.m., returning to Euston at 5:30 p.m., or if you wish, go to the theater or take Guide Friday's Cotswolds Country Inns Tour, catching the train back to London at 11:40 p.m., arriving in the capital in the early hours. Ask for a Shakespeare Connection ticket at London's Euston Station or any British Rail London Travel Centre. British Rail pass holders using the service simply pay the coach fare from Coventry Station to Stratford-upon-Avon.

CAUGHT WITHOUT A ROOM?: During the long theater season, the hotels in Stratford-upon-Avon are jam-packed, and you may run into difficulty if you arrive without a reservation. However, if you should visit from April to October during regular office hours (9 a.m. to 5:30 p.m. weekdays, 2 to 5 p.m. on Sunday) you can go to the **Information Centre** at the Judith Shakespeare House, 1 High St. (tel. Stratford-upon-Avon 293127).

Here a staff person, who has had much experience with travelers on all budgets, will get on the telephone and try to book a room for you in the price range you are seeking.

It is also possible to reserve accommodations if you write well enough in advance. By writing to the Information Centre, you'll be spared having to get in touch with several hotels on your own and running the risk of getting turned down. If you do write, specify the price range and the number of beds required. The centre often gets vague letters, and the staff doesn't know whether to book you into a private suite at the Shakespeare Hotel, or else lend you a cot to put in front of the Royal Shakespeare Theatre. Don't be surprised. Stratford-upon-Avon visitors are a varied group. Recently a young man not only slept in front of the theater, but was seen frying an egg there over an open fire the next morning.

WHERE TO STAY: For my hotel recommendations, I'll lead off with the most expensive in:

The Upper Bracket

Alveston Manor Hotel, Clopton Bridge (tel. Stratford-upon-Avon 4581), is a black-and-white timbered manor, conveniently placed for attending the theater, just a two-minute walk from the Avon. It has more chimneys and gables than one can count—a hodgepodge of styles, everything from an Elizabethan gazebo to Queen Anne windows. Tracing the building's ancestry involves one in early English history, as its origins predate the arrival of William the Conqueror. A ping-pong game of ownership has been played with Alveston, mentioned, by the way, in the Domesday Book. Perhaps any other manor would have become frayed at the edges, but under the Trusthouse management, a well-directed program of expansion is being carried out, making for a top-level accommodation that combines the past with the comfort of today.

Rooms in the Manor House are for those who enjoy an atmosphere of old slanted floors, overhead beams, and antique furnishings. However, in the new block, attached by a covered walk through the rear garden, rooms are fully modernized with skillfully designed built-in pieces, baths with showers, heated towel racks, telephones, radios, bedside lamps, dressing tables, and a color-coordinated decor. The price of lodgings varies according to the season, peaking from June through September. In a single room, the rate is £28 ($54.60), increasing to £39 ($76.05) in a double or twin. Breakfast is extra, but service charge and VAT are included. In the new block, a number of large rooms are rented to three or four persons.

The lounges are in the manor; and guests gather in the Cedar Room for relaxation, enjoying the view of the centuries-old tree at the top of the garden—said to have been the background for the first presentation of *A Midsummer Night's Dream.* In the main living room, with its well-preserved linenfold paneling, logs burn in the Tudor fireplace. The bar-lounge is another cozy spot, with its stone fireplace, Tudor bench, and Windsor armchairs. Good food is served in the softly lit Tudor Restaurant, with its oak beams and leaded-glass windows.

Hilton International, Bridgefoot (tel. Stratford-upon-Avon 67511). It had to happen: a Hilton in Stratford. On five landscaped acres of lawns and gardens, laid out in a semi-Tudor style, this complex of red brick and stone stands right on the Avon, within walking distance of the theater. In fact, not since the construction of the theater back in the 1930s has a building sparked such controversy, and attracted so many defenders and detractors. It's only four stories high—the top floor semidisguised by a mansard roof—and it's spread out, much like a hospital. Each of its 253 rooms contains individually controlled heating and air conditioning, plus views of the river, the theater, and the surrounding countryside. Each has a private bath and shower, with direct-dial telephones, taped music, color TV. High-season rates apply from April 1 to October 1; singles range from £31.85 ($62.11) to £39.35 ($76.73), doubles from £43.15 to ($84.14) to £52.10 ($101.60). Tax and service are included in the tariffs. The hotel has an Actors Bar, an unusual octagonal-shaped cocktail lounge, with windows overlooking the gardens and the Avon. A live group plays for dancing here from 10 p.m. to 2 a.m. It is joined to the main building by an enclosed walkway. Guests can reach the theater via a ten-minute boat ride on a barge docked in front on the canal. The Tavern restaurant is a coffeeshop open for lunch and dinner, serving a buffet of cold meats, salads, and desserts, plus at least two hot dishes, costing from £5.25 ($10.24) per head. The Warwick Grill, the prestige restaurant of the hotel, offers a wide range of international and English cuisine. A specialty is roast rib of Scottish beef.

Welcombe Hotel, Warwick Road (tel. Stratford-upon-Avon 295252), is one of England's great Jacobean country houses, placed about a ten-minute ride from the heart of Stratford-upon-Avon. The home once belonged to Sir Archibald Flower, the philanthropic brewer who helped create the Shakespeare Memorial Theatre. Converted into a hotel, and run by the British Transport Hotels Ltd., it is surrounded by 120 acres of grounds. It is reached by a formal entrance on Warwick Road, a winding driveway leading to the main hall. There's even an 18-hole, 6300-yard course on the estate. Guests gather on fair days for afternoon tea or drinks on the rear terrace, with its Italian-style garden and steps leading down to flower beds. The public rooms are heroic in size, with high mullioned windows providing views of the park. Although the antiques have been removed, the furnishings are suitable. The bedrooms—some big enough for tennis matches—have pleasant pieces. A single room with bath rents for £36 ($70.20). A double with bath costs £55 ($107.25), including a full breakfast, service charge, and VAT. There is an elaborate à la carte menu, plus a good wine list. The management tries to provide tickets for theater performances and serves pretheater suppers.

The **Shakespeare Hotel,** Chapel Street (tel. Stratford-upon-Avon 294771), a 16th-century building, now redecorated and run as a Trusthouses Forte Hotel, lies within a few minutes of the theater, the poet's grammar school, and New Place, where the Bard died. It's easy to spot, with its nine gables, black-and-white timbering, leaded diamond windows, bays, and hanging baskets of red geraniums. In 1769, David Garrick, the famous actor, named most of the lounges and bedrooms after plays or characters of Shakespeare. You may be assigned the Ophelia Bedroom or the Romeo and Juliet Bedroom. There's even a private Hamlet suite. Room rates are higher between April 1 and November 1, with a single going for £30 ($58.50). Double rooms rent for an inclusive £42 ($81.90). All meals are extra. The rooms are centrally heated and contain private bath, radio, and TV.

Meals are served in the "As You Like It" dining room, where the old beams have been preserved. While there is an extensive à la carte menu and a fine wine list, the bargain is the table d'hôte dinner starting at £8 ($15.60). The table d'hôte luncheon begins at £6 ($11.70). "The Measure for Measure" bar, with its Windsor chairs and pine settles, and Frank's Bar, with its winged chairs and open fireplace, lure one to the Shakespeare.

The Medium-Priced Range

The Falcon, Chapel Street (tel. Stratford-upon-Avon 5777), is a blending of the very old and the very new. At the rear of a black-and-white timbered inn, licensed a quarter of a century after Shakespeare's death, is a contemporary bedroom extension, joined by a glass-covered passageway. In the heart of Stratford, the Falcon faces the Guild Chapel and the New Place Gardens. The bedrooms in the mellowed part have oak beams, diamond leaded-glass windows, antique furnishings, and good reproductions. One arrives at the rear portion to unload luggage, just as horse-drawn coaches once dispatched their passengers. All bedrooms have private bathrooms, radio, television, telephone, electric trouser press, and tea- and coffee-making equipment. Rates include accommodation, full English breakfast, space for your car, VAT, and service charge. A single with bath is £40 ($78); a double or twin with bath, £45 ($87.75).

The social lounges are tasteful and comfortable—some of the finest in the Midlands. In the intimate Merlin Lounge is an open copper-hooded fireplace where coal and log fires are kept burning under beams salvaged from old ships (the walls are a good example of wattle and daub, typical of Shakespeare's day). The Oak Lounge Bar is a forest of weathered beams, and on either side of the stone fireplace is the paneling removed from the poet's last home, New Place. A set luncheon costs £5.50 ($10.73), a set dinner going for £7.50 ($14.63), both tariffs including three courses, service, and VAT.

The **Arden Hotel**, Waterside (tel. Stratford-upon-Avon 294949), is frankly your best choice if you're really devoted to the Shakespeare theater. A Regency brick house, with its own acre garden right on the Avon, the hotel sits diagonally across from the theater. The management knows how to spell hospitality, going out of their way to obtain seats for guests, providing tea and refreshments in their English garden, with its arbor of white roses, fruit trees, and views of the swan-studded river. Constantly returning guests have created a space problem, which has been solved by building a 20-bedroom wing. All the rooms contain private baths and overlook the Avon and the garden. There is a residents' lounge, opening onto the herb garden, plus a TV room. The rooms are pleasant, all with central heating and hot and cold running water. Bathless singles rent for £17 ($33.15), increasing to £24 ($46.80) with bath. Bathless doubles cost £30 ($58.50), the price going up to £38 ($74.10) with bath, these tariffs including an English breakfast, service, and VAT. Meals are served in the front dining room, where two large bay windows open toward the river. Nonresidents should note the inexpensive and good-tasting meals here: lunches and dinners are served carvery style and you pay only for what roast you select, around £6 ($11.70) per head at lunch, from £8 ($15.60) at dinner. The food is typical English fare, and includes boiled York ham with a parsley sauce, stuffed Norfolk turkey, roast beef with Yorkshire pudding, and fresh Wye salmon. The latest addition is an open-air terrace overlooking the river where one can eat or drink.

Haytor Hotel, Avenue Road (tel. Stratford-upon-Avon 297799), is the domain of the Branston family, whose Edwardian-style house at the edge of a residential sector is an offbeat private hotel. Planned by a French architect in Edwardian times, it is surrounded by a garden, scheduled under the National Gardens Scheme. Most rooms contain private baths, and all are individually furnished and fully carpeted. In the Green Onyx room is an antique four-poster bed. Charges are from £13 ($25.35) per person in a room with wash basin only, from £15.50 ($30.23) per person with private bath. A full English breakfast is included, but not VAT. Good meals are served in an attractive dining room decorated with English antiques and a number of old maps. The hotel lies only 900 yards from the Royal Shakespeare Theatre, and the family offers a free theater-booking service for its guests.

Grosvenor House Hotel, Warwick Road (tel. Stratford-upon-Avon 69213), is a Georgian residence converted into a hotel of 57 bedrooms (53 with private shower or bath), run by the Adcock family and friendly staff. Lawns and gardens to the front and rear of the hotel lend additional character. In high season (March through October), singles rent from £16 ($31.20); doubles, £25 ($48.75)—including service, VAT, and a big English breakfast. Rooms are centrally heated, and all have radio, telephone, and color TV. There is a comfortable bar, open till midnight.

Stratford House, Sheep Street (tel. Stratford-upon-Avon 68288), is a pleasant Georgian house 100 yards from the Avon River and the Royal Shakespeare Theatre. A small hotel of only ten bedrooms (seven of which have private baths or showers), the agreeable B&B establishment is run by Peter and Pamela Wade, who extend a fond welcome for their North American clients. The house is furnished tastefully and with style, somewhat like a private home, with books and pictures along with a scattering of antiques. Everything is spotlessly maintained. On the side is a small walled courtyard, with flowering plants. A double with private bath rents for £19.25 ($37.54) per person, only £17 ($33.15) if bathless. Families can rent a room for four with private bath at a cost of £14.25 ($27.79) per person. Children under 9 are granted reduced prices. Singles, however, are charged from £27.50 ($53.63). No service charge is included. Rates quoted include a full English breakfast, VAT, and early morning tea. Color TV, incidentally, is provided in every bedroom.

The Budget Range

Stratheden Hotel, Chapel Street (tel. Stratford-upon-Avon 297119), is a small, tuck-away hotel, in a weathered building dating back to 1673, with a tiny rear garden and top-floor rooms with slanted, beamed ceilings. Owned by Mr. and Mrs. Wells (she's from Northern Ireland, he's a native of Warwickshire), the house has improved in both decor and comfort, with fresh paint, new curtains, and good beds. The charge for B&B ranges from £8 ($15.60) to £11 ($21.45), plus VAT. Some rooms have private showers and toilets, and all contain tea- and coffee-making facilities.

The entry hallway has a glass cupboard, holding family heirlooms and collector tidbits. The house is sprinkled with old pieces. The dining room, with a bay window, has an overscale sideboard that once belonged to the "insanely vain" Marie Corelli, the eccentric novelist, poet, and mystic who wrote a series of seven books, beginning with *A Romance of Two Worlds* and ending with *Spirit and Power and Universal Love.* Queen Victoria was one of her avid readers. The Victorian novelist (1855–1924) was noted for her passion for pastoral paintings and objets d'art. You can see an example of her taste in bedchamber furniture: a massive mahogany tester bed in one of the rooms.

WHERE TO EAT: The **Box Tree Restaurant,** the Royal Shakespeare Theatre, Waterside (tel. Stratford-upon-Avon 293226), has dibs on the best position in town, in the theater, with walls of glass providing an unobstructed view of the Avon and its swans. You can also dine on the outer terrace where tables are placed in fair weather. The meals and service are worthy of its unique position. The restaurant is open on matinee days and Sunday from 12:30 to 2 p.m., and in the evenings from 6 to 11 p.m. A three-course pretheater dinner begins at £8.50 ($16.58), going up to £12 ($23.40). Lunches start at £6 ($11.70). After each evening's performance, you can dine by flickering candlelight. Such items are featured as duckling à l'orange, grilled sirloin steak, coq au vin, escalope of veal. Be sure to book your table in advance, especially on the days of performances (there's a special phone for reservations in the theater lobby).

In the **River Terrace Restaurant,** (tel. Stratford-upon-Avon 293226), an assortment of snack meals, homemade pizzas, quiches, pâtés, pies, soups, and hamburgers, all with salads, is offered. With dessert to finish off your meal, expect to pay around £6 ($11.70).

Marianne, 3 Greenhill St. (tel. Stratford-upon-Avon 293563), is a bistro-like restaurant, providing an authentic French cuisine. The small two-story dining room has an open wooden staircase leading to additional tables on the mezzanine. The best value here is the table d'hôte dinner, which includes an appetizer, main course, and cheese or dessert. On the à la carte menu, appetizers are likely to include gratinée lyonnaise, a tasty onion soup or perhaps escargots in sauce à la bourguignonne. The menu selections vary according to the season since the owner, Pierre Denervaux, makes every effort to obtain only fresh ingredients for his dishes. When you visit, you may find such items listed as scampi à l'estragon, a savory shrimp dish in a delicate tarragon sauce, or caneton au cassis, duckling served with a fragrant cassis glaze. Entrees range from £4 ($7.80) to £6.50 ($12.68). For dessert, you might like to sample one of the pastries prepared by the chef and costing about £1.20 ($2.34). Marianne's is open Monday through Saturday for dinner, and also offers a daily set lunch for £3.50 ($6.83) from 12:30 to 2 p.m.

Christophi's, 21–23 Sheep Street (tel. Stratford-upon-Avon 293546), is a bit of old Athens set down in the middle of Shakespeare's hometown. Owned by Nicos Christophi, the restaurant is laid out in Greek fashion, with an indoor courtyard. You may dine on both Greek and Cypriot dishes while live Greek music plays in the background. A number of items of standard British fare are included on the menu for the less adventurous. To begin your meal you might try the dolmadakia, a meat and rice ball wrapped in vine leaves, for £2.50 ($4.88), or the popular avgolemono, a chicken soup heavily laced with lemon juice, for £1.40 ($2.73). The entree portion of the menu includes moussaka, a casserole of chopped beef, eggplant, and potatoes, crowned with a wonderful cheese-flavored cream sauce, and priced at £5.50 ($10.73). Christophi's features the meze, a typical Greek "taverna" dinner, consisting of a variety of individual dishes, including various hors d'oeuvres and a main course "to satisfy the most adverturous palate." The restaurant is open for dinner from 5:30 p.m. to midnight. Closed Sunday.

Mr. Christophi also operates the **Bancroft Garden Hotel and Restaurant,** Waterside (tel. Stratford-upon-Avon 0789), just opposite the Royal Shakespeare Theatre. Here single rooms rent for £17 ($33.15) and doubles for £27 ($52.65). All rooms are equipped with private shower and toilet. Rates include a continental breakfast, VAT, and service.

Da Giovanni, 8 Ely St. (tel. Stratford-upon-Avon 297999), is an intimate spot, favored by actors at the theater. The yellow brick cottage is graced with white bay windows. Up front is a sophisticated cocktail lounge with antiques. Da Giovanni is in the trattoria style, its cuisine beginning fittingly enough with minestrone. The classic Italian menu includes such pasta dishes as lasagne and cannelloni, and such main dishes as escalope Pietmontese and spezzato di pollo alla casalinga (casserole of chicken cooked in wine with tomatoes and mushrooms). A good Italian dessert is the zabaglione, although at least two persons must order it. A selection of excellent continental ices is also featured, everything from Italian cassata to mela Stregata. Expect to pay from £10 ($19.50) for a complete dinner. A 10% service charge is added. It's closed on Sunday, but open other days from 12:30 to 2 p.m. and from 6 to 11:30 p.m.

Cobweb Restaurant & Confectionery, 12 Sheep St. (tel. Stratford-upon-Avon 292554), is a black-and-white timbered building, with a high gabled wing, dating from the early 16th century. It's steeped in associations with the days of Shakespeare. On the ground floor are cases of goodies for sale, but you may want to go to the second floor, where there's a maze of three rooms filled with antique oak tables, Windsor chairs, and settles. The shop is noted as one of the finest in England for its cakes, pastries, cream cakes (especially chocolate and sherry ones), meringues, apple strudel, and cheesecake.

The light luncheons are excellent, and the kitchen provides the traditional English roasts. The soups are most tasty, each costing 50p (98¢). A full lunch of three courses is from £3.50 ($6.83). After morning coffee and luncheon, the next major event is teatime. A good-size pot of tea is 50p (98¢) and the Cobweb offers at least 60 varieties of English and continental cakes from 30p (59¢) upward. The Cobweb is also open for teas on Sunday from 3 to 6 p.m. It also serves snacks and bistro-style meals in the evening.

The Dirty Duck, Waterside Street (tel. Stratford-upon-Avon 297312), was formerly known as the Black Swan. By whatever bird it's called, it's been popular since the 18th century as a hangout for Stratford players. The autographed photographs of its patrons, such as Lord Laurence Olivier, line the wall. The front lounge and bar crackles with intense conversation. In the spring and fall an open fire burns moodily.

In the Dirty Duck Grill Room meals are served from noon to 2:30 p.m. and from 6 p.m. to midnight. An à la carte menu is offered. Typical English grills are featured from £5 ($9.75). In fair weather, you can drink while sitting in the front garden, and watching the swans on the Avon glide by.

The Garrick Inn, High Street (tel. Stratford-upon-Avon 292186), is a black-and-white timbered Elizabethan pub named after one of England's greatest actors, David Garrick. It has its own kind of unpretentious charm. The front bar is decked out with tapestry-covered settles, an old oak refectory table, and an open fireplace where the locals gravitate. The back bar has a circular fireplace with a copper hood, plus a buffet bar serving "ploughman's lunches."

The Hall's Croft Festival Club, in the Old Town, makes an ideal headquarters during your stay in Stratford-upon-Avon. This skillfully preserved, timbered Elizabethan building can become your private club, where you can congregate with fellow Shakespeare enthusiasts, and dine inexpensively. Hall's Croft was the original town house of Susanna, daughter of William Shakespeare, and her husband, Dr. John Hall. Parts of the authentically furnished house may be visited on your £2.20 ($4.29) ticket which admits you to five Shakespeare Trust Properties. The house lies about two blocks from the Royal Shakespeare Theatre, and a block from the Avon.

The cost of membership is £1.50 ($2.93) weekly. As a member, you'll be entitled to use the facilities of the club, including the comfortable rooms for lounging, lunching, or reading, as well as the garden. Lectures and poetry readings are held, books and pamphlets sold—and you can even get your mail here.

Eating at the club is inexpensive, and the food is quite good. A typical luncheon selection might include oxtail soup, roast lamb with mint sauce, roast potatoes, carrots, cabbage, followed by apple crumble and custard—all for approximately £4.50 ($8.78) including coffee. Luncheon is served from noon to 2 p.m. After these hours, snacks are available. The club is open from April till the end of October, six days a week, from 10:30 a.m. til 6 p.m. (later in the summer).

ATTENDING THE THEATER: The **Royal Shakespeare Theatre** on the banks of the Avon is the number one theater for Shakespearean productions. The season runs for nine months from March to January, with a winter festival of music and ballet in February. The present theater was opened in 1932, after the old Shakespeare Memorial Theatre, erected in Victoria's day, burned down in 1926. The theater employs the finest actors and actresses on the British stage. In an average season, five Shakespearean plays rotate in repertory.

Usually, you'll need reservations: there are three successive booking periods, each one opening about two months in advance. You can best pick these up from a North American or an English travel agent. If you wait until your arrival in Stratford, it may be too late to get a good seat. In summer the stall (orchestra) seats range in price from £6 ($11.70) to £12 ($23.40), and if you're not subject to nosebleed, you may want to anchor in the high-altitude balcony in a seat that goes for £3 ($5.85) to £4 ($7.80).

Tip: Don't despair completely if you should arrive in Stratford without a ticket. The theater box office always holds back a block of £4 ($7.80) stall seats that go on sale the day of each performance at 10:30 a.m. An alternative course is to buy standing room at the same time for £1 ($1.95).

In the Victorian wing of the old Memorial Theatre—spared by the fire—is a Picture Gallery and Museum, filled with portraits of the Bard, oils of performances from his various classics showing 18th- and 19th-century costume designs, portraits of actors in memorable characterizations of Shakespearean roles, such as Lord Laurence Olivier as Macbeth and Dame Edith Evans as Volumnia. The gallery is open April to October weekdays from 10 a.m. to 1 p.m. and 2 to 6 p.m.; matinee days, 10 a.m. to 6 p.m.; Sunday, 2 to 6 p.m. December to March, open Sunday only. Admission is 45p (88¢) for adults, 25p (49¢) for children.

BOOK BROWSING: Although it seems ironic to call this shop at 21 Chapel St. the **Chaucer Head Bookshop**, it is still an interesting place to visit, offering both new and secondhand editions. A friend of Shakespeare's, Julius Shaw, who was one of the executors of his will, lived at this address from 1597 to 1629. It is owned and run by Dorothy Withey, who has opened a second-floor art gallery exhibiting current books on Shakespeare and the Elizabethan period, a room for displaying the work of living artists, and for prints and engravings as well.

STAYING AT WILMCOTE: **Swan House Hotel**, The Green (tel. Stratford-upon-Avon 67030), lies in the heart of the tiny hamlet of Wilmcote, where Shakespeare's mother, Mary Arden, lived. Really an upgraded village pub-hotel, the white-painted Swan is tranquil, restful, and gracious, offering not only attractive and fresh bedrooms at low prices, but good meals as well. It's owned by Mr. and Mrs. Paul Knight, who have made the little inn homelike. You'll find bright colors and antiques, as well as an attractive staff. Bathless singles rent for £12 ($23.40), bathless doubles for £22 ($42.90). The charge is £25 ($48.75) in a double with private bath, VAT and service included. Drinks are offered in the little bar, with its log-burning fireplace, a bay window with a view of the Mary Arden cottage which you can visit, and tiny rear courtyard and old well.

The beamed dining room at the rear provides a good setting for an excellent English cuisine with some French overtones. You might start with an apple filled with a creamy mixture of Stilton cheese. Bar lunches are from noon till 2 p.m. and dinner from 7:30 to 9:30 p.m. (last orders). At Sunday dinner, only residents are served

---

Most travelers approach our next stopover, Warwick, via route A46 from Stratford-upon-Avon, eight miles away. The town is 92 miles from London, and is on the Avon.

2. Warwick

Visitors seem to rush through Warwick to see Warwick Castle; then they're off on their next adventure, traditionally to the ruins of Kenilworth Castle. But the historic center of medieval Warwick deserves to be treated with greater respect. It has far more to offer than a castle.

In 1694, a fire swept through Warwick, destroying large segments of the town, but it still retains a number of Elizabethan and medieval buildings—along with some fine Georgian structures. (Very few traces remain, however, of the town walls, except the East and West Gates.) Warwick looks to Ethelfleda, daughter of Alfred the Great, as its founder. But most of its history is associated with the Earls of Warwick, a title created by the son of William the Conqueror in 1088. The story of those earls—the Beaumonts, the Beauchamps (such figures as "Kingmaker" Richard Neville)—makes for an exciting episode in English history, but is too detailed to document here.

WARWICK CASTLE: Perched on a rocky cliff above the Avon, this magnificent 14th-century fortress encloses a stately mansion in the grandest late 17th-century style.

The importance of the site has been recognized from earliest times. The first defense works of significance at Warwick were built by Ethelfleda, daughter of Alfred the Great, in A.D. 915. Her fortifications were further developed by the construction of a motte and bailey castle on the orders of William the Conqueror in 1068, two years after the Norman Conquest. There are now no remains of the Norman castle, as this was sacked by Simon de Montfort in the Barons' War of 1264.

The Beauchamp family, the most illustrious medieval Earls of Warwick, are responsible for most of the castle as it is seen today, and much of the external structure remains unchanged from the mid-14th century. When the castle was granted to Sir Fulke Greville by James I in 1604, he spent £20,000 (an enormous sum in those days) converting the existing castle buildings into a luxurious mansion. The Grevilles have held the Earl of Warwick title since 1759, when it passed from the Rich family.

The State Rooms and Great Hall house fine collections of paintings, furniture, arms, and armor. The armory, dungeon, torture chamber, ghost tower, clock tower, and Guy's tower give vivid insights into the castle's turbulent past and its important part in the history of England. Surrounded by gardens, lawns, and woodland, where peacocks roam freely, and skirted by the Avon, Warwick Castle was described by Sir Walter Scott in 1828 as "that fairest monument of ancient and chivalrous spendor which yet remains uninjured by time.

The castle is open daily, except Christmas Day, March 1 to October 31, 10 a.m. to 5:30 p.m.; November 1 to February 28, 10 a.m. to 4:30 p.m. Admission is £2.50 ($4.88) for adults, £1.50 ($2.93) for children.

OTHER SIGHTS: Other nearby sights worth exploring include the following:

St. Mary's Church

Destroyed, in part, by the fire of 1694, this church with its rebuilt battlemented tower and nave is considered among the finest examples of the work of the late 17th and early 18th centuries. The Beauchamp Chapel, spared from the flames, encases the Purbeck marble tomb of Richard Beauchamp, a well-known Earl of Warwick who died in 1439 and is commemorated by a gilded bronze effigy. The most powerful man in the kingdom, not excepting Henry V, Beauchamp has a tomb considered one of the finest remaining examples of Perpendicular-Gothic as practiced in England in the mid-15th century. The tomb of Robert Dudley, Earl of Leicester, a favorite of Elizabeth I, is against the north wall. The Perpendicular-Gothic choir dates from the 14th century.

The Norman crypt and the 14th-century Chapter House are also fine examples of this period. For more information, get in touch with the Rectory, Warwick (tel. Warwick 491132).

Lord Leycester Hospital

At the West Gate, this group of half-timbered almshouses was also spared from the Great Fire. The buildings were erected in about 1400, and the hospital was founded in 1571 by Robert Dudley, the Earl of Leicester, as a home for old soldiers. It is still in use by ex-servicemen today. On top of the West Gate is the attractive little chapel of St. James, dating from the 12th century, although much restored. The hospital may be visited weekdays from 10 a.m. to 5:30 p.m. (closed Sunday) for 75p ($1.46) for adults, 25P (49¢) for children. Off-season, it closes at 4 p.m.

Warwickshire Museum

At the Market Place, this museum was established in 1836 to house a collection of geological remains, fossils, and a fine grouping of British amphibians from the Triassic period. There are also displays illustrating the history, archeology, and natural history of the country, including the Sheldon tapestry map. It is open weekdays from 10 a.m. to 5:30 p.m., and on Sunday in summer from 2:30 to 5 p.m.

St. John's House

At Coten End, not far from the castle gates, there is a display of folk life, craft, and costumes, and the house in which these exhibitions are displayed is a fund of beauty itself, dating from the early 17th century. A Victorian schoolroom, recently opened, is furnished with original 19th-century school furniture and equipment. During term time, Warwickshire children, dressed in replica costumes, can be seen enjoying Victorian-style lessons. An important collection of musical instruments is on view, including a Tabel harpsichord and three Stanesby recorders dating from the 18th century and a 16th-century lute by Hans Frei. On the first floor is a military exhibition, tracing the history of the Royal Warwickshire Regiment from 1674 to the present day.

Warwick Doll Museum

Housed in one of the most charming Elizabethan buildings in Warwick, Oken's House, the Warwick Doll Museum keeps alive the memory of childhood. It contains an extensive collection of dolls—be they wood, wax, or porcelain. Of particular interest is a swivel-necked, double-headed doll that moves from tears to smiles. The house is on Castle Street, near St. Mary's Church. It was the birthplace of Thomas Oken, a bailiff in Warwick in Tudor days, whose reputation rests largely on his philanthropic work. The dolls, however, are from the collection of Joy Robinson. The house is open weekdays from 10 a.m. to 6 p.m. (on Sunday from 2:30 to 5 p.m.), for 50p (98¢) for adults, 25p (49¢) for children.

WHERE TO STAY: Many prefer to seek lodgings in Warwick, then commute to Stratford-upon-Avon. If you're one of them, here are my hotel recommendations:

Tudor House Inn & Restaurant, West Street (tel. Warwick 495447), was built in 1472. It's at the edge of town, on the main road from Stratford-upon-

Avon leading to Warwick Castle. It is a stunning black-and-white timbered inn, one of the few buildings to escape the fire that destroyed the High Street in 1694. Off the central hall are two large rooms, each of which could be the setting for an Elizabethan play. In the corner of the lounge is an open turning staircase, waiting for the entrance of a minstrel player. The minstrels' gallery is dominated by a large inglenook. A regular meal in the restaurant and steak bar costs about £9 ($17.55). The inn has nine bedrooms, all with wash basins, although some have baths en suite. The cost ranges from £12 ($23.40) to £25 ($48.75) per room nightly. Two of the rooms have doors only four feet high! There's the usual resident ghost—an old man who gets up early in the morning, leaving the front door open and heading toward Stratford-upon-Avon, without paying his bill. In addition, the old priest's hiding hole has become the Priest Hole Bar.

Lord Leycester Hotel, Jury Street (tel. Warwick 491481), is a remake of what was once the country house of the Earl of Leicester. Extensively renovated, it now accommodates guests comfortably in its 50 bedrooms, some of which have private baths. Its position is most central, within walking distance of the castle and other historic buildings of Warwick. A bathless single goes for £16 ($31.20), £19 ($37.05) with bath. In a bathless double or twin, the price is £25 ($48.75), £29 ($56.55) with bath. Prices include a full English breakfast, service, and VAT. A nicety is the inclusion of early-morning tea and a newspaper (if you state your preference the night before to the porter). The bedrooms are furnished with moderately modern pieces, neat and attractive. Lord Leicester's former stables have been transformed into the Tavern, where imbibers sit on cobblers' stools at trestle tables. In the dining room a table d'hôte dinner is from £5.50 ($10.73).

3. Kenilworth Castle

In magnificent ruins, this castle—the subject of Sir Walter Scott's romance *Kenilworth*—once had walls that enclosed an area of seven acres. It lies five miles north of Warwick, 13 from Stratford-upon-Avon. In 1957, Lord Kenilworth presented the decaying castle to England, and limited restoration has since been carried out.

The castle dates back to the days of Henry I, having been built by one of his lieutenants, Geoffrey de Clinton. Of the original castle, only Caesar's Tower, with its 16-foot-thick walls, remains. Edward II was forced to abdicate at Kenilworth in 1327, before being carried off to Berkeley Castle in Gloucestershire, where he was undoubtedly murdered. Elizabeth I in 1563 gave the castle to her favorite, Robert Dudley, Earl of Leicester. The earl built the Gatehouse, which was visited on several occasions by the queen. After the Civil War, the Roundheads were responsible for breaching the outer wall and towers, and blowing up the north wall of the keep. This was the only damage caused following the Earl of Monmouth's plea that it be "Slighted with as little spoil to the dwellinghouse as might be."

From March 15 to October 15, the castle is open Monday to Saturday from 9:30 a.m. to 6:30 p.m. Otherwise, hours are from 9:30 a.m. to 4 p.m. In summer, the Sunday visiting hours are 2 to 6:30 p.m. (from 2 to 4 p.m. off-season). The castle is closed on December 25 and 26, and on January 1, as well as the first Monday in May. Admission charges are 50p (98¢) for adults, 25p (49¢) for children under 16.

FOOD AND LODGING: The Clarendon House Hotel, High Street (tel. Kenilworth 54694), is a family-run hotel and restaurant in the old part of Kenilworth. The oak tree around which the original ale house was built in 1538 is still supporting the roof of the building today. The present owners, the Lea family, welcome guests to spend the night in any of the 14 bedrooms, all of which are tastefully decorated. Prices range from £15.50 ($30.23) for a single with shower to £28 ($54.60) for a double with private shower, toilet, and four-poster bed. Tariffs include a full English breakfast and VAT.

Before the evening meal, guests gather in the timbered lounge. The hotel's restaurant is housed in what was once the inn stable. The oddly timbered room is decorated with antique maps and armor, constant reminders that a Cromwellian garrison once stayed at the inn during a seige of Kenilworth Castle.

Game is a specialty at the Clarendon House, and in season you may dine on such specialties as pigeon Normandy, casseroled in cider with onions, venison casserole, and mallard (wild duck cooked in red wine). A complete dinner, inclusive of VAT, is available for around £7 ($13.65) per head. Lunch, costing from £3.50 ($6.83), is served Tuesday to Friday from noon to 2 p.m., and dinner is offered Sunday to Thursday from 7 to 9 p.m. (until 9:30 p.m. on Friday and Saturday). The Leas also have an interesting collection of small antiques and old maps for sale.

Restaurant Bosquet, Warwick Road (tel. Kenilworth 52463), is a tiny terraced town-house restaurant—only eight tables—run by Noreen Groves and her daughter Marian. The cooking is done by David Groves, Noreen's husband, who is a skillful master of French cuisine. The impressive à la carte menu features game and a number of meat and fish dishes. Included are chevrenil forestière, local venison marinated in red wine and sauteed with mushrooms and bacon, or sauté d'agneau Romarin, a lamb steak sauteed with fresh rosemary and served in a white wine sauce. Fish dishes include two poached salmon dishes, one served with a delectable hollandaise sauce and the other poached in white wine and tomato and served with sour cream. Other dishes include salmon quenelles, beef portugaise, and guinea fowl. You may begin with an hors d'oeuvres assortment or a "petite entree." Desserts feature such delightful specialties as banana soufflé and a delicate Bavarian cream laced with Curaçao. The average meal here will run about £14 ($27.30) per head, plus wine. Restaurant Bosquet is open for dinner from 7 to 10 p.m. daily, except Sunday and Monday. It is closed ten days at Easter, ten days at Christmas, and four weeks during July and August. Reservations here are absolutely essential.

Tudor Cottage (tel. Kenilworth 56702), is a 450-year-old half-timbered structure right across the street from the castle. Its little restaurant is a delightful spot for a refreshing afternoon tea following a tour of Kenilworth. The friendly owner, Frank Hart, is happy to share his wealth of knowledge about the interesting history and the sights of the area. If you decide to spend the night, B&B will cost you a modest, all-inclusive £8 ($15.60). Both lunch and dinner are served in his tiny restaurant which is open for coffee at 10:30 a.m., then for lunch between 12:30 and 2:30 p.m., and for dinner from 7:30 p.m. "until the last person leaves." Traditional English dishes are accompanied by fresh vegetables. A three-course lunch with choice of dishes costs £2.50 ($4.88). Dinner selected from the à la carte menu is priced from £5 ($9.75) for three courses. The restaurant is closed on Monday.

4. Coventry

Although the Midlands city of Coventry, home of motorcar and cycle manufacturing, is principally industrial, you'll want to pay it a visit to see Sir

Basil Spence's controversial **Coventry Cathedral,** consecrated in 1962. The city was partially destroyed during the blitz in the early '40s, but the rebuilding was miraculous. No city more than Coventry seems to symbolize England's power to bounce back from adversity.

Before the war, Coventry was noted in legend as the ancient market town through which Lady Godiva made her famous ride, giving birth to a new name in English: Peeping Tom. The Lady Godiva story is clouded in such obscurity that the truth has probably been lost forever. It has been suggested that the good lady never appeared in the nude, but was the victim of scandalmongers, who, in their attempt to tarnish her image, unknowingly immortalized her.

The cathedral grew up on the same site as the 14th-century Perpendicular building. Many Coventry residents have maintained that the foreign visitor is more likely to admire the structure than the Britisher, who perhaps is more attached to traditional cathedral design.

Outside is Sir Jacob Epstein's bronze masterpiece, St. Michael slaying the Devil. Inside, the outstanding feature is the 70-foot-high altar tapestry by Graham Sutherland, said to be the largest in the world. The floor-to-ceiling abstract stained-glass windows are the work of the Royal College of Art. The West Window is most interesting, with its engraved glass, rows of stylized saints and monarchs with jazzy angels flying around between them.

Coventry is 19 miles from Stratford-upon-Avon, and only 11 from Warwick and 6 from Kenilworth.

The **Museum of British Transport,** on Cook Street, lies about a six-minute taxi ride from the heart of Coventry and houses the largest and most representative collection of its kind in England. The oldest car is an original Daimler, dating from 1897 (the first Daimler was built in Coventry only the year before). The museum also displays the most antique vehicle still running, an 1898 Daimler. Curiosities include a 1910 Humber taxi whose mileage is listed at one million.

Exhibits are diversified, as the museum has the ambitious task of covering the total history of transport in the British Isles. Among the military vehicles is the staff car Montgomery rode into Berlin after the defeat of the Nazis. The museum is open daily, except Monday, from 9 a.m. to 5 p.m., charging adults an admission of $3. Children and senior citizens are admitted at half price. For more information, telephone the Director of Libraries, Coventry City Council, Bayley Lane, Coventry (tel. Coventry 25555, ext. 2315).

FOOD AND LODGING: De Vere Hotel, Cathedral Square (tel. Coventry 51851), is strikingly modern, designed to relate architecturally to the adjoining cathedral. Just off the Coventry inner ring road, it stands in the center of the city. For such a provincial hotel, it has an international first-class standard of comfort and service. Attracting a large business clientele, the hotel sounds an elegant tone in its public rooms, including the Terrace Room, a coffeeshop-restaurant where, in summer, glass doors slide back to give access to the terrace forming one side of Cathedral Square. In addition, the Taverna, the hotel's biggest bar, is decorated in an Italianate style, and the Three Spires Restaurant specializes in classical British and continental cookery, with prime Scottish beef a specialty. Bedrooms are spacious and equipped with rosewood furnishings, and each unit was designed as a twin-bedded studio with private baths and double-glazed windows to keep out traffic noises. Twins range in price from £51 ($99.45) to £56 ($109.20), and singles pay from £38 ($74.10) to £43 ($83.85), the latter in the "executive" class. These rates include breakfast and VAT.

Leofric, Broadgate (tel. Coventry 21371), named for Lady Godiva's husband, is the major hotel in the city, attracting, I suspect, far more business people than tourists. However, if you're overnighting in Coventry, it's the best choice, lying only two or three minutes from the cathedral, overlooking the famous statue of Lady Godiva. Each of the 90 bedrooms has a private bath, TV, phone, and central heating. The regular rate in a single is £27 ($52.65), increasing to £35 ($68.25) in a double or twin. Tariffs include a continental breakfast, service, and VAT. The Leofric's Carving Room is perhaps the best value in Coventry and serves traditional English food. A three-course meal is offered for £5.95 ($11.60). The coffeeshop, Peep-in Tom's, is named after the legendary figure who took a look at Lady Godiva. For a predinner drink, I'd recommend one of the specials in Ray's Bar.

The **Post House,** Rye Hill, Allesley, near Coventry (tel. Allesley 402151), is a motor hotel, built in rural surroundings three miles to the west of the center of Coventry, overlooking the main A45 road. There are nine floors and 200 bedrooms, each with wide-view window, private bath, radio, telephone, color TV, and central heating, as well as tea- and coffee-making facilities. You pay £26 ($50.70) in a single, £32 ($62.40) in a double, including service and VAT. Meals are rapid in the Buttery, more leisurely in the restaurant.

5. Hereford and Worcester

The Wye Valley contains some of the most beautiful river scenery in Europe. The river cuts through agricultural country, and there is no population explosion in the sleepy villages. Wool used to be its staple business, although fruit growing and dairy farming are important today.

The old country of Herefordshire has now combined with Worcestershire to form "Hereford and Worcester"-shire. Worcestershire's name, of course, has become famous around the world because of its sauce familiar to gourmets. It is one of the most charming of Midland counties, covering a portion of the rich valleys of the Severn and Avon.

Herefordshire's Black Mountains border the Welsh Brecon Beacons National Park, and between the two cathedral cities of Hereford and Worcester the ridge of the Malverns rises from the Severn Plain.

HEREFORD: One of the most colorful old towns of England, the ancient Saxon city of Hereford, on the Wye River, was the birthplace of both David Garrick and Nell Gwynne. Dating from 1079, the red sandstone **Hereford Cathedral** (tel. Hereford 59880) contains all styles of architecture, from Norman to Perpendicular. One of its most interesting features is a library of chained books—more than 1600 copies—as well as one of the oldest maps in existence, the Mappa Mundi of 1290. There is also a newly established Treasury in the crypt.

Hereford is surrounded by both orchards and rich pasturelands. Hence, it has some of the finest cider in the world, best sampled in one of the city's mellow pubs. Hereford cattle sold here are some of the finest in the world, too.

The **Old House,** High Town, is preserved as a Jacobean period museum, with the appropriate furnishings. The completely restored half-timbered structure was built in 1621. The house is open all year on Monday and Saturday from 10 a.m. to 1 p.m. On other days, hours are 10 a.m. to 1 p.m. and 2 to 5:30 p.m. It is closed on Sunday. Admission is 20p (39¢) for adults, 10p (20¢) for children.

Food and Lodging

Green Dragon, Broad Street (tel. Hereford 2506), hides behind an 18th-century Georgian facade, although the former coaching inn is considerably older. Convenient to the cathedral, the inn has a large, pillared main hall. It's warm and inviting, made especially so by the traditional old features which remain, including some early 17th-century paneling of Herefordshire oak. Next to the restaurant is a paneled cocktail bar, and there's also the Offa Bar on the ground floor.

Many of the bedrooms are spacious, and all are pleasantly decorated—93 units in all, mainly with private baths. Depending on the plumbing, singles begin at £24 ($46.80), and doubles go from £28 ($54.60), including VAT, service, and a continental breakfast. The paneled restaurant is a room of character. Good food, including both English and continental dishes, are featured by the chef. Expect to pay about £3 ($5.85) for a buffet lunch, from £9 ($17.55) for an à la carte dinner.

WORCESTER: This historic cathedral city, known for its gloves and porcelain, stands 27 miles from Birmingham and 26 miles from Stratford-upon-Avon.

Offering views of the Malvern Hills, **Worcester Cathedral** stands on the banks of the Severn River. Dating from 1084, it contains the Quire (rebuilt in 1224) which shelters King John's Tomb from 1216. The Chapter House, with its massive central supporting column, is considered one of the finest in England. The cathedral is open from 7:30 a.m. to 6 p.m. daily (in summer until 7:30 p.m.).

A visit to the **Royal Worcester Porcelain Factory** (tel. Worcester 23221) is worthwhile. A tour costs £1.20 ($2.34) for adults, 50p (98¢) for children, allowing you to see the crafts people at work. Unfortunately it's necessary to book ahead if you wish to take a tour, but everyone can enjoy browsing in the shop at the factory. There you can buy examples of their craft. Many pieces are "seconds," all marked as such and sold at low prices. Most of the time you won't be able to tell why! There is a magnificent museum as well.

The city is rich in other sights as well, including the **Commandery,** a fine 15th-century timber-framed structure which was originally founded about 1085 as a hospital. Purchased by the City of Worcester in 1973, it contains a great hall with a hammer-beam ceiling and oriel window. It features displays on the city's history from Roman times. It's open Tuesday to Saturday from 10:30 a.m. to 5 p.m. (Sunday in summer only, 2:30 to 5 p.m.) Admission is 40p (78¢) for adults, 15p (29¢) for children and senior citizens.

If time remains, see **King Charles' House,** where Charles II stayed before the Battle of Worcestershire in 1651; **Queen Elizabeth's House,** and the **Queen Anne Guildhall,** built in 1723 (outside, the Royalists honored Charles I and II with statues); and **St. Helen's,** the nation's oldest church, which may date back to 680.

On Sunday in summer, guided walking tours, lasting 1½ hours, leave at 11 a.m. and again at 2:30 p.m. from the Lychgate Precinct at a cost of 25p (49¢) per person.

Food and Lodging

Giffard Hotel, High Street (tel. Worcester 27155), is a modern hotel in the center of the city, built in a new shopping district, which contains a multistory car park. In the lounge, guests can gaze through picture windows which frame a view of the cathedral. Often used as a conference center, the hotel has more than 100 well-furnished bedrooms, each with private bath, radio, TV, phone, and coffee-making equipment. The cost is from £26 ($50.70) in a single, from £36 ($70.20) in a double, including both service and VAT. The pleasantly efficient staff will make your stay comfortable. Adjoining the Royal Worcester Room, the elegantly furnished restaurant, is a cocktail bar. A second bar, elegantly finished in marble and deep mahogany, is named the Royalist, its theme based on the Royalist connections in Worcester. The hotel is easily accessible from the M5 Motorway (exit 7).

For meals, I'd suggest the **King Charles II**, 29 New St. (tel. Worcester 22449), a mellow old half-timbered building where Charles II was believed to have hidden out following the Battle of Worcester. The paneled dining room is elegantly decorated with two open fireplaces. The specialties—continental with mainly Italian dishes—are enjoyable prepared from good ingredients. Expect to pay about £14 ($27.30) per person for dinner on the à la carte menu. The restaurant, however, serves a set lunch for £7.50 ($14.63). It is closed on Sunday and for the last three weeks in July.

Bottle's Wine Bar & Bistro, 5 Friar St. (tel. Worcester 21958), is a favored rendezvous right in the historic center. The decor is handsomely subdued, with black painted wickerwork tables, and the selection of cold foods is very good. I prefer the clove-studded freshly baked ham, along with a nice crisp salad, costing £2.50 ($4.88) per platter. In addition, the good-tasting soups are also homemade, going for 50p (98¢) a bowl. The roast joints, seafood dishes, and at least one hot specialty every day are also recommended. You might end your meal with cheesecake or gâteau, or even with brie or Stilton cheese at 75p ($1.46). The wine bar is open from noon to 2:30 p.m. (last orders are taken at 2 p.m.) and from 6:30 to 10:30 p.m. (until 11 p.m. on Friday and Saturday; last orders a half hour before closing). Closed Sunday.

A Museum on the Outskirts

Avoncroft Museum of Buildings, Stoke Heath, Bromsgrove, Worcester (tel. Bromsgrove 31886), is 11 miles from Worcester and 21 miles from Stratford-upon-Avon. It is open daily from March 1 to November 30 from 10:30 a.m. to 5:30 p.m. Admission is £1.10 ($2.15) for adults, 60p ($1.17) for children. You can hire a guide for £3 ($5.85) per party. The museum's cafeteria is open from 11 a.m. for coffee, lunch, and afternoon tea. Snacks are available from 50p (98¢), and tea or coffee costs 35p (68¢). The museum is an open-air site where a variety of historic buildings have been saved from destruction and reconstructed. There is a windmill in working order, a timber-framed merchant's house from the 15th century, an Elizabethan house, chain- and nail-making workshops, and a blacksmith's forge. This gives one a fascinating insight into the construction of those buildings as done by our forefathers. The 14th-century Guesten Hall roof from Worcester has been reconstructed at ground level so that you can see how the joints were made by the skill of artisans of the past. Recent additions include a cockfight theater, a stable, and a wagon shed, all of the 18th century. These are just a few of the exhibits on display at this ten-acre site. Free car parking is available, and there is also a picnic area.

GREAT MALVERN: A holiday spa and splendid walking center, Great Malvern is the best spot for your headquarters if you want to tour the beautiful, historic Malverns, once part of the ancient kingdom of Mercia. Great Malvern became important in the 19th century as a spa town, and much of the Victorian splendor remains. The Malvern Hills stretch for nine miles, with six townships lying along their line.

A Farm Cottage Holiday

   Whitewells Farm Cottages, Ridgeway Cross, near Malvern (tel. Ridgeway Cross 607), are just one example of the country cottages offered in the heart of England. Peter and Lynne Bennett have turned their farm buildings into unique holiday accommodations. The old hop kiln has a circular kitchen and bedroom; saddlestones and haywain have bedrooms on the ground floor, a lounge and kitchen in the old hayloft. The cottages have antique oak beams and country-style furnishings. An old stone barn has been turned into a cottage named Cider Press, which sleeps from two to four persons. In addition an old pigs' cot alongside the pony stables now provides a laundry room, with an automatic washing machine and dryer for the use of guests. The old pony stables act as the reception. Milk, bread, and newspapers are delivered here, and you'll find a telephone, a library of books, and local information. All cottages are well furnished with refrigerator, cooker, central heating, color TV, and electric blankets, plus little extras such as hair-dryers, toasters, and irons. They will willingly tell you where to buy provisions and will make you welcome to their part of the country. Prices range from £100 ($195) per week for two, £125 ($243.75) for four to £135 ($263.25) for six persons. During the early spring, winter, and autumn, shorter rentals are possible.

LODGINGS NEAR EVESHAM: **Salford Hall,** Abbots Salford, near Evesham (tel. Evesham 870561). Part of the original building dates back to the 15th century but, as with so many country houses of those times, it has been added to in the 17th century and later restored to provide ten bedrooms, six with baths. The Abbots Bar (this was once a nunnery) is oak paneled, and the lounge is full of comfortable chairs. The restaurant provides a lunchtime carvery on Sunday for £6.50 ($12.68). At other times an ample three-course meal will cost around £9 ($17.55) per person. A single room with bath is £16 ($31.20) a night, a double or twin renting from £25 ($48.75) to £27 ($52.65) a night, including a full breakfast. All rooms have tea and coffeemakers. VAT is included.

WEOBLEY: This small medieval village of old timbered houses lies west of the A49 Hereford–Ludlow road, only a few miles east of the border of Wales.
   Red Lion Hotel (tel. Weobley 220) is a charming village inn, more than 500 years old, which has been carefully restored to offer seven rooms, all with private bath or shower, color TV, warm furnishings, and comfortable beds.
   Mr. and Mrs. Gordon Bryan run the place most efficiently, and everything is kept spotlessly clean. Rooms go for £20 ($39) in a single, from £26 ($50.70) in a double, including service and VAT. Breakfast, featuring cooked dishes, is included. A daily set luncheon is featured for £5.50 ($10.73). On Sunday, the traditional English luncheon of roast meats and vegetables with all the trimmings goes for £6 ($11.70). Lunch is served from 12:30 to 2 p.m., dinner from 7 to 10 p.m. (till 9 p.m. on Sunday). Aside from the bar occupied in the evenings by locals, there is a cozy lounge with a roaring fire and soft armchairs where your orders for dinner are taken. You dine in the elegant dining room, selecting your choice from a wide menu of moules (mussels) marinières, deep-fried mushrooms filled with pâté or Stilton cheese, a casserole of wild duck with brandy, veal Cordon Bleu, or chicken cooked with brandy, white wine, cream,

and peppers. Expect to spend from £10 ($19.50) for an evening meal. Service is good and friendly, and passersby are welcomed.

6. Salop (Shropshire)

Immortalized by A. E. Housman's "A Shropshire Lad," this hilly county borders Wales, which accounts for its turbulent history. The bloody battles are over today, and the towns of Salop, with their black-and-white timbered houses, are peaceful and quiet. Salop makes a good base for touring in the Welsh mountains.

SHREWSBURY: Lying within a horseshoe bend of the Severn River, Shrewsbury is the capital of Salop. The river almost encloses the town. Known for its cakes and ale, Shrewsbury contains one of the best known schools in England. It was also the birthplace of Charles Darwin.

Considered the finest Tudor town in England, Shrewsbury is noted for its black-and-white buildings of timber and plaster, including Abbot's House from 1450 and the tall gabled Ireland's Mansion from 1575 standing on High Street. It also has a number of Georgian and Regency mansions, some old bridges, and handsome churches, including the Abbey Church of Saint Peter and St. Mary's Church.

Shrewsbury Castle is 900 years old and was saved from destruction in 1790 when an engineer, Thomas Telford, had it restored as a private house. Built of red sandstone on a hill dominating the town, it is now a visitor center with permanent displays of the history of Shrewsbury. Called the **Information Centre**, it stands on the Square (tel. Shrewsbury 52019).

Rowley's House on Barker Street has a fine collection of Roman artifacts from Viroconium (Wroxeter), and is open weekdays from 10 a.m. to 1 p.m. and 2 to 5 p.m. This building is adjacent to **Rowley's Mansion**, which opened as a museum in 1982, covering art, local history, numismatics, Roman archeology, geology and minerals, prehistory, costumes, and natural history. The great treasures of these museums are the Hadrianic inscription (second century) and silver mirror (third century), both from Wroxeter.

Clive House Museum, on College Hill (tel. Shrewsbury 54811), has displays of local ceramics, industrial archeology, art, costumes, and a Georgian room, besides being the regimental museum of the Queen's Dragoon Guards. Hours are from 10 a.m. to 1 p.m. and 2 to 5 p.m., except Monday when hours are from noon to 1 p.m. and 2 to 5 p.m.

At **Coleham Pumping Station**, Longden Coleham, you can see displayed compound rotative pumping engines from 1900, on Wednesday and Friday from 2 to 5 p.m.

Food and Lodging

Prince Rupert Hotel, Butcher Row (tel. Shrewsbury 52461), is a hotel of character—part of it dating from the 15th century—right on a quiet side street in the center of town. Its front has four peaked gables and, in summer, a wealth of flower boxes full of petunias and geraniums. The facade is characterized by peaked gables on the Old Church Street entrance. Even though the interior has been modernized, it still has exposed beams and uneven floors. A favorite gathering spot is the lounge, which is tapestried. There are three restaurants in all, including the Cavalier. The rooms are bright and fresh, with compact, well-maintained baths found in 47 of the 66 units. Singles range in price from

£19 ($37.05) to £23.50 ($45.83); doubles or twins go from £27.50 ($53.63) to £33.50 ($65.33).

Lion Hotel, Wyle Cop (tel. Shrewsbury 53107), is a simple red brick structure, once a well-known posting inn, standing on the outskirts of town on the Telford road. In part the hotel dates from the 15th century, and oak beams and paneling from that period remain. Many famous people have stayed here, including Dickens, Jenny Lind, and De Quincey, who described the hotel's Adam-style ballroom in his *Confessions of an Opium Eater.* Bedrooms are simply furnished, and many are quite small. Depending on the plumbing, singles range from £24 ($46.80), and doubles cost from £36 ($70.20), including both VAT and service. Forty-four of the 64 bedrooms contain private baths. The Dickens Suite boasts a "half-tester" bed in which the Victorian novelist is reputed to have slept. The restaurant with its Victorian decor is named after him, and it serves both table d'hôte and à la carte meals. A set lunch goes for £5.50 ($10.73), increasing to £7 ($13.65) for a table d'hôte dinner. The hotel has two bars, the Tudor one featuring a buffet at lunchtime.

OSWESTRY: Near the Welsh border, this interesting old market town has some Yale monuments in its St. Oswald's Church and a 17th-century Griddle Gate nearby. At Old Owestry, an Iron Age hill fort with multiple ramparts can be seen.

LUDLOW: Looking down on the Teme River, this is a mellow old town with a historic Norman castle. Many Georgian and Jacobean timbered buildings stand on its quiet lanes and courts. The most colorful street is known as "Broad," rising from the old Ludford Bridge to Broadgate, the one remaining gateway from walls erected in the Middle Ages. See, in particular, the Church of St. Laurence, Butter Cross, and Reader's House.

Food and Lodging

The Feathers, Bullring (tel. Ludlow 2919), is one of England's most famous Elizabethan inns. Built in 1603 as a private residence, it is characterized by its half-timbered front and richly decorated interior. Bedrooms are bright and cheerful, and all of them contain private baths en suite, as well as phones, radios, television sets, and tea- and coffee-making facilities. Colors are in perfect harmony, with Welsh tapestry bedspreads. Singles go from £26 ($50.70), and doubles cost from £23 ($44.85) to £26 ($50.70) per person, including an English breakfast. If possible, ask for one of the units with a four-poster bed. The Richard III restaurant, with its original fireplace, is in the old-world style, serving good food and drink. Set meals go for £9.50 ($18.53), but there will be an à la carte menu as well. There are also two fully licensed bars, and polished brass and copper set the right decorative tone. In the James I lounge, you can enjoy a carved mantelpiece and an elaborately ornamented plaster ceiling.

For lunch, I'd suggest the **Bull Hotel,** Corve Street (tel. Ludlow 2962). Close to the castle, it's an old coaching inn which you enter under a typical arch into the courtyard. The oldest parts of the building are early Tudor. There is a large bar with roaring open fire where bar snacks are served, including the day's special hot soup at 35p (68¢) or salads at £1.50 ($2.93). In summer you can take your drink and food into the courtyard, but in winter, far better to hog the fire.

TUTBURY: Once a stronghold of the Anglo-Saxon kings of Mercia, and mentioned in the Domesday Book, Tutbury is a small town on the Dove River, lying four miles north of Burton-upon-Trent. It has a fine Norman church and the ruins of Tutbury Castle.

Ye Olde Dog and Partridge, High Street (tel. Tutbury 813030), has been a colorful village inn for so long there is no clear record of its beginnings. Charming in appearance, is has an ornate black-and-white timbered facade, bay windows, and leaded glass, surviving elements from the 15th century. A popular coaching house in the 18th and 19th centuries, it offers a more modernized hospitality today. New luxury bathrooms have been installed for each bedroom, and singles rent for £25 ($48.75) a night, doubles going for £32 ($62.40), including a full English breakfast.

Inside, the inn still has a wealth of old timbering and fireplaces, maintaining a traditional character. On a more incongruous note, it has a French restaurant which is open from Monday evening through Saturday evening (Saturday lunches excepted). The à la carte menu, costing about £9 ($17.55) for a meal, is changed weekly. In addition, the inn also has a wine bar and carvery open seven days a week.

7. Staffordshire

Stoke-on-Trent is the name of the five towns known as the Potteries, the "Five Towns" of Arnold Bennett's novels. The Potteries are known throughout the world for the excellence of their fine porcelain and china.

The so-called "Black Country" of steelworks and coal mines has almost disappeared, although you can visit a coal mine and descend in the "cage" to the worked-out seams.

Within easy reach of the industrial town of Dovedale is a valley with some of English's most beautiful scenery, forming part of the Peak District National Park.

STOKE-ON-TRENT: Because of the worldwide interest in the making of pottery, this town has found itself something of a tourist attraction. It's the home of the pottery made famous by Josiah Wedgwood, along with other well-known names such as Coalport, Minton, and Spode.

The **Wedgwood Visitor Centre,** at Barlaston (tel. Barlaston 4141), at present charges no admission and is open from 9 a.m. to 5 p.m. Monday to Friday except over Christmas. In the demonstration hall you can watch the slip, the clay, built up on the potter's wheel, see how the raised motifs so well known on Wedgwood Blue pottery are made and added to the pieces, as well as witness how delicate flowers are made and painted and plates turned and fired, then painted.

The young people working at the benches are often apprentices, but the work they produce is of the highest quality. They are happy to answer your questions about their special occupation.

There's a continuous film show in the large cinema, and the beginning of the movie is announced on the public address system. In the shop you can see samples of all the sorts of items made at the factory, and purchase souvenirs. Prices are the same as elsewhere, but they do sometimes have items of discontinued lines and some "seconds" available at reduced prices.

The fascinating museum has exhibits of more than 200 years of craftsmanship, showcases of old bills, working details, experimental pots and goblets, and drawings of machines invented by Josiah Wedgwood two centuries ago and still used daily in the factory.

When you need a rest, there's a lounge with a snack cafeteria where for under £1 ($1.95) you can get a bowl of soup, a sandwich, or some steak-and-kidney pie with a glass of wine. Here you can write your postcards home and have them franked with a special stamp to say they were mailed at the Wedgwood Centre.

Afterward, a visit to the past is in order. The **Gladstone Pottery Museum,** Uttoxeter Road at Longton (tel. Stoke-on-Trent 319232), is an old building with a paneled hallway leading to rooms piled with ancient machines and equipment used in the pottery trade. Tiles and saggers (something to do with the piling of plates in kilns) are stacked everywhere. There's a marvelous exhibit of washstand bowls and jugs, plus toilets of all shapes and sizes, including the original flush toilet made for Queen Elizabeth I in 1596. Called the Harrington Water Closet, it is still in working order. It was here that the tiles used in the Capitol in Washington were made, and they have examples displayed on the floor. Outside is a replica of a typical potter's home, plus a working pottery with its old Victorian bottle ovens, the last few in the area where there used to be several thousand. The area around the museum is known as Potters Acre because of the number of shops specializing in rejects and discontinued lines. Here you may be able to replace that broken cup. Admission to the museum is £1 ($1.95). It is open from Monday to Saturday from 10:30 a.m. to 5:30 p.m. (closed Monday in winter). It is also open on Sunday in summer from 2 to 6 p.m.

The **Stoke-on-Trent City Museum,** on Broad Street in Hanley (tel. Stoke-on-Trent 29611), surely must contain the most comprehensive collection of ceramics in the world. The enthusiastic curator tells me that they have twice as much stored away as they can possibly show at any one time. Even those who aren't museum buffs must find this a beautiful collection. There are also exhibitions of modern art as well as prehistoric local remains, all housed in a delightful contemporary building. The museum is open Monday to Saturday from 10:30 a.m. to 5 p.m.

Afterward, sustenance is required, and where better than at **Heath's Wine Bar,** Albion Street at Hanley (tel. Stoke-on-Trent 272472), almost opposite the museum? The long bar groans beneath great dishes of pâté, cold meats, pies (veal, ham and egg, steak and kidney, grosvenor), chili, salads (several varieties), dressed crab, and hot soup. Mounds of french bread are stacked up, and jacket potatoes are a favorite item. For dessert, try the cheesecake or a fruit salad. Everything is fresh, and there is much that's homemade. Order and collect your meal and repair to one of the low coffee tables surrounded by sofas or the wheelbacked chair-surrounded tables. The music is soft, and the atmosphere is warm and red. A two-course meal will cost around £1.60 ($3.12) to £2.40 ($4.68). Wine is 50p (98¢) and 75p ($1.46) a glass, or else you can order tea or coffee.

The **New Minton Museum,** at London Road, Stoke-on-Trent (tel. Stoke-on-Trent 47771), is the starting place for a 1½ hour tour through the major departments of this factory, where they specialize in heavily decorated work. A phone call or a letter in advance is needed to join the 50p (98¢) tour, but your understanding of the processes will be complete when you have seen how to raise patterns and scour and burnish gold relief. It takes 45 minutes to finish the decoration on one plate, so you can see how much a dinner service should cost.

Free-hand painting from some 1800 patterns is also shown during the tour. It is here that you can get that unique souvenir, a personalized free-hand-painted plate or other piece of china. Simply arrange to discuss with one of the artists the photo or picture you wish to have, and they'll do the rest. The cost of a plate can be as much as £130 ($253.50), and it'll take from 2 to 12 months to complete, depending on the demand for orders. But you'll have an elegant and totally different souvenir. For more information, see Mrs. Joan Jones, the museum's curator.

The **Chatterley Whitfield Mining Museum,** at Tunstall, Stoke-on-Trent (tel. Stoke-on-Trent 813337), is the only place in England where you can visit a coal mine, going down to the coal face. You are "kitted out" with lamp and helmet, and you can get overalls to cover your clothes. Stout shoes are also recommended. This mine was the first to produce one million tons of coal in a year. Coal was mined for 140 years, but the mine has been closed now for five years. The 700-foot shaft is 80 years old, and it takes 1½ minutes to descend to the face. Each party is accompanied by a retired miner. Mine was Joe, who was born in Poland, but settled in England in the '40s. He explains the techniques of mining, feeding you much information, including how the steam-winding engines work. The tour takes about an hour and costs £2 ($3.90).

Food and Lodging

For those who wish to visit the Potteries and stay overnight in this industrial part of the country, I offer the following suggestions.

The **Crown Hotel,** High Street at Stone (tel. Stone 813535), is a solid 18th century coaching inn, built on the site of a far more ancient staging post, one of the most important in the country in the reign of Charles II. Today the coach yard is roofed in to provide for the lofty paneled dining room. The sleek "carriages" of today's travelers are housed in a large yard behind the hotel.

Some of the accommodations are in the main hotel, reached by a fine galleried oak staircase; others are in a new extension at the back of the building. All units have bath (shower only in the newer part), color TV, and coffee- and tea-making facilities. Prices run from £15.50 ($30.23) per person in a double with bath to £17 ($33.15) per person in a room with a sitting room. Singles run from £18 ($35.10) in a room with shower to £19.50 ($38.03) with bath. All prices include VAT, service, and an enormous breakfast.

Dinner in the magnificent paneled dining hall includes roasts at £3 ($5.85), salmon steaks at £5 ($9.75), and steaks from £5.50 ($10.73) to £6.50 ($12.68). Portions are huge, and you may not even want to think of an appetizer. I just managed to finish my main course and had to skip dessert on my latest rounds. If you want dessert, you face a choice from the groaning trolley, priced from 75p ($1.46) to £1.20 ($2.34) per serving. At lunch, a buffet provides substantial meals, including cold meats, quiche, and chicken-and-ham pie, along with an assortment of salads.

Haydon House Hotel, 5–9 Haydon St. at Basford (tel. Basford 629311), is a turn-of-the-century house in a quiet part of Basford, one of the Five Towns that make up Stoke-on-Trent. It has a pleasant Victorian bar and a dining room with wheelback chairs and a clubby atmosphere. Bedrooms run from £12.50 ($24.38) per person in a double with bath or shower, although singles are charged £13.50 ($26.33) without tub, £19.50 ($38.03) with. All units have color TV, radio, and phone, and prices include a large breakfast and a newspaper.

A three-course luncheon chosen from the ample list of dishes will cost £5.15 ($10.05). You are likely to be given deep-fried mushrooms with cucumber sauce, roast of the day, or braised duck, then a dessert. The table d'hôte dinner at £6.50 ($12.68) has a choice of four appetizers and four hot main dishes, plus a dessert or cheese, then coffee.

STAFFORD: The county town was the birthplace of Izaak Walton, the British writer and celebrated fisherman. Its main industry is boot making, and it contains many historic buildings, notably St. Chad's, the town's oldest church; St. Mary's, with its unusual octagonal tower; and the William Salt Library, with its interesting collection of folklore.

Food and Lodging

Tillington Hall Hotel, Eccleshall Road (tel. Stafford 53531), which has been extensively remodeled and renovated, stands in its own grounds just a mile from the center of the county town, yet less than half a mile from the M6 Motorway (junction 14). The attractive paneled reception lounge, where you are likely to stand next to Midlands business people checking in, leads to a modern bar and a lounge with an open fire on nippy nights. Eighty bedrooms, each furnished in a contemporary idiom, come equipped with private bath, radio, phone, color TV set, and coffee-making equipment. The cost is £30 ($58.50) nightly in a single, £38 ($74.10) in a double, including a full English breakfast, VAT, and service. Good food is served in the Izaak Walton Restaurant, where meals begin at £7 ($13.65).

LICHFIELD: Fans of Samuel Johnson pay a pilgrimage here to this historic city where he was born in 1709, son of an unsuccessful bookseller and parchment maker. The city is noted for its cathedral, whose three spires are known as "Ladies of the Vale." The tallest spire rises more than 250 feet, and the west front of the cathedral was built from about 1280. You can walk around the beautiful Close and see a bit of the Vicars Close, with its half-timbered houses, along with the 17th-century Bishops Palace.

Dr. Johnson's Birthplace on Breadmarket Street contains mementos and pictures of the author and his contemporaries. It is open from 10 a.m. to 5 p.m., closing at 4 p.m. off-season and Sunday afternoons in the summer. The admission charged is 40p (78¢) for adults, 20p (39¢) for children.

Across the street from Dr. Johnson's Birthplace stands the **Heritage Centre & Treasury,** in Lichfield's Market Square. Adults pay an admission of 50p (98¢), and children are charged only 25p (49¢). Hours are daily from 10 a.m. to 5 p.m. (except Monday). Exhibits depict everything from burnings at the stake to plagues. Wax models are displayed of many of the city's galaxy of visitors, including David Garrick, the actor. The treasury displays goldsmiths and silversmiths over the centuries.

You can also visit the **Guildhall** (across the road from the Heritage Centre). Over the city dungeons dating from the Middle Ages, the Guildhall was rebuilt in 1846. Prisoners were jailed here before they were burned at the stake in Market Square.

Incidentally, market days are Friday and Saturday in Lichfield.

READER'S HOTEL SELECTION: "In Newcastle-under-Lyme, I can heartily recommend the **Grove Court Hotel,** 100 Lancaster Rd. (tel. Newcastle-under-Lyme 614406). It is a large, old house, with a rose garden and a lounge for sitting, a small bar in the office, and the hostess is a superb cook (a caterer in her not very plentiful spare time). For £30 ($58.50), my husband and I enjoyed a room with a private bath, drinks, dinner, lodging, and breakfast" (Anne S. Short, Garden City, N.Y.).

CAMBRIDGE AND EAST ANGLIA

"WE ARE FARMERS—great animal lovers," say two sisters who run a small farm in Essex. They delight in receiving paying guests at their old farm, feeding them fresh vegetables and home-grown fruit. They are not atypical of the East Anglians. The four counties of East Anglia—Essex, Suffolk, Norfolk, and Cambridgeshire—are essentially low-lying areas, where the bucolic life still reigns supreme.

East Anglia was an ancient Anglo-Saxon kingdom, under heavy domination of the Danes for many a year. Beginning in the 12th century, it was the center of a great cloth industry that brought it prosperity, as the spires of some of its churches testify to this day. Essentially, it is a land of heathland, fens, marshes, and broads in Norfolk.

Cambridge is the most visited city in East Anglia, but don't neglect to pass through Suffolk and Essex, Constable country, containing some of the finest landscapes in England. Norwich, the seat of the Duke of Norfolk, is less visited, but the fortunate few who go that far toward the North Sea will be rewarded.

1. Cambridge

A young couple lying in an open green space between colleges, reading the Romantic poets . . . rowing under the Bridge of Sighs . . . spires and turrets . . . drooping willows that witness much punting . . . dusty secondhand bookshops . . . daffodils swaying in the meadows . . . carol singing on Christmas Eve in King's College Chapel . . . dancing till sunrise at the May balls . . . the sound of Elizabethan madrigals . . . the purchase of horse brasses at the corner stall in the open market . . . narrow lanes where Darwin, Newton, and Cromwell once trod . . . The Backs, where the lawns of the colleges sweep down to the Cam River . . . the tattered black robe of an upperclassman, rebelliously hanging by a thread to his shoulder as it flies in the wind.

We're in the university city of Cambridge, which, along with Oxford, is one of the ancient seats of learning in Britain. The city on the banks of the Cam River is also the county town of Cambridgeshire, 55 miles northeast of London, 80 miles from Oxford. In many ways, the stories of Oxford and Cambridge are similar—particularly the age-old conflict between town and gown (impoverished scholars vs. rent-gouging landlords). But Oxford is an industrial city, sheltering a thriving life beyond the campus. Cambridge has some industry, but if the university were removed, I suspect it would revert to an unpretentious market town.

There is much to see and explore in Cambridge—so give yourself time to wander, even aimlessly. For those pressed, I'll offer more specific direction.

CAMBRIDGE UNIVERSITY: Oxford University predates the one at Cambridge. But in the early 13th century scholars began coming up to Cambridge, as opposed to being "sent down." The choice of the market town as a seat of learning just happened—perhaps coming about as a result of a core of important masters, dissatisfied with Oxford, electing to live near the fens. Eventually, Cambridge won partial recognition from Henry III, rising and slumping with the approval or disdain of subsequent English monarchs. Cambridge consists of 29 colleges for both men and women. If you have time for only one sight, then make it:

King's College Chapel

The teenaged Henry VI founded the college on King's Parade in 1441. But most of its buildings today are from the 19th century. It is the Perpendicular Chapel which is not only the crowning glory, but one of the architectural gems in England inherited from the Middle Ages. The chapel, owing to the chaotic vicissitudes of English kings, wasn't completed until the early years of the 16th century. Its most characteristic features are its magnificent fan vaulting—all of stone—and its Great Windows, most of which were fashioned by Flemish artisans between 1515 and 1531 (the west window, however, dates from the late Victorian period). The stained glass, in hues of blues, reds, and ambers, reflects biblical stories. The long range of the windows, reading from the first on the north side at the west end right around the chapel back to the first on the south side, tell the story of the Birth of the Virgin, the Annunciation, the Birth of Christ, the Life, Ministry, and Death of Christ, the Resurrection, the Ascension, the Acts of the Apostles, and the Assumption. The upper range contains Old Testament parallels to these New Testament stories. The rood screen is from the early 16th century. Henry James called King's College Chapel "the most beautiful in England." It is open during vacation time on weekdays from 9 a.m. to 5 p.m., and on Sunday from 10:30 a.m. to 5 p.m. During term time the public is welcome to choral services which are at 5:30 p.m. on weekdays (service said on Monday), and at 10:30 a.m. and 3:30 p.m. on Sunday. In "term" the chapel is open to visitors from 9 a.m. to 3:45 p.m. on weekdays, from 2 to 3 p.m. and from 4:30 to 5:45 p.m. on Sunday. Closed December 26 to January 1. It may be closed at other times for recording sessions.

Peterhouse

This college on Trumpington Street is visited largely because it is the oldest Cambridge college, having been founded as early as 1284. The founding father was Hugh de Balsham, the bishop of Ely. Of the original buildings, only the Hall remains, but this was restored in the 19th century and now contains stained-glass windows by William Morris. Old Court was constructed in the 15th century, but refaced in 1754, and the chapel dates from 1632. Ask permission to enter at the porter's desk.

Trinity College

On Trinity Street, Trinity College—the largest at Cambridge (not to be confused with Trinity Hall)—was founded in 1546 by Henry VIII from a number of smaller colleges that had existed on the site. The courtyard is the most spacious one in Cambridge, built when Thomas Nevile was master. Sir Christopher Wren designed the Library. For admission to the college, apply at the porter's lodge, or telephone Cambridge 58201 for information.

Emmanuel College

On St. Andrew's Street, Emmanuel was founded in 1584 by Sir Walter Mildmay, a chancellor of the exchequer to Elizabeth I. It is of interest at least to Harvard men, as John Harvard, founder of that university, studied here. With its attractive gardens, it makes for a good stroll. You might even visit the chapel designed by Sir Christopher Wren and consecrated in 1677. Both the chapel and college are open daily from 9:30 a.m. to 12:15 p.m. and from 2 to 6 p.m.

Queens' College

On Queens' Lane, Queens' College (tel. Cambridge 65511) is considered by some as the loveliest in the architectural galaxy. Dating back to 1448, it was founded, then "refounded" by two English queens—one the wife of Henry VI, the other the wife of Edward IV. Its second cloisters are the most interesting—flanked with the half-timbered President's Lodge, dating from the first half of the 16th century. Normally, the college is open to visitors between 2 and 4:30 p.m. Entry and exit is by the Old Porters' Lodge in Queens' Lane only. The college is closed between mid-May and mid-June. An admission fee of 25p (49¢) is charged, and in return a short printed guide is issued.

St. John's College

On St. John's Street, the college was founded in 1511 by Lady Margaret Beaufort, mother of Henry VII. A few years earlier she had founded Christ's College. Before her intervention, an old monk-run hospital had stood on the site of St. John's. The impressive gateway bears the Tudor coat-of-arms, and the dining room, one of the largest in Cambridge, is handsome, dating from the early 16th century. But its best known feature is the Bridge of Sighs, crossing the Cam, built as late as the 19th century and named after the bridge in Venice.

It connects the more dated part of the college with New Court—a Gothic revival—on the opposite bank. Wordsworth was an alumnus. The college may be visited any time before dusk, except during the summer examination period, May to early June.

Other College Sights

The above are only a representative selection of some of the more interesting colleges. **Magdalen College** on Magdalene Street was founded in 1542; **Pembroke College** on Trumpington Street was founded in 1347; **Christ's College** in St. Andrew's Street was founded in 1505; and **Corpus Christi College** on Trumpington Street dates from 1352. Only someone planning to stop in Cambridge for a long time will get around to them.

A Word of Warning: Unfortunately, because of the disturbances caused by the influx of tourists to the university, Cambridge has regretfully had to limit visitors, and even exclude them from various parts of the university altogether, and, in some cases, even charge a small fee for entrance. Small groups of up to six persons are generally admitted with no problem, and you can inquire from your local tourist office about visiting hours here.

OTHER SIGHTS: However, colleges aren't the only thing to see in Cambridge, as you'll assuredly agree if you explore the following attractions.

The Fitzwilliam Museum

On Trumpington Street, near Peterhouse, this museum was the gift of the Viscount Fitzwilliam, who in 1816 gave Cambridge University his paintings and rare books—along with £100,000 to build the house in which to display them. He thereby knowingly or unknowingly immortalized himself. Other gifts have since been bequeathed to the museum, and now it is one of the finest in England. It is noted for its porcelain, old prints, archeological relics, and oils (works by Titian and Rembrandt).

The museum is open weekdays from 10 a.m. to 5 p.m., on Sunday from 2:15 till 5 p.m. Closed Monday, Good Friday, December 24 to 31, and New Year's Day.

Great St. Mary's

Great St. Mary's, opposite King's College Chapel on King's Parade, is the university church (tel. Cambridge 350914). It is built on the site of an 11th-century church, but the present building dates largely from 1478. It was closely associated with events of the Reformation. The cloth which covered the hearse of King Henry VII is on display in the church. A fine view of Cambridge may be obtained from the top of the tower.

BOAT RENTALS: Scudamore's, at Granta Place adjacent to the Anchor Pub, has been in business since 1910. Costs are by the hour: £2.60 ($5.07) for a punt, £2.40 ($4.68) for a rowboat, or £2.20 ($4.29) for a canoe. A deposit of £15 ($29.25) is required, and it is refundable if you don't wreck the boat. Upriver you can go all the way to Grantchester, about a distance of two miles, made so famous by Rupert Brooke. Downstream, you pass along the Backs behind the colleges of the university.

PERSONALIZED TOURS: The person to know if you're in the Cambridge area is **Mrs. Isobel Bryant,** who runs Heritage Tours from her 200-year-old cottage, Manor Cottage, Swaffham Prior, Cambridge (tel. Newmarket 741440). A highly qualified expert on the area, she will arrange tours, starting from your Cambridge hotel to, say, Saffron Walden, Thaxted, and Audley End, for example, or to the U.S. military cemetery at Madingley, then Ely, and Anglesey Abbey, or to the charming timbered houses of Lavenham. Lunch is often organized in beautifully furnished private manor houses, so that you have the change of meeting local people. The day's trip costs around £30 ($58.50) for three people. Lunch and admission charges are extra—probably about £5 ($9.75) per person more.

Mrs. Bryant can also arrange accommodations with local families in their lovely country houses. The charges range from £16 ($31.20) to £20 ($39) for two persons per night in double rooms with private baths, these tariffs including a full English breakfast. Often dinner with the family can be arranged at around £5 ($9.75) per person, including wine. Rooms without private baths rent from £6 ($11.70) per person.

There are also walking tours around the colleges of Cambridge and, if you can make up a party of 15 or more persons, a fascinating tour of Newmarket, center of the horse-racing industry. On that tour, you visit a racecourse, the sales paddock, and watch a training gallop and visit stables and a stud farm. A whole day costs £12 ($23.40) per person; a half day £6.50 ($12.68). If you want lunch arranged at a private house with Cordon Bleu cookery, the cost is around £5 ($9.75) per person. All prices include **VAT.**

A SELF-GUIDED TOUR: The center of Cambridge is closed to cars. There is good parking at the Anchor Pub in Silver Street, so why not leave your car there and then go for a walk around to some of the colleges?

Cross Silver Street Bridge, and you'll see the entrance to Queens College. Go into the college, crossing over the mathematical wooden bridge, so called because of its geometrical design. Then enter the older part of the college into the center of a quadrangle, and you'll see much of the beautiful Elizabethan architecture and also the doors around the quad, leading to the "staircases" of tiny studies and bedrooms for undergraduates within the college itself. Those who cannot get an accommodation here are boarded out around the city.

Leave through the fine Elizabethan arch into the new part of the college; turn right and, just past the chapel, take the doorway open to the road. Turn left and at the end of the road the archway leads to King's College Chapel and the college itself. Just inside is a very well-defined "staircase." This is also a beautiful college with lawns sweeping to the Cam. Visit the chapel to see the *Adoration of the Magi* by Reubens hanging over the High Altar. You can attend evensong at King's most every night at 5:30 p.m. There are services every Sunday at 10:30 a.m., 3:30 p.m., and again at 6 p.m.

Leave by the Porter's Lodge and walk to the Church Tower of the 800-year-old parish church of St. Edward Saint and Martyr. Within its walls the reformers of the 16th century preached and ministered the gospel. Turn right into the main Market Square where there is a daily market for fruit, vegetables, and other produce.

Leave on Wheeler Street, leading on to Benet Street. Opposite St. Benet's Church in St. Benet's Lane you will see two doors leading to a passage which will bring you to the **Eagle Pub** on the grounds of Corpus Christi—arguably the only galleried inn in Cambridge. It is little known by tourists but much frequented by locals. The usual bar snacks are provided to mop up the beer.

Totter back to Benet Street and you'll be back where you started at the Anchor where you left your car. Without stopovers, this walk will take you about one hour of leisurely observation.

This tour is best done when the colleges aren't in session. Otherwise, many colleges at term time are, of course, closed in the mornings.

WHERE TO STAY: Accommodations are limited in scope and facilities, although generally adequate for the purpose. Much of the overload in summer is siphoned off by little guest houses, filled at term time with scholars, but otherwise freed when most visitors arrive in July and August. I'll begin with a general survey of the best hotels in:

The Medium-Priced Range

University Arms Hotel, Regent Street (tel. Cambridge 51241), is a successful blending of the old and new. It originated late in Victoria's day as an inn operated by Marcus Dennis Bradford, grandfather of the present owner, William Bradford. One portion is traditionally designed, although a new wing was added in 1965, offering 58 modern bedrooms, all with private bath and tasteful decorations. Sliding glass doors open onto private balconies, with views of the cricket grounds of Parker's Place, known for its associations with cricketer Sir Jack Hobbs. The rooms opening onto Regent Street have soundproofed double-glass windows.

Each bedroom has its own telephone, central heating, private bath, electric razor outlets, radio, and color TV. The single rate is £24.50 ($47.78), and a twin-bedded room is £36 ($70.20). These rates include service, VAT, and a full English breakfast. Meals are served in the wood-paneled dining room, opening toward the lawn and trees. The charge for a table d'hôte luncheon is from £5.50 ($10.73), rising to £6.50 ($12.68) for a set dinner. The older octagonal lounge, with its stained-glass dome, is still the best place to gather at teatime. Tip: The hall porter can arrange for a guide to show you the nearby colleges.

The **Royal Cambridge Hotel,** Trumpington Street (tel. Cambridge 51631), may be the answer to England's hotel problem. The facade of a row of town houses has been preserved, but the inside has been gutted and redesigned in a tasteful modern way. The 86 rooms are compact and handsomely appointed. The bedrooms use many of the built-in techniques of motel design. Rates depend on the season, plumbing, and floor. Singles range from £16 ($31.20) to £21 ($40.95); twins, £26 ($50.70) to £31 ($60.45)—including service and VAT. Each room is centrally heated, and has both radio and telephone. A lot of extras are found here, including a hairdressing salon. Meals are à la carte.

Cambridgeshire Hotel, Bar Hill (tel. Crafts Hill 80555), is four miles from Cambridge city center. It's a modern, four-star hotel with heated swimming pool, a sauna, three squash courts, two outside tennis courts, and an 18-hole championship golf course. The 100 bedrooms are spacious and furnished in a functional way, including private bathroom/shower, color TV, radio, early-morning call system, and tea- and coffee-making facilities. Singles are £31 ($60.45); doubles £45 ($87.75). The main dining room, with a hammerbeamed ceiling, is overlooked by the lounge/cocktail bar in the Minstrels' Gallery. The food is traditionally English, including roast beef and Yorkshire pudding, steak-and-kidney pie, and grilled Dover sole. Bar lunches are also offered daily.

Blue Boar Hotel, Trinity Street (tel. Cambridge 63121), has an innkeeping fame that stretches back at least to the late 17th century. The most central of all my recommendations, it is run by Trusthouses Forte, attracting international visitors as well as parents of Cambridge students. Since its early days, it has been considerably modernized, with hot and cold running water added to every room (11 with private baths), as well as central heating and well-maintained furnishings. A pleasant brick building, directly opposite the Trinity Great Gate, it still keeps its original Blue Boar inn sign hanging over the arched doorway. Room prices are £22 ($42.90) for a single, from £29 ($56.55) to £36 ($70.20) in a double, including VAT and service, although breakfast is extra. Being a small inn, the hotel offers a limited lounge area. The Athene Bar draws an interesting crowd of people. It couldn't be handier for visiting the colleges, and there's a public car park a few blocks away.

Gonville Hotel, Gonville Place (tel. Cambridge 66611), stands on its own grounds, opposite Parkers Place, only a five-minute walk from the center of the city. It's not unlike a country house—ivy covered, with shade trees and a formal car entry. In 1973 it was gutted and rebuilt as a commercial hotel, intending to attract business people as well as tourists in summer. Singles go for £26 ($50.70), doubles for £37 ($72.15). Prices include VAT, service charge, and an English breakfast. Special three-bedded family rooms rent for £44 ($85.80). Central heating is provided throughout, plus air conditioning in the restaurant, where you can get a set lunch or dinner for about £7 ($13.65). The quality of comforts is good, the furnishings stylish.

WHERE TO EAT: The Pentagon, 6 St. Edwards Passage (tel. Cambridge 355246), is in the center of Cambridge, overlooking medieval cottages and the historic churchyard. Cold buffet meals and four hot specialties are served daily, the price per dish being about £3.50 ($6.83). There is a fine wine list, and fully licensed bar. Connected to and run by the Arts Theatre, the restaurant has a strong artistic atmosphere and is patronized by many stars of the English stage. It's open for lunch Monday to Saturday from noon to 2 p.m. and for supper from 6 to 10:30 p.m.

The **Arts Roof Garden Buffet,** perched above the theater, is popular in summer as it offers alfresco meals, self-service lunch, afternoon tea and supper, with a view of the Cambridge spires. You select from an array of hot and cold dishes, with meals averaging around £2.50 ($4.88). Wines are available by the glass, and there's a fully licensed bar. Local artists, incidentally, exhibit their work upstairs. It's open Monday to Saturday from 9:30 a.m. to 8 p.m.

Nettles, 6 St. Edward's Passage, is a tiny health-food bar, offering a wide variety of homemade soups, tossed salads, crusty whole-meal rolls, and a range of homemade pies—spinach, curry, lentil, cheese, and mushroom among them. It also makes different dishes of the day such as whole-meal spaghetti, vegetable hot pot, and curried rice and vegetables. Nettles is run by Miss Marks, who came from Cranks in London, and has brought renewed life to this popular place. The dish of the day costs £1 ($1.95); a salad is 50p (98¢); soup, 80p ($1.56); and apple pie, 50p (98¢). Hours are from 10 a.m. to 3 p.m. Monday to Saturday. The food bar is busy with undergraduates at term time.

Just off St. Benet Street in Free School Lane, a narrow passage past Friar's House Gift Shop, is the **Eros Restaurant,** 25 Petty Cury (tel. Cambridge 63420), fully licensed and offering an interesting menu. Specialties include roast duckling with stuffing and orange sauce, roast lamb peperoni with cream cheese, kebab indienne with ginger and curry, marinated lamb and rice, all served with vegetables and a salad. There are many good appetizers, and crème caramel, cheesecake, and sorbets finish off the menu. The Greek coffee is thick and sweet. A three-course Greek meal costs about £6 ($11.70), and the Cypriot, Italian, and English dinners go for about the same price. Hours are from noon to 3 p.m. and from 5:30 to 11 p.m. Monday to Friday, from noon to 11:30 p.m. on Saturday and Sunday. It's very popular with undergraduates who know they are getting good value for their money and who enjoy listening to the Greek music on weekends.

Shades Wine Bar & Restaurant, opposite King's College on Kings Parade (tel. Cambridge 354907 for the restaurant), gives you a choice of having either a full meal or bar snacks. The wine bar does pâtés, salads, quiches, and well-filled rolls (sandwiches), to be washed down with a selection of excellent wines. It's open Monday to Saturday from noon to 2:30 p.m. and from 6 to 10 p.m. It's closed on Sunday and bank holidays.

The restaurant, on the other hand, is open from 7 to 10 p.m. daily except Sunday. It's wise to reserve a table. Homemade soup is usually good, followed by prawns in a shell with garlic mayonnaise, escargots, Mediterranean chicken casserole, sukiyaki, or cold beef or smoked ham with a choice of a variety of salads. There is as well a tasty selection of desserts or fresh fruit. The menu is not only good but imaginative, and the portions are ample. A meal costs around £5 ($9.75), including wine, although the dish of the day usually goes for £2 ($3.90).

The **Anchor Pub,** Silver Street (tel. Cambridge 353554), right beside the Silver Street Bridge, has a bar and terrace right on the waterside, where you can get snacks—a ploughman's lunch, french bread and pâté, ham salad, and various cold meats in sandwiches.

Upstairs is a restaurant where you can enjoy a prawn cocktail, soups, lamb cutlets with mint sauce, peas, jacket potato, plus vanilla meringue surprise, or grilled rump steak with potatoes, followed by dessert. A beefburger is another popular item. A three-course meal will cost about £6.50 ($12.68) per person. Below the pub is the Rock Revival snackbar where you can buy the makings of a picnic lunch to be taken on a boat on the River Cam. The pub is by Scudamore's where you rent boats.

READER'S RESTAURANT SELECTION: "**La Taverna 76,** 72 Regent St. (tel. Cambridge 53942), is at the top of our list for agreeable atmosphere, prompt and friendly service, fresh, well-seasoned food, and reasonable prices. The menu offers a wide choice, but we often took the daily special for £2 ($3.90) and were never disappointed. One example: A dish listed as steak and vegetables, a wonderful Italian beef stew, lives on in memory. We especially appreciated the variety of vegetables served with entrees from day to day. Desserts are Italian and luscious, but one should not overlook the ice creams. And Taverna's coffee, with a fluff of cream and a shake of powdered chocolate, is a special way to end your meal. Closed Sunday, it is fully licensed" (L. Davidson, Charlottesville, Va.).

THE ARTS THEATRE: The outstanding attraction in Cambridge is the Arts Theatre, with its entrance on Peas Hill, squeezed among lodging houses and shops. It provides Cambridge and the surrounding area with its most important theatrical events. Almost all the leading stars of the British stage have performed here at one time or another. Call Cambridge 352000 to find out what's playing. The cheapest seats cost £3 ($5.85); the most expensive ones range from £3.50 ($6.83) to £5 ($9.75).

Nearby, on Market Passage, you'll find the principal **movie house,** the **Arts Cinema,** which usually has separate showings daily. Seats for the evening performances are "bookable" by telephoning Cambridge 352001.

2. Ely

The top attraction in the fen country, outside of Cambridge, is Ely Cathedral. The small city of Ely lies 70 miles from London, only 16 miles north of Cambridge. Ely used to be known as the Isle of Ely, until the surrounding marshes and meres were drained. The last stronghold of Saxon England, Ely was defended by Hereward the Wake, until his capitulation to the Normans in 1071.

ELY CATHEDRAL: The near-legendary founder of the cathedral was Etheldreda, the wife of a Northumbrian king, who established a monastery on the spot in 673. The present structure dates from 1083. Seen for miles around, the landmark octagonal lantern tower is the crowning glory of the cathedral. It was erected in 1322, following the collapse of the old tower, and represents a remarkable engineering achievement.

You enter the cathedral through the Galilee West Door, a good example of the Early English style of architecture. The already-mentioned lantern tower and the Octagon are the most notable features inside, but visit the Lady Chapel. Although it's lost much of its decoration over the centuries, it still is a handsome example of the Perpendicular style, having been completed in the mid-14th century.

The city, really a market town, is interesting—at least momentarily so—as it seems to be living in the past. If you choose to lodge or dine at Ely, here are my recommendations.

WHERE TO STAY AND EAT: The **Lamb Hotel** (tel. Ely 3574), right in the center of Ely, with ample car parking space available and in the shadows of Ely Cathedral, is a Grand Metropolitan hotel offering all bedrooms with private baths and showers, televisions, and tea- and coffee-making facilities. The bed-and-breakfast rate in a double or twin is £23 ($44.85), £18.40 ($35.88) in a single. Tariffs are inclusive of an English breakfast and VAT. A table d'hôte lunch costs £4.50 ($8.78); dinner, £6 ($11.70).

The **Old Fire Engine House**, St. Mary's Street (tel. Ely 2582), opposite St. Mary's Church, is one of the finer restaurants in East Anglia, worth a detour. It enjoys an interesting setting in a walled garden, in a complex of buildings with an art gallery. The restaurant was converted from a fire station. It is open for lunch from 12:30 to 2 p.m. and for dinner from 7:30 till 9 p.m. (closed Sunday). Reservations are required.

All the good English cooking is the result of the staff, a harmonious combination of unusual people who really care about food preparation. Materials are all fresh. Soups are served in huge bowls, and accompanying them is a coarse-grained crusty bread. Main dishes include duck with orange sauce, jugged hare, and steak-and-kidney pie. Main courses cost from £3.80 ($7.41) with vegetables at lunchtime, and from £4.95 ($9.65) at dinner. The soups mentioned go from 80p ($1.56), and appetizers such as pâtés begin at £1.15 ($2.24). Desserts, costing from 80p ($1.56) include fruit pie and cream, although I'd recommend the syllabub at £1.15 ($2.24). In summer, you can dine outside in the garden, even order a cream tea. The young and attractive Anne Ford owns the place, and not only does some of the cooking and serves but still has time to talk to customers.

A TOUR TO GRIME'S GRAVES: On the B1108, off the main A1065 from Swaffham to Mildenhall road east of Ely, you can visit **Grime's Graves.** This is well worth the short detour, as it is the largest group of Neolithic flintmines in the country. This is fir-wooded country with little population, and it's easy to imagine oneself transported back to ancient times.

The mines are well signposted, and you soon find yourself at a small parking lot presided over by a bearded enthusiast and his aging labrador. Because the mines have no head machinery and are spread around a common area, they are all securely enclosed. But, on your arrival, the custodian will open up one or several of the shafts, allowing you to enter ancient Britain.

Climb down the ladder of the pit and imagine what must have been going on even before the time of the Anglo-Saxons. Restoration has been carried out during the intervening years, and it is now possible to see where work took place and, if you're lucky, you may find a worked flint of your own to present to the custodian. He has a vast knowledge of the working methods and the implements used in those far-off days.

The location is close to the air force bases so well known to countless American air crews during World War II.

The place is open for most of the year from 9:30 a.m. to 4 p.m. (longer in summer), charging adults an admission of 50p (98¢); children, 25p (49¢).

AN AIRCRAFT MUSEUM: The **Imperial War Museum** (tel. Cambridge 833963), on the A505 Newmarket–Royston road, is housed appropriately at Duxford Airfield, the former Battle of Britain station. In airport hangars which date from World War I, you'll find a huge collection of historic civil and military aircraft, including the B17 Flying Fortress, the Super Sabre and Concord 01, Britain's preproduction specimen of the controversial jet. Other exhibits include midget submarines, British and German tanks, and a variety of field artillery pieces. Duxford was also a U.S. Eighth Air Force fighter station in World War II. There are now more than 70 aircraft on display, including the only B-29 Superfortress in Europe, plus a BE2c and an RE8 from World War I. Other exhibits include a giant 140-ton coastal artillery gun from Gibraltar and a special historical display on the U.S. Eighth Air Force in World War II.

The museum is open daily from March 13 to October 31 from 11 a.m. to 5:30 p.m., charging an admission of £1.20 ($2.34) for adults and 60p ($1.17) for children. Parking is free.

ESSEX

Even though it borders London, and is heavily industrialized in places, Essex still contains unspoiled rural areas and villages. Most tourists pass through it on the way to Cambridge. What they find, after leaving Greater London, is a land of rolling fields. In the east are many seaside towns and villages, as Essex opens onto the North Sea.

The major city is **Colchester**, in the east, known for its oysters and roses. Fifty miles from London, it was the first Roman city in Britain, the oldest recorded town in the kingdom. It's a rather dull-appearing city today, although parts of its Roman fortifications remain. A Norman castle has been turned into a museum, containing a fine collection of Roman Britain. Among the former residents of Colchester were King Cole, immortalized in the nursery rhyme, and Cunobelinus, the warrior king, known to Shakespearean scholars as Cymbeline.

However, Colchester is not the pathway of most visitors—so I have concentrated instead on three tiny villages in the western part of Essex: **Saffron**

Walden, Thaxted, and **Finchingfield,** all three representative of the best of the shire. You can explore all of them quite easily on your way to Cambridge or on your return trip to London. Roughly, they lie from 25 to 30 miles south of Cambridge.

A BASE OUTSIDE LONDON: Moat House, London Road, Brentwood (tel. Brentwood 225252), stands on the London side of Brentwood, about three-quarters of a mile from the center of town and only 22 miles from London's West End. A remarkably well-preserved and modernized country mansion, this early 16th-century hotel claims associations with Henry VIII and Catherine of Aragon.

It's a handsome black-and-white timbered structure with a great hall for dining and a minstrels' gallery. Nowadays modern extensions give you a wide choice of accommodations, although traditionalists will gravitate to one of the original Tudor bedrooms which have maintained their character, complete with four-poster beds. Singles with bath rent for £28 ($54.60), going up to £36 ($70.20) in a double, including VAT and service.

Bargains are the house rooms, which, true to their original Tudor character, have no baths, costing from £22.50 ($43.88) in a single, from £28.50 ($55.58) in a double. Breakfast is extra. The restoration of the public rooms has been skillful, and you're invited to enter a world of heavy old beams, oak paneling, inglenooks, and ceilings of carved plasterwork.

3. Thaxted

Some 43 miles north of London, the Saxon town of Thaxted sits on the crest of a hill. It contains the most beautiful small church in England, whose graceful spire can be seen for miles around. Its bells are heard throughout the day, ringing out special chimes to parishioners who attend their church seriously. Dating back to 1340, the church is a nearly perfect example of religious architecture.

Thaxted is well known to newspaper and magazine readers because of the late iconoclastic Conrad Noel, the Red Vicar, whose son-in-law, the Rev. Jack Putterill, carries on in the traditions of the elder.

The Rev. Putterill has brought back to the church a sense of drama, which he feels has been gradually eliminated elsewhere. The parishioners often enter the church in a processional, carrying a banner or a long branch of leaves. Gay and colorful flags hang from the heights of the church; flowers are everywhere; the rare and ancient chairs are meant to be used. There are candles in great brass stands, and incense billows up as the purple-robed vicar and his assistants proceed with the ceremony. The choir kneels and sings at the rear of the church, near the bell tower. On a banner you'll see Picasso's dove of peace.

During the summer, folk dancing is performed by the townspeople, both in and out of church. The London Philharmonic Orchestra comes down to play. The vicar has encouraged the church to use music, and you can hear both the old and the experimental. The denizens of Thaxted are divided about the activities of the church, but one thing they like: their town is alive and flourishing because of it.

Thaxted also has a number of well-preserved Elizabethan houses and a wooded-pillared Jacobean guildhall.

WHERE TO STAY AND EAT: The Swan Hotel, Watling Street (tel. Thaxted 830321), is a 14th-century coaching inn, right in the middle of everything.

From several of the bedroom windows you can see the church—even have a box seat if a processional should pass by. For many centuries, the townspeople have patronized the Swan for drinks and gossip. It is owned by Michael Ainsworth, who respects the heritage of the inn. His B&B rate is £14 ($27.30) for two persons, plus service and VAT, based on double occupancy. Singles rent for £10 ($19.50). If you're just passing through for the day, you may want to consider the three-course lunch for £6 ($11.70), plus service and VAT, consisting, say, of cream of mushroom soup, roast leg of pork with apple sauce, and a lemon mousse with cream for dessert. You can also have a three-course dinner from £7.50 ($14.63), plus service and VAT.

4. Saffron Walden

In the northern corner of Essex, a short drive from Thaxted, is the ancient market town of Walden, renamed Saffron Walden because of the fields of autumn crocus that used to grow around it. Although it lies only 44 miles from London, it still hasn't succumbed to heavy tourist traffic. Residents of Cambridge, 15 miles to the north, escape to this old borough for their weekends.

One mile west of Saffron Walden (on the B1383) is **Audley End House** (tel. Saffron Walden 23207), considered one of the finest mansions in all of East Anglia. This Jacobean estate was begun in 1603, built on the foundation of a monastery. It is open from April 1 to September 30 except Monday bank holidays and on Good Friday, from 1 to 5:30 p.m., for an admission of £1.80 ($3.51) for adults, 90p ($1.76) for children. The grounds close at 6:30 p.m. James I is reported to have said, "Audley End is too large for a king, though it might do for a lord treasurer." At the north end of the hall is a screen dating from the early 17th century and considered one of the most ornamental in England.

Many of the houses in Saffron Walden are distinctive in England, in that the 16th- and 17th-century builders faced their houses with parget—a kind of plasterwork (sometimes made with cow dung) used for ornamental facades.

WHERE TO STAY: The **Saffron Hotel**, 10 High St. (tel. Saffron Walden 23286), stands in the center of the Cromwellian market town. Dating from the 16th century, the Saffron combines modern comforts with old-world charm, as reflected by its individually designed and decorated rooms. The hotel was completely refurbished in 1981 by its new owners. All rooms have color TV, telephone, central heating, and most have private baths. Most units overlook the High Street or the inner courtyard with its patio garden and small carp pool. Stories abound locally about the Saffron Hotel ghost which several of the staff claim to have seen in recent years. B&B rates are £12.50 ($24.38) in a bathless single, £18.50 ($36.08) with shower. For a bathless double the rent is £21 ($40.95), £30 ($58.50) with a private bath. Children are welcomed at reduced prices. The hotel's restaurant is renowned locally and is in a Regency style. Dining is by candlelight overlooking the flood-lit patio garden. A three-course menu with several choices on each course ranges from £4.95 ($9.65) to £6.25 ($12.19). The cuisine at the Saffron is among the best in the area, combining traditional dishes with more ambitious specialties.

5. Finchingfield

This little village, only a short drive east of Thaxted, puts in a serious claim for being the model village of England. Even though you may have another personal favorite, you still must admit it's a dream village, surrounded by the quiet life of the countryside. If you're staying in either Saffron Walden or Thaxted, you might want to motor over here. It makes for an interesting jaunt.

WHERE TO STAY: The **Fox Inn** (tel. Great Dunmow 810151), two hours from London airport, stands near the edge of the pond on the village green. It's an attractive old pub, run more or less as an inn by John and Joan Plester. Note the authentic pargeting (raised plaster) design on the facade. They are enthusiastic about their food, especially the steak-and-kidney pie and other English dishes. Lunches are served every day from noon to 2 p.m., providing a real fill-up for £5 ($9.75), including coffee. A Sunday roast dinner is served with all the trimmings for about £4 ($7.80).

Near to the Fox, Joe King runs the little eight-room **Old Manse** (tel. Great Dunmow 810306), all accommodations with central heating, wall-to-wall carpeting, hot and cold running water, and shaving points. Two rooms have private baths, and most of them overlook the village pond. There is a lounge with color TV, plus a large garden as well. Terms, including a full English breakfast consisting of farm produce, are £11 ($21.45) in a single, £20 ($39) in a double, including VAT and service.

6. Dedham

Remember Constable's *Vale of Dedham*? In this little Essex village on the Stour River, you're in the heart of Constable country. Flatford Mill is only a mile farther down the river. The village, with its Tudor, Georgian, and Regency house, is set in the midst of the water meadows of the Stour. Constable immortalized its church and tower. Dedham is right on the Essex-Suffolk border, and makes a good center for exploring both North Essex and the Suffolk border country.

In the village is **Castle House** (tel. Colchester 322127), home of Sir Alfred Munnings, the president of the Royal Academy (1944–1949) and painter extraordinaire of racehorses and animals. The house and studio contain sketches and other works, and are open from May 9 to October 10, Wednesday and Sunday from 2 to 5 p.m., charging adults an admission of 50p (98¢); children, 15p (29¢).

WHERE TO STAY: **Maison Talbooth** (tel. Colchester 322367), is small and exclusive, each of its ten bedrooms really a spacious suite. This Victorian country house has been given a facelift, and each accommodation has been distinctively furnished by one of England's best known decorators. High-fashion colors abound; antiques are mixed discreetly with reproductions—and the original architectural beauty has been preserved. The super-luxury suite, with a sunken bath, goes for £60 ($117) nightly for two persons, and has a draped bed. Other suites, each with its own theme, start as low as £40 ($78) for two. One person pays from £32 ($62.40) to £45 ($87.75). When you arrive, you're greeted with a bowl of fresh fruit and an array of soft and hard drinks on the mantelpiece, even a bowl of ice cubes. A continental or cooked breakfast is brought in the morning. In an informal, yet stylish, drawing room, guests mingle with the hostess making you feel as if you're a guest in her country home. Although the Maison Talbooth doesn't have a restaurant on its premises, it does own one nearby. **Le Talbooth** (tel. Colchester 323150 for reservations), a 16th-century timbered weaver's house set in beautiful gardens on the banks of the River Stour in Constable country. The owner, Gerald Milsom, has brought a high standard of international cooking, backed by good wines. Dinner is served from 7:30 to 9 p.m. You can dine here for about £15 ($29.25) per person.

Dedham Vale, Gun Hill (tel. Colchester 322273), is a handsome, Virginia-creeper-covered 19th-century residence, with tall windows overlooking spacious lawns, flowerbeds, and trees, plus a view of the Stour River. Mr. and Mrs. Milsom run it graciously and well. Even though the house isn't furnished with fabulous antiques, it is pleasant and comfortable, each bedroom different in character. Singles rent for £30 ($58.50), doubles for £45 ($87.75), and a family room for £50 ($98), tariffs including **VAT** and a continental breakfast, plus 10% for service. Dinner will be a rotisserie and priced at less than the Talbooth. Some of the specialties are cooked at your table. The hotel is within easy reach of Felixstowe and Harwich for journeys to the continent.

SUFFOLK

The easternmost county of England—a link in the four-county chain of East Anglia—Suffolk is a refuge for artists, just as it was in the day of its famous native sons, Constable and Gainsborough. Through them many of the Suffolk landscapes have ended up in museums on canvas.

A fast train can make it from London to East Suffolk in approximately an hour and a half. Still, its fishing villages, dozens of flint churches, historic homes, and national monuments remain relatively unvisited by overseas visitors.

The major towns of Suffolk are **Bury St. Edmunds,** the capital of West Suffolk, and **Ipswich** in the east, a port city on the Orwell River. But to capture the true charm of Suffolk, you must explore its little market towns and villages. Beginning at the Essex border, we'll strike out toward the North Sea, highlighting the most scenic villages as we move easterly across the shire.

7. Clare

Lying 58 miles from London, but only 26 east from Cambridge, the small town of Clare holds to the old ways of East Anglia. Many of its houses are bathed in Suffolk pink, the facades of a few demonstrating the 16th- and 17th-century plasterwork technique of pargeting, discussed previously. The Stour River, which has its source a few miles away, flows by, marking the boundary of Suffolk and Essex. The little rail station has fallen to the economy axe. The nearest station is now at Sudbury, where Gainsborough was born. The journey by road from London takes about two hours, unless you succumb to the scenery and the countryside along the way. For accommodations in Clare, I have the following recommendations in the budget range.

FOOD AND LODGING: The **Bell Hotel** (tel. Clare 277741) is considered one of the oldest inns in England. Once known as the Green Dragon, it served the soldiers of Richard de Clare, one of William the Conqueror's barons. Later it became a posting house, but in time the old stable gave way to a car park. Its owners, Hugh and Daphne Jones, are responsible for its recent facelift. Both of them maintain a friendly give-and-take with their guests. B&B rates range from £28 ($54.60) for a single, £36 ($70.20) for a double, plus service and tax. The rooms have a fresh, pleasant style to them, and the beds are soft. The beamed dining room, with its high-back chairs and large brick fireplace, is ideal for winter dining. Lunch costs £6 ($11.70); dinner, around £8.50 ($16.58).

"You might mention the **Ancient House Museum,** directly across from the churchyard. The house is a splendid example of pargeting and has many notable architectural features and numerous fascinating exhibits. One comes away from the Ancient House with a deeper understanding and appreciation of the rural life of Suffolk. Rates are 20p (39¢) for adults, 10p (20¢) for children. The museum is open from 2:30 p.m. to 4:30 p.m. on Monday, Tuesday, Friday, Saturday, and Sunday, as well as from 11 a.m. to 12:30 p.m. from Easter Saturday until the end of October" (David and Jackie Allswang, Oakland, Calif.).

8. Long Melford

Long Melford has been famous since the days of the early clothmakers. Like its sister, Lavenham (coming up), it grew in prestige and importance in the Middle Ages. Of the old buildings remaining, the village church is often called "one of the glories of the shire." Along its High Street are many private homes erected by wealthy wool merchants of yore. While London seems far removed here, it is only 61 miles to the south.

WHERE TO STAY: Bull Hotel (tel. Sudbury 78794) provides another fortunate opportunity to experience life in one of the great old inns of East Anglia. Built by a wool merchant, it probably is Long Melford's finest and best preserved building, dating back to 1450. The improvements and interior modernization have been undertaken by Trusthouses Forte Ltd., who have shown a tasteful respect for the beauty of the old beams. Incorporated into the general hotel is a medieval weavers' gallery and the open hearth with its Elizabethan brickwork. The bedrooms are a goodly mixture of the old and new—each centrally heated, with telephones and radios—a nice ambience. A single room with bath rents for £28 ($54.60), a double with bath for £38 ($74.10). The dining room is the outstanding part of the Bull, with its high beamed ceilings, trestle tables, settles, and handmade chairs, as well as a ten-foot fireplace. You can order a set three-course lunch for £7 ($13.65), a table d'hôte dinner for £9 ($17.55).

WHERE TO EAT: Jason's Carving Room, Hall Street (tel. Long Melford 226), is housed in a converted 15th-century building, warmed with oak beams, natural wood tables, flowers, and copper pots. At a set price, you dine bountifully: all the roast beef, lamb, or pork you want, and as many vegetables and salads as you wish. The carving room is run by Maurice Signorini. Lunch weekdays costs £3.50 ($6.83), going up to £3.80 ($7.41) on Sunday. The weekday dinner tab is £4 ($7.80). It's closed on Sunday evening and Monday.

9. Lavenham

Once a great wool center, Lavenham is considered a model village of East Anglia. It is filled with a number of half-timbered Tudor houses, washed in the characteristic Suffolk pink. Be sure to visit its church, with its landmark tower, built in the Perpendicular style. Lavenham lies only seven miles from Sudbury, 11 from Bury St. Edmunds. For accommodations or meals, there is the following medium-priced recommendation.

WHERE TO STAY AND EAT: Swan Hotel, High Street (tel. Lavenham 247477), is linked to the Middle Ages—a lavishly timbered inn, probably one of the oldest and best preserved buildings in this relatively unmarred village. Its success has necessitated incorporating an adjoining ancient Wool Hall, which provides a high-ceilinged and timbered guest house and additional raftered, second-story bedrooms, opening onto a tiny cloistered garden. The Garden Bar opens onto yet another garden, with old stone walls and flowerbeds. Londoners often visit on September-to-March weekends for dinner and chamber music concerts. All the accommodations contain private baths. A single rents for £26 ($50.70), doubles from £38 ($74.10). The bedrooms vary greatly in size, according to the eccentricities of the architecture. Most have beamed ceilings and a mixture of traditional pieces which blend well with the old. There are nearly enough lounges for guests to try a different one every night of the week.

Meals in the raftered, two-story-high dining room have their own drama, as you sit on leather and oak chairs with brass studding. Even if you're not spending the night, you can sample the three-course luncheon priced at £6 ($11.70). Evening table d'hôte dinners go for £8 ($15.60). From the à la carte menu, you can order such specialties as Norfolk duckling in a sauce with almonds and raisins or boned English saddle of lamb with artichokes. Expect to spend from £9 ($17.55). In World War II, Allied pilots (who made the Swan their second home) carved their signatures in the bar, a longish room with a timbered ceiling and a fine weapon collection—with placards advertising everything from the Huntingdon Steeplechase to a wine and cheese party for the Young Conservatives.

A Dining Event in Hintlesham

Hintlesham Hall (tel. Hintlesham 268) is the personal statement of Robert Carrier, of cookbook fame. After a smash success with his London restaurant (Carrier's), he decided to tackle the country, and selected one of England's fine old estates in East Anglia. The hall was begun in the reign of Henry VIII and completed during that of Elizabeth I. There are two ghosts—a Lady in Gray and a crying baby. Two moats are all that remain of the original medieval structure, dating from the 13th century, and laurel hedges lead to a Queen Anne orangery.

Mr. Carrier has not only found a stylish background for his creative cookery, but he's tied it in with a music and art festival. On any night of the week, dining is a dramatic event. You're ushered into the Red Room or the Blue Room, where you can order an apéritif and make your selections from the menu. Meals are served in either the China Room, the Justice Room, or the Great Saloon with its trompe-l'oeil decorations. A set lunch costs £10 ($19.50), a set dinner from £12 ($23.40), certainly one of the finest values in East Anglia, considering the quality of the cuisine. Specialties of the house, carrying supplements, include Mr. Carrier's super sirloin, with a béarnaise sauce; charcoal-grilled guinea fowl with juniper berries; a paupiette of sole with champagne sauce. A not-so-simple starter is a brandade of smoked mackerel, and "your just desserts" include Elizabeth Moxon's lemon posset.

The hall also sponsors a seminar of cooking, where you learn to cook as you eat and drink. Each course starts off with a kitchen buffet party on Sunday evening, and there is a five-course gala gourmet banquet every Thursday.

Hintlesham Hall stands in 18 acres of parkland just off the A12, 5 miles from Ipswich, 15 miles from Colchester, and 50 miles from Cambridge.

Truly, this is one of Britain's exciting restaurants.

10. Woodbridge

A yachting center, 12 miles from the North Sea, Woodbridge is a market town on a branch of the Deben River. Its best known resident was Edward FitzGerald, the Victorian poet and translator of the *Rubáiyát* of Omar Khayyám (some critics consider the Englishman's version better than the original). The poet died in 1883 and was buried four miles away at Boulge.

Woodbridge is a good base for exploring the East Suffolk coastline and excursions to Constable's Flatford Mill, coming up. But first, a look at my medium-priced accommodations and dining recommendation, which is some 1½ miles from the Woodbridge rail station.

WHERE TO STAY: Seckford Hall, A12 Road near Woodbridge (tel. Woodbridge 5678), captures the spirit of the days of Henry VIII and his strong-willed daughter Elizabeth (the latter may have held court here). The estate is built of brick, now ivy covered, and adorned with crow stepped gables, mullioned windows, and ornate chimneys—pure Tudor. The hall was built in 1530 by Sir Thomas Seckford, a member of one of Suffolk's first families. You enter through a heavy studded Tudor door into a flagstone hallway with antiques. The butler will show you to your bedroom. Owners Mr. and Mrs. M. S. Bunn have seen to it that your stay is like a house party. A single room rents for £20 ($39) nightly, increasing to £26.50 ($51.68) with bath. A double or twin without bath costs £31 ($60.45) per night, increasing to £37.50 ($73.13) with bath. At least one room is high-ceilinged with a monumental four-poster, costing from £38 ($74.10). In summer, reservations are helpful for those desiring bed, breakfast, and evening dinner. (Nonguests can stop by for dinner, which is à la carte. Best to phone first.)

If you arrive before sundown, you may want to stroll through a portion of the 34-acre gardens. As you proceed to the side and rear, you'll come upon a rose garden, herbaceous borders, and greenhouses. At the bottom of the garden is an ornamental lake, complete with weeping willows and paddling ducks. At four o'clock, you can have a complete tea in the Great Hall. Sip your brew slowly, savoring the atmosphere of heavy beams and a simple stone fireplace. Your chair may be Queen Anne, your table Elizabethan. Dinner will be announced by the butler. Good English meals are served in a setting of linenfold paneling and Chippendale and Hepplewhite chairs. After-dinner coffee and brandy are featured in the Tudor Bar.

FOOD AND DRINK: Sherlock's Wine Bar, 17 The Thoroughfare (tel. Woodbridge 2557). The owner, Douglas Wilmer, who portrayed Holmes in a B.B.C. TV series, littered his upstairs wine bar with memorabilia of the famous detective. The food has a homemade taste, and the menu is changed daily. However, you are likely to be offered a cognac pâté a very spicy sausage meat quiche, and, in summer, a spinach-and-crab quiche. There's also a good wine choice, and you might prefer a glass from France, Germany, Italy, or Spain. For a meal, expect to spend from £3 ($5.85). Food is served from noon to 2:30 p.m. and 7:30 to 11 p.m. daily, except Sunday and Monday.

11. Aldeburgh

Pressed against the North Sea, Aldeburgh is a favorite retreat of the in-the-know traveler, even attracting some Dutch tourists who make the sea crossing via Harwich, the British entry port for those coming from the Hook of Holland. The late composer Benjamin Britten (*Peter Grimes, The Rape of*

Lucretia), used to live in the area. But the festival he started at Aldeburgh in 1948 is held at Snape in June, a short drive to the north.

Less than 100 miles from London, the resort was founded in Roman times, but legionnaires have been replaced by fishermen, boatmen, and fanciers of wildfowl. A bird sanctuary, Havergate Island, lies about ten miles offshore. Some take time out from their sporting activities (a golf course stretches 3½ miles) to visit the 16th-century **Moot Hall.**

WHERE TO STAY AND EAT: In August, the time of the regatta, accommodations tend to be fully booked. I'll survey the pick of the lot:

Brudenell Hotel, The Parade (tel. Aldeburgh 2071), is Aldeburgh's prestige hotel, right on the waterfront. Built at the beginning of the 20th century, it was remodeled and decorated by its owner, Trusthouses Forte Ltd. An attractive and comfortable accommodation awaits the visitor exploring the East Anglian seacoast. The interior is most successful and pleasant, and from many of the bedrooms there's a view of the churning sea. All of the rooms contain private baths. A single begins at £22 ($42.90), a double at £34 ($66.30) to £38 ($74.10). During the months of October to May, many bargain-break offers are available, with golfing breaks and jazz weekends as specialties. Every room has TV, telephone, radio, tea and coffee makers, and central heating, as well as good, soft beds. The dining room with an all-glass wall overlooking the coast is an ideal spot for a three-course luncheon costing £5.50 ($10.73). A set dinner costs £7.50 ($14.63). There are à la carte selections also, a dinner averaging around £9 ($17.55). Excellent bar snacks featuring local fish are available, at a price range starting at £1.25 ($2.44).

Uplands Hotel, Victorian Road (tel. Aldeburgh 2420), is as untouristy a retreat as you're apt to find. It's more like a private home run by good friends (Mr. and Mrs. Barrett) who take in paying guests. The inn dates from the 18th century; at one time it was the childhood home of Elizabeth Garrett Anderson, the first woman doctor in England. Uplands provides personally decorated bedrooms and excellently planned and well-served meals. Once inside the living room, you sense the informality and charm. They have furnished it with some good antiques, a few comfortable upholstered chairs, paintings, and books. The prices range from £12 ($23.40) to £16 ($31.20) per person for an overnight stopover. There are seven twin-bedded chalets in the garden, with TV and private bathrooms. The chef, with a stack of cooking awards, offers an à la carte dinner for approximately £7 ($13.65). A typical offering might include escalope de veau Uplands and roast Aylesbury duck. You can have coffee in front of the fireplace or, in fair weather, in the garden.

The Local Pub

Ye Olde Crosse Keys, Crabbe Street, is a genuine 15th-century pub, with the real atmosphere of a Suffolk seaside local. In the summertime, everyone takes his or her real English ale or lager out and sits on the seawall, sipping, talking, and thinking. The pub is rustic—favored by local artists, who in the cooler months sit beside an old brick fireplace and eat plates of oysters or smoked salmon. Sandwiches, and very good ones, are available at from 75p ($1.46). Ye Olde Crosse Keys is easy to spot, a short walk from Ye Olde Curiosity Shoppe.

12. East Bergholt

The English landscape painter, John Constable (1776–1837), was born at East Bergholt. Near the village is **Flatford Mill** (tel. Colchester 298283), subject of one of his most renowned canvases. The mill, in a scenic setting, was given to the National Trust in 1943, and since has been leased to the Fields Studies Council for use as a residential college. Weekly courses are arranged on all aspects of the countryside and the environment. None of the buildings contains relics of Constable, nor are they open to the general public, but students of all ages and capabilities are welcome to courses. The fee for one week is around £95 ($185.25), inclusive of accommodation, meals, and tuition. Details may be obtained from the warden, Flatford Mill Field Centre, East Bergholt, Colchester CO7 60L.

THE LOCAL PUB: **Red Lion Inn,** Gaston Street (tel. Colchester 298332), traces its ancestry back to around 1500. Numerous authors have written of the Red Lion, citing it as one of the unmarred inns of East Anglia.

The hosts keep an immaculate, friendly place. Bowls of soup are available in the bar, along with a ploughman's lunch. Also offered are scampi, sausages with fried potatoes, and fruit pie. Snacks are in the £1 ($1.95) to £3 ($4.85) range. A short stroll from Flatford Mill, the inn is reached by turning off the A12, the Colchester–Ipswich road. An Eastern National Coach, no. 87 or 87A, comes here from Colchester.

NORFOLK

Bounded by the North Sea, Norfolk is the biggest of the East Anglian counties. It's a low-lying area, with fens, heaths, and salt marshes. An occasional dike or windmill makes you think you've been delivered to the Netherlands. One of the features of Norfolk is its network of Broads, miles and miles of lagoons—shallow in parts—connected by streams.

Summer sports people flock to Norfolk to hire boats for sailing or fishing. From Norwich itself, **Wroxham**, the so-called capital of the Broads, is easily reached, only eight miles to the northeast. Motorboats regularly leave from this resort, taking parties on short trips. Some of the best scenery of the Broads is to be found on the periphery of Wroxham.

EN ROUTE TO NORWICH: If you're searching for a place to dine near the Suffolk/Norfolk border, before driving on to Norwich, you'll find none better than the recommendation below.

The Fox and Goose, Fressingfield, near Diss, Norfolk (tel. Fressingfield 247), is a charming old building with a wide gravel courtyard and a pond with ducks. It was the old guildhall, and is the only remaining inn I could find in England still owned by the church and originally provided by the church for the refreshment of parishioners instead of their eating in the nave after services. The place is a delight. It's open daily from noon to 1:30 p.m. and from 7 to 9 p.m., except Tuesday and from December 21 to December 28.

The Clarke family runs it, and its members have been here for longer than a decade, serving lunches and dinners to locals (London is only 80 miles of fast road away so some come from there) and passersby.

If you can plan ahead, telephone and reserve a table. The Clarkes will send you the menu and you can select your meal in advance. The kitchen staff prefers one party to order the same entree if possible, as this place is very much a family concern. The selection is made from a wide variety of fresh fish and local meat dishes. Featured are smoked eel, mackerel, salmon and trout, sole normande, coquille St. Jacques, king prawns, lobster, and crab, followed by beef or pork en croûte, five sorts of steak, tournedos provençale, three duck dishes, venison in season or game, all served with a variety of vegetables. Desserts include fresh fruit dishes and sorbets and ices laced with liqueurs.

Mr. Clarke used to be a wholesale butcher, and the quality of the meat reflects his interest. Adrian, his young son, hated school but had a knack for cooking. He presides in the kitchen. The kitchen staff bakes its own whole-meal crusty bread to serve with masses of yellow butter.

The dining room seats only 26 "at a pinch," and punctuality is essential. But once you're there, the table is yours to enjoy your meal in comfort. Start in the bar with an apéritif. The wine list is long and excellent, although you can order a bottle of the house wine for £4.50 ($8.78). Service is unobtrusive in the simple dining room, with its low ceiling and wooden tables and chairs. A meal, not including wine, will cost from £11 ($21.45) to £16 ($31.20).

13. Norwich

Some 20 miles from the North Sea, Norwich still holds to its claim as the capital city of East Anglia. The county town of Norfolk, Norwich is a charming and historic city, despite encroachments by industry and its position as a market town for the shire. Besides its cathedral, the city has more than 30 parish churches, some of which were built in the 15th century of flint.

Norwich is a city of narrow and cobbled streets, with endless baffling one-ways. The big open-air market place, with stalls with canvas roofs, comes alive with fruit, vegetable, and trinket peddlers on Wednesday and Saturday. The city also boasts a thriving art colony: the Norwich Players long ago revived the 18th-century Maddermarket Theatre (built in the style of an Elizabethan playhouse), whose predecessor had been ordered shut down by Cromwell. In addition the Norwich School of Painting is a good rallying center for East Anglian artists.

THE CASTLE: In the center of Norwich, on an artificial mound, sits the castle, formerly the county gaol (jail). Its huge 12th-century Norman keep and the later prison buildings are used as a civic museum and headquarters of the county-wide Norfolk Museums Service (tel. Norwich 611277). The museum houses an impressive collection of pictures by artists of the Norwich School, of whom the most distinguished were John Crome, born 1768, and John Sell Cotman, born 1782. The Castle Museum also contains a fine collection of Lowestoft porcelain and Norwich silver. These are shown in the rotunda. There are two sets of dioramas, one showing Norfolk wildlife in its natural setting, the other illustrating scenes of Norfolk life from the Old Stone Age to the early days of Norwich Castle. You can also visit a geology gallery and a permanent exhibition in the keep, "Norfolk in Europe."

The Castle Museum is open weekdays from 10 a.m. to 5 p.m. (on Sunday from 2 to 5 p.m.). Charges from the spring bank holiday until September are 50p (98¢) for adults, 10p (20¢) for children, and 25p (49¢) for students. The rest of the year, adults pay 25p (49¢); children, 10p (20¢); and students, 15p (29¢). There's a coffee bar, plus the licensed Buttery which is open from 10:30 a.m. to 2:30 p.m.

THE CATHEDRAL: Principally of Norman design, the cathedral dates back to 1096. It is noted primarily for its long nave, with its lofty columns. Its spire, built in the late Perpendicular style, rises 315 feet, and shares distinction with the keep of the castle as the significant landmarks on the Norwich skyline. On the vaulted ceiling are more than 300 bosses (knoblike ornamental projections) depicting biblical scenes. The impressive choir stalls with the handsome misereres date from the 15th century. Edith Cavell—"Patriotism is not enough"— the English nurse executed by the Germans in World War I, was buried on the cathedral's Life's Green. The quadrangular Cloisters go back to the 13th century, and are among the most spacious in England.

The cathedral Visitors' Centre includes a refreshment area and an exhibition and film room with tape/slide shows about the cathedral. Admission is free.

A short walk from the cathedral will take you to **Tombland,** one of the most interesting old squares in Norwich.

SAINSBURY CENTRE FOR VISUAL ARTS: In 1973 Sir Robert and Lady Sainsbury gave their private art collection to the University of East Anglia, and their son David gave an endowment to provide a building to house the collection. The center, designed by Foster Associates, was opened in 1978, and since then the building has won many national and international awards. A feature of the structure is its flexibility, allowing solid and glass areas to be interchanged, and the superb quality of light which allows optimum viewing of works of art. The Sainsbury Collection is one of the foremost in the country, including modern, ancient, classical, and ethnographic art. Other displays at the center include the Anderson collection of art nouveau and the university aggregation of 20th-century nonfigurative art. There is also a regular program of special exhibitions.

The center (tel. Norwich 56161) is open from noon to 5 p.m. from Tuesday to Sunday. Admission to the permanent collections is 50p (98¢) for adults, 25p (49¢) for students.

The restaurant offers a self-service buffet from 10:30 a.m. to 2:30 p.m. Monday to Friday. Meal service is available from 12:30 to 2 p.m., also Monday to Friday. In the coffee bar, snacks are served from 2:30 to 4:30 p.m. from Tuesday to Friday and from noon to 4:30 p.m. on Saturday and Sunday.

WHERE TO STAY: The **Post House,** Ipswich Road (tel. Norwich 56431), is built in the motel style, two miles from the center of the city on the A140 Ipswich road and one mile from the A11 London road. Free parking space is provided for 200 cars. Run as a Trusthouses Forte hotel, it charges £27 ($52.65) in a single, £34 ($66.30) in a double, VAT and service charge included. Each of the 120 bedrooms has a private bath, telephone, TV, radio, central heating, tea- and coffee-making equipment, and a small refrigerated bar. The rooms have combined sitting areas, with sofas and armchairs. The coffeeshop, which stays open till 10:30 p.m., reflects Norfolk's ties with agriculture (sturdy farming tools decorating the walls); the main restaurant specializes in traditional English fare, such as game in season, smoked fish, and potted meats. The modern Punch Bar is decorated with early *Punch* cartoons and drawings.

The **Maid's Head Hotel,** Tombland (tel. Norwich 28821), claims to be the oldest continuously operated inn in England, circa 1272. Opposite the cathedral, in the most interesting district of Norwich, it has a dual personality architecturally: one portion an Elizabethan black-and-white timbered inn with four gables, the other a modernized Georgian section with a prim white entry and small-paned windows. The interior—83 bedrooms with private baths—is joined by a glassed-in courtyard, with many flowering and hanging plants and vines.

The resident general manager, Derek B. Cooke, charges £27 ($52.65) in a single, £32 ($62.40) in a double, including service. The bedrooms vary according to their location—some are contemporary, some traditional, others in between. The lucky ones get the Queen Elizabeth I bedroom, where the Tudor monarch allegedly slept. It is furnished with an ornate carved four-poster. Meals, basically English with continental influences, are served in the formal paneled dining room, where you can have a set lunch for £6.50 ($12.68), dinner for £8 ($15.60)

Santa Lucia Hotel, 38–40 Yarmouth Rd. (tel. Norwich 33207), is one of the best for value of the hotels outside Norwich, only 1½ miles from the center. The combined hotel and guest house offers not only inexpensive rooms, but an attractive setting and a friendly atmosphere.

You pay £7.50 ($14.63) nightly for B&B. The food is quite good, too, costing £4 ($7.80) for a dinner. Each of the rooms has running water and a radio. There are sun terraces for relaxing, modern bathrooms, and plenty of parking space. Three buses pass by the door heading for the center of the city.

WHERE TO EAT: The **Assembly House,** Theatre Street (tel. Norwich 26402), is a good example of Georgian architecture. You enter the building through a large front courtyard, which leads to the central hall, with its columns, fine paneling, and crystal chandelier. The restaurant is administered by H. J. Sexton Norwich Arts Trust.

On your left is a high-ceilinged room, with paneling, fine paintings, and a long buffet table—ready for self-service. After making your selection, take your plate to any one of the many tables. Often you'll share—perhaps with an artist, or else a woman who owns an estate in the country. You'll find an unusually varied selection of hors d'oeuvres. A big bowl of homemade soup is nutritious. Hot entrees are homemade, too, prepared with fresh ingredients. The prices, like the food, are simple. For example, a home-cured ham and salad meal goes for £1.75 ($3.41), an omelet for £1.20 ($2.34). The restaurant is open from 10 a.m. to 2 p.m. and from 3 to 8 p.m.

After dining, you may want to stroll through the rest of the building. Art exhibits are usually held regularly in the Ivory and Hobart Rooms, open from 10 a.m. to 5:30 p.m. Concerts are sponsored in the Music Room, with its chandeliers and sconces. There's even a small movie house.

The **Britons Arms Coffee House,** 9 Elm Hill (tel. Norwich 23367), overlooks the most beautiful cobbled street in Norwich, in the heart of the old city. Over the years, it's had several names, and traces its history back to the days of Edward III. Now it's one of the least expensive eating places in Norwich—certainly the most intimate and informal. The coffeehouse has several rooms, including a back one with an inglenook. You'll find old beamed ceilings, Tudor benches, and pink-washed walls.

It's open every day except Sunday, Thursday afternoons, and evenings, serving mostly lunches and coffee. Lunch begins at 12:15 p.m. (the staff is strict about that), ending at 2:30 p.m. Generally, you can have tea from 3:30 until 5 p.m.

The procedure here is to go to the little counter, where you purchase your lunch and bring it to the table of your choice. Everything I've tried was tasty, and the items are homemade. In summertime the food is cold; in winter, hot. You'll find an assortment of soups, quiches, flans, fruit pies, and cheeses, a meal costing around £3 ($5.85). It's a good place to stop after your inspection of the cathedral, only a block away.

14. Tottenhill

This village can be a center for exploring some stately homes and gardens, the seaside resorts and fens and broads of East Anglia. Within a day's drive are the historic old port of King's Lynn, the country home of Queen Elizabeth (Sandringham), the lavender fields of Heacham, the tulip fields of Spalding, as well as the large man-made forest at Thetford and the neolithic flint mines at Grime's Graves. The following private hotel is recommended as a stopover.

Oakwood House, on Route A10 near Tottenhill, just four miles south of King's Lynn (tel. King's Lynn 810256), is a country house of Tudor origin with all the amenities of a modern hotel. The house was enlarged some 200 years ago and refaced with a typical Georgian exterior. Within a short drive of the Norfolk coast, Oakwood House offers visitors a peaceful alternative to the bustling seaside resorts and market towns.

Nestled in its own two acres of gardens, the hotel has guest rooms with color TV, tea- and coffee-making facilities, hot and cold running water, individually controlled heating, and pleasant views over the Norfolk countryside and the gardens. Some rooms are equipped with private showers en suite. The comfortably furnished guest lounge contains a color TV, and the spacious dining room adjoins the well-stocked period bar.

The menu is carefully chosen to make the best use of local and home-grown produce whenever possible, and all cooking is under the personal supervision of Marjorie Rhodes, who, with her husband Geoff, sees that the needs of their guests are attended to. Rates per person for B&B begin at £11 ($21.45). The four-course dinner will cost you an additional £6 ($11.70). VAT is included in the price, and no service charge is made. Ample parking facilities are maintained within the grounds.

15. North Norfolk

This part is already well known by members of the American Eighth Air Force, for many Liberators and Flying Fortresses took off and landed from this corner of the country. Their captains and crews sampled most of the local hostelries at one time or another. Now it is just feathered birds that fly overhead, and the countryside is quiet and peaceful.

THE SIGHTS: This area is of considerable scenic interest, having some very good value in its offering of accommodations and food. Norfolk especially provides an alternative to the vastly overcrowded West Country in summer, and it's extremely convenient for a weekend out of London, as it lies only a three-hour drive away.

Sandringham

Some 110 miles northeast of London, Sandringham has been the country home of four generations of British monarchs, ever since the Prince of Wales (later King Edward VII) purchased it in 1861. The son of Queen Victoria, along with his Danish wife, Princess Alexandra, rebuilt the house, standing on 7000 acres of grounds, and in time, it became a fashionable rendezvous of British society.

The red brick Victorian Tudor mansion consists of more than 200 rooms, and in recent times some of these rooms have been opened to the public, including two drawing rooms and a dining room. Sandringham joins Windsor Castle and the Palace of Holyroodhouse in Edinburgh as the only British royal residences which can be examined by the public. Guests can also visit a lofty saloon with a minstrels' gallery.

A group of former coach houses has been converted into a museum of big-game trophies, plus a collection of cars, including the first vehicle purchased by a royal, a 1900 Daimler Tonneau that belonged to Edward VII. The house and grounds are open Tuesday to Thursday from Easter to May 1. After that, they are open Sunday through Thursday until about the end of September, except for a period in late July and early August when members of the royal family are likely to be in residence.

The grounds and the house are open from April until the end of September Monday through Thursday from 10:30 a.m. to 4:45 p.m. (on Sunday from 11:30 a.m. to 4:45 p.m.). The house is closed July 19 to August 8, and the grounds are closed from July 23 to August 4. Admission is £1.10 ($2.15) for adults, with a reduction for children. If you want to be admitted only to the gardens, the charge is 80p ($1.56) for adults, less for children. The 70-acre gardens, incidentally, are richly planted with azaleas, rhododendrons, hydrangeas, and camellias.

Sandringham lies 50 miles from Cambridge and 10 miles from King's Lynn. There is bus service between King's Lynn and Sandringham.

Blickling Hall

A long drive, bordered by massive yew hedges towering above and framing your first view of this lovely old house, leads you to Blickling Hall, near Aylsham (tel. Aylsham 733471). A great Jacobean house built in the early 17th century, it is, perhaps, one of the finest examples of such architecture in the country. The Long Gallery has an elaborate 17th-century ceiling, and the Peter the Great Room, decorated later, has a fine tapestry on the wall. The house is set in ornamental parkland with a formal garden and an orangery. Meals and snacks are available. It is open from April 1 until the end of October, except Monday and Friday, from 2 to 6 p.m. The house is also open from 11 a.m. to 1 p.m. daily, except Monday and Friday, from June to September. Admission is £1.40 ($2.73) for adults, 70p ($1.37) for children.

Norfolk Lavender Ltd.

At Caley Mill at Heacham (tel. Heacham 70384), you can see how lavender is grown, the flowers harvested, and the essence distilled before appearing prettily packaged as perfume, aftershave, potpourri, and old-fashioned lavender bags to slip between your hankies. The mills are open from 10 a.m. to 6 p.m. May to September, from 9 a.m. to dusk in winter. Admission is 30p (59¢) for adults, 15p (29¢) for children. The Miller's Cottage Tearoom serves cream teas with homemade cakes, scones, and buns, as well as light lunches. The best time to see the lavender in bloom is mid-July to early August. You will be able to discuss the merits of the various varieties and their suitability for your own particular garden.

Alby Crafts Ltd.

This brainchild of Valerie Alston, on Cromer Road, Erpingham (tel. Hanworth 761590), is open from Easter to Christmas, daily, except Monday, from 10 a.m. to 5 p.m. The craft center is housed in an old Norfolk stone farmhouse and its outbuildings. Mrs. Alston scours the country to find genuine articles of country craft, including leatherwork, woodcarving, and ceramics. A rocking chair model, perfect in every detail, yet only four inches high, costs £18 ($35.10). A woodcarving of a Bedfordshire farmer and his pig goes for £58 ($113.10). Bronze and wrought-iron work can be made to order, a piece costing from £3 ($5.85) to £500 ($975). There are sometimes demonstrations and specialist exhibitions, and several of the workshops are made available to local craftspeople. The delight of this place is that the articles come from all over the country and are entirely genuine craftware. Homemade dishes and cakes are served throughout the day in the tearoom.

Sutton Windmill

At Sutton (1½ miles south east of Stalham off the A149) is the tallest mill in the country. But its main claim to fame, in a county where many windmills still work, is the exceptional quality and interest of the working machinery. Chris Nunn, the young man who owns the mill, decided it was time he put something back into the country instead of taking it out. So he left the construction business and now devotes his days to restoring the mill. When money runs short, he works on the North Sea oil rigs for a time. He hopes shortly to be grinding corn again, but the lower floors—there are nine in all—house a collection of tools and bygones reflecting the mill's 100 years of history. The mill is open from the beginning of April until the end of September, from 9:30 a.m. to 6 p.m. Admission is 50p (98¢) for adults, 25p (49¢) for children. There is a telescope on the top floor, and the view over the countryside is magnificent. Crafts, pottery, books, and gifts are on sale. Telephone Stalham 81195 for more information.

The Thursford Collection

Just off the A148 which runs from Kings Lynn to Cromer, at Laurel Farm, Thursford Green, Thursford, near Fakenham (tel. Thursford 238), George Cushing has been collecting and restoring steam engines and organs for more years than you'd care to remember. His collection is now a trust, and the old painted giants are on display, a paradise of traction engines with impeccable pedigrees such as Burrells, Garretts, and Ruston Proctors. There are some static engines, the sort that run merry-go-rounds at funfairs, but the most flamboyant exhibits are the showman's organs, the Wurlitzers and concert organs with their brilliant decoration, moving figures, and mass of windpipes. The organs play at 3 p.m. There is a children's play area, and a Savages Venetian Gondola switchback ride with Gavoili organ, which operates daily. It was built at nearby Kings Lynn, and Disneyland has been after it for years. On many days during the summer, the two-foot gauge steam railway, the Cackler, will take you around the wooded grounds of the museum. There is a refreshment café and a souvenir shop to buy photographs, books, and records of the steam-organ music. The collection is open daily from 2 to 5:30 p.m. from the beginning of April until the end of October. On Sunday it is open throughout the year. Admission is £1.20 ($2.34) for adults, 60p ($1.17) for children.

The North Norfolk Railway

This steam railway plies from Sheringham to Weybourne. The station at Sheringham is open daily from 10 a.m. from Easter to October. Admission is 30p (59¢) for adults; children pay 15p (29¢). There are two museums of railway paraphernalia, steam locomotives, and historic rolling stock. The round trip to Weybourne by steam train takes about 45 minutes through most attractive countryside. Days and times of departures vary so you should telephone Sheringham 822045 between 10 a.m. and 5 p.m. before you go there. The round-trip journey will cost £1 ($1.95) for adults; children, 50p (98¢).

FOOD AND LODGING: The Maltings, Weybourne, near Holt (tel. Weybourne 275). Almost on the edge of the sea but protected from its worst ravages, the Maltings is a delightfully friendly, family-run country "pub" in the best tradition. It is under the watchful eye of Chris Trueman and his wife Elizabeth, who are aided and abetted by James and Lillian, Chris's mother and father. Bedrooms are simple and comfortable with color TV and radio. They go from £15.50 ($30.23) to £20 ($39) in a single, and from £28 ($54.60) to £32 ($62.40) in a double, depending on whether or not you have a private bath. Rates include a large breakfast, VAT, and service.

The original building dates back to the 16th century, and the flint walls and stout plain exterior bear witness to those times. The elegant restaurant has a sophisticated à la carte menu, including most of those haute cuisine dishes that you crave—coquilles St. Jacques frites, veal escalope with rosemary, beef filet with parsley butter—along with a Taste of England menu when a succulent three courses will cost you £7 ($13.65). There are some interesting variations such as jugged hare cooked in red wine.

If you feel unable to sustain a whole meal, drift down the yard to the Inn and the Buttery where, in another solid old stone building, you can sup off a variety of salads complemented by fresh-caught seafoods, home-cooked meats, and, the main attraction, hot baked jacket potatoes, with a wide variety of fillings. John Byle rules over the kitchens, but he has a superb team of chefs with him. To crown it all, Myles Nolan, headwaiter of the restaurant, and the Trueman family make sure you will be greeted with a smile.

The **Blakeney Hotel,** The Quay, Blakeney, near Holt (tel. Cley 740797). As its address indicates, the hotel is right on the quay overlooking the harbor and across the flats from Blakeney Point where migrating birds rest on their way south. The village and neighboring Cley built many of the Elizabethan sailing ships, and the hotel bars are named for them—Jacob, Revenge, and Mayflower. Rooms are cozy, have tea- and coffee-making facilities, as well as telephones and radios. Most have baths and color TVs.

For half board, expect to pay from £22 ($42.90) to £26 ($50.70), in a double including VAT. The cheaper rooms are without bath, the more expensive with private bath and color TV. If double rooms are rented for only one person, a supplement is levied. Children under 12 sharing an accommodation with their parents will be charged for meals only.

There is an indoor swimming pool, and the lounge has panoramic windows with superb views over the flats to the sea. Table d'hôte meals are offered: £6 ($11.70) for lunch, from £8 ($15.60) for dinner, both with three courses. There is a good à la carte menu, but if you just want a snack, the Blakeney Bar offers real ale with which to wash down your selection.

The **Buckinghamshire Arms Hotel,** Blickling, near Aylsham (tel. Aylsham 2133), is a pleasant 17th-century village inn with roaring fires in the bars. Offered are comfortable rooms—some with four-poster beds, others with half-tester beds (the canopy reaches over the sleeper's head only). Some come with just ordinary divans, although all have TV and coffee- and tea-making trays. The charge for the night, plus a large and satisfying breakfast, is £24.50 ($47.78) for two, including VAT. A real country-style dinner will cost £9.50

($18.53). The soup comes from an aromatic stockpot, and Norfolk duckling and chicken are served with fresh vegetables. During the winter they hold special feasts once or twice a month with lobster, venison, and pheasant among the main dishes. Robert Dawson-Smith leases the inn from the National Trust, which owns the nearby Blickling Hall. Real ale, featured in the bar, is often so strong that it only comes in "nips."

The **Old Rectory,** Great Snoring, Fakenham (tel. Walsingham 597). The history of this old house is shrouded in mystery, but in 1500 it was believed to be hexagonal with stone-mullioned windows and heraldic shields of the then owners, the Shelton family, carved on the oaken front door. The Victorians did their bit to restore the house, but it still remains a solid part of medieval village life.

Rosamond Scoles and her family have six comfortable and elegantly furnished rooms for guests. Overnight is £16 ($31.20) to £18.50 ($36.08) in a single, from £35 ($68.25) in a double, the latter with bath, including a leisurely and substantial breakfast. There is a large lounge for guests, where an open woodstove burns, and the light flickers on antique woodwork.

Dinner is three courses, cheese, and coffee for £7 ($13.65) per person. Picnic hampers are provided for luncheon alfresco if you wish. The Old Rectory has a residential license so you can enjoy a sherry before dinner or a nightcap by the fire before retiring to your bed. It's an entirely elegant, relaxed experience, an insight into comfortable country life.

Gasche's Swiss Restaurant, Weybourne (tel. Weybourne 220), has been going on for about 40 years. These days it is run by Edgar Steiner, nephew of the original Herr Gasche. Nigel Massingham, the chef, trained here and has picked up those Swiss touches in the preparation of the dishes. The beamed dining room of the flint and thatch cottage is warmed by a log fire. You will be greeted as warmly by the staff as you partake of the set lunch, costing £6 ($11.70) for three courses. You have a choice of seven appetizers, a homemade soup, and eight main courses including wienerschnitzel. Dinner for £9 ($17.55) is chosen from a similarly large menu, including roast Norfolk duckling. There is an à la carte menu where a meal will cost around £14 ($27.30), but I think you will find enough choices on the set menus to satisfy all tastes. The restaurant is open daily except Monday throughout the year (except for dinner on Sunday).

16. English Country Cottages

"England's most exclusive and individual self-catering holiday homes," they claim, and it could well be so. These cottages are the dream-child of Maj. G. M. S. Bowlby, who controls the operation. His idea originated at Vere Lodge, where he lives, tucked away in the Norfolk village of South Raynham, and at one time the cottages at Vere Lodge were the only ones owned and rented as self-catering properties by Major Bowlby. Since then, English Country Cottages has expanded beyond all expectations and now offers a choice of some 600 properties, ranging from mini-apartments to converted boathouses, farmhouses, and stately homes in most parts of England and Wales, all of which are inspected by a senior member of the staff before acceptance.

Visitors therefore have a choice not only of a wide range of types but also of a variety of locations. They can choose to take their holiday either in the upland moorland of Yorkshire; in the spacious corn-growing country of East Anglia; in Dorset, where Thomas Hardy lived and wrote; or in the lush pastureland of Devon and Cornwall, with their tall, bright-red cliffs, narrow lanes, the high banks of which are bright with wildflowers, and hundreds of pretty fishing villages. This part of England is the mecca of vacationers and provides everything one could possibly want—surfing, sailing, pony trekking, riding, old-world inns, high-class restaurants—all in a climate which is the kindest and softest England has to offer.

The cottages sleep from 2 to 14 persons. A brochure provides full details of all the properties available, with a color photograph of each. Prices range from £60 ($117) per week in low season (April 1 to May 24) to £390 ($760.50) for the high season (July and August). The interior appointments range from the simple to the luxurious. Prices, of course, depend not only on the quality of the decor but also on the location of the property and the amenities which accompany it, such as a heated swimming pool, a hard tennis court, or a barbecue patio.

The great advantage of this type of holiday is that visitors can do their own thing in their own way in their own time. They can get up when they like, eat when like, wear what they like. A self-catering vacation with English Country Cottages offers outstanding value for the money, complete freedom from all restrictions, and an opportunity of sampling English country life in its many and varied aspects.

A word of advice: Most cottages are in villages or else on the grounds of mansions and farms. Most are quite difficult to find. Don't worry, however. When you reserve, the major will send you detailed instructions on how to get there. The head office is Claypit Lane, Fakenham, Norfolk, and the phone number for reservations is (0328) 51155.

Chapter XIII

EAST MIDLANDS

1. **Northamptonshire**
2. **Leicestershire**
3. **Derbyshire**
4. **Nottinghamshire**
5. **Lincolnshire**

THE EAST MIDLANDS contains several widely varied counties, both in character and scenery. This part of central England, for instance, offers miles of dreary industrial sections and their offspring row-type Victorian houses, yet the district is intermixed with some of Britain's noblest scenery, such as the Peak District National Park, centered in Derbyshire. Byron said that scenes there rivaled those of Switzerland and Greece. There are, in short, many pleasant surprises in store for you, from the tulip land of Lincoln to the 18th-century spa of Buxton in Derbyshire, from George Washington's ancestral home at Sulgrave Manor in Northamptonshire to what remains of Sherwood Forest.

1. Northamptonshire

This sprawling county in the middle of England is rather undistinguished in scenery, although its meadows are pleasant in summer. The county town is—

NORTHAMPTON: This has long been an important shoe-making center, and the **Central Museum** on Guildhall Road commemorates that fact. In its collection it traces footwear through the ages, some of which dates back to Roman times. It can be visited from Monday to Saturday from 10 a.m. to 6 p.m. Admission is free. Most visitors pass through here en route to Sulgrave Manor, previewed below.

Food and Lodging

Saxon Inn, Silver Street (tel. Northampton 22441), is a concrete-and-glass structure, attracting mainly the business client, drawn to its good location just off the Inner Ring Road (West). A first-class motor hotel, it checks you in and out smoothly and efficiently. The atmosphere isn't stiff at all—in fact, it's rather informal, and the public lounges are attractively decorated. Portraits of sporting personalities decorate the Sportsman Bar, and light meals are served in the Little Mermaid coffeeshop. Or else you can dine in a coaching-house atmosphere in the Saddle Room, with its large stone fireplace and heavy beams. The menu is international, and guests dine by candlelight, enjoying soft music from a piano player. A resident band entertains on Saturday nights. Rooms are well furnished and comfortable, each with private bath, shower, and toilet en suite, along with color TV, radio, phone, and wall-to-wall carpeting. Singles range in price from £28 ($54.60), and doubles cost from £38 ($74.10).

Westone Hotel, Ashley Way, Weston Favell (tel. Northampton 406262), is a big 19th-century mansion that has seen much modernization. My favorite spot here is the cocktail lounge, which has a calm elegance, its windows opening onto the terrace and grounds. All of the 63 bedrooms have private baths, color TV, radio, and telephone. Depending on the facilities, singles range from £25.30 ($49.34) nightly, with twins costing from £33.92 ($66.14). Traditional English dishes are among the offerings in the restaurant which has good food, fine service, and a bright, cheery decor.

SULGRAVE MANOR: On your way from Oxford to Stratford-upon-Avon, you can visit Sulgrave Manor, the ancestral home of George Washington. First, you'll come to **Banbury,** a market town famed in the nursery rhyme, immortalizing the lady upon the white horse. The old Banbury Cross was destroyed by the Roundheads, but was replaced in Victoria's day. Eight miles northeast of Banbury will take you to Sulgrave Manor, a small Tudor manorial house, built in about the mid-16th century. Follow the A422 east from Banbury toward Brackley. Go left on the B4525 toward Northampton until you pick up the signs to Sulgrave.

As part of Henry VIII's plan to dissolve monasteries, he sold the priory-owned manor in 1539 to Lawrence Washington, who had been mayor of Northampton. George Washington was a direct descendant of Lawrence (seven generations removed). The Washington family occupied Sulgrave for more than a century. In 1656, Col. John Washington left for the New World.

In 1914 the manor was purchased by a group of English people in honor of the friendship between Britain and America. Over the years, major restoration has taken place (a whole new wing had to be added), with an eye toward returning it as much as possible to its original state. The Colonial Dames have been largely responsible for raising the money. From both sides of the Atlantic the appropriate furnishings were donated, including a number of portraits—even a Gilbert Stuart original of the first president. On the main doorway is the Washington family coat-of-arms—two bars and a trio of mullets—which is believed to have been the inspiration for the "Stars and Stripes."

The manor is open daily except Wednesday from April 1 to September 30, 10:30 a.m. to 1 p.m. and from 2 to 5:30 p.m. From October to March the hours are from 10:30 a.m. to 1 p.m. and from 2 to 4 p.m. It's closed in January. Admission is 70p ($1.37) for adults, 35p (68¢) for children. For more information, telephone Sulgrave 205.

Food and Lodging

Across from Sulgrave Manor is the **Thatched House Hotel** (tel. Sulgrave 232), a long, low group of thatched 17th-century cottages, with a front garden full of flowers. It's a good place to stop for afternoon tea, served at a table in either the beamed living or dining room, furnished with antiques. You'll get a pot of tea with homemade scones, jam, thick cream, and cakes £1.35 ($2.63). In season, a tea with strawberries and thick cream may be served for an additional cost.

The owners, Eileen and Ron Walpole, offer three-course lunches in the £4 ($7.80) to £6.50 ($12.68) price range, and dinners from £6.50 ($12.68) to £10 ($19.50). A former hotel consultant, Mr. Walpole will rent you one of his well-furnished singles with bath for £16 ($31.20) or a double with bath for £25 ($48.75), including an English breakfast and VAT.

OUNDLE: A good stopover after Cambridge, if you're driving north, is Oundle in Northamptonshire, 80 miles from London. It's a pleasant old stone town with a fine church dating back to the 14th century. Its Latham almshouses date from 1611. Those motorists moving between East Anglia and Northeastern England will find a warm welcome at—

The **Talbot Hotel,** Oundle, Northamptonshire (tel. Oundle 3621), an ancient inn last reconstructed in 1626. An arch from the street leads to the yard and a pleasant garden in the rear. At this busy country-town pub, with its many beams and old pictures, the oak staircase is reputed to have come from Fotheringhay Castle where Mary Queen of Scots was imprisoned and then executed in 1587. Most of the bedrooms have private bath, color TV, and radio. Singles without bath rent for £19.50 ($38.03), that rate going up to £25 ($48.75) with bath. Bathless doubles are priced at £29 ($56.55), that rate going up to £38 ($74.10) with bath, these tariffs including breakfast and VAT. The hotel is warm and well furnished. Meals are quickly and efficiently provided from a wide menu of grills and roasts. This is a typical country-town inn, catering to local business people, but welcoming strangers, too, in their long tradition as a coaching inn.

WANSFORD-IN-ENGLAND: Instead of staying at the George Hotel in Stamford, an ideal alternative lies just off the A1 road to the north in a pleasant village of stone houses with a wide, typical English main street.

It's the **Haycock Hotel,** at Wansford, near Peterborough (tel. Stamford 782223). A stone in the garden dates the present building from 1632, although an inn has existed on this site for many years. The inn is built around a courtyard with stone archways and mullioned windows. It is said that Mary Queen of Scots, on her way to imprisonment in 1586 at Fotheringhay, visited the inn. In later years, Queen Victoria stopped by when she was still a princess. Many stories of bygone times exist, and you need to visit the place to discover more of its history.

Many of the bedrooms have four-posters, some have private baths, and all contain phones and color TVs. Your overnight charge includes early-morning tea and a newspaper, then a full English breakfast. Depending on a private bath or the lack of one, the per-person rate ranges from £15.75 ($30.71) to £21.25 ($41.44) in a double. Singles go from £19 ($37.05). Reductions on room rates are granted on weekends except during the peak season, ranging from July to September.

Downstairs the busy bar caters to locals and guests alike. If you don't want to order a full meal in the dining room, you can eat heartily from a wide range of bar snacks. A three-course meal in the dining room will cost around £8 ($15.60) per person. For that, you are likely to be served pâté, or a prawn, pineapple, and cucumber cocktail, followed by roast beef and Yorkshire pudding. For dessert, you can make a selection from the trolley. However, I prefer Melton Mowbray Stilton cheese, as this is the homeland of that famous English cheese.

AT WEEDON: The **Crossroads Hotel,** High Street, Weedon (tel. Weedon 40354), is a true crossroad hotel, off the M1, the A5, and A45. The owners, Richard and Wendy Amos, have created a little nook where imagination and good taste reign. The clock tower of the hotel, standing in the garden, is a sign of hospitality. Inside there is a fascinating collection of old clocks throughout the dining room and lounges. The antique collection in the dining room is enhanced with stuffed fish, horse prints, birds in cages, a Victorian carved sideboard, old bicycles hanging from the ceiling, and etched mirrors. There's a large brick oven, and best of all, excellent meals are offered. The house specialty is "Wendy's famous steak, kidney, and mushroom pie," served with vegetables for £5.50 ($10.73). The bedrooms, with color TV sets, are handsomely decorated, singles renting for £19.25 ($37.54) bathless, £22 ($42.90) with bath. Bathless doubles are £29.25 ($57.04) going up to £33 ($64.35) with bath. Included is an English breakfast.

2. Leicestershire

Virtually ignored by most North American tourists, this eastern Midland county was the home of King Lear and is rich in historical associations.

LEICESTER: Although the county town is a busy industrial center, it was once a Roman settlement and has a forum and other sites that remind one of those days.

It also has a Norman castle-hall, a period museum, a 15th-century Guildhall (Shakespeare is said to have played here), and many interesting gardens. On its abbey park and grounds are the remains of Leicester Abbey, Cardinal Wolsey's grave, a boating lake, paddling pool, riverside walks, a miniature railway, ornamental gardens, and an aviary.

You can ask at the Information Bureau on Bishop Street (tel. Leicester 20644) for details of guided walks around the city or inquire of the **City Transport** on Rutland Street (tel. Leicester 24326) about double-decker bus tours.

Food and Lodging

Grand Hotel, Granby Street (tel. Leicester 555599), is aptly named indeed. Built in the days when no expense was spared, the interior decoration is truly magnificent, oak and mahogany paneling abound, and the friendly welcome matches the setting, with the emphasis placed on making your stay as comfortable as possible and offering you good value for money. In the Grand Carving Room, you can choose from succulent joints of meat generously carved by the chef to satisfy the heartiest appetite. The completely refurbished bedrooms have a bright, cheery decor, and all have private bathrooms and color TV. Singles cost from £24 ($46.80), twins from £31 ($60.45).

Holiday Inn, St. Nicholas Circle (tel. Leicester 531161), is smart and stylish, much warmer on its interior than its rather plain facade would suggest. Its enclosed swimming pool is a special feature, and plants and flowers throughout the hotel soften the modernity. Bedrooms, for the most part, are well furnished, with good, large beds, carpeting, private baths, radios, color TV sets, in-house movies, direct-dial phones, and individually controlled air conditioning. Rates begin at £28 ($54.60) in a single, going up to £36 ($70.20) in a double. I'd suggest a meal in the Hayloft Restaurant, with its collection of rustically decorated small lofts. The menu is wide ranging, and the dishes are well prepared and presented, a complete dinner costing about £12 ($23.40) per person.

STAMFORD: Lady Anne's Hotel, 37–38 High St., St. Martins (tel. Stamford 53175), is named after Lady Anne Cecil, a young and favorite sister of the ninth Earl of Exeter. She lived in the original building for many years, but it has seen many changes before emerging as a pleasant country hotel. Bedrooms come in a wide range—some have very small showers, while others are light and airy with baths and toilets en suite. Prices range from £11 ($21.45) per person in a double without bath to £16.50 ($32.16) per person in a double with bath. Single occupancy starts at £17.50 ($34.13), these rates including tea or coffee, a morning paper, and a large English breakfast. Outside is a good car park, and inside there's a welcoming log fire in the bar. Bedrooms have individual TV sets, although there's a large one in the chintzy lounge.

The cottagey dining room has a pleasant but simple menu of grills and fish dishes, including, for example, trout cooked in white wine and butter, scampi provençale, and ham with pineapple or duckling with orange sauce. You can also order a large grilled steak. In season, venison pie and quail in wine sauce are specialties. You can pick your trout from the pond, and the venison is local. All dishes are garnished with home-grown herbs, and the desserts are luscious and homemade. Anne Hastings supervises the kitchen and makes the desserts herself. Expect to spend from £10 ($19.50) for a meal. It's also possible to order snack meals. Her husband, Geoffrey, runs an outside catering company. Together they offer barbecues in the garden during summer, and, in winter, dinner-dances on Saturday nights.

TOURING THE COUNTRY: As long as people continue to read Sir Walter Scott's *Ivanhoe,* they will remember **Ashby-de-la-Zouch,** a town that retains a pleasant country atmosphere. Mary Queen of Scots was imprisoned in an ancient castle here.

If you're in the area, you might want to dine at the **Fallen Knight Restaurant,** 16 Kilwardby St. (tel. Ashby-de-la-Zouch 2230), a small place that takes its name from a resident suit of armor. A rustic decor is created by the plain wooden tables and ladderback chairs. The menu is like a "taste of England," with some good, country-style cookery and some imaginative dishes. Joints are carved from the trolley, and an extensive à la carte menu is available. The hospitable staff adds to the pleasant stopover—lunch till 2 and dinner from 7 to 10:30 p.m. No lunch is served on Saturday, no dinner on Sunday. Meals are from £8 ($15.60) per person. The Fallen Knight is also a hotel, offering single rooms with bath from £12.50 ($24.38) and doubles, also with bath, from £21.50 ($41.93). Units contain color TV, a tea or coffee maker, central heating, and shaver points.

On the northern border of Leicestershire, **Belvoir Castle** has been the seat of the Dukes of Rutland since Henry VIII's time, overlooking the Vale of Belvoir. Rebuilt by Wyatt in 1816, the castle contains paintings by Holbein, Poussin, and Gainsborough, as well as tapestries in its magnificent state rooms. The location is seven miles west-southwest of Grantham, between the A607 to Melton Mowbray and the A52 to Nottingham. It is open from Easter to the end of September on Wednesday, Thursday, and Saturday from noon to 6 p.m., on Sunday from 2 to 7 p.m. (except in June, July, and August when Sunday hours are noon to 7 p.m.), and bank holiday Mondays from 11 a.m. to 7 p.m. Special events, such as medieval jousting tournaments, mock battles, and hawking and falconry displays, are held most Sundays throughout the summer months. Admission is £1.50 ($2.93) for adults, 80p ($1.56) for children. Full details can be obtained from Jimmy Durrands, Estate Office, Belvoir Castle, Grantham, Lincolnshire (tel. Knipton 262).

Other interesting towns to visit in Leicestershire include **Melton Mowbray,** a fox-hunting center and market town which claims to be the original home of Stilton cheese and is renowned for its pork pies.

For a sample of this town's gastronomy, I'd recommend **Dickinson & Morris Ltd.,** 10 Nottingham St., in Melton Mowbray, a 17th-century structure. By tradition, the first Melton pork pie was baked here, and you can sample it today, based on an old recipe, costing from £1.30 ($2.54). The Melton Hunt cake (rich fruit) is made in the bakery shop to the rear, going for 45p (88¢) a serving.

3. Derbyshire

The most magnificent scenery in the Midlands is found within the borders of this county, lying between Nottinghamshire and Staffordshire. Derbyshire has been less defaced by industry than its neighbors. The north of the county, containing the **Peak District National Park,** is by far the most exciting for touring, as it contains waterfalls, hills, moors, green valleys, and dales. In the south the land is more level, and the look becomes, in places, one of pastoral meadows.

Some tourists avoid this part of the country, because it is ringed by the industrial sprawl of Manchester, Leeds, Sheffield, and Derby. To do so, however, would be a pity, and this part of England contains the rugged peaks and leafy dales which merit a substantial detour, especially Dovedale, Chee Dale, and Millers Dale.

Chatsworth House, home of the Dukes of Devonshire, and **Haddon Hall,** home of the Duke of Rutland, are worth a visit. Melbourne Hall, Kedlestone, and Hardwick Hall are also open to view.

OTHER PLACES TO SEE: In addition to majestic scenery, you may want to seek out the following specific sights.

Tramway Museum, Crich, near Matlock (tel. Ambergate 2565). One young 65-year-old whom I know spends as much of his free time as his wife will allow in the paradise of trams—electric, steam, and horse-drawn. Your admission ticket is £1.50 ($2.93) for adults, 80p ($1.56) for children. This ticket allows you to ride on the tram which makes a round trip to Glory mine with scenic views over the Derwent Valley, then back through Wakebridge where a stop is made to visit the Peak District Mines Historical Society display of lead mining. It also includes admission to the tramway exhibition. It is open every Saturday and Sunday from April to October, and daily, except Friday, from Easter to September. Hours are from 10:30 a.m. until some time in the late afternoon.

Peak District Mining Museum, The Pavilion, Matlock Bath (tel. Matlock 3834), is open year round, daily (except for Christmas Day) from 11 a.m. to 4 p.m. Admission is 85p ($1.66) for adults, 50p (98¢) for children. The main exhibit of this display of 2000 years of Derbyshire lead mining is a giant water-pressure engine, used to pump water from the mines and itself rescued from 360 feet underground by members of the society before being brought to the museum. The most popular feature is the children's climbing shaft, a twisting tunnel through which they crawl.

The **Royal Cave** at Matlock Bath (tel. Matlock 3654) is just off the A6 main road beside the Pavilion. Before going underground, you are given a brief audio-visual explanation of man's activities under the earth. Then you descend into the cavern, with its series of sound-and-light shows depicting the life of the earliest cavemen through hardships and disasters, as well as the life of the first Romans in Britain and on to the present day. There's a mineral museum, and after the tour the Gallery Cafeteria will revitalize or sustain you. The cave is open daily from Easter until the end of September from 11 a.m. to 4:30 p.m. (sometimes closed on Friday).

Magpie Mine, at Sheldon, near Bakewell, has been the site of much desperate toil, murders, vendettas, and enormous financial losses. In summer the surface remains of the lead mine (the underground workings are dangerous) are open to view from 2:30 to 4 p.m. The cost is 50p (98¢) for adults, 40p (78¢) for children. This is definitely a specialist tour, but it is representative of conditions which existed in the 18th- and 19th-century English countryside.

The **Red House Stables,** Old Road, Darley Dale, near Matlock (tel. Darley Dale 3583). Caroline Dale's father collected coaches and carriages as a hobby, restored them, and used them for his own pleasure, driving through the Peakland countryside. Today, the carriages and horses are available for the pleasure of anyone who wants to learn to drive a four-in-hand (as Prince Philip does), a pair or a tandem. An introductory course of three days costs £75 ($146.25), but if you already have some experience in driving, an intermediate course is available for £100 ($195). A special unaccompanied child's course of English riding and some driving costs £115 ($224.25), plus VAT for seven days, including full board. No previous experience is necessary, and the course caters to the 8- to 16-year-old age group, learners and more advanced pupils alike.

If you would rather someone else drove so that you could enjoy the scenery, Mrs. Dale operates special drives through Chatsworth Park with halts at local inns for refreshment in traditional style. A stagecoach—yes, a real one—or a four-in-hand which seats 14 people costs £160 ($312). For a party of four, a landau and pair is more suitable at £60 ($117). These prices include the use of the coach and the services of the coachman, but your meal and drinks are at your expense.

Two or three times a year, a luxury three-day tour of the Peak District in the Stagecoach Gay Gordon leaves the stables with a fanfare of posthorns. Overnights are spent in traditional coaching inns, and meals during the day, plus your overnight accommodations, will cost £200 ($390) per person.

These tours are very popular, and the coaches are often busy with film and television work, weddings, and private parties, so it is worth booking early. Mrs. Dale also has riding horses at livery. An hour will cost £4 ($7.80); a day's trek, £20 ($39) (bring your own picnic basket and bad-weather clothing).

The **Clock Warehouse,** London Road, Shardlow (tel. Darby 792844), was built in 1780 on the Trent and Mersey Canal at the junction with the navigable River Trent. It became part of the inland port where merchandise was stored on arrival by narrow boat and river barge. Nowadays, the old building houses the Canal Story exhibition which fills its three floors. There are life-size models of boats and barges, historic photographs, artifacts, and a diorama showing the history of the canal system and the flourishing trade carried on along the waterways. The Canal Shop will sell books, souvenirs, and mementos. Look out for the authentic canal boat painted buckets, jugs, and boxes. The Lace Plate Restaurant is a simple beamed room decorated with dozens of authentic "lace-plates" peculiar to the canals. It serves snacks and refreshments throughout the day. You may be lucky enough to be able to take a short trip on the canal in an authentic narrow boat. Admission is 50p (98¢) for adults, 30p (59¢) for children. The warehouse is open during most of the year, but telephone to make sure.

BUXTON: One of the loveliest towns in Britain, Buxton was built in the 18th century to rival the spa at Bath. Although it eventually fell into a decline, it is now being considerably revived. The 18th-century opera house, for years the local movie palace, is being restored, and will be the centerpiece for a festival featuring Britain's National Theatre. Buxton is 20 miles southeast of Manchester and 163 miles northwest of London.

Of its old buildings, the finest is the Crescent, built by the fifth Duke of Devonshire between 1780 and 1784. The Pump Room, opened in 1894, now houses the Tourist Information Centre, in which you may drink the water from Buxton's natural springs.

ASHBOURNE: This old market town has a 13th-century church, a 16th-century grammar school, and ancient almshouses.

For accommodations, I recommend—

Green Man Hotel (tel. Ashbourne 42017), in the town center, has many historical connections going back to 1710. In 1777, Dr. Samuel Johnson and his biographer, James Boswell, stayed at the inn, and Boswell writes, "I took my post-chaise from the Green Man, a very good inn." In the Tap Room you can still see the chairs of Boswell and Johnson. Even Princess Victoria and her widowed mother, the Duchess of Kent, halted here and gave the inn the right to add "Royal" to its name. This red brick posting inn has retained its traditional character, although modern amenities have been added. You can get a bathless double for £22.50 ($43.88); with bath, £28 ($54.60). Bathless singles are £15.50 ($30.23); with bath, £18 ($35.10). There are 17 rooms, each well decorated, and all tariffs include breakfast, early-morning coffee, and VAT. Service is extra. At lunch, you can enjoy the bar buffet, costing from £4 ($7.80) for three courses. Evening dinners are offered in the Shrovetide Restaurants, selections made from an à la carte menu.

On the Outskirts

Pervil of the Peak, Thorpe, near Ashbourne (tel. Thorpe Cloud 333), is a low, rambling hotel which may have been the Thorpe rectory. Offering 29 handsomely furnished bedrooms, it stands at the foot of Thorpe Cloud, a 900-foot peak guarding the gateway to Dovedale, an area preserved by the National Trust which incorporates 5000 acres of the Peak District. A Trusthouses Forte hotel, it charges from £22.50 ($43.88) daily in a single with bath, including breakfast, service, and VAT. Doubles go for £32 ($62.40) with bath. All units have private plumbing.

The interior is paneled in natural pine, combined with local stone walls, and large picture windows open onto the big country garden, where a hard tennis court is situated. The attractively decorated hotel restaurant offers both table d'hôte and à la carte meals, a set luncheon going from £5.70 ($11.12), a set dinner costing from £7 ($13.65).

DOVEDALE: Overhung by limestone crags, this beautiful wooded valley forms part of the Peak District National Park, with its views of Thorpe Cloud, a conical hill 900 feet high. It's best explored on foot. Fishermen know of its River Dove trout stream, because of its associations with such anglers as Izaak

Walton and Charles Cotton. One is honored by the hotel named after him (previewed below).

The **Izaak Walton Hotel**, Dovedale (tel. Thorpe Cloud 261). Even the telephone exchange—Thorpe Cloud—has a romantic ring about it. This is a very comfortable hotel in what was originally a 17th-century farmhouse. Most of the rooms have private bathrooms, and the views over the dales and peaks of Derbyshire are unsurpassed. This is ideal rambling country, with Dovedale spreading before you.

A single room with bath will cost £26 ($50.70); in a double with bath, £38 ($74.10)—including service, an English breakfast, and VAT. A table d'hôte luncheon costs £5.50 ($10.73). A set dinner at £8 ($15.60) offers an excellent variety of appetizers, three entrees, and a cold buffet, followed by dessert and coffee. Or else you can make selections from a pleasant country menu where a meal will cost around £11 ($21.45).

This is the country for the fisherman, as the name implies, but if that is not your scene, it is an excellent center for touring, with Haddon Hall, Chatsworth House, and Hardwick Hall, to name but a few, lying within easy reach.

FOOD AND LODGING ELSEWHERE IN DERBYSHIRE: The **Howard Hotel**, Friar Gate, Derby (tel. Derby 43455), is a small elegant city house run by Charles Price as a pleasant hotel, ideally situated for visitors to the peaks and dales or those just passing along the M1 from London to Scotland. Bedrooms are warm and comfortable, with radio and wash basin, and go for £12 ($23.40) in a single, £15 ($29.25) in a double. There is a TV in the small lounge. Room rates include a full English breakfast, and there is a pleasant dining room where a set meal costs from £5 ($9.75). In the cellars, reputedly part of the old Derby jail, lurks or burgeons the Judge Jeffreys, with music and dancing nightly until 2 a.m. Meals in the basket are served until 11 p.m.

Peacock Hotel, Rowsley, near Matlock (tel. Darley Dale 833518), is a charming old house with a creeper covering the front door, where fishermen gather with tales of catches in the nearby Wye and Derwent Rivers. Just up the valley is Chatsworth House and down the road is Bakewell, where the tarts (a sort of macaroon with jam) come from. Accommodations reflect the informal country atmosphere, with patterned curtains, deep beds, and well-appointed baths. The lounge and dining room gleam with well-polished woods. The reception area is informal, decorated with trophies from bygone battles. A single room will cost £18 ($35.10) to £25.50 ($49.73), £26 ($50.70) to £30 ($58.50) in a double. Lunch is £5 ($9.75); dinner, £9 ($17.55). Meals are served beneath low beams in the dining room by friendly local waitresses. Details of nearby walks and other attractions are available, and the hotel has fishing rights on local waters.

Rutland Arms, The Square, Bakewell (tel. Bakewell 2812), is a lovely old hotel on the edge of town, offering comfort and good food. There are a comfortable lounge and bar, plus a dining room that has an excellent local reputation. Dinner includes such delicacies as chicken suprême, wienerschnitzel, fresh seafood from the East Coast, and scotch roast beef. A special three-course luncheon is offered for £6.60 ($12.87), or in the Buttery you can order a two-course meal for about £3.50 ($6.83). Rooms are well equipped and have private bathrooms. To keep costs down, there is no porterage or room service. Overnight will cost £22 ($42.90) in a single, £30 ($58.50) in a double, including VAT. Families can avail themselves of a three- or four-bed unit for £36 ($70.20).

Cavendish Hotel, Baslow, near Bakewell (tel. Baslow 2311), is the most select choice for food and hotel accommodations in the entire Peak District. It's a well-preserved Georgian stone manor house, part of the estate of the Dukes of Devonshire. Under the supervision of the duchess, this gem of a house was completely redecorated. The hotel is small, only 13 rooms, and it's owned and managed by Eric Marsh and a small team of professional colleagues. The style and standard are comparable to the most highly rated of British inns, including Chewton Glen and Gravetye Manor. Some of the furnishings of the house came from Chatsworth, home of the Cavendish family for four centuries.

All guest bedrooms face due south, with a wide view of the park and encircling hills. Twin- or double-bedded rooms rent for £30 ($58.50) nightly. Singles aren't available; however, sole occupancy of a double costs from £25 ($48.75). All units feature an en suite private bath with shower, phone, color TV, and a mini-bar. Peter's cocktail bar is a sophisticated rendezvous, and after a drink you can go to the Paxton Room where classical cookery, beautifully served, is presented. The menu includes many unusual dishes such as game specialties.

4. Nottinghamshire

"Notts," as it is called, was the county of Robin Hood and Lord Byron. It is also Lawrence country, as the English novelist, author of *Sons and Lovers* and *Lady Chatterley's Lover,* was also from here, born at Eastwood. Although Sherwood Forest isn't the green wood paradise it used to be, it did provide in its time excellent cover for its world-famous bandit and his band, including Friar Tuck and Little John.

Sherwood Forest is probably the most famous woodland in the world, yet very little of it was forest, even in the days of Robin Hood and his men. The area consists of woodland glades, fields, and agricultural land, along with villages and hamlets. The **Sherwood Forest Visitor Centre,** Sherwood Forest National Park at Edwinstowe, near Mansfield (tel. Mansfield 823202), has been opened in the area just by the Major Oak, known popularly as Robin Hood's tree. It's the center of many marked walks and footpaths through the woodland. There's an exhibition with life-size models of Robin Hood and the other well-known outlaws, as well as a shop with books, gifts, and souvenirs. Robin Hood's Larder offers light snacks and meals, with an emphasis on traditional English country recipes. It is open daily except Monday from 11 a.m. However, it is closed on Friday in winter. There is no admission charge to the center which is on the B6034 north of Edwinstowe village, seven miles north of Mansfield.

Nottinghamshire is so rarely visited by foreign tourists that its beautiful landscapes could almost be called "undiscovered," although British trippers know of its hidden villages and numerous parks.

NOTTINGHAM: The county town is a busy industrial city, 121 miles north of London. On the north bank of the Trent, Nottingham is one of the most pleasant cities in the Midlands.

Overlooking the city, **Nottingham Castle,** was built by the Duke of Newcastle on the site of a Norman fortress in 1679. After restoration in 1878, it was opened as a provincial museum, surrounded by a charmingly laid-out garden. See, in particular, the collection of medieval Nottingham alabaster carvings. The works of Nottingham-born artists are displayed in the first-floor gallery. The admission-free castle is open all year, except Christmas Day, from April to September, daily from 10 a.m. to 5:45 p.m. Otherwise, its hours are daily from 10 a.m. to 4:45 p.m. from October to March.

For 35p (68¢), 20p (39¢) on Sunday and bank holidays, you'll be taken on a conducted tour at the castle of **Mortimer's Hole** and underground passages. King Edward III is said to have led a band of noblemen through these secret passages, surprising Roger Mortimer and the queen, killing Mortimer, and putting his lady in prison. A statue of Robin Hood stands at the base of the castle.

More recently opened, the **Brewhouse Yard Museum** consists of five 17th-century cottages at the foot of Castle Rock, presenting a panorama of Nottingham life in a series of furnished rooms. Some of them, open from cellar to garret, have much local history material on open display, and visitors are encouraged to handle these exhibits. The most interesting features are in a series of cellars cut into the rock of the castle instead of below the houses. This is not a typical folk museum, but attempts to be as lively as possible, involving both visitors and the Nottingham community in expanding displays and altering exhibitions on a bimonthly basis. Open all year, the admission-free museum (tel. Nottingham 411881, ext. 48) may be visited from 10 a.m. to 5 p.m. (except during the lunch hour from noon to 1 p.m.). It is closed Christmas.

An elegant row of Georgian terraced houses, the **Museum of Costume and Textiles** at Castle Gate, presents lace, textile, and costume collections of one of the city's great industries. You'll see everything from the 1632 Eyre map tapestries of Nottingham to "fallals and frippery." The admission-free museum is open daily from 10 a.m. to 5 p.m.

On the outskirts of Nottingham, at Linby, **Newstead Abbey** was once Lord Byron's home. It lies 11 miles north of Nottingham on the A60 (the Mansfield road). Some of the original Augustinian priory, bought by Sir John Byron in 1540, still survives. In the 19th century the mansion was given a neo-Gothic restoration. The poet's bedroom is somewhat as he left it. Mementos, including first editions and manuscripts, are displayed inside, and, later, you can explore a parkland of some 300 acres, with waterfalls, rose gardens, a Monk's Stew Pond, and a Japanese water garden.

The gardens are open all year from 10 a.m. to dusk. Adults are charged 60p ($1.17) for admission; children pay 20p (39¢). The abbey is open from Easter to September 30, daily from 2 to 6 p.m. adults pay an admission of 50p (98¢); children, 10p (20¢). There is a tearoom open during the summer.

Also on the outskirts of Nottingham, **Wollaton Hall** is a well-preserved Elizabethan mansion, housing a natural history museum, with lots of insects, invertebrates, and British mammals, along with reptiles and crustaceans, some a long way from their former home in the South Seas. The mansion is open, April to September, daily from 10 a.m. to 7 p.m., on Sunday from 2 to 5 p.m. From October to March daily, hours are 10 a.m. to dusk, from 1:30 to 4:30 p.m. on Sunday; closed Christmas Day. Admission is free. The hall is surrounded by a deer park and gardens.

Food and Lodging

Albany Hotel, St. James's Street (tel. Nottingham 40131), a Trusthouses Forte hotel, is a large tower block of 160 bedrooms in the heart of the city. Flanked by multistory car parks, it offers good rooms, each with private bath, double-glazed windows, air conditioning, and central heating, as well as a color TV, radio, direct-dial phone, and coffee-making facilities. Singles rent for £36 ($70.20) nightly, doubles going for £45 ($87.75).

In the hotel's Carvery, guests can carve as much as they wish from prime hot and cold joints, or else patronize the more elegant Four Seasons, which, in honor of its namesake, changes its menu and floral decorations quarterly. Along with seasonal specialties, continental dishes are featured. The Forum, the lounge and cocktail bar, is a sleek rendezvous.

Savoy Hotel, Mansfield Road (tel. Nottingham 602621), stands on the A60 Nottingham–Mansfield road, a little less than a mile from the city center. A bustling, modern hotel, it is immaculately maintained and efficiently run, and there's plenty of room to park your car. Attracting business people (and likely to be heavily booked on weekdays), it offers well-furnished, streamlined rooms for £26 ($50.70) daily in a single, £34 ($66.30) in a double, including private baths (some have showers), color TVs, radios, and phones. Have a predinner drink in Fagin's Bar, its decor inspired by the Dickensian atmosphere of the 19th century, before dining in one of two steak bars or else the Colonial Restaurant. A five-course meal in the Colonial Restaurant goes for about £6.50 ($12.68); however, an average meal in the Steak Bar ranges from £3.50 ($6.83) to £6 ($11.70).

Strathdon Hotel, 44 Derby Rd. (tel. Nottingham 48501), a favorite of traveling business people, lies about five miles from the M1, in the center of the city. Of the 67 bedrooms (the majority of which are singles), 23 come with private and pleasant tiled bath, the rest with shower, although all have color TV, phone, radio, and coffee-making facilities. The rate for either a twin- or double-bedded room is £34 ($66.30) from Monday to Thursday, the tariff lowered to £27.50 ($53.63) from Friday to Sunday. Breakfast is extra. Drinks are ordered in the dark-paneled Mariners Tavern, decorated with fishing nets, ropes, ships' wheels, and portholes. In the hotel's restaurant, a good table d'hôte evening meal goes from £8 ($15.60), a set luncheon for £4.50 ($8.78). The cookery is acceptable, and some international dishes are featured along with traditional English fare.

Farmhouse Dining on the Outskirts

Grange Farm, Toton (tel. Long Eaton 69426), is an old English farmhouse, built in 1691, serving traditional English fare and run by the Ackroyd family. This busy Nottinghamshire restaurant serves lunch Monday to Saturday from noon to 2 p.m., a set meal costing £6.50 ($12.68), inclusive of VAT, service charge, and coffee. The chefs prepare an excellent choice of interesting appetizers and many homemade English dishes—for example, steak-and-kidney pudding, venison pie, braised steak in Burgundy sauce, followed by a large variety of desserts and cheeses. Dinner is served in two sittings, 7 and 8:30 p.m., a set meal costing £10 ($19.50), inclusive. Dinner is similar to lunch with an addition of an extra course. For example, you may also enjoy battered mushrooms in sweet-and-sour sauce or fried whitebait. It is advisable to telephone for a reservation to avoid disappointment. Saturday nights, the restaurant has a dinner-dance, which is popular. There is a fine collection of porcelain and ivories in the lounges which should be seen. Grange Farm has excellent car parking facilities and is six miles from Nottingham.

About a half-hour's drive from Lord Byron's Newstead Abbey leads to—

SOUTHWELL: This ancient market town is a good center for exploring the Robin Hood country. Byron once belonged to a local amateur dramatic society here. An unexpected gem is the old twin-spired cathedral, **Southwell Minster,** which many consider the most beautiful church in England. James I found that it held up with "any other kirk in Christendom." Look for the well-proportioned Georgian houses across from the cathedral.

Saracen's Head, Market Place (tel. Southwell 812701), is a historic coaching inn, where both Charles I and James I dined. In fact, Charles I was made a prisoner here before the Scots handed him over to the Parliamentarians. After he was beheaded, the name of the inn was changed from King's Arms to Saracen's Head. Commanding the junction of the main ancient thoroughfares of the town, the old hostelry also frequently entertained Byron. Today, your hosts are Joanna and René Koomen, who are proud of its old atmosphere, such as cozy bars with exposed beams and fine old paneling. The redecorated and refurbished bedrooms are up-to-date, however, each containing a private bath, TV, radio, and phone. Doubles cost from £38 ($74.10), and singles begin at £28 ($54.60). This includes a full English breakfast and VAT. The oldest part of the inn has been redeveloped, providing another 11 rooms, featuring oak beams and traditional furnishings. From the well-stocked cellar emerges a good selection of wines to complement a meal, with both an à la carte and a table d'hôte menu.

East of Southwell, near the Lincolnshire border—

NEWARK-ON-TRENT: Here is an ancient riverside market town, on the Roman Fosse Way, lying about 15 miles across flatlands from Nottingham. King John died at **Newark Castle** in 1216. Constructed between the 12th and 15th centuries, the castle—now in ruins—survived three sieges by Cromwell's troops before falling into ruin in 1646. From its parapet, you can look down on the Trent River and across to Nottingham. The delicately detailed parish church here is said to be the finest in the country. The town contains many ancient inns, reflecting its long history.

THE DUKERIES: In the Dukeries, portions of Sherwood Forest, legendarily associated with Robin Hood, are still preserved. These are vast country estates on the edge of industrial towns. Most of the estates have disappeared, but the part at **Clumber**—covering some 4000 acres—is administered by the National Trust, which has preserved its 18th-century beauty, as exemplified by Lime Tree Avenue. Rolling heaths and a peaceful lake add to the charm. You can visit Clumber Chapel, built in 1886–1889 as a chapel for the seventh Duke of Newcastle. It is open April 5 to September 30 Monday to Friday from 2 to 7 p.m. On weekends its hours are noon to 7 p.m. Off-season hours are daily, 1 to 4. There is no admission charge, but car entry charge to the park is £1 ($1.95). The location is at Clumber Park, five miles southeast of Worksop.

A few miles south of Clumber stands the greatest Victorian house in the Midlands, **Thoresby Hall.** Built by Salvin in 1864, it is the only mansion in the Dukeries still occupied as the home of the original owners. Barton & Skills run tours from Nottingham. The hall is open to the public during June, July, and August. It lies four miles north of Ollerton, just west of the Bawtry road (A614).

EASTWOOD: Because of the increased interest in D. H. Lawrence these days, many literary fans like to make a pilgrimage to Eastwood, his hometown. The English novelist was born there on September 11, 1885. Mrs. Brown, a member of the D. H. Lawrence Society, conducts parties of visitors around the "Lawrence country." Hopefully, at the end, you'll make a donation to the society. If you're interested in taking a tour, write her in advance—Mrs. M. Brown,

D. H. Lawrence Society, c/o 8A Victoria St., Eastwood, Nottingham (tel. Langley Mill 68139).

SCROOBY: This is a tiny village of some 260 inhabitants where in 1566 William Brewster, a leader of the Pilgrim Fathers, was born. His father was bailiff of the manor and master of the postes, so it may have been in the Manor House that the infant Brewster first saw the light of day. The original house dated from the 12th century, and the present manor farm, built on the site in the 18th century, has little except historical association to attract.

Brewster Cottage, with its pinfold where stray animals were impounded, lies beside the village church of St. Wilfred. But it's uncertain whether the Pilgrim father ever lived there.

The village also contains Monks Mill on the River Ryton, now almost a backwater but once a navigable stream down which Brewster and his companions may have escaped to travel to Leyden in Holland and on to their eventual freedom.

In the 18th century the turnpike ran through the village, and there are many stories of highwaymen, robberies, and murders. The body of one John Spencer hung for more than 60 years as a reminder of the penalties of wrongdoing. He'd attempted to dispose of the bodies of the keeper of the Scrooby toll-bar and his mother in the river.

5. Lincolnshire

This large East Midlands county is bordered on one side by the North Sea. Its most interesting section is Holland, in the southeast, a land known for its fields of tulips, its marshes and fens, and windmills reminiscent of the Netherlands. Although much of the shire is interesting to explore, time is too important for most visitors to linger long. Foreign tourists, particularly North Americans, generally cross the tulip fields, scheduling stopovers in the busy port of Boston before making the swing north to the cathedral city of Lincoln, lying inland.

BOSTON: This old seaport in the riding of Holland has a namesake that has gone on to greater glory, and perhaps for this reason it is visited by New Englanders. At Scotia Creek, on a river bank near Boston, is a memorial to the early Pilgrims who made an unsuccessful attempt in 1607 to reach the promised land. They were imprisoned in the Guildhall in cells that can be visited today. A company left again in 1620—and fared better, as anybody who has ever been to Massachusetts will testify. Part of the ritual here is climbing the Boston Stump, a church lantern tower with a view for miles around of the all-encircling fens. In the 1930s, the people of Boston, U.S.A., paid for the restoration of the tower, known officially as St. Botolph's Tower. Actually, it's not recommended that you climb the tower, as the stairs aren't in good shape. The tower, as it stands, was finished in 1460. The city fathers were going to add a spire, making it the tallest in England. But because of the wind and the weight, they feared the tower would collapse. Therefore, the tower became known as "the Boston Stump." An elderly gentleman at the tower assured me it was the tallest in England—that is, 272½ feet tall. Boston is 116 miles north from London, and 34 miles southeast of Lincoln.

Food and Lodging

White Hart Hotel, High Street (tel. Boston 64877), is a gleaming white hotel, built against the high wall of a canal embankment. A bathless single rents for £13 ($25.35); a bathless double is priced at £23 ($44.85), going up to £27 ($52.65) with bath. These tariffs include a full breakfast, service, and VAT. Rooms are pleasantly furnished, with central or electrical heating and a radio, and are kept immaculate. A bonus is the free car park at the rear of the hotel (you drive through an old coaching alleyway).

The White Hart contains half a dozen bars, each one decorated differently, serving draft sherries and beer, as well as spirits and food. Of the two restaurants, one features duck and steak dishes; the other, fish and chicken specialties. A meal costs around £6 ($11.70) to £8 ($15.60), and hours are from noon to 2:30 p.m. and 6 to 11 p.m.

LINCOLN: One of the most ancient cities of England, and only 135 miles north of London, Lincoln was known to the Romans as Lindum. Some of the architectural glory of the Roman Empire still stands to charm the present-day visitor. The renowned Newport Arch (the North Gate) is the last remaining arch left in Britain that still spans a principal highway. For a look at the Roman relics excavated in and around Lincoln, head for the **City and County Museum,** Broadgate (tel. Lincoln 26866), open daily from 10 a.m. to 5:30 p.m. (2:30 to 5 p.m. on Sunday).

Two years after the Battle of Hastings, William the Conqueror built a castle on the site of a Roman fortress. Used for administrative purposes, parts of the castle still remain, including the walls, the 12th-century keep, and fragments of the gateway tower. In addition, you can visit the high bridge over the Witham River, with its half-timbered houses (you can have a meal in one of them). This is one of the few medieval bridges left in England that has buildings nestling on it.

Lincoln Cathedral

Towering over the ancient city, the Minster forms a grand sight, with its three towers. The central one is 271 feet tall, making it the second tallest in England, ranking under the Boston Stump, mentioned earlier. However, the central tower at Lincoln was once the tallest spire in the world (525 feet) until it blew down in 1549. There are regular summer trips up the tower on weekdays, costing 60p ($1.17) for adults, 35p (68¢) for children. The Norman cathedral was consecrated in 1092, but only the west front remains. The cathedral represents the Gothic style, particularly the Early English and Decorated periods. The nave, in its present form, was built in the early 13th century. In the Early English Great Transept, you can see a rose medallion window, known as the Dean's Eye. The rose window at the opposite end of the transept—in the Decorated style—is known as the Bishop's Eye. The Angel Choir, in the eastern end, consecrated on October 6, 1280, is named after the sculptured angels displayed in it. The exquisite carving in the choir dates from the 14th century. The black font of Tournai marble is from the 11th century.

In the Seamen's Chapel is a window commemorating Lincolnshire-born Capt. John Smith, one of the pioneers of early settlement in America and the first governor of Virginia.

The Library, in the Cloister, was built in 1674 by Sir Christopher Wren. It contains many fine books and manuscripts, some of which are on view in the adjoining Medieval Library (1422), together with one of the four remaining original copies of the Magna Carta of 1215, the Cathedral Charter of 1072, and the Foresters' Charter of 1225. The Library is open Monday through Saturday, from 10:30 a.m. to 4:30 p.m. Easter through September, and in winter by appointment (tel. Lincoln 21089).

In the Treasury (open weekdays 2:30 to 4:30 p.m., Easter through September), there is fine gold and silver plate from churches in the diocese.

Suggested donation to the cathedral is 60p ($1.17) for adults, 35p (68¢) for children.

Where to Stay

Eastgate Post House, Eastgate (tel. Lincoln 20341), should put to shame those critics who resist contemporary architecture, especially in old English cathedral cities. A hotel attached to a Victorian mansion (now the Eastgate Bar), the Trusthouse occupies a historic site: in fact, when workmen were digging its foundations in the mid-'60s, they discovered the remnants of the north tower of the East Gate of Roman Lincoln. Many of the large bedrooms, 16 with balconies, offer unimpaired views of the cathedral. The airy main lounge, with its high slat ceiling and overscale windows, is spacious, furnished with compact, tasteful pieces. The modern bedrooms, each with a private bath, telephone, radio, picture window, and Nordic-style appurtenances, are inviting and rent for £27 ($52.65) in a single, from £36 ($70.20) in a double, all with private baths. The rates include service and VAT. The wood-paneled dining room, warmed by vibrant colors, offers an extensive à la carte menu, plus a set lunch for £7 ($13.65), a set dinner for £9 ($17.55). An average à la carte dinner will cost £14 ($27.30). In addition, the Eastgate runs a good coffeeshop, serving the usual grilled and fried dishes, plus one specialty every day. In addition to a coffeeshop meal, you'll get a fine view of the cathedral.

The **White Hart,** Bailgate (tel. Lincoln 26222), is a red brick Georgian inn, with its corner clock and miniature figure of a white hart, right in the shadow of the cathedral, within the range of its chimes. On Lincoln's historic mile, the inn is unpretentious, and skillfully operated by a well-trained staff. Oldtimers respect the ambience, as reflected in the large living room opening onto a hothouse and patio garden. High mahogany cabinets hold a collection of old silver and porcelain; overstuffed chairs are set around tables for after-dinner coffee; and there are antiques in the reception lounges and corridors, including the more intimate upstairs residents' lounge. The bedrooms have nice old furnishings, with such pieces as a pedestal swivel mirror or a mahogany table. Each has a telephone and radio, and many have private baths.

Depending on the facilities, singles range in price from £21 ($40.95) to £27 ($52.65), and doubles go from £28 ($54.60) to £41 ($79.95). In the olive and red dining room, you'll be served some of the finest English fare in Lincoln. Very good sandwiches are served with coffee or tea in the lounge throughout the day, and you can also enjoy the same in a patio and garden bar known as the Orangery, a bright and cheerful place to meet friends and enjoy a selection from the buffet of hot and cold dishes and from the self-service salad bar. Prices are around £2.50 ($4.88) for a plate and coffee.

Grand Hotel, St. Mary Street (tel. Lincoln 24211), is a good bet for the seeker of economy, as it's an extensively remodeled hotel, top-heavy with contemporary amenities and a cooperative staff. You'll pay around £30 ($58.50) for a double with a private bath. Singles go for £20 ($39) with bath. The Grand's program of redecorating has given it a pleasant, spacious look. The West Bar and the lounges are streamlined, but the Tudor Bar pays homage to the past. The bedrooms are compact, with many built-in features and coordinated colors. The Grand is easy to spot, as it lies opposite the bus depot. It's a long walk to the cathedral, however, but you can hop a bus. Its food is a top-notch bargain, both in price and taste. From 7 to 8:30 p.m., a table d'hôte dinner is offered for £5 ($9.75). Meals are inclusive, priced according to the entree. The food is not only good and typically English, but the portions are ample. You can also lunch at the Grand from noon to 2 p.m. A buttery is open from 11 a.m. to 10 p.m. Bargain breaks are offered on weekends if you stay a minimum of two nights.

READER'S HOTEL SELECTION: "The **D'Isney Place Hotel,** Eastgate (tel. Lincoln 38629), should be recommended. Not only is the location excellent, but the accommodations are superb. Each room is uniquely decorated, with an extra-large bath, comfortable beds, color television, and private tea service. The rates are quite reasonable at £27 ($52.65) for a double, considering the quality of the rooms and the fact that breakfast is served in your room at the time you specify. The proprietors, David and Judy Payne, are splendid people who give their utmost attention to the care and comfort of their patrons. The D'Isney Place Hotel is the perfect example of the pleasure of traveling in England" (Michael K. Lafferty, Riverside, Calif.).

Where to Eat

Harveys Cathedral Restaurant, 1 Exchequergate, Castle Square (tel. Lincoln 21886), lies in the heart of the old town, a short walk from the cathedral and the castle. My favored dining spot in the city, it is run by Adrianne and Bob Harvey, whose children may occasionally be glimpsed helping in the background. It is housed in a stately Georgian building which, until recently, was reputed to be haunted, but the cozy modern decor has routed any dismal spirits. The motto of the Harveys is "Simple lunches—superb dinners," and they live up to this with a lunch menu offering traditional English dishes such as farmhouse chicken pie for £2.60 ($5.07) and beef in Guinness, £2.85 ($5.56), followed by Victorian sherry trifle, 95p ($1.85). Coffee is good value at 50p (98¢) for a bottomless cup. Start with Bob's homemade pâté at £1 ($1.95), or warming soup, always freshly made, 75p ($1.46).

In the evenings the restaurant is candlelit and bubbles with a romantic atmosphere (reservations are essential on weekends). The Harveys offer a table d'hôte gourmet menu at £12 ($23.40), fully inclusive. This consists of a special soup or fruit dish, followed by the appetizer course, with a choice of fish, savory dishes, or pâté. Then there is a selection of seven main dishes, including French and "Taste of England" specialties. A massive choice of cheeses follows, with a finale of diet-beating homemade desserts and ice creams, plus the bottomless coffee cup and mints. Almost everything the Harveys serve is homemade, and all ingredients are fresh.

Finally, if you're in Lincoln over a weekend, take in a traditional Sunday lunch here. You won't taste better roast beef anywhere, but remember to reserve your table. The restaurant is open for lunch daily except Monday in winter, from noon to 1:45 p.m. Dinners are from 7:30 to 9:30 p.m. Tuesday through Saturday. **Green Dragon,** Broadgate (tel. Lincoln 24950, near the river, about a block from The High, is one of Lincoln's most attractive buildings, sheltering both pubs and a dining room. Actually, it is comprised of a row of 16th-century houses, black-and-white timbered, joined together and heavily reconstructed to create an inviting ambience.

A set lunch is featured for £3.50 ($6.83). If you're ordering à la carte, you'll find a wide menu selection, with a meal costing from £6 ($11.70).

Chapter XIV

CHESHIRE, LIVERPOOL, AND THE LAKES

ONE OF ENGLAND'S most popular summer retreats in Victoria's day was the Lake District in the northwest. It enjoyed vogue during the flowering of the Lake Poets, including Wordsworth, who was ecstatically moved by the rugged beauty of this area. In its time, the district has lured such writers as S. T. Coleridge, Charles Lamb, Shelley, Keats, Alfred Lord Tennyson, Matthew Arnold, and Charlotte Brontë.

The Lake District is a miniature Switzerland condensed into about 32 miles, principally in Cumbria, although it begins in the northern part of Lancashire.

As an added bonus, I've included Liverpool, plus Cheshire, a county that lies south of Lancashire. I suggest that you make a pilgrimage to the ancient city of Chester, with its medieval walls, near the border of Wales.

The northwest of England is one of the special parts of the country, yet it is rarely visited by the agenda-loaded foreigner, who considers it too far removed. In many ways, however, its remoteness is part of its charm. Have you ever seen one of those English-made films depicting the life of the Lake District? A soft mist hovers over the hills and dells, sheep graze silently on the slope of the pasture—and a foggy enchantment fills the air.

But first—

CHESHIRE

This county is low lying and largely agricultural. The name it gave to a cheese (Cheshire) has spread across the world. This northwestern county borders Wales, which accounts for its turbulent history. The towns and villages of Cheshire are peaceful and quiet—forming a good base for touring North Wales, the most beautiful part of that little country. For our headquarters in Cheshire, we'll locate at:

1. Chester

Chester is ancient, having been founded by a Roman legion on the Dee River in the first century A.D. It reached its pinnacle as a bustling port in the 13th and 14th centuries, declining thereafter following the gradual silting up of the river. The upstart Liverpudlians captured the sea-trafficking business. The other walled medieval cities of England were either torn down or badly fragmented, but Chester still retains two miles of fortified city walls intact.

The main entrance into Chester is Eastgate, itself dating back to only the 18th century. Within the walls are half-timbered houses and shops. Of course, not all of them came from the days of the Tudors. Chester is freakish architecturally in that some of its builders kept to the black-and-white timbered facades —even when erecting buildings during the Georgian and Victorian periods, with their radically different tastes.

The Rows are double-decker layers of shops—one tier on the street level, the other stacked on top and connected by a footway. The upper tier is like a continuous galleried balcony. Shopping upstairs is much more adventurous than down on the street. Rain is never a problem. Thriving establishments operate in this traffic-free paradise: tobacco shops, restaurants, department stores, china shops, jewelers, even antique dealers. For the most representative look, take an arcaded walk on Watergate Street.

At noon and at 3 p.m. daily at the City Cross, the world's champion town crier issues his news (local stuff on sales, exhibitions, and attractions in the city) at the top of his not-inconsiderable voice, to the accompaniment of a hand bell—at the junction of Watergate(!), Northgate, and Bridge Streets.

After exploring The Rows, focus your attention on:

CHESTER CATHEDRAL: The present building founded in 1092 as a Benedictine abbey was created as a cathedral church in 1541. Considerable architectural restorations were carried out in the 19th century, but older parts have been preserved. Notable features include the fine range of monastic buildings, particularly the cloisters and refectory, the chapter house, and the superb medieval wood carding in the quire (especially the misericords). Also worth attention are the long south transept with its various chapels, the consistory court, and the medieval roof bosses in the Lady Chapel. A free-standing bell tower, the first to be built in England since the Reformation, was completed in 1975 and may be seen southeast of the main building. For more information, telephone Chester 25920.

HERITAGE CENTER: The **Chester Heritage Centre** is housed in the former St. Michael's Church in Bridge Street Row (tel. Chester 317948). It is open from April to September, Monday to Saturday (closed Wednesday) from 10 a.m. to 5 p.m.; on Sunday from 2 to 5 p.m. From October to March, it is open every day except Wednesday from 1:30 to 4:30 p.m. Admission for adults is 50p (98¢); children pay 25p (49¢). The center contains an audio-visual display on the character of Chester and its historic buildings, an excellent introduction to the city for visitors. There is also a permanent exhibition on the conservation of the city's heritage, and the continuous program of restoration work which is arranged by Chester City Council.

The City Record Office has the responsibility of the administration of the Heritage Centre, and the city archivist arranges for special temporary exhibitions to be shown there. These generally have a local and historical theme but can also include the work of local artists and craftspeople. Souvenirs and publications of general and special interest are on sale.

WHERE TO STAY: Blossoms Hotel, St. John Street (tel. Chester 23186), has been in business since the mid-17th century, although the present structure was rebuilt late in Victoria's day. Each of the 70 traditionally furnished bedrooms is equipped with central heating, and all private baths. Each room has a telephone and radio, as well as color TV and coffee maker. The price for B&B in a single is from £27.50 ($53.63); in a twin or double, from £40 ($78). The old open staircase in the reception room sets the tone of the hotel. Dinner is served in the Egerton Room from 7 to 9:30 p.m., both table d'hôte at £6.50 ($12.68) and à la carte. The Snooty Fox coffeeshop offers salads and seafoods in the 75p ($1.46) to £1.75 ($3.41) price range.

Rowton Hall, Whitchurch Road (tel. Chester 35262), is a stately home, two miles from the city center, which offers overnight accommodation for motorists. The gracious house, built in 1797, with a later wing added, is nearly covered with green ivy, and stands on its own eight-acre garden, with a formal driveway entrance. The Hall has comfortable traditional and semicontemporary pieces. A bathless single goes for £20 ($39), for £24 ($46.80) with bath. A bathless double is £30 ($58.50), £34 ($66.30) with bath. Breakfast, service, and VAT are included. A set lunch or dinner costs from £5.50 ($10.73), although you are likely to spend more than £8 ($15.60) if you order from the à la carte menu. The good English meals are served in the oak-paneled dining room, with its Tudor fireplace. On Saturday nights, a dinner dance is staged, costing £8 ($15.60) per person. The hotel stands on the site of the battle of Rowton Moor, which was fought in 1643 between the Roundheads and the Cavaliers.

Ye Olde King's Head, 48/50 Lower Bridge Street (tel. Chester 24855), is a 17th-century museum piece of black-and-white architecture. From 1598 to 1707, it was occupied by the well-known Randle Holme family of Chester, noted heraldic painters and genealogists (some of their manuscripts have made it to the British Museum). Since 1717, the King's Head has been a licensed inn. The host rents out a dozen handsome bedrooms at £19 ($37.05) for a single room, from £13.50 ($26.33) per person in a double, for B&B, VAT, and service. The bedchambers are linked with the past; many of the walls and ceilings are sloped and highly pitched, with exposed beams.

The residents' lounge, with its massive beams overhead, boasts a Tudor fireplace, and authentic furnishings, including an elaborate grandfather clock, an octagonal card table, high-backed Jacobean oak chairs, and soft upholstered pieces. The main lounge has a number of wall settles, barrel tables, wood paneling, and a Tudor fireplace. The 17th-century dining room is also a showcase of timberwork, with old furnishings, such as a Welsh cupboard and pewter and copper pieces. A set lunch costs £4 ($7.80). Dinner is served from 6:30 to 9 p.m. every day, costing from £6 ($11.70).

The Belgrave Hotel, City Road (tel. Chester 312138). Derek and Alma Wood have concentrated on friendly service in their Victorian-era hotel, within a stone's throw of the railway station and within easy walking distance of the city center. They charge around £10 ($19.50) a night for B&B.

WHERE TO EAT: The Courtyard, 13 St. Werburgh St. (tel. Chester 21447), was originally a stable courtyard, opposite the south transept of the cathedral. Today, it's been turned into one of the finest dining spots in Chester. The narrow entrance, with its black-and-white decorative motif, sets the stage for a two-in-one restaurant. Opening into the inner courtyard is the ingeniously designed split-level bistro, which offers a luncheon buffet from noon to 2:30 p.m.

A smörgasbord lunch is individually priced with hot dishes, cold meats, and salads. Prices range from £1.50 ($2.93) per helping. From 6 to 10 p.m., the restaurant offers a bistro dinner where one serves one's self for an inclusive price of £6.60 ($12.87). It's good value. A more elaborate à la carte menu costing from £9 ($17.55) is available from 7 to 10 p.m., including items such as veal in orange and rum sauce. A specialty appetizer is Raymond's homemade pâté, or you might try mushroom Armenienne cooked in red wine, bacon, and garlic. The chef's desserts include walnut fudge.

The Courtyard cellar is open nightly for dancing Monday to Friday. The restaurant is open Monday to Saturday and is closed on bank holidays.

The Witches Kitchen, Frodsham Street (tel. Chester 311836), is in the center of town, just a short walk from the station. It seats 100 and has old-world charm and good service. The ground-floor restaurant is 15 yards from the city walls and Chester Cathedral. It is open every day for luncheon (11:30 a.m. till 5:30 p.m.), afternoon tea (3 to 5 p.m.), and dinner (7 to 10:30 p.m.). Quick-lunch main-course dishes begin at £1.80 ($3.51). An à la carte menu with a wide variety of traditional dishes is served throughout the day—for example, roast beef and Yorkshire pudding and other roasts, beginning at £2.80 ($5.46). Included in the price is a selection of fresh vegetables in season. Desserts are excellent as well. On Sunday you can enjoy the traditional roast beef lunch, and on Saturday night a carvery with succulent roasts. A children's menu is always available, and the restaurant has a fully licensed cocktail bar.

Jean's Kitchen, 1 Newtown Close, St. Anne Street (tel. Chester 381313), offers a table d'hôte luncheon that continues up to 7 p.m. at a cost of around £3 ($5.85). Dinner from the à la carte menu will cost about £5 ($9.75) per person. Specialties include mushrooms cooked in wine, seafood salad with rice, thin steak smothered in a cheese and tomato sauce, or boeuf bourguignon, followed by the richest desserts in Chester. Wine is French, a small bottle costing from £1.70 ($3.32).

The **Royal Oak,** Foregate Street (tel. Chester 314336), is a 17th-century building with a nice old paneled dining room where a set three-course lunch with two or three choices for each course will cost £3.50 ($6.83). Or else a meal chosen from the à la carte menu will go for £6.50 ($12.68). Choose from spicy tomato soup with cream, then chicken schnitzel with sweet corn relish, a jacket potato and vegetables, or lamb cutlets with peas and fried potatoes, grilled plaice with chips, followed by a large slice of Black Forest cake. Steaks, grilled to your specification and served with jacket or fried potatoes, peas, and tomato, are also served. Peter and Anne Flaig supervise everything and also provide bar snacks in the Long Bar if you don't have time to stop for a meal.

Some Local Pubs

The **Bear & Billet Inn,** Lower Bridge Street (tel. Chester 21272), with its intricately timbered and highly decorative facade from the mid-17th century, is one of the best known buildings in Chester. The well-preserved pub, once a city house belonging to the Earls of Shrewsbury, still preserves its traditional atmosphere. Snacks available include a ploughman's lunch, ham and pineapple salad, cheese and beetroot salad, homemade soup, and fresh Dee salmon in season.

An alternative for drinking is the **Boot Inn,** Eastgate Street, established in 1643, making it even older than the Bear & Billet. It's the smallest and most unspoiled pub in Chester. Only oldtimers and those on the "in" know about it. It's reached by entering a passageway along the upper Rows of Eastgate Street. The publican has a multitude of mementos cluttering the walls—horse brasses, steins, curios from everywhere, even brass crocodiles and castanets.

AN EXCURSION TO CONWY CASTLE (WALES): The most popular excursion from Chester is to the castle and walled town of Conwy in Wales, a distance of some 48 miles. The town contains many interesting old buildings, including the National Trust property of Aberconwy, Plas Mawr, and what is said to be the smallest house in Britain.

However, the major interest, of course, centers on **Conwy Castle,** built between 1283 and 1289 and considered a perfect specimen of medieval fortifications in Britain. Following the contours of a narrow strip of rock, the eight towers of the castle dominate the estuary of the River Conwy. The castle stands at the harbor where the river finds its way to the sea. From these old walls you can see the small fishing fleet at anchor in the sheltered harbor. Fishermen bring in their catch of mussels and Conwy dabs here.

The castle (tel. Conwy 2358) is open from 9:30 a.m. to 6:30 p.m. from mid-March to mid-October. Otherwise, it is open weekdays from 9:30 a.m. to 4 p.m. and on Sunday from 2 to 4 p.m. The summer admission charge is 60p ($1.17) for adults, 30p (59¢) for children and senior citizens. In winter, charges are reduced to 40p (78¢) and 20p (39¢), respectively.

The town wall, which protected the borough laid out by Edward I below the castle, is still nearly intact. It is flanked by 21 towers and pierced by three twin-towered gateways.

2. Nantwich

The old market town on the Weaver River lies only 15 miles southeast of the county town of Chester, and can easily be tied in with a visit to that city. The town is particularly outstanding because of its black-and-white timbered houses. The most spectacular one, Churche's Mansion, is one of my dining recommendations.

WHERE TO STAY: Crown Hotel and Restaurant, High Street (tel. Nantwich 625283), is a black-and-white timbered structure, with leaded windows and an archway for carriages. The hotel was rebuilt in 1583 after a fire. Most attractive, the Crown offers guest rooms where you can immerse yourself in the charm of old England for £10 ($19.50) in a bathless single, £12.50 ($24.38) in a single with bath. In a twin or double without bath, the rate is £18 ($35.10), going up to £19 ($37.05) with bath, these tariffs including breakfast and VAT. The plank floors are so slanted you have to be careful not to lose your balance. The tavern and lounge blend antiquity with charm. The unique Georgian Assembly Room attached to the Crown has been restored, redecorated, and refurnished in the style of the period, and is now used as a dining and ballroom. The new restaurant is really a coffeeshop, serving steaks, grills, scampi, hamburgers, and pizzas throughout the day. There is no proper restaurant and no set lunches or dinners. Everything is quick service at an average price of £5 ($9.75). If you only want a light snack, try the fully licensed Lounge Bar.

WHERE TO EAT: Churche's Mansion Restaurant, Hospital Street, is the most enchanting old restaurant in Cheshire, lying in Nantwich at the junction of Newcastle Road and the Chester bypass. Many years ago, Dr. and Mrs. E. C. Myott learned that this historic home of a wealthy Elizabethan merchant had been advertised for sale in America, and asked the town council to step in and save it. Alas, no English housewife wanted such a gloomy and dark home, so the Myotts attended the sale and outbid the American syndicate who wanted to transport it to the United States. Dr. Myott said that "our friends thought we were mad." They sought out the mysteries of the house; a window in the side wall, inlaid initials, a Tudor well in the garden, a long-ago love knot with a central heart (a token of Richard Churche's affection for his young wife). Today the house is widely known and recommended for its quality meals. A table d'hôte luncheon is offered for £6 ($11.70), and a set dinner for £12 ($23.40). You need to reserve a table, especially for dinner (tel. Nantwich 65933). Guests dine at candlelit tables. The mansion is "open to view" throughout the day for 40p (78¢), and refreshments are available.

3. Liverpool

Liverpool, with its famous waterfront on the Mersey River, is a great shipping port and industrial center that gave the world everybody from Fannie Hill to the Beatles. King John launched it on its road to glory when he granted it a charter in 1207, and it quickly became a port for shipping men and materials to Ireland. At the time Victoria came to the throne, Liverpool had become Britain's biggest port.

Liverpudlians, as they are called, are rightly proud of their city, with its new hotels, two cathedrals, shopping and entertainment complexes (as exemplified by St. John's Centre, a modern pedestrian precinct), and the parks and open spaces (2400 acres in and around the city, including Sefton Park with its Palm House). Liverpool's main shopping street, Church, is traffic free for most of the day.

Consecrated in 1967, the **Metropolitan Cathedral of Christ the King** contains more stained glass than any other, 25,000 square feet in 300 shades. It was built in only four years.

Among Liverpool's historic buildings, **St. George's Hall,** designed by a 24-year-old architect who never saw it realized, was completed in 1854. It has been called "England's finest public building." It contains law courts, and in the rear are pleasantly laid-out gardens.

Many visitors head for Liverpool these days just to see one attraction, the great new Anglican edifice, the **Cathedral Church of Christ,** completed 74 years after it was begun in 1903. On a rocky eminence overlooking the Mersey River, the cathedral might possibly be the last Gothic-style one to be built on earth. Dedicated to Queen Elizabeth in 1979, it is the largest church in the country (the fifth largest in the world). England's poet laureate, Sir John Betjeman, hailed it as "one of the great buildings of the world." Its vaulting under the tower is 175 feet high, the highest in the world, and its length of 619 feet is second only to that of St. Peter's in Rome. The architect who won a competition in 1903 for the building's design was Giles Scott. He later went on to rebuild the House of Commons, gutted by bombs after World War II. He personally laid the last stone on the highest tower pinnacle.

Want to visit the early Liverpool beginnings of the Beatles? In Mathew Street, just a few yards from the former site of the Cavern, their original stomping ground, is **Cavern Mecca,** the Beatles museum, information center, and souvenir shop.

Further information about Liverpool and souvenirs of the city are available from the Tourist Information Centre, opposite Lime Street Railway Station.

WHERE TO STAY: **Adelphi Hotel,** Ranelagh Place (tel. Liverpool 7097200), a British Transport hotel, is "the grand hotel" of Liverpool, known for its good rooms and fine cuisine. Past the elegant entrance, you enter a world of marble corridors, molded ceilings, and dark polished wood. However, these traditional features are complemented by a range of modern facilities, including a swimming pool, squash courts, sauna, and sun-bed.

The new Radleys Restaurant is open seven days a week until 10 p.m. for breakfast, lunch, and dinner. For dinner here, you can pay from £5 ($9.75) to as much as £20 ($39) for two persons. In the basement of the hotel is Steiners Hairdressing Salon for both men and women. Nearly all the hotel bedrooms have private bath, color TV, and phone, and are well furnished and attractively maintained, costing from £21 ($40.95) to £33 ($64.35) in a single, from £30 ($58.50) to £40 ($78) in a twin or double, the more expensive tabs for units with private baths.

Holiday Inn, Paradise Street (tel. Liverpool 7090181), is large and modern, just what you'd expect. In the center of the city, it is one of the most comfortable hotels in Liverpool, if you like its particular brand of plush modernity. Close to the shopping and commercial area, the hotel offers 273 bedrooms, each with private tiled bath, color TV (showing free in-house movies), radio, and direct-dial phone, plus individually controlled heating and air conditioning. Each of the roomy bedrooms has two double beds. Rates are £29.50 ($57.53) in a single, from £39 ($76.05) in a double, including a full English breakfast. There's a spacious lounge bar that is most inviting, and, in addition, guests can enjoy a heated indoor pool, complete with its own mini-gymnasium and sauna. Guests gravitate to either the Spyglass or the Warehouse for a drink before dinner in the well-appointed Chez Jacques.

St. George's Hotel, Lime Street (tel. Liverpool 7097090), a Trusthouses Forte hotel, was opened in the early 1970s in a modern shopping district, known as the St. John's Precinct development scheme, directly opposite Lime Street Station. In the heart of Liverpool, it is well run and of an international high standard, with color-coordinated bedrooms, 155 in all, each with a private bath, color TV, razor socket, phone, and coffeemaker. Singles range in price from £30 ($58.50), and doubles go from £38 ($74.10). The large restaurant on the second floor has a modern look and an impressive menu of international dishes. There's also a coffeeshop for quick snacks or grills.

WHERE TO EAT: In food, **Jenny's Seafood Restaurant,** the Old Ropery, Fenwick Street (tel. Liverpool 2360332), is consistently good. In the vicinity of the harbor, it has a basement room that is both pleasantly decorated and softly illuminated. All this forms a backdrop for the good-tasting fresh seafood which is brought in daily. Everything we've sampled has been of fine quality and well prepared. The service, on our latest rounds, was excellent. Expect to pay about £12 ($23.40) to £14 ($27.30) per person. The restaurant is closed for lunch on Saturday and all day on Sunday, but is open otherwise until 2:30 p.m. for lunch, serving dinner from 6 to 9:30 p.m.

In a much more elegant, luxurious bracket, the **Oriel**, Oriel Building, Water Street (tel. Liverpool 2364664), presents a large menu of superb dishes, mainly fish, but with some excellent game and meat dishes as well. The special dishes of the place are lobster, turbot, scampi, and sole. You can choose from about ten different sorts of sole. The vegetables are always the freshest possible. Good ingredients are competently cooked, and the service is attentive. The backdrop consists of silver silk-textured wallpaper and a water garden lit at night. A set luncheon costs £9 ($17.55), but in the evening you can expect to pay from £16 ($31.20) per person. The Oriel doesn't service lunch on Saturday, and is closed all day on Sunday and for three weeks in August. Otherwise, it is open for lunch until 2 p.m., serving dinner until 10 p.m.

CUMBRIA

Driving in the wilds of this northwestern shire is fine for a start, but the best activity is walking, which is an art—practiced here by both young and old with a crooked stick. Don't go out without a warning, however. There is a great deal of rain and heavy mist. Sunny days are few. When the mist starts to fall, try to be near an old inn or pub, where you can drop in for a visit and warm yourself beside an open fireplace. You'll be carried back to the good old days, as many places in Cumbria have valiantly resisted change. If you strike up a conversation with a local, just make sure you know something about hounds.

The far northwestern part of the shire, bordering Scotland, used to be called Cumberland. Now part of Cumbria, it is generally divided geographically into a trio of segments: the Pennines dominating the eastern sector (loftiest point at Cross Fell, nearly 3000 feet high); the Valley of Eden; and the lakes and secluded valleys of the west—by far the most interesting. The area, so beautifully described by the Romantic Lake Poets, enjoys many literary associations. Wordsworth ("when all at once I saw . . . a host of golden daffodils") was a native son, having been born at Cockermouth.

The largest town is Carlisle in the north—not a very interesting tourist center, but possible as a base for explorations to **Hadrian's Wall.** The wall stretches from Wallsend in the east to Bowness on the Solway, a distance of about 75 miles, It was built in the second century A.D. by the Romans.

4. Kendal

A simple market town, Kendal contains the ruins of a castle where Catherine Parr, the last wife of Henry VIII, was born. With its 13th-century parish church, Kendal makes for a good stopover en route to the lakeside resort of Windermere, about nine miles away. Kendal is 270 miles from London.

The town was also associated with George Romney, the 18th-century portrait painter (Lady Hamilton his favorite subject) who used to travel all over the Lake District trying to get someone to sit for him. He held his first exhibition in Kendal, married and had children there. He deserted them in 1762, not returning until the end of his life. He died at Kendal in 1802.

WHERE TO STAY: **Woolpack Hotel,** Stricklandgate (tel. Kendal 23852), offers every modern convenience in this sprawling, motel-like establishment.

Many of the 58 rooms are equipped with private bath, and some are suites which are ideal for families of three or more. Children under 12 are accommodated at no charge when sharing their parents' rooms. All the rooms are decorated in bright colors to add to the already cheerful atmosphere. Convenient parking is provided just outside. Singles range upward from £23 ($44.85), while doubles begin at £35 ($68.25). VAT, service, and a full English breakfast are included in the tab.

5. Windermere

The grandest of the lakes is Windermere, the largest one in England, whose shores wash up against the adjoining towns of **Bowness** and **Windermere.** Both of these lakeside resorts lie on the eastern shore of Windermere. A ferry service connects Hawkshead and Bowness. Windermere, the resort, is the end of the railway line. From either town, you can climb up Orrest Head in less than an hour for a panoramic view of England's lakeland. From that vantage point, you can even see Scafell Pike, rising to a height of 3210 feet—the peak pinnacle in all of England.

Windermere Steamboat Museum, Rayrigg Road, Windermere (tel. Windermere 5565), is one of the most delightful working museums it has been my lot to visit for many years. It was founded and developed by George Pattinson, who discovered the fascination of steam many years ago and now has probably the best and most comprehensive collection of steamboats in the country. The wet boatsheds house some dozen boats, including the Veteran *Dolly,* probably the oldest mechanically powered boat in the world, dating from around 1850. It was raised from the lake bed in the early 1960s and run for several years with the original boiler and steambox.

Also displayed is the *Espérance,* an iron steam yacht registered with Lloyds in 1869, as well as many elegant Victorian steam launches and ferry boats. Attached to the boathouses is the speedboat *Jane,* dating from 1938, the first glider-plane to take off from the water in 1943, and the hydroplane racer *Cookie*—all jostling Beatrix Potter's rowing boat and other Lakeland craft for position.

There's a small shop selling books, postcards, and souvenirs of the historic craft. The museum is open from Easter to October, charging an admission of 95p ($1.85) for adults and 50p (98¢) for children. The *Osprey* is regularly in steam, and visitors can make a 40-minute trip on the lake for £1.50 ($2.93) for adults and £1.20 ($2.34) for children.

It's also possible to make trips on Ullswater and on Coniston, and there is regular steamer service around Windermere, the largest of the lakes, which serves the outlying villages as well as operating for visitors in summer. Ken Crowther is curator. He retired there in recent times, and is totally absorbed in the craft and concept of the museum.

WHERE TO STAY AND DINE: Miller Howe Hotel, Rayrigg Road (tel. Windermere 2536), serves theatrically presented meals with dramatic flourish. This inn bears the unique imprint of its creator, former actor John Tovey. At the beginning of the 1970s, he selected a country estate overlooking Lake Windermere, with views of the Langdale Peaks, and converted it to provide stylish accommodations and an exquisite cuisine.

His large, graciously furnished rooms have names—no number—and he treats each guest as if he or she were invited to a house party. Each accommodation is provided with binoculars to help absorb the view better, and even copies

THE LAKE DISTRICT

NORTHUMBERLAND

CARLISLE

DURHAM

PENRITH

MARYPORT

WORKINGTON

KESWICK

CUMBRIA

GRASMERE

GOSFORTH

HAWKSHEAD

CONISTON

KENDAL

WINDERMERE

RAVENGLASS

GRANGE OVER SANDS

NORTH YORKSHIRE

BARROW

LANCASTER

HEYSHAM

LANCASHIRE

W. YORK-SHIRE

BLACKPOOL

BURNLEY

PRESTON

BLACKBURN

ENGLAND

WALES

LONDON

GREATER MANCHESTER

MERSEYSIDE

of *Punch* from the 1890s. Antiques are used lavishly throughout the house. Rates per person, including a full English breakfast and dinner, range from £40 ($78) to £57 ($111.15), depending on the plumbing and the view. The hotel is closed from mid-December to mid-March. The public rooms, such as the lounge and library, are lushly decorated, evoking London sophistication.

Dinner at Miller Howe is worth the drive up from London. It's a joyful and satisfying experience. While Tovey is famed as a pastry chef, he is equally known for his original appetizers and main dishes. Even if you can't stay the night, at least consider a meal here. The set meal costs £15 ($29.25). Regional dishes using local produce are a special feature. You might try Lake District lamb, fresh salmon, game pies (in season), Lancashire cheese, and Cumbria sausage. The lettuce and fennel soup with bacon is superb. Coats and ties are worn in the dining room. Dinners are served at 8:30 p.m. only; at 7:30 and 9:30 on Saturday. You're allowed half an hour for menu selections and apéritifs.

Overnight guests can request a picnic lunch, packed with goodies, including homemade rolls and quiches.

Langdale Chase Hotel, on the A591 between Windermere and Ambleside (tel. Ambleside 2201), is a great old lakeside house—built for grandeur—comparable to a villa on Lake Como, Italy. The story goes back to 1930 when the dynamic Ms. Dalzell and her mother took over the country estate, with its handsomely landscaped gardens, and decided to accept paying guests while retaining an uncommercial house-party atmosphere. Waterskiing, rowing, lake bathing, tennis, croquet on the grounds, and fishing attract the sports-minded. The per-person rate for B&B ranges from £18 ($35.10) to £25.75 ($50.21). The bedrooms are skillfully furnished, with excellent pieces.

The interior of the Victorian stone château, with its many gables, balconies, large mullioned windows, and terraces, is a treasure house of antiques. The main lounge hall looks like a setting for one of those English drawing-room comedies. The house was built in part with bits and pieces salvaged from the destruction of a nearby abbey and castle—hence, the ecclesiastical paneling. On the walls are distinctive paintings, mostly Italian primitives, although one is alleged to be a Van Dyck.

The dining room ranks among the finest in the Lake District—with guests selecting tables which are good vantage points for lake viewing. The cuisine is highly personal, mostly a liberated English fare, supported by a fine wine list. Open to nonresidents, the dining room charges £6.50 ($12.68) for a set lunch, £12 ($23.40) for a set six-course dinner. Next to the dining room is a cocktail bar, opening onto the terrace through two French windows. In this room are some old prints of the Lake District which have been collected over the years.

If you'd like a holiday apartment, I'd suggest **The Heaning** (tel. Windermere 3453), a fabulous place to stay just outside the village. The housekeeping units are well designed, well furnished, and well equipped, and the couple who run it, Mr. and Mrs. Coates, are delightful. Their country residence is set in its own grounds on some six acres of land, including formal gardens. Surrounded by Lakeland farms, the house provides unspoiled views of the Fells and Pennines. The Heaning lies only one mile from Windermere station, and it's approached by a secluded minor lane off the A591.

Self-contained apartments are tastefully furnished and spacious, costing in high season from £73 ($142.35) to £151 ($294.95) weekly. The lower price is for two persons, the higher price for anywhere from four to six persons.

Visitors can enjoy the gardens, and there's a separate play area for children. Fresh farm milk is delivered daily.

LAKE DISTRICT TOURS: Mountain Goat Tours, Victoria Street, Windermere (tel. Windermere 5161), is one of the most enterprising ideas I have come across. Begun in 1972 by Chris Taylor, who had a strong desire to start his own business after spending some years in Australia, it has become firmly established in the Lake District as the fell-walking tours. For the less energetic, Mountain Goat has minibus tours that take you to many of the otherwise inaccessible beauty spots of the area.

For a full day's tour to the homes of the poet Wordsworth, the cost is £9 ($17.55) per person and includes the entrance fees. You retrace the poet's life and places he has lived. This is called the In the Steps of Wordsworth Tour.

Another possibility for the more energetic is the tour up Hardknott and Wrynose Passes to Eskdale, following the old Roman route to Hardknott Roman Fort, where a pub lunch can be had in Eskdale. You can take a ride on the miniature Ravenglass-Eskdale railway before having tea at Ravenglass and returning over the fells to Duddon Bridge, Coniston, and Windermere. The cost is £8 ($15.60) per person.

Other tours visit Hawkshead and the home of Beatrix Potter for £4.75 ($9.26) for a half day, increasing to £8 ($15.60) for a full-day tour of Grasmere, Keswick, and Buttermere.

Mountain Goat Tours will also arrange two- or three-night stopovers in the Lakes, including a special discount rail ticket from London or wherever. Excluding travel to the lakes, the cost of two nights in a guest house, a full-day tour by minibus, a boat trip on Windermere, and taxis to and from Windermere coach or bus station is £55 ($107.25) per person. An experienced guide can be hired for this tour. For a hotel with a bath or shower, the cost rises to £82 ($160) per person. Both tariffs are for half board.

There are also week-long walking tours available, providing you are properly clad and reasonably fit, from £128 ($249.60). Required equipment can be hired locally. However, if you arrive without a suitable kit for this tour they will not take you out, for it is an area that calls for proper equipment. I suggest you inquire about what you will need for these specialized tours directly from Mountain Goat.

6. Ambleside

A good and idyllic retreat, Ambleside is one of the major centers attracting pony-trekkers, fell-hikers, and rock-scalers. The charms are essentially there year round, even in late autumn when it's fashionable to sport a mackintosh. Ambleside is superbly perched, at the top of Lake Windermere. Traditions are entrenched, especially at the Rushbearing Festival, an annual event.

WHERE TO STAY AND DINE: Rothay Manor, Rothay Bridge (tel. Ambleside 3605), at the edge of Ambleside, is like a French country inn, where the sparkling star is the cuisine, combined with a dedicated chef in the kitchen, well-selected French wines, and 12 comfortable, centrally heated bedrooms with bath or shower, phones, and color TVs. All this is possible because of a very special person, Mrs. Bronwen M.G. Nixon, who has installed herself in this gracious Regency house, bringing her energy, imagination, and taste to bear on its operation. She charges from £24 ($46.80) to £27 ($52.65) per person for B&B. The rooms are individually decorated, with a free use of vibrant colors. Most of them have shuttered French doors opening onto a sun balcony, with a mountain view. Throughout the estate you'll find an eclectic combination of antiques (some Georgian blended harmoniously with Victorian), flowers, and "get-lost" armchairs.

The manor is also a restaurant open to nonresidents. Mrs. Nixon's spacious dining room is decked with antique tables and chairs. Her appointments are flawless, and incorporate fine crystal, silver, and china. At night candles burn in silver holders. Lunches seven days a week feature soup, cold meats, a variety of salads, desserts, cheeses, and coffee.

Dinners, from 7:30 till 9 p.m., are more ambitious, costing £14 ($27.30). Here is a typical selection: homemade chicken liver pâté laced with brandy, celery and almond soup, filet Talleyrand (beef filet rolled in a mirepoix of vegetables, baked in a flaky pastry case and served with a rich Espagnole sauce), an exciting selection of homemade desserts, fresh fruit, and a cheese trolley. Afterward good coffee awaits you in the lounges. All prices include VAT.

In the kitchen Mrs. Nixon directs everything herself with a wise and loving eye, and has trained a friendly young staff to produce the meals. I've saved the best news for last: that is, Mrs. Nixon herself, a forthright conversationalist and (that rarity) a sensitive listener—a winning combination.

Riverside Hotel, Gilbert Scar, Under Loughrigg (tel. Ambleside 2395), is a small country hotel beautifully situated in a lovely and peaceful riverside setting. It's secluded on a quiet lane away from traffic noise and yet is only a few minutes' walk to the center of Ambleside. Loughrigg Fell climbs behind the hotel, providing walking for the enthusiast amid superb scenery. The Riverside accommodates up to 20 guests, and bedrooms go for approximately £20 ($39) per person, inclusive of dinner and a full English breakfast. The hotel is owned by Gillian and Alan Rhone. Gillian cooks the meals, specializing in traditional English cooking with generous portions. Breakfast is served at 9 a.m. and dinner at 7 p.m.

READERS' GUEST HOUSE SELECTION: "We were treated to the finest hospitality we've found throughout our entire six-month visit to Europe, when we discovered a truly fantastic place to stay with John and Sue Horne at **Horseshoe Guest House,** Rothay Road (tel. Ambleside 2000). An architect from London by profession, John has left the big city life behind and is creating an enviable lifestyle for Sue and himself in the Lake Country. For £16 ($31.20) per night for a double, you can stay in a large and immaculate room, bath down the hall, in a former church-owned residence which is undergoing a complete restoration by the Hornes. Five new bedrooms, all with private shower, toilet, and balcony, have been added, and another £1 ($1.95) is charged for these units. John, an avid outdoorsman and member of the local Mountain Rescue Squad, has a complete knowledge of the surrounding area and he will gladly direct you to places of interest. Sue was up bright and early in the morning to fix us a fine breakfast of eggs, bacon, and sausage, all included in the room cost" (Phil Pritulsky and Pauline Dainty, Norfolk Va.).

7. Rydal

Between Ambleside and Wordsworth's former retreat at Grasmere is Rydal, a small village on one of the smallest lakes, Rydal Water. Wordsworth lived at Rydal Mount, overlooking the lake, from 1813 until his death in 1850. The house is now a museum. The village is noted for its sheepdog trials at the end of summer.

WHERE TO STAY: Rydal Lodge (tel. Ambleside 3208), beside the roadway between Ambleside and Grasmere, is a good center for walking and touring the whole of the Lake District. The Rothay River runs beside the pleasant and secluded gardens; and Rydal Water, a beautiful lake, is at the end of the garden. Mr. and Mrs. Warren provide meals of high quality, and the menus are well planned. Strawberries and other fruit from the garden are provided in season, and the lodge has a license to serve wine with main meals. The bedrooms are equipped with hot and cold running water, shaving points, electric blankets, heaters, and innerspring mattress, and there are two bathrooms and a shower room. There is also a private car park. Terms are from £11 ($21.45) for B&B, with dinner costing from £6.50 ($12.68), including VAT and service. Rydal Lodge is of historical interest. Matthew Arnold stayed here, and it is connected with Harriet Martineau. The older part of the house was an inn in 1655.

8. Grasmere

On a lake that bears its name, Grasmere was the home of Wordsworth from 1799 to 1808. The nature poet lived with his sister, Dorothy (the English writer and diarist) at **Dove Cottage,** which is now a museum administered by Dove Cottage Trust. Wordsworth, who followed Southey as poet laureate, died in the spring of 1850, and was buried in the graveyard of the village church at Grasmere. The other tenant of Dove Cottage was Thomas De Quincey *(Confessions of an English Opium Eater).* For a combined ticket costing £1.50 ($2.93) for adults, half price for children, you can visit both Dove Cottage and the **Wordsworth Museum,** with its collection of his manuscripts and memorabilia, as well as a collection of portraits of the Wordsworth Circle, including Lamb, Coleridge, Keats, and Hazlitt, from the National Portrait Gallery. The trust property is open weekdays from 9:30 a.m. to 1 p.m. and from 2 to 5 p.m., Easter to October. Off-season, the properties open at 10 a.m. and close at 4:30 p.m. and remain shut entirely from mid-November to March 1.

A SHOPPING RECOMMENDATION: It isn't often that you get the opportunity to watch the material that you will later purchase being made. But at **Chris Reekie's,** in the Old Coach House at Grasmere (tel. Grasmere 221), you can see Mr. Reekie or one of his sons, perhaps young apprentices, working at the traditional fly-shuttle loom which Mr. Reekie brought from his own apprenticeship employers in Selkirk. For about the last 30 years, he has been weaving tartans and fine woolens for direct sale, thus keeping the prices down. His charges are below those in Scotland. Apart from a vast range of ready-made cloths and clothing, he will make to measure a garment within 14 days. If that is too long to wait, he will send articles anywhere in the world, so you can buy for relatives and friends.

FOOD AND LODGING: In this hiking and rock-scaling center, you'll find the following recommendations, beginning first with the most expensive, then descending in price level.

Michael's Nook, outside Grasmere (turn off the A591 at the Swan Hotel; tel. Grasmere 496), is a country-house hotel, once a private residence, standing in its own secluded garden of three acres. A Lakeland home of stone, it contains much fine mahogany woodwork and paneling, exemplified by its elegant staircase. Throughout the house, owned by Mr. R. S. E. Gifford, are many fine antiques, which are only enhanced by the mellow glow of log fires or the discreetly placed vases of flowers.

The handsomely decorated bedrooms, ten in all, are individually furnished with grace and care. All are equipped with phones, private baths or showers, and TV sets. The minimum booking is usually three nights. The tariffs range from £36 ($70.20) to £45 ($87.75) per person per night and include a five-course dinner, bed, early-morning tea, and an English or a continental breakfast, and VAT. After only a few hours here, guests become acquainted with Mr. Gifford's cats and other pets. The feeling is very much that of living in a private home.

A limited number of guests can be accommodated in the dining room, and advance reservations are essential. Great care and an attention to detail go into the excellent English cooking, and the best of fresh ingredients are used whenever available. An attractive young staff serves the fine food, which costs from £11.50 ($22.43) for lunch, £14 ($27.30) for dinner, VAT included. The menus change, but you might have an appetizer of quiche of guinea fowl and asparagus, a first for me. Main courses include such dishes as home-baked Cumberland ham with mustard sauce, loin of lamb with green-pepper stuffing, and poached Loch trout with hollandaise sauce.

The **Wordsworth Hotel** at Grasmere (tel. Grasmere 592) stands right in the middle of the village. Mr. Gifford of Michael's Nook has a new venture, and this is it. An old stone Lakeland house (once the 19th-century Rothay Hotel) has been gutted and rebuilt to provide large bedrooms with views of the fells and river, as well as modern bath, TV, phone, and "comfy" chairs. The rate of £18.50 ($36.08) per person includes a full breakfast and VAT. They even have a four-poster bedroom at £28.50 ($55.58) in the modern part of the building which looks older than the new, with its beams and dormer windows. The original master bedroom has a gorgeous Victorian bathroom, with a brass towel rail and polished pipes and taps.

There are several lounges, with sink-in armchairs grouped around log fires. A buffet lunch is served in the cocktail lounge, including the chef's hot dish of the day—perhaps ragoût, lasagne, or curry. The most expensive item is only £2.25 ($4.39).

A set dinner at £8.75 ($17.06) is likely to include a light fruit or vegetable appetizer, then soup, a choice of two meat dishes, then dessert or cheese, along with coffee and mints. The à la carte menu is more ambitious, and a three-course meal of, say, camembert and mushroom crêpe, medallions of beef filet cooked with mustard, shallots, and beer, or liver with avocado and apple flambéed in Calvados, followed by black cherries flamed in brandy on ice cream, will cost around £8.50 ($16.58). Each dish is carefully explained on the menu so you know what you're getting.

After all this food, the hotel has a heated swimming pool, quite large, and there's also a sauna and a solarium.

White Moss House, Rydal Water (tel. Grasmere 295), is an old Lakeland cottage off the main A591 between Grasmere and Rydal Water. It overlooks the lake and the fells, where you're welcomed as a house guest to be pampered with morning tea in bed, your bedcovers turned down at night, and your culinary preferences remembered and adhered to.

The rooms are comfortably furnished and well heated in nippy weather. In all there are only five accommodations, so advance booking is essential. These units have baths en suite and go for £32 ($62.40) per person nightly including an elegant, if large, breakfast and a dinner to satisfy a gourmet.

There's also Brockstone, their cottage annex, a five-minute drive along the road, where two, three, or four guests can be accommodated in utter peace.

Dinner is a leisurely affair beginning at 7:30 p.m. You're served five courses—perhaps a celery and almond soup, then a fish soufflé, followed by a roast of lamb with an orange and red currant sauce, or quail with a chicken and brown rice stuffing, accompanied by a selection of intriguing vegetable dishes, cheesey potatoes, eggplant with lime, and cauliflower with herb cheese. For dessert, I hope Mrs. Beeton's chocolate pudding is featured, or the homemade brown bread ice cream, followed by English cheese and homemade "oat biscuits," coffee, and mints.

If you're not a resident, dinner will cost from £12 ($23.40) without wines, but you must reserve a table early for, as you can imagine, residents very rarely pass up a chance to eat in. There isn't much space in the dining room.

Mrs. Butterworth has been in charge of the kitchen for some years now, and her cookery has made her renowned throughout the country. You may be lucky enough to catch one of her rare appearances on TV, discussing and promoting English country cuisine. All of the above rates include VAT, but service is left to the discretion of the guest. They don't take dogs, and they make no reductions for children.

Red Lion Hotel (tel. Grasmere 456) is a 200-year-old coaching inn in the heart of the village, owned by the Fawthrops, Mr. John and Mr. Stewart. It's only a short stroll to the waterside cottage once occupied by Wordsworth, and it's assumed that the poet often stopped in for a meal, a drink, or to warm himself by the fire. A rambling informal structure, it is imbued with a sophisticated rustic decor. In the spacious residents' lounge, the rugged stone fireplace is two-sided. Two of the three bars are paneled in mahogany, with refectory tables and chairs. In the dining room, you will be served some of the finest fare in the district: a set meal costing from £5 ($9.75) to £9 ($17.55). A twin ranges from £32 ($62.40) without bath, from £36 ($70.20) with bath, and a single room is priced from £17 ($33.15) without bath to £24 ($46.80) with bath. Breakfast is included in the room rates, as are VAT and service. There is an elevator serving all 36 bedrooms, 21 of which contain private baths. As a family-run hotel, the Grasmere Red Lion maintains a personal atmosphere.

Swan Hotel (tel. Grasmere 551) has been renovated so that only the shell of the old building remains. However, there have been inns on this site for 300 years. Wordsworth mentioned it in *The Waggoner*. In fact, in one of the lounges is the poet's tapestry chair. The 31 rooms contain built-in furniture and good beds. Singles without bath rent for £21 ($40.95), going up to £24 ($46.80) with bath. Bathless doubles cost £29 ($56.55), rising to £33 ($64.35) with bath, these tariffs including service and VAT. The restaurant provides both table d'hôte and à la carte meals. A set luncheon goes for £6.50 ($12.68); dinner, £9 ($17.55).

Meadow Brow (tel. Grasmere 275) is an old country house perched halfway up a hillside just a mile from the center of the village. Commanding superb views of the surrounding hills, the stone-and-timber building stands in two acres of secluded gardens nourished by a tiny stream. The house is furnished with antiques, and on cooler evenings you can relax by the open fire in the sitting room. The small library is stacked with books on the history and geology of the Lake District. All the bedrooms are comfortably and thoughtfully furnished, right down to the electric blankets for those colder nights. Every evening except Wednesday, the hosts, Mr. and Mrs. Bateman, serve a four-course dinner, along with good conversation and enjoyable wines. The cost for dinner, bed, and breakfast is £16.50 ($32.16) per person per night.

9. Hawkshead and Coniston

Discover for yourself the village of Hawkshead, with its 15th-century grammar school where Wordsworth went to school for eight years (he carved his name on a desk that still remains). Near Hawkshead, in the vicinity of Esthwaite Water, is the 17th-century **Hill Top Farm**, former home of Beatrix Potter, the author of the Peter Rabbit books, who died during World War II.

At **Coniston,** four miles away from Hawkshead, you can visit the village associated with John Ruskin. Coniston is a good base for rock climbing. The Coniston "Old Man" towers in the background at 2633 feet, giving mountain climbers one of the finest views of the Lake District.

Ruskin moved to his home, **Brantwood,** on the east side of Coniston Water in 1872 and lived there until his death in 1900. The house today is open for visitors to view much Ruskiniana, including some 175 pictures by him. Also displayed is his coach and boat, the *Jumping Jenny.*

An exhibition illustrating the work of W. J. Linton is laid out in his old printing room. Linton was born in England in 1812 and died at New Haven, Connecticut, in 1897. Well known as a wood engraver and for his private press, he lived at Brantwood, where he set up his printing business in 1853. He published *The English Republic,* a newspaper and review, before emigrating to America in 1866, where he set up his printing press in 1870. The house is owned and managed by the Education Trust, a self-supporting registered charity. It is open daily from Easter to the end of October from 11 a.m. to 5:30 p.m.; closed on Saturday. The admission is £1 ($1.95) for adults, 50p (98¢) for children. Part of the 250-acre estate is also open as a nature trail, costing 35p (68¢) for adults, 20p (39¢) for children. A special £2.50 ($4.88) family day ticket (mother and/or father and children up to the age of 16) covers the house and nature trail. There is a gift and Ruskin book shop, and tea and coffee are available.

Literary fans may want to pay a pilgrimage to the graveyard of the village church, where Ruskin was buried; his family turned down a chance to have him interred at Westminster Abbey.

ACCOMMODATIONS: **Ivy House Hotel,** Main Street (tel. Hawkshead 204), is a friendly Georgian house that warms the austere Lake District. It's an ideal headquarters from which to branch out for visits on Lake Windermere. If you stay anywhere from one to three days, the B&B rate is £10 ($19.50) per person daily. Cheaper terms are quoted for longer stays. Dinner, bed, and breakfast cost £13.50 ($26.33). The hospitable proprietors, Mr. and Mrs. Williams, are used to welcoming overseas visitors, and Mrs. Williams tries to take a personal interest in all her lodgers. But because of her charming house and lovely situation, she is heavily booked—so it's imperative that you reserve well in advance. Some other points worth noting: All the rooms are centrally heated and have hot and cold running water. A modern, motel-type annex, with unrestricted electric heating, handles overflow guests. The house is open March to the end of October only. Log fires blaze in the lounge in early and late seasons.

10. Keswick

Lying 22 miles north of Windermere, Keswick opens onto Derwentwater, one of the loveliest lakes in the district. Robert Southey, poet laureate, lived for four decades at Greta Hall, and was buried at Crosthwaite Church. Coleridge lived here, too, depending on Southey for financial aid. Sir Hugh Walpole, the novelist, in a different era also resided near Keswick. Keswick is a good center for touring the northern Lake District.

WHERE TO STAY: **Royal Oak Hotel** (tel. Keswick 72965) dates back to the days of Queen Elizabeth I, although the present building more accurately reflects the architecture of the 18th century. As a posting house, it was a favored lakeland retreat of Sir Walter Scott, who is said to have written a section of *Bridal of Triermain* here. The famous hunter, John Peel, and authors Alfred Lord Tennyson and Robert Louis Stevenson also patronized the inn. Now redecorated and modernized under Trusthouses Forte auspices, the hotel is a cheerful and atmospheric place at which to stay. Rates are £16.50 ($32.16) for a bathless single, £23 ($44.85) for a single with bath. A bathless double or twin-bedded room costs £26.50 ($51.68), £33 ($64.35) with bath. Breakfast is extra, but service and VAT are included.

Borrowdale, Borrowdale, near Keswick (tel. Borrowdale 224), is a typical lakeside stone building with log fires—even in summer—to welcome you. Its rooms are comfortable, many opening onto lovely views. All have private baths and showers, going for £23 ($44.85) per person, including dinner, bed, breakfast, service, and VAT. The management likes you to stay just one or two nights or for more than a week; otherwise, the charges are increased a little.

The main attraction of Borrowdale is its restaurant. Lunches are offered only on Sunday, costing from £5.80 ($11.31); and on other days you can order bar snacks in the £1.50 ($2.93) to £4 ($7.80) range. Dinner at £10 ($19.50) might begin with avocado and crab salad, then local roast pheasant or a specialty dish such as wienerschnitzel, piccata milanese, or marha gulyas, all served with the appropriate vegetables or a salad, and potatoes. For dessert, the choice is bewildering—French peach flan, chilled Bavarian cream, profiteroles, to name only a few. You dine by candlelight on silver service, attended to by an efficient, friendly staff. The restaurant is run by Gunter Fidrmuc and his wife, Jean.

Skiddaw Hotel (tel. Keswick 72071) has a bone-white, clean-cut facade, and is built right onto the sidewalk in the heart of Keswick. The owners, Mr. and Mrs. Kitchin, have used natural elements in the interiors with walls of simple pine or rugged fieldstone. The meals are totally English, well prepared. The bedrooms are compact and eye-catching, renting at prices that vary according to the season and the view. The B&B rate ranges from £13 ($23.35) to £16.85 ($32.86) per person, the top price for a unit with bath, including VAT. Every room has hot and cold running water; the beds are bouncy soft, and the linen as clean as the lake air. Guests gather in the stone-walled lounge, or else in the pine-paneled cocktail bar.

A set four-course dinner goes for £5 ($9.75), the price going up to £6.50 ($12.68) for a six-course meal. A three-course Sunday lunch (always a roast) is £4.50 ($8.78). Lunch on other days is à la carte, but there is always a chef's special such as Lancashire hotpot, lamb cutlets, or pork chops, each platter costing from £2 ($3.90), including a vegetable.

The George Hotel, St. John Street (tel. Keswick 72076), is a wayside tavern that has bedded down many a traveler who pulled in on a horse-drawn coach. Once associated with Coleridge, it brings a comfort and pleasure to the modern pilgrim. Guests still gather for a warming hot punch in the bar where Wordsworth and Southey met for quiet talks in high-backed settles in front of the fireplace. Modern amenities have been sneaked in, including central heating, electric razor outlets, and hot and cold running water. Six have private baths. Singles rent for £13 ($25.35), the cost going up to £23 ($44.85) in a double, including VAT and a full English breakfast. There is no service charge. Throughout the inn, modern furniture is blended harmoniously with well-chosen antiques.

WHERE TO DINE: The Bay Tree Restaurant and Guest House, 1 Wordsworth St. (tel. Keswick 73313), is an old house on the main Penrith road, lying outside Keswick and overlooking the river and parkland. It has white walls with brown canopies over the windows, plus a glass door through which lights twinkle invitingly. The owner is Mrs. Joyce Shepherd, who is assisted by her sons. Her B&B rate is £7.50 ($14.63) nightly, rising to £10.50 ($20.48) per person for half board.

A few tables in the tiny dining room are open to nonresidents who should reserve a table for dinner between 6:30 and 7 p.m. The cost of a meal is £6.50 ($12.68), and dishes are likely to include ham steaks with a green salad and sauteed potatoes, or else lamb cutlets with a red currant and orange sauce. Appetizers always include a soup or pâté, and for dessert, such delights as black cherries in brandy with fresh cream. Coffee is served in the lounge.

READERS' RESTAURANT SELECTION: "While in Keswick, we chanced upon the **Yan, Tyan, Tethera**, 70 Main St., where we not only had a tasty meal, but a delightful time as well. Simone Boddington is the owner of this small, cozy place, and the feeling is one of being a guest in her house rather than a customer in a restaurant. The cooking and preparing of food is one out in the open, and Simone cuts up and prepares a fresh salad for your table right before your eyes, all the while chatting, joking, and bantering with customers. Summer hours are from noon to 3 p.m. and Tuesday through Sunday evening. In winter it's open from noon to 2:30 p.m. and Thursday, Friday, and Saturday evening, when reservations are necessary. The specialty of the house is shrimp. There are several sauces to accompany it, as well as rolls and that crispy salad already referred to. Featured is casserole of local venison. A typical à la carte dinner, which might include an appetizer of pâté, jumbo shrimp, tossed salad, rolls, cherry pie, and beverage, costs about £9 ($17.55) per person. For lunch, the restaurant serves delightful dishes to satisfy either large or small appetites. Weight watchers and vegetarians will find many satisfying dishes also. Especially popular specialties include savory cheese and prawn platters or a stockpot soup and roll. Draft sherry, lager, and wines are sold at reasonable prices. Reservations for the evening are advisable by telephoning Keswick 72033" (Dave and Jan Gelman, East Longmeadow, Mass.).

11. Bassenthwaite

With its fine stretch of water in the shadow of the 3053-foot Skiddaw, Bassenthwaite makes a good center for exploring the western Lakeland. In the village I have a choice recommendation.

The **Pheasant Inn**, Bassenthwaite Lake, Cockermouth (tel. Bassenthwaite Lake 234), is a 16th-century inn with a neat exterior set against a wooded mountain backdrop. Inside, the bar is wood-paneled and smoke-mellowed. Old hunting prints dot the walls, and real ale is on tap. The beamed dining room is bright and cheerful, with spotless white tablecloths and a menu of good-quality roasts, fish, and poultry with fresh vegetables. A set lunch is £6 ($11.70), a set dinner is £8.50 ($16.58), and the staff will pack you a lunch for £3 ($5.85). There are three pleasant lounges with an open log fire, and fresh flowers abound. The bedrooms are spotless and bright with chintz. Eleven have a bath or shower room attached, and there are electric blankets on the beds. There are also three bedrooms in the annex, which is a bungalow on the grounds. A single without bath is £17 ($33.15), going up to £18.50 ($36.08) with bath. A double without bath costs £33 ($64.35), rising to £35.50 ($69.23) with bath, including VAT, service, and an English breakfast.

12. Ullswater

A seven-mile sheet of water, stretching from Pooley Bridge to Patterdale, Ullswater is the second-largest lake in the district. Incidentally, it was on the shores of Ullswater that Wordsworth saw his "host of golden daffodils." The market town of Penrith lies seven miles to the east, and while housed in the area it is easy to explore several places of archeological interest, such as Hadrian's Wall, east of Carlisle, or Long Meg stone circle near Penrith.

WHERE TO STAY AND EAT: Sharrow Bay Country House Hotel, Howtown, Lake Ullswater, near Penrith (tel. Pooley Bridge 301483). Francis Coulson rules in the kitchen, Brian Sack in the dining room. Mr. Coulson bought this unusual Victorian house in 1949, and, up to then, it'd been a private house, similar to those one might find on Lake Maggiore, with a low angled roof and wide eaves. Sleeping on the floor during restoration work, he had the place rebuilt, turning it into one of England's finest country dining places, and offering accommodations as well, with daily terms in the range of £37 ($72.15) to £55 ($107.25) per person for room, dinner, breakfast, service, and VAT.

The atmosphere is relaxed, the lounges comfortable and handsomely decorated. From the picture window in the drawing room, a view opens across the lake to the Martindale Fells.

The six-course, £19 ($37.05) set menu contains a formidable list of choices. I recently counted 28 appetizers, including the chef's specialty, mousseline of fresh salmon with hollandaise sauce. The carefully chosen main courses seemed designed to make the best of home-grown food items, including roast Lancashire guinea fowl, a roast stuffed shoulder of young English lamb, or even a Cumberland ham from a cold table selection. The dessert selections are among the best you'll find in northwest England, including a fresh strawberry hazelnut brandy cream roulade. A feature as well is the Sharrow homemade cream ices, including prune and armagnac.

Brian Sack is a delightful host, and his staff is friendly and efficient which makes Mr. Coulson's food all the more delectable.

If you're motoring through the area, and not stopping over for the night, I suggest you call in advance and make a reservation for the £15.50 ($30.23) set luncheon.

The hotel offers 29 antique-filled bedrooms, 17 of them in the lodge annex and cottages. In the main hotel, seven rooms have private baths, and 13 of the bedrooms in the cottages have private baths as well. Some rooms open onto views of the lakes, others onto fells and trees. Each of the individually decorated bedrooms has been given a name rather than a number, a nice touch.

Also write or telephone in advance, either for a meal or room. Closed December, January, and February.

COUNTRY LIVING: In the small hamlet of Armathwaite, lying off the M6, between Carlisle and Penrith, **Armathwaite Castle** (tel. Armathwaite 287), is the private home of two brothers, Lloyd and Charles Francis. Lloyd is a history teacher at the local private school, and Charles is a freelance chef. Their house, which is 13th, 14th, 17th, or 19th century, depending on which part you are in, is filled with antiques and lovely furniture. The setting is on 50 acres of parkland, and reached by way of a potholed drive designed to deter all but the most determined.

You must write in advance to reserve for B&B, as they don't take casual visitors. The reason for this is that they must organize the old house for your arrival. There is no central heating, but huge log fires warm the main rooms.

This is real English rural life, where you live an energetic outdoor existence in daytime, relaxing by the fire in the evening. The brothers charge around £17 ($33.15) per person for dinner, bed, and breakfast.

Chapter XV

YORKSHIRE AND NORTHUMBRIA

1. York
2. North Yorkshire
3. West Yorkshire
4. Durham
5. Tyne and Wear
6. Northumberland

UNLESS YOU ENJOY untamed scenery and perhaps a visit to an ancient city or two, such as York, then this huge hunk of northeastern England may hold little interest for you. Many of its towns carry the taint of the Industrial Revolution, but once you've bypassed them, you'll discover heather-covered moors, comprising some of the most dramatic scenery England has to offer.

Let's begin our travels through this area of northeast England in its major historical and ecclesiastical center—

1. York

Few cities in England are as rich in history as York. It is still encircled by its 13th- and 14th-century city walls—about 2½ miles long—with four gates. One of these, Micklegate, once grimly greeted visitors coming up from the south with the heads of traitors. To this day, you can walk on the footpath of the walls of the Middle Ages.

The crowning achievement of York is its Minster or cathedral, which makes the city an ecclesiastical center topped only by Canterbury. In spite of this, York is one of the most overlooked cities on the cathedral circuit. Perhaps foreign visitors are intimidated by the feeling that the great city of northeastern England is too far north. Actually, it lies about 195 miles north of London on the Ouse River, and can easily be tied in with a motor trip to Edinburgh. Or, after visiting Cambridge, a motorist can make a swing through a too-often-neglected cathedral circuit: Ely, Lincoln, then York.

There was a Roman York (Hadrian came this way), then a Saxon York, a Danish York, a Norman York (William the Conqueror slept here), a medieval York, a Georgian York, a Victorian York (the center of a flourishing rail business), and certainly a 20th-century York. A surprising amount of 18th-century York remains, including Richard Boyle's restored Assembly Rooms.

THE SIGHTS: The best way to see York is to go to the **Tourist Information Centre,** DeGrey Rooms, Exhibition Square (tel. York 21756) at 10:15 a.m. and 2:15 p.m. daily from Good Friday to the end of October, where you'll be met by a voluntary guide who will take you on an 1½-hour walking tour of the city, revealing its history and lore through numerous intriguing stories. There is no charge. Additional tours are made at 7:15 p.m. daily during June, July, and August.

At some point in your exploration, you way want to visit **The Shambles,** once the meat-butchering center of York, dating back before the Norman Conquest. But this messy business has given way, and the ancient street survives. It is filled with jewelry stores, cafés, and buildings that huddle so closely together you can practically stand in the middle of the pavement, arms outstretched, and touch the houses on both sides of the street.

Recently, special interest has been focused on discoveries of the Viking era, from 867 to 1066, when the city was known as Jorvik, the Viking capital and a major Scandinavian trade center. During excavations under York's Coppergate prior to development, a wealth of artifacts was unearthed in the late 1970s and early 1980s, including entire houses and workshops of the Viking age. For information on the period of history and treasures found in the excavations, inquire at the **Vikings in England Information Office,** 3 Kings Court, Kings Square (tel. York 32342).

Incidentally, the suffix "gate" used for streets and sites in York is from the Scandinavian word for "street," a holdover from the era when Vikings held sway here.

York Minster

One of the great cathedrals of the world, York Minster traces its origins back to the early seventh century. The present building, however, dates mainly from the 13th century. Like the minster at Lincoln, York Cathedral is characterized by three towers, all built in the 15th century. The central tower is lantern shaped, in the Perpendicular style.

Perhaps the distinguishing characteristic of the cathedral is its medley of stained glass from the Middle Ages—in glorious Angelico blues, ruby reds, forest greens, and ambers. See in particular the large east window, the work of a 15th-century Coventry glass painter. In the north transept is an architectural gem of the mid-13th century, the "Five Sisters," with its lancets. The choir screen, from the late 15th century, has an impressive line-up—everybody from William the Conqueror to the overthrown Henry VI.

The undercroft is open Monday to Saturday from 10 a.m. to dusk (on Sunday from 1 to 4 p.m.), charging adults 40p (78¢) for admission; children 20p (39¢). The central tower is open Monday to Saturday, April to September, from 10:30 a.m. to 7 p.m. (October to March, 10:30 a.m. to 3:30 p.m.), costing adults 75p ($1.46) and children 50p (98¢). The chapter house is open Monday to Saturday, May to October, from 10 a.m., costing adults 20p (39¢); children, 10p (20¢). The crypt is shown during conducted tours only. At an Information Desk in the south aisle of the Minster parties can be put in touch with a guide, if one is available, for a conducted tour. No charge is made, and the guides do not accept gratuities. Gifts toward the maintenance of the Minster are, however, always welcome. For information, telephone York 24426.

York Castle Museum

On Tower Street, the York Castle Museum (tel. York 53611) is one of the finest folk museums in the country. Its unique feature is the shop-flanked Kirkgate, the recreation of a cobbled street, with authentic facades moved to the site (including a silversmith). The present exhibition was inspired mainly by a Dr. Kirk who on his travels through Yorkshire acquired a large collection of antiques and old relics.

Upstairs rooms range from a formal, neoclassic Georgian interior to an overstuffed and heavily adorned Victorian living room. In the debtors' prison, former prison cells have been converted into workshops, such as one cubicle where a blacksmith plies his trade.

On the main floor, a collection of costumes ranges from a gown a Georgian debutante would have worn to a fancy-dress ball all the way to the grandmother of the mini in the post–World War I era. Firearms and armor are also displayed.

Part of the debtors' prison is the Half-Moon Court, a recreation of an Edwardian street, with a gypsy caravan, a sheriff's coach, and a pub that would have attracted the eye of Dickens. Finally, you can visit a mill powered by the water of the Foss River. The museum is open April to September, Monday to Saturday, 9:30 a.m. to 6 p.m.; Sunday, 10 a.m. to 6 p.m. From October to March, hours are from 9:30 to 4:30 p.m. weekdays, 10 a.m. to 4:30 p.m. on Sunday. Admission is £1.20 ($2.34) for adults, 60p ($1.17) for children.

National Railway Museum

The first national museum to be built away from London, the National Railway Museum (tel. York 21261) has attracted millions of visitors. Adapted from an original steam locomotive depot, the museum gives visitors a chance to look under and inside steam locomotives or see how Queen Victoria traveled in luxury. In addition, there's a full-size collection of railway memorabilia, including an early 19th-century clock and penny machines for purchasing tickets to the railway platform. On display are more than 20 full-size locomotives. One, the *Agenoria*, dates from 1829 and is a contemporary of Stephenson's well-known *Rocket*. It's almost identical to the first American locomotive, the *Stourbridge Lion*, brought over from England in 1828. Items on exhibition change from time to time, but a popular display is the *Mallard*, the fastest steam locomotive in the world. Of several royal coaches, the most interesting is the century-old Royal Saloon, in which Queen Victoria rode until her death. It's like a small hotel, with polished wood, silk, brocade, and silver accessories. The museum, on Leeman Road, can be visited weekdays from 10 a.m. to 6 p.m. and on Sunday from 2:30 to 6 p.m. It is closed on bank holidays and some public holidays. Admission is free.

The Treasurer's House

In the Minster Yard, the Treasurer's House stands on a site which dates from Roman times. But the main part of the house was erected in the early 17th century when it became the official residence of the treasurer of York Minster. The house contains much fine furniture and an exhibition with tape and slide shows, illustrating the traditions and some of the interesting people associated with the city and the house. It is open from April until the end of October from 10:30 a.m. to 6 p.m., except on Good Friday. Admission is 90p ($1.76) for adults, 40p (78¢) for children. On some evenings in summer, the house is open from 8 to 10 p.m., when you can enjoy coffee by candlelight in the main hall, then music in the drawing room.

Theatre Royal

Finally, Theatre Royal, St. Leonard's Place (tel. York 23568), is an old traditional theater building with modern additions to house the box office bars and restaurant. It is worth inquiring about the current production as the Royal Shakespeare Company includes York in its tours, the Arts Council presents dance, drama, and opera, and visiting celebrities appear in classics. There is also an excellent resident repertory company.

Seats go from around £1.50 ($2.93) to about £4 ($7.80) when there are visiting celebrities. The glass-walled, ground-floor restaurant does pre- and postperformance meals. The ground-floor snackbar serves coffee, along with such fare as soup, baked potatoes with cheese, ham and baked beans, priced from 80p ($1.56). Upstairs the Salad Bowl does a variety of cold dishes, costing from £1.55 ($3.02) to £2.10 ($4.10). A three-course businessmen's lunch is featured for £1.95 ($3.80), and evening specialties begin at £2.25 ($4.39). You don't have to buy a seat to eat here, and it's quite a relaxing experience to sit inside with your drink and a snack, looking out on the world passing by.

Brass Rubbing

In College Street, formerly Vicarage Lane, is the Treasurer's House which stands on the site of a Roman villa. Nearby is St. Williams's College and the **York Brass Rubbing Centre,** which is open from 10 a.m. to 5 p.m. daily (on Sunday from 12:30 to 5 p.m.). The lovely old building was once the home of William Fitzherbert, great-grandson of William the Conqueror. Now a hive of activity, it offers rubbings ranging in price from 20p (39¢) for a small dog to £2 ($3.90) for an elaborate medieval lady. Or else you can purchase readymade rubbings.

Afterward you can go to **The Restaurant,** across the courtyard, for coffee and homemade cakes and scones, served from 10 a.m. to noon. Lunch is from noon to 2 p.m., and teas follow from 2 to 4 p.m. At lunch, costing from £2.50 ($4.88), you can order such dishes as homemade soups, herb-flavored quiches, steak, kidney, and mushroom pie, chicken paprika, and wine by the glass. Among the more delectable desserts are lemon or chocolate mousse, honey pie, or a butterscotch tart.

An Unguided Walk-About

Starting from York Minster, walk down past Young's Hotel, the birthplace of Guy Fawkes. Turn right into Stonegate, a pedestrian area with lovely old shops, a 12th-century house on the right, and some old coffeehouses. Continue across Davygate into St. Helen's Square to see the Guildhall and Mansion House, then go left into Coney Street, taking a right into Lower Ousegate.

At the beginning of Ouse Bridge, take the steps down to Kings Staithe with a pub on the left for refreshment before continuing on into South Esplanade and St. George's Gardens beside the river.

At the bridge, join the road again, turning left and in front of you stand the Castle Museum, the Assize Courts, and Clifford's Tower. Walk up Tower Street and Clifford Street to Nessgate. Turn right into High Ousegate and continue across Parliament Street to the beginning of the Shambles on the left.

Walk up the Shambles past the attractive shops and ancient buildings to Kings Square, then bear right into Goodramgate. Walk down Goodramgate and, at the end, cross Deangate into College Street with St. William's College on the right. At the end a narrow road leads to the Treasurer's House.

You're now behind the east end of the Minster. Walk around to the west end and then up Bootham Bar, through the city gate and turn left into Exhibition Square. The Art Gallery is on the right, the Tourist Information Centre to the left, and beside it, York's Theatre Royal. Continue down St. Leonard's Street to the crossroads, turning right into Museum Street. Cross the river and go right to join part of the old Roman wall.

A Horse-Drawn Carriage Tour

While in York, what about a 15-minute trip in a horse-drawn Danish carriage around the city? One or two horses pull up to five persons, and an umbrella protects you in case it rains. The cost is 90p ($1.76) for adults and 45p (88¢) for children. Call Mr. B. W. Calam (tel. York 769490) for more information, or else just turn up at the cathedral's west doors where he is likely to be found. He's also available for private rentals, including day country trips for four to six persons, costing about £26 ($50.70) per person up to eight hours. You can stop at country pubs for drinks and farmhouses for tea. He also takes visitors on evening trips, with lantern lights, the price depending on the time.

WHERE TO STAY: My recommendations for rooms and meals follow.

The Upper Bracket

Viking Hotel, North Street (tel. York 59822), is a nine-floor, ultramodern hotel, built in 1968, with a four-story extension completed in 1981. It takes its name from the Viking kingdom of York of 867, but that's the only thing ancient about it. On the banks of the River Ouse, many of the bedrooms and public rooms overlook not only the water but also the Minster in the distance. Douglas Bamber, general manager, has set the following minimum rates: £31.05 ($60.55) for a single room, £43.70 ($85.22) in a double, including breakfast, service, and VAT. The 187 bedrooms, all with private bath, contain such services as TV, tea- and coffee-making facilities, radio, and direct-dial telephone. Breakfast, luncheon, and dinner are available in the Regatta Restaurant and the Carvers' Table. Light snacks and afternoon tea are served all day in Plumes. The three dining areas have adjacent bars.

The Judges Lodging, 9 Lendal (tel. York 23587). The earliest historical fact about this charming house is that it was the home of a certain Dr. Wintringham in 1710. At the beginning of the 19th century it is listed as having been a judges' lodging, used when they traveled north from the London Inns of Justice. In 1979 it was bought by Gerald C. Mason, M.B.E., Her Majesty's consul in Biarritz, and his delightful Hungarian countess wife. Mme la Comtesse was brought up in Paris and has had a very wide experience of hotels. Her touch is evident throughout the elegant building. Drive around the sweeping drive, then up the broad stone steps to the stout front door. You will be greeted by the butler who will register your name and then lead you up a magnificent circular wooden staircase, the only one of its type in the United Kingdom, to one of the bedrooms. All have four-poster beds. If you want to spoil yourself, you can book the large Prince Albert suite, a twin-bedded room with three large windows overlooking the Minster. Prince Albert actually slept in the room once. Hand-embroidered sheets and French embroidered linen in the bathrooms are an additional elegant touch. Each room has a different decor and is named accordingly. One is known as the Queen Mother Room and, in fact, it is with her blessing that the coffee cups you will use at dinner come from Clarence House.

There are two dining rooms, where candles flicker and the carefully trained French staff will attend to your every need. Dinner will cost around £8.50 ($16.58) for four courses, and the experience is worth it. All meat, fish, and vegetables are brought in fresh, and the countess does much of the selecting and cooking. The menu is a mouthwatering selection. Down in the old cellars where they found all sorts of bits of Roman pottery, antique pieces of glass, and other relics of the house's varied past, there is the Cocktail Bar, open to the public. Bar snacks at lunchtime include quiche Lorraine and smoked salmon with brown bread, from £1 ($1.95) to £2.50 ($4.88). Your room will go from £46 ($89.70) a night, for two, to £55 ($107.25), including breakfast and VAT. You may be lucky enough to see one of the three ghosts—the countess has—that of Elizabeth Deltrey who was shut in to stop her eloping with her lover.

Royal Station Hotel (tel. York 53681), outside the city, was built when it was fashionable to stop for the night at a railway station hotel. Owned by British Transport Hotels, it is a mammoth building, not unlike a palace. Most of its 129 bedrooms have private baths. The most expensive rates apply from April 1 to October 31, when a bathless single rents for £20 ($39), a bathless double for £33 ($65.33). With bath, a single goes for £32 ($62.40), a double for £42 ($81.90), including a full breakfast, service, and VAT. The rooms are generally spacious, well furnished, and comfortable. There's an elaborate garden with a central fountain, and surrounding woods. York Minster is only a five-minute walk from the hotel. The public rooms were designed for Victorian grandeur, with high ceilings and miles of carpeting. In the lofty dining room, you can order an à la carte dinner from £7 ($13.65), including VAT and service. With a separate entrance at the side of the hotel, Bess's Coffee Shop offers steaks, omelets, curries, hamburgers, and salads, a good meal costing around £6 ($11.70).

The annex of the Royal Station is the **Friars Garden Hotel** (tel. York 53681), which offers 22 comfortably furnished bedrooms, all with private baths and tea- and coffee-making facilities. Including a full breakfast, service, and VAT, a single rents for £20 ($39), a double for £33 ($64.35).

The Medium-Priced Range

The **Post House,** Tadcaster Road (tel. York 67921), is a Trusthouses Forte enterprise, built on the grounds of a former manor house. Only a mile and a half south of the center of York, it is on the A1036, the main approach to York from the A1 and the south. Although contemporary in design, with picture windows in each bedroom, there are many traditional touches as well. The entrance hall and living room, for example, have authentic York flagstones and a montage of old prints and local family crests. A single in summer rents for £26.50 ($51.68), a double for £38 ($74.10). Service and tax are included, but breakfast is extra. Each room has a single color theme, with such amenities as air conditioning, color TV, radio, and tea- and coffee-making facilities. The Cedar Restaurant has wide-view windows overlooking a magnificent cedar of Lebanon planted many years ago. An international cuisine is offered. Light meals and snacks, as well as breakfasts, are served in the coffeeshop. Predinner drinks are to be had in the bar, where the wall cabinets are filled with heavy leather-bound books, such as one finds in a country house.

Mount Royale Hotel, The Mount (tel. York 56261), is excellent value for the money, and the food is good, too. Run by Richard and Christine Oxtoby, the Mount Royale is only minutes from the city center. Built in 1833, it is carefully furnished with some beautiful antiques blended with modern pieces. They have taken over the house next door, increasing their bedroom capacity to 18 units, each with bath, costing from £32 ($62.40) for two persons, including VAT and a large breakfast. The hotel has a swimming pool. The menu consists of roast joints with interesting accompaniments—grilled York ham with eggs and spinach, fresh halibut with mushroom sauce, roast duckling with black cherry and brandy sauce, duckling with green pepper and corn sauce. The extensive set menu, costing £10 ($19.50), carries supplements for such items as fresh out-of-season asparagus or strawberries. The dining room opens onto an attractive garden.

Justifiably popular with locals, the restaurant requires advance reservations. As one local habitué told me, "I suppose that now my son is a week old, it's too late to book for his 21st birthday!" It's still worth the effort trying to get in, however.

Dean Court Hotel, Duncombe Place (tel. York 25082), is an ancient building lying right beneath the towers of the Minster. All rooms have bathroom or shower, telephone, radio, and color TV. Ian Washington, the owner, has done a lot recently to bring facilities up to the standards expected these days. B&B is £26 ($50.70) per person nightly. Lunch will cost £7 ($13.65); dinner, £9 ($17.55), for a meal from a well-chosen table d'hôte. VAT and service are included in all prices. There is a coffee lounge where snacks are served from 10 a.m. to 10 p.m. A salad will cost around £2.50 ($4.88), or there are sandwiches at about 75p ($1.46) a serving.

The Budget Range

Lady Anne Middleton's Hotel, Skeldergate House, Skeldergate (tel. York 32257), is a delightful 17th-century house, originally built as a hotel for the widows of York's freemen. On the river right opposite the Castle Museum, it is run by Andrew Clark and his wife Kathe, who have lovingly restored the building and created a very comfortable overnight hostelry. There's good car parking, and close by is the world's largest O-gauge railway exhibition. And in the nearby Quaker burial ground lie John Woolman and Linley Murray, two well-loved American Quakers.

If you approach by car you should head toward Harrogate, then turn right to the back of Cromwell House and the car park. Rooms in the new building are cheerful and warmly decorated. Only two bedrooms have private facilities, although there are adequate public baths and toilets. The hotel consists of two separate buildings with extensions added. The overnight cost is £10.20 ($19.94) per person, including an English breakfast, but not VAT.

The restaurant is converted from an old sawmill. The dining rooms offer à la carte dinners such as ham with apricots, roast chicken, and lamb cutlets. The restaurant has a good local reputation, even though the menu is limited. Meals average around £8 ($15.60).

Beechwood Close Hotel, 19 Shipton Rd. (tel. York 58378). On the A19, north of the city, Beechwood is a large house surrounded by trees, a garden with a putting green, and free parking space. Mr. and Mrs. Bulmer have converted it into a hotel, with all modern comforts, such as hot and cold running water in the rooms (most with showers) and central heating. The charge for a bed and a good Yorkshire breakfast is £14.50 ($28.28) to £15.50 ($30.23), including VAT. With its friendly atmosphere, Beechwood attracts many North Americans. It's a 15-minute walk to the Minster, either by road or along the river. However, a bus stop is close by.

Galtres Lodge, Low Petergate (tel. York 22478), is a Georgian brick building, presided over by Mr. and Mrs. Adams, who have completely redecorated it, and, in so doing, found three priest holes, one Adam fireplace, and two Georgian fireplaces which have greatly added to the charm of the hotel. The tariff is £11 ($21.45) per person for B&B, including VAT. Some of the rooms open onto a view of the rose window of the cathedral, and a few contain private showers and four-poster beds. Lunch is offered à la carte from noon to 2 p.m. The location of the Galtres is faultless, lying only a hop from the Minster, and in the vicinity of the railway station. Historical note: There is a plaque attached to the wall outside the hotel, showing that the street was once the "via principalis" of the old Roman fortress of Eboracum.

Bootham Bar Hotel, 4 High Petergate (tel. York 58516), is a charming place, a scrupulously clean, 18th-century house with bedroom views over various city sights. Right by the Minster, it is well situated for walking in the evening. Mr. and Mrs. M. Warren offer ten bedrooms at a rate of £8.25 ($16.09) per person nightly, including an English breakfast, although VAT is extra. A £5 ($9.75) deposit will secure a room. All the accommodations, incidentally, are heated and contain wash basins and radios. There is a small lounge with TV. Mrs. Warren's tiny staff is pleasant and helpful.

Granby Lodge Hotel, Scarcroft Road (tel. York 53291), is a family-run hotel lying about a ten-minute walk from the historical "downtown" of York. Centrally heated, the hotel, run by the Jacksons, offers 57 pleasantly furnished bedrooms which contain hot and cold running water, shaver points, radios, and tea- or coffee-making facilities. Some of the units are equipped with private baths or showers. The cost is £12 ($23.40) per person nightly, including VAT, although you'll pay £15.50 ($30.23) per person with bath. The licensed restaurant, seating 200 diners, offers good English food, a reasonably priced dinner served between 6 and 7 p.m. A full English breakfast is included in the tariff quoted. The cozy cocktail bar provides an attractive old-world atmosphere, and private parking is available.

WHERE TO EAT: Betty's Restaurant, St. Helen's Square (tel. York 22323), is a good all-around eating house in York, regardless of the price range in which you travel. First, at its second-floor self-service restaurant, well-prepared luncheons are served from 11:30 a.m. till 2 p.m., averaging £2.50 ($4.88) for a meal consisting of a main course, including vegetables, plus dessert for 55p ($1.07). The food is traditionally English, including roast beef and steak-and-kidney pie. All dishes are attractively served. There's no skimping on the portions either, and the restaurant is licensed.

In the Oak Room in the basement, with bar and waitress service, a set lunch is featured for £4 ($7.80). Dinner is à la carte only. Main courses average around £4 also, and desserts are priced from 80p ($1.56). On the ground floor is a confectionery, gift section, and coffee lounge. The restaurant is closed on Sunday.

Kooks Bistro, 108 Fishergate (tel. York 37553), is an informal, relaxed eating place run by the owners, Stephanie Cooke and Richard P. Thiel, whose idea is "If *you* don't enjoy it, we don't." Pleasantly decorated in fresh greens and browns with plants and flowers, it features a varied and unusual menu of English, American, Mexican, French, and vegetarian dishes. All main courses are served with a choice of baked potato, french fries, or a side salad included in the price. Kooks Cheapies range from £1.50 ($2.93), while the most expensive, Posh Kooks, is only £5.25 ($10.24). Special features include help-yourself french bread and unlimited coffee. The service is friendly and the atmosphere relaxed, with interesting background music and handmade jigsaws, games, and puzzles on every table. Kooks is fully licensed and open daily except Monday from noon to 3 p.m. and from 7 p.m. to midnight. It is within walking distance of the city center, and there is also plenty of easy parking.

Lew's Place, Kings Staithe (tel. York 28167), is an old wharfside gathering place, run with sprightly charm by Lewis Speight, who admits, "We try to cater for most tastes." Even some of his rival restaurant and café owners drop in whenever they're free, it's that relaxed and friendly. The food is good, too, certainly hardy. The menu changes daily. Main-course lunch prices average £3 ($5.85), increasing to £4 ($7.80) in the evening. The fare is likely to include a homemade moussaka, a savory seafood crêpe, a lamb steak (marinated in red wine, herbs, and garlic), even chili con carne. Usually a homemade soup is offered for a beginning course. Meals are served Monday to Saturday from 11:30 a.m. to 2 p.m. and from 6:30 to 10 p.m. The place is smartly painted a black and white, and it's cheerful inside with checked cloths on small tables jostling for room. It's a good atmosphere, and the service is efficient and friendly from the "wenches" in Lew's Place T-shirts.

Le Girondin, 30–32 High Petergate (tel. York 55344), is owned and operated by Pierre Dufau, who does most of the cooking along with his two assistants. His is probably the closest catering establishment to the Minster. The place opens at 9:30 a.m. for coffee, expanding to lunches from noon to 2:30 p.m. From 6 to 8:30 p.m., they do set dinners. However, they are also open in the afternoon for snacks as well.

A set lunch or dinner at £4.50 ($8.78) includes a choice of four appetizers and about six main dishes. The evening's à la carte menu features such exotic delicacies as snails and frog legs, mingled with the usual steaks and grills. You should escape for about £7 ($13.65) for a meal.

Pierre's cousin owns a vineyard in his native Bordeaux region, and he imports his own label wine from his kinsman. A glass will cost about 55p ($1.07).

Restaurant Bari, 15 The Shambles (tel. York 33807), stands in one of York's oldest and most colorful streets, originally the street of the butchers and mentioned in the Domesday Book. In a continental atmosphere, you can enjoy a quick single course or a full leisurely meal. Ten different pizzas are offered from £1.60 ($3.12) up. Lasagne and cannelloni at £1.90 ($3.71) are superb. Lunch can cost as little as £2.50 ($4.88) and dinner from about £3 ($5.85). A main-dish specialty is escalope Sophia Loren (veal cooked with brandy and cheese with a rich tomato sauce). The restaurant is open seven days a week from 11:30 a.m. to 2:30 p.m. and from 6 to 11 p.m.

Thomas's Wine Bar and Bistro, Museum Street (tel. York 54494). On a site where in the 1870s Eldrige's Royal Hotel was offering "a high standard of comfort and service to the nobility and county gentry," Thomas's now offers very good, economical meals or just a snack to sustain anyone who wants to stop. Downstairs, the wine bar has bare wooden floors and country-style wooden furniture; wine and sherry are dispensed from casks behind the bar. Pâtés, cheeses, pies, and salads are available at lunchtime. The bar is open seven days a week from noon to 2:30 p.m. and from 7 to 10:30 p.m.

The cheapest way to dine here is to order the set meal at £3.50 ($6.83), including VAT. For this you are likely to get a main course such as poached salmon or steak-and-kidney pie. Bistro dinners are likely to cost from £8 ($15.60). For this you might be served an appetizer such as deep-fried mushrooms or stuffed peppers, followed by pork Stroganoff with onions or beef with

Stilton sauce. Duck with orange sauce is another specialty, as are kidneys turbigo. The very pleasant atmosphere is created by Pam and Ian Postlethwaite, who run the place.

Plunkets, 9 High Petergate, is a bright, cheerful, busy place right beneath the shadow of the Minster yet seeming to fit in with its ancient surroundings. Hamburgers are served with french fries, salad with choice of dressing, and the relish tray. All the usual ones are there from plain quarter-pounder at £1.80 ($3.51) to Plunket Burger, a half-pounder with cheese or chili topping. A large club sandwich is £1.70 ($3.32), and a rump steak goes for £5 ($9.75). There are milkshakes, ice creams, cheesecake, chocolate fudge cake, and banana splits, all costing around 90p ($1.76). A three-course meal will cost about £5.80 ($11.31). At peak hours—lunch and suppertime—you must eat, but at other times just a coffee or milkshake is all you need have. There are several smaller rooms upstairs where you cannot hear the musak and be a little more intimate if you wish to. The place is open from 11 a.m. to 11 p.m. daily, although in winter they close from 3 to 5 p.m.

The **Kings Arms,** King Street, started life as a hostelry in 1534 when the cobbled street was called Kergate. Right beside Ouse Bridge and the river, the place has flood marks in the bar recording times when the whole place must have been under water for days at a time. On less damp days you can watch coasters unloading their cargo at the wharfs opposite the pub. The King's Arms is bright and cheerful, with geraniums in the window. Your host is Derick Bragg, and most of the beer he sells is brewed in local breweries. He features some very strong real ales. Sandwiches are available for around 40p (78¢). Steak-and-kidney pie, a country pâté, and salads cost about £1 ($1.95) to £1.30 ($2.54) each, and the day's special, perhaps shepherd's pie or else steak pie, served with chips, goes for £1.25 ($2.44).

Jeeves, 39 Tanner Row (tel. York 59622), is a family-run bistro with polished tables and winking candlelight. It is open only in the evening from 7 to 10 p.m. (closed on Sunday in summer, on Monday in winter). The kitchen does a three-course set dinner for £8.50 ($16.58). Appetizers include homemade soup, fresh pâté, taramasalata, or a more inventive crab à la pomme (an apple filled with crabmeat and dressing). Main dishes are likely to be chicken chasseur, sirloin steak, sirloin paupiettes with sauce, and fish dishes in season—all served with a selection of fresh vegetables. The meal is rounded off with a choice of dessert from the trolley and coffee. VAT is included, but not the 10% service charge.

Taylors in Stonegate, 46 Stonegate (tel. York 22865). Downstairs, the bow-windowed shop is filled with bags and jars of coffee. The old-fashioned till bears the prices of the various teas for sale. They boast 36 varieties of teas and coffee. When you see the shop, you'll know that is no idle boast. Teas come all the way from China and India, including exotic Moroccan mint and passion fruit. Upstairs, the coffeeshop dispenses these same beverages at 48p (94¢) for a pot of tea for one, 78p ($1.50) for a pot of coffee for one. They advertise a late breakfast for £1.75 ($3.41). You can also order Welsh rarebit, Yorkshire ham, and omelets with various fillings, costing around £2 ($3.90). Spiced Yorkshire teacakes and cinnamon toast are also on the menu. Service is from 9 a.m. to 5:15 p.m.

LODGINGS IN THE ENVIRONS: Just about 30 miles southeast of York lies a small market town, Beverley, in North Humberside. There are several medieval buildings in the town, and many travelers prefer to stay here instead of in York proper.

The **Beverley Arms Hotel,** North Bar Within, Beverley, North Humberside (tel. Hull 869241), is, in part, more than 300 years old. A wing has been added to provide bedrooms with bath, radio, phone, TV, and tea- and coffee-making equipment. A double room costs £33.50 ($65.33) a night, including VAT. The restaurant features many seafood and fish dishes, using produce caught daily in the North Sea and landed at Hull. There is also the Ridings Coffeeshop, constructed in the old kitchens, with a stone-flagged floor and high-backed chairs where snacks and light meals are served from 10 a.m. to 10 p.m. The North Bar serves traditional ales, and good food.

Kings Head Hotel, Market Place, Beverley, North Humberside (tel. Hull 868103), is a Georgian inn where a double room will cost you £23 ($44.85); a single, £12.65 ($24.67)—including a full Yorkshire breakfast. This is a typical small-town place where standards have to be kept up otherwise you lose your regular customers. Lunch at £3.25 ($6.34) includes a choice of three appetizers, then from two roasts, steak-and-kidney pie, or several other hot dishes, plus dessert. Dinner at £6 ($11.70) includes such substantial dishes as lamb cutlets and braised steak with carrots and onions. There is also an à la carte menu with dishes, grills, and salads at around £8.50 ($16.58). But who wants it when such succulent local dishes are available?

A CHANCE TO STAY WITH BRITISH ARISTOCRACY: Although not

in Yorkshire itself, I've included the following place because of its proximity.

Gunnerside Lodge is the family seat of the Earl and Countess Peel, a rambling house in Swaledale where Lord Peel (that is how you address him) owns and farms some 35,000 acres deep in the heart of the Herriot country and bordering on the Brontë country near the ancient city of York. The earl and countess have opened their home to small parties of six or more, who want to stay for at least three nights and learn something of this part of the country and the English way of life as lived here.

There are eight large double bedrooms with downy beds, modern literature, *The Sporting Life* and *Horse and Hound* on the bureau, and gorgeous views for miles over the dale. Four bathrooms are down the hall. Downstairs, the marble-floored main hall leads to the large drawing room, with the biggest set of antlers you'll ever see over the fireplace where a log fire often flickers. Beyond, the billiard room winds to the Orangery, with more views over the countryside.

Lady Peel supervises the kitchen, so if you have a particular dislike or dietary problem, it can be coped with. Breakfast in the paneled dining room is a leisurely, help-yourself-from-the-sideboard affair. Dinner is a candlelight occasion, with the earl and countess. The conversation flows—the conservation of land and wildlife, world affairs, or the latest debate attended by Lord Peel in the House of Lords.

During your days there's a trip to York, accompanied by the earl or the countess, including visits to the sights, lunch, and a drive through the Dales, with a lucid and enthusiastic Dalesman as your guide.

The cost of £500 ($975) for two people, inclusive of all food and drink for three days, as well as tobacco and other incidentals, is somewhat of a bargain if you figure that the same amount of time in a deluxe London hotel will set you back far more.

You must make up your own group, but that should be the least of your problems. Incidentally, for those history buffs, the earl is descended from Sir Robert Peel (his great-great-grandfather), once prime minister of England and the founder of the First Force to Protect Life and Property, the Peelers or Peelersmen, soon to become the policemen, bobbies, and rozzers.

For those worried about meeting the English aristocracy, chances are that within 24 hours you'll be on a first-name basis, inviting them to visit you.

For reservations and inquiries, write to the Secretary, the Gunnerside Estate Office, 8 Main St., Kirkby Lonsdale, Carnforth, Lancashire LA6 2AF; tel. (0468) 71114.

A SIDE TRIP FROM YORK: The most interesting day trip from York is to:

Castle Howard

In its dramatic setting of lakes, fountains, and extensive gardens, the 18th-century palace (tel. Coneysthorpe 333) designed by Sir John Vanbrugh is undoubtedly the finest private residence in Yorkshire. The first major achievement of the architect who later created the lavish Blenheim Palace near Oxford, Castle Howard was begun in 1699 for the third Earl of Carlisle, Charles Howard, whose descendants still call the place "home." The striking facade is topped by a painted and gilded dome, reaching more than 80 feet into the air. The interior boasts a 192-foot "Long Gallery," as well as a chapel with a magnificent stained-glass window by the 19th-century artist, Sir Edward Burne-Jones. Besides the collections of antique furniture, tapestries, porcelains, and sculpture, the castle contains a number of important paintings, including a portrait of Henry VIII by Holbein, and works by Rubens, Reynolds, and Gainsborough.

The seemingly endless grounds around the palace also offer the visitor some memorable sights, including the domed Temple of the Four Winds, by Vanbrugh, and the richly designed family mausoleum by Hawksmoor. There are two rose gardens, one with old-fashioned roses, the other featuring modern creations. The stable court houses the Costume Galleries, the largest private collection of 18th- to 20th-century costumes in Britain. The authentically dressed mannequins are exhibited in period settings. Castle Howard is just 15 miles northeast of York. The grounds are open from 11 a.m., and the hours for the house and Costume Gallery are from 11:30 a.m. to 5 p.m. Admission is £2 ($3.90) for adults, £1 ($1.95) for children, including entrance to the house, gallery, Costume Galleries, and grounds.

Castle Howard had the "title role" in "Brideshead Revisited," the popular television mini-series.

2. North Yorkshire

Yorkshire, known to readers of *Wuthering Heights* around the world, is now divided into three counties—West Yorkshire, South Yorkshire, and North Yorkshire. For those seeking legendary untamed scenery, I'd recommend a tour of North Yorkshire, which also takes in the historic cathedral city of York.

North Yorkshire contains England's most varied landscape. Its history has been turbulent, often bloody, and many relics of its rich past are still standing, including ruined abbeys. Yorkshire is little known to the average North American visitor, but many an English traveler is familiar with its haunting moors, serene valleys, and windswept dales.

The hospitality of the people of Yorkshire is world renowned, and if a pudding which originated there doesn't accompany a slab of roast beef, the plate looks naked to the British. The people of Yorkshire, who speak an original twang often imitated in English cinema, are, in general, hard-working and industrious, perhaps a little contemptuous of the easy living of the south. But they are decidedly open and friendly to strangers, providing you speak to them first.

HARROGATE: If you head northeast from York for 20 miles, you reach Harrogate, North Yorkshire's second-largest town after York itself. In the 19th century, Harrogate was a fashionable spa. Most of its town center is surrounded by a 200-acre lawn called "The Stray." Boutiques and antique shops—which Queen Mary used to frequent—make Harrogate a shopping center of excellence, particularly along Montpellier Parade. Harrogate is called England's floral resort, deserving such a reputation because of its gardens, including Harlow Car Gardens and Valley Gardens. The former spa has an abundance of guest houses and hotels, including the expensive Swan where Agatha Christie hid out during her mysterious disappearance—still unexplained—in the 1920s.

Food and Lodging

The Old Swan, Swan Road (tel. Harrogate 504051). This is the spot where the late mystery writer, Agatha Christie, suddenly surfaced after a mysterious 11-day disappearance that was the subject of the film *Agatha,* starring Dustin Hoffman. One of the most famous hotels in northern England, the Old Swan commemorates that long-ago event by naming its restaurant the Agatha Christie Library, which, incidentally, serves a chocolate cake known as "Delicious Death" which was featured in one of her novels. The Old Swan certainly predates Ms. Christie—in fact, it goes back to 1700.

Its 140 rooms are well-furnished, and each has a private bath. The basic tariff for a twin-bedded room is £45 ($87.75) per night, and in a single, £30 ($58.50)—both rates including VAT and an English breakfast. The public rooms are spacious and pleasantly grand, often with Victorian design.

Yorke Arms Hotel, Ramsgill, near Harrogate (tel. Harrogate 75243), is surrounded by moody moorland scenery, and is an ideal center for excursions. It's a widely spread manor house, with many well-preserved architectural features, plus a selection of antiques. The dining hall, for example, with its black oak sideboard, holds a collection of pewter, and you dine on Windsor armchairs in front of a time-blackened fireplace. The lounge has tufted velvet sofas drawn up around a stone fireplace. The exterior is stately, built of stone, with creeping ivy covering part of its gables and mullioned windows. The rooms are comfortably furnished and well maintained, and some contain private baths. The cost of half board here is about £30 ($58.50) per person nightly.

In this attractively furnished town house, built back in Victoria's day, **Number Six,** 6 Ripon Rd. (tel. Harrogate 502908), is one of the finest dining rooms at the spa, and I recommend that you skip a meal at your hotel to patronize this fine and well-run establishment with its outstanding wine list. The Di Silvestro brothers have hired a well-trained staff to serve their beautifully prepared dishes, which are likely to include such delicacies as quenelles of sole, quails en cocotte with raisins, fresh lobster thermidor, roast duckling with orange sauce, or roast mallard.

As you enter the restaurant you can head for the intimate bar to enjoy an apéritif, and, while sipping it, make menu selections from an imaginative choice of dishes, mostly continental in flavor and presentation. Ingredients are well chosen, and the wine list is above average. The price of most dishes, beginning at £10.50 ($20.48) and going up, includes appetizer, soup, and dessert, the latter most often a mouthwatering, rich concoction. Expect to pay at least £12 ($23.40) per person, plus the cost of your wine. Only dinner is served, except Monday, and hours are from 7 to 10 p.m., when reservations are essential.

MOORS AND DALES: The rural landscape is pierced with ruins of once-great abbeys and castles. North Yorkshire is a land of green hills, valleys, and purple moors. Both the Yorkshire Dales and the Moors are wide open spaces, two of Britain's finest national parks, with a combined area of some 1200 square miles. However, the term "national" can be misleading, as the land is managed by foresters, farmers, and private landowners. In fact, more than 90% of the land is in private ownership. The Dales rise toward Cumbria and Lancashire to the east, and the Moors stretch to the eastern coastline.

Of course, York, the major center, has already been previewed. But those with the time may want to explore deeper into the rural roots of England. From Harrogate, our last stopover, you can enjoy the wildest scenery of the region by heading out on day trips, anchoring at one of the inns coming up if you don't want to return to the old spa.

After leaving Harrogate, you can discover white limestone crags, drystone walls, fast-rushing rivers, and isolated sheep farms or else clusters of sandstone cottages.

Malhamdale receives more visitors annually than any dale in Yorkshire. Of the priories and castles to visit, two of the most interesting are the 12th-century ruins of **Bolton Priory,** and the 14th-century pile, **Castle Bolton,** to the north in Wensleydale.

Richmond, the most frequently used town name in the world, stands here at the head of the Dales as the mother of them all. Here the Norman towers of Richmond Castle, the county's best known fortress, dominate the cobbled market town.

In contrast, the Moors, on the other side of the Vale of York, have a wild beauty all their own, quite different from that of the Dales. They are bounded by the Cleveland and Hambleton Hills. The white horse of Kilburn can be seen hewn out of the landscape.

Both **Pickering** and **Northallerton,** two market towns, serve as gateways to the Moors. Across the Moors are seen primordial burial grounds and stone crosses. The best known trek in moorland is the 40-mile hike over bog, heather, and stream from Mount Grace Priory inland to Ravenscar on the seacoast. It's known as **Lyke Wake Walk.**

In your tour of the Moors, a good center is **Helmsley,** the key to Ryedale and the mother town of the district, standing as it does at the junction of the roads from York, Pickering, Malton, Stokesley, and Thirsk. Beyond the main square at Helmsley are the ruins of the castle with its impressive keep. This castle was built between 1186 and 1227.

Three miles to the north of Helmsley, the ruins of **Rievaulx Abbey** are among the most impressive in England, charging an admission of 60p ($1.17) for visits. Rievaulx was the first large Cistercian church to be built in England. Construction began in 1131, and work continued until its completion in 1175. In its heyday, it was a stunning example of the English Gothic style.

Coxwold is on the southern border of the park, one of the most attractive villages in the Moors.

Along North Yorkshire's 45 miles of coastline are such traditional seaside resorts as **Filey, Whitby,** and **Scarborough,** the latter claiming to be the oldest seaside spa in Britain, standing on the site of a Roman signaling station. It was founded in 1622, following the discovery of mineral springs with medicinal properties. In the 19th century, its Grand Hotel, a Victorian structure, was acclaimed "as the best in Europe." The Norman castle on big cliffs overlooks the twin bays.

At Helmsley

The **Black Swan** (tel. Helmsley 70466) has stood since the 16th century overlooking the marketplace. Part Tudor, part Georgian, part modern, this Trusthouses Forte hotel offers 38 well-furnished bedrooms, each with private bath, radio, TV, phone, and coffee-making facilities. These rent from £27 ($52.65) in a single, from £36 ($70.20) in a double, including service and VAT. Breakfast is extra. A new wing of bedrooms has been added at the rear. Public rooms are full of character, with open fires, paneling, and time-aged beams. In the traditionally furnished restaurant, you can enjoy unusual Yorkshire dishes, such as Wensley fowl stuffed with dale cheese or jugged venison, a dinner costing from £8 ($15.60) per head. The hotel also has three bars.

Crown Hotel, Market Square (tel. Helmsley 70297), is of undetermined age, but at least from 1550. It's built of stone, standing at the edge of the village square, and the walls are covered by creepers, giving it charm. The owners, Mr. and Mrs. Mander, have spared no effort to make every room not only attractive, but comfortable. Nine of their bedrooms now have showers, all have hot and cold running water, and, wherever possible, in the restoration old beams have been left exposed. The dining room is well furnished; there are two bars, one public and one better furnished for residents. In addition, there are two living rooms. B&B is priced according to the plumbing you get, £12.70 ($24.77) to £14.10 ($27.50) per person, including VAT. For dinner, bed, and breakfast, the cost is £17 ($33.15) to £18.50 ($36.08). Set lunches are from £5 ($9.75), dinners from £8 ($15.60), and the food is typically English.

Near Skipton

The **Buck Inn**, Malham, near Skipton (tel. Airton 317), is a Victorian stone inn where Dale explorers can find excellent ale, a comfortable and cozy room, and a good breakfast and dinner. There are two bars, one especially for hikers, the other for residents. The inn offers ten centrally heated bedrooms, each with a wash basin, only one with a private bath, which costs £1 ($1.95) extra per night. The charge is £12 ($23.40) for B&B, £17.50 ($34.13) for half board, including VAT, between July 1 and mid-October, and after that, tariffs are reduced. You can order bar lunches noon and evenings if you don't want a full meal.

At Thornton-le-Dale

The **Hall**, Thornton-le-Dale, near Pickering (tel. Pickering 74789), is a stately 16th-century manor house with a formal facade and an informal rear garden. A fully licensed residential hotel, it stands in the center of what had been called "the prettiest village in Yorkshire," on the main Pickering–Scarborough road. The interior has been adapted for modern comfort, and all of the comfortable bedrooms have private baths. The B&B tariff ranges from £22 ($42.90) per night in a single to £32 ($62.40) in a double. Dinner costs yet another £8 ($15.60). A riding school is attached to the hotel.

Ripon

A cathedral city on the Ure River, Ripon is the second-oldest incorporated community in the country, dating from A.D. 886. It still maintains the ancient custom of the "Sounding of the Horn" at 9 o'clock every evening. The Curfew Bell and the Corn Bell are also still used.

Of its many fine old buildings, none is better known than its cathedral, with its fine Saxon crypt dating from A.D. 674. Across from the Market Square is the Wakeman's House, one of the oldest and most interesting buildings of its kind in England, containing a tiny museum.

The **Unicorn Hotel,** Market Square (tel. Ripon 2202), is a coaching inn and posting house. It has welcomed travelers for some 400 years with true Yorkshire warmth and hospitality, and the same is true today. It's directly on the Market Square opposite the obelisk where the 1000-year-old tradition of setting the watch by blowing the horn takes place each evening. The facade of the inn is in Victorian style, with square bay windows and an elaborate front entrance. All of the 28 bedrooms have private facilities, central heating, tea- and coffee-making equipment, and phones. Singles rent from £16 ($31.20) and doubles or twins from £28 ($54.60), these tariffs including VAT and a full English breakfast. The cuisine in the Pykestolle Restaurant is Cordon Bleu, and, in addition, bar lunches are served in the Tom Crudds bar, a typically English pub with locally brewed real ale.

The **Nordale,** 1 North Parade (tel. Ripon 3557), is a bargain at the daily per-person rate of £8.25 ($16.09), which includes not only a complete full-course breakfast but VAT. There are no "private facilities" except the hot and cold running water in your room. However, adequate baths are in the halls. Consider having a Yorkshire dinner as well, and this costs £12.50 ($24.38) per person, including your room and breakfast. The owners are John and Barbara Richmond. She will pack a picnic lunch for you if you are making a day trip. All their bedrooms are attractively furnished, with twins and doubles, according to your wish. Children can stay at reduced rates. The Nordale is a good center for exploring the Yorkshire Dales.

Black-a-Moor Inn, Risplith, near Ripon (tel. Sawley 214), is a stone country inn well known for its hospitality and convivial atmosphere. It's on the Ripon to Pateley Bridge road, the B6265, five miles from Ripon, just perfect for visits to Fountains Abbey, the Brimham Rocks, and the Dales. Owners Byron and Patricia Brader have decorated the three bedrooms with taste, installing central heating as well as hot and cold running water. They charge £12 ($24.30) in a single and £18 ($35.10) in a double for B&B, including VAT and the service charge. Their breakfasts are "as you want it." In addition, Patricia can prepare evening meals—simple country fare—such as homemade steak-and-kidney pie. The Braders' son, Martin, presides over the bar.

3. West Yorkshire

HAWORTH: In West Yorkshire, this ancient stone village lying on the high moors of the Pennines—45 miles west of York via Leeds and 21 miles west of Leeds itself—is world famous as the home of the Brontë family. The three sisters—Charlotte, Emily, and Anne—distinguished themselves as English novelists. They lived a life of imagination at a lonely parsonage at Haworth.

Anne wrote two novels, *The Tenant of Wildfell Hall* and *Agnes Grey,* and Charlotte's masterpiece was *Jane Eyre,* which depicted her experiences as a governess and enjoyed popular success in its day.

But, of course, it was Emily's fierce and tragic *Wuthering Heights* which made her surpass her sisters, as she created a novel of such passion, intensity, and primitive power, with its scenes of unforgettable, haunting melancholy, that the book has survived to this day, appreciated by later generations far more than those she'd written it for.

From Haworth, you can walk to Withens, the "Wuthering Heights" of the immortal novel. In Haworth, Charlotte and Emily are buried in the family vault under the church of St. Michael's.

The parsonage where they lived has been preserved as the **Brontë Parsonage Museum** (tel. Haworth 42323). Emily and Charlotte died there. It may be visited daily from April 1 to September 30 on weekdays from 11 a.m. to 5:30 p.m., and on Sunday from 2 to 5:30 p.m. In winter it is open from 11 a.m. to 4:30 p.m. weekdays and on Sunday from 2 to 4:30 p.m. The admission is 50p (98¢) for adults, 25p (49¢) for children.

On the Haworth Moor stands a Brontë landmark, **Ponden Hall**, Stanbury, near Keighley (tel. Haworth 44154), a distance of some three miles from Haworth. It lies half a mile from the main road on a wide rough track which is the Pennine Way. An Elizabethan farmhouse built in 1560 and extended in 1801, this reputedly is the model for Thrushcross Grange, Catherine's home after her marriage to Edgar Linton.

Today the hall provides a farmhouse accommodation, a hand-loom weaving studio, a residential weaving course, a bunkhouse accommodation, as well as camping.

The hall is restricted to accommodating only six guests, and supplies evening meals for residents only. For B&B, the charge is only £7 ($13.65) per person nightly, with subsequent reductions for longer stays. The food is good, log fires burn brightly, and guests often gather around the piano for spontaneous entertainment.

To fulfill the needs of Pennine Way walkers, Roderick Taylor has converted a traditional, two-story farm cottage in the yard above the hall to provide simple self-catering accommodations for nine. You need your own sleeping bag, however. Booking isn't really necessary, and the charge is £2.50 ($4.88) per person nightly. However, between Easter and October, there's a maximum stay of two nights. An evening meal goes for £3.50 ($6.83).

For a tour of the many sights of the Brontë country—far too numerous to mention here—you can get in touch with Norman Raistrick, curator of the Parsonage Museum, or the U.S. representative of the Brontë Society, Katherine Reise, 335 Grove St., Oradell, NJ 07649.

Food and Lodging

The **Tourist Information Centre,** at 2–4 West Lane in Haworth (tel. Haworth 42329), offers an accommodation-booking service, and the office is open daily from 10 a.m. to 5:30 p.m. from Easter until the end of October, from 10:30 a.m. to 4:30 p.m. from November to March. Otherwise, you might stay at one of the recommendations below.

The **Old White Lion Hotel** (tel. Haworth 42313) stands at the top of a cobbled street. It was built around 1700 with a solid stone roof almost next door to the church where the Reverend Mr. Brontë preached and to the parsonage where the family lived. Phyllis and Don Wolstenholme welcome Brontë buffs and others in their warm, cheerful, and comfortable inn. They charge them £11 ($21.45) per person in a double, £13 ($25.35) in a single. For an additional £1.50 ($2.93) per person, you'll be given a room with a bath or shower. VAT is included, but service is extra. Dinners, except Sunday, are à la carte, and good local meats and fresh vegetables are used at a cost of £5 ($9.75) per person. A set Sunday lunch costs £4 ($7.80), usually featuring a roast. Bar snacks include the usual favorites—ploughman's lunch, hot pies, fish, and sandwiches. Prices range from sandwiches at 60p ($1.17) to meat pies at £1.70 ($3.32).

The Black Bull, Main Street (tel. Haworth 42249), owned by Ron and Kath Bennett, stands close to the parish church where Patrick Brontë was incumbent for 41 years and is closely associated with the son, Branwell Brontë. Although renovated and improved since Branwell's day, it is still interesting to spend time within the walls that drew him so strongly and even to sit in the chair which he occupied on his many visits to the place, still on the premises. Today the Black Bull is as comfortable an inn as you will find.

Conversion of the restaurant, which seats 40, has made use of a thick stone wall in forming a central arch. This is the room where Branwell's chair sits, and here is the original bell pull and bell which he used to ring for his many drinks. Luncheon and bar snacks are served from noon until 2:30 p.m. A three-course lunch with roast beef and Yorkshire pudding costs around £5 ($9.75). Snacks and assorted sandwiches are served in the lounge area. Chicken, scampi, and haddock with chips and peas or homemade steak pie are offered for around £2.50 ($4.88). Dinner is served from 7 until 10:30 p.m. The cuisine is excellent, and the à la carte menu, with a good supporting wine list, gives an ample choice. Morning coffee and high tea are served on Sunday. The Bennets charge £20 ($39) for a double room, including a good breakfast.

Keepers Restaurant, The Fold, Haworth, near Keighley (tel. Haworth 42919). Four cottages make up this delightful place presided over by Mrs. Starr, while her daughter, a qualified chef, and her husband do all the cooking. Although the present structure is not all that old (just a couple of hundred years), the original cottages date from the 15th century, and the decor reflects the period. More than 300 watercolor paintings decorate the walls, and they serve a variety of simple dishes, such as roast beef and Yorkshire pudding, but they also do korma or hot Bengal curry with sambals (side dishes of relish). The dessert specialty of the house is a chocolate brandy cake made with fresh cream. A meal will cost around £5 ($9.75).

In the evenings, they like to have warning of your arrival for dinner (from 8 p.m.). A homemade soup followed by sirloin steak, beef Stroganoff, or chicken cooked with a sauce of cream, asparagus, and sherry, dessert, and coffee costs around £10 ($19.50). They bake all their own cakes and pastries, and are open from 11:30 a.m. to 7 p.m. daily in summer, noon to 6 p.m. in winter, when they also close on Friday. They do not have a liquor license, but will happily provide glasses without a corkage charge if you produce your own bottles. They also have a couple of rooms available in their cottage next door and charge £7 ($13.65) per person for B&B (you have to come along to the restaurant). The units are spotlessly clean and comfortable.

The Brontë Bookshop, 1 Church St. (tel. Haworth 42243), was the post office in the Brontës' time. Today, Mrs. Tricia Richmond runs a spotlessly clean B&B accommodation at the address, charging £8 ($15.60) per person, including a truly enormous Yorkshire breakfast. She and her husband spent many years in Africa before returning to Haworth. Mrs. Richmond admits to being from Lancashire, but "as my father was from Yorkshire, they let me in."

HAREWOOD HOUSE AND BIRD GARDEN: In West Yorkshire, at Junction A61/659, midway between Leeds and Harrogate and five miles from the A1 at Wetherby, stands Harewood House, home of the Earl and Countess of Harewood. It's one of the "magnificent seven" homes of England, which includes Blenheim Palace and Beaulieu Abbey. The 18th-century house was designed by Robert Adam and John Carr and has always been owned by the Lascelles family. It contains superb plasterwork, beautiful Chippendale furniture, and collections of Sèvres and Chinese porcelain, and of English and Italian paintings.

Harewood Bird Garden borders the lake and blends successfully with the fine landscape, created by Capability Brown. It houses some 180 exotic species from all over the world, including penguins, macaws, snowy owls, and flamingos, and has an undercover area housing tropical birds and small mammals. The extensive grounds offer terrace and lakeside walks, shops, a cafeteria, a picnic area, occasional exhibitions, a Courtyard Restaurant, and an Adventure Playground for the children.

Harewood is open daily from April 1 to October 31 and on Sunday, Tuesday, Wednesday, and Thursday in February, March, and November. Gates open at 10 a.m. (house at 11 a.m.). The bird garden and playground only are also open from December 26 to the first Sunday in January. Admission rates vary during the year, but a summer Freedom Ticket, admitting the bearer to all facilities, is approximately £2.50 ($4.88) for adults, with reductions for children under 15. Call Harewood 886225 for recorded information, available 24 hours.

Incidentally, Harewood is on a regular bus route (Leeds/Harrogate/Ripon), but the stop is about one mile from the house. Summer excursions run on varying days from those cities served by the regular buses and from York and Bradford, among other places. Ask at local tourist information centers and at your hotel for details.

4. Durham

This densely populated county of northeast England is too often pictured as a dismal, foreboding place, with coalfields, ironworks, mining towns, and shipyards. Yet it contains valleys of quiet charm and a region of wild moors in the west.

DURHAM: The county town is built around a standstone peninsula. It possesses a Norman **cathedral** which ranks as one of the most important in England. Adjoining the cathedral is **Durham Castle** (tel. Durham 65481), a Norman structure of the prince bishops which has been used by Durham University since 1832. Except on the occasion of university or other functions, the castle is open to visitors from 10 a.m. to noon and 2 to 4:30 p.m., daily during the first three weeks in April and during all of July, August, and September; 2 to 4 p.m. on Monday, Wednesday, and Saturday the rest of the year. Admission is 75p ($1.46) for adults, 35p (68¢) for children.

Food and Lodging

The **Royal County Hotel**, Old Elvet (tel. Durham 66821), is a Georgian hotel tracing its origins back to Cromwellian times. In its well-conceived modernization program, this antique riverside coaching inn blends yesteryear with contemporary design, and does so effectively. The owner has decorated the public rooms with mementoes depicting the checkered history of the place. There are 126 bedrooms in the hotel, all with private baths, and you're given a choice of accommodations in the older building, with its traditional furnishings, or else in the new block of rooms overlooking the river. Most units are fully equipped with TV set, radio, phone, and coffee-making facilities. Food is served in the Light Infantryman Restaurant, and the coffeeshop provides light snacks. Rates range from £28.50 ($55.58) in a single, from £38 ($74.10) in a double, including an English breakfast. In the foyer is an aviary, and there is sunken seating in the bar.

BARNARD CASTLE: Near the Tees River, in the town of Barnard Castle, stands **The Bowes Museum** (tel. Teesdale 37139), at the eastern end. It was built in 1869 by John Bowes and his wife, the Countess of Montalbo, to house and display their art collection. Here you'll find masterpieces by Goya and El Greco, plus many fine tapestries and porcelains. There are also collections of French and English furniture, superb costumes, musical instruments, a children's gallery, and many other exhibits of interest. A tearoom and ample parking are found on the premises. It is open all year, weekdays from 10 a.m. to 5 p.m., on Sunday from 2 to 5 p.m., charging 70p ($1.37) for adults, 15p (29¢) for children. It closes at 4 p.m. from November to February.

Where to Dine

Blagraves House Restaurant, The Bank (tel. Teesdale 37668), occupies a 15th-century house with a dining room which has been richly, warmly decorated by Mr. and Mrs. Davidson. They invite you to come by and "taste our food," which I've found to be excellently prepared and very wholesome. Fresh local produce and friendly service characterize the establishment. A fixed-price meal is offered for £12 ($23.40). Main dishes are likely to include rounds of filet of beef with a roquefort herb butter, duckling with peach and lemon sauce, or chicken breasts stuffed with asparagus in a white wine and cheese sauce. Our favorite beginning, if featured, is a "very fine fish soup," made with lobsters, crab, prawns, plaice, cream, and brandy. Only dinner is served, and it's offered nightly from 7 to 9, except Sunday. Call for a reservation.

BLANCHLAND: Near Consett, the village of Blanchland dates from the mid-12th century. It's a cobbled square with houses and little village shops. The post office still shows the arms of Queen Victoria over the mailbox.

The Lord Crewe Arms Hotel (tel. Blanchland 251) was the priory of the now-destroyed Abbey of Blanchland, and the bars are to be found in the crypt of the old building. You can walk through one of the enormous chimneys with a priest's hole above your head. It is easy to imagine the ghost of Dorothy Foster stalking the narrow passages.

Many of the rooms have baths, costing from £16 ($31.20) in a single or £26 ($50.70) in a double, including a traditional cooked breakfast, VAT, and service. A four-course dinner is likely to include such intriguing dishes as consommé profiteroles, collops of beef, and a traditional Sunday lunch. There are also bar snacks for those who want to stop for a short while en route to Hadrian's Wall or Scotland.

5. Tyne and Wear

In the newly created county of Tyne and Wear, industrial Newcastle upon Tyne is the dominant focus, yet outside the city there is much natural beauty. Cattle graze on many a grassed-over mining shaft. There is such scenic beauty as moors and hills of purple-blue. The rugged coastline is beautiful. Americans like to pass through because of their interest in the ancestral home of George

Washington (see below), and Newcastle itself also merits a stopover, particularly from motorists heading to Scotland.

The National Trust administers two sights in the region surrounding Newcastle:

Gibside Chapel, built in the classical style of James Paine in 1760, is an outstanding example of Georgian church architecture. A stately oak-lined avenue leads to the door of the chapel, which is the mausoleum of the Bowes family. The interior is decorated in delicate plasterwork and is furnished with paneled pews of cherrywood and a rare mahogany three-tiered pulpit. Hours are from 2 to 6 p.m. every day except Tuesday from April 1 to September 30. The entrance fee is 50p (98¢) per person. The location is six miles southwest of Gateshead and 20 miles northwest of Durham between Rowlands Gill and Burnopfield.

Washington Old Hall is the ancestral home of the first president of the United States, and the place from which the family took its name. President Carter visited the manor house in 1977. The interior of the house, whose origins date back to 1183, is furnished with period antiques and a collection of Delft ware. Relics of the Washingtons are also on display. The hall is open from March to October daily, except Thursday, from 1 to 6 p.m. From November to February, it is open on Saturday and Sunday, and by appointment, from 2 to 5 p.m. Admission is 60p ($1.17) for adults, 30p (59¢) for children. The location is in Washington on the east side of the A182, five miles west of Sunderland (two miles from the A1). South of Tyne Tunnel, follow signs for Washington New Town District 4 and then Washington Village.

At Stanley, just a few miles south of Newcastle upon Tyne is **Beamish,** the North of England Open Air Museum. Here the way of life of the people of this area around the turn of the century is being recreated. You can visit an old railway station and ride behind a steam locomotive, see bread being baked in a coal-fired oven in a row of furnished pit cottages, and go down a "drift" mine to witness how coal was worked around the turn of the century. You can also visit Home Farm to see animals and exhibitions and Beamish Hall in its beautiful parkland for a drink in the Victorian bar (summer only). For further information, telephone Stanley 31811. The museum is open throughout the year, except on Monday in winter.

NEWCASTLE UPON TYNE: Although an industrial city, Newcastle is graced with some fine streets and parks, as well as many old buildings. After crossing its best known landmark, the Tyne Bridge, you enter a steep city which sweeps down to the Tyne, usually on narrow lanes called "chares." Once wealthy merchants built their town houses right on the quayside, and some of them remain.

For years Newcastle has been known as a shipbuilding and coal-exporting center, and gave rise to the expression of suggesting the absurdity of shipping coals to Newcastle.

Dominating the skyline, the **Cathedral of Newcastle** rises to a beautiful Scottish crown spire. It is England's most northerly cathedral, lying on a downward sweep between the Central Station and the quay. Its provost admits, "We're not on the cathedral circuit, like York Minster and Lincoln, but foreigners still seek us out." The cathedral's date of construction is unknown, although its recorded history predates 1122. The church was rebuilt in the 14th century, and John Knox preached from its pulpit.

The keep of the so-called New Castle, built by Henry II in 1170, contains the **Keep Museum,** on St. Nicholas Street, with a collection of medieval relics.

It's open April to September, Monday from 2 to 5 p.m.; Tuesday to Saturday, 10 a.m. to 5 p.m. From October to March, its Monday hours are from 2 to 4 p.m.; Tuesday to Saturday, 10 a.m. to 4 p.m.

Food and Lodging

Royal Station Hotel, Neville Street (tel. Newcastle 320781), was built back in the days when the big, grand hotels were connected to the railway station by a covered way. This well-kept hotel has two restaurants, the main one called the Victoria, where an extensive à la carte menu is served. Otherwise, you can dine more inexpensively at their Oscars Viking Restaurant, which is on the lines of a coffeeshop/grill room with an interesting self-service cold table also available. Of the three bars, the Lord Mountbatten is the most recent. It has two sides, a nautical theme being used in one and an empire theme in the other.

Most of the bedrooms have been kept up to date, although some still have their heavy Victorian-style furniture. Bathless singles rent for £21 ($40.95), the rate increasing to £33.50 ($65.33) with bath. Twins and doubles with bath cost £42.75 ($83.36). Reductions are given on Friday, Saturday, and Sunday. The tariffs quoted include a full English breakfast, service, and VAT.

6. Northumberland

Most motorists zip through this far-northern county on their way to Scotland. Because it lies so close to Scotland, Northumberland was the scene of many a skirmish. The county now displays a number of fortified castles which saw action in those battles.

Wallington, at Cambo, 12 miles west of Morpeth (take the A696 north from Newcastle), dates from 1688, but the present building reflects the great changes brought about in the 1740s when Daniel Garrett completely refashioned the exterior of the house. The interior is decorated with rococo plasterwork and furnished with fine porcelains, furniture, and paintings. Visitors may also visit the museum and enjoy an extensive display of dollhouses. The Coach House contains an exhibit of ornate carriages. The main building itself is surrounded by 100 acres of woodlands and lakes, including a beautifully terraced, walled garden and a conservatory. The grounds are open all year; the house, from April 1 to September 1 from 1 to 6 p.m. daily except Tuesday. Admission to the house and grounds is £1.70 ($3.32); to the grounds and gardens only, 60p ($1.17). Children pay half price. For more information, telephone 067-074-283.

Seaton Delaval, the enormous country house off Whitley Bay, represents the architecture of Sir John Vanbrugh at its most forbidding. It looks like the stage settings for 14 Roman tragedies piled one on top of another. Walk over and look through a window in the east wing, and you can almost imagine knights and wenches feasting at long tables and drinking mead. The house is open to view from May to September on Wednesday and Sunday from 2 to 6 p.m., charging adults an admission of 50p (98¢); children, 25p (49¢).

The **Farne Islands** are a group of small islands off the Northumbria coast, which provide a summer home for at least 20 species of sea birds as well as for one of the largest British colonies of gray seals. St. Cuthbert died here in 687, and a chapel built in the 14th century is thought to be on the site of his original cell. Only Inner Farne and Staple Island are open to the public. Visiting season extends from April through September, but access is more controlled during the breeding season. From mid-May to mid-July, you can visit Staple Island from 10:30 a.m. to 1:30 p.m. each day, and Inner Farne from 2 to 5 p.m. daily. From April 1 to mid-May and from mid-July until the end of September hours for both Staple Island and Inner Farne are from 10 a.m. to 6 p.m. Tickets are obtained on the island. During the peak season, adults pay £1.60 ($3.12), and children are charged 80p ($1.56). During the rest of the season, the admission is £1 ($1.95) for adults and 50p (98¢) for children.

The best way to get to this most famous bird and animal sanctuary in the British Isles is to telephone or write Billy Shiel, the Farne Islands boatman at 4 Southfield Ave., Seahouses, Northumberland (tel. Seahouses 720308). He has been taking people in his licensed boat for the past 40 years, so he knows the tides and the best places to film seals, puffins, and guillemots. He runs 2½-hour trips in his 40-passenger craft at a cost of £2.50 ($4.88) per person.

Incidentally, these are the islands where Grace Darling and her father made their famous rescue of men from a foundered ship.

HOLY ISLAND: The site of the Lindisfarne religious community during the Dark Ages, Holy Island is only accessible for ten hours of the day, high tides covering the causeway at other times. For crossing times, check with local information centers.

Lindisfarne Castle, built on the island about 1550, is open from April until the end of September, daily, except Friday, from 11 a.m. to 1 p.m. and from 2 to 5 p.m., charging an admission of £1 ($1.95).

At Lindisfarne, you can stay at the **Lindisfarne Private Hotel** (tel. Holy Island 89273). This is a fine, substantial frame building with a trio of tall chimneys. It's run by members of the Massey family, who conduct it more like a private home than a hotel. Centrally heated bedrooms contain hot and cold running water (a few with private baths) and are decorated with personality, providing a homelike atmosphere. The charge ranges from £15 ($29.25) to £18 ($35.10) per person daily for bed, breakfast, and evening dinner. Boating excursions can be arranged to the Farnes.

READER'S SIGHTSEEING TIP: "**Bamburgh Castle** guards the British shore along the North Sea. Legend has it that Lancelot and Guinevere fled here. It is open Easter until the end of October, daily at 1 p.m. Admission is 90p ($1.76) for adults, 45p (88¢) for children. For more information, telephone Bamburgh 208" (Paul W. Ware, New Providence, Pa.).

HADRIAN'S WALL: This wall, which extends across the north of England for 73 miles, from the North Sea to the Irish Sea, is particularly interesting for a stretch of 3½ miles west of Housesteads. Only the lower courses of the wall are preserved intact; the rest were reconstructed in the 19th century with the original stones. From several vantage points along the wall, you have incomparable views north to the Cheviot Hills along the Scottish border, and south to the Durham moors.

At Housesteads you can visit a **Roman fort** (tel. Bardon Mill 363), built about A.D. 130 to house an infantry of 1000 men. Called Vercovicium in Latin, the fort housed a full-scale military encampment, the remains of which can be seen today. The fort is open in April daily from 9:30 a.m. to 5:30 p.m., from May to September the hours are 9:30 a.m. to 7 p.m. daily, and in October it is open weekdays from 9:30 a.m. to 5:30 p.m. (on Sunday from 2 p.m. to 5:30 p.m.); in November through February, the hours are 9:30 a.m. to 4 p.m. weekdays (on Sunday from 2 p.m. to 4 p.m.). Price of admission in summer is 80p ($1.56) for adults, 40p (78¢) for children.

Just west of Housesteads is **Vindolanda,** another fort south of the Wall at Chesterholm. The building is very well preserved, and there is also a recently excavated civilian settlement outside the fort with an interesting museum of artifacts of everyday Roman life. Admission is 80p ($1.56) for adults, 40p (78¢) for children.

HALTWHISTLE: About 20 miles east of Carlisle lies the town of Haltwhistle. There the **Grey Bull Hotel** (tel. Haltwhistle 20298) would be a good base of operations for seeing the best section of Hadrian's Wall and its Roman garrisons. These include Housesteads, Vindolanda (the largest site in Europe), the Chesters, and the Carvoran Roman Army Museum, all within 15 minutes' drive from the hotel. The Grey Bull has been modernized and reequipped. There are 11 bedrooms, each with its own wash basin with hot and cold running water. The inclusive price is £10.50 ($20.48) per person, including an English breakfast, service, and VAT. Packed lunches are available on request. The bar at the hotel is a lively gathering place for the local people.

HEXHAM: Above the Tyne River, this historic old market town is characterized by its narrow streets, old Market Square, a fine abbey church, and its Moot Hall. It makes a good base for exploring Hadrian's Wall and the Roman supply base of Corstopitum at Corbridge-on-Tyne, the ancient capital of Northumberland. The Tourist Office has masses of information on the wall for walkers, drivers, campers, and picnickers.

The **Abbey Church of St. Wilfred** is full of ancient relics. The Saxon font, the misericord carvings on the choir stalls, Acca's Cross, and St. Wilfred's chair are well worth seeing.

For accommodations, try the **Beaumont Hotel,** Beaumont Street (tel. Hexham 602331), a family-run place across from the village park. It offers excellent facilities, including handsomely furnished and pleasantly decorated bedrooms, which are in the modern style, the effect livened by bright colors. Nearly all 20 bedrooms have private baths or shower units tucked in. A bathless single room costs £15 ($29.25), rising to £20 ($39) with bath. Doubles or twins with baths or showers rent from £24.50 ($47.78). Tariffs include VAT and service. Guests have a choice of two bars. Lunch is from £5 ($9.75), and dinner is à la carte.

The **Hadrian Hotel,** Wall, near Hexham (tel. Humshaugh 232), is the ideal place to stay when visiting Hadrian's Wall. It's an ivy-covered building erected of stones taken from the wall. The lounge has a collection of antiques, swords, guns, and curios, excellent for after-dinner coffee in front of the blazing fire. The dining room with three window walls has red tablecloths with white lace overcloths. You can look across the meadow toward the wall. There are eight bedrooms, all with hot and cold running water, innerspring mattresses, and electric blankets. The daily tariff in a single room is £14.50 ($28.28), from £24 ($46.80) in a double. Lunches are table d'hôte, costing from £5 ($9.75), and dinners begin at £8 ($15.60).

As a luncheon stopover, I'd suggest the **Country Kitchen,** 23 Market Pl. (tel. Hexham 603835), where you can order a good-tasting homemade soup, followed by, perhaps, sugar-baked ham with a salad or vegetables, or smoked haddock flan. Desserts include the likes of baked banana sponge pudding. Expect to pay from £2.50 ($4.88), plus the cost of your drink. The kitchen is open daily except Sunday and Monday from 10:30 to 11:30 a.m. for coffee, then from noon to 2:15 p.m. for lunch.

Next door is an intriguing shop, selling all sorts of local crafts, exotic food, and souvenirs.

If you're spending the night in town, try dinner at the **Abbey Flags,** 19 Market Pl. (tel. Hexham 3252). As the name suggests, it stands in the forecourt of the abbey, and it's open for dinner from 7 to 10 p.m. from Monday to Saturday.

Chilled honeydew melon or fresh pineapple or mushroom salad, along with fried sprats or homemade chicken liver pâté, jostle various cold and hot soups as appetizers. Main dishes include fish, pork with ginger sauce, turkey-and-walnut pie, or liver of lamb with Dubonnet. The whole meal, including dessert and coffee, VAT, and service, is likely to cost from £8.50 ($16.58) per person. Close the door as you go out, or the rubber plant at the bottom of the stairs complains. Look out if you try to pay by credit card, as a fee of 5% is charged.

On the Outskirts

The **George Hotel,** Chollerford, Humshaugh, near Hexham (tel. Humshaugh 446), stands on the banks of the Tyne, an ingratiating, creeper-covered country hotel with well-tended gardens leading down to the riverbank. It's a convenient base for visiting the whole of the wall. The age of the hotel is unknown, and its drawing room maintains a country-house style, with ornate white woodwork including an original fireplace. Brightly colored chintz armchairs are drawn up for after-dinner coffee. Out the bay window you can see the river at the bottom of the garden. The bedrooms are small, nicely equipped, and come with private baths or showers and TV sets. Many of the units have been recently modernized, refurnished, and decorated. Adjoining the restaurant is a cocktail bar and lounge, and locals gather in the Fisherman's Bar, which has the atmosphere of a country inn. Sandwiches are freshly made here. A set luncheon goes for £5.50 ($10.73), including a choice from three or four appetizers, three or four main courses, then fresh fruit salad, dessert, or cheese, climaxed by coffee. There's a very good wine list. In the lounge, except for Sunday, a salad bar dispenses pie, sausage, scotch eggs, along with mixed green and vegetable salads. For £1.25 ($2.44), your plate will be heavily laden. A single rents for £23.50 ($45.83) nightly, a double or twin for £34 ($66.30), including a large cooked breakfast, VAT, and service.

OTTERBURN: This mellowed old village on the Rede River was the scene of the famous Battle of Otterburn in 1388. It makes a good base for touring the Cheviot Hills.

Otterburn Tower Hotel (tel. Otterburn 20673) stands in a quiet, tree-edged hollow in the hills. It's reached by crossing over a tiny bridge, past the Otterburn Mill. Once Sir Walter Scott was a guest at the tower in 1812, and the hotel still retains many fine architectural details, including 16th-century paneling in the dining room as well as stained-glass family crests. Guests dine while seated on Windsor chairs, and in the dining lounge is an Italian marble fireplace. The bedrooms are large and traditionally furnished. A single rents for £15 ($29.25), rising to anywhere from £24 ($46.80) in a bathless double to £32 ($62.40) in a twin with private bath. All tariffs include VAT and a full English breakfast. A lunch costs from £5 ($9.75); a dinner, £6.75 ($13.16).

ALNMOUTH: A seaside resort on the Aln estuary, Alnmouth attracts sporting people who fish for salmon and trout in the Coquet River or else play on its good golf course.

The **Schooner Hotel**, Northumberland Street (tel. Alnwick 830216), is a well-preserved Georgian coaching inn, only a few minutes' walk to the water. The hotel is adjacent to the nine-hole Village Golf Course, the second oldest in the country, and also lies near an 18-hole course. The hotel has a squash court. A single room with breakfast is £12.50 ($24.38), £11 ($21.45) per person in a double, including VAT. Guests count on the good meals prepared and served at low prices. Set luncheons are £4 ($7.80); set dinners, £7 ($13.65); or you can also stay here on the full-board rate of £20 ($39) per person daily, which includes either a packed picnic or bar luncheon. There are 24 bedrooms, a grill room, dining room, the Sea Hunter bar, the Chase Bar, and the Long Bar, as well as a resident's lounge with color TV.

On the outskirts, the **Dunes Hotel**, Seahouses (tel. Seahouses 720378), is a 30-bedroom establishment, from which you can view the Farne Islands with their bird and seal sanctuaries, Bamburgh Castle, and the sand dunes and Seahouses Harbour. Rooms are well kept and pleasantly furnished, and five doubles contain private baths. In a double or twin with bath, the B&B rate is £30 ($58.50), dropping to £26 ($50.70) without bath. Singles go for £12 ($23.40) without bath, £15 ($29.25) with, and all these tariffs include breakfast. There are three large lounges and a sun parlor overlooking the front lawn, plus a bright, sunny smoking room opening onto a flower garden. In the paneled restaurant, a good and varied cuisine is served. The Dunes Hotel is an excellent center for exploring the Farne Islands, Holy Island, the Roman Wall, and the Border Country. The hotel lies just half a mile from Seahouses itself, 14 miles from Alnmouth.

ALNWICK: Set in the peaceful countryside of Northumberland, this ancient market town has had a colorful history. A good center for touring an area of scenic beauty, Alnwick is visited chiefly today by travelers wanting to see—

Alnwick Castle

In the town of Alnwick, 30 miles north of Newcastle, Alnwick Castle (tel. Rothbury 20333) is the seat of the Duke of Northumberland. This border fortress dates from the 11th century, when the earliest parts of the present castle were constructed by Yvo de Vescy, the first Norman Baron of Alnwick. A major restoration was undertaken by the fourth duke in the mid-19th century, and Alnwick remains relatively unchanged to this day. The rugged medieval outer walls do not prepare the first-time visitor for the richness of the interior, decorated mainly in the style of the Italian Renaissance.

Most of the castle is open to the public during visiting hours. You can tour the principal apartments, including the armory, guard chamber, and library, where you can view portraits and landscapes painted by such masters as Titian, Canaletto, and Van Dyck. You may also visit the dungeons and the interesting Museum of Early British and Roman Relics. From the terraces within the castle's outer walls, you can look across the broad landscape stretching over the River Aln.

Alnwick is open to the public daily, except Saturday, from 1 to 5 p.m. from May to September. Admission is £1.50 ($2.93) for adults and 75p ($1.46) for children. For an additional 20p (39¢) you can also visit the Regimental Museum of the Royal Northumberland Fusiliers, within the castle grounds.

Cragside, designed in the late 19th century by architect Richard Norman Shaw for the first Lord Armstrong, is a grand estate stretching across 900 acres on the southern edge of the Alnwick Moor. Here groves of magnificent trees and fields of rhododendrons frequently give way to peaceful ponds and lakes. The Victorian house is open only for part of the season, but the grounds alone are well worth the visit. At Rothbury, the house is just 13 miles southwest of Alnwick. The park is open from April to the end of September from 10:30 a.m. to 6 p.m.; in October, daily from 10:40 a.m. to 5 p.m.; November to the end of March, Saturday and Sunday from 10:30 a.m. to 4 p.m. Admission to the park only is 60p ($1.17). The house is open from April to the end of September daily except Monday (open bank holidays) from 1 to 6 p.m.; in October, on Wednesday, Saturday, and Sunday from 2 to 5 p.m. Admission is £1.60 ($3.12), including the park. Children are admitted at half price. For more information, telephone Rothbury 20333.

Dunstanburgh Castle, on the coast nine miles northeast of Alnwick, was begun in 1316 by Thomas, Earl of Lancaster, and enlarged in the 14th century by John of Gaunt. The dramatic ruins of the gatehouse, towers, and curtain wall stand on a promontory high above the sea. You can reach the castle on foot only, either walking from Craster in the south or across the Dunstanburgh Golf Course from Embleton and Dunstan Steads in the north. The castle is open daily from 9 a.m. to 6:30 p.m., except Sunday. Admission is 50p ($1.95).

Food and Lodging

White Swan, Bondgate Within (tel. Alnwick 602109), has a history going back to medieval days when it entertained highwaymen and passengers on the Edinburgh to London stagecoaches. A neoclassic-style coaching inn, just inside an ancient town gate, the Hotspur, it has also become the permanent home of the music room of the S.S. *Olympic,* sister ship of the *Titanic.* This beautiful paneled room was removed from the ship and completely reconstructed at the hotel. The hotel has 40 bedrooms, with bath and shower, and some of these are in a modern block and others in the older, more traditional part of the inn. Singles begin at £26 ($50.70), and doubles peak at £36 ($70.20), including a full breakfast, service, and VAT. The pleasant restaurant offers traditional dishes from a large table d'hôte menu.

CORNHILL-ON-TWEED: This border village, on the Tweed River, faces Coldstream on the Scottish shore.

Tillmouth Park Hotel (tel. Coldstream 2255), built in 1882, is an imposing Victorian mansion, occupying a secluded position in its own parkland gardens overlooking the Till River at the heart of a 1000-acre estate. It stands about nine miles from Berwick, three miles from Cornhill-on-Tweed, and four miles from Coldstream. Monumental and impressive, it rises four stories high, with many wings, gables, and chimneys, including a porch emblazoned with heraldic devices.

In spite of its size, there are only 14 bedrooms, each one exceptionally comfortable, seven containing private baths. Ask for the Sir Walter Scott room, with its stunning four-poster and private bath. Often Edwardian furnishings grace the private chambers. B&B costs from £17 ($33.15) to £23 ($44.85) in a single, from £13 ($25.35) to £17 ($33.15) per person in a double room.

Modernity, as reflected by a cocktail bar, has been blended with tradition, as represented by a galleried lounge with a massive stone fireplace. Spacious lawns adjoin the hotel.

Part Two

Scotland

Chapter XVI

SOUTHERN SCOTLAND

**1. The Border Country
2. Ayr, Prestwick, and District
3. Dumfries and Galloway**

FROM NEWCASTLE-UPON-TYNE, the A68 heading northwest takes you to where Scotland meets England, an area long known as Carter Bar. At this point, all of Scotland lies before you, and an unforgettable land it is.

In this country of clans and bagpipes, you'll find some of the most dramatic scenery in Europe. Stretching before you will be Lowlands, but in the far distance, the fabled Highlands loom.

If you traverse all the country; you'll discover lochs and glens, heather-covered moors, twirling kilts and tam o'shanters, pastel-bathed houses and gray-stone cottages, mountains, rivers, and sea monsters, as well as the sound of Gaelic, Shetland ponies, scotch whiskey, and misty blue hills, to name only some of its attractions.

I'd recommend to many visitors that they approach the Border Country after a stopover in the York area of England. That way, they can start exploring Scotland in the east with Edinburgh as their goal, then go up through Royal Deeside and on to Iverness, crossing over and down the west side to Glasgow, emerging at Gretna Green, near Carlisle in England's Lake District.

The Border Country is a fit introduction to Scotland, as it contains many reminders of the country's historic and literary past. A highlight of the tour is a visit to Abbotsford, the house Sir Walter Scott built on the banks of the salmon river, the Tweed.

However, if you're approaching Scotland from the west of England, you'll travel through Ayrshire—the Land of Burns. This is the former home of Scotland's most famous novelist and her national poet, Robert Burns.

Burns knew so well the southwestern corner of Scotland, which is bounded by an indented coastline of charm which attracts many artists who prefer the quiet, secluded life that prevails there. Distances aren't long, but many motorists have taken two or more days to cover some 100 miles.

The southwestern Lowlands are often called Galloway, their ancient title, and they contain some of the most impressive scenery in all the country.

At Ayr, Troon, and Prestwick (with its international airport), you'll find sandy beaches and golf courses; and you'll also find that the fishing is good in southern Scotland, as is the pony trekking.

SCOTLAND

This map is taken from *Historic Houses, Castles & Gardens* with permission of ABC Historic Publications, a Division of ABC Travel Guides Ltd., Oldhill London Road, Dunstable LU6 3EB

1. The Border Country

Castles in romantic ruins and Gothic skeletons of abbeys stand as reminders, in this ballad-rich land of plunder and destruction, of interminable battles that raged between England and the proud Scots. For a long time, the so-called Border Country was a no-man's land. And, as mentioned, this is also the land of Sir Walter Scott, that master of romantic adventure in a panoramic setting, who died in 1832. Today he is remembered for such works as *Rob Roy, Kenilworth, Ivanhoe,* and *The Bride of Lammermoor.*

Southeast Scotland contains the remains of the four great abbeys built by David I in the mid-12th century: Dryburgh (where Scott was buried), Melrose, Jedburgh, and Kelso. "The Borders" are also home of the famous "Common Riding" gatherings celebrating major events in the past.

JEDBURGH: Jedburgh lies 325 miles from London, 48 from Edinburgh. This royal burgh and border town is famous for its ruined **Jedburgh Abbey,** founded by King David in 1147, and considered one of the finest abbeys in Scotland. The town lies on the River Jed. The abbey is open daily except Thursday and Friday from April to September, charging 30p (59¢) for adults, 15p (29¢) for children (under 16) and senior citizens.

On Queen Street, you can visit the **Mary Queen of Scots House,** where she resided in the year 1566 from October 9 to November 9. After a long ride to Hermitage Castle where the wounded Earl of Bothwell was, the queen suffered a stomach hemorrhage which nearly killed her. The house, containing articles which once belonged to the queen (her watch, communion service, documents, and paintings), is open from March 1 to October 31 daily from 10 a.m. to 5:30 p.m. Admission is 30p (59¢) for adults, 15p (29¢) for children.

Food and Lodging

Mrs. A. Richardson, 124 Bongate (tel. Jedburgh 62480), is more a private home than a guest house—in fact, it's an apartment in a block of four buildings. The Richardsons have two bedrooms, one with double bed, the other with a double and single, which is classified as a family room. The per-person cost for an adult is £7 ($13.65) nightly. Mrs. Richardson gives you a hot beverage and cookies before you go to bed, and in the morning, a big breakfast. She'll also cook an evening meal, if asked beforehand, which she serves at 6:30 ("so I can go for a walk afterward").

The Carters' Restaurant (tel. Jedburgh 3414) is a pub with downstairs dining room built of old abbey stones. The building has had a colorful history—a local grammar school from 1779, before finding its present role. This is the favorite gathering place of the people of Jedburgh who know that its owner, Michael Wares, serves good food and drink. Soups, bar snacks, and coffee are served daily in the lounge bar. The restaurant offers either British or continental dishes daily from £5 ($9.75). Lunches are served Monday to Saturday from noon to 2 p.m. Dinners are more elaborate, presented Monday to Thursday from 6 to 9 p.m. (till 10 on Friday and Saturday). Fish is fresh from Eyemouth, and plates begin at £3 ($5.85), accompanied, if you wish, by a tomato and cole slaw salad at £1 ($1.95).

If you follow the A698 northeast of Jedburgh, the road will lead to:

KELSO: Another typical historic border town, Kelso lies at the point where the Teviot meets the Tweed. **Kelso Abbey,** now in ruins, was the earliest and the largest of the border abbeys. In the town's marketplace, the "Old Pretender," James Stewart, was proclaimed king, designated James VIII.

Kelso is also the home of the Duke of Roxburghe, who lives at **Floors Castle,** built in 1721 by William Adam. Part of this border house is on view to the public, which is allowed to tour through it, admiring the tapestries, French antiques, Chinese porcelain, and paintings by such artists as Gainsborough, Reynolds, and Landi. Afternoon tea is served in the Courtyard Restaurant. Floors is open daily, except Friday and Saturday, from early May to late September. The house is open at 1:30 p.m., the last guests shown through at 4:45 p.m. The grounds and gardens may be visited from 12:30 to 5:30 p.m. The Garden Centre is open daily from 10:30 a.m. to 4:30 p.m.

Food and Lodging

Kelso makes a good base if you're planning to overnight in the Borders. There you'll find the **Woodside Hotel,** Edenside Road (tel. Kelso 2152), a mansion standing on its own immaculately kept grounds. Some guests find that the best bedrooms are the modern ones, with showers, in a converted stable. However, we prefer the comfortably fitted bedrooms in the main house. Singles range in price from £20 ($39), doubles from £26 ($50.70). The restaurant is particularly recommendable. Many guests visit from all over "Scott country" to enjoy the fine continental dishes. A set dinner costs £8 ($15.60), served from 7 to 9:30 p.m. The pleasantly traditional dining room overlooks the garden.

Ednam House Hotel (tel. Kelso 24168) is a delightful conversion of a Georgian house into a 34-room hotel often referred to as "that lovely place beside the river." The hotel, lying on the fringe of Kelso, has a good atmosphere, and the bedrooms are well kept, some with river views. Built in 1761, the hotel was purchased by the Brooks family from the Duke of Roxburghe in 1928, and it is one of the finest examples of Georgian architecture in the Border Country. Still family owned, the hotel at present is managed by R. Alastair Brooks, grandson of the original purchaser.

A few of the bedrooms are spacious and airy, although late arrivals might be given the more cramped quarters. At least half the accommodations come equipped with private baths, and you pay more for these, of course. Singles range in price from £15.25 ($29.74) to £18 ($35.10), doubles from £30.50 ($59.48) to £35.50 ($69.23). Rates include a full Scottish breakfast and VAT, although service is extra. For those wanting to chance it with the highly unreliable Scottish sun, there is a terrace.

From Kelso, it is only a short drive on the A699 to—

DRYBURGH: Scott himself is buried at **Dyrburgh Abbey.** These Gothic ruins are surrounded by gnarled yew trees and cedar of Lebanon, said to have been planted there by knights returning from the Holy Land during the years of the Crusades. Near Dryburgh is "Scott's View," over the Tweed to his beloved Eildon Hills, considered one of the most beautiful views in the region.

The adjoining town is—

ST. BOSWELLS: This old village, 40 miles from Edinburgh, stands on the Selkirk–Kelso road, near Dryburgh Abbey. It lies four miles from Melrose and 14 miles from Kelso. Because of the following hotel, many motorists prefer to make St. Boswells their headquarters for touring "the Borders."

Dryburgh Abbey Hotel (tel. 22261) actually stands beside the ruins from which it takes its name. On the outskirts of St. Boswells, the red sandstone hotel is surrounded by lovely grounds, made all the more so by the gently flowing Tweed River. Built in the Scottish baronial manor, the abbey hotel has all the amenities associated with the traditional country house hotel, including large, extensive grounds. Modern conveniences have been slipped in, however. About 30 rooms are offered, with singles renting from £23 ($44.85), doubles from £26 ($50.70), these tariffs including a full English breakfast. You have a choice of several lounges and a handsome dining room, plus a cocktail bar. The hotel is open all year. Good Scottish fare is served, and that means fresh local salmon or perhaps roast gigot of "Borders" lamb, with its traditional accompaniment, red currant jelly. Soups are good, too, especially the homemade ham and lentil broth.

Four miles from Dryburgh Abbey is—

MELROSE: Lying 37 miles from Edinburgh, Melrose enjoys many associations with Scott. This border town, as mentioned, is also famous for its ruined **Melrose Abbey,** in the Valley of the Tweed. You can visit the ruins of the abbey in which the heart of Robert Bruce is said to have been buried. Look for the beautiful carvings and the tombs of other well-known Scotsmen buried in the chancel. In Scott's *The Lay of the Last Minstrel,* the abbey's east window received rhapsodic treatment, and in *The Abbot* and *The Monastery,* Melrose appears as "Kennaquhair." It is open Monday to Saturday from 9:30 a.m. to 4 p.m. (from 2 to 5 p.m. on Sunday), charging an admission of 35p (68¢) for adults, 20p (39¢) for children.

The leading hotel in Melrose is **George & Abbotsford,** High Street (tel. Melrose 2308), a 19th-century coaching inn built overlooking the ruins of Melrose Abbey. The hotel is unpretentious, with well-equipped bedrooms, about half of which contain private baths. Singles range in price from £14 ($27.30) to £16 ($31.20), and doubles rent from £27 ($52.65) to £30 ($58.50). Breakfast is extra. In the garden you can admire the roses—and think about the brave heart of the Scottish hero, Robert Bruce. Later on, you can fortify yourself for another day's exploration in one of the two lounges or bar, meeting a congenial blend of visitors and locals.

At sunset you can stroll along the banks of the River Tweed, perhaps walk along a public footpath on a hill overlooking the town.

The next morning, you can drive three miles to—

ABBOTSFORD: This was the home of Sir Walter Scott that he built and lived in from 1812 until he died. It contains many relics collected by the author. Especially interesting is his study, with his writing desk and chair. In 1935 two secret drawers were found in the desk. One of them contained 57 letters, part of the correspondence between Sir Walter and his wife-to-be. The Scott home is open from March 22 to October 31, weekdays from 10 a.m. to 5 p.m., on Sunday from 2 to 5 p.m., charging £1 ($1.95) for adults, 50p (98¢) for children.

After leaving Scott's house, you can continue along the Tweed to—

TRAQUAIR HOUSE: At Innerleithen, a few miles east of Peebles, Traquair is considered the oldest inhabited and most romantic house in Scotland. Dating back to the tenth century, it is rich in associations with Mary Queen of Scots and the Jacobite risings. Its treasures include glass, embroideries, silver, manuscripts, and paintings. Of particular interest is a brewhouse equipped as it was two centuries ago. The great house is still lived in by the Stuarts of Traquair.

The house and grounds are open from Easter Saturday until about the last week in October, daily from 1:30 to 5:30 p.m. In July and August, hours are from 10:30 a.m. to 5:30 p.m. (last admittance is at 5 p.m.). Rates are £1.20 ($2.34) for adults, 60p ($1.17) for children.

There are five craft workshops in the grounds as well as a tearoom, home bakehouse, playground, woodland and River Tweed walks, and a newly planted maze. Tennis and croquet can be played by arrangement, and trout fishing is available on a private stretch of the Tweed. To make inquiries, telephone Innerleithen 323.

Innerleithen is a modest little mill town, but the unmarred beauty of the River Tweed valley as seen from the town's surrounding hillsides remains constant. The famous Ballantyne cashmeres are manufactured here, and annual games and a Cleikum ceremony take place here in July. Scott's novel, *St. Ronan's Well,* is identified with the town.

From Innerleithen, it's only a six-mile ride to—

PEEBLES: This royal burgh and county town, 23 miles from Edinburgh, is a market center in the Valley of the Tweed. Scottish kings used to come here when they went to hunt in Ettrick Forest. The town is noted for its large woolen mills, although the **Scottish Museum of Wool Textiles,** where you can see how tartans and fine woolens are dyed and spun, and where you can buy lengths of cloth and garments to take home, lies nine miles west in the town of Walkerburn.

Peebles is also known as a "writer's town." John Buchan Tweedsmuir, the Scottish author and statesman who died in 1940 and is remembered chiefly for writing the Stevensonian adventure story *Prester John* in 1910, lived here. He was also the author of *The Thirty-Nine Steps* (1915), the first of a highly successful series of secret-service thrillers. In 1935 he was appointed governor-general of Canada. Robert Louis Stevenson once lived at Peebles, and drew upon the surrounding countryside in *Kidnapped,* which was published first in 1886.

On the north bank of the Tweed stands **Neidpath Castle,** its peel (tower) dating from the 13th century. Cromwell besieged and took it in 1650.

Food and Lodging

If you'd like to spend the night instead of heading on to Edinburgh, a good bet is the **Tontine Hotel,** High Street (tel. Peebles 20892), which has a Scottish lion on a fountain in its forecourt. The hotel was built in 1808 by subscription—hence its name. It has been recently redecorated and restyled, and in the comfortable main lounge is a fine display of silver belonging to the hotel. An extension has been added, housing a block of modern, studio-style rooms, all equipped with private baths. Singles rent for £21 ($40.95), doubles for £32 ($62.40), including VAT and service. The staff is efficient and friendly. The restaurant, the Adam Room, has good views overlooking Glensax Hills. One bar is known as the Tweeddale Shoot Bar, named after the long-established Shooting Club of Peebles. The second bar, the Beltane, is decorated in pine and named after a local festival. It has one of the finest displays of working-horse harnesses in the country. Bar snacks are available at lunch, and there's always a hot chef's specialty, costing from £1.95 ($3.80).

The **Cringletie House Hotel,** at Eddleston, near Peebles (tel. Eddleston 233), is an imposing country hotel, with towers and turrets, standing on 28 acres of private grounds. It's like a small French château, built of red sandstone and lying slightly more than two miles from the center of Peebles, set back from the A703. Your hosts, Mr. and Mrs. Maguire, receive you as if you were a private guest in their baronial mansion.

Most of the bedrooms, 16 in all, are spacious, and all of them are comfortably appointed. Nine have private baths. Singles range in price from £16.50 ($32.16), and doubles go from £17.50 ($34.13) per person with private bath. Top-floor bedrooms without private baths cost £14.50 ($28.28) per person. The public rooms are rich in character and style, as befits a Victorian mansion. There was, to our surprise, an elevator as well. The bar is well stocked, and guests gather there before dinner, exchanging introductions.

Mrs. Maguire is in charge of the hotel's restaurant. In elegant surroundings, you are given a limited but extremely well-selected choice of dishes. The food is made even more enjoyable by the attentive service. In season the vegetables come fresh from Mrs. Maguire's garden. She has her own style of cooking, and her special dishes include a delectable smoked haddock mousse. A set luncheon is offered from 1 to 1:45 at £6 ($11.70), and a four-course dinner is from 7:30 to 8:30, going for £10 ($19.50). You must be punctual, because of the short hours of serving (the food is freshly cooked), and you'll need a reservation, of course, particularly if you aren't a guest of the hotel. The restaurant and hotel are closed from mid-November to mid-March.

MELLERSTAIN: Seat of the Lord Binning, Mellerstain lies in "the Borders," although it is most often visited on a day trip from Edinburgh, 37 miles away. One of Scotland's famous Adam mansions, it lies near Gordon, nine miles northeast of Melrose and seven miles northwest of Kelso (tel. Gordon 225). It's open from May to September daily, except Saturday, from 1:30 to 5:30 p.m.

Mellerstain enjoys associations with Lady Grisel Baillie, the Scottish heroine, and Lord Binning is her descendant. William Adam built two wings of the house in 1725, although the main building was designed by his more famous son, Robert, some 40 years later.

You're shown through the interior, with its decorations and ceilings by Robert Adam, and are allowed to view the impressive library as well as paintings by old masters and antique furniture. Later, from the garden terrace, you can look south to the lake, with the Cheviot Hills in the distance, a panoramic view. Afternoon tea is served, and tweeds and souvenir gifts are on sale.

2. Ayr, Prestwick, and District

As Sir Walter Scott dominates the Borders, so does Robert Burns the country around Ayr and Prestwick. There are, in addition, a string of famous seaside resorts stretching from Girvan to Largs. Some of the greatest golf courses in Britain, including Turnberry, are found here, and Prestwick, of course, is one of the major airports of Europe.

AYR: Ayr is the most popular resort on Scotland's west coast. A busy market town, it offers 2½ miles of sands and makes for a good center for touring the Burns Country. This royal burgh is also noted for its manufacture of fabrics and carpets, so you may want to allow time to browse through its shops. With its steamer cruises, fishing, golf, and racing, it faces the Isle of Arran and the Firth of Clyde.

Ayr is full of Burns associations. The 13th-century **Auld Brig o' Ayr,** the poet's "poor narrow footpath of a street,/ Where two wheelbarrows tremble when they meet," was renovated in 1910. A Burns museum is housed in the thatched **Tam o'Shanter Inn** in Ayr High Street, an alehouse in Rabbie's day.

The **Auld Kirk** of Ayr dates from 1654 when it replaced the 12th-century Church of St. John. Burns was baptized in the kirk.

Ayr is also the birthplace of the famous road builder, John L. MacAdam, whose name was immortalized in road surfacing.

In Tarbolton village, 7½ miles northeast of Ayr, is the **Bachelors' Club**, a 17th-century house where in 1780 Burns and his friends founded a literary and debating society, now a property of the National Trust for Scotland. In 1779 Burns attended dancing lessons there, against the wishes of his father. There also, in 1781, he was initiated as a Freemason in the Lodge St. David. Eleven months later, he became a member of Lodge St. James, which continues today in the village. Samuel Hay, 7 Croft St. (tel. Tarbolton 424), says the Bachelors' Club is open for visitors any time of day from April until October, and he will arrange to show it at other times if you telephone. Admission is 30p (59¢) for adults, 15p (29¢) for children. Tarbolton is six miles from Prestwick Airport.

For centuries, Ayr has been associated with horse racing, and it now has the top racecourse in Scotland. One of the main streets of the town is named Racecourse Road for a stretch near the town center.

Where to Stay

Pickwick Hotel, 19 Racecourse Rd. (tel. Ayr 60111). It may seem ironic to have a hotel commemorating a character in a Charles Dickens novel in a town noted for its memories of Rabbie Burns. But this early Victorian hotel, set on its own grounds, does just that. The Pickwick is really a large-size house, renting out 15 well-furnished private bedrooms which contain either a private shower or else a complete bath. The B&B rate is £19 ($37.05) per person, including a full breakfast, VAT, and service. Each room bears a Dickensian title. All rooms have private bathroom facilities, color TV, radio, drinks dispenser, trouser presser, and tea- and coffee-making equipment. In the paneled Pickwick Club you can soak up much Dickensian atmosphere. The food itself is simple but well prepared, a dinner costing from £7.50 ($14.63). The hotel is personally supervised by Sheila and Edward Lynas, the proprietors, who endeavor to make everyone who stays at the Pickwick feel welcome.

Caledonian Hotel, Dalblair Road (tel. Ayr 69331), occupies a convenient central location, offering comfortable although certainly not luxurious bedrooms, all 122 of which contain functional, compact private baths or showers plus TV. Singles rent for £27 ($52.65), doubles for £40 ($78). Flight crews from various international carriers stay here, a fact acknowledged by the Flight Deck Bar. The food is good, particularly in the hotel's theme restaurant, Chaplin's. There is also a sauna, souvenir shop, and a disco which is open five nights a week. A dinner-dance is held every Saturday night.

Marine Court, Fairfield Road (tel. Ayr 67461), has long been a favorite with travelers. A substantial building, in a cul-de-sac, it offers good, solid comfort, and many of its rooms open onto a sweeping view of the Firth of Clyde. The hotel also lies about 200 yards from the beach, and it makes for a charming oasis, especially as you wander through its garden. The bedrooms are well furnished and immaculately maintained, and almost all of them come equipped with private bath. Singles peak at £18.50 ($36.08), and doubles are rented for a top £28 ($54.60), including a full breakfast, service, and VAT. The food is well prepared and handsomely served. A normal set lunch goes for £2.75 ($5.36), going up to £6.50 ($12.68) for the weekday set dinner. On

Saturday a band plays for a dinner-dance at a special price. The hotel has cable TV with a better-than-average choice of programs.

The Local Pub

By all means, pay your respects to Burns by going to **Rabbie's Bar**, Burns Statue Square (tel. Ayr 262112), right in the heart of town. A colorfully decorated pub, this place is, of course, dedicated to the memory of the poet. On the walls you'll find a selection of some of his most famous lines. In addition to the good drink which Burns enjoyed, you can also order simple fare such as snacks and grills. Guests sit near a thatched bar counter. One reader reports that disco music wasn't what she expected to hear in a bar honoring Burns.

ALLOWAY: Some three miles from the center of Ayr is where Robert Burns, Scotland's national poet, was born on January 25, 1759, in the gardener's cottage—the "auld clay biggin"—his father, William Burns, built in 1757. More than 100,000 people visit the **Burns Cottage** annually, and it still retains some of its original furniture, including the bed in which the poet was born. Chairs displayed here were said to have been used by Tam o'Shanter and Souter Johnnie. Beside the cottage in which the poet lived is a museum, open all year from 9 a.m. to 7 p.m. during summer (shorter hours in the off-season). Admission to the cottage and the Burns Monument is 50p (98¢) for adults, 25p (49¢) for children.

The Auld Brig over the Ayr, mentioned in "Tam o'Shanter," still spans the river, and Alloway Auld Kirk, also mentioned in the poem, stands roofless and "haunted" not far away. The poet's father is buried in the graveyard of the kirk.

The **Land o' Burns Centre** near the monument is a good place to stop. You can watch the multiscreen presentation of highlights of Burn's life, his friends, and his poetry. Information is available from the friendly personnel, and a well-stocked gift shop is there. The Russians are particularly fond of Burns and his poetry, and many come annually to visit the cottage and pore over his original manuscripts.

Where to Stay

The **Burns Monument Hotel** (tel. Alloway 42466) is a 185-year-old inn which looks out onto the Doon River and the bridge, "Brig o'Doon," immortalized in "Tam o'Shanter." The inn is an attractive, historical place, with riverside gardens and a whitewashed bar. The rooms are pleasantly and attractively decorated, bright and cheerful, opening onto river views. All bedrooms have private baths. B&B averages around £12.50 ($24.38) in a single and from £26 ($50.70) in a double.

The **Balgarth Hotel** (tel. Alloway 42441), two miles south of Ayr on the A719 coastal road to the fishing village of Dunure, is within easy reach for touring the Burns Country and southwest Scotland. The hotel stands within its own pleasant grounds, complete with beer garden overlooking the Clyde and Carrick Hills, and offers special rates to golf enthusiasts with access to Royal Troon, Turnberry, and other scenic courses on the Ayrshire coast. The 15 rooms are bright and well furnished, with TV, telephone, and private baths. The tariff per person for B&B is £11 ($21.45), including VAT. Dinner is from £5.50 ($10.73). The Balgarth is open all year.

CULZEAN CASTLE: One of Robert Adam's most notable creations, although built around an ancient tower of the Kennedys, Culzean (pronounced Cullane), 12 miles south-southwest of Ayr, dates mainly from 1777 and is considered one of the finest Adam houses in Scotland. The castle, with a view of Ailsa Craig to the south and overlooking the Firth of Clyde, is well worth a visit and is of special interest to Americans because of General Eisenhower's connection with it and its National Guest Flat. In 1946 the guest flat was given to the general for his lifetime in gratitude for his services as Supreme Commander of Allied Forces in World War II. Culzean stands near the golf courses of Turnberry and Troon, a fact which particularly pleased the golf-loving Eisenhower.

An exhibition of Eisenhower memorabilia includes sound and audio-visual spectacles, and is seen by more than 100,000 people a year. The exhibition is sponsored by the Scottish Heritage U.S.A., Inc., and Mobil Oil. To illustrate his career, there is a capsule history of World War II demonstrated with wall maps. Mementos of Eisenhower include his North African campaign desk and a replica of the Steuben glass bowl given him by his cabinet when he retired from the presidency.

The castle is open April 1 through September daily, 10 a.m. to 6 p.m. (last admission at 5:30 p.m.); October 1 through October 31 daily, 10 a.m. to 4 p.m. Admission to the castle is £1.30 ($2.54) for adults, 65p ($1.27) for children.

In the castle grounds is **Culzean Country Park,** which in 1969 became the first such park in Scotland. It has an exhibition center in farm buildings by Adam. The 565-acre grounds include a walled garden, an aviary, a swan pond, a camellia house, an orangery, a deer park, miles of woodland paths, and beaches. Cars can drive through the Culzean Country Park at a cost of £1.20 ($2.34). For information, telephone Kirkoswald 269.

After leaving Culzean Castle, you might want to take a short drive to **Kirkoswald** near Maybole. This is the thatched cottage which was the home of the village cobbler, John Davidson (Souter Johnnie), at the end of the 18th century. Davidson and his friend Douglas Graham of Shanter Farm were immortalized by Burns in his poem "Tam o' Shanter." The cottage contains Burnsiana and contemporary cobblers' workshop and tools. In the churchyard are the graves of Tam o'Shanter and Souter Johnnie, two of his best known characters. The cottage is open April 1 to September 30, daily except Friday, noon to 5 p.m. (other times by appointment). Admission is 40p (78¢) for adults, 20p (39¢) for children. Telephone Kirkoswald 603 for more information.

GIRVAN: About eight miles south of Culzean Castle on the A77, Girvan is the leading coastal resort of southwest Scotland, with sandy beaches and good fishing. A whisky distillery offers guided tours (and samples) for visitors.

In summer entertainment is offered at the **Beach Pavilion,** featuring music, dancing, children's shows, variety shows, and concerts.

Ailsa Craig, a 1110-foot-high, rounded rock ten miles offshore, is a nesting ground and sanctuary for seabirds and formerly provided granite for stones used in the Scottish game of curling. You can sail out to the rock for a modest charge.

Three miles northeast of Girvan is the 16th-century **Kilochan Castle,** stronghold of the Cathcarts of Carleton in the valley of the Water of Girvan.

Six miles north of Girvan are the scant remains of **Turnberry Castle,** where many historians believe Robert the Bruce was born in 1274.

The **Westcliffe Hotel,** Louisa Drive (tel. Girvan 2128), is on the seafront and overlooks the Promenade, putting greens, and a children's boating lake.

This is a family hotel, and the resident proprietors, Mr. and Mrs. Robert Jardine, have carried out extensive alterations, adding six ground-floor bedrooms, all with private bathrooms, at the back. Some bedrooms in the original building have showers. All bedrooms have hot and cold water and electric shaving points, and are carpeted. Rooms without bath rent for £9 ($17.55) per person for B&B. With bath, the rent is £10 ($19.50). The Westcliffe is licensed, with a new lounge bar and a small service bar at the end of the dining room which looks out over the seafront and Ailsa Craig. Mrs. Jardine personally supervises preparation of the food, which is very good. There are tea- and coffee-making facilities in the reception area.

PRESTWICK: Prestwick is the oldest recorded baronial burgh in Scotland. But most visitors today aren't concerned with that ancient fact—rather, they fly in, landing at Prestwick's International Airport, which is, in itself, a popular sightseeing attraction, as spectators gather to watch planes take off and land from all over the world.

Behind St. Ninian's Episcopal Church is **Bruce's Well,** the water from which is reputed to have cured Robert the Bruce of leprosy. The **Mercat Cross** still stands outside what used to be the Registry Office and marks the center of the oldest part of Prestwick, whose existence goes back to at least 983. Prestwick is a popular holiday town, and is considered one of Scotland's most attractive resorts, with its splendid sands and golf courses. Prestwick opens onto views of Ayr Bay and the Isle of Arran.

Where to Stay

Carlton Motor Hotel, 187 Ayr Rd. (tel. Prestwick 76811), is a good stopover point if you're waiting for your plane at Prestwick. On the Prestwick-Ayr road, right in the vicinity of the international airport, the hotel is built in a straightforward modern design which offers all the amenities you'd expect in such a place—coffee-making equipment, full baths with all rooms, color TV, and attractive furnishings. Singles begin at £18 ($35.10), and doubles rent for £28 ($54.60), including breakfast, service, and VAT. A trio of bars is offered, and there are plenty of lounges in which to relax. Some of the windows open onto a garden. A set dinner costs £6.50 ($12.68), and you can dance to a live band on Friday and Saturday nights at no extra charge.

Adamton House Hotel, Monktown, near Prestwick (tel. Prestwick 70678), is an 18th-century, 30-bedroom hotel with views of the Isle of Arran and Ailsa Craig. As it lies only a few miles from Prestwick Airport, it provides an excellent opportunity to get over jet-lag. All rooms have bath or shower, tea-making equipment, and TV and radio. The beautiful curved wooden staircase leads down again to a quiet, comfortable lounge, the restaurant, and the cocktail bar. In the Secret Room beneath the house, the hotel stages nightly a historical banquet with candlelight and medieval entertainment. Including food and wine, the banquet costs £11 ($21.45) per person and lasts three hours. Singles with shower are £23 ($44.85), and doubles and twins with bath cost from £40 ($78), including breakfast and VAT, although service is extra.

Towans Hotel, Prestwick Airport (tel. Prestwick 79691). The original building faces a side lawn and then looks out over the Firth of Clyde to the Isle of Arran. Much of the accommodation is in a new hotel/motel block which blends successfully with the old. The Martin family, conscious of the needs of international travelers passing through Prestwick Airport, are geared to catering for early and late arrivals. Rooms have private baths, and tea and coffee makers. Breakfast is served from 4 a.m., and the dining room has a good local reputation for well-cooked meals. A bed will cost you from £14 ($27.30). All meals are extra, but you can make as much tea and coffee as you want in your room.

The **Parkstone,** Esplanade (tel. Prestwick 77286), is more suited for a beach holiday center, as it opens onto the sea. Catering to families, it is handsomely perched, receiving guests all year in one of its many bedrooms, some of which contain a private bath and a color TV. The single tariff is £14.50 ($28.28), rising to £25 ($48.75) in a double, including a full breakfast, VAT, and service. Rooms are comfortably and pleasantly furnished. A two-course luncheon goes for £3.75 ($7.31), a set dinner for £6.75 ($13.16), and high tea from £3.35 ($6.53).

TROON: This holiday resort looks out across the Firth of Clyde to the Isle of Arran. It offers several golf links, including the "Old Troon" course. Bathers in summer find plenty of room on its two miles of sandy beaches, stretching from both sides of its harbor. The broad sands and shallow waters make it a safe haven also. From here you can take steamer trips to Arran and the Kyles of Bute.

Troon is mostly a 20th-century town, its earlier history having gone unrecorded. It takes its name from the curiously shaped promontory that juts out into the Clyde estuary on which the old town and the harbor stand. The promontory was called "Trwyn," the Cymric word for nose, and later this became the Trone and then Troon.

Fullarton Estate, on the edge of Troon beyond the municipal golf course, is the ancestral seat of the Dukes of Portland.

A massive statue of **Britannia** stands on the seafront as a memorial to the dead of the two World Wars. On her breastplate is the lion of Scotland emerging from the sea.

Where to Stay

Marine Hotel, Crosbie Road (tel. Troon 314444), is a large deluxe hotel which is enveloped by about 20 miles of seaside golf courses. One of the principal hotels along the Clyde coast, it offers a wide range of accommodations —70 rooms in all, each with bath, and each differing in style, space, and furnishings. The single rate is £28 ($54.60), rising to £45 ($87.75) in a double, including VAT, service, and a full breakfast. Not only are the views from the windows spectacular, but the hotel is most agreeable and makes a good base for touring the Burns Country. The helpful staff gives personal attention—if you come back a second time they'll know your name. The noise from Prestwick—three miles away—is kept out by double-glazed windows.

The hotel's restaurants offer excellent fare, although I prefer L'Auberge de Provence, where the French cookery is superb, as is the selection of fine burgundies. The auberge is decorated in a rustic style, serving dinner only, from 7 to 10:30 p.m. daily except Sunday, charging about £16 ($31.20) per person. The lounges are spacious, and there are two stylish bars.

Sun Court, Crosbie Road (tel. Troon 312727), was once the home of an industrialist, and it offers all the grand style of the Edwardian era. Like the Marine, it looks out onto golf courses and the sea. Its most delightful feature is a conservatory filled with flowers. The hotel also contains a Real Tennis Court, one of of the few in Britain. A sandy beach along the Firth of Clyde is about a 100-yard walk away.

Open all year, the Sun Court offers 20 handsome bedrooms, 17 of which contain private baths. The single tariff ranges from £20 ($39) to £23 ($44.85), the double rate going from £30 ($58.50) to £34 ($66.30). There is as well a beautiful walled garden. The lounges are stylish and decorated in a conservative fashion. Try to get one of the more old-fashioned bedrooms, although you may be assigned a more modernized one. From a well-stocked cellar emerges a fine collection of wine, and the food at Sun Court is well prepared and served.

KILMARNOCK: This inland town is the site of the largest whisky-bottling concern in the world. Johnnie Walker, a grocer in King Street, started to blend whisky in Kilmarnock in 1820, and the product is known all over the world today.

The town also has Burns associations. The first edition of his poems was printed here in 1786. Burns published the poems to raise money to emigrate to Jamaica, but they were so successful he decided to remain in Scotland. In Kay Park, the **Burns Monument** is a red sandstone temple surmounted by a tower, which contains a good museum of Burnsiana.

Dundonald Castle, 4½ miles southwest of Kilmarnock, is a notable landmark high on an isolated hill. It was built by Robert II, the first Stuart king, who died there in 1390, as did Robert III in 1406. East along the River Irvine are the three lace-making towns of Galston, Newmilns, and Darvel where Dutch and Huguenot immigrants settled in the 17th century.

3. Dumfries and Galloway

Southwestern Scotland is often overlooked by motorists rushing north. But this country of Burns is filled with many rewarding targets—a land of unspoiled countryside, fishing harbors, artists' colonies of color-washed houses, and romantically ruined abbeys and castles dating from the days of the border wars.

It's a fine touring country, and the hotels are generally small, of the Scottish provincial variety, but that usually means a friendly reception from a smiling staff and good traditional Scottish cookery, using the local produce.

I've documented the most important centers below, but have included some offbeat places for those seeking a more esoteric trip.

LOCKERBIE: A border market town, Lockerbie lies in the beautiful valley of Annandale, offering much fishing and golf. It's a good center for exploring some sightseeing attractions in its environs.

Lockerbie was the scene in 1593 of a battle which ended one of the last great Border family feuds. The Johnstones routed the Maxwells, killing Lord Maxwell and 700 of his men. Many of the victims had their ears cut off with a cleaver, a method of mutilation which became known throughout the Border Country as the "Lockerbie Nick."

Of interest are the remains of **Lochmaben Castle**, 3½ miles west of Lockerbie, said to have been the boyhood home (some historians say the birthplace) of Robert the Bruce. This castle, on the south shore of Castle Loch, was captured and recaptured 12 times and also withstood six attacks and sieges. James IV was a frequent visitor, and Mary Queen of Scots was here in 1565. The ruin of the early 14th-century castle is on the site of a castle of the de Brus family, ancestors of Robert the Bruce. However, the charming little hamlet of Lochmaben, with its five lochs, is reason enough to visit, regardless of who was or was not born there.

Rammerscales lies five miles west of Lockerbie and 2½ miles south of Lochmaben on the B7020. It can easily be visited on your tour of Lochmaben and its lakes. Rammerscales is a Georgian manor house, dating from 1760. Set on high ground, it offers beautiful views of the Valley of Annandale. You can visit a walled garden of the period. It is open from June 29 to September 2 on Tuesday, Wednesday, and Thursday (also alternate Sundays from July 4), from 2 to 5 p.m. (other days by appointment), charging an admission of 60p ($1.17) for adults, 35p (68¢) for children. For more information, telephone 038-781-361 in office hours.

If you're heading north to Lockerbie on the A74, I'd suggest a stopover in the village of Ecclefechan. There you can visit **Carlyle's Birthplace,** five miles southeast of Lockerbie on the Lockerbie–Carlisle road. Even though the historian, critic, and essayist Thomas Carlyle isn't much read these days, the "arched house" in which he was born in 1795 is interesting in itself, containing mementoes and manuscripts of the author. It's open from Easter until the end of October, daily except Sunday, from 10 a.m. to 6 p.m., charging an admission of 40p (78¢) for adults, 20p (39¢) for children. For more information, telephone Ecclefechan 666.

In Lockerbie, you'll find the best accommodations at the **Dryfesdale House Hotel** (tel. Lockerbie 2427). The house was built in 1831 and was originally a Church of Scotland manse. This quiet hotel offers traditional comfort with log fires and tranquil surroundings. There is a choice of 15 bedrooms, seven of which have private bathrooms. Several of the bedrooms are quite spacious, and you can stay either in the main building or in an annex. Singles range from £15 ($29.25) to £17.50 ($34.13) and doubles run from £20.50 ($39.98) to £27.50 ($53.63). The hotel, known for its good food and wines, is fully licensed with two old-world bars. The sun lounge and elegant dining room open onto good views. The owners are always available to help.

MOFFAT: An Annandale town, Moffat thrives as a center of a sheep-farming area, symbolized by a statue of a ram in the wide High Street, and has been a holiday resort since the mid-17th century, because of the curative properties of its water. It was here that Robert Burns composed the drinking song "O Willie Brew'd a Peck o' Maut." Today people visit this border town on the banks of the Annan River for its good fishing and golf.

North of Moffat is spectacular hill scenery. Five miles northwest is a huge, sheer-sided 500-foot-deep hollow in the hills called the **Devil's Beef Tub,** where Border cattle thieves, called reivers, hid cattle lifted in their raids.

Northeast along Moffat Water, past White Coomb, which stands 2696 feet high, is the **Grey Mare's Tail,** a 200-foot hanging waterfall formed by the Tail Burn dropping from Loch Skene. It is under the National Trust for Scotland.

Food and Lodgings

Annandale Hotel, High Street (tel. Moffat 20013), has been a coaching inn since the 18th century, housing travelers who crossed through the Border Country en route to Glasgow. However, the inn has been modernized and the amenities provided around here have improved considerably since the old days. Still, only five of the nearly 30 bedrooms contain private baths, and none of these has a shower. But the rates in the bathless rooms, to compensate, are low—from £12 ($23.40) in a single, from £23 ($44.85) in a double. In the more expensive chambers, expect to pay £16 ($31.20) in a single, from £27 ($52.65) in a double. The rooms, including the public ones, are kept immaculately. The proprietors have built up a good reputation for their cuisine which includes both British and German specialties. The last dinner is served at 8:30 p.m., and the cost is from £8 ($15.60). Although it's in the center of town, Annandale provides ample car parking on its own grounds.

Beechwood Country House Hotel & Restaurant, off Harthope Place (tel. Moffat 20210), has built its reputation more as a restaurant than a hotel. However, it does offer eight rooms, six of which contain private baths. The bedrooms are adequate for a short stay, costing from £14 ($27.30) in a single to £24 ($46.80) in a double, although the best doubles go for £28 ($54.60). All bedrooms are equipped with tea- and coffee-making facilities and radios, and most have telephones.

The owners, Mr. and Mrs. McIlwrick, serve some of the finest food in the area and offer a wide choice from an extensive wine list. A set luncheon is offered from 12:30 to 1:30 p.m. for £5.50 ($10.73), and it features a good-tasting, homemade soup, including, on one occasion, curried apple. When weather permits, you can take your coffee or afternoon tea in the garden. Dinner is served between 7:30 and 9:30 p.m., when reserving a table is essential. Mrs. McIlwrick sparkles as the chef. A set meal will run £7.20 ($14.04), although you will more likely spend about £10 ($19.50). The dinner offers four courses, and the dishes are nearly always imaginative, certainly well prepared, and everything is made more enjoyable by the enthusiasm of the staff of local country girls. The freshly caught sea trout is a favorite, but if you arrive at the right season you are likely to find venison, even guinea-fowl, on the menu. The produce is fresh, the vegetables tasting as if they had just been picked in the garden. For breakfast, you may enjoy oatcakes. The house is closed in January.

Mercury Motor Inn (tel. Moffat 20464) makes a good place to stop off for the night as you're traveling through the Border Country. At the southern end of town, each of its compact, functional bedrooms contains a private bath, toilet, and coffee-making equipment. Some rooms open onto a public park with a boating pond. Bunk beds for children can also be rented, and there is ample car parking. The staff is helpful and friendly, and you'll be charged from £21 ($40.95) in a single, from £28 ($54.60) to £36 ($70.20) in a double, and you pay extra for breakfast and VAT. The charming licensed bar is bedecked in an 1890s mauve, and the grill room provides good and reasonably priced meals—including such treats as grilled Scottish trout—until about 10 p.m. Dinner costs from £8 ($15.60). In the restaurant, three table d'hôte menus are offered, priced at £7.50 ($14.63), £8.50 ($16.58), and £9.50 ($18.53).

READER'S SHOPPING RECOMMENDATION: "We visited the Moffat weavers at **Ladyknowe Mill,** High Street (tel. Moffat 20134), a perfect place to purchase the least expensive tweeds, tartans, kilts, and knitwear that can be found in Britain. Wool kilts can be found for as little as £14 ($27.30). At the mill you can also watch the kiltmakers busy at work" (Anita T. Taylor, Hartsdale, N.Y.).

A Castle Hotel at Beattock

On the outskirts of Moffat, near the village of Beattock, the most luxurious accommodations in the area are found at **Auchen Castle Hotel** (tel. Beattock 407), a Victorian mock-castle, really a charming country house, built on the site of Auchen Castle. It's one of the most tranquil oases in the Scottish Lowlands, with terraced gardens, a trout-filled loch, and vistas from its windows. Beginning with your arrival at the reception desk, you are treated with graciousness and courtesy, and much effort is extended to make your stay a pleasant one.

The bedrooms, although lacking in fanciful decor, are often spacious and invariably comfortable, and each has a private bath or shower. Rates are £19.50 ($38.03) in a single, from £32 ($62.40) in a double, including a full breakfast, VAT, and service. The rooms in the main building are preferred over those in the annex.

The lofty dining room is exceptional for the area, its windows looking out over flowering ornamental grounds in late spring. Simple dishes are appetizingly good because of the excellent materials used. Roast Scottish beef is superb. The well-appointed tables and efficient staff complement the atmosphere of the peaceful country house. Lunch is from 12:30 to 2 p.m. and dinner from 7 to 8:30 p.m. Bar lunches only are offered, and a table d'hôte dinner goes for £9 ($17.55). Closed mid-December until mid-February.

DUMFRIES: A county town and royal burgh, this Scottish Lowland center enjoys associations with Robert Burns and James Barrie. In a sense it rivals Ayr as a mecca for admirers of Burns. He lived in Dumfries from 1791 until his death in 1796, and it was here that he wrote some of his most famous songs, including "Auld Lang Syne" and "Ye Banks and Braes of Bonnie Doon."

In **St. Michael's Churchyard,** a burial place for at least 900 years, stands the **Burns Mausoleum.** The poet was buried there along with his wife, Jean Armour, as well as five of their children. Burns died in 1796, although his remains weren't removed to the tomb until 1815. In the 18th-century church of St. Michael's you can still see the pew used by the Burns family.

The poet died at what is now called the **Robert Burns House,** a simple, unpretentious stone structure, which can be visited by the public, as it contains personal relics and mementoes relating to Burns. His death may have been hastened by icy dips in well water which the doctor prescribed. The house is on Burns Street (formerly Mill Vennel). The **Town Museum,** the **Globe Inn,** and the **Hole in the Wa' Tavern** all contain Burns relics, and a statue of him stands in the High Street. You can stroll along **Burns' Walk** on the banks of the River Nith.

St. Michael's is the original parish church of Dumfries and its founding is of great antiquity. The site was probably sacred before the advent of Christianity. It appears that a Christian church has stood there for more than 1300 years. The earliest written records date from the reign of William the Lion (1165–1214). The church and the churchyard are interesting to visit because of all its connections with Scottish history, continuing through World War II.

From St. Michael's, it's a short walk to the Whitesands, where four bridges span the Nith. The earliest of these was built by Devorgilla Balliol, widow of John Balliol, father of a Scottish king. The bridge originally had nine arches but now has six and is still in constant use as a footbridge.

The Tourist Information Office is near the bridge. The wide esplanade was once the scene of horse and hiring fairs and now is a fine place to park your car and explore the town. Tour buses park here.

The **Mid Steeple** was built in 1707 as municipal buildings, courthouse, and prison. The old Scots "ell" measure of 37 inches is carved on the front of the building. A table of distances on the building includes the mileage to Huntingdon, England, which in the 18th century was the destination for Scottish cattle drovers driving their beasts south for the markets of London.

At the **Academy,** Barrie was a pupil, and he later wrote that he got the idea for *Peter Pan* from his games in the nearby garden.

Where to Stay

Cairndale Hotel, English Street (tel. Dumfries 4111), is most reliable, a fine and substantial choice. Its bedrooms have been attractively decorated, with special care paid to modern amenities (at least the ones I inspected). Most of the color-coordinated chambers contain private baths, although there are a few bathless bargains offered. Depending on the plumbing, singles range from £16.50 ($32.16) to £21 ($40.95), and doubles go from £28 ($54.60) to £30 ($58.50), including VAT and service. You have a choice of a trio of bars, and guests quickly decide which one they'll make their local. The public lounges are handsomely decorated, and you can select your own favorite nook, perhaps a comfortable chair upholstered in velvet. Dinner, served until 9 p.m., is generally quite good, including such dishes as Galloway beef and grilled scampi. A three-course table d'hôte lunch goes for £6.50 ($12.68), a four-course dinner costing £7.75 ($15.11).

Station Hotel, 49 Lovers Walk (tel. Dumfries 4316), has been improved in recent years and now offers one of the best of the moderately priced accommodations in Dumfries. Rooms come in a variety of styles with differences in plumbing. The atmosphere is modest, although pleasant, and the hosts are most agreeable. Nearly 15 of their rooms contain private baths. Singles range from £18 ($35.10) to £21 ($40.95), and doubles go from £24 ($46.80) to £27 ($52.65), including VAT and a full breakfast. Meals are well prepared, and the service is efficient and polite. A set lunch costs £3.50 ($6.83), a table d'hôte dinner going for £6.50 ($12.68).

Newall House, 22 Newall Terrace (tel. Dumfries 2676), is owned by Charlie and Sheila Cowie. Together they run a friendly place, and do so cheerfully and well. Their rooms are clean and comfortable and include tea- and coffee-making facilities. They charge £8 ($15.60) for a single and £7.50 ($14.63) per person for double occupancy. The tariffs include a well-cooked breakfast. Mrs. Cowie will also prepare an appetizing dinner, if given fair warning, for just £4 ($7.80).

Fulwood Private Hotel, Lovers Walk (tel. Dumfries 2262), is run by congenial, friendly hosts, Mr. and Mrs. J. B. Rowland, who believe in giving wayfarers pleasure, cleanliness, and comfort in their tiny home, containing only five bedrooms (the bath must be shared). They have a wealth of information about touring in the area, and, on one occasion, Mr. Rowland drove a reader from San Jose, California, to some scenic spots. Their rate is £7 ($13.65) per person, including breakfast, VAT, and service.

The Mayfair Hotel, St. Mary's Street, top of English Street (tel. Dumfries 4588), is another good bargain, close to the station, about a five-minute walk to the center of town. It's small, but fully licensed, and there is central heating. The owners, David Solley and his son, offer 15 bedrooms, with hot and cold running water, shaving points, electric blankets, and floor lamps. Some family rooms are available, and there is a reduction for children sharing their parents' room. Singles cost from £10.50 ($20.48), and doubles are rented for £19 ($37.05), including VAT and a full breakfast. Drinks can be enjoyed in the Windmill Cellar Bar. In the evenings a "high tea" menu is available, giving you a choice of steaks, salads, fish, and bacon and eggs, a meal starting at £3 ($5.85). Everything tastes homemade in the attractively decorated, although petite, dining room.

Where to Eat

Bruno's, 5 Balmoral Rd. (tel. Dumfries 5757). It may seem ironic to recommend an Italian restaurant in the seat of Rabbie Burns, but Bruno's serves some of the best food in town. It is most unassuming, and that is part of its charm. Its minestrone is first rate, and its pastas such as lasagne are homemade. The chef doesn't serve the most imaginative Italian dishes ever sampled—in fact, the repertoire is most familiar, such as saltimbocca alla Romana and pollo alla diavola, but it's done with flair. The veal is particularly tender, and the tomato sauce well spiced and blended. Steak au poivre is also excellent. The waiters are friendly and skillful and offer good advice. Bruno's serves only dinner, from 6:30 to 10 p.m. nightly except Tuesday and it will cost you about £12 ($23.40) per person, and it's worth it.

If you're looking for a place to have lunch or tea, go to **Barbour's Department Store,** Buccleuch Street, where you can get tasty dishes in the dining room on the second floor, for prices ranging from 60p ($1.17) for an open sandwich to £3 ($5.85) for a full lunch. The dining room is licensed, and there's an elevator to take you up. Naturally, it's open only during store hours.

Several carry-out delicatessens are along the street across from the Tourist Information Office. The **Merry Chef,** for one, has a variety of goodies if you're in a hurry.

The Local Pub

The **Globe Tavern** was a favorite haunt of Burns. It was one of the "howffs" (taverns) where he imbibed. The location is on a little side street, so ask at your hotel for directions before heading out for your nightly game of "skittles."

Excursions from Dumfries

Based in Dumfries, you can set out on treks in all directions to some of the most intriguing sightseeing goals in the Scottish Lowlands.

South on the 710 leads to the village of **New Abbey,** dominated by the red sandstone ruins of the Cistercian abbey founded in 1273 by Devorgilla, mother of John Balliol, the "vassal king." When her husband, John Balliol the Elder, died, she became one of the richest women in Europe. Most of Galloway, with estates and castles in England and land in Normandy, belonged to her. Devorgilla founded Balliol College, Oxford, in her husband's memory. She kept his embalmed heart in a silver and ivory casket by her side for 21 years until her death in 1289 at the age of 80, when she and the casket were buried beside Balliol in the front of the abbey altar. So the abbey gained the name of "Dulce Cor," Latin for "sweet heart," which has since become a part of the English language.

Built into a wall of a cottage in the village is a rough piece of sculpture showing three women rowing a boat—an allusion to the bringing of sandstone across the Nith to build the abbey.

Directly south from New Abbey on the 710 to Southerness leads to the **Arbigland Gardens and Cottage** at Kirkbean, 15 miles southwest of Dumfries. This is where John Paul Jones, one of the founders of the American navy, was born. You can visit the woodland with its water gardens arranged around a secluded bay, walking in the pathways where the great admiral once worked as a boy. The gardens are open, May to September on Tuesday, Thursday, and Sunday from 2 to 6 p.m., charging adults 50p (98¢); children, 25p (49¢).

Or, alternatively, you can head south from Dumfries on the 725 to **Caerlaverock Castle,** near the mouth of the River Nith, two miles south from Glencaple. Once the seat of the Maxwell family, this impressive ruined fortress dates back to 1279. In 1300 Edward I laid siege to it. In 1640 it yielded to

Covenanters after a 13-week siege. The castle is triangular with round towers. The interior was reconstructed in the 17th century as a Renaissance mansion, with fine carving. Near the castle is the Caerlaverock National Nature Reserve between the River Nith and Lochar Water. It is a noted winter haunt of wildfowl, including barnacle geese.

After leaving the castle, continue east along the 725 to the village of **Ruthwell,** about ten miles southeast of Dumfries. There at the early 19th-century Ruthwell Church, you'll see one of the most outstanding crosses of the Dark Ages. Standing 18 feet high, the cross is believed to date from the eighth century. Engraved with carvings, it bears the earliest known specimen of written English (a Christian poem in Runic characters).

North from Dumfries on the A76 takes you to **Lincluden College,** two miles away. This is the richly decorated remains of a 15th-century collegiate church.

Four miles away, still following the A76, is **Ellisland Farm,** where Robert Burns made his last attempt at farming, renting the spread from 1788 to 1791. The present occupants of the house will show you through the Burns Room. It was at this farm that Burns wrote "Tam o'Shanter."

Continuing north, still on the A76, you reach **Thornhill,** a country resort —familiar to Burns—overlooking the River Nith. From here, it's possible to branch out for excursions in many directions.

The main target is **Drumlanrig Castle,** the seat of the Dukes of Buccleuch and Queensberry, built between 1679 and 1689. It lies three miles north of Thornhill, off the A76. This exquisite pink castle contains some celebrated paintings, including a Rembrandt and a Holbein. In addition, it is further enriched by Louis XIV antiques, silver, porcelain, and relics related to Bonnie Prince Charlie. The castle stands in a parkland ringed by wild hills, and there's even an "Adventure Woodland Playground." On Easter weekend (Friday to Monday) it is open weekdays from 12:30 to 5 p.m. and on Sunday from 2 to 6 p.m. In May and June it keeps the same hours, but only on Monday, Thursday, Saturday, and Sunday. In July and August it is open daily except Friday on weekdays from 11 a.m. to 5 p.m. (on Sunday, until the last Monday of August, from 2 to 6 p.m.). The last entry to the castle is 45 minutes before closing time. Admission charges are £1.20 ($2.34) for adults, 70p ($1.37) for children. For information, telephone 0848/30248.

Of almost equal interest, **Maxwelton House** (tel. Moniaive 384) lies three miles south of Moniaive and 13 miles north of Dumfries on the B729. It was the stronghold of the Earls of Glencairn in the 14th and 15th centuries. But it is more remembered today as the birthplace (1682) of Annie Laurie of the Scottish ballad. From Maxwelton you can see that the braes are just as bonnie as ever. The braes, of course, refer to the neighboring hills. The house, garden, chapel, gift shop, and an agricultural museum can be visited from May to September on Wednesday and Thursday from 2 to 5 p.m. and every fourth Sunday of those same months. Admission is £1 ($1.95) for adults, 30p (59¢) for children.

Back on the A76, you can branch northwest on the B797, heading in the direction of Mennock Pass. There, at **Wanlockhead,** you'll be in the highest village in Scotland. Once this village was a gold-mining center and known as "God's Treasure House." Gold was mined here for the Scottish crown jewels.

CASTLE DOUGLAS: A cattle and sheep market town, Castle Douglas makes a good touring center for Galloway. It lies about eight miles southwest of Dumfries, at the northern tip of Carlingwark Loch. On one of the islets in the loch is an ancient lake dwelling known as a "crannog."

The favorite excursion is to **Threave Castle**, 1½ miles west on an islet in the River Dee west of town, the ruined 14th-century stronghold of the Black Douglases. The four-story tower was built between 1639 and 1690 by Archibald the Grim, Lord of Galloway. In 1455 Threave Castle was the last Douglas stronghold to surrender to James II, who employed "Mons Meg" (the famous cannon now in Edinburgh Castle) in its subjection. Over the doorway projects the "gallows knob" from which the Douglases hanged their enemies. The castle was captured by the Covenanters in 1640 and dismantled. Owned by the National Trust, the site must be reached by a *lengthy* walk through farmlands and then by small boat across the Dee.

Threave Gardens, around Threave House, a Scottish baronial mansion 1½ miles west of Castle Douglas, off the A75, is under the protection of the National Trust for Scotland which uses it as a school for gardening and a wild fowl refuge. The gardens are open daily from 9 a.m. to 5 p.m. From April 1 to October 31, a Visitor Centre is also open. Admission is 90p ($1.76) for adults, 65p ($1.27) for children.

Back in Castle Douglas, I'd recommend the following selections for food and lodging.

Douglas Arms, King Street (tel. Castle Douglas 2231), was once an old coaching inn, but it has been turned into a modernized hotel, right in the center of this hamlet, situated at a busy crossroads. Therefore, it's not the most tranquil choice, but it is still inviting—made all the more so by the gracious hospitality extended by the owners, Mr. and Mrs. Wylie. Behind a rather stark, two-story facade, the public rooms are bright and cheerful, giving you a toasty feeling on a cold night. Bedrooms have color-coordinated schemes, and such new gadgets as razor sockets. At least 11 out of the 27 rooms contain private baths. Single rates go from £12.50 ($24.38) to £15 ($29.25), and doubles from £22 ($42.90) to £26 ($50.70), including VAT and service. Dinner is served until 9 p.m., and, of course, trout and salmon are featured along with good beef and lamb, of which the hamlet has plenty. A three-course set dinner goes for £6.50 ($12.68), rising to £7.75 ($15.11) for four courses.

King's Arms, St. Andrew's Street (tel. Castle Douglas 2097), is a good place at which to stop over, enjoying either a room or a meal or drink in the trio of tartan-clad bars, featuring the malt whisky collection of Mr. Iain Mac-Donald. The restaurant serves good, simple meals, using the freshest of fish and tender beef, a set meal costing from £8 ($15.60). It is attractively decorated, and the staff is most helpful. Bedrooms are comfortable, although modest, and four chambers contain private baths and toilets and two are equipped with showers and toilets. For these, the rate is £19 ($37.05) per person daily. However, in a bathless room, the tariff is £13.50 ($26.33) per person, including a full breakfast, VAT, and service. There is an attractive, sheltered, and secluded sun garden at the rear of the hotel which is a favorite rendezvous for coffee, tea, or a sundowner. Everything is maintained immaculately, and parking is provided. The hotel is under the personal management of the proprietors, Iain and Betty Macdonald.

An excellent hotel choice lies south of Castle Douglas, near Dalbeattie, in the hamlet of—

ROCKCLIFFE: An attractive seaside village, Rockcliffe has a bird sanctuary on its offshore Rough Island. From its sand and rock beach, you can look out to the Lake District mountains on the distant horizon.

Baron's Craig Hotel (tel. Rockcliffe 225) is a stately country home, built of granite, and set back from the shoreline of Solway Firth. Because of its sheltered position from the cold north wind, its gardens bloom profusely in season. Lawns and grounds—nearly 12 acres—are well manicured. The public rooms are spacious and airy, brightly decorated and most welcoming. In the modern bar you can select at leisure your favorite whisky. The owners have paid special attention to the bedrooms, decorating them in warm, pleasing colors to suggest in summer a holiday atmosphere. From April to October, it rents singles (bathless) for £20.90 ($40.76), going up to £29 ($56.55) with bath. A bathless double costs £38 ($74.10), rising to $52 ($101.40) with bath, including breakfast. At least 21 of the rooms contain private baths, which are spotlessly clean.

Even if you're not staying here, you might want to drive down to enjoy the hotel's fine cookery. The dining room overlooks the water, and table appointments have flair and style. At lunch the menu is considerably shortened, but still quite good, a simple meal costing from £2.50 ($4.88). A cold table is invariably featured. In the evening, however, a four-course table d'hôte is offered at £10 ($19.50) between the hours of 7 and 9 p.m. The menu is based on good local ingredients, and all dishes are acceptably prepared. The service is exceptional.

KIRKCUDBRIGHT: Stewartry's most ancient burgh, Kirkcudbright (pronounced Kir-coo-bree) lies at the head of Kirkcudbright Bay on the Dee Estuary. This intriguing old town contains color-washed houses inhabited, in part, by artists. In fact, Kirkcudbright has been called the "St. Ives (Cornwall) of Scotland."

In the old town graveyard are memorials to Covenanters and to Billy Marshall, the tinker king who died in 1792 at the age of 120, reportedly having fathered four children after the age of 100.

Maclellan's Castle, built in 1582 for the town's provost, Sir Thomas Maclellan, easily dominates the center of town. Kirkcudbright is an attractive town which is the center of a lively group of weavers, potters, and painters who work in the 18th-century streets and lanes.

The **Tolbooth,** a large building, dates back to the 16th and 17th centuries, and in front of it is a **Mercat Cross** of 1610. The Tolbooth is a memorial to John Paul Jones (1747–1792), the gardener's son from Kirkbean who became a slave trader, a privateer, and in due course one of the founders of the American navy. For a time, before his emigration, he was imprisoned for murder in the Tolbooth.

Art exhibitions are regularly sponsored at **Broughton House,** a 17th-century mansion which once belonged to E. A. Hornel, the artist. The house contains a large reference library with a valuable Burns collection, along with pictures by Hornel and other artists, plus antiques and other works of art. You can stroll through its beautiful garden. Broughton is open April to October seven days a week, from 11 a.m. to 1 p.m. and 2 to 5 p.m.; and November to March on Tuesday and Thursday from 2 to 5 p.m. Admission is 30p (59¢).

In addition, the **Stewartry Museum** contains a fascinating collection of antiquities, depicting the history and culture of Galloway and its many and varied associations with John Paul Jones. It is open daily, except Sunday, from 10 a.m. to 5 p.m., charging adults 40p (78¢) and children 20p (39¢). It's open from Easter to October.

North of town is the ruined **Tongland Abbey,** one of whose abbots, John Damian, once tried to fly from the battlements of Stirling Castle wearing wings of bird feathers, in the presence of James IV. He landed in a manure pile.

Dundrennan Abbey, seven miles southeast of Kirkcudbright, the ruins of a rich Cistercian house founded in 1142, include much late Norman and Transitional work. Dundrennan is a daughter abbey of Rievaulx Abbey in Yorkshire and the mother abbey of Glenluce and Sweetheart Abbeys. The small village is partly built of stones "quarried" from the abbey. Mary Queen of Scots, after escaping from Loch Leven and being defeated at the Battle of Langside, spent her last night in Scotland at the abbey in May 1568. She went to England to seek help from Elizabeth who imprisoned her instead. The transept and choir, a unique example of the Early Pointed style, remain.

In accommodations, I'd suggest the **Selkirk Arms,** Old High Street (tel. Kirkcudbright 30402), where Robert Burns stayed when he composed the celebrated Selkirk Grace. (The grace was actually given on St. Mary's isle, the seat of the Douglases, Earls of Selkirk, and, in part, it went as follows: "But we ha'e meat, and we can eat, And sae the Lord be thankit.") The hotel has 27 bedrooms, and the furnishings are in keeping with the character of the house. It has a homey atmosphere and a friendly staff, making it a pleasure to stay in such charming surroundings. The neighborhood evokes memories of John Paul Jones, and there are little art galleries displaying the works of local painters. In all, you'll enjoy a restful, tranquil atmosphere. You have a choice of rooms in the main building or in the annex. Depending on the plumbing, singles range from £14.50 ($28.28) to £17 ($33.15) and doubles from £23 ($44.85) to £26 ($50.70), including breakfast. Dinner costs £8.50 ($16.58). The hotel is open all year. It has both a TV lounge and a cocktail bar, and there is ample parking.

GATEHOUSE-OF-FLEET:

GATEHOUSE-OF-FLEET: This sleepy former cotton town, on the Water of Fleet, was the **Kippletringan** in Sir Walter Scott's *Guy Mannering,* and Burns composed "Scots Wha Hae wi' Wallace Bled" on the moors nearby and wrote it down in the Murray Arms Hotel there.

The town's name probably dates from 1642 when the English government opened the first military road through Galloway to assist the passage of troops to Ireland. In 1661 Richard Murray of Cally was authorized by Parliament to widen the bridge and to erect beside it an inn which was to serve as a tollhouse, with the innkeeper responsible for the maintenance of a 12-mile stretch of road. This is believed to have been the original house on the "gait," or road, which later became known as the "gait house of Fleet," and by 1790 it was being written in its present form and spelling. This ancient "gait house" is now part of the Murray Arms Hotel, used as a coffeeroom, and is therefore probably the oldest building still in existence in the town.

West of Gatehouse, on the road to Creetown, is the well-preserved 15th-century tower of the McCullochs, with its sinister "murder hole" over the entrance passage. Through this trapdoor, boiling pitch was poured onto attackers. **Cardoness Castle** was originally the seat of the McCulloch family, one of whom, Sir Godfrey McCulloch, was the last person in Scotland to be executed, at Edinburgh in 1697, by the "Maiden," the Scots version of the guillotine.

For accommodations, we recommend the following:

Cally Palace Hotel (tel. Gatehouse 341) is a large 18th-century mansion standing in 100 acres of beautiful gardens and wooded parkland. Especially popular with more mature readers, it is an oasis of peace and quiet—most comfortable, more suited for someone who wishes to spend a few days in

Galloway than the fleeting overnight motorist. The public lounges are overscale with some fine period pieces, and a sun patio looks out onto a swimming pool. Amenities include two bars, table tennis, billiards, in addition to a hard tennis court, putting, croquet, a sauna, game fishing, loch boating, and dancing at certain times of the year. All of its 90 rooms contain private baths or showers, costing from £20 ($39) in a single, from £30 ($58.50) in a double. Some of the bedrooms have balconies opening onto the grounds. Rooms come in widely varying styles and sizes, but all have color TV and tea- and coffee-making facilities.

Murray Arms (tel. Gatehouse 207) is a long, low, white-painted building that was once a posting inn in the 18th century, its coffeehouse dating back even earlier, 1642. Burns wrote his stirring song, "Scots Wha' Ha'e" while staying at the inn, the occasion still commemorated to this day by the Burns room with its Leitch pictures. The inn has been considerably updated and modernized by the laird of the Cally Estate, and that is as it should be, since it was James Murray of Cally who made the Murray Arms into a coaching inn so long ago. Now it's back in the same family after a long departure.

Standing by an old clock tower, the inn has long been known for its food and hospitality. In addition to three bars, the house has a sun lounge opening onto a roof terrace. The rooms are modestly furnished, and singles range from £16 ($31.20) to £23 ($44.85), doubles from £28 ($54.60) to £44 ($85.80), plus VAT. Nearly half of the rooms contain private baths.

You can stop in for a complete dinner in its attractively decorated restaurant opening onto the garden. Between 12:30 and 2 p.m. typical bar lunches are offered. But at dinner, from 7:30 to 9 p.m., you can order a table d'hôte meal for £9 ($17.55). Specialties include Galloway beef and fresh Solway Firth salmon.

CREETOWN: "The Ferry Toon," as Creetown is called, lies west of Gatehouse-on-Fleet, on the road to Newton Stewart. There are two ruined 16th-century castles about midway along the road, **Carsluith** and **Barholm.** Up the Kirkdale Burn from Barholm are the 4000-year-old standing stones and chambered tombs of Cairn Holy.

NEWTON STEWART: Sometimes called "the gateway to Galloway" and the "heart of Galloway," this small town on the River Cree was made a burgh or barony in 1677 after a son of the second Earl of Galloway built some houses beside the ford across the river and gave the hamlet its present name. When the estate was later purchased by William Douglas, he changed the name to Newton Douglas, but it didn't stick. The town has a livestock market and woolen mills. Cree Bridge, built of granite in 1813 to replace one swept away by a flood, links the town with **Minnigaff** where there is an old church with carved stones and some memorials.

Newton Stewart is associated with Scott, Stevenson, and Burns. Today it is chiefly a center for touring, especially north for nine miles to the beauty spot of **Loch Troolin** in the Glen Trool Forest Park, 200 square miles of magnificently preserved splendor. On the way to Loch Trool, you go through the village of Glentrool where you'll find the first car park for those wanting to take the Stroan Bridge walk, a distance of 3½ miles. The hearty Scots, of course, walk the entire loch, all 4½ miles of it.

Food and Lodging

Newton Stewart has a wide range of accommodations, making it one of the best bases for touring Galloway.

Bruce, Queen Street (tel. Newton Stewart 2294), is an exemplary up-to-date hotel. Although not lavish in appointments, it is completely modern and efficiently run, maintaining a high standard of comfort, but keeping its prices reasonable—from £17 ($33.15) in a single, from £34 ($66.30) in a double. The decor is bright, and the bedrooms well designed. All of the 20 bedrooms contain private baths. Guests enjoy a pleasant bar and congenial company, composed mainly of locals who frequent the Bruce. The restaurant, also in the modern style, offers a cold table at lunch from 12:30 to 2 p.m., costing £3.50 ($6.83). Dinners, when the menu is more varied, is quite interesting, and everything tastes as if it were home cooked from fresh produce. A table d'hôte, served from 7:30 to 9 p.m., goes for £8 ($15.60).

Kirroughtree (tel. Newton Stewart 2141) is an impressive manor house, once the seat of the Herons of Galloway, built in 1719 and full of traditional character. Lying about a mile east of the town, it borders a golf course. The hotel is ideal for those who want complete peace and quiet, as it is surrounded by some nine acres of private grounds with beautiful views of the Galloway countryside and Solway Firth. The hotel is fully licensed with two cocktail bars and an extensive wine list, central heating, and many amenities. The 25 bedrooms all have private bath, color TV, radio, and tea- and coffee-making facilities.

The chefs have built up a reputation for producing the finest food in the region. Rates range from £15.50 ($30.23) to £19 ($37.05) per person for B&B. Dinner, bed, and breakfast is from £88 ($171.60) to £106 ($206.70) per person for four days, including VAT and free golf at the local nine-hole course. There are many other golf courses nearby, pony trekking, and beautiful walks. Permits for salmon or trout fishing are available at the hotel.

WIGTOWN: This former county town of the district is still a center for fishing and wildfowling although its harbor is silted up. Two market crosses, an 18th-century one topped by a sundial and another which was erected in 1816, stand in the town's central square. In 1685 two women, Margaret Maclauchlan and Margaret Wilson, Covenanters who were accused of attending meetings of their sect, were tied to stakes at the mouth of the River Bladnoch and drowned by the rising tide after refusing to give up their beliefs. An obelisk marks the traditional site of their martyrdom. A monument to all Covenanters stands on Windy Hill back of the town.

Three miles northwest of Wigtown, near Torhouskie Farm, are the Bronze Age **Stones of Torhouse,** 19 standing stones in a circle with three in the center.

The remains of **Baldoon Castle** are one mile from Wigtown. This was the setting for Sir Walter Scott's *The Bride of Lammermoor.* It was the home of David Dunbar and his wife, supposed to be the principal characters of the *Bride.* The castle was captured by Wallace in 1297.

WHITHORN: Ten miles south of Wigtown, you come upon Whithorn, a modern town with a museum containing ancient crosses and tombstones, including the fifth-century **Latinus Stone,** the earliest Christian memorial in Scotland. St. Ninian, the son of a local chieftain, founded a monastery here in A.D. 397 and built his "Candida Casa" or "White House," probably the first Christian church in Scotland. In the 12th century Fergus, Lord of Galloway, built a priory. The church and monastery were destroyed in the 16th century. Excavations in the ruins have revealed fragments of wall covered in pale plaster believed to be from Ninian's Candida Casa. The ruins are entered through the Pend, a 17th-century arch on which are carved the Royal Arms of Scotland.

A moorland walk to the west coast 2½ miles away leads to **St. Ninian's Cave** in Port Castle Bay, used by the missionary as a retreat.

The **Isle of Whithorn,** three miles southeast of the town, is where St. Ninian landed about A.D. 395 on his return from studying in Rome; to bring Christianity to Scotland. The ruins of a plain 13th-century chapel are here but no signs of an earlier church. On the point of the promontory are the remains of an Iron Age fort and a late 17th-century tower.

Chapel Finian, near the shore road on the way from Whithorn to Glenluce, is a small chapel or oratory probably dating from the 10th or 11th century, in an enclosure about 50 feet wide.

An excellent place to stay just outside Whithorn is the **Castlewigg Hotel** (tel. Whithorn 213), a small licensed country hotel under the personal supervision of its owners, Sam and Bett Christie. Castlewigg is two miles north of Whithorn on the A746, with views to the north toward Newton Stewart and to the east to Fleet Bay. More than 200 years old, the hotel building was the dower house of Castle Wigg, which lies in ruins, not open to the public, a mile or so off the road. The hotel has two singles, two doubles, and one family room, which rent for £9.50 ($18.53) per person for B&B. Guests may enjoy the resident's lounge with color TV, the spacious, colorful dining room, and the lounge bar. Dinner costs from £6 ($11.70). From the à la carte menu you can order such delicacies as prawn cocktail, venison in red wine and port, and rainbow trout. The Castlewigg sits in seven acres of grounds, about 150 yards from the main road, so there's ample parking. It's open all year.

PORT WILLIAM: On Luce Bay, this little holiday resort is a center for tennis, golf, and swimming.

By taking the 714 west, you'll reach **Drumtrodden Stones,** a cluster of ring and cup markings from the Bronze Age on a rock face. Just 400 yards to the south is an alignment of three adjacent surviving stones. It's hardly Stonehenge, but interesting, nevertheless.

While still on an antiquity search, you can drive directly south of Port William a short distance to **Barsalloch Fort,** the remains of a fort dating from the Iron Age.

In the pleasant village, you can stay at the **Monreith Arms Hotel** (tel. Port William 206), a big stone building at the roundabout where you will find immaculate bedrooms, innerspring mattresses, and comfortable public rooms, as well as a good garage accommodation for your car. Mr. and Mrs. A. R. Jardine, in their fully licensed hostelry, offer B&B for £10.50 ($20.48) per night per person. Dinner costs from £6 ($11.70). All prices include VAT and service charge. The hotel is open all year.

GLENLUCE: Lying on the Water of Luce near its estuary in Luce Bay, Glenluce is another attractive village. **Glenluce Abbey,** one mile northwest, is a ruined Cistercian house founded about 1190, which has intact a 15th-century vaulted chapter house of architectural interest. The border "wizard," Michael Scott, is said to have lured the plague to the abbey in the 13th century and shut it in a vault. **Castle of Park,** a 16th-century mansion, overlooks the village from the brow of a hill across the river.

A convenient and pleasant place to stay in Glenluce is the **Judge's Keep,** in the center of town (tel. Glenluce 203), where Mr. and Mrs. William Atkinson receive guests in their fully licensed hotel for £9 ($17.55) per person for B&B. Dinner, prepared under Mrs. Atkinson's close supervision in the immaculate kitchen on the ground floor, costs £6 ($11.70), and it's well worth it. There is a TV lounge for guests, as well as public and lounge bars and ample car parking. Snacks are served in the bar for those who don't want a large meal, and Bill Atkinson will keep your glass, as one patron said, "topped up with your choice of tipple." The hotel is open all year.

PORTPATRICK: Until 1849 steamers sailed the 21 miles from Donaghdee in Northern Ireland to Portpatrick, which became a "Gretna Green" for the Irish. Couples would land on Saturday, have the banns called on Sunday, and marry on Monday. When the harbor became silted up, Portpatrick was replaced by Stranraer as a port.

Commanding a clifftop to the south are the ruins of **Dunskey Castle,** a grim keep built in 1510 by John Adair.

Ten miles south of Portpatrick is the quiet little hamlet of **Port Logan.** In the vicinity is **Logan House,** the seat of the McDouall family, which could trace their ancestry so far back that it was claimed they were as "old as the sun itself." This family laid out the world-famous gardens at Logan which are visited by people from all over the world. **Logan Botanic Garden,** an annex of the Royal Botanic Garden, Edinburgh, contains a wide range of plants from the temperate regions of the world. Cordylines, palms, tree ferns, and tender rhododendrons grow well in the mild climate of southwest Scotland. The garden is open from 10 a.m. to 5 p.m. Admission is 50p (98¢). The site is 14 miles south of Stranraer off the B7065 road. Restaurant facilities are available.

Nearby is **Ardwell House,** with gardens which are at their best in April and May.

The ancient church site of **Kirkmadrine** lies in the parish of Stoneykirk, south of Portpatrick. The site now has a modern church but there is an ancient graveyard and early inscribed stones and crosses, including three of the earliest Christian monuments in Britain, showing the chi-rho symbol and inscriptions dating from the fifth or early sixth century. There was an early Christian monastery and in the Middle Ages a parish church.

Instead of going to the larger town, Stranraer, you might stay at the **Knockinaam Lodge** (tel. Portpatrick 681471), a Victorian house with view looking out over the sea to Northern Ireland. People come to Knockinaam for the peace and relaxation, as the lodge stands in 30 secluded acres of private grounds right on the sea. It's run in the best country-house tradition by the resident owners Simon and Caroline Pilkington. In the heat of World War II, Churchill, who met Eisenhower here, enjoyed a long hot bath (in a tub which remains) while smoking a cigar. The hotel contains only ten rooms, most of which have private bath or shower. The rate is from £16 ($31.20) per person, including VAT and a full Scottish breakfast. The lodge serves the best food in the area. All ingredients used in the kitchen are fresh, and dishes on both the à la carte and table d'hôte menus are cooked to order. Service is polite and efficient, and the views open onto the water. Lunch from noon to 2 p.m. is offered, along with dinner from 7 to 9 p.m., when a set meal costs £10.50 ($20.48), including VAT. The lodge is closed from mid-January until the end of February.

STRANRAER: The largest town in Wigtownshire, Stranraer is the terminal of the 35-mile ferry crossing from Larne, Northern Ireland. An early chapel, built by a member of the Adair family near the 16th-century **Castle of St. John** in the heart of town, gave the settlement its original name of Chapel, later changed to Chapel of Stranrawer and then shortened to Stranraer. The name is supposed to have referred to the row or "raw" of original houses on the "strand" or burn, now largely buried beneath the town's streets. The Castle of St. John became the town jail and in the late 17th century held Covenanters during Graham of Claverhouse's campaigns of religious persecution.

To the east is **Lochinch Castle,** a late 19th-century Scots baronial mansion. In the grounds are White and Black Lochs and the ruins of **Castle Kennedy,** built during the reign of James IV, but burned down in 1716. Restored in the middle of the 19th century, the gardens contain the finest pinetum in Scotland. Go in the right season and you can wander among rhododendrons, azaleas, and magnolias. The gardens are open daily, except Saturday from April to September from 10 a.m. to 5 p.m. (open Easter Saturday and on May and August bank holidays), charging adults £1 ($1.95) for admission; children under 16 and senior citizens, 50p (98¢).

The leading hotels are as follows:

North West Castle, Royal Crescent (tel. Stranraer 4413), overlooks Loch Ryan and the departure quay for Northern Ireland. The oldest part of the house was built in 1820 by Capt. Sir John Ross, R.N., the Arctic explorer. Of course, to honor the brave man, your bedroom window should face northwest, an allusion to his search for the "North West Passage." The hotel owners will give you a brochure which relates the exploits and disappointments of the explorer. The original building has been altered and extended to meet the hotel's increasing popularity. At last count, a total of 83 rooms are offered, all with private bath. Singles go from £15 ($29.25) and doubles from a low of £20 ($39) to a high of £30 ($58.50) for the well-appointed suites. Many of the best rooms are in the two more modern wings.

The lounges are cozy and pleasantly furnished, and the dining room is impressive, serving mainly continental fare with Scottish overtones. Fresh local ingredients are used. The bars downstairs are well stocked—I prefer the Explorers' Lounge with its views of the harbor. Further amenities include a garden, a sauna, and a solarium, plus a curling rink, game room, buttery, indoor swimming pool, and dancing to a live band on Saturday night.

George Hotel, George Street (tel. Stranraer 24878), stands right in the heart of town. I first stayed there many, many years ago, and, on my most recent visit, found it considerably improved, a lot of money spent, in fact, to provide the latest up-to-date comforts for its guests, many of whom are embarking for Northern Ireland in the morning. Less than half the bedrooms contain private baths. Singles cost from £15 ($29.25) to £18 ($35.10) nightly, and doubles go for £25 ($48.75) to £30 ($58.50), including VAT, service, and a full breakfast. Most of the rooms contain such amenities as razor sockets and radio. Color-coordinated schemes are used in the bedrooms, and the baths are spotlessly clean. A friendly, cooperative staff is expert at giving touring advice. The hotel's restaurant is also good, the cooking and service quite acceptable. The lighting is subdued and the ingredients fresh, the emphasis placed on "Taste of Scotland" dishes, costing £6.50 ($12.68) for three courses, £7.75 ($15.11) for four courses.

Chapter XVII

EDINBURGH AND CENTRAL SCOTLAND

1. Edinburgh
2. Day Trips from Edinburgh
3. The Kingdom of Fife
4. Glasgow and the Clyde
5. The Trossachs and Loch Lomond

SCOTLAND HAS OFTEN been compared to a sandwich in that the central belt is considered the meatier part. Within a relatively small compass of land, you can visit not only the capital at Edinburgh but enjoy such beauty as the Trossachs (the Scottish lake district), the silver waters of Loch Lomond, or take in the cragginess of Stirling Castle. Central Scotland should be treated as far more than just a gateway to the Highlands.

Edinburgh, often called the fairest city in Europe, is our first stopover. While based there you can take many day trips, such as to the seaside and golfing resort of North Berwick. The Scots suggest you take a "look aboot ye."

From Edinburgh, on the opposite shore of the Firth of Forth, reached by bridge, the Kingdom of Fife is rich in treasures, such as Falkland Palace, the hunting retreat of the Stuart kings, and the unspoiled fishing villages along the coast, collectively known as "East Neuk."

To the west of Edinburgh, a distance of some 40 miles, the industrial city of Glasgow is a target for some, although, to me at least, it has none of the charm of the capital. However, from Glasgow you can set out on a tour in many directions, including the glens and hills associated with the outlaw Rob Roy. Also on Glasgow's doorstep is the scenic estuary of the Firth of Clyde. You can cruise down the Clyde on a paddle-steamer.

But, assuming you're still back in the Lowlands, you can begin your descent upon—

1. Edinburgh

Scotland's capital city is Edinburgh, off the beaten path for those doing the mad whirlwind tour of Europe, as it lies 373 miles north of London.

The city is associated with John Knox, Mary Queen of Scots, Robert Louis Stevenson, Sir Arthur Conan Doyle (creator of Sherlock Holmes), David Hume, Alexander Graham Bell, Sir Walter Scott, and Bonnie Prince Charlie—to name-drop only a bit.

From the elegant Georgian crescents of the New Town, to the dark medieval "wynds" of the Old Town, down the wide, magnificent Princes Street (Stevenson's "liveliest and brightest thoroughfare"), Edinburgh lives up to its reputation as one of the fairest cities in Europe. Of course, it's not as sophisticated as Paris, nor as fast-paced as London. And it's banal to call it the Athens of the North, although the Greek Revival movement of the 19th century made many of the buildings look like pagan temples.

What Edinburgh has to offer is unique. It's Scottish (scotch is a drink—so play it safe and refer to the hearty, ruddy-faced people as Scots)—and that means it's different from English. It wasn't sameness that made these two countries fight many a bloody border skirmish.

Most travelers know that since World War II Edinburgh has been the scene of an ever-growing International Festival, with its action-packed list of cultural events. But that shouldn't be your only reason for visiting the ancient seat of Scottish royalty. Its treasures are available all year. In fact, the pace the rest of the time—when the festival-hoppers have gone south—is more relaxed. The prices are lowered, and the people themselves, under less pressure as hosts, return to their traditional hospitable nature.

Before looking closer at the attractions of Edinburgh, we'll tackle the question of finding a hotel. In the Scottish capital that doesn't have to be a problem.

WHERE TO STAY: Searching for a suitable hotel isn't too difficult in Edinburgh, as the city offers a full range of accommodations at different price levels throughout the year. However, during the three-week period of the festival, the establishments fill up with international visitors, so it's prudent to reserve in advance. To take care of emergency lodging 360 days a year, the **Edinburgh Tourist Information & Accommodation Service**, at 5 Waverley Bridge (tel. 226-6591), compiles a well-investigated and lengthy list of small hotels and guest houses. The emphasis is on well-managed, clean, comfortable, and hospitable guest houses, usually catering to anywhere from 2 to 12 visitors, some for as little as £6.50 ($12.68) per person. The bureau's hours during the peak season, May 1 to September 30, are from 8:30 a.m. to 8 p.m. Monday through Saturday, and from 11 a.m. to 8 p.m. on Sunday (open till 9 p.m. during July and August). A 60p ($1.17) booking fee is charged. There's also an information and accommodation desk at Edinburgh Airport, with a telephone link to the center. It's open according to the frequency of incoming flights.

The **City of Edinburgh Public Relations Department**, 9 Cockburn St. (tel. 226-6591), will also assist visitors in obtaining accommodations, charging a 40p (78¢) booking fee. You can write in advance, enclosing your requirements and the fee, but you should allow about four weeks' notice, especially during the summer and particularly during the festival weeks.

Assuming you arrive in Edinburgh when the hotels aren't fully booked or that you will reserve a room in advance, I've prepared a representative sampling of the leading candidates, from the upper bracket to the budget range.

The Upper Bracket

The **Caledonian**, Prince Street and Lothian Road (tel. 225-2433), is the king of the hotels in Edinburgh, standing opposite its queen, the North British, at the other end of Princes Gardens. A British Transport hotel, it is the first choice for those who demand the best against an elegant background where service is keyed to personal tastes. It occupies the entire end of a block, with

views of the castle and the parklike grounds. The interior is prestigious, drawing on some of the classic decorative and architectural features of both France and Scotland. The entrance hall achieves dignity with oyster-white paneled walls and desks, brass chandeliers, and a vibrant ceiling mural; and the main lounge is graced with neoclassic columns, a grand staircase, and chandelier.

The rates at the hotel in high season—May 1 to October 31—range from £37 ($72.15) in a single room with shower to £68 ($132.60) in a twin-bedded room with bath. In the low season, tariffs are sharply reduced, to £23 ($44.85) in a single, from £36 ($70.20) in a double. A full breakfast is included. The bedrooms are freshly decorated and pleasantly furnished.

For drinks, try the cavelike American Bar, with a curvy ceiling of cedar and walls of marble, spiked with flame-red accents. The Caledonia's Pompadour Restaurant, with its bona fide French cuisine, is such a highlight of the Edinburgh scene that I've featured it separately in the dining section, coming up. The most recent addition is Laird's Lodge Coffee House, featuring such items as Arbroath smokie mousse at £1.20 ($2.34), grills and griddles from £2.30 ($4.49). All prices quoted are inclusive of service and VAT.

North British Hotel, Princes Street (tel. 556-2414), is the queen of Edinburgh's hotels, at the eastern end of Princes Street, opposite the Caledonian. It's a great old structure, designed for grand living and administered by British Transport Hotels. It is constantly being renewed and freshly decorated. Its lounges are impressively 18th and 19th century, the basic architecture classic. The finest is the residents' lounge, all in soft aqua and white, with a tall, formal fireplace, an elaborately carved ceiling and woodwork, and sky-high windows draped in gold. The cost of staying here is £25 ($58.75) in a bathless single, £35 ($68.25) with a private bath. In a bathless double, the rate is £40 ($78); it's £60 ($117) for two persons in a room with bath. Off-season reductions are granted. Most rooms are furnished with a combination of traditional and modern—most comfortable.

The main dining room, with its blue tile columns, is neoclassic—just right for your best bib and tucker. Guests usually take advantage of the £8.50 ($16.58) table d'hôte luncheon or set dinner. A typical meal might include crème Longchamps, salmon Véronique, roast turkey and stuffing with vegetables, followed by lemon pancakes.

On the lower floor, you'll find the Cleikum, featuring many national dishes. Ever had cock-a-leekie soup? Scottish trout fried in oatmeal? Haggis and champit neeps? Collops in the pan (rump beef, with onion, butter, and walnut catsup)? A good meal averages around £8 ($15.60). At one recent meal, I resisted the "Piggy Wigglies"! If you have the courage, you can order "stovies" and "rumbledethumps" as vegetables. Overlooking the castle, the Gourmet Restaurant is open in summer only. A meal here will cost around £20 ($39), but it will be quite an experience.

The **Roxburghe Hotel,** Charlotte Square (tel. 225-3921), is an Adam building of dove-gray stone, trimmed in white, with a stately town house opening directly onto a tree-filled square. While not elaborately equipped, and only four floors high (including a row of dormered mansard windows), it is, nevertheless, the first choice for a number of discriminating people who prefer a dignified place at which to stay. Within five minutes of the British Airways Terminal, the hotel is central, a short walk from Princes Street. The atmosphere is genteel and traditional, as reflected in the drawing room, with its ornate ceiling and woodwork, and tall arched windows opening toward the park. The furnishings are mostly antique, with groups of Chippendale chairs.

Most of the 75 bedrooms, reached by elevator, have private baths or showers. The rooms are handsomely traditional, a favorite scheme being Wedgwood blue-and-white Adam-style paneling. There are a few bathless singles for £22 ($42.90); with shower or bath, it's £29 ($56.55). The bathless doubles go for £42 ($81.90) for two persons, the price rising to £56 ($109.20) with bath, service and VAT included. A smart place to congregate for drinks is the Consort Bar, with its festive decor of chinoiserie and bistro tables. A modern dining room serves not only good meals, but gives diners a view of the square.

Howard Hotel, Great King Street (tel. 556-1393). Three Georgian terrace houses have been skillfully combined to create a comfortable resting place. Singles renting for £24 ($46.80) contain showers, and doubles or twins have complete baths, costing from £35 ($68.25), including a full breakfast, VAT, and service. The decor is a combination of both traditional and modern. Units have tea- or coffee-making equipment, color TV, radio, and direct-dial phones.

After relaxing in the pleasant lounge, you might want to patronize an elegant restaurant in the basement, known as No. 36. Decorated in browns and cream, it has linen tablecloths and shining glassware. A two-course luncheon goes for £5.50 ($10.73), increasing to £6.25 ($12.19) for three courses. Specialties include such dishes as Highland game casserole and lamb sweetbreads in garlic butter with herbs and bacon. At dinner, two courses from a wide selection of dishes will cost from £9.50 ($18.53), and you are likely to be served grilled salmon filet or venison escalope with orange.

Across the passage in the basement is the Claret Jug, with paneled walls and touches of red, along with dark wood wheelback chairs. At lunchtime a very popular cold buffet is served in the bar, with ample portions of cold poultry and meat. You can help yourself, too, to a selection of salads. The cost is from £2.50 ($4.88), and they have a good selection of wines by the glass, in addition to the usual pub ales. At the back is a car park, a blessing in busy Edinburgh.

The **George Hotel,** George Street (tel. 225-1251), is concentrated quality. A great deal is compressed into a comparatively small space. A member of the Grand Metropolitan Hotels Group, the George is only two short blocks from Princes Street, in the midst of a number of boutiques, bus, rail, and air terminals. Between April 1 and October 1 the highest rates are in effect: £41 ($79.95) in a single with bath, £56 ($109.20) in a twin- or double-bedded room, also with bath. All of the bedrooms have been refurnished and redecorated, but the public rooms have retained the style, elegance, and old-fashioned comfort of a country house. The Carvers Table offers a selection of prime Scottish beef, roast lamb, or roast pork, including vegetables, an appetizer, a dessert, and coffee, all for £6.50 ($12.68). Le Chambertin, the hotel's new and exclusive French restaurant, is open Monday to Saturday, inclusive (refer to my dining recommendations).

The Medium-Priced Range

Carlton Hotel, North Bridge (tel. 556-7277), is in a unique position, just off the Royal Mile at the entrance to the North Bridge, with views of Princes Gardens. It's pure Victorian, with brick towers and turrets, reached by an unimpressive entrance from North Bridge. Even the public lounges give no clue to the quite up-to-date bedrooms that evoke Scandinavia in their design. Each pleasant bedroom has its own bath and costs £25 ($48.75) single, £43 ($83.85) for a double or twin, including a full breakfast, service, and tax. In the Carving Room, you can carve as much as you want, either at lunch or dinner, for £9 ($17.55). The hotel is 100 yards from Waverley Station (you can enter via a station-level doorway in Jeffrey Street).

The **Old Waverley Hotel,** 43 Princes St. (tel. 556-4648), can be an ideal stopover for those desiring a central, clean, and comfortable establishment. The

Old Waverley's world is that of the turn of the century, although a great deal of modernization has made it serviceable and fairly streamlined inside, with a friendly personnel providing efficient service. All of the bedrooms have hot and cold running water, and only a few are fitted with private baths. The B&B rate in a bathless single is £19.15 ($37.34), £23 ($44.85) with a private bath. In a bathless double, the B&B charge is £30.30 ($59.09), rising to £37 ($72.15) with bath. The lounges on the second floor have been given that contemporary look. The Waverley is a pleasant place to unwind after a day of sightseeing across loch and dale. Some of the rooms look onto Princes Street and at night the floodlit castle. The Waverley has a good restaurant serving à la carte meals at around £8 ($15.60) for a lunch or dinner.

The **Mount Royal Hotel,** Princes Street (tel. 225-7161), is right in the middle of the famed thoroughfare, complete with exclusive shops. A modern world emerges as you climb the spiral staircase or take an elevator to the second floor, with its reception rooms and lounges, and ceiling-to-floor windows opening onto views of the Old Town. In reality, Mount Royal is a remake of an old hotel, providing streamlined bedrooms with a view. The emphasis is utilitarian —not on frills, although the comfort is genuine. In summer, singles with bath go for £28 ($54.60) and up; twins with bath begin at £38 ($74.10). Prices include a continental breakfast, service, and VAT. The main dining room serves reasonably priced lunches and dinners.

The lounge on the second floor, with floor-to-ceiling windows offering views over the Scot Memorial and Princes Street, provides a wide variety of sandwiches and snacks throughout the day and night.

King James Hotel, 107 St. James Centre (tel. 556-0111), at the end of Princes Street, is a large modern hotel with functional bedrooms, each equipped with bath, color TV, radio, telephone, and double-glazed windows to protect against the roar of traffic. Singles rent for £32.50 ($63.38), doubles for £39.50 ($77.03), including VAT and service, although breakfast is extra. The hotel, well run by Mr. Deeson, is directly connected to the St. James Centre, with its wide variety of shops and good parking for cars.

Crest Hotel, Queensferry Road (tel. 332-2442), stands on the road leading to the airport and the Forth Road Bridge. A modern building, it is easily accessible in a city where you may find parking difficult. It offers lovely views over the Firth of Forth to the floodlit cathedral. Well-furnished bedrooms come with color TV, radio, phone, bath, and plenty of hanging space to catch up on your laundry. The standard rate is £26.50 ($51.68) in a single, from £33 ($64.35) in a double.

The Rendezvous Écossais Restaurant offers the chef's table at lunch, a full menu in the evening. You can also obtain sandwiches and hot drinks from the porter throughout the night if you don't want to travel the five minutes or so downtown to Princes Street by bus or taxi. A three-course lunch costs from £6.50 ($12.68), and dinner is from £7.50 ($14.63). An à la carte meal will run about £11 ($21.45) per person, but the set meals are very good value and totally adequate, with such typically English fare as roast joints and fish or meat pies.

The Budget Range

Belmont Hotel, 10 Carlton Terrace (tel. 556-6146), is right in the midst of a row of classic town houses, dating from the 18th and 19th centuries. A 15-minute walk from the center of Edinburgh, with views of the parks and rooftops from most of the windows, it is really two houses joined together by Mr. and Mrs. Stanley, who accept paying guests year round, charging them £10.50 ($20.48) per person in a double, £11 ($21.45) in a single in high season.

These rooms are bathless. If you want a double or twin with bath, the rate increases to £13 ($44.85) nightly, plus VAT. The price includes breakfast. Your bed will be soft, the sheets freshly laundered, the furnishings comfortable. The dining room is as old-fashioned as the rest of the place, in typical Georgian style. The hotel was awarded a commendation prize by the Edinburgh New Town Conservation Committee for the extensive renovations to the dining room, restoring it to its natural Georgian splendor. The Belmont is ideal for those who want a simple, uncluttered life in a homelike atmosphere.

Georgian Hotel, 5–6 Dean Terrace (tel. 332-4520), is a small, family-run hotel in central Edinburgh, and from it you can walk alongside the Water of Leith to historic Dean Village or to the Botanical Gardens. This Georgian house, under the direction of Mr. and Mrs. Frank Tomney, has many fine Adam architectural features and tall, wide windows. The owners have a variety of nicely decorated bedrooms, renting from £11.22 ($21.89) in a single without bath, rising to £14.60 ($28.47) with bath. Doubles cost £20.24 ($39.47) without bath, £25.30 ($49.34) with bath. All these tariffs include breakfast, VAT, and service. Many of the units have their own shower and toilet en suite, and all have TV, radio, intercom, and a baby-listening service. Guests can enjoy drinks and the company in the hotel's bar, later going to the hotel's dining room which serves a dinner for £6.50 ($12.68).

Golf View Hotel, Marchhall Road (tel. 667-4812); along Dalkeith Road, just past Commonwealth Swimming Pool, turn down Marchhall Place into Marchhall Road. There, Joseph and Margaret d'Ambrosio have run a spotlessly kept, comfortable private hotel for the past 14 years. Most of their bedrooms have private baths or showers, and some have views over the golf course. The accommodations are well furnished, and there is a lounge with TV for a peaceful evening. The d'Ambrosios have been in catering for many years, and their breakfast is large and well cooked. They also provide a door key so that you can come and go at will. They offer singles, twins, and doubles, and all their twins have both a double bed and a single bed, making them ideal as family rooms. The charge is from £8 ($15.60) per person, depending on the type of room and time of year. Children sharing a room with parents are given a reduced rate. Most of the bedrooms have private baths or showers and tea- and coffee-making facilities. Some have views over the golf course. The hotel has a residents' lounge where drinks are served.

Hotels on the Outskirts

These hotels in the environs might be useful if Edinburgh gets heavily booked—at festival time and during the summer. Both are in the medium-priced range.

The **Royal Scot Hotel,** 111 Glasgow Rd. (tel. 334-9191), is close to EDI airport to the west of the city. It's a modern hotel with its own helicopter pad and good parking, yet it lies within easy reach of the city center. Large lounges and bars lead to your pleasant room, where you have tea- or coffee-making facilities, color TV, and phone, plus private bath and shower. Singles rent for £25.30 ($49.34) to £27.85 ($54.31), doubles for £36.40 ($70.98) to £40 ($78), including a traditional cooked breakfast, VAT, and service.

Kings Manor Hotel, 100 Milton Rd. East (tel. 669-0444), is owned and run by the Solley family. The hotel lies within a ten-minute walk of the beach on the Firth of Forth, but still is within easy reach of the city center. It's a pleasant old building, comfortably modernized to provide most rooms with private baths. There is a bar and a lounge with a roaring fire. Rooms have color TV, radio, and phone. Singles rent for £13.50 ($26.33) without bath, £22

($42.90) with bath. Bathless doubles are priced at £19 ($37.05), rising to £32 ($62.40) with bath, including VAT and service. A set luncheon is provided for £4.50 ($8.78), a table d'hôte dinner costing from £6.50 ($12.68), giving you a choice of 15 main dishes. However, if you want a filet steak, you'll pay slightly more.

Castle Hotels

To fulfill your fantasy, you might want to spend your first night in Scotland in a real castle surrounded by gardens and spacious grounds. If so, I have the following recommendations:

Dalhousie Castle, Bonnyrigg (tel. Gorebridge 20153), dates back to the 12th century. It lies off the A7 Carlisle–Edinburgh road, just outside the village of Bonnyrigg, only nine miles from Edinburgh. It is now run by Miss E. J. McIlroy, who welcomes guests to this historic old castle. A turreted and fortified house, with ramparted terraces and battlements, it offers such delights as a dungeon lounge and restaurant where meals are served, including many local Scottish dishes. The rooms are large and traditionally furnished, with private baths and plenty of space to sit and relax. One of the suites has a four-poster bed. The cost per night ranges from £40 ($78) to £45 ($87.75), depending on the room's location and including breakfast for one or two persons. A suite goes for £55 ($107.25) per night, plus service and VAT.

Borthwick Castle, North Middleton (tel. Gorebridge 20514), lies 12 miles south of Edinburgh on the A7. This 15th-century structure recently celebrated its 550th anniversary and was the last refuge of Mary Queen of Scots and the Earl of Bothwell in 1567. Her apartments, the small chapel where she prayed, and the bedchamber once occupied by Bothwell are available to guests. Both bedchambers have four-poster beds. All the bedrooms have shower and toilet en suite and are centrally heated. Guests dine in the magnificent stone-vaulted Great Hall by roaring log fire and candlelight. On special evenings, pipers, dancers, and traditional entertainment are enjoyed. Borthwick Castle has become internationally famous for the excellence of its cuisine and personal service, its authentic medieval ambience, and the recreation of a gracious lifestyle which is unrepeatable. Miss Helen Bailey, the chatelaine of the castle, and the members of her household provide warm hospitality to all who enter this stately home. The rates are: £47 ($91.65) for a twin or double, £37 ($72.15) for single occupancy (no single rooms), including a full Scottish breakfast. VAT and service are extra. A five-course menu is available for £16 ($31.20).

WHERE TO DINE: The Scots are hearty eaters—and you'll like the sizes of their portions as well as the quality of their fare, with choices from river, sea, and loch. You can dine on a cock-a-leekie soup, fresh Tay salmon, haggis, neeps, tatties, and whisky, Aberdeen Angus filet steak, potted hough, poacher's soup, and good old stovies and rumbledethumps. If none of the above tempts you, you'll find that the French cuisine has made an inroad at many of the first-class hotels.

The Upper Bracket

Prestonfield House, Priestfield Road (tel. 667-8055), offers gourmet meals in the setting of a Jacobean country estate, in the midst of a 17-acre garden. King James II often visited before students burned down the house. Rebuilt, it was later to host Benjamin Franklin, then American ambassador, as well as Boswell and Johnson. The architect was William Bruce, who designed the

Palace of Holyroodhouse. No matter which room you enter, you'll find fine furnishings and paintings, including two Ramsays over the dining room fireplace. Have a predinner toast in the Old Bar (drinks served from a Sheraton bookcase), while perusing the menu. If you arrive early enough, you can stroll through the gardens and pay your respects to the peacocks. The manager will guide you to one of the early 19th-century candlelit dining rooms, with their exquisite table settings.

All meals are à la carte, and the cuisine is essentially French. With so many fine dishes to recommend, I hesitate to point out a small group. Nevertheless, specialties include smoked haddock mousse and pâté maison. The Scottish national soup, cock-a-leekie, is also featured. Another local treat is trout fried in oatmeal. Main courses are likely to include escalope of pork. You can have after-dinner coffee in the second floor Mortlake Tapestry Room, with its ornate ceiling, Persian carpets, and antiques, or in the Leather Room, with its panels from Còrdoba. Expect to spend from £15 ($29.25) for dinner. Meals are served between 12:30 and 3 p.m. and between 7 and 10:30 p.m., including Sunday. It's essential to call ahead for a reservation.

Five bedrooms are available for those who book well in advance. The rooms are large and well furnished, with pieces from the 18th and 19th centuries. The rate for B&B, including VAT and service, is £35 ($68.25) for a single, £47 ($91.65) for a double. Two rooms have shower units, and the others have baths within easy reach. The breakfast is most generous, complete with Scottish oatmeal.

Pompadour Restaurant, Caledonian Hotel, Princes Street (tel. 225-2433), serves the haute French cuisine. At least 60 classic Gallic specialties are offered, augmented by an extensive wine list. The setting is convincing, in a drawing room atmosphere of pale blue and white, with ornate bas-relief plaster paneling, fruitwood provincial armchairs, cerise draperies, and half-moon windows overlooking Princes Street. For your à la carte opening you might prefer escargots or smoked trout. Main dishes include chicken marechal and sole Caledonian. Various specialty dishes are also offered, including filet d'angus chemise au poivre. Desserts range from ices to crêpes suzette.

In addition to the French dishes, there's always a Taste of Scotland selection. Try, for example, scallops in wild Highland garlic butter or, for the more sophisticated, chicken suprême filled with scampi and creamed leeks. An average meal costs from £20 ($39) per person. The restaurant is open for dinner in summer from 7:30 to 10:30 p.m. (in winter from 7 to 10:30 p.m.). Closed Sunday.

Le Chambertin, George Hotel, 21 George St. (tel. 225-1251), provides a top-level French cuisine in intimate surroundings, between 12:30 and 2:30 p.m. Monday through Friday. A meal, inclusive of unlimited wines, is available for £9.50 ($18.53), £11.50 ($22.43), or £12.50 ($24.38).

In the evening, guests can select from a wide choice of wines, including some special bottles from the Chambertin district of France. The à la carte menu is well balanced and features many traditional French dishes and also, subject to availability, lobster, mussels, oysters, and many other dishes.

The Medium-Priced and Budget Range

The Consort, Roxburghe Hotel, Charlotte Square (tel. 225-3921), provides intimate dining in a plush atmosphere at one of Edinburgh's leading hotels. It and its adjoining cocktail bar attract sophisticated residents, artists during the festival weeks. Through its separate entrance on George Street, you descend a stairway into an almost theatrical setting. Lunch is served between

12:15 and 2:30 p.m., dinner from 7 to 10 p.m. (Sunday till 9:30 p.m.). For appetizers, you might prefer either smoked Scottish salmon or escargots bourguignons. Many attractively prepared main dishes are offered, including the mixed grill and steak Diane. A set lunch goes for £5.50 ($10.73), a fixed-price dinner for £7 ($13.65), plus coffee.

Henderson's Salad Table, 94 Hanover St. (tel. 225-3400), is a Shangri-la for healthfood lovers as well as those who want an array of rich, nutritious salads—some of the most imaginative and original I've known. It's self-service, and you can pick and choose at 55p ($1.07) per mammoth dollop, or pay a flat £1.60 ($3.12) for a representative plate. The ingredients are combined ingeniously—eggs, carrots, grapes, nuts, yogurts, cheese, potatoes, cabbage, watercress, you name it. A variety of cosmopolitan international dishes is served on request, including stuffed eggplant or chop suey. For around £1.80 ($3.51), you can have a number of hot plates, such as stuffed peppers with rice and pimiento. The soups are fabulous, costing 50p (98¢). Desserts are homemade, so rich and pure you'll strain trying to choose between them. Settle for a fresh fruit salad or a gâteau with double whipped cream and chocolate sauce. Average price is 75p ($1.46).

Henderson's is open regularly from 8 a.m. to 11 p.m. Monday through Saturday (on Sunday from noon to 9 p.m.). The scene takes place in a semibasement; and the furnishings are appropriate: pine-wood tables (often shared) and crude box-stools. The Vegetarian Society raises a provocative question: "Have you ever thought that killing for food is not necessary?" At Henderson's it certainly isn't. The Sherry Bar serves Spanish tapas (hors d'oeuvres). The wine cellar provides a choice of 50 wines, some 20 of which may be had by the glass. Live classical music is played most evenings. The bar may be reached by the same entrance as the Salad Table. Exhibitions of batik, sculpture, and ceramics by up-and-coming local artists add to the evening's entertainment.

Casa Española, 61–65 Rose St. (tel. 225-5979), is a Spanish restaurant, the best of its type in Edinburgh. Its owners, Mrs. Pascual and Mr. Hernanz, specialize in paella, a savory offering, costing £11 ($21.45) for two persons. Or perhaps you'd have their fish stew, zarzuela, going for £11 also, for two persons. The gazpacho is very tasty and strongly flavored, £1.40 ($2.73). A shrimp cocktail with garlic at £2 ($3.90) is another appetizing opener. The best bargain is a three-course luncheon offered for £4.50 ($8.78). Matador capes, bullfight posters, and wine bottles enliven the decor. Lunch is served until 2 p.m., and dinner is from 7 to 10:30 p.m. The bar is open until 11:30 p.m., serving tapas (light Spanish snacks) with your drinks. Closed Sunday.

Denzler's, 80 Queen St. (tel. 226-5467), offers appetizing Swiss dishes, skillfully prepared, using high-quality ingredients. Portions are generous, and service is efficient, although informal, the waiters contributing to the relaxed atmosphere. Air-dried Swiss ham with melon is the most enticing opener, costing £2.50 ($4.88). For a main course, choose from slices of venison at £5 ($9.75), or else the pièce de résistance, fondue bourguignonne, £10 ($19.50) for two persons. For dessert, I'd endorse the apfelstrudel at £1.30 ($2.54). Dinner is served nightly, except Sunday, from 6:30 to 10. At lunch, offered from noon to 2 p.m., main dishes range in price from £2.75 ($5.36) to £6 ($11.70).

Madogs, 38a George St. (tel. 225-3408), evokes a touch of American sophistication and flair in the Scottish capital. With its menu and movie posters (heavy on Bogart), it suggests someplace in California. Although English beer is very good, it's more chic here to order an American variety, such as Budweiser. The New England clam chowder at £1.20 ($2.34) is often very good, and better than you're likely to get at many places in New England these days. The kosher pastrami at £2.40 ($4.68) is popular, however most guests prefer the hamburger with french fries and a salad at £3.20 ($6.24). Chili con carne at £1.45 ($2.83) is another favorite. Eggs Benedict (the menu writer has to translate this for local diners) costs £2.30 ($4.49). At dinner the menu has a continental range—teriyaki steak at £5 ($9.75); Long Island duck, £5 also; even Bahamian grouper, £4.80 ($9.36). The split-level restaurant is graced with hanging baskets and potted palms, and the slim-hipped waitresses are attired in jeans. Lunch is until 3 p.m., and dinner is from 6 to 11:30. Closed Sunday.

Cosmo, 58a North Castle St. (tel. 226-6743), is one of the most heavily patronized Italian restaurants in the Scottish capital. Courtesy, efficiency, and good cookery are featured here. Cosmo Tamburro is your host. In season you can ask for mussels as an appetizer, costing £2.40 ($4.68). Soups and pastas are in the £1.40 ($2.73) to £2.50 ($4.88) range. However, remember that the cost of your pasta is doubled if you order it as a main course. On the other hand, the portions are also doubled. I've found the veal dishes the best cooked and a good value, ranging from £5.50 ($10.73), although you may be attracted to the seafood at £5.50 also. The cassata Siciliana, £1.10 ($2.15, is well made and not unbearably sweet. Closed Sunday and Monday, the restaurant serves otherwise until 2:15 p.m. for lunch and until 10:30 p.m. for dinner.

Luckpenny's, 88–90 Hanover St. (tel. 225-2227), next to Henderson's, caters to a leisurely clientele of visitors and shoppers. The downstairs restaurant is bright with polish, flowers, and the intoxicating smell of herbs. There's a long salad bar where you can choose from a choice of some ten different mixtures to go with cold pie, sausage, and meats. There are also several hot dishes, such as Irish stew, boiled York ham, and savory pie. Desserts include fruit salad and trifle, along with the mousee of the day. A meal will cost about £2.50 ($4.88), including a glass of wine. Incidentally, there's a no-smoking area. The establishment is open daily from 10 a.m. to 8 p.m., but closed on Sunday in winter.

The Witchery by the Castle, 352 Castle Hill, Royal Mile (tel. 225-5615), lies in a tiny court where James Boswell and Samuel Johnson are reputed to have met in 1770. Within 50 yards of the castle entrance, the dimly lit cellar restaurant is just the sort of place where the 17th-century witches of the city met with the devil and practiced their craft.

Present-day witches are asked to park their broomsticks at the door before lunching on hot-pot, scampi, finnan haddie, or broomstick pie. Duck with orange and venison in red wine and port sauce are available throughout the day. In the evening a soup is ladled from a bubbling cauldron, and later you might prefer White Witches (peaches stuffed with cottage cheese, walnuts, and raisins), or else Black Cat's Dream (seafood cocktail). The curried chicken is tasty, as is the chili con carne. Expect to spend from £7 ($13.65). The place is good fun, and the food is good, too. It's very convenient for the hungry sightseer who can visit any time from 10 a.m. to 11 p.m.

Cousteau's Bar and Seafood Restaurant, 109 Hanover St. (tel. 226-3355), is reached down wide stone steps decorated by a mammoth pair of flippers and a diver's mask. Polished tables and green plants make for a simple but inviting decor. Obviously the emphasis is placed on the freshness and quality of the fish. Oysters are often available, and a savory opener would be the mussels marinière au gratin or perhaps crab en chemise. For a main course, I'd suggest the seafood platter. You might also order turbot, grilled or poached salmon, or trout. Most seasonal fish are available, and the prices vary with weather conditions. Expect to pay from £8.50 ($16.58) per person for a meal. There are simple desserts and a good wine list which is perhaps a little expensive.

The Best of the Pubs

Deacon Brodie's Tavern, 435 Lawnmarket, is the neighborhood pub along the Royal Mile. It perpetuates the memory of Deacon Brodie, good citizen by day, robber by night. Mr. Brodie, it is believed, was the inspiration for Robert Louis Stevenson's *The Strange Case of Dr. Jekyll and Mr. Hyde.* Brodie ended up on the gallows on October 1, 1788. The tavern and wine cellars contain a cocktail and lounge bar—decked out in Jacobean and tartan decor. It offers a traditional pub setting and lots of atmosphere, making it popular with visitors and locals alike. The tavern provides inexpensive snacks between 11 a.m. and 2:30 p.m. (every day except Sunday), with prices averaging around £2.10 ($4.10). Among the selection: cottage pie, Scottish eggs, cheese, and the ploughman's special.

The **Guildford Arms**, West Register Street, dates back to the "mauve era" of the 1890s. This Victorian-Italianesque corner pub, still harboring its oldtime memories, has one of the most intriguing decors of any pub in Edinburgh—or Scotland for that matter. It lies near the King James Hotel. It still has seven arched windows with etched glass, plus an ornate ceiling, as well as a central bar and around-the-wall seating. It's large and bustling, with plenty of character.

Restaurants on the Outskirts

At least once you should get out into the countryside surrounding Edinburgh. One way to do this is to take bus 41 for about five miles from the West End to the little Scottish village of Cramond. Few visible traces remain today of its Roman occupation.

Quietly nestling on a sloping street is the **Cramond Inn,** on Cramond Glebe Road, which has been serving food and drinks to wayfarers for 300 years (it was known to Robert Louis Stevenson). Picture upholstered booths, opera-red carpeting, some beerbarrel upholstered chairs, a collection of local watercolors, a low ceiling, large foot-square old beams, dark oak and creamy-colored walls, recessed windows, a small stone fireplace—and you'll begin to get the feel of the inn.

The restaurant can serve 60 diners, but you'd better call in advance (tel. 336-2035), as it's most popular. The prices are quite reasonable, considering the quality of food—some of the finest of Scottish dishes. The steak-and-kidney pie is delicious, but I'm drawn to the haggis, the famed dish of Scotland, made with an assortment of chopped meats, oatmeal, and spices. For an appetizer, the Scottish game soup is a favorite. A specialty of the house is roast duck. Desserts are extremely tasty. The inn serves lunch from noon to 2:30 p.m., dinner till 10:30 p.m. The minimum charge is £2.50 ($4.88), although most meals, excluding drink, begin at £6 ($11.70), ranging upward. Cramond Inn is closed Sunday.

THE TOP SIGHTS: Before leaving the Scottish capital, you'll want to take a look at both the Old Town and the New Town. Both have their different attractions—the Old Town's largely medieval; the New Town, Georgian. We'll begin our exploration on the Royal Mile of the Old Town, a collective term for Canongate, Lawnmarket, and The High. At one end on Castle Rock sits—

Edinburgh Castle

It is believed that the ancient city grew up on the seat of the dead volcano, Castle Rock. History is vague on possible settlements, although it is known that in the 11th century Malcolm III (Canmore), and his Saxon queen, Margaret, occupied a castle on this spot. The good Margaret was later venerated as a saint. St. Margaret's Chapel was built in the Norman style, the present oblong structure dating principally from the 12th century. The five-ton **Mons Meg,** a 15th-century cannon which formerly sat outside the tiny chapel, is now to be found in the French Prisons.

Inside the castle you can visit the **State Apartments**—particularly Queen Mary's Bedroom—where Mary Queen of Scots gave birth to James VI of Scotland (later James I of England). The Great Hall with its hammer-beam ceiling was built by James IV. It displays armaments and armor, although Scottish Parliaments used to convene in this hall.

The highlight, however, is the Crown Chamber, which houses the Honours of Scotland, used at the coronation of James VI, along with the sceptre and the sword of state of Scotland. Unseen by the public for 15 years, the French Prisons have been reopened. Turned into a prison in the 18th century, these great storerooms housed hundreds of Napoleonic soldiers during the early 19th century. Many of them made wall carvings which you can see today.

The castle may be visited from January 5 to April 30 and November 1 through December, weekdays from 9:30 a.m. to 5:05 p.m. (on Sunday from 12:30 to 4:20 p.m.). From May 1 to October 31, hours are weekdays from 9:30 a.m. to 6 p.m. (on Sunday from 11 a.m. to 6 p.m.). The price of admission ranges from 70p ($1.37) to £1.30 ($2.54) for adults and from 35p (68¢) to 65p ($1.27) for children under 16 and senior citizens.

The **Camera Obscura,** Castlehill (tel. 226-3709), is right beside the castle at the head of the Royal Mile. It's an Outlook Tower and on the rooftop terrace the Camera Obscura depicts the panorama of the Edinburgh skyline so that you can pinpoint the main landmarks of the city. Afterward you can use the telescopes on the rooftop to identify the sights. It is open daily from 9:30 a.m., charging an admission of 60p ($1.17) for adults, 30p (59¢) for children.

The **Scottish United Services Museum** (tel. 226-6907) is the National Museum for the Armed Forces of Scotland. It has the most unique, comprehensive, and longest established collections of British armed forces historical material in the United Kingdom. It has, in addition, a major research and archival function and specialist library. The galleries on the west side of Crown Square contain uniforms, weapons, and equipment of the Lowland and Highland Scottish regiments and also those of artillery units and other support corps. The sections which occupy the east side of the square deal with cavalry, the Royal Navy, and the Royal Air Force. The exhibits include many unique items of costume and equipment worn by the Scottish regiments of the British army at all periods, as well as items connected with Scottish factors in the history of the navy and air force. Material from the museum's collections associated with the Jacobite rebellions is shown in a room adjoining Queen Mary's apartments.

Entry to the museum's public galleries is included in the admission charge to the castle, and open hours are the same as those of the castle.

Along the Royal Mile

Ideally, if you have the time, you should walk the full length of the Royal Mile—all the way to the Palace of Holyroodhouse at the opposite end. Along the way, you'll see some of the most interesting old structures in Edinburgh, with their turrets, gables, and towering chimneys. Of all the buildings that may intrigue you, the most visited are John Knox's House and **St. Giles' Cathedral.**

Although it still bears the name "cathedral" which it once was, St. Giles' is now properly titled the High Kirk of Edinburgh. Founded in 1120, the interior dates mainly from the 15th century. It contains the Thistle Chapel, designed by Sir Robert Lorimer and housing beautiful stalls and notable heraldic stained-glass windows. The chapel is open from 10 a.m. to 5 p.m. and may be visited for 30p (59¢). John Knox, the leader of the Reformation in Scotland, was minister of St. Giles' from 1560 to 1572.

Farther down the street at 45 High St. is **John Knox's House,** whose history goes back to the late 15th century. Even if you're not interested in the reformer who founded the Scottish Presbyterian Church, you may want to visit his house, as it is characteristic of the "lands" that used to flank the Royal Mile. All of them are gone now, except Knox's house, with its timbered gallery. Inside, you'll see the tempera ceiling in the Oak Room, along with exhibitions of Knox memorabilia. The house may be visited daily (except Sunday) from 10 a.m. to 5 p.m. for 50p (98¢) for adults, 30p (59¢) for children and senior citizens.

READER'S SIGHTSEEING TIP: "An unusual attraction is the **Museum of Childhood,** 38 High St. (tel. 225-2424), on the Royal Mile, opposite John Knox's House. Three floors are devoted to every facet of childhood, ranging from antique toys and games to exhibits on health, education, costumes, juvenile 'arsenals,' and many other items representing the childhood experience of different nationalities and periods" (Ralph M. Stein, Flushing, N.Y.).

Author's Note: The museum is open weekdays from 10 a.m. to 5 p.m. (to 6 p.m. from June through September; on Sunday from 2 to 5 p.m. during the Edinburgh Festival), charging 50p (98¢) for adults, 40p (78¢) for children.

The Palace of Holyroodhouse

At the eastern end of the Royal Mile, the palace was built adjacent to an Augustinian abbey, established by David I in the 12th century. The nave, now in ruins, remains today. James IV founded the palace nearby in the early part of the 16th century, but, of his palace, only the north tower is left. Much of what you see today was ordered built by Charles II.

In the old wing occurred the most epic moments in the history of Holyroodhouse, when Mary Queen of Scots was in residence. Mary, who had been Queen of France and widowed while still a teenager, decided to return to her native Scotland. She eventually entered into an unsuccessful marriage with Lord Darnley but spent more time and settled affairs of state with her secretary, David Rizzio. Darnley plotted to kill the Italian, and he and his accomplices marched into Mary's supper room, grabbed Rizzio over her protests, then carried him to the Audience Chamber, where he was murdered by 56 stab wounds. A plaque marks the spot of his death on March 9, 1566.

Darnley himself was to live less than a year after, dying mysteriously in a gunpowder explosion. Mary, of course, was eventually executed on the order of her cousin, Elizabeth I. One of the most curious exhibits in Holyroodhouse is a piece of needlework by Mary, depicting a cat-and-mouse scene (Elizabeth's the cat).

The State Apartments also contain some fine 17th-century Flemish tapestries, especially a whole series devoted to Diana, as well as some Gobelins. In the Great Gallery are 89 portraits, depicting Scottish kings, including Macbeth, painted by a Dutchman, de Wet.

The palace suffered long periods of neglect, although it basked in glory at the ball in the mid-18th century thrown by Bonnie Prince Charlie. The present Queen and Prince Philip live at Holyroodhouse whenever they visit Edinburgh. When they're not in residence, you can visit the palace weekdays from 9:30 a.m. to 5:15 p.m. (on Sunday from 11 a.m. to 4:30 p.m.). In the off-season, the palace is closed on Sunday. Adults pay £1 ($1.95) to enter, but when the State Apartments are closed, the cost is 50p (98¢) for the Historical Rooms tour. Children, students, and senior citizens are admitted at half the adult rate. Light refreshments are available only in the summer months.

The New Town

At some point, the Old Town became too small. The burghers decided to build a whole new town across the valley, the marsh being drained and eventually turned into public gardens. Princes Street is the most striking boulevard. Architecturally, the most interesting district of the New Town is the north side of Charlotte Square, designed by Robert Adam. It was young architect James Craig who shaped much of the Georgian style of the New Town, with its crescents and squares.

At No. 7 Charlotte Square, a part of the northern facade, is the restored building known simply as the **Georgian House** (tel. 225-2160). It is a prime example of Scottish architecture and interior design in the zenith of the New Town. Originally the home of John Lamont XVII, known as "the last of the patriarchs and the first of the moderns," the house has recently been refurbished and reopened to the public by the National Trust for Scotland. The furniture in this Robert Adam house is mainly Hepplewhite, Chippendale, and Sheraton, all dating from the 18th century. In a ground-floor bedroom is a sturdy old four-poster with an original 18th-century canopy. The dining room table is set for a dinner on fine Wedgwood china, and the kitchen is stocked with gleaming copper pots and pans. The house is open April to October from 10 a.m. to 5 p.m. (on Sunday from 2 to 5 p.m.). In winter its hours are from 10 to 4:30 on Saturday (on Sunday from 2 to 4:30 p.m.). Admission is 90p ($1.76) for adults, 45p (88¢) for children.

As an Old Town complement to the New Town Georgian House, the National Trust for Scotland has opened in a 1620 tenement in the Royal Mile, **Gladstone's Land,** Lawnmarket (tel. 226-5856), an upstairs apartment of four rooms furnished as it might have been in the 17th century. On the ground floor, reconstructed shop booths display replicas of goods of the period. It is open April through October, Monday through Saturday from 10 a.m. to 5 p.m. (on Sunday from 2 to 5 p.m.). Admission is 70p ($1.37) for adults, 35p (68¢) for children.

The Gothic-inspired **Scott Monument** lies in the **East Princes Street Gardens.** It is the most famous landmark of Edinburgh, completed in the mid-19th century. Sir Walter Scott's heroes are honored by small figures in the monument. You can climb the tower weekdays from May to October from 9 a.m. to 6 p.m. for 25p (49¢). Off-season, you must scale the monument before 3 p.m. Closed Sunday. At **West Princes Street Gardens** is the first ever **Floral Clock,** which was constructed in 1904.

ART TREASURES: For the art lover, Edinburgh has a number of masterpieces, and many visitors come here just to look at the galleries. Of course, the principal museum is the **National Gallery of Scotland,** on The Mound (tel. 556-8921), in the center of Princes Street Gardens. Although the gallery is small as national galleries go, the collection came about with great care and was expanded considerably by bequests and loans. A few paintings are of exceptional merit. I'll highlight a representative sampling.

Among recent acquisitions is Giulio Romano's *Vierge à la Légende.* Other Italian paintings are Verrocchio's *Madonna and Child,* Andrea del Sarto's *Portrait of a Man,* and Domenichino's *Adoration of the Shepherds.* However, perhaps the most acclaimed among them is Tiepolo's *Finding of Moses.*

The Spanish masters are less well represented but shine forth in El Greco's *Saviour,* Velázquez's *Old Woman Cooking Eggs,* an early work by that great master, and *Immaculate Conception* by Zurbarán, his friend and contemporary.

The Flemish School emerges notably in Rubens's *Feast of Herod* and the Dutch in Rembrandt's *Woman in Bed.* The recent purchase of Hans Holbein the Younger's *Allegory of the Old and New Testaments* adds a new dimension to the representation of early northern painting in the gallery.

Among the paintings on loan to the gallery since World War II, from the Duke of Sutherland, are two Raphaels: *The Holy Family with a Palm Tree* and *The Bridgewater Madonna.* Titian gives us his favorite subject, Venus, this time rising from the sea, but he's even more masterly in his Diana canvases. A rare feature of the gallery: the *Seven Sacraments* paintings by Poussin, the 17th-century French painter, are also on loan.

The most valuable gift to the gallery since its founding, the Maitland Collection, includes Cézanne's *Mont St. Victoire,* as well as works by Degas, Van Gogh, Renoir, Gauguin, and Seurat, among others. Gauguin's *Vision of the Sermon,* a key work in the development of modern painting, is one of the gallery's masterpieces and a notable new acquisition is an early Monet, *Shipping Scene—Night Effects.*

The great English painters are represented by excellent examples—Gainsborough's *The Hon. Mrs. Graham,* Constable's *Dedham Vale,* along with works by Turner, Reynolds, and Hogarth. Naturally, the work of Scottish painters decks the walls, none finer than Henry Raeburn, at his best in the whimsical *The Rev. Robert Walker Skating on Duddingston Loch.*

The gallery is open from 10 a.m. to 5 p.m. weekdays (2 to 5 on Sunday). During the festival, hours are from 10 a.m. to 6 p.m. weekdays and from 11 a.m. to 6 p.m. on Sunday. Admission is free.

It may be typical of Edinburgh that it houses the only museum collection in Britain solely of 20th-century art, the **Scottish National Gallery of Modern Art,** in an 18th-century house, Inverleith House, on an eminence in the Royal Botanic Garden looking up to the skyline of the old city, a uniquely beautiful situation. But it is too small, and the gallery will move to a much larger but still old building, the former John Watson's School. Meanwhile, in the garden outside the gallery are major sculptures by Bourdelle, Epstein, Marini, Moore, Hepworth, Reg Butler, and William Turnbull, and a sundial by Ian Hamilton Finlay. The galleries contain works by Picasso, Matisse, Braque, Léger, Rouault, Derain, Miró, Magritte, Kirchner, Nolde, Kokoschka, Giacometti, Arp, Schwitters, Popova, and many others of the major creators of the 20th century, with a sound representation of English and, particularly, Scottish modern art. Works are also displayed from the studios of Otto Dix, Roy Lichtenstein, Louise Nevelson, Max Ernst, Ben Nicholson, Henri Gaudier-Bozeska, Richard Long, Jackson Pollock, Joseph Beuys, Balthus, Soutine, Duane Hanson, and John de Andrea. Bus routes passing the Royal Botanic Garden are 8, 9, 19/39, 23, and 27. Hours are from 10 a.m. to 5 p.m. (or dusk if earlier) on weekdays, and 2 to 5 p.m. (or dusk if earlier; opening at 11 a.m. during the Edinburgh Festival) on Sunday.

THE FESTIVAL: The highlight of Edinburgh's year—and the time of the greatest tourist invasion—is when the world-famous Edinburgh International Festival takes place. The annual festival is usually staged around mid-August to mid-September. Artists in all fields—music, drama, opera, ballet, painting—contribute their talents, and "Auld Reekie" takes on a cosmopolitan air.

One of the best attended spectacles is the military tattoo on the floodlit Esplanade in front of Edinburgh Castle. This is a chance for the spectator to witness some Highland dancing of the Scots and to watch a parade of Scottish regiments. In addition to operatic and dance presentations, choral and orchestral concerts, soloists, chamber concerts, and recitals (expect at least half a dozen every evening), there is a large number of dramatic shows and, to top it off, a widely attended film festival.

During these busy days, it's smart to make your headquarters at the **Festival Club,** a rendezvous for people participating in and witnessing the events. The club's headquarters are in the Edinburgh University Staff Club, 9–15 Chambers St. The licensed club operates a reasonably priced restaurant, cafeteria, snackbar, and lounges. The daily membership costs £1 ($1.95); a seven-day membership, £4 ($7.80); and for the season, £9 ($17.55).

For festival tickets, write to Festival Box Office, 21 Market St., Edinburgh EH1 1BW (tel. 226-4001). For accommodations, write to Tourist Accommodation Service, 9 Cockburn St., Edinburgh EH1 1BR.

THE SCOTTISH EXPERIENCE: This popular tourist attraction stands at West End Princes Street (tel. 228-2828). It is open from May to October, daily from 10 a.m. to 7 p.m. (in winter, Thursday to Saturday from 10 a.m. to 5:30 p.m.). Hourly shows are presented. A 40-foot relief model of Scotland shows at the press of a button the well-known places associated with the history of the country—the home of Sir Walter Scott at Abbotsford, Eilean Donan Castle, the cliffs of St. Kilda. It's a vision and sound presentation. There's also a multi-image screen presentation with stereo sound effects of the dramatic history of Edinburgh.

The Scottish Craft Shop is open daily except Sunday from 10 a.m. to 5:30 p.m., selling Scottish souvenirs of good value.

Also at the same address, Alison's Kitchen is open daily except Sunday from 10 a.m. to 5 p.m., offering homemade soups, quiches, flans, and savory tarts, with side salads, at around £1.20 ($2.34) to £1.50 ($2.93) a portion. They also do coffee, tea, cakes, patties, and biscuits.

LOW-COST TOURS: If you want a quick introduction to the principal attractions in and around the capital, then consider one or more of the inexpensive tours offered by the **Lothian Region Transport,** 14 Queen St. (tel. 556-5656). You won't find a cheaper way to hit the highlights, and, later, you can go back on your own if you want a deeper experience. The luxury-type coaches leave from Waverley Bridge, near the Scott Monument. The tours start in April and run through late October. A winter program is also offered. A half-day coach tour (which takes about 3½ hours) leaves daily at 9:30 a.m. and 1:30 p.m. (Sunday at 1:30 p.m. only), costing £4 ($7.80) and visiting the castle, the Palace of Holyroodhouse, and St. Giles' Cathedral. Operating throughout the day are half a dozen shorter tours that show you some of the environs—such as Scott and Stevenson Country. These tours are priced from £1 ($1.95). Also available is a wide selection of journeys which operate away from Edinburgh. These are on a special program called the "Waverley Series," composed of full-day and half-day excursions to destinations throughout Scotland and northern England.

SHOPPING: There are big and beautiful stores along Princes Street, facing the gardens and the castle, but there is just as much opportunity for seeking out souvenirs along the Royal Mile.

There you'll find the **Scottish Craft Centre**, Acheson House, Canongate, an exhibition of Scottish crafts—and everything is for sale. It is open Monday to Saturday from 10 a.m. to 6 p.m. At your leisure you can browse among all sorts of typically Scottish products, knitwear, pottery, glass, and jewelry. Everything is reasonably priced.

J. & R. Glen Ltd., 497 Lawnmarket (tel. 225-8065), is one of the oldest Highland bagpipe makers. They will furnish a set for £125 ($243.75) or more and a starter kit for learners at £21 ($40.95), complete with tutor book and cassette.

John Morrison, 461 Lawnmarket (tel. 225-8149), is a marvelous place at which to shop for a tartan. A woman's authentic hand-tailored kilt will cost around £70 ($136.50), but a semi-kilt or kilt skirt can be purchased for as little as £29 ($56.55). They will also provide evening sashes and stoles to match your skirt at £12 ($23.40) and £15 ($29.25).

For men, the tradition is far more complicated—kilts go for £85 ($165.75) to £165 ($321.75) for a heavy hand-woven worsted in your favorite tartan. To go with it, there are doublets and jackets, barathea at £75 ($146.25) and velvet at £98 ($191.10). That's followed up with accessories, a jabot and cuffs, £9 ($17.55) for the set, along with kilt hose at £7.25 ($14.14), a tie at £3.50 ($6.83), and plain green undertrews at £2.25 ($4.39) to answer the eternal question.

A belt with a sterling silver buckle is £21.50 ($41.93), and sporrans range from £15 ($29.25) for plain pig grain hide to £55 ($107.25) for a white sealskin evening model with silver mounts and skean dhus to tuck into your hose. Orders can be mailed throughout the world if you can't take personal delivery of your Highland dress.

The **Scottish Stone and Brass Rubbing Centre**, Canongate Tolbooth, 163 Canongate (tel. 225-1131), is open Monday to Saturday from 10 a.m. to 5 p.m. (also on Sunday during the festival from noon to 5 p.m.). Amateurs will be shown how to make their first rubbing, and professionals will have a vast selection of subjects to chose from. Ready-made rubbings, rubbing kits, booklets, and postcards are also on sale.

NIGHTLIFE: The **Dalhousie Banquet** takes place most evenings during the season at Dalhousie Courte, Cockpen, near Bonnyrigg, a few miles south of Edinburgh. A Jacobean feast of five courses is washed down with mead and wine at long candlelit tables to the tune of medieval songs and the strumming of old string instruments. A typical evening rounds off the meal, presented by the court chamberlain and the ladies and gentlemen of the court dressed in traditional costume. A cheerful, harmless family evening awaits you. Advance reservations are essential; telephone 663-5155. A free coach runs from central Edinburgh at 6:45 p.m. and will bring you back at the end of the evening.

2. Day Trips from Edinburgh

Within easy reach of Edinburgh lie some of the most interesting castles and mansions in Scotland, the most important of which follow.

STIRLING: Almost equidistant from Glasgow and Edinburgh, Stirling is dominated by its impressive castle, perched on a 250-foot basalt rock. From

Edinburgh, a bus takes about an hour and a half, traveling a distance of 37 miles.

This ancient town, with its turbulent history, was the scene of several battles, notably the Battle of Bannockburn in 1314, in which the Scots routed the army of Edward II. On the right bank of the Forth, the castle dates from an unknown age, although its main gateway was built by James III. At one time the castle was considered the "key to the Highlands," and is today the head-quarters of the Argyle and Sutherland Highlanders, one of Britain's most famous regiments.

The castle is open daily in April, May, and September from 9:30 a.m. to 6:15 p.m. (on Sunday from 11 to 6); June, July, and August, daily from 9:30 a.m. to 7 p.m. (on Sunday from 11 to 7); and October to March, daily from 9:30 a.m. to 4 p.m. (on Sunday from 1 to 4), charging adults 50p (98¢); children, 25p (49¢).

Other places of interest to visit in Stirling include the 15th-century **Church of the Holy Rude,** in which Mary Queen of Scots was crowned in 1543 at the age of nine months; the **Auld Brig** over the Forth, dating from the 14th century; and the **palace** built by James V in the 16th century.

Just outside the town is the **Robert Bruce Memorial and Museum.** Admission is 20p (39¢) for a continual audio-visual presentation of stories of Bruce's times and history.

Food and Lodging

Portcullis Hotel, Castle Wynd (tel. Stirling 2290), is my favorite place to stay in the area. It's a tall, 14th-century, rugged stone building hugging the walls of the castle. You enter through a lower courtyard of shrubbery and trees, protected by a high old stone wall. The inviting bar, which is colorful, is on the ground floor. You ascend to the second-floor lounge with stone walls, a cathedral ceiling, and a fireplace at one end. It's furnished with a mixture of antiques and comfortable chairs. The dining room has encircling windows offering a spectacular view. The finest Scottish china is used for meals. Snacks include "mince and mash" at £1.60 ($3.12), although upstairs a lunch will cost £6.50 ($12.68). The bedrooms are personal, each furnished informally and comfortably. The per-person rate is £14 ($27.30), including VAT, service, and a full breakfast.

If you're a Scottish history buff and would like to spend the night in this historic town, creaking with memories of time gone by, you might try to find a room at the tiny **Heritage Hotel,** containing only four bedrooms, all of which have private baths and showers.

It's at 16 Allan Park (tel. Stirling 3660). You're welcomed by the owner, Monsieur Marquetty, a Frenchman who married "a Scottish lassie" and settled in this unlikely spot. Their "hotel" is really like a private residence, and they have outfitted it as such, discreetly using antiques, paintings, and personal objects to make it warm and homelike. Their single rate is £14 ($27.30) per night, and two persons are charged from £28 ($54.60).

Monsieur Marquetty also offers a good cuisine in his adjoining restaurant, which features a set lunch at £5 ($9.75), served between noon and 3, and a table d'hôte dinner, four courses, for £9 ($17.55), offered between 6:30 and 11 p.m., the latter a surprisingly late hour for provincial Stirling.

La Romantica, 4 Viewfield Pl. (tel. Stirling 64521), is a trattoria with a good bar, Valentino's Lounge, near the Royal Hotel. It offers well-prepared, familiar, and enjoyable Italian dishes, including the chef's pasta specialty, spaghetti Romantica at £2.75 ($5.36). All pasta dishes, ordered as a main course, cost £3.50 ($6.83). Instead of pasta, you might begin with minestrone at 90p ($1.76). Recommendable main courses include chicken suprême "Romeo and Juliet," £4.80 ($9.36), and veal alla Romantica, £4.90 ($9.56). The smoothest finish is the zabaglione at £1.65 ($3.22). The restaurant is closed on Sunday, although open otherwise until 11 p.m.

DOUNE CASTLE: At Doune, on the banks of the Teith River, four miles west of Dunblane, stands this 14th-century castle, once a royal palace. Now owned by the Earl of Moray, it was restored in 1883, making it one of the best preserved of the medieval castles of Scotland. It is open daily from April through October, charging adults 70p ($1.37) for admission; children pay 40p (78¢). It's closed on Thursday in April and October.

After visiting the castle, guests can drive 1½ miles to the **Doune Motor Museum,** which charges £1.20 ($2.34) for adults, 60p ($1.17) for children. The motor museum contains about 40 vintage and postvintage motor cars, including the second-oldest Rolls-Royce in the world. It is open daily from April 1 to October 31. In April and May, the last admissions are at 4:30 p.m. From June to August, the hours are from 10 a.m. to 6 p.m., and in September and October, the last admissions are again at 4:30 p.m. For more information, telephone (078-684) 203.

South of Doune is the highly popular **Blair Drummond Safari Park.** It's open from mid-March to the last Sunday in October, from 10 a.m. (tel. Doune 456). Apart from the zebras, you are likely to meet the typical safari-park cast of lions, giraffes, elephants, and Highland cattle, and there's even a Pet's Corner. Meals are offered in the Ranch Kitchen, and free picnic areas are provided. Cars are admitted for £4.50 ($8.78), including a guidebook. Safari buses, costing £1.30 ($2.54) for adults, 90p ($1.76) for children, are available for those without their own transport. A Safari boat trip is offered at a cost of 50p (98¢) for adults, 30p (59¢) for children. Take exit 10 off the M9 onto the A84.

Food and Lodging

The Woodside (tel. Doune 237) is a pleasant stone structure standing on the A84 main Stirling–Oban road. In the heart of Perthshire, it was originally a coaching inn and dates back to the 18th century. It contains 14 well-furnished bedrooms, mostly with private baths. Singles rent for £16 ($31.20) and doubles go for £28 ($54.60), including a full breakfast. You can stay three nights for the price of two. The lounge is brightened by red plush seating, and in addition there are two simply decorated bars. You can enjoy a selection of traditional salad dishes on the bar luncheon menu with soused herring and homemade pâté salads, costing from about £1.50 ($2.93). Grilled Aberdeen angus steaks are priced about £4 ($7.80). The dining room overlooks the garden, and you sit in high-backed carved Edwardian chairs, enjoying such specialties as venison, grilled rainbow trout, and fresh lobster in season. Dinner is likely to run about £7 ($13.65).

Deanston House Hotel (tel. Doune 248) is a Georgian building dating from 1820 and standing on 56 acres of private woodland and park, with the River Teith running along one side of the property. The manor was later given an Italianate style, and a three-story tower and conservatory were added. Owned by Denzil S. Crawford, the hotel has a wide variety of rooms, with and without private baths. The decor honors the era, and there are many fine antiques and paintings. A double or twin rents from £16 ($31.20) per person nightly without private bath, increasing to £22 ($42.90) per person with private bath (these latter rooms often contain four-poster beds). Singles without bath rent from £17 ($33.15) nightly. Good Scottish food is served, a set dinner costing from £7 ($13.65), although you may prefer to order à la carte. Before your meal, you may want to have a drink in the ornate Ormonde cocktail bar, with its original wooden ceiling.

LINLITHGOW: In this royal burgh, a county town in West Lothian, 18 miles west of Edinburgh, Mary Queen of Scots was born. The roofless **Palace of Linlithgow,** site of her birth in 1542, can still be viewed here today, although it is but a shell of its former self. Once a favorite residence of Scottish kings, the palace was built square-shaped. In the center are the remains of a royal fountain erected by James V. The queen's suite was in the north quarter, but this was rebuilt for the homecoming of James VI in 1617. The Great Hall is on the first floor. Gen. Henry Hawley's dragoons burned the palace in 1746, destroying one of the gems in the Scottish architectural crown. It is open daily from 10 a.m. to 5 p.m. (on Sunday from 2 to 5 p.m.).

South of the palace stands the medieval kirk of **St. Michael the Archangel.**

From Linlithgow, it is but a 3½-mile drive east on the Queensferry Road (A904) to the **House of the Binns,** the historic home of the Dalyells. The mansion, with its fine Jacobean plaster ceilings, portraits, and panoramic vistas, receives visitors Easter Week and then from May 1 to September 30—daily, except Friday, from 2 to 5:30 p.m. The parkland is open from 10 a.m. to 7 p.m. Admission is 90p ($1.76) for adults, 45p (88¢) for children.

For dining, **Champany,** on the A904, three miles northeast of Linlithgow (tel. Philpstoun 532), was once a farmhouse built of stone, but it has been handsomely converted into one of the finest places for dining in the area. The dining room is circular, with a steep hexagonal ceiling. Victorian mahogany furniture adds a sedate touch. My happiest experience was discovering the chef's specialty, a chicken breast suprême, made royal with its clever use of hazelnuts, port, and tasty apples. It's a remarkable dish and I recommend it highly, although the escalope of veal, prepared in the Roman style, is almost as good. All in all, it's personal cookery at reasonable prices. The set luncheon goes for £7.50 ($14.63), and a complete dinner on an à la carte menu runs around £14 ($27.30) per head. The menu changes twice yearly. The restaurant is open daily except Sunday from 12:30 to 2:15 p.m. and from 7 to 10 p.m. Apart from the restaurant, there is the charming Country Life Bar, serving a tasty bar lunch at around £2.25 ($4.39) and specializing in real ales.

HOPETOUN HOUSE: This is Scotland's greatest Adam mansion, that fine example of 18th-century architecture. It is the seat of the Marquess of Linlithgow, whose ancestors were once the governor-general of Australia and the viceroy of India. Set in the midst of beautifully landscaped grounds, laid out along the lines of Versailles, the mansion lies near the Forth Road Bridge at South Queensferry, off the A904. On a tour you're shown through splendid reception rooms filled with 18th-century tapestries, unique Cullen furniture, paintings, statuary, and other works of art. From a rooftop viewing platform, you look out over a panoramic view of the Firth of Forth. Even more enjoyable, perhaps, is to take the Nature Trail, explore the Deer Parks, investigate the Stables' Museum, or stroll through the formal gardens, all on the grounds. In the Ballroom Suite is a licensed restaurant that serves coffee, lunch, afternoon tea, and high tea. Hopetoun is open Easter weekend, then daily from May to the end of September, from 11 a.m. to 5:30 p.m. Admission to the house and grounds is £1.50 ($2.93) for adults and 70p ($1.37) for children under 16. For more information, telephone 331-2451.

NORTH BERWICK: This royal burgh, created in the 14th century, was once an important Scottish port. In East Lothian, 24 miles east from Edinburgh, it is today a holiday resort popular with the Scots and an increasing horde of foreigners. Visitors are drawn to its golf courses, beach sands, and colorful harbor life on the Firth of Forth. You can climb the rocky shoreline or else enjoy the heated outdoor swimming pool in July and August.

At the tourist office (tel. North Berwick 2197), you can pick up information on how to take boat trips to the offshore islands, including **Bass Rock,** a breeding ground inhabited by about 10,000 gannets and one or two crusty lighthouse keepers. The volcanic island is one mile in circumference. It's possible to see the rock from the harbor. The viewing is even better at Berwick Law, a volcanic lookout point surmounted by the jawbones of a whale.

Some three miles east of the resort stand the dramatic ruins of the 14th-century diked and rose-colored **Tantallon Castle,** rising magnificently on cliffs. This was the ancient stronghold of the Douglases.

The favorite choice for accommodations in North Berwick is the **Marine Hotel,** Cromwell Road (tel. North Berwick 2406), one of those grand seaside resort establishments, standing in its own garden looking across the West Link golf course to the Firth of Forth. After a slumber, it has now blossomed out into a summer holiday hotel of the finest standing, ideal for families. In its modernization, all 85 of its bedrooms now contain private baths. An airiness and freshness prevail. Rates vary according to the length of your stay. However, expect to pay from £20 ($39) per person in a room with bath, rising to £25.50 ($49.73) with bath, these terms including dinner, bed, and breakfast, as well as VAT and service. Tennis courts and a putting green are on the hotel's grounds. A resident orchestra plays for dancing on Saturday evening. The public rooms are spacious and nicely furnished. The hotel also has a heated outdoor pool in use from May to September, as well as squash courts and a sauna.

If you're seeking something less expensive, **Blenheim House** (tel. North Berwick 2385), is, I understand from readers' reports, a good bet, although I've never stayed there. It's tiny, offering only two singles (and these go fast), eight doubles, and a couple of family rooms. Rates are £12.50 ($24.38) in a single, from £22 ($42.90) in a double. The food—again, according to reports—is also good. Service is until 9 p.m. The hotel is very popular in summer, so reservations will be essential. In addition, Mr. and Mrs. Wight rent a garden apartment, consisting of two double bedrooms and one single room, at a rate of £115 ($224.25) per week.

DIRLETON: Another popular excursion from North Berwick is to the rose-tinted **Dirleton Castle,** with its surrounding gardens, at Dirleton on the Edinburgh–North Berwick road (A198). This 13th-century castle is well preserved, receiving visitors at a cost of 50p (98¢) for adults, 25p (49¢) for children under 16 and senior citizens. Visitors are welcome in season on weekdays from 9:30 a.m. and on Sunday from 2 p.m. Dirleton vies for the title of "the prettiest village in Scotland."

For dining at Dirleton, the **Open Arms** (tel. Dirleton 241) will receive you in keeping with the promise of its name. This old stone hostelry has been transformed into a handsome restaurant, serving the finest food in the area. It lies off the A198, 2½ miles southwest of North Berwick. Overlooking the castle ruins, the hotel is owned by Arthur Neil, who has built up an enormous local reputation for serving Scottish dishes. Try, for example, cranachan (served with shortbread, this is a concoction of oatmeal, heavy cream, and brambles). Cold Scottish salmon is served encased in pastry, and is one of the inn's specialties. Another specialty is a stew made of fresh mussels and onions. On one recent occasion, the luncheon menu featured a first for me—smoked mackerel with gooseberry cream sauce. Before having, say, a venison casserole in red wine sauce, you might begin with a real "Taste of Scotland" specialty, lentil broth with oatmeal, in which, as the Scots say, you can "stand up your spoon in it." The people who serve are quiet, informed, and skillful. A table d'hôte luncheon is offered for £7.50 ($14.63), although you can order à la carte as well, paying from £10 ($19.50). Hours are from 12:30 to 2:15 p.m. In the evening, between 7 and 10, a three-course set dinner is offered for £11 ($21.45), plus service.

The Open Arms will also receive you as an overnight guest. However, it's small, only eight bedrooms, each with private bath, and, joy of joys, room service available at no extra cost. In a single, charges range from £23 ($44.85) to £24 ($46.80), from £35 ($68.25) in a double, including a full breakfast, service, and VAT. Log fires crackle and blaze, and it must surely be a golfer's paradise, as it's surrounded by eight courses.

DUNBAR: In East Lothian, southeast of North Berwick, Dunbar, another royal burgh, is a popular seaside resort at the foot of the Lammermuir Hills. On a rock above the harbor are the remains of **Dunbar Castle,** built on the site of an earlier castle that dated from 856. Mary Queen of Scots fled there with Darnley in 1566, immediately after the murder of her secretary, Rizzio. Today the kittiwakes live where once the "Black Angus of Dunbar," the Countess of March, held off the English. The Battle of Dunbar was fought in 1650 between Cromwell's army and the Scots led by David Leslie. The Scots, fighting valiantly, lost and nearly 3000 were killed in one day.

Roxburghe Hotel, Queen's Road (tel. Dunbar 62755), is a rather old-fashioned hotel of much comfort. A large, 40-bedroom establishment, it stands in a sheltered position on the seafront, adjoining the Dunbar golf course. Bedrooms are often roomy and most comfortable, a large proportion containing private baths. B&B, depending on the plumbing, ranges from £15 ($29.25) to £20 ($39) per person, including VAT, service, and a full breakfast. The public rooms are furnished in a homey fashion, often with open fires. The cocktail bar is modernized, and in the sea-view dining room the good food, using fresh produce, is supervised by Mr. Marcel, a well-known chef de cuisine.

The **Battleblent Hotel** (tel. Dunbar 62234) lies just outside Dunbar on the road to Edinburgh, 26 miles away. Jim and Faye Ferguson own the castle-like home set on a hill surrounded by three acres of their own land overlooking the Balhaven Bay on the Firth of Forth. The bedrooms are large, high-ceilinged, and comfortable, with electric heaters and facilities for making tea and coffee. Assisted by their sons, Martin and Kevin, the Fergusons have a disco and lounge bar downstairs, and a small, charming, bright dining room on the first floor. The bar and disco are popular with the people of Dunbar, so you can get acquainted with the local affairs of the day. Get Mr. Ferguson to show you his collection of international coins in the downstairs lounge bar. The tariff is £11 ($21.45) for bed and a continental breakfast, or £12 ($23.40) for bed and a big Scottish breakfast.

DALKEITH: This small burgh in Midlothian, seven miles southeast of Edinburgh, is the site of **Dalkeith Palace,** rebuilt and redesigned by Sir John Vanbrugh, circa 1700. Such monarchs as George IV, Victoria, and Edward VII have stayed here during visits to Edinburgh.

Visitors flock here for **Dalkeith Park,** to explore the woodland and riverside walks in and around the extensive grounds of the palace. Luring guests are natural trails and an adventure woodland play area, a tunnel walk, and an Adam bridge. The park is open daily from 11 a.m. to 6 p.m., April 2 to October 31. During November, the park is open only on Sunday from 11 a.m. to dusk. To reach the park, go seven miles south of Edinburgh on the A68. The price of admission is 50p (98¢).

On the same tour, it's easy to explore—

3. The Kingdom of Fife

North of Forth from Edinburgh, the county of Fife still likes to call itself a "kingdom." Its name, even today, suggests the romantic episodes and pageantry during the reign of the early Stuart kings. Fourteen of Scotland's 66 royal burghs lay within this shire. Many of the former royal palaces and castles, either restored or in colorful ruins, can be visited today, and I've previewed the most important ones coming up.

As Edinburgh is so near, the temptation is to set up headquarters in one of the city's many elegant hotels or B&B houses and explore Fife from that base. However, serious golfers may want to stay at one of my recommended hotels in St. Andrews.

DUNFERMLINE: This ancient town was once the capital of Scotland. It is easily reached by ferry or by the railway crossing the Forth Bridge. Dunfermline lies five miles northwest of the Forth Bridge, a distance of 14 miles northwest of Edinburgh.

In **Dunfermline Abbey** lie many of Scotland's royal dead, including Robert the Bruce, who gave the town its charter in 1322. His skeleton was rediscovered in 1818 during excavations. Queen Victoria commanded that the tomb of St. Margaret be restored.

The **Royal Palace** witnessed the birth of Kings Charles I and James I. Only the southwest wall remains of this once-gargantuan edifice. The last king to reside here was Charles II in 1651.

Andrew Carnegie, the American industrialist and philanthropist, was born here in 1835. The **Andrew Carnegie Birthplace,** a former weaver's cottage, lies at the junction of Priory Lane and Moodie Street and may be visited weekdays, May to August, from 11 a.m. to 1 p.m. and 2 to 5 p.m. From September, it's open from 11 a.m. to 1 p.m. and 2 to 4 p.m.; on Sunday from 2 to 5 p.m. all year.

After he retired from steelmaking and finance, Carnegie gave away $400 million for charitable purposes, mainly in Britain and America. Dunfermline received the first free library of many thousands, public baths, and **Pittencrieff Park,** rich in history and natural charm. Run by the trust which still provides extra benefits for his native town, the birthplace museum gives a glimpse of his humble origins and his benefactions.

From Dunfermline, you can take an excursion six miles west to—

Culross

This old royal burgh has been renovated by the National Trust for Scotland, and is one of the most beautiful in the country. As you walk its cobbled streets, admiring its whitewashed houses, you'll feel you're taking a stroll back into the 17th century. Many of the cottages have crow-stepped gables and red pantiled roofs.

Set in tranquil walled gardens, **Culross Palace** was built in the village between 1597 and 1611, containing a series of paintings on its wooden walls and ceilings. It has been restored and may be visited, April to September, daily from 9:30 a.m. to 7 p.m. (on Sunday from 2 to 7). From October to March, it's open daily from 9:30 to 4 (on Sunday from 2 to 4). Admission is 40p (78¢) for adults, 20p (39¢) for children.

For food and lodging, the **Red Lion Inn** (tel. New Mills 880225) stands on the north side of the Forth River midway between Forth Road Bridge and Kincardine Road Bridge. Both ancient and modern, the little pub has a few rooms which owner Findlays Sinclair rents out at £9 ($17.55) per person per day, including breakfast. There is a pine-paneled pub and a lounge with a fireplace, where you can have bar snacks. The pub is easy to spot, a blue and stucco building with a slate roof in the center of the village. There's parking in the rear—next to the stone wall, overlooking the river. A mixed crowd frequents the Red Lion, the rich, the poor, locals blending with visitors. The cooking is above average, and you'll have a wide choice of whiskies, including Royal Culross.

FALKLAND PALACE: Now owned by Queen Elizabeth, Falkland was once the hunting retreat of the Stuart kings. This royal burgh of cobbled streets and crooked houses lies at the northern base of the hill of East Lomond, 21 miles north of Edinburgh.

Since the 12th century, it has been connected with Scottish kings. Originally a castle stood on the site of today's palace, but it was replaced in the 16th century. Falkland then became a favorite seat of the Scottish court. A grief-stricken James V died here. Mary Queen of Scots used to come to Falkland for "hunting and hawking." It was also here that the Earl of Bothwell was arrested, accused of a plot against her. Cromwell's forces occupied Falkland in 1654.

The royal chapel and apartments are open from April 1 to October 31, weekdays from 10 a.m. to 6 p.m. and on Sunday from 2 to 6. The gardens, incidentally, have been laid out to the original royal plans. At Falkland is the oldest royal tennis court in the United Kingdom. For a ticket to both the palace and gardens, adults pay £1.10 ($2.15); children, 55p ($1.07).

Food and Lodging

Covenanter Hotel (tel. Falkland 224) has been a popular inn since the early 18th century. With modest modernization, it offers a good standard of accommodation. It's built ruggedly of local stone, with high chimneys, wooden shutters, and a Georgian entry. The location is on a tiny plaza, opposite the church and castle. You enter a gleaming white entry hall with a circular staircase leading to the lounges and bedrooms. The dining room is strictly "old style" and for predinner drinks there is an intimate pub, the Covenanter Cocktail Bar. B&B costs £10 ($19.50) per person, including service and VAT, and luncheons go for £5 ($9.75), a set evening meal for £6.95 ($13.55).

Kind Kyttock's Kitchen, Cross Wynd, stands right near the palace and welcomes you most of the year with a stone fireplace where logs burn brightly.

The "kitchen" is also an art gallery, displaying local crafts and paintings. A specialty is four oatcakes with cheese at £1 ($1.95). The bread is always homemade, very fresh tasting, as you'll discover if you order an open sandwich at £1.25 ($2.44). Locally grown potatoes in their jackets are served with a variety of fillings for £1.10 ($2.15). For a tea, I'd suggest the homemade pancake with fruit and fresh cream at 60p ($1.17). Even better, however, are the homemade tarts with fresh cream at 75p ($1.46). Salads are good tasting, costing from £1.55 ($3.02) a plate. A cup of Scottish broth, served with a slice of home-baked wholemeal bread, costs 50p (98¢). The Kitchen now serves wine at 65p ($1.27) a glass or by the carafe at £2.25 ($4.39). The women who run the place serve from 10:30 a.m. to 5:30 p.m. Off-season, it is open only on weekends.

Back at Dunfermline you can connect with the coastal road, heading east to:

Largo

Alexander Selkirk, the original Robinson Crusoe, was born here in 1676. This Scottish sailor, son of a shoemaker and tanner, was once charged with "indecent behavior in church," but he never had to pay the penalty, whatever it was, as he was away at sea. He disappeared in the South Seas, but was discovered in 1709. He returned to Largo in 1712. A statue in the village honors this hometown boy, who was clearly the inspiration for the Daniel Defoe classic. A house Selkirk purchased for his father is still standing.

THE EAST NEUK: Within a half hour's drive of St. Andrews are some of the most beautiful and unspoiled fishing villages of eastern Scotland:

Pittenweem

If you're here in the morning, try to get caught up in the action at the fish auction held under a large shed (except Sunday). The actual time depends on the tides. Afterward you can go for a walk through the village, taking in the sturdy stone homes, some of which have been preserved by the National Trust for Scotland.

Anstruther

This is an important fishing port and a summer resort, with the **Scottish Fisheries Museum** down by the harbor. Tracing the history of the fishing industry in Scotland, it charges 75p ($1.46) admission for adults, 25p (49¢) for children. The museum is open from April 1 to October 31, Monday to Saturday, from 10 a.m. to 6 p.m. (on Sunday from 2 to 5 p.m.). From November 1 to March 31, it may be visited every day except Tuesday, from 2 to 5 p.m. The museum also has a tearoom and a marine aquarium. It has restored two large sail fishing boats in Anstruther Harbor. One, the 70-foot *Fifie*, is open to the public. From the museum, you can walk to the tiny hamlet of Cellardyke which is really Old Anstruther, with many charming stone houses.

The **Craw's Nest Hotel**, Bankwell Road (tel. Anstruther 310691), was originally an old Scottish manse before its conversion to a popular hotel, with beautiful views over the Firth of Forth and May Island. To the original building, many extensions were added under the direction of the owners, Mr. and Mrs. Edward Clarke, and their son-in-law, Ian Birrel. The black-and-white building is step-gabled, standing behind a high stone wall. Bedrooms are handsomely equipped and well appointed, costing from £22 ($42.90) per person nightly for B&B. Each of the units contains a private bath. Public areas are simply decorated and cozy, including a lounge bar as well as a bustling public bar. The food is good, and the wine is priced reasonably in the hotel's dining room.

Smuggler's Inn, High Street (tel. Anstruther 310506), stands in the heart of town, a warmly inviting inn that evokes memories of smuggling days around here. The original inn that stood on this spot dates back to 1300. In Queen Anne's day, it was a well-known tavern. The ceilings are low, the floors uneven, and, of course, the stairways are winding. Overlooking the harbor, rooms are rented for £14.75 ($28.76) per person if bathless, rising to £16.25 ($31.69) with bath. All rates include VAT, service, and a full breakfast. There is no table d'hôte lunch, but bar snacks are priced from £1 ($1.95) to £5 ($9.75). Dinner, served between 7 and 9:30 p.m., is à la carte, prices for a meal ranging between £8.50 ($16.58) and £10 ($19.50). If featured, ask for the local Pittenweem prawns. Otherwise, you are likely to have a choice of fried fish, lobsters, chicken, and local Scottish steak. All food is fresh except, as the owner, Mr. McSharry, said, the tomato soup. "We just can't catch the flavor like Heinz."

READER'S RESTAURANT SELECTION: "I recommend highly the **Cellar,** just back of the Fisheries Museum (tel. Anstruther 310378). The place is attractive, and the food is outstanding. The owner has a floor show on Saturday night" (David L. Chalmers, Chevy Chase, Md.).

Elie

With its step-gabled houses and little harbor, this is my favorite village along the coast. Nearby is a good golf course, and there are rock-ribbed sands for bathing.

If you're passing this way, I'd suggest you drop in at the **Ship Inn** on the Toft, there to enjoy a pint of lager. In summer you can sit out in fair weather, overlooking the water. In colder months, a fireplace burns brightly. The pub has a nautical atmosphere, and doesn't do much in the way of food, but the friendly woman who runs it will prepare a sandwich if you're hungry.

For more substantial dining, I'd suggest **Upstairs/Downstairs,** 51 High St. (tel. Elie 330374), a pleasant little place to eat, opposite a small triangular park. For a menu of standard dishes, you are charged £7 ($13.65) for an evening's dinner. During the day, snacks and bar lunches are also offered, followed by high teas and suppers. The restaurant, incidentally, is licensed. A bar lunch averages around £2.25 ($4.39), and wine by the glass goes for 65p ($1.27). If you'd like to stay overnight, you can request one of the simple, pleasant bedrooms, costing only £6 ($11.70) per person nightly.

Mrs. Barbara Walker, Dalmore, The Toft (tel. Elie 330583), is the village librarian. She wisely began to accept guests so she could afford to keep her bayfront home. Since then, she's won all sorts of new friends, especially among Americans, and she feels she's expanded her own horizons. "We feel less isolated—now we are a part of the world," Mrs. Walker told me. Her Tudoresque, tall and stylish 19th-century villa is on a grassy terrace, just 20 steps up from the harbor. It's still a private-seeming home, with many antiques in the sitting-breakfast room, the entry, and bedrooms. She personalizes the breakfasts, and charges £7 ($13.65) per person nightly. She also serves a beverage and cookies around 9 p.m. If you ask, she'll serve an evening meal for £3.50 ($6.83). If possible, it's wise to phone for a reservation and to get directions to the house.

Crail

Considered the pearl of the East Neuk of Fife, Crail is an artists' colony, and many painters have found cottages around this little harbor. Natural bathing facilities are found at Roome Bay, and there are many beaches nearby. The Balcomie Golf Course, in good condition, is one of the oldest in the world.

Croma Hotel (tel. Crail 239) is near the harbor with ten bedrooms. It's the "home base" of famed all-American ball player Jack Healy and his attractive wife Rosemarie, originally from Ireland. Brooklyn-born Jack is a strapping, handsome former Pan Am executive. From Samoa he brought handicrafts and trinkets, and has hung them against the wall-size geographic maps from Pan Am. This, the Chart Room, is fully licensed, and it's Jack's domain. Rosemarie has decorated the dining room in green and white and used Windsor chairs set in front of the bay window. Many of the artists who live in this little fishing village come here for drinks and evening meals. Mr. and Mrs. Healy have hired an excellent local chef, who wisely uses farm-fresh vegetables, as well as local lobster, crab, and beef. The Healys charge £10 ($19.50) per person for B&B. They serve a table d'hôte lunch for £3 ($5.85), and an evening meal for £6.50 ($12.68).

ST. ANDREWS: On a bay of the North Sea, St. Andrews is sometimes known as the "Oxford of Scotland." Founded in 1411, the **University of St. Andrews** is the oldest in Scotland and the third oldest in Britain. At term time you can see the students in their characteristic red gowns.

The university's most interesting buildings include the tower and church of St. Salvator's College and the courtyard of St. Mary's College, dating from 1538. An ancient thorn tree, said to have been planted by Mary Queen of Scots, stands near the college's chapel. The church of St. Leonard's College is also from medieval days. The Scottish Parliament in 1645 met in the old University Library, now the Psychology Department. A new library building was opened in 1976 and contains nearly half a million books, with many rare and ancient volumes.

The historic sea town in northeast Fife is also known as the home of golf in Britain. The world's leading golf club, the **Royal & Ancient,** was founded here in 1754. All of St. Andrew's four golf courses—the Old, the New, the Jubilee, and the Eden—are open to the public. Of course, the hallowed turf of the Old Course is the sentimental favorite. The clubhouse is not open to nonmembers, but in common with the rest of Scotland there's no problem in playing a round on the Old, New, Jubilee, or Eden courses. It is advisable to reserve with the starter, however, or you may not get on, especially with the Old Course. It will cost around £6 ($11.70) for greens fees, and a caddy will charge another £5 ($9.75) or so. Of course, he'll expect a tip and deserves one if he knows the hazards and spots well. But do negotiate first, as they have a bit of a reputation—be warned. Club hire from the Pro Shop is £4 ($7.80) for an up-to-date set.

The old gray royal burgh of St. Andrew is filled with many monastic ruins and ancient houses; regrettably, they represent but a few mere skeletons of medieval St. Andrews.

St. Andrews Cathedral and Priory. The earliest part is the church and tower of St. Rule, although in 1160 a much larger cathedral was started and eventually consecrated in 1318. Built in both the Romanesque and Gothic styles, it was the largest church in Scotland, establishing St. Andrews as the ecclesiastical capital of the country. Today the ruins can only suggest the former beauty and importance of the cathedral. The east and west gables and a part of the south wall remain, and standing still is "the Pends," part of the old main gateway of the priory.

The **St. Andrews Cathedral Museum** contains a collection of early Christian and medieval monuments, as well as artifacts discovered on the cathedral site. It is open April to September daily from 9:30 a.m. to 7 p.m. (on Sunday from 2 to 7 p.m.). Admission is 30p (59¢) for adults and 15p (29¢) for children under 16 and senior citizens.

The **Holy Trinity Church** ("the Town Kirk") is a beautifully restored medieval church, founded in 1410. John Knox preached his first sermon here. The stained glass, sacramental plate, Archbishop Sharp's tomb, and the Boyd memorial pulpit are of special interest. The original tower houses a 23-bell carillon. The 12th-century St. Regulus Tower stands in the grounds of a ruined cathedral, the largest church in Scotland before the Reformation (founded 1160, consecrated 1318). There is access to the tower of the church which is 108 feet high.

You also can visit the ruined 13th-century castle, fortress, and residence of the bishops of St. Andrews. Notable features are a "bottle dungeon" and secret passage, a mine and countermine of 1546.

Food and Lodging

In hotels, many dedicated golfers prefer the **Old Course Hotel** (tel. St. Andrews 74371), as it stands right in the middle of this legendary 17th-century fairway—hence, the protective net covering the hotel's entrance. Fortified by finnan haddie and porridge, a real old-fashioned Scottish breakfast, you can face that diabolical stretch of greenery where nearly all of the world's golfing greats have played and the Scots have been whacking away since early in the 15th century.

The hotel is not ancient—far from it; it's bandbox modern, its balconies affording top preview seats at all tournaments. The bedrooms are well equipped and always spotlessly maintained, renting for £40 ($78) in a single, from £47 ($91.65) to £58 ($113.10) in a double. All 80 bedrooms contain private baths.

Try to pay a predinner visit to the Jigger Inn adjoining the hotel. In a former stationmaster's house, this pub evokes days of yore in sharp contrast to the modernity of the hotel.

The main dining room, the Road Hole, on the top floor opens onto views of the links. The menu is continental although many Scottish specialties are featured. A table d'hôte dinner is offered for about £10 ($19.50). Fresh produce is used whenever possible. The restaurant serves dinner from 7:30 to 9:30 p.m.

For lunch, check out the Fife & Forfar on the ground floor, where an average lunch goes for £5 ($9.75) from 11:30 a.m. to 6 p.m. Other golfers prefer the cozier retreat of **Rufflets Hotel,** on the B939, about a mile and a half from St. Andrews (tel. St. Andrews 72594). Of the 21 bedrooms, all are equipped with private baths or showers, phones, radios, and alarm clocks, and all are well furnished in a warm, homelike way. Set in a garden of about ten acres, this is a substantial country house. The furnishings throughout are tasteful, as is the decor. The more modern bedrooms are in an annex, although traditionalists request space in the handsome main building, and those in the know reserve well in advance, as Rufflets is very popular with the British. Singles rent from £21 ($40.95), and doubles from £39 ($76.05). The hotel is closed from mid-January to mid-February.

Even if you aren't staying here, you may want to call and reserve a table at the Rufflets Hotel Restaurant, a trio of dining rooms overlooking a well-laid-out garden. Excellent, fresh ingredients are used in the continental and British dishes, and everything I've sampled here has been accurately cooked. The service, too, is polite and friendly. A set luncheon costs £4.50 ($8.78), a table d'hote dinner from £8 ($15.60, although there is also an à la carte menu. Lunch is served from 12:30 to 2 p.m. and dinner from 7 to 9 p.m. Like the hotel, the restaurant shuts down from mid-January to mid-February.

If you're seeking less formality, a favorite eating spot for years has been the **Grange Inn,** at Grange, about a mile and a half from St. Andrews on the A959 (tel. St. Andrews 72670). In this country cottage, with its charming garden, an old-fashioned hospitality prevails. In such a homey atmosphere, tempting dishes are served, some of them continental in flavor, but all of them well cooked and pleasantly served. The fresh produce tastes homegrown. The proprietors are justly proud of the reputation they have acquired for food. Lunch is served from 12:30 to 2 p.m. and dinner from 7 to 10 p.m. Be sure to reserve and expect to pay about £11 ($21.45) per head for a very large meal, everything included.

Argyle House Hotel, 127 North St. (tel. St. Andrews 73387), is a substantial renovated hotel in the center of town. While it has the rates of a simpler guest house, it offers many of the amenities of a larger hotel. There are three lounges—one for watching color TV, another where you can have a predinner drink, and the third for games such as chess, "snakes and ladders," backgammon, and bridge. Owners Tom and Joan Dowie and their courteous staff can make this an excellent stay. Their rooms have hot and cold water, good firm beds, and if you waken early you'll find each room has an electric kettle for making your own coffee. The rate per person, including VAT, for B&B is £8 ($15.60) to £9 ($17.55). Evening meals are offered for £5 ($9.75).

Number Ten, 10 Hope St. (tel. St. Andrews 74601), is run by Mr. and Mrs. Featherstone who have set reasonable rates per person for B&B—£8 ($15.60). With an evening meal, which I strongly recommend, it's £11.50 ($22.43) per person. They invite parents to bring their children along, as they charge half price for them, providing they share their parents' room and are under 12. Prices include VAT, and there is no service charge. Every room has hot and cold water, and you are invited to watch the color TV set in the lounge. There are ample shower or bath facilities. The hotel, which is of great architectural interest, is only 400 yards from the first tee on the Old Course.

4. Glasgow and the Clyde

Forty miles west of Edinburgh, Scotland's largest city stands on the banks of the River Clyde, which was the birthplace of the *Queen Mary* and *Queen Elizabeth,* plus many other ocean-going liners. Here is housed half of Scotland's population. The Firth of Clyde is one of the loveliest waterways in the world, with its long sea lochs, islands, and hills.

GLASGOW: The commercial capital of Scotland, and Britain's third-largest city, Glasgow is very ancient, making Edinburgh, for all its wealth of history, seem comparatively young. The village that became the city grew up beside a ford 20 miles from the mouth of the River Clyde, which is famous for its shipbuilding, iron and steelworks. Glasgow was a medieval ecclesiastical center and seat of learning. The ancient city is buried beneath 19th-century Glasgow, which is now undergoing vast urban renewal. Glasgow was founded by St. Kentigern, also called St. Mungo, who selected the site 1400 years ago for his church.

GLASGOW

In 1136 a cathedral was erected over his remains; in 1451 the university was started—the second established in Scotland. Commercial prosperity began in the 17th century when its merchants set out to dominate the trade of the western seas. The Clyde was widened and deepened, and the city's expansion engulfed the smaller towns of Ardrie, Renfrew, Rutherglen, and Paisley, whose roots are deep in the Middle Ages.

The smoking industrial city of Glasgow is blighted, in parts, by the "Gorbals," some of the worst slums in Europe which are now giving way to urban development schemes.

Glasgow does contain some sightseeing attractions—enough to make the city a worthy goal for many visitors. But mainly it's a good center for touring central Scotland. For example, you can sail on Loch Lomond and Loch Katrine on the same day, and the resorts along the Ayrshire coast are only an hour away by frequent train service. From Glasgow you can also explore the Burns Country, the Stirling area, Culzean Castle, and the Trossachs.

The Sights

In Glasgow, the center of the city is **George Square,** dominated by the City Chambers which Queen Victoria opened in 1888. Of the statues in the square, the most imposing is that of Sir Walter Scott on an 80-foot column. Naturally, you'll find Victoria along with her beloved Albert, plus Robert Burns. The Banqueting Hall, lavishly decorated, is open to the public on most weekdays.

The **Cathedral of St. Kentigern,** first built in 1136, was burned down in 1192 but rebuilt soon after. The Laigh Kirk, the vaulted crypt said to be the finest in Europe, remains to this day. Visit the tomb of St. Mungo in the crypt where a light always burns. The edifice is one of mainland Scotland's few complete medieval cathedrals, dating from the 12th and 13th centuries. Formerly a place of pilgrimage, 16th-century zeal purged it of all "monuments of idolatry." For the best view of the cathedral, cross the Bridge of Sighs into the necropolis, the graveyard containing almost every type of architecture in the world. The graveyard is built on a rocky hill and dominated by a statue of John Knox. It was first opened in 1832, and the first person to be buried there was a Jew—typical of the mixing of all races in this cosmopolitan city where tolerance reigns until the rival local football teams meet. The necropolis is full of monuments to Glasgow merchants, among them William Miller (1810–1872) who wrote "Wee Willie Winkie."

The **Art Gallery and Museum,** at Kelvingrove Park (tel. 334-1134), is the finest in Britain outside London. The gallery contains such a superb collection of old masters, including Dutch and French painters, that one first-time woman visitor questioned their authenticity—she could not believe her eyes. Displayed are works by Giorgione *(Adulteress Brought before Christ),* Rembrandt *(Man in Armour),* Rubens, and Bellini, including four galleries of British paintings from the 16th century to the present. The gallery of 19th-century French paintings includes all the famous names. Even Salvador Dali gets in on the act with his *Christ of St. John of the Cross.* Scottish painting, of course, is also well represented.

In 1944 Sir William Burrell presented a splendid collection of paintings, tapestries, and other objets d'art. A new gallery is being built for the collection in Pollok Park. One highlight of the Burrell bequest are nearly two dozen drawings and paintings by Degas.

The museum has an outstanding collection of European arms and armor, displays from the ethnography collections featuring the Eskimo peoples,

Africa, and Polynesia, as well as a large section devoted to natural history. There are also small, regularly changing displays from the decorative art collections of silver (especially Scottish), ceramics, glass, and jewelry. The museum and gallery are generally open weekdays from 10 a.m. to 5 p.m., on Sunday from 2 to 5 p.m. However, you should telephone to verify this as the museum, as of this writing, was closed for major structural repairs.

Haggs Castle is a branch museum for children, with displays showing the history of the castle, temporary exhibitions, and a workshop for activities. It is open from 10 a.m. to 5 p.m. daily (from 2 to 5 p.m. on Sunday). For information, telephone 427-2725.

St. Enoch Exhibition Centre is a gallery for temporary exhibitions of contemporary film and decorative arts.

If time remains, **Provands Lordship,** 3 Castle St., is the oldest house in Glasgow, built in 1471. Mary Queen of Scots is said to have written the notorious "Casket letters" there. The house contains 17th- and 18th-century furniture and domestic utensils. It is now in the care of Glasgow Museums and Art Galleries. Entrance is 25p (49¢) for adults, 10p (20¢) for children; open Monday through Saturday from 11 a.m. to 4 p.m., Sunday from 2 to 4 p.m.; closed Christmas and New Year's Day. For information, telephone 554-0223.

Glasgow also offers a number of branch museums, including the **Museum of Transport,** 25 Albert Dr. (tel 423-8000). Once Glasgow's trams were famous. You can see seven displayed here, dating from 1894. Many Scottish-built vintage cars are also exhibited, along with railway locomotives. The most recent extensions house a magnificent display of nearly 200 ship models and a reconstruction of the old Glasgow underground. Hours are weekdays from 10 a.m. to 5 p.m., on Sunday from 2 to 5 p.m. There is a self-service tearoom and also a souvenir shop.

Pollok House in Pollok Park was built around 1750, with additions in 1890 to 1908 designed by Sir Robert Rowand Anderson. It houses the Stirling Maxwell Collection of Spanish and other European paintings, as well as displays of furniture, ceramics, glass, and silver, mostly 18th century. The house may be visited weekdays from 10 a.m. to 5 p.m. and on Sunday from 2 to 5 p.m.

Finally, **People's Palace,** Glasgow Green, provides a visual record of the rise of Glasgow. The palace was built originally as a cultural center for the people of the East End of Glasgow, and it was constructed between 1895 and 1897. Exhibitions trace the foundation of the city in 1175–1178. Such turbulent interludes as the reign of Mary Queen of Scots are represented by the personal relics of the queen. The bulk of the collections are from the 19th century, representing Victorian Glasgow, including posters, programs, and props from the music hall era. The city museum may be visited weekdays from 10 a.m. to 5 p.m. and on Sunday from 2 to 5 p.m.

The park in which the palace is situated, **Glasgow Green,** is the oldest public park in the city. Once a common pasture for the early town, it has witnessed much history. Seek out, in particular, Nelson's monument, the first of its kind in Britain; the Saracen Fountain, opposite the palace; and Templeton's Carpet Factory, modeled on the Doge's Palace in Venice.

The principal shopping district is **Sauchiehall Street,** Glasgow's fashion center, containing many shops and department stores where you'll often find quite good bargains, particularly in woolen goods. The major shopping area, about three blocks long, has been made into a pedestrian mall.

Although it's blighted by much industry and stark commercial areas, Glasgow contains many gardens and open spaces.

Chief among these is **Bellahouston Park,** Paisley Road West, 171 acres of beauty with a sunken wall and rock gardens as well as wildlife. It's open all year, daily, from 8 a.m. to dusk.

Glasgow's **Botanic Gardens,** Great Western Road, covers 40 acres, an extensive collection of tropical plants and herb gardens. It, too, is open all year, daily, including Sunday, from 7 a.m. to dusk.

Linn Park, on Clarkston Road, is 212 acres of pine and woodland, with many lovely walks along the river. There's also a nature trail. The park is open all year, daily from 8 a.m. to dusk.

Greenock is an important industrial and shipbuilding town on the Clyde Estuary a few miles west of the center of Glasgow. It was the birthplace in 1736 of James Watt, inventor of the steam engine. A huge Cross of Lorraine on Lyle Hill above the town commemorates Free French sailors who died in the Battle of the Atlantic during World War II.

Upper-Bracket Hotels

Albany, Bothwell Street (tel. 248-2656), is a contemporary tower block hotel in the heart of Glasgow, rising nine stories and offering a total of 250 well-furnished rooms, all with private baths. The rate in a single is £39 ($76.05), rising to £48 ($93.60), including service and VAT. Windows are double glazed against the noise, and air conditioning and color TV sets are what you'd expect in a hotel of this standing. However, in spite of its modernity, the Albany is efficiently and beautifully run in the grand tradition of Scottish hospitality. The staff extends a friendly welcome, and you don't feel part of a computer. The restaurant, Four Seasons, exudes formality, offering a well-chosen French menu, although you may prefer the Carvery, typical of such places already recommended in London. At any hour of the day, you can order drinks and sandwiches brought to your room. The public rooms are well appointed, of a first-class international standard, and there are ample bars, including a Scandinavian-style Cabin Bar if you want to sneak away to the cellar for a light snack.

The **North British Hotel,** George Square (tel. 332-6711), is an old-fashioned and handsome hotel looking out over the green trees and lawns of the square in the center of this busy, commercial city. It is close to the Queen Street Station where trains depart for the north of Scotland. There is a comfortable lounge bar for a quiet rest or the Devil's Elbow, a bright and lively pub. The addition of a new wing means that you will almost certainly get an accommodation with private bath. Singles go for £20 ($39) to £28 ($54.60), and doubles or twins from £35 ($68.25) to £39 ($76.05). Over the weekends the rates are often cheaper by about £8 ($15.60) or so. The dining room, open from 7 to 10:30 p.m., is enormous and discreet, and the food is standard, although quite good.

Central Hotel, Gordon Street (tel. 221-9680), still retains its Victorian aura, although it has been completely updated to meet modern demands. Owned by British Railways, the hotel stands at the Central Station where it has been welcoming train travelers for more than a century. Its rooms, some of which are cavernous, are comfortable and well appointed, and of the 211 accommodations available, at least 150 contain their own private baths. Singles range in price from £36.50 ($71.18), and doubles go from £48 ($93.60). I've saved the best for last—the Malmaison Restaurant, serving what, in my opinion, is the finest food in Glasgow (see my dining recommendations, immediately following).

Excelsior Hotel, Glasgow Airport (tel. 887-1212), stands at the Glasgow Airport at Abbotsinch, and is not to be confused with the international Prestwick Airport. The Excelsior is modern, and, like many other concrete-and-glass buildings these days, is absolutely geared to the needs of today's traveler. All rooms, for example, contain private baths with shower, and there are radio and TV sets as well. The 24-hour room service promised by the hotel really works. I asked for sandwiches and drinks at 3 a.m. and got them promptly and cheerfully. In the rooms are coffee-and tea-making equipment for do-it-yourselfers. Singles rent for £34 ($66.30) and doubles for £45 ($87.75), including VAT and service. There are the usual lounges and bars, plus a well-designed and pleasantly paneled dining room with quite a wide menu of international and Scottish dishes, as well as a cut-and-come-again Carvery. All meals are extra, but not expensive.

The Middle-Bracket Hotels

Tinto Firs, 470 Kilmarnock Rd. (tel. 637-2353), is a modern, two-story building in a residential sector away from the city center. It's small, only 30 rooms, of which 25 contain private baths. It is efficiently run, but the welcome from the staff is almost old-fashioned and personal. The bedrooms are well designed and compact—pleasantly, although not lavishly, decorated, costing from £25 ($48.70) to £30.50 ($59.48) in a single, from £35 ($68.25) in a double, but you must pay extra for breakfast. The food is of a good standard, competently served.

Lorne, 923 Sauchiehall St. (tel. 334-4891), is a modern hotel, with compact, functional bedrooms that are, nevertheless, attractively decorated and most comfortable. It's best suited for a stay of only one or two nights. Of its 86 chambers, only 50 contain private baths. Singles rent for £20 ($39) to £25 ($48.75) going up to £30 ($58.50) to £34 ($66.30) in a double. The hotel serves dinner till around 9:30 p.m., offering such specialties as chicken Devonshire and steak tartare, although grills are the main feature. One of the Lorne's cocktail lounges stay open until the last resident has departed, and sometimes that means all night.

Bellahouston, 517 Paisley Rd. (tel. 427-3146), a modern, three-story hotel, is especially preferred by business people, as it's convenient to the Glasgow Airport, although about a ten-minute ride from the center of the city. It is also quite near Bellahouston Park, from which it takes its name. There's plenty of parking which makes the hotel even more alluring. Each of its 50 functional bedrooms contains a private bath, renting for £19 ($37.05) to £24 ($46.80) in a single, from £25 ($48.75) to £35 ($68.25) in a double, including a full breakfast. The fully licensed hotel has central heating, an elevator, TV lounge, and cocktail bar, as well as a restaurant serving a set lunch for £5 ($9.75). In winter there is dancing on Saturday night.

The Glasgow Centre Hotel, Argyle Street (tel. 248-2355), is a modern block of 120 bedrooms, all with bath, standing in the heart of the city, within easy reach of the main railway stations. Somewhat stark in appearance, it offers rooms which have been equipped with many conveniences, such as auto-dial telephone, electric alarm clocks, color TVs, tea- and coffee-making facilities, and individually controlled central heating. Opened in 1974, the hotel charges £26 ($50.70) in a single, from £33 ($64.35) in a double, these tariffs including a continental breakfast, although a full Scottish breakfast costs extra. The Centre (not to be confused with the Central) also features a specialty restaurant, plus two bars.

A Budget Hotel

Hazelcourt Hotel, 232 Renfrew St. (tel. 332-7737), is small and quiet, a pleasantly furnished hotel in the heart of the city, convenient to bus depots, the rail and air terminals, plus shops and theaters, even the Kelvin Hall and Art Galleries. The comfortable rooms are centrally heated, containing hot and cold running water, shaver sockets, and electric radiators. The Hazelcourt contains only eight bedrooms, none with private bath, charging from £8 ($15.60) in a single, from £16 ($31.20) in a double, these tariffs including breakfast. Dinner, served between 6 and 7 p.m., can also be ordered if requested in advance.

The Leading Restaurant

Malmaison Restaurant, Gordon Street (tel. 221-9680), takes its name from the villa that once housed Josephine and Napoleon outside Paris. The Malmaison in Scotland is actually in the previously recommended Central Hotel, that Victorian building that forms part of one of the city's principal railway stations.

Of course, you dine here in your best jacket and tie (if you're a man), because the Malmaison is clearly the most luxurious dining choice in town—the aura enhanced by the fresh flowers, the soft piano music, and the stern portraits.

Both simple and complex dishes are virtually without flaw, and the sauces are light and well balanced. In addition to the decor, the lavishness is evident in the presentation. On one recent occasion, the highly trained waiter gave me a veritable lesson in cookery when I inquired about a particular dish.

The food is perhaps the best in Scotland of an international nature. Chef James F. Anderson is a master. His specialties are a dream, including queues de langoustine promenade des Anglaise, suprême de fletan Mentonaise, escalope de veau Roscoff, and noisettes de chevreuil aigre doux.

Over the years I've had some of my finest meals in Scotland here, including on one memorable night, grouse. Although chefs have come and gone, the standards have remained consistent.

Lunch is from 12:30 to 2:30 p.m. and dinner from 7 to 10:30 p.m. A set luncheon goes for £9 ($17.55), and an à la carte dinner for £20 ($39) and up. It is essential to make a reservation. The restaurant is closed for lunch on Saturday, shuts down all day on Sunday, and is closed for all of August.

Other Favorites for Dining

Fountain, 2 Woodside Crescent, Charing Cross (tel. 332-6396), attracts a clientele of gourmets and Glasgow's most fashionable people. It is sophisticated and formal, and the cookery is almost invariably good.

Against an attractive backdrop, you can enjoy some fine French cooking between the hours of noon and 2:30 p.m., and 7 and 10 p.m. One of the all-time favorite dishes here is crayfish tails. Ever had a "casserole des gourmets"?

The restaurant shuts for lunch on Saturday and all day on Sunday. The two-course table d'hôte luncheon costs about £6 ($11.70), although you can easily pay as much as £17 ($33.15) per person in the evening. However, a £9 ($17.55) fixed-price dinner is offered. The wine list is excellent, and the staff makes a conscious effort to find wines from different regions, as well as the traditional clarets and burgundies. For some reason, it seems out of place in Glasgow, but that's part of its charm.

Ambassador, 19 Blythswood Square (tel. 221-2034), is a cellar restaurant specializing in continental dishes, including such specialties as scampi Ambassadeur (in a white sauce served with rice), tender escalope de veau, and, of course, the finest rib of roast Angus beef on the bone. The licensed restaurant features dancing to a live band, and the service by the waiters is polite and attentive. Lunch is from 12:30 to 2:30 p.m., costing £6 ($11.70) if you order from the set menu. A speical lure of the Ambassador is its pretheater set meal, costing the same price as the lunch. However, if you dine à la carte, any time before 11 p.m., expect to pay about £14 ($27.30) per person. The restaurant closes on Sunday and bank holidays.

Rogano Restaurant, 11 South Exchange Pl. (tel. 248-6687), is famous for its seafood and crustaceans, serving some of the most superbly prepared and fresh-tasting fish dishes in Glasgow. The oysters (if you're there on the right night) are delectable. Most definitely, Rogano is one of the best known eating places in Scotland, and night after night you'll see some of the same customers pondering the long, varied menu, which also has steak, veal, and chicken dishes. Specialties include smoked eel and scrambled egg and Helford oysters. Owner Donald Grant carefully supervises everything, both in the kitchen and in the dining room. For a complete meal, expect to pay as much as £17 ($33.15) per head, although you can dine much cheaper, of course. Lunch is from noon to 2:30 p.m. and dinner from 6 to 10:30 p.m. It's advisable to reserve a table. Closed Sunday and bank holidays.

Vesuvio, 15 St. Vincent Pl. (tel. 221-0355), seems run pretty much like an Italian family business. It is a praiseworthy, unassuming restaurant, where the service is brisk and efficient. The feature of the place is its dinner-dancing to a live orchestra about six nights a week. Although Italian cookery is the attraction, the chef does not limit himself to the cuisine of that country, but offers a full range of continental dishes. Specialties include chicken Vesuviana, prepared in a tomato sauce with green peppers, and saltimbocca, a veal and ham dish, and, for dessert, a delectable zabaglione. If you visit for lunch, you can order a set meal, costing £6 ($11.70) per person, although your à la carte tab in the evening is more likely to tally up to £15 ($29.25). Closed Sunday. Hours are from noon to 3 p.m. and from 5:30 p.m. to 1 a.m.

Danish Food Centre, 56 St. Vincent St. (tel. 221-0518), offers what you'd expect, the celebrated Danish cold table and those delectable open-face sandwiches known as smørrebrød. You are rarely disappointed here. The smoked fish, in particular, is fresh and most reliable—so good, in fact, I've often made an entire meal of it. If you have the appetite for it, a hot "plat du jour" is featured daily. The service is friendly and efficient. Arrive between noon and 2:30 p.m. and between 6 and 10:30 p.m. and expect to pay about £7.95 ($15.50) per person for a really filling menu and a change of pace from typically Scottish fare. Closed on bank holidays.

A Few Pubs

The **Horseshoe Bar and Restaurant,** 17 Drury St., is worth taking a look at even if you don't stop for a drink or a pub lunch or dinner. Drury is a narrow, short street, probably little changed for a century or so. There's lots of highly polished brass edging the door, and frosted glass door panels. The pub has dark wood paneling and a real pub flavor. Lunches are served from noon to 2:30 p.m., and meals, costing from £5 ($9.75), are available in the public bar from 5 to 7:30 p.m.

Rogano's, 11 South Exchange Pl. (tel. 221-5677). Landlord Donald Grant serves a good pint of ale in his well-cared-for 1930s pub. The main bar is large and majestic, with a good lunchtime buffet counter, offering a hot dish of the day, kebabs, and omelets, in addition to sandwiches. They also do a very good, real Scots broth. The price of the average dish is £1.80 ($3.51). You can also order from the menu of their seafood restaurant (see my previous recommendation). The pub is closed on Sunday and on bank holidays.

Rock Garden, 73 Queen St. (tel. 221-6381). Rock music and walls covered with posters have changed this pub into more of an American-style bar than you are likely to find in the States. They offer more than a dozen different cocktails, all the uusal drinks. From noon to 9 p.m. on Monday through Saturday, they also serve good wholesome dishes such as beef casserole, chili and beans, sandwiches, pâté and bread, along with salads, an average meal costing £1.80 ($3.51).

Living on the Outskirts

Gleddoch House Hotel, at Langbank in Renfrewshire (tel. Langbank 711), is the former residence of Sir James Lithgow, which was converted in 1974 to a deluxe hotel set on enormous grounds, including farmlands, riding stables, golf course, and gardens. The 18 rooms are named for birds—Golden Eagle, Mallard, Osprey—and have good bathrooms, radio, color TV, and coffee- or tea-making equipment. Fresh milk and shortbread biscuits are provided as well. A single room, including a Scottish breakfast, is £32.50 ($63.38), a double going for £45 ($87.75).

The paneled hallway is bright with a roaring fire, and there's a cozy bar. The residents' sitting room is upstairs. Breakfast is a leisurely, help-yourself affair. Dinner is a five-course meal, costing £10 ($19.50), more on Saturday. Appetizers are likely to include smoked Argyll trout or pheasant consommé, followed by a small fish course, then a choice of lamb cutlets, duckling, or beef, all served with fresh vegetables and the appropriate sauces. A vast array of desserts awaits you on a central table, and you can wallow in lemon mousse, chocolate cake, and trifles.

There's also a set luncheon or à la carte grills, but the more energetic repair to the Golf Club House to mingle with sportsmen, who usually order the hot dish of the day.

Glenddoch House is a perfect place to unwind after a transatlantic flight. There are a sauna and a plunge pool, as well as horseback riding. Trout fishing is available on the 250-acre estate and, of course, golf.

To get there, drive west along the A8/M8 from Glasgow and the Erskine Bridge toward Greenock and Gourock. Turn left at the sign for Langbank on the B789, going left again under the railway bridge and then steeply up the hill to the hotel entrance on the right.

5. The Trossachs and Loch Lomond

"The Trossachs" is the collective name given that wild Highland area lying east and northeast of Loch Lomond. Both the Trossachs and Loch Lomond are said to contain Scotland's finest scenery in moor, mountain, and loch. The area is famed in history and romance ever since Sir Walter Scott included vivid descriptive passages in *The Lady of the Lake* and *Rob Roy.*

In Gaelic, the Trossachs means "the bristled country," an allusion to its luxuriant vegetation. The thickly wooded valley contains three lochs—Vennachar, Achray, and Katrine. The best centers for exploring are the village of the Trossachs and the "gateways" of Callander and Aberfoyle.

Legendary Loch Lomond, the largest and most beautiful of Scottish lakes, is known for its "bonnie banks." Lying within easy reach of Glasgow, the loch is about 24 miles long. At its widest point, it stretches for five miles. At Balloch in the south the lake is a Lowland loch of gentle hills and islands. But as it moves north, the loch changes to a narrow lake of Highland character, with moody cloud formations and rugged steep hillsides.

CALLANDER: For many, this small burgh, 16 miles northwest of Stirling by road, makes the best base for exploring the Trossachs and Loch Katrine, Loch Achray, and Loch Vernachar. For years, motorists—and before them passengers traveling by bumpy coach—stopped here to rest up on the once-difficult journey between Edinburgh and Oban.

Callander stands at the entrance to the **Pass of Leny** in the shadow of the Callander Crags. The Teith and Leny Rivers meet to the west of the town. British TV viewers know of Callander as the "Tannochbrae" of the B.B.C. "Dr. Finlay's Casebook."

For miles beyond the Pass of Leny, with its beautiful falls, lies **Loch Lubnaig** ("the crooked lake"), divided into two reaches by a rock and considered fine fishing waters. Nearby is **Little Leny,** the ancestral burial ground of the Buchanans.

More falls are found at **Bracklinn,** 1½ miles northeast of Callander. In a gorge above the town, Bracklinn is considered one of the most scenic of the local beauty spots. Other places of interest include the **Roman Camp,** the **Caledonian Fort,** and the **Foundations of St. Bride's Chapel.** The tourist office will give you a map pinpointing the above-recommended sights. While there, you can also get directions for one of the most interesting excursions from Callander, to **Balquhidder Church,** 13 miles to the northwest, the burial place of Rob Roy.

The leading hotel is **Roman Camp** (tel. Callander 30003), once a 17th-century hunting lodge with pink walls and small gray-roofed towers, built on the site of what was believed to have been a Roman camp. The Dukes of Perth once came to this turreted establishment, lodging here for "hunting and hawking." Entering through a gate, the modern-day traveler drives up a splendid driveway, enjoying the gardens along the way with their well-manicured yew hedges. The setting, as in the cliché, is like a picture postcard, with peacocks roaming the grounds. Naturally, a river runs through the 20-acre estate. Inside a walled garden, vegetables and fruit—used in the hotel's kitchen—are grown. In summer flowerbeds are in full bloom.

Once inside, you are welcomed to a country house furnished in a gracious manner. The hotel contains 11 bedrooms, most of which have their own baths, as well as another five bedrooms in the cottage standing on the grounds. Singles start at £22 ($42.90), doubles at £42 ($81.90), plus service and VAT. The bedrooms vary in size and furnishings, but all are comfortable, spotless, and cozy. I prefer the rooms in the main house to those in the annex across the drive.

The hotel has a small cocktail bar, but the library, with its plasterwork and paneling, remains undisturbed. The meals—"Scottish country-house fare," as one reader described them—are served until 9 in the evening.

For the tradition-minded, the Roman Camp is one of the finest choices in the Trossachs, and by all means treat yourself to "tea and scones" in the afternoon. The hotel closes down from November to early April.

ABERFOYLE: Looking like an Alpine village, in the heart of the Rob Roy country, this small holiday resort is the gateway to the Trossachs, near Loch

Ard. A large crafts center contains a wealth of gift items related to the Highlands.

Bailie Nicol Jarvie Hotel (tel. 087-72202) is an old-fashioned hotel on the road between Loch Ard and Aberfoyle. If you're passing through the Trossachs, it makes a suitable overnight stopover. The hotel takes its name from Nicol Jarvie, the Glasgow magistrate who used to visit the outlaw, Rob Roy, at a former inn on this site. The hotel is one of character, somewhat dated in appeal.

Many of the rooms have high ceilings and are furnished in "comfy" pieces. The B&B rate is £12.50 ($24.38) per person nightly, increasing to £16 ($31.20) per person for half board. All 39 rooms contain private baths. Lovers of antiquity are drawn to Bailie Bar, a cocktail lounge hung with weaponry. The hotel serves good country meals, using farm produce when available. It's open from April to October.

THE TROSSACHS: The Duke's Road (A821) north from Aberfoyle climbs through the Achray Forest, past the **David Marshall Lodge** information center, operated by the Forestry Commission, where you can stop for snacks and a breathtaking view of the Forth Valley. The road runs to the Trossachs—the "bristly country"—between Lochs Achray and Katrine.

Loch Katrine, at the head of which Rob Roy was born, owes its fame to Sir Walter Scott who set his poem *The Lady of the Lake* there. The loch is the principal reservoir of the city of Glasgow. A small steamer, S.S. *Sir Walter Scott*, plies the waters of the loch which has submerged the Silver Strand of the romantic poet.

Sailings are between May 14 and September 24, between Trossachs Pier and Stronachlachar at a round-trip fare of £1.75 ($3.41) for adults, £1 ($1.95) for children. Complete information as to the sailing schedules is available from the Strathclyde Water Department, Lower Clyde Division, 419 Balmore Rd., Glasgow, Scotland G22 6NU.

Trossachs Hotel, Trossachs (tel. Trossachs 232), became famous in Victoria's heyday. Built on the site of one of the old posting inns of Scotland which dated from the 18th century, it was erected by Lady Willoughby as a castle in 1826, converting to a hotel in 1852. After a long career, the hotel, now mellowed with time, is still going strong, although it's rather shabby, which accounts for its low rates. Rooms come in a variety of styles with a wide range of plumbing, costing about £11 ($21.45) to £13 ($25.35) per person for B&B, plus VAT. Usually you pay another small supplement for a single room or for the privilege of private bath. The Shield Hung Dining Room is draped with the plaids of the ancient clans and has a timbered ceiling, serving dinners for about £6.50 ($12.68). Bar snacks are around £2 ($3.90) for the hot dish of the day, and you can also take lunch in the dining room for about £4 ($7.80). The location is right in the heart of the Trossachs, two miles from Loch Katrine where you can sail on the loch steamship *Sir Walter Scott*.

On Loch Achray, lying between Lochs Venachar and Katrine, stands the **Loch Achray Hotel,** Trossachs (tel. Trossachs 229), run by Mr. Penny and Mr. MacDonald. The hotel stands in an estate of 45 acres between Callender and Aberfoyle on the A821. From the hotel you can step directly into the Achray Forest, part of the vast. Queen Elizabeth National Park, which abounds in wildlife, including roe deer. The original building of the hotel dates from Jacobean times. The Achray Burn is an overflow of Loch Katrine and runs through the hotel grounds. This hotel is a good stopping place for a two-day tour out of Edinburgh or for those on their way north. A pleasant hotel, it offers views over the loch. Rooms are comfortable—only two have private baths—and the first-floor lounge is well furnished. They charge from £10.50 ($20.48) per person for B&B, or else you can stay here on half-board terms of £15.50 ($30.23) per person nightly.

LOCH LOMOND: This largest of Scotland's lochs was the center of the ancient district of Lennox, in the possession of the branch of the Stewart family from which sprang Lord Darnley, second husband of Mary Queen of Scots and father of James VI of Scotland, who was also James I of England. The ruins of Lennox Castle are on Inchmurrin, one of the 30 islands of the loch—one having ecclesiastical ruins, one noted for its yew trees planted by King Robert the Bruce to ensure a suitable supply of wood for the bows of his archers. The loch is fed by at least ten rivers from west, east, and north. On the eastern side is Ben Lomond, rising to a height of 3192 feet.

The song "Loch Lomond" is supposed to have been composed by one of Bonnie Prince Charlie's captured followers on the eve of his execution in Carlisle Jail. The "low road" of the song is the path through the underworld which his spirit will follow to his native land after death more quickly than his friends can travel to Scotland by the ordinary high road.

The road from Dumbarton to Crianlarich runs along the western shore of the loch, but the paddle steamer *Maid of the Loch* is an interesting, if slower, way to see the "banks and braes." It sails daily during the summer from Balloch Pier which is reached by the railway. There is a large car park serving the pier.

Traveling around Loch Lomond from the east, you'll find:

ARROCHAR: At the head of the sea-arm of Loch Long, 1½ miles west of Loch Lomond, this village, easily reached by road and railway from Glasgow, is a center for climbers.

A pleasant accommodation is the **Lochside Guest House** (tel. Arrochar 467), a small place with a garden overlooking the shores of Loch Long. There Mrs. Bishop will welcome you to one of her singles for £8 ($15.60), or in a double for £15 ($29.25), including breakfast. For £11.50 ($22.43) per person, she'll include not only your room and breakfast, but a good, hearty dinner as well, quite a bargain. Receiving guests year round, Mrs. Bishop can arrange for a small-boat rental (also chartered sea fishing). Naturally, anglers flock to Lochside.

Heading west from Loch Long and Loch Lomond on the A83 toward Inveraray and Loch Fyne you'll come to:

CAIRNDOW: Barely visible from the main highway, the A83, this little town nestles between a hill and Loch Fyne, on the loch's eastern shore. It is a peaceful haven with a view of the loch and the high mountains. **Strone Gardens,** open on Sunday from April 1 to September 30 and by arrangement otherwise, has in its pine forest the tallest tree in Great Britain.

The **Cairndow Inn** (tel. Cairndow 286) is a fully licensed, stone gem of an old stagecoach inn overlooking the loch. The present building is only about 200 years old, the original having been destroyed by fire in the 1700s. There's a residents' lounge with a piano for sing-alongs and bar. The stone staircase, with a low ceiling, leads to nine immaculate and cozy bedrooms on the second and third floors, one with private bath. You'll pay £8.50 ($16.58) per person daily, plus VAT, for B&B. Lunch is £3.50 ($6.83); dinner, £6 ($11.70). The stables left over from the old coaching days have been converted to a fine restaurant overlooking Loch Fyne.

Chapter XVIII

NORTHEAST SCOTLAND

1. Exploring Tayside
2. Aberdeen and Royal Deeside

COVERING THE REGIONS of Tayside and Grampian, Northeast Scotland beckons the visitor with much scenic grandeur, although some come just to hit the Whisky Trail.

Three of Scotland's most important cities, Dundee, Aberdeen, and Perth, are tucked away in this corner, and the section also contains three of the country's best-known salmon rivers, the Dee, the Spey, and the Tay.

The land is riddled with historic old castles, and will give you a view of Highland majesty—imposing, grand, tumultuous, including Queen Victoria's favorite view. The best-known of the traditional Highland gatherings takes place at Braemar.

1. Exploring Tayside

The trouble with exploring Tayside is you may find it so fascinating in scenery you'll never make it on to the Highlands. Carved out of the old counties of Perth and Angus, Tayside is named for its major river, the 119-mile Tay. Its tributaries and dozens of lochans and Highland streams are some of the best salmon and trout waters in Europe. One of the loveliest regions of Scotland, Tayside is filled with heatherclad Highland hills, long blue lochs under treeclad banks, and miles and miles of walking trails.

It is a region dear to the Scots, a symbol of their desire for independence, as exemplified by the Declaration of Arbroath and the ancient coronation ritual of the "Stone of Destiny" at Scone. In cities, Perth and Dundee are among the leading six centers of Scotland.

Tayside also provided the backdrop for many novels by Sir Walter Scott, including *The Fair Maid of Perth, Waverley,* and *The Abbot.*

Its golf courses are world famous, ranging from the trio of 18-hole courses at Gleneagles to the open championships links at Carnoustie.

We'll begin our trip in an offshoot southern pocket of the county at Loch Leven, then take in Perth and its environs, heading east to Dundee, and later along the fishing villages of the North Sea, cutting west again to visit Glamis Castle, and, finally, ending our journey of exploration even further west in the lochs and glens of the Perthshire Highlands.

LOCH LEVEN: "Those never got luck who came to Loch Leven." This proverbial saying sums up the history of the ruined **Loch Leven Castle,** on Castle Island, dating from the late 14th century. Among its more ill-fated prisoners, none was more notable than Mary Queen of Scots. Within its forbidding walls, she signed her abdication on July 24, 1567. However, she effected her escape from Loch Leven on May 2, 1568. Thomas Percy, seventh Earl of Northumberland, supported her cause. For his efforts, he, too, was imprisoned and lodged in the castle for three years until he was handed over to the English, who beheaded him at York.

Lying to the north of Dunfermline (head toward Kinross), the loch has seven islands. Loch Leven Castle, of course, is in ruins. So is the **Priory of Loch Leven,** built on the site of one of the oldest Culdee establishments in Scotland, and lying on St. Serf's, the largest of the islands in the loch.

In Kinross, 25 miles north of Edinburgh, you can make arrangements to visit Loch Leven Castle by boat, the only means of access.

For dining or lodgings I offer **Nivingston House,** on the B9097, two miles south of Kinross at Cleish (tel. Cleish Hills 216), which serves some of the finest food in Tayside. The hotel's chef, Michael Thompson, maintains a high culinary standard. The place is run by Ann and Jim Hill, who offer only three bedrooms for £16 ($31.20) per person nightly for B&B, including VAT and service.

However, most visitors arrive to sample the wares of the kitchen. I've never had the same meal here twice, as one must depend on the inspiration of the chef. But that's hardly a problem.

Lunch or dinner, costing £9 ($17.55) for an average meal, is made up principally from local produce, such as fish, Scottish lamb and beef, and veal, as well as charcoal-grilled sardines. Try, if featured, his fish terrine and the king prawns, or the delectable house pâté. Desserts are luscious and velvety, your selection made from a trolley wheeled to your table. Hours are from 12:30 to 2 p.m. and from 7:30 to 9 p.m. The hotel shuts down on Monday and is closed sometime in the autumn for vacations. Always reserve a table, and men should wear a jacket and tie in the evening. The hotel stands on ten acres of grounds.

Hawthorn Vale (tel. Kinross 63117) has a picture-postcard look to it, a small stone house set in a garden, with a stone wall along the road, overlooking Loch Leven. It's the private home of Mrs. P. Warder, who has three double rooms, one with twins, which she rents reasonably at £7 ($13.65) per person for B&B. Each of her rooms is acceptably attractive and comfortable, with hot and cold running water. Along the hall is a separate toilet. In Mrs. Warder's guest lounge is a TV set and a radio at your disposal. Two of her rooms overlook her garden (and she's rightly proud of how well kept it is). Her breakfasts are filling and done as you like them. It's best to stay here on the half-board plan, sampling one of her dinners in the evening, the tariff for all this, including your room and breakfast, only £8.50 ($16.58) per person.

Kirklands Hotel, High Street (tel. Kinross 63313), is a village hotel, all glistening white with bright shutters and a modernized interior. It has Georgian touches in its entry, and the pillars in the residents' lounge. Warm colors have been used throughout; even the bedrooms carry out the autumnal theme. Each bedroom is pleasant, with hot and cold water. What makes people from all over the country, and England as well, show up at the doorstep is the exceptional chef, William Kerr. He is considered by many critics as the finest chef in Scotland, and has walked away with Scotland's top cooking awards for the past five years.

Along with his wife, Diana, they charge £9.50 ($18.53) per person for B&B, including VAT and service. And what a breakfast—properly made porridge with Drambuie and cream, finnan haddock with an egg on top, among the other dishes.

At lunch £3.50 ($6.83) buys you a light meal of homemade soup, pâté, and steak pie served in the bar. Dinner is a delight—homemade cream soups, Stilton and port wine pâté, a whole lemon sole cooked in pastry, rabbit casserole in red wine, an array of exciting dishes. A set meal of five courses with coffee wil go for £9.50 ($18.53), and you'll understand why Bill Kerr has created so much excitement in Britain. Always reserve a table, of course. The hotel is 30 minutes from Gleaneagles and St. Andrews golf courses.

PERTH: From its majestic position on the Tay, the ancient city of Perth was the capital of Scotland until the middle of the 15th century. Here the Highland meets the Lowland. Sir Walter Scott immortalized the royal burgh in *The Fair Maid of Perth.* On Curfew Road you can still see the house of Catherine Glover, the fair maid herself.

The main sightseeing attraction of "the fair city" is the **Church of St. John the Baptist,** of which the original foundation, it is believed, dates from Pictish times. However, the present choir dates from 1440 and the nave from 1490. In 1559 John Knox preached his famous sermon here attacking idolatry, and it caused a wave of iconoclasm to sweep across the land. The church was restored as a World War I memorial in the late 1920s. In the church is the tombstone of James I, who was murdered by Sir Robert Graham.

Food and Lodging

Royal George, Tay Street (tel. Perth 24455), is royal because it once listed on its guest list the illustrious name of Queen Victoria. But since that monarch's day, the hotel has been considerably updated with the latest amenities. Now run by Trusthouses Forte, the Royal George opens onto views of the River Tay and the Bridge of Perth. All of its roomy, solidly furnished bedrooms contain private baths, renting for £26 ($50.70) in a single, from £34 ($66.30) to £38 ($74.10) in a double. The lounges are still large enough to evoke if not Victoria's day, then Edward's. The food is—well, solid. The Ox and Claret restaurant serves à la carte meals, costing from £8.50 ($16.58), and the Riverside Buffet features a set three-course meal for £4.95 ($9.65).

The **Station Hotel,** Leonard Street (tel. Perth 24141), also evokes Queen Victoria, although she never, to my knowledge, stayed there. However, like the Royal George, it has been considerably updated, and its bedrooms are well equipped and maintained. Some of the bathrooms, at least the one I had, would have pleased Lillie Langtry at least, as it was as large as most bedrooms in many modern hotels. The lounge is faithful to the old style, and the drinks in the bar seem generous if you order enough of them. You can even stroll in the garden, inspecting the lime trees. Singles pay from £18.50 ($36.08) to £26 ($50.70), doubles from £34 ($66.30) to £45 ($87.75). All units have color TV and bedside controls. A set lunch is offered for £8 ($15.60), and dinner costs the same.

Another good choice is the **City Mills Hotel,** West Mill Street (tel. Perth 28281), which is so named because it was once an oldtime watermill. It has been cleverly adapted to its present function, that of a modern hotel in the center, containing 40 rooms, all with private baths. Singles range from £22 ($42.90), doubles from £35 ($68.25), including VAT and a full breakfast. The rooms, although not large, are well furnished, conservative in tone, and warm and comfortable if you're not planning to stay too long. Again, the City Mills has a garden for your pleasure. As for the millstream, you're given a view through panels of glass. On Saturday nights, the merchants of Perth bring their wives, or whomever, here for dancing.

For dining, I recommend **Timothy's** 24 St. John St. (tel. Perth 26641), which has a convivial informality, and also serves the best food in this ancient city, far superior to that I've encountered in the dining rooms of the staid Victorian hotels. Ever had a Scottish smörgåsbord? If not, then try the table offered by the owner, Timothy Norman. Roast beef (served rare and tender), smoked trout, tasty sausages, crabmeat wrapped in smoked salmon, and truly homemade soups are well prepared and pleasantly served here. Meals are from noon to 2:30 p.m. and from 7 to 10 p.m., and it's necessary to call for a reservation, as the restaurant can fill up rapidly, particularly in summer. For a complete meal, expect to pay £6 ($11.70) per head. Closed Sunday and Monday.

SCONE: On the River Tay, Old Scone was the ancient capital of the Picts. On a lump of granite, the "Stone of Destiny," the monarchs of the Dark Ages were enthroned. The British sovereign to this day is still crowned on the stone, but in Westminster Abbey. Edward I removed the stone there in 1296. Charles II was the last king crowned at Scone; the year: 1651.

Scone Palace (tel. Scone 51416), the seat of the Earl of Mansfield, was largely rebuilt in 1803, incorporating the old palace of 1580. Inside is an impressive collection of French furniture, china, ivories, and 16th-century needlework; including bed hangings executed by Mary Queen of Scots. A fine collection of rare conifers is found on the grounds in the Pinetum. Rhododendrons and azaleas grow profusely in the gardens and woodlands around the palace. To reach the palace, head north of Perth on the A93. It lies half a mile west of Old Scone. The site is open April 27 to October 13 on weekdays from 10 a.m. to 6 p.m. (on Sunday from 2 to 6), charging an admission of £1.50 ($2.93) for adults, 75p ($1.46) for children, including entrance to both the house and grounds.

GLENEAGLES: This is a famous golfing center on a moor between Strath Earn and Strath Allan, and, in addition, it provides a good, although lethal in expense, base from which to explore the major attractions of Central Scotland. The center gets its name from the Gaelic Gleann-an-Eaglias, "glen of the church." The golf courses here are said to be unrivaled anywhere in the world.

Gleneagles Hotel Restaurant, Gleneagles, Auchterarder (tel. Auchterarder 2231), is one of the showcases of Scotland. From golfers to gourmets, the hotel has catered to everybody from the Duke of Edinburgh to Richard Burton to the late Noel Coward. Opened in 1924 in the Scottish hills, this is a self-contained resort, with four championship golf courses, plus an indoor swimming pool, sauna, and tennis courts. Gleneagles even has its own bank and post office, not to mention a helipad for your spectacular arrival. You'll also find game fishing, horseback riding, croquet, and pitch-and-putt. There is dancing nightly, plus a shopping arcade.

The food offered is French and international—and quite good, with a set lunch going for £12 ($23.40), a table d'hôte dinner for £15 ($29.25). These meals are totally adequate, so you need not venture into the à la carte.

The hotel is clean and warm, but service is lacking in most departments. Gleneagles is under the general management of Mr. J. Bannatyne, and he hopes to stay open all year from now on, with the development of conference facilities.

The location is 37 miles out in the country northwest of Edinburgh. The stone monument to the good life offers 210 luxuriously appointed rooms, costing sky-high prices; from £110 ($214.50) in a double, from £50 ($98) in a single, including service and VAT.

CRIEFF: At the edge of the Perthshire Highlands, Crieff makes for a pleasant stopover, what with its possibilities for fishing and golf. This small burgh, 18 miles from Perth, was the seat of the court of the Earls of Strathearn until 1747. Once gallows in its marketplace were used to execute Highland cattle rustlers.

Three miles south of Crieff, you can visit the gardens of **Drummond Castle**, the seat of the Earl of Ancaster. The second Earl of Perth laid out these ten-acre gardens in 1662 along continental lines. The grounds are open from April 1 to October 31 on Wednesday and Sunday from 2 to 6 p.m. Admission is 60p ($1.17) for adults, 30p (59¢) for children.

In accommodations, I recommend the following:

If you're like most people and can't afford the tariffs at the nearby Gleneagles Hotel, you might prefer to anchor instead at Crieff's **Murraypark Hotel,** Connaught Terrace (tel. Crieff 3731). It's small, offering ten rooms with private baths, but its standards are first rate. Each year the hotel seems to improve a bit. The bedrooms have a pleasing decor and are comfortably furnished. Singles rent for £15 ($29.25) for B&B, doubles going for £28 ($54.60). Before dinner you can meet in one of two bars, after having strolled around the hotel, enjoying views across Strathearn. Meals are based on country-house fare, costing from £9 ($17.55) for four courses.

Gwydyr, Comrie Road (tel. Crieff 3277), now a century old, is a fine house about a five-minute walk from the center of the burgh. Ian and Christine Gillies, along with their warm and hospitable staff, welcome you to this friendly and gracious hotel. The B&B charge is about £8.25 ($16.09) per person nightly, and all of their accommodations contain hot and cold running water. The beds are comfortable, and, as an added convenience, you're given facilities for making tea or coffee. The dining room serves well-prepared food, using local ingredients whenever possible. They offer a selection of dishes, all reasonably priced. The dining room is open from 7 to 8 p.m. Prices range from about £5 ($9.75) for a set dinner. The cellar is well stocked with wines, beers, and liquors. In the residents' lounge, guests gather around a color television. Gwydyr stands on its own grounds, almost an acre of charming garden overlooking MacRosty Park. You'll have an uninterrupted view of Ben Vorlich and Glen Artney to the south.

COMRIE: An attractive little village in Strathearn, 25 miles from Perth, Comrie stands at the confluence of the Earn, Ruchill, and Lednock Rivers. The A85 runs through the village to Lochearnhead, Crianlarich, Oban, and the Hebrides in the west. It's convenient as an overnight stop for travelers crossing Scotland. Waterskiing, boating, and sailing are available on Loch Earn.

The **Royal Hotel,** Melville Square (tel. Comrie 70200), was awarded the "royal" after the visit of Her Majesty, Queen Victoria. It's not, as you might imagine, a Victorian hotel, but rather an L-shaped stone inn dating back to 1765, with white trim and six bedroom dormers. Its cocktail bar with coppertop tables, furnished and decorated in the proprietor's own Gordon tartan, is noted for its selection of malt whiskies, and on the walls are framed prints and photographs with signatures of numerous famous guests who have stayed here over the years, including that of "Monty," Lloyd George, actress Sarah Bernhardt, and Queen Victoria's faithful servant, John Brown. The dining room is equally attractive, with an open log fire and autumnal colors. The bedrooms are most comfortable, consisting of a three-room suite with one four-poster bed, plus 13 bedrooms of which 10 have private bathroom or shower, and all have telephone, TV, radio, tea- and coffee-making facilities, electric blanket, and self-selection heating control. The lounge offers color television in comfortable and well-appointed surroundings. The charge per person nightly for B&B is £14 ($27.30), rising to £15.50 ($30.23) per person with private bath. Dinner prices start at £8.50 ($16.58), although you can also choose à la carte.

DUNDEE: This royal burgh and old seaport is an industrial city, one of the largest in Scotland, lying on the north shore of the Firth of Tay. It's noted for its flax, jute, and marmalade. Spanning the Firth, the Tay Railway Bridge was opened in 1888. It's nearly two miles long, one of the longest in Europe.

In the suburbs, at **Broughty Ferry,** 3½ miles from Dundee, the **castle** dates from 1498. For a spectacular view, go to **Dundee Law,** a 572-foot hill just a mile north of the city.

Most visitors pass through Dundee en route to Glamis Castle, 12 miles north. However if you'd like to stop for the night, there is the—

Angus Hotel, 101 Market Gait (tel. Dundee 26874), the best equipped hotel in the heart of town, a glass-and-concrete structure. On my most recent stopover, I encountered a number of businessmen from Pakistan who export raw materials to Dundee used in making jute. Don't stay here seeking historical romance. But if you want a comfortable accommodation, you'll find all the amenities. The furnishings throughout are well maintained, and most bedrooms contain private baths. In a single the rate is £26 ($50.70). A double with bath rents for £30.50 ($59.48), including VAT, service, and a continental breakfast. The hotel also possesses three bars and a main dining room serving a standard cuisine.

CARNOUSTIE: This seaside resort, 61 miles northeast of Edinburgh, is celebrated for its championship golf course. Lying between Dundee and Arbroath (eight miles away), Carnoustie opens onto the North Sea. In summer its five miles of sand give plenty of beach space to it visitors.

The **Bruce Hotel,** 1 Link Parade (tel. Carnoustie 52364), is preferred by golfers, who book up its most desired accommodations in peak season. Mr. Kenneth Hood, who heads a dynamic, hearty staff, welcomes you to one of the well-kept clean bedrooms which vary in size and furnishings as well as plumbing. The hotel comfortably evokes Edwardian seaside days, and from its windows you can look out onto views of the North Sea—rather rugged the last time I stopped by. The hotel also offers views of the already-mentioned golf course. B&B is £23 ($44.85) in a single, from £38 ($74.10) in a double, including service and VAT. The plumbing has been modernized, and 25 of the bedrooms contain private baths. I've found the food quite good, and the portions are so ample that few leave the dining room hungry. The hotel is owned by the Edward family and is a member at Best Western hotels.

ARBROATH: Samuel Johnson wasn't that much impressed with Scotland on his jaunt there, but he did say that the view of Arbroath repaid him for some of the hardships suffered in his journey. Arbroath is a popular coastal resort with a colorful fishing harbor and rugged, red sandstone cliffs weathered into grotesque shapes. Smugglers once used the sandstone caves along the coast.

Arbroath "smokies" (smoked haddock) are one of the fish delicacies along the east coast of Scotland.

The "Fairport" of Sir Walter Scott's *The Antiquary,* the royal burgh of Arbroath lies 17 miles northeast of Dundee. On its High Street are the ruins of a red sandstone abbey, once the richest in Scotland. It was founded by William the Lion in 1178, and the king was buried in its precincts in 1214. The Scottish Parliament met there in 1320 and sent the pope a famous letter asserting the independence of their country. In the abbey a historical pageant is presented every year.

Two miles to the west stands **Kellie Castle** (tel. Arbroath 72271), built in 1170 and restored in 1679. Of pink sandstone, the castle is noted for its unique countyard and left-handed spiral stairway. Robert the Bruce once came into possession of it, during the "Black Parliament." It is open from April until October 1, daily except Tuesday, from 10:30 a.m. to 5:30 p.m., charging adults £1.50 ($2.93) for admission to both the castle and grounds, although children pay half price.

Hotel Seaforth (tel. Arbroath 72232) has been modernized and refurnished, a stone structure that is made inviting by the pleasant staff, the fine service, and the good food. The hotel overlooks the sea with a southern exposure, standing some 200 yards from the beach and within minutes of the center of town. Roomy, comfortable bedrooms rent for £12 ($24.30) in a single without bath, from £22 ($42.90) in a double if bathless; increasing to £15 ($29.25) in a single and £27 ($52.65) in a double with private bath. Tariffs include VAT, service, and a full breakfast. The cuisine consists of a concise, balanced range of popular standard dishes. Good, fresh ingredients are used. A three-course set lunch goes for £3.75 ($7.31), a four-course dinner for £5.35 ($10.43), including coffee.

MONTROSE: Instead of heading immediately for Glamis Castle, I suggest you continue along the coastal road from Arbroath toward Montrose. Along the way you'll pass stretches of rugged beauty. Sandstone cliffs rise sharply out of the water, and little slate-roofed cottages house the families who make their living from the often turbulent sea.

Montrose stands on a bottleneck of Montrose Basin, a broad estuary inhabited by hundreds of wild birds, notably pink-footed geese. This harbor town, with its well-known golf links, is a North Sea coastal resort for holiday makers. Its spired church and town hall date from the 18th century. David I granted Montrose its charter, and in 1352 it became one of Scotland's many royal burghs. Montrose lies 30 miles northeast of Dundee by road.

The Links Hotel (tel. Montrose 2288) is modern and attractive, the successful adaptation of a grand old house with interesting stained glass. Latter-day additions have been made, and central heating has been added. The bedrooms are brightly furnished and spotlessly kept, and the service provided by the friendly, helpful staff is excellent. A single room costs about £22 ($42.90) per night, a double goes for £30 ($58.50), and a triple for £36 ($70.20), these prices including a private bath en suite and breakfast as well. Lunch is served from a table d'hôte menu, costing from £5 ($9.75), and dinner from £7 ($13.65) is likely to include salmon from its own fisheries and Aberdeen angus rib roast. There is entertainment every evening in the Toffs Disco and a dinner-dance every Friday and Saturday in the Kingfisher Restaurant.

Central Hotel, High Street (tel. Montrose 2152), is one of the Welcome Inn chain which gives one assurance of a well-run hostelry. It's in the heart of town, where you can get all the necessities and sleep in peace. A bathless single with breakfast is £10.50 ($20.48), and a double or twin is £19.50 ($38.03) to £21 ($40.95) nightly. If you want a private bath, the tariff rises to £22.50 ($43.88). In the Steakhouse, lunch starts at £3.50 ($6.83), high tea from £2 ($3.90), and dinners from £5 ($9.75). When in the bar, you can have a simple lunch at a low tab. All prices include VAT.

KIRRIEMUIR: This town of narrow streets is the birthplace of Sir James Barrie, the "Thrums" of his novels. The Scottish dramatist and novelist, whose best loved play is *Peter Pan,* was born here in 1860, the son of a father who was employed as a hand-loom weaver of linen. **Barrie's Birthplace,** a National Trust property, contains manuscripts and mementos of the writer, and is open May 1 to September 30 on weekdays from 10 a.m. to 12:30 p.m. and from 2 to 6 p.m. (on Sunday from 2 to 6 p.m.), charging 50p (98¢) for admission for adults, 25p (49¢) for children. For information, telephone Kirriemuir 2646.

From Kirriemuir, it's a four-mile drive south to—

GLAMIS CASTLE: After Balmoral Castle, most visitors to Scotland want to see Glamis Castle at Glamis (pronounced Glaams), for its architecture, its Shakespearian link (Macbeth was Thane of Glamis at the beginning of the play), and its link with the Crown. For ten centuries it has been connected to British royalty. Her Majesty, Queen Elizabeth, the Queen Mother, was brought up here; her daughter, now Queen Elizabeth II, spent a good deal of her childhood here; and Princess Margaret, the Queen's sister, was born here, becoming the first royal princess born in Scotland in three centuries. The existing castle dates in part from the middle of the 15th century, but there are records of a castle's having been in existence in the 11th century, at which time it was one of the hunting lodges of the kings of Scotland. King Malcolm II was carried there mortally wounded in 1034 after having been attacked by his enemies while hunting in a nearby forest.

Glamis Castle has been in the possession of the Lyon family since 1372, when it formed part of the dowry of Princess Joanna, daughter of King Robert II, when she married John Lyon, secretary to the king. The castle was altered in the 16th century and restored and enlarged in the 17th, 18th, and 19th centuries. It contains some fine plaster ceilings, furniture, and paintings.

The present owner, the Queen's cousin, is the 17th Earl of Strathmore and Kinghorne. He lives at the castle with his wife and three children. He is the direct descendant of the first earl.

The castle is open to the public, who have access to the Royal Apartments and many other rooms, and also to the gardens and grounds, daily except Saturday, May 1 to October 1, from 1 to 5 p.m. (also Easter weekend). Admission to the castle and gardens is £1.50 ($2.93) for adults, £1.10 ($2.15) for senior citizens, and 70p ($1.37) for children. If you wish to visit the grounds only, the charge is 50p (98¢) for adults and 30p (59¢) for senior citizens. Children are admitted free.

Also in Glamis, you may want to visit the **Angus Folk Museum, Kirkwynd Cottages,** run by the National Trust for Scotland. From the former county of Angus, rich in folklore, were collected domestic utensils, agricultural implements, furniture, and clothing. The museum is open May 1 to September 30 from noon to 5 p.m., charging adults 60p ($1.17); children, 30p (59¢). Last entry is at 4:30 p.m.

DUNKELD: A cathedral town, Dunkeld lies in a thickly wooded valley of the Tay River, at the edge of the Perthshire Highlands. Once a major ecclesiastical center, it is one of the seats of ancient Scottish history. It was an important center of the Celtic church, for example.

The National Trust for Scotland has been effective in restoring many of the old houses and shops around the marketplace and cathedral that had fallen into decay.

The **Cathedral of Dunkeld** was founded in 815. David I converted the church into a cathedral in 1127. The 14th and 15th centuries witnessed subsequent additions. The cathedral was first restored in 1815, and at that time traces of the 12th-century structure clearly remained, as they do to this day.

Finally, Shakespeare fans may want to seek out the oak and sycamore in front of the destroyed **Birnam House,** a mile to the south. This was believed to be a remnant of the Birnam wood to which the Bard gave everlasting literary fame in *Macbeth*. In Shakespeare's drama, you may recall, the "woods of Birnam came to Dunsinane."

The **Dunkeld House Hotel** (tel. Dunkeld 243) offers the quiet dignity of life in a Scottish country house. Built for the seventh Duke of Atholl in the 19th century, the house was erected on the banks of the Tay, and the surrounding grounds were planted with trees and flowering bushes, making for parklike setting. You reach the house by going down a long drive. Guests can fish for trout and salmon on the grounds.

The house is well preserved and beautifully kept, and, as befits such a place, accommodations come in a wide range of styles, space, and furnishings. Overnight stays start at £14.30 ($27.98) per person without bath, rising to £24.20 ($47.19) per person in a suite in low season. However, in summer prices go up to £15.95 ($31.10) to £30.80 ($60.06) per person, respectively, these tariffs including VAT, service, and a full breakfast.

The people of Dunkeld come here on Saturday nights for dancing, with dinner at £11 ($21.45). The dining room opens onto a Tayside vista, and the owners have established a reputation for continental dishes, including some original offerings, plus good wines from their cellar. Service is exemplary. Lunch is served from 12:30 to 2 p.m., costing £6 ($11.70) for a table d'hôte, and dinner is from 7 to 9 p.m. It closes half an hour earlier on Sunday, when a buffet dinner goes for £11 ($21.45). The price for the set evening meal is £9 ($17.55). The hotel and restaurant are closed from the first of November to mid-January.

Cardney House (tel. Butterstone 222) is an elegant 18th-century manor on a private estate outside Dunkeld, three miles from the town on the A923 Blair Gowrie road. The house is surrounded by hills, forests, and lochs, and on the grounds rare and beautiful shrubs are grown, as well as orchids, stephanotis, and lemon and orange trees. Here you are received like the guest at a private party at a country home by the charming and hospitable hosts, Lieutenant Commander (retired) and Mrs. MacGregor, who because of "crippling taxes" now receive paying guests. The gracious home is well furnished, often with antiques, and the atmosphere is one of refinement and tranquility, a style set so admirably by the proprietors.

They have available now only two singles and six doubles, charging £14 ($27.30) per person for B&B, £20.50 ($39.98) per person for half board, including VAT. Dinner, often a Cordon Bleu cuisine, is served until 8 in the evening, and you definitely feel you are dining family style. The food is well prepared and beautifully served, and meals are complemented by a first-class wine cellar. Men are expected to change into lounge suits or dinner jackets; women, long or short dresses. Guests relax freely in the lounges, which are furnished with family treasures, often antiques. Surprisingly, there's an elevator. During the day, shooting and fishing expeditions can be arranged. Mrs. MacGregor is an active concert singer, and musical evenings are given regularly at Cardney.

PITLOCHRY: After leaving Edinburgh, many motorists stop here for the night before continuing on the Highland road to Inverness. However, once they discover the charms of Pitlochry, they want to linger. This popular holiday resort center is a touring headquarters for the Valley of the Tummel.

It is particularly renowned for its **Pitlochry Festival Theatre,** Scotland's "theater in the hills." Telephone Pitlochry 2680 for information. Founded in 1951, the festival theater draws people from all over the world to its repertoire of plays, usually presented from early April until late October. Performances in the evening begin at 8 p.m., and on Wednesday and Saturday there is a matinee at 2:15 p.m. A new theater next to Pitlochry's dam and salmon ladder opened in 1981.

The **Pitlochry Dam** was created because a new power station was needed, but in effect the engineers created a new loch. The famous "Salmon Ladder" was built to help the struggling salmon upstream. An underwater portion of the ladder—a salmon observation chamber—has been enclosed in glass to give fascinated sightseers a look.

Pitlochry doesn't just entertain visitors, although it would appear that way in summer. It also produces scotch whisky and tweeds.

Food and Lodging

Green Park (tel. Pitlochry 2537) lies about half a mile from the center, at the northwest end of Pitlochry, and it's one of the best hotels in the area, the preferred choice of many. Against a backdrop of woodland, the white-painted mansion with its carved eaves enjoys a top scenic position, its lawns reaching to the shores of Loch Faskally, the only hotel so situated. Visitors who reserve well in advance get one of the half dozen or so snappy modern rooms in the garden wing, each with a private bath and all enjoying a view of loch and woodland. The more antiquated rooms, however, are still good, with old-fashioned furniture. Depending on where you anchor, singles range from £18 ($35.10) to £20 ($39), doubles from £36 ($70.20) to £40 ($78), the higher tariffs for rooms with private baths. Guests enjoy drinks in a half-moon-shaped lounge overlooking the water. Many diners come here during festival season to enjoy not only the good food and wine, but the panoramic views. The hotel is closely supervised by Anne and Graham Brown. Dinner is served until 8 p.m., and many traditional Scottish dishes are featured. The Green Park is open from mid-March until November 1.

Hydro Hotel, Knockard Road (tel. Pitlochry 2666), was originally known by the English gentry who came here in summer to enjoy the fresh air of the Perthshire Highlands. Built in the Scottish baronial mansion style, the hotel has kept up with much-needed modern improvements, and now ranks with Green Park as the preferred choice of accommodations in Pitlochry. The hotel stands on large, well-manicured grounds, offering tennis and a nine-hole golf course, as well as a solarium, putting green, and croquet lawn. The merchants of Pitlochry and their wives come here on Saturday nights for dancing.

At latest count, the hotel had nearly 70 rooms and at least 40 of them contained private baths. Hopefully, you'll be given one of the turreted corner rooms, although you should request such space when making a reservation. Depending on the perch you're given, rates in a single range from £18.50

($36.08) to £23 ($44.85), and in a double from £30 ($58.50) to £36 ($70.20), plus VAT.

The lounges have been considerably improved since I first stayed there in 1973. The Hydro shuts down from October to the middle of April.

The Pine Trees, Strathview Terrace (tel. Pitlochry 2121), is a mansion built in the 1890s and now converted into a charming country-house hotel, set high above the main Pitlochry Road. Deer and squirrels roam the tranquil grounds, 14 acres of bucolic bliss, about a ten-minute walk from the center. Mr. White owns this fine Scottish home of character and charm, and he and his staff are most hospitable. Of the roomy 30 bedrooms offered, 25 have private baths, for which you pay extra, of course. The high-season rates are £17 ($33.15) in a single, £31 ($60.45) in a double, including breakfast. It's best to take the half-board rate of £23 ($44.85) per person nightly. Nonresidents are welcome to drop in for dinner, enjoying not only the bountiful cuisine, but a view of the Valley of Tummel. For guests, Mr. White can also provide exclusive salmon fishing.

Moulin Hotel (tel Pitlochry 2196) is an old Highland coaching inn converted to a comfortable hotel, lying less than a mile from the center of Pitlochry in the attractive old-world village of Moulin. It is within easy reach of the theater and all the attractions of Pitlochry. A detached annex at the Moulin contains more modern rooms. Nine of the pleasantly furnished bedrooms contain private baths. For B&B one person pays £12.50 ($24.38) to £14.70 ($28.67); two persons, from £19 ($37.05) to £23 ($44.85). The food is good. The dining room opens onto beautiful views of the hills. In summer umbrella-shaded tables are set out for drinks, although when the wind blows, patrons prefer the modern lounge bar, where they can also order snacks and sandwiches. Tariffs include VAT, but service and breakfast are extra. A lunch at the hotel or else a packed lunch are à la carte, and dinners start at £7.50 ($14.63). The hotel is closed from October to April.

Excursions from Pitlochry

From the town you can take excursions in almost any direction. Heading northwest for four miles, you come to the **Pass of Killiecrankie,** where "Bonnie Dundee" and his Jacobites won their victory over the armies of General Mackay fighting for King William in 1689. This is one of the scenic highlights of the area.

If time remains, try to see another attraction, **Queen's View,** where Victoria herself picnicked. The view is reached by taking the road alongside Loch Tummel. At the eastern end, Victoria looked down the length of the loch toward Schiehallion.

BLAIR ATHOLL: Eight miles to the northwest of Pitlochry stands the gleaming white **Blair Castle** (tel. Blair Atholl 355), the home of the Duke of Atholl, on the A9. Built in the Scottish baronial style, and dating from 1269, the castle allows you to view some 30 rooms. Inside is an impressive collection of Jacobite relics, china, lace, and armor, along with many family portraits. It is open Sunday and Monday in April, and then again daily from May 1 until the second Sunday in October. Hours are weekdays from 10 a.m. to 6 p.m. (on Sunday from 2 to 6).

For both food and lodging, you might prefer a stopover in Blair Atholl to Pitlochry. If so, I'd recommend **Atholl Arms** (tel. Blair Atholl 205). Once lords and ladies who couldn't find room at Blair Castle stayed here, and some of the grand balls of old Perthshire were held here. Now the Atholl Arms is a roadside inn, built of stone and gabled with large bays, attracting motorists en route to Inverness. A cocktail lounge has been redecorated, and there's a public bar as well, attracting the locals. The ballroom has been turned into an arched-roof restaurant, complete with a minstrels' gallery. There's also a more intimate dining room with antiques and mahogany chairs. Both rooms offer a substantial menu. The bedrooms are individually styled and well fitted, and each one we inspected had a completely different character. The B&B price is around £10 ($19.50) per person, or else you can take half board for £16.50 ($32.16) per person daily.

ABERFELDY: The "Birks o' Aberfeldy" is one of the beauty spots made famous by Robert Burns. Once a Pictish center, this small town makes a fine base for touring Perthshire's glens and lochs. Loch Tay lies 6 miles to the west; Glen Lyon, 15 miles west; and Kinloch Rannoch, 18 miles northwest.

General Wade in 1733 built the bridge spanning the Tay. In the town's shops you'll find good buys in tweeds and tartans, plus other items of Highland dress.

The **Cruachan Hotel**, Kenmore Street (tel. Aberfeldy 20545), stands at the edge of town in about three acres of flowery gardens and greenery. The hotel is small and immaculately kept, renting out only three singles, six doubles, and one family room, each containing hot and cold running water. Some of the rooms contain private baths, for which the charge is an additional £2 ($3.90) per person nightly. Evening meals, and well-prepared ones at that, are served from 7 to 8 p.m. It's best to take the half-board arrangement, costing from £16.50 ($32.16) per person daily. At lunch, it's possible to order those open-face Danish sandwiches. The centrally heated, fully licensed, private hotel is closed in December, January, and February. On the grounds is a nine-hole putting green for the use of guests.

KILLIN: Just over the border from Tayside in the Central Region, Killin is a village on the Dochart at the lower end of Loch Tay. Lying 45 miles west of Perth by road, Killin is both a summer holiday resort and a winter sports center. The **Falls of Dochart** are world famous, but the town is also noted for beauty spots, and there are sights of historical interest as well.

Killin Church contains a font more than 1000 years old. Less than a quarter of a mile from the church stands an upright stone, said to mark the grave of Fingal. An island in the Dochart was the ancient burial place of the MacNab Clan.

The ruins of **Finlarig Castle** contains a beheading pit near the castle gate which was written about in Scott's *The Fair Maid of Perth*. Perched 1000 feet above the loch, the castle was the seat of "Black Duncan of the Cowl," a notoriously ruthless chieftain of the Campbell Clan.

For accommodations or meals, I recommend **Bridge of Lochay** (tel. Killin 272), which retains some of its 16th-century character, although it has seen many alterations and additions since that time. Half a mile from **Killin**, the "bridge"—an attractive, rambling, white-painted building—lies on the banks of the Lochay River, at the tip of Loch Tay. A. G. Symon, the owner, welcomes you to one of his 17 bedrooms, simply but comfortably furnished, each containing hot and cold running water. The overnight charge is £11 ($21.45) per person for a bed and a large Scottish breakfast. Guests can enjoy good drinks in the bar or else sit in front of peat and log fires in the lounges. The food is plain Scottish cooking, quite good. If you stay at least three nights, you'll be quoted a half-board tariff of £18 ($35.10) per person daily. The hotel is open from April to October.

Morenish Lodge (tel. Killin 258) is now a small Highland hotel, although formerly it was the shooting lodge of an earl, lying 200 feet above Loch Tay and less than three miles from Killin (on the A827 Aberfeldy road). The hotel, run by William C. Barr for nearly a quarter of a century, offers only a dozen bedrooms, with hot and cold running water, a few with private bath. Furnishings are comfortable and old-fashioned. It's best to stay here on a half-board arrangement, costing from £20 ($39) per person nightly. Many of the public rooms face the loch, and you can enjoy a good meal with wine in the Tay View room; and in the Laird's Bar, scotch whisky, both blended and malt, is served.

Dall Lodge Hotel (tel. Killin 217) is a 19th-century stone house overlooking the River Lochay on the outskirts of Killin. The hotel specializes in serving many traditional Scottish foods, such as salmon, trout, venison, haggis, Aberdeen angus beef, Scottish hill lamb, cloutie dumpling, and Scottish raspberry shortcake. The tariff, VAT included, for B&B is £8.50 ($16.58) per person, and the five-course dinner is £6 ($11.70). The hotel carries a wide range of fine wines and a comprehensive choice of Scottish malt whiskies. All bedrooms have hot and cold water and do-it-yourself tea- and coffee-making facilities, and offer splendid views.

2. Aberdeen and Royal Deeside

Traveling north from the lochs—previewed in the section above—heading toward Royal Deeside, you can't help but go through Glen Shee and Glen Clunie, a most spectacular route which will give you your first taste of Highland scenery.

As you journey across uncrowded roads into Scotland's northeast, you'll pass heather-covered moorland and peaty lochs, wood glens and salmon-filled rivers, granite-stone villages and fishing harbors, even North Sea beach resorts.

This is the Grampian region, with such centers as Aberdeen and Braemar, and such sights as Balmoral Castle and the "Whisky Trail." Even the Queen comes here for holidays.

BRAEMAR: This little Deeside resort is the site of the **Royal Highland Gathering**, which takes place there annually, either in late August or early September. It is usually attended by Queen Elizabeth. The "royal link" dates from the 1840s when Queen Victoria first attended the games.

The capital of the Deeside Highlands, Braemar is overrun with foreign visitors, as well as the British, during the gathering. Anyone thinking of attending would be wise to make application for accommodation anywhere within 20-mile radius of Braemar not later than early April.

The gathering in Braemar is the most famous of the many Highland games. The spectacular occasion is held in the **Princess Royal and Duke of Fife Memorial Park.** Competitions include tossing the caber, throwing the hammer, sprinting, vaulting, a tug-o'-war, the long leap, Highland dancing, putting a 16-pound ball, sword dancing, relay races, and, naturally, a bagpiping contest. At a vast refreshment tent, Scottish lassies serve tea, coffee, buns, and other refreshments.

The romantic 17th-century **Braemar Castle** (tel. Braemar 224) lies half a mile northeast of Braemar on the A93. A private residence of architectural grace, scenic charm, and historical interest, it is the seat of Capt. A. A. Farquharson of Invercauld. It can be visited from early May until the first Monday in October—daily from 10 a.m. to 6 p.m., costing adults 90p ($1.76); children under 13 pay 45p (88¢).

Food and Lodging

Invercauld Arms Hotel, Braemar (tel. Braemar 605), is a lovely old stone Highlands house converted to welcome guests. Its main building dates back to the 18th century. In cool weather they're greeted by a roaring fire in the hearth and shown to a comfortable armchair. In this friendly atmosphere one can really relax. This is a perfect part of the country for walking and fishing, and, in winter in nearby Glenshee, skiing. When you return to the hotel, you can have a dram in the bar called Colonel's Bed, named after a local gentleman who escaped the Battle of Killiecrankie with his mistress and hid out near the hotel. A single room goes for £22.50 ($43.88) without bath, going up to £32 ($62.40) with bath. Bathless doubles rent for £18.50 ($36.08) per person; with a shared bath, £22.50 ($43.88) per person; and with a private bath, £26.50 ($51.68) per person. All tariffs include a full Scottish breakfast. Half-board terms are also available. You'll sample a taste of Scotland here in the salmon and trout fresh from the River Dee, or perhaps succulent angus beef, Highland venison, and grouse. For breakfast you might dare to order kippers and porridge, and you can even try haggis. The staff will pack a lunch for you if you're going on a walking trip. This is a thoroughly pleasant place, well run by Mr. Lock, the owner.

Fife Arms Hotel, Mar Road, near the center of Braemar (tel. Braemar 644), is a pleasant stone building surrounded by gardens. It contains a comfortable lounge with two bars to slake your thirst. Many of the bedrooms have baths and cost from £17.50 ($34.13) per person nightly, based on double occupancy. That becomes quite a bargain when you realize it also includes a full breakfast plus a good-tasting dinner that evening. Mr. Harris, the owner, runs a busy, bustling place. During the day he does bar meals and set lunches from noon to 2 p.m. There is a more ambitious menu in the evening, going for £5 ($9.75) and likely to include Scottish salmon or trout. However, either of these delicacies is likely to run the tab up another £2 ($3.90). Coffee is served later in the lounge.

Braemar Lodge Hotel (tel. Braemar 617) is run by the delightful Mrs. McKay, who is frightfully apologetic that on reservations in advance she must insist on a £5 ($9.75) deposit. The house is an old hunting lodge but has been converted into a friendly hotel with a small lounge for guests. The bedrooms are warm and neat, and there are adequate bathroom facilities. B&B costs £10 ($19.50). Dinner, served at 7 p.m. (and don't be late), costs £7 ($13.65). You can sit afterward in the lounge, ordering coffee and Drambuie if you wish. Local information is willingly given, and the small staff will go out of their way to make you feel at home. Mrs. McKay spends a lot of time in the kitchen, and the food is plain and excellent, served by attractive young women. When booking, say whether you plan to be there for dinner, as that helps Mrs. McKay plan the meals. Opposite the hotel is the cottage where Robert Louis Stevenson wrote *Treasure Island*.

THE WHISKY TRAIL: Extending north from Braemar, from Grantown and Dufftown to Elgin, are many distilleries of scotch whisky. Many are open for visits only by appointments—collect the list of telephone numbers from the local tourist office at Braemar. However, **Glenfiddich Distillery** in **Dufftown**

is open Monday to Friday from 10 a.m. to 12:30 p.m. and from 2 to 4:30 p.m. Visitors are shown around the plant, and the process of distilling is explained by charming young women in tartans. At the finish of the tour, you're given a free dram of malt whisky—and the whole tour is free.

BALLATER: On the Dee River, with the Grampian mountains in the background, Ballater is a holiday resort center where visitors flock to attend one of Scotland's most popular sightseeing attractions, Balmoral Castle (see below).

The town still centers around its **Station Square,** where the royal family used to be photographed as they arrived to spend holidays. The railway has since been closed.

From Ballater you can drive west to view the magnificent scenery of **Glen Muick** and **Lochnagar,** where you'll see herds of deer.

Food and Lodging

Tullich Lodge, on the A93, 1½ miles east of Ballater (tel. Ballater 55406), is a turreted country house built in the Scottish baronial style, standing in five acres of its own gardens and woods above Royal Deeside and Ballater. The attractive hotel is tastefully decorated and furnished, often with antiques, its brass fittings and wood paneling providing the traditional touches. Your pleasant hosts, Hector Macdonald and Neil Bannister, offer only ten bedrooms, but they're of generous size and are beautifully furnished. At least eight contain private baths, the rest showers. Rates are £34 ($66.30) in a single, from £30 ($58.50) per person in a double. The lodge closes from December through March.

Its dining room commanding panoramic views of the "royal valley," serves some of the finest food along Royal Deeside. One of the chef's specialties is casseroles, although he does all the standard dishes with above-average flair, including locally caught trout and salmon, game and especially venison in season, as well as crab and lobster. The homemade soups are particularly enjoyable. A table d'hôte dinner, served from 7:30 to 9 p.m., goes for about £10 ($19.50). A bar luncheon is at 1 p.m. with no fried foods. It's essential to make a reservation. In an amusing bar, with a model railway, you can order from a good selection of malt whiskies. For guests to get the most out of the surrounding countryside, as well as this special hotel, I'd recommend whenever possible that they stay a minimum of two nights. In this way, they won't have to live out of suitcases all the time and will have a chance to settle in.

The **Invercauld Arms** (tel. Ballater 55417) is a whitewashed Victorian hotel right in the heart of Royal Deeside. Queen Victoria used to visit it when at court at Balmoral. Mr. and Mrs. Alistair R. Norrie, the proprietors, will welcome you most kindly, offering good food, comfortable bedrooms, and solid service. He greets guests resplendent in his kilt. The atmosphere is informal, and visitors quickly get to know each other. Nearly half the bedrooms contain private baths. A single without bath costs £14 ($27.30), rising to £20 ($39) with bath. Doubles, depending on the plumbing, go from £24 ($46.80) to £36 ($70.20). A Scottish breakfast is another £2.50 ($4.88) per person, and VAT is included, although there is a 10% service charge. In some of the more traditionally furnished bedrooms the antiques were made by Victoria's cabinet-maker.

The fully licensed hotel was built as a coaching inn in the early 1800s, and offers a wide range of pursuits such as game fishing, tennis, bowling, and golf. The hotel's spacious restaurant is especially fine, not only opening onto beautiful views, but serving a country-house fare of standard dishes that are well prepared, using fresh ingredients. The roasts are especially good. Lunch is served from noon to 2:30 p.m., dinner from 7:30 to 9:30 p.m. Expect to pay about £10 ($19.50) for a four-course dinner. Lunch served in the bar is from a cold buffet table, with the hot dish of the day priced at £3 ($5.85). The hotel is open all year.

Balmoral Castle

"This dear paradise" is how Queen Victoria described this castle, rebuilt in the Scottish baronial style by her beloved Albert. It was completed in 1855. Today Balmoral, eight miles west of Ballater, is still a private residence of the British sovereign. Albert, the prince consort, acquired the property in 1847, and the royal family first arrived there in 1848. As the small castle left by the Farquharsons proved too small, the present castle was rebuilt. Its principal feature is a 100-foot tower. On the grounds are many memorials to the royal family. Only the grounds, incidentally, can be visited—daily, except Sunday in May, June, and July from 10 a.m. to 5 p.m. However, no visits are allowed if the royal family is in residence. Admission is 85p ($1.66) for adults, 45p (88¢) for children.

BANCHORY: On lower Deeside, this pleasant resort is rich in woodland and river scenery. From this base, you can take excursions to two of the most popular castles in the Grampian region.

The Sights

Crathes Castle and Gardens, (tel. Crathes 525) two miles east of Banchory, is a fine early Jacobean building which is celebrated for its gardens with sculptured yews dating from 1702. Just north of the A93 on the north bank of the Dee, this baronial castle contains remarkable painted ceilings. Gardens and grounds are open all year from 9:30 a.m. to sunset. The castle is open at Easter, then May 1 until September 30 Monday through Saturday from 11 a.m. to 6 p.m. (on Sunday from 2 to 6 p.m.). Admission to the grounds is as follows: cars, 60p ($1.17); minibuses, £1.50 ($2.44); and coaches, £5 ($9.75). To visit just the castle, adults pay 85p ($1.66); children, 40p (78¢). If you desire to see only the gardens, the charge is 45p (88¢) for adults, 20p (39¢) for children. A combined ticket costs adults £1.40 ($2.73); children, 70p ($1.37). There is a licensed restaurant serving light meals during the hours the castle is open.

Structurally unchanged since its completion in 1626, **Craigievar Castle** (tel. Lumphanan 635) is an example of Scottish baronial architecture at its greatest height. Original molded plaster ceilings are to be seen in most rooms. The castle has been continually inhabited by the descendants of the builder, William Forbes, and is now preserved by the National Trust for Scotland. It is open daily except Friday from May to September, from 2 to 7 p.m., charging an admission of £1.10 ($2.15) for adults, 55p ($1.07) for children. The grounds are open all year from 9:30 a.m. to dusk, and admission is by donation.

A mile from the castle is **Macbeth's Cairn,** where, according to legend, Macduff put an end to **Macbeth.**

Food and Lodging

Raemoir House (tel. Banchory 2846) is an 18th-century manor standing on 3500 acres of grounds with such sporting attractions as shooting, fishing, and riding. It is a journey into nostalgia, with its ballroom, antiques, and fine tapestries, and log fires burning in the colder months. The rooms are handsomely decorated, most of them quite large, and at least 17 of the 23 bedchambers contain private baths. What is so lovely about Scotland is its curious mixtures—in this case, an 18th-century manor house with its own helipad. This place is run by two of the most charming ladies you could find anywhere. Mrs. Kit Sabin and Mrs. Peggy Jordan have been there since 1942, and they and the house have grown together. Meals are served in an attractive Georgian dining room, featuring a standard repertoire of familiar dishes, rather well done. Service is informal and prompt. Depending on the plumbing, the B&B rate ranges from £18 ($35.10) to £19 ($37.05) per person daily. Dinner is £9 ($17.55) per person. Lunch is usually £4 ($7.80), although the bigger traditional Sunday meal goes for £7 ($13.65).

The hotel is run just like a private house—no keys to bedroom doors, but you can bolt yourself in for privacy. The office is an old desk in the cubbyhole under the splendid staircase. The adjoining Ha' Hoose with rentable rooms was once used by Mary Queen of Scots. The place is unique, its special character not recommended for Hilton/convenience food/21st-century fans.

Tor-Na-Coille, Inchmarlo Road (tel. Banchory 2242), is a country house hotel—really a Victorian mansion—standing on its own wooded grounds of about six acres. Public rooms are suitably spacious, most comfortable, and the whisky always tastes better in the modern bar. If you're on your way to see Balmoral Castle or else to attend the Highland gathering at Braemar, you will be able to relax here, enjoying the gracious hospitality of Mr. Graham. The bedrooms, many quite large, are restful, 60% of them have private baths, and all of them have color TV, radio, phone, and coffee-making equipment. Singles cost from £18 ($35.10) with private bath and doubles begin at £31 ($60.45) with private bath, including a full breakfast and VAT. A half-board rate applies for stays of more than three nights. The hotel is interesting architecturally, and the room you may be assigned could have much character.

Lunches are light meals in the bar, including smoked venison sausage blended with rum and red wine. Sunday lunch is a grander affair, when the main dishes include roast beef, turkey, and leg of pork. Food at night is by candlelight, and here might be your chance to try real Scottish salmon (the salmon leap at the Falls of Feugh nearby). Dinner is likely to feature the chef's special pheasant. The hotel has a high reputation for its food. A set lunch of two courses goes for £4.60 ($8.97), increasing to £8.50 ($16.58) for a four-course dinner. If ordering an à la carte dinner, expect to pay from £4 ($27.30) per person.

Banchory Lodge Hotel (tel. Banchory 2625), built in 1738, was once the home of a well-known Deeside family. But when Maggie and Dugald Jaffray took it over, it was almost derelict. With dedication and hard work, they transformed it into the pleasant country house it is today, with much Georgian charm. On its own grounds, on the bank of the Dee, where it is joined by the Water of the Feugh, the lodge is open all year, accommodating guests in some 29 bedrooms, many of which overlook the river; 23 have private baths. The B&B rate is about £20 ($39) per person, increasing to £26 ($50.70) for half board. In the dining room, overlooking the river, furnishings and decor are in period style. Maggie Jaffray supervises the kitchen, where specialties include fresh Dee salmon and Aberdeen angus roast beef. Guests can fish from the lawn or in one of the hotel's boats by arrangement.

ABERDEEN: The harbor in this seaport in the northeast of Scotland is one of the largest fishing ports in the country, literally infested with kipper and deep-sea trawlers. The **Fish Market** is well worth a visit, as it's the liveliest in Britain.

Bordered by fine sandy beaches (delightful if you're a polar bear), Scotland's third city is often called "the granite city," as its buildings are constructed largely of granite, in pink or gray, hewn from the Rubislaw quarries.

Aberdeen has become the capital of the oil workers pouring into northeast Scotland to help harvest the riches from six North Sea oilfields. The city lies on the banks of the salmon- and trout-filled Don and Dee Rivers. Spanning the Don is the world-famous **Brig o' Balgownie,** a steep Gothic arch, begun in 1285.

In Castlegate is the **Mercat Cross,** a hexagonally shaped structure, built in 1686, and considered the most handsome of the old crosses in Scotland.

Aberdeen University is a fusion of two separate colleges. King's College is older, dating from 1483, and it contains the oldest school of medicine in Great Britain. The chapel of King's College is crowned by a stately tower from 1505. Marischal College, founded in 1593, is recognized as one of the finest granite buildings in the world.

The university is in Old Aberdeen, as is the **Cathedral of St. Machar,** founded in 1131, although the present structure dates from the 15th century. Its splendid heraldic ceiling contains three rows of shields representing the kings and princes of Europe along with the Scottish ecclesiastical and aristocratic hierarchy. The modern stained-glass windows are magnificent, the work of Douglas Strachan.

Provost Skene's House, 45 Guestrow, is named for a rich merchant who was Lord Provost of Aberdeen during 1676–1685. Off Broad Street, it is now a museum with period rooms and artifacts of domestic life. Admission is 10p (20¢) for adults, 5p (10¢) for children, and it can be visited Monday to Saturday from 10 a.m. to 5 p.m.

Food and Lodging

Because of the increasing numbers of tourists and business visitors to the Granite City, now established as Europe's Offshore Oil Capital, hotels are likely to be heavily booked any time of the year. In that case, it's best to go to the **Tourist Bureau,** St. Nicholas House, Broad Street (tel. Aberdeen 23456). A member of the staff there will assist with hotel or guest house reservations. If you're calling on a Saturday, use a different telephone number (tel. Aberdeen 24890).

For those willing to reserve in advance, here are my favorite selections:

Holiday Inn, Oldmeldrum Road, Bucksburn (tel. 0244/713911), is especially popular with business people from the oil-related concerns flocking to Aberdeen. Even though Laird's Bar is done up in a Highland baronial flavor, you're likely to hear customers ordering Jack Daniel's and Old Grand-Dad as much as malt scotch. The 99-unit Holiday Inn is a fresh package, all accommodations containing fully tiled private baths. In decor the tone is traditional rather than modern. Singles rent for £34 ($66.30), doubles for £38 ($74.10), and breakfast is extra. The Mariner Restaurant, serving until 10:30 p.m., evokes the nostalgia for the days of the Aberdeen clipper ships.

Prince Regent Hotel, Waverly Place (tel. Aberdeen 55071), is a small, attractive, and well-kept hotel run by Mr. and Mrs. Ashdown. Their little oasis lies only yards from the West End of Union Street. The public rooms have a Regency decor, and the bedrooms, although simply furnished, have all the necessities, and most of them come with private baths. Singles begin at £17 ($33.15), and doubles or twins rent for about £35 ($68.25), including bath or shower, VAT, service, and a full Scottish breakfast. The cookery is quite fine and is handsomely presented, the hotel offering both table d'hôte and à la carte menus. A table d'hôte lunch goes for £4 ($7.80), the set dinner price going up to £7 ($13.65). Guests can enjoy apéritifs in the Regency Buck or drinks in the Jug.

Malacca Hotel, 349 Great Western Rd. (tel. Aberdeen 28901), is one of the best of the small hotels of Aberdeen. Actually, it offers only eight bedrooms, seven of which contain private baths and showers. Singles rent for £27 ($52.65) nightly, doubles going for £36 ($70.20). The granite town-house hotel, with its surrounding stone wall and trees, is much better known for its restaurant, an attractively decorated dining room with bentwood caned chairs, a sophisticated setting for the international dishes served here, everything from bouillabaisse to chicken jubilee to duck in orange sauce. You can dine here for about £15 ($29.25) per person. Lunch is served until 2 p.m. and dinner until 10:30 p.m.

On the outskirts, if you're heading for Royal Deeside, I'd suggest a dining stopover at **Marycutler House** (tel. Aberdeen 732124), about six miles from Aberdeen on the South Deeside Road. World traveler Mrs. Martin purchased this 17th-century house beside the river, imaginatively decorating the dining rooms with treasures brought back from her trips. The baronial bars has an eclectic collection—an African mask, an Early English settle, a Victorian sofa, and Adam bar. In addition to the bar are two handsome dining rooms as well as one with a glass roof, evoking memories of Marrakesh. The menu is likely to change by the time of your visit, but it's international in scope—tagliatelle Florentine, Stilton soup, quail with grapes and almonds, port venison, or Greek salad, perhaps topped by peaches in wine or, a favorite, brown bread ice cream. Expect to spend from £10 ($19.50), plus the cost of your drink, for a complete meal. Lunch is until 2 p.m., and dinner (make a reservation) is from 7:30 to 9:30 p.m. If you're stopping in for lunch, you can have a light pub meal in front of the fireplace. Closed Sunday. The house is likely to be closed for dinner from January until April.

Excursions in "Castle Country"

Aberdeen is the center of "castle country," as 40 inhabited castles lie within a 40-mile radius. Two of the most popular castle excursions are previewed below. For others, refer above to Banchory.

Drum Castle: The handsome mansion (tel. Drumoak 204) was added in 1619, but the great square tower dates from the late 13th century, making it one of the three oldest tower houses in the country. Historic Drum lies ten miles west of Aberdeen, off the A93. The castle is open May to September, Monday to Saturday from 11 a.m. to 6 p.m. (on Sunday from 2 to 6), charging adults 75p ($1.46) for admission; children pay 55p ($1.07). The grounds are open all year from 9:30 a.m. to dusk, and admission is by donation.

Muchalls Castle: Built by the Burnetts of Leys in 1619, this castle is now lived in by Mr. and Mrs. Maurice A. Simpson. It is noted for its elaborate plasterwork ceilings and fireplaces. The castle lies five miles north of Stonehaven, nine miles south of Aberdeen. It is open May to September on Tuesday and Sunday from 3 to 5 p.m., charging adults 40p (78¢); children, 10p (20¢).

Chapter XIX

HIGHLANDS AND ISLANDS

1. Aviemore, Speyside, and Elgin
2. Inverness and Loch Ness
3. Fort William and Lochaber
4. Kyle of Lochalsh and Skye
5. Oban, Mull, and District
6. Kintyre, Arran, and Islay

FROM ITS ROMANTIC GLENS and its rugged mountainous landscapes, the Highlands suggest a timeless antiquity. Off the coast, mysterious islands, such as Skye with its jagged peaks, rise from the sea, inviting further exploration. These lands are sparsely inhabited even today, and much wildlife, such as the red deer, still flourishes.

As the unofficial capital of the Highlands, Inverness is the terminus of that rail journey from London, a distance of some 570 miles. As such, many visitors use it as a base for Highland adventures.

From Inverness, you can journey along Loch Ness (especially if you're a monster watcher) to Fort William, dominated by Ben Nevis, the highest mountain in Britain. Oban is the main resort on Scotland's West Highland coastline. It is also one of the major ports for journeying to the Hebridean islands.

If at all possible, try to explore some of these islands, the largest of which is Lewis, where the Standing Stones of Callanish, a prehistoric monument, evokes Stonehenge. Numerous interisland air services allow you to go "island hopping."

Many pleasure trips are possible to the islands in the Firth of Clyde, Scotland's greatest yachting center. Dominated by the peak of Goat Fell, Arran is the largest of these Clyde islands.

1. Aviemore, Speyside, and Elgin

Aviemore is the winter sports capital of Britain, but it also enjoys mass popularity in summer, too. Aviemore Centre, previewed below, is Scotland's most modern holiday resort, an all-year, all-weather center, endowed with a multitude of outdoor pursuits, such as golfing, angling, skiing, or ice skating.

Those seeking a more traditional Scottish ambience will gravitate to one of the many Speyside villages, each with its own attractions and atmosphere. Ranking next to Aviemore, Grantown-on-Spey is another major center.

The Spey is the fastest flowing river in the British Isles, famed not only for its scenery but also for its salmon and ski slopes.

Finally, on your way to Inverness, you might care to stop off at the old cathedral city of Elgin.

Our first stop up the Spey follows.

NEWTONMORE: This Highland resort on Speyside is a good center for the Grampian and Monadhliath Mountains, and it offers excellent fishing, golf, pony trekking, and hill walking. Most motorists zip through it on the way to Aviemore, but sightseers may want to stop off and visit the **Clan MacPherson House & Museum** (tel. Newtonmore 332), at the south end of the village. Displayed are clan relics and memorials, including the Black Chanter and Green Banner as well as a "charmed sword," and the broken fiddle of the freebooter James MacPherson—a Scottish Robin Hood. Sentenced to death in 1700, he is said to have played the dirge "MacPherson's Rant" on his fiddle as he stood on the gallows at Banff. He then offered the instrument to anyone who would think well of him. There were no takers, so he smashed it. The museum is open from May to September on weekdays from 10 a.m. to noon and from 2 to 6 p.m.

A track from the village climbs past the Calder River to Loch Dubh and the massive Carn Ban (3087 feet), where eagles fly. Castle Cluny, ancient seat of the MacPherson chiefs, is six miles west of Newtonmore.

A good place to stay is the **Pines Hotel**, Station Road (tel. Newtonmore 271), on a hill overlooking the Spey Valley, with the Cairngorms, the Grampians, and the Monadhliath Mountains all in view. The resident proprietors, John and Fran Raw, offer seven rooms in their attractive stone house, all with heaters and hot and cold running water. They charge £8.50 ($16.58) for B&B per person in low season, £9.50 ($18.53) in high season (June, July, and August). I recommend taking the dinner, bed, and breakfast at £12 ($24.30) per person in low season, £13 ($25.35) in high season, because of the excellent cuisine. Such choices as trout, salmon, venison, beef, and lamb are offered, all locally supplied. All the food is home-cooked, and a substantial wine list is offered. The hotel has a pleasant residents' lounge where guests enjoy malt whisky and fine liqueurs. As its name implies, the hotel is in the middle of a pine grove.

KINGUSSIE: Your next stop along the Spey might be at this little summer holiday resort and winter ski center (it's pronounced King-youcie), the so-called capital of Badenoch, a district known as "the drowned land" because the Spey can flood the valley when the snows of a severe winter melt in the spring. There you can visit the six-acre **Highland Folk Museum**, on Duke Street, just off High Street, with its comprehensive collection of artifacts, including weaponry, bagpipes, and fiddles illustrating more than two centuries of Highland customs, plus the work of crafts people. Naturally, there are tartans. A furnished cottage with a mill and a farming shed stand on the museum grounds. It is open all year from 10 a.m. to 3 p.m. but stays open as late as 6 p.m. from April to October. The admission is 60p ($1.17) for adults, 20p (39¢) for children.

If you'd like to stop here instead of at Aviemore, I'd recommend the following establishments:

Scott's Hotel (tel. Kingussie 351) is more personal than the leading hotel at Kingussie, the Duke of Gordon. Scott's is really more of a B&B house, under the personal supervision of its resident proprietors, Mr. and Mrs. Patrick John

Cook, who are most hospitable. Rooms are comfortable and well appointed. One reader wrote, "Our stay here was the happiest in Scotland." The hotel has mostly double rooms, charging £15 ($29.25) to £18 ($35.10) for two persons for an overnight's stay, this tariff including a good dinner and a mammoth breakfast. The hotel has a residential license, and its cuisine is home-cooking, family style. Dinners are only £4.50 ($8.78), and bar lunches go for £2 ($3.90). In winter this hotel is very busy housing skiers.

If you're not dining at a hotel, try the **Wood'n Spoon,** 3 High St. (tel. Kingussie 488), on the A9, run by Mr. and Mrs. David Russell. It is considered by some the only "real pub" in the Highlands, and it serves excellent home-cooked food. For lunch (11:30 a.m. to 2:30 p.m.) there is a cold display and numerous hot dishes made to order. In the evening from 5:30 to 9:30 p.m. (Highland dining is early), a more extensive selection is available. Dishes offered are, as much as possible, made from local produce including fish from the Spey and venison from the nearby glens. The Russells also offer a large selection of homemade jams and chutneys for sale. Expect to pay £8 ($15.60) for a meal. Try their stovie potatoes (that is, diced potatoes with onions and minced beef), or else the venison casserole. Appetizers include smoked fish pâté, and there's always a soup of the day made from a real stockpot so it's always different. Desserts feature a Scottish trifle. A meal ranges in price from £6 ($11.70) to £8 ($15.60).

AVIEMORE CENTRE: This year-round holiday complex on the Spey was opened in 1966 in the heart of the Highlands, at the foot of the historic rock of Craigellachie. This rock was the rallying place for Clan Grant.

In winter, ski runs are available for both beginners and experts (four chair lifts and seven T-bar tows). Après-ski activities include swimming in a heated indoor pool 82 feet long, folk singing, table tennis, or else just relaxing and drinking in one of the many bars in the complex.

The ice rink is the second-largest indoor ice rink in Britain, with seven curling lanes and ice skating on a separate 4000-square-foot pad. At night younger people are attracted to the discos, although others seek out one of the Scottish nights, country dancing, supper dances, or else dancing in the large Osprey Ballroom with a sprung maple floor.

In summer, sailing, canoeing, pony trekking, hill walking, and mountain climbing, as well as golf and fishing, are just some of the many activities. The **Speyside Theatre,** seating 720, changes its film programs every day, and often is host to live shows and concerts. The center's shopping precincts cover a wide range of services, ranging from banking to hairdressing to car-rental offices.

Children always like to visit **Santa Claus Land,** set on a six-acre site, with a log cabin, toy factory, dollhouse, and a permanently frozen "North Pole" in peppermint colors. It also includes pony rides, cowboy trail, veteran cars, and a gingerbread house. Since it's Scotland, there is also Santa Shortbread.

Adjacent to Santa Claus Land is the **Highland Craft Centre,** where wood-carvers, potters, jewelers, weavers, blacksmiths, and engravers maintain the ancient skills and crafts of the Highlands. Their products are offered for sale.

Later, you can visit **Alan Keegan's Craft Shop,** where you can see 135 different kinds of scotch whisky from 65 different distilleries. He doesn't sell drinks. Collecting scotch whisky is his hobby. He's good at it, too, as his collection is considered the largest in Scotland. The most expensive is a Spring-bank whisky. Only one cask was ever produced.

Food and Lodging

The following hotels in the complex are recommended:

Strathspey (tel. Aviemore Centre 810681). The tower block of this hotel recalls the design of the traditional Scottish keep. The 90-bedroom, six-story hotel dominates the approach to Aviemore Centre. This well-organized hotel was built with a purpose—to provide a comfortable nest in both summer and winter for sports-minded holidaymakers. Its public lounges are large, with picture windows opening onto views of the Cairngorms.

Bedrooms come in a variety of styles and amenities, containing private bath and color TV. Some rooms, for example, are booked by families, as they contain bunk beds for children. Others are large, airy, and pleasantly decorated. Singles rent for £28 ($54.60), twins for £22 ($42.90) per person, including a full cooked breakfast, plus VAT. Coffee makers are provided, and there is suitable storage space for sports equipment. In addition, the hotel offers bars, a restaurant, plus a sauna bath, and there is, as well, ski instruction in winter.

Post House (tel. Aviemore Centre 810771) is one of the increasingly popular post houses belonging to Trusthouses Forte. (At a post house, you don't get room service, but every other amenity seems to be there.) The hotel is spread informally over a hillside, which often causes a split-level effect. The style here is most casual and informal, a holiday atmosphere. The spacious layout is balanced effectively by a warm color scheme. Picture windows and terraces open onto country views. The staff is most helpful and friendly. The bedrooms are all equipped with private baths, and some family rooms are available. Singles rent for £26 ($50.70), the tariff increasing to £35 ($68.25) in a double, including VAT and service.

You can drink in the Illicit Still Bar, with its shiny copper-topped tables and a copper whisky still, or else in the White Lady Bar, named after one of the Cairngorm ski runs. The Coffee Shop is for light meals, and the main restaurant is crowned by a tall pyramidal ceiling, from which a quartet of chandeliers hangs. The service and the food are first class. I'd highly recommend the roast ribs of Scottish beef. In the game room is a resident nanny—so, if you have children, you're free to hit the slopes without them.

Badenoch Hotel (tel. Aviemore Centre 810261) overlooks the Craigellachie Nature Reserve and its much-photographed rock. The hotel gives summer and winter holidaymakers a choice of both luxury and economy rooms. In this starkly modern Highland building, 60 rooms are streamlined and functional, all large size, all with the modern amenities. For these you pay £19 ($37.05) in a single, from £26 ($50.70) in a twin. But there are as well about 16 more "raw-boned" accommodations, with bunk-type beds and adjacent bathrooms and showers, going for £16.40 ($31.98) in a single, from £14.70 ($28.67) in a twin. The hotel is well stocked with facilities—a nursery, cocktail bar, disco, a game room, ski equipment, rover touring, a Norseman bar, even an attractive restaurant with a view of heather-covered grounds in summer or snow caps in winter.

Aviemore Chalets Motel (tel. Aviemore Centre 810618) offers comfortable, moderately priced double-story chalets with four units on each floor. Each chalet is centrally heated, carpeted, and adequately furnished with double-tiered bunks, two wash basins with hot and cold running water, private showers, toilets, and heated drying cupboards. Based on four persons in a room, the rate is from £6.60 ($12.87) per person. The reception chalet offers a snackbar, large lounge, and an attractive licensed lounge bar, the Craigellachie. For meals, the Pinewood is a cafeteria (self-service) restaurant, but in Das Stübel, an Austrian-style grillroom, friendly waitresses serve your meals. There are also seven self-catering apartments, each sleeping six, with cooking facilities and color television. The latest addition is a collection of eight deluxe twin-bedded rooms, with private shower, toilet, drying cupboard, color TV, and tea- and coffee-making facilities. These rent for £12.50 ($24.38) per person.

The Rank organization has the following offering:

Coylumbridge Hotel, Rothiemurchus (tel. Aviemore Centre 810661), suggests northern Sweden rather than northern Scotland. Christened by the Duke of Edinburgh, the Coylumbridge stands on 65 acres of tree-studded grounds, facing the slopes of the Cairngorms. The bedroom decor is chalet style, with pinewood used profusely. Cheerful appointments evoke both a summer and a winter holiday atmosphere. All rooms have private bathroom, color TV, radio, telephone, and coffee maker. Singles are £25 ($48.75) and doubles go for £38 ($74.10), including VAT.

The Coylumbridge is geared for the winter skier, with instruction and equipment available. In summer, pony-trekkers, fishermen, and golfers check in. On some nights there is disco dancing. It's really a self-contained unit, with a game room, hairdresser, 24-hour coffeeshop, plus a pleasant modern restaurant, the Epicure, offering a continental cuisine in the evening, a set dinner costing from £8 ($15.60). As well as the restaurant, the hotel has a Chieftain Grill, open seven days a week.

Another leading hotel in the area is the **High Range** (tel. Aviemore Centre 810636), standing above the main Perth–Inverness road. This chalet hotel enjoys a wooded setting of natural birch. From the windows of the single-story chalets, you look out onto the Rothiemurchus Forest and the snow- or heather-covered slopes of the Cairngorms.

In the main block, built of western red cedar, are housed a restaurant, a cocktail bar, and public lounges, all evoking the atmosphere of a ski lodge. The rooms are pleasantly and attractively decorated, offering single, double, twin, and family rooms, each with bath or shower and the majority with bidet. Singles range from £10 ($19.50) to £15 ($29.25), doubles from £20 ($39) to £30 ($58.50). Winter is higher. For dinner, add £6 ($15.60) per person to the room tariff. Rates include VAT, service, and a Scottish breakfast.

The restaurant at High Range is one of the best at Aviemore, serving dinner only, from 7:30 to 10:30 p.m. The attractive modern dining room draws a lively, youthful crowd to its capable bistro cooking. On my last visit, in summer, the vegetables were garden fresh, and the fish, salmon from the Spey, was exquisitely tender. The soups were interesting, too, and the service alert and efficient but definitely not rushed. Expect to pay £8 ($15.60) for the set dinner, or perhaps £12 ($23.40) if you're ordering à la carte and selecting some good-tasting French specialties (the chef, Peter Morris, does lamb especially well).

Fish 'n' Chips

At the **Happy Haggis Chip Shop,** Grampian Road (tel. Aviemore Centre 810430), you can get fish and chips to take out.

GRANTOWN-ON-SPEY: This holiday resort, with its gray granite buildings, stands in a wooded valley and commands splendid views of the Cairngorm mountains. It is a key center of winter sports in Scotland. Fishermen are also attracted to its setting, because the Spey is renowned for its salmon. Lying 34 miles southeast of Inverness by road, it was one of Scotland's many 18th-century planned towns, founded on a heather-covered moor in 1765 by Sir

James Grant of Grant, becoming the seat of that ancient family. Grantown became famous in the 19th century as a Highland tourist center, enticing visitors with its planned concept, the beauty of surrounding pine forests, the Spey River, and the mountains around it.

From a base here you can explore the valleys of the Don and Dee, the already-mentioned Cairngorms, and Culloden Moor, scene of the historic battle in 1746.

In hotels, the leading recommendations follow:

Grant Arms, The Square (tel. Grantown-on-Spey 2526). When Queen Victoria stayed here in 1860, she is reported to have said, "My bed was hard, but at least it was clean." Her old room with its four-poster is still there—and still clean—although not at all hard. Into its second century of hospitality, the Grant Arms is still the best place to stay at the resort. The hotel has been considerably modernized, yet it retains traditional touches. The color-coordinated bedrooms are well maintained, and some of them are deluxe in their appointments. At least 40 of the 55 units contain private baths, and another 15 come equipped with showers. In the peak season, the overnight charge ranges from £16 ($31.20) per person, based on double occupancy, this rate including a full Scottish breakfast. The inclusive daily rate, with all meals, begins at £34 ($66.30) per person daily. There's about a £3 ($5.85) daily supplement for single rooms.

At the Grant Arms a former ballroom has been converted into the Balmoral Restaurant, where tour groups often dine. It serves what is perhaps the best food in Grantown-on-Spey, not only the national dishes of Scotland, but fresh salmon and trout and venison in season. The service is expert even when the Balmoral seems crowded. Lunch is from noon to 2:30 p.m. and dinner from 7 to 8:45 p.m.

Craighlynne, Woodland Terrace (tel. Grantown-on-Spey 2597), is spacious and sprawling, standing on its own grounds overlooking the wooded valley and the hills beyond. Resident ski instructors—and equipment for renting—are on hand in winter, and in summer pony-trekkers check in. Accommodations come in a variety of styles, plumbing, and space. The bedrooms are pleasant and bright, well maintained, although some are somewhat spartan in decor. Most rooms have private bath or shower (only four without). Singles range in price from £12 ($23.40) to £17.50 ($34.13); doubles from £23.50 ($45.83) to £35 ($68.25)—including VAT, service, and a Scottish breakfast. The tartan bar with its peat fire is the center of après-ski life. In season there is entertainment every evening. The dining room is light and airy, serving good country fare, including such Scottish dishes as haggis and malt gravy.

ROTHES: A Speyside town with five distilleries, Rothes lies just to the south of the lovely Glen of Rothes. You can stay in Rothes and explore "The Whisky Trail," detailed earlier. It is but a short ride from here to **Dufftown,** containing at least seven distilleries, including **William Grant's Glenfiddich Distillery,** operating a reception room from March to October and showing visitors how malt whisky is produced.

After your career up "The Whisky Trail," **Rothes Glen Hotel** in Rothes (tel. Rothes 254) may appear to be a mirage. The old turreted house, with many of its original pieces of furniture, stands back from the road, surrounded by about 40 acres of fields with grazing Highland cattle—how can they see to eat with all that shaggy hair? This historic castle-like building was designed by the architect who built Balmoral. Inside the house a warm fire greets you. Bedrooms are well furnished and relaxing. Owner Donald Carmichael charges from £22.20 ($43.29) in a single without bath to £24.50 ($47.78) in a single with bath. Doubles with bath cost £45 ($87.75), including VAT and a full breakfast, although service is extra. The dining room is paneled in wood, and good wholesome meals are served in true Scottish tradition. The bar lunches are very popular, with a wide choice offered, including fried fresh haddock, a three-course meal with coffee going for about £4.80 ($9.36). A set dinner costs £9.75 ($19.01). A favorite specialty is mince, tatties, and skirlie (fried oatmeal and onions). This goes very well with roast pheasant for dinner, a local delicacy. Lunch is from 12:30 to 2 p.m. and dinner from 7 to 8:30 p.m. The hotel shuts down from mid-November to March 1.

FOCHABERS: This village, on the Inverness–Aberdeen road, dates from 1776 and was created as one of the early planned towns by John Baxter, for the fourth Duke of Gordon. Most of the buildings along High Street are protected and have not been changed much in 200 years. On the Spey, Fochabers is distinguished by its **Market Cross** and **Tower of Gordon Castle**.

The **Gordon Arms** (tel. Fochabers 820508) is a well-known 18th-century coaching inn, run by Mr. and Mrs. Pern, who are justly proud of the hospitality they offer wayfarers of today. Bedrooms are both traditional and modern, either in the old wing or the new. Singles without bath cost £30 ($58.50), rising to £33 ($64.35) with bath, and doubles cost from £31 ($60.45) to £36 ($70.20), including a full breakfast and VAT. Only 7 of the 17 rooms contain private baths. Fishermen are fond of the place, as revealed by the "salmon house" for the storing of rods and tackle.

The Perns are noted for their catering, and their food is some of the best along Speyside, including many national dishes Mrs. Pern cooks for her visitors, such as herring rolled in oatmeal and grilled. The Moray beef and salmon are rarely equaled. Sometimes continental dishes appear on the menu. A table d'hôte luncheon goes for £5 ($9.75) a set dinner for £11 ($21.45). Meals are served from 12:30 to 2 p.m. and from 7 to 9:30 p.m. It's important to make a reservation, incidentally. On the wall are paintings by local artists. If you're stopping on a summer afternoon, you might have tea in the garden.

ELGIN: The center of local government in the Moray district, an ancient royal burgh, this cathedral city lies on the Lossie River, 38 miles from Inverness by road. Once called the "lantern of the north," the **Cathedral of Moray** is now in ruins. It was founded in 1224 but almost destroyed in 1390 by the "wolf of Badenoch," the natural son of Robert II. After its destruction, the citizens of Elgin rebuilt their beloved cathedral, turning it into one of the most attractive and graceful buildings in Scotland. The architect's plan was that of a Jerusalem cross. However, when the central tower fell in 1711, the cathedral was allowed to fall into decay. But a faithful cobbler still respected its grandeur, and he became its caretaker. By the time of his death, in 1841, he had removed most of the debris that had fallen. Today visitors wander among its ruins, snapping pictures. Best preserved is the 15th-century chapter house.

Samuel Johnson and Boswell came this way on their Highland tour, reporting a "vile dinner" at the Red Lion Inn in 1773.

Hopefully, you'll fare better at the **Eight Acres Hotel**, Sheriffmill (tel. Elgin 3077), a modern, low-lying, motel-type unit, all 40 of its streamlined, functionally furnished rooms offering a private bath or shower. Standing on spacious grounds, the hotel lies on the western approaches to Elgin on the main A96 Inverness road. The public rooms are spacious, and the restaurant attracts a lot of motorists bound for Inverness. Rates in a single are £23 ($44.85), rising to £39 ($76.05) in a double, including breakfast. The hotel offers quite a bit of entertainment at various times of the year, not only a disco and dinner—dancing to a live band, but occasional Scottish folk evenings. However, entertainment is not on a regular basis.

Less expensive is the **Royal Hotel,** corner of Station Road and Moss Street (tel. Elgin 2320), a pleasant, privately owned hotel standing on its own grounds about a four-minute walk from the center of Elgin. It lies adjacent to the railway station and in close proximity to golf, bowling, swimming, and tennis courts. The owners, Mr. and Mrs. Iain Grant McAllister, ask £10 ($19.50) per person per night for bed and a traditional Scottish breakfast. There are ten rooms, each with hot and cold water, shaver points, gas fires, electric blankets, tea- and coffee-making facilities, and comfortable furnishings. High tea, with a variety of menus, is served between 5 and 7 p.m. at reasonable prices. Guests are invited to relax in the TV lounge, where a beautiful antique fireplace is a focal point. The double staircase with old-fashioned wrought-iron banisters and a mahogany rail is a striking feature leading from the front hall. The house was constructed in 1865 by James Grant, founder of the Glen Grant Distillery, who also built all the railways in northern Scotland. This three-story structure is surrounded by a garden and car parking space.

The McAllisters also have a beautifully situated **Hotel St. Leonards** around on the next street, Duff Avenue. It is slightly more expensive, as bedrooms with private baths are available.

FINDHORN: As you travel westward from Elgin to Forres, a turn to the right and then to the left will bring you to Findhorn, a tiny village whose name has become internationally known through its connection with the University of Light in Forres and as a gathering place for persons seeking a place where communal living and creativity have burgeoned. Actually, a caravan park just before you arrive in Findhorn is the center of these activities. Findhorn is on a unique tidal bay at the mouth of the River Findhorn, which makes it ideal for yacht racing, sailing, and waterskiing. Across the bay from Findhorn is the Culbin Sands, under which lies a buried village.

In Findhorn, a good place to stay is the **Culbin Sands Hotel** (tel. Findhorn 2252), which has panoramic views of the Moray Firth across to Ross and Cromarty, Caithness, Sutherland, Findhorn Bay, and the Culbin Forest. There are eight miles of sandy beach within two minutes' walk of the hotel. Owned by R. M. Sinclair, the hotel has 15 bedrooms, all with hot and cold water, renting nightly for £10.50 ($20.48) in a single, £18.50 ($36.08) in a double for B&B, including VAT. Children under 12 pay half price, and cots are available. The hotel boasts three well-stocked bars, a pleasant dining room, and a color TV lounge. Bar lunches are served seven days a week, and high teas and dinners are also offered to guests. The hotel, open all year, is a mile from the Findhorn Foundation and is the home of the Royal Findhorn Yacht Club. There are ample facilities for fishing, pony trekking, waterskiing, and sailing. It's best to reserve well in advance if you plan to visit Findhorn in the high season.

FORRES: This ancient burgh, mainly residential in character, stands on the Aberdeen–Inverness road, between Elgin and Nairn (ten miles to the east). Near the mouth of the Findhorn, it is one of Scotland's oldest towns. Once a castle associated with Duncan and Macbeth stood here. Nearby is **Sueno's Stone,** a 23-foot sandstone monolith containing 10th- and 11th-century Celtic carvings with intricate figures of men. **The Witches' Stone,** in the same vicinity, marks the site of the burnings of persons accused of witchcraft.

The best hotels include the **Ramnee,** Victoria Road (tel. Forres 72410), a charming house set back from the road and entered through well-kept gardens. Mrs. Jill Martini personally supervises the day-to-day running of the place, keeping it spotless. There is a lounge plus a pleasant dining room with wood panels and gleaming napery where meals are served. A full breakfast is included in the overnight cost, and dinner consists of simple grills, steak, and fish. There is as well a bar for the use of residents. The bedrooms are large and, where bathrooms have been added, the workmanship has been professional—you don't feel that your toilet has been carved out of a corner of your room. The charge is £15 ($29.25) per person, £2.50 ($4.88) extra for a room with bath. A set dinner costs from £8 ($15.60).

Built in an informal 19th-century style, the hotel is sited within a garden in the Laigh of Moray. To reach it, pull off the A96 Aberdeen–Inverness road on a clearly marked driveway leading to the hotel. The view from the front of the hotel is the richly wooded Cluny Hill of *Macbeth* witches fame. To the rear the view stretches out many miles over Findhorn Bay and the Culbin Sands Forest.

Nearby, the **Park Hotel,** Victoria Road (tel. Forres 72328), is very much the same sort of house. Set on spacious, well-kept grounds, it overlooks Findhorn Bay and the Moray Firth. The bedrooms are comfortable and well appointed, containing hot and cold running water. In season fresh fruit and vegetables come from the garden, the produce used in the hotel's kitchen. Mr. and Mrs. Leslie welcome guests, charging them £13.50 ($26.33), for B&B, including VAT, service, and a full Scottish breakfast. Bar lunches are served. The hotel also has a cocktail bar, drawing room, and television lounge.

2. Inverness and Loch Ness

After Glasgow, most motorists wanting to explore the Highlands head for Inverness, its ancient capital. From its doorstep, one can explore a romantic land of hills, lochs, and lots of myths.

Of course, the most popular excursion is to Loch Ness, where one sets up an observation point to await the appearance of "Nessie," the Loch Ness monster. But even if the monster doesn't put in an appearance, the loch itself has splendid scenery. I have a scattering of recommendations around the loch for those wanting to base there.

Finally, visitors going east may want to explore the old town of Nairn, and those adventurous readers wanting to venture into the forlorn and relatively uninhabited section of northwest Scotland may want to do so from a base at the old spa of Strathpeffer.

INVERNESS: The capital of the Highlands, Inverness is a royal burgh and seaport, at the north end of Great Glen, lying on both sides of the Ness River. It is considered the best base for touring the north. At the Highland Games, with their festive balls, the season in Inverness reaches its social peak.

The city has a new and luxurious theater complex on the bank of the Ness, the **Eden Court Theatre,** Bishops Road, which has a superb restaurant, bars, and an art gallery. Included in the repertoire are variety shows, drama, ballet, pop music, movies, opera, rock and folk concerts, and a summer-season traditional Scottish show with top stars. The theater, which opened in 1976, was constructed with an ingenious use of hexagonal shapes and has a horseshoe-shaped auditorium. Programs are advertised in most hotels and guest houses. The box office is open from 10:30 a.m. to 8 p.m., Monday through Saturday (tel. Inverness 221718).

Inverness is one of the oldest inhabited localities in Scotland.

On **Craig Phadrig** are the remains of a vitrified fort, believed to date from the fourth century B.C., where the Pictish King Brude is said to have been visited by St. Columba in A.D. 565. The old castle of Inverness stood to the east of the present Castlehill, the site still retaining the name **Auld Castlehill.** Because of the somewhat shaky geography of Shakespeare in dramatizing the crime of Macbeth by murdering King Duncan, some scholars claim that the deed was done in the old castle of Inverness while others say it happened at Cawdor Castle, 4½ miles to the south where Macbeth held forth as Thane of Cawdor.

King David built the first stone castle in Inverness around 1141. The **Clock Tower** is all that remains of a fort erected by Cromwell's army between 1652 and 1657. The 16th-century **Abertarff House** is now the headquarters of An Comunn Gaidhealach, the Highland association which preserves the Gaelic language and culture.

Inverness today has a castle, but it's a "modern" one—that is, dating from 1835. Crowning a low cliff of the east bank of the Ness, the **Castle of Inverness** occupies the site of an ancient fortress blown up by the Jacobites in 1746. The castle houses county offices and law courts. Mary Queen of Scots was denied admission to the castle in 1562, and she subsequently occupied a house on Bridge Street. From the window of this house, she witnessed the execution of her cousin, Sir John Gordon. For not gaining admission to the castle, she took reprisals, taking the fortress and hanging the governor.

Opposite the town hall is the **Old Mercat Cross,** with its **Stone of the Tubs,** an Inverness landmark said to be where women rested their washtubs as they ascended from the river. Known as "Clachnacudainn," the lozenge-shaped stone was the spot where the early kings were crowned.

Inverness Museum and Art Gallery, at Castle Wynd (tel. Inverness 37114), contains displays of the culture of the Highlands, including silver and an exhibition called "The Life of the Clans." Hours are weekdays from 9 a.m. to 5 p.m.

West of the river rises the wooded hill of **Tomnahurich,** known as "the hill of the fairies." It is now a cemetery, and from here the views are magnificent.

In the Ness are wooded islands, linked to Inverness by suspension bridges and turned into parks.

From Inverness, you can visit **Culloden Battlefield,** six miles to the east. This is the spot where Bonnie Prince Charlie and the Jacobite army were finally crushed at the battle on April 16, 1746. A cairn marks the site on Drummossie Moor where the battle raged. **Leanach Cottage,** around which the battle took place, still stands and was inhabited until 1912. A path from the cottage leads through the Field of the English, where 76 men of the Duke of Cumberland's forces who died during the battle are said to be buried. Features of interest include the **Graves of the Clans,** communal burial places with simple stones bearing individual clan names alongside the main road and through the woodland; the great memorial cairn, erected in 1881; the **Well of the Dead,** a single stone with the inscription: "The English Were Buried Here"; and the huge **Cumberland Stone** from which the victorious "Butcher" Cumberland is said to have reviewed the scene. The battle lasted only 40 minutes; the prince's army lost some 1200 men out of 5000 and the king's army 310. A visitors' center and museum are open all year.

Between Inverness and Nairn, also about six miles to the east of Inverness, are the **Stones of Clava,** one of the most important prehistoric monuments in the north. These cairns and standing stones are from the Bronze Age.

Back in Inverness, we'll investigate—

Food and Lodging

Culloden House, at Culloden Moor, six miles from Inverness (tel. Inverness 790461), is a Georgian mansion with extensive gardens and parkland. It stands on the ruins of the Renaissance castle in which Bonnie Prince Charlie slept the night before the last great battle on British soil, the Battle of Culloden. Superbly isolated, it is perfect for a relaxed Highland holiday. Public rooms, furnished in the grand style, are suitably spacious and comfortable. The bedrooms are cheerful, cozy, and agreeably furnished. All 21 of them contain private baths. Depending on your room assignment, singles pay from £34.50 ($67.28), doubles, from £45 ($87.75) to £69 ($134.55), the latter double tariff for a suite—plus service and VAT.

The hotel maintains pleasantly traditional ideas of personal service. The food, in my opinion, is of exceptional quality, and it's served against an impressive backdrop of refinement and elegance. Simple and complex dishes are virtually flawless, and the finest of fresh local ingredients are used. Ordering à la carte, expect to pay about £15 ($29.25) per person.

Station Hotel, Academy Street (tel. Inverness 31926), adjacent to the railway station, offers a high standard of first-class service, comfortable accommodations, and well-prepared food. The occupants of those baronial Highland mansions like to stop here when they're in Inverness on shopping or social expeditions, gathering for somewhat lively chats in the conservatory lounge, there ordering their tea and scones. Grandly Victorian, the bedrooms are tastefully decorated and welcoming, costing from £27.75 ($54.11) to £31 ($60.45) in a single, from £32 ($62.40) to £47 ($91.65) in a double. The majority of rooms contain fully equipped private baths.

The dining room is one of the finest in Inverness, serving good-quality Scottish dishes, plus some excellently cooked continental favorites. Courteous waiters create a friendly atmosphere. Lunch is served from 12:30 to 2 p.m. and dinner from 7 to 9 p.m. A table d'hôte evening meal costs £8 ($15.60) but expect to pay £12 ($23.40) if you're ordering à la carte, sampling the French specialties.

Dunain Park, 2½ miles southwest of Inverness (tel. Inverness 30512), stands in six acres of garden and woods, between Loch Ness and Inverness. This 18th-century house was opened as a hotel in 1974, and is furnished with fine antiques, china, and clocks, allowing it to retain its atmosphere of a private country house. Although Dunain Park has won its fame mainly as a restaurant, it does offer six bedrooms, four of which contain private baths and one of which has an antique four-poster bed. The rates range from £30 ($58.50) to £50 ($97.50) in a double or twin, plus VAT and service. A host of thoughtful details and pretty, soft furnishings have gone into the bedrooms. The breakfast served here is exceptional—in fact, the homemade marmalade was the best I've ever tasted, and you can buy some to take with you.

You can order a simple lunch (in the garden, if you prefer). Snack meals are served from 12:30 to 1:30 p.m. But it is at dinner that the chef really delivers, offering a set meal for about £15 ($29.25), fully inclusive. This menu changes daily, depending on the availability of high-quality produce, fish, and meat. The chicken with ginger and honey and cod's-roe pâté are particular favorites. The restaurant and hotel are closed from mid-November until mid-March.

Kingsmills Hotel, Culcabock Road (tel. Inverness 37166), is an 18th-century house of much charm set in four acres of woodland garden only a mile from the center of Inverness. Once a private mansion, it stands adjacent to an 18-hole golf course, and the hotel has its own private squash courts. Angus and Lillian MacLeod have carefully maintained a country-house atmosphere, with a small, pleasantly informal, and most hospitable Highland staff. Furnishing throughout the hotel is of a high quality, and all 54 bedrooms have private bath, radio, color TV, and telephone. Single room rates range from £25 ($48.75) to £35 ($68.25), and doubles go from £30 ($58.50) to £48 ($93.60), according to location and season. Bed-sitting rooms and family rooms are also available. The rates include a full Highland dinner, offered from 7 to 10 p.m. nightly and costing from £8.50 ($16.58). The fish dishes are exceptionally good. Bar lunches and snack meals offer a wide choice, including Scottish fare. Centrally heated, the hotel remains open all year.

Mercury Motor Inn, Nairn Road, at the junction of the A9 and the A96 (tel. Inverness 39666), is without surprises, each uniform room well furnished with a high degree of comfort, an ideal center for those who want to tour the Highlands. Accommodations come with private baths, toilets, color TV, radio, and tea- or coffee-making facilities. In all, 108 rooms are offered, ranging in price from £30 ($58.50) to £35 ($68.25) in a single and from £40 ($78) to £46 ($89.70) in a double. Breakfast is extra. The inn offers a conically shaped grill and two fully licensed bars.

Glen Mhor, 10 Ness Bank (tel. Inverness 34308), looks out onto the River Ness. A house of gables and bay windows, it is a hospitable, family-run hotel with an enduring charm in spite of its creaky quality. The Manson family has provided many thoughtful touches, such as a log fire blazing in the entrance lounge. From many of the individually styled bedrooms, you have views of the river. The staff is informal and friendly. The hotel offers seven single rooms and 20 doubles. Some of these are family rooms, and most of the units contain private bathrooms, along with such amenities as a baby-listening service and color TV. The B&B rate in a single is £20 ($39), rising to £24 ($46.80) in a double. The half-board tariff is £26 ($50.70) per person. In a restaurant overlooking the river, both table d'hôte and à la carte menus are served. You are likely to enjoy fish caught by the local fishermen, along with Scottish lamb and prime steaks. The wine list is considered one of the best in Scotland. There's a charming "Parisian bistro" called Nico's, which is open for food and drinks all day in the summer months. The hotel is a good center for angling, golf, horseback riding, and hunting.

Redcliffe, 1 Gordon Terrace (tel. Inverness 32767), is a small hotel set on its own grounds, commanding a peaceful perch above the Ness and the castle, yet lying within a three-minute walk of the main shopping district. Your hosts, Mr. and Mrs. West, have completely modernized the interior, but have kept the traditional stone facade intact. The bedrooms are pleasantly decorated and have hot and cold running water. The B&B rate is £12.50 ($24.38) per person, increasing to £14 ($27.30) if you request a private bath. VAT is extra. In a spacious, comfortable lounge, guests gather to watch TV. At the hotel is a permanent exhibition of the work of local artists, with all art for sale. The hotel also serves excellent Highland dinners with pheasant, haggis, venison, and salmon (the latter should be requested in advance when making a reservation). My latest à la carte meal, including coffee later in the lounge, cost about £7.50 ($14.63) per person.

In the Environs

North of Inverness is a fertile peninsula known as the **Black Isle** because it is seldom whitened by snow. Here tropical plants flourish, and **Cromarty,** at the northeast tip, has fine sandy beaches. The cottage there where Hugh Miller, noted geologist, was born in 1802 is now a geological museum. **Fortrose,** an ancient town facing the Moray Firth, has a sheltered bay for yachting.

Dingwall is a town in Easter Ross district near the mouth of the River Conon. The town arms, a starfish, are displayed on the tolbooth (originally a booth for collecting tolls), dating from 1730. In front of this is the shaft of a former Mercat Cross, and beside it is an iron gate of the old town jail.

Strathpeffer, about six miles west of Dingwall, is a good center for touring Easter Ross, where the countryside is dominated by the 3433-foot summit of Ben Wyvis. If you'd like to stop over, I have the following recommendation:

Rosslyn Lodge (tel. Strathpeffer 281) is a stone hotel dating from 1898 and standing on its own well-maintained grounds. Family run, it is personally supervised by the MacLeods. Comfort, good food, and a friendly atmosphere attract clients to its 15 well-furnished bedrooms, each with hot and cold running water. A reader, G. O. Beckwith of Mount Waverley, Australia, wrote: "Deathly quiet, tremendously respectable, and with a somewhat older clientele —it was hard to believe it wasn't 1920." B&B is provided for £8.50 ($16.58) per person, including VAT. One of the owners, Patricia MacLeod, does the cooking, serving local game and meat produce whenever possible, and vegetables fresh from the garden. Dinner is £6 ($11.70).

Heading back toward Inverness, an interesting stop is at **Beauly,** 12 miles west of the city, where you can visit the ruins of a Valliscaulian priory built in 1230. On the south bank of the River Beauly southwest of the town is **Beaufort Castle,** a 19th-century baronial mansion which is the seat of the Frasers of Lovat whose ancestor was the "Lovat of the Forty-five." The original seat of the Lovats was Castle Dounie, built about 1400, but it was destroyed by "Butcher" Cumberland after his victory at Culloden.

ULLAPOOL: Northwest of Inverness, on an arm of the sea called Loch Broom, the little town of Ullapool is an embarkation point for travelers crossing The Minch, a section of the North Atlantic separating Scotland from the Outer Hebrides. The road from Inverness takes you through the wild Northwest Highlands, and a car-ferry from Ullapool will deposit you in Stornaway on Lewis, one of the Western Isles.

Altanaharrie Inn, at Ullapool, Wester Ross (tel. Dundonnell 230), is one of those places that you feel you should not tell anyone about, as it is small (only three bedrooms). But it is one of those places which calls for inclusion because of its uniqueness and total integration into the life of the region. The Altanaharrie was once a drovers' inn on the banks of Loch Broom. There is no access by road so guests are brought over the loch by private launch. Tell them what time you are arriving at Ullapool, and they'll come and meet you.

Once you're landed, Fred Brown greets you with a warm log fire in a bar for a dram before dinner which is likely to consist of locally caught seafood. Much meat, local venison, and fish such as trout and lobster are obtained locally. They make their own bread, and they like to know beforehand if you are eating "in" so that they can cater accordingly.

Overnight will cost you £20 ($39) per person, including dinner, VAT, and breakfast.

Fred also has canoes and small dinghies available free, or else motorized dinghies and sailing craft for rent at £10 ($19.50) a day. He also operates

Summer Isles Charters for cruising among the offshore islands or, for the more ambitious, to Skye or the Outer Hebrides, with or without skipper. This is a serious business, and you should write to Fred before you embark on such a venture, giving details of your experience. Otherwise he may not let you take a boat out.

NAIRN: A favorite family seaside resort on the sheltered Moray Firth, Nairn is a royal burgh, lying at the mouth of the Nairn River. Its fishing harbor was constructed in 1820, and golf has been played here since 1672, as it still is today. A large uncrowded beach, tennis, and angling draw a horde of vacationers in summer.

At **Cawdor Castle** (tel. Cawdor 666), to the south of Nairn, you encounter 600 years of Highland history. Since the early 14th century it's been the home of the Thanes of Cawdor. The castle has all the architectural ingredients you associate with the medieval: a drawbridge, an ancient tower (this one built around a tree), and fortified walls. The severity is softened by the handsome gardens, flowers, trees, and rolling lawns. As I mentioned earlier, even the Scots can't agree as to where Macbeth, who actually was made Thane of Cawdor by King Duncan, committed his foul deed of murdering the king—at Cawdor or in the castle which once stood on Auld Castlehill in Inverness, if at all. The castle is open to the public from 10 a.m. to 5:30 p.m. every day from May 1 to October 3. Admission is £1.50 ($2.93) for adults, 75p ($1.46) for children. It's a member of "The Grand Tour of Scotland" group of Historic Houses.

Food and Lodging

Clifton, Viewfield Street (tel. Nairn 53119), reflects the dynamic personality of J. Gordon Macintyre, the owner of this honey-colored sandstone, vine-covered Victorian mansion. The Clifton has been owned by the same family probably longer than any other hotel in the north of Scotland. Fully licensed, it stands on the seafront, three minutes from the beach and golf links.

Mr. Macintyre has spent a lot of time, trouble, and money in decorating the house, often with interesting prints, and in selecting the furnishings, as exemplified by the Clifton's old-fashioned parlor. The collection of pictures, paintings, prints, engravings, etchings, and drawings is unusual and extensive, not only in public rooms, the drawing room, the writing room, and the bar and restaurant, but also in the long corridor. The bedrooms on the first floor are better equipped, each pleasantly appointed, while those on the second floor are more spartan, yet the view from this higher perch seems to compensate. Singles rent for £16.50 ($32.16), doubles from £30 ($58.50). All bedrooms have baths, except one which has a shower; some, however, do not have toilets. Musical and theatrical performances are often staged in the hotel.

The Clifton also serves the best food in Nairn, in fact, it's some of the best in the north of Scotland. The cooking is often in the hearty Highland tradition —that is, game pie, pigeons in wine, lamb in a mustard sauce—although French specialties also tempt. The bar serves snacks at lunchtime. Dinner hours are from 7 to 9:30, when an à la carte order is likely to run between £7 ($13.65) and £10 ($19.50). Bar snacks at lunchtime go for around £2.75 ($5.36) for an ample plateful. Breakfast is very special. There is no menu as such. Since the hotel is stocked with all the necessary ingredients, guests are asked what they would like cooked. The ultimate aim is to try to make guests feel they are staying in a well-run private house. The emphasis is on good taste, without making things too overly refined or too "precious." The hotel and restaurant are shuttered from November until February.

Newton, Inverness Road (tel. Nairn 53144), a castle-like hotel, stands just outside town in an attractive park of 35 acres, offering views across sweeping lawns and the golf course to the sea. Considered one of the finest of the "manor house" hotels of Scotland, it is spacious and sumptuous, drawing a clientele likely to include everybody from a prime minister to a Glasgow industrialist. Prices have a pedigree, too: a single rents for £27 ($52.65) and a double goes for £52 ($101.40), including VAT, service, and a full breakfast. It's also possible to stay here on the half-board rate, at £32 ($62.40) per person, plus 10% for service. The public rooms are furnished with taste, and the Moray Firth, viewed on a day when the sun is shining brightly, forms a spectacle of beauty from many of the Newton's windows. The bedrooms have many fine appointments— sedate, comfortable, although unpretentious. All 34 of them contain private baths. There is a high standard of maintenance and personal service.

The **Windsor Hotel,** Albert Street (tel. Nairn 53108), is a fine sandstone building which has been renovated and refurbished to good effect. The resident proprietors, Mr. and Mrs. Charles Woolley, see to it that the hotel provides a comfortable family atmosphere and first-class cuisine. The hotel is centrally heated, and each bedroom contains its own basin with hot and cold running water. There are numerous bathrooms, showers, and toilets throughout the hotel. The color TV lounge, residents' lounge, and fully licensed cocktail bar add to the guests' enjoyment. A single without bath costs £12.65 ($24.67), rising to £15 ($29.25) with bath. A bathless double costs £25.50 ($49.73), going up to £30 ($58.50) with bath, including VAT, service, and a full breakfast. Special rates are allowed for children. A four-course dinner costs £8.50 ($16.58). The hotel is close to centers of transportation and sports facilities. It is open all year.

DRUMNADROCHIT: This pleasant little hamlet lies about a mile from Loch Ness at the entrance to Glen Urquhart. The ruined **Urquhart Castle,** one of Scotland's largest castles, is a mile and a half southeast on a promontory overlooking Loch Ness. The chief of Clan Grant owned the castle in 1509, and most of the existing building dates from that period. In 1692, the castle was blown up by the Grants to prevent its becoming a Jacobite stronghold. It is here at Urquhart Castle that sightings of the Loch Ness monster are most often reported.

In the vicinity stands the **Lewiston Arms,** Lewiston, near Drumnadrochit (tel. Drumnadrochit 225), an old whitewashed coaching inn, lying just off the principal road in the village of Lewiston. Many motorists prefer to stop off here instead of going on to Inverness. The inn offers only one single and seven doubles, none with private bath. The tariffs are £10 ($19.50) in a single, £18 ($35.10) in a double. You might ask for the dinner, bed, and breakfast rate of £16 ($31.20) per person. Bedrooms are simply but adequately furnished. Outside is an attractive garden. In all, it's a good center for exploring the Loch Ness district. The place is owned and run by Nicholas and Helen Quinn, a team with a spotless little inn off the fast A82, right beside the castle.

FORT AUGUSTUS: This Highland touring center stands at the head (the southernmost end) of Loch Ness. The town took its name from a fort named for the Duke of Cumberland. Built after the 1715 Rising, the present Benedictine Abbey stands on its site.

In accommodations, it offers the **Inchnacardoch Lodge** (tel. Fort Augustus 6258), a family-run, two-star hotel in a beautiful setting overlooking Loch Ness. From one of the bedroom windows, you can monster-watch. The old-fashioned house of many gables offers comfortable and well-equipped bedrooms, charging from £9.40 ($18.33) to £10.80 ($21.06) in a single, from £18.80 ($36.66) to £21.60 ($42.12) in a double, including a full breakfast, service, and VAT. Of the 17 bedrooms, 6 contain private baths. You can enjoy mellow scotch whisky in the lounge bar and then succulent Scottish steak in the fully licensed Highland restaurant, where a dinner with some choices averages about £6 ($11.70). Bar lunches cost from 85p ($1.66) to £3 ($5.85). Open all year, the hotel is owned and run by a former London architect, Alan Anderson, and his wife, Val, who enjoy meeting their guests as much as they hope their guests enjoy their stay. Music for dancing is provided on Friday and Saturday nights in season.

INVERGARRY: A Highland center for fishing and deer stalking, Invergarry is noted for its fine scenery. It, too, is a good center for exploring Glen More and Loch Ness. At Invergarry is the beginning of the road through the West Highland glens and mountains, forming one famous "Road to the Isles" that terminates at Kyle of Lochalsh.

Near Invergarry, you can visit the **Well of the Heads,** on the west side of Loch Oich near its southern tip, erected in 1812 by MacDonnell of Glengarry to commemorate the decapitation by the family bard of seven brothers who had murdered the two sons of a 17th-century chief of Clan Keppoch, a branch of the MacDonnell Clan. The seven heads were washed in the well before being presented to the chief of the MacDonnells at Glengarry.

The **Glengarry Castle Hotel,** at Invergarry (tel. 254), stands on the River Garry, which runs into Loch Oich. The castle hotel is privately owned and run by Mr. and Mrs. MacCallum and Mrs. Paterson. Their 100-year-old house lies on extensive grounds and has recently been modernized to provide comfort to the passerby or to be a pleasant base for a week or so of country holiday with fishing, tennis, walking, and rowing. On the grounds are the ruins of **Glengarry Castle,** the historic seat of the MacDonnells.

There are two spacious lounges where drinks can be served to residents, and the dining room offers excellent meals made from local produce. They charge £13 ($25.35) per person in a bathless room, £15.25 ($29.74) per person with bath. Lunch costs from £4.75 ($9.26); dinner, from £6.50 ($12.68); and tariffs quoted include VAT and service.

SPEAN BRIDGE: This village is a busy intersection of the Fort William–Perth and Fort William–Inverness roads, as well as having daily train service to Fort William, Glasgow, and London, and bus service to Inverness and Fort William. Two miles outside the town, in Glen Spean, is the striking **Commando Memorial** by Scott Sutherland which the Queen Mother unveiled in 1952. In this area many commandos were trained during World War II. Numerous war movies have been filmed here.

On the outskirts of the village on the A86 going toward Newtonmore and Perth is **Coire Glas** (tel. Spean Bridge 272), a motel-style guest house with 15 bedrooms. Mr. and Mrs. MacFarlane have added onto the back of their one-story home, to come up with an attractive and convenient place for visitors to stay overnight or for long periods. All the rooms are equipped with hot and cold running water, and ample bathroom facilities are provided. Three bedrooms have shower and toilet en suite. The MacFarlanes charge £7.50 ($14.63) per person per night for B&B. Dinner costs from £5 ($9.75), and the house is licensed to sell alcohol with meals. A lunch will be packed for you upon request. Spean Bridge is a central area for touring the loch country, and from Coire Glas, looking across a wide, grassy lawn, you can see Ben Gurry, which is a part of the Ben Nevis range.

3. Fort William and Lochaber

Fort William, the capital of Lochaber, is the major touring center for the western Highlands. Wildly beautiful Lochaber, the area around Fort William, has been called "the land of bens, glens, and heroes."

Dominating the area is **Ben Nevis**, Britain's highest mountain, rising 4418 feet. In summer when it's clear of snow, there's a safe path to the summit. Fort William stands on the site of a fort built by General Monk in 1655, which was pulled down to make way for the railroad. This district is the western end of what is known as Glen Mor—the Great Glen, geologically a fissure which divides the northwest of Scotland from the southeast and contains Loch Lochy, Loch Oich, and Loch Ness. The Caledonian Canal, opened in 1847, linked these lochs, the River Ness, and Moray Firth. It provided sailing boats a safe alternative to the stormy route around the north of Scotland. Larger steamships made the canal out of date commercially, but fishing boats and pleasure steamers still use it. Good roads run the length of the Great Glen, partly following the line of General Wade's military road. From Fort William you can take steamer trips to Staffa and Iona.

The ruins of **Old Inverlochy Castle,** scene of the famous battle in 1645, can be reached by driving on the A82 two miles north of Fort William. At a point just one mile north of Fort William is **Glen Nevis,** one of the most beautiful in Scotland.

About 15 miles west of Fort William, on the A830 toward Mallaig, at Glenfinnan at the head of Loch Shiel is the **Glenfinnan Monument,** which marks the spot where Bonnie Prince Charlie unfurled his proud red-and-white silk banner on August 19,1745, in the ill-fated attempt to restore the Stuarts to the British throne. The monument is topped by the figure of a kilted Highlander. At a Visitors' Centre one may learn of the prince's campaign from Glenfinnan to Derby and back to the final defeat at Culloden.

FORT WILLIAM: The name evokes redcoats billeted in rough barracks to keep the Highlanders of Lochaber under control. Fort William today is a busy tourist town on the shores of Loch Linnhe. Although it stands in the shadow of Ben Nevis, the mountain can't be seen from town. While the town is most often used as a touring center, in Fort William itself you can visit the **West Highland Museum,** on Cameron Square, containing all aspects of local history, especially the 1745 Jacobite rising, plus sections on tartans and folk life. The museum is open Monday to Saturday, September to June, from 9:30 a.m. to 1 p.m. and from 2 to 5 p.m.; in July and August its hours are from 9:30 to 9 p.m. Admission costs 30p (59¢) for adults, 10p (20¢) for children.

Where to Stay

In Fort William, I'd recommend the following accommodations, beginning first with a deluxe suggestion:

Inverlochy Castle (tel. Fort William 2177) is another one of the places where Queen Victoria stayed. In her time it was newly built (1863), a Scottish baronial mansion belonging to Lord Abinger. The monarch claimed in her diary, "I never saw a lovelier or more romantic spot." I do not wish to detract from that long-ago sentiment. In fact, Inverlochy Castle today remains one of the premier places of Scotland for food and accommodations.

Against the scenic backdrop of Ben Nevis, the castle hotel has a mood inside of elegance and refinement, luxurious appointments and antiques, artwork and crystal, plus a profusion of flowers. Danish-born Mrs. Hobbs, the owner, is a delight, equally at home in welcoming a prime minister or an American couple from the Midwest.

Only 14 bedrooms, each with private bath, are offered, and all of them are beautifully furnished. The prices reflect the opulence, however—from £65 ($126.75) in a single, from £90 ($175.50) in a double, including VAT, a full Scottish breakfast, and service.

The cuisine is one of the finest in all of Scotland. Every dish emerging from the kitchen of Mr. Ken MacPhee is cooked to order and served on silver platters. Sparkling crystal and fine china are placed on hand-carved polished tables where the fortunate guests enjoy such fare as salmon from the Spean or crayfish from Loch Linnhe, even produce from the hotel's own garden. Mr. MacPhee is a natural-born cook, an unusually gifted one at that, adding a creative touch to food yet instinctively preserving its natural flavor. His orange soufflé Grand Marnier makes for spectacular dining. Only dinner is served, and reservations are mandatory. It is likely you'll spend about £21 ($40.95) per person, including tax and service charge, before leaving the table a most satisfied diner. The hotel and restaurant are closed from mid-November to March.

Alexandra (tel. Fort William 2241) is a familiar sight, a hotel with tall gables and formidable granite walls, so common in this part of the Highlands. But the hotel is no antiquated mansion—rather, it has been completely modernized, offering 76 double rooms and 11 singles that are pleasantly and attractively furnished. The rate in a bathless double or twin is £26 ($50.70), rising to £37 ($72.15) in a double or twin with bath. A single, depending on the plumbing, ranges in price from £15 ($29.25) to £23 ($44.85). These tariffs include VAT, service, and a Scottish breakfast. Service and housekeeping standards are good. The chef makes excellent use of fresh fish, and the wine cellar is amply endowed. The vegetables are simply cooked with enjoyable results. Bar lunches range from £1.50 ($2.93) to £2 ($3.90) per dish, a set dinner costing £7.60 ($14.82).

Croit Anna (tel. Fort William 2268) lies on the A82, the Inverness–Glasgow road, 2½ miles southwest of Fort William. Somewhat like a Scottish motel, it commands views of loch and hills. Croit Anna is a good-size establishment, containing a total of 115 bedrooms, and is owned and run by the same Watt family which designed and built it on a croft that was in the family's possession for more than 250 years. At present it's run by Mr. Watt's married daughter, Elizabeth Morgan, and her family. The rooms are pleasant, the service competent. Don't come here expecting luxury, just a good "average standard." A single rents for £11 ($21.45), a double for £21 ($40.95), and all units contain private baths.

Open all year, the hotel offers a large dining room serving good food, plus a lounge bar, a resident's lounge, and even a first-floor panoramic lounge with a dance floor. A set dinner costs £7.50 ($14.63), although a four-course à la carte meal is likely to run about £10 ($19.50).

Where to Dine

Like its counterpart in Oban, **McTavish's Kitchen** and the **Tweeddale Restaurant,** under the same management, on the High Street (tel. Fort William 2406), is dedicated to preserving the hearty Scottish cuisine. The kitchen is a self-service cafeteria, which is open from mid-May until the end of October. Light meals are served throughout the day and evening. A homemade soup of the day is offered, although you may prefer poacher's broth or even pheasant consommé with burgundy. Main courses include Scottish crab with hot cheese and smoked salmon with chips and brown bread. Smoked fish, traditionally cooked in milk, is always featured. You can dine well for around £4.50 ($8.78).

If you'd prefer waitress service, try the Tweeddale, but first have a drink at the adjoining Laird's Bar, a snug tavern with photographs of a Scottish laird. The licensed restaurant is open from mid-May until the end of September, seven days a week. Specialties include haggis and neeps, Scotland's national dish, Loch Fyne kippers (smoked herring), Scottish crab with hot cheese sauce and duchesse potatoes, when available, and a deep-dish apple pie with thick cream. A budget special, including a homemade soup, a main course (served with vegetables), and a dessert, is priced at £4.25 ($8.29). However, for the "Taste of Scotland" menu, with the main specialties, the price is £7 ($13.65), including as a conclusion a Drambuie syllabub.

A feature of the restaurant is folk cabaret, offered Easter and every evening from mid-May until the end of September from 8:45 to 10:45 p.m., with singers, a piper, and a Highland dancer. Children are welcome. Admission is £1.45 ($2.83) for adults, 80p ($1.56) for children.

ONICH: On the shores of Loch Linnhe, this charming little village lies to the north of the Ballachulish Bridge. It's a good center if you're taking the western route to Inverness, or going to Skye and Fort William. My favorite hotels in the area follow.

Creag Dhu Hotel (tel. Onich 238) was once the country home of Lady McPherson and takes its name from the rallying cry of her clan. Now a family-run hotel, it lies between Ben Nevis and Glencoe, with expansive lochside and mountain views. The loch views are of prawn-filled Linnhe and Leven. Creag Dhu is an imposing country home with modern additions. More than half the rooms contain private baths. B&B rates range from £14 ($27.30) per person in low season to £16 ($31.20) per person in high season, plus another £2.50 ($4.88) supplement for each room with a private bath. The half-board rate runs from £20 ($39) per person in low season to £23 ($44.85) in high season, including a full breakfast, service, and VAT. Ceilidhs, evenings of Scottish music and song, as well as talks and slide shows are among events held at the hotel. Special musical weekends take place in the spring and autumn, and there are courses in painting, spinning, and other crafts. Available locally are such activities as boating, sailing, waterskiing, and aqualung diving, along with good sea and freshwater fishing, pony trekking, riding, golfing, swimming, and tennis. Receiving guests from April to October, the hotel has a loyal repeat clientele.

Onich Hotel (tel. Onich 214) is handsomely perched on the shores of Loch Linnhe, commanding views of the Ardgour and Glencoe Mountains and the Firth of Lorne. Its gardens slope down to the water. Under family management, the hotel definitely reflects a personal touch, both in its welcome of real Highland hospitality and in the appointments of its bedrooms and lounges. The hotel is owned by Ian and Ronald Young, brothers who have run the inn since 1964. They have a very loyal band of guests who return over and over again. Their cookery enjoys a good reputation for its consistency. Ronald cooks, incidentally, and Ian looks after the administration of the hotel. The bright, airy bedrooms have been modernized—25 in all, renting for £12.50 ($24.38) per person for B&B. The bed, breakfast, and evening meal rate is £20 ($39) per person. Rooms do not contain private baths, however. The hotel attracts the athletic-minded, as it's a center for walking, climbing, loch bathing, putting, fishing, sailing, and pony trekking. The cuisine is of a good standard, backed up by a fine wine list. Guests gather either in the Clan cocktail bar or the Deerstalker lounge bar. The hotel is open only from April to October.

BALLACHULISH: This small village enjoys a splendid scenic position on the shores of Loch Leven at the entrance to Glencoe. The Ballachulish Bridge links North and South Ballachulish. A good center for touring the western Highlands, the village has the following recommended hotel:

Ballachulish Hotel (tel. Ballachulish 239) stands right on the shores of Loch Leven, at the point where hills split Leven from Loch Linnhe. Built in the style of a Scottish manor house, it offers hospitality, warmth, relaxation—just what you're seeking in a Highland hotel. The bedrooms have a high standard of comfort and convenience, although they vary considerably in style and plumbing. A single without bath goes for £15 ($29.25), rising to £19 ($37.05) with bath. A double without bath rents for £28 ($54.60), increasing to £36 ($70.20) with bath, these tariffs including VAT, service, and a full breakfast. Receiving guests from April to October, the hotel also serves good food, handsomely presented, with fresh ingredients. There are very good bar snacks, ranging in price from 60p ($1.17) to £3 ($5.85). The fare offers everything from sandwiches to pizzas, from fish and fresh chips to hot and cold meat dishes. Set dinners go for £7 ($13.65), although you are likely to spend £8 ($15.60) if you order à la carte. Residents from nearby gather in the hotel's bars, mingling with foreign visitors (and by that I mean the English). From the windows of the hotel you can look out onto views of hill and loch. The staff will arrange boat trips on the lochs or fishing expeditions.

GLENCOE: On the shores of Loch Leven, near where it joins Loch Linnhe, the Ballachulish Bridge now links the villages of North and South Ballachulish, at the entrance to Glencoe. The bridge saves a long drive to the head of the loch if you are coming from the north, but many visitors enjoy the scenic drive to Kinlochleven to come upon the wild and celebrated Glencoe from the east.

Glencoe runs from Rannoch Moor to Loch Leven between some magnificent mountains, including 3766-foot Bidean nam Bian. Known as the "Glen of Weeping," Glencoe is where, on February 11, 1692, Campbells massacred MacDonalds—men, women, and children—who had been their hosts for 12 days. Although massacres were not uncommon in those times, this one shocked even the Highlanders because of the breach of hospitality. When the killing was done, the crime of "murder under trust" was regarded by law as an aggravated form of murder, and carried the same penalties as treason.

The glen, much of which now belongs to the National Trust for Scotland, is full of history and legend. A tiny lochan is known as "the pool of blood" because by its side some men are said to have quarreled over a piece of cheese, and all were killed.

This is an area of massive splendor, with towering peaks and mysterious glens where you can well imagine the fierce battle among the kilted Highlanders to the skirl of the pipes and the beat of the drums.

Splurge into History

Almost where Glen Etive joins Glencoe, under the jagged peak of Buchaille Etive Mor dominating the road (A82), lies the **King's House Hotel** (tel. King's House 259), several miles from the village of Glencoe. A building has stood here since the time of the Jacobite Rising of 1745, when it was required to accommodate troops on their way south from Fort William. It is now a center for skiing and attracts thousands from far and near.

Believed to be the oldest licensed inn in Scotland, **King's House Hotel** has been enlarged and modernized. Whichever way you drive through Glencoe, from the rolling east or the dramatic and narrow west, the hotel lying to the north of the road, is a welcoming outpost. Simple yet comfortable bedrooms go for £12 ($23.40) per person if bathless, rising to £13.75 ($26.81) per person with bath, including breakfast.

A set dinner is £4.50 ($8.78), and they'll pack you a lunch at £1.75 ($3.41) for your next day's touring. Lunchtime snacks in the bar, ranging in price from £1.20 ($2.34) to £2.10 ($4.10), include plaice or scampi with chips and a large plate of salad. You can also order hot meat pies. Sandwiches vary according to the filling, and all portions are large and very satisfying. The bar is decorated with antlers and paintings of the Glen and surrounding area.

A ski lift is almost opposite the hotel. The Buachaille Etive Mor guards Glencoe's eastern end. This mountain provides a challenge for climbers and was the training ground for Sir John Hunt and the party he took to the top of Everest in Coronation year. This is great climbing and walking country, and rescue techniques evolved and taught here have been widely used.

Besides access from the Glasgow–Inverness highway, guests at the King's House Hotel can be met at the Bridge of Orchy railway station by arrangement. **Glen Orchy**, to the south, is well worth a visit, too, with the wild river and mountain scenery being beautiful and photogenic. It was the birthplace of the Gaelic bard Duncan Ban MacIntyre, whose song, "In Praise of Ben Doran," is considered a masterpiece.

In Glencoe Village

As you turn away from Loch Leven to enter the historic glen, you will find a number of accommodations available in the village of Glencoe, including—

Glencoe Hotel (tel. Ballachulish 245) is a spruce and stucco building with a slate mansard roof, dominating its area. In the hotel are 13 rooms, including one with a double bed and a private bathroom, one twin-bedded with a private bath, while the other doubles, twins, and singles have hot and cold running water. The hotel charges from £9 ($17.55) off-season to £11.50 ($22.43) in high season per person for B&B. Snack lunches are available in all public rooms, and dinner is offered from £5.50 ($10.73). VAT is included in all charges. The hotel is open all year.

MALLAIG: This small fishing village is a good touring center for the western Highlands and the islands. Steamers call here for the Kyle of Lochalsh, the Isle of Skye, the Outer Hebrides, and the sea lochs of the northwest coast. At the tip of a peninsula, Mallaig is a bustling little fishing village, and it is surrounded by moody lochs and hills. The distance between Morar and Mallaig is just three miles.

In the village you can find food and lodging at the **West Highland Hotel** (tel. Mallaig 2210), Mallaig's major hotel, situated above the port, its bedroom windows looking upon the harbor and the Isle of Skye. The hotel is antiquated, but it offers good old-fashioned comfort and pleasant Highland hospitality. Only a handful of rooms contain private baths, however. Depending on room assignment, singles rent for £14.50 ($28.28) to £18.50 ($36.08), and doubles for £23 ($44.85) to £33 ($64.35) including breakfast. The bed, breakfast, and evening meal rate is £22.50 ($43.88) to £25 ($48.75) per person. The hotel is open from May to September.

Less expensive is the **Marine Hotel,** near the railway station and ferry terminal (tel. Mallaig 2217), a family-owned operation which has passed to the third generation. The hotel has been brought up to date, offering some rooms with private baths, hot and cold running water in all rooms, heaters, shaving points, and tea- and coffee-making facilities. The cost is £9 ($17.55) in a single, from £16 ($31.20) in a double, although you'll pay £2 ($3.90) extra for a private bath. Unlike the West Highland, the Marine is open all year. There is a small garden below. The location is above shops and a bank.

4. Kyle of Lochalsh and Skye

From the Kyle of Lochalsh you can take a ferry to the mystical Isle of Skye, off the northwest coast of Scotland. The island has inspired many of the best loved and best known of Scottish ballads such as "Over the Sea to Skye" and "Will Ye Not Come Back Again." On the 48-mile-long island, you can explore castle ruins, duns, and brochs, enjoying a Highland welcome. For the Scots, the island will forever evoke images of Flora Macdonald, who conducted Bonnie Prince Charlie to Skye. She disguised him as Betty Burke after the Culloden defeat.

Once on Skye, you'll find ferry service back to Kyle or to Mallaig from Armadale. The Armadale ferry transports cars, but the service is less frequent than the one to Kyle. If you're planning to take your car, reservations are recommended.

Caledonian MacBrayne, The Pier, Gourock, near Glasgow (tel. Gourock 34664), runs ferry services to Skye and to Mull. The company also offers inclusive tours for people and cars to island-hop, using their services between islands. This is an ideal opportunity to visit places well away from the beaten track. The information office at Gourock is most helpful, and someone there will assist you in planning a trip if you wish to make up your own journey.

The largest island of the Inner Hebrides, Skye is separated from the mainland by the Sound of Sleat on its southeastern side. At Kyleakin, on the eastern end, the channel is only a quarter of a mile wide and thus the ferry docks there. Dominating the land of summer seas, streams, woodland glens, mountain passes, cliffs, and waterfalls are the Cuillin Hills, a range of jagged black mountains. The Peninsula of Sleat, the island's southernmost arm, is known as "The Garden of Skye."

DORNIE: This small crofting village on the road to the Isle of Skye is the meeting place of three lochs—Duich, Long, and Alsh. On a rocky islet stands **Eilean Donan Castle,** Wester Ross at Dornie, eight miles east of Kyle of Lochalsh on the A87. This romantic castle was built in 1220 as a defense against the Danes. In 1719 it was shelled by the British frigate *Worcester.* In ruins for 200 years, it was restored by Colonel MacRae of Clan MacRae in 1932 and is now a clan war memorial and museum, containing Jacobite relics, mostly with clan connections. It is open April to September 30, daily, including Sunday, from 10 a.m. to 12:30 p.m. and from 2 to 6 p.m., charging 50p (98¢) for admission.

South of Dornie and Eilean Donan Castle is Shiel Bridge. From here, an "unclassified road" leads to **Glenelg**, after a twisting climb over Ratagan Pass with a fine view of the mountain range known as the **Five Sisters of Kintail,** which is dominated by Sgurr Fhuaran, 3505 feet high. In summer a car-ferry crosses the Sound of Sleat to Skye. It was from Glenelg that Dr. Johnson and James Boswell crossed to Skye in 1773. In Gleann Beag, two miles to the southeast, stand two of the best preserved Iron Age brochs on the Scottish mainland—**Dun Telve** and **Dun Troddan.** Brochs are stone towers with double walls, probably built more than 2000 years ago by the Picts for protection against raiders. The walls of the two brochs are more than 30 feet high.

Just outside Dornie, across Loch Long and at the end of Loch Duich, the **Loch Duich Hotel,** Ardelve, near Kyle of Lochalsh (tel. Dornie 213), is among my favorite hotels, in a dream location overlooking one of the Highland's most photogenic castles, Eilean Donan. It's now owned by Rod and Gerry Stenson, a young couple who have brought their enthusiasm and energy to the place. They lived for two years on the island of Rhum, running the castle and guest house there where they learned to be self-sufficient.

Gerry cooks—really cooks! She turns out bread, oatcakes, cakes, scones, shortbread, pâtés, broth, and even makes yogurt from their own goat's milk as well as cream cheese from the same herd. Vegetarians are welcome—just give them fair warning, as Gerry is adept in balancing a suitable diet and producing appetizing meals.

Behind the hotel is a pub, reached through the hallway or outside-and-round-the-corner. It's well patronized by locals and guests alike in the evenings.

At lunch, bar snacks include a hot dish costing around £1 ($1.95) a portion, along with a substantial soup and homemade bread, plus freshly made, well-filled sandwiches.

The hotel has a small lounge and bar where you can wait for dinner at £6.50 ($12.68). It's likely to be a magnificent meal of fresh chowder or pâté, followed by local venison (melt in your mouth) or perhaps a brown trout farmed by a shy American in a forgotten loch, 1½ pounds in weight at the end of the season and superb. Rod's worry is that in winter they can't always provide fresh vegetables in this wild part of the island. But you can rest assured that everything that possibly can be is fresh.

Bedrooms are simple, and many overlook Eilean Donan and the loch. Including an enormous freshly cooked breakfast with porridge and eggs and bacon—you name it—they charge only £12 ($23.40) per person.

They also have a boat which you can rent to go fishing (Gerry will cook your catch for supper). For those so inclined, the National Trust for Scotland Ranger Service, 5 Charlotte Square, Edinburgh EH2 4DU (tel. Edinburgh 226-5922), will arrange for you to make the six-mile guided hike through some of Scotland's wildest country along the Seven Sisters Kintail. Advance reservations are necessary, as this is no country stroll, and you must be suitably clad and fit.

From Dornie, it is a short drive to the—

KYLE OF LOCHALSH: This popular center for touring the western Highlands is also a good jumping-off point to the islands. A car-ferry leaves for Kyleakin on the Isle of Skye. There is no need to book in advance. The journey is only ten minutes, costing 65p ($1.27) for each person, £2.30 ($4.49) for a standard car. The ferry shuttles back and forth all day, and you will have plenty of time to drive the length of Skye in a day, returning to the mainland by night if you want to. If that is your intent, you might register at:

Lochalsh Hotel (tel. Kyle 4204) occupies a choice situation right beside the loch where the ferry to Skye sails in front of the windows. Rooms have been modernized, a single renting from £17.65 ($34.42) to £22 ($42.90), a double from £27.75 ($54.11) to £35.25 ($68.74), including a Scottish breakfast, although VAT and service are extra.

Lunch is served in the Ocean Bar, a choice of snacks including grilled mussels in garlic, smoked fish mousse, homemade soup, fisherman's kebab, grilled herrings in oatmeal, omelets, and a hot dish of the day. These dishes will cost from £1 ($1.95) to £2.75 ($5.36) per portion, the latter for the cold fresh salmon and salad. Homemade apple pie with cream is another 80p ($1.56).

If you happen to be on the "Road to the Isles" on a nippy day, try afternoon tea here with pancakes and scones, covered with jam, along with buttered toast and pastries, served with coffee or tea for around £1.50 ($2.93) per person. This will amply fill you and revive your spirit.

A set dinner at £7.75 ($15.11) is likely to include a choice of four appetizers such as mackerel and horseradish sauce, followed by a selection of five main dishes, including grilled or roast meat, a fish dish, plus a choice from the dessert trolley. The chef does a number of interesting house specialties—scallops, collops, and venison, all at around £7 ($13.65) per dish.

BALMACARA: Those planning to stay in the Kyle of Lochalsh district, taking the car and passenger ferry to Skye, may prefer a more peaceful oasis for a day or two. In the Balmacara estate, now the property of the National Trust for Scotland, the **Balmacara Hotel** (tel. Balmacara 283) is a quiet, unassuming choice. On the road along Balmacara Bay, facing the Cuillins of Skye, it has been preferred by many readers, although I personally have not stayed there. Guests are received all year and charged from £12.50 ($24.38) without bath, £15.50 ($30.23) with bath in a single, from £30 ($58.50) to £34 ($66.30) in a double, including breakfast. An evening meal will cost from £8 ($15.60). A fishing party can be arranged.

A hotel courtesy bus can be arranged to meet you at Kyle Railway Station when coming from Inverness, or at the Skye ferry terminal.

ISLE OF SKYE: Skye is the largest of the Inner Hebrides, 48 miles long and between 3 and 25 miles wide. It is separated from the mainland by the Sound of Sleat (pronounced Slate). There are many stories as to the origin of the name, Skye. Some believe it is from the Norse "ski," meaning a cloud, while others say it is from the Gaelic word for winged. There are Norse names on the island, however, as the Norsemen held sway for four centuries before 1263. Overlooking the Kyle is the ruined Castle Maol, once the home of a Norwegian princess.

For those who want to overnight or else spend a longer holiday on the island, I offer the following suggestions, scattered in the various hamlets. However, in summer be sure to reserve in advance, as accommodations are extremely limited.

There are coach tours three or four times a week in summer from Kyleakin where the ferry lands to Dunvegan Castle or to the north end of the island. They generally start at 10 a.m., returning to Kyleakin around 6 p.m., so you need not take your car across with you. Telephone Kyle 4328, **Clan Coaches,** for further information.

If you're staying at Portree in the center of the island, **W. J. Sutherland,** Glenbrittle, Skye (tel. Carbost 267), operates a round trip from Portree to

Sligachan, then Carbost where the Talisker Whisky Distillery is. Then it goes on to Portnalong and Fiskavaig on the west coast where there is a sandy beach for a day of relaxation before the return journey at 5 p.m. The round trip costs £2.50 ($4.88).

Kyleakin

The ferry from Kyle of Lochalsh docks at this tiny waterfront village. For those seeking a quiet, well-kept place to stay, I'd recommend:

Dunringell Hotel (tel. Kyle 4180) sits in 4½ acres of extensive lawns in which rhododendrons, azaleas, and other flowering shrubs provide a riot of color from March to July. Dunringell is a spacious structure, built in 1912, with large bedrooms and public rooms. Mr. and Mrs. MacPherson charge £10.35 ($20.18) per person for B&B. For half board, the tariff is £16.10 ($31.40) per person. Both a smoking and no-smoking lounge are maintained for guests. For those who wish to participate, the MacPhersons hold a short worship service in one of the lounges each evening. Some of the bedrooms are in the lodge, a stone building about 100 yards from the main house.

Broadford

This town is the meeting point for the ports of Armadale, Kylerhea, and Kyleakin.

Broadford Hotel (tel. Broadford 204) is a venerated old inn dating from 1611, when it was established by Sir Lauchlin MacKinnon. It was here that a descendant of his first came up with the secret recipe for Drambuie liqueur, now a symbol throughout the world of Highland hospitality.

The Broadford has seen a lot of changes since those days, and it's been completely modernized and brought up to date, both in its bedrooms and public facilities. The inn lies by the waters of Broadford River, and guests are allowed to fish for salmon and trout. If you'd like this congenial center for exploring the southern part of Skye, you can request a double room for £28 ($54.60) to £32 ($62.40), the latter with bath, or a single for £15 ($29.25) to £19 ($37.05), depending on the plumbing. If you're traveling with a child, it costs £10 ($19.50) extra to have a bed added to the room. Rooms are comfortable and unpretentious.

The old inn offers good Scottish cooking, making fine use of the local produce. A dinner goes for £7.50 ($14.63). You can stop in for a drink in the cocktail bar. The inn lies four minutes from the Skye airfield, where there is direct daily service to Glasgow. Nearby are the ruins of the farmhouse where Samuel Johnson and his companion, Boswell, spent a night on their tour of the Highlands.

Sligachan

Sligachan Hotel (tel. Sligachan 204) stands in the middle of the islands on its own moorland at the head of a beautiful loch, affording views of water and hills. As such, the hotel is the most convenient center from which to explore the entire island. Climbers who love "to go up in the heather" book its 23 simply furnished bedrooms, only nine of which contain private baths. From April to October, they cost from £16 ($31.20) to £18.50 ($36.08), including a big Scottish breakfast that often features kippers and porridge. The meals are excellent, comprising, for example, homemade soups, steak-and-kidney pie with a flaky crust, salmon, followed by fresh fruit and cream, ending with good coffee. A complete dinner costs from £8.50 ($16.58). At Sligachan guests in their classic tweeds (which have been well broken in) mingle freely in good companionship, and the talk is of fishing for trout and salmon and of motorboat excursions through the Outer Hebrides.

Portree

Skye's capital, Portree, is the port for steamers making trips around the island and linking Skye with the 15-mile-long island Raasay. Sligachan, nine miles south, and Glenbrittle, seven miles farther southwest, are centers for climbing the Cuillin (Coolin) Hills.

Royal Hotel (tel. Portree 2525) stands on a hill facing the water and is said to have offered hospitality to Bonnie Prince Charlie during his flight in 1746. In less dramatic and rushed circumstances, you can book one of its comfortable bedrooms, the preferred ones opening onto the sea. A double- or twin-bedded room costs £23 ($44.85) if bathless, increasing to £31 ($60.45) with private bath. Singles, if bathless, rent from £12 ($23.40) nightly, rising to £16 ($31.20) with bath, these tariffs including VAT, service, and a full Scottish breakfast. A set lunch ranges from £3.75 ($7.31) to £4.25 ($8.29). Dinner is from £7.25 ($14.14). The hotel is open all year.

Rosedale Hotel, Beaumont Crescent (tel. Portree 2531), lying in one of the more secluded parts of Portree, opens directly onto the sea. Owned and run by the Andrews family since 1950, it is a warm and friendly place. Offered are 20 bedrooms decorated in the modern style, some of which have private baths. The Rosedale is open only from May to October, charging £12.50 ($24.38) per person in a bathless room, the rate increasing to £15 ($29.25) per person with bath. These tariffs include a big Scottish breakfast. In a new lounge, you can be served a good range of Highland malt whiskies. The food is good, too.

Uig

This village is on Trotternish, the largest Skye peninsula, and ferry port for Harris and Uist in the Outer Hebrides. It is 15 miles north of Portree and 49 miles from Kyle of Lochalsh. **Monkstadt House,** a mile and a half north, is where Flora MacDonald brought Prince Charles, in the guise of a girl named Betty Burke, after their escape flight from Benbecula. In **Kilmuir** churchyard, five miles north, Flora was buried, wrapped in a sheet used by the prince. Her grave is marked by a Celtic cross.

Uig Hotel (tel. Uig 205) has been furnished with warmth, imagination, and creativity. In homelike comfort, guests are welcomed and shown to the lounge with its pleasant, harmonious colors. The hotel stands on a hillside overlooking a small bay and a tiny fishing harbor. The food, excellently prepared Scottish fare, is served in a cheerful dining room with a view of the bay. The 24-room hotel comes equipped with private bath or shower in every chamber. Rates range from £15.50 ($30.23) to £19.50 ($38.03) for singles, £31 ($60.45) to £39 ($76.05) for doubles, including a full Scottish breakfast and VAT. Half-board rates go from £23 ($44.85) to £27 ($52.65) per person. The hotel is open from April to the end of September.

Dunvegan

The village of Dunvegan grew up around **Dunvegan Castle,** the principal man-made sight on the Isle of Skye, seat of the chiefs of Clan MacLeod who have lived there for 700 years. The castle, which stands on a rocky promontory, was once accessible only by boat, but now the moat is bridged and the castle open to the public. It holds many fascinating relics, including a "fairy flag."

It is reputed to be the oldest inhabited castle in Britain. It is open from March 31 to mid-May from 2 to 5 p.m.; from mid-May to the end of September, from 10:30 a.m. to 5 p.m.; and for most of October from 2 to 5 p.m. It is closed all day Sunday. Adults pay £1 ($1.95) for admission; children, 50p (98¢).

The **Black House museum**, four miles from Dunvegan on the Glendale road (tel. Glendale 291), contains implements and furniture of bygone days and has a peat fire burning throughout the day. A replica of an illicit whisky still can be seen behind the museum, which is open daily from 10 a.m. to 7 p.m.

There's also a pottery and silversmith in Glendale, along with a watermill and an art gallery specializing in local views. **Skye Venture Cottage Industry,** 18 Holmisdal, Glendale-by-Dunvegan (tel. Glendale 316), specializes in hand-and machine-made sweaters, waistcoats, hats, and scarves, with a wide range of Arran, Fair Isle, and Icelandic garments. The store is open Monday to Saturday from 10 a.m. to 6 p.m.

At **Trumpan,** nine miles north of Dunvegan, are the remains of a church which was set afire in 1597 by MacDonald raiders while the congregation, all MacLeods, were inside at worship. Only one woman survived. The MacLeods of Dunvegan rushed to the defense, and only two MacDonalds escaped death.

Atholl House Hotel (tel. Dunvegan 219) lies right in the village of Dunvegan, only half a mile from Skye's most popular sightseeing attraction, Dunvegan Castle. The owner of Atholl House, Ena McPhie, a Gaelic singer, welcomes guests seeking a B&B accommodation from April to October. She charges from £8 ($15.60) per person, including a hearty Scottish breakfast that will fortify you for the day. She offers only 12 rooms, including a trio rented to families. The rooms are clean and pleasantly furnished. There is a spacious, comfortable lounge which adds to the comfort.

Skeabost Bridge

Eastward from Dunvegan is Skeabost Bridge, with an island cemetery of great antiquity. The graves of four Crusaders are here.

Nearby is the **Skeabost House Hotel** (tel. Skeabost Bridge 202), one of the most comfortable, refreshing, and inviting country homes of Skye, receiving paying guests from May 1 to mid-October. Thoroughly modernized, it is interesting architecturally with its dormers, chimneys, tower, and gables, everything a weather-worn beige. Inside, the taste level is high, with wood paneling and carpets. Once a private estate, it has been converted into a lochside hotel, standing on beautiful grounds that in summer are studded with flowering bushes. The location is 35 miles from Kyle of Lochalsh and 5 miles from Portree.

Sportsmen are attracted to the hotel, gathering in the firelit lounge for a mellow scotch whisky. The atmosphere is of hardy tweeds with the distinctive aroma of a good cigar. The loch outside is well stocked with salmon and trout.

Of the 27 handsomely furnished rooms, 11 contain private baths. Singles are accepted at a rate of £13.70 ($26.72) to £17.50 ($34.13), and doubles cost from £11 ($21.45) to £17.50 ($34.13) per person, including a big Scottish breakfast. The Scottish fare, including smoked salmon, is served on fine china and elegant silver, a dinner costing from £8 ($15.60).

5. Oban, Mull, and District

Oban (meaning "small bay") is the great port for the Western Isles and a center of Gaelic culture. It is the gateway to Mull, largest of the Inner Hebrides; to the island of Iona, the cradle of Scottish Christianity; and to Staffa, where Fingal's Cave inspired Mendelssohn to write his Hebridean overture. The ferries to the offshore islands run only twice a day until summer; then there are cruises to Iona from early June to late September. For information about island ferry services to Mull, Iona, and the Outer Hebrides, get in touch with **MacBraynes Steamers** at their office in Oban (tel. Oban 62285).

Back on the mainland, I'll include a number of colorful sites, such as Fort Appin and Inveraray, for those who prefer to soak up atmosphere away from the major towns.

OBAN: One of Scotland's leading coastal resorts, the bustling port town of Oban is set in a sheltered bay that is almost landlocked by the island of Kerrera. A yachting center and small burgh, it lies about 50 miles south of Fort William.

From Pulpit Hill in Oban there is a fine view across the Firth of Lorn and the Sound of Mull. Overlooking the town is an unfinished replica of the Colosseum of Rome, built by a banker, John Stuart McCaig, in 1897–1900 as a memorial to his family and to try to curb local unemployment during a slump. Its walls are two feet thick and from 37 to 40 feet high. The courtyard within is landscaped and the tower is floodlit at night. It is known locally as **McCaig's Folly.**

In September the Oban Highland Games are held, with massed pipe bands marching through the streets. The Oban Pipe Band plays regularly throughout the summer, parading up and down main street. Paul W. Ware, New Providence, Pennsylvania, writes: "During evening, the promenade is traversed by little dogs pulling their masters who are wearing tweed jackets and smoking pipes. But the town also attracts young people."

On the island of Kerrera stands **Gylen Castle,** home of the MacDougalls, dating back to 1587.

Near the little granite **Cathedral of the Isles,** one mile north of the end of the bay, is the ruin of the 13th-century **Dunollie Castle,** seat of the Lords of Lorn who once owned a third of Scotland.

You can visit **Dunstaffnage Castle,** 3½ miles to the north, which was believed to have been the royal seat of the Dalriadic monarchy in the eighth century. The present castle was probably built in 1263. "The Stone of Destiny," now in Westminster Abbey, was kept here before its removal to Scone.

In Oban, Gaelic is taught in schools as a "leaving certificate subject."

Where to Stay

As a holiday resort, Oban has a number of good hotels and guest houses within easy reach of the seafront and the piers from which cruises to the offshore islands can be booked.

Alexandra, Esplanade (tel. Oban 62381), is a stone hotel with gables and a tower, plus a Regency-style front veranda, enjoying a sunny perch on the promenade. From its public rooms, you can look out onto Oban Bay. Two sun lounges overlook the seafront. The bedrooms are substantial and pleasing, offering comfort and conveniences at a rate in a single that ranges from £17.65 ($34.42) to £20.65 ($40.27), in a double from £27.30 ($53.24) to £34.50 ($67.28), including VAT, service, and a full breakfast. Of the 60 bedrooms, nearly half contain private baths. The restaurant, serving good food, also opens onto the panorama. Bar lunches are available for around £2.50 ($4.88), a complete dinner in the evening averaging around £8 ($15.60). The hotel is open from April to October.

Lancaster, Esplanade (tel. Oban 62587), is distinguished by its attractive pseudo-Tudor facade. On the crescent of the bay, it commands views from its public rooms of the islands of Lismore and Kerrera, even the more distant peaks of Mull. Open all year, the hotel is managed by its resident owners, Mr. and Mrs. J. T. Ramage, who welcome you to one of their well-furnished bedrooms, charging from £13 ($25.35) in a single, from £13 also per person in a double, including breakfast. For bed, breakfast, and evening meal, the charge is £18 ($35.10) per person nightly. A number of rooms offer central heating, and a few have private baths or showers. The fully licensed Lancaster is the only hotel in Oban featuring a heated indoor swimming pool, a sauna bath, and a solarium.

Wellpark Hotel (tel. Oban 62948) is a substantial stone house with a gabled bay window, positioned on the seafront and commanding views of the bay and the islands of Kerrera, Mull, and Lismore. It's also one of the best bargains in Oban. Mr. and Mrs. R. B. Dickison welcome you, charging £13 ($25.35) per person nightly for bed, dinner, and a full Scottish breakfast, based on double occupancy. Their rooms—simple, pleasantly comfortable—contain hot and cold running water and are equipped with electric blankets. The hotel receives guests from April to October, and there is full central heating.

Where to Dine

McTavish's Kitchens, George Street (tel. Oban 63064), like its cousin in Fort William, is dedicated to preserving the local cuisine. Downstairs is a self-service restaurant providing à la carte breakfasts from 9 to 11:30 a.m., and light meals starting at 11:30 a.m. and served throughout the day and evening, seven days a week. There are, in addition, Laird's Bar, opening onto a beautiful view over Oban Bay, and the Mantrap Bar with a "real Mantrap."

The licensed second-floor restaurant has a more ambitious Scottish and continental menu with higher prices. It's open only from mid-May until the end of September, from 9 to 11 p.m. Specialties include a poacher's broth, and haggis and neeps (Scotland's national dish). Main courses are genuinely Scottish, too—smoked salmon with brown bread, Scottish crab with hot cheese sauce and duchesse potatoes, and Loch Fyne kippers (smoked herring). The way to have many of these dishes is to order a "Taste of Scotland" menu, costing £7 ($13.65) per person. For dessert on this menu, you can order a Drambuie syllabub. If you're on a strict economy binge, ask for the "Budget Special" at £4.25 ($8.29) per head, which includes, say, a homemade soup, filet of haddock, and apple pie and fresh cream.

A feature of the restaurant is folk cabaret, with singers, a piper, and a Highland dancer, 8:30 to 10:30 p.m., offered at Easter and each evening from mid-May to the end of September. Children are welcome. Admission is £1.05 ($2.05) for adults, 60p ($1.17) for children. Some of the best folk and contemporary music in Scotland is heard here. Recordings of these concerts are available at the restaurant. The bagpipes provide haunting melodies, new and old.

On the Outskirts

The Isle of Eriska Hotel, Ledaig, Connel, near Oban, is Strathclyde (tel. Ledaig 371), is a glorious Victorian house which welcomes you at the end of a winding drive. From the main road it takes about five minutes to reach the house, which must remind one of a clan castle with the house flag flying strongly from the tower. A magnificent front door leads to the paneled entrance hall, with a log fire to back up the central heating.

A wide staircase leads to the spacious bedrooms which are well furnished with wax-polished furniture, comfortable beds, and warm, cheerful draperies. Modern bathrooms with showers as well as tubs have been installed, and thoughtful touches include nail brushes, large cakes of soap, and bath crystals. Fresh fruit is presented, and conveniences include phone and radio. Dinner, bed, and breakfast is around £45 ($87.75) per person, including VAT and service. The Isle of Eriska is owned and very personally run by Mr. and Mrs. Robin Buchanan-Smith.

Settled in, you're expected to wear jacket and tie for dinner, as you descend for a drink in the bar before embarking upon a six-course meal. You get no choices, except for appetizers. The main course is nearly always a roast joint. If you're worried, you have only to discuss your diet with the chef, who will arrange something else. Nonresidents are charged £13.50 ($26.33) per person for dinner. Afterward, you repair to the lounge or the hall for coffee.

Breakfast is an adventure, a step back into the past. Silver dishes on the sideboard contain kippers, haddock, bacon, sausages, kidneys, tomatoes, eggs, you name it. If it's not usually there, it will be by the next morning. Try porridge the proper way, that is, cooked slowly for more than 12 hours on the stove.

After breakfast, you can charter the seven-ton Bermudian rig yacht for fishing or visiting the islands on the loch. Or else you can ride a Highland pony across the countryside, play tennis, or just walk in the beautiful gardens. It's also possible to visit the home farm from whence much fresh produce comes to the kitchens.

Lunch is an informal buffet meal of cold meats, salads, and cheese, costing £5.50 ($10.73). On Sunday a traditional lunch is served, and that evening supper is a relaxed meal set out on the sideboard for you to help yourself. Morning coffee and afternoon tea are served free to residents.

MULL: The largest island in the Inner Hebrides, Mull is rich in legend and folklore, a land of ghosts, monsters, and the wee folk. Over log fires that burn on cold winter evenings, the talk is of myths and ancient times. The island is wild and mountainous, characterized by sea lochs and sandy bars.

The capital is **Tobermory,** lying on a bay guarded by **Duart Castle,** restored in 1912 and still the seat of the once-fiery MacLeans, who shed much blood in and around the castle during their battles with the Lords of the Isles. In the bay—somewhere—lies the *Florencia,* the Spanish galleon that went down laden with treasure. Many attempts have been made to bring it up, but so far all of them have failed.

To the southeast, near Salen, are the ruins of **Aros Castle,** once the stronghold of the Lords of the Isles.

On the far south coast at Lochbuie, **Moy Castle** has a water-filled dungeon. The wild countryside of Mull was the scene of many of David Balfour's adventures in *Kidnapped* by Robert Louis Stevenson.

Roads on Mull are few and can be quite rough. If you're taking a bus tour, the driver often has to stop to let sheep and cattle cross.

From Oban you can take one of the car-ferry services to Mull, operated by **Caledonian MacBrayne.** For information in Oban, telephone Oban 62285. In Tobermory, on Mull, you can reach the steamer office by telephoning Tobermory 2017. The cost of taking a car to Mull from Oban is about £16 ($31.20) for a single journey. A round-trip excursion is around £20 ($39). Passengers are charged £1.70 ($3.32) for a single trip or £2.75 ($5.36) for a round-trip excursion. There are reductions in the off-season and also an "Island Hopscotch" for those who wish to visit several islands.

Always make a reservation if you're planning to spend the night on Mull.

I'll follow with a selection of hotels scattered across the island, beginning first at—

Tobermory

Western Isles (tel. Tobermory 2012) has a beautiful location above the harbor, looking out upon the bay. The hotel is plain and simple, rather conventional, although the atmosphere is made most gracious by the hospitality and helpfulness of the owners. Singles go from £16 ($31.20), doubles from £23 ($44.85) to £31 ($60.45), including a full Scottish breakfast. Here you get good meals with excellent fish, the chef equally adept at both Scottish and French cuisine. Lunches in the bar range from £2 ($3.90) to £3.50 ($6.83), and a four-course dinner goes for £7.50 ($14.63), The hotel receives guests all year.

Carnaberg Hotel, 55 Main St. (tel. Tobermory 2479), lies right on the quay, overlooking the harbor and the Sound of Mull. The house has been pleasantly redecorated, and the rooms are comfortable. Ian MacLean charges £14 ($27.30) for two persons, this tariff including a Scottish breakfast and VAT. The dinner, bed, and breakfast rate is £21 ($40.95) for two persons. If you're there on a cold night, you might be given a hot water bottle to take to bed with you, but only after you've been offered a snack before retiring. And what a snack! On one recent occasion, it consisted of four different kinds of cake, including chocolate, and three types of cookies (the oatmeal ones are especially good).

Mishnish Hotel (tel. Tobermory 2009) is a personal favorite. It's small, only 15 rooms, but its owners, the "MacCleod clan," have run it for four generations, giving island hospitality and creating a congenial atmosphere for guests. They never seem too busy that they can't stop and give advice and directions for exploring both Mull and Iona. Open all year, the Mishnish charges from £17 ($33.15) to £19 ($37.05) per person nightly, including a full Scottish breakfast, service, and VAT. The food is simple but the portions are ample, the ingredients fresh. The hotel contains many low ceilings and narrow passageways, and many of its furnishings have been polished with years of loving care. Residents can ask about boats for rent. In all, the Mishnish is a plain, simple, and friendly choice.

Suidhe Hotel, 59 Main St. (tel. Tobermory 2209), was originally recommended by readers Joseph and Elizabeth Mooney, and I agree fully with their point of view. Suidhe is Gaelic for "sit, rest, or a break in a journey," and that's exactly what this place is. Jim and Christine Scott, delightful people, run this clean, friendly little hotel charging £16 ($31.20) per person nightly, including bed, breakfast, and evening dinner. The meals are well prepared and good tasting. All rooms have hot and cold water. Trout fishing, sea angling, and pony trekking are available locally. Suidhe is in a village off the western coast, right on the harbor, facing mountains covered with all shades of rhododendron in spring. In the village is a very good craft shop in a former church.

Craignure

Isle of Mull (tel. Craignure 351) is a first-class hotel which opened in 1971. It stands near the ferry and the meeting point of the Sound of Mull and Loch Linnhe. From the picture windows of its public rooms you'll have panoramic vistas of mountains and the island of Lismore. Each of its 60 bedrooms, all handsomely furnished, comes equipped with private bath and good views. The single rate is £22 ($42.90), increasing to £36 ($70.20) in a double, plus VAT. The food is good and pleasantly served in the attractive dining room, which faces both sea and hills. The chef does both British and continental dishes. The sea trout is superb. Hopefully, you'll be there on a night when the specialty is roast haunch of venison with gooseberry sauce. A set lunch costs about £5 ($9.75), a dinner going for around £8 ($15.60). Bar lunches begin at £2.20 ($4.29). Other facilities include a cocktail bar and a residents' television lounge. The hotel is open from the first of May until the end of September.

Dervaig

Bellachroy (tel. Dervaig 225) is a small hotel, consisting of only eight rooms. But it remains open all year, welcoming visitors and charging them £10.50 ($20.48) per person nightly for a comfortable bed and a hearty Scottish breakfast the next morning. You can also stay here on half-board terms of £16 ($31.20) per person nightly. The Bellachroy is run by resident proprietors Andrew and Anne Arnold. The hotel was recently mentioned in *Gourmet* magazine for its good food. Free permits for the Western Isle golf course are provided, and loch and river trout and salmon fishing are available, plus sea angling locally.

IONA: Iona has been known as a place of spiritual power and pilgrimage for centuries. It was the site of the first Christian settlement in Scotland. A remote, low-lying, and treeless island now owned by the National Trust for Scotland, Iona lies off the southwestern coast of Mull and is only one mile by 3½ miles in size. It is accessible only by passenger ferry from the Isle of Mull (cars must remain on Mull). The ferry to Iona is run by local fishermen, and it's very informal in service, depending in large part on the weather.

Iona is known for its **"graves of the kings."** A total of 48 Scottish kings, including Macbeth and his victim Duncan, were buried on Iona, as were four Irish kings and eight Norwegian kings.

Today the island attracts nearly 1000 visitors a week in high season. Most of them come here mainly to see the **Abbey of Iona,** part of which dates back to the 13th century. But they also visit relics of the settlement founded there by St. Columba in 563, from which Celtic Christianity spread through Scotland. The abbey has been restored by an ecumenical group called the Iona Community, which conducts workshops on Christianity, sponsors a youth camp, offers tours of the abbey, and leads a seven-mile hike to the various holy and historic spots on the island each Wednesday.

Although there are many visitors to the abbey, the atmosphere on the island remains very rare, peaceful, and spiritual. It's possible to walk off among the sheep that wander freely everywhere to the top of Dun-I, a small mountain, and contemplate the ocean and the landscape as if you were the only person on earth.

There is much to do on Iona, but perhaps best of all, you can simply do nothing and absorb the kind of atmosphere that has drawn people on pilgrimages here for centuries.

One reader, Capt. Robert Haggart, Laguna, California, described his experience this way: "I was enchanted by the place. It really has a mystic atmosphere—one *feels* something ancient here, something spiritual, sacred, long struggles and wonderment about the strength of religion."

Most of the islanders live by crofting and fishing. In addition, they supplement their income by taking in paying guests in season, charging usually very low or at least fair prices. You can, of course, check into the hotel recommended below, but a stay here in a private home may be an altogether rewarding travel adventure. If you don't stay on Iona, you must catch one of the ferries back to Mull, and they rarely leave after 5 p.m.

The **St. Columba Hotel** (tel. Iona 304) stands right outside the village, in the vicinity of the cathedral. Offering a total of 29 simply furnished rooms (only two of which have private baths), the hotel accepts guests from March to October. Singles range in price from £12.42 ($24.22) to £13.57 ($26.46), doubles from £11.27 ($21.98) to £16.10 ($31.40) per person, including a full Scottish breakfast. The half-board rate ranges from £17.25 ($33.64) to £21.85 ($42.61) per person, including service and tax. There are reduced rates for guests staying four nights or longer. The food is good, especially the fish dishes, but, remember, the last order for dinner is taken at 7 p.m. People turn in early on Iona. Try to get a room overlooking the sea, but know that it's virtually impossible to secure an accommodation here in season without a reservation made well in advance.

STAFFA: Fingal's Cave, on Staffa, a 75-acre island in the Hebrides off Scotland's west coast, has been attracting visitors for more than 200 years. It has been the inspiration for music, poetry, paintings, and prose. No less a personage than Queen Victoria visited the cave in the 19th century and wrote: "The effect is splendid, like a great entrance into a vaulted hall. The sea is immensely deep in the cave. The rocks under water were all colors—pink, blue and green." The sound of the crashing waves and swirling waters caused Mendelssohn to write the "Fingal's Cave Overture." Turner painted the cave on canvas, and Keats, Wordsworth, and Tennyson all praised it in their poetry.

The cave is unique in that it is the only known cave in the world formed of basalt columns. Over the centuries, the sea has carved a huge cavern in the basalt, leaving massive hexagonal columns to create the "vaulted hall" effect which enchanted Queen Victoria.

The Gaelic name of the cave is An Uamh Ehinn or the musical cave.

Although the island of Staffa has not been inhabited for more than 160 years, visitors can still explore the cave, thanks to the Laird of Staffa, Alastair de Watteville. In his hydrojet-equipped boat, *Fulmar,* the laird makes three trips a day from the quay at Ulva Ferry on the Isle of Mull to the rocky shores of Staffa. After docking, visitors are led along the basalt path and into Fingal's Cave. Inside, the noise of the pounding sea is deafening.

Another cave, **Clamshell Cave,** can also be visited, but only at low tide. Appropriately named, **Boat Cave** is accessible only by water.

Kenway Travel operates a range of excursions, cruises, and tours from Oban and Argyll. There are daily sailings in summer (May to September) to Staffa, Iona, Mull, and a variety of beauty spots on the Argyll coast. Visits to Staffa include opportunities to land on this unique island, explore Fingal's Cave, and study the remarkable sea caves formed in the hexagonal basalt. All trips present views of dramatic, beautiful scenery and sights of varied marine and seabird life. Puffins, cormorants, gannets, kittiwakes, fulmars, and many kinds of gull are frequently seen, as are seals and porpoises.

Kenway Travel Centre is at 13 Stafford St., Oban (tel. Oban 64747).

PORT APPIN: To the north of Oban lies a beautiful lochside district, including Lismore Island. On an islet nearby is a landmark, **Castle Stalker,** the ancient seat of the Stewarts of Appin, built in the 15th century by Duncan Stewart, son of the first chief of Appin. Dugald, the ninth chief, was forced to sell the estate in 1765, and the castle slowly fell into ruin. It was recently restored and is once again inhabited. According to myth, there's a subterranean undersea passage at Port Appin where a piper supposedly entered with his dog. Only the dog returned, and he was hairless. Port Appin itself is a small hamlet of stone cottages.

Airds Hotel (tel. Appin 236) is an old ferry inn, one of the most outstanding in its classification, dating from 1700, in one of the most beautiful spots in the historic district of Appin. You're assured of serenity if you take a room at this tranquil choice on Loch Linnhe, midway between Oban and Fort William. The hotel overlooks not only Loch Linnhe, but the island of Lismore and the mountains of Morvern, an ideal center for touring this area of the country. You can take forest walks in many directions, or else go pony trekking, sea angling, or trout fishing. Boats can be rented and trips arranged to see the seals and to visit the island of Lismore.

The resident proprietors, Mr. and Mrs. Allen, welcome you to one of their comfortably furnished bedrooms, five of which contain private baths (in the new addition). Depending on your room assignment and plumbing, rates range from £14.50 ($28.28) to £17 ($33.15), including a full Scottish breakfast. Dinner costs from £10 ($19.50). The food is excellent, using fresh produce when possible. By all means try to return to the inn for a bountiful Scottish tea in the late afternoon, with home-baked scones and cakes. Guests are received from March to October. The hotel has a cocktail bar, a public bar, and residents' lounges.

SEIL: Those seeking a truly hidden oasis in the district south of Oban can leave town on the 816, turning west at Kilninver on the 844 until you reach Clachan Bridge. The locals claim, somewhat whimsically, that this is "the only bridge across the Atlantic Ocean." Easdale is an attractive, tiny slate village, nestling under the cliffs of Seil Island, with a view of Mull. Here you have complete serenity.

The **Dunmor House,** Seil, near Easdale (tel. Balvicar 203), is a licensed country-house hotel, enjoying a beautiful setting on its own 1000-acre hill farm, with panoramic views over the Atlantic and Hebridean islands. The house was built by a steward of the Bredalbane Campbells, who considered it much too big for a steward and promptly fired him. Today, the resident owners, Lieutenant Commander and Mrs. H. D. Campbell-Gibson, welcome you to one of their simply furnished, but comfortable, rooms, for which they charge £12 ($23.40) per person, including breakfast, service and VAT.

The real reason for recommending such an out-of-the-way place is the cookery of Mrs. Campbell-Gibson, who uses produce from her own garden. She even grows her own fresh herbs. At lunch typical Scottish pub fare is featured from 12:45 to 2 p.m., and you are likely to spend no more than £3 ($5.85) for food and a bottled beer. However, at dinner, from 8 to 9 nightly, any array of delectable continental dishes is offered. The ingredients are fresh, the results enjoyable. Easdale salmon is a specialty. Your tab is likely to run around £9 ($17.55). Dunmor shuts down the third week of October, reopening on May 1. Trout fishing in 12 lochs is available, and special day excursions by boat to offshore islands are available.

LOCH AWE: Twenty-two miles long and in most places only about a mile wide, Loch Awe for years acted as a natural moat protecting the Campbells of Inveraray from their enemies to the north. Along its banks and on its islands are many reminders of its fortified past. There is a ruined castle at Fincharn, at the southern end of the loch, and another on the island of Fraoch Eilean. The **Isle of Inishail** has an ancient chapel and burial ground, and at the northern end of the loch are the ruins of **Kilchurn Castle,** built by Sir Colin Campbell in 1440. The bulk of Ben Cruachan, 3689 feet, dominates Loch Awe at its northern end and attracts climbers. On the ben is the world's second-largest hydroelectric power station, which pumps water from Loch Awe to a reservoir high up the mountain. Below the mountain are the **Falls of Cruachan** and the wild **Pass of Brander,** where Robert the Bruce routed the Clan Mac-Dougall in 1308.

In this area, the Forestry Commission has vast forests, and a new road now makes it possible to travel around Loch Awe, so that it is more than ever a popular angling center. Sharp-eyed James Bond fans may even recognize some scenes which appeared in one of the films.

The Pass of Brander where Loch Awe narrows was the scene of many a fierce battle in bygone times, and something of that bloody past seems to brood over the narrow defile. Through it the waters of the Awe flow on their way to Loch Etive. This winding sealoch is 19 miles long, stretching from Dun Dunstaffnage Bay at Oban to Glen Etive, reaching into the Moor of Rannoch at the foot of the 3000-foot Buachaille Etive (the Shepherd of Etive), into which Glencoe also reaches.

Taychreggan Hotel, Lochaweside, near Taynuilt (tel. Kilchrenan 211), is a delightful old house nestling in firs beside the loch. John Taylor and Tove, his Danish wife, have furnished the place with great simplicity, skillfully joining the old with the new by using pinewood and stonework. They have created a friendly country-house atmosphere, providing comfortable, warm rooms, soft armchairs to sink into the lounge, and dinner cooked from local produce, including freshly caught fish. This is an excellent center for walking and relaxing, but there are many interesting things to do in this area, where good hotels are few and far between. The charge is £19 ($37.05) per person with bath. Without bath, the per-person rate ranges from £17.50 ($34.13), including a large breakfast. Most guests prefer to take the half-board arrangement, costing from £24 ($46.80) to £26 ($70.20) per person nightly. A high tea can be provided for children who do not stay up for dinner. Lunch at £5 ($9.75) is a smashing Danish cold table. Packed lunches are available as a matter of course, and afternoon tea or coffee, with crackers, goes for £1.50 ($2.93). You can hire a boat for the day for £6 ($11.70).

THE CRINAN CANAL: The nine-mile-long canal, constructed between 1793 –1801, was designed to provide water communication between the Firth of Clyde, Argyll, the western Highlands, and the islands. It runs roughly north from Ardrishaig and curves gradually to the west before reaching Loch Crinan on the Sound of Jura. Four miles north of **Cairnbaan,** on the canal, is the ruined hill-fort of **Dunadd,** once capital of Dalriada, kingdom of the Scots. There are numerous Bronze Age stone circles in the vicinity, and **Kilmartin churchyard,** five miles north of Cairnbaan, has a carved cross dating from the 16th century. **Carnasserie Castle,** also to the north of the canal, built in the late 16th century, was the home of John Carswell, the first post-Reformation bishop of the isles, whose translation of John Knox's liturgy into Gaelic was the first book to be published in that language.

Crinan, a yachtsman's haven on the Sound of Jura, is overlooked by the early 11th-century **Duntrune Castle,** one of the oldest castles in Scotland, and still inhabited by the descendants of the original owners, the Clan Malcolm. Crinan is a charming little village.

Lochgilphead, a pleasant little town sitting just where the canal turns westward, is the address of my recommendation for a stopover in this area:

The **Cairnbaan Motor Inn** (tel. Lochgilphead 2488). Formerly an old coach inn and now a privately owned hotel, this is an excellent base for touring Argyll and the islands. Nearby are safe beaches, and for the sportsman there is loch fishing, sea angling, and salmon fishing on the River Add. The motor inn has comfortable, modern bedrooms, some with private bathrooms and verandas. All bedrooms have built-in wardrobes, wash basins, razor sockets, radios, intercoms, and baby listening service. The tariff in a twin-bedded room without bath is £11.50 ($22.43) per person; with bath, £14 ($27.30) per person. The same charges apply in a single room.

The split-level dining room has a superb view southward down the busy canal. Emphasis for the cuisine is on Scottish dishes. There is a handsome cocktail bar and a comfortable sun lounge with a patio beyond.

Crinan Hotel (tel. Crinan 235), off the B841, seven miles northwest of Lochgilphead, is an inn with a bright, attractive decor and modern comforts and conveniences. Because of its location on a canal and yacht basin, it is naturally a favorite with yachtsmen, who book its 24 rooms with private bath in July and August, the peak sailing months. If you're reserving (and I highly recommend that you do), ask for one of the rooms with private balconies opening onto mountains and lochside sunsets.

The hotel is managed by Nicolas Ryan, who once worked as a bellboy on the old *Queen Mary,* later rising rapidly within the Cunard organization. Bedrooms rent for £20 ($39) in a single, from £30 ($58.50) to £33 ($64.35) in a double, including a breakfast that often features oatcakes and hot croissants.

Open all year, the hotel serves exceptionally good food—dishes such as fresh salmon, Crinan clams mornay, roast duckling in black cherry sauce, and Scottish sirloin. Meals are served from noon to 2 p.m. and from 7 to 9 p.m. A table d'hôte luncheon goes for £6 ($11.70), a set dinner for £11 ($21.45), although you are likely to pay £14 ($27.30) if you order from the à la carte menu. Luncheon in fair weather is served alfresco. The hotel is one of the best run in the area. As efficient as Mr. Ryan's staff is, they never overlook old-fashioned Scottish hospitality and friendliness.

INVERARAY: This small resort and royal burgh occupies a splendid Highland setting on the upper shores of Loch Fyne. The hereditary seat of the Dukes of Argyll, **Inveraray Castle** has been headquarters of the Clan Campbell since the early 15th century. In 1644, the original village was burned by the Royalist Marquess of Montrose. The third Duke of Argyll built a new town and castle between 1744 and 1788. The present laird, the 12th Duke of Argyll and 26th MacCailein Mor, chief of the Clan Campbell, has opened the castle to the public, with a special welcome for anyone who is related to Clan Campbell. The castle is among the earliest examples of Gothic revival in Britain, and offers a fine collection of pictures and 18th-century French furniture, old English and continental porcelain, and a magnificent Armoury Hall, which alone contains 1300 pieces. There is a castle shop for souvenirs and a tearoom where home-made cakes and scones are served. The castle is open daily from April 3 to October 10, charging £1.50 ($2.93) for adults, 75p ($1.46) for children. The castle is closed on Friday from the opening date until the end of June each year and in September and October.

At one end of the main street of the town is a Celtic burial cross from Iona. The parish church is divided by a wall enabling services to be held in Gaelic and English at the same time.

Auchindrain, six miles southwest of Inveraray, is a museum of farming life over the past 200 years. It is a unique survival of the past, whose origins are so far back as to be a subject for archeology. The farming township stands more or less as it was in the late 1800s, but studies are showing at least two centuries before that. One description states, "Auchindrain avoided progress." Open daily during the summer, Auchindrain and mid-Argyll are in an area crammed with things and places of interest for historians, antiquarians, and archeologists.

A fine woodland garden may be visited at **Crarae Lodge,** four miles southwest of the village.

Vacationing fishing enthusiasts may want to visit the **Castle Fisheries** (tel. Inveraray 2233), two miles north past the castle on the Oban road. Primarily a farm providing trout for the table, facilities are set up so that visitors can try their luck in one of the trout ponds, while the children play in the playground area or enjoy snacks from the refreshment stand. Other facilities include a baby deer park and even a hospital for sick fish. Admission is 75p ($1.46) for adults, 40p (78¢) for children, with an additional charge to those who go fishing. It's open 10 a.m. to 6 p.m., from April to October (fishing all year). A rod to fish with costs £1 ($1.95) for two hours, and you pay 60p ($1.17) per fish you catch. There is a minimum size, of course.

For food and accommodations in Inveraray, I'd suggest the **George,** Main Street (tel. Inveraray 2111), which is a small inn, open all year. The overnight rate is £10 ($19.50) to £12 ($23.40) per person, including a full Scottish breakfast, service, and VAT. The rooms are simply furnished, with a minimum of plumbing, decidedly old-fashioned. The dining room, however, is attractively modern with bright furnishings. A four-course dinner costs from £6 ($11.70), and bar snacks for lunch range from bacon rolls at 60p ($1.17) to fresh salmon salad at £3 ($5.85). Downstairs there's a public bar with stone walls and a flagstone floor, a part of which was connected with the stables when the George was a stagecoach inn. Here you can order snacks at lunch along with your lager. The George also owns the cheaper Loch Fyne Guest House, 500 yards up the road.

6. Kintyre, Arran, and Islay

For many foreign visitors, the Atlantic seaboard of the old county of Argyll will represent a journey into the unknown. For those who want to sample a bygone age, this is one of the most rewarding trips off the coastline of western Scotland. My recommendations lie on islands, easily reached by ferries—except the Kintyre Peninsula which is a virtual island in itself. You'll soon discover that the Gaelic traditions of the islands endure. Peace and tranquility prevail.

ISLE OF ARRAN: At the mouth of the Firth of Clyde, this island is often described as Scotland in miniature, because of its wild and varied scenery, containing an assortment of glens, moors, lochs, sandy bays, and rocky coasts for which the country is known. Ferry services, making the 50-minute crossing, operate from Ardrossan to Brodick, the major village of Arran, lying on the eastern shore. There are also ferry connections linking the northern part of Arran with the Kintyre Peninsula and the Highlands. Once on Arran, you'll find buses take you to the various villages, each with its own character. A coast road, 60 miles long, runs the length of the island.

Arran contains some splendid mountain scenery, notably the conical peak of **Goatfell** in the north, reaching a height of 2866 feet. It's called "the mountain of the winds."

Students of geology flock to Arran to study igneous rocks of the Tertiary Age. Cairns and standing stones at **Tormore** intrigue archeologists as well.

Arran is also filled with beautiful glens, especially **Glen Sannox** in the northeast and **Glen Rosa**, directly north of Brodick. In one day you can see a lot, as the island is only 25 miles long, 10 miles wide.

After the ferry docks at Brodick, you may want to head for Arran's major sight—**Brodick Castle**, 1½ miles north of the Brodick pierhead. The historic home of the Dukes of Hamilton, the castle dates from the 13th century and contains superb silver, antiques, portraits, and objets d'art. It is open in April after Easter on Monday, Wednesday, and Saturday from 1 to 5 p.m. From May 1 to September 30, hours are daily from 1 to 5 p.m. The award-winning gardens and the new Country Park are open all year, daily from 10 a.m. to 5 p.m. Admission to both the castle and gardens is £1.05 ($2.05) for adults, 50p (98¢) for children.

South from Brodick lies the village and holiday resort of **Lamlash**, opening onto Lamlash Bay. From here a ferry takes visitors over to **Holy Island**, with its 1000-foot peak. A disciple of St. Columba founded a church on this island.

One of the best-known centers on the western coast is **Blackwater Foot**, which offers pony trekking and golfing.

Finally, in the north, **Lochranza** is a village with unique appeal. It opens onto a bay of pebbles and sand, and in the backdrop lie the ruins of a castle that reputedly was the hunting seat of Robert Bruce.

Brodick

Glenartney (tel. Brodick 2220) is a two-story, 20-bedroom rough-cast hotel commanding a hilltop perch overlooking the bay. The hotel offers comfortable rooms and good food, plus a congenial atmosphere. Singles peak at £10 ($19.50); doubles, £19 ($37.05)—including breakfast. A lunch by arrangement goes for £4 ($7.80), a complete dinner costing from £6 ($11.70). None of the rooms contains a private bath, and you have to get to the dining room between 7 and 7:30 p.m. The hotel is closed from October to February. There is no advance reservation accepted for stays of only one or two nights. You just arrive and take a chance on finding a room available.

Whiting Bay

Whiting Bay Hotel (tel. Whiting Bay 247) is a substantial, well-heated hotel, its windows looking out over the bay and the Firth of Clyde. The hotel is immaculately maintained, and the staff is most hospitable. They will welcome you all year in one of their comfortable bedrooms, of which only 6 out of 22 contain private baths. Rates range from £15 ($29.25) to £16 ($31.20) in a single, from £28 ($54.60) to £31 ($60.45) in a double, including a full Scottish breakfast. The half-board rate goes from £23 ($44.85) to £25 ($48.75) per person nightly. The cook prepares Scottish specialties, among other dishes, very well. The hotel is fully licensed, and it has ample parking as well as a cocktail bar, lounge bar, and a ballroom with regular entertainment. A piper pipes guests to dinner most evenings. The hotel receives visitors from April to October only.

Lamlash

Although I missed this on my latest rounds, the **Carraig Mhor**, Lamlash, Arran (tel. Lamlash 453), continues to get accolades by food writers and has been awarded rosettes. This highly spoken-of restaurant is open nightly except Sunday and Monday, and you can expect to pay from £8.50 ($16.58) for a meal. Always telephone ahead for a reservation, however.

KINTYRE PENINSULA: The longest peninsula in Scotland, Kintyre is more than 60 miles in length, containing much beautiful scenery, pleasant villages, and magnificent gardens on the Isle of Gigha, which lies off its western shores. The largest center on Kintyre is Campbeltown, although Tarbert in the north is also popular. In the evening you just might hear the music of the "ceilidhs" in hotels and village halls.

The major sight is an excursion to Gigha's famous gardens. They're called **Achamore** and are located a quarter of a mile from Ardminish on the Isle of Gigha. The island is reached by ferry boat which picks up passengers at the Tayinloan jetty on Kintyre. Weather permitting, sailings are four times daily. It is advisable to check times with Cal/Mac Ltd. (tel. 088-073-253).

These extensive gardens contain roses, hydrangeas, rhododendrons, camellias, and azaleas. They are open March to October from 10 a.m. to dusk, charging adults 40p (78¢); children, 20p (39¢).

At Carradale, near the ruins of Aird Castle on the eastern coast, you can visit the **Carradale Forest Centre** and the gardens of Carradale House.

TARBERT: A sheltered harbor protects this fishing port and yachting center which lies on a narrow neck of the northern tip of the Kintyre Peninsula, between West Loch Tarbert and the head of herring-filled Loch Fyne. Nearby is the finest accommodation on the Kintyre Peninsula.

Stonefield Castle Hotel (tel. Tarbert 207), occupying a commanding position, is a luxuriously appointed and magnificent hotel on 100 acres of wooded grounds and parklike gardens on Loch Fyne, two miles outside Tarbert. The grounds are studded with rare shrubs, and from the gardens come the flowers for the exquisite arrangements inside the house. Extended from the central square tower are tall step-gabled wings, with highly pitched windows and rows of dormers. From this impressively handsome building are seemingly unlimited views. Older readers especially find it a tranquil oasis. The castle was formerly owned by a member of the Campbell clan. Nowadays the proprietor is James H. Scot, whose son, Graeme, is the manager. Both are still in constant attendance. Its public rooms are lofty, decorated, in part, with antiques.

Try to get one of the well-furnished bedrooms in the main building, although you may be assigned an accommodation in the more modern wing. In all, there are 34 rooms, 29 with private bath. Singles range from £22 ($42.90) to £25 ($48.75), doubles from £44 ($85.80) to £48 ($93.60), including a full Scottish breakfast, service, and VAT. Meals utilize produce from the hotel's own garden. In the kitchen the staff does their own baking. The paneled dining room is decorated in a formal style, and the service is superb.

Lunch in the bar costs about £3 ($5.85), and dinner ranges from £12 ($23.40). The hotel has many excellent facilities, including a spacious drawing room overlooking the loch, a cocktail bar, tennis court, putting green, a large library, an outdoor swimming pool, a sauna, even yacht anchorage. Sea fishing can be arranged. It's imperative to book well in advance, as Stonefield has a large repeat clientele. It remains open all year.

Considerably less expensive, the **Tarbert Hotel** (tel. Tarbert 264) stands on the quayside where the Kintyre fishermen anchor with their herring-filled boats. The hotel is really like a pub, painted in white, and the frugal Scots book the comfortable and simply furnished rooms which cost from £11 ($21.45) per person. Dinner is an additional £9.50 ($18.53), and a lunch goes for £4.50 ($8.78) per person. If you don't dine in the main room, you'll find a goodly assortment of snacks. The lounge bar is usually well stuffed with the local people, enjoying their Scottish & Newcastle.

The **West Loch Hotel** (tel. Tarbert 283), a small, family-managed hotel, is also good, although it contains only six bedrooms, renting for £17.50 ($34.13) in a single, from £27 ($52.65) in a double, including a full breakfast. The rooms are immaculately maintained, furnished in an old style. The main building dates back to old coaching days. You really should take the half-board rate of £23 ($44.85) per person, or else drop in for a meal, because the cookery is first rate. Fresh ingredients are used whenever available, and the fish dishes are superb. In season game is featured. Hot and cold snacks are served both in the bar and dining room at noon, costing from £2.50 ($4.88) to £3 ($5.85). The black-and-white inn overlooks West Loch—hence its name. It lies one mile south of the village on the Campbeltown road. It's popular with yachtsmen from the east harbor. The hotel is conveniently situated for ferries sailing to Arran, Islay, and Jura. A nine-hole golf course, pony trekking, forestry walks, and the sandy West Coast beaches are all within easy reach.

ISLE OF ISLAY: The southernmost island of the Inner Hebrides, Islay lies 16 miles west of the Kintyre peninsula and less than a mile southwest of Jura, from which it is separated only by a narrow sound. At its maximum breadth, Islay is only 15 miles wide (25 miles long).

Called "the Queen of the Hebrides," it is a peaceful unspoiled island of moors, salmon-filled lochs, sandy bays, and wild rocky cliffs. Islay was the ancient seat of the Lords of the Isles, and today you'll see the ruins of two castles and several Celtic crosses.

Near Port Charlotte are the graves of the U.S. seamen and army troops who lost their lives in 1918 when their carriers, the *Tuscania* and *Otranto,* were torpedoed off the shores of Islay. There's a memorial tower on the Mull of Oa, eight miles from Port Ellen.

The island is noted for its distilleries, producing single-malt Highland whiskies by the antiquated pot-still method.

MacBrayne Steamers operate a daily service to Islay—you leave West Tarbert on the Kintyre peninsula, arriving at Port Askaig on Islay.

The island's capital is Bowmore, on the coast across from Port Askaig. There you can see a fascinating round church—no corners for the devil. But the most important town is Port Ellen, on the south coast, a holiday and golfing resort as well as Islay's principal port.

As accommodations are limited on Islay, always arrive with a reservation in your pocket.

Port Askaig

Port Askaig Hotel (tel. Port Askaig 245) is a genuine old island inn, dating from the 18th century, built on the site of an even older inn. It stands on the

Sound of Islay overlooking the pier where a MacBrayne steamer berths daily. The hotel is quite charming, offering island hospitality and Scottish fare, including broiled trout, cock-a-leekie soup, roast pheasant, smoked Scottish salmon, and, of course, haggis. The hotel is a major destination for anglers on Islay, and the bar at the inn is popular with local fishermen. All year the friendly staff welcomes you to one of its modestly furnished bedrooms, costing from £16 ($31.20) in a single and from £26 ($50.70) in a double, including a continental breakfast. Dinner costs from £8 ($15.60). The hotel, incidentally, offers only nine rooms, half of which contain private baths.

Port Ellen

White Hart (tel. Port Ellen 2311) is modest, but pleasantly situated, standing on a tiny promenade on the skirttails of Port Ellen. The furnishings are in good taste, offering unassuming comfort. The hotel rents out 19 rooms, of which only 5 contain private baths. All year singles cost from £13 ($25.35) to £16 ($31.20); doubles, £27 ($52.65) to £33 ($64.35)—including a full breakfast. The half-board rate is £25 ($48.75) per person. Meals are good, although simple, and are served in a dining room opening onto a view of the water. Log fires burn in the attractive lounge. If given proper notice, the staff will arrange fishing expeditions for guests.

Bridgend

Bridgend Hotel (tel. Bowmore 212) is a good base if you're crossing Islay, making your headquarters around the capital at Bowmore. All year the resident owners of this hotel will welcome you to their quiet retreat, opening onto Loch Indaal. The hotel is plainly furnished, although a nice touch is added by the pictures of wild bird life on Islay and the seascape paintings of local artists. The Bridgend offers only nine doubles and two singles, none of which contains a private bath. Singles range in price from £18 ($35.10) to £20 ($39), with doubles priced from £36 ($70.20) to £40 ($78), including VAT, service, and a full Scottish breakfast. Meals—good, simple, unassuming cookery—are served between 7 and 7:30 p.m. The hotel also has a fully licensed cocktail bar.

ISLE OF JURA: This is the fourth-largest island in the Inner Hebrides. It perhaps takes its name from the Norse *Jura,* meaning "deer island." The red deer on Jura outnumber the people by about 20 to 1. At four feet high, the deer are the largest wild animals roaming Scotland. The hardy islanders number only about 250 brave souls, and most of them live along the east coast. The west coast is virtually uninhabited.

The capital, **Craighouse,** is hardly more than a hamlet. It is connected by steamer to West Loch Tarbert on the Kintyre peninsula. If you're already on Islay, you can journey to Jura by taking a five-minute ferry ride from Port Askaig, docking at the Feolin Ferry berth.

The breadth of Jura varies from two to eight miles, and at its maximum length it is 27 miles long. The island's landscape is dominated by the **Paps of Jura,** reaching a peak of 2571 feet at Beinn-an-Oir. An arm of the sea, **Loch Tarbert** nearly divides the island, cutting into it for nearly six miles.

As islands go, Jura is relatively little known and explored, although its mountains, soaring cliffs, snug coves, and moors make it an inviting paradise—nowhere is there overcrowding. The island has actually lost population drastically.

The square tower of **Claig Castle** is now in ruins, but once it was the stronghold of the MacDonalds until they were subdued by the Campbells in the 17th century.

Literary historians may be interested to know that George Orwell in the bitter postwar winters of 1946 and 1947 lived at Jura. Even then a sick and dying man, he wrote his masterpiece, *1984,* a satire on modern politics. He almost lost his life on Jura when he and his adopted son ventured too close to the whirlpool in the Gulf of Corryvreckan. Orwell and his son were saved by local fishermen, and he went on to finish *1984,* only to die in London of tuberculosis in 1950. His life span hardly matched that of Gillouir MacCrain, said to have been 180 when he died on Jura in the days of Charles I.

In accommodations, the **Jura Hotel** (tel. 243) at Craighouse is the only licensed premises on the island. Overlooking the sea, it actually has palms growing on its grounds, thanks to the benevolence of the Gulf Stream. All year it rents 18 bedrooms, 4 of which contain private baths. The single tariff is £18 ($35.10); the double rate, £36 ($70.20)—including breakfast. The half-board terms are from £26 ($50.70) per person daily. Rooms are simply although agreeably furnished. However, bring along some mosquito repellant to deal with the pest of the islands.

Chapter XX

THE ABC'S OF BRITAIN

THE AIM of this "grab bag" section—dealing with the vital minutiae of your stay—is to make your adjustment to British ways of life easier. It is maddening to have your trip marred by an incident which could have been avoided, had you but been tipped off earlier. To prevent this from happening, we'll try to anticipate the addresses, data, and information that might come in handy on all manner of occasion.

ACCIDENT COMPENSATION: There is no automatic compensation. Some auto insurance companies operate a "knock for knock" cover. All other claims are settled by the courts. We would advise you to carry good personal accident and "third party" insurance. If you consider it necessary in the United States or Canada, the same rules apply in Britain.

AIRPORTS: London has two main airports—**Heathrow** and **Gatwick.** It takes 45 to 60 minutes by underground train from Heathrow and 60 minutes by train from Gatwick to central London. Buses and taxis go from both airports. Taxis from Heathrow charge by a meter; those from Gatwick have a set fee which should be confirmed before departure. There's also a bus service between the two airports, leaving every hour; the trip takes about 70 minutes. In addition, there's an expensive helicopter service that takes only 15 minutes between the airports. For flight information, telephone Heathrow (01) 759-4321. For Gatwick, telephone Crawley 31299. Airline phone numbers are listed in the telephone directory.

AMERICAN EXPRESS: The main office is 6 Haymarket in London, S.W.1 (tel. 930-4411). There are some ten other London locations.

BABYSITTERS: These are very hard to find, and the only safe way would be to get your hotel to recommend someone—or, possibly, a staff member. Expect to pay around £5 ($9.75) an hour and, often, the cost of travel home by taxi.

BANKS: Hours, generally, are 9:30 a.m. to 3:30 p.m., Monday to Friday. There are also Bureaux de Change, which charge for cashing travelers' checks or personal checks (United Kingdom ones only), or for changing dollars into sterling. Bureaux are often open seven days a week, 12 hours a day.

BUS TERMINALS: Victoria Coach Station, Victoria, S.W.1 (tube: Victoria) in London is the main bus terminal. For departure times and general information, telephone (01) 750-0202.

CIGARETTES. Most U.S. brands are available in major cities and towns. Expect to pay more than $2 (U.S.) for a package of 20. Warning: there is an increasing number of places where smoking is banned. Make sure you enter a "smoking carriage" in the train or underground, and only smoke on the top of buses, or in the smoking sections of single deckers, cinemas, or other public places. Some restaurants post "no smoking" signs.

CLOTHING SIZES: Women will find the size of stockings the same in Britain as in America. Likewise, men will find suits and shirts the same size. However, there are some exceptions.

For women

Dresses, Coats, and Skirts											
American	7	8	9	10	11	12	13	14	15	16	17	18
British	9	10	11	12	13	14	15	16	17	18	19	20

Blouses and Sweaters					
American	10	12	14	16	18	20
British	32	34	36	38	40	42

Shoes											
American	4½	5	5½	6	6½	7	7½	8	8½	9	9½	10
British	3	3½	4	4½	5	5½	6	6½	7	7½	8	8½

For Men

Shoes						
American	7	8	9	10	11	12	13
British	6	7	8	9	10	11	12

CRIME: Theft is not as bad, perhaps, as in the U.S. Mugging is limited in the main to the poor areas. As for murder and assault, reports say that most of these occur within families and related groups. The best advice is to use discretion and a little common sense.

CURRENCY EXCHANGE: As we go to press, Britain's pound sterling is worth about $1.95, and the price conversions in this book have been computed at that exchange rate. Since the pound is far from stable, however, it's always wise to check with a bank before you set off for Britain.

Each pound breaks down into 100 pence, making each penny worth just under 2¢ U.S.

CUSTOMS: Overseas visitors may import 400 cigarettes and one quart of liquor. But if you come from the EEC area, you're allowed 300 cigarettes and one quart of liquor, provided you bought them and paid tax in that EEC country. If you have obtained your allowance on a ship or plane, then you may only import 200 cigarettes and one liter of liquor. There is no limit on money, film, or other items which are for your own use. Obviously commercial goods, such as video films and nonpersonal items, will require payment of a bond and will take a number of hours to clear and deal with. Do not try to import live birds or animals. You may be subjected to heavy fines, and the pet will be destroyed.

CLIMATE: British temperatures can range from 30° to 110°F. It is, however, a temperate country with no real extremes, and, even in summer, evenings are cool. No English person will ever really advise on the weather—it is far too uncertain. However, if you come from a hot area, bring some warm clothes. If you come from the cooler climes, you should be all right.

DENTIST: In London, telephone (01) 584-1008 for the name of the nearest dentist. Expect to pay £15 ($29.25) for treatment unless it is a genuine emergency. Or else get in touch with the **Royal Dental Hospital,** 32 Leicester Square, London, W.C.2 (tel. 930-8831). Outside London, ask the nearest, sympathetic local, a hotelier for example.

DOCTORS: Hotels have their own list of local practitioners for whom you'll have to pay. (Look under "Hospitals" for 24-hour emergency service.) If out of town, dial "0" and ask the operator for the local police, who will give you the name and address of a doctor in your area, along with his or her telephone number. Emergency treatment is free, but treatment for existing conditions is liable to require payment, although this will be at the doctor's discretion.

DRUGSTORES: Here they are called "chemist" shops. Every police station in the country has a list of emergency chemists. Dial "0" and ask the operator for the local police.

DOCUMENTS FOR ENTRY: Every U.S. citizen needs a valid passport. Generally, a U.S. driving license is sufficient to rent a car.

ELECTRICAL APPLIANCES: The current is 220 volts, AC. Plugs are normally three-pin square.

EMBASSY AND HIGH COMMISSION: The U.S. Embassy is at 24 Grosvenor Square, London, W.1 (tel. 499-9000), and the **Canadian High Commission** is at Canada House, Trafalgar Square, London, S.W.1 (tel. 629-9492).

EMERGENCY: In London, for police, fire, or ambulance, dial 999. Give your name and address, plus the telephone number and state the nature of the emergency. Misuse of the 999 service will result in a heavy fine. Cardiac arrest, yes. Sprained ankle, no. Accident injury, yes. Dented fender, no.

ETIQUETTE: How many chapters? Be normal, be quiet. The British do not like hearing other people's conversations. In pubs you are not expected to buy a round of drinks unless someone has bought you a drink. Don't talk politics or religion in pubs.

FILM: All types are available. Processing takes about 24 hours, although many places in London will do it almost while you wait. There are almost no restrictions on the use of your camera, except when notices are posted as in churches and theaters. If in doubt, ask.

FOOD AND CUISINE: Again, a separate book is needed. A continental breakfast consists of rolls or croissants or toast, coffee or tea, and jam or marmalade. An English breakfast can include porridge, kippers, smoked haddock, eggs, bacon, sausages, tomatoes, and mushrooms, tea or coffee. National dishes range from steak and kidney pie or pudding, roast beef and Yorkshire pudding, to more exotic concoctions such as starry-gazey pie, haggis and neaps, collops and mash. Desserts are trifle, apple pie and cheese, rhubarb fool, summer pudding, and a host of others.

GAS: It's called "petrol" here. Prices are rising. As of this writing, it is selling for £1.65 ($3.22) a gallon. Watch out for where it is sold in liters, but they usually have a comparative list of prices.

HAIRDRESSING: Ask your hotel. You should tip the "hairwasher" 20p (39¢) and the stylist 50p (98¢) or more if you have a tint or permanent.

HITCHHIKING: It is not illegal and is normally quite safe and practical. It is, however, illegal for pedestrians to be on motorways. The cleaner and tidier you look, the better your chance. Have a board with your destination written on it.

HOLIDAYS AND FESTIVALS: Christmas Day, Boxing Day (December 26), New Year's Day, Good Friday and Easter Monday, May Day, spring and summer bank holiday. Scotland also takes January 2 as a holiday, but does not recognize the summer bank holiday, taking the first Monday in August instead of the last for a holiday. Scotland does not take Easter Monday as a bank holiday.

HOSPITALS: The following offer emergency treatment in London 24 hours a day, and it's free under the National Health Service. If you have an existing condition, it may not be treated free. **Royal Free Hospital,** Pond St., N.W.3 (tel. 636-8333); **Middlesex Hospital,** Mortimer St., W.1 (tel. 636-8333); **New Charing Cross Hospital,** Fulham Palace Rd. (tel. 748-2040); **St. Bartholomew's Hospital,** West Smithfield, E.C.1 (tel. 600-9000); **St. Stephen's Hospital,** 369 Fulham Rd., S.W.10 (tel. 352-8161); **St. Thomas's Hospital,** Lambeth Palace Rd., S.E.1 (tel. 928-9292); **University College Hospital,** Gower St., W.C.1 (tel. 387-9300).

INFORMATION: There are more than 650 tourist information offices in England and Wales and 160 in Scotland. All are well sign-posted in their cities, and some are closed in winter. The **British Tourist Authority,** Queens House, 64 St. James's St., London, S.W.1 (tel. 629-9191), will answer most questions about the country. You might also consult the **English Tourist Board,** 4 Grosvenor Gardens, London, S.W.1 (tel. (01-730-3400); the **Scottish Tourist Board,** 23 Ravalston Terrace, Edinburgh EH4 3EU (tel. (031-332-2433), and the **Welsh Tourist Board,** Brunci House, 2 Fitzalan Rd., Cardiff CF2 1UY (tel. 0222-49-99-09). The regional boards will answer questions of a more detailed nature, providing data on accommodations and local sights. They'll also give you the addresses of the tourist offices in the local towns.

LAUNDRY AND DRY CLEANING: There are plenty of establishments around. Most places take two days to complete the job.

LIBRARIES: Every town has a public library, and as a visitor you can use the reference sections. The lending of volumes is restricted to local citizens.

LIQUOR LAWS: No alcohol is served to anyone under the age of 18. Children under 16 aren't allowed in pubs, except in special rooms. Pub hours *vary,* but as a general guide they are open from 11:30 a.m. to 2:30 p.m. and from 6 to 10:30 p.m. Monday to Saturday. Sunday hours are noon to 2:30 p.m. and from 7 to 10 p.m.

LITERATURE: If you're really dedicated in your exploring, we'd suggest Churchill's *History of the English Speaking Peoples* and Trevelyan's *History of England.* These tomes will help you understand a lot more about what you'll be seeing. Otherwise, just read the guidebook and use a good map if you're touring.

MAIL DELIVERY: Any letter sent "Poste Restante," London, is available for collection at the **Head Post Office,** St. Martin-le-Grand, London, E.C.1 (personal callers only, near St. Paul's Cathedral). Otherwise, have your mail addressed Poste Restante at any of the big towns or give your hotel address. A letter generally takes about seven to ten days to arrive in the U.S.

MEASURES: At present Britain uses miles and inches but probably soon will switch to metric.

1 inch	2.54cm.	1 mile	1.61km.
1 foot	0.30m.	1 yard	0.91m

Weights, for the most part, are already metric.

1 ounce	28.35gm	1 pint imp.	0.56 liter
1 pound	0.45kg	1 gallon imp.	4.54 liters

NEWSPAPERS: *The Times* is the top, then the *Telegraph,* the *Daily Mail,* and the *Guardian,* all papers carrying the latest news. Others have some news, but rely on other gimmicks to sell. The international edition of *The Herald Tribune,* published in Paris, is available daily. *What's On* and similar publications appear weekly and are sold at all bookstalls in London.

OFFICE HOURS: Business hours are 9 a.m. to 5 p.m., Monday to Friday. The lunch break lasts an hour, but most places stay open all day.

PETS: See Customs. It is illegal to bring in pets, except with veterinary documents. They are subject to a quarantine of six months. Hotels have their own rules, but generally they do not allow dogs in restaurants or public rooms and often not in the bedrooms either.

POLITICS: There are two main parties, Conservative and Labour. The Conservatives believe in free enterprise and freedom of the individual to make his or her own decisions with some government support. Labour believes in state ownership and control, with the state providing maximum support for the individual. Other parties are the Liberals and the Social Democratic Party; they are somewhat similar and presently have no great strength in government or as opposition.

POLICE: The best source of help and advice in emergencies is the police, dial 999. If the local police cannot assist, they will have the address of a person who can. Losses, theft, and other crime should be reported immediately to the police.

POST OFFICE: Post offices and sub-post offices are centrally situated, and are open from 9 a.m. to 5 p.m., Monday to Friday (from 9 a.m. to noon on Saturday).

RADIO AND TV: There are some 24-hour stations on the radio in London, mostly pop music and talk shows. TV starts around 7 a.m. with educational programs. Lighter entertainment begins around 4 to 5 p.m., after the children's programs and continues till around midnight. There are, at present, three TV channels, one commercial and two B.B.C.

RAILROAD INFORMATION: In London, personal callers are welcome at **British Rail/Sealink**, Lower Regent Street, S.W.1, and at **Victoria Station.** Or else they can call the various stations, all listed under British Rail in the telephone directory. Elsewhere, get in touch with the local station or a travel agent who holds a British Rail license.

RELIGIOUS SERVICES: Times of services are posted outside the various places of worship. Almost every form of worship is catered to in London and other large cities, but in the smaller towns and villages you are likely to find only Anglican (Episcopalian), Roman Catholic, Baptists, and Nonconformists. **The American Church** is on Tottenham Court Road, W.1, London.

REST ROOMS: These are usually found at signs saying "Public Toilets." Expect to pay from 2p (4¢) to 5p (10¢) tip for women; men are free. Hotels can be used, but they discourage non-residents. Garages (filling stations) also have facilities for use of customers only, and the key is often kept by the cash register. There's no need to tip except in hotels where there is an attendant.

SENIOR DISCOUNTS: Only available to holders of a British pension book.

SHOE REPAIRS: Many of the large department stores of Britain have "Shoe Bars" where repairs are done while you wait.

SHOP HOURS: In general, stores are open from 9 a.m. to 5 or 5:30 p.m. Monday through Saturday. Late shopping in London is on Thursday, when stores close at 7 p.m. There are very few all-night stores, mostly in the Bayswater area of London.

SUBWAY INFORMATION: There is a map at the entrance to each Underground station. If you ask for the "subway," you may end up in a tunnel for pedestrians beneath a road. In the Underground, you pay according to the distance you travel; posted by the ticket office is a list of fares showing the cost to most stations. There are also ticket machines for certain fares to destinations shown on the machines.

TELEPHONES: To make a phone call from a call box, you'll need 5p (10¢) and 10p (20¢) coins. Phone numbers in Britain don't have any consistency or pattern. It's what the British call a "real hotch-potch." Next-door neighbors may have a six-figure number and an eight-figure number. In some cases you have an exchange name, in others a set of figures. You'll need all the figures, which can vary from ten down to six figures.

Consider **Directory Enquiries** to aid you. Dial 192, give the operator the town where you want the number, the subscriber's name, and then the address. A guide to telephone costs—a call at noon from London to Reading, 40 miles away, lasting three minutes, goes for 84p ($1.64). A local call within a radius of one mile can cost 21p (41¢) for three minutes. These costs are roughly halved between 6 p.m. and 8 a.m. You will have to pay far more if you use a hotel operator at any time.

TIPPING: Many establishments add a service charge. If service has been good, it is usual to add an additional 5%. If no service is added to the bill, give 10% for poor service; otherwise, 15%. If service is bad, tell them and don't tip!

TAXES: There is no local sales tax. For Value Added Tax, refer to the front of this guide.

TELEGRAMS: Send from any main (not sub) post office or by telephone.

TELEX: These are mostly restricted to business premises and hotels. If your hotel has a telex, they will send for you. It is less common in the U.S. than in Europe, and you may need to arrange for receipt of a telex message.

TIME: England and Scotland are based on Greenwich Mean Time with BST/ British Standard Time (GMT + 1) during the summer (roughly April to October). When London is 12 noon, New York is 7 a.m., Chicago 6 a.m., Denver 5 a.m., and Los Angeles, 4 a.m.

WEATHER INFORMATION: There is continuously updated information available by telephone. In London dial 246-8091.

USEFUL TELEPHONE NUMBERS: These are for London. Outside London, dial Directory Enquiries, 192. For Directory Enquiries in London, dial 142. For the operator, 100; for telegrams, 100; international calls to the U.S. and Canada, 157. For the time, telephone 980-81; for motoring information, 246-8021. For Teletourist information (recorded), dial 246-8041 in London, 246-8041 in Edinburgh. Want to hear a bedtime story? In London, dial 246-8000.